Frederick George Lee

The history, description and antiquities of the prebendal church of the Blessed Virgin Mary of Thame, in the county and diocese of Oxford : including a transcript of all the monumental inscriptions remaining therein; extracts from the registers and c

Frederick George Lee

The history, description and antiquities of the prebendal church of the Blessed Virgin Mary of Thame, in the county and diocese of Oxford : including a transcript of all the monumental inscriptions remaining therein; extracts from the registers and c

ISBN/EAN: 9783337201869

Printed in Europe, USA, Canada, Australia, Japan

Cover: Foto ©ninafisch / pixelio.de

More available books at **www.hansebooks.com**

The history, description and antiquities of the prebendal ...
Frederick George Lee

HISTORY AND ANTIQUITIES

OF

The Church of the Blessed Virgin Mary of Thame.

To face the Title Page

Exterior of Thame Church.
from the South-East looking North-West.

THE HISTORY, DESCRIPTION, AND ANTIQUITIES OF THE PREBENDAL CHURCH OF THE BLESSED VIRGIN MARY OF THAME,

In the County and Diocese of Oxford,

INCLUDING A TRANSCRIPT OF ALL THE MONUMENTAL INSCRIPTIONS REMAINING THEREIN; EXTRACTS FROM THE REGISTERS AND CHURCHWARDENS' BOOKS; TOGETHER WITH DIVERS ORIGINAL PEDIGREES, COPIOUS ANTIQUARIAN, ARCHITECTURAL, PERSONAL, AND GENEALOGICAL NOTES AND APPENDICES, RELATING TO, AND ILLUSTRATIVE OF, THE TOWN, ITS HISTORY, AND INHABITANTS: IN WHICH IS INCLUDED SOME ACCOUNT OF THE ABBEY OF THAME PARK, THE GRAMMAR SCHOOL, AND THE ANCIENT CHAPELRIES OF TOWERSEY, TETTESWORTH, SYDENHAM, NORTH WESTON, AND RYCOTT.

BY THE REV. FREDERICK GEORGE LEE, D.D., F.S.A.,

VICAR OF ALL SAINTS', LAMBETH, ETC., ETC.

WITH NUMEROUS ILLUSTRATIONS.

Ave Maria  gratia plena.

Enter these aisles, and note thou all they teach.
This is God's House, and here of yore He dwelt:
Shrine, lamp, and Presence; while, to eye of Faith,
Grace, like the dew, fell from His throne above;
Warmed the chill heart and cooled the feverish glow:
For His delights are with the sons of men.
Herein crowds gathered to adore His Name
And glorify His Saints. The blessed Dead
Repose in peace within these sacred walls,—
Good Christ, have mercy; Lady Mary, help!
Herein angelic hosts bowed down with awe,
When Sacrifice was had and Silence reigned:
The Garden-plot of Lily and of Rose—
Type of our City of Eternal Peace.

GODEFRIDUS.

LONDON:

Printed and Published by Mitchell and Hughes, 140 Wardour Street, W.

MDCCCLXXXIII.

"Search your Pedigrees, collect the scattered monuments and histories of your ancestors, and observe by what steps your worthy progenitors raised their houses to the height of gentry or nobility."—Bishop Sanderson's *Sermons*, p. 197. 1674.

"There is no subject more difficult to be dwelt on than that of honourable descent, none on which the world are greater sceptics, none more offensive to them; and yet there is no quality to which every one in his heart pays so great a respect."—*Autobiography* of Sir Egerton Brydges, p. 153.

TO

The Right Honourable

MONTAGU ARTHUR,

Baron Norreys of Rycott,

Heir to the Lordships of Old Thame,

New Thame, and Priestend,

etc., etc., etc.,

This Volume,

BY HIS LORDSHIP'S PERMISSION,

IS

VERY RESPECTFULLY

DEDICATED.

'Tis but a simple record of the Past,
Scarce worthy of your note. Yet there are names
Of good men and of true enshrined here;
With some blurred pictures of an age long dead,
And humble records of the days gone by,
When God was honoured year by year in faith;
While every rank, bonded in links of trust,
Made our loved Country—where the smiles of Heaven
On Spring-time's buds and Autumn's golden fields
Fell in rich benediction—blest and great.

GODEFRIDUS.

THE dappled kine that graze the herbage brown,
And chew the scantly-honied clover flower,
And whisk the teasing flies from hour to hour,
While in the distance looms the murky Town
Wearing a haze of purple heat for crown,
And livid lands look heavenward for the shower,—
These are not sights to stir the heart with power
Or cheat the wrinkled forehead of a frown:—
But I, who long have ceased to seek the Great,
Prize every lesser gift that Nature yields,
And o'er the leaden prospect linger late
Beneath the drowsy elm-trees' dense green shields,
And love the more—perhaps more duly rate—
The homely beauty of my native fields.

JOHN CHARLES EARLE, B.A. Oxon.

✠ Fide et  constantiâ.

AS withereth the primrose by the river,
As fadeth Summer's sun from gliding fountains,
As vanisheth the light-blown bubble ever,
As melteth snow upon the mossey mountains:
So melts, so vanishes, so fades, so withers
The rose, the shine, the bubble, and the snow,
Of praise, pomp, glory, joy (which short life gathers),
Fair praise, vain pomp, sweet glory, brittle joy!
The withèred primrose by the mourning river,
The faded Summer's sun, from weeping fountains,
The light-blown bubble vanishèd for ever,
The molten snow upon the naked mountains,
Are emblems that the treasures we uplay,
Soon wither, vanish, fade, and melt away.

HENRY KING (of Thame), Bishop of Chichester.

PREFACE.

NLY those who have undertaken a Work like the present, mainly based on facts, can realize the amount of personal enquiry and often prolonged research which is involved in collecting the various materials for such a production. Of course I have set forth such information as I myself have gathered, or that with which I have been so kindly supplied by others. Those few persons who declined to afford any assistance may possibly be amongst the first to blame me for being dull, or inaccurate, or imperfect, or prosaic, or partial, or ignorant. So be it; every writer is, of course, open to criticism. I do not court it, but I do not fear it.

My single endeavour has been to give a simple History of the Church—the chief building in a country Town; to group round its chequered history and to interweave with its mutilated memorials, such details of events and records of persons as have sufficed to enable me to systematize such information and complete the present book. In unfolding this History, and setting forth facts, plain-spoken comments on certain deeds done during the Reformation and Great Rebellion will be here and there found,—without which it might have been pointless. I have, however, only said what I meant, and meant what I said. An author who is ashamed of his convictions and afraid of plain-speaking is in serious danger of becoming despicable. It must be frankly admitted that the advice of Terence has not been altogether followed:—

Facile omnes perferre ac pati,
Cum quibus erat cunque una: his sese dedere,
Eorum obsequi studiis, advorsus nemini,
Nunquam præponens se aliis: ita facillime
Sine invidia invenias laudem, et amicos pares.

Some of my remarks may appear partial or severe. Rightly understood, however, they are neither the one nor the other. For it will have been noticed by the watchful that almost every modern treatise regarding the Philosophy of History is now carefully written in the interests of a bald theory of Democracy, easily enough set forth when historical facts are ignored and principles passed by; but inherently and utterly unsound. No system of government can be complete which does not culminate in a legitimate monarchy based on hereditary succession. Let the Head of any State be but the product of Election, and he is, by consequence, only the leader of a party; neither the Father nor representative of the whole people, nor the authoritative Guardian of their rights and liberties.

In popular assemblies the predominance of party becomes unavoidable; so that, even from an utilitarian standing-point, the only practicable counterpoise and compensation for the radical evil of party-rule is to be found in the recognition of an hereditary sovereign whose title is superior to party intrigues.

Modern political writers, however, seem blind to such considerations, and almost universally treat Monarchy as an antiquated but worthless excrescence, to be tolerated for the sake of sentiment, or for the mere avoidance of such strife and turmoil as its abolition would involve. And what is true as regards authority in the State is equally true of Ecclesiastical authority; destroy the latter and the former is found to have been both weakened and placed on an inclined plane. Under the Tudors the Church of England—as the following pages abundantly shew—was first deprived of all relations with its spiritual Head, duly enslaved by Henry VIII. and the State, and then made so impotent by internal factions and divisions that its ancient position and privileges are at length in direct danger of being lost. In the Historical Drama which has been played during the last three centuries, the second act—the disastrous Civil War of the seventeenth century—followed speedily upon the Tudor changes; the Revolution of 1688, as a consequence, succeeded to the Civil War. We are now living on the mere attenuated Christian traditions of the Past—daily squandered and being purposely eliminated from public political life.

The Puritans of 1650, it should be noted, were the legitimate successors of Thomas Cromwell and Hooper, of Bale, Somerset, and Lord Williams, of a previous century; the "dissenting interest" of the present day—both socially and ecclesiastically destructive—is the direct outcome of the Civil War and of the dangerous principles of the subsequent Revolution. Now almost every country-town or village meeting-house is not only a focus of democratic agitation, but both the preachers and presiding authorities of each send Petitions to Parliament for the direct abolition of the Almighty's Name in the work of legislation. The last act of the drama—to judge by popular sentiment—may too soon be played out here. As in France, at the close of the last century, so in England ere long, the final scenes will no doubt end in sedition, disorder, and savagery, possibly in chaos and gloom.

The History of the most obscure place, though it may sometimes commemorate dishonour and degradation, may at the same time serve to present examples of dignity, self-denial, and integrity in the Past, as well as to provide warnings for the Present and Future. So much as to the Philosophy of History. Now as to facts, and my method. The Inscriptions which have been copied from Tombs, as regards the use of capital letters, spelling, and punctuation, as well as the Extracts from Registers and the documents generally, are reproduced as they remain, except where otherwise mentioned.

As regards the Pedigrees, some of them have been supplied by members of the families whose descents are thus set forth; but much use has been made in all of Wills, Memorial Inscriptions, and official entries in Parochial Registers and Family Records. Many of these Pedigrees might have been considerably enlarged by the addition of collateral branches and descendants in the female lines, but a certain limit had to be made in the adoption of such additions.

I have endeavoured to avoid over-burdening the book with foot-notes, except where explanations seemed to be required, or authorities specifically mentioned. Several are appended, and to these it would have been easy enough to have made considerable additions; but where acknowledged facts are being dealt with, detailed references have not been provided.

For courteous answers to enquiries and for information kindly vouchsafed, I am indebted to many. In the first place to His Grace the Duke of Buckingham, G.C.S.I., to the Marquis of Bath, to Lord Mount-Temple, to the late Archdeacon Clerke, to the late Sir W. H. Clerke, and to the late Sir Philip Rose. I am also under obligations to General Sir William Knollys, K.C.B., to the Hon. and Rev. A. Bertie of Albury, and to the Hon. Harold Dillon. Several members of the College of Arms have likewise assisted me with their valued aid, *e.g.*, Mr. Cockayne, Mr. Murray Lane, General de Havilland, and Mr. Charles A. Buckler. The late Colonel J. L. Chester likewise rendered me efficient help. In the Town and neighbourhood of Thame I am specially indebted to several, for trouble taken and facts provided. Firstly, to the Vicar, the Rev. E. B. Corbett, whose courtesy and kindness during my researches have been unvarying. Also to Mr. Wykeham of Tythorpe House, Mr. A. H. Clerke Brown of Kingston Blount, Mr. Henry Birch, Mr. William Parker, Mr. William Lightfoot of the Prebendal House, Mr. Greenwood of Easington Manor; to the Revs. Canon J. H. Ashhurst, Thomas Hayton of Crendon, and John Hempsted of Ickford; to Mr. Whitehouse Griffin of Towersey Manor, to Mr. J. Kirby Hedges of Wallingford Castle, and Mr. Charles Hedges of Newnham Murren House. Also to the President of Magdalene College, to the Warden of New College, and to the President of Corpus Christi College, Oxford; to Canon Estcourt of Leamington, to Canon J. E. Jackson of Leigh Delamere, to Dr. Parker Deane, Q.C., to Miss Cottrell-Dormer of Rousham, to Professor Montagu Burrows and Mr. James Parker of Oxford, the Rev. W. H. Thompson, D.D., Master of Trinity College, Cambridge, to Mr. William Cozens of Bishop's Court, Dorchester, to Canon T. P. Phelps of Ridley, to Mr. Herbert Wakeman of Warminster, to Brother Henry Foley, S.J., to the Rev. A. H. de Romestin of Freeland, the Rev. W. D. Macray of Ducklington, the Rev. Dr. Higgs of Handborough, Miss Mary Custis Lee of Virginia, Mr. Harry Lupton of Stratford-on-Avon, Mr. R. Gibbs of Aylesbury, Mr. E. W. Greenfield of Southampton, to Mrs. Francklin of Westlington House, to Mr. Richard Rose of Aylesbury, and to several others. My son, Mr. Ambrose de Lisle Lee, has rendered me efficient help with his pencil, and my daughter has given me constant aid in carrying the Work through the press. Messrs. Mitchell and Hughes, the Printers and Publishers, deserve my best acknowledgments for the care taken in their part of the Work; and Mr. Clarke Irons and Mr. Barton, as Engravers on Wood, have also aided me.

I am sincerely grateful to all.

F. G. L.

ALL SAINTS' VICARAGE, LAMBETH.

May, 1883.

TABLE OF CONTENTS.

Chapter the Fourth.

The Cistercian Abbey of Thame Park, and its Chartulary; with some account of the Grammar School of Lord Williams of Thame.

Chapter the Fifth.

The Town of Thame and its Inhabitants.

Appendices.

LIST OF FULL-PAGE ILLUSTRATIONS.

LIST OF WOODCUTS.

ℭ HISTORY AND ANTIQUITIES

of the Prebendal Church of the Blessed Virgin Mary of Thame.

CHAPTER THE FIRST.

The Church, its History and Antiquities.

HE market town of Thame, in the County and Diocese of Oxford, is situated thirteen miles east of Oxford, about forty-four and a half miles, in a north-westerly direction, from London; and comprises the townships of Old Thame, New Thame, and Priest End (which make up the town itself), together with Moreton, North Weston, and Thame Park. It stands in a pleasant country, on a gentle declivity upon the eastern bank of the river Tame or Thame. This stream, rising beside the Buckinghamshire hills, at no great distance from Stewkley and Whitchurch, is joined near Quarrendon and Nether Winchendon by other streams from Long Marston and Hulcott, and lower down by another from Aston Moleyns and Haddenham. At Thame it divides Oxfordshire from Buckinghamshire for a few miles, and so winding its way westwards, through Shabbington, Waterperry, and Waterstock, and southwards through Wheatley, Chiswelhampton, and Drayton, joins the Cherwell and the Isis (flowing together from Oxford) at Dorchester, and there and thus becomes the Thames.

The town of Thame is believed, though on somewhat scanty evidence, to have been of Roman origin. It is certainly a fact, however, that several Roman coins, specimens of pottery and metal-work, have from time to time been discovered in the neighbourhood;* and there can be little doubt that a military road was made to go through the place at an early period, and so gave it a certain importance, though this characteristic declined during the later years of our island's Roman occupation.

In 1821 the population of the town amounted to 2479; during the next half century, that is in 1871, it had risen to 3229; while at the Census of 1881 it had only slightly increased, then consisting exactly of 3267 souls. In earlier periods, prior to the Tudor changes, Thame cannot have been otherwise than a town of considerable importance,† for its sacred edifices give abundant evidence of this,—the Parish Church at the northern end, and the once grand, but now utterly destroyed, monastic Church of the Abbey of Thame Park, at the south-western portion of the parish, harmonizing with an official record made during the episcopate of Henry Beaufort, Bishop of Lincoln A.D. 1401, viz. that in Thame, during his day, there were no less than "a thousand and three hundred houselling-folk,"

---

* A golden coin of the Emperor Honorius was found about forty years ago upon the property of the late Mr. Harry Lupton; and the Author possesses a small collection of Roman coins which from time to time have been dug up in the neighbourhood.

† Thame itself had its Parish Church; inhabitants living near the south-east part of the town could attend divine service at the Chapel near the Abbey gateway in Thame Park; and there were also Chapels at North Weston and Moreton, as well as a daily offering of the Christian Sacrifice at the Chapel of the Prebendal House.

B

i.e. those who received the Sacrament at least every Easter. Many persons of rank and family unquestionably resided there during the fourteenth, fifteenth, and sixteenth centuries—their presence of course directly benefiting the inhabitants.

The town itself consists mainly of one long, broad, and spacious street, having a slightly foreign appearance, with other streets to the north and east. Several of the old gabled houses have been removed or altered, though many remain. The Market-place, in the centre of the town, was once far more picturesque* than it is now. Its public Well has long been closed. The ditch and water-course on either side of the street, over which here and there were planks and hand-rails, with at intervals an oil lamp or lantern placed at the head of a pole, are all gone. So, too, are the trees, planted in rows, which here and there protected some of the houses of the gentlefolk. Originally the upper part of the Town Hall, supported on pillars of oak, consisted of timber and pargetting, effectively arranged and constructed; but many changes have been made in it, and Common-place has long ago stamped upon it an indelible impression. For the character and vigour so generally displayed in ancient buildings are too frequently wanting in a majority of those of recent date. The trade of the town still depends greatly on agriculture. Old families of the rank of yeomen, of which in the seventeenth century there were many; gentle people of moderate estates, living on their own property, and the heirs of popular squires of the last century, have, to a great extent, passed to other places, secured higher rank, sunk into poverty and obscurity, emigrated, or become extinct. These changes, however, are common everywhere, and are not peculiar to Thame or its neighbourhood.

The Parish Church, dedicated to God, in honour of the Blessed Virgin Mary, stands at the extreme north end of the town, and at no great distance from the bridge over the river Thame, which there separates the county of Oxford from that of Bucks. The ground upon which this house of prayer was erected no doubt formed a slight and suitable eminence naturally, but the interments in the churchyard, during many centuries, have raised it considerably, more especially on its southern side, so that there is a notable descent on entering the church by the south porch, while at that door, now bricked up, by which the south transept was originally entered from the west, the descent was greater.

The building, of different styles of pointed or Christian architecture, from whatever aspect or standing-point it may be surveyed or examined, is seen to be thoughtfully and artfully planned, remarkably well proportioned, dignified and effective in all its ancient details, forming a notable feature in the landscape. It can be seen from Cuddesdon on the one hand to Cuddington on the other; while, from the Chiltern Hills, its massive and striking tower serves to enable those who contemplate the varied natural beauties of Oxfordshire and Buckinghamshire—taking in at a single glance the vale of Aylesbury, with the slopes of Whitchurch beyond, to the hill of Shotover—to distinguish the exact position of the town of Thame, flanked on the north by the hills of Crendon, Chilton, and Brill.

The church, to describe it generally, is a cruciform building—a hundred and fifty-one feet and a half long, and fifty-four feet broad, inclusive of its aisles*—consisting of chancel, clerestoried nave, north and south transepts, north and south aisles, with a lofty and well-proportioned tower† in the centre, a chantry chapel to the east of the south transept, a south porch, groined in stone and having stone sediles on either side, with a parvise over it, a small, modern, ill-designed vestry to the north of the north aisle, and a room or loft,‡ one on either side, over both the north and south transepts. That over the latter was originally known as "the almery," more recently as the "old vestry." In the chancel there is a low first-pointed archway and priests' door on the north side: opposite to this, though hidden by the panelling, is another door thus concealed, leading by a stone staircase to the almery alluded to. On the east side of the north transept is a third door, now blocked up, which led anciently both to the rood-loft, to the vestry over the transept, to the ringing chamber in the tower, to the leads, and to the belfry. The doorway, up above, by which the rood-loft was directly entered, is now stopped up. There is a separate external entrance to this north transept in its north wall. Until within the last twenty years the south transept was entered from without by a door on its western side, but this likewise has been blocked up in order

* There exists an old engraving of the Market-place, which was issued in 1745, in which the ornamental paragetting-work is very distinctly shewn.

* Measured within the walls, the length of the nave is 64 feet, and, including the tower, measured east and west, 96 feet. The width of the church across the aisles is 54 feet 8 inches; across the transepts, 72 feet. Its total length within being 151 feet 6 inches. The east end of the chancel, however, is not perfectly rectangular.

† At the recent Government Survey it was found that the Church Tower measured from the ground at the door of the belfry turret to the top of the battlement exactly ninety-two and a half feet, and ninety-five feet from the floor of the church.

‡ Though these were repaired and largely reconstructed during the sixteenth century, it is clear from the Churchwardens' "Accounts" that there were similar rooms existing and in use over the two transepts for keeping the vestments and ornaments of the church in the fifteenth century.

that a warming apparatus with its internal chimney—a construction in brick, compo, and cast-iron, perfectly hideous—might be built. This is a sore and great disfigurement to the church, and, in its present position and form, ought never to have been erected.

It is, of course, quite impossible to determine when Christianity was first introduced into this part of the country. There can be little doubt, however, that the influence of St. Birinus, first Bishop of Dorchester, a city only sixteen miles from Thame, was directly felt here. Thirty-seven years after the mission of our holy Apostle of England, St. Augustine, that is about the year A.D. 634, Birinus, a Benedictine monk, was consecrated Bishop at Genoa, by Asterius, Bishop of Milan, and soon afterwards came hither to continue the good work already begun by others. Here, in this part of the country, as one important and direct result, Cynegils, King of the West Saxons, was baptized, many of his subjects following him in submission to the dominion of the Gospel; here, too, by the devotion of Birinus, Oswald, a pious King of the Northumbrians, took the newly-baptized monarch under his protection, and the two regal authorities, in thanksgiving for grace thus bestowed, founded this ancient See—*Sedes Dorecastrensis*.* As the Venerable Bede has put on record, Birinus planted Christianity in all the adjacent parts, and built many churches. It is also related that about three centuries and more afterwards, Thame actually formed a part of the diocese of Dorchester. Here, it is on record in the *Saxon Chronicle*, lived Oskytel, sometime Bishop of that See (consecrated A.D. 950), but afterwards, in A.D. 958, translated to York; and here, on All Saints' Day A.D. 971, "in his mansion house at Thame," he is said to have departed to his rest.* It is highly improbable, therefore—notwithstanding the devastations which the Danes had made throughout the whole of this part of the country in the previous century—that no church then existed in Thame. It may not even have been of stone, but merely of timber, mortar, and rubble: rough, simple, without architectural characteristics, but still it may be reasonably concluded that there was some building in which the sacrament of regeneration was administered, where the chrism was drawn on the foreheads of the

* The following valuable account of this bishopric is from the pen of Mr. Freeman, the historian, of Somerleaze:—

Dorchester, in Oxfordshire, has been at different times the seat of two distinct bishoprics, the one West Saxon, the other Mercian.

The first bishopric of Dorchester was that which began under Birinus in 634. Dorchester was then a central point of the West Saxon dominions, which spread a long way north of the Thames, while it did not stretch nearly so far westward as it did afterwards.

This diocese lasted till the division of 705. Dorchester then ceased to be an episcopal see (the see was removed by Headda to Winchester), and it did not become one again till late in the ninth century. Then Mercia had long reached to the Thames, and Dorchester became the seat of that Mercian diocese whose seat was removed by Remigius to Lincoln.

In A.D. 705, the one West Saxon diocese, whatever may have been its previous boundaries to the west and north, was divided between Winchester and Shirburn.

A.D. 777. In about seventy years after the removal of the see to Winchester, Dorchester became part of Mercia, being absorbed into the rising power of the great King Offa.

A.D. 870. When Leicester was taken by the Danes, Dorchester became the seat of an united bishopric, *i.e.* of Dorchester, Leicester, and Lindsey.

From A.D. 869 to 897, we find Aldheard Bishop of Dorchester; he died, with many other Saxon nobles, after the Danish invasion of that year.

A.D. 909. Ceolwulf was consecrated bishop.

A.D. 926-934. The name of Winsey occurs in charters.

A.D. 950. Oskytel was consecrated Bishop of Dorchester, and in 956 translated to the see of York.

A.D. 974. In this year the name of Leofwyn, Bishop of Dorchester, occurs in a charter of King Edgar to the Monastery of Malmesbury.

A.D. 975. That of Eadnoth I.

A.D. 979-1002. That of Escwy. In 992 all the ships of war were gathered together at London to resist the Danes. The King committed the forces to the leading of Elfrid the Ealdorman, and of Thorold the Earl, of Bishop Elfstan of London, and of Bishop Escwy of Dorchester.

It is his effigy which is supposed to be in the south aisle, in episcopal robes, though executed at a much later date.

A.D. 1002-1005, occurs the name of Bp. Alfhelm.

A.D. 1006-1016. That of Eadnoth II.

When Archbishop Elphege of Canterbury was murdered by the Danes, it was Bishop Eadnoth who aided Bishop Ælfhun of London in removing the body to London, and having it buried with all reverence in St. Paul's minster.

Bishop Eadnoth was slain at Assingdon in Essex, in the battle fought between King Edmund Ironside and Canute.

A.D. 1016-1034. He was succeeded by Bishop Ethelric.

A.D. 1034-1049. He was succeeded by a third Bishop Eadnoth, a man so renowned for his piety as to be called the Good Bishop. He is recorded to have rebuilt the minster at Stow, in Lincolnshire, for the use of the northern diocese, after the Byzantine or apsidal form.

This Church of St. Mary of Stow and the Abbey of Ramsay, erected in 969, are said to be the only examples known of the Greek cruciform style. But it is highly probable that the minster of Dorchester, which the requirements of the united sees must have called for, formed a third; and that the nave with the transepts, traces of which are still extant, is part of the original building.

Bishop Eadnoth died in 1049, and was buried at his minster in Dorchester.

A.D. 1049. King Edward gave the bishopric at his death to Ulf, his priest, a most unworthy successor of Eadnoth. He sided with Earl Godwin in his rebellion against the King, and fled with Archbishop Rodbert. He narrowly escaped degradation by Pope Leo IX. Ulf had come to England with Emma, wife of King Ethelred, who afterwards married Canute.

A.D. 1053. Wulfwig obtained the bishopric while Ulf was yet living.

A.D. 1067. He died, and was buried at Dorchester.

A.D. 1067. Remigius, his successor, owed his appointment to his offering of a single ship and twenty knights at the time when William was fitting out his fleet to invade England. He was then almoner to the house of Fécamp, in Normandy.

A.D. 1085. The seat of the see of Mercia was transferred to Lincoln, of which Remigius became the first bishop, by virtue of a decree of a council held under Archbishop Lanfranc (A.D. 1075).

* "Anno 970, Oskytel, Archbishop of York, who like his predecessor Wulstan had been translated from his see of Dorchester, resided now at Tame in this county, and dying there on All Saints' Day was buried at Bedford by his cousin Turketil, Abbot of that place."—Kennet's *Parochial Antiquities*, p. 43. Oxford: 1695.

baptized, and where the Christian sacrifice was duly offered with solemnity and devotion. And no doubt such sacred sanctuary stood where the present church stands.

No traces, however, even of Norman architecture remain visible in Thame Church. The most ancient style existing is first-pointed. But when the old church of Tettesworth was taken down, about forty years ago, it was found that in the lower part of the north-west corner there were distinct and evident remains of Anglo-Saxon masonry. Moreover, there can be no doubt that the churches at Tettesworth and Towersey,* and possibly that of St. James at North Weston (now destroyed), were originally of Norman character, probably built in the eleventh century. If then these three daughter chapelries of Thame Church were thus substantial buildings of stone at that period—buildings on which the masons' and carvers' arts had been employed, traces of which still remain—may it not be reasonably concluded that upon the sacred site of the present church there had always been a suitable and worthy sanctuary of the Most High, even from the days of Birinus of Dorchester, or his more immediate successors?

For Thame is thought by some to be the Roman station "Thamesis," and it is known that under King Edward the Elder, A.D. 921, it was a fortified place, for the Danes, taking their way thither from Huntingdon, laid siege to it, were successful in their assault, massacred many of the people, and partly destroyed the fortifications, though King Edward, as it is chronicled, soon afterwards triumphantly reversed the defeat.†

But to proceed. Under King Henry I. several examples of Christian zeal and munificence are on record, and many events serve to shew that amid the wars and turbulence of that period, the progress of the Church of God was, on the whole, onwards and forwards. St. Anselm in 1103 had firmly and successfully opposed the King in the interest of the Church's freedom (for it was impossible that the bishops should receive investiture from the monarch, as the King desired, though their "act of homage" may have been reasonably due); and Anselm's saintly influence remained potent with those still on earth long after his soul had passed to rest. The see of Ely, in the Eastern Fens, was founded in 1108, and that of Bangor was filled up twelve years afterwards, having been vacant no less than eleven years. The see of Carlisle was founded in the spring of 1132, and Adelulph, its first occupant, consecrated at York by Archbishop Thurstan in the autumn of the following year. Again, clerical discipline was improved, owing to the beneficial influence of the Synods of London held in 1125 and 1129, and several grave scandals and painful disorders were consequently remedied. Many of the prelates—men of principle and renown—were zealous, active, and influential; so that, under their guidance, the blessings and influence of *true* Religion were extended, faith was deepened, and charity abounded. Many religious houses were either founded or enlarged, and these became a permanent advantage to the various localities in which they had been established. Their size and dignity, their beauty of design, completeness of plan, and splendour, as regards everything relating to the worship of God and the well-being of the community, were remarkable, and exercised due influence.

Amongst those called to rule the Church at this period was Alexander, Bishop of Lincoln, known as "the munificent," who succeeded Robert Bluett in that see, and was consecrated at Canterbury 22 July, 1123, by William de Corbeuil and four other prelates, and who died in 1148. He is said to have been educated at Oxford, and thus may there have learnt something of the needs of the town and neighbourhood of Thame. At all events, after his consecration he soon shewed his interest in the monks of Ottley-on-Otmoor by giving up to them his ancient Park at Thame—an official possession of his see, when their own unfinished House was found to have been planted in so low, damp, and unfavourable a locality as that first selected on the sedgy and unhealthy Oxfordshire moors.

These monks were Cistercians—so called from Citeaux or *Cistertium* in Burgundy, within the diocese of Châlons—a branch of the ancient and venerable Benedictine Order. They began their pious labours by observing a stricter rule than had then been customary, in fact they aimed at following the exact enactment of their wise and saintly founder. An Englishman, Stephen Harding, a monk of Sherborne Abbey, had already led the way in zeal, self-denial, and devotion, and subsequently became the third Abbot of Citeaux. The popularity with which these changes for the better were viewed and regarded in England led that devoted prelate William Giffard, Bishop of Winchester, to found a monastery at Waverley in Surrey. The work was commenced in the Name of the Blessed Trinity, and the foundations were solemnly laid on 24 November, 1128.* This house, like all others of the Order,

* The piscina still existing in the church of Towersey, to the south of the sanctuary, and which is represented on a later page, was no doubt carved and put up in the reign of King Stephen *circa* 1140.

† It is conjectured that the White-Lead Cross, near Prince's Risborough, was made as a memorial of some victory by King Edward the Elder over his enemies.

* "1128. Hoc anno fundata est Abbatia de Waverleia a domino Willelmo Giffard, Episcopo Wintoniensi VIII. Kal. Decembris. Et ipse episcopus eodem anno obiit, et Henricus Blesensis successit.

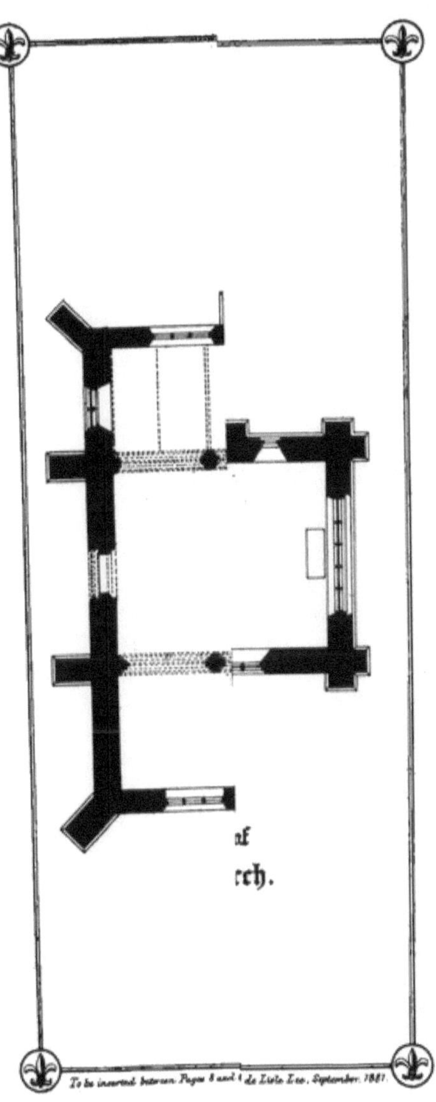

To be inserted between Pages 8 and 9 de Lisle Leo, September 1881.

was placed under the powerful patronage of the Blessed Virgin. In due course twelve monks were brought from the Abbey of Aumone (*Elemosina*) in Normandy to occupy it; and three years later, under similar invocation, Tintern Abbey in South Wales was founded.

From Waverley were set up the House of Garendon in Leicestershire, founded in 1133; Ford Abbey, in the county of Devon, founded three years afterwards; Combe in Warwickshire, about the same time; and the Abbey of Thame Park likewise.

Further particulars concerning the history of this sacred house of prayer will be given later on: its rise and fall will be then briefly sketched, while the present condition of that portion of the building still remaining will be carefully described. Here it is only necessary to set forth exactly at what period the Town became so directly benefited by the establishment of so magnificent an Abbey, with all its spiritual blessings and temporal advantages. Those prelates and pastors of the Church of God who then bore rule in England—and the Bishop of Lincoln was amongst the most notable—were obviously earnest and zealous, as well for their Master's honour and glory as for the advantage and behoof of the flocks committed to their keeping. They had the fear of God in their minds, and the love of God in their hearts. All this is recorded in the deeds they did, and the benefits, both spiritual and temporal, they conferred on their fellows. They made roads and built bridges; they taught their flocks a pure faith and good manners; they stood forward as arbiters between the weak and the strong; as occasion arose, they rebuked the arrogant and withstood the tyrannical, while they jealously protected the outcast, poor, and friendless.

The present church* was built during the reign of Henry III., in or about the year 1241, under the patronage and with the efficient aid of Robert Grostête, Bishop of Lincoln,† who was a most remarkable and distinguished prelate, notable alike for his personal influence, zeal, and devotion. The churches of Aylesbury, Crendon, Monk's Risborough, Haddenham, and Great Milton were probably either altogether rebuilt, or substantially altered, under his beneficial rule; at all events, it is known that both Aylesbury and Thame Churches were then attached to Prebends in Lincoln Minster,—dignities which were terminated three centuries afterwards under the imperious personal domination of the Tudors. The ground plans of the churches of Aylesbury and Thame are very much alike. Each has a broad nave, narrow aisles, short transepts, a lantern tower, and a deep long chancel.* Moreover, the mouldings and architectural details and characteristics of the oldest work in each when carefully examined are often found to be the same. In both churches several alterations and additions have been made from time to time, but the special features referred to, if carefully sought after, still remain and can be seen.

In the chancel of Thame Church,—which, with the western side of the north transept and the south porch, is the oldest part of the building,†—the four lancet windows on the north side still remain as when inserted, under Bishop Grostête, in the thirteenth century. No doubt there was originally a triplet of similar windows (after the plan of those in the eastern wall of the chapel of the Prebendal House) at the east end of the choir. The first-pointed window of three lights at the western part of the north wall of the chancel, having three well-designed quatrefoils in its head, was possibly inserted about the year 1258. Its design and mouldings are admirable. Next in point of antiquity comes the present early second-pointed east window of the chancel. This, which is of five plain well-proportioned lights, without cuspings, has a large circle in the head, divided somewhat quaintly and originally by one horizontal and two perpendicular mullions; and there are two well-moulded quatrefoils within plain circles—one on either side of the large circle, but below it. The window is placed somewhat high up in the wall, under a first-pointed hood-moulding, and is in itself severe, original, and effective. It was, no doubt, designed by some cleric of

frater Regis Stephani, qui fuit abbas apud Glastoniam. Et Iohannes, primus abbas Waverleiæ, qui venit cum conventu, hoc anno mortuus est apud Midehurst, rediens a capitale. Successit Gilbertus abbas II. Obiit Ranulphus, Dunelmensis episcopus."—*Annales Monasterii de Waverleia* (MSS. Cotton, Brit. Museum, A. xvj.).

* The author is indebted to the courtesy of Mr. William Moss, of the Old Palace, Lincoln, for the following information:—"There are no Registers in this Registry of the date of Bishop Alexander; and the Registers of Bishop Grostête do not contain the documents and information you are seeking:" viz., the deed of consecration, or an official transcript of it, and the deed elevating the Church to the dignity of a Prebendal Church.

† Robert Grostête was consecrated at Reading on 17 June 1235, by St. Edmund [Rich, Archbishop] of Canterbury, assisted by Roger Niger, Bishop of London; Jocelyn Troteman, Bishop of Bath; Robert Bingham, Bishop of Salisbury; Hugh Norwold, Bishop of Ely; and Ralph [of Maidstone], Bishop of Hereford. The following occurs in *Annales de Oseneia*:—"MCCXXXV. Obiit Hugo secundus Lincolniensis episcopus mense Februarii; et electus est Robertus Grossetete, *vir bene morigeratus et magnæ literaturæ*, in Episcopum Lincolniensem ad annunciationem Sanctæ Mariæ, et consecratus est sequenti die Sanctæ Trinitatis."—*Annales Monastici*, vol. iv., p. 82. London: 1869.

* In some respects, likewise, the church of Crendon is of the same character. There are certain architectural features in Great Milton Church, too, which indicate its old connection with Lincoln, Aylesbury, and Thame. For the skill and ability of the Lincoln masons—evidently experienced architects—were known throughout the whole diocese.

† Mr. John Henry Parker, C.B., Keeper of the Ashmolean Museum, informed me that in his judgment the choir of Thame Church was erected between 1200 and 1275, the nave and aisles between 1325 and 1375, and the tower and transepts between 1425 and 1515.

Lincoln, and carried out by skilled artificers of that city, under direct ecclesiastical authority. For, in that day, the clergy were foremost in the arts, and often very accomplished. In all substantial structural changes direct sanction was almost invariably sought for, and, after examination and approval, formally given.

Twenty years later, in the reign of Edward III., considerable alterations were made to the sacred edifice, more especially by the insertion of three new windows on the south side of the choir, in lieu of those of the first-pointed style. These windows—each of three lights with flowing tracery in the head, though not at all original in their design, yet well proportioned, pleasing, and effective—were most probably inserted about the year 1358, at a period when Edward the Black Prince was so distinguishing himself in France. About the same time, or possibly a little earlier, the north aisle received substantial restoration; second-pointed windows of a somewhat similar character being likewise there inserted. Perhaps at this period that aisle was entirely rebuilt. The windows on the opposite side, in the south aisle, each consisting of three lights, with a sexfoil in a circle in the head, and with very graceful and flowing tracery on either side, were obviously designed with skill and freedom, and were probably inserted early in the reign of King Richard II., about the year 1378. Their design, as regards this tracery, is somewhat peculiar, possibly unique. The accompanying woodcut faithfully represents one of these windows.

Window in the South Aisle.

Some persons believe that they were planned to receive a series of special subjects in stained glass. Anyhow, when a watercourse close to the fabric was being repaired about the year 1839, several fragments of rich stained glass, very much destroyed, were found buried in the earth; so that these windows, whether under the Tudors or the Usurper, were probably broken from within. The pillars of the nave—and it may be the arches they bear, though these own second-pointed features—are possibly coeval with the church as built on its present ground-plan in the thirteenth century; but the clerestory and its windows above are of a later date—erected, no doubt, in the early part of the fifteenth century, under Henry IV., about 1404, when the upper portions of the tower were added to that which very probably carried originally only a small spire, and when the chantry of St. Bartholomew was thrown out eastwards of the south transept. These additions served to alter greatly the character of the building. In the first-pointed church there was probably a very high-pitched roof, and no clerestory, or one of narrow lancet lights in couplets or triplets; and it is obvious that the four substantial piers which carry the tower were efficiently strengthened, and entirely re-cased with ashlar at the time these additions were made. Possibly it may have been then rebuilt from the base of its lantern storey.

About the same period, as some maintain, or it may be twenty or twenty-five years earlier, the south porch had been repaired, new windows inserted, and the room above it reconstructed, or at least considerably altered. The external crown or coping of the stone staircase—which leads to this parvise by a door from the interior of the building on the western side of the porch, and close to where the font originally stood—is of excellent second-pointed work. At the present time this place, with its dilapidated fire-place, rough walls, and uneven floor, is unquestionably in a scandalous state of decay and neglect. The buttresses at the angles of the porch are solid, yet graceful, the caps being particularly so; and its general effect exceedingly pleasing. It harmonizes completely both as regards position, proportion, and general architectural character with the adjoining parts of the fabric. Immediately over the external door a tabernacle or niche in stone remains, which once contained an image of the Blessed Virgin, holding Her Divine Child in the act of imparting a blessing. This was partly destroyed in Edward VI.'s time, for the heads of the figures were then knocked off; and its destruction was completed during the Usurpation of Cromwell and the disastrous Civil Wars, by which Thame and its neighbourhood were specially cursed.

It may be asked, "What is a parvise? To what uses were this place put in the times that are gone?" Such questions may thus be answered. The parvise of a church was no doubt originally used for various purposes. Sometimes it was the residence of the custodian—*Custos Ecclesiæ*—an office occasionally endowed; sometimes the Sacrist or Sacristan, not residing there, made use of it for the work of his office. Herein, it may be, the sacred vessels and precious MS. Service books were often kept, when there was no Treasury or other dry and secure place in the church: and here the fire was probably lighted by which the thuribles were kindled for use during the more solemn ceremonies of divine service. Sometimes an Anchorite or "*Inclusus*,"* as he was technically termed, inhabited the parvise; if a layman, officiating as custodian of the church in general, or of some chantry-chapel, shrine, or image in particular; if a priest, saying mass daily, possibly at some specially privileged or indulgenced altar. Here, too—unless there were special aumbries for them—would be preserved all things necessary for the due celebration of the sacraments and rites of the church, the sacred chrism, the oil for anointing the sick; the altar-breads, the wine, and the various sacred vessels for the same.

Under two energetic churchwardens, John Manyturn and Thomas Bunce or Buns, a very important reconstruction of the north transept was commenced in the reign of Henry VI., A.D. 1442. The ability, forethought, and good taste displayed by them in their undertaking can be very accurately gathered from the records of the proceedings, and are not devoid of interest. These officials appear to have not only planned the needful reparation and desirable improvements, but to have gathered money from the townspeople and others to defray the costs.

The actual list of donations being in existence, has been carefully copied, and is here inserted. To some it may appear a mere batch of uninteresting names. Others, however, may hold it to be worthy of preservation and reproduction.

Receyt.

The yer of howr lorde a m cccc xliiij yere the viij day of Julius y Jo' manyturne & Tomas bonste Schyrcheche Wardeyngs of the new towne of tame We haue reseyvede to the Werke of the norte ele.

	s.	d.
of Io' tayler		vj
halson mulschofe		ij
haneys Klerke	xviij &	iiij
Rycharde Karlese		xij
Jon' Golde		viij
Jon' godyndon		iiij
Jon' Powlyn		iiij
Jon' doddeley		iiij

	s.	d.
Tomas prymens'		xij
Jon' dowge		iiij
harry dorel		vj
Jon' polglas		iiij
Jon' botte		xij
Tomas Wellys	vj	viij
Tomas lukenore		xij
Tomas flyote		vj
Jon' haywarde		iiij
Tomas Sadelere		iiij
felyppe barbere		xii
Harry Spe'sere	ij	
Jon' mexbery		xii
Hysbel flyote		iiij
Wyllya' lukenore	ij	
Jon' benet	ij	
Jon' chapman		xx
Tomas felde		viij
Jon' towers		ij
halyson beschope		xviij
Tomas horner		viij
Jon' buske		xij
Wyllya' Walschefe	ij	
Tomas Worschepe		viij
Jon' kyng		xij
Roseber dyere		iiij
Wyllya' prentyse		vj
Jon' browne		xx
Wyllya' benet		xij
Jon' trewe		xx
Hew benet	xij	
Jon' bascheby		vj
Harry baker	ij	
Jon' rossel	vj	
Jon' Elys	xij	
Jon' sowe*		xij
Jon' belle		xx
Rychard myngge		viij
Hew Powlyn		iiij
Roberde bam'eto'		viij
Roberde velledew		iiij
Reddeward babbot		xij
Benet krosvale		iiij
Jon' Stretzley		iiij
Beruyrte lukenore		iiij
Gylys Jaket		iiij
Jon' morche		iiij
Tomas bolte		viij
Wyllya' tan'er		vj
Perse wefer		xvj
Thomas baker	ij	
Jon' Pers		iiij
Rycharde derby		iiij
Hemu'de carelese		iij
Thomas longg	ij	viij
Rycharde botelere		xij
Tomas turnepase	ij	
and of money that was y^s a house xvj^d thereof we haue reseyued x^s vj^d ys behy'de of the same tomas.		
Tomas bonste	vj	viij
Jon' borcher		viij

* The Anchorite or "*Inclusus*" differed from the Hermit. The former never left his cell or enclosed-limit: the latter was free to travel hither and thither, often lighting travellers over a ford or across a ferry; and sometimes he was engaged in collecting alms from wayfarers to maintain and repair some bridge, highway, or wayside shrine or chapel. There was anciently a Hermitage at Tetsworth—traditions concerning which are not even now altogether lost.

	s.	d.
Nekol mersche		xij
helsever Jake		viij
Hew grene		xx
Harry Peynter		
Kat'ne Sadeler		viij
Jon' Wyttelefe		viij
Jon' skyn'er		xvj
Jon' derley		iiij
Wyllys' kosyn		viij
Rycharde barbor		xx
Rycharde boyse		viij
Rychard hesy		xx
Rychard gylbard		xij
han'yse karp'nter		ij
Jon' Walshefe		iiij
Perse mapuld'ra'	iij	ij
Jone Warborow		ij
Rychard lokema'		vj
Wyllys' Kowper		xx
Thomas halle	vi	viij
Rocher boches		vi
Jone tebarde and Jone lokeyer		iiij
Robert Smyrth		vi
Rychard tayler		vi
Wyllys' Bate	xiij	iv
Maystyr Jon' appulto'	vi	viij
Jon' tamworth		iiij
Jon' mesbery the beldyr		vi
Jon' halyday		iiij
Ser Wyllym ye preste	iij	iv
Rychard hydnemere		ij
Jon' Bo'ke		iiij
Rychard skyn'er		ij
Nykol' of Sedon'		iiij
Nykol' Fowler		
Tomas Merston		ij
Tomas nefel		ij
Jon' Taylar		i
Tomas tan'er		xij
Rychard sandon		iiij
Wyllys' frogmore		viij
Nykol' beddyn		iiij

The churchwardens already named, themselves acted as architects. In the neighbouring Abbeys of Thame Park and Notley—buildings of great magnificence—architecture was evidently not unstudied; and it may have been under the tuition of some accomplished religious—the "Custodian of the Fabric"—or the celebrated Lincoln masons, or some member of the Minster Chapter who devoted himself to architecture, that these church officers of a country town acquired so sound a taste. They appear to have gone off to Teynton, beyond Burford, for stone of the best quality and the choicest grain, and to Headington and Crendon for ordinary stone; to adjoining parks to select, mark, and buy the needful timber; and to have gathered the best and most skilful carvers, masons, and carpenters from the neighbouring towns and villages round about. John East, from Finchhampstead, constructed the new roof; a skilled mason came from Cadmer End to carve the more delicate mouldings; labourers came from Iekeford; plumbers from Abingdon and Wycombe. Already, a competent artist in window-construction, Mason by name, had drawn the plans and mouldings, and had made wooden models—"modys" they are termed—from which the hewers and carvers were to work. Beckley of Headington supplied stone for the walls and buttresses, but appears to have died during the progress of the work, and then his widow continued to send cartload after cartload to Thame for its completion. Laurence, Warren, Sharpe, and Walkeleyne, all masons, were the chief local workmen who executed these restorations. They first removed the original roof, the dignified and effective pitch of which can be known from the weather-moulding still remaining on the tower; then the north gable wall was taken down, with its triplet of first-pointed windows; then the new wall rose steadily with the new grand north window of five lights,—an admirable example of early third-pointed work inserted in their place.* The wall completed, the gable finished, the side walls "rered" or heightened, and the loft above in due course erected, they left the work complete. The cost of all this amounted exactly to £28 : 15 : 3—a sum equivalent to about £320 at the present day.

The following Extracts from the Churchwardens' "Accounts" will throw some further light on the work then accomplished :—

(A.D. 1443.) Hn ex expensys of ye sam yere.

	s.	d.
ffor ij lods of stone fro' hedyndon to Jon' machel of remborow	ij	ij
Wyllys' hallered for ij quarter of lyme and vj boschel	iij	iiij
the weke aftyr syntemaryday Jon' mas'n and rychard scharpe v dayys	v	
a laborar Jon' Walkeleyne v dayys	ij	i
Jon' Mason and rychard scharpe vi dayys	vj	v
Harry Stokys vi dayys	ij	vj
Tomas Knygtewyn for ii lods of sonde		iij
Jon' mason and rychard scharpe iij dayys	iij	
Jon' Walkeleyne iij dayys		xij
halleso for sawyng of ccc fote and a halfe of borde	iiij	iiij
ffor ij lods of stone from hedyndon to Jon' borne of Yckeford	ii	iv
Rychard lavender for ij lods from hedyndon	ij	vi
hallered for a quarter of lyme		xvj
Jon' Kyng for one lode from hedyndon		xij
Rychard lavender ij lods from hedyndon	ij	vj

* It is probable, looking to its design and mouldings, that a window on the east side, over the altar of the Blessed Trinity, had been inserted about twenty years earlier, *circa* 1420. This window, which had been several times repaired, was blown in and destroyed by a serious gale in the early part of the present century, but re-erected, as it had stood, by the advice of the Rev. Henry Quartley, who represented the Visitor.

	s.	d.
Harry pede of weston for a lode		xiiij
Jon' borne ij lods from bedyndon	ij	iiij
Gone uppe* for vij boschel of lyme		vij
Jon' mason and rychard scharp v days	v	
Harry stoke vj days	ij	
Jon' yreche v dayys		xx
Jon' mason and rychard schape vi days	vj	
Jon' yreche vj days	ij	
Jon' borne a lode from bedeyndon		xiiij
ffor a barre to yᵉ wyndow yn yᵉ gabul a bore, to tomas smygth		viij
Jon' Mason ii days	ij	
Wyllyam ballerede for xix boschel lyme	ij	iij
Jon' borne a lode from bedyndon		xiij
Jon' Mason ii days		xij
Jon' borne ii lods from bedyndon	ii	iv
Jon' mason iii days and halfe		xv
Jon' yresche i day and a halfe		vj
Wyllyam ballered iv quarter lyme	iiij	iiij
To make klene the rodeseler* yn vyse and vernesche	iij	
Tomas yresche fo' caryage of iii lods sonde		iij

Here occurs a record, omitted, of the ordinary Church expenses chiefly relating to waxlights.

	s.	d.
Jon' mason and Jon' stowe iij days	iij	vi
Jon' Polglas ij days and a halfe		x
Jon' mason a weke	iij	iv
Jon' Polglas ij days		viij
* * * * * *		*
Jon' mason a weke	iij	
Jon' Polglas i day		iiij
Jon' Plommer of habyndon, to make yᵉ pypys of yᵉ nory* ele and hele yᵉ fyse	iij	iiij
And sowdyr vᴵᴵ and a halfe		xvj
Wyllyam Plommer of Wykombe for lede that weste to yᵉ pypys and to hele the fyse v C the C vij s. v d., the sum of halle	xxxvij	i
And for ij krompys of yrnᵉ to bere the pypys, to tomas smygth		vj
And for nayle		iiij
Rychard lavender for workema'schepe of the rofe of the fyse, and for tymbyr borde and nayle		xx
And for ij dorys borde bokys and chystys, and nayle		xv
We reseyuede of rychard stone for vij boschel of lyme and sonde		vij
And for iij boschel of lyme of Jo. grene		iv ob.
And for iv boschel of lyme of a masone of hyckeford		vj

Amongst those† who further contributed to the rebuilding of the north transept, were :—

	s.	d.
Thomas fernam		iiij
Pet' towysey		vi
Wyllm' Yrostrer		ij
The geneylms' at pers mapuld'rs'	ij	iiij
Jone orpe		ij
Tomas ffayre		iiij
Tomas nefel		ij
Joh' Kyng		ij
Joh' frangkelayn of scherysley*		ii
Rychard gylbarde ye elder		ij
Tomas flente		ij
Pers Cowper		ij
Of Joh' Rose yᵉ testement		xiiij
Wyllya' byeben		iij
Joh' halyday		iiij

No better conception of the influence which in times gone by True Religion exercised upon the people can be obtained, than by a study of the documents which record so many evidences of their self-denial and devotion. There were voluntary collections twice a year for carrying on the daily services of the Church, to which most liberal gifts from time to time were added for particular requirements. Every Easter the parochial gathering produced a substantial sum, which was devoted to paying the ordinary expenses of Divine service. At Christmas-tyde another "gadering" took place. Before every chief or locally-popular festival, collections were made throughout the townships, so that such festivals might be duly observed. Those of Our Lady, St. George, St. Hugh of Lincoln, and All Saints' were very popular. In almost all large churches placed under the protection of the Mother of God, the doles given away on her festivals—to which the parishioners in general, or special benefactors had contributed—were sometimes called "Mary-bred," "Ladye-mete," and "Seynt Marie's-loaf." Occasionally a special alms'-dish was placed near her altar on the Sunday before the festival specially commemorated, into which the parishioners dropped their gifts, to be laid out on the feast itself in bread for the poor and aged distributed after mass,—a custom duly observed here. Traces of it are distinctly on record. The costs for tapers and lamp-oil at such great feasts were always considerable. Such details as "washyng the chyrch gere," repairing the altar-cloths and vestments, mending the lamps and candlesticks—"a basyn and harneyse to a lampe, v s. iij d."—and providing sacred vessels for the sacraments are continually found. The Bells were evidently a constant source of expense, and very large sums were spent in their re-casting and re-hanging. Scarcely a

* "Gone uppe," evidently a familiar nickname of one of the tradespeople.

† Amongst the above are several members of local families of repute and rank, *e.g.* :—The Towerseys of Towersey, Farnham, Hester —so curiously spelt in the quotation above,—Neville, Franklin, Cowper, and Rose.

* A brass to the memory of this man, his wife and seven children, still remains in the chancel of Chearsley Church, with the following inscription :—

Here lyth John Frankelyn and Margarete hys wyff which ordeyned lyvelode to thys Chirche, & [illegible] to be named every holy day in the per' [illegible]. On whos' soulis' God have mercy. Amen.

year passed without some new bell-wheel, bawdricke, rope or clapper being required. Sometimes the whole six bells had to be taken away and re-cast. All this involved very heavy charges—duly put on record. Lead for the roof and for the glazier, stone for substantial repairs to the fabric or needful alterations, and lyme for daubing the church walls are again and again entered in the "Accounts." As early as the year 1445 the clock was put up; and though its making and erection was costly, and its repair likewise involved considerable expense from time to time, it still tells the hour, four hundred and thirty-seven years after its first erection—a good testimony to the admirable materials and honest workmanship of our forefathers' days.

♣♣♣♣♣♣♣

Various Altars in the Parish Church.

ANCIENTLY there were at least ten altars in the church. Documentary evidence to this effect still exists. (1) THE HIGH ALTAR, dedicated in honour of the Blessed Virgin Mary, stood on a stone elevation or *predella* of three steps at the east end of the chancel. It was itself of stone with a large and solid *mensa*, and was flanked with curtains* of rich damask embroidered, hung on brass rods. Behind it was a reredos of carved stone. Over it was erected an elaborate and costly canopy of carved wood, under which hung a silver-gilt *ciborium* in the form of a dove, containing the Blessed Sacrament. From the east wall of the choir, on the north and south of the east window, projected carved stone brackets with crocketed canopies for two large sacred images. One of these represented Our Lady, and before it stood a brass candlestick of many branches for tapers, provided and offered by the worshippers.† That on the south side may possibly have represented St. Thomas the Apostle. Two other large brass candlesticks were placed, one at each western corner of the altar-platform or stone elevation, with tall wax-candles in each. These candlesticks, together with the six bowls with prickets, which held tapers on the rood-screen, were, as the Churchwardens' "Accounts" shew, regularly scoured before each of the chief Church festivals. Two lecterns of brass for the Epistle and Gospel (the last-named facing north) stood, one on either side of the choir, with lanterns near them. There was also another large lectern, "with braunches,"* covered with a hanging of "sattyne embroidered with sters and crownes" "in the myddst of of ye quere;" two tall lanterns, a paire of organs, small and moveable,† and three "crownes of lyght" suspended from the roof. There was likewise a "deske for the rector"—*i.e.* for the chief singing-man, *Rector Chori*—and there were "stooles" for the clerks and singing-boys.‡ The Prebendary of Thame had his place within the choir to the left of the chancel door, "Master Vicar" had his to the right. (2) ST. JOHN THE BAPTIST'S ALTAR stood against the east wall of the south transept, near the south-east pillar of the tower, and at the east end of the two Quartermain tombs, before they were removed. (3) In the chantry chapel, which was built eastward of this south transept, stood the ALTAR OF ST. CHRISTOPHER.§ Its piscina, or water-drain, of very plain architectural features, still remains in the south wall, under a large bas-relief,

* "Item, for a dozen curten ryngs and ye settyng on to
ye ij wyngs of ye hye awter........................ ijd ob."
Churchwardens' "Accounts," 1496.

† The Blessed Virgin Mary was called *Stella matutina*, and held in great honour as the highest of created beings. This point is set forth in *The Pilgrimage of Perfection*, in the following quaint but forcible language:—"The thyrde interpretacion of this holy name Maria is *illuminatrix*, that is to say an illumyner or a gyver of lyght. And like as the *morenynge* comyth before the sonne rysynge, and divideth the night from the day; so the Virgin Mary rose, as the morenynge before the Sonne of justyce and divided the state of grace from the state of synne, the childer' of God from the childer' of darkness. Wherupon the Chirche syngeth to her prayse that her gloryous lyfe gave lyght to the worlde and illumyned all the chirche and congregacions of faythfull people."—*The Pilgrymage of Perfection*, fol. class. Imprinted by Wynken de Worde, A.D. 1531.

* *I.e.* with branches of brass for tapers with which to light the Chanters or *Rectores Chori*, as they stood thereat to chant the antiphons or commence the psalms, etc.

† From the Churchwardens' "Accounts" it is certain that there must have been a soler, loft or gallery for the organs, evidently an erection of wood, made in the fifteenth century, and put up in the north aisle. The cost of it, together with the materials are set forth in detail. Peter Marmion supplied the wood, William Smith the ironwork, and William Carpenter the labour. Then John the organmaker put up the organs, with the advice and co-operation of Edward Jonson. The erection of this gallery or loft cost exactly 24 shillings and two pence halfpenny, which was divided between Old and New Thame. John King and John Benet made a collection or "gadering" throughout the parish and secured 18 shillings and three pence halfpenny in response.

‡ These all received liberal payments in money at certain great festivals; and on special occasions when the services were long, *e.g.* "Palme Sonday," they had "bred and ale." Entries of these frequently occur in the Churchwardens' "Accounts." In Holy Week, when the "Passion" was sung, such "mete and dryncke" seems to have been invariably provided.

§ The altar of St. Christopher *had* been indulgenced: that is, all who fulfilled the conditions of the indulgence granted through the Bishop by the Holy Father and said a *Pater noster* and *Ave Maria*, secured for themselves a remission of forty days' suffering in purgatory.

much decayed, and without inscription, of a priest or prelate in Eucharistic vestments. Little is known of Saint Christopher, and much that is possibly lengendary has gathered round his name. It is generally believed, however, that he suffered martyrdom under Decius, in Lycia, and his feast-day occurs on July 25 in the ancient MS. *Martyrologium*, which bears St. Jerome's name. The Greeks, however, commemorate him on the 9th of May, and the Copts in June. His name—the "Christ-bearer"—was no doubt either taken, or bestowed, to indicate the ardent devotion with which he bore his Saviour in his heart—the sole object of his affection and desires. He is often depicted as old and almost always represented as of great stature, sometimes wading through water and bearing our Lord as a Child on his shoulder—an obvious allegory, touching and telling, however; and readily understood. In England he was remarkably popular, and many altars were erected to his honour. I cannot myself see that the bas-relief of a gigantic priest vested for the Eucharistic Offering, on the south wall of the chantry at Thame, represents St. Christopher; for it is not generally believed that the saint was in orders. Nevertheless, on the principle that some license was often taken in art, it may represent him. Our Christian forefathers, who undoubtedly held him in great reverence, asked his intercession against plagues, pestilences, and distempers. His name occurs in the "Litany of the Saints" in a MS. Horae B.V.M. of the Salisbury or Lincoln Use in my possession, and "Christopher" seems to have been very often selected as a baptismal name amongst our Catholic ancestors. (4) In the north transept THE ALTAR OF THE MOST BLESSED TRINITY stood on a stone platform against the east wall. Over it was an image of the Adorable Trinity—God the Father crowned with tiara, seated on a throne holding an orb and a crucifix, with the dove, a symbol of the Holy Ghost, descending on the suffering Son of God. To the immediate west of the chancel skreen, on either side of its doors and underneath the carved oaken rood-loft, which curved outwards and westwards, stood two altars, one (5) dedicated in honour of OUR LADY OF PITY on the north or gospel-side, and another (6) in honour of ST. LOUIS OF FRANCE on the epistle-side. Each of these, raised on stone platforms, had their own *ornamenta*, cross, candlesticks, cushion, cruetts, chalice, paten, and *ciborium*. Louis was born at Poissy in the diocese of Chartres, 25 April, 1215. He was the son of Louis VIII., by Blanche, daughter of Alphonsus the IX. King of Castile. He came to the throne of France at the age of twelve years, and was crowned at Rheims by the Bishop of Soissons. During his minority affairs both home and foreign were in an exceedingly turbulent state. He married, at Sens, 27 May, 1234, Margaret, eldest daughter of Raymund Berenger, Count of Provence, and assumed the reins of government two years afterwards. His laws, founded on Christian principles, are rife with wisdom; and justice was administered with the strictest impartiality. He was the greatest, noblest, and most Christian King that ever ruled over France, and on his death, 25 August, 1270, was universally regarded as a saint. Many miracles wrought at his tomb were formally and conclusively proved before the examiners appointed to investigate them to have taken place, and he was duly canonized by Boniface VIII. in 1297. The popularity of St. Louis throughout Christendom was remarkable. In him were united qualities which formed a perfect hero and a wonderful Christian, attracting the admiration of thousands. He possessed remarkable qualifications for governing, excelling both in the arts of peace and in those of war. A lofty intrepidity, indomitable courage, and a calm elevation of mind appear to have been his ruling characteristics. His evident motives for action were the Christian Religion, the spiritual and temporal welfare of his subjects, and the glory of God. Though the two Crusades in which he took part were not successful, yet they distinctly served to bring out the beauty and nobility of his character; for his goodness and piety shone forth all the more clearly through the cloud of afflictions which encompassed him. (7) There was also an ALTAR OF "OUR LADY IN JESAN," with a representation of the Nativity (possibly a painting on panel) above it. This was evidently what would now be termed an altar of "Our Lady of the Crib"—almost always found in the chief churches dedicated in honour of the Blessed Virgin Mary. The term "*in jesan*" or "*de gesina*" (as it stands in the "Accounts" of Salisbury Cathedral, now in the Library of Jesus College, Oxford) appears to be of French origin, and means "lying-in" or "being brought to bed for child-birth." This seems to have stood where the existing pulpit* is now placed. (8) ALL HALLOWS,† OR ALL SAINTS' ALTAR stood against a skreen which originally separated the north aisle from the north transept, under the arch still

* Originally the pulpit was placed against the easternmost pillar on the north side of the nave. It was removed about the middle of the last century, and has been twice shifted since that period. The monument of Richard Leaver was formerly placed where the pulpit now stands, but was removed to the north aisle to make way for it. The reading desk, which originally stood facing southwards close to the north-west pier of the tower, was first made to face the congregation about the year 1843.

† "It'm payde to the paynter ffor the steadyng off All halow, xij^d."—Churchwardens' "Accounts," 1520. From this it seems probable that the representation of All Saints' was not in sculpture but by a painting on panel. In 1877 I inspected a representation of this subject near Venice, in which the Blessed Virgin Mary was

existing; while (9) the ALTAR OF ALL SOULS', at which an annual commemoration of the benefactors* of the church was made, appears to have stood under the arch which separates the south aisle from the south transept. Here too was an ancient skreen of carved oak, older than that in part still existing, destroyed no doubt when the gallery was put up, or possibly earlier. (10) There was likewise an ALTAR OF ST. MICHAEL;† but its position cannot be determined. It is not improbable, however, that the south aisle, where All Souls' Altar stood, was known as St. Michael's aisle.

A painting of St. Hugh of Lincoln, the Carthusian; another of St. Nicholas, and a third of St. Crispin, each most probably on panel, were placed on the walls, and a large representation of the Day of Judgment hung high up at the east end of the nave, facing the west. There was likewise some picture in which representations of Gog and Magog‡ appeared, in the northern part of the church--possibly on the north side of the north aisle. There was furthermore an image of St. Thomas the Martyr, before which a lamp was kept continually burning, and another of St. George, the Patron Saint of England.§ Independent of these, the many spaces between the windows contained paintings of sacred subjects; and the splays of the windows, the string-courses, arches, and pillars of the fabric were richly decorated.‖ Black, blue, yellow, vermilion, and a dark red or chocolate seem to have been the predominant colours used throughout the church.* The chancel walls were very richly adorned; and the roof coloured mainly with gold and vermilion.

Before every altar, image, or shrine hung lamps—those in honour of the Blessed Sacrament and the Patron Saint of the Church being probably kept always burning. The fire with which they were first kindled was blessed year by year with the appointed rites on Holy Saturday. Along the front of the rood-loft stood six bowls of latten, or brass, with prickets in the centre—three on either side of the Rood—on which were placed large tapers of wax lit at great solemnities: probably at the High or Parish Mass every Sunday, and on all the principal festivals of the year, viz.:—Christmas, Easter, Ascension Day, Whitsun Day, Trinity Sunday, Corpus Christi, the Feasts of the Annunciation, St. Michael, Lady Day in Harvest, the Conception of the Blessed Virgin Mary, and during the services of the Parish Feast. Independent of these, however, there was a lamp, furnished with oil, always burning before the Rood—"the lampe in ye myddst of ye chirche"—and another in the chantry chapel of St. Christopher. These had been provided for by regular endowments—gifts of lands and tenements; just as the lamp before the Rood appears to have been supplied by the annually-collected gifts of the parishioners for the honour and worship of our Divine Lord; and that for All Souls' Altar by those of the faithful whose friends had recently passed away, and whose wishes, memories, and needs were thus piously regarded.

The first public service, a Low Mass, sometimes began as early as five o'clock in the morning on Sundays and great feasts. This was followed by others at six, seven, or eight. Then Mattyns was chanted in public. The Parish Mass, or chief service of the day, rendered by singing-men and with organs, commenced at nine. Prior to this there was a procession of clergy, singing-men and boys, to which the people were called by what the Churchwardens' "Accounts" term "the holy water bell," because during such procession the assembled worshippers were sprinkled with hallowed water; and at its close,—before the officiants with their ministers and attendants passed into the choir and up to the high altar,—prayers in English for all estates of men, living and departed, (called "bidding the bedes") were made by one of the

depicted sitting on a throne in the central panel of an altar-reredos of wood, with the Four Doctors of the West, and thirty-eight other saints, each with his or her symbol, represented in twenty-one panels on either side.

* At the "obit of ye benefactores," a book of vellum or stout paper leaves, frequently bound in embossed silver or with carved ivory sides, containing the names of those departed persons who had benefited the Church, was placed on the altar—out of which the officiant (or if at High Mass, the Deacon from the rood-loft or pulpit), at or about the Offertory, recited their names so that prayer might be made on their behalf. On other occasions it was customary that the book in question (sometimes called *Liber Defunctorum*, sometimes the "Bead Roll," and sometimes, as at Durham, *Liber Vitæ*) lay on the altar, like the Dyptychs of a more ancient period, to remind the Priest to remember the departed generally before God. In a MS. *Sacramentary of St. Gregory the Great* of the ninth century, preserved in the Treasury of Cologne Cathedral, the commencement of the *Canon Missæ* has this sentence referring to this custom written on the margin,—"Et eorum quorum nomina ad memorandum conscripsimus ac super sanctum Altare Tuum scripta adesse videntur."

† "It'm. Will'm owthe to the Churche *ffor* lythemony of Sent Michelles ele, iij^s."—Churchwardens' "Accounts," 1509-10.

‡ "It'm. sol. p^r una asxia ad le *stoppyng* fenestre *retro* Gogmagog et factur *ejusd^m* in p^te boreali *eccl'ie*."—Churchwardens' "Accounts," 1488-9.

§ "It'. rec. of Nicholas Perywale for settyng up of his *sete* before Sey^t George, iij^d."—Churchwardens' "Accounts," 1496.

‖ In the early part of Henry VII.'s reign there was a local "pargiter" at Buckingham, who appears to have had a great reputation. The family of Dormer were his patrons. He was employed at Thame on more than one occasion, and the high fees paid to him shew that his work occupied some time, was carefully done, and elaborate. In 1480 he supplied a Picture of the Blessed Virgin

* When the church was under repair about forty years ago, and the north aisle was rebuilt, several distinct traces of the original colouring were discovered. The splays of the windows had been evidently adorned with figure-subjects, placed one above the other; while the north wall, in parts, was divided by representations of bands of stonework in red paint, having alternately conventional lilies and roses on each rectangular figure.

clergy standing in the nave in front of the great Crucifix. High Mass—to judge by entries and incidental records—appears to have been completed sometime before noon: possibly about half-past ten. Vespers were sung soon after midday; and thus the services of Sunday and festival came to an end, leaving the latter part of the day for rest and reasonable recreation. The church was open every day from sunrise to noon. It was the House of Prayer and the place of meditation and devotion both for rich and poor. There were daily offerings of the Christian sacrifice by the Prebendary, the Vicar, and the Chantry Priest—the "Mass of Our Lady" being said either at the High Altar within the choir or at that of Our Lady of Pity just outside the chancel doors on the north or gospel side, every morning throughout the year.

Most probably the Scribe of the Church,—who was sometimes likewise the Sexton or Sacristan, and had the care of the books, bells, vestments, and ornaments, or it may have been one of the inferior clerks—taught poor children their letters and prayers—the Our Father, the Belief, and the Memorial of the Incarnation,—in some skreened-off portion of the edifice. Of old the floor of the church was strewn with rushes, the doors were covered with hangings, the windows were rich with pictured glass; while the whole interior had that furnished look which would present so marked a contrast to the cold and whitewashed churches, or to the unused, chilly, empty, lampless buildings as "restored" at the present day.

♣♣♣♣♣♣♣

Extracts from the Churchwardens' Accounts.

What were exactly the yearly Receipts and Expenses of the Church, how they differed, and to what extent, may be readily seen from the following Extracts from the Churchwardens' "Accounts," transcribed *verbatim et literatim*. The first extract, comprising the accounts of one year, relates, as will be noted, to the fifteenth century; the second to the sixteenth:—

No. I.

Recep. Joh'is Mangtorn & Thome Bone yconomor. Eccl'ae De Thame ab undecimo die Octbr' Anno D'ni mcccc°lxvij usq. quindecim' die Octbr. tunc p'x. sequen't. vij E' iv. sup'rd'a.

	s.	d.
In prim's at Ester for the E'st' taper and the trendell	x	
It. for Rent of lond at Chelyndon		iij
It. of hos Grene for yᵉ lampe in ye myddes of yᵉ chyrch	iii	
It. Off Agnes Ffrogmore to yᵉ Rode lyght		xij
It. off Peres evens for wast iiij torches		viij
It. of yᵉ same Peres to yᵉ Rode lyght		iiij
It. Receyvyt at Cristynmas for yᵉ Rode lyght	xiij	vj
It. off John Elys to yᵉ Rode lyght		xij
It. ffor lond at Chalyndon		iij
It. off Thomas Prynsham		xij
S'm. recep't. p'dict.	xxxj s.	

Expens' dict. Joh'is Mangtorn & Thome p. tempus p'd'i'm.

	s.	d.
In primis at Est' ffor the taper & the trendell	iij	xj ob.
It'm for besomes to yᵉ chirch		j
It. ffor mendyng of yᵉ grete bell whele		j
It. a pond off wex candell to yᵉ Rode lyght		vij
It. ffor mendyng of the clok to Robert Smyth		x
It. for a pond off wex candell on Bertlemele ys day		vij
It. for ij pond off wex on seynt mary day		xiiij
It. for j pond wex on seynt luke day		vij
It. att Cristynmas xiij ponds wex	vj	vj
It. for makyng xxiiij pond of wex		xij
It. for wrytyng of dyv's thynges in this Boke		viij
It. for makyng of Baudrikkes		vj
It. for mendyng ye chirch yarde gate		j ob.
Sm' expens' p'dict.	xvij s.	

No. II.

Comp'us Joh'is Goodwyn Johis Mo'tymere Sen' Will'i Alen & Joh'is Baby procurator. sive yconomo'r. eccl'ie p'bendal b'te Marie de Thame tam p. p'te nove Thame q'm p. p'te vet's Thame vid. a' d'm'ca. p'x' ante Ascens'o'm D'ni' Anno D'ni mill'mo quingentesimo p'mo usq. eand'm d'm'cam A° D'm' M° quingentesimo secundo vid. p'mo anno integro.

Recepts.

	s.	d.
In primis the said proctours byn charged of ye fote of the last accompte as it apperith there	iiijli.	vjs.
Itm. rec'. of the may ale and of the gaderyng of Robyn Hodde in new Thame att whitsontyed clere	xx	
Itm. rec. the same tyme of the may ale in old Thame	xiiij	
Itm. rec. of the p'yshonys for the rode light at Cristmasse	xiij	
Itm. rec. of the p'yshonys for the rode lirt at Ester	xxj	
Itm. rec. of John Rede for rent of his howse the hole yere		ij
Itm. rec. of Robert Ffrankelyn behynde of all sollyn lirt		xx
Itm. rec. of Thomas barne for chirche lond in prest ende		vij
Itm. rec. for the sepulture of Pawlyn A Brigge in the chirche	vj	viij
Itm. rec. for the wastyng of torchys the same tyme		viij
Itm. rec. of cart's wyf for wastyng of torchis		iiij
Sum. tot. rec.	vij li. v s. xj d.	

EXPENS.

	s.	d.
In primis paid to Robert Mortym' for ii li. wex ageyn Whitsontide		xiiij
It. paid to Thomas Powlen for mendyng of ij bawderikke		ij
It. paid to Thomas Ive for mendyng of the clokke		ij
It. paid to Thomas Hawthorne for rydyng to my lorde of lyncolne to Banbury for the sealyng of the chirch dorys		xx
It. paid to Cristofer Briggeman for the kepyng of the clokke for midsomer quarter		xx
It. paid to Robert mortym' for j li. wex ageyn Relike sonday*		vij
It. paid to the same Robert for j li. wex ageyn the Assu'pcyon of our lady		vij
It. to Thomas Powlen for the mendyng of the litell bell whele		iiij
It. for nayles to the same whele		ob.
It. paid to Thomas Swadlyng for castyng of ij brasis one of the litell bell and A noth' to the iij^d belle	iij	iij
It. paid to A carpenter of Risborugh for leying of the same brasis		ij
It. paid to ij men of Abendon for the levelyng of ij bellys		xij
It. paid to Prentise for makyng of a corpys of a bere and mending of A nother corpys		xj
It. paid to Willm. Holden Smythe of Bisseter for the mendyng of the clok in full payment of A bargen wt hym made	iij	viij
It. paid to Thomas Ive for A locke and ye tu'yng of the dore in the vyce goyng in to the stepull and nayles		vij
It. paid to Robert Mortym' for ij li. wex ageyn ye natiuite of or lady		xiiij
It. paid to John Goodwyn for plate to the cherche lanterne		ij
It. paid for ye mendyng of the same lanterne		iiij
It. paid to Thomas Powlen for the mendyng of A bawdryk		ij
It. paid to John hille for white lethyr		ij
It. paid to Robert Mortym' for iii sisys age'st all halou day		vij
It. paid to Water Prett for iii talow candell to the quere		j
It. paid to ye Pewterer for ye mendyng of ij candilstikke yat stondith uppon ye hy awter and for iiii sowdyr to ye same		viij
It. paid Ric. plumer of Oxford for j day labor and A half		viij
It. paid for xiij sowdyr to ye northsyde of ye chirche and to ye stepull A bove	iij	iv
It. paid for ij bs. coles		ij
It. to ye plum'. syvaunt A day and A half		vj
It. to Robert Frankeleyn for A rope to ye litell peyse of ye clokke		xij
It. to the Sexten for michaelmas quarter for ye clokke		xx
It. paid to John Gathorppe for A galon and an half of oyle agenst Cristmas	ij	
It. paid to ye same John for vi li wex the same tyme	iij	vj
It. paid to ye same John for makyng of the same wex		x ob.
It. paid for vij lampys		vj
It. paid to Robert Mortym' for v li sises ye same tyme	ij	xj
It. paid to Margery Clerk for wasshyng of A sirples		j
It. paid to Willia' Triplad for i li candyl in ye quere		j
It. paid to Thomas Smythe for iiij boke iiij sconsis		ij
It. paid to Keteryn Tillisery for mendyng of vij surpleys		xij
It. paid to Will'm millborne for mendyng of ye lede on seynt cristofer and ij li sowdyr		xij
It. paid to ye sexten for cristmas qrt' kepyng ye clokke		xx
It. paid for bredd and ale on palme sonday		iij
It. paid to John hill for white lether for bawderikke		ij
It. paid for makyng of bawdricke		iij
It. paid for ii li sises at Ester		vij
It. paid John Gathorppe for vij li wex to the trendill and iij li to the paschale and font taper	vi	
It. paid to John Wellington for a cofer		xij
It. paid to the somner for his fee		viij
It. paid to Ric. millborne for ix li sowdyr remaynyng in oure hand		xvj
It. paid to Will'm. lewkenore for the orgens ye hole yere	xiij	iv
It paid in costs on sheer thursday		xij
It. paid for wesshyng of surples albys amyses towell and awter clothis and mendyng of the same		xx
It. paid for wasshyng of surples agenst michaelmas		viij
It. paid to ye Sexten for kepyng of ye clok at Ester		xx
It. paid to Mr Vycare for ye bedd rolle		iiij
It. paid to engrose this accompte		viij
It. paid in bred and ale at oure accompte		iij

S'm. tot'l. expens. ....iij li. xj s. v d.

S'm. remanens de claro...iij li. xiiij s. vij d.

* Relic-Sunday was the Sunday after the Feast of the Translation of the Relics of St. Thomas of Canterbury (July 7th).

The importance which was anciently attached to rendering the service of God with dignity, regularity, and devotion may be in some degree apprehended on studying the following Inventories. They also serve to shew how liberal the people were in supplying the House of Prayer with everything needed for Divine worship, and how rich the ancient churches were. They also prove that the raid subsequently made, under the Tudors, upon the plate and ornaments of the monasteries, chantries, and churches must have been made by those who well knew what they were about, and that their confiscation produced a very large sum. Nor will these particular inventories be wanting in interest to the archæologian and ecclesiologist; for they indicate with sufficient exactness what the ecclesiastical colours in use were in the diocese of Lincoln—a diocese where the old local rite was only second in dignity, grandeur, and interest to that of the illustrious Church of Sarum.

♣♣♣♣♣♣♣

List of Service Books, Vestments, & Sacred Ornaments.

p'tinentes Eccl'e p'och. de Thame Hic intitulant' sive notant' Om'es Libri & Vestimenta ac div'sae res p. Joh'em Mangtorn' & Thoma' Buns & alios comp'curatores necno' proconomos Ecc'e p'ochial' de Thame Incipient' xxv° die mensis Febr. A° D'ni. m° cccc^mo xlvii°. In Primis*

Una' Antiphon'r. ex dono ven'viri Willi' Kynnewolmersh Thes'd'ni Reg. & p'ben. d'ce Ecc'e p'bendal. de Thame. s'c'do folio Incipient' l nig° *Marie semp. Virginis.*

It' ex dono d'ci ven. viri duo g'dal. quor' p'mu' incip' l s'c'do fo. l rubio p' *Totu'* Et s'c'd'm in s'c'do fo. *Tuas d'ne.*

It' ex dono d'ci ven. viri ij p'cessional. In s'c'do fo. vni° incip. *A deo* Alterius s'c'do fo. incipient' *lius dei.*

It'm aliud processi^le s'c'do fo. incipient' *virtute sp'z s'ti.*

It'm magnu' portiforiu' ex dono ven. p'ris Ep'i d'm. d'm. Wakeryng Ep'i Norvic' et quond' d'ce Ecc. Rector. S'c'do folio incipient' *D'n'z vobiscu'.*

It'm duo nova missalia q^r' p'mu' incip. in s'c'do fo° *vobis me.* & co'tine's l p'n° kalendar'. It'm s'c'd'm incip. l s'c'do folio & l rubio *p'i'q^m a pascha.* & co'tine's l inic'o kalendar'.

It'm aliud g^dal. ex dono Thome Wodegrene s'c'do fo. incipient. l nig° *qui venit.*

It'm portifor'm ex dono Agnet' Clerk s'c'do folio incipient. *de femore* usq' do'c° p'ma advent°.

It'm legend' s'c'do fo. incipient. *pullus asine.*

It'm novu' manual' s'c'do fo. incipient. *fessa p' d'nm.*

It'm psalt'm s'c'do fo. incip. *adversus.*

It'm aliud psalt'mi s'c'do fo. incip. *Miser' mei d'ne* cu' s'uic' de A'p'lis & m^r'b's &c l fine.

It'm ij missalia vs' linc. q^r' vnu' incip. s'c'do fo. *ka'ris pacientes.* S'c'd'm incip. s'c'do folio *se orbi.*

It'm aliud Missale antiq'u' s'c'do fo. incipient. *suscipiam'.*

It'm duo g'dal' q^r' p'mu' incip. l s'c'do fo. *lutar' tua'.* Alt'um incip. s'c'do fo. *Populus Syon.*

It'm iij Antiphonar' p'mu' incip. l s'c'do fo. *Rer' creator.* S'c'd'm l s'c'do fo. incip. *Si tu es ipse* T'ciu' l s'c'do fo. *Pro. pr.*

It'm legend' de s'c'a maria p. annu' cu' s'uic' corp'is' x' & s'i Thome Marteris s'c'do fo. incipient. *est regnu'.*

It'm Collectar' in s'c'do fo. incip. *Ecce Virgo co.*

I'tm manuale antiqu' s'c'do fo. incip. *nib' sit.*

It'm libru' de laudib' cu' s'uic' s'ci' hugonis s'c'do fo. incip. *loquar i amaritudie.*

It'm aliud Missale incipiens in fo. s'c'do *p' quem.*

Hic notant' vestimenta ornamenta & cet'a pertinentia Eccle' de Thame p' Joh'em Mangtorn Thomam Buns & socios suos Anno D'n'i mill'imo cccc^mo xlviij.

Ffyrst a sute of Blew imbroudyd Wt gold wt Antlopp & byrdes of gold the Orffrayes wt crockays & sterres of gold. That ys to say ij copes wt all the Aparell ffor Prest Dekyn and Subdekyn. The which wer° of the gyft of Will'm Bates & Crystyn his wyffe. Delyverd & beyng in the kepyng of W. Bates the which by assent off the Paryssh sy'vyth for Witsonday.

It'm ij copes the grond off Rede Sylk wt white Byrdes and white Branches Wt a Cope of Rede Sylk the grond wt white ffloewers & skalabes off gold.

It'm A chesebyll the grond off Rede Sylk wt Byrdes & Branches off gold wt aube amys stole and ffanon. the orffray co'teynyng A & M yerchyat and p'teynyth to Seynt John Aut'.

It'm an auter' Cloth off Rede Sylk wt Byrdes and Branches off Blew wt a ffrontell and a corporas purse of the same p'tenyng to Seynt John ys Aut'. It'm ij Pedell of Rede Sylk wt rays to the saide Aut'.

It'm A croce of tre gylt wt a clothe of Sylk to kepe hit.

It'm A sute off grene & Black wt White bundys and Chapletys of gold and Egylles of the Same. that ys to say A cope wt all the App'ell for prest Dekon & Subdekyn wt a clothe to keep hem to sy'ue for holy Thorsday & Trynyte Sonday off the gyfft off John Crouche.

It'm A sute of White damask cloth off gold wt Orfrayes of grene Welwet with buddes of gold pouder° and blak & red. Wt a hole corporas of the same s'rib with a Cope off the same sute. That ys to say wt al that p'tenyth for Prest dekyn & Subdekyn & Remayneth now in ye keping of Jhon At hylle.

It'm a ffrontell of Blew & grene baudkyn Wt floures of White and Rede. Wt a cloth of the same to heng ondw the same frontell with a Reredose of the same to heng abow the Aut' wt a Crucifyx. And ij Custos redler for the

* This passage sets forth the old method of drawing up a Catalogue of MSS. The first folio of any volume is described either by an account of its large initial letter, or by the subject-matter of its commencement; and the second folio by its first word or portion of a word. By this means any MS. could be readily identified, though its first page were worn, damaged, or lost. When a book was particularly remarkable or precious, the first word or syllable in half-a-dozen or a dozen consecutive folios was set forth in the Inventory or Catalogue in order still further to identify any volume.

same Aut' o' of blew Tartryn And of the gyft of Henry Clerk & Agnes his wyffe And Remayneth ye kepyng of the saide Agnes to sy'ue for the v. dayes off our lady & Remayneth in ye keping of Jhon At hille.

It'm ij towellis yt sy'ue to besill wt at Ester & j chaleyse.

It'm A cope off Rede embrowdyd Wyth gold and wt ymages off the Assumpcon off our lady the Orfraies off grene Sylk embroudyt With gold. Off the gyft off Mayst. Nicholas Bobewyth Byshupp off Bath.

A sute off grene Sylk & Rede for the Preste wt ymages of gold & Rede Saten. And for the dekyn wt Orffrayes of gold the grund of rede sylk wt Archangles off gold. And for the Subdekyn the orffray of welvet grene welvet & Rede wt lyones & Roses of white. Wt a cope of the same sute. Wt a stole & fanon of clothe wt Byrdes And a stole & fanon of Rede thik Sylk. Wt an Amyse amyte of grene wt a sterr & crownes of gold. wt a clothe of sylk to kepe hem. And remaynes wt W. Inkenore.

A sute off greene Satayn wt Skalappes mones & sterres of gold for Prest dekyn & Subdekyn. a cope wt orfrayes onely of the same sute wt ij clothes to keep he'. And a frontell of cheker velvet.

It'm a chesebyll the groud rede Sylk wt Aube fanon & stole wt beres & byrdes of gold & an Amyte of the same to sy'ue for Mydsom' day & other dayes of Apostles.

A hole sute of Blewe yalow colo' the grunde except ij stoles & a ffanon Wt a cope of the same sute.

A chesebyle the grund of White Sylk wt popynjays of gold the orfrayes of grene weluat wt ymages of gold in tabernacles wt Stole ffanon Albe & Amys. the orfrayes of the same Wt a cope the grund rede Sattayn wt ymages of gold the orfrayes of grene Sattayn y set wt byrdes & chaplets of gold. Off the gyft of Bugebyth.

A chesebyle of yaloe Sylk wt orfrayes of gold of wt Albe Stole & ffanon of Bordalysander wt an Amyte of Sylk Rede & Grene.

It'm ij Sencers of copyr gylt wt a Shyppe of copyr gylt ij crowets of sylu' wt a croce of Sylu' & gold and a shafft syluyt & gylt wt a Baner off grene Sylk wt Armys and Schochens

Al so ij clothes of gold the grund of Rede Baudkyn wt pyne-applyes of gold contenyng in lenght x yardes of the gyfte of Dame John Bechame lady of Burgewny. And remaynes wt John Manytorn.

It'm ij copyes of Rede Sylk worken wt grene Sylk and Dragownes off gold the orfrayes of cheker veluet wt strakys of gold of the gyft off Robt. Checom.

A parell for the Aut' off grene Ray Tartren & A ffrontell wt a clothe Sowyt y to of Crysomys & a cloth before the Aut' of the same and A Reredose wyth a crucyfyx & ij custos of the same de dono mag'ri Johis' Wakeryng.

It'm A parell for the Aut' of Steyned wark of the Natyvyte of our lord wt a clothe befor the Aut' and a Reredose of the same wt ij custos wt angels off the gyfte of Will'm Kyllyngwolnesh.

It'm A parell made of crysomes for lent wt Ihc wt ij custos and all y't pteyth y'to off the gyft of Sr John Dormor som tyme Vicar of Thame.

It'm ij Reredose of Sylk for an Aut' palyd wt yelow & grene wt ij custos of Sylk wt blew Ray.

It'm ij chesebill and j tonakyll of white. I'tm ij tonakles of Rede.

It'm a chesabyl of Bordaly sander wt stole & fanon of the same.

It'm A ffrontell off Grene Ray Sylk. It'm A ffrontell of grene & Rede.

It'm A Chalyce gylt only wtynforth off the gyft of henry clerk & Agnes his wyffe, being in kepyng wt the saide Agnes.

It'm a chalyce gylt wt out and wt yn of the gyfte of Thos. Nasshe Rector de Chynnor.

It'm ij chalyce gylt wtyn & wtout.

It'm a Chalice gylt wtynforth onely.

It'm a purse of gold wt ymages for a corpase.

It'm iiij corp'as wt vj pursys p'teynyng to the hye Aut'.

It'm vij pyllowes off Sylk.

It'm iiij candylstykes off laton two moche & two lytell syr'vng for the hye Aut. also off the ordnance of Robert Marney knyght.

It'm ij lytill candylstykke of laton for precession.

It'm A croce off Sylv' and gold for the Sacrament to be born wt a case off ledere de ordina'cn Rob'ti marney milit.

A longe Bann' wt an Antlopp cheyned. It'm iij Bann' of Tartryn Rode & grene.

A nor. of Rede & Blewe y peyntyd. It'm ij Bann' of Rede & White.

A Bann' off the Trynyte.

It'm ij Bordeclothes of ynglyssh werk. It'm ij towayles of ffrensh werk.

It'm iij towayle of Diaperwerk. It'm iiij wesshyng towales.

It'm two latton Wesselys to bere holy wat' p.m. wt ij ysopes off latton off the which oon ys of the gyft off the saide Robt. Marney. and the tother ys of the gyft & ordnans of Thomas Bryggewell & Agnes ux' eius.

It'm a croce off cop' gylt off the gyft off John Wakering sometyme p'son off Thame.

It'm ij croces off laton wt ij Shafftes.

It'm sensers off latton. And a Shypp of cop'. And also a Dysshe off cop'.

It'm iiij hand Belles ffor s'vyse off dede pepull.

It'm a lytyll Bell off laton of the gyft off Agnes Bryghtwell for visitacon off seke men.

It'm v grete Belles wt so many clappe honging in the Stepull off the said church.

It'm a lytell Belle for the hy Aut' to ryng to Sacring wyth.

It'm a lytell Belle hongyng in the chauncele by the quere dor for to ryng Sacryng.

It' a Belle hongyng in the saide Stepull for to ryng to holyewat' wyth Sondayes.

It' a lavv'r off latton wt a cheue off S yrne honging by the churche dore.

It' ij grete lau't'nes. It. ij lectenes standyng in the chauncelle.

It'm ij paxbredes oon of latton and ano'r off lede ygylt & clesit in tre.

It'm ij ffrontell oon of blew silk w. white hartys. And ano' off Ray wellvet chekeryd.

It' a white weyle for the Croce in lent tyme. And ano' white weyle to be hangyng in the chauncell be for the hy Aut' in lentyn tyme.

It'm ij steyned clothes ffor the lectenes oon wt an ymage of our lady & a no'r of Seynt hew of ye gift of John Croke. iij steyned clots wt ymags at ye quere dore of the gift of the same.

It' ij old steyned clothes for lectnys wt ymages off our lady.

It' a payre off old Organes beyng in the chauncelle.

It'm a knyffe wt tew haffies to kut holy brede.

It'm ij stayned clotes for ye lecturn one wt an ymage of o' lady & the other of saint Katrine of ye gift of Isabell Elys.

It'm a croce off tre wt Mary & John all y gyllyd & beyng in the kepyng off W Batten.

Notant' hic omnia ornamenta ac bon'ae tre p'tinent' Gild'e S'te Trinit' temp. Wetor. yconomor'.

ffyrst A chesebyll off white wt an Albe for lent. It. A pax brede of the Resurexcon of Crist.

It'm ij crowet of tyn. It'm ij manutergia v towayles. It'm a Sacrynbelle.

It'm A chesebyll an Albe & amyte off blak silk with rebannes of gold embrowdyd.

It'm a ffrontell wt a bordcloth off the same sute. It'm an Autclothe wt a bordclothe off the same sute. And of the gyft of Will'm Bate & Cry'tyne hys wyffe.

It'm j chalyse gylt wt yn and wt out of the gyft of Sr John Locas su'tyme Vikery.

It'm a chesybille with Albe Amyte stole and ffanon of grene and blew mixsyt with littel rede Rosys.

It'm an aut' clothe steyne wt an image of the Trynyte yn the mydds ymages of seynt Clement & Seynt Laurens beying in the Sydes.

It'm ij aut' clothes of crysomes for Lent tyme.

It'm i bord clothe wt a ffrontell of rede & grene.

It'm iiij bordclothes for the Aut' of which i ye brokyn & torn.

It'm i corpax in a purse wt Rosys of white.

It'm candelabru' o' a candlestick of latton, of the ordnance of John Manytorn.

It'm i hongying candlestick of latton wt v lyrtes of the ordenance of the sayde Mr.

It'm i aut' cloth steyned.

It'm i vestment of blew damask, wt orfray of cloth of gold wt the t'in'te on ye bak of the gyfte of Isabell Chapman other wise called Crokk.

Hic intitulant' Que p'tinent' Gilde S'ti Joh'is temp'e p'd'tor' yconomor' sive Procurator'.

Ffyrst, a masbok, ye gyfte of Will'm Bate & Cristyne hys wyffe.

It' A cheseble of rede sylke wt byrdes and Branches of gold wt Aube amyte stole & fanon of the same the Orfray co'ta'nyng A & M crownyt And off the gyfte of Rob. Chacombe and leticie ux' sue.

It'm an aut' cloth of Rede sylk wt Byrdes and branches of blew With a frontell & corpas purse of the same.

It'm ij Pedell of rede sylk, with rayes.

It'm j cheseble of bordalisander wt Albe stole ffanon & Amyte of the gyfte of Agnes Brightwell.

It'm i corpas wt a p'se of blew grene & white.

It'm ij Bordclothes, wt a towayle. It'm j paxbrede.

It'm j stanyd clothe wt ymages of Sent Kat'ine Sent John Baptist, & Sent Nicholase.

It'm ij crewets off tyn And a sacryn belle.

It'm a letteyne for a mas boke.

It'm a lampe wt a basyn of laton.

It'm a hangying candlestick of laton wt v lyrtes.

Her om'ia Subscripta sunt que p'tinent' sive Gild'e Beate Marie in le sesan Anno D'ni mill'mo ccccc° xlvii° d'ctor. yconomor' sive p'curator'.

Ffyrst a palle of rede wt lyonnes of gold embroidyd.

Al so a cheseble of blew wt orfrayes of white wt an amyte of bordalisander and Albe with orfreys of Rede with ymages of gold.

Al so an aut' clothe steynet wt an ymage of our lady & an ymage of Gabriell with ij custos of the same sute.

Al so a clothe of blew card to cu're the ymagen in lent wt ij curtos of the same.

Al so iiij bordclothes and iiij towelys for the aut'.

Al so a pelow of grene and another of rede wt byrdes of yelow.

Al so a nother pelow of Rede blew and grene chekeryd.

Al so a paxbrede of cop' wt a crucifyx and Mary & John. Also a sacrynbell.

Al so a pax brede of copr and a crucyfix and Mary and John. Al so a sacryn belle.

* * * * * *

The following is recorded at the commencement of the "Accounts" for A.D. 1498-1499.

Memorand'. That in the day of the Apostells Symon and Jude, in the yere of our Lord God MCCCCLXXXXVII, Ales Goodchilde and X'tofer her sonne, executors unto Willyam Goodchyld, husbonde unto the seid Ales, and fader unto the said X'tofer, haue gevyn and delyv'd unto the Chirch of Thame, in the honore of the blessed Marye Virgine and all Seyntes A seute of vestyments wt A cope the coler rede veluet, orfraryd of clothe of golde, powdred with Imagery, the bodies of the seute, wt angelys and flowrys of golde braunched, in the saide Chirche to remayne for ev', to the honore and laud of all myghty god and the blessed Marye the Virgyne and all Seynts in Whome his sowle may rest. Amen.

The following analysis of the various colours of the vestments may be of interest to the ecclesiologist and antiquary:

GREEN.—Two sets of chasuble, dalmatic and tunic. One cope. One frontell (*for St. John's altar*).

WHITE.—Three sets of chasuble, dalmatic and tunic.

RED.—Six copes. One chasuble (*for St. John's altar*). One chasuble (*for Midsummer and days of Apostles*).

BLUE.—One chasuble, dalmatic and tunic. Two copes (*used on Whitsunday*).

GREEN AND BLACK.—One chasuble, dalmatic and tunic. One cope (*for Holy Thursday and Trinity Sunday*).

GREEN AND BLUE.—One chasuble, dalmatic and tunic. A frontell. An antependium. A reredos.

YELLOW.—A chasuble.

TRINITY AISLE.—One white chasuble (*for Lent*). One black chasuble. One green chasuble. One blue chasuble.

ST. JOHN'S AISLE.—One red chasuble.

OUR LADY OF THE CRIB.—One blue chasuble. A red velvet set of the gift of the Goodchild Family, &c. &c.

A brief account and explanation of the various service books* belonging to the church in the preceding Inventory, may also not be out of place here. It is clear that they were preserved with great reverence,† and kept in good repair; for entries in the Churchwardens' "Accounts" are found, from time to time, of payments for such reparation. New volumes likewise appear to have been provided as occasion demanded. The monks at Notley Abbey and at Thame Park were evidently very often the trusted scribes of the neighbourhood for providing, amending, or renewing these precious MSS., their assistance being often sought after. Sometimes some local parish priest, like the Vicar of Saunderton, obtained a good reputation for writing such books, and was at no loss for purchasers. The Prior of Notley rebound old *Psalters* and *Manuals* for the moderate sum of two shillings, with extra charges for eight brass bosses and two pairs of hammered clasps. The work of binding was sometimes called "stryngyng." Defective leaves were supplied at a cost of from one shilling and eightpence to two shillings and twopence, with an additional charge for illuminated letters or borders. There was a notable binder in Cat Street, in Oxford, John Pratt, who enjoyed a great reputation during the middle part of the fifteenth century, and worked with artistic efficiency. Later on, under the Tudors, William Forrest, of Thame Park Abbey, was found to be a most accomplished scribe—a good writer of old English letters and illuminations, and a clever draughtsman, as much of his remaining handiwork, both on vellum and paper, abundantly testifies. These monks, and such as these, wrote out from authorized standard copies of the various service books belonging to their respective houses, fresh MSS., which local churchwardens from time to time required, or which the

* When Pope St. Gregory sent to St. Augustine the Pall (a vestment symbolizing jurisdiction), he also sent various sacred relics, and many books (*codices*), evidently intended for public worship. One of these, a MS. Book of the Gospels, now in the Bodleian Library, is believed to be part of the donation in question. In the twenty-first of Ælfric's Canons a list of service books is given as necessary for the spiritual work of the parish priest, and the same prelate in his Pastoral Letter enumerates the Mass Book, the Book of Evangelical Canticles, the Psalter, the Legendium, the Manual, and the Penitential. Numerous Injunctions and Constitutions issued by Church authority during the ages of faith, testify to the care which was taken, not only to have suitable volumes—substantially the same as those enumerated, in every church, but such as were neither deficient in the true and authorized text nor disfigured by wear and tear, or by unseemly illuminations, or by local and peculiar additions which were not recognized by authority.

† In the fourth chapter of the third book of Archbishop Egbert's *Penitential*, is set forth his opinion as to the reverence due to books made use of in the service of God: "Sacerdotes Dei, et diaconi," he wrote, "et alii Dei ministri quos in Dei templo Deo servire oportet, et reliquias et sacros libros manu tractare, castitatem suam usque servare debeat." This prelate was a contemporary and friend of the Venerable Bede, and no doubt this accurately represented the sentiment of his age.

gentlepeople and yeomen of the neighbourhood were glad to purchase and possess. The *Hours of the Blessed Virgin** was a most popular and comprehensive volume, and few families were without one or more copies. In such, as in the large Family Bible of later generations, entries of births, baptisms, lists of "gossips," "bishoppings," marriages, and deaths of the members of the family were frequently entered. All such volumes, however, were so generally destroyed under the Tudor changes, and this in the most barbarous and ruthless manner, that, comparatively speaking, few examples remain. To have possessed one would, under Queen Elizabeth, have probably secured for its owner prompt and severe punishment.

In the Churchwardens' Inventory there are two specimens of the *Portiforium* enumerated. A large volume, the gift of John Walkeleyne, Bishop of Norwich, who had been previously one of the clergy of Thame Church, and a second given by Agnes Clerk.

The *Portiforium*, or Portuary, was the title commonly made use of in England to describe and designate the Breviary, *Breviarium*. This latter name (which is said to have been first used by Micrologus about the year 1080) may have been adopted from the fact that such volumes contained an authorized and official *abbreviation* of the services commonly recited in choir by the clerks. These volumes consisted of the whole of the offices, completely set forth, of the Canonical hours for every day in the year, Sundays, ferias and feast-days, and in their old MS. form were commonly divided into two parts, the *Pars Estivalis* and the *Pars Hiemalis*.

The author possesses two separate leaves of a twelfth-century *Portiforium*, which Tradition asserts once belonged to Thame Church. They may have formed part of one of these volumes. They were taken from beneath the wooden and pig-skin binding of a merchant's Account Book, which had previously belonged to a member of the family of Ballowe, of Thame. Other leaves of the same MS. had been evidently used for strengthening the back of the volume, on part of one of which the words "*ecclesie de Thama*" were written. The two leaves in question, measuring exactly eleven inches and a third, by eight inches and two-thirds, contain part of the office for Holy Week, and are written with full musical notation, and illuminated with capital letters. The letters A and D are designed and executed with remarkable skill and good effect, and are very fine specimens of the illuminator's art. The former represents our Lord washing the Disciples' feet: the other Moses and the Burning Bush. Of this latter a woodcut is here inserted:—

Illuminated Letter from ancient manuscript.

The *Missale*, or Mass-book, contained all that was needful for saying mass day by day. Anciently it was sometimes called *Sacramentarium*, or *Liber Mysteriorum* (though such MSS. occasionally comprised other than the services for the altar). The Missal consisted of a Kalendar, the Common and Proper Services for Saints, masses to be said every day in the week, votive masses, mass for the dead; and the Ordinary Service and unalterable Canon, which parts were almost invariably placed in the middle of the volume, generally following the service for Easter-day, and preceding those for the various Saints' days.

The *Manuale*, or Manual,* generally contained those services and ceremonies which the ordinary parish priest was constantly being called upon to perform, viz. —baptism, churching of women, matrimony, visitation of the sick, extreme unction, and burial. But other forms were often contained in this volume, *e.g.* the Blessing of salt and water, of holy bread, of tapers for Candlemass day, of flowers and branches *in dominica palmarum*, and of various other objects; together with forms for grace before and after taking food, for proclaiming banns of marriage, for making a will, and various rules for the due observance of all commemorations of the departed.

The *Legendum* contained the Lections to be read in the office for Mattins, mainly consisting of extracts from the Holy Scriptures, with, on special occasions, portions of Homilies of the Fathers, passages from the

* Amongst the Appendices will be found reprinted a "Litany of the Saints," which presents features of liturgical interest. It is taken from a *Hora B.V.M.* in my possession—a MS. which is very probably an example of "the old Use of Lincoln."

* Abroad the *Manuale* was sometimes termed *Rituale*. For example, that of the Church of Chalons is so termed—"Rituale seu Manuale ecclesiae Catalaunensis;" and the same was the case with a printed volume issued officially for the diocese of St. Quintin.

Lives of the Saints, and approved and authorized accounts of the sufferings of the Martyrs. But the contents were seldom or never quite uniform. This volume was often divided into three, sometimes into four or five parts. The first part invariably contained passages from Scripture; the second part sermons of the Fathers and Doctors of the Church; and the third part special lessons for the commemoration of Saints, recounting their dignity and recording their deeds. Local uses, or uses peculiar to a diocese, were sometimes superadded.

The *Antiphonarium* contained all the antiphons orderly arranged and musically notated, which were chanted at the Canonical Hours throughout the year. These antiphons were generally short sentences either from the Psalms and Canticles therein sung to give a tone and character, joyous or penitential, sad or exultant, as the case might be, suitable to the day or season in which the office was being recited. To these antiphons, however, were often added Invitatories, Versicles and Responses, and "Little Chapters" as they were technically called. Sometimes those parts of the mass which might reasonably come under the head of "antiphons" were likewise included in this volume, which often lay upon a large lectern standing in the midst of the choir, facing the high altar—at which the *Rectores chori* stood to give the keynote, or intonation, of psalm or canticle, and to commence each particular part of the divine office.

The *Graduale*, Gradale or Grayle, contained those parts of the service of the high or chanted mass, which if sung at all were sung antiphonally, and the book was so named from containing the "Graduals," short antiphons directly following the Epistle. Such a volume, however, often comprised much more than these—in fact, all the ordinary and special parts of the solemn mass in which the singing-clerks and children were wont to take part. Its contents varied somewhat, commencing sometimes with the *Officium aspersionis aquae benedictae*, and concluding with the *Communio*.

The *Psalterium* contained the Psalms of David divided into daily portions, so as to be said or sung throughout in the course of a single week. The divisions of the Psalms were herein substantially like the divisions of the *Portiforium*, but not exactly, differing slightly and occasionally, but immaterially. Sometimes the proper antiphons were prefixed to the Psalms, and occasionally the Canticles and the Litany of the Saints were added.

The *Collectore*, or *Collectarium*, was a volume often found in our old churches, and no doubt was so called because originally, and in the main, it consisted of a collection of collects used in divine service. Ducange in his "Glossarium" thus defined it: "Liber Ecclesiasticus in quo *Collectæ* ad quævis officia dicendæ continentur." So great, however, has been the destruction of all such books, that not a single English specimen is known to exist. There are, of course, several MSS. which contain collects, but not exclusively such. Antiphons, hymns, Short Chapters, and versicles and responses, have been added, so that such volumes, not exclusively containing collects, might often receive some other designation.

The *Processional* contained various Litanies, Rubrical directions, forms for blessing the seeds for the ground, the fruits of the earth, cattle; and very frequently the accustomed forms for baptism, visitation of the sick, extreme unction, the commendation of a departing soul, and the burial of the dead.

But to proceed with the quotations.

There are many incidents recorded in the Church "Accounts," set forth in quaint language, for the words are often spelt as pronounced, and sometimes with a very provincial pronunciation, which, nevertheless, are quite worthy of being here preserved, and serve to enable a true conception of the services and the influence of a parish church upon the religiously-united people of a mediæval country Town and its Hamlets, to be readily made and accurately realized. The care which was taken of the fabric, the bells, and the ornaments, the regularity and reverence with which divine service was conducted, the self-sacrifice and liberal alms of the people both by gift and bequest, the respect paid to the successor of St. Gregory, who had founded the National Church, and whose dues, as "Peter's Pence," were paid year by year, as well as the harmony and good feeling which existed amongst all classes, bound together as they then were by the valuable and potent bonds of True Religion, are features worthy both of admiration and imitation.

The quotations from the Churchwardens' "Accounts," beginning anew in the reign of Henry VI., are now continued:—

* * * * * *

(1446.) **Receipts.**

	s.	d.
Halso of Wyllys' Rose for waste of to torchys ...		iiij
Halso for syr Tomas the pryste for waste of ij torchys ...		ij
Halso for harry lauender to the nory ele ...		viij

* * * * * *

Expences.

	s.	d.
Halso for modys* of a wyndow yn yᵉ norre ele		xiij
Halso for modys of the klokke to roberd smyrt		iij
Halso for modys of the keverer of the vante to Richard lavender ...		ij
Halso for a kevr to yᵉ hey awter ...		viij ob.

* A model from which the artificer worked, carrying out the designer's plan

Candles were made at St. Mary Maudlin-tyde, at Bartholomew's-tyde, at St. Mary's-tyde, as also before all the great Festivals. This appears to have been an occasion upon which the makers invariably expected and always received "mete and drynke" at the cost of the church.

* * * * * *

	s.	d.
Halso for iij hawbys & iij hamyse and stolyss & fannyus to halys'n towersey	iiij	ix
Halso for warshyng of klorys to the same halys'n		iiij

* * * * * *

Receipts.

	s.	d.
Of Sir tomas the prest		iiij
Of harry tanner of haddens'		ij
Of Syr Wylly'm Schyttyrne		ij

(1449.) Receipts.

	s.	d.
We have res' of halle the parryshe at Estyr to the tryndyl and to the Estyr tapur	x	ij ob.
We resd wyt a nale y made at Wytsuntyde halkostys recued	xj	viij
Halso we resd of Wylys' redhed of Wykombe for ye fadyr ye bequyst	iij	iiij
It' of Agnes Klerke to ye Rode lyght	x	
It' of Thomas prymsham to ye Rode lyght	xiiij	vij
It' of roberde langsdale for ye testemente of petyr mapuldra'		xx

Expences.

	s.	d.
For a manuel to the Vyke' of Saundyrdon as for howr part	xj	viij*
It' to Wyllyam Karpynter of schylton, for makyng of ye setys yn ye nory' quarter of the chyrch at seynt reme ye tyde	xiij	iv
It' to Roberd Smyrt for ye makyng of ij new keyys to ye dor yn seynt jone ye elle as for howr part & for mendyng of ye lokke hallso		viij
It' to Joh'is Pradte, bokebynder of Oxford, dwellyng yn katstrete, for mendyng of the bokys, as for howre pard	v	
It' to Roberdd watyr for a bord of hokke to mende wyt ye bokys, as for howr part		ij
It' to Wyllyam Karpynter of schylton, for makyng of the setys at seynt bew ye tyde	xiij	iv
It' to Wyllyam plommer of Wykombe, for mendyng of the rofe of the stepul, as for howr parte		xiij
It' to Wyllyam Karpynter at hocketyde	xiij	iv
It' for bed and bord ix dayys, hym and ye schylde	j	v
It' yn bred and hale to . . ere to helpe hym to dryue the setys to the walle		ij

	s.	d.
It' to on of ye neyberys for the karyage of the tymbyr from schylton bedyr wenyt was y framede	j	v
It' for nayle		j

In 1449 there appears to have been a general collection for "the worke of ye setys"—possibly the first occasion upon which any permanent pews or benches were put up—to which a large number of the parishioners contributed. The principal donors were—John Mason, Richard Flynte, William Lukenor, Thomas Flynte, Robert Water, John Manyturne, John Kyng the yr, William Kosin, John Reve, Richard Barbor, John Walkeleyne, Harry Spenser, John Myles, John Elys, John Benet, and John Kyng the elder. (The surnames are spelt as written.)

* * * * * *

Expences.

	s.	d.
It' to the walow for the bryng of a payr vestements of the quest of ye beshope of lynkole*		xij
It' to halyson towersey for a begke to a grete boke		ij
It' to ye plomer of Kodysdon for a watyrtabyl of ledde yt weyyt xiiij li. & mete & drynke & settyng ynto ye walle		xiiij
It' to cocke haren for me'dyng of ye bellys howr parte	v	vj
It' for hys kostys of mete & drynke hym & ye ma' & ye hors		xvj
It' we reseyerede a kofyr of ye bequeste of John Elys the werthe ye at ye howse yt wasse su' tyme Wyllya' frogmore yt ye in ye halle a hole sute of festement that wer at hold lukenor.		
It' of Ph. Edwarde for ye beqoest of thomas loogg		vj
It' for ye beryyng of Jho. Mylton† in trenty ele	iij	iv

* * * * * *

(1452.) Receipts.

	s.	d.
It'm of Barklet of morton for his modur testame't	iij	iv
It'm of ye testament of ye same Barklot ye modor the bequere to ye rode lyrt		xij
It'm we reseyved of ye Testament of Jone Tebard of Morton‡	iiij	iv

* The Rector of Saunderton was Thomas Haryn, who had been presented in the previous year, 1448,—very probably of the family of that name of Thame; to one member of which, Valentine Harris, the last Prior of Notley Abbey, Valentine Bownde, left a legacy.

* This appears to have been William Alnwick, some time Bishop of Norwich, but translated to Lincoln in 1436, who died 5th Dec., 1449.

† It may be interesting to note that families of Milton and Powell were both flourishing at Thame in the middle of the sixteenth century. And it is clear from the above entry—comprising a high fee or donation—that the "John Milton" buried in the north transept must have occupied a good social position.

‡ Of this family was William Tebard presented to the Rectory of Saunderton 18 Feb. 1459.

	s.	d.
It'm we reseyfyd for wast of iiij torchys at ye beryying of Styrfyng		viij
It'm we reseved for John Manytorn vj s. viij d. for hys graue.		

Expensys.

	s.	d.
It'm half C latheys to stope owt ye dowffis of ye stepull		iij ob.
It'm for to make clene ye stepull & ye bellys		iij
It'm for ye mendyng of v corpys		xv
It'm for mending of ye whyrt Pewter		iij
It'm for ye makeyng of ye wedirkoke*		ij
It'm for settyng up of ye same koke		j
It'm for mendyng of a frontell to ye hy awter		iij
It'm at seynt how ye tyde ilb wexe		vj
It'm we payd to ye makyng of ye crucifix owr part	ij	iiij
It'm for mendyng of ye glasse ye glarsyer had to houyer part	iiij	
It'm ffor mendyng of the west dore ower parte		xij
It'm for ilb wex agens ouyr lady day† before crestmas		vj
It'm crystmas last was in wex xilb prys	v	vj

	s.	d.
It'm for makyng of ye same xilb wex		v ob.
It'm for makyng of viijlb of holde wex to tapur candylle		viij
It'm for ilb & a hafe of talow candell ye preys		j ob.

* * * * * * *

(1455.) Recepts.

	s.	d.
It'm we reseyved on Ester day to the paschall & to ye font tapyr and to ye trendyll*	ix	j ob.

* * * * * * *

(1456.) Expens.

	s.	d.
It'm for a buke yt we boght of John Mason ye pte	ix	
It'm for ye mendyng of ij mess bukys & j grayll	iij	iv
It'm for ye repayr of ye vestymentys & for ye womans hyr & hyr bord		xxij ob.

* * * * * * *

	s.	d.
It'm for i lyre to ye canopye		j
It'm for ye mendyng of a crosse yt lyeth at John Batyst†		iij
It'm for ladyng of ye stepull to ye plumer	xlij	viij
It'm for ye repayr of j chalence late chaunged	iij	vj
It'm for caryage off lede fro' Aylysbury to Thame for ye stepull		vj
It'm for on Amyse		iij
It'm for ye amendyng of a claspe of ye mess-buke of ye hye awter		iij ob.
It'm for ye ledder & mendyng of ye messbuke of seynt John yle		ix

* * * * * * *

(1457.) Receipts.

	s.	d.
Also we resseryd of hockmoney‡ of ye womanys Gaderyng of ye tyme iij qrs	ij	vij

* William Durandus, the distinguished liturgical writer of the thirteenth century, thus quaintly writes in his *Rationale Divinorum Officiorum*:—"The cock which is placed thereon (*i.e.* on the spire) representeth preachers. For the cock in the deep watches of the night, divideth the hours thereof with his song; he arouseth the sleepers; he foretelleth the approach of day; but first he stirreth up himself to crow by the striking of his wings. Behold ye these things mystically: for not one is there without meaning. The sleepers be the children of this world, lying in sins. The cock is the company of preachers, which do preach sharply, do stir up the sleepers to cast away the works of darkness, crying, *Woe to the sleepers: awake thou that sleepest;* which also do foretell the coming of the light when they preach of the Day of Judgement and future glory. But wisely before they preach unto others do they rouse themselves by virtues from the sleep of sin, and do chasten their bodies. Whence saith the Apostle, *I keep under my body and bring it into subjection.* The same also do turn themselves to meet the wind when they bravely do contend against and resist the rebellious by admonition and argument, lest they should seem to flee when the wolf cometh. The iron rod, upon which the cock sitteth, sheweth the straight-forward speech of the preacher; that he doth not speak from the spirit of man, but according to the Scriptures of God: as it is said, *If any man speak, let him speak as the oracles of God.* In that this rod is placed above the Cross, it is shewn that the words of Scripture be consummated and confirmed by the Cross: whence our Lord said in His Passion, *It is finished.* And His Title was indelibly written over Him. The ball (*tholus*) upon which the Cross is placed doth signify perfection by its roundness: since the Catholick Faith is to be preached and held perfectly and inviolably: Which Faith except a man do keep whole and undefiled, without doubt he shall perish everlastingly. Or else the ball doth signify the World redeemed by the Price of the Cross: on which account the Cross is placed over it. The cock being set over the Cross signifieth that the preacher ought to make sure this point, that Christ redeemed the world by His Cross."—*Symbolism of Churches and Church Ornaments*, etc., pp. 199, 200. London: 1843.

† *I.e.* the Feast of the Immaculate Conception observed on 8th December. "Our Ladyday in Lent" was the Annunciation; "our Lady Day in Harvest" the Assumption in August, or possibly the Nativity B.V.M. in September. "Our Lady Day upon Mid-summer" was the Visitation.

* A certain number of large wax candles—the cost of which was considerable—were made once or twice a year. When burnt at the obsequies of any parishioner (rich people had many, poor persons few, all had some, at least two) a uniform charge, entered as "waste of wax," was made for the same. The charge varied in amount. At the font stood "the font taper" often referred to in connection with the making of "the Easter taper" or Paschal candle. For that, lighted at baptisms, no charge was made; but the people whose children were christened almost invariably made special offerings both to the officiant and to the church. Baptism was then celebrated with many more expressive and instructive ceremonies than is the case now, and was consequently a service to which many flocked, as they were forcibly taught by its administration.

† This man was no doubt a kinsman of Mr. William and Christian Bates, great benefactors to the Church and Town, who had been munificent in their gifts. The name is remembered by the fact that certain lands in Thame are still known as "Bates's Leys." This and other similar entries show that valuable *ornaments* were often left in the keeping of the living representatives of those families which had originally bequeathed or given them.

‡ "Hock money," *i.e.* money collected at Hock-tyde, on the Hock-days. These days were the Monday and Tuesday following the Second Sunday after Easter. The money then collected was used to celebrate King Etheldred's victory over the Danes A.D. 1002, a custom sanctioned by the Laws of King Edward the Confessor.

Expences.

	s.	d.
Also we haue payd for ij Gadyrings to Rychard Sydlokke	ij	ij
Also we haue payd for mendyng of Bates Grayle		xiiij
Also we haue payde for ij Torches y^t weyed xxxij pou'de	xiij	
Also payde to ye mason for makyng of ye cherche style		v

(1458.) Receipts.

	s.	d.
Imprimis We reseyyd of Wylls' Teberd for rent of land	iiij	
It'm we resseyved of a ma' y^t deyde at Benet lambys to ye rode lyrt	ij	vj
It'm we resseryd of John East for ye beryyng of ye fadyr	iij	iv
It'm we resseyuyd of John Verdyr* for ye howse y^t was John a bryge de weston	xxiij	iv

* * * * * *

Expends.

	s.	d.
It'm payd un to John Harriys yoman bedill of Oxunford for dedis delivirydd		xx
It' payd for A man y^t mendit ye iij bells at mydsale tyde		vj
It' for me'dyng of iiij brasys to Pers tyngker ...	iiij	x
It' for wrytyng of ye dedys of Edward ye howse and possessyon takyng		xvj
It' in spensis for makyng of ye legger† be for ye Veker	ii	vj
It' for makyng of ye lant'n ye grete lant'ne		ix
It' for byndyng of ye Grayle		xv
It' for makyng of A Bagge for ye grete legger be for ye Pr'sh p'st		vj

	s.	d.
It' ffor John Dawns* y^e to Oxford ffor owyr proktor		iiij
It' ffor John Dawns to Woxford ffor ye proktor y^e sekond tyme		vj
It' ffor y^e prokter y^e last day wen wer in losuyng	iij	j

(1464.)

In this year legacies to the church were received from the following:—John Miller 4^d, and other gifts amounting in value to $3^s\ 4^d$. John Bartlot gave barley to the value of 6^d. The wife of William Tebard left 2^d. From John Bartlet for the work of the church $3^s\ 4^d$ was received. John Sadeler bequeathed $3^s\ 4^d$ and $6^s\ 8^d$; and William East, sen^r, of West Wycombe, left $3^s\ 4^d$.

* * * * * *

(1465.) Receipts.

	s.	d.
It' we have resseryd of John Dau'on in y^e name of y^e p'son for strawyng of y^e chirch		xx

Expens.

	s.	d.
It' we payd for a halywat' stycke of latyn†		ix
It' we payde for heggyng of y^e chyrch howse & for a locke to y^e hall dor		x
It' we payde for a corn for ye claspe of ye best mas boke & wasshyng of ye hye aut' cloyis		v
It' we payde for a pype locke‡ to ye trenite ele dore in ye loft		x
It' for Rydyng to Newelme to fet a ma' to mende ye bellys		ij ob.
It' for Rydyng to Oxford to speke w^t ye abbot of Osney for ye chyrch howse		iiij
It' for Rydyng to Bryghtwel to speke w^t my mayst' Rede for ye chyrch howse		ij ob.
It' we payde for makyng of ye poleys§ for ye crowne w^t ye lampis		j

* * * * * *

(1465.)

	s.	d.
It' we haue resseryd of Will'm Coryn for duetees y^t he owyt to ye chyrche		xx
It' we haue resseryd of Will'm Coryn for ye sam duete & yit a^s y^t be hynde		xl

* * * * * *

* "Ville Dieu" corrupted to "Verder."

† The "Leger" was a MS. book containing entries of various kinds relating to the Church either of interest or importance. The names of the benefactors were therein recorded; of those who held the church lands, the lands for lamp-lights, and of all personal gifts, dues, and donations, and the recorded conditions upon which they had been bestowed. It contained directions for the carrying on divine service, special rules not found in the service books, but traditionally regarded and observed by the clergy; the days and dates for obits or commemorations of the dead; copies of grants, wills, letters, dispensations, and other official documents or directions from the bishop and ecclesiastical authorities of the diocese; and it, no doubt, in some respects served the purpose of the modern Kalendar and Directory. How festivals which "concurred" were to be observed; on what days processions took place; when commemorations of the dead had been made, or masses said, the character and details of funerals for the different degrees of rank, were all recorded, under the hand and authority of the Vicar and "Churchmen," *i.e.* Churchwardens, or else by the hand of the scribe. Occasionally the advent of some local nobleman or abbot, the coming of the diocesan on his visitation of churches, the passing of the King with his court and retinue through the town, were recorded. In the universal destruction of books under the Tudors—some of which were intentionally made away with in the suppression of evidence regarding Church property—almost all such Legers were destroyed. Similar volumes were similarly used at the Religious Houses, and must have contained most interesting and important information.

* A son of this John, of the same name, who was knighted by King Henry VIII., was Chief Steward of the demesne lands of Notley Abbey at the period of its suppression, and is mentioned in the "Accounts" later on.

† This was technically termed *Aspergillum*, "aspergill;" and was used for sprinkling the people with holy water during the procession before High Mass.

‡ *I.e.* a bolt.

§ *I.e.* poles or sticks, round the head of which pieces of thin wax taper were twisted and fastened with which to light the *coronæ*, or crowns, suspended from the roof.

	s.	d.
It' we resseryd of Elyzabeth Milton to ye rode lyght		ij
It' a geyne Estur we lete set Ryngs upon ye cloth yt hangyth a geyne ye Rode........		j ob.
It' for washyng of ye to clotheys yt hangyn agayne ye Rode loft we payde		j ob.
It' for washyng of a vestme't ageyne good fryday & settyng on of ye aubs........		ob.
It' we payde for beryng hom of ye organs fro' owr pley........		ob.
It' we haue payde for mendyng of the crowns in ye Rode-loft		ij
It' we have payde for oyle to ye lampus in ye rode loft........		ij
It' we have payde for byndyng of ye Rode loft wt yron at both ends		iiij
It' we have payde for a pot to ber in owr oyle		ob.
It' we have payde for skowryng of ye lampys in ye rode loft........		ob.
It' we payd for washyng of ye long cloth* yt hangyth be for ye hye aut'........		j
It' we payd for makyng of ye sepulcere† at Ester		ob.
It' we spende when we Rode to Oxford to spake wt Mayst' Will'm Raffe to wete wen ye dene of lyncoln wer at lyncoln......		iiij
It' we payd to Mayst' Quat'mans clerke for makyng of ye bille to ye dene of lyncoln ...		vj
It' we haue payde to John Cowp' for fotyng of ye clocke & for makyng of a flor by to save ye rode loft yif ye peyse fall for ij dayes labor		v
It' we payde for hys mete & drynke........		ij ob.
It' we payd to Thoms Smyth for gret nayles ...		ob. q'
It' we payd for tymb' for ye clocke fete		j ob.
It' we payd for ij new Gyistys‡ for ye new flor		ij

* This was a long white cloth of fine linen, attached to the temporary hand-rail or moveable support, placed as occasion required, in front of the altar, at which the people knelt on being communicated. Each person received the Holy Sacrament in his mouth, and held the cloth with both hands during reception, so that, if by any mishap an accident happened, no irreverence need take place. "To housel" was to give the Blessed Sacrament; "to be houselled" was to receive it; and this cloth was consequently termed "the houselling cloth."

† The "sepulchre," as it was called, was frequently a slight temporary erection of wood, placed on the north side of the choir, sometimes in a stone recess, at no great distance from the High Altar, and hung with rich palls and coverings of cloth of gold. This was certainly its form at Thame. Its hangings, which must have been rich and valuable, were sold to William Bebyngfeld for the considerable sum of forty shillings and eightpence by Edward VI.'s Commissioners, or at their suggestion, in the year 1550. In it the Blessed Sacrament was reserved from Maundy Thursday until Easter Even, to set forth and symbolise the Burial of our Lord. Often an image of an angel, or more than one, was placed near: it was always surrounded with lighted tapers, and watchers praying near in appointed relays, worshipped with devotion, rich and poor taking their turn. Sometimes this "sepulchre" was a substantial and permanent construction in stone. Often figures of sleeping soldiers, representing the Roman guard, were introduced; while the whole construction was most elaborately adorned in colours and with gilding. Examples of such still remain at Hawton in Nottinghamshire, at Bampton in Oxfordshire, and at Stanton St. John's. It is believed that the Founder's tomb in St. Mary Magdalen College, Oxford, was used for the "sepulchre."

‡ *I.e.* joists.

(1465.)

	s.	d.
It' we gave to childryn to gad' yvy		ob.

(1466.)

	s.	d.
It' we payde to Wandylbrorth for a yron ladyl to ye sylour sens'		iiij
It' we lete washe ageyn Estur a hole sute & a ferial vestme't & a surplice		ij ob.
It' we payde to ye Glasyer for mendyng of ye stepul wyndowes & ye body of ye chyrch & led		xxj
It' we payde to ye Glasyer for mendyng of ye wyndowes in ye trenite ele & ye Northe syde & led		xvij

(1468.) **Expensys.**

	s.	d.
It' we haue payde to John Garthorpe for rydyng to lyncoln ij tymes........	xiij	iv
It' we have payde to John Garthorpe to ryde to lyncolne		xl

(1469.) **Receptis.**

	s.	d.
We haue resseryd of Thomas Tybbarde for rent of ye howse yt Conyn dwellyth in........	iiij	viij
We have resseryd of John Chapma' for bakers place	xxvij	viij

(1474.) **Receptis.**

	s.	d.
It' receyvyd of geferey Dorm' for owr part for strawyng of ye chyrche	iij	iv

Expensys.

	s.	d.
It' we payd for mendyng of ye grene cope & ye canape	iij	iv
It' for owr part of ye rope yt drawyth up the kanape of ye fant		iij ob.
It' for owr part of the holy bred basket		ij ob.
It' we payd for brewyng of the Ale at Wyt Sondy		xij

The following details relating to the erection of two "organ-lofts" or "solars" are of interest. It is possible that these erections were placed one on either side of the west end of the choir, which, as a matter of convenience, would have been found a suitable position for a pair of organs, or it may be that these are the actual "Solars" or "Lofts" referred to elsewhere in the "Accounts," as being situated in "Master Dormers Ile."

(A.D. 1477-80.)

CUSTUS SOLAR. P. ORGAN.

	s.	d.
It'm sol. Thome Carpenter s.p' factura ij solarior p. organis situand' in gross'	viij	viij
It' sol. Petro marmyon p. i magno ligno maeremij p. dict' solario	iij	iv
It' sol. p. vij p'uis peciis meremij pre ca ij		xiiij
It' sol. p. ij lignis meremii ad dict' opus		x

	s.	d.
It' sol. p. ij plankes ad id'm opus		xij
It'm in cert' clavis vis iiij peny nayle & vd nayle		viij
It'm in asseribus vis. CC & i qrt' ad idem opus	vj	
It' sol. Will'm' Smyth p' heng' hoks & ij barres ferri ad id'm op'		xxij ob.
S'ma	xxiiij	ij ob.
Et sic p. p'te noue Thame	xij	i jq'
S'm' Solar. p' organ. p. noba Thame	xij	i jq'

The following extracts relating to the latter years of the fifteenth century are reproduced as they appear in the "Accounts:"—

	s.	d.
(1494.)		
It' (and again in 1498) to Mr Vycare for the bedrolle for Robert hegurston		iiij
(1496.)		
It' rec' of money gadered by Robyn Hood at the same tyme clerely	xiiij	
It' rec' of Thom's Striblehill for rent of his ten' for j yere	iiij	
(1498.)		
It' paide to John Wellington for ye mendyng of i candelstykke the schepe wt mose' ye lever and ye belowys of the organ	v̄	
It' to John Wellington for ye mendyng of the canopie and ye scoryng of ij grete standard and ye iiij candilstykks on ye hye awter ...		xvj

A few more notes and extracts in detail, several of them serving to illustrate the customs of our ancestors, and throwing a light on those services and rites of the Church then commonly said and observed, may here be given. In the "Accounts" for 1503, "Shere Thursday" is mentioned, and the Vicar received the sum of fourpence for reciting the accustomed Bede Roll and for praying for the dead. At Master Richard Fowler's burial a like sum was paid for the waste of torches. He had become the heir of the Quartermains of Weston. Again, at the burial of Geoffrey Dormer, his widow Alice paid the usual sum of six shillings and eightpence "for the berying of her husband," as the entry stands. Julian Bocher paid a similar fee for a like occurrence in the same year. A rochet, that is a linen vestment without sleeves, or possibly with tight sleeves, was provided for the Sexton at a cost of twenty-two pence. Christopher Bridgeman,* the Sexton and Scribe, received five shillings for writing some additions to a mass-book. In the same year, 1503, probably in course of his ordinary visitation of a very large diocese, William Smith, Lord Bishop of Lincoln, twice came into the town, when the ringers welcomed him with a peal on the bells from the church tower. The veil-cloth which hung between the choir and nave, still used in the Oriental Church, is mentioned in the "Accounts" for this year; and so is the Bede Roll for Master Nicholas Hagarston, who had been a liberal benefactor to the church. The Bellman and the "Clerke of Old Thame" each had a new rochet provided, which together cost two shillings and eightpence. The Bishop's "Somner," or Summoner, brought the sacramental oils, episcopal documents and written authorities, year by year, and received eightpence for his accustomed annual fee. The steple was cleaned at least every year, and the leads of the church, and the gutters of the roof, swept; while sometimes an entry occurs for removing the snow. In 1510 the details of a solemn and impressive funeral are recorded, of one "Master Piers,"* and about the same time Elizabeth Pratt bequeathed six shillings and a penny to the Rood Light. In the same year the Ordinary, the Lord Bishop of Lincoln, again visited the church. On every Palme Sunday the singers who chanted the Passion of our Lord received a gift of "brede and ale." In 1511, under the heading of "Detts owing to the Chirche," it is recorded that "Thomas Strippulhyll owithe to the chirche ffor the beryng off his wyff vj s. viij d.," and for the "waste of torches" on that occasion the sum of two shillings. The Abbot of Notley is in arrears for rent. There are also other debtors. "Master Parson owithe to the chirche for strewing the quer and the setts by the yer iij s. iv d. wiche ys onpayde xi yere sum' xxxvj s. viij d." "Robert Pereson owithe to the chirche in mony iiij li. vj s. iij d." In 1512 the Bishop of Lincoln again visited Thame, and at his visitation blessed a chalice; and the young King, Henry VIII., passed through the town the same year, when his Highness was welcomed by the ringers. Little enough did the people then imagine what changes were in store for them in matters ecclesiastical. It is also on record that one penny was paid for Rushes "agayne the feast of Pentecost." In 1513 "Mistress Dormer," the widow of Mr. Geoffrey, was buried in the church, at the liberal cost of six shillings and eightpence; "Jerom Holt for his office,"—evidently that of "Somner"—received the customary fee of eightpence, and two shillings and twopence were expended in "paving tyle for Mastr Dormers modres grave." In 1516 a representation of the Resurrection Play "produced xxj s. vj d." Here occurs an *hiatus* of five years in the "Accounts."

* Christopher Bridgeman was the Sexton or Sacrist in 1496. John Bridgeman, his father—who originally termed himself "John A Brigge de Weston," or "John-at-the Brigge"—had filled the same office before him; his original name occurring in the Churchwardens' "Accounts" as early as the year 1458. The inscription upon the memorial brass of Christopher is given later on.

* This may have been either "Piers Marmyon" or "Piers Powlyn"—both persons of family and substance.

In 1520 the following entries are on record:—

	s.	d.
It' rec' of the lyghtmen of the sepulchre	iii li	
It' rec' of the lyghtmen of the trinitie yle	vj	viij
It' rec' of the lyghtmen of saynt Johns yle	iij	iv
It' rec' of the lyghtmen of our lady in jesus ...	xiij	iv
It' rec' of the same light men A golde rynge recd	vj	iv
It' rec' of the light men of All Sowlys light	x	
It' rec' of X'ofer Brystwyke for Maister Adryan late p'bendary for A yere endyd at Witsontyde for strawing of the church	iij	iv

It appears from the "Accounts" for the same year, that two linen altar-cloths for the high altar were then provided at a cost of 4s. 6d., and two others for side altars at a cost of 4s. 4d. These were hallowed by the Bishop of Lincoln's suffragan—"Suferingan to my Lord of Lincol'," "the Abbot of Dorchester,"* as the entry stands, when a fee of 6d. was paid.† John Hayward "for carying of the seid clothis to halowying" also received 6d. At that time it seems that the church (the solemn services of which must have been rendered by many priests and clerks) possessed at least twenty-one linen albes and two rochets, for these were then mended and washed. These linen garments were independent of surplices,—of which there appear to have been more than three dozen of various sorts and sizes.

In the year 1521 there occurs a remarkable and touching entry, thus:—

	s.	d.
It' recd of a man that will not be named for fynding of a candyll brennyng before the rode in the rode loft eu'y Sonday in the yere at the sakering of hye masse............		xvj

The "Leger" and the "Church Book" were again mended, increased in size by the addition of many skins of parchment, and newly bound at this time. Here are the entries concerning them, affording a good idea of the cost of such work early in the sixteenth century:—

	s.	d.
It' paied for p'chment thred and glew to the byndiug of the Church book		vj
It' paied for borde to the same boke		iij
It' payed for borde to the grete lygger before Mr Vicar		iv
It' payed to Will'm Chadlok for claspe lether to the same boke		iv
It' paied for iiij bonys of bras to set on the same boke		viij
It' paid for iij buck skynnys to the kou'yng of the same boke	iiij	
It' paid for A dosyn of red skynnys to the same boke	iiij	
It' paid for A dosyn of white skynnys to the same boke	iij	
It' paid to the boke bynder for byndiug of the same boke	xvj	viij

The "Accounts" for 1522 are lost. In those for the following year this entry stands:—

	s.	d.
It' recd of Thom' Stribillyll toward the new making and bylding of A charnall howse in the Church of Thame for a hole yere endyd at our lady day in Lent in the yere abouesaid in p'te of payme't of...............	xl	

And immediately afterwards the following:—

	s.	d.
It' recd for the sepulcre of John Awger	vj	viij
It' receyved of the bequest of the same John to certayn lyghts in the church and to the bying of A cope	x	
It' recd of the p'son of Staunton for the old organs in p'te of payme't of ls. xliijs ivd rest	vj	viij

The following extracts relate to the various lights in the Church, and are taken from the "Records" of the same year:—

		s.	d.
In the hands of Robt' Mortym' & Geoffrey Stockdale to th' use of the sepulcre.........	vi li	iiij	iiij
It' in the hands of Thom' Modersby & Robt Tyler kep'rs of the trin'tie Ile		x	x ob.
It' in the handes of Alexander Glou' & John Bunse kepr of Saynt Johns Ile		viij	ix
It' in the honds of Nic'ase Morley & Richard Oldfeld kepr's of or lady pew		ix	iij ob.
It' in the hoods of Richard Bunse & John Tomlynson kepr of All Sowlys lyght		viij	ob.

There are two entries under the year 1523, which deserve special notice, as they serve to shew something of the nature of the annual plays which were performed, either in the Church or Churchyard, on the Tuesday in Easter week, and occasionally at other seasons, as at the Epiphany, May day,* or Corpus Christi day. These entries stand thus:—

* This was Richard Beauforest, Abbot of Dorchester, Oxon, and a Bishop of some See *in partibus infidelium*. He belonged to a good old Oxfordshire family resident in the city of Dorchester, which had sprung from Deane in Gloucestershire. He died in the spring of 1525, and was buried in the choir of the Abbey Church, where his memorial brass still remains. He is represented with hands joined in prayer, in the choral habit of an Augustinian wearing the almuce, *almutium*, the choral cope, *cappa choralis*, and having the pastoral staff encircled by his right arm. On a label coming out of his mouth stands the following—**O dulcis mater virgo virginu' ora pro nobis.**

And beneath the following—

Here lyeth Sir Richard Beauforreste
Pray thee give hys sowle good Rest.

† On another occasion the following record occurs:—

It' payed for the halowing of iij awter clothis............... xxd
A.D. 1521.

* Compare with the above extracts those given later on in the "Accounts" for the year 1557, under Queen Mary of happy memory, when the May Ale was restored, and the minstrels and other performers were housed, fed, and well rewarded for their labours by the Churchwardens.

	s.	d.
It' payed for writing of the p'cells of the iij kings of Colen & Herod on Corp' X'ti day		viij
It' payed to X'fer Myxbury for keping of the yernaments and chevelers for the Resurrection played in the Church of Thame ...		xvj

The first relates to a then popular play or "mystery" in which the coming of the Eastern Kings to the Shrine at Bethlehem, the murder of the Innocents, and the preservation of our Divine Lord, afforded scope for touching incidents, tragic effects, and picturesque representations. The "parcells" were the different written parts for the various performers to recite. "The Interlude of the Bitter Passion of Chryste Jhesus" was another subject of great interest, and was often represented. These miracle-plays, as they were called, were of very special use in effectually teaching the people great religious truths and interesting historical facts through the eye, and were exceedingly popular. With nine out of every ten persons born in a country town, it was probably the case that such never in the whole of their uneventful lives went any greater distance than twenty or twenty-five miles from their homes; and consequently were entirely dependent upon the resources of the town itself for any innocent and rational amusement, which, from time to time, they might enjoy. Then, to the behoof of the nation, everything gathered round the Church. The ancient faith was a reality. God's sanctuary was the common home of all. Men themselves content to dwell in timber houses or cottages of wattle, gave freely of their best to furnish worthily the House of God the Trinity—the principal building of the village or town. Therein, rich and poor, high and low, knelt side by side, or stood shoulder by shoulder, in the worship of the Almighty. The clergy were the natural teachers of the people, the obvious leaders amongst the multitude; while True Religion stamped its beneficent influence on all, and tinctured their every thought. In sorrow and in joy, in sadness, and when rejoicing, in their ordinary work, and during their times of recreation and amusement, our English forefathers had God before their eyes, while the beautiful island in which they dwelt was accurately described as "merrie England."

Various kinds of entertainments were given. Some were dramas, or directly dramatic in their substance, others were like the Ober-Ammergau Passion-Play of Bavaria—a series of set scenes made up of living figures: others, again, were a combination of dialogue and action, with musical interludes and explanations by a *Magister* or *Director*. But they were all at once instructive or amusing, according to season and circumstance. They set forth some religious fact, described the heroic fortitude and patience of some great saint, or recorded certain details of past history of national importance; and were keenly appreciated. A temporary stage was erected, about six feet from the ground, covered with canvas, enclosed with wings, and hung with tapestry, where sometimes incidents were depicted in dumb show by the performers, and sometimes with appointed dialogue and pre-arranged action. Under the stage their dresses were assumed and changed. On one occasion, at least, the organs of the Church were lent for the performance, and their return to the Church duly put on record. The players very frequently were members of a religious guild—of which the Warden was sometimes a clerk of rank and learning, and which always owned several Chaplains. These dignitaries, by instruction, advice, and careful drilling, superintended the literary part of the entertainment; while officers, specially appointed for the purpose and known as "Wardens of the Play," made arrangements for engaging competent players, erecting the platform, preparing the dresses and accompaniments, providing the minstrels, and housing and feeding them all during their temporary sojourn in the town. The players, if not members of a religious guild, were occasionally a well-drilled band in the service of some nobleman or knight of influence, whose patronage was proclaimed; and thus secured for them various engagements in and about the locality in which their abilities were known and recognized. The "ornaments," —spears, armour, surcoats and shields, of which Christopher Myxbury of Thame was the official custodian on the part of the townspeople, were used for that particular miracle-play almost invariably represented on Easter Tuesday; and probably on Easter Sunday afternoon.

Some weeks before the event, the Town Crier gave notice of the Play to be rendered every market-day, so that people of all ranks from the villages and manors round about flocked into the town to witness the exhibition—the pecuniary result of which was that the Parish Churchwardens, after all expenses had been paid, very often received several pounds,* which were appropriated to the ordinary needs of the Church—substantial repairs, and other similar work. Records of such receipts still remain.

In Edward the Sixth's reign, the various local players, minstrels and miracle-men, following popular taste, sharply and sorely satirized the innovators throughout the kingdom. Cranmer's foreign intermeddlers were severely handled, and the changes in religion deprecated. Sir John Cheke complained of

* For example, at the May Ale of New Thame, in 1532, Richard Ray, John Benet, Christopher Brystwycke and John Renner, the Churchwardens, received no less than £4 13s. 0d.; and from that of Old Thame, £2 1s. 0d.

this increasing and almost irreverent inconvenience, and brought it before the Council. By consequence a Proclamation of the most severe and arbitrary nature, dated 6th of August, 1549, was issued. All miracle-plays, mysteries, interludes, and similar exhibitions were distinctly and sternly forbidden. The document in question maintained that these and such-like entertainments too often arraigned the government and brought authority into contempt: that many disturbances and disorders had arisen in various places by consequence of the liberty of speech and action hitherto enjoyed; and that consequently, to avoid such offences in future, no stage performances in English of any sort or kind were to take place on any plea or under any circumstance between the day on which the Proclamation was issued, and the feast of All Saints, then next ensuing. The penalty for disregarding this was imprisonment on bread and water, and further punishment at the King's pleasure and discretion.

During the reign of Queen Mary, as has been pointed out, the miracle-plays were again restored; while under Elizabeth dramas of a classical character —neither over-refined nor very edifying—became very popular, first with the upper classes, and subsequently with those below them. The same taste prevailed during the reign of King James I. But one or two fragments of the more ancient religious plays have been occasionally represented—though with many barbarous corruptions and undesirable changes—year by year during the intervening generations. The text of a "Christmas Miracle-Play," to which a few remarks of the author's are prefixed, still occasionally performed in the Town and neighbourhood, is given amongst the "Appendices."

Other extracts from the "Accounts" now follow. Many of the details of these later "Accounts," however, require exceedingly little explanation or annotation. They tell their own story simply and plainly. Here and there it may be, a quaint expression, a word spelt eccentrically, or an unusual entry may require a little careful attention ere its meaning be self-evident. Otherwise the various details are perfectly plain, and full of interest to the antiquary, the historian, and the ecclesiologist:—

(1530.) Expences.

* * * * * *

	s.	d.
It'm p^{d} for the obbytt holden for the benefactors by ye yere	x	vj
It'm p^{d} to Geffrey Brasher for kepyng of the churche		j
It'm p^{d} to Jone Baker for scowryng of ij greatt candellstycks standing yn the channell		iij
It'm p^{d} to Mast' Standiche for pet' pens	viij	iiij
It' p^{d} to Sur Umfrey and to Will'm Barett gyyng to the Lord Abbott of Thame * for halowyng of xij corporals		xij
It' p^{d} to the clarke of hadenh'm for mendyng of the bewlys of the organs		vj

(1531.)

* * * * * *

	s.	d.
It' p^{d} for a present of wyne to Sur John Dewnes	ij	
It' p^{d} for th'obbytte of ye benefactors †	x	ij
It'm p^{d} for v propes to kepe the carps upryght yn the rood loft		iiij

(1532.) Receipts.

Receved att the may ale of newe Thame clerely	iiij li.	xiij s.
	s.	d.
Received att the maye ale of the old Thame clerely	xlj	
Received of the churchmen of Toursely for peters pens due thys seyd yere	ij	
Receved of the churchmen of Sydenham for peters pens due this seme yere	ij	
Receved of the churchmen of Tettesworth for peters pens		xviij
Receved of Weston for peters pens		
Receved of Morton for peters pens	ij	
Re^{d} of new Thame old Thame and pr'stynd for peters pens	iiij	ij

(1533.) Receipts.

* * * * * *

	s.	d.
Receved of Master Doctor Mortemar of the gyfth of Master Archdeacon	vj	viij
It'm gevyn to Master Michell Dormer and Mr Richard Dormer a bottell of wyn		vj

(1534.) Receipts.

* * * * * *

	s.	d.
Receved for the sepulture of W^{m} hellys	vj	viij
It'm Rec^{d} off Betrywe Edryche for waste of iij torches ‡		vj

* *I.e.* Robert King, or Kynge, Bishop of Rheon and Suffragan to the Bishop of Lincoln.

† Mass was said at least yearly for the repose of the souls of all the benefactors of the Church, whose names and gifts were always carefully recorded and preserved. On such occasions their living representatives (if such remained) were present, with many of the parishioners. A Dole of Bread, or other gifts in kind and money, was generally made at the funeral and often repeated year by year. In 1535 the cost of Bread provided by the Wardens out of funds for that purpose amounted to four shillings. In 1534, the expenditure on this anniversary amounted to 13s. 2d.

‡ Anciently at funerals, not only were torches carried before the corpse when borne to burial, headed by the processional cross without its staff, but four or six large tapers on standards were placed at the four corners of the bier, during the funeral service. For these (though provided by the Church Authorities, and paid for originally out of the church funds) there seems to have been no uniform charge at Thame of so much for each taper. The amount paid for burial within the Church was for several centuries an unvarying sum—six shillings and eightpence.

Expences.

	s.	d.
It'm paid to a Tynkker ffor mendyng of the holy water stocks * and for the lattyn censures		iiij
It'm p'd ffor iij lb. of talow candells ffor crismas day yn the mornyng		ix
It'm paied to Maister Vicar for the wast of some torches at the Beryall of Will'm herres ...		ij
It'm p'd for xx elles of lynnen clothe for to make thre surples for the churche	xij	vj
It'm p'd for the makyng of the same surples ...	v	
It'm to John Bennett ffor lampe oyle and for lampes for the Rood lyght and for his labour	iiij	viij
It'm paied to Clayes wyffe ffor scowryng of the candellstycks in the roode loft		vj
It'm paied ffor the anniversary for the benefactories of ye church	xiij	ij
It'm p'd to Ric'd Clay ffor hs halfe yeres wages		viij
It'm p'd for the scowryng of the candelstyckes yn the quere before the his awter		iiij
It'm payed to Thomas Bloxham for ffooting of a stole in the quere		iiij
It' payed to Syaley Whyte for mendyng of iiij baner clothis		vj
It'm p'd for makyng of vijli of syses at dyrge tyme and for the rood lyght		viij
It' p'd for xijli and ½ of wax for the same lyght	vij	iiij
It' p'd for iiijli and q' of wax and for makyng of the paschall tap'	ij	viij
It' p'd for oon li. wax and for makyng of the ffont tap'		viij
It' p'd for vili of wax to the trendell	iij	vj
It' p'd to Will'm Barett for kepyng of the clocke for mydsom' quarter		xx
It' p'd to Ric'd Clay ffor swepyng of the church stepull and the churche leeds		iiij
It'm p'd for alle on palme Sonday		j ob
It'm p'd for tymb' for a Beres		viij
It' p'd to maryon Jacson ffor washeshyng of surples	ij	

(1535.) Receipts.

* * * * * *

	s.	d.
It'm receyveyd off John Cole ffor the sepultre of ys wyffe	vj	viij
It'm Receyvyd at the ffeast of th'anativitie of our Lord Jh'u Cryst of the p'rche for the Rood lyght	xiij	
It'm Rec'd of Thomas Tylar for the Rent of the Churche Ten't for oon hoole yere endyd at the feast of th' annunciacon of o' lady	viij	
It'm receyved at Est' of the parishe for the Rood lyght	xxiij	x
It'm Rec'd off the per'che at the feast off th' annunciation of our blessed lady V'rgyn last towards the clarks waygs	vj	j
Rec'd at the Resurreccion play de Clay	xxvj	viij

Expences.

	s.	d.
Imprimis paied to Thomas Cannon of Crendon ffor the Rent of a Ten't in the sowthe q'rtr off New Thame that Thomas Tyler whelar holdyth of the churche		xij
It'm paied to Richard Clay for hys q'ters wagys		iiij
It'm paied to Symon Synclere for hys wagys for midsom' q'rter	xx	
It'm paied to the same Symeon for his wagys at Michelmas	xx	
It'm p'd to John Burns for the beryng of holy and Ivy ffor the Churche agaynst Cristmas		ij
It'm p'd for vili of candells that were Burned yn the mattyns tyme at dyvers seasons ...		x
It'm p'd for bred at the anniversary of the benefactores* of this churche	iiij	
It'm p'd for ij dosen of systenes ye ale	ij	vj
It'm p'd to p'ste clarke and children	iiij	vij
It'm p'd for wast of wax		vj
It'm p'd for a cord for the vayle		ij

* * * * * *

(1536.) Receipts.

	s.	d.
It'm recevyd of Thomas Tylar the whyle maker ffor a hoell yere rent of a Ten't latte Thomas Byrtts of Shabendon	viij	

Expences.

* * * * * *

	s.	d.
Item paied for bred and ale on palme Sonday		j
It' p'd to Maryan Jacson for washyng the churche ger this ye'	iij	iv
It' p'd to Will'm Baret for mendyng of albys wt a amys		vj

(1547.) Expences.

* * * * * *

	s.	d.
It' payd to ye paynt' for payntynge ye vayle before ye rood and ye rectors stool		viij

(1548.) Expences.

* * * * * *

	s.	d.
It'm to Master Dormer for to by colorys for ye paynting		
It'm payd to ye pargitor for xxxix days work in whitt lynyng of the church after ye rat of vijd ye daye ffyndyng himself meat and drynke	xxij	ix

* The Holy Water was blessed every week, and bread which was distributed after mass—the Holy Loaf—was hallowed likewise. At the Sunday aspersion on two occasions, viz.:—Easter morning and Whitsuntide, however, water hallowed on the previous days, Easter Even and Whitsun Eve, was often used, and the stone vessels which are sometimes found hacked and mutilated at the entrances of churches were filled with Holy Water week by week for the use of the faithful. The form for blessing the bread—"the Holy Loaf," *Eulogiæ*, often stands immediately after that for blessing holy water in the ancient "Manuals."

* Doles of Bread and Ale, as has been pointed out, were given to the poor at the anniversary of all the benefactors of the Church; and in some cases inhabitants of Thame had bequeathed lands and tenements, from the proceeds of which similar gifts were publicly bestowed after divine service every Sunday. The Quartermains of Weston had been liberal benefactors, and the oldest of their tombs is still called "The Poor Stone."

*   *   *   *   *

	s.	d.
It'm payd to harry Cowper for xv C. bords for to mak ye loft on Master Dormer's Ile ……	xj	
It'm for meadynge ye pulpyt and a desk for the Byble with Jemyes nayles and workemanshippe……		xij
It'm for iijlb candle for ye queyre ……		vj
It'm for bred for ye holy lofe……		j
It'm for ye expens at ye weynge of ye playt……		viij
It'm recd of Mr Will'm Dormer for ij cruetts of Sylvr weying xj unces after the rat of iiijs xd ye unce—Sum ……	lv	vij

It thus appears that at a very considerable cost the old decorations of walls and window-splays were washed out at this period—the second year of the reign of Edward VI. It is recorded that Mr. William Dormer superintended the work. Although some members of this family clung to their ancient faith, others apparently were quite prepared to co-operate with the advocates of change, and, when occasion offered, to benefit by it. Various entries shew that much of the church plate and many of the ornaments were about this period abstracted, that no sufficient account was ever provided of their original value or of the amount derived from their sale;—that the rage for change and confiscation had become so remarkably powerful, that every person of influence who believed himself likely to secure any personal advantage by approving the new policy, did so; while the confiscatory principle involved in taking a portion of the proceeds of the sale of the Church goods in order to mend the causeway at the southern part of the Town, appears to have been tacitly accepted as perfectly right and reasonable. Any regard for the memory of those who, through several centuries, had been benefactors to the church, and had bequeathed lands and money for the honour and worship of God, had evidently ceased to exist; or else (which is more than probable) the ferocity of the Tudors and the resolution of their official tools so overawed the people, that they were afraid to speak out.

In order to understand the true state of national affairs, which in every town and village led to practical changes of a somewhat revolutionary character as regards Religion, the consequences of which are still felt, it is necessary to realize the situation, as it was slowly unfolded after the unmourned death of King Henry VIII. upon 28 January, 1547. The child who succeeded him, Edward VI., by reason of his youth, of course exercised exceedingly little influence on public events. The real rulers were first his astute uncle, the Duke of Somerset, and afterwards the bold and unscrupulous John Dudley, Duke of Northumberland—two persons of exceedingly little principle. From purely political motives they allied themselves with Cranmer and the innovating party; who, uprooting much and pulling down more, laboured incessantly to set up Protestantism and to render the clergy mere creatures of the State. These latter, it is to be feared, were already too pliable, and pliable because of want of sound principle, and for the lack of means for active co-operation either with other. Monastic corporations had already been rudely crushed out of existence; could "corporations sole" withstand the pressure from above? Ridley and Poynet were appointed bishops by Letters Patent, and readily consented to become mere stipendiaries of those who appointed them; while the revenues of their sees were appropriated for secular purposes by order of the Council. The Bishoprick of Durham was altogether suppressed, and that of Gloucester was united to Worcester. In lieu of the ancient service books a Prayer Book in English was compiled in 1548, and ordered to be everywhere used on Easter Sunday 1549. At the same time the Lords of the Council issued Proclamations against observing the old Christian rites common to Candlemass Day and Ash Wednesday. Later on a general Visitation of Churches was carried out, the Visitors being laymen, for the purpose of breaking down images, removing altars and pictures, and enforcing the new rites and service-book on the dazed and astonished clergy. All the old books were to be delivered up on pain of severe punishment. A new and somewhat bold Form for the consecration of bishops, and the ordering of priests and deacons, was put forth in 1549, a compilation which has proved a source of continual controversy from that day to the present. A copy of the "Bishops' Bible" and the *Paraphrase* of Erasmus were ordered by Royal Injunction to be procured, for which the clergyman was bound to pay half the cost, and the parishioners the other half.*

A book of "Homilies" was issued by authority embodying in somewhat coarse and violent language the crude opinions of the innovators. Peter Martyr, Fagius, Bucer, and other communistic foreigners, were invited to England to assist the new authorities, by pen and voice, in breaking down the powerful opposition which was everywhere being experienced; while official Visitors were sent to the two Universities in order to

* "They shall provide within three monethes next after this Visitation, one book of the whole Bible, of the largest volume in English. And within one twelve moneths next after the said Visitation the *Paraphrasis* of Erasmus, also in English, upon the Gospels, and the same set up in some convenient place within the said church, that they have care of, whereat their parishioners may most commodiously resort unto the same and read the same. The charges of which books shall be notably born between the Parson or Appropriatary, and Parishioners aforesaid, that is to say, the one half by the Parson or Proprietary, and the other half by the Parishioners." "Injunctions given by the Most Excellent Prince, Edward the Sixth," etc. London: Printed by R. Grafton, 1547.

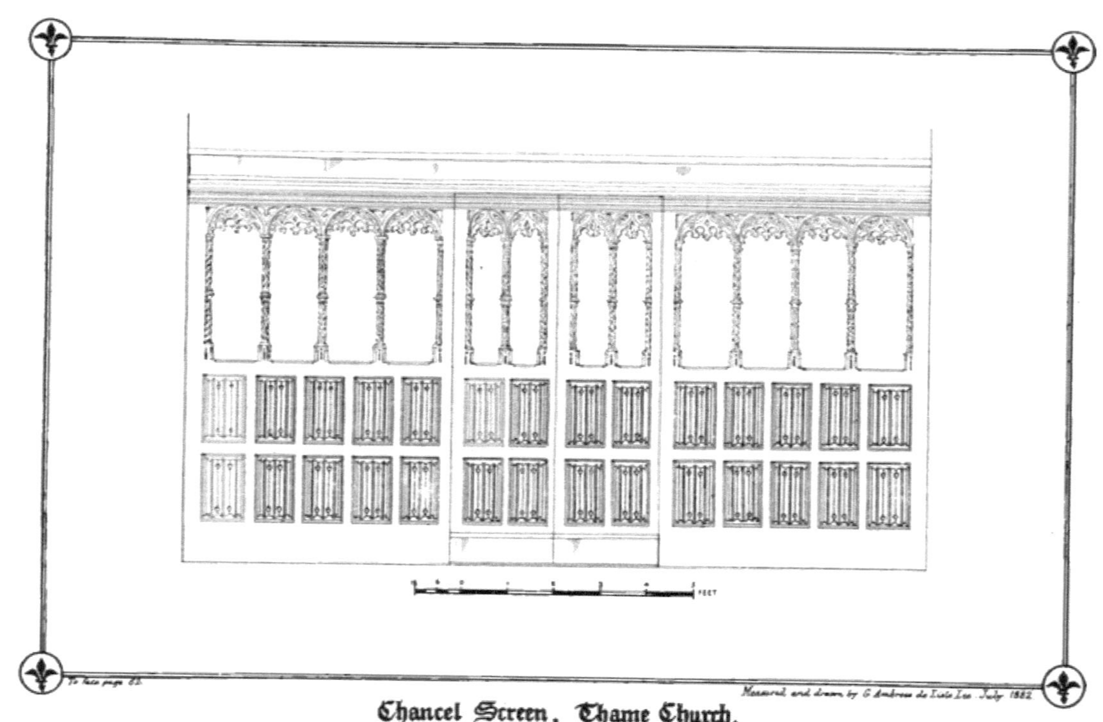

To face page 62.

Measured and drawn by G. Ambrose de Lisle Lee. July 1882.

Chancel Screen. Thame Church.

destroy the influence of those persons who were resisting the innovations. In 1549, at the suggestion of Somerset and Cranmer, Commissioners visited the parish churches in order to take Inventories of the plate, jewels, bells, vestments and other *ornamenta*, nine-tenths of which were then either confiscated or stolen. Englishmen generally were heartily opposed to the innovators and their policy, as the rising under Humphrey Arundell, in Somerset, Devon and Cornwall, once again so truly proved. But the Council ordered all who had been found in active opposition to be promptly punished under martial law. So that hereupon priests and people were "strung up" without a trial, and many of the clergy were strangled and their dead bodies hung upon the steples of their own parish churches, for daring to prefer the Catholic religion to the new opinions. In a later year of Edward's reign, *i.e.* in 1550, the new Prayer Book, which, as its compilers asserted, had been drawn up under the express guidance of the Holy Ghost, was revised under the suggestion of the imported foreigners, and made more unorthodox and bald. What its compilers and admirers termed "worship in spirit and in truth" without body, sacred sanctuary or altar, appears to have been the dream of the more active part of these foreign sectaries. The parish church was to be henceforth looked upon as a mere place of assembly; no longer the gate of Heaven, nor even the Holy of Holies, but a convenient meeting-place, a synagogue to wranglers, or a mere preaching-room for pedants. Into this latter so many of our old parish churches were deliberately turned. A stringent Act of Uniformity was passed in 1552, and the observance of fast days and holy days was regulated by statute.

As generally throughout the country, so at Thame, the influence of the innovators was soon practically and powerfully experienced. It is to be feared, however, that apathy, indolence, and in many places a deep-seated corruption, which served to paralyze resistance, enabled those who were anxious for change to effect their object by bearing down and crushing out all opposition. Too many of the shepherds both failed to feed their flocks, and left the fold open to the incursions of wild beasts. Too many of the old nobility and ancient knightly families had died out, or become impoverished. The new men were often of quite a different stamp,—greedy, pushing, selfish, and rapacious. Moreover the bad example which had been frequently set by those in high places, who had already secured for themselves the spoils of monastery, shrine, and chantry, was soon eagerly followed by persons in a less elevated social position. New peers had been created in order to support and uphold the innovators in their policy; and such were endowed with lands and possessions which had for centuries belonged to the Church and to the poor. It being clearly perceived, therefore, that the adherents of the new order of things were thus heaping to themselves much of the confiscated properties, and were had in honour at Court, many knights and yeomen, many tradesmen and country gentlemen, in every shire, hankering after that which did not belong to them, began with wistful hope to lean towards the daring and successful innovators.

Before the religious changes of the Tudor era come under consideration, it may be well to call to mind how thoroughly and completely this Church was furnished; and how utterly unlike its interior was in the early part of the sixteenth century to what it has ever since remained.

Of old, looking eastwards, the great Rood in the centre of the chancel-skreen, with images of Our Lady and St. John, could not fail to impress the worshipper with awe and gratitude. By it the work of Calvary, the redeeming love of God-made-Man, was set before the eyes of the simplest and least-instructed with far greater force and power than by any combination of words—brief or elaborate—in the most touching or descriptive sermon. Representations of events recorded in Scripture, drawn rudely, it may have been, but effectively, often full of incident, and always both conceived and carried out in a truly religious spirit, and telling their story well and forcibly, were depicted on the walls. Statues of those saints whose names in accordance with prediction and pledge were to be had in everlasting remembrance, stood in tabernacles rich with carved crockets and bright with colour and gilding. Here then, as in every other church throughout the land, open day by day, the people were taught through their eyes as well as through their ears, and were thus taught both wisely and efficiently.

Sometimes an inscription was placed along the skreen, *e.g.* :—

(1) "**Amor meus Jh's Christus, crucifixus est.**"

Or—

(2) "**Effigiem Christi, quam transis, pronus honora:**
Non tamen effigiem, sed Quem designat, adora."

Or again—

(3) "**Nec Deus est, nec homo, quam praesens cernis imago;**
Sed Deus est et Homo, Quem Sacra figurat Imago." *

* Thus rendered into English :—
(1) "Jesus Christ, my Love, is crucified."
(2) "What time thou passest by the Rood, bow humbly evermore;
Yet not the Rood, but Him Who there was Crucified adore."
(3) "The Form is neither God nor man, which here thou dost behold:
He very God and Man, of Whom thou by that Form art told."

All shewing that the vulgar and superficial notions on the subject of idolatry were only the result of want of information or obstinate prejudice.

A veil depended from within the chancel arch separating the choir and sanctuary from the rest of the church. The chapels in the transepts were shut off by skreens.* Most of the altars had canopies to them, and were flanked by silken hangings and enclosed by low rails. The choir, as has been already pointed out, was richly furnished. When—after the surrender by Abbot King, the Prior and the monks—the splendid church of the Abbey of Thame Park was dismantled, the Prebendary of Thame purchased the stalls belonging to it and set them in the Parish Church. The bench ends—carved in oak which no doubt had grown in Thame Park—represent archaically various forms of Indian Corn. Here is a representation of one of them. The others are equally bold and effective.

Stall End, Choir, Thame Church.

And now to revert to public events, as they directly bore upon Thame Church, its officers and its parishioners. Without so doing several of the "Records" to be here introduced, might be wanting in point and meaning. In the latter part of the year 1548 Parliament, after great opposition on the part of many influential Catholics, formally decreed that "all books called Antiphoners, Missales, Grailes, Processionales, Manueles, Legendes, Pies, Portuasses, Primers in Latin or English, Couchers, Journalles, Ordinalles, or other books or writings whatsoever, heretofore used for service of the Church, written or printed in the English or Latin tongue, other than such as are or shall be set forth by the King's Majesty, shall be by Authority of this present Act clearly and utterly abolished, extinguished, *and forbidden for ever to be used or kept in this realm, or elsewhere within any of the King's dominions.*"

"It is further enacted," the statute continues, "that all images, of whatsoever materials, taken out of churches or chapels, or yet standing in any such places, should be destroyed and defaced." As for the books, they were to be delivered to the Mayor, Bailiffs, Constables, or Churchwardens, in their respective towns, who within three months after such came to their hands, were to deliver them over to the Archbishop, Bishop, Chancellor, or Commissary of the diocese, in order to be by them *either openly burned, or otherwise defaced and destroyed.* And that in case any of the persons above mentioned kept any of the books, and did not bring them in to the Archbishop, Bishops, etc., they were for the first offence to forfeit ten shillings, four pounds for the second, and for the third to suffer imprisonment at the King's pleasure.

And if the Archbishop, Bishops, etc., failed to execute the act, and did not *burn, deface, and destroy,* all the said books, within forty days after they received them, they were to forfeit forty pounds, half of which sum was for the King, and the other moiety for the informer. The violence and wickedness of this outrageous enactment, serves to shew, that those in authority were quite conscious of the fact that any injunction or decree less sweeping and severe would certainly have failed of its purpose. The vulgar idea,—hitherto fostered by so many so-called "historians,"—that our English ancestors were anxious for such changes as those thus effected, is merely founded on prejudice, imagination and ignorance.

By this singular and barbarous statute, worthy rather of Huns and Goths than of so-called "Christian statesmen," it was provided, first, that "any figure, or picture, upon any tomb, in churches, or chapels, might stand, *in case the person represented had not the character of a saint.*" Thus, while all images of saints were distinctly forbidden, the images of sinners were tolerated and allowed to remain. How this frightful work of destruction and devastation was carried on; how, like all others, the Church of Thame was efficiently rifled, sacred and artistic treasures destroyed or sold for the cost of an old song, may be read of in the "Accounts" here printed. "Old iron," "old banner clothes," "old wood

* That between the Tower and the South Transept was removed in 1549, and was probably described in the "Accounts" as "old wood sold." Those at the east end of the two aisles were likewise taken down at the same time.

solde," "brasse and lattayns sold," "timber-work about the high altar," "certain playte sold," are amongst the various terms and entries, which sufficiently describe the devastation effected. The canopy of one of the altars was disposed of to William Etheridge, who was a Catholic; a pair of "cruetts of silver" were sold to Mr. William Dormer; the "coverlid that lay before the high altar" to a member of the family of Hester; "the great Bell to Ap Powell the bell-founder of Buckingham, for a very large sum—nearly £24; the hangings of the Easter sepulchre to another man. "Certain stones sold in the church" were no doubt altars, tabernacles, imagery in alabaster, and reredoses. With the exception, therefore, of the font, the two tombs of the Quartermains in the south transept, Sir John Clerke's in the choir, and that of Geoffrey Dormer in the north transept, everything was cleared out and carried away,—either sold, embezzled, or destroyed.

In 1548, at Thame, as elsewhere, great and palpable ecclesiastical changes had been effected, some by Parliamentary enactment, others by mere Orders in Council, or by Proclamation. Those in authority ruled with a rod of iron. No one could predicate to what extent change might be carried. Already an "Ecclesiastical Visitation," as it was called—mainly composed of persons who were certainly *not* ecclesiastics—had been carried out for the purpose of maintaining the new Tudor dogma of the Royal Supremacy, and for compelling the immediate use of the vernacular in the public services. Special preachers—many of them gifted with rude eloquence and rough tongues—had been previously sent round to prepare the people for the changes designed. But in many instances these orators were often received by the populace with derision and occasionally with execration. A book of "Homilies," embodying the new opinions in somewhat coarse and profane language, was issued; and the clergy and their parishioners were bound not only to purchase it at their own cost, but to see that its contents were read out from the pulpit. Bishops were henceforth to be appointed like judges and other secular offices, by Letters Patent. Against the expelled monastics,—who were most determined and pertinacious opponents of the innovations and innovators, and who seldom received the pensions which had been promised to them,—a statute was passed * ordering all such homeless wanderers to be branded on the breast with a hot iron, and the letter V for "vagabond;" † and enjoining further that if they

* 1 Edward VI., cap. 3.

† Twenty years later, under Queen Elizabeth, it is on record that "at Thame in Oxfordshire some 'proper stoute abbey-men' were convicted and punished as vagabonds . . . . . On Sep. 8, 1571, they took their stocking and whipping verie ill. So they were sore bloodied, and one thereafter died, no long while thereupon."—*The Church under Queen Elizabeth*, vol. i., p. 198. London; 1880.

dared to abscond from any master, whose absolute slaves they were to become for two years,—and who was to feed them "on bread and water and such small drink and refuse of meat" as he might think fit to bestow, they were to be branded anew with the letter S and reduced to a state of perpetual slavery.

All colleges, chantries, and free chapels were to be given to the King; the old ceremonies and sacred rites for Candlemass Day, Ash Wednesday, Holy Week, Good Friday, and the Rogation Days were utterly abolished; and certain communistic foreigners—men who maintained principles subversive of all Law and Order both in Church and State—were invited over to England to aid Archbishop Cranmer and his fellow-reformers in carrying out their projects. At the same time those in authority, led by the Duke of Somerset, induced the young King to make peers of some of the lowest, least scrupulous, and most dishonourable of their tools, and to provide them with the necessary means of maintaining their new dignity by further robbing the Church and the Poor.

Sir William Barentyne,* of Haseley Court, and Mr. John Pollard (afterwards knighted, and subsequently Recorder of Oxford), were two of the Commissioners appointed, on the 14th of February, 1549, to visit the Oxfordshire churches, in accordance with a recent Act,†

* This Sir William Barentyne (whose wife's name was Anne, and who died 27 December, 1522) had no male issue. His only daughter, Mary, who died 15 May, 1581, and was buried at Great Haseley, married Anthony Huddlestone, Esq., in consequence of which alliance Haseley Court passed to the Huddlestones. Their son, Richard Huddlestone, was High Sheriff of Oxon in 1579. This Barentyne was of an ancient race and of a knightly family. Drogo Barentyne, his collateral ancestor, had been Sheriff of Oxfordshire in A.D. 1321-26; Thomas Barentyne, in 1378, in 1382, in 1386, and in 1394; John Barentyne, in 1456; and possibly his son, another John Barentyne, in 1484; William Barentyne, in 1511; Sir William, in 1525. The family had property at Thame, at Great and Little Haseley, at Churchill, and at Chalgrove. Their armorial bearings, formerly in the Church of Thame, were—Sable, three eagles displayed argent, armed or. The Roll of Arms of Henry III.'s time gives identically the above blazon; but that of Edward II., under the head of "Buckinghamshire," sets forth that "Sire Dru de Barentin" bore "de sable, a vj egles de argent." There is a fine monument to their memory in the choir of Great Haseley Church, of which parish John Leland, the antiquary, was sometime the Rector, having been presented by Henry VIII. in 1542.

† What was exactly enjoined to be carried out may be accurately gathered from the text of the statute which follows:—

"The said Commissioners shall, upon their view and survey taken, cause due Inventories to be made, by bills or books indented, of all manner of goods, plate, jewels, bells, and ornaments, as yet remaining, or any wise forthcoming, and belonging to any churches, chapels, fraternities, or gilds; and the one part of the same Inventories to send and return to Our Privy Council, and the other to deliver to them in whose hands the said goods, plate, jewels, bells, and ornaments, shall remain to be kept preserved: and they shall also give good charge and order that the same goods, and every part thereof, be at all times forth-coming to be answered; leaving, nevertheless, in every parish church, or chapel, of common resort, one, two, or more, chalices, or cups, according to the multitude of the people in every such church or chapel, and also such other orna-

and they came to Thame for that purpose in the summer of the same year. They were enjoined to obtain Inventories of all church ornaments, jewels, shrines, vestments, hangings, bells, and other property, it having been determined to seize and appropriate everything which was of any value, on behalf of the Crown. The principle which underlay this strange desire to appropriate property to which the Crown had no rightful claim, was one, as dangerous in itself, as it was still more dangerous in the impetus it gave to misappropriation, robbery, and rascality of all sorts.

The Churchwardens' "Accounts" which immediately follow illustrate the work of the period very forcibly. Everything was sold, belonging to the sacred fabric and parishioners, which would produce even a groat.

(1549.) Receipts.

	s.	d.
It'm rec' for candelstyckks of latayn that were sold	iiij	
It'm rec' for the great crosse sold at London weyinge lxxxiij unces viij dw. after the rat of v^s^ iiij^d^ le unc. Som. xxij li iiij s.		

Expens.

	s.	d.
It'm for a Book of the parafrase of Erasmus of the largest volome	x	
It'm for a chayne and a haspe to ye same		vj
It'm for ij Books of the newe Service in Englyshe	x	
It'm for iiij sawlters in Englyshe	iij	viij
It'm to Symon Synckler for his cost in rydynge to London when we sold the great crosse by ye space of iij days ffyndynge hymself and his horse	iij	
It'm for his labor and payns therein	ij	
It'm for a book of the homyles		xviij
It'm for sylk for regesters for ye newe books		viij
It'm for a potele of Muskadle gevyn to Sir Will'm Barradyn and Mr Pollard		viij

Whereas Master Will'm Dormer Esquier was charged as it dothe appere in the state of the last accompt in the some of lxxvj li. xij s. iiij d. Whereof he hath payd to the hands of John Collens at ye sevrall tymes xv li. It'm to Will'm Hunt and Edmund Cornyshe, l s. It'm to John Smythe and Thomas Audefeld for the poore men and towards ye makynge of the newe Cawsey at the Towne end at dyvers payments, xx li. xij s. viij d. It'm to Symon Synckler xxxj s. It'm to Bell the paynter, l s. The hole some as y^t^ dothe appere by his byll brought on to this accompt y^t^, xlj li. xviij s. viij d. & so remaunyeth in the hands of ye sayd Mas. Will'm Dormer xxxiv li. xiij s. viij d.

(1550.) Receipts.

	s.	d.
It'm for ix^li^ of olde Irone sold		x
It'm for iij^li^ do of Irone		iiij
It'm for olde Banner clothes y^t^ were sold	iij	iv
It'm for olde wood solde		xij
It'm for an olde clothe sold to Careways	ij	
It'm for lxxxi^li^ of Brasse and lattayns sold to Young the Brasyer after the rat of ij d. p^r^ pound	xiij	vj
It'm for one Coffer sold to Richard Childe	iij	iv
It'm for one Coffer sold to John Playsted		iiij

It'm receavy^d^ for certayne playt sold at London that y^e^ to saye in Gylt playt one pyx and ij chalices weying xlvj unce at v s. viij d. le unce. It'm xiij li. iij s. also ij payre of sencers weynge lv unces at v s. iiij d. le unc. It'm xiiij li. xij s. and vj d.

Some of ye hole ys xxvjli. xvj s.

Expenses.

* * * * * *

	s.	d.
It'm p^d^ to Mast. Dormer for a Booke of the Newe Service	vj	

ments as by their discretion shall seem requisite for the Divine service, in every such place for the time.

"And, because we be informed, that in many places great quantities of the said plate, jewels, bells, and ornaments, be embezzled by certain private men, contrary to Our express commandments in that behalf; the said Commissioners shall substantially and justly inquire, and attain the knowledge thereof, by whose default the same is, and hath been, and in whose hands any part of the same is come. And in that point the said Commissioners shall have good regard, that they attain to certain names and dwelling-places of every person and persons, that hath sold, alienated, embezzled, taken, or carried away, and of such also as have counselled, advised, and commanded, any part of the said goods, plate, jewels, bells, vestments and ornaments, to be taken or carried away, or otherwise embezzled. And these things they shall, as certainly and duly as they can, cause to be searched and understanded.

"Upon a full search and inquiry whereof, the said Commissioners four or three of them, shall cause to be called before them, all such persons by whom any of the said goods, plate, jewels, bells, ornaments, or any other the premises, have been alienated, embezzled, or taken away, or by whose means or procurement the same, or any part thereof, hath been attempted, or to whose hands or use any of the same, or any profit for the same, hath grown; and by such means as to their discretion shall seem best, cause them to bring into their the said Commissioners' hands, to Our use, the said plate, jewels, bells, and other the premises so alienated, or the true and just value thereof, certifying unto Our Privy Council, the names of all such as refuse to stand to, or obey their order, touching the re-delivery and restitution of the same, or the just value thereof, to the intent, that as cause and reason shall require, every man may answer to his doings in this behalf.

"Finally, Our pleasure is, that the said Commissioners, in all their doings, shall use such sober and discreet manner of proceeding, as the effect of this commission may go forward, with as much quiet, and as little occasion of trouble or disquiet of the multitude as may be; using to that end such wise persuasions, in all places of their sessions, as in respect of the place, and disposition of the people, may seem to their wisdoms most expedient; giving also good and substantial order for the stay of the inordinate and greedy covetousness of such disordered people as have, or shall go about, the alienating of any the premises, so as, according to reason and order, such as have or shall contemptuously offend in this behalf may receive reformation, as for the quality of their doings shall be requisite." See Fuller's *Church History*, where the enactment is given at length. Book VII., p. 417.

	s.	d.
It'm for a bottell for the prest to puttyn wyne		iij
It'm to the poore prest Sr Robt. Bold	iij	iiij
It'm for a quart of Malvesey for the clerks upon Christmas Day in ye quere		iiij
It'm for a mat to knele upon at the communion		iij
It'm for the carriage of the Books to the Byssoppe to Thame Park*		iiij
It'm for a corple of capons geryn unto Mastres Symons at London		xxij
It'm for the expences costs and charge of John Collens, Heyster, Thomas Andfeld and Richard Child in sellynge of certayne playt at London	xiij	iv
It'm pyd to harry Carpentr for mendyng the seatts within ye churche and makynge the stepps by the Bible		viij
It'm for the hangyngs belongyng unto the sepulcure sold to Will'm Bekyngfeld	xlvj	viij
It'm for a coveled yt laye before the hye altar sold to John Hester	vij	
It'm for lxxxlb of old Iron sold to ye sayd John	vj	viij
It'm for the Canarpie sold to Will'm Etherige	xxvj	viij

(1551.)

In this year the churchwardens were John Spens, Richard Bunse, William Mynchard, and Richard Etherige, the last of whom either died or declined office, as appears.

Receipts.

* * * * * *

	s.	d.
It'm for the second crosse and a chalyce sold at London weyinge lxv unces after the rat of vj s. the unc. Sum. xix li. x s.		
It'm for certayne stones sold in the Churche ...	vj	viij
It'm for the great bell, sold unto John Appowell weyinge xxc iij q'rters at xxxviij s. c. xxiij li. xiij s. xj d.		

Expens.

	s.	d.
It'm to Thomas Perry for his yere's wages	x	
It'm pd to Thomas Geyt for pullynge downe the Tymber work about the hye aulter ...		iiij
It'm for or charges to London on sellynge of certayne playt for the behove of ye church	xiij	iv
It'm for a lb of candle on Cristemas daye		ij
It'm ye xxv day of January pd to the Joniers for makynge of the Table and ye fformes for the Communion†		viiij
It'm pd for iij bords for the same	ij	
It'm pd to George Andesley for torpyngel‡ up the walls where ye seats were made.........		viij
It'm pd to Habgrow for ryngynge of curfewe...	ij	
It'm the thyrde day of Maye p'd for sendynge for ye Crowner to sitt uppon Habgrow that fell out of the Rood loft and dyed		viij

	s.	d.
It'm p'd for ye act of Obedience*		iiij
It'm p'd for a book called The Omyles	xviij	
It'm the xxth daye of December payd to George Ansley in pt of payment for takynge downe of the aulters	x	iv
Item to his smith		viij
It'm p'd for the cariage of a load of payvynge tyle ffrom Mr Dormer's..............................		vj
It'm payd to Gernesaye for makynge and mendynge of seats in the churche	iiij	iv
It'm p'd to Geyt for workynge in ye Churche and other thyngs		xviij
It'm p'd to hym for takyng downe certayne thyngs in the Churche		xij
It'm payd to Spyer for makynge and mendynge of seats	iiij	
It'm p'd to George Thornton for payvynge in the Church..	iiij	x
It'm payd for a newe beam	ij	iv
It'm for the makynge of mor surplices		xvj
It'm payd for the payvynge about the Com'on Well in the Market place as yet doth appere by ther Bill hereunto anyxed iij li. xiij s.		

1552. William Forrest, sometime a Cistercian monk, was ministering in the Parish Church at this period. He had seen many changes during the thirteen years which had passed since the Abbey of Thame Park had been surrendered to the Royal Commissioners on a dull November day. The Abbey Church had been razed to the ground, while the extensive and once magnificent buildings were fast going to ruin. Needy tenants occupied the dilapidated Grange, and were unable to pay the high rents demanded of them by the Duke of Somerset's Steward. Bishop King had already alienated the Manor by licence from the Monarch. The residents thereabout and in the southern part of Thame, having, therefore, no church near them to attend, ceased to worship. Thus the contrast between the state of Religion in the Town in the past and present must have been depressing.

To revert now for awhile to public events, full of interest to the inhabitants of Thame. Not a few Englishmen rejoiced at the death of Edward the Sixth, which took place at Greenwich on the 6th of July, 1553. The Council, or at least that portion of it which was under the Duke of Northumberland's influence, wished to conceal the King's departure hence from the public,

* *I.e.* Robert King, Bishop successively of Rheos, Osney, and Oxford.

† See footnote on p. 79.

‡ *I.e.* daubing.

* This was evidently the Second Act of Uniformity, which states that the newly-revised Book of Common Prayer had been "perused, explained, and made fully perfect," and that henceforth it alone was to be used under the heaviest penalties. Any one speaking or writing against it was liable to be fined for the first and second offences, and to forfeit all his goods and chattels and to be imprisoned for life for a third offence;—sufficient proof that the changes made were directly in the face of public opinion, and were only effected by the stringency of enactments like that referred to.

in order to further their design of securing the crown for Lady Jane Grey. But Mary had at once been apprized of it—some assert by a confidential letter from Sir John Williams, others by a secret communication from the Earl of Arundel—and lost no time in issuing the following Proclamation, which was read three times at the Market Place of Thame, and received with acclamation and rejoicing by many of the inhabitants:—

"MARIE THE QUEEN,—

"Knowe ye, all the good subjects of this Realme, that yr most noble Prince, yr Souraigne Lord and Kinge, Edward the VIth is upon thursday last dep'ted this world to God's mercie. And that now the most exullent Princes, his sister Marie, by the grace of God ye Quene of E and Y and verie owner of the crown Government and tytle of E and Y and all things thereunto belonging, to God's glory, the honor of the royalme of England, and all yr comfortes. And her Highness ye not fledd thys royalme, ne intendethe to do, as ye most contraly surmysed."

Though the Duke of Northumberland, with his active allies, Sir John Gates and Sir Thomas Palmer, had taken several precautions, had secured a fleet in the River Thames, and an army in the Isle of Wight; though Archbishop Cranmer, Thirlby the Lord Chancellor, and twenty-one other members of the Council, had advised the Queen to submit to Lady Jane Grey, it was very soon found that this discreditable scheme was rejected and repudiated both by the nobility in general and by the people. Bishop Ridley's dishonest and offensive sermon at St. Paul's Cross before the Lord Mayor and Alderman, maintaining that Mary was illegitimate and idolatrous, did more harm than good to the failing cause which this episcopal traitor had disastrously espoused. In the east of England the Earl of Essex, Lord Thomas Howard, with the Pastons, Bedingfields and Jerninghams of those parts had risen in behalf of their lawful sovereign. The Earls of Bath and Sussex had loyally done the same some days previously. From Oxfordshire and Buckinghamshire, Sir Edward Peckham, Sir John Williams, and Sir Robert Drury had levied and co-operated in equipping nearly ten thousand men, who were assembled at Lord Paget's suggestion near West Drayton. From Thame more than a hundred sturdy yeomen and others marched thither under the command of Captain William Lee, prepared to dare and do on behalf of their rightful Queen.

Here is one record of what exactly took place. The wit and wisdom, the discretion and foresight, displayed by the influential knight of Rycott, in taking care to be found walking politically upon the sunshiny side of the street, will no doubt be appreciated by all those enlightened and benevolent persons who look upon self-seeking and selfishness as natural virtues.

(1552.) **Expenses.**

It'm pd into the hands of Will'm Lee by the com'andement of Sr John Williams Knyght, for the goynge fforth of the sowldyers in the behalf of or Sowaryne lady Quene Marye	x li.

The following further extracts—taken from the "Accounts" of Mr. William Ballowe and Mr. William Lee in the first year of Queen Mary—shew that some attempt was at once made to repair the devastations of the "Gospellers" and fanatics of the previous reign; and to restore the Parish Church to something like its previous state. The second entry at the foot setting forth the additional cost of the soldiers who were furnished from Thame, will be noticed.

	s.	d.
Imprimis. for ye carriage of a load of stones for the hye aulter		iiij
It'm for a padelock for ye parafrase		iiij
It'm for iiij yerds of hearclothe* for ye hye aulter	ij	iv
It'm payd to George Anesley for makynge of ye hye aulter	iiij	
It'm pd for lynnen clothe to mend an albe		vj
It'm for ye caryinge and recavyng of the church gere to Oxford	vj	iv
It'm for bryngynge of ij books ffrom Thame Park		ij
It'm for the Tryndle upon Candlemas daye		iiij
It'm for ye makynge of the Canypie		x
It'm for makyng the Judas and ye sepulcre		iij
It'm for Colles for ye halowed fyer		iiij
It'm for a paten of silvr for a chalice weyyng iiij unces and an half at v s. ij d. once	xvij	vj
It'm for a pyxe and the clothe	vj	iiij
It'm for a lyne to the same		j
It'm for a Corporas case		xvj
It'm for ijlb of sixes for ye Judas light		xxij
It'm for a Basket for the holy bread		ij
It'm for ij tapers for the sepulcre		xxij
It'm for the Pascall tapr and the font tapr	iij	ix
It'm pd to William Lee that he layd forth above ye money that he receavyd for ye souldyers as dothe appere by his bill brougt in to this accompte	xiij	iv

(1556.) **Receipts.**

	s.	d.
Imprimis Receaved of Will'm Ballowe and William Lee w'ch was the remayne of their last account in the yere of or lord God A thousand and five hundred ffyftye and foure	vj	iiij
It'm of John Hester for olde Iren	vj	iij
It'm for the hole yere's rent of ye houses in ye churchyard	iiij	iiij

* "Haircloth," i.e. what would be now called "baize," for a cover to protect the altar from dust.

Expences.

* * * * * *

	s.	d.
It'm p'd to the Belman for his hole yeres wage		xvj
It'm p'd for a nell and a half of lynnen clothe toward the ffurnyshyng of a surples and for the makyng of the same	iiij	
It'm for a masse book	vj	viij
It'm pd toward ye bying of the holy wat' pot ...		xij
It'm for a payre of censers	iiij	iiij
It'm for il of syses for Judas light		xj
It'm for pack thred occupied about ye sepulcrye		j
It'm for Collis		ij
It'm for ffranckyncens		ij
It'm for skowrynge of candelstecks wt the lavor and crismatory		ij
It'm for the paschall and fount tap' weynge il iij q'rt'rs and for ye makyng	ij	
It'm paid to the Somner for beyngng ye holy oyle		iiij
It'm p'd to harry Batys for whit lynynge the wallis and for lyme		vij
It'm p'd for a Rode wt Mary and John	xviij	
It'm p'd to the paynter in pt of payment	iij	iiij
It'm p'd to Marks for a Cross and a foot to the same of cop' and gylt	x	

(1557.) Receipts.

* * * * * *

	s.	d.
It'm Receyvyd for the sepulture of Annes Beckynfeld	vj	viij
It'm Rec. in money gathered in ye churche for the Rood	viij	x
It'm Rec. for the sepulcrye of John Newman ...	vj	viij
It'm Gevyn by ye lady john to the Churche Payments		xij

Expenses.

	s.	d.
p'd for meat to dyvers p'sons, viz., Will'm Beckynffeld iij s. vj d. John Morley ij s. x d. Richard Cotton xviij d. Raphe Pollen ij s. iij d. to Olyver Crotson xxiij d. Thomas Page ij s. viij d.		
It'm pay'd for xiij yards of grene for mens cotts*	xiij	
p'd for ij yards and halfe of yalow cotton		xx
p'd for v pear of say	iij	iiij
p'd for colorred threed		iiij
p'd for makynge of the cotts	vj	x
p'd for ix dozen dansyng Bells	iij	vj
p'd for makynge of the lord hyways and for pap'	iij	vj
p'd for playing cards		v
p'd to ye lord of the Maye ale	v	
p'd to the Mynstrells for their wags	xx	
p'd for ther costs and charges	viij	
p'd for ther bedds	vj	
p'd for wood	vj	viij
p'd for the exchaunge of the Roode and for ye Image of o' lady at ye hye awter end	xvj	iiij

	s.	d.
p'd to a carpenter for v dayes worke	iiij	ij
p'd for a staple and a pyne put throught the cross and Nayle		x
p'd to harry Goodrige for helpynge the man that mendyd the great Bell		xvj
p'd for iij Bushells Colles		vj
p'd for ffrankynsens and Besoms		iii
p'd to ye Belman for his half yeres wags		viij
p'd for th' expences to henley upon ye visitacion		xiiij
p'd for th' expences to Oxford wt ye presentement		x
p'd to Thomas Andefeld for vll waxe & for makynge of the Roode lyght	iiij	ij
P'd to Thomas Hore for pricks that the tappers stand on		viij
p'd for payntynge the Image of o' lady	ij	
p'd for iiij tappers wt flowers that stand before the sayd Image	iij	
p'd for mendynge of the churche gayt, for nails and settynge upe the Tab'nacle before o' lady		vij
p'd for mendynge of the crosse		v
p'd to Thomas joyner for mendynge ye Roode loft	iiij	viij
p'd to Will'm Etherige for C Borde	iij	viij
p'd to the Glasier	xxv	vj
p'd for hangynge upe the sakrynge bell at the chancell Dore		xviij
p'd for ale for the quere at Est'		vij
p'd for naile in settynge upe the sepulcrye		j
p'd for mendynge of the second bell and for dresshynge and hangynge of ye great bell...	xliij	iiij
p'd for il of sizes for Judas light		xiiij
p'd for the pascall tapper weyinge iijll	iij	vj
p'd for a taper for the fount weying ill		xiiij

(1558). Expenses.

* * * * * *

	s.	d.
P'd for skowrynge the boolls of the candlestikks before the Roode		iiij

In 1560 another set of Visitors arrived in the Town commissioned by the Queen and Council. Already in the previous year the ancient jurisdiction of the Crown over "the estate ecclesiastical and spiritual," as it was termed, had been restored, and "all foreign jurisdiction repugnant to the same"* abolished. Oaths were enjoined to be taken by officials, both of Church ann State, affirming this fact, and severe punishments, including death, were inflicted on those who declined to take them. The Churchwardens of Thame officially received the Visitors of the supreme Governess of the National Church, and refreshed them during their labours with a gallon of wine. As one direct consequence of their visit, all the altars which had been set up again under Queen Mary, were finally taken down

* This and the following twelve entries have already been referred to in the footnote on p. 52.

* 1 Eliz., cap. 2.

and removed; while all the ornaments of the Church, with the exception of those which were old, tattered, or worthless, either scheduled, handed over to partisan officials, or there and then taken away. The new Communion Book, that is the slightly-revised version of that in Edward VI.'s Second Prayer Book, was purchased for use. Two small "Processioners"—that is what would now be called "A Book of Occasional Services," though the old term was still applied to them—were procured. A second book of the "Homilies" was also provided, together with the Queen's comprehensive and celebrated "Injunctions."* In 1562 the table of the Commandments was set up, and a desk for reading the Lessons provided in the body of the church. This stood under the pulpit against the second pillar from the tower on the north side of the nave. The new Prayer Book—which made the third issued since the first "reform" of the Old Religion thirty years previously—was procured by the Churchwardens, as were also four English Psalters. In 1564 some side altar which had been allowed to remain, probably that of the Blessed Trinity in Dormers' Aisle, was also finally removed. Three years later, one surplice and one "table-cloth" were probably all that remained to the Church, these being all that were then washed; for many of the new ministers—more especially those who were fanatically earnest in behalf of the innovations—distinctly refused to wear any surplice.† In 1569 Archbishop Parker held a Visitation. Twenty years afterwards, in 1589—the intervening years were times of religious desolation—John Trinder, just instituted as Vicar, evidently endeavoured to secure some few decent *ornamenta* for divine service, for a new table-cloth for the communion-trestles was obtained at a cost of 5s. Four cushions were likewise procured, and a new fringed pulpit-cloth. At this period it appears that the chancel, and possibly the north transept,‡ were boarded off and unused, and that the Pulpit had become the centre of interest and the place of importance in this old Prebendal Church. Ever since the importation of foreign innovators—more particularly during the later years of Elizabeth, as also under the Stuarts, until the better influence of Archbishop Laud was experienced—and the spread of their immoral teaching, controversies and wranglings, wearisome disputations and trumpery pulpit-dissertations, too often formed the only spiritual *pabulum* which was popular and acceptable.

* Injunctions given by the Queen's Majesty concerning both the Clergy and Laity of this Realm. London: 1559.

† It will have been noticed by the ecclesiastical antiquary that, with very unique exceptions—those of Parglove, at Tideswell, co. Derby, and Hunt, of Denham, co. Bucks, being amongst the most notable—that no Elizabethan ministers are ever represented on memorial brasses in surplices. They all appear in academical gowns.

‡ The south side of the skreen of the north transept has evidently been boarded over, for its once beautiful carvings have been rudely hacked away for this purpose.

Although the extracts which follow are, perhaps, of less intrinsic interest than those already produced; it appears desirable to make a few more quotations from the Churchwardens' "Accounts," not only to explain and justify comments already made, but also in order to provide, as far as may be, an official record of what has taken place since the middle of the sixteenth century:—

(1560.) **Receipts.**

* * * * * *

	s.	d.
It'm Rec' of Anthony Bostock in p^t of payment for the Cotteons that dyd hange in ye churche at the Buriall of my lorde Williams of Thame,* w'ch were gevyn by his executors to ye works of the churche	xlvj	viij

Expenses.

	s.	d.
Imprimis pay^d for ye Communion book and iij small processioners	vj	vj
It'm pay^d for the Clarks wags	xxvj	viij
It'm p^{d} to John Hoare ye clark for his quarters wage due at Michelmas	xx	
It'm p^{d} to Henry Goodridge belman for his qr'ts wags due at Michelmas	x	
It'm p^{d} for a gallon of wyne for ye Visitors	ij	
It'm p^{d} to the under officers beynge parators		xij
It'm p^{d} for swepynge of the churche agaynst the comynge of the Visitors		vj
It'm pay^{d} to Gybbens for pullynge downe ye Roode lofte		ij
It'm payde to Prest for takynge downe the aulters in the churche	iij	iv
It'm p^{d} to hugh Puller for certayne work about ye churche at ye buryinge of my lorde Williams		vj
It'm p^{d} more toward the clarks wags than we could rec. of ye last yeres Easteryuges		vij
It'm p^{d} for the book of the homyles		xij
It'm pay^d for the Iniunctions		vj
It'm pay^d to Thomas Hester for the bible †	xx	

* Lord Williams' funeral took place at 8 A.M. on the morning of Wednesday, 15th Nov., 1559, in Thame Church. A detailed account of it from the MSS. of Dugdale is printed on a later page.

† The following Pedigree of Hester is taken from fol. 27 of a MS., No. 129, recording the Visitation of the County of Oxford, by John Philipot and William Ryley, A.D. 1634, in the Library of Queen's College, Oxford.

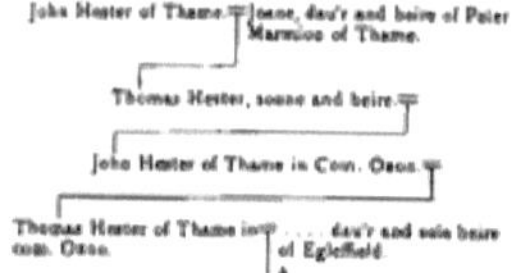

	s.	d.
It'm pd for wyne at ye lyon for ye time of Ester	iij	vj

(1561.) **Payments.**

*   *   *   *   *   *

	s.	d.
It'm pd to John Appowell for xv small barrs of Iron for the west wyndow in the churche	iij	j
It'm payd for wyne at Ester viz. xv quarts of claret wyne v s. and iij quarts of Malvesly at xviij d.	vj	vj

(1562.) **Payments.**

	s.	d.
It'm pd to Hugh Fuller for goynge for the clockmaker to Dorchester and Nettlebed...		xiiij
pd for the Table of the Commandments		xx
pd for or charge goynge to Watlyngton to the Ordinare		vj
pd to Spryngolde for ropes for the clok	vj	iv
pd to the plomber for castinge of payses for the Cloke		xvj
payd to the Clockmaker for makinge ye cloke...	xx	
It'm pd for the Makynge of the Deske in the body of the Churche for Readinge ye lessons *	vij	

(1563.) **Payments.**

	s.	d.
Payd for a Booke of Common prayer	vj	
Payd for mendynge the style in the church-yard in ye layne next the Court Close		iiij
Payd for iiijn Candle		ix
Payd for iiij Englyshe salters	viij	
Payd for wyne at Estr	vij	

a

John Hester of Thame = Katherine, dau'r of Will'm Umfreuile.

William Hester of Thame. = Elizabethe, eldest dau'r of William Hyde of Hurst, Com. Berks, Esq.

John. William. Elizabeth. Katherine. Tho. Hester, 1 son. Jane. Mary.

Thomas Parsons of Great Milton married Katherin, daughter of Mr. Hester of Sidenham near Thame. Harl. MSS., Brit. Mus., 1412, fol. 32.

Peregrine Wilcox of Creswell (aged 41, 28 March, 1663), son of Thomas Wilcox of Creswell in Bray, co. Berks, by Mary, dau. of Robert Scroope, married Mary, dau. to William Hester of Thame in com. Oxford. Add. MSS., Brit. Mus., 14,284; Visit. Berks, fol. 134; and Harl. MSS. 1483.

A coat of Arms of Hester is tricked in "Arms of Sundrie Counties," Harl. MSS. Photo LV. F.

* In 1548, the pulpit had been mended and a desk or lectern set up for the great Bible. In the same year the church plate had been weighed, and part of it sold. Mr. William Dormer bought two silver cruetts. The great silver cross, which weighed nearly eighty-four ounces—a magnificent specimen—was taken to London by Simon Synclere and sold for £22 4s. So vast an amount of the church goods had been already sold under Edward VI. that, as the "Accounts" shew, very little then remained for any person either to covet or to steal.

	s.	d.
Payd for breade		xiij
Payd to Cornelis for iij Keys and for platts for the Deske where ye lesson be redd	ij	iiij

(1564.) **Payments.**

	s.	d.
Imprimis Payd to George Annesley for Rough Castinge the Churche	iij	
pd for pulling down the aulter		viij

(1565.) **Payments.**

	s.	d.
Payd for ij spalters and one psalme booke	vj	viij
Payd for halfe the paraphrase *	vj	vj

(1566.)

	s.	d.
Payd to George Andesley for roughe castynge of the Churche	viij	

(1567.)

	s.	d.
It'm pd for washinge the surplice and Table Cloth		vj
Payde to John Appowell of Buckingham the bellfounder for Castinge of the Bell	xliij	iiij

(1568.) **Receipts.**

	s.	d.
It'm Rec. of Johanne Rowbothome for the sepulture of her husband	vj	viij

(1569.) **Payments.**

	s.	d.
It'm payd at my Lord of Cantorbery Visitacon †	ij	x

(1570.)

	s.	d.
Payd to Hobcrofte and his man for bording the steple wyndows and makinge ij seates	v	vj

(1575.) **Receipts.**

	s.	d.
Item a cope sold by Richard Benson which was given by Mr. Peter Dormer ‡ of Newbottall in the countie of Northampton for iij li.		
Item given by Mrs. Cecilia Ballowe wyfe to William Ballow of Thame to the behofe of the poore v li.		
Item given by Mr. Will'm Place	xx	

(1589.)

A new pulpit was made in this year.

Payments.

	s.	d.
It'm payde for ij eles d of hollande for the Communion clothe	iv	ix
It'm for making it		iij
It'm payde for makinge iiij cushones	iij	iv
It'm for vi ounce iij dt of fringe for the pulpitt clothe	ij	iij

* *i.e.* the "Paraphrase" of Erasmus.

† Archbishop Matthew Parker.

‡ The fourth son of Geoffrey Dormer, whose wife was Agnes Cowper.

	s.	d.
It'm payed Mr Hall at the Visitation for the iiij churchwardens and the sidesmen and putting in the Bill	ij	ij
Item for ij prayer bookes		iiij

In the latter part of Queen Elizabeth's reign there occurs a remarkable entry in the Churchwardens' "Accounts" evidently relating to the manner in which the Communion was then celebrated, as elsewhere, so at Thame. Under recent changes, instead of remaining a mystery it had evidently become a mere solemn meal. The rash and fanatical persons, headed by Bucer, who had been imported from the continent to carry out what are termed "reforms," having so well succeeded in degrading True Religion, opened wide the flood-gates of impiety, which no authority, even now, has as yet succeeded in closing. Amongst other institutions they both revived "love feasts," and sometimes ate and drank to surfeiting round the new communion-board; while the presiding minister with weighty words and ponderous sentences blessed them with sermons or "exercises" of two hours' duration—the interested listeners sustaining themselves during the operation with wafers of fine flour, passed from hand to hand, or bunches of bread served up on platters, and with copious draughts of potent Malmsey* or Red Burgundy in the new "communion-cups" of the period.

Here is the entry in question :—

(1591.)

May 2nd. Item delivered unto Will'm Tippinge two cupps for the Communion Table ij dozen and an half of Platters one pamt six spoones and halfe a dozen of Trenchers ij Table Clothes iiij curteons.

The era of the Tudors, as may be gathered from the preceding extracts, was notoriously an age of destruction. As regards any work of building up, if we look for such, except during Mary's too short reign, we shall certainly look in vain. Not only was no substantial reparation or improvement of any sort or kind made of the fabric of the Church, but it was often left uncared for and neglected. All that could be taken away of its ancient treasures had been duly carried off either under Henry VIII. or his son. All that may have been found during the reign of Elizabeth, in a well-nigh deserted building, was the least valuable of the Church's ancient treasures,—tattered vestments, pewter stoups, and broken carvings. Manuscript service books of rare beauty and great antiquity had been deliberately destroyed; ledger books, full of precious records, with details of local and personal history; chartularies and sacramental registers were utterly lost; *ornamenta* of silver and gold, choice in design and artful in construction, for obvious reasons, had been promptly hurried off to the melting-pot.

The wandering Commissioners, duly authorized by parchment, signature and seal, set the example of legally robbing the House of God on behalf of the Crown; taking sacred vessels to augment the King's Treasure-house, chalice for drinking cup at homely meals or personal carousal, cope for couch-coverlid, altar-canopy for bed-tester; while the townsmen and local gentlemen of influence too often followed the bad example thus set them. Between the two everything graspable, portable, and moveable was grasped and carried off; little remaining but the bare walls, four altar-tombs, cracked bells, decayed roof, broken windows, and such skreens, stalls, and fittings as were then thought to be comparatively worthless.

* Note likewise the entry, already quoted, under the year 1561, when no less than eighteen quarts of wine were provided for the Easter "Supper."

† The following extract shews that the custom was not by any means singular :—"8 Eliz. 1565-6. St. Martin's, Leicester. For four quarts of Malmsey at the Communion, 2s."—Nichols's *Leicester*, vol. i., pt. 2, p. 573. Four quarts of wine would, of course, require a large "pann" to hold it.

Robert Cooke, one of the Gentlemen of the Queen's Chapel, wrote : "My remarks relate to the Last Supper of Christ, in the administration of which a mistake is made now-a-days, and ever has been almost from the time of St. Paul, since he placed before the Corinthians a supper to be eaten; we, only a morsel of bread in mockery of a supper. They used a variety and abundance of meat and drink, so as to depart satisfied; we return hungry." Robert Cooke to Rodolph Gualter, *Zurich Letters*, 2nd Series, Letter 95.

"The 'Lord's board,' as it was called, was brought down with its trestles from the east end of the chancel, and placed, as for a domestic meal, with benches round, in the middle of the choir. It was covered with an ample table-napkin of Damascus cloth. A large leathern bottle of wine, a loaf of bread, and a knife, sometimes a pewter plate and flagon, or occasionally a wooden platter and a tin cup, were by the sexton then placed upon it. A cushion and a Prayer Book of the latest revision completed the *ornamenta*. The proceedings began by the singing of a hymn. Round the table the people sat or stood. The minister, though ordered to go to its north end by the direction of the Rubric, often stood at the eastern part, or seated himself in an armchair, where he alternately preached and prayed. When the service was over, what remained of the bread and wine was passed round again to the congregation, who helped themselves, and so were communicated, after a fashion, twice over; the bottles and flagons were then taken away, the cloth removed, and the table often lifted back again to its place under the east wall.

"Such was the ordinary rule and custom with reference to what was termed 'the Supper.'

"Some of the more fanatical and mad of the innovating party, however, adopting the Protestant method of interpretation of Scripture, maintained that even such practices were wrong, and without Biblical authority, and that the Lord's Supper ought to be something very different—a well-prepared and substantial meal, at which the faithful could satisfy the cravings of hunger with 'a variety and abundance of meat and drink.' Ever since the days of St. Paul, the Catholic Church, as they so modestly maintained, had been in blind error. It was thus reserved to certain infallible innovators of the sixteenth century, mad-men, fanatics, and demon-possessed, to redeliver the lost Truth. One fool often makes many. There were several who enthusiastically embraced this new and remarkable idea."—*The Church under Queen Elizabeth*, vol. i., pp. 89-91. London: 1880.

In 1606 xviijs. were due from John Striblehill for the rent of the porch for xviij years.

In 1608 a legacy of xx s. left by Edmund Tomlinson was paid by John Tomlinson.

(1609.)

John Striblehill rents the church porch for x s.

(1610.)

	s.	d.
Mr Saunders' child buried	vj	viij
Mrs Ellis' grave	vj	viij
Mr Way's grave	vj	viij

A few more extracts are given; but they lack the interest attaching to those of previous times, already set forth:—

(1613.)

	s.	d.
Paid John Adams for a seat in the pulpitt		xviij
Paid to the Vicar for writing the booke	ij	

(1613.)

Recd xiiij s. for the rent of the church porch on the north side of the church.

(1616.)

	s.	d.
In this year the pulpit was mended at a cost of	vj	viij

(1617.)

	s.	d.
Paid to Cowden for the desk	x	

(1624.)

"ij li. iv s. viij d." were delivered to Mr. Hall and Mr. Lee.

In place of William Heybourne and Henry Vivers Mr. Hugh Robotham and John Smith of North Weston were chosen Churchwardens. Amongst the "Accounts" of William Hall and Richard Lee, A.D. 1625, are the following payments:—

	s.	d.
To Bartholomew White for making the frame of the houre glasse	ij	vj
For the Communion table *	xxx	
For a Communion book	viij	
For the pulpit cloth	xl	vj

Chosen in the place of Mr. Hall and Mr. Richard Lee, Churchwardens, Peter Tomlinson and Thomas Wildgoose.

* This Communion Table—which had taken place of the old trestles and loose "communion-board" of Elizabeth's reign—still remains. It is of oak, carved, well made, of a Jacobean design, with four solid supports, bulbous ornaments on each support, and, though small in proportion to the sanctuary, is not altogether unsuitable for its sacred purpose. Fourteen years previously, *i.e.* in 1611, "Mastr Edw'd Lee Minister here (*i.e.* Curate of Thame) gave unto this Church for the use & behoofe of the Parson, a Communion-booke of poppie velvet, to the lawde & Honor of Allmighty God." (*MS. Note in Register.*)

1624. With the consent of the Parish in the place of Mr. Robotham and Jo. Smith, are chosen Thomas Bryan and Jerome Messenger.

1627. Thomas Wildgoose and Peter Tomlinson are Churchwardens.

	s.	d.
Humfry Jemot's grave cost	vj	viij
Marmaduke Saunders for a grave paid	vj	viij

* * * * * *

It' a legacy given by Mr Richard Butcher to the Church of Thame in his last will iiij li.

Laid out to Jerom Henly * xxv li.

To Knight the bell-founder x li. x s.

And now to revert briefly once again to public events. Whether the Kingdom of England in general or some parts of it in particular—an out-of-the-way diocese, or a remote country-town—be contemplated, it will be found that the fundamental changes of the Tudor era had too certainly produced indifference to Religion, self-pleasing, fresh divisions, a revolting fanaticism, and much social disorder. Those who had feebly dreamt that there was a finality in applying the principle of Church Reform soon found out their error: those who fondly imagined that other minds would be satisfied with the changes which their own minds had been led to approve, soon admitted their grave mistake. If one person could reform, so could many. If one Reformation was urgently required, in due course half a dozen might be needed. Thus the dangers and disorders which were threatening under King Charles I. were only the reasonable results of destructive work commenced nearly a century before. Oliver Cromwell, the Usurper, and his deeds of blood and rapine—sent as a just punishment for the Nation's sins—were the natural consequences of the schemes and actions of Thomas Cromwell, the daring but despicable beggar-on-horseback of Henry VIII.'s day.

In matters ecclesiastical—as every page of history, truly written, proves—a want of due zeal, an absence of self-denial, the towering principle of indifference, and a pitiable fanaticism, were almost everywhere apparent. The Town of Thame, it is to be feared, formed no exception whatsoever to the general rule.

In the early part of the reign of King Charles I. the Ornaments of Thame Church—to judge by an existing Inventory—were of no very great value, and present a somewhat remarkable contrast to those which were so carefully catalogued nearly two centuries previously and have been already reproduced on a previous page.

* *I.e.* Church money lent on a bond or other security.

On the 30th of May, 1630, only the following *Ornamenta* existed:—

Imprimis, One brass pott.
Four Tabel Clothes.
One old surples.
One key of the Colidge Chest.
One Cushine.
A greene Pulpitt Clothe.
One Damask Clothe.
Three other cushines.
One Table Clothe for the Communion-table.
Three yards of p'ticoulered fringe.

P^r me, Thos Hennant,
Vicar.

At this period the Holy Communion was only administered at Christmas, Easter, and Whitsunde; and the number of those who "approached the table" in the early part of the sixteenth century varied from less than thirty to more than fifty. Later on, when the Civil War, preceding the Usurpation, was at its height, it appears that all regular services were suspended. Prayer-meetings, preachings, and prolix controversies were alone tolerated. From the year 1644, it became "an offence against the Parliament" to use the "Prayer Book;" so that only such *extempore* prayers and long sermons in favour of the Revolution and Rebellion were popular or permitted.

Baptism, if administered at all, was administered stealthily and in private. Of course, those of the clergy who denied the value or importance of that sacrament* could not be depended on to minister it with any great care, or with any special regard to its virtue or validity. Fanaticism had effectively undermined Faith, and the Old Religion of our pious forefathers had been deliberately and utterly banished. No confirmations were held. Women were never churched: the sick were not communicated, nor were the dead buried with any appointed service. The fabric of the Church, already much dilapidated, shewed signs of decay in several parts. As to the choir of Thame Church, it was little more than a barn-like ruin—unfurnished, empty, desolate. The old chancel roof then existing—not almost flat as at present—was of a very fair pitch (as the hood-moulding on the east side of the Tower indicates), but the roof itself was everywhere much decayed. No substantial repairs had been then done for more than a century and a half.* The gutters and spouts were not water-tight, the wall-plates consequently rotted, and the principal timbers began to give way. It appears to have remained in this state until Lord Viscount Weymouth repaired it during the reign of Queen Anne.

But to return. In the month of January, 1641, the House of Commons—following the important and well-remembered precedents of the Tudor era—ordered that "Commissions † be sent into all the counties for the defacing, demolishing, and quite taking away of all images, altars, or tables turned altar-wise, crucifixes, superstitious pictures, monuments, and relics of idolatry out of all churches or chapels."

At Thame little enough remained. The Somersets, the Williamses, the Pollards, the Barentynes, the Norrises, and others of the same grasping spirit, had already made a tolerably clean sweep of all that was worth taking. These distinguished persons, however, had not been much benefited by their acquisitions: while the townspeople had been spiritually starved. As to "superstitious pictures" the east windows of the choir and the two transepts had already suffered in the previous "Reformation;" having been "sore broken" and damaged by "riotous usages" under Edward VI. The chancel itself, when Charles I. reigned, presented an appearance of utter desolation. In its centre, the handsome tomb of Lord Williams was not allowed to remain undamaged, though his representatives by the marriage of his two daughters lived near; but the chief personal inscription in brass upon it was then removed; while the monumental altar-tomb of Sir John Clerke did not suffer further than that two brasses were then wrenched from the back of it and have never been recovered nor replaced; nor were the choir-stalls taken down. The personal influence of Mr. Hennant the Vicar, who, connected by marriage with several Puritan

* During the Great Rebellion, as the Thame Registers abundantly testify, Religion was neglected and the religious services of the Established Church despised. Whether the unbaptized in this town received baptism after the Restoration of Charles II. or not is uncertain. In another Oxfordshire Parish, Handborough, the following record occurs in the Church Registers:—"The names of such as were born in the time of Mr. Rogers [the intruded Minister] many of them not being baptized, but only named by their parents." Then follow seventy-four names. In 1662, the same Register shews that whole families were then christened.

* Adrian de Bardis had expended a large sum on the church in the latter part of the fifteenth century, and Dr. Prebendary Mandelay had added to its internal fittings about A.D. 1525.

† "That the Chancell-ground of every such church or chappel, raised for any altar or communion-table to stand upon, shall be laid down and levelled; and that no copes, surplices, superstitious vestments, hoods or roodlofts or holy-water founts shall be, or be any more used, in any church or chapel within this Realme; and that crosse, crucifix, picture or representation of any of the Persons of the Trinity, or of any angel or saint shall be or continue upon any plate, or other thing used, or to be used in or about the worship of God. And that all organs, and the frames or cases in which they stand, in all churches and chappels aforesaid shall be taken away and utterly defaced, and none other hereafter set up in their places, and that all copes, surplices, superstitious vestments, and founts aforesaid be likewise utterly defaced—whereunto all persons within this kingdom whom it may concern are hereby required at their peril to yield due obedience."—Original Proclamation, "The Ordinance for the further demolishing of Monuments of Idolatry and Superstition. Die Jovis, 9 May, 1644."

families,* was a quiet ally of the revolutionary party, may have been found useful throughout this period in preventing further depredations and destruction.

When in 1641, 1642, and 1643 the Parliamentary Commissioners commenced their labours hereabouts—enjoined, as they were, to proceed against all "scandalous ministers," all those who were "lazy, non-resident, idle, ignorant, and ill-effected to the Parliament,"—Mr. Hennant evidently came off scot-free. He may have been admonished, if, in the judgment of the Commissioners, he needed it: but he was certainly allowed to remain in his official position.

About this period "the great principles of the Reformation" were still further extended and applied.†

In the early part of the year 1644, on 21st of January, the Covenant was formally imposed on all classes, by Parliament, while all official persons who refused to subscribe to it suffered sorely. The Judges and every lawyer, all physicians and surgeons, the soldiers and all who held any public office of any sort or kind, were bound to obey, or at once forfeit their positions. About a year later, by the same authority, the "Directory for Public Worship" was substituted for the "Book of Common Prayer." No preaching was allowed, (so that all opponents—whether they liked it or not—were gagged, and all criticism silenced,) except to those ministers who had obediently obtained a special Parliamentary licence. There was what was termed a "Grand Committee of Religion," divided into Sub-Committees, *e.g.* that of "Scandalous Ministers," that of "Plundered Ministers," and others. These took care not only to fill the benefices—from which the lawfully-instituted clergy had been forcibly ejected—with the lowest and most ignorant of the rabble, who believed themselves to be "elect of God, and specially precious:" but to reward their own political allies by whatever of goods and property, under the form of "law," they could lay their hands on. A little later "Episcopacy"—as it then came to be called—was abolished, and the Presbyterian system set up in its stead. The Bishops themselves, for many years very unpopular, were soon "rabbled"—as the expressive phrase stood: a process more pleasant and amusing for the mob of fanatics who did the work or witnessed it, than for those dignified persons thus forced to make the sport.* The Bishop's lands and manors were everywhere confiscated; while the neediest and most daring and demonstrative amongst the fanatical "saints" affectionately grasped the plunder. One of these, a Leicestershire man, named Arthur Hasilrigge, obtained the mock title of "Bishop of Durham" because, by cant and lying, he had secured such a considerable and substantial portion of the possessions of that see.

In 1648—as a consequence of the universally-applied Puritan zeal, which resulted in the destruction of almost all coloured glass—the sum of £1 16s. 11d.

* The following outline Pedigree will shew the exact connection between the families of Cromwell, Hampden, Waller, Petty, Burte, and Hennant:—

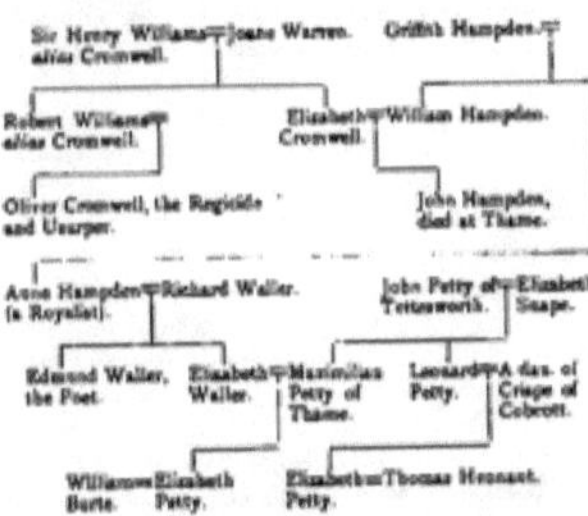

In September of the year 1645, Anthony à Wood thus wrote:—

"That which A. W. observ'd was that the Vicar and his wife were alwaies more kind to the parl. soldiers or rebells, than to the cavaliers, as his master W. Burt and his wife were, having been alwaies acquainted with and obliged to the families of the Ingoldesbies and Hamdens in Buckinghamshire and other puritanical and factious families in the said countie; who, while yong, had been mostly bred in the said school of Thame, and had sojourned either with the Vicar or Master; but as to the Usher Dav. Thomas, a proper stout Welshman, A. W. alwaies took [him] to be a good loyalist, as indeed he was."

And again, twelve years later:—

"In his [*i.e.* Anthony à Wood's] rambles [14 Aug., 1657] about the country he went to Dorchester, seven miles distant from Oxon, to see his old master David Thomas, who, from being Usher of Thame School, was now the Head Master of the Free School at Dorchester, founded by Joh. Feteplace, Esq., an old bachelaur. He had succeeded in that office Joh. Drope, lately fellow of Magd. Coll., who was the first Master appointed by the Founder."—*Life of Anthony à Wood.*

† "On the beginning of October, 1641, at St. Leonard's Eastcheap, being our church, the Idol in the wall was cut down, and the superstitious pictures in the glass were broken to pieces, and the superstitious things and prayers for the dead in brass were picked up and broke; and the picture of the Virgin Mary on the branch of candlesticks was broke, and some of those pieces of broken glass I have, to keep for a remembrance, to shew to the generation to come what God hath done for us, *to give us such a Reformation that our forefathers never saw the like.* His Name ever have the praise."—"The MS. Journal of Nehemiah Wallington," *in loco*, British Museum.

* "O lamentable!—what times do we live in? when the Church is without true discipline, God's lawes quite taken from us: no Lord's Prayer, no Creed, no Common Prayer allowed; but Master Presbyter to do as his fickle brain serves him: the Sacrament of the Lord's Supper not administered once in halfe a yeare, and when it is delivered, wonderful out of order it is; the Sacrament of Baptism administered as any would have it that is in fee with Master Parson; the dead body buried with five or six words at the most; no decency in the churches, no manners nor order."—*A Dirge for the Directory*, p. 2. Oxford: 1645.

was paid by the Churchwardens to William Eeles for glazing the Church windows, and twenty-two shillings were expended in cleaning the church—in which certain Royalist soldiers, who had been taken prisoners, had been kept.

The following are the chief entries of interest recorded by the Churchwardens during twenty years:—

(1629.)

	s.	d.
For keeping doggs out of the Church		ij

(1630.)*

	£	s.	d.
Paid for ye minister's surples	1	12	
Item to Jo. Toms for whipping ye doggs this quarter			6
Paid to John Greene for enlardging ye minister's pue		6	

(1633.)

	£	s.	d.
It'm paid for our hower glasse			8
It'm give to Jo. Busur a grat whose Father was take by ye Turkes			8

(1635.)

	£	s.	d.
Givin to a poore minister whose name was Griffith Tomson who traveld towards Wales		1	

(1637.)

	£	s.	d.
Imprimis laid out for ye use of ye church for making ye railes before ye communion Table for reparation and other necessary things	14	5	5

(1639.)

	£	s.	d.
Received of Mr Barry for his child's grave		6	8

[In this year two shillings and sixpence was gived to the Ringers for ringing on the 5th of November.]

(1641.)

	£	s.	d.
Paid to a maimed soldier y^{t} was sent by Mr Hennant			10
Received for John Tomlinson's wife's grave		6	8

* A House then standing in the Churchyard, possibly that which in previous entries had been described as "The Church House," was granted by the Parish on 6 July, 1630, to Mr. Hennant for his life, in return for the work of writing and keeping the Church Accounts.

(1648.)

	£	s.	d.
For making cleare ye Church after ye prisoners were here		1	2

Memorandum (made in 1652) that £20 of Mr Almond's gift (then received) was laid out the same yeare for mending ye way at Lashbrooke. At the same time (*i.e.* 11 June, 1654) there remained in the hands of Stiven Cooke one bond of Mr Basse for £10.

Thus much as regards certain momentous occurrences of the sixteenth and seventeenth centuries. The state of the Church during the past two centuries, and in recent times, will be dealt with later on. It will be found that throughout the years in question the influence of Change has been great, and that its direct effect even now has not yet ceased to be felt. For, as we have seen, there is no finality in reform. Until quite recent years, however, those who were born were baptized and lived within hearing of the bells of their Parish Church—though sometimes perverted by irreligious factions and cankered with political bitterness—have almost invariably felt some affection for the Church's sacred walls and hallowed associations. The chief building of the Town, as it unquestionably is—pleasant memories, tinged it may be with sadness and sometimes darkened with sorrows, have clustered around its consecrated aisles and stately tower. Nevertheless the days are gone for ever, when the voices which of old spake within its aisles, spake with no ambiguous meaning. Unity amongst Christians has been long ago broken up. Authority has lost its power, and, alas! that so it should be! Discord and Dissensions reign. With half the population it appears that no such interest in the Church is now taken. Some have built for themselves tabernacles of their own, where modern calves of Dan and Bethel have been set up.

On later pages of this book will be given miscellaneous notes and records of families, of every grade and rank, belonging to the Town; so that varied traditions still lingering and memorials gradually becoming effaced may not be altogether lost; for those social and archæological traditions which are directly connected with the Church itself are frequently pleasant to dwell upon; and it cannot be out of place to deal with them in its formal History.

CHAPTER THE SECOND.

The Church, its Monuments and Officers.

F sculptured effigies*—that is of figures either in low relief or complete—there are none remaining in Thame Church except those of Lord and Lady Williams in the chancel, and the much-damaged representation of a Priest in Eucharistic vestments—traditionally known as "St. Christopher"—on the south wall of the chantry chapel in the south transept. The destruction already referred to and partly described, which took place under Edward VI. and Elizabeth; the still further devastation which the sacred fabric underwent during the Great Rebellion, may in some measure account for the absence of other figures. For, as has been pointed out, though it was permitted that brasses and representations of persons "not reputed to be saints" should still be tolerated, even personal monuments, which contained figures of the canonized, or depicted records of their deeds, were cast out and swept away at the two periods of "reform" already referred to.

Incised slabs—of which there remain three late specimens, viz.: that of Richard Boucher or Butcher, on dark marble, A.D. 1627, and those of Simon and Merrial Coates, on white marble, A.D. 1644, all by one engraver—were very popular in certain localities of England, and gave scope to artists for a display of their taste and ability. These specimens in the chancel of this Church are not remarkable, but they are simple in conception, fair in execution, and by no means to be despised. Of course when compared with the magnificently-engraved slabs of foreign churches, they lose by comparison.

This Church, however, was especially rich in memorial brasses—made of a composition known as lattyn or latton*—but the wanton and wicked destruc-

* Occasionally in England effigies wrought in other materials are found: *e.g.* at Burford, co. Salop, there is a leaden plate engraved with a figure of Lady Corbet, A.D. 1516. Iron memorials—sometimes cast, sometimes wrought—are found in Surrey, Sussex, and Cornwall: while wooden effigies—easily cut, damaged, and defaced—were far more common than they are now. In ancient times, prior to the Reformation, the cross, in some form or other, was constantly introduced; and while the churchyard cross of stone commonly stood near the south porch, at the head of almost every grave was placed another cross of stone or of wood, with some simple and touching prayer for the departed, that God's mercy, for Christ's sake, might be known.

* Latten, letton, or lattyn, is a mixed metal which was used largely in the making of mediæval church ornaments, such as candlesticks, lecterns, crosses, and memorial brasses. Fuller points out that the largeness of the ransom demanded for Richard I. was so great, that church plate was very generally sold to provide it; and that subsequently latten was used for all but the vessels of the altar in making ecclesiastical ornaments. See Fuller's *Holy Warre*, book iii., c. 13, and *Archæologia*, vol. xxi., pp. 261, 262.

tion of everything which to the destroyers appeared to savour of what they termed "superstition," has swept away many such monumental memorials. Even the slabs which contained them have been taken up, and some, as I discovered, had been used as paving-stones for the space near the south-western gate of the churchyard. A few brasses, however, remain, some of which are of great interest to the antiquary and archæologist, and are now described:—

1. On an altar-tomb in the south transept are those of Thomas Quartermain of North Weston, his wife Katherine, and their son Thomas. This lady was the daughter of Guy de Breton and his wife Joane, who was the daughter and heiress of Thomas de Grey, son of Sir Robert, fifth Lord Grey of Rotherfield, co. Oxon.* Thomas Quartermain and his wife died in one year, 1342. Their son Thomas is represented by an effigy, the lower portion of which has been broken off and is lost, and his wife Joane stands on a kind of bracket. These figures were engraved about the year 1420. The greater part of the marginal inscription is lost.

The inscription, however, has been thus preserved in the Cottonian MS. Cleopatra, C. iii., folio 3 b, in the British Museum:—

Hic jacent Thomas Quatremayn de North Westene Kath'rna uxor eius que fuit filia Guidonis Breton' et Joh'e uxor' eius filie et heredis Tho'e de Grey, filii Roberti D'ni de Grey Retherfeld' qui obier'nt vi die Junii Anno D'ni millesimo C.C.C.xlij. Similiterque hic jacent Thomas filius predicti Thome Quatremayn et Johanna uxor eius qui quidem Thomas obijt vj die Maij Anno D'ni Millesimo ccclxxxxvi quorum an'mab's p'pitietur Deus. Amen.

In these two military figures it will be found that plate armour has entirely superseded the mail of a previous generation. The bascinet, called by the Italians *cervelliera*, from *cervella*, a skull, is also less acutely pointed, while the part over the forehead, as well as the edges or cuffs of the gauntlets, are effectively ornamented with trefoils side by side. The spurs of the figure are guarded by a thin plate of steel over the rowels to prevent both entanglement and too great punishment for the horse. In one figure, roundels in front of the arm-pits are represented; in the other, a shield-like palette on either breast. The simple veil of one of the female figures, worn over a tight-fitting kirtle, gives much grace and dignity to this part of the memorial; the bold and expressive lines of the outer mantle in which render it artistically very effective. The other figure wears the kirtle likewise, with a turned-down collar and an ornamental zone below the breasts, and also a flowing mantle. The hair is dressed in careful and somewhat formal plaits on either side of the face, with a roll or wreath above, over which a transparent and light veil is placed. The lines of the drapery are here likewise well arranged. All the figures have the palms of their hands joined, as in prayer.

2. Then comes Richard Quartermain, Esq., Councillor to Richard, Duke of York, and Edward IV., with Sibyl, daughter of Nicholas Englefield, his wife, and one son, in armour like that of his father. Both father and son are represented bareheaded, with hands joined in prayer, and with their hair cut close. Their armour is of a mixed kind. Here a zig-zag collar of mail hangs over the breast-plate round the neck; but the chief peculiarity of that on these two figures is the size and angular shape of its elbow-plates and pauldrons, which are attached to the arms and shoulders by arming-points or by spring-pins, and the use of ridges to strengthen the various pieces of the armour, especially the pauldron of the left shoulder. The lady of Quartermain wears a close-fitting kirtle, open at the neck, with a short tunic over it, and a mantle fastened together in front with cords and tassels. A veil covers her head, and depends therefrom. These figures in brass are on the upper slab of a very handsome and elaborate freestone altar-tomb in the south transept, the sides of which are beautiful with elaborate carvings, quatrefoils, tabernacles, and heraldic shields.*

* "In the same year (1361), John de Grey, [third] Baron of Rotherfeld, settled upon his son, on his marriage, his manors of Shobiston (Shabbington), com. Bucks, and Somerton, com. Oxon, with a rent-charge of sixty pounds per annum, out of his lordship of Rotherfeld, which from this family took the name of Rotherfeld-Greys, as the other Rotherfeld did that of Pipard, being held of the Honor of Wallingford, as a part of six knights' fees granted upon homage to William, son of Roger Pipard, in 9 Henry III."—*History of Wallingford*, by J. K. Hedges, p. 8. London: 1881.

* The family of Quartermain remained at Thame for many generations, though the particular branch here commemorated, terminated. "Thomas Quartermain of Thame, gentleman," made his will 28 Feb. 1630, and it was proved 12 Feb. 1631. The witnesses were Hugh Robotham and William Welsh. His wife's name was Bridget. He left three sons, 1. Edward; 2. Windsor; 3. Richard; and four daughters, the eldest, Margaret, married to Mr. Lee; the second, Rebecca, married to Mr. Herbert; and the two younger, Sarah and Eleanor, were then unmarried. He "desires to be buried in the Church of Thame in an ile there called Quartermain's Ile, if it pleases God I die of this sickness." (Will enrolled in Audley, 15.)

In the Record Office, amongst the Chancery Bills and Answers, under the letter Q, bundle I., are the following:—15. Quartermain v. Smith; 16. Q. v. Martin; 26. Q. v. Chibnall; 46. Q. v. King; 50. Q. v. Quartermaine; and in bundle II.: 89. Q. v. Heybourn, and 90. Q. v. Martin.

William, son of Walter Quartermain of Thame and Shabbington, gent., having received his grammar education at Thame School, matriculated from B. N. C. 10 Oct. 1634, aged 16. He became Physician to King Charles II. His first wife was buried in Westminster Abbey 15 July 1661. He married, secondly, Mary, dau. of Sir Thomas Dyke and granddaughter of Sir John Bramston, Chief Justice of the King's Bench. He was buried in St. Martin's-in-the-Fields 11 June 1667.

The inscription round the edge of the slab of this altar-tomb stands thus:—

O certeyn deth that now hast overthrow, Richard Quartremayns Squyer and Sibil his wife that lie here now lowe. That with rial Princes of Counsel was true and wise famed To Richard Duke of York and after with his sone Kyng Edward the iiii named. That founded in the Church of Thame a chantrie vi pore men and a fraternytie In the worship of Seynt Cristofere to be releved in p'petuyte. They that of her almys for ther Soulis a Paternoster and Ave devoutly wul Sey of holy Faders is graunted they pardon of dayes forty alwey. Which Richard and Sibil oute of this Worlde passid in the yere of oure Lord mcccclx. Upon theyr Soules Jhu have mercy. Amen.

3. A civilian and his wife, with three sons and six daughters, are represented on the floor of the Nave, much worn. The personal inscription and a device of the Holy Trinity are lost; but a label coming out of the woman's mouth stands thus, **Fili redemptor mundi De' miserere nobis.** The man, dressed in a plain gown or tunic, girdled, reaching to the ankles, stands with hands joined in prayer turned towards his wife, in a similar devotional attitude turned towards him. He wears the *gypciere* or girdle-pouch at his left side, and his shoes are rounded. The lady wears a plain kirtle—with ample folds, and with cuffs of fur at the wrists—gathered in at the waist with a buckled girdle. Round her neck is a simple turned-down collar. Upon her head is an angular-shaped folded covering, with formal lappets, quite plain, but graceful. The children are placed below; the boys under their father, and the girls under their mother. The latter have no head-dress.

4. In the north wall of the north transept, towards the eastern part of it, stands east and west, under a third-pointed arch of plain character, an altar-tomb of stone, with a Purbeck marble slab, in commemoration of Geoffrey Dormer and his two wives; one with five sons and eight daughters underneath, and the other with seven sons and five daughters. At the corners of the slab are the four Evangelistic symbols in circles. There are also two coats of arms and a shield bearing the merchant's mark of Geoffrey Dormer. He is represented in a long gown, lined with fur, the sleeves and collar of which are also trimmed with fur. His under garment, shewn below the neck, is embroidered, and his hair is parted down the middle. His two wives are dressed alike, in plain kirtles, almost close round the neck, and with cuffs of fur. Handsome buckled girdles, with ornamental ends, bind their waists. They both likewise wear the same kind of angular head-dress, and their hands are joined, as if in prayer. Round the edge of the tomb the following inscription in brass still remains:—

Orate pro animab's Galfridi Dormer, mercatoris stapule ville Calis et Margere et Alicie uxores eius qui quidem Galfridus obiit nono die Marcii Anno D'ni Mil's'mo quingentesimo secundo quor' a'i'ab' propicietur Deus. Amen.

5. Before the entrance to the choir is a memorial stone on which are effigies of Christopher Bridgeman and Maude his wife, with their children, all of whom seem to have predeceased their parents. The brass of the ten sons has been removed; that of the two daughters remains. He is represented in a long gown, lined and cuffed with fur, a belt round the waist, to which is attached at his right side the purse or *gypciere*. His wife wears a tight, close-fitting dress, flowing below the waist, which is confined by a girdle, the whole of which is either embroidered or otherwise ornamented. The following inscription remains:—

Pray for ye sowle of Cr'stofre Bridgman which deceased on holy Rode day next before Mighelmas in the yere of our lord mdiij on whose soule jh'u have mercy. Also pray for ye soulys of Maude late ye wife of the said Cristofer & of all ye children cristofre john edward geffrey rychard Will'm thomas Edward Rich'as thomas ye sonnes & iohane & iohane ye doughters wich children be deceasid on whois soulis jh'u have m'cy.

6. On the floor of the nave is a memorial brass to Walter Prat and Isabell his wife, who are represented full-faced, with their hands joined in prayer, and in the costume of the period. Four sons are under the representation of the man, and five daughters under that of the woman. The four evangelistic symbols in circles were originally placed at the corners of the slab, but one of these—that relating to St. Matthew—is now lost. The inscription below is partly destroyed; while that fragment which remains is reversed. A label above, on which has been engraved a petition for those departed, **Qui venisti redimere perditos, noli damnare redemptos,** is also partially lost, and the whole memorial is very much worn and defaced. It was first placed here in 1508, and the inscription stood thus:—

Pray for the soules of Walter Prat and Isabel his wife which Walter died the xx'o day of August in the yere of our lorde mdviii and the said Isabel deceased —— on whose sowles ye Lorde have mercy.

7. At the back of an altar-tomb of Purbeck marble, on the south side of the choir, and over the family vault, is a representation of Sir John Clerke of Weston. He is represented kneeling on a cushion at a prayer

desk, with joined palms. On a label above stands the prayer on a scroll—**Sancta trinitas unus de' miserere.** Before him lies an open book. Over his armour he wears a tabard adorned with his armorial bearings.* The artistic character of the figure is decidedly inferior to that of the earlier brasses. Breadth of design and vigour of drawing have given place to a certain weakness, by no means atoned for by a greater attention to

BRASS OF SIR JOHN CLERKE, KNT.

detail, and the introduction of inexact perspective and cross-hatching to obtain effect. The inscription stands thus:—

Here lyeth Sr John Clerk of Northe Weston, Knyght, whyche toke Louys of Orleans duk of longuevile & marquis of Roteline prysonr at ye iorney of Bomy by Terouane ye xvj day of August in ye vth yere of ye Reigne of ye noble & victorius kyng henry ye viii whych John deceasyd ye vth day of Apl'l Ao D'ni 1·5·3·9 whose soule god p'do'n.

* On the wall above, a helmet, surmounted with a ram's head, the crest of the Clerkes, remains suspended on a projecting rod. Late in the last century there were three banner-poles remaining, with tattered fragments of funeral ornaments, and several eschocheons and hatchments, but these latter have all been lost. The present baronet, Sir W. F. Clerke, possesses his ancestor's sword—large, but plain, and having no sheath. Anciently, the dignity and degree of a person of rank was duly and carefully acknowledged at his funeral; and in the case of barons, knights, and esquires it was the custom to suspend armour, shield, surcoat, helmet, and sword over the place of sepulture or the monumental memorial. As knights of old received their swords, duly blessed, from the altar; so no doubt the custom arose of their thus bequeathing them to the church of their parish. In later times, however, instead of the actual military armour being suspended, special armour, used in the funeral obsequies, was made for the purpose. I possess one of the gauntlets of Lord Paget, father of the lady of Sir Henry Lee, K.G.

Two other representations or inscriptions have been wrenched off, and are lost. Below, on the face of the tomb, in the centre of each panel, the arms of Clerke with the canton still remain.

8. Between Sir John Clerke's tomb and the choir skreen, on the floor, is the figure of a civilian, John Caley, with an inscription below. He is habited in a long furred gown with open sleeves, and wears large broad-toed shoes with a strap across the instep. His hands are joined in prayer. The head of this figure is broken off, and the representation of his wife is altogether lost. The inscription, partly gone and much worn, stands thus:—

[Orate pro animabus*] Johannis Caley gen'osi et Johanne uxoris sue qui quidem . . . . xxx die Marcii Ao D'ni mlo'xliii cui' a'i'e p'picietur deus.

9. On the south wall of the choir near is a brass memorial of Edward Harris, Fellow of New College, and the first Head Master of Thame Grammar School. Habited in an university gown, with braid on the long sleeves, he is kneeling facing eastwards, with joined hands. The figure is well designed, and the head fine. He wears mustachios and a pointed beard. Round his neck is a small ruff. The following are the inscriptions:—

MEMORIÆ EDOVARDI HARRIS NOVI COLLEGII OXON. QUONDAM SOCIJ, ARTIVM MAGISTRI ET SCHOLÆ THAMENSIS A IOHANNE WILLIAMS MILITE DOMINO WILLIAMS DE THAME FVNDATÆ MODERATORIS PRIMI, ET PRIMARIJ, POST AN'OS 30 IN EADEM SVMMÃ CVM FIDE ET INDVSTRIÃ INSVMPTOS, IBIDEM ANNO SALVTIS 1597° ÆTATIS SVÆ FERE 63° DIE NOVEMBRIS 3° PIE DEFVNCTI.

* The three words within brackets are now wanting, and so are others below.

Hic sitvs es qva sedisti; locvs vnvs, et idem
Et cathedram, et tumvly' dat tibi (docte senex).
Hic pveros vivens docvisti, mortvvs omnes,
(Nvnc magis exemplo, quam privs arte) doces,
Disce docenda cohors, vivum integritatis amore,
Defvnctvm meritis, et pietate seqvi.

A Gulielmo Ballowe ex testamento hærede
Optimi præceptoris desiderio positvm.

The author possesses three fragments of an inscription on brass presumed to have belonged to Thame Church. These are so broken and defaced, however, that the legend is imperfect. As far as it can be decyphered, it stands thus:—

O blessid trinite .... e us from payne eternall & we pray you .... schall red or se this .... have i memory the date of our lorde a.m.ccccli .... yet as on this ston .... tha' dep'tid as herafter doith apperiѕ upon the day of ....

Purbeck marble. South side of Choir.

Altar Tomb of Sir John Clerke, Knt.

(*From a Sketch by the Author.*)

Ten years ago the Library of the Archæological Institute possessed two rubbings of brasses from Thame Church, which are now mislaid, and cannot be found. The brasses appear to have been removed or lost about the year 1843. One of these is said to have represented a civilian of the fifteenth century, and the other was an inscription in black letter to the memory of John Benet, *circa* 1460. Two persons of this name were Churchwardens of Thame during the fifteenth century; and their vault, as Tradition affirms, is near the middle aisle, where the font now stands.

There are two modern brasses with the following inscriptions on the north-east pillar of the Tower, near the entrance of the Chancel :—

1. **Ad Majorem Dei Gloriam. In the year 1876 Richard Lee, Surgeon of this Town, raised a Fund by subscription amounting to £240 for re-casting the six old bells of this House of Prayer. A peal on eight new bells hung in the Tower was first rung upon August 11th of the aforenamed year. May God the Trinity bless and have mercy upon all the donors. Amen.**

2. THE GATES AT THE ENTRANCE OF THE SOUTH PORCH ARE ERECTED TO THE MEMORY OF MARIA THE BELOVED WIFE OF RICHARD LEE, WHO DIED DECEMBER 30TH, 1878, AGED 69 YEARS.

And a third on the splay of the easternmost window of the south side of the Chancel :—

3. **This window is offered by Anne Reynolds to the Glory of God, and in loving memory of her husband, Henry Wells Reynolds, who entered into rest January 12th, 1875, aged 72 years.**

From the Collections of Francis Thynne the herald,* who visited Thame Church on the 22nd of September, 1582, the following inscriptions, now lost, are taken :—

Pray for the sowle of Master John Aldersonne, prieste, late Vicar of Thame who died the tuesday next after Passion Sondaye in the yeare of our lorde mcccciij; on whose sowle Jhesus have mercy. Amen.

Pray for the soule of Henry Bowler and Elizabeth his wyfe the w'ch Elizabeth died the x daye of Marche in the yere of or lorde mcccclv on whose soule Jesus have mercye. He had four sonnes and six daughters.

So much for the brasses in Thame Church. Now follow exact copies of all the monumental inscriptions, whether found on the walls, or upon the floor, beginning with those of the family of Clerke of North Weston. The arbitrary spelling and often irregular punctuation of the various inscriptions are followed carefully. Every existing monument, both on wall and floor, has been noticed, and each personal record duly transcribed. Several on the floor were destroyed about forty years ago.

Choir Floor.

M. S.
Hic sepultus est
Familia conjuge Prole
Suaq' magis adhuc virtute
Præclarissimus Vir Iohan'es Clerke
Eques Auratus & Baronettus.
Qui Majorum Fortitudinem et Liberalitatem
Suo, hoc est, maximo decorabat
Ingenio et comitate.
Uxorem qua' vnica qua' Semp^{er} Charissima habvit
Nobili orta' Carreorv' Stem'ate
Animi Corporis Fortvnæ Dotibus ornata'
Sibiq' Parem
Iuvenis Ivvenem Duxit
Qvalem tanti Parentes Sobolem Peperere
Læti Celebrabunt Posteri
Nil vitra nvmervm Memorabit
Iners Marmor.
Nempe Eliberis novem Editis Quinq' svpersunt
Paternæ Virtuti Maternæ pulchritudine
Compares.
Propriu' Vivunt Encomium
Seroq' (Precetvr Candidvs Lector)
Inscribantvr Epitaphio

Mortem Obijt { Mens: Octob^{is} / Anno / Die vii. } { Ætat: svæ xlv. / Salut^{is} nost^{ræ} / ciↄiↄclxvii.

---

* Cotton MSS., Brit. Museum, Cleopatra, C. iii., fol. 4, 5.

Choir. South wall. Black and white marble.

H. S. E.
juxta patrem,
EDVARDUS CLERKE, IOHAN'IS CLERKE
de NORTH WESTON in agro Oxon. Baronetti,
et Philadelphiæ conjugis ejus superstitis filius
ordine nascendi et moriendi tertius qui diem
obiit 24° April' A'no Dn' 1677 Ætatis suæ 24°
fatali variolarum morbo abreptus, quo
IOHANNES frater ejus proxime natu major
Decem ante annis peregre Madritij
interierat.

South wall. White marble.

Near this Place, lyeth yᵉ Body of
Dame PHILADELPHIA CLERKE
Widow of Sʳ JOHN CLERK of
North Weston in yᵉ County of Oxford, Kᵗ
and Baronet,
Daughter of Sʳ EDWARD CARR
of Hillingdon in yᵉ County of
Middlesex, Knight,
who during yᵉ space of one and thirty years
lived a widow in great credit & reputation;
and, as she was most deservedly beloved
by all her children, so she was most
justly esteemed by all that knew her;
who departed this life yᵉ 9ᵗʰ day of
August Anno Dom' 1698
In yᵉ 72ᵈ year of her age.

Choir Floor. Black marble.

HERE LIETH THE BODY OF
RICHARD CLERKE THE 5ᵀᴴ
SONNE OF IOHN CLERKE ESQ
BY PHILADELPHIA HIS WIFE
OF WESTON IN THE PARISH OF
THAME
HEE LIUED 13 MONTHS AND
DYED YE 3ᴿᴰ OF FEB. AN. DOM.
1658.

Choir Floor. Black marble.

EDVARDVS
CLERKE OBIJT
1677.

Floor of Choir. Freestone.

CHRISTOPH'
FILIVS GILBERTI
ET MARGARETE TROWE
OBIJT FEB. 22 1680
ÆTATIS SVÆ
24 ANN'

EDUARDVS
FILIVS GILBERTI
ET MARGARETE TROWE
OBIJT DECEMB. 23 1679
ÆTATIS SVÆ
20 ANN'

North wall of Choir. White marble.

Chancel Floor. Preestone.

In hope of yᵉ Resurrection
Under this Tombe lyeth yᵉ body of Margaret
Wife of Gilbert Trowe* of this par. Gent. (with
whome she liued a most deare & louinge
Wife nere 40 yeares,) and by him had issue five
Sonnes (two of which lye here interr'd) & three
Daughters. She dyed lamented of all Decemb.
yᵉ 30. 1690 aged 55 yeares & 10 months.

Hail sacred dust, premit a mournfull sonne
To dropp some tears for roses on your urn!
In holy writ renowned are the names
Of Sarah and Rebecca, worthy dames.
Reader, such was th' enshrined in all her life—
A tender mother & a loueing wife:
She's gonne alas, but cease all tears for see
She's gonne to blisse: her seat's eternity.
And till both soule and body meet again
Unmov'd may her sweet ashes here remain.

Sic sperat votaque sua . . . .
Trowe filius mœrens qui piæ
memoriæ matris suæ charissime
dedi . . . .

Chancel Floor. Preestone.

H. S. E.
Corpus Hannæ, Henrici Bruges Thamensis
Scholæ magistri, uxoris Quæ Trigesimum
Secundum ætatis suæ annum agens obiit
Nono Junii MDCCIII.

Sub eodem lapide jacet Kethrana, Henrici
et Annæ Bruges Filia natu minima,
Quæ, unum mensem et quatuor dies nata,
Occidit quarto die Julii A.D. MDCCIII.

On the marble and alabaster tomb in the midst of the Chancel.

Epitaphium† Domini Iohannis Williams, equitis aurati, Baronis a Thame, qui obiit xiv die Octobris Anno Domini 1559.

PARVA TEGIT CINERES GULIELMIDES URNA IOHANNIS,
NULLA TEGENT TANTI SECULA FACTA VIRI;
QUEM DOTES ANIMI FORTUNÆ DOTIBUS ULTRO
ORNAVIT, SORTIS MUNERE PLUS MERITUM;
NAM POTUIT VIRTUS MERITIS SI ACQUIRERE FORTIS,
MUNERA, DIVITIAS, VIR BONUS ECCE TULIT.

* Sir Richard Combes, of Hemel Hempstead, Knt., married for his second wife Anne, daughter of Gilbert Trowe, of Thame, Oxon.

† The personal inscription was wrenched off by the Parliamentary soldiers during the Civil War, and has not since been discovered.

TAM BONUS, UT MERITO CUNCTIS CHARISSIMUS ESSET
ORDINIBUS, TITULUS MAJOR ET ILLE SUIS.
SI QUAERIS STIRPE, SATUS NON VILIS: EQUESTRI
FACTUS EQUES; PROCERUM POST PROCER UNUS ERAT;
REGUM ÆRI QUAESTOR, REGALI EX INDE CUBILI,
POSTREMUM CAMBRO PRÆFUIT ET POPULO.*

Marble monument. North side of Sanctuary.

LECTOR
HEIC JUXTA CORPUS
MAXIMILIANI PETTY, ARMIG.
ELISABETHA FILIA PRIMOGENITA
CONJUX GUL' BURTE S. T. P. DOCTISS.
SCHOLÆ THAMENSIS & WINTON: INFORMATORIS
ISTIUS ETIAM COLLEGII CUSTODIS DIGNISS.
DEPOSUIT QUOD ERAT MORTALE. CAVE
ENIM CREDAT INGENTES, QUIBUS ORNATA
ERAT, ANIMI DOTES HEIC QUOQUE TUMULARI
VIVUNT IN ORE, OCULIS MEMORIÂ OMNIUM
QUI EAM NO'RUNT (NOR'UNT AUTEM OMNES, QUIB'
IGNOTA NON ERAT VIRTUS) ET AD CŒLUM
AD QUOD DUM VIXIT VERE ANHELAVIT
ANIMÂ TAM VENUSTUM CORPUS ÆQRÈ
RELINQUENTE, TANDEM ABÎERE; ITERUM
VISENDÆ, & HUIC MONUMENTO FIDEM
CONCILIATURÆ, IPSIQUE PREMIUM
IN DIE ILLO
ELISABETA FILIA MŒRENS P.
A'NO D'NI MDCLXXXIII ÆTATIS LXIJ.

* The following translation of this remaining portion of the epitaph into English blank verse is from the pen of my eldest son:—

The Epitaph of John, Lord Williams, Kt., Baron of Thame, who departed this life the 14th of October, Anno Domini 1559.

John Williams' body, a small urn doth hide.
No age can hide the merits of that man
Whom willingly great Fortune to her gifts
Has added no mean talents; and by lot
These gifts came, not by merit. If a man
Riches by chance has gained, much he will do
If virtue be but added to his wealth:
So noble that all others be excelled,
And rightly too, his title made him that.
Ask you his birth? Of no mean stock was he,
A knight was made, and afterwards became
The noblest of the noble; guardian
Of all his country's wealth; from thence advanced
To dignity the highest in the land.

F. REGINALD B. D. LEE.

Chancel Floor. Freestone.

HIC JACET HUGO WILLIS FILIUS 2dus HUGONIS WILLIS QUI NATUS EST DIE JOVIS 9 FEB. 1659 AT OBIIT DIE JOVIS 19o APRILIS 1660 HORAM CIS CITER OCTAVAM MATUTINAM.

HIC JACET ETIAM ELIZABETHA WILLIS FILIA 2da HUGONIS WILLIS. QUAE OBIIT 24o NOV. 1661.*

White marble monument. South side of Sanctuary.

In Memory of
HENRY WARNER
An attorney of this town,
Eminent for his integrity & skill in his profession,
Who died Feb. 17th 1750. Aged 70 years.
ELIZABETH his wife (Daughter of
THOMAS and SARAH HODGKINS of Stoke
Goldington, Bucks)
Who died May 30th 1733. Aged 53.
And their Issue
THOs WARNER died Dec. 20th 1734, aged 21,
unmarried,
HENRY WARNER June 5th 1746, aged 36,
And
SARAH WARNER spinster Nov. 27. 1771. Aged 59,
All interred in a vault near this Place;
Where are also Buried
EST'ER, wife of the said HENRY WARNER, Junr
(and daughter of THOMAS NEWELL of Postcomb,
Oxon.)
who died Feb. 19th 1765. aged 58 years.
JAMES-WARNER WAY died Sepr 2d 1769 Aged
3 Months,
And was Son of JAMES WAY of this Town, Gent.
By SARAH his wife Only Child
Of the said HENRY and EST'ER WARNER,
And Sole surviving Heir of the first
HENRY WARNER abovenamed.
Also SARAH WAY, Spinster,
Who died Feb. 29th 1849. Aged 79 years.

Wall. South side Choir. Black and white marble.

[The arms in the shield above appear to be those of Ellis of Glasdryn, co. Carnarvon, with three quarterings, impaling Petty of Tetlesworth and Stoke Tallmache.]

M. S.

HERE LYETH Ye BODIE OF Mrs REBECCA ELLIS Ye DAVGHTER OF Mr IOHN PETTIE OF STOKE, ESQ. AND LATE WIFE TO Mr JOHN ELLIS OF WHITFIELD, CLERK, WHO LIVED MOST RELIGIOUSLY & DIED IN A MOST GODLY MANNER VPON SUNDAY THE SIXT OF NOVEMBER, 1631, IN THE 7TH YEARE OF KING CHARLES & OF HER AGE ABOUT THE NINETEENTH.

In memorie of whose vertues her husband caused this to be erected.*

Black marble, in a frame of white alabaster. Choir wall, south-west corner.

RICHARDVS BOVCHER LL.BACCALAUREVS NOVI COLLEGII OXON' QUONDAM SOCIVS ET ARCHIDIDASCALVS SCHOLÆ THAMENSIS CVI PER 30 FERE ANNOS SUMMA CVM LAVDE PRÆFUIT QUO NON ALTER LATINIVS GRÆCIS LITERIS FELICITER EDOCENDIS MAGIS DEXTER SEDVLVSVE FUIT VIR CASTUS SOBRIV' DOCTUS INTEGER DEO' REPVBLICA LITERARIÂ OPTIMÈ MERITVS IVLII 14. Ao D'NI 1627 MORTALITATEM CVM ÆTERNITATE FELICITER COMMVTAVIT.

[Here is represented a standing figure of a man in a ruff, with beard, trunk hose, and bachelor's gown. His hands are joined in prayer.]

Quem Morum exemplar Thama est venerata honoru'
Dum regit annexam bis tria lustra scholam
Quem schola per cultæ subsellia densa juventæ
Mirata est Latio dum docet ore loqui
Parcentem flagris, ut amatas traderet artes
Fingeret et placidis mollia corda modis
Otia jam sibi longa dedit Boucherus et isthinc
(Flebitis ô Pueri) non rediturus abit.

✠ { THOMAS BOUCHER CHARISSIMVS
FRATER SUIS IMPENSIS POSUIT } ✠

---

* Some commemorative verses in Latin, under each of the inscriptions, have been originally engraved on this stone; but they are now so much worn and obscured that their meaning is not evident.

* The following inscription on brass, with four shields of arms, to the memory of Mrs. Rebecca Ellis's grandfather, remains in the

White marble. South wall of Choir.

S. I.
IOH'ES STRIBLEHILL
de THAME in Com. OXON. Gen. ex
Antiquâ satis familiâ apud Thame'ses
oriundus, quam suâ ipse industriâ plurimu'
erexit ex FRANCISCA uxore (Filiâ THO.
CARTER de NORTHWESTON Gen:) Tres
Reliquit filias Superstites, MARTHA' (nunc
uxore' CAROLI HOLT de STOKE in Com' OXON
Armig.) FRANCISCA' et ELIZ' Obiit 24 die Augusti
A° Ætatis Suæ 49° Salutis Humanæ 1692
Juxta Patrem Sita Est
Francisca Filiarum dicti IOHAN^{e} natu s'c'da,
quæ quasi patrem sui amantissimum vel
ad umbras usq' sequi Festinaret, infra
unius ab illo mensis spatium morte
obiit Repentina 25° Die mensis
Sept' A° Ætatis Suæ 17° Salutis
Humanæ, 1692.

Choir Floor. Freestone.

Here
Lyeth the Body
of HANNAH the WIFE of
STEPHEN COOK Who
Departed this Life September
the 13th 1717 Aged
35 years.

Choir Floor. Freestone.

Here
Lyeth the Body of
STEPHEN COOK Senior
Who departed this Life
April the 13th 1707
Aged 83 years.

Choir Floor. White marble.

Here
Lyeth the Body of
ANN the Wife of EDWARD
GURDON, Gent. who died ye 7th
July 1691 aged 31 years
& 8 months.

church of Stoke Tallmarhe, co. Oxon:—"Hic jacet Johannes Pettie, armiger, qui obiit xxmo die Aprilis Anno Regni Dnae Reginae Elizabeth' Tricesimo primo relictis ex Elizabetha uxore illa et herede Thome Snapp gen: Johanne, Leonardo, Maximiliano, Christophero, et Georgio filiis: Maria, Joanna, Anna, Alicia et Phillippa, filiabus." A grant of arms had been made to John Petty of Tettesworth, by Ralph Cooke, Clarencieux, on 10 May, 1570, thus: Quarterly or and az., over all on a bend vert three martlets of the first.—Harl. MS. "Armes of Severall Counties," fol. 6.

Choir Floor, south side. Freestone.

Here
lyeth the Body of
Susanna the wife of John
Hebern, junior, who died
September y^{e} 26, 1704
Aged 34 years.

Choir, south wall, white marble.

In Memory of
Timothy Newmarch Lee, gent.
(eldest son of John Lee, of Pocklington
in the county of York, gent. and great-grandson of
Francis Lee of Spelsbury in this county, esq^{r})
who died Nov. 20. 1794 aged 49,
leaving issue by his wife Elizabeth a son and a
daughter, the former Vicar of this parish.
his daughter Abigail died in infancy.

ALSO OF CORNELIUS LEE, ESQ.
SECOND SON OF THE REV. T. T. LEE, BY ELIZABETH
3RD DAUGHTER OF RICHARD SMITH ESQ. J.P. & D.L.
HE MARRIED CHARLOTTE LOUISA WYKES,
AND DIED WITHOUT SURVIVING ISSUE
FEB. 10. 1843, AGED 47 YEARS.

ALSO OF FRANCES [M.A.
ELDEST DAUGHTER OF THE REV. FREDERICK LEE,
VICAR OF STANTONBURY BUCKS,
AND RECTOR OF EASINGTON IN THIS COUNTY;
SHE DIED IN INFANCY.
REQUIESCANT IN PACE.

Brass on the east wall of Choir.

In affectionate remembrance of
Rachel Lyne, daughter of B. Tucker
Esq. of Trematon Castle, Cornwall, and
wife of George Lee Esq. of Kentons near
Henley-on-Thames; 6th son of a former Vicar of
This Parish. She died 22 Dec. 1877, aged 78.

Black and white marble. East wall of Choir.

In Memory of
THE
REV. TIMOTHY TRIPP LEE, B.A.
VICAR OF THIS PARISH 46 YEARS,
AND MASTER OF
THE FREE GRAMMAR SCHOOL IN THIS TOWN
26 YEARS
HE DIED THE 29TH OF DECR 1840,
IN THE 72ND YEAR OF HIS AGE.
ALSO TO THE MEMORY OF
ELIZABETH
WIFE OF THE ABOVE
WHO DIED JANUARY 25TH 1854
AGED 79.

Black and white marble. East wall of Choir.

HIC JACET CORPUS
FREDERICI LEE, ART. MAG.,
PRIMUM E COLLEGIO S. MARIÆ MAGDALENÆ
DEINDE MERTONENSIS ALUMNI,
ISTIUS ECCLESIÆ PER ANNOS OCTODECIM
QUONDAM SACERDOTIS,
QUI OBIIT DIE IV. NOV.
ANNO SALUTIS MDCCCXLI.
JUXTA PORTAM MERIDIONALEM
DORMIT MARIA UXOR EJUSDEM,
QUÆ OBIIT DIE MAII XXVII., A.S.MDCCCLIII.
QUORUM ANIMABUS
ET OMNIUM FIDELIUM DEFUNCTORUM
PROPITIETUR DEUS. AMEN.*

Choir, south side. Black marble.

Beneath
are deposited
the Remains of
EDWD. ROSE, Attorney,
Who died 7th March 1776, Aged 78 years.
Also of ANN his Wife
(Daur of John Burrows, Gent.)
and three of their
Children.

Choir Floor, south side. White marble.

Hic jacet
Reverendus Vir
THOMAS MIDDLETON
Tam exemplo quam Doctrina
Vere Christianus
Noui Collegii Oxoniensis olim Socius
Vocatus inde ad Scholam Thamensem
Quam quanto omnium favore tenuit
Tanto omnium dolore reliquit
Obiit 22 April
Anno { Domini 1694
{ Ætatis suæ 51.

Choir Floor. White marble.

HIC JACET
THOMAS MIDDLETO'
FILIVS THO: MIDDLETON, A.M.
OBIIT NONIS DECEMBRIS
Ao { ÆTATIS SUÆ 8o
{ SALUTIS HUMANÆ
1684.

Choir Floor, south side. White marble.

In Memory of
ANNE the Wife of the
Reverend Mr BUERDSELL
and Daughter of the Reverend
Mr MIDDLETON, who died
November the 4th 1749
Aged 71 years.

Choir, north wall. White marble.

Near this place
lye interr'd the Bodies
of MATTHEW WILKINS, Gent.
who, after an Industrious And
Honest Practice of the Law above
THIRTY YEARS in this PARISH,
Departed this Life on the 9th of
APRIL 1722 Aged 63 years,
As also
of GRACIANA His loving wife,
who was Remarkably
PIOUS, Humble
& Charitable
And died on the 11th of DECEMber
1699 Aged 36 years.
He had issue by her Only two
Daughters who have Erected
this Monument.

---

* On this monument the arms are those of Lee, with a mullet for difference, impaling Ellys of Aylesbury. "There is handed down to us," writes Mr. Robert Gibbs of that town, "from a seventeenth-century transcript of 'Francis Thyn's *Notes*,' in the Library of Hartwell House, a copy of a memento once existing in the chancel, and bearing the ancient name of Ellys (Ellis, Ellia). Thyn describes it as a 'boryall shocheon in ye Chyrch of Ailesburgh'—Argent a chevron verte, between three estoiles or mullets gules." To which the following footnote is appended: "The name of Ellys is met with as early as the third of Henry VI. (1424), at which period Robert Ellis, clerk, was one of the incumbents of the chantry, or brotherhood, founded by John Singleton and John Baldwin, inhabitants of Aylesbury."—*History of Aylesbury*, by Mr. Robert Gibbs. Aylesbury: 1885.

Choir Floor. White marble.

Here
lies interr'd
the Body of ANN
Daughter of the Rev^d
JOHN NEWBOROUGH
Vicar of this Parish, who died Octr 6th 1784.
requiescat in pace.
Also
The Body of the Rev. WILLIAM NEWBOROUGH, A.M.
FELLOW of PEMBROKE COLLEGE OXON,
And Minister of Long Crendon, Bucks,
who departed this Life
Nov. 15, 1787.

Choir, north wall. White marble.

Below
Rest the Remains of
SACKVILLE BALE LUPTON
late Surgeon of this Place
He died June 3rd 1840
Aged 85 years.
And also of his mother LETITIA,
His wife, JANE THEODOSIA,
Of His Sons
THOMAS, SACKVILLE, WILLIAM
ARTHUR and WILLIAM
And of his daughter DECIMA.
His eldest daughter LETITIA
Died, and was buried at
Lamberhurst, Sussex.
His only surviving son HARRY
placed this tablet
As a small tribute of affection
To their Memory.

Floor, North Transept.

Here lie the Remains
of
HARRY STYLE, Gent.
Who died the 8th day of Dec^r.
1798 aged 89 years
Also of THEODOSIA STYLE, Widow
of the said HARRY STYLE,
Who died the 21 day of September
1806 aged . . . . years
Also of CHARLOTTE THEODOSIA HOLLAND
Daughter of the above named
HARRY & THEODOSIA STYLE
and wife of the
REV. JOHN HOLLAND,

Choir, north side. Marble.

Near this Place
Lies Interr'd ye Body
of Frances ye Wife of
IOHN STRIBLEHILL, Gen^t
who departed this Life
October ye 10th 1722.
Aged 82 years.

Choir Floor. Marble.

H. I.
FRANCESCA STRIBLEHILL
1692.

White marble. North wall of North Transept.

The afflicted Parents of
CHARLES THEOPHILUS DORRINGTON*
Bowing with humble submission to the Divine
Providence
which removed him (their only child,)
From their fond embrace,
Erect this monument to his memory.
He died 13th September 1821, aged 15 years.

"Thy will be done." Though tears profusely flow,
To Thee we yield our dearest hope below,
For Faith adoring waits to see him rise
(From this dark tomb emerging,) to the skies;
While Hope benignly wipes the gushing tear,
And bids us strive to join our offspring there.

White marble. East wall of North Transept.

In Memory
of
SAMUEL WOLLASTON, Apothecary
who dyed Oct. 2nd 1741. Aged 63.
And of MARY his wife
who dy'd Augt 8th 1752 aged 61.
And also of John and George
their sons who dy'd in their Infancy.†

---

* A deed exists, dated 1677, relating to houses in Sherborne Lane in the City of London, between the Company of Haberdashers and a member of this family, "Theophilus Dorrington, Merchant Taylor." Another between William Hayward and the aforesaid Theophilus Dorrington is dated 1694. A "Theophilus Dorrington," who was "bred a Dissenter," possibly the same person, was inducted to the Rectory of Wittersham, Kent, in Nov. 1698. He was an author, and wrote in favour of Infant Baptism and against the Dissenters. Some of his sermons were published in 8vo, to which his portrait, painted by Franck and engraved by Bouttats, was prefixed. He likewise compiled a *Familiar Guide to the Right Receiving of the Lord's Supper*, 12mo, published in London in 1718. The University of Oxford conferred upon him the honorary degree of M.A. by decree of Convocation on the 9th March 1710. He died in 1715.

† Prior to the year 1843, a stone lay in the north transept, having upon it the arms of Wollaston of Shenton, co. Leicester. Argent, three mullets sable pierced of the field, with a mullet for difference.

North wall, North Transept. Marble.

In Memory of
PHILIP HERBERT Esqr
of KINGSEY, near this place,
Member of Parliament for the City of Oxford.
He was a disinterested lover of his Country
without any affection for Popularity,
And was belov'd by all,
not because he sought it but because he deserv'd it.
He was a most tender and indulgent Husband,
A sincere and steady Friend.
He dyed July 22nd 1749 in the 32 year of his Age.
He married MARY only Daughter and sole Heiress
of EDWARD BUTLER LL.D.
who was President of Magdalene College, OXFORD
and Member of Parliament for that University.
His disconsolate Widow
As a testimony of her Gratitude and Affection
And in justice to so deserving a Character
Caused this Monument to be Erected.

South Transept. Pillar.

Neare this Place
Lieth the Body of
ROBERT CREWS
who died Jan. ye 7th 1731
In the 60th year of his age.
He was an Humble Obsequious Son,
A Tender affectionate Brother,
A Peaceable Benevolent Neighbour;
He kept up the Good Old Hospitality,
His Liberal Table was spread to ye Hungry
His Purse open to the Necessitous:
Generous without affectation,
Just in His action & Sincere to his friend,
A Pattern of Patience, Humility,
Charity, Good Nature and Peace.*

South Transept, Floor. White marble.

. . . .
. . . . . Body of IANE . . . . .
THOMAS CREWES . . . . .
Nov. 15, 1709.
. . . . . THOMAS their Son
. . . . . . Nov. 20
1769.

South Transept, East wall.

[Arms of Simons of Thame, Harl. MSS., Brit. Museum, No. 1483.]

In memory
of Mr WILLIAM SIMONS
who died (universally lamented,)
Sep. 19th 1764, aged 42 years.
Also of ANN his wife who died
Oct. 2^d 1792, aged 68 years.

No single virtue we could most commend
Whether the wife, the mother or the friend,
For she was all in that supreme degree
That as no one prevailed so all was she.

South Transept, South wall.

Near this Place
Lies interr'd the Body
of THOMAS BAYLEY,*
who departed This Life
March ye 20th 1747
Aged 51 years.
Death was to me a fri^nd:
Let this your joys increase
To change a World of trouble
For a World of peace.

South Transept, East wall White marble.

Near this place
lyeth interred
the Body of
WILLIAM PECK, Senior†
of this Town, Ironmonger
who departed this life
The 12th of September 1717.
Aged 70 years.

---

* At the end of this inscription the following had been painted:—

"In the morning when sober, in the evening when mellow,
You scarce ever met such a jolly good fellow."

This, however, was duly obliterated at the special direction of the late Dr. Samuel Wilberforce, sometime Bishop of Oxford.

* A member of this family had evidently been a benefactor to the Church, as the following entry in the "Accounts" for 1542 proves:—

Mem'dum. That yn this p'sent yere in the p'sens of the hole P'yshe Mast^r Iohn Balye hath delyv'd and geeyn to the Church of Thame ij garnyshes of rought Puther Vessell to the use of the Churche that is to saye one garnyshe for the olde Towne & y^e other garnyshe for the Newe towne. God off his Infinyte goodnesse Rewaryd hym in heven for hys good gyftis.

† The following is from a will:—

Robert Pecke, bapt. 2 Sept., 1604; will made 2 Aug., 1686, proved 12 Feb. of the following year.

John. = ... — Robert. = ... — William, sole executor. = ...

Robert. — Robert. — William.

South Transept, East wall. White marble.

Near Here
Lyeth the Body of
DOROTHY
The Wife of William Peek
who died Febr. yᵉ 26
1713
aged 60 years.

South Transept, South wall. Stone.

Near this Place
Lies interred the Body of
John Rose, he departed this
life February yᵉ 7ᵗʰ 1726, aged
75 years and 11 Months.
Elizabeth Rose his wife
Departed this Life April yᵉ 3ᵈ
1690 Aged 37 years &
11 months.

South Transept, Floor. White marble.

Spe Resurgendi
Sub hoc marmore sepulta jacent
Ossa VINCENTII BARRY de Thame*
Armigeri, qui obiit decimo nono
die Julii Anno D'ni 1666
ætatis suæ 69.

South Transept, West wall. Stone.

Near to this Place
Lyeth the Body of
Thomas Crewes
who departed this Life
January yᵉ 26ᵗʰ 1727 Aged 60
years. Matthew his
Son dyed Decembʳ ye 25ᵗʰ
1778 aged j yeare
32 days.

South Transept, West wall. White marble.

To the Memory of
FRANCES wife of
Mʳ THOMAS BAILEY, who departed
This Life August the 24ᵗʰ 1749
Aged 46 years.

From floods of tears to hills of joys
The Lord hath set me free,
And crownèd me with heavenly joys,—
A happy change for me.
My Friends and my Relations all
That I have left behind,
Preparèd be to follow me
And bear me in your mind.

South Transept, West wall. Freestone.

Here lieth the Body of WILLIAM
the Son of THOMAS and ELIZABETH
MESSENGER, who dyed Nov. yᵉ 30, 1684,
aged 21 years.

Reader improve the precious talent Time;
Death cut me off when I was in my prime;
Occasion bald behind, you can't recall
A minute's time once past. When God doth call
Poor man must go: but whither is he bound?
Unto the place from whence he came—the ground.

---

* Barry of Eynsham and Thame.

Arms: Per pale az. and gules, two lions passant guardant or.

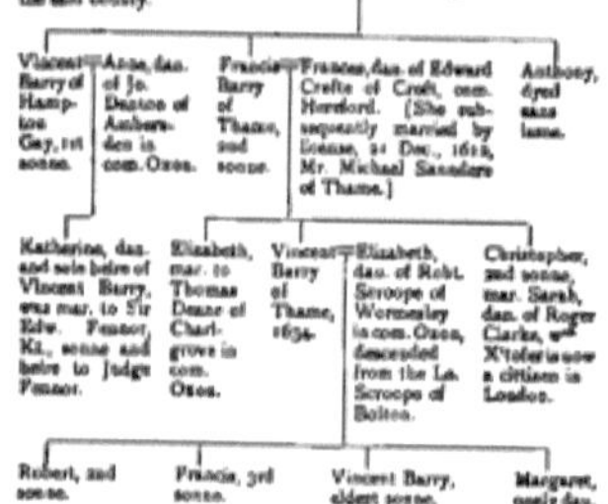

—Visitation of Oxfordshire by Richard Lee, Portcullis, A.D. 1574, and in 1634, by John Philipott and William Ryley, etc., pp. 198 and 326. London: 1871.

Mr. Vincent Barry, besides those children recorded in this pedigree, had by Elizabeth Scroope his wife: 1, Adrian, bapt. 12 Feb., 1634. 2, Elizabeth, bapt. 7 June, 1637, and buried 17 June, 1639. 3, Sarah, bapt. 29 Oct., 1640. Francis was baptised at Thame 10 May 1632, was of Oriel College, Oxford (tutor to John Holt, afterwards Lord Chief Justice), and Vicar of Kingsey, co. Bucks. He died 25 Jan., 1694-5, æt. 62. M.I. in Kingsey Church. Mr. Barry resided in the old-fashioned brick and timber house close to the south side of the churchyard, which once contained some large and oak-panelled rooms, and is still a picturesque building. His eldest son, Vincent Barry, married Jane, daughter of Thomas Southby of Stamford, by Mary, daughter of Sir William Gardiner. (Visit. of Berks in 1665; MS., Brit. Museum, No. 14,284, fol. 7.)

South Transept.

Elizabeth wife of William Mead
daughter of Thomas Messenger
dyed May ye 11 1705 aged 39 years.

Our Life's the subject of anxiety,
Our death the prodrom of felicity:
A happy change whose change is for the best,
To live in ease, & die and go to rest.

Thomas Messenger
jun^r died Octob. ye 11th 1708
aged 49
years.

Thomas Messenger, Gent.
died March 25, 1712 aged
78 years.

South Transept. White marble.

H. S. E.
Richardus Cowley*
hujus Parochiæ Pharmacopola,
qui obiit 21 die Junii
A.D. 1710 æt. suæ
57.

Middle Aisle or Nave Floor. Freestone.

Reliquiæ
Johannis Nott, A.M.†
Collegij SS. Trinitatis Cantab: quondam Socij
Verbi Divini Ministri
Qui
Annum agens LXXIII
a laboribus requievit
Decemb. 20
MDCCII.
Necnon
Elizabethæ Nott,
quæ ejus
annos supra L
uxor
mensesque supra VIII
vidua
In Christo obdormivit
Sep 6
MDCCIIJ
Spe beatæ Resurrectionis.

Black marble. Floor.

H. S. E.
THOMAS CARTER, DE NORTH WESTON, GENEROS.
ET
CATHERINA UXOR EJUS:
OBIIT ILLE 22 DIE SEPTEMBRIS ANNO
DO'NI 1687
ILLA 29 DIE AUGUSTI ANNO DO'NI 1689
ET ÆTATIS SUÆ 78
In memoria Æterna erit justi.

Nave, near Pulpit, N.W. pillar of Tower. White marble.

Near this Place
Lies Interr'd ye Body
of THOMAS CARTER Esqr,
who departed this Life
March ye 8th 1719
Aged 78 years.

Freestone. Floor. Middle Aisle or Nave.

In Memory of
THO: PRICKETT
who died August
26, 1816 in the 55
year of His age.

Middle Aisle. Floor. Black marble.

The
Body of IANE
LEAVER wife of
EDWARD LEAVER
Gent. was here interr'd Septr ye 24
1683 Aged 55 years.
The Body of EDWARD LEAVER Gent.
was here interr'd Decemb'r
the 9th 1697 aged
74 years.

---

* Richard Cowley, second son of William Cowley of Thame, yeoman, and Mary his wife. The aforesaid William Cowley made his will 12 April, 1680, and it was proved 6 May, 1683.

† The following concerning this clergyman, which occurs in the admission-book of Trinity College, Cambridge, was courteously communicated to me by the Master, the Rev. W. H. Thompson, D.D.:—"Nott [admitted from Emmanuel] May 29, 1645, pupil to Mr Akehurst"—and the following from the Register of Fellows:—"1647, Ioannes Nott, Vigorniensis, juratus et admissus in numerum Sociorum minorum." The Master adds, "It does not appear that he was ever sworn as Socius major; and, if not, he would by the Statutes forfeit his fellowship when of M.A. standing..... He may have declined *conscientiæ causâ* to take the oath as Major Fellow, or more probably to subscribe the Declaration of Allegiance to the Commonwealth of England imposed on all Fellows, etc., by Parliament in 1649." In the Thame Register of Burials he is described as a "Non-conforming minister." His will, dated 6 April, 1695, was proved 12 April, 1703, by Elizabeth Nott, relict and executrix. He left three unmarried daughters, Elizabeth, Sarah, and Penelope; and one daughter married to Mr. Richard Mayo.

Middle Aisle. Floor.

The
Body of ANN LEAVER
WIFE of RICHARD LEAVER
GENT. WAS HERE INTER'D
NOVEMBER THE 9, 1710
AGED 54 years.

Nave Floor. Marble.

M. S.
Here rest the bodies of Thomas
Bryan, Gent. Sonne of Richard Bryan* of
Henley upon Thames, Esqr, which Thomas
changed this life the 16th of July 1643
Aged 42 years. And of Anne his wife
daughter of John Tomlinson of this
Parish Gent. which Anne deceased the
2nd of August 16 . Aged 40 years.
They had issue six daughters, Mary, Anne,
Bridget, Elizabeth, Frances† & Margaret:
one son, Thomas, who layd this marble
stone, and caused this memorial of His
dear & virtuous parents to be Heere-
on engraved.

North Aisle, North wall. White marble.

HERE
Lieth the Body
of THOMAS HAYNES
of THAME, Boddes
Macker, he Dyed
Nov. ye 8th 1731
aged 68
years.

* This family was of considerable antiquity at Henley, Gilbert Bryan having been an important personage as early as the first year of King Edward I. (*i.e.* 1272). On the 15th of June, in the 3rd year of Henry VIII., Richard Bryan and five others were elected "to tax all the inhabitants for the apparel of four men to be found and sent with the lord the King." On the Subsidy Roll of Fifteenths and Tenths (*circa* 1550) one return stands thus:—"John Bryan, in goodes xv^li." In 1589 "Richard Bryan, gentleman," was one of the farmers of the Corporation property. In 1609, and again in 1633, a "Richard Bryan" is found to be the Mayor; and the name of "Mistress Brydget Brian," probably his wife, occurs in a rent account of the year 1629. The will of Thomas Bryan, of Thame, "beer-brewer," son of Richard, was made 13 July, 1643, and proved on 20 September of the same year. By it he left £50 to his son Thomas on coming of age, and all his goods and chattels to his wife Anne Bryan, sole executrix. His son Thomas had been admitted a Commoner of Trinity College, Oxon, in 1647, aged 16; and when certain questions were put to him regarding the authority of the Parliamentary Visitors he replied in writing: "I never studied state policie, and therefore cannot give any answer to so hard questions."

† Anthony, son of Anthony Spier, of Holcombe Grange, co. Oxon, by Barbara, eldest daughter of Sir Francis Castillion, of Benham Valence, co. Berks, Knt., married Frances, daughter of Thomas Bryan, of Thame (*vide* Harl. MSS. No. 1483, Visitation of Berks, A.D. 1664). Of this noble Italian Family (Castillion) was the great St. Bernard, Abbot of Clairvaux, who was the son of Tesselinus Castiglione, Lord of Fontaine in Burgundy. Another member, Rinaldo Castiglione, after great exploits in the Holy Land, married Constance, sister of Baldwin, King of Jerusalem, by whom he was made Prince of Antioch, but died by the hand of Saladin after the fatal battle of Tiberias. Pope Urban II., who was beatified, and Pope Celestine IV. (Geoffrey de Castiglione), who died eighteen days after his coronation, were of this family. Christopher, Count Castiglione, the celebrated lawyer called the "Prince of Doctors," who died in 1425; Branda Castiglione (Judge of the Roman Rota, and Cardinal of St. Clement, who died in 1443); and John Castiglione, sixth Bishop of Vicenza, who died in 1409, belonged to this same stock. So too did Franchino, a great civilian, who died in 1462; John, Cardinal of Pavia; and George, Auditor of the Roman Rota, each likewise great civilians and judges. Baltazar, born at Mantua, of Count Christopher Castiglione and Aluigia Gonzaga (a lady of the sovereign House of Mantua), an elegant poet, and excellent prose writer, is best known in England. He was Ambassador of the Duke of Urbino to Henry VIII., and subsequently to Louis XII., King of France. Eventually he received Holy Orders, and was elected Bishop of Avila, in Spain. This dignitary left one son, by his wife Hippolita, who married Katherine, daughter of the Marquis of Malaspina, and his son, Peter Castiglione, was father of John Baptist Castillion of Benham Valence in the county of Berks. This, the eldest, line is now extinct, and the English branch of this family is represented by the descendants of Douglas Castillion, fifth son of John Baptist Castillion, and sometime Fellow of Magdalen College, Oxford; his eldest son, John, Dean of Rochester, married Margaret, daughter of Thomas Digges, Esq., of Chilham Castle, Kent, and granddaughter of Sir Dudley Digges, Master of the Rolls, and their only child and heir, Mary Castillion, was married to Herbert Randolph, Esq., Recorder of Canterbury, who died on 14 March, 1725. The Castillions were represented by the late Rev. Herbert Randolph, M.A., of Balliol College, Oxon, fourth in direct descent from the Recorder, whose only child and heir, Martha-Jane, was married, in 1860, to the Rev. Francis Charles Hingeston-Randolph, M.A., Rector of Ringmore, Devon, in whose possession are several remarkable heirlooms of this ancient and distinguished race. The most interesting of these is a copy of the "*Elogi Historici di Alcuni Personaggi della Famiglia Castigliona*," containing on a flyleaf the following inscriptions:—

"In the yeare of our Lord 1600 I sent a ma' of purpose wth two forishe dogges, both white, lardge and fierse, wth a letter of mine in Italien, the copy of wch letter I have, meaning once to have made a voyage unto Mantua to visite the Counte.

"1600.—This booke was sent me fro' Mantua in Italie, 1610, from the Counte Baldazar Castillion, with his Picture, and a letter of thankes unto me for the forish dogges I sent him for a present to hunt the wulfe.

"Also he sent me ye Armes of that Familie, wch is Gules, a Lion Rampant *argent*, a Castell *or*, fro' a younger of which House we are descended, as may appeare by a Pedegree I have.

"FRAUNCIS CASTILLION."

"Coute Baldassar Castiglione
che vivo adesso' 1600
un Caualiero del' ordine' di St Stephano
Di Florenza.
A Crosse gules ✠ ingrayled w^t or."

This book is bound in red velvet, and is in excellent preservation. The "Pedegree" and the portrait of the Count, referred to above, are also among these heirlooms, the former being a very fine vellum roll, with arms beautifully illuminated, and the latter, a half-length figure, admirably painted on an oak panel, and in perfect condition. There are also a portrait of a lady of the family, which is supposed to represent Mary Castillion, but cannot now be identified, and a most interesting and beautiful Italian ebony cabinet, fitted up with a "Shrine" and numerous secret drawers, and most richly inlaid, both inside and out, with marble and with varied woods.

North Aisle. White marble.

Spe beatæ Resurrectionis
Infra sitæ sunt Exuviæ mortales
MATTHÆI LODER*
unacum trinis Uxoribus
Et Prole non superstí
Quanto hic cum sagaci Genio
Quanto cum ludifesso labore
Quanta perspicasi Scientiâ
Artem chirurgicam coluit et exercuit
Bene nôrunt & experii sunt
Nostrates et indigenæ
Palam omnibus supremus ille Dies
indicabit
Obdormivit in Christo
Vicesimo Octavo Octobris
Anno Domini
1763.
Ætatis
77.

West End. North Aisle.

Vincenti Dabitur
I. H. S. S.
Reliquiæ
ANNÆ, MATT: LODER, Chyr.
Uxoris
Quæ immortalitatem induens
Jul. 8. 1734
Anno Ætatis suæ 27
Magnum sui Omnibus Desiderium
Æque ac Propinquis
Maximum Omnino reliquit
Dolorem.

Farewell awhile, thou joy & half my Life,
Thou Tenderest Mother & thou Dearest wife.

South wall, South Aisle. White marble.

In Memory of
Robert Heath of THAME,
Mason, who died y^e 28th
day of January, Anno
Domini 1694
Aged 58 yeares.

Let's live with labour, whilst time we have,
For there's no work nor acting in the grave.

South Aisle, wall. Freestone.

Near this place lie
interred y^e Bodies of
y^e Rev. Mr ROBERT HEATH*
& Mary his wife. He
died Decr ye 15 1743
aged 52 years
She died Dec. y^e 9th
1744, aged 51 years.

South Aisle, wall. Freestone.

Neare this place
lyeth interred
ye Body of
M_r ROBERT HEATH
jun^r died January
y^e 28, 1765.
aged 31
years.

When upon Earth
I much afflictions bore,
But now am I launched
Into a happy shore.

---

* A tradition exists that Mr. Matthew Loder came of a Berkshire family. A miniature of him in the possession of Mrs. Bennett (his great-great-great-granddaughter) represents him, as a handsome regular-featured man, in a blue naval uniform. The following Pedigree of Loder of Berks stands on fol. 36 in the "Visitation of Berks, A.D. 1664," in the British Museum:—

John Loder, second son of John Loder, of Balston Park,
by Mary, daughter of Thomas Barrett, had issue.

John, 2nd son.	Thomas Loder, 1st son, æt. 12, 1664.	Jane. Mary.

In the Church of Hinton, in the same county, there are monuments to "Charles Loder, Esq., Lord of the Manor of Hinton, Longworth, &c.," who died 1 Sept., 1727, aged 61. There is also another to John Loder, Esq. The late Mrs. Loder-Symonds wrote to the author as follows, on 28 Aug. 1871: "She is sorry that she cannot give him any information with regard to Matthew Loder, of Thame. She considers it very likely that he may have been one of the Loders of Lechlade, from whence the family came to Hinton: but the lineal descent is now extinct by the death of her husband, John Loder-Symonds, who, in right of his mother, Miss Loder, became possessed of the Loder estate. There were some Loders of Harwell in Berkshire, but they passed away before the marriage of Mrs. Loder-Symonds." "John King of Harwell and Martha Loder, of the parish of Thame, were married by License 4th of April 1757."—*Thame Register.*

* Robert Heath, of St. Edmund Hall, graduated B.A. 4 February, 1707, M.A. 16 November, 1710. The following is from the Register Book of the Parish of Chearsley, co. Bucks:—" 1731, Mr. Robert Heath, of Thame, and Mary Cannon, of Long Crendon, marryd April 19, 1731."

Wall, North Aisle. White marble.

Juxta S. E.
Corpus Richardi Leaver, gen.*
qui duplici suggesto Precum et concionum
officiis accommodato propriis sumptibus
hanc ornavit ecclesiam:
amicis multa, plura pauperibus,
plurima consanguineis irrogavit.
Mortuus est tricesimo Augusti
CIƆƆCCXIII
Ætatis suæ LXVIIJ.
Nec non
Corpus Annæ uxoris suæ Thomæ Carter
Gen. filiæ natu minimæ
Quæ pii in Deum, Materni in cognatos
Benigni in omnes animi nota,
variolarum morbo laborans,
Obiit nono die Novembris
CIƆƆCCX
Ætatis suæ LIV.
Abi (Viator,) et fac simile.

North-east pillar of Tower. Black and white marble.
Sacred to the Memory of
THOMAS HEDGES
for upwards of eighty years a Resident in this Town
Born March 24th 1767. Died May 7th 1847
His remains lie interred in a vault near this spot.
Also of
SOPHIA, his Widow
who died January 29th 1861
aged 81 years.

---

* The will of Richard Leaver was made 14 June 1723, a codicil having been added afterwards. He desires to be buried near his wife in Thame Church, and directs that a marble monument of the value of £35, with his coat of arms displayed on it, be put up in the church. He mentions, amongst others, his cousin, William Phillips, his nephew, Samuel Turner, and Mrs. Martha Holt; also the Reverends Thomas Ward and Robert Heath. He gives mourning rings, value a guinea each, to Francis Knollys, Esq., and to Mr. Richard Knollys. He leaves property to his god-daughter Martha, then under age, daughter of Arthur Day, of Tiddington, and appoints her aunt, Elizabeth Day, to be her guardian. He refers to his relations the Phillipses of Ickford; and furthermore leaves a charge on the Blue Man, in Friday Street, Thame, to provide gowns for two poor men and women, the materials for the same "to be bought of a draper in communion with the Church of England and not a Dissenter." The Rev. Henry Bruges is the executor of the will, which is witnessed by Henry Bruges, junr.

South Aisle, South wall. Freestone.
Deus noster Refugium.
Near this Place
Lieth Interr'd
The Body of
EDWD BURNARD
who died 4 Nov.
1777. In the 53
Year of His
age.

In my life afflicted was
With grievous pains full sore;
Yet hope to find a place of rest
With Christ for evermore.

South Aisle, South wall.
Neare this place
Lyes Interr'd
ye Body of EDWARD
PHILLIPS of this Town,
Draper, who Died
May ye 5th 1719
Aged 86 years.

South Aisle, South wall.
Near this Place
Lyeth ye Body of
FRANCES ye Daughter of
WILLIAM PHILLIPS
who departed this Life
Iuly 30th 1724
Aged 26 years.

South Aisle, South wall. White marble.
ABIGAIL
EDOUARDI PHILLIPS
UXOR HIC JUXTA SCITA EST
ÆTATIS SUÆ
62.

South Aisle, Floor. Black marble.
Here
Lyeth the Body of
ELIZABETH the wife of
WILLIAM PHILLIPS. She
Died October the 7th
Anno Dom' 1703
aged 33 years & 7
Months and 10 days

Here lyes a mouldering body that did once contain
A soul breath'd in by God, to God return'd again:
For my all-wise Creator thought it best
To take me hence to an eternal rest.

North-east pillar of Tower. Black and white marble.

In Memory of
HENRY REYNOLDS
of Thame, Solicitor
second son of Mr. HENRY REYNOLDS
of Notley Abbey, Bucks,
who died 14th May 1806
in the 29th year of his age.
Beloved and lamented,
on the 28th of July 1846, died
ANN
Fourth daughter of
EDWARD WELLS, Esqre
of Wallingford, Berks,
and wife of HENRY WELLS REYNOLDS
of Thame, Surgeon,
in the 36th year of her age.

East wall, South Transept. Black stone.

Near this Place
lies all that was mortal
of ELIZABETH Daughter of
WILLM and MARGARET TRIPP
of this Town, and Wife of
Mr James Stubbs
late of Watlington, draper.
She died Decr the 22nd 1749.
Aged 28.

She was obliging to all without flattery;
An enemy to nothing but wt was vicious & base;
A friend only to Virtue & Truth.
I LECTOR & IMITARE.

South Aisle, Floor. White marble.

H. S. E.
RICHARDUS SMITH, Arm.*
Com. Buck: Vice-Prolegat:
Obiit die XVo Septembris
A. S. MDCCCVIII.
R. I. P.

* Mr. Richard Smith's will was made 2 September, and proved 1 December, 1808. He bequeaths to his daughter Juliana £500, to Amelia Wood £500, to Frances Wood "all my right and title to Hodsdon estate now in the occupation of Thomas Oliver, and £500 of lawful money," and to Mrs. Elizabeth Lee £50. His son, Spencer Smith, was appointed sole executor and residuary legatee.

The following record of heraldic stained glass is taken from an original MS., "The Gatherings of Oxfordshire by Richard Lee, Portcullis," preserved amongst Anthony à Wood's MSS. in the Bodleian Library, numbered 14 D. It refers to families of repute and distinction, which belonged to the Town and its hamlets prior to the sixteenth century, and is of special value now that so many memorial inscriptions are lost, and every fragment of old glass has been utterly destroyed:—

In Thame Church.*

1. Or, a bend fusillée gules within a bordure gobony argent and azure [Bardis]. Over it written **Je ay ben cause.**
2. Bardis, impaling az. three pairs of stags' horns arg. in chief, an annulet or for a difference.
3. Or, a bend fusillée gu. in the sinister chief three lions passant of the 2nd. Over the coats 2 and 3 is written **Me Adrian de Bardis.**
4. Bardis, impaling arg. three buckles gules [? Marmion of Thame].
5. Or, a bend fusillée gu. in sinister chief a castle arg.
6. Bardis, impaling arg. three chevronels sa.
7. Or, a bend masculée arg. in each mascle a fleur-de-lys or, within a bordure gobony arg. and az.
8. Bardis, impaling arg. a tiger looking at her face in a glass.† Over these coats [5-8] is written **Adrian de Bardis p'ben' ist' ec'le'e.**

* To avoid repetitions the monumental inscriptions reproduced in Richard Lee's MS. are here omitted, and the omissions indicated. Where there can be little doubt as to the families to which the arms belong, the names have been added within brackets. The armorial bearings Nos. 1 to 8 were in the north windows of the chancel; those from 9 to 15 were on tombs in the south transept; and those from 16 to 30 were in the south window of that transept.

In 1611 Nicholas Charles visited the church, and has preserved fourteen coats, as then existing. These may be found in the Lansdowne MS., No. 874, thus:—I. Quartermain, impaling quarterly 1 and 4 Bretton, and 2 and 3 Grey of Rotherfield; II. Quartermain, impaling Fitz Ellis; III. Quartermain, impaling 1 and 4 Bretton, 2 and 3 Grey of Rotherfield; IV. De Bardis, impaling az., three pairs of stags' horns arg.; V. De Bardis, impaling vaire argent and gules, three lozenges voided or (? Hester of Thame, Harl. MSS., Brit. Museum, Plate LV. F.); VI. De Bardis, impaling or, three chevrons gules, De Clare; and the following single coats—VII. Arg., on a chevron sable three fleur-de-lys of the field; VIII. Azure, an eagle displayed argent, legged or; IX. and X. Arg., a chevron between three escallops, Lyttelton of Frankley; XI. Erm., on a bend azure three cinquefoils or; XII. Wykeham; XIII. Or, three bends sable, a canton ermine; XIV. Argent, on a chevron sable between three pellets, as many vanes of the field (old arms of Baldington of Thame).

Some of the arms given in the text above remained in the church as late as Anthony à Wood's day, for amongst his own personal MSS., viz., in No. E. 1, folio 251, he reproduces the eight shields as still existing which Richard Lee had described half a century previously.

† "Argent *A Tiger Passant Regardant*, gazing in a mirror or looking-glass, all proper. This *coat-armour* standeth in the chancell of the Church of *Thame*, in *Oxford-shire*, in a *Glasse window* of

(The inscription on Sir John Clerke's tomb, copied by Richard Lee, has been already given at length on p. 95 from the original.)

9. Arms: arg. on a bend between three ogresses gu. three swans of the field, on a canton sinister az. three fleurs-de-lys or, a bendlet arg.

Crest: on a wreath arg. and sa. a bird gu. winged and legged or, holding a branch in its mouth or.

On a square tomb of marble the following arms stood:—

10. Barry of six arg. and az. over all a bend gu. [Grey of Rotherfield], impaling, Quarterly, 1 and 4, gu. a fess az. between four dexter hands couped at the wrist arg. [Quartermain], 2 and 3, arg. two hounds passant palewise [Bretton].

11. Quartermain, impaling vairée or and gu. [Gresley].

(The inscription around the verge of the tomb has been already given on p. 93.)

On Anoth^r Tombe of Marble.

[On which are the effigies of two men armed, one of them having his wife on his right hand, and the other his on his left, each having arms over their heads, Nos. 12 to 15. The inscription has already been given from the original on p. 91.]

12. Quarterly, 1 and 4, Grey of Rotherfield; 2 and 3, Bretton.

13. Quartermain, impaling Bretton, quartering per fess Grey.

14. Quarterly—I. Quartermain. II. Quarterly, 1 and 4, Grey; 2 and 3, Bretton. III. Bretton. IV. Grey of Rotherfield.

[These arms are over the head of the second woman.]

15. Quartermain, impaling arg., on a bend between six fleurs-de-lys gu. a quatrefoil. [Fitz-Ellis.]

In a Window.

16. Quarterly, 1 and 4, checky or and az.; 2 and 3, gu. a lion rampant or, impaling Grey of Rotherfield.

17. Az. a fess dancettée between ten billets or.

18. Quarterly, 1 and 4, Barry nebulée of six or and gu.; 2 and 3, Az. semée of fleur-de-lys gu. a lion rampant arg.

19. Arg. a cross moline sa.

20. Gu. a lion rampant, arg. within a bordure engrailed.

21. Quarterly, 1 and 4, A chief, over a bend; 2 and 3, checky a chief erm. (untinctured). [Tateshale.]

22. The same, impaling Grey of Rotherfield.

23. Grey of Rotherfield, impaling arg. a maunche sa. [Tony?]

24. Quartermain, impaling . . . . (broken).

25. Quartermain, impaling . . . . (broken).

26. Bretton, impaling Grey of Rotherfield.

27. Quartermain, impaling, Quarterly, 1 and 4, Bretton; 2 and 3, Grey of Rotherfield.

28. Quarterly, arg. and az. in the 2nd quarter a mullet arg.

29. Quarterly, 1 and 4, Quartermain; 2 and 3, vairée arg. and gu. [Gresley.]

30. Quarterly, az. and arg.

In a oth^r window.

31. Arg. on a chevron sa. three fleurs-de-lys of the field.

32. Arg. a chevron engrailed* between three escallops sa. [Lyttelton of Frankley.]

33. Az. an eagle displayed arg. legged or. [Cottesmore.]

34. Or, three bends sa. a canton ermine.

35. Arg. two chevrons sa. between three roses gu. a mullet for a difference. [Wykeham.]

36. Erm. on a bend az. three cinquefoils or pierced of the second.

37. Arg. on a chevron sa. between three ogresses, three roses of the field.† [Baldington.]

38. Or, three crescents gu.

39. Az. a cross patonce between five martlets or, impaling, Quarterly, 1 and 4, France (ancient); 2 and 3, England. The whole within a bordure gobony arg. and az.

40. Sa. three garbs arg.

Church and Parochial Charities.

The following statements concerning the Ecclesiastical and Parochial Charities of the Town are painted and set forth on boards framed and fastened up in South Transept, two of them being so sunburnt and disfigured that they are illegible and cannot be here reproduced:—

Benefactors belonging to the Parish and Church of Thame. An Estate of Eight Acres called Buttle [*i.e.* Butwell] Leys for the use of the Church.

A tenement in the occupation of Marg^t Pim. Opposite to the White Hound pond.

---

the same chancell, Impaled on the *sinister* side with the *Coate-Armour* properly pertaining to the Family of *De Bardis*. Near to this *Escocheon* is placed this inscription, *Hadrianus De Bardis Prebendarius istius Ecclesiæ*."—*A Display of Heraldry*, by John Gwillim, Sixth Edition, p. 198. London: 1666.

* Nicholas Charles points out that the chevron should be plain.

† In the northern transept the arms of the Baldingtons of Baldington, an ancient manor in Thame, were represented with their alliances. Those given in the text are not the most ancient arms. One of the Dormers married the heiress of this family; and so, when the afore-mentioned name thus died out, the property long

Land held by Robert Cotton in Priest End Field, Ten Shillings a Year. A Message given by Mr. Nicholas Almond of Thame in the occupation of Mr. Cock, one sixth part of the Rent for the Repairs of the Church; Another sixth part for ye Repairs of the High way Towards Had'nam Bridge. One third for ye Poor of Thame Parish on Easter Monday. The Remaining third part to Apprentice out a Poor Boy. Mr. Robert Hall of New Thame gave 10s. a Year to the Poor of Thame Payable on Easter Monday out of Pages House scituate in ye North Quarter of New Thame. Mr. Richard Bracy gave 2s. 6*d*. a year to be spent by ye Ch. Wardens on Easter Monday.

A messuage in the occupation of Thomas Bailey in the Sheep Market in New Thame 6s. 8d. a year to be disposed of at St. Thomas's Day. Four Cottages belonging to ye Poor scituate in Friday Street over against the Place House.

Mr. John Hart of Cotsford Oxfordshire left a Rent charge of £10 a year to Apprentice out 3 Goal Boys Payable out of a farm called Easingdon in Oxfordshire. Mr. George Benson gave £6 a year to Purchase Eight Suits of Clothes for the Poor of Thame. The Persons who are to have the said suits to be appointed the 1st Sunday in October and to appear in them at Church the 6th of November: the said sum payable out of the Gray-hound-Close houses adjoining.

South Transept, on Wood.

Mrs. Robotham Gave £50: Mrs. Martha Burrowes Gave £160: The Trustees made an Addition of £3 4s. 6*d*. with wch sum of £213 4s. 6*d*. A House and Land and ye Tyths of the s'd Land were Purchased at Piddington & Ambersden in Oxford shire for the uses following (viz.) ⅕ part to be given for the relief of 4 Poor People of New Thame; The Remaining ⅘^{ths} to purchase 7 suits of Clothes Coats and Hose for men & Gowns for women.

Mr. George Burrowes Gave £50 to the poor of Thame, the Interest of which was to buy suits of Clothes yearly. Mr. Richard Leaver secured to the Church Wardens of Thame the Yearly Clear Rent of £7 10s. out of a Pasture Ground at Oakly Bucks in consideration of £105 of Charity Money which he had then Received and which was given and disposed of in manner following (viz.) Mrs. Lettice Stowell of Chesham Bucks Gave £100 of the said money the interest of which was to Apprentice Poor Children of Thame. Mr. William Atkins Gave £30 of ye said Money to Purchase Coats yearly with ye interest thereof for two Poor People Born in Thame Parish. Mr. Tho. Cannon of Long Crendon and others gave the Remaining Thirty five Pounds Out of wch there was to be given Yearly 4^d apiece to 30 Poor Widows of Thame Parish and ye remaining Interest to be divided among ye Poor. The s^d Richard Leaver gave a Tenement called ye Blew Man to the Poor of Thame to be laid out yearly in suits of Clothes. Mr. Wm. Peck of New Thame Gave £10 to the intent that 30 groat loaves of Bread might be Purchased with the Interest of the said sum and distributed Yearly on Candlemas day. Mrs. Phillis Burrowes Gave £100 to the Poor of Thame, the Interest whereof to be yearly laid out in shirts and shifts for Men and Women.

West wall, South Transept, on Wood.

Mr Thomas Funge
late Citizen of London and a
Native of this Town,

Did by His Will dated ye 20 of August 1766 give to the Churchwardens & Overseers of ye Poor of this Parish for the time being £600 Old South Sea Annuities upon Trust to lay out all the dividends or interest thereof in Threepenny Loaves of Household Bread and Distribute the same at their discretion every Sunday morning after Divine Service amongst Poor Housekeepers belonging to, and not receiving Alms of, this Parish.

South Transept on Wood.

Ewstace May,
of this Town,
Gentleman,

By Deed inrolled in Chancery 24th April 1793, granted to John Eeles, Draper and Willm Claridge, Grocer and their Heirs, an Annual Rent charge Yearly of ye sum of £8 issuing out of his Freehold Estate at Towersey, in the county of Bucks, to be paid to the Churchwardens for the time being, and by them laid out in bread and distributed on the Sunday after the 26^{day} of Dec. Yearly among such poor persons Parishioners of this Parish whom they shall think proper objects of the said Charity.

South Transept on Wood.

Martha May of this Town,

Spinster, by her Will dated 3rd Oc^r 1811, proved in Doctors Commons, Bequeathed £700 Stock £3 Per Centum Consolidated Bank Annuities, unto Edward Payne, Wool-stapler, and William Claridge, Grocer, upon trust, to pay the Yearly dividends and interest thereon, to the Minister, Churchwardens, and Overseers of this Parish for the time being, to be by them laid out

connected with it passed to the heirs of Geoffrey Dormer. On the floor of the chapel, where their altar-tomb stands, may still be seen a few half-defaced tiles, some with the fleur-de-lys of Baldington upon them (the old arms), and others with the arms of the Staple of Calais.

in the purchase of Linen for Shifts, Gowns, and Petticoats, for the use of poor women inhabitants of this parish, and given made up amongst such poor women as they, the Minister, Churchwardens, and Overseers, shall think proper Objects of Charity, Yearly on the Sunday morning after Christmas Day.

South wall, South Transept, on Wood.

SOPHIA BULL,
of this Town,

Spinster, by her will dated 30th July 1801, proved in Doctors Commons, bequeathed to John Eeles, Draper, and John Hollier, Gent., £200 upon trust to invest the same in their names in old South Sea Annuity Stock, and to pay the dividends thereof to the Churchwardens and Overseers of the Poor of Thame, for the time being, to be laid out in 3d loaves of Wheaten Bread, and distributed at their discretion Weekly, on Sunday mornings immediately after Divine Service, among Poor Housekeepers of the parish of Thame who receive no Alms or Collection of the Parish.

The above £200, after deducting £12 for Legacy Duty, was laid out in the names of the above Trustees, 15th Augst 1804, in the purchase of £327 13s. 5d. Old South Sea Annuity Stock.

Prebendaries of Thame.

A Prebend, from *prœbenda*, which signifies originally "provender" or "a stated allowance of food." Hence in its ecclesiastical sense, and when applied to the officer of a Cathedral or to a Church, it means that a stated and appointed income has been legally and regularly attached to some member of the same in return for the due and proper discharge, at some special place, of certain acknowledged and recognized ecclesiastical duties. The Prebendary was primarily and directly responsible for the due performance of all the sacraments, services, and rites of the Church. At Thame it seems tolerably certain that the whole of the tithes, dues, and fruits of lands were devoted to the maintenance of the Prebendary—for the Advowson was the endowment of the dignity. The duties of his responsible office were of course formally delegated to him by his superiors; and he was bound to be ordinarily in residence. Within a certain district, he owned a peculiar but clearly-defined ecclesiastical jurisdiction:—in order to exercise which, he would of course have a Court, with its customary officials—Summoner, Crier, Clerk, Notary, Registrar, and official seal.* At Thame this Court was often held in the Great Hall of the Prebendal House. Moreover, he would be authorized to hear and determine ecclesiastical causes and disputes, to punish wrong-doers according to Canon, to pronounce public absolution, to exercise the power of excommunication; to prove wills, to grant letters of administration, to issue marriage-licenses, and—subject to superior authority, *i.e.* of the Archdeacon, and possibly of the Dean of Lincoln—to represent the Bishop of the Diocese by delegation. Under him were the Vicar of the parish, the Perpetual Curates of the various Chapelries connected with the Parish Church, the Chantry-priests, the Custodians of the privileged altars and sacred shrines, the Clerks in minor orders, the Sacristan, Bellman, and Singing-boys, and lastly the Churchwardens and Synodsmen. His duties, therefore, were considerable: his position of importance.

This Prebend of Thame,—like others in the Cathedral Church of Lincoln,—as has been already pointed out, was founded by Robert Grostête, the distinguished bishop who presided over that see for nineteen years, viz., from A.D. 1235 to 1254. A prelate of vast energy, considerable independence, and singular influence, a very special benefactor to Thame, he left the impression of his wisdom, learning, and general ability on many parts of his extensive diocese. By the establishment of Prebendal Churches in various important towns, and centres of life and activity, he was enabled not only to attach the people of those places to the spiritual ruler of the diocese and his coadjutors; but

* "There are," wrote Mr. Swan fifty-two years ago, "twenty-four parishes in the county of Lincoln, over which the Dean and Chapter of Lincoln exercise jurisdiction; and there are several other separate parishes, over which the respective Prebendaries who derive the name of their prebends from those parishes, separately exercise jurisdiction. The jurisdictions of the Dean and Chapter and Prebendaries were originally granted to them by Robert, Bishop of Lincoln, about the year 1160 [the grant will be found amongst the "Appendices"—F. G. L.], to exempt them from Archidiaconal jurisdiction; and their appeal is, by the statutes of the Church of Lincoln, reserved to the Bishop. The present practice is in accordance with the original grant, and their jurisdictions are inhibited for three months once in every three years, at the time of the Bishop's primary and triennial visitations, and all jurisdiction in them is, during the inhibition, exercised by the Bishop and his Chancellor; but, during the remainder of the three years, the Dean and Chapter and Prebendaries exercise jurisdiction in their respective parishes" (pp. 64, 65).—*A Practical Treatise of the Jurisdiction of the Ecclesiastical Courts, etc.* By Robert Swan, Registrar of the Diocese of Lincoln. London: Sweet, 1830.

As regards Thame the following is extracted:—

Style of Court.	Extent of Jurisdiction.	Places where Wills are deposited.	Person in whose Custody.
Court of the Dean and Chapter of Lincoln in the Peculiar of Thame.	The Parishes of Thame, Tetsworth, Siddenham, and Great Milton, in the county of Oxford, and Towersey in the county of Buckingham.	In the office of the Deputy Registrar at Aylesbury.	Edward Pricket, Deputy Registrar.

—*Ibid.*, p. 111.

to secure both a due exercise of authority and a unity of action amongst those who were responsible for the progress of True Religion, which certainly produced many great and most beneficial results.

He objected to the too-common practice of bestowing some of the best-endowed preferments of the English dioceses upon foreigners, and specially upon Italians and Frenchmen. On one occasion he distinctly refused to induct a youth from Mantua, in minor orders only, to a valuable benefice in the diocese. Abuses such as these were rightly and righteously opposed by him: for, as a rule, no one should be promoted to a post of honour and responsibility who is unable to perform its duties and fulfil the required obligations. On the other hand, it should never be forgotten that the actual Unity of the Catholic Church must have been eminently declared and efficiently made known by the consoling and undeniable fact that, in the One Church of God, all persons,* of every nationality and race, were welcomed to office and to honours. Within a century of the period in which Grostête flourished, Nicholas Breakespere, the son of a Hertfordshire husbandman, had become, firstly, Bishop of Albano; secondly, a papal legate of high rank; and subsequently the Chief Bishop and honoured Ruler of the Church Universal: while, as regards Divine Service, the same rites were practically observed at Lincoln and Liège, at Milan and Durham, at Rheims and Westminster. No Italian would have found himself a stranger within the aisles of Osney or Peterborough; no Englishman an alien at the shrine of St. Mark in Venice, or bending in worship on the marble floors of the Basilicas of Rome.

This practical truth must have been well known to Bishop Grostête, ere Nationalism had become rampant and divisions had been sealed.

To sum up his character: he is said to have been a lover of the Truth, a corrector of prelates, a director of priests, a preacher to the people, a maintainer of scholars, and of a pure and blameless life. He delighted much in Church music and in listening to the harper.

"Next bys chaumber, besyde his studye
His harper's chamber was fast by;
Manys the tymes by nights and days
He had him solace of notes and lays."

He was the author of several ecclesiastical treatises, and had the reputation of being both a scholar and a theologian. He was held in great admiration by the people, who flocked to greet him upon his Visitations. When he died—as has been the case with other great and saintly servants of God—angelic music was heard round his chamber; and it was for long generations a tradition, and is still on record, that the bells of Thame and Aylesbury Churches tolled of their own accord, without human instrumentality, to tell the faithful of their loss. He was buried at Lincoln, with all the old Catholic and consoling rites, with mass and dirge and expressive psalm; and his body rests in the southern part of the lesser transept of that glorious Minster, where once a noble tomb and a representation of him in brass, in full pontificals, drew wanderers who had known him personally or by repute, from time to time, to kneel down and say the *Pater noster* and *De profundis*, for the repose of his soul; as they called to mind examples of his wisdom and zeal; and there, before God Incarnate, blessed his memory because of his good and righteous deeds. Of him it may be truly said, "*Ecce Sacerdos magnus!*"

During the last three centuries, and in consequence of the great and general work of destruction under the Tudors, (when Church funds and goods were seized, and the robbery of God was looked upon as a virtue,) Decrepitude and Decay have too generally left their impress on the towns and villages of England as regards religion. The mere form is left, but the spirit is found to have fled: the scaffolding remains, but the once-fair building has fallen into ruin. Streams have been dammed up: wells have been poisoned. And so, while the people languish, our enemies—legions officered by Unbelief and Indifference—come in like a flood. Again and again during the last three centuries the sound and accumulated wisdom of our Christian ancestors has been wholly ignored, or foolishly bartered away for the random and haphazard experiments of rash and ill-instructed contemporaries, often without honour, without justice, without religion.

The endowment of this Prebend was perhaps the richest of any in the Cathedral Church of Lincoln, excepting that of Sutton-cum-Bucks. It consisted of the Impropriation and Advowson of the parish of Thame. In the year 1535 the clear value of this was £82 12s. 2½d.; for which it stood rated for first-fruits and tenths* before its dissolution in 1547.

The following names of Prebendaries are on record:—

Simon de London held this Prebend, it having been given to him by Robert Grostête, Bishop of Lincoln, about 1241; but the Pope, Gregory IX. (Conti), is said to have bestowed it upon

John Mansel, who held it at this period.

* "Ye have put on the new man; which is renewed in knowledge, after the image of Him that created Him; where there is neither Greek nor Jew, circumcision nor uncircumcision, Barbarian, Scythian, bond nor free: but Christ is all and in all."—Col. iii. 10, 11.

* Valuation of the Prebend and Vicarage of Thame, A.D. 1535 (King's Books, vol. ii., page 168). Diocese of Oxford, formerly Lincoln. Oxford, Deanery of Aston. [See over-leaf.

WILLIAM FRERE or FERRY appears to have died possessed of it in 1292.

THOMAS DE SUTTON was collated to it on "the third Ides of September 1292." He had been collated to the Archdeaconry of Northampton 9 January 1290, and, dying in 1315, was succeeded by

HUGH DE NORMANTON,* who was appointed Prebendary in 1315, but exchanged it for that of Leighton Buzzard, with

GILBERT DE MIDDLETON, in the year 1316. This ecclesiastic was subsequently made Archdeacon of Northampton 8 June 1316, and died in the year 1330. He had founded a college for a Warden and four Priests at Wappenham, co. Northampton, where he himself was buried.

PETER DE ST. STEPHEN [or de Mortuomare], Cardinal de Cœlio Monte, succeeded to the Prebend in 1330, and died possessed of it.

CARDINAL DE PELEGRINI was Prebendary of Thame in 1340; but, on his taking part with the French King against Edward III., the King deprived him and gave it to

WILLIAM DE KILSDERSBY, who had possession of it in 1343.

TALAIRANDUS DE PETAGORICIS, "Cardinalis Beati Sancti Petri ad Vincula," another Cardinal, was possessed of it in 1348. He was appointed Dean of York, and died 17 January 1366.†

JOHN, BISHOP OF ALBANO, and a Cardinal-Priest, held the Prebend from 1348 to 1363.

HUGH, a Cardinal-Deacon, held it in 1376. He was never in residence, and a deputy represented him.

STEPHANUS, a Cardinal, held it in 1378, when it was valued at 200 marks by the year.

NICHOLAS, a Cardinal, said to have been a kinsman of Pope Gregory XI. (Pierre Roger), had the profits of the Prebend in 1381.

HENRY BEAUFORT, third son of John of Gaunt, Duke of Lancaster, by Katherine Swinford, was installed Prebendary of Thame 7 January 1389, quitted it for the Prebend of Bucks, was consecrated Bishop of Lincoln 14 July 1398; and translated to Winchester in March 1405. He was a Cardinal of the Holy Roman Church, Chancellor of the University of Oxford, and Lord High Chancellor of England; and died 11 April 1447.

RICHARD FIELD, collated 16 February 1389. He was Rector of Ringwood, co. Hants, and died in 1400.

NICHOLAS BUBWITH or BUBBLEWITH,* collated to the Prebend of Thame in the year 1400, was consecrated Bishop of London at Mortlake, 26 September 1406, by Thomas Arundel, Archbishop of Canterbury, assisted by Henry Beaufort, Bishop of Winchester, and Richard Clifford, Bishop of Worcester; afterwards translated to Sarum, then to Bath. He died 27 October 1424.

RICHARD COURTENAY, installed Prebendary of Banbury 25 November 1394, resigned the same when he was collated Prebendary of Thame in 1404, was consecrated Bishop of Norwich at Windsor, 17 September 1413, by Thomas Arundel, Archbishop of Canterbury. He died 15 September 1415.

JOHN WAKERING or WALKELYNE, sometime Vicar and Prebendary of Thame, born at Thame and educated at Oxford, was consecrated Bishop of Norwich at St. Paul's Cathedral, 31 May 1416, by Henry Chicheley, Archbishop of Canterbury, assisted by Henry Bowett, Archbishop of York, and seven other prelates. He died 9 April 1425.

WILLIAM KILDWOLDSMERSH succeeded to the Prebend in 1416, and died in 1422.

ROBERT LEEKS was collated to it 16 December 1422, and died in 1434.

WILLIAM GREY, Rector of Amersham, co. Bucks, was collated to the Prebend in 1434. He was consecrated Bishop of Ely at Mortlake, 8 September 1454, the feast of Our Lady's Nativity, by Thomas Bouchier, Archbishop of Canterbury, and the Bishops of Worcester and Ross. He died August 4, 1478, at Downham, and was buried in Ely Cathedral.

GEORGE NEVILLE, Prebendary of Thame, 17 August 1454, was consecrated Bishop of Exeter 3 December 1458; translated to York in 1464, and died 8 June 1476.

JOHN CHEDWORTH, Archdeacon of Northampton

	£	s.	d.
THAME.—Sir John Rayne prebendary	90	8	9
Thereof deducted for the payment of the Chaplain of Lincoln in common years .	7	3	2½
Also to Richard Cryppe steward for his fee .	0	13	4
Sum .	82	12	2½
10th part	8	5	2¼

	£	s.	d.
Sir John Parker vicar there	18	0	0
10th part	1	16	0

* This man died possessed of the Prebend of Leighton Buzzard in 1344.

† Drake's *Eboracum*. London: 1736.

* According to the Account Book of the Church for the year 1448, *temp.* Henry VI., this prelate had given a red cope embroidered in gold, representing the Assumption of the Blessed Virgin Mary, with orphreys of green and gold embroidery: also a white silk chasuble with popinjays of gold embroidered upon it, and images of gold in tabernacles on its cross and pillar, together with stole, maniple, alb and amice; as also a red satin cope, with images of gold, the orphreys of green satin set with birds and chaplets of gold. He was admitted to the freedom of the Merchant Taylors' Company when Bishop of London. Stowe states that he was "Chancellor of the King's Exchequer."

19 August 1457, Prebendary of Thame 4 September 1458, Archdeacon of Lincoln 27 April 1464, Provost of St. Mary's and St. Nicholas, Cambridge; was consecrated Bishop of Lincoln 18 June 1452, installed 7 September of the same year; and died 23 November 1471.

Thomas Bonifaunt, S.T.P., succeeded, having been collated 1 May 1465. He died in 1470, and was succeeded by

Peter Courtenay, LL.D., Prebendary of Thame 7 November 1470, who was consecrated Bishop of Exeter at St. Stephen's Chapel, Westminster, on the Octave of All Saints, 8 November 1478: was translated to Winchester in 1487, and died 22 September 1492.

Lionel Woodeville was installed Prebendary 28 November 1478, but resigned it in 1480; he was consecrated Bishop of Salisbury by Thomas Bouchier, Archbishop of Canterbury, on 21 April 1482. He died in 1484.

Adrian Tebarde* or de Bardis, born at Moreton near Thame, educated at Florence, was presented on Woodeville's retirement, and installed 20 September 1480. He was a great benefactor to the church, repaired it substantially, improved the choir, put up much stained glass, and left his armorial bearings in stone in several places upon its exterior. He likewise repaired the Chapel of Tettesworth, and adorned it considerably. In Anthony à Wood's time the arms of De Bardis remained in five of the chancel windows; and the same was the case in two of the north windows of the choir of the Thame Church up to the year 1840. He was likewise a benefactor to the Chapel of Rycott.

Richard Maudelay, M.A. and LL.D., who had been installed Archdeacon of Leicester 29 May 1518, was instituted Rector of Sherrington, co. Bucks, 7 December 1518, and installed Prebendary of Thame in 1519. He had the reputation of being a great canon lawyer and good theologian. He took part in discussing and determining the question of the validity of Henry VIII.'s marriage, when that subject was under the consideration of the University of Oxford; and, in conjunction with Doctors Moreman, Mortimer, Holyman, Cooke, Aldridge, and Charnock, delivered an opinion in favour of the marriage with Katherine. Maudelay was against the innovations and usurpations of the King; and evidently looked with suspicion and fear upon the dangerous policy which Cardinal Wolsey and Bishop John Longland of Lincoln had inaugurated. He provided the stalls for Thame Church in 1529.* In his will, dated 15 March 1530, and proved 17 November 1531, he ordered a priest to sing for him in his Prebendal Church, left a legacy to it, and desired to be buried therein. It is said that a brass representing him, with an inscription and prayer, were removed by order of the Edwardian Commissioners.

On the death of Archdeacon Maudelay, Dr. John Rayne was collated to the Prebend on 18 March 1531. He died early in the year 1543, and left a legacy to the Church. Amongst the "Expenses" of the year 1543, in the "Churchwardens' "Accounts," the following entries occur relating to this:—

	s.	d.
It'm P'd for the costes of me & my ffellows and John Brige riding in the Northe for the legaice of Doctor Rayne p'bendare of Thame	x	
It'm P'd to John Brigge for his p'ment		xij
It'm P'd for the making of an obligacion for the legacie of Dr. Rayne P'son of this Church ...		iiij

Two years afterwards the following entry is found:—

	s.	d.
It'm Rec'd of the legacie of Doctor Rayne lat P'son of Thame	xiij	iv

George Henneage, LL.B., was installed Prebendary in 1543. He was also Treasurer of Lincoln, Archdeacon of Taunton, and Archdeacon of Lincoln. He was appointed Dean of Lincoln in 1528. He resigned the Deanery for a pension in 1542. He was a willing and active tool of the innovators, a great pluralist, and very obsequious to the State authorities. He surrendered this Prebend of Thame, with all its rights and appurtenances, to Sir John Thynne, Knt., and Robert Keylway, Esq., on 16 November 1547; died in 1548, and was buried in Lincoln Minster.

The following abstracts of deeds and notes from documents existing at Longleat, co. Wilts, belonging to the Marquis of Bath, and relating to the Prebend of Thame, have been supplied to me by the Rev. Canon J. E. Jackson, M.A., to whom, as well as to Lord Bath, my best acknowledgments are due and are here tendered for the same:—

1 Aug., 1 Edw. VI., A.D. 1547. License of alienation by K. Edw. VI., to Henry, Bp. of Lincoln, to aliene to the Duke of Somerset the Manor of Thame.

* The following entry, most probably relating to work undertaken for the May Ale, is noteworthy:—

"It' payed for making of ale to Mr Adryan Tebarde late p'bendary ij^d."—Churchwardens' "Accounts," 1520.

* The following entry occurs in the "Accounts," A.D. 1529:—

"M'dom That mayster Ric^d Maudelay, doctor off dyuinitie preb'endary of this Churche of Thyame & archdeacon Leycestre hath given unto this church a corpe of clothe of tyssu col^r Redd and also made the quere setts in the Channselle. Whose soule All myghtie god p'don."

21 Aug., 1 Edw. VI., A.D. 1547. Henry, Bp. of Lincoln, among other manors, granted to Edw., D. of Somerset, the Manor of Thame, Northweston, Mortone, & Ensworth Hardwicke, co. Oxon. Confirmed by the Dean and Chapter.

16 Nov., 1 Edw. VI., A.D. 1547. George Henage, Prebendary of Thame, sold to Sir John Thynne & Robert Keylway, All Manors &c., in Thame, Weston, Tettesworth, Towersey, Sydenham, Priestend, & Mortone.

21 Jan., 2 Edw. VI., A.D. 1548. Sir J. Thynne & Keylway in performance of certain covenants dated 2 July, 2 Edw. VI., Between Edw., Duke of Somerset, & John Williams, Kt, & Eliz., his wife, grant unto sd Williams All Tithes in Weston, N. Weston, part of the Prebend of Thame. Also manors, &c., of Thame, Towersey, Sydenham, &c., belonging to same Prebend.

16 Feb., 2 Edw. VI., A.D. 1548. Henry, Bp. of Lincoln, Patron of the Prebend of Thame, reciting the conveyance made by said Henry to Sir John Thynne & Keylway, confirms the same.

3 June, 7 Edw. VI. (*sic*, but shd be 2 Edw. VI., 1548). Sir J. Williams & Elizth his wife, being seised of said Tithes and sd Manor, & Sir Edw. Seymour pretending by an indenture of 24 Feby, 4 Edw. VI., to have an interest in sd prebend & lands wh. Hennage had granted to Thynne & Keylway, & claiming same unto his heirs. And Thynne & Keylway having by sd indenture confirmed the claim of Sir Edw. Seymour in the Mansion House & other premises, & Thynne & Keylway had released the same to Sir Edw. Seymour. In consideration thereof Sir Edw. Seymour confirms to Sir J. Williams & his wife the estate in the Tithes of N. Weston & some others.

21 April, 3 Eliz., A.D. 1561. Sr Edw. Seymour sells to Sir John Thynne & his heirs the Prebend & Parsonage of Thame & all his Manor, &c., in Thame, Weston, Tettesworth & Towersey, Sydenham, Priestend & Mortone, which ye sd Sir John Thynne then late had by gifte of Sir Edw. Seymour.

30 March, 8 Eliz., A.D. 1566. Sir John Thynne grants to Sr Henry Nevell, Sir Giles Poole & others the Manor of Kingswood, in Wilts & Glouc., & the Prebend & Rectory of Thame with Tythes, & all Tythe in Tettesworth, &c., Habendum to said feoffees to use of Sir John T. & Dorothy his wife & heirs male.

Indenture, 4 July, 3o & 38o James, A.D. 1606. Sr Thomas Thynne leased to Sir Thos. Knevett & Sir Wm Bowyer, the Parsonage & Prebend of Thame as enjoyed from the death of old Sir John Thynne. To Hold for 150 y'rs immediately from the death of Lady Dorothy Ralegh [widow of Sir J. T.], if John Thynne, brother of sd Sir Thomas, or his 1st wife or eldest son, & in default of such son, his eldest dau., shall so long live, yielding £5 yearly, upon Trust for behoof of himself, his 1st wife, his eldest son, & eldest dau.

NOTES FROM SOME OLD DOCUMENTS AT LONGLEAT.

A.D. 1535. John Rayn, Clerk, Prebendary of Thame, in ye Cath. Ch. of Lincoln, leased to John Pate, gent., servant to John Longland, Bp. of Lincoln, the tithes of Thame, Weston, Tettesworth, Towersey, Sydnam, & Mortone. Also the Hall, Chapel, &c., & the Patronage of the Vicarage of the Prebend of Thame, for 50 yrs.

The Parsonage of Thame was exchanged by Sir Edw. Seymour, with Sir John Thynne, for lands in Devonshire, Somerset, 11 June, 4 Edw. VI.

A dispute between Sir John Thynne, *temp.* Eliz., & Dean & Chapter of Lincoln, about an annual payment of £7 3s. 2d., which they claimed out of the Prebend of Thame.

The Prebend of Thame was held by John Thynne, youngest son of Sir John Thynne (the builder of Longleat), in satisfaction for an annuity of £100 a yr for his life.

1653, 20 May. John Thynne, of Thame, surrenders a lease of the Prebend to Sir James Thynne, great-grandson of the first Sir John T., in order that a recovery may be suffered.

1704. Madam Jane Thynne, of Egham, co. Surrey, widow of John Thynne, leases the Prebend to Mr John Rose, of New Thame.

1704. Madam Thynne leases to Mr. Leaver Priestend & Moreton Parsonage for 7 years, at £100 a yr.

1751. Lord Weymouth leases the Prebend of Thame to Lord Carteret.

The property belonging to the Thynne family was sold many years ago.

Vicars of Thame.

As regards the cure of souls the Vicar, *Vicarius*, is the substitute or delegate of the authorized chief ecclesiastic of the parish or district; in the case of Thame Church, he was the appointed substitute or delegate of the Prebendary. His office was sometimes specifically endowed, but, as old law-suits shew, the Endowment often passed through the hands of his immediate ecclesiastical superior. Ordinarily, however, the voluntary oblations of the faithful formed the leading portion of the Vicar's income. His were the offerings at baptism, marriage, churching, and burial,* his too were the customary Easter-dues, and he was furnished with a suitable residence and glebe. In many cases the parishioners of all grades and classes remembered him when they were making their last testament. For the

* At Thame the hire of the parish coffin (for corpses were commonly only swathed with linen and shrouded), the bier, the palls, the Eucharistic vestments for mass for the dead, the lanterns for funerals, and the large wax tapers for the burial services, went to increase the Church moneys in the keeping of the churchwardens.

facts here given, and for others of a collateral character, nearly five hundred local wills of Peculiars have been carefully examined by me. Husbandmen often bequeathed the Vicar 1s., artificers and tradesmen 3s. 4d., yeomen and gentlemen 6s. 8d., those of a still higher rank 13s. 6d., or even larger sums. Occasionally these Easter-dues had been withheld or forgotten, and persons often, honestly and wisely, made up for the omission by a testamentary bequest.

Anciently the Vicar could be dismissed by his superior; but, for three generations or more prior to the Tudor changes, his office was perpetual, for life; and, if he performed his accustomed duties, by himself, or when absent, or infirm, or sick, by delegation (approved by authority), he could not be easily removed.

His choir dress was a cassock, a flowing surplice with sleeves, and a black choral sleeveless cope, or mantle, in the summer months; but in lieu of this cope it was often a furred almess (*almutium*) covering the neck and shoulders in the winter. In some dioceses, however—where Custom ruled—the almess was confined to dignitaries, to the Prebendary or Rector. The clergy likewise wore in choir a black skull-cap.

The relations between the Prebendary and the Vicar—often the subject of canon, enactment, and special decree—are not now easily defined. The latter, however, was never in the same position as the modern curate. He was essentially independent. Each officer had his own clearly-marked rights and duties, and these were carefully and duly remembered and recognized. It is believed that the right of preaching at the High or Parish Mass belonged, by local canon or general custom recognized at Lincoln, to the Prebendary, upon Christmas Day, Easter Day, Whitsun Day, as well as on the Feasts of the Annunciation and the Assumption of our Blessed Lady. Whether it was the Prebendary's duty so to preach, and if absent or non-resident to provide and reward a substitute, seems doubtful. It was, however, the Vicar's duty to see that all the appointed services were said, the sacraments administered, the anniversaries observed, and that the various chantry-priests fulfilled their obligations.

When the Prebend was suppressed, and its ample endowments confiscated, the Vicar of Thame appears by custom to have obtained certain unimportant privileges which had belonged to his predecessors' superiors. These, however, were abandoned or lapsed in the course of time, probably during the Great Rebellion; for at present the endowment is comparatively small, and no adequate provision exists even for the due reparation of the fabric of the Church.

1273. William de Langford, upon the presentation of Richard Meopham, the Dean of Lincoln, as Prebendary of Thame, was Vicar.

1293. Jacobus de Freston or Alfreston, on the presentation of Thomas de Sutton, Prebendary of Thame and Archdeacon of Northampton.

1318. William de Romeseye, upon the presentation of Gilbert de Middleton, Prebendary of Thame and Archdeacon of Northampton.

1324. Robertus Leuce, upon the same presentation, on 6 March 1324.

1326 or 1329. Richardus de Conyngesby, upon the same presentation, 19 Kalends Jan. 1326 (?).

1361. Nicholas Bricklesworth, presented by Hugh Pelegrini, proctor of the Bishop of Albano, Cardinal and Prebendary of Thame.

1376. In this year Nicholas Bricklesworth exchanged his benefice with William Weltone, Rector of Surfleet, in Lincolnshire, 27 March 1376.

1415. John Dormer, in February 1415, upon the presentation of John Walkelyne, Prebendary of Thame.

1440. Sir John Lucas, "Vicar."

1448. Sir John Dormer.

1452. Robert Sybford, upon the presentation of William Chedworth, proctor on behalf of John Chedworth.

1454. John Mason, "Parson."

1469. John Alderson, Vicar, died in 1503, buried in Thame Church.*

1503. George Perey, on the presentation of Adrian de Bardis, Prebendary of Thame.

1503. John Parker, presented 7 March 1503, by Adrian de Bardis. He was living in 1535.†

1520. Richard Martyn, "Chantry Priest" until 1520.‡

1536. William Goodrich, collated 1 February 1536, by John Longland, Bishop of Lincoln, by reason of a grant from the Prebendary of Thame.

1541. Robert Willerton, collated 7 April 1541, upon the presentation of George Heneage, Prebendary of Thame and Dean of Lincoln.

1546. Edward Daiborne, upon the same presentation. He was collated 27 November 1546.

1547. John Collyns, "Chantry Priest," so appointed this year.

1550. John Lamnott, instituted Vicar in 1550.

1551. William Forrest, ministering at Thame this year.

1552. Edward Fellowes, instituted Vicar in 1552.

* "It. rec. for waste of torches at Mr Vicars beryng, viijd."—Churchwardens' "Accounts," 1503.

† In the King's Books, or the Valor of Henry VIII. of all benefices taken in 1535, John Parker was the Vicar of Thame.

‡ "It' rec' of harry Byrte of Chylton for the sepulcre of Sr Richard Martyn late chantry p'st, vjs viijd."—Churchwardens' "Accounts," 1520.

1559. Francis Hall, instituted Vicar in 1559,* signs Vicar in 1577.

1588. Thomas Hall, "Minister" in 1588.

(Autograph of Thomas Hall from the Register.)

1589. John Trinder, was instituted in 1589, acted as Surrogate 1602; received a legacy in 1615; was buried at Thame 5th November 1629.

(Autograph of John Trinder from the Register.)

1631. Thomas Hennant, sprung from the Hennants of Arbour, in Herefordshire,† was educated, as Anthony à Wood states, at Trinity College, Oxford. He married Elizabeth, daughter of Leonard Petty, of Thame and Tettesworth, gent., on the 17th of January 1630, at Tettesworth, and was instituted Vicar of Thame on the presentation of Sir John Thynne in 1631.‡ He retained his position throughout the whole of the Civil War and Rebellion.§ At the period in question—notwithstanding the disorganized state of public affairs—the Grammar School enjoyed a high reputation. The sons of many of the nobility and gentry round about were educated there. Some of those who favoured the Puritans and Cromwellites were received, boarded, and lodged by the Vicar, who evidently enjoyed to some extent the confidence of the party of Rebellion. Under Cromwell, however, the School steadily languished and was subsequently closed. Hennant died at Thame, 2 January 166$\frac{4}{5}$, and was buried in the chancel. His widow died at Great Milton in the house of her kinsman, John Cave, Vicar of that parish, 22 November 1670, and was buried in the church there.

(Autograph of Thomas Hennant from the Register.)

166$\frac{4}{5}$. Hugh Willis, son of John Willis, of Winchester, *pleb.*, born *circa* 1625. Admitted to Winchester School in 1640, matriculated from St. Alban's Hall 2 June 1647, aged 22. Became a member of New College in the following year, where, when the Parliamentary visitors endeavoured to impose their authority on that Society, he replied in writing, being a staunch Royalist—"I humbly desire that I may not be forced to perjure myself by submission to the authoritie for this visitation, which to do were to violate my conscience." This occurred on 14 July 1648. On the death of Mr. Hennant he was presented by Sir John Thynne, and instituted, to the Vicarage of Thame in February 166$\frac{4}{5}$. His wife's name was "Mary," and two of his children,* Hugh and Elizabeth, were buried in the chancel.

* A "Francis Hall" had been appointed Rector of Aston Sandford, 9 March 1558, but was deprived, under Queen Elizabeth, for "favouring the old order," though he was presented again, 17 September 1560, by John Vere, Lord Badlesmere and Viscount Bulbeck.

† (1664, Jan. 22.) "Thom. Hennant, M.A., Vicar of Thame, in whose house A. W. sojourned when he went to school there, died. He was buried in the chancel there, and was descended from the Hennants of Henant in the Arbour, in Herefordshire."—*Life of Anthony à Wood.*

‡ The Lincoln and Oxford certificates are in the Record Office for this date, the former commencing in 1586; but they contain no record of the institution of Thomas Hennant. His appointment and those of the four succeeding Vicars are taken from the Composition Books, there being no certificate of institution for Lincoln for the period when they were instituted.

§ Theophilus Weston was "Minister," possibly Curate, in 1650, for there can be little doubt that Hennant succeeded in retaining undisturbed possession of his benefice during the Great Rebellion.

* Francis Willis, son of Hugh Willis, was born at Thame Vicarage, first educated at the Grammar School, and in due course entered at Winchester College in 1675. Being of Founder's kin he became Perpetual Fellow of New College, Oxford, having matriculated A.D. 1680, æt. 17. He graduated B.A. 17 June 1685, M.A. 30 May 1689, M.B. 16 June 1691, and M.D. 25 June 1694. He was an author of considerable distinction and repute, a poet of no mean ability, and a physician of much skill and renown. Amongst other tractates, he wrote "Synopsis Physicæ, tam Aristotelicæ, quam novæ, ad usum Scholæ accommodatæ," 8vo.—London: 1690. He contributed to a volume, entitled "Miscellany Poems and Translations, by Oxford Hands (foolscap 8vo).—London: Printed for Anthony Stephens, Bookseller near the Theatre in Oxford: 1685." The British Museum copy belonged to Robert Harley, Earl of Oxford, and has an impression of his autograph stamped in gold, and his bookplate placed on the back of the title-page. The book contains pp. viij, 206. In a MS. note on the flyleaf the following stands:—"From p. 64 to p. 90 by John Smythe, Servitor, afterwards Usher of Magdalene School. The compositions from p. 1 to p. 37, including Pindarick Odes (inscribed to the Right Hon. James, Earl of Abingdon), are by Francis Willis." Humphrey Hody, of Wadham College, contributed some Verses "To His Chamber-Fellow, Mr. Thomas Creech, on his translation of Lucretius." Then follow a "Song set by Dr. Blow," signed T. B. (*i.e.* Thomas Brown) of Christ Church; "Upon the Slighting of his Friends' Love," by Mr. C. S., of Wadham College; "Ovid's Amours," by J. G.; "The Golden Age," by H. W.; and a poem "To His honoured Friend and Relation Mr. Francis Willis, Merchant in Greenwich, upon his discovery of a Weed in Virginia, which is a present remedy against the venom of Rattlesnakes there, by F. Willis, Fellow of New College, Oxon." The book concludes with Seneca's Agamemnon, Act I., Chorus by J. Glanvil, of Trinity College.

1675. William Clerke, born *circa* 1646, son of Henry Clerke, of Enford, co. Wilts, Esq. Matriculated from Trinity College, Oxford, 16 July 1664, aged 18. He graduated B.A. 15 October 1668, and M.A. from Hart Hall 23 June 1671. Of this Society he was for some time the Vice-Principal. On the presentation of John Thynne he was instituted to the Vicarage of Thame, 29 October 1675, by Bishop Barlow, of Lincoln. He married five years afterwards. "Mr. William Clerke, Vicr of Thame, and Mrs Joan Burnham, of Crendon, were marryed August ye 8 at Tetsworth, 1680."—*Register of Marriages, Tetterworth.* He was also instituted to the Vicarage of Crendon, co. Bucks, in 1693. His daughter, Frances, married Thomas Fanshawe, of Parsloes, co. Essex, Esq.* His wife "Jone" was buried at Thame on the 24 June 1719. He himself was buried at Thame 10 January 1721.

(Autograph of William Clerke from the Register.)

1722. Samuel Thornbury, born *circa* 1696, son of Joseph Thornbury, of Leek, co. Stafford, *pleb.* Matriculated from University College, Oxford, 24 June 1715, aged 19. He graduated B.A. from Christ Church 17 October 1719, and M.A. from Magdalene Hall 2 July 1723. He was instituted, on the presentation of Carteret, Earl Granville, 18 April 1722. He married, 15 January 1745, Mary, daughter of William Tripp, of Thame, gent. He died on the 9th, and was buried in the choir of Thame Church on the 15th July 1751. His widow married at Thame, 4 October 1755, by license, Hugh Barker Bell, Esq.*

1761. John Newborough, born *circa* 1722, son of Page Newborough, Rector of Onibury, co. Salop (by Rebecca Harris, his wife, whom he married, by license, at St. Anne's, Soho, 16 October 1617). Matriculated from Balliol College, Oxon, 28 March 1740, æt. 18. He graduated B.A. 13 December 1743, and M.A. 11 July 1747. He married Catherine, sole heiress of William Pigott, of Broadhurst, co. Sussex, gent. (by Jane, daughter of the Rev. William Needham, S.T.B. of Emmanuel College, Cambridge, Rector of Old Alresford, co. Hants), and had issue a son, William, in Holy Orders, Vicar of Crendon (who was buried at Thame 4 November 1787), and five other children. He was presented by Carteret, Earl Granville, and instituted to the

---

* The following sets forth the issue of this marriage:—

Thomas Fanshawe, of Parsloes, co. Essex, Esq., born 18 Sep. 1696 (son of John Fanshawe, Esq., Auditor of the Duchy of Lancaster, by Mary, dau. of John Coke, of Melbourne, co. Derby); died 21 August, 1738, buried at Barking, co. Essex, August 27th. = Frances, "dr of the Rev. Mr. Clarke, of Oxfordshire." Died in childbed. [Burials at Barking:—"1725, Aug. 4th, Frances, wife of Thomas Fanshawe, Esq."]

- 1. Alice Fanshawe, born 5 May, bapt. at Thame 25 May, 1719; buried at Thame 24 July of the same year.
- 2. Frances, bapt. at Thame 23 June, 1720.
- 2. John, died young.
- 3. Maria.
- 1. Thomas, son and heir, born at Thame 4 January, and bapt. 28 of the same month, 1721.

Nearly a century earlier Roger Fanshawe, of Thame, had married Anne Towns, 10 April 1634.

The following note from a MS. in the handwriting of Mr. Clerke, is obviously an official record, possibly part of a Terrier:—

Thame is a Vicarage; Patron, Lord Carteret.

1. Thame, St. Mary.
2. North Weston capella sive cur' St. James.
3. Sidenham cur. St. Mary.
4. Tettesworth cur. St. Giles.
5. Towersey cur. (Pars in Com' Bucks).

} All of exempt jurisdiction from the Archdeacon, and under the Prebendary and Abbot of Thame.

} Dissolved Prebend of Thame in Lincoln Cathedral.

Will' Clerke, Vic'.

---

* The following Pedigree sets forth this alliance:—

BARKER AND BELL, OF AYLESBURY AND THAME.

Arms of Barker.—Argent, three bears' heads, erased gules, muzzled or. In chief three ogresses.

Arms of Bell.—Sable, a fesse erm. between three bells.

Robert Barker, Esq., of Culworth, co. Northampton. = Mary, dau. of William Danvers, Esq., of Culworth, by Elizabeth, dau. of Richard Fienes, son and heir of Henry, Lord Saye and Sele.

Robert Barker, 3rd son, died 6 July, 1676, aged 70; brother of Dr. Hugh Barker, Chancellor of the Diocese of Oxon and Dean of the Arches' Court. = Mary, dau. of William Smith, of Brickhill, co. Bucks, LL.D.; died in 1653, aged 75.

Hugh Barker, of Newbury, co. Berks, M.D., 2nd son; died 1683. = Joanna, dau. of Mr. Goddard, of Woodbery, co. Hants, 2nd wife; died 1667.

Hugh Barker, of Great Horwood, co. Bucks, Esq., eldest son; died 1704. = Elizabeth, dau. of Richard Whitehead, of Tidderley, co. Hants.

Richard Barker, of Great Horwood, Esq., eldest son. Will dated 1718, died 1719. = Ann Peck, of Thame. She survived him, and died in 1753.

Cœlia Barker. = Joseph Bell, of Aylesbury, gent.

Anne. (1st wife.) = Hugh Barker Bell, Esq., of Thame and Aylesbury; mar. by license at Thame 4 October, 1755. = Mary, dau. of William Tripp, of Thame, gent., and widow of the Rev. Samuel Thornbury. (2nd wife.)

Hugh Barker Bell, Esq., of Thame, Fellow of New Coll., Oxford, Registrar of the Archdeaconry of Bucks; died s.p. May, 1792.

Elizabeth Bell. = Rev. William Walker.

Vicarage of Thame, 21 October, 1761. He was also for some time Vicar of Crendon, co. Bucks, having been thereto instituted 11 July 1747. He was likewise Vicar of Aston Rowant. He died in 1795.*

John Newborough

(Autograph of John Newborough from the Register.)

1795. Timothy Tripp Lee, born 22 Dec. 1770, only son and heir of Timothy Newmarch Lee, of Thame, gent., by Elizabeth, eldest daughter of Mr. William Simons, or Symeons, of the same place. He was educated at Winchester in 1782, and matriculated at Oxford from Pembroke College, 26 November 1787, æt. 17.† He was admitted a scholar of that Society, and subsequently graduated B.A. 23 June 1791. He was presented by John Blackall, of Haseley, co. Oxon, Esq., and instituted to the Vicarage of Thame, on 1 September 1795, by Bishop George Pretyman, of Lincoln. He was appointed Head Master of the Grammar School in 1814. He had married, 2 February 1792, Elizabeth, the third daughter of Richard Smith, Esq., J.P. and D.L., of Thame, and had issue a large family. One of his Sermons, "On the Eternity of Punishment," appears in *Miscellaneous Sermons by Clergymen of the Church of England.* London: 1860. He died 29 December 1840, and was buried in a vault near the Communion Table of Thame Church.

1841. James Prosser was born 30 March 1790, and commenced life in commerce, but subsequently resolved to prepare for the ministry of the Established Church, and with that object entered St. Katherine's College, Cambridge, where he graduated B.A. in 1832 and M.A. in 1835. He was ordained Deacon in 1832 and Priest in 1833 by the Bishop of Lincoln. For ten years he was Perpetual Curate of the Chapel of Loudwater, co. Bucks, having been thereto presented on the death of the Rev. William Price in 1833. On the presentation of Richard Barry Slater, of Wycombe, M.D., who had purchased the advowson, he was presented to the Vicarage of Thame, and instituted 11 June 1841. At this time the chapelries of Towersey, Tettesworth, and Sydenham were formally and legally separated from the mother-church, and made into separate benefices; the patronage of each being vested in certain trustees appointed by Dr. Slater. Mr. Prosser married, firstly, Rebecca Charlotte Hammond, who died 6 March 1856, aged 60, and was buried in the churchyard on the south side of the church. He married, secondly, Caroline, daughter of Mr. John Eeles, of Thame, by Eliza, daughter of Mr. William Cox. He was the author of *A Key to the Hebrew Scriptures, &c., with an Index, To which is prefixed a short but compendious Hebrew Grammar, without Points, &c.*, and of *The Primitives of the Greek Tongue*, together with other minor publications. He likewise edited Parkhurst's *Hebrew and Chaldee Grammar, without Points*. Mr. Prosser resigned his benefice in the spring of 1872, and dying without issue at his residence "The Elms" 15 July 1877, aged 87, was buried in the churchyard of Thame.

1872. Elijah Bagot Corbett, born 28 April 1837, was admitted an Associate of King's College, London, in June 1862, in which year he was also ordained Deacon and became Curate of Shere, co. Surrey. He was ordained Priest in 1863, and has likewise been Curate of Oswestry, co. Salop. He married, 18 November 1863, Mary Anne Davies, and has issue four sons and five surviving daughters. He was instituted to the Vicarage of Thame 3 March 1872.

♣♣♣♣♣♣♣

* His Will, dated 7 April, 1791, gives and grants unto his wife, Catherine, "all and singular my goods, chattels, corn and cattle," after her death "to be equally divided between my daughters absolutely." No executor is named. Administration was granted to Catherine the widow, 19 September, 1795.

† From the Register of the Matriculation of the University of Oxford: "1787, Novbris 26to, Coll. Pemb.—Timotheus Tripp Lee, 17, Timothei de Thame, Com. Oxon. Gen. Fil."

In the year 1811 a Return made to the House of Lords to certain queries contained in a Letter to the Bishop of Lincoln, by the Archbishop of Canterbury, respecting the Places of Divine Worship within the diocese of Lincoln, which was ordered to be printed 5 April, 1811. The following embodied the Vicar's replies:—

Parishes.	No. of Churches according to the Rites of the Church of England.	No. of Persons each is capable of containing.	Other Places of Worship.
Thame	Four, Thame	2000	Two Dissenting Meeting Houses.
	Tettesworth Chapel	400	
	Towersey Chapel	400	
	Sydenham Chapel	400	

Surrogates.

FROM various sources—*e.g.* Parish Registers, Wills, and private documents—the following names of Surrogates acting for the Peculiar of Thame, and of clergy who were from time to time Curates, have been obtained:

1602. John Trinder.
1619. Anthony Maunde.
1631. Giles Sweet.
1634. Thomas Hennant.
1647. Gregory Ballard.
1662. Thomas Bouchier.
1679. Nicholas Villette.
1687. Thomas Middleton.
1808. William Stockins.
1832. Frederick Lee.
1842. James Prosser.
1878. Elijah Bagot Corbett.

Curates.

1606. William Jones.
1611. Edward Lee.*
1614. Francis Lee.†
1629. Richard Rastall.
1660. Francis Hearne.
1665. Joseph Urmaston.
1666. Edward Fellowes.
1702. John King.
1713. Thomas Harris.
1714. Nicholas Maunde.*
1718. Henry Bruges.
1720. Robert Heath.
1721. Thomas Whorwood.
1722. Thomas Ward.
1724. Peter Waldo.†
1728. Robert Hughes.
1730. John Kipling.
1744. John Higson.
1752. Richard Hickson.
1754. Robert Style.‡
1756. William Yates.§
1757. John Newborough.
1763. Charles Kipling.
1764. Morgan Reynolds.
1769. William Newborough.‖
1771. Thomas Gibbons.
1773. Samuel Thomas.
1774. William Cooke, sen.
1777. Robert Style.
1779. Edward Williams.
1782. John Holland.¶
1789. William Harrison.
1790. Joseph Rose.**
1791. John Williams.
1792. Thomas Cripps.
1792. Edward Evans.
1793. Thomas Evans.
1795. Thomas Williams.
1796. Edward Ellerton.††
1804. James Way.
1813. Isaac Dupuy Akers.
1814. Frederick Spring.
1815. Robert William Williams.
1817. Thomas A. Jones.
1821. Frederick Lee.‡‡
1825. Charles Lee.§§
1829. William Henry Mavor Roberson.
1859. Nathan Challis.
1866. Charles Abdiel Seaton.
1870. William Toovey.‖‖

* Abstract of the Will of Edward Lee (subsequently Rector of Hardwicke—*i.e.* 2 March, 1613), proved in the Court of the Archdeacon of Bucks in 1641. He leaves to the Poor of Hardwicke and Weedon £6 13s. 4d. To the Poor of Aylesbury 40s. To Mr. Barlin, Minister of Aylesbury, to preach a Funeral Sermon at his burial, 20s. He bequeaths St. Augustine's *Works* to Merton College, Oxford; to Sir Nathaniel Brent a mourning Ring; to "Lady Lee, late wife to Sir Francis Henry Lee, baronett, my nephew deceased, my guilded Bible in octavo." .... "I give unto her my seale ring of our ancestors' arms, humbly intreating her to keep it for the use of the heire of our house and to deliver it to him at the age of one and twenty years." To sister Lake, now wife of Mr. Henry Lake of Buckland, bedstead, bedding, and furniture. To Lucy Lake, god-daughter, 20s. To nephews George and Harry Lee, sons of brother George deceased, and to their two sisters my nieces, 10s. each for ring. To my sister Mrs. Mary Hall a bedstead. To Mr. George Pickering and to Mr. John Cary 10s. each for ring. To wife of William Thead of Whitechurch 20s. for a ring. Residue to William Hall and Lee Hall, nephews. Sole executor, William Hall. In a codicil 10s. each are left to Sir Edward Tyrrell, to Lady Tryon, and "to Mrs Anne Lee, dr of my brother Sir Henry Lee."—The marriage and issue of George, a younger brother of the testator, are thus given on fol. 78 of Harl. MS. 1533: George Lee of Highgate (son of Sir Robert of Hulcott, by Lucy his wife) married Judith daughter of Basil Nicholls of London and widow of — Sasby of London, merchant. Mr. George Lee died 13 June, 1637, leaving issue Robert, George, Henry, Judith, and Lucy.

† Perpetual Curate of Crendon, co. Bucks, 1612-1628.

* Perpetual Curate of Chearsley, co. Bucks, 1713.

† Rector of Aston-Clinton, co. Bucks, 1716.

‡ Rector of Syresham, co. Northampton.

§ Perpetual Curate of Crendon, 1673.

‖ Perpetual Curate of Crendon, 1781.

¶ Vicar of Aston-Rowant, co. Oxon.

** Minister of the Chapel of Ease, Islington.

†† Fellow of Magdalen Coll., Oxon, and Vicar of Horsepath, co. Oxon.

‡‡ Rector of Easington, co. Oxon, 1832.

§§ Vicar of Yaxley, co. Hunts, 1836.

‖‖ Rector of Newton Blossomville, co. Bucks, 1880.

1873. Edward Greensill.
1876. Humphry Donald Creaton.
1881. Richard Paul Cudmore.

Churchwardens

FROM A.D. 1442 TO A.D. 1750.

THE office of Churchwarden is of great antiquity,—the name of that office being derived from the chief duty of those who filled it, viz. that of being custodians or guardians of the fabric, of the lands and tenements belonging to each parish church, as well as of all the goods and property of the House of God,—the ornaments and vestments used in divine service.

Anciently, when the founders had not bequeathed lands or gifts for that particular purpose, the duty of providing means for keeping the fabric in repair devolved exclusively on the Churchwardens. The parishioners met,—yearly as a matter of custom, or as necessity arose, or when any particular work of reparation or improvement seemed to be required;—and, having voluntarily assessed themselves, according to their means and opportunities, the Wardens made gatherings amongst all the parishioners of the amounts agreed upon to be provided for the repairs or improvements in question.

Synodsmen or Sy'dsmen were grave and influential laymen of the parish, selected from the most experienced and best educated, summoned by the Bishop or Archdeacon, when the parochial visitation was made, to report upon oath as to its moral and religious condition, and to give the spiritual rulers an accurate idea of its needs and necessities.

Persons eligible for each of these offices were the chief and most respectable and influential resident householders of the parish; not absentees, but those who by active personal co-operation were able to perform the duties of their office, and, for the general good, were ready and willing to do so. They were ordinarily chosen, after mass, on Easter Tuesday morning annually, and in the south transept before the altar of St. Christopher. In Thame the number seems to have varied. Sometimes for several years one Churchwarden was chosen for Old Thame, another for New Thame; a third for Weston, and a fourth for Priestend and Mureton. At one time the Prebendary of Thame appears to have chosen the Churchwarden for Old Thame; the Vicar for New Thame; and the parishioners to have chosen the other two. At another period only two Churchwardens were chosen, with two Sy'dsmen: one by the Parson, the other by the people. Custom, here as elsewhere, seems to have varied at different times: though it was always respected and had the force of law. The Churchwardens were admitted to their office by the Bishop of the Diocese, or by one of his suffragans, the Abbot of Thame, the Dean of Lincoln, or the Abbot of Dorchester; and sometimes by the Archdeacon of Lincoln. As a study of the following list will shew, it appears to have been a custom here for many years that two of the four Churchwardens retired at every Easter vestry-meeting, and that two others were elected in their place, so that each couple served for two years. This custom is referred to again and again in the "Accounts." These officers kept the fabric in repair, provided bells and organs; let the church lands, and received the rents thereof. Moreover, they gathered the accustomed dues and duties of the parishioners; in ancient times they provided candles and lamp-oil for the lights; they kept the floor well paved, and had it strewed with dry rushes week by week; they saw that the custodians of the various altars, shrines, and images, (who acted under them,) did their duty; and generally speaking, in co-operation with their fellow churchmen, provided all that was necessary for the due and solemn performance of divine service. A study of the extracts already given from the "Accounts" will shew how thoroughly these elected officers of our ancestors were devoted to their religious duties; how carefully they kept a record of receipts and expenditure; how self-denying many of them were in their gifts, and how they co-operated together to offer the best they could give to Almighty God—of whose earthly temple and its treasures they were the appointed and privileged custodians.

To some persons it may seem that the following extended list of Churchwardens—which has been made with very great care—is but a record of names long forgotten, and nothing more. This is not so, however. Many of those names belonged to the leading families of the town for three centuries—to persons who were true benefactors to the Church and parish, who served God to the best of their ability in important offices of trust and dignity, and many of whom are still deservedly had in remembrance.

KING HENRY VI.

1442. Peter Mapledurham and Richard Higecosx.*
1445. John Manytorn and Thomas Bons.
1446. The same.
1447. The same.

* In this list the spelling of the original names has been scrupulously followed, even where the same name is spelled in different modes.

1448. This year the Accounts of the aforesaid Proctors or Stewards for eight years were passed and the payments sanctioned, in the presence of William Bates and other parishioners, John Manytorn and Richard Saunders being churchwardens.
1449. Thomas Bons and John Chapman.
1451. John Walkleyn and Thomas Ivys.
1452. John Edwards and John Walkelyn.*
1453. John Edwards and Robert Butler.
1454. The same.†
1457. John Chapman and John Walkelyne.

King Edward IV.

1461. John Benet and William Daynale.
1463. John Dawnse and John Benet.
1462. The same.
1464. John King and Richard Orpyn.
1465. John King and John Benet.
1468. John Walclene and John Kyng.
1469. John Kyng and John Garthrope.
1474. John Benet and John Garthrope.
1480. John Benet jun. and John Chapman.
1481. John Chapman sen' and John Garthorpp.
1482. John Chapman sen' and Nicholas Peryvall.

King Henry VII.

1489. Peter Ffrankeleyn and William Triplade.‡
1491. William Baker and Peter Ffrankelyn.
1492. William Baker (deceased) and Peter Ffrankelyn.
1494. Peter Ffranklyn and Thomas Hylle.
1495. John Cokkys and Thomas Hyll.
1496. John Cokkys and Nicholas Peryvale.§
1497. William Goodchyld, Walter Prat, Reginald Brystwyk, and John Erys.

* At the top of the leaf of the "Accounts" for this year stands the exclamation (O lesus Jhu).

† John Manytorn, who had taken so prominent a part in rebuilding the north aisle twelve years previously, died and was buried within the church in 1454, at a cost of 6s. 8d. He had already (two years previously) provided himself with a grave.

‡ In this year John Walkelyn and Edmund Tournay were appointed "Custodians" of the Trinity aisle; Thomas Hill and Harry Clerec "Custodians" of St. John the Baptist's aisle; William Yong and Peter Powlyn of Our Lady's altar; and Thomas Ive and William Butler of the lamp before the Image of St. Thomas the Apostle. It is evident that the living representatives, if such remained, of the donors of lights, vestments, benefactions, or endowments, were allowed to have personal charge of such gifts, to see that the wishes of their departed friends were duly observed; to take care that all *ornaments* bestowed or bequeathed were carefully preserved, and that the various altars, shrines, pictures, and images were kept clean and in good order.

§ Geoffrey Simeons, or Symonds, son of Geoffrey of Thame, and Margaret his wife, daughter of Nicholas Peryvale, "Churchman of Thame," *i.e.* Warden of the Church, was sometime Rector of Colerne, co. Wilts, and subsequently Dean of Lincoln 1505-1508. He died and was buried at the Charter House, London.

1498. Nicholas Rouse, William Triplad, Thomas Tebard, and William Yonge.
1499. William Triplade, Hugh Eylyn, William Yonge, and John Mortymer.
1501. John Goodwyn, John Mortymere, William Alen, and John Davy.
1502. John Mortymer sen', William Woodbrigge, John Davy, and William Yonge.
1503. The same.
1504. William Woodbrigge, Robert Mortymer, William Yonge, and Thomas Tebarde.
1505. John Goodwyn,* William Woodbrigge, Thomas Tebarde, and John Alen sen'.
1506. Walter Pratt,† Robert Pearson, John Mortymer, and Peter Pollyn.
1507. William Ross, William Saulter, John Mortymer, and John Auger sen'.
1508. Robert Holland, Giles Yonge, John Mortymer, and Peter Powlyn.

King Henry VIII.

1509. William Saulter, Robert Holland, John Mortymer, and John Auger.
1510. William Ross, William Saulter, John Myxbery, and John Auger.
1511. Robert Holland, William Yonge jun', John Mortymer, and Peter Pawlyn.
1512. William Yonge, John Funteyn, Peter Pawlyn, and Thomas Tybarde.
1513. John Ffuntene, Thomas Tybbarde, John Benet, and William Chadlock.
1514. John Benet, William Chadlock, John Tybbard, and John Mathew.
1515. John Elys and Christopher Bristwyk.
1520. Richard Elys, Thomas Edrich, John Myxbury, and John Tybbard.
1523. Richard Smarte, Thomas Smythe, John Yong, and Peter Powlyn.
1524. Richard Marker, Thomas Church, Thomas Hester, and John Myxbury.‡
1529. Thomas Benett, John Smythe, Thomas Church, and Robert Smythe.
1532. Richard Way, John Benet, Christopher Brystwycke, and John Renner.

* This churchwarden was a benefactor to the Church, as the following entry shews:—"M'd'm. That John Goodwyn and Elizabeth his wyffe haue geyn unto the Churche of Thame a payre of vestments of grene saiyne w^t th' appurtenances for to be occupied at the aulter of o^r Ladye of pite. A° D'ni mcccccxxiv."

† The memorial brass commemorating this man, his wife, and children still exists, and has been already described at p. 94.

‡ The following entry occurs in the "Church Accounts" for the year 1524:—"It'm. paid to Thomas Benet for his costs and expenses in fetchyng from London a payer of vestments of the gyfte of Sr John Dormer conveyed away fro' the Church of Thame by X'ofer Myxbury of the same town, vj^s."

1533. Richard Way, John Benet, Christopher Brystwycke, and John Strybelhyll.

1534. Robert Jones,* John Thomlynson, Thomas Andfeld, and John Strebylhyll.

1535. John Thomlynson, Robert Jones, Thomas Andfeld, and John Strebylhyll.

1537. William Yong, James Watson, Robert Jones, and John Hester.

1542. James Roose the younger, James Belford, Harry Gardiner, and Thomas Bredon.

KING EDWARD VI.

1549. John Collens, John Heister, Edward Cornishe, and William Hunte.

1551. John Spense and Richard Bunse.†

QUEEN MARY.

1553. William Lee and William Ballowe.

1554. Mr William Lee and William Ballowe.

1556. John Spens, Thomas Symeon, Robert Coorpe, Nicholas Eule.

1557. Thomas Symeon,‡ William Hardynge, John Strebelhill, and William Scott.

QUEEN ELIZABETH.

1558. John Tatnell, William Hardynge, John Stribblehill, and William Scott.

1559. John Tatnell and Walter Thame of New Thame.*
John Stryblehill and John Playsted of Old Thame.

1560. Oliver Robotham,† Thomas Strebelhill, Walter Thame, and Thomas Andfelde.

1561. Thomas Andfelde and Thomas Page.

1562. Thomas Helys and Richard Pitman for New Thame.
John Child *alias* Barnes for Old Thame.
Thomas Garnet for Priestend, and Thomas Addams for Moreton.

1563. Richard Pitman, William Smythe, Thomas Springolde, and Robert Springolde.

1564. William Smythe, Henry Greenod, Thomas Springolde, and Robert Springolde.

1565. Henry Greenod and John Bedford.

1566. John Bedford and Raphe Pollen for New Thame.
William Mynchard and Thomas Streblehill of Old Thame.

1567. Ralph Pollen and Phillip Byrde.

1568. Phillip Byrde and Robert Phillipps *alias* Coxe.

1569. Robert Phillipps *alias* Coxe and Hugh Ives for New Thame.

1570. Hugh Ives and Richard Benson for New Thame.
John Barnes *alias* Child for Old Thame.

1571. Richard Henson and Cornelius Carden for New Thame.
John Helyar and Robert Adams for Old Thame.

1572. Cornelius Carden and Peter Wylmote.

---

* Lady Bulmer (Margaret Cheyne).—"Upon Whitmonday, at breakfast, certain company was in the chantry at Thame, when was had speech and communication of the state of the north country, being that proditors against the King's highness should suffer to the number of ten; amongst which proditors the Lady Bulmer should suffer. Then being Robert Jones said it is a pity that she should suffer. Then to that answered John Strebilhill, saying it is no pity if she be a traitor to her prince, but that she should have after her deserving. Then said Robert Jones, let us speak no more of this matter; for men may be blamed for speaking of the truth."—*Rolls' House MS.*, first series, 1862.

† A note is amongst my MS. Collections from which it appears that James Bunce, member of the Fishmongers' Company and Sheriff of London in 1643, sprung from Thame, and may have been a descendant of the Thomas Buns, Churchwarden in 1445, who co-operated in restoring the church and in rebuilding the north transept, or of Richard Bunse, Churchwarden in 1551. In the year 1648 James Bunce boldly refused to publish in the City of London the illegal Act for the extradition of the Royal line of Stuart, for abolishing monarchy and for setting up a Commonwealth, for which he was committed to the Tower. In 1660 he was knighted at the Hague by King Charles II., and was soon afterwards created a baronet. Sir James Bunce, his grandson, whose mother was "Eleanor Simeons," was living at Thame in 1695.

‡ In 1573 a son of this Churchwarden was one William Symeonds, "an Oxfordshire man and Demy of Magdalene," as Anthony à Wood styles him. Afterwards he was elected a Fellow of that Society, and was subsequently Vicar of Halton Holgate in Lincolnshire, and Preacher of St. Saviour's, Southwark, and D.D. in 1613. Collateral branches of this family, which can be traced back at Thame to the reign of Henry VI., flourished at Stoke Talmache, Tetsworth, and Baldwin Brightwell. Mr. Christopher Bothom, son of Nicholas of Crendon, married Margaret, daughter of Edmund Symeons, of Pyrton, and by her had issue—1, Nicholas; 2, Robert; 3, Hugh; and two daughters, Elizabeth and Joane.

* By indenture of feoffment, dated the 10th of August 5th and 6th of Philip and Mary, John Collins granted to John Tatnell and Walter Thame, Churchwardens, a messuage and garden in the east of Thame, near White Hound pond, for the maintenance of God's service.

† The following contains three descents of this family:—

Hugh (son of Oliver Robotham of Thame, by Joane his wife), b. *circa* 1575; matriculated from Merton College, Oxon, 15 October, 1590. =

Hugh Robotham of Thame; disclaimed right to arms at Oxford, September 1634. = ...

Francis, b. *circa* 1604; matriculated from St. Mary Hall 17 October, 1623; presented to the Rectory of Horsendon, co. Bucks, in 1632, by the Guardians of Anne Cotton, a minor. = Elizabeth dau. of William Hester, mar. at Thame, by lic., 24 Aug. 1637.

Oliver, b. *circa* 1615; matriculated from St. Alban's Hall 16 October, 1635.

Hugh Robotham, bap. 28 September, 1625; matriculated from Magdalene College 4 December, 1640.

Francis.

Of this family Oliver Robotham was buried at Thame in 1588. The Will of Joane Robotham, his widow, dated 28 October, 1595, contained a bequest to Thomas Ballowe of £10 for the benefit of the church and parish; and Richard Robotham was presented to the vicarage of Lavendon, co. Bucks, 10 July, 1629, by Robert Eccleston and Anthony Elcock.

1576. William Hester and Edmond Aymotte.
John Striblehill and Leonard Grene.
1577. Edmund Alnotte and Thomas Newcome.
Leonard Grene and John Whitney.
1578. Thomas Newcome and William Wethered of New Thame.
John Wytney and Thomas Collet of Old Thame.
1589. John Lylington.
1590. William Typping and John Adams.
1591. John Adams and William Typpinge.

[Here the records are wanting.]

King James I.

1603. Mr. George Walpoll.
1604. Richard Brasey.*
1608. Roger Burges and William Heybourne.
1609. Francis Carter and John Striblehill.
1610. Peter Wilmot and Richard Molinux.
John Calcott,† Thomas Messenger, and John Pecke.
1611. Mr. Francis Carter, John Calcott,
Thomas Messenger, and John Pecke.
1612. Mr. Marmaduke Saunders* and John Parkins.
1613. John Pitman, Richard Smith,
John Burte, and Robert Baker.
1614. Thomas Springall, John Groom,
Richard Bennett, and Humphrey Jemmot.
1623. Henry Vivers and William Heybourne.
1624. Mr. Hugh Robotham.
John Smith of North Weston, and afterwards
Mr. Thomas Bryan and Jerom Messenger.

King Charles I.

1625. William Hall.
Mr. Richard Lee.
1626. Peter Tomlinson and Thomas Wildgoose.
1627. Edmund Littlepage and Edward Gurdon.
1628. Edward Curson and Edmund Brookes.
1629. Edmund Page and William Smith.
John Woodbridge† and Thomas Wetmore.
1630. William Phillips and Richard Springall.
John Woodbridge and Thomas Wetmore.
1631. William Phillips and Richard Springall.
Matthew Warters and Stephen Cosens.
1632. Robert Parkins, Stevin Cosens.
Matthew Waters, and Robert Ratford.
1633. Henry Cowley, William Norris,
Robert Parkins, and Stephen Cozens.
1634. Thomas Springall, James Roberts,
Henry Cowley, and William Norris.
1635. John Tomlinson, Robert Maunde,
Thomas Springall, and James Roberts.
1636. John Calcott, Richard Messenger of Moreton,
John Tomlinson, and Robert Maunde.‡
1637. Philip Burde, Thomas Stribblehill,
John Calcott, and Richard Messenger.

---

* The following Pedigree of Brasey of Thame stands on fol. 25 of Harl. MS. No. 1480:—

John Brasey of Haikfield, in com. Worcester.=

Richard Brasey of Thame, free of the Vintners in London. = Mary, dau. of Richard Dandridge of Berkshire.

Alexander Crooke, sonne and heyre of William Crooke, Esqr, which William is brother to Judge Crooke. = Anne, sole dau. and heyre of Richard Brasey.

Richard Crooke, only child.

Richard Brasey of Thame, Esq., by Will dated 1642, proved in 1647, bequeathed the manor of Little Kimble *alias* Bolbeck's to his grandson, Richard Croke, then of Chilton, co. Bucks, but subsequently of Adwell, co. Oxon, son of Alex^r Croke of Studley, by Anne, dau. and sole heiress of the said Richard Brasey.

Anne Brasey herself died young, and was buried at Chilton, co. Bucks. Here is the inscription, on a brass fillet round the tomb:—

Here lyeth Anne Croke wife of Alexander Croke Esquire, daughter and heire of Richard Brasey of Thame, in the County of Oxon gent, who dyed the 22nd day of March, An^o D'ni 1622, and in the 22^d yeare of her age.

On a brass plate in the middle—

God's love and favor is not known always
By earthly comforts, nor by length of days;
For often times we see whom He loves best
He soonest takes unto His place of rest.
Long life on earth doth but prolong our pain,
In happy death there is the greatest gain.

† This man is mentioned in the Will of his mother-in-law, "Alse Cotton of Thame," made 22 November, 1602. "I bequeath my soule to Allmightie God and my bodie to be buryed in the Church of Thame, as near to my husband as may be, *without anie coffin.*" Mentions sons Robert and Richard, and sons-in-law John Calcot and Dickenson, daughter Mary Sydbury; bequeaths to the Poor of Thame, 20s., "to be distributed in bread at the day of my burial."—From Wills of the Peculiar of Thame, etc.

* Minchard, formerly Saunders.—The Will of Ann Minchard was made 10 August, 1615. To Luke, son of John Saunders deceased, she bequeathed £40 and "the joined bedstead whereon I usually do lye." To Anne Saunders, daughter to Marmaduke my son, £40. To Elizabeth, dau. to Marmaduke, £10. To Mary, dau. to Marmaduke, £20, "a silver spoone, and my goald ringe with the stone in it." To Sarah, dau. to Marmaduke, £30 and "my best goulde ringe but one." To Rachel, dau. to Marmaduke, £20. To Abigall, dau. of Marmaduke, £20. To Samuel, son of Marmaduke, £20 and "my best silver goblet," etc. To all my godchildren who will come to demand it, 12d. To poor of Thame, 40s. To John Trinder, Vicar of Thame, 10s. Rest of goods, etc., to Marmaduke Saunders, sole executor.—From Wills of the Peculiar of Thame, etc.

† The inventory of the goods and chattels of John Woodbridge of North Weston in the co. Oxon, a wealthy yeoman, was taken in 1647, by Thomas Carter of Weston, gent.; by William Tipping of Wor'sall, yeoman; by William Burte, of Crendon, yeoman; and by Thomas Phillips of Ickford, gent. This inventory amounted to the very large sum of £1739 5s. 6d.—From Wills of the Peculiar of Thame, etc.

‡ At the Whitsun Ale held this year, as the "Accounts" testify, the large amount of £29 12s. 7d. was gathered.

1638. John Sheerley and Samuel Coster of North Weston.
John Calcot and Richard Messenger.

1639. Thomas Stribblehill, Robert Cooke,
Hugh Hester, and Thomas Cursons.

1640. Robert Hall, William Bigge,
Hugh Hester, and Thomas Cousins.

1641. Robert Hall, William Bigge,
William Heybourne,* and Thomas Crewes.

1642. William Bigge, Robert Hall,
John Eares, and Edward Kent.

1643. Peter Tomlinson, John Powell of Priestend,
Edward Kent, and John Eares.

1644. Thomas Carter, William Sumner,
Peter Tomlinson, and John Powell.

1645. William Roper and Thomas Stone of Moreton.

1646. Thomas Stone, William Roper,
Robert Pecke, and William Greene.

1647. Henry Cope, Henry Edwards,
William Rey, and Thos. Stone.

1648. Richard Springall, John Cole,
Henry Coope, and Henry Edwards.

King Charles II.

1649. Thomas Calcott, John Yonge,
Richard Springold, and John Calcott.

1650. John Stribblehill, Philip Cotton,
John Calcott, and John Yonge.

1651. Roger Eustace, Edward Batys,
John Stribblebill, and Philip Cotton.

1652. Steven Cooke, Christopher Barnes,
Roger Eustace, and Edward Batys.

1653. William Ffoide of New Thame, John Messenger of Moreton,
Steven Cooke, and Christopher Barne.

1655. Richard Cotton and Leonard Greene.

1656. John Woodbridge of Weston, William Parslowe,
Mr. John Barton, and Jeremy Appowell.
[Instead of the latter, "who is gone out of the p'rish," is chosen John Carter of Old Thame.]

1657. John Higgons, Henry Tryppys,
William Parslowe, and John Woodbridge.*

[The records are here wanting for five years.]

1663. Robert Waters and Thomas Stribblehill.

1664. Thomas Messenger of Old Thame and Thomas Baker.
Thomas King and Henry Jemott.

1665. Thomas Baker, Thomas Messenger,
Richard Horne, and John Messenger jun^r^.

1666. Richard Horne and John Messenger jun^r^ of Moreton.
Robert Coles and Johan Springall.†

1667. Robert Coles and John Springall.
William Evans of New Thame, Philip Grene of Priestend.

1668. William Evans, Philip Greene,
Edward Phillips, and William Maunde.

1669. Edward Phillips and Wm. Maunde.
John Harris and William Towne jun^r^.

1670. George Burrows of Thame and Thomas Dorrell the elder, gent.

1671. Thomas Dorrell gent., George Burrows,
Thomas Reeve of New Thame, and Thomas Gibbons of North Weston.

1672. Thomas Reeve, Thomas Gibbons,
Richard Atkins of New Thame, and William Coope of Old Thame.

1673. Richd. Atkins, William Coope,
John Roberts, and George Yonge.
Note. John Dearinge nominated by the Vicar because John Roberts has "listed in the militia of the kingdom and soe exempted from bearinge any office in ye p'rish." Dated "April 5th being ye Saturday in Easter week, 1673."

1674. John Dearing, George Young,
John Knappe, and Mr. Hugh Dorell.

1675. John Knappe, Mr. Hugh Dorell,
Thomas Price of North Weston, and George Ingrom.

---

* The Will of William Heybourn of Thame Park Grange, made 13 July 1659, proved 24 May 1660. To each of his children, Anne, William, John, Richard, and Mary, £20. To wife, Thomasine, sole executrix, rest of goods and chattels. Loving brother Richard of Thame Park Grange and Thomas Piggott of the Pound, in the Tything of Plomridge, overseers.—The Will of Richard Hayburne of Siddenham, yeoman. "To Agnes my wife the house I live in for her life, and then to cosin William, son of William. But if testator dies before his wife, then it shall go to my cosin Thomas, my brother Thomas Hayburne's son. To brother Thomas and his son Thomas my house in Friday Street, Thame. To brother Christopher £10, to his four children £5 apiece. To Richard, son of William, £10; the same amount to Mary, wife of Thomas King. To Anne, wife of Thomas Gibbons of North Weston, £5, and the same amount to brother John of Postcombe; to sister Jane Umphry, 10s. To cosins James and Jonas, sons of Jane, £5 each. To cosin William Haybourn, the drawer-table in the Hall." To William Keene and Jeffrey North, witnesses, 5s. each. All the rest of goods and chattels to Agnes, wife, and brother Thomas, sole executors. Will proved 18 June 1677. Inventory £571 19s. 0d.—From Wills of the Peculiar of Thame, etc.

* The following entry occurs in the "Accounts" for this year:—"Gave to ye ringers whe' ye Lord Richard was pr'claimed p'tector, 2s. 6d."

† It appears from the entries of this year that it was then the custom for the Vicar to choose one churchwarden and the parishioners another; and that, when once chosen, they were expected to serve for two years.

1676. George Ingrom, Thomas Price,
William Gibson, and John Parteridge.
1677. William Gibson, John Parteridge,
John Gerey of New Thame, and William Fryer of Priestend.
1678. John Crews, William Fryer,
Nicholas Larkcom, and Edward Bouvier.
1679. Nicholas Larkcom of New Thame, Edward Bouvier of Old Thame,
William Webb, and John Yong.
1680. William Webb, John Young,
Matthew Crews, and William Wheeler.
1681. Matthew Crews, William Wheeler,
William Jemmot, and John Bew.
1682. William Jemmet, John Bew,
Mr. Edward Smythe of New Thame, and Mr. Edward Cooke of Priestend.
1683. Mr. Edward Smythe, Mr. Edward Cooke,
Steven Kent, and Richard Jordan.
1684. John Jordan, Steven Kent,
Robert Heath, and Anthony Price.

KING JAMES II.

1685. Robert Heath, Anthony Price,
Francis Webb, and Steven King.
1686. Stephen King, Francis Webb,
Mr. Robert Barry, and Mr. Andrew Parslow.
1687. Mr. Robert Barry, Mr. Andrew Paslow,
William Munt, and Edward Gurdon.
1688. Mr. Gourden, William Munt,
John Rose of New Thame, and Mr. Robert Cotten.

WILLIAM OF ORANGE, KNOWN AS WILLIAM III.

1689. Mr John Rose, Robert Cotton,
John Wilkins, and Richard Bowles.
1690. John Wilkins and Richard Bowles.
John Egerton of New Thame, and Richard Pimm.
1691. John Egerton, Richard Pimm,
Geffrey Alnut senr, and Richard Inet.
1692. Geffrey Alnut and Richard Inet.
William Simmonds of Old Thame, and Richard Cotton of New Thame.
1693. Richard Cotton, William Simons,
Edward Burnard, and William Peck junr.
1694. William Peck junr, Richard Burnard,
Joseph Darwell, and John Eystace.
1695. Joseph Darwell, John Eustace,
John Prickett, and John Heburne.
1696. John Pricket of New Thame.
John Heybourne of Priestend.
Thomas Druce of Old Thame.
John Ewstace of New Thame.
1697. Thomas Druce of Old Thame.
Mr. John Ewstace of New Thame.
Richard Jordan of New Thame.
John Young of Moreton, sen.
1699. Mr. John Burrows of New Thame.
Henry Parker of Old Thame.
Stephen Smyth of North Weston.
John Younge of New Thame.
1700. John Young of New Thame.
Steven Smyth of North Weston.
Edward House of Old Thame.
John Low of New Thame.

QUEEN ANNE.

1701. John Low of New Thame.
Edward House of Old Thame.
Mr. Richard Leaver.
Samuel Horn.
1702. Mr. Richard Leaver of Old Thame.
Samuel Horn of New Thame.
Nathanael Saywell.
Richard Tanner.
1703. Nathaniel Saywell of Old Thame.
Richard Tanner of New Thame.
William Phillips of New Thame.
William James of Moreton.
1704. Mr. William Phillips, William Jones,
Richard Cotton, Thomas Crips of Old Thame.
1705. Richard Cotton of New Thame, Thomas Crips of Old Thame.
John Alnut, Jonas Humpherye.
1706. John Alnut of New Thame, Josiah Humphrey of Weston.
William Tripp, John Aeres.
1707. John Aeres of Old Thame.
William Tripp of New Thame.
Mortimer Druce of Priestend.
Thomas Tomkins of New Thame.
1708. Thomas Tomkins of New Thame.
Abraham Trescher of Priestend.
John Sheen of New Thame.
Thomas Heabourne of Old Thame.
1709. John Sheen of Old Thame.
Thomas Heibourne of New Thame.
Peter Burton.
William Way.
1710. Peter Burton of New Thame.
William Way of Moreton.
Christopher Walkland of New Thame.
Robert Maund of Old Thame.
1711. Christopher Walkland of New Thame.
Robert Maund of Old Thame.
Thomas Haines.
Edward Triplet of North Weston.

1712. Thomas Haines of New Thame.
Edward Triplet of Moreton.
Richard Deely.
William Horrod.

1713. William Horrod of New Thame.
Mr Deely of Old Thame.
John Knapp.
Mortemore Druce of Priestend.

KING GEORGE I.

1714. John Knapp of New Thame.
Mortemore Druce of Priestend.
John Williams.
William Loosely.

1715. John Williams of New Thame.
William Looseley of Old Thame.
Benjamin West of Moreton.
Thomas King of New Thame.

1716. Thomas King of New Thame.
John Knapp of Old Thame.
John Bouvier of Old Thame.
Edward Jordane.

1717. Edward Jordane of New Thame.
John Bouvier of Old Thame.
John Acres of New Thame.
Francis Tombs of Weston.

1718. John Acres of New Thame.
Francis Tombs of Weston.
Thomas Heath of New Thame.
Thomas Greene of Priestend.

1719. Thomas Heath of New Thame.
Thomas Green of Priestend.
Thomas Eversage.
Thomas Stanley.

1720. Thomas Eversage of New Thame.
Thomas Stanley.

1721. Mr Dorrell of Old Thame.
Thomas Rose of New Thame.
Richard Burges of New Thame.
Jeffrey Crips.

1722. William Tripp of New Thame.*
Thomas Hedges of North Weston.

1723. (No record.)

1724. Mr Henry Warner of New Thame.
Mr Joshua Ovey of Old Thame.

1725. Richard Gibbard of Old Thame.
Robert Crewes of New Thame.

1726. Richard Deeley of Old Thame.
Francis Randal of New Thame.

KING GEORGE II.

1727. William Cox of New Thame.
William Simons of Old Thame.

1728. Richard Talbot of New Thame.
Joseph Friday of Old Thame.

1729. William Eustace of New Thame.
Robert Cotton of Old Thame.

1730. Samuel Peck of New Thame.
John Gibbins of Morton.

1731. Richard Way of New Thame.
William Burnard of North Weston.

1732. Edward Phillips of New Thame.
Umphrey Eaton of Weston.

1733. Thomas Treacher of Old Thame.
Robert Quartermaine of New Thame.

1734. Thomas Cowper of Old Thame.
Henry Jemett of New Thame.

1735. Thomas Juggins of Moreton.
William Field of New Thame.

1736. Thomas Smith of New Thame.
Thomas Green of Old Thame.

1737. Thomas Cozens of Weston.
Thomas Barnes of New Thame.

1738. Thomas Deeley of Old Thame.
John Humphries of New Thame.

1739. John Burnard of Old Thame.
John Stephens of New Thame.

1740. Isaac Wheeler of Old Thame.
David Bristow of New Thame.

1741. Henry Tharpe of Old Thame.
George Sheen of New Thame.

1742. Thomas Hedges of North Weston.
Richard Lane of New Thame.

1743. Richard Head of Weston.
James Horseman of New Thame.

1744. William Webster of North Weston.
Thomas Kent of Old Thame.

1745. Thomas Crews of Old Thame.
William Hester of Thame Park.

1746. Walter West of Priestend.
John Hunt of New Thame.

1747. Francis Clerk, Esq., of North Weston.
Edward Phillips of New Thame.

1748. William Wheeler of New Thame.
Robert Howland of Old Thame.

1749. Timothy Maunde of the Liberty of Old Thame.
Simon Ostridge of New Thame.

1750. John Foster of New Thame.
Henry Humphrey of the Liberty of Priestend.

* The Will of William Tripp, made 9 March, 1675, was proved 18 June, 1677. "To loving wife Elizabeth Tripp, sole executrix, all goods and chattels." Witnesses Jane Cruse and Matthew Cruse. Inventory £148 14s. The Will of the above Elizabeth Tripp, widow, made 19 February, 1686, was proved 13 June, 1689. To daughter Elizabeth £40 and other goods, likewise two gold rings. All the rest to son William, sole executor. Witnesses, Matthew Cruse, sen., and Matthew Cruse, jun. Inventory £234 9s.—From Wills of the Peculiar of Thame, etc.

To be inserted between Page ?. C. Buckler, Esq.

And now, having reproduced the monumental inscriptions, and furnished the lists of ecclesiastical officers already set forth, let a survey be taken of the sacred edifice as it at present stands; with a few explanatory remarks, notes, and comments.

As regards its general plan, walls and windows, tower, nave, transepts, aisles and porch, the Church remains substantially very much as it appeared to onlookers three centuries and a half ago. Nevertheless Reform has played sad havoc with all its interior fittings, and both Change and Decay have done their steady work of destruction thoroughly. However, notwithstanding the fact that Thame was in the very thick of some of the battles between the King and the Rebels during the Great Rebellion, several memorials of archæological interest are still happily in existence.

The drawing of the interior here reproduced, by Mr. John C. Buckler, taken from the south transept looking towards the north-east, is most exact, picturesque, and admirable—giving a very accurate idea of the character of the sacred building, before the alterations of 1845. The two remaining skreens of the choir and north transept are seen beyond the two ancient tombs of the Quartermains; that in the foreground having been known from time immemorial as "the Poor Stone," because upon it the gifts and charities to the poor were placed prior to their due distribution. A memorial brass represented on the left hand side of the floor is gone; and so have several inscriptions in the same part of the Church. In this drawing the general dignity of the interior of the Church is represented with all the taste and adroit touch of a true artist: while the later tomb of the Quartermains, rich with canopy, quatrefoil and imagery, together with other details of interest, are most accurately depicted. Though the *Piscina*, remaining in St. Christopher's chantry, is but of slender architectural interest, a woodcut of it is here provided, because it is the only *piscina* now visible throughout the Church.

Piscina in St. Christopher's Chantry.

As the reader has already remarked, the names of several old families—of the nobility and gentry, as well as of honest yeomen and substantial merchants (some of them persons of distinction)—still likewise remain commemorated by inscriptions on the walls of the Church and on the tombs in God's Acre around.

However, it cannot be denied that, from the period of what is frequently termed "the Reformation" almost to the time in which we live, the epitaphs or monumental inscriptions commonly put up in our churches have steadily deteriorated as regards their religious character. This has certainly been the case at Thame. The simplicity and beauty of the earlier and more ancient inscriptions—"he who runs may read"—soon passed away; while in their place were too frequently chosen long and inflated compositions, rife with bad taste, exaggeration, pomposity, and pride. The Paganism displayed in certain of those quoted, the self-confidence and want of humility which are manifest in others, the almost utter absence of the Christian instinct, will at once strike any properly-informed observer. The better traditions of Catholicism, however, were not all forgotten or banished at once;* some of them lingered on, here as elsewhere, for several generations, and a certain number of distinct examples of definite prayers for the departed,†—the doctrine of "the communion of saints" put into practice—still remain at Thame, as models worthy of imitation.

Not the least interesting records, however, are those already set forth, of which the originals remain in the south transept,—where from time immemorial deeds of Christian charity have been periodically exercised round the ancient tombs of the Quartermains;—records in which old towns-people of substance and good feeling are shown to have had due care for the House of God

* "Above all the Signe of the Crosse is most superstitiously amongst them abused, for when they shut their windowes, they will make a crosse. When they leav their cattell in Houses or in the feilds, they will make a crosse. When they go out of their Houses in the Morninge they make crosses on their foreheads; they lay crosses upon the dead as they carry them to be buried; and when they are buried they lay crosses upon their graves."—Thomas Hearne's Edition of Leland's *De Rebus Anglicanis Opuscula varia*, p. 630, vol. ii. London: 1770.

† Theophilus Higgons, born at Chilton, Bucks, son of Robert, his mother a woman from Thame, was educated at the Thame Grammar School under Mr. Harris, its first Master, up to the year 1592, when he became a student of Christ Church. He took his M.A. degree in 1600. He was appointed Chaplain to Dr. Thomas Ravis, firstly Bishop of Gloucester (1605), and afterwards Bishop of London (1607), but subsequently joined the Catholic Church, and wrote a remarkable treatise entitled *Detectio falsitatis in Doctoribus quibusdam Protestantibus in controversiâ de Purgatorio et Oratione pro mortuis*. This book, which is remarkable, as well for its sound learning as for the force of its arguments and the pointed nature of its comments, created considerable interest amongst the Oxfordshire clergy, and served to keep alive old traditions with regard to the departed. Higgons was for awhile at St. Omer's and Rouen; but was afterwards induced to return to the Church of England. He then became Rector of Hunton near Maidstone; but during the Great Rebellion, his benefice being sequestered, he suffered much and died at Maidstone in 1659.

and to have blessed and benefited their poorer brethren and those who have come after them.

It is, however, an extremely pleasant feature to note, as old names and ancient families are passed in review, that, from the time of the Reformation to the period of the Commonwealth, almost all the well-to-do inhabitants of the Town, in making their Wills, charitably left donations both to the Church and the poor. Occasionally they gave a generous donation to the Mother Church of Lincoln. Some persons, in addition, bequeathed small legacies to the alms-people, gifts for repairing the neighbouring bridges, and for keeping the roads of the town in repair. From squires and gentlemen and yeomen of good estate forty shillings seems to have been the ordinary sum given to the Church; and twenty shillings to the poor, commonly distributed in gifts of four-pence, or in numerous doles of loaves of bread at the funeral. The husbandman and the artizan, each according to his ability and possessions, likewise did the same; while the religious tone and devout expressions in some of the different Wills long retained certain of their pre-Reformation characteristics; and when now inspected serve to shew that, in the practice of Will-making, the striking contrast between the Present and the Past now existing, was scarcely effected in less than six or seven generations.

The dilapidated state into which the choir, and indeed the whole fabric and fittings of the Church, had been permitted to be brought, was a scandal to all concerned.* The "Reformation," of course, commenced the great work of robbery and destruction; the Civil War, with all its horrors and curses, continued it; and the almost universal apathy as regards Church restoration, which amongst so many consequently ensued under Charles II., James II., and William of Orange, completed it. In those times pleasure-seeking, selfishness, scepticism, and general irreligion were all far too common. As regards Thame Church, things external (the House of God neglected and decaying, the services few, carelessly rendered, and ill-attended,) only too accurately shadowed forth things not seen. The timbers of the choir roof were rotting on the wall plates; the rain, when rain descended, poured down the walls, both within and without, and damaged the foundations. Many windows were unglazed, so that pigeons and starlings built their nests amongst the carved timbers above; it had been proposed to board up the choir arch and all the windows and let the choir take its chance; while the accumulation of earth round the external walls of the Church had long previously choked up and destroyed the rain-courses, and made the interior of both choir and transepts green with *fungi*, and moist because of the continued wet and damp. A formal report delivered at Buckden Palace to William Wake, Lord Bishop of Lincoln, made in the spring of 1707, which I have inspected, describes only too truly the terrible state of dilapidation and neglect into which the Church of Thame had thus been permitted to fall.

The nobleman who repaired the Chancel in Queen Anne's reign was Thomas first Viscount Weymouth—the successor of Sir John Thynne, to whom, a century and a half before, the Prebend had been granted. He was the second son of Sir Henry-Frederick Thynne (who had been created a baronet by King Charles I. on 15 June, 1641,) by Mary, daughter of the first Lord Coventry. Thomas, Lord Viscount Weymouth, who had been also so created by King Charles II. on 11 December, 1682, was a staunch Churchman, and sympathized with the clergy—then beginning, in a certain way, to assert their position and to regain something of their old influence. A few, here and there,—a little disappointed with the blessings of Puritanism and Presbyterianism, and somewhat weary of the practical application of the Cromwellian principles of disorder, revolution, robbery, and anarchy—had discreetly and wisely turned back to truer and more ancient principles; and in their preaching and teaching had partly adopted them. These clergy were anti-Erastians, who professed to base their faith and practice on the writings of the Fathers, the decrees of Councils, and the faith and profession of the Primitive Church. They were, generally speaking, consistent and often competent opponents of the school of Burnet, Tillotson, and their allies: and so prepared the minds of many of the more thoughtful Englishmen for the subsequent fruitless action of the Nonjurors. One of these, who had sometime filled the office of Vice-Principal of Hart Hall, Oxford, was the Rev. William Clerke at that time Vicar.

The arms of Lord Weymouth, painted on glass, still remain in the lower portion of the East window, with the following imperfect inscription below:—

Thomas	. . . .	Weymouth
Patron of	. . . .	repaired
this Chan	. . . .	decayed
& ruined	. . . .	1707.

As regards the choir, little has been done since Lord Weymouth restored it, except that a few coats of paint have from time to time been added to the panelling around, and to the oaken stalls, which would be far better without any paint at all. Many old encaustic tiles were removed about the year 1849, and their places supplied by others of quite a plain character.

* On a subsequent page will be found an original account from the pen of Dr. Burte, Head Master of Thame School, describing the destruction which had been wrought on Lord Williams' tomb

To face Page 170

Encaustic Tiles from Thame Church.

From drawings by the Author

The accompanying print of certain specimens, selected from several fragments which exist, are of interest. These six examples vary both as regards antiquity and artistic merit. Some are as early as the thirteenth century: others of the fifteenth and perhaps even later.

The Parson's external door on the north side of the chancel is practically blocked up, while the space between it and the door of the interior panelling is used as a receptacle for lumber.

The old stalls, panelled in front with the well-known linen-pattern, boldly carved, are of late third-pointed or perpendicular work, are returned; and would seat twenty-four clerics. The stall heads are eight in number, and all vary in pattern. Behind them, the upper part of the panelling is of the linen-pattern likewise,—there being thirteen of such panels on the north side, and fourteen on the south. Below them are low *subsellæ* on either side near the floor.

But the altar tomb of Lord and Lady Williams in the midst of the chancel, is, with the exception of that of Sir John Clerke, the most remarkable monument therein remaining. It is of marble and alabaster, of fair design and proportions, and of excellent, most probably of foreign, workmanship. On the top is represented a carpet or covering spread out and fringed. The figures of Lord Williams and his lady (Elizabeth, his first wife, who was not buried here, however, but at Rycott, grand-daughter of "Thomas Bledlow, citizen and grocer" and "relict of Andrew Edmonds, of Cressing Temple, co. Essex, gent.") are carved with considerable skill. The position of each, with hands reverently joined as in prayer, is most suitable and appropriate. Lord Williams, who is bearded and has a full and lofty brow, is represented in the armour of the period, his head resting on a helmet, and his lady's on a cushion. Her features are handsome and regular; but a little coarse. Both the pairs of hands are large. At his feet is a greyhound; at hers an unicorn; each artistically placed and most spiritedly carved. She wears a kirtle, covered with a mantle, tied at the neck with long cords and tassels. On her head is a close-fitting cap, and round her neck a tightly-fitting frill. Their heads are placed towards the east and their feet towards the west—an unusual and almost unprecedented position for lay-persons. Whether this was done intentionally or by inadvertence by those who actually erected the monument cannot now be determined. At the period in question, however, changes of this kind were sometimes made for the mere sake of change* to set forth and shew the profound contempt of the irreligious innovators for the Faith of their forefathers and the customs and Religion of Christendom. There were originally two brass plates, engraved with inscriptions, one on the north side and the other on the south; but both were wrenched off during the Civil Wars,* and though, in the year 1661, these were reported to be respectively in the safe custody of Mr. Willis, at that time the Schoolmaster, and of the Earl of Lindsey, only one of these inscriptions (that already given on p. 103) remains. The other is lost. The tomb is rich with armorial bearings. At the west end are the arms of Williams and Moore quarterly, with the crest above, but no baron's coronet, and with greyhounds as supporters, finely and boldly carved.

On the south side of the tomb, towards the eastern-most portion, are the arms of Wenman—1st and 4th Wenman, 2nd Giffard, 3rd Staveley—impaling Williams, quartering Moore; and towards the west those of Norris, with many quarterings (set forth in detail below), impaling Williams, quartering Moore again.

The following are the arms represented:—

I. Williams. Az. two organ pipes in saltier, the sinister surmounted of the dexter, between four crosses patée ar.

Moore. Arg. a moor-cock sable.

Supporters. Two greyhounds arg. collared or.

Crest of Williams. A fish-weir basket fessewise proper.

II. Wenman. Sa. on a fesse arg. between three anchors or, as many lions' heads erased gu.

Giffard. Gu. three lions passant in pale arg.

* "The well-known 'rule of contraries' was duly applied by those who made these changes. For example, in the Mass there was always an altar of stone used: in the new service of the Supper a table of wood. At the former the priest was enjoined to stand before the altar: at the latter, by way of contrast, the minister was directed to go to the north end of the table. In the Mass the priest invariably began the service on the epistle side, and the *Gloria in excelsis* was said or sung at its commencement: in the Supper the minister began on the gospel side, while in this new service the *Gloria in excelsis* was placed at its close."—*The Church under Queen Elizabeth*, vol. i., p. 42. London: 1880.

* A tradition existed at Thame, preserved in writing by Mr. John Kidman, an artist and schoolmaster, whose MSS. were bequeathed to the late Mr. Harry Lupton, that on one occasion when the Cromwellite garrison at Thame was surprised by the King's troops, the former fled into the Church and took shots at their opponents from behind the Tower battlements. It was also handed down that when their bullets were exhausted they opened Lord Williams' vault, and, finding the outer coffin with its silver fittings decayed, appropriated the leaden coffin to the making of bullets. It is further said that the corpse was treated with marked and revolting indecency. Anyhow, when one side of the vault was necessarily opened about forty-five years ago, in order to repair an adjoining vault, the former was found to be perfectly empty.

John Kidman of Thame, schoolmaster, Will made 13 May, and proved 17 December, 1835. Leaves to his grandmother, Elizabeth Mears, widow, for life all his freehold estates: afterwards the same to his brother James. To Harry Lupton, surgeon, his MS. Volumes, Poetical Dictionary, and Original Verses. James Kidman and Thomas Stone, executors.—From Wills of the Peculiar of Thame, etc.

Staveley. Arg. on a chevron azure between three lozenges sa. as many bucks' heads caboshed or.

The above impaling Williams quarterly with Moore.

III. 1. Norris and Fermor.* 1 and 4, Norris. Quarterly arg. and gu., in the 2nd and 3rd quarters a fret or, over all a bend az. 2 and 3, Fermor. Arg. a chevron sa. between three ravens' heads erased of the last.

2. Lovell of Oxfordshire. Barry nebulée of six or and gu.

3. Deyncourt. Az. a fesse indented, between ten billets or.

4. De la Plaunche, of co. Bucks. Arg. within a bordure az. a lion rampant sa. crowned or.

5. Holland. Az. a lion rampant guardant, between six fleurs-de-lys or.

6. Beaumont. Or, semée de fleurs-de-lys a lion rampant or.

7. Comyn (Earl of Buchan). Az. three garbs or.

8. Bardolph. Az. three cinquefoils or.

9. . . . . . Quarterly gu. and arg. on the first and fourth an eagle displayed or.

The above nine coats stand impaling Williams quarterly with Moore.

On the north side of the choir, below the second platform, and near the tomb of Lord Williams, a Purbeck marble remains in the floor, which probably covers the tomb of Archdeacon Maudelay, who was also Prebendary of Thame. Originally—to judge by the hollow places remaining—it had received a brass of a priest in a cope, with armorial bearings below and an inscription remaining round its edge. Not a fragment of metal now remains on it, except the original pins fastened by solder, while the stone itself has been much battered. It is possibly to this stone that Mr. Francis Thynne made reference when he visited the Church in the latter part of the sixteenth century.

On the same side of the chancel, the four first-pointed, or lancet, windows have been recently filled with excellent and effective stained glass, rich and brilliant in colour, consisting of figures of the Four Evangelists, with their accustomed emblems, standing under archaic and well-designed canopies. They were executed by Messrs. Clayton and Bell of London; and, though of a later character than the original windows, the figures and accessories not being over-weighted with too deep or staring colours, are well suited for the place they occupy.

* On the tomb the herald-painter has made some obvious mistakes. Fermor is incorrectly represented in the first and fourth quarters; and the arms of Norris in the second and third are altogether wrong.

At the foot of each stands the following inscription:—

1. In loving memory of Harry Lupton, late
2. Surgeon of this place, who died June 18, 1861,
3. In his 76th year, by his affectionate
4. Daughters. He being dead yet speaketh.

The easternmost of the three windows on the opposite or south side, has been filled with stained glass by the same artists in memory of the late Mr. Reynolds, surgeon, of Thame. The subject is "The Wise and Foolish Virgins." The archaic representation of the subject is carried throughout the three lights. Above, Our Blessed Lord as a King is crowned, and the five wise virgins, with their lamps trimmed and burning, find themselves near Him. Below, the door is shut, and the five virgins with their oil-less lamps are groping in sadness and gloom.

"'No light, so late, and dark and chill the night;
O let us in that we may find the Light!'
No, no! Too late, ye cannot enter now."*

The subject is reverently and well designed, and has been executed with much artistic taste and excellent effect. The colours, artfully arranged though not too strong or deep, have a sparkling brilliancy which is striking, while the incidents of the subject are powerfully told. In the head of the window are three angels in albs, one with a scroll—"Watch ye therefore," and the other two, similarly apparelled, with trumpets. In the window itself stands the following inscription: "Be ye also ready, for in such an hour as ye think not the Son of Man cometh. Watch therefore, for ye know neither the hour nor the day when the Son of Man cometh." An inscription on brass on the left-hand splay of the window has been given on page 99. The subject thus represented is, on the whole, a very beautiful work of art; and it is to be hoped that ere long the other windows of the chancel may be filled with corresponding subjects, by the same artists, and be equally well treated.

The Sanctuary has been panelled, but in a very commonplace and unsuitable style. This panelling, no doubt, hides *piscina*† and *sedilia* on the south side, and

* "Idyls of the King," by Alfred Tennyson, D.C.L.

† The *piscina* was a stone drain, frequently placed under an arch in the wall, on the south side of every altar, at which the officiating mass-priest washed his fingers, after receiving the oblation, and before going on with the sacrifice. The *sedilia* were three (or sometimes fewer) seats on the same side, often under arches or canopies in the wall, where the clergy ministering at the altar sat at certain periods during mass. In the aumbrey on the north side the sacred vessels, chalice, paten, cruets, ciborium, bason, etc. were

aumbrey, and perhaps the Easter sepulchre (or what remains of it) on the north. At the east end is a debased reredos of wood, in a classical style, divided into four panels, on which the Creed, the Lord's Prayer, and the Ten Commandments have been painted.

The Communion-table, already referred to, of massive oak carved, and of the Jacobean or early Caroline era, is of the sort handsome. It had a cover of green Genoese velvet, fringed with gold, early in the eighteenth century; but in more recent years its covering has been one of crimson velvet. In front of this the well-known device of the Society of Jesus, the sacred monogram I.H.S. within a glory, was admirably embroidered in gold thread. A modern and very inferior covering is upon it now.

Two large silver candelsticks, with wax tapers, formerly stood on the Communion-table, said to have been presented by a member of the noble family of Thynne, but these are traditionally reported to have been stolen in the latter years of Mr. Newborough's incumbency, when they were replaced by two others of a much smaller size, and not of precious metal. These, however, have been disused, though I have been informed that they were generally placed on the Holy table at Communion-time until the year 1828 or 1829. These last-named are still in the Vicar's custody, but are not used.

As early as the year 1636, at Archbishop Laud's instigation, an order had been somewhat reluctantly sent by John Williams, Bishop of Lincoln, to enclose the sanctuary, and not to allow the Holy Table to be moved from its position at the east wall under the east window. The churchwardens received this direction with respectful consideration, and in the following year erected sanctuary rails at a cost of about £14.

From the ceiling of the nave, on a chain, depends a handsome seventeenth-century brass *chandelier*, consisting of a globe of brass, from the sides of which twelve symmetrical branches, spreading out in graceful curves, bear sockets and sconces for tapers or wax candles. Until the last fifty years evening service was always said at 3 P.M., and I have been informed that the tapers in this *chandelier* were invariably lighted both in summer and winter, a custom dropped only during the present century. Over the *chandelier* is a dove, symbolical of the Spirit of Light and Truth.

On the floor of the north aisle, westward of the passage from north to south, lies a large Purbeck marble slab, placed east and west, and probably in its original position, from which two brasses and an inscription round its margin have been torn. These vacant spaces no doubt contained figures of a man and his wife, and there appears to have been a representation of the Holy Trinity, or of Our Lord in glory, or perhaps of Our Lady with Her Divine Child at the head of it.*

Between the spandrils of the arches of the nave, as also on the walls of the aisles and elsewhere, were texts of Scripture written up in bold Roman capitals, surrounded by ornamental borders of red, green, and yellow. These, of considerable antiquity, possibly as early as the reign of Elizabeth, had been evidently often repaired, but they retained their ancient quaint character, and were only finally obliterated about forty years ago.

The roof of the nave, of good second-pointed work, is now hidden by a wretched artificial construction of lathe and plaster, put up about the same time, and colour-washed in imitation of stone. Six freestone corbels on each side serve to support the main timbers and principals, oaken pendant posts resting upon them. These corbels, varying in subject, but all most effective in design and telling in execution, as fresh and sharp as when they first passed out of the carver's hands, may be thus described:—

North side, beginning at the West.

1. A woman veiled, probably a religious, and possibly St. Osyth of Quarrendon, holding an open book.
2. An angel, in an alb, playing upon a zither.
3. The head of a crowned king, possibly David.
4. An angel, in an alb, with hands joined in prayer.
5. The head of a crowned king, possibly Ethelbert.
6. A crowned king, with a sceptre holding a ring, St. Edward the Confessor.

kept. The Easter sepulchre, on the same side, was often a permanent construction for the Reservation of the Blessed Sacrament, one of the most impressive and important ceremonies of Holy Week.

* This may have covered the tomb of the Marmions of Thame. I have a MS. note stating that some members of this family were buried in the north aisle, and that fragments of brass upon a Purbeck marble slab, with the words **Marmion & M'gery hys wyffe, and blessid mother of grace**, were to be read about the year 1629. This family appears to have died out at Thame in the fifteenth century, the last heiress of the same having married John Hester. (See p. 76.) But there were Marmions of the same blood at Oxford and at Ellingdon, in Gloucestershire, during the sixteenth century; and again at Thame, as well as at Aynhoe, co. Northampton, in the seventeenth century.

Arms of Marmion in Christ Church, Oxon.—Vairée arg. and az. over all three lozenges gules 2 and 1.

The same arms quartering Cottesmore (viz., an imperial eagle, on the breast an escutcheon charged with a leopard's face). Over it "**Will'm Marmyon, Esq., & Margaret.**"

Though commemorated by the putting up of armorial bearings in stained glass at Oxford, it is by no means improbable that this William and his wife were buried in Thame Church.

Anthony Marmyon, died 6 December 1549 at Ellingdon in Gloucestershire.

3. Isabella=John Parker. 1. John Marmyon.=a 2. Arthur. Marmyon.

1546.—Arthur Marmyon, aged 16 years, admitted Demy of Magdalene.

South side, beginning at the East.

1. A male figure with hands crossed on the breast.
2. The head of a prelate, mitred; possibly St. Birinus, first Bishop of Dorchester.
3. The angel of the Passion.
4. The head of a prelate, mitred; possibly St. Hugh, Bishop of Lincoln.
5. An angel, in an alb, playing on two kettle-drums.
6. A male figure in a cassock, holding a ring.

The various galleries of the Church not only disfigure it greatly, but render the possibility of appreciating the fine proportions of its interior quite out of the question. The oldest of these galleries in the south aisle, blocking up three arches, was erected for the use of the Grammar School, during the seventeenth century, and its oaken front is obviously of late Jacobean work. That which stands at the west-end of the nave—a still more hideous erection—was put up a little later. Another gallery which projected northwards from the south-west pillar of the tower, and was painted in squares of black and white, was sometime used by the Lords Wenman, of Thame Park. However, when the desecrated chapel (near which stood formerly the gate of the Monastery) was restored for worship, the gallery in question in Thame Church was first abandoned and then happily removed. Other galleries—two monstrous and vulgar erections, one in the south transept and another blocking up the east end of the north aisle,—are terrible eye-sores; and, as if the singing-gallery at the west end of the nave had not been large and hideous enough, two others, at the west end of the north and south aisles, have since been projected and erected, to the still further disfigurement of the Church, and to the discredit of the taste and judgment of those who were allowed to put them up.

Under the west window of five lights, at its base, below the splay, stands an inscription thus:—"Thomas Reeve, Thomas Gibbins, Churchwardens, 1672." This indicates its exact age, its style being debased pointed work. The heads of the lights of the window are perfectly plain without any cusps, while the mouldings of the mullions are coarse and poor. The officials mentioned deserve commendation for having done their best in a tasteless age.

On the outer panels of the wooden door of the south porch stands the date at which it was made, viz. 1682; and there is also a date, on the small external door of the north transept: but this is not easily discernable.

With the best intentions, no doubt, with a generally-expressed desire to remedy previous defects and to improve the interior of the Church, a public meeting of the inhabitants was called in the summer of the year 1843, with a view to raising funds for re-seating the whole of the area of the nave, aisles, the space under the tower, and the south transept.

It is true that pews of all shapes and sizes, some of them erected a century before the Tudor changes, had been put up by persons of rank and influence. Nicholas Peryvale, a gentleman of the parish, erected a seat for himself and his family in the year 1449. To give another example, the Dormer family, succeeding by the marriage of an heiress to the manor and lands of the Baldingtons, succeeded likewise to certain ancient and acknowledged rights of worship and sepulture in

Altar-Tomb of Mr. Geoffrey Dormer in the North Transept.

(From a Sketch by the Author.)

the north transept, known as "Baldington's," and afterwards as "Dormer's Aisle." Here they too had put up a private pue. In the vault beneath, members of these families had from time to time been interred. Under a depressed arch in the north wall, the widow of Mr. Geoffrey Dormer, in the early part of the sixteenth century, had erected an altar-tomb,* still remaining, but with crumbling carvings, surrounded by tokens of neglect and decay—not very creditable to those who, representing the discreet wool-stapler of Thame and Calais, and benefiting by his thrift, allow their ancestor's burial-place to remain in such a forlorn and unhonoured state.

In that transept these Dormers had secured a "pue" for their own personal use, as early as the year 1477. This no doubt stood at the western side of the transept, and consisted in all probability of a raised bench, with carved ends, placed north and south immediately opposite to the Altar of the Blessed Trinity, which was under the east window.† The platform or *predella* of the thrown-down and destroyed altar still remains, enclosed by an iron grille, with a gate on the south side: evidently not the original enclosure, but no doubt occupying the same place and taking in the same area.

The Quartermain family owned similar rights in the south transept—rights which seem to have been claimed by, and allowed to, collateral descendants. There was a dispute about a pue, "kept locked to the great let and hindrance of many," in the reign of Elizabeth; about the right of burial in an ancient vault in the reign of King James; while the body of a Mr. Thomas Quartermain of Thame was certainly buried there in the year 1631.

The subject of pues—here incidentally introduced—is one of considerable practical interest. Of late years a great prejudice has been created against them by a somewhat unreal and artificial agitation which certainly owns certain communistic features. For example, if the original founder and benefactor, by endowment, of a Church, of a Chapel, or of a Chantry, reserved to himself and his heirs for ever the right to have and enjoy some special pue or bench in sight of the altar which he himself had been the means of setting up, who could say that the lawful ecclesiastical authorities had exceeded their powers, if, in return for such foundation and benefaction, they, by special deed—signed, sealed, delivered, and enrolled—formally granted a particular pue for his and his successors' use and benefit? Those who give should get. And so long as there are ranks and gradations in society, rank and benefactions by people of rank should be duly regarded. A like principle will hold good with other classes: and it is quite unreasonable and unjust that those who contribute the least to the fabric and services of the Church should be permitted to monopolize the chief seats.

Anyhow in Thame Church the old customs and rights of people have not been as yet taken away. And, although no one would rejoice more sincerely than the Author if the galleries were removed, it stands to reason that those who have secured certain rights, should not be robbed of them by the hasty judgment of a perverted Public Opinion, without due and just compensation.

The following exact transcript of the Original Faculty granted to Mr. John Eustace by Dr. Bouchier, the Official Principal of the exempt Jurisdiction of Thame, etc., is worthy of reproduction. Incidentally it proves that at Thame, so late as the eighth year of the reign of King James II., the men sat on the north or gospel side of the church, and the women on the south or epistle side—a tradition inherited from time immemorial:—

Thomas Bouchier Docto' of Laws and Officiall or Co'm'ssary of the Peculiar and exempt Jurisdicions of Thame and Milton in the County of Oxon with the members to the same belonging lawfully appointed To all to whom these p'sents shall come sendeth greeting in the Lord everlasting.

Whereas it hath been alleaged unto us by John Eustace of Thame aforesaid Maulster That ffrances his now wife is destitute of some convenient Seat or Pew in the Church of Thame aforesaid to sitt in, to hear divine service and sermons And that the uppermost Pew of the Women's

* Two coats of arms remain on the tomb, here reproduced. It seems doubtful, however, if when this memorial was erected the family bore arms; and this opinion is supported by the absence of the Pedigree of Dormer in the earlier Oxfordshire Visitations.

Ancient Arms of Baldington of Thame.

Arms of the Staple of Calais.

† "Previously to the separation of Thame as a Peculiar of the Dean and Chapter of Lincoln, at a period when the Rev. Henry Quartley was Visitor, it happened that the eastern window of the northern transept was blown in and totally demolished; and the Churchwardens for the time being proposed to brick it up, and thus spoil the general character of the Church. It is a remarkable fact that two lads of the town waited on the Visitor as soon as he arrived, and stated the intention of the Wardens. 'Well done, my lads,' was his reply, 'I thank you. It shall be my care that the window be restored, as it before stood.' And it was restored."—*History of Thame*, by Henry Lupton, pp. 81, 82. Thame: 1860. I may here very properly add that, to his credit, Mr. Lupton himself was one of the lads referred to. He was a gentleman of much good taste and archæological feeling, greatly attached to the place of his birth; and had gathered an interesting collection of local antiquities during a long and honoured life.

Pews Westward being five foot wide and ffive foot Nine Inches long from North to south scituate and being under the South Gallery in the said Church was enjoyed upon an exchange for some other seat in the said Church by the said John Eustace's predecessors being owners and proprietors of a certaine Messuage or Tenem^t in Thame aforesaid now in his possession And that the said Pew or Seat may be appropriated to the use of the said ffrances Eustace and one more under such limittac'ons as are hereinafter expressed and hath desired our Licence or ffaculty for the quiet enjoyment of the same as aforesaid. Wee therefore the Officiall or Co'missary abovenamed having ffirst issued out our Proclamacon and upon due return thereof in Court having duely Weighed and maturely considered the premises at the mocon and instant request of the said John Eustace have adjudged and decreed the said Pew or Seat soe exchanged as aforesaid to be appropriated and imployed for the proper use of the said ffrances Eustace (saving and reserving liberty and power to the Churchwardens of Thame for the time being of placing any one Woman in the said Pew or Seat untill the same shall be more fully disposed, And saving also liberty to Grace Wilkins wife of Mathew Wilkins of Thame aforesaid, Gent- of sitting in the said Pew or Seat in time of divine Service and Sermons soe long as she shall live in the said Parish of Thame the right of the said Eustace being always saved and reserved) And We do hereby adjudge and decree the same to the said use Soe that from henceforth it shall and may be lawfull to and for the said ffrances Eustace and any One Woman of the said Parish which shall be placed there by the Churchwardens for the time being and the said Grace Wilkins for soe long time as she shall live in the said Parish to be and remaine in the said Pew or Seat to hear divine service and Sermons and to exercise all Christian Duties fit and requisite for the same place (All other Inhabitants of the said Parish excluded) Inhibiting further and Wee doe hereby Inhibit and admonish all other the Inhabitants and Parishion'rs of the said Parish that neither they nor any of them doe attempt or presume to molest disturbe or disquiett the persons aforenamed or any of them in her or their quiet possession and enjoym^t of their said places in the said Pew or Seat in the said Church to the uses aforesaid.

In Witness whereof wee have caused the seals of our office to be hereunto sett this Third day of July Anno D'm'i One Thousand Six Hundred Ninety & Three,

Richard Cotton, William Simbons,
Church Wardens.

Will' Clerke, Vic'.

A Committee of townspeople was formed, on the 29th of June 1843, to carry out the proposition already referred to for reseating the Church, and it was determined to enlist the services of Mr. H. B. Hodson,—who about that period had been engaged in what was called "restoring" the Prebendal House,—to prepare plans and superintend the work. The various existing pues were of all sorts, shapes, sizes, and heights, many of them lined with coloured baizes of different tint and varying antiquity. A few of the old, well-designed, pre-Reformation benches remained, upon most of which loftier structures owning no uniformity had been from time to time long ago erected; and it is to be regretted that these said old benches were not restored and others of a similar pattern made to correspond with them. This, however, was not attempted. The plans submitted and carried out can hardly be commended, nor can the pues themselves which were then erected be admired. They are unecclesiastical, commonplace, ill-arranged, and inconvenient.

Moreover the removal of the Font, from its original and appointed position near the south-western entrance —where it duly symbolized admission to the Family of Christ by baptism—was a grave mistake and a great blunder. The Font, the proportions of which are

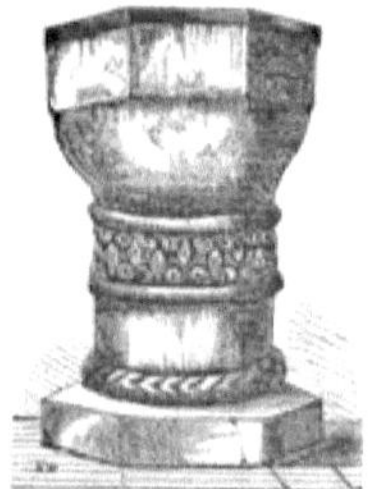

The Font.

not uniform, now stands in the centre of the nave where the pathways join and cross each other; it efficiently obstructs the carrying of corpses through the western door, on a level with the churchyard, without ascent or descent; it bars the progress both of marriage and funeral processions, and is altogether in its wrong place. The two stone steps upon which it previously stood were removed; the socket of the branch for the "font-taper" extracted, put aside, and lost; the old oaken lid with which the Font was covered was taken away and never replaced; the drain for the blessed water, when used, to be let off, was of purpose stopped up, so that ever since the period in question the Font has never been filled, but a small crockery dish is apparently used in its stead. The Font is of rare antiquity and interest, carved in close-grained freestone, and probably not less than six hundred and fifty years old. Octagonal in shape as regards the bowl, it now stands exactly three feet and six inches in height. The bowl itself is two feet and a half in diameter, measured from edge to edge, but the hollow circle containing the leaden basin measures only two feet and one inch. On one side the stone is shattered, from which part the fastening which formerly secured the hinge to the cover has evidently been wrenched.

Nor was the removal of the two ancient tombs of

the Quartermains from the position in which they had been originally placed, east and west, close to the eastern wall of the south transept, where they are now huddled up as worthless lumber, at all to the credit either of the Church authorities or of the architect who had advised their removal. Had the late Lord Lyttelton, who, in the female line, represented this old and knightly race of Thame and North Weston, been made aware of the indignity illegally and unjustly proposed to be offered to the memorials of his ancestors, he would, as on the best authority I happen to know, have refused his permission for their unjustifiable removal.

At this period nearly £400 were spent on making these changes and erecting the new seats, while at the same time many other remains of antiquity and of archæological interest were either deliberately or carelessly destroyed. The Prayer-desk for the minister, which had hitherto faced southwards, was then turned towards the west, so that prayers and lessons were henceforward read facing the congregation. Several brasses were then lost, as has been already pointed out, and at least three ancient *piscinæ*—one in the north transept, another in the north aisle near to the pulpit stairs, and a third in the south aisle (below the Heath monuments)—were chipped off level with the wall, broken, filled up with stones and mortar, and then carefully plastered over. Holy-water stoups at the south-west porch and at the west door of the south transept, were likewise purposely destroyed; while the doorway of the roodloft, near to the north-east pillar of the tower, was also duly blocked up and plastered over.

These changes having been effected, and the new seats finished and put up, the Committee responsible for the work met in the autumn of the year 1845 and assigned the same to the parishioners, according to their rank, rights, and requirements.

Again, the blocking-up of the west door in the south transept was a great mistake, while the erection of a heating-apparatus of the nature and character of that now existing in the south-west corner of the same, was a greater. This latter is a disfigurement and an eyesore. Any competent architect, or even an experienced builder, would have discountenanced the introduction of such a coarse brick-and-compo monstrosity. It is to be hoped, therefore, that the day may soon arrive for a thorough and systematic restoration of the Church; when past changes for the worse may be unmade; when all the old features may be carefully renewed; and when it may be gathered from the result of such an improvement that the spirit, generosity, and self-sacrifice of our ancestors are not yet dead and gone.

As regards the Bells, it is evident from existing "Accounts" that there was no greater source of expense year by year. There is scarcely a single annual record of moneys expended, from the middle of the fifteenth century to the middle of the sixteenth, in which the costs of re-casting, re-hanging, or re-arranging them, their wheels and their baldricks, do not appear. In recent times likewise the bells have proved a costly item. Some of the expenses incurred at Thame, prior to the Tudor changes, were very considerable; and the timbers and machinery appear to have been constantly needing reparation.

In 1450 Thomas Swadling was the bellfounder employed. But his locality is not specified in the document in which his name occurs. Two years later these entries appear:—

	s.	d.
For yᵉ lyttull Bell wheele making		iiij

In 1452:—

	s.	d.
For yᵉ making of yᵉ grete bell clapur	vj	viij
For yᵉ mendyng of yᵉ grete bell whele		j

In 1465 "a man from Ewelme" was engaged in similar work. In the "Accounts" for 1480 are many entries relating to re-hanging and arranging the bells, and occasional expenses incurred with regard to the same are entered almost every subsequent year. In 1530 the Abbot of Notley received 6s. 8d. for "tymber for the great bell-frame;" from oaks which had long flourished in the well-watered, fertile, and fruitful valley of the Thame. In the same year £10 2s. 3d. were paid to the Bellfounder "for changing of two bells." In 1531 Thomas Bloxam and others "fynyshed the frame of yᵉ grete Bell," and were paid 26s. and 8d. for their labour. When first rung, however, the tenor bell was found to be cracked; so in 1539 it was again recast. In 1557 the great bell was once again "dressed and hanged," and the second bell was mended. Ten years later, John Ap Powell of Buckingham cast a large bell for the Church of Thame; and re-hung others. There was a bell foundry at Reading in the latter part of the fifteenth and in the early part of the sixteenth century, of which a certain John Saunders, some of whose relations lived at Thame* and supplied the "bawdrickkes," was the owner. He likewise was employed by the churchwardens. His marks on bells made by him were—(1) The arms of the See of Winchester in a circle surrounded with fleurs-de-lys archaically arranged; (2) A device made of four fleurs-de-lys placed crosswise; (3) A lion's head; and (4) A bell with the letter S on either side of it. He re-cast some of the Thame bells in Henry VIII.'s reign, and was succeeded by a man, White by name, who was engaged at Thame in the year 1539, and whose reputation for a time was considerable. The apathy of the post-Reforma-

* A presumed descendant of his was a bellfounder at Bromsgrove, co. Worcester, in the early part of the eighteenth century.

tion people was, however, so great, that while so many bells were taken down and sold at that eventful period,* few were put up.

The Powells or Ap-Powells of Buckingham had been likewise employed at Thame as early as the year 1503. They continued to act as bellfounders in their native place until about the year 1570, possibly later, and appear to have been succeeded by Bartholomew Atton, bailiff of that town in 1604. A family of the name of Chandler is believed to have succeeded Atton.

Here is another account from the Churchwardens' Book :—

	s.	d.
P'd for a breakfast mayd at Will' Wayes for White of Redynge and the men of London, w^t other of o^r neybors for the seconde makyng for the g^t belle whyche were at charges upon us before........		ij

From this entry it appears that the cracked bell was very probably re-cast at Thame,† by the bell-founder's men who had come from Reading and London to superintend the work. At that period, when roads were bad and locomotion—with such weighty objects to carry—was difficult, there can be no doubt that bells were sometimes cast in the precincts of religious houses or in churchyards.

Again in 1545 this entry appears :—

	li.	s.	d.
It'm p'd to the Belfoundre as doth appere by a Byll indented........	iij	xiij	iv
It' p'd to the Cartter for caryage of the Bellis...		xxvj	viij

In 1548, when God's House was being robbed instead of furnished, certain bells were disposed of :—

	li.	s.	d.
It'm Rec^d for ye grete Bell & iij littel hand bells, sold to Richd Hylton, weying xxviij c. after the rat of xxvj^s ye c........	xxviij	viij	

Bell-metal, it may be here observed, consists ordinarily of one portion of tin to three of copper. The popular notion that silver was often used is not accurate. It was no doubt sometimes a custom to throw a few coins into the furnace; but of silver, more than this, there was none. Before the bell, when cast, was lifted up to its appointed place, it was formally blessed, consecrated, and named. A custom arose of there being sponsors at this blessing—which was sometimes loosely termed its "baptism." And the name of a saint or angel was commonly given to it. As regards this rite, more than a thousand years old—the grand and beautiful Litany of the Saints* was first sung, with psalms, antiphons, and prayers. The bell was then washed with hallowed water, and afterwards anointed with chrism and holy oil for the sick, after which it was incensed and solemnly blessed in the Name of the Holy Trinity by the Bishop.

There is an entry recording such an impressive and appropriate solemnity in the Churchwardens' "Accounts" of St. Lawrence, Reading, which stands thus :—

		s.	d.
1499.	It'm payed for halowing of the grete bell named Harry........	vj	viij
	And Mem' that Sr Will'm Symys, Richard Clerk and Maistres Smythe beyng godfadurs & godmoder at the consecracyon of the same bell, & beryng all o^r costys to ye suffryogan.		

A printed paper, not devoid of interest, which was circulated amongst the subscribers to a "Fund for Re-casting the Bells" in the year 1876, will be found amongst the Appendices, as it contains all the information concerning the work then voluntarily and enthusiastically undertaken by a true old-fashioned Churchman.

We now pass from the interior of the Church to the exterior—the character of which may be accurately judged from the illustrations embodied in this book. Later on, several additional notes and facts relating to persons long passed away, will serve to further set forth the history of the building and those who have worshipped God within its sacred walls. For of old all were baptized there, all who were married were joined together in its sanctuary; while those, who, from time to time, have ended their period of probation upon earth, were borne to Church and Churchyard to be laid at rest with Christian rites and solemn prayer, and wait for the Resurrection morning.

And firstly I remark that nothing can be finer nor more effective and dignified than the exterior of Thame Church—no matter from what point of view it is approached. This, let it be noted, is one of the unvarying features of old buildings. They look well from all sides and quarters. Unlike so many modern

* "In the two hundred years succeeding the Reformation—and more especially in the eighteenth century—as churches fell into decay in rural districts, a very common way of raising money to pay for the repairs was to petition the Bishop to grant a faculty empowering the parishioners to sell some of the bells, which they represented as being unnecessary, or as cracked, and so unfit for use."—*The Church Bells of Northamptonshire*, by Thomas North, F.S.A., p. 18. Leicester: 1878.

† Mr. Thomas North, F.S.A., in his most interesting *Bells of Northamptonshire* (pp. 10, 11), points out that such casting took place in mediæval times at St. Alban's Abbey, as also at Scalford in Leicestershire, and Empingham in Rutlandshire. Great Tom of Lincoln was cast in the Minster Yard in 1610, and the Great Bell of Canterbury in the Cathedral Yard there in 1762.

* See a local example of this Litany—that used in the old diocese of Lincoln—amongst the Appendices.

erections, built only to be seen from a single standing-point,* both the Church and the Old Grammar School are effective from every point of view. The tower, with its turret at the north-east angle, is of excellent proportions, and is seen for miles around. The building generally, though of different styles of architecture, is on the whole perfectly harmonious in its character, and rises from its ground-plan of a Latin cross, with great effect. The transepts are finely proportioned and well placed; the addition of the Chantry of St. Christopher was evidently made by a true artist and clever architect: the choir is perhaps the weakest point, because of its painfully depressed roof, which sadly needs amending and restoring to its ancient pitch. Such a restoration would add dignity to the building in general. The south porch, with its circular stone staircase or "vyse," capped with stone, and the parvise above the porch, is quite picturesque. The buttresses are admirably formed and well placed. Here, too, however, as elsewhere, the need of reparation and restoration is great. The mouldings of the outer door are decayed, and the niche above is empty. But this restoration should be effected by a thoroughly competent architect, whose tastes and feelings are in harmony with the sacred buildings of our Catholic forefathers, and not by any uneducated adventurer, ready at a moment's notice to build either a mansion, a drinking fountain, a meeting-house, or a garden wall; and in the "restoration" of churches to destroy, without thought, every feature of architectural interest and every existing object of archæological value.

In the year 1856 it was wisely resolved to add to the Churchyard. Because of the interments for so many centuries this need became apparent, and had to be at once supplied. Some persons desired a cemetery. The Earl of Abingdon, however, having been applied to, generously consented to sell an acre of land out of Court Close, for the nominal sum of £100, situated to the direct east of the old Churchyard. This part, having been cut off by a sunken fence, was set apart by prayer and the reciting of psalms by the Bishop of the Diocese, and has since been used. The expenses of making this addition—provided for both by rate and gifts—were very considerable, and out of all proportion to the cost of the land itself, amounting as was the case to the sum of £393 11s. 6d. Thus the proposal, which had been made, to have a cemetery was overruled, and the necessity for it removed. The cutting down of so many trees to the east of the Church, however, was no improvement.

Some of the various tombstones in the Churchyard are old; a few perhaps of the latter part of the sixteenth century: but all these, and most of those of the seventeenth century, are so much worn that their inscriptions cannot be deciphered. Prior to the Tudor changes a stone* or wooden cross was commonly erected at the head of the graves of the poor, with some such simple words as "Jesu mercy," "Miserere mei," "Ladye help," "May he rest in peace," "God be merciful to us." Such inscriptions, however, were ordered to be erased by some of the innovating prelates under Edward VI. and Elizabeth; and the crosses, which were distinctly and directly forbidden,† gave place to a long plank of wood, supported by two posts one at each end, at the head and foot of the grave,—on which plank the commemorative inscription was rudely painted. This kind of memorial remained popular for three centuries and more; but it has now gone of fashion. The once popular stone urns—which imply the use of cremation and the preservation of ashes; the inverted torches which appear to indicate annihilation, and the broken pillars which do not even teach the immortality of the soul, much less the Christian doctrine of the Resurrection of the body,—are still popular with some; but the use of the Cross—the sign of the Son of Man, the symbol of the World's redemption, and the distinguishing mark of a Christian, is now being very generally restored in the memorials of the departed.

Various Dissenters from the Established Church in times now passed, professed such a horror of consecrated ground, and of the Service for the Burial of the Dead, that—handing on the traditions of the Puritans, when the bodies of Christians only received "the burial of an ass"‡—they preferred to be buried elsewhere, in ground not consecrated. Katherine, the wife of John Geary, and Katherine Geary their daughter, and some others of their children, had been interred in a garden on the west side of Friday Street; but in the year 1761 their bodies were taken up and re-interred on the north side of the churchyard—to which removal an allusion is

* As the late Mr. Welby Pugin put this fact tersely, and in verse, regarding a dissenting meeting-house:—

"They reared a front of stone, all grand,
Just like Westminster Abbey:
But go to side or end, and stand,—
You'll find the back part shabby."

* An example of a stone cross with a coped head still remains in Handborough Churchyard, co. Oxon, a little to the left of the chief entrance; but it has no inscription now visible.

† "That there bee no crosses of wood made and erected in sundrie places, where thei vse to rest with the corpse; and especially that no Wodden Crosses be set vpon the Crosse in yᵉ Churchyard, or vpon, or about his grave.

* * * * * * *

"Item that there be no praiers made for the dead either in the house or vpon the waie, or els where; whiche thyng superstitiously hath been frequented and tollerated by the Ministers."—Bishop Middleton's *Injunctions*, A.D. 1583.

‡ "He shall be buried with the burial of an ass, drawn and cast forth beyond the gates of Jerusalem."—Jeremiah xxii. 19.

made on their monument. An "Independent Minister," the Rev. W. H. Whiffin, was also buried in front of a little meeting-house in the High Street; but his remains, literally his bones, were within the last twenty years dug up by some of his followers and removed to the Churchyard. Again, a certain Mr. William Burnard* desired to be buried in his own garden, with rites and ceremonies excogitated by himself; and expressed his desire in detail in his last Will and Testament; but some of his friends interfered after his death, and he too was buried in the Churchyard.

Here are now added a few of the oldest and most legible inscriptions remaining upon the tombstones. The destruction of these which has taken place, however, has been very great, as the following extracts, two from letters to myself testify:

One correspondent† writes as follows:—

"The Rose family owned a vault in the chancel near the burial-place of the Clerkes; but this was quite full at the beginning of the present century. Many of my relations were buried in the yard, to the right of the chief entrance, near the north side of the old mansion-house (now in ruins); and the coat of arms I bear was both cut and painted on two or three headstones."

Another, Professor Burrows of Oxford, who is sprung from a Thame family of the seventeenth century, has put the following, to the same effect, on record:—

"There was certainly a family vault (of the Burrows') in Thame Churchyard; and the remains of a score or more of our ancestors are lying there; but it cannot now be found. The gravestones have become entirely defaced by Time; and the most liberal promises to the Sexton, who has spent hours in rubbing the ancient inscriptions on the south side of the Church, where the stone was many years ago pointed out to my brother Henry, have produced no result."‡

And a third, who represents a very old family of the Town and its Hamlets,§ writes to the same effect:—

"The family of Hedges of Weston had a very large vault in Thame Churchyard, with a high iron-railing around it, and many inscriptions upon the tomb. It was quite full; but some alterations in the churchyard since the incumbency of your ancestor, necessitated its removal; and nothing now remains to mark the spot but a slab."

Here follow certain of the inscriptions referred to:—

South side.

. . . . . BODIE OF
RICHARD STRIBLEHILL
. . . . DIED . . . .
1765,
IN Y^E^ 40TH YEAR OF
HIS AGE.

✠ A friende to rich, a frende to poor,
God reste his soul for evermo'
And graunt him uppon Abram's breaste
A home of peace, a house of rest,
Thro' Christ Who dyed, but rose once more,
Thus opening wide high Heav'^ns^ door
That man might liue for ivermo' ✠

South side.

Here lyeth the Bodie
of
WILLIAM ROSE,
Gent,
Who died Ju 1638
Aged 41 yeeres.

North side.

In Memory of JOHN GEARY
Who was interred in this vault Sep. 27th
1761 by whose desire the remains of his Wife
KATHARINE GEARY
Who died Feb. 16th 1737 were with those of their
Children removed from their Burial Place
and Here deposited.
Also KATHERINE GEARY their Daughter
interred in this vault.

* Will of William Burnard of Thame, Schoolmaster:—"I direct that on the day of my interment my Body be removed into the schoolroom attached to my dwelling-house and placed on two Tressels without a Pall & that a Funeral Oration be pronounced over it by some able & well-educated Minister; that my dear friends Mr. Caterer & Mr. Howlett speak the dictates of their consciences, & offer up appropriate prayers: Hymns are to be sung and then my Body to be quietly removed into the Garden belonging to my dwelling-house, & there deposited in a brick grave prepared for the purpose, the relations only following. After a few words spoken at the grave they will return to the schoolroom,—the whole to be conducted in the most solemn manner, the three officiating ministers to be supplied with silk hatbands & gloves & paid their travelling expenses."—Will made May 17, 1834; proved June 19, 1835. From "Wills of the Peculiar of Thame," etc.

† Letter from Mr. J. Burrows Rose to the Author, dated 26 Sept., 1876.

‡ *History of the Family of Burrows of Sydenham and Long Crendon*, by Montagu Burrows, R.N., M.A., p. 10. (For Private Circulation only.) Oxford: 1877.

§ Letter of Mr. J. Kirby Hedges, J.P., to the Author, dated 6 June, 1882.

East side.

In Memory of
MARY Wife of
JOHN BESTON
who died April 2^{d} 1781 in
the 55 Year of her Age.

West side.

HERE LIETH THE BODY OF
RICHARD EYNOT
WHO DYED MARCH THE 4
1720 AGED 80 YEARS.

South side.

Here lieth the Body
of ELIZABETH TRIPP
who departed this life
January 12, 1731.
Aged 78 years.

In Memory
of JOHN TRIPP, died
May ye 21st 1765
In ye 30 Year of His Age.

Also SARAH His
daughter, died Jan. 23,
1770.

South side.

Here
lieth the body of
FRANCES the Wife of
THOMAS GIBBINS
Who Departed this Life
October the 31th
1746 Aged 64
Years.

South side.

HERE LIETH THE BODY OF
THOMAS THE SON OF
THOMAS & FRANCES
GIBBINS WHO DYED
JANUARY Y^{E} 22: 1730-1
AGED 15 YEARS 10 MONTHS.

South side.

In Memory of
FRANCES POWELL,
who departed this Life
the 11th of February 1726.
R.I.P.

South side. Altar-tomb of Freestone.
Claridge's tombe.

To the Memory of
WILLIAM CLARIDGE
who departed this Life
the 17th of July 1821
in the 64th Year of his Age.

In Memory of
WILLIAM C. HARDING
Born Dec. 20, 1793
Died June 23, 1870.

To the Memory of
ANN, Wife of
WILLIAM CLARIDGE,
who departed this life
April 23, 1844
Aged 78 Years.
Blessed are the dead
which die in the
Lord.
Rev. 14 Chap. 13 Vrs.

South side.

HERE LIETH Y^{E} BODY OF
MARY Y^{E} WIFE OF WILLIAM
DOBINSON. SHE DYED APRIL
Y^{E} 29TH 1713 AGED 39
YEARS 8 MONTHS 3 WEEKS.

South side.

In affectionate remembrance of
THE REVEREND JAMES PROSSER, M.A.
For 30 years Vicar of this Parish
He passed from this world to a brighter on the 15th
July 1877 in the 88th year of his age,
Of him it may be truly said that he believed the record that God gave
Of His Son "and this is the Record that God hath given to us Eternal Life,
And this Life is in His Son." 1 John v. 11.
His Life and his lips agreed in declaring:—
"In God is my salvation and my glory.
The Rock of my strength and my Refuge is in God." Ps. lxii. 7.
Clear in his views of Scripture Truth, firmly attached to the doctrines of
Sovereign grace, and a faithful preacher of Christ, a diligent and devoted
Pastor, sound in judgment, gentle in manners, and truly kind in heart. "To
him to live was Christ and to die was gain."

Sacred to the Memory of
REBECCA CHARLOTTE
The beloved wife of THE REVEREND JAMES PROSSER
Vicar of this parish:
She departed this Life March 6th 1856, aged 60 years.
Blessed and Holy are they that have part in the First Resurrection. Rev. xx. 6.

South side.

In Memory of
WILLm BOWLER
Who died Octr 2
1818 Aged 71
Years.

West side.

Payne's Monumt

To the Memory
of
HANNAH the Wife of
EDWARD PAYNE
who died 27th September 1814
Aged 60 Years.
Of
EDWARD PAYNE
who died 3rd October 1824
Aged 75 Years.
Of
JOB PAYNE his Brother
who died 29th March 1826
Aged 71 Years.

West side.

Of
EDWARD son of EDWARD
and HANNAH PAYNE
who died 9th February 1839
Aged 55 Years.
Of
EDWARD Son of EDWARD
and HANNAH PAYNE
who died 28th June 1848
Aged 37 Years.
And of
MARY the Widow of
EDWARD PAYNE
who died 30 April 1858
Aged 70 Years.

Stone. West end of Church exterior.
Removed from the South side near the South Porch.

HERE LYES THE BODY OF JOHN MAUND THE SON OF Mr ROBERT AND KATHERINE MAUND WHO DEPARTED THIS LIFE JANUARY 31, 1722. AGED 40 YEARS. ALSO HERE LYETH THE BODY OF WILLIAM MAUND THE SON OF Mr ROBERT AND KATHERINE MAUND WHO DEPARTED THIS LIFE JUNE 19, 1715, AGED 70 YEARS.

HERE LYETH THE BODY OF KATHERINE THE WIFE OF Mr ROBERT MAUND WHO DEPARTED THIS LIFE JANry 24, 1708. AGED 69 YEARS. ALSO THE BODY OF THEIR ELDEST SON ROBERT MAUND WHO DEPARTED THIS LIFE MARCH ye 15, 1708. AGED 44 YEARS.*

HERE LYETH THE BODIES OF VVILLIAM AND MARY WEBB HEE DEPARTED THIS LIFE DECEMBIR ...... 1588 .... AGED 79 YEARES SHEE DEPARTED THIS LIFE APRIEL THE 15 1589 AGED 76 YEERES.†

South side.

Here lyeth ye
Body of WILLIAM
FRIER of MORETON
Who departed
this life ye 24th day of
June 1679.

---

* There is another monument to the Maundes, adjoining those reproduced above, but it is so defaced by age and weather that its inscription is illegible.

† "In wandering about our churchyard some days ago, I discovered a stone which tells me it has been there three hundred years. I have had it cleaned, and taken the enclosed rubbings. Some of the letters are obliterated, and consequently imperfect. I thought you might like to know its antiquity."—Letter from the late Mr. Richard Lee, to the Author, dated 23 March, 1882.

South side.

The following Coat of Arms of the Loders appears on a stone without any remaining inscription :—

[Arms of Loder. Sable, six annulets, three, two, and one.]

South side.

In Memory of
JAMES WAY
who died Oct. 18
1823 Aged 63.
Also RUTH Wife
of JAMES WAY
who died Feby 3 1823
Aged 67 Years.

South side.

In Memory of
WILLIAM Son of
WILLIAM & MARY
WOOD
Who departed this life
Sept 25, 1816 Aged 20 Years.
Also ELIZn, GEORGE and MARY
Who died in their Infancy.

South side.

HENRY PALMER
FOOKES
Died Jany 16th
A.D. 1845
Aged 3 Years.
Of such is the Kingdom
of God.

West side.

In Memory of
JOHN BRAZELL
who died March 26th
1844
Aged 80 Years.
Also MARTHA
Wife of the above
died March 5th 1847
Aged 75 Years.

West side.

Sacred
to the Memory of
FRANCES THORP
who departed this life
March 4th 1843 Aged 44
Years.
Also of JOHN THORP
who departed this life
June 21st 1849 Aged 54 Years.

JANE youngest Daughter
of the above, died Novr 13, 1854
Aged 20 Years.

North side.

Sacred
to the Memory of
ROBERT HOWLAND
who Departed this life
Oct. 15th 1851
Aged 63 Years.
And of
ELIZABETH HOWLAND
His Wife
who died Feb. 28th 1878
in the 87th year of her age.
Also of
ELIZTH MARY FIELDING
His Grand-daughter
who died Oct. 16, 1865
Aged 22 Years.

Sacred
to the Memory of
ALFRED ROBERT,
son of ROBERT and
ELIZABETH HOWLAND,
Born February 5th 1828
Died May 6th 1879.

North side.

In Memory of
JOHN HOWLETT
who departed this life
January 17th 1845
Aged 81 Years.

In Memory of
ANN Widow of
JOHN HOWLETT,
who departed this life
February 28th 1846
Aged 78 Years.

West side.
ROBERT STAPLES
Born A.D. 1743
Died 26th April 1820.
MOLLY STAPLES
Born April 10th A.D. 1761
Died 8th Decr. 1844.
JANE STAPLES
Born 5th Novr A.D. 1789
Died 21st Decr 1840.
MARY SHRIMPTON
Born 9th April A.D. 1785
Died 7th March 1859.

Church exterior. West end.
Near
Lieth the Body of John Kent
Of Peace, Probity, Sobriety and
Industry, an Example Worthy
of Imitation.
Having acquired a Suitable Competency
He Retired from Business
Allowing himself those Necessarys
too Sparingly
which he Bounteously Bestowed
on his Friends and Relations.
Seduced by False Glosses and
Wrong Notions
He for some Time Ioyned a
Dissenting Congregation:
Till Awakened and Convinced
Of his Error: He Returned to the Church
of Whose most Excellent Devotions,
Doctrine, and Sacraments
he was a Constant and Zealous Attendant.
He died Dec. 21, 1737.
Aged 63.*

West side.
In Memory of
THO. LAWRANCE
Infant Son of
THOMAS & JANE
CASTLE
who died Nov. 17th
1848
Aged 6 Months.

North side.
In
Memory of
THOMAS SHEEN
who died Febry 6th
1826, Aged 67
Years.

Also
MARY his Wife
who died Sep. 13th
1827 Aged 70
Years.

Churchyard. Altar-tomb. South side.
In Memory of
ANN Wife of
JOHN JEMMETT
who died Nov. 21st 1783
in the 21st year of her Age.
Also of ANN their daughter
who died an infant 2d of
Jan. 1785
and JOHN their son
who died an infant
31st of Oct. 1785.

* The Will of John Kent of New Thame, Hatband-maker, made 20 Dec. 1737, proved 7 Feb. 1738.—"First and principally I commend my soul into the hands of Almighty God my Creator and most merciful Father, hoping through the merits, death & passion of my Blessed Lord & Saviour Jesus Xt to have full pardon and remission of my sins, and after this life to enjoy eternal happiness in His heavenly kingdom." He leaves £10 for the Lecturer of Thame (the Rev. John Kipling); also unto Mary Payne, daughter of William Payne of New Thame, £10. To Edward Randolph, yeoman, of Long Crendon, bond for £10. To Elizabeth, wife of Thomas Horne, £5. To the wife of Joseph Clark of Thame, one guinea; and to her son Joseph Clark, one guinea. Joseph Clark, John Emmerton, John Timothy, and James Eustace, "do carry me to Church," for their trouble to each is to be given one guinea. To Elizabeth Gibson, who lately lived with the Rev. Mr. Higgins, £5. To Susanna, wife of Isaac Claydon of Longwick, £5. To Charles Russell of Old Thame, one guinea; to the widow of Thomas Roberts, 50s.; to the widow of Stephen Prickett deceased, 50s. To wife of Daniel Eustace, one guinea. To Marian, Phillips and James Roberts, three of the children of Thomas Roberts deceased, one guinea. To John Timothy the elder, one guinea. To Hugh Allbright of Stony Stratford, £5. To Michael Penn of Stony Stratford, £5. To Mathew Loder of Thame and Thomas Crewe Executors and Trustees, each £10. Rest and residue to Thomas Russell of Priestend, and others.—From "Wills of the Peculiar of Thame," etc.

Churchyard. Altar-tomb. South side.

In Memory of
ELIZA (eldest) daughter of
WILLIAM and ELIZABETH
JEMMETT
who died 4 June 1798
Aged 19 Years.

O hastening Death and Heeling Time
To crop young flowers in their prime,
My days on earth run out apace
To win I hope a better place.

Churchyard. Altar-tomb. South side.

To the Memory of
Elizabeth Wife of
William Jemmett, Esqr
of Little Milton,
Who died July 28, 1804,
Aged 48 years.

Within this silent tomb lies buried here
A neighbour good, a tender mother dear;
For unto all she was both good and kind,
Which is well known to many left behind.*

* Thomas Jemmett of Little Milton, co. Oxon, Esq., was High Sheriff of the County in 1788.

Amongst other names, in addition to those already given, the following may be traced in various parts of the Churchyard; but the stones on which they appear are so decayed, overgrown with lichen, worn with rain and exposure, and sunk into the ground, that in almost every case little or nothing more than the bare names can be read; while any attempt to set forth the effaced inscriptions would be vain and misleading. Some names, however, are still perfectly legible: others with great care can be decyphered; as, for example, those of Talbot, Beston, Pettie, Smith, Mears, Stone, East, Peck, Sheen, Field, Prickett, Dobinson, Quartermain, Phillips, Sheldon, Wray, Greene, Wakeman, Willis, Phillips, Munt, Way, Cowper, Brasier, Bowdray or Bowdrey, Dorell, Crooke or Croke, Randolph, Saunders, Malins, Winslowe, Styles, and Cotton. But in most cases little more than the names remain.

To the left of the chief path leading to the southern porch—under the shadow of the lime-trees—were buried the Striblehills. A row of dilapidated tombstones, some put up as early as the year 1630, some as late as the year 1720, still stand, with illegible inscriptions.

Many of the above-enumerated families belonged to Thame for several centuries, and others were of a good position, of rank and substance. In some cases they have died out: in others their representatives have either migrated, or apparently ceased to take any interest in the preservation of their ancestral memorials. So true it is that the names of one generation are too readily blotted out of the memories of those who follow; and the departed are too soon forgotten.

Tota pulchra es, Maria,  et macula non est in Te.

CHAPTER THE THIRD.

The Churches of Tettesworth, Sydenham, Towersey, and North Weston; with Some Account of Rycott Chapel.

HESE Churches, or, as they were anciently styled, Chapelries (except the last-named), were originally attached to Thame Church, and were under the jurisdiction of the Prebendary and the Vicar—served, however, by Curates. About the year 1841 Tettesworth, Sydenham, and Towersey were disconnected from the Parish of Thame, and made into separate benefices.

Tettesworth.

THE Parish of Tettesworth is situated about three miles and a half, in a south-westerly direction, from Thame, and eleven miles and a half from Oxford. It is purely an agricultural village, old fashioned and picturesque, with several seventeenth-century houses here and there, lying on the main road from London, through Uxbridge and Wycombe, to Oxford. There are two good Inns in the place, which in the old coaching days was a village of considerable importance. It is said that within the memory of those living twenty-eight coaches passed through the place every day, and that more than two hundred coach and post horses were kept at the various hostels and inns. The place, however, has now a deserted and forsaken appearance; but being situated in a country where the grazing land is rich, and the landscape undulating, well wooded, and commanding extensive views, this village, though out-of-the-way and retired, is pleasant, for the air is pure, the drainage effectual, and the water good.

Here, as early as the eleventh century, lived the family of Chevauchesul, great benefactors to the Abbey of Thame Park. One of the daughters of this house, Matilda Chevauchesul, married Peter Talmache, of the neighbouring village of Stoke, afterwards called Stoke Talmache or Tallmache. Richard, of this last-named family, married Amicia, sister of Richard Taillard; Claricia, his sister, married Alan Clerke, of Tettesworth, and had issue Roger Clerke. From Richard and Amicia came Peter, Richard, Robert, and Ralphe Talmache. This last was a Cistercian monk of Thame Park.

In later times, amongst others, the families of Clerke, Danvers, Walkleyne, Deane, Sparrowhawke, Pettie, Cosens, Cave, Latham, and Cornish have been amongst the chief proprietors.

The old Church of St. Giles consisted of a nave and chancel with a square wooden bell-cote at the west end, and was very plain; originally no doubt Norman, but most of it of the first-pointed style, with later windows, some being of debased third-pointed work, inserted here and there in the nave. The old south doorway, within a wooden porch, was rude and bold, with a semi-circular tympanum* of stone, curiously carved, representing an *Agnus Dei* placed within a circle in the centre, with a

* An engraving of the *tympanum* of this doorway is given on p. 17 of the *Gentleman's Magazine* for January, 1790.

mitred Bishop bearing his pastoral staff of the old Tau-shape, and giving his blessing, on the dexter side, St. Birinus no doubt, and St. John the Baptist, or it may have been a religious or tonsured priest, pointing to the symbol of Our Lord, and bearing a book in his left hand, on the sinister. The hinges and iron-work of the old oak door were very rude and antique, the oaken porch being of fifteenth-century work, much dilapidated. At the north-west corner of the nave the masonry, indisputably of Anglo-Saxon character, was much loosened and decayed. But in construction it presented features characteristic of a very early period. A north door of the nave, exactly opposite that in the south porch, was of plain Norman work, with a Tau cross represented on a surface diapered with a design like fish-scales upon the semi-circular tympanum. This door had been long ago stopped up and plastered over, but was discovered when the building was demolished.

Amongst the stone fragments here found embedded in the wall, some of them belonging to the substantial *ornamenta* of the old Romanesque Church, were portions of what appeared to be an arcading of interlaced semi-circles, possibly a shrine, or more probably the reredos of some altar. The capital of an ancient *piscina*, with a bowl* and a drain, was also discovered. Of this I took a sketch, from which the accompanying woodcut has been made:—

Ancient Piscina, Ettesworth Old Church.

The chancel was certainly very ancient, probably of the early part of the twelfth century, Romanesque in character, the east window, of three lights, being second-pointed, but the chancel-arch and the north window were of Norman work. The east window of the chancel, of three plain lights, cusped in their heads, with two small trefoil-like openings between, was of good design, and of late first-pointed work. In its centre light were the arms of Adrian de Bardis, sometime Prebendary of Thame.† There was also a curious Romanesque semi-circular headed window on the north side of the sanctuary, very plain and severe, which contained several examples, now all lost, of an almost unique pattern of flowered quarries.* An engraving of one of these is given on the next page.

There was likewise a curious early Romanesque stoup for Holy Water, at the right hand side of the entrance, in the wall of the nave.† It consisted of an arch of interlaced carved-work of stone, with a projecting bason of very hard granite.‡ On either side there was a rude pillar of granite supporting the arch, and the whole stood very near to the floor, thus shewing that the ancient levels had been much altered. One cross-marked gravestone remained in the chancel, of which a representation is here given, and there were several slabs, from which the brasses had been removed, remaining in the chancel until the Church was pulled down.

Fragment of a Monumental Slab, Chancel, Ettesworth Old Church.

In the Harleian MSS. in the British Museum, No. 6365, the following record occurs. The brass referred

* I am disposed to think that the sculptured bowl is of a later period than the piscina itself.

† Harl. MSS., Brit. Museum, 6365. "Arms: Or, a bend lozengy gu., a border gobony."

* A Quarry, or "flowered quarry," is "a diamond-shaped piece of glass, with some monogram, motto, rebus, or device painted upon it. The word is probably derived from the French *carré*, a four-sided figure; although some maintain that it comes from quarrel (*quadrellum*, a small square). Quarries are said to be "flowered" when on each a flower is represented, or a floral device conventionally treated. Some are found of a first-pointed character, examples of which occur at Lincoln Cathedral, Stanton Harcourt, Oxfordshire, and Little Chigwell, Essex. These all contain an oak or other leaf very conventionally and boldly drawn. Fleurs-de-lys, single flowers, stars, floriated crosses, sprays of ivy, broom, lilies, roses, birds, beasts, monograms, mushrooms (as at Ockham Church, Surrey), inscriptions, short legends, and other devices, are very numerous. Quarries were largely used in church windows, as well as in those of religious houses.—*Glossary of Liturgical and Ecclesiastical Terms*, pp. 308-9. London: 1877.

† This is represented in my *Glossary of Liturgical and Ecclesiastical Terms*. But the engraving on p. 152 of that work was made from the very imperfect drawing of a mere youth, and inadequately represents the curious Holy Water stoup in question.

‡ Its position, and the fact that it had no drain, prove that it was a Holy Water stoup.

Flowered Quarry, Chancel, Tettesworth Old Church.

to is believed to have remained in the Church until the latter was pulled down in 1841.

"On a brass on the ground in the body of the Church [is] the picture of a man and his wife praying, under them this inscription :—

Pray for ye soules of John Greying & Alys his wife ye which John deceased ye xiii day of July in ye year of our Lord Mccccxxiii. On whose soules Jesu have mercy. Amen.

Under are two boys and a girl praying."

The following, from the original document, shews how completely Tettesworth Church had been cleared out of all its *ornamenta* and goods as early as the sixth year of King Edward the Sixth, *i.e.* in 1553.

Queen's Remembrancer, Miscellanea, Church Goods, Record Office.

Hundred of Thame.— . . . . . . ys indented and made the xvij . . . . . . in thys vj yere of the Rayne of our . . . . . . lorde Kyng Edwarde the vj^th . . . . . . chalice and surplesses of the p'rish above written delivered by Sr Franc^s Knolly^s, Sr Willia' Rainforde, Knights, Leonard Chamberlayne, Thomas Brigge, Edmunde Ashefild, Thomas Douloy, Esquires, unto the custody of Sr Christofer Annet, clerke, Christofer Grening, church^ward', to the use of our souevayne lorde the Kynge at all tymes when it shall please hym to receave the same.

Imp'mis one chalice of sylver w^tout a cou^r.

It' iij bells. — Chris'fer Allnot.

It' one surplesse. — Christofer Greyning.

The new Church, built a little more towards the north than the old, consists of a nave, a south aisle of five bays, without clerestory; a chancel, with a vestry on its north side; and a tower and spire over the south porch. It is of Early English or first-pointed work, and is of fair design and proportions, though not remarkable in any way as regards its architectural features; save that its tower and graceful spire are picturesque features in the landscape, and can be seen from a considerable distance. Designed by Mr. John Billing, of 38, Parliament Street, Westminster, its nave is sixty-two feet long by twenty-six feet broad. The chancel is twenty-six feet long by eighteen feet broad; while the length of the building is eighty-eight feet, and its breadth, including nave and south aisle, is exactly thirty-eight feet—proportions which are good. The east window of the chancel is of three lights. The chancel is raised by three steps at the chancel arch, and the sanctuary by a single additional step, further eastward. There are two pues placed stall-wise in the choir. The Communion-table and the pulpit are of pine-wood. The latter is too cumbersome: the former too small. There is no reredos, nor stained glass, and the sanctuary, consequently, is very bald and bare, while the building generally has a cold and desolate appearance. On the north side of the nave there are five double lancet windows; and the style of the other windows are throughout in harmony with the general plan. The roof of the south aisle, however, is ill designed, very heavy as regards its timbers, and an eyesore.

The font, of freestone and octagonal, standing on a slender shaft, and not raised upon steps, placed near the south-west door, is small and without any remarkable characteristics—of third-pointed character. It is certainly not the original font—"round and plain," which existed in 1793.

The Church accommodates 422 worshippers. Of the pine-wood seats in general, well designed and convenient enough, exactly 164 are appropriated; there are 153 free sittings, and there is further accommodation for 105 children. So that the population of the village, as far as the number of sittings is concerned, is here abundantly and well supplied with means for public worship. At the last Census it amounted to exactly 428—indicating a steady and considerable decrease.

The Communion plate consists of a modern silver chalice, of poor and debased workmanship, seven inches and three-quarters in height, and three inches and three-quarters across the bowl. There is a stoup or flagon of pewter of the eighteenth century, but of very poor design, and there are also two common pewter plates, one dated 1773.

I find the following old memorandum amongst my Collections, in a hand-writing of the last century:—

"At Tettesworth there is a peal of six bells, of which the tenor bell weighs five hundredweight. One bell is very old, and has the inscription **In Honor' Sancti Egidii** upon it. Three of these six bells were re-cast by Lester and Pack of Whitechapel, near London, and were re-hung by Samuel and Robert Turner, bell-hangers, *circa* 1770."

There are five bells and a saints' bell still remaining: but one of these is cracked, and only three are ordinarily used. That with the inscription relating to St. Giles is gone.

The Rev. John Witherington Peers, M.A., of St. Katherine's College, Cambridge, was the first Perpetual Curate of Tettesworth, on its being made a separate benefice in 1841. There is an excellent parsonage-house to the south-west of the Church, which was built about that period. The income of the benefice, however, is only £150 per annum. On the death of Mr. Peers, in 1876, he was succeeded by the Rev. William Edward Hancock, B.A., Cantab., who resigned the appointment in 1878. To him succeeded, in the same year, the Rev. John Armstrong Coghlan, M.A., Dublin, who is the present Vicar.

The Registers and Parochial Books of the Church, in very fair preservation and order, are kept in an iron safe in the vestry. From these the following extracts have been taken:—

The Churche Booke of Tetsworth

with all the names of those that were baptized, & of those that were dead, & of those that were married: it is truly compared with the old booke & it begins from the yeere of our Lord God one thousand six hundred & four as followeth:—

Agnes Dormer the daughter of Rich'd Dormer was baptized May 1, 1604.

Maximilian Pettie the son of Joh' Pettie was baptized June 3, 1617.

Leonard Pettie the son of John Pettie was baptized March 2, 1620.

Anne Pettie the daughter of Charnell Pettie was baptized June 2, 1619.

Anno D'ni 1658.

Eleoor Deane the daughter of Aaron Deane was borne Jan. 19, 1658.

1660. Henry Deane the son of Aaron Deane was Borne July 4, 1660.

1663. Joan Deane the daughter of Aaron Deane was borne ffeb. 4, 1662.

1665. Mary Dean the daughter of Aaron Dean was baptized September ye 29th 1665.

1668. Aaron Deane son of Aaron Dean was baptized July 3, 1668.

Edwd Rose ye son of Will' Rose & Jone his wife Baptized May ye 22, 1698.

Meary Cosons the dafter off Thomas Cossons and Meary his wiffe was baptiesed the 5 day off September in 1714.

Elesabeth Cossons the dafter off Thomas and Maary Cossens his wiff was baptyesed the 23 day of Desember in 1716.

Ann Cosense the dafter off Thomas Cossons and Meary his wiffe was baptyesed the 8 day of May in 1719.

hester Cossons the dafter off Thomas Cossons and Meary his wiffe was baptiesed the 25 day of October in 1721.

(Baptisms continued.)

Katherine Cosens d^r of Thomas Cosens & Hester his wife.

Robert & Mary twin son & daughter of Thomas Cosens & Hester his wife, August 20, 1749.

Hester ye D^r of Thomas Cosens & Hester his wife Aug. 26, 1750.

1753. Oct. 25. Thomas son of Thomas & Hester Cosens.

1754. June 25. John S. of Thomas & Hester Cosens.

1756. May 2. Judeth daughter of Thomas & Hester Cosens.

1758. Aug. 6. William Son of Thomas & Hester Cozens.
1759. Dec. 23. Olife d. of Tho's & Hester Cozens.
1761. March 7. Honour d. of Thos & Hester Cozens.
1777. Dec. 25. Thomas son of John & Ann Cozens.

Marriages. Anno D'ni.

1625. Thomas Widmer & ffrances pettie were married Oct. 8, 1625.

1626. William Davis & Elenor Pettie were married Decemb' 18, 1626.

An'o D'ni.

1675. Mr Richd Playstow of West Wickham in the county of Bucks & Mrs Elenor Gibbons of Chipping Wickham in the county of Bucks, were married at Tetsworth by virtue of a license June 12, 1675.

1680. Mr William Clerke Vicr of Thame & Mrs Joan Burnham of Crendon were marryed August ye 8 at Tetsworth 1680.

The two married the 25th of August 1709 are Richard Aston, son to Sir Willoughby Aston & Elizabeth Warren of Wantage, Daughter of Mr John Warren of same place.

1747. Wellbore Ellis, Esq., of St. Martin's in the Fields, & Elizabeth Stanhope of St. George's Hanover Square, Middlesex, Nov. 21, 1747.

(*Note.*) July 9, 1751. The Rev. Mr Thornbury died, & was succeeded by Sampson Letsome, M.A.

Thomas Gadbury
Ann Cornish } married by License 14 Nov. 1757.

John Allen
Mary Cornish } married by License 29 Dec. 1757.

Humphrey Briaris
Elizabeth English } married by License 21 Feb. 1758.

Thomas Ward of Long Compton
Mary Latham of Tettesworth } married by License 16 Feb. 1706.

Adam Ballenger of New Woodstock
Ann Hobday of Tetsworth } married by License 2 Aug. 1760.

Charles Millward of Reading
Hannah Allen of Tetsworth } married by License 18 July 1762.

John Biggerstaff of St. Mary's, Islington
Ann Latham } married by License 14 Aug. 1762.

John Latham
Catherine Cozens } married by License 19 April 1766.

Gamaliel Hodgkinson Bobart of New Woodstock
Sarah Hobday } married by License 28 May 1767.

Robert Leaver of Wallingford
Hester Cozens } married by License 18 May 1776.

John Cozens of Tetsworth
Ann Hester of Dormer's Leys } married by License 26 Dec. 1776.

John Eeles of Thame
Judith Cozens } married by License 16 Aug. 1781.

William Cox of Eythorpe
Olive Cozins } married by License 4 Sep. 1783.

Burials.

Aaron Deane was buried March 9, 1676.
1685. Joan Dean the daughter of Aaron Dean was baryed September ye 5th.
1739. Elizabeth Cursons the wife of Thomas Cozens was Burd May 9th 1739.
1748. Richard Deane, Sep. 14, 1748.
1797. Sep. 20. Robert Cozens, farmer.
1806. 19 June. Esther Cozens, widow.

Only the following monumental memorials remain in the Church. Great destruction has taken place in the past:—

South side of Chancel. Black and white marble.

Beneath lie the Remains of
Mr THOMAS COZENS
who died 29th of August 1789,
in the 77th year of his age.

In Memory of
ROBERT COZENS,
who died Sepr 17th 1797,
aged 48 years.

Also ESTHER Wife of the above
THOMAS COZENS,
died 16 June 1806. Aged 88.

THOMAS COZENS,
born Nov. 14, 1755,
Died Decr 20th 1834, aged 81.

North side of Chancel. Black and white marble.

SACRED
TO THE MEMORY OF
CHARLOTTE,
WIFE OF JOHN COZENS
WHO DIED MARCH 18TH 1860,
AGED 35 YEARS.

"BLESSED ARE THE DEAD
WHICH DIE IN THE LORD."
REV. C. XIV. V. 13.

ALSO OF THE ABOVE
JOHN COZENS,
WHO DIED AUGUST 29TH 1879
AGED 64 YEARS.

"WHETHER WE LIVE THEREFORE
OR DIE, WE ARE THE LORD'S."
ROM. C. XIV. V. 8.

North side of Nave. White and black marble.

THIS TABLET
IS ERECTED BY THE PARISHIONERS
OF TETSWORTH,
IN AFFECTIONATE REMEMBRANCE OF
JOHN WITHERINGTON PEERS, M.A.,
WHO LOVINGLY MINISTERED AMONGST
THEM FOR 34 YEARS.
HIS DEEP SYMPATHY IN ALL THEIR
NEED,
HIS COURTEOUS BEARING,
AND HIS FAITHFUL TEACHING,
ENDEARED HIM TO ALL.
HE LEFT HIS FIELD OF LABOUR HERE
TO ENTER INTO
HIS OWN QUIET HOME,
TO BE WITH CHRIST WHICH IS FAR BETTER,
ON THE 28TH OF MARCH 1876,
AGED 71 YEARS.

WHILE I DRAW THIS FLEETING BREATH;
WHEN MY EYELIDS CLOSE IN DEATH;
WHEN I SOAR TO WORLDS UNKNOWN,
SEE THEE ON THY JUDGMENT THRONE;
ROCK OF AGES CLEFT FOR ME,
LET ME HIDE MYSELF IN THEE.

As regards the Churchyard, it certainly must be admitted that the work of destruction has been excessive. Nearly forty ancient gravestones have been removed from their places, and used as paving-stones for the pathway between the south gate and the south porch. Some of these, in their original state, were deeply and elaborately carved; and here and there remains of armorial bearings may be distinguished. There are, nevertheless, several handsome altar-tombs remaining in the Churchyard, to the memory of the families of Cozens, Hobday, Latham, and others. The following are a few of the existing inscriptions:—

West side.

In Memory of
JOHN MORRIS Who died
July 4th 1798 aged 34 years.
Also ELIZ. his Wife Who died
May 4th 1796 aged 32 years.

South side.

Sacred
To the Memory of
JOHN youngest Son of JOHN and ANN COZENS,
Who departed this life
The 23rd Day of April 1836,
in the 48th Year of his age.

Sacred
to
the Memory of
THOMAS COZENS,
Who departed this life
March 28th 1857 Aged 79
years.

Also ANN PRISCILLA,
Wife of the above-named
THOMAS COZENS,
Who died Dec. 17th 1863
Aged 83 Years.

Sacred
to the Memory of
ROBERT COZENS,
Who departed this
life Novbr 22nd 1858
Aged 77 years.

Sacred
To the Memory
of MARY Relict of
ROBERT COZENS,
Who departed
This life Dec. 20th
1868. Aged 84
Years.

Sacred
to the Memory
of BETSY, Daughter of
ROBERT and MARY
COZENS,
Who died the 18th of Jan.
1870, Aged 60
years.

In Memory of
ANN COZENS,
Wife of JNo COZENS,
Who died
19 March 1811
Aged 52 Years.

Also the before named
JOHN COZENS,
Who died June 1st 1836
Aged 81 Years.

South-east side.
Sacred
To the Memory of
JOHN GRINELL,
Who died Feb. 10th
1837
Aged 60 Years.

Sacred
to
the Memory of
MARY Wife of
JOHN GRINELL
who died May 7th
1842
Aged 70 years.

Here
lyeth the Body of
IOHN FETTYPLACE,
who dy'd Augst ye 4th 1763,
Aged
49 Yeeres.

His Bodie here in dust dothe reste,
Sin caus'd that Earth claim'd it as dve:
God give Him peace in Hearn bleste,
Christ give him light; make all things new.

In Memory of
ELIZABETH,
Wife of JOHN
COPPOCK,
Died August 10, 1809
Aged 68.

Also
JOHN COPPOCK
Who died April 9th
1835 aged 84.

High tomb. South side.
In Memory of JOHN DALE,
Who died April 25th 1848
Aged 65 years.

In Memory of
MARY WEST,
Who died March 21
1845
aged 78 years.

In Memory of
SARAH, Wife of
RICHARD TRAY,
Who died April 7th
1802 Aged 83.

In Memory of
FRANCES the Wife
of JOSEPH KEELY,
Who departed this life
Aug. ye 21st 1780
Aged 36 years.

Hughes monument.
Sacred to the Memory of
JAMES FLEET SHRIMPTON,
Who suddenly departed this life
Oct. 24th 1852 aged 48.

May thy dear Spirit rest in peace
Till the great day of Christ shall come;
Then may'st thou dwell in endless bliss
With the Eternal Three in One!

In Memory of
EDWARD SHRIMPTON,
Who died May 22, 1848
Aged 75 years.

Also of SARAH
SHRIMPTON his Wife
Who died July 24th 1852
Aged 85 years.

In Memory of
MARY, Daughter of
THOS. and MARY
SHRIMPTON,
Who died Febry 9, 1859
Aged 15 years.

Altar-tomb. Churchyard.
Sacred to the Memory of
Mrs ANN HUGHES late of Thame
Who died Dec. 19th 1847 Aged 70
Years.
Her end was peace.

Also of
Mrs ANN SHRIMPTON
Daughter of the above and Wife of
Mr JAMES SHRIMPTON of this parish,
She died May 22nd 1848 Aged 38 years.

She soon left this transient scene,
But she shall live again Oh Death!

To
the Memory of
MARY, Wife of
THOS. SHRIMPTON,
Who died Dec. 13th 1843
Aged 34 years.

Also of
THOS. SHRIMPTON
the beloved Husband
of the above,
Who died March 17, 1851
Aged 42 years.

South side.
In Memory of
JOHN LINDARS,
Who died 30 June
1801 aged 47.

In Memory of
THOs LATHAM,
Who died 5 June
1800 Aged 44
Years.

In Memory of
ALICE, Wife of
THOs LATHAM,
Who died Nov. 8th
1839
Aged 92 years.

All these various memorials, as will be seen, relate to recent times. Neglect and destruction have caused the loss of many of those which formerly existed. The family of *Greening*, two members of which have been already referred to, possessed property here in the sixteenth century, having come hither from Haseley, where several monuments to them recently remained; and there was an altar-tomb standing about two centuries ago, in memory of certain members of the family belonging to this village. To the north of the Church, on the road to Thame, is a field of about twenty acres still called "The Hermitage," indicating, no doubt, the residence of a hermit as early as the reign of King John. It is a tradition that Peter of Talmache (A.D. 1207) granted certain lands in the exact locality in question, to enable a religious to guard a ford, maintain a foot-bridge, recite the divine office, and keep a lamp burning before an image of the Blessed Virgin; and that this gift was confirmed by Richard, the son of the aforesaid Peter, and testified to by Ralph Ffoliot and Richard, his son, by William de Bruges, Nicholas D'Oili, Herbert Quatermain, Alan Clerke, and others. In the time of Adrian de Bardis the Shrine or Hermitage Chapel, having fallen into decay, was repaired on the same occasion that the chancel of Tettesworth Church underwent reparation. Whether the hermit was a clerk in orders, or only a member of some religious order, or whether he was in any way attached to, or under the jurisdiction of, the Abbot of Thame, seems uncertain. His pious labours, however, tended both spiritually and temporally to benefit his fellow Christians.

At Horsendon, between Tettesworth and Thame, a family which took its name from the place, de Horsendon, resided for several generations. The following descent is taken from the Chartulary of Thame Abbey:

Richard de Horsendon of Horsendon, = Matilda.
co. Oxon.

1. Richard de Horsendon of = Cecilia.
the same place.

2. John de
Horsendon.

The son, Richard, granted forty acres to Serlo, Abbot of Thame, at the instigation and request of his mother; and John, her younger son, also gave a grant of lands, subsequently confirmed by the Lord of the demesne. "Horsendon-hill" is the name given to a considerable rise in the ground in the locality described, though no remains of any important residence or mansion can now be traced.

THE following Pedigrees of the Family of Pettie or Petty are now set forth. As will be seen, the Petties have intermarried with members of many of the most ancient houses of this part of Oxfordshire.

Pedigree of Pettie or Petty.

No. I.

[These Pedigrees are founded on that compiled by Anthony à Wood, and preserved amongst his MSS. in the Bodleian Library. They have been modernized in their spelling, and many considerable additions have been made to them.]

"John le Petite vel Pety vel Pettie de Tettesworth in Co. Oxon; ob. mense Feb. 1529, sepultus in cœmeterio de Tettisworth sub muro chori vel cancelli eccl'æ ejusd."—*Anthony à Wood.* = Alice, sister to John Sparhauke, Gent. She died about the latter end of August 1546 (*ult. ann. Hen. VIII.*), and was buried by her husband in Tettesworth Church.

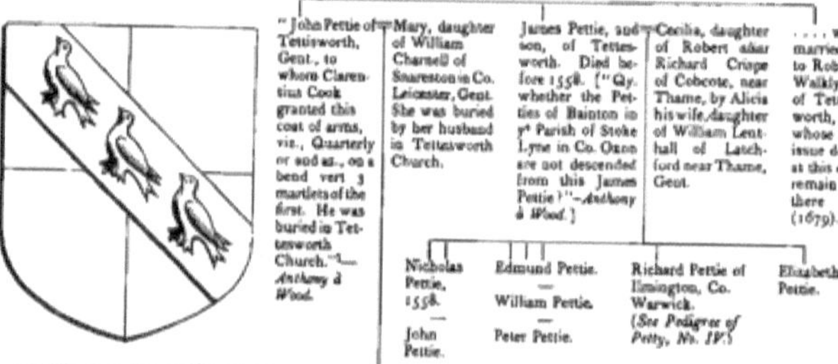

- "John Pettie of Tettisworth, Gent., to whom Clarentius Cook granted this coat of arms, viz., Quarterly or and az., on a bend vert 3 martlets of the first. He was buried in Tettesworth Church."—*Anthony à Wood.* = Mary, daughter of William Charnell of Snareston in Co. Leicester, Gent. She was buried by her husband in Tettesworth Church.
- James Pettie, 2nd son, of Tettesworth. Died before 1558. ["Qy. whether the Petties of Bainton in yᵉ Parish of Stoke Lyne in Co. Oxon are not descended from this James Pettie?"—*Anthony à Wood.*] = Cecilia, daughter of Robert alias Richard Crispe of Cobcote, near Thame, by Alicia his wife, daughter of William Lenthall of Latchford near Thame, Gent.
  - Nicholas Pettie, 1558. — John Pettie.
  - Edmund Pettie. — William Pettie. — Peter Pettie.
  - Richard Pettie of Ilmington, Co. Warwick. (*See Pedigree of Petty, No. IV.*)
  - Elizabeth Pettie.
- . . . . was married to Rob't Walklyne of Tettesworth, whose issue doth at this day remain there (1679).

Issue of John Pettie of Tettisworth and Mary Charnell:

- John Pettie of Stoke Talmache, near Tettesworth, in Co. Oxon, eldest son. Died 9 April 31 Q. Eliz., *i.e.*, 1588. Buried at Stoke Talmache. = Elizabeth, daughter and heir of Thomas Snape or Snapp of Fawler, near Witney, Co. Oxon, by his wife . . . . Annesley of Mapledurham. This Elizabeth Snape was buried in Thame Church. = John Browne, M.A., Rector of Loughborough, Co. Leicester. Was 2nd husband to Elizabeth Snape, having been married to her in St. Peter's Church in the East in Oxford, 21 Dec. 1611. Died s.p.
- Christopher Pettie of Tettesworth, 2nd son. Married . . . . daughter of . . . . Lamborne of Lambourne, Co. Berks.
- Robert Pettie of Wivold, near Reading, Co. Berks, 3rd son. (*See Pedigree of Petty, No. II.*)
- George Pettie. A scholar of Christ Church, Oxford. Vide *Hist. Oxon*, vol. ii., p. 167. Died s.p. — Henry Pettie of Thame.
- Frances, was first married to John Ray of Hagbourne, Co. Oxon, and afterward to Leonard Lydcott of Checkendon, Co. Oxon, son of Christopher Lydcott of Rushcombe, Co. Berks, by Catherine, daughter of Sir Robert Cheney of Chesham Bois, Co. Bucks, Knt.

Issue of John Pettie of Stoke Talmache and Elizabeth Snape:

Anne, daughter of Stephen Breise or Brice of Witney, Co. Oxon, by Maude, daughter of Thomas Yate of the same place. "Norton was named after this Family Breise-Norton." = John Pettie of Stoke Talmache aforesaid, 1 son. = Anne, daughter of . . . . Johnson of Witney, widow of Thomas Webley of the same place, clothier, and wife. She died 1622, and was buried in Witney Church.

A | B | C

A | B | C

John, Robert, Stephen, and other children. } Died s.p.

Thomas Pettie. Sold his lands, lived at Witney, and died a poor man, Anno 1660. Buried in Witney Churchyard, aged 63.

Elizabeth Pettie, was married to Richard Hale of Staffordshire, son of Edward Hale of Compton in the same county.

Anne Pettie, was married to .... Cox of Staffordshire.

—

Alice Pettie, was married to .... Chamberlaine of Kirtlington in Co. Oxon.

Dorothy Pettie, was married to William Gore of Sandwell Chapel, near London.

Mary Pettie, was married to .... Kettlesby of Staffordshire, brother to Edmund Pettie's wife.

Maud Pettie, the 2nd daughter, was married to Robert Bowman of Haly, near Witney, Co. Oxon.

—

Frances Pettie, was married to .... Grey of London, Civil Lawyer.

Edmund Pettie. Married the daughter of .... Kettlesby of .... Co. Stafford.

Maximilian Pettie. Married Mary, daughter of his uncle Leonard Pettie.

Leonard. Died s.p.

Rebecca. Born A.D. 1612. Was married to John Ellis, Rector of Wheatfield in Co. Oxon. She died 6 Nov. 1631, aged 19, s.p. Buried in Thame Chancel.

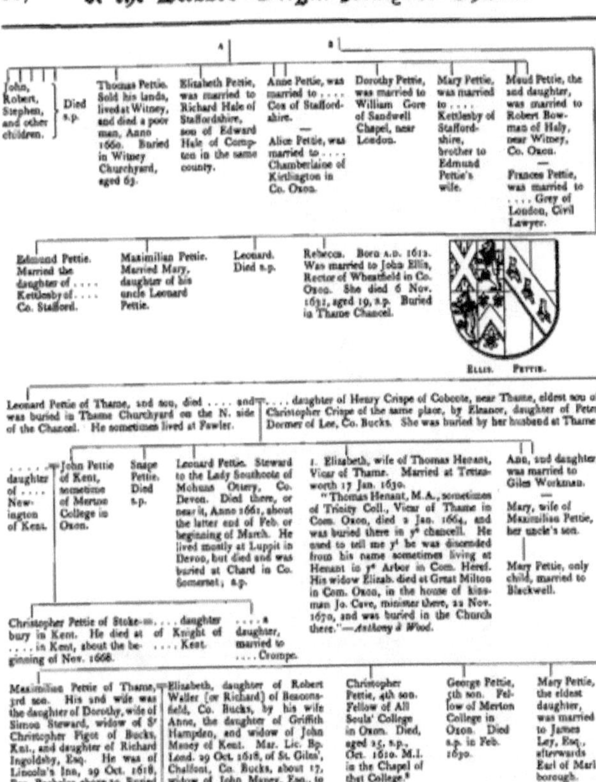

Ellis. Pettie.

Leonard Pettie of Thame, 2nd son, died .... and was buried in Thame Churchyard on the N. side of the Chancel. He sometimes lived at Fawler. = ... daughter of Henry Crispe of Cobcote, near Thame, eldest son of Christopher Crispe of the same place, by Eleanor, daughter of Peter Dormer of Lee, Co. Bucks. She was buried by her husband at Thame.

.... daughter of .... Newington of Kent. = John Pettie of Kent, sometime of Merton College in Oxon.

Snape Pettie. Died s.p.

Leonard Pettie. Steward to the Lady Southcote of Mohuns Ottery, Co. Devon. Died there, or near it, Anno 1661, about the latter end of Feb. or beginning of March. He lived mostly at Luppit in Devon, but died and was buried at Chard in Co. Somerset; s.p.

1. Elizabeth, wife of Thomas Henant, Vicar of Thame. Married at Tetsworth 17 Jan. 1630.

"Thomas Henant, M.A., sometimes of Trinity Coll., Vicar of Thame in Com. Oxon, died 2 Jan. 1664, and was buried there in ye chancell. He used to tell me y^t he was discended from his name sometimes living at Henant in ye Arbor in Com. Heref. His widow Elizab. died at Great Milton in Com. Oxon, in the house of kinsman Jo. Cave, minister there, 22 Nov. 1670, and was buried in the Church there."—*Anthony à Wood.*

Ann, 2nd daughter, was married to Giles Workman.

—

Mary, wife of Maximilian Pettie, her uncle's son.

Mary Pettie, only child, married to Blackwell.

Christopher Pettie of Stokebury in Kent. He died at .... in Kent, about the beginning of Nov. 1668. = ... daughter of Knight of .... Kent.

.... a daughter, married to .... Crompe.

Maximilian Pettie of Thame, 3rd son. His 2nd wife was the daughter of Dorothy, wife of Simon Steward, widow of Sr Christopher Pigot of Bucks, Knt., and daughter of Richard Ingoldsby, Esq. He was of Lincoln's Inn, 29 Oct. 1618, Esq. Bachelor, above 30. Buried at Thame 26 Aug. 1639. = Elizabeth, daughter of Robert Waller (or Richard) of Beaconsfield, Co. Bucks, by his wife Anne, the daughter of Griffith Hampden, and widow of John Maney of Kent. Mar. Lic. Bp. Lond. 29 Oct. 1618, of St. Giles', Chalfont, Co. Bucks, about 17, widow of John Maney, Esq., to marry at St. Leonard's, Foster Lane.

Christopher Pettie, 4th son. Fellow of All Souls' College in Oxon. Died, aged 25, s.p., Oct. 1610. M.I. in the Chapel of that College.[8]

George Pettie, 5th son. Fellow of Merton College in Oxon. Died s.p. in Feb. 1630.

Mary Pettie, the eldest daughter, was married to James Ley, Esq., afterwards Earl of Marlborough.

Joane Pettie, 2nd daughter. Married 1st to George Lee of North Aston, Co. Oxon; 2ndly to Thomas Darcell of London, Barbary Merchant, by whom she had issue; 3rdly to John Brookes of Lewknor, Co. Oxon, by whom she had issue, Nicholas Brookes, s.p.; and 4thly to .... Ives of Great Milton, Co. Oxon.

Anne Pettie, 3rd daughter. Married to Hugh Bethom, Gent., 3rd son of Christopher Bethom of Adwell, Co. Oxon, by Margaret, daughter of Edward Symeons or Simons of Pyrton Manor, sometimes living at Wheatfield in Co. Oxon, and at Adwell.

Alice Pettie, 4th daughter. Married to William Peesley of Ascott-under-Whichwood, Co. Oxon. She had Elizabeth Peesley, married to Humphrey Lewes of Chesterton Grange, near Bicester (but born in Wales), who had John Lewes, *cœlebs* 1679.

Phillippa Pettie, 5th daughter (yet older than Maximilian her brother), was married to William King of Great Milum, Co. Oxon, Gent., where she died in Feb. 1663, aged *circa* 86, and was buried in the Church. Her son, Philip King of Thame, died s.p. about the time his said mother died.

D

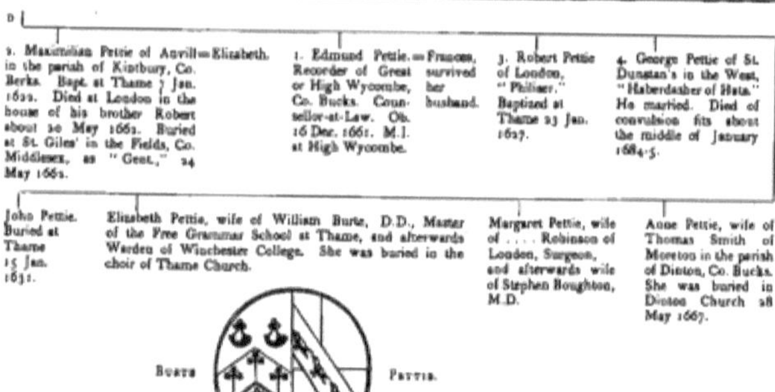

D

2. Maximilian Pettie of Auvill = Elizabeth. in the parish of Kintbury, Co. Berks. Bapt. at Thame 7 Jan. 1622. Died at London in the house of his brother Robert about 20 May 1662. Buried at St. Giles' in the Fields, Co. Middlesex, as "Gent.," 24 May 1662.

1. Edmund Pettie. = Frances, survived her husband. Recorder of Great or High Wycombe, Co. Bucks. Counsellor-at-Law. Ob. 16 Dec. 1661. M.I. at High Wycombe.

3. Robert Pettie of London, "Philiser." Baptized at Thame 23 Jan. 1627.

4. George Pettie of St. Dunstan's in the West, "Haberdasher of Hats." He married. Died of convulsion fits about the middle of January 1684-5.

John Pettie. Buried at Thame 15 Jan. 1631.

Elizabeth Pettie, wife of William Burte, D.D., Master of the Free Grammar School at Thame, and afterwards Warden of Winchester College. She was buried in the choir of Thame Church.

Margaret Pettie, wife of .... Robinson of London, Surgeon, and afterwards wife of Stephen Boughton, M.D.

Anne Pettie, wife of Thomas Smith of Moreton in the parish of Dinton, Co. Bucks. She was buried in Dinton Church 28 May 1667.

BURTE — PETTIE.

♣♣♣♣♣♣♣♣♣♣♣

Pedigree of Pettie or Petty.

No. II.

Richard Taverner, Lord of the Manor of Woodeaton, Co. Oxon, Esq., Clerk of the Signet to King Henry VIII. and King Edw. VI. High Sheriff of Oxon Anno 12 Eliz., *i.e.* 1568. Buried at Woodeaton 19 July 1575. = Mary, one of the daughters of *Sir* John Harcourt of Stanton Harcourt, Co. Oxon, Knt. (2nd wife.) Married in Feb., 6th year of Q. Eliz. Remarried Cromwell Lee, Esq., of the family of Lees of Ditchley, Co. Oxon, but had no issue by him. (See Vol. i., *Athenæ et Fasti Oxon.*, *sub Anno* 1601.)

Penelope Taverner. Baptized at Woodeaton 8 Sept. 1566. Died Nov. 1641 at Charlemont, Ireland, the seat of her nephew William, Viscount Caulfeild. = Robert Petty of Wiveold, Co. Oxon, Gent. Captain of the Trainband in Oxford. Third son of John Petty of Stoke Talmach and Tetterworth, Esq. Buried at Cotsford 10 May 1612.

Harcourt Petty. Matriculated at Corpus Christi College, Oxon, 30 Oct. 1607, aged 16, afterwards M.A. of Gloucester Hall. He hath had two wives and several children. He died at Bicester 18 June 1660. Buried at Bicester Church.

Francis Petty. Matriculated at Corpus Christi College, Oxon, 30 Oct. 1607, æt. 14. Died on the seas without issue. He was called by some "Jock Petty."

Mary Petty. = Thomas Wood. Born at Islington 1580. Subsequently of the parish of St. John the Baptist, in Oxford, Gent. Ob. 19 Jan. 1643. Mary Petty Ob. 28 Feb. 1669, aged 65.

Anthony à Wood, 4th son. Born 17 Dec. 1632. Educated at Thame Grammar School. M.A. of Merton College, Oxon. Author of *Athenæ Oxonienses*, etc. Ob. 28 Nov. 1695, æt. 64.

♣♣♣♣♣♣♣♣♣♣♣

Pedigree of Pettie or Petty.

No. III.

Christopher Pettie, Lord of the Manor of Tettesworth. 2nd son of John Pettie, Gent. Died Anno 1614, and was buried in Tettesworth Church. = ... daughter of . . . . Lambourne of Lambourne, Co. Berks. Buried in Tettesworth Church. = John Pettie (son of James Pettie). "Her 1st husband, as I have been informed."—*Anthony à Wood.*

Charnell Pettie of Tettesworth. High Sheriff of Co. Oxon 1653. Died at Stoke Lyne, near Bicester, Co. Oxon, in the house of Ralph Holt, his grandson, on 11 Feb. 1660-1, and was buried in the chancell there, aged 82 or more.[3] = Ellen, daughter of Edmund Wilson of . . . . Co. Essex, Gent. Died at Stoke Lyne 10 March 1661, and was buried by her husband, aged 85 and more. The said Edmund married Gertrode, daughter of . . . . After Wilson's death she was married to . . . . Wade.

A daughter, married to . . . . Crispe, son of Christopher Crispe of Cobcote, near Thame, by Eleanor Dormer, his wife.

Dorothy, daughter of Sir Richard Moore of Bledlow, Co. Bucks, 1st wife, s.p. Buried in the chancel of Stoke Lyne, near to the door. Sir Richard Moore was Master of the Chancery, and the said Dorothy was widow of . . . . Keyt or Kate. = Christopher Pettie, eldest son. Died at Stoke Lyne about Michaelmas Anno 1651, and was buried at Stoke Lyne in the north aisle of the Church. = "Judith, daughter of Nicholas Bost of Bicester, sister of John Bost of Woodead in Cumnore, Co. Berks. She died in her brother Bost's house in Grandpoole, in Oxford, 6 Dec. 1661, and was buried in the upper end of St. Aldate's chancel in that city. She had formerly been a servant maid to her husband's 1st wife."—*Anthony à Wood.*

George Pettie, a younger son. Died circa 1643, aged 24, and was buried in Stoke Lyne Church, s.p.

Christopher Pettie of Tettesworth. "Aged 30 or thereabouts A.D. 1679. He sold part of his lands at Tettesworth to his kinsman Christopher Wood in April 1680. The Manor House and other lands there to the said Christopher Wood in the beginning of 1683, at which time he sold more of his lands, worth £2000 and above, to Thomas Phillips of Ickford, Co. Bucks, Attorney-at-Law. Went away from Milton to seek his fortune about Lent 1687-8."—*Anthony à Wood.* Buried at Thame 7 Jan. 1739.[4] = Hester, daughter of Robert Parsons of Great Milton, Co. Oxon, Gent. Baptized there 9 Jan. 1650. Married 21 April 1674. Buried 10 June 1697.

Ellen Pettie, was married to George Cave, her first cousin, a younger son of John Cave, Clerk, M.A., Vicar of Great Milton. George Cave's Will was made 20 April, and proved 31 May, 1704.

Charnell Pettie. Baptized at Great Milton 21 Feb. 1674-5.

Hester. Baptized at Great Milton 18 June 1676.

Frances. Married at Tettesworth 8 Oct. 1625. = Thomas Widmere of Hughendon, Co. Bucks.

William Davies, sen., proprietor of Great Milton. (1st husband.) = Eleanor Pettie. Married at Tettesworth 18 Dec. 1626. Died 20 March 1685-6, aged 80 or more, and was buried in Great Milton Church. = John Cave, M.A., Vicar of Great Milton, Co. Oxon. Sometime Rector of Middleton Cheney, Co. Northampton. Eldest son of Sir Richard [or Sir Brian] Cave.

Aylesworth Major of Cowley in the parish of Preston Bisset, Co. Bucks, son of Edmund Major, by Ann his wife. Died 23 Nov. 1664, and was buried near his wife and ancestors at Preston Bisset.[5] = ... Pettie. Died 6 June 1659, and buried in Preston Church.

Charnell Major. A silkman in Paternoster Row, London, of St. Faith's, London. Bachelor, aged 24 at time of marriage. Called "Mercer of Ivy Lane" in the record of his daughter's baptism. = Mary, daughter of Richard Royston of London, stationer. Married 10 Feb. 1661, being then Shrove Tuesday. Mar. Lic. Fac. 10 Feb. 1661-2, Spinster, aged 17, to marry at St. Paul's Cathedral (father alleged).

Edmund Major, M.A., and sometime Fellow of Lincoln College. Rector of Whitchurch, Co. Oxon, also Minister of Turweston, near Brackley, Co. Northampton. Died at Whitchurch 17 Oct. 1685. M.I. at Preston Bisset, where he was buried. = Susan, daughter of Thomas Holt of Stoke Lyne, Esq. She was her husband's first cousin.

Mary. Born and baptized at St. Faith's, London, 5 Aug. 1663.

A

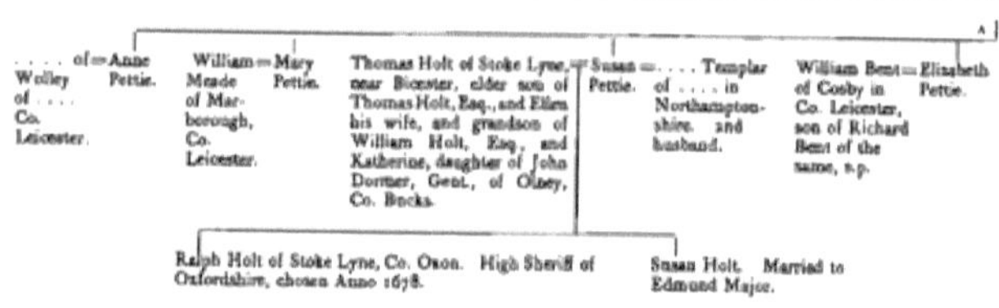

♣♣♣♣♣♣♣♣♣♣♣

Pedigree of Pettie or Petty of Warwickshire.

No. IV.

(Harl. MSS. No. 1167, Visitation of Warwickshire, by William Camden.)

Arms.—*Quarterly or and azure, on a bend vert three martlets of the first.*
Crest.—*Out of a ducal coronet an elephant's head argent, armed and eared gules.*

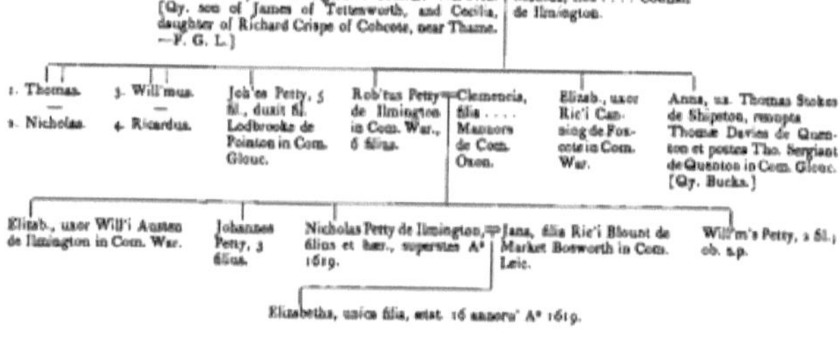

SOME EXPLANATORY NOTES OF THE FOREGOING PEDIGREES.

[1] For the inscription to the memory of John Petty, see footnote p. 107. The arms granted to John Petty of Tettesworth, by Ralph Cooke, Clarencieux, on the 10th of May, 1570, occur on folio 6 of the Harleian MSS., "Arms of Several Counties."

Arms of Petty in the Church of Stoke Talmache: Quarterly or and azure, on a bend vert three martlets of the first.

Petty, impaling Charnell—Azure, a cross engrailed or.

Petty, impaling Snappe or Snape—Gules, a buck's head caboshed argent, attired or, between the antlers a cross crosslet fitchée of the last.

Charnell, impaling Lord Williams of Thame—Azure, four crosses pattée, and in saltire two organ-pipes or.

Stoke Talmache—"This manor formerly belong'd to the Pettys, who sold it to the Simmons', of whom the Barkers bought it ab't 1630—the Lady Lydcott and Sr Wm Barker, of Sonning."—*Rawlinson's Collections for Oxfordshire, Bodleian Library*

There is a Pedigree of Petty on folio 26 of the Harleian MSS. No. 1557.

Various degrees at Oxford of the Petty family:—

Petty, Alexander, Magd. Hall, B.A., 31 May, 1673; Hart Hall, M.A., 26 April, 1676.

Petty, John, New Coll., B.A., 10 Oct. 1685.

Petty, Thomas, C.C.C., B.A., 26 March, 1666; Magd. Hall, M.A., 9 July, 1668.

[a] All Souls' College Chapel, Oxford:—

Hic jacet Christopherus Petty, quartus filius Johannis Petty, nuper de Stoke Talmage in com. Oxon, arm. Juris civilis Baccalaureus, hujus Collegii socius, qui obiit mense Octobris anno dom' Millesimo Septentisimo decimo, anno ætatis suæ, vicesimo quinto.

The arms hereon depicted are the same as those which appear upon the monument at Stoke Talmache.

[b] Charnell Pettie, Esq., Lord of the Manor of Tettesworth, and High Sheriff of the County of Oxford in 1653, was buried in the Church of Stoke Lyne.

The following inscription is on a white free-stone gravestone in capitals:—

February the 14th, 1661. Here lyes the body of Charnell Pettie, Esq., aged 82. The Righteous shall bee in everlasting Remembrance.—Ps. 112, v. 6.

They who full threescore years in one bed lay
Doe here rest sweetly in one bed of clay.

[c] This family were owners for a long time of the Manor of Tettesworth, and were related by marriage to Anthony à Wood, the Oxford Antiquary. In Delafield's manuscript *Account of Great Milton* is the following:—"Christopher Pettie, who left his name on one of the bells in Tetsworth Church, a lasting memorial of his unthriftiness, folly, and extravagance. For being much addicted to ringing, he carried about with him a set of silken ropes (as I have heard it often affirmed), and a train of idle fellows for his accommodation of that exercise, till he had rung away a good estate and dyed very old, and extremely reduced, at Thame, in the year 17 . ."

"Mr Petty had £800 per annum; now keeps an ale-house at Thame."—*Rawlinson's Collections for Oxfordshire*, vol. ii.

Thame Register of Burials. 1739, Jan. 7th, Christopher Petty, Esq.

The Pettys of Heath are descended from Henry Petty of Thame, son of John of Tettesworth:—

Joane, d^r of Alexander Petty of Heath, co. Oxon, died April 12, 1690, aged 8; and Elizabeth Wyatt, d^r of Alex^r Petty, died Aug. 23, 1700, lieth buried in St. Anne's Aldersgate churchyard, aged 25.

Elizabeth, wife of Richard Petty, died July 30th 1696, aged 77.

Richard, son of Alexander Petty, died May 2, 1686, aged 14.—*Rawlinson's Collections*, etc.

[d] The Advowson and Rectory of Preston Bisset, co. Bucks, belonged to the Langstons of Caversfield, who became Patrons, and presented to the living from the year 1426, until the time of Queen Elizabeth, when they sold their right to the family of Major, who held likewise considerable demesnes at Cowley, a hamlet always united to Preston Bisset, where the following memorials of this family remain:—

Here lyeth the body of Ann Maior, late the wife of Edmund Maior the yonger, gent. daughter to Edward Aylsworth of Aylsworth in the County of Glocester Esq. who lived vertuously & died Christianly ye 24th of February 1613, leavinge behinde her two sonns and fower daughters. Aetatis suae 30.

Exuviæ Edmundi Major, Clerici, Eccl. de Whitchurch, in Com. Oxon, et Turweston, in Com. Bucks, nuper Rectoris; Filii Aylworth Major, Generosi, de Cowley prope adjacentis hujus Parochiæ parte. Obiit 17 Octobris A.D. 1685.

Arms: A fess between six billets, impaling, on a bend engrailed three fleurs-de-lis.

♣♣♣♣♣♣♣♣♣♣♣

THE family of Cosyns, Cosens, Cursons, Cozens, or Cussens—for the name is variously spelled—is of considerable antiquity in the town and neighbourhood of Thame. At Waterperry they held a distinguished rank, intermarrying with noble and knightly families, *e.g.*, Tufton, Dormer, Digby, Hampden, Belson, Brown, Burrough, Giffard, and Towneley. At Crendon, North Weston, Shabbington, and Ickford, branches of the family have existed, being of the rank of gentlepeople as well as that of yeomen. At Thame, William Cosyn, in 1443, contributed the sum of eightpence to the work of repairing the north transept; and again in 1449, to certain seats then put up. Another William Cosyn is referred to, as renting certain Church lands, in the Churchwardens' Accounts for the year 1464. Nearly a hundred and seventy years afterwards, in 1628, Edward Curzon was one of the Churchwardens. The Will of another William Cosens of Thame, yeoman, was made 20 September, 1630. His "loving wife Ann Cosens" was sole executrix, and he left a substantial legacy to "Ann Wildes my kinswoman." Steven Cosens filled the office of Churchwarden from 1631 to 1633; Thomas Cursons in 1639 and 1640; and another of the same name, of North Weston, was Churchwarden in 1737. When the property of the Petty family was disposed of in the year 1656, the estate called "Harlesford" was sold amongst others.* This was purchased by Thomas Cozens in 1729. Other lands and tenements were so obtained in the year 1760, by another Thomas Cozens, and still further additions were made to the properties of this family at Tettesworth in 1794, by Mr. Robert Cozens. In the year 1838 Thomas Cozens made other purchases of lands, as did also the late Mr. John Cozens of Harlesford, in the years 1871 and 1876. A ledger stone of the seventeenth century, with the same arms as those borne by the family of Cursons of Waterperry, lay in the nave of the old Church; but it is now lost—though the arms in question are represented in deep carving at the east end of one of the altar-tombs in the Churchyard.

* From information given to me by Mr. William Parker, solicitor, of Thame, who adds, "The late Joseph Cornish of Tettesworth was the owner, by purchase from the Matthews family, of the Manor or reputed Manor of Tettesworth. The present owner (1882) is a son of Mr. Cornish."

Of this family of Matthews of Tettesworth, was Dorothy Matthews of Thame, whose Will was made 11 Feb. 1642. Therein she sets forth a desire to be buried in the Parish Church, "as neare as may be to the bodie of my first husband." To her son Michael Cooke she leaves the rent of a copyhold house, and other bequests to son-in-law Thomas Lambourne, to Anne Gadbury, and to Mary Warren. "I give and bequeath unto my cousin William Basse my deske. . . . . I leave and give unto my above-named son Michael Cooke and Dionis his wife all the rest of my goods and chattels."—"Wills of the Peculiar of Thame," etc.

Pedigree of Cozens of Tettesworth.

ARMS.—*Argent, on a bend sable, three popinjays or, collared gules.*

William Cozens of Thame, yeoman. Will made 10 Sept. 1630. = Ann Dormer.

Thomas Cozens of Thame and Tettesworth, yeoman. = Elizabeth.

Thomas Cozens of Tettesworth, aforesaid, yeoman. Churchwarden of Thame in 1737. Died 1744. = Mary.

Thomas Cozens of Tettesworth aforesaid, Gent. Born *circa* 1713. Will proved 4 Sep. 1789 at London. Died 29 Aug. 1789, aged 76. Buried at Tettesworth. M.I. in the Church. = Hester. Born *circa* 1718. Will made 7 April 1801; proved 1 Nov. 1806.[1] Died 16 June, buried at Tettesworth 19 June, 1806, aged 88. M.I. in the Church.

Mary Cozens. Baptized 5 Sept. 1714.

Elizabeth Cozens. Baptized 23 Dec. 1716.

Ann Cozens. Baptized 8 May 1719.

Hester Cozens. Baptized 25 Oct. 1721.

1. Robert Cozens. Baptized 20 Aug. 1749. Of Tettesworth, yeoman. Died 17, buried 20 Sep. 1797 at Tettesworth. M.I. in the Church.

2. Thomas Cozens. Baptized 25 Oct. 1753.

3. John Cozens. Baptized 25 June 1754. Of Lobb, Co. Oxon, and Great Marlow, Co. Bucks, Gent. Died 1 June 1836, aged 81. Will dated 22 Jan. 1835; proved in 1836. Personalty sworn under £35,000. Buried at Tettesworth. M.I. in Churchyard. = Anne Hester. Born *circa* 1759, daughter of Mr. Hester of Dormer's Leys, near Thame. Married by Licence at Tettesworth 26 Dec. 1776. Died 19 March 1811. Buried at Tettesworth. M.I. in Churchyard. [Pedigree of Hester of Thame[2] entered at the Visitation of Oxon in 1634.]

4. Thomas Cozens. Born 14 Nov. 1755. Died 20 Dec. 1834, aged 81. M.I. in Tettesworth Church.

John Lathom. = Katherine Cozens. Baptized 19 July 1747. Married by Licence at Tettesworth 19 April 1766.

1. Thomas Cozens. Baptized 25 Dec. 1777. Of Tettesworth and Thame. Died 18 March 1857, aged 79. Will proved 3 June same year. Admon. granted to his brother Robert. Buried at Tettesworth. M.I. in Churchyard. = Ann Priscilla. Born *circa* 1780. Daughter of .... Wells of Little Milton and Wallingford. Married 11 Nov. 1811. Died 17 Dec. 1863. Buried at Tettesworth. M.I. in Churchyard.

2. Robert Cozens. Born *circa* 1781 at Ewelme Park, Co. Oxon. Of Upton Grey and Northington, Co. Hants, and of Winterbrook, near Wallingford. Died 22 Nov. 1858. Buried at Tettesworth. M.I. in Churchyard. = Mary, daughter of .... Newton. Died at Winterbrook aforesaid 20 Dec. 1868. Buried at Tettesworth. M.I. in Churchyard.

1. Robert Cozens. Born 28 Aug. 1804. Of Norton in the parish of Wonston, Co. Hants, Gent. Died 5 Sept. 1854. = Jane, daughter of John Hoare of Sutton Courtenay, Co. Berks. Born Feb. 1814. Married 19 Oct. 1837. Died 15 Sept. 1848.

Charlotte, daughter of William Cozens and Elizabeth Parsons his wife. Born *circa* 1825. Died 18 March 1860. Admon. granted to her husband. Buried at Tettesworth. M.I. in Church. (1st wife.) = 2. John Cozens of Tettesworth aforesaid, Gent. Born *circa* 1815. Died 29 Aug. 1879. Buried at Tettesworth. M.I. in Church. = Ellen, born at Uckfield, Co. Sussex, fourth daughter of Richard Hart of Falmer, Esq., by Sarah Gibbs his second wife, and niece to Admiral Sir Henry Hart, Knight of the Guelphic Order, one of the Commissioners of Greenwich Hospital. She married at Broughton, Co. Southampton, 23 Sept. 1863. Living 1882. (2nd wife.)

ARMS OF HART.—*Per chevron azure and gules, three harts trippant or.*

1. John Robert Cozens. Born 25 March 1839. Died 21 Nov. 1879.

2. Thomas Cozens. Born 18 May 1843. Died 9 March 1844.

Mary Jane Cozens. Born 5 Oct. 1841. Married at Broughton, Co. Southampton, 28 April 1864. = Herbert Grove Lee of Thame, M.D.

ARMS OF LEE.—*Argent, a fesse between three crescents sable.*

Mary Elizabeth Cozens.

Charlotte Beatrice Cozens.

Margaret Ellen Cozens.

A B C

A | B | C

Joseph Bailey of Cole Henleigh, Co. Hants. = Mary Ann Cosens.
Two sons and one daughter.

Esther Cosens.

William Newton of Twyford, Co. Hants. = Emma Cosens.

Joseph Franklin of Ewelme, Co. Oxon. = Ellen Cosens.
One son and three daughters.

George Gater of West-end, Co. Southampton. = Sarah Cosens.
One son and six daughters.

John Lawrence of Odiham, Co. Hants. = Louisa Cosens.
Three sons and three daughters.

---

3. William Cosens. Born *circa* 1783. Of East Hendred, and subsequently of Mackney, Co. Berks. Died 23 June 1845. Buried at Little Wittenham, Co. Berks. = Elizabeth, daughter of Richard Parsons[2] of Knighton, Co. Berks. Born *circa* 1788. She died 13 March 1866, aged 78. Buried at Little Wittenham.
Arms of Parsons.—*Gules, two chevronells ermine, between three eagles displayed or.*

4. John Cosens. Born *circa* 1788. Died 23 April 1836. Buried at Tettesworth. M.I. in Churchyard.

Esther Cosens.

---

1. William Cosens of Little Wittenham, Co. Berks, yeoman. Born 2 Sept. 1810. Died 14 Jan. 1842. Buried at Little Wittenham. = Sarah. Born 17 June 1808. Fourth daughter of James Hazell of Sotwell, Co. Berks, yeoman. Married 7 July 1835. Died 3 Sept. 1841. Buried at Little Wittenham.

- William Cosens, Gent. Born 24 April 1839. Living at Bishop's Court, Dorchester, Co. Oxon, 1882.
- Emily Cosens. Born 14 June 1836. Authoress of *Original Poems*, *Bertha*, *The Miser's Dream*, etc. Died 13 Jan. 1879. Buried at Little Wittenham aforesaid.

2. Wellington Cosens of Mackney aforesaid, yeoman. = Harriett daughter of Stephen Hughes of Wheatfield, Co. Oxon.
Five sons and two daughters.

3. Thomas Cosens, yeoman, deceased. Buried at Nuffield, Co. Oxon. = Helen Mary, 2nd daughter of Thomas Stevens of Blount's Court, Mapledurham, Co. Oxon.
Two sons and five daughters.

4. George and 6. Robert Cosens, yeomen. Living unmarried at Sotwell, Co. Berks, in 1882.

---

5. John Cosens of Little Wittenham, Co. Berks. = Jane, daughter of Henry Wilmot of Dorchester, Co. Oxon.
One son and two daughters.

1. Eliza Cosens.

2. Ann Cosens.

John Moore of Warwick. = 3. Hester Cosens.

4. Charlotte Cosens. Married her cousin John, 2nd son of Robert and Mary Cosens.

Mary Cosens Baptized 20 Aug. 1749.

Robert Leaver of Wallingford, Co. Berks. = Hester Cosens. Baptized 26 Aug. 1750. Married by Licence at Tettesworth 18 May 1776.
Arms of Leaver.—*Argent, two bends gules.*

John Eeles of Thame. = Judith Cosens. Baptized 2 May 1756. Married by Licence at Tettesworth 4 Sept. 1783.

William Cosens of Watlington, Co. Oxon, Banker. Bapt. 6 Aug. 1758. Died 13 Feb. 1844. Personalty sworn under £45,000. Buried at Watlington. M.I. in Church.[4] = Ann, born *circa* 1769. Sole daughter of Paul Blackall of Pyrton, Co. Oxon, Esq., by Miss Hester his wife. She died 18 Nov. 1825, aged 56. Buried at Watlington. M.I. in Church.
Arms of Blackall.—*Argent, a greyhound courant sable, on a chief dancetté of the second three bezants.*

William Cox of Eythorpe, yeoman. = Olive Cosens. Baptized 23 Dec. 1759. Married by Licence at Tettesworth 4 Sept. 1783.

Honour Cosens. Baptized 7 March 1761.

Edward Wells. Born *circa* 1749. Of Wallingford, Esq., J.P., and Captain of the Volunteers. Died 13 Feb. 1811. M.I. in the Church of St. Leonard, Wallingford. = Charlotte Cosens. Born *circa* 1753. Died 4 June 1824, aged 71. M.I. in the Church of St. Leonard, Wallingford. (2nd wife.)
Arms of Wells.—*On a field argent a chevron voided azure between three flames proper.*
Crest.—*A flame proper.*

---

1. Robert Cosens of Watlington, Gent. Died without issue 7 Dec. 1844. = Charlotte Butcher.

2. Thomas Cosens. Died unmarried.

James Lathom of Abingdon, Co. Berks. (1st husband.) = 1. Ann Cosens. Married firstly in June 1813. = ... Langston. (2nd husband.)

.... Biggerstaff. (1st husband.) = 2. Esther Cosens. = Captain Ackham. (2nd husband.)

.... Leaver. = 3. Charlotte Cosens.

.... Webb. = 4. Elizabeth Cosens.

SOME EXPLANATORY NOTES OF THE FOREGOING PEDIGREE.

[1] Will of Esther Cosens of Tettesworth, widow, made 7 April 1801, proved 1 Nov. 1806. She leaves £500 to each of her sons Thomas and John, and a like sum to each of her daughters. Her sons are executors. The witnesses to the Will are H. Reynolds, and J. Hedges, attorney, Wallingford.

[2] The arms of Hester of Thame are set forth in the "Arms of Sundrie Counties," Harleian MSS., Photo LV. F. Their Pedigree is given from the Visitation of Oxfordshire in 1634, on pp. 76 and 77 of this book. The yeoman family of Hester occupied a position of importance at Thame as early as the reign of Henry VII. Some of its members were then merchants in the town, but had intermarried with gentle families of the locality, *e.g.*, the heiress of the Marmions and an Umfraville, and were consequently people of good means, certain rank, and considerable influence. Later on they appear to have taken an active part in parochial affairs; and held office as churchwardens during the Tudor changes. They supplied the new service books under Edward VI. and Elizabeth, and became very wealthy in the succeeding reign.

[3] The following Pedigree of Parsons of Great Milton is taken from Harl. MS., No. 1412, fol. 32:—"These are the Armes and Discent of Thom' Parsons of Great Milton in the County of Oxford, gentellman, as appeareth by the Visitation of that County remayneinge uppon Record in the office of Armes, examined and testified under the common seale of the said office the 28 day of June, 1638:"—

Arms: Gules, two chevronells ermine, between three eagles displayed or.

Crest: On a wreath argent and gules a leopard's face of the second, surmounted by an eagle's claw erased or.

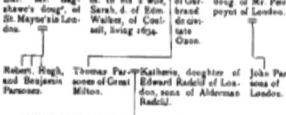

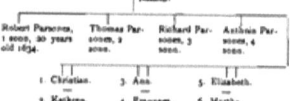

Thomas Parsons of Great Milton, in the com. Oxon. = Katherin, daughter of Mr. Heaster [of] Sidenham, near Thame.

Hughe Parsones of Sandford, 2 sone, mar. Mr. Bagshawe's doug[r], of St. Mayne's in London. | Thom's Parsones, of Great Milton, m. to his 2 wife, Sarah, d. of Edm. Walter, of Coolsell, living 1634. = Judeth, daugh. of Gerbrand de civitate Oxon. | Richard Parsones, 3 sone, mar. Martha doug. of Mr. Peirpoynt of London.

Robert, Hugh, and Benjamin Parsones. | Thomas Parsones of Great Milton. = Katherin, doughter of Edward Radcliff of London, sone of Alderman Radcliff. | John Parsons of London.

Robert Parsones, 1 sone, 20 years old 1634. | Thomas Parsones, 2 sone. | Richard Parsones, 3 sone. | Anthonie Parsones, 4 sone.

1. Christian. 3. Ann. 5. Elizabeth.

2. Kathren. 4. Frauncees. 6. Martha.

[4] Inscriptions on marble tablets upon the wall of Watlington Church, co. Oxon:—

Ann Cosens, Wife of William Cosens, died Nov[r] 18th, 1825, aged 56.

William Cosens, born July 31st, 1758, died Feb[y] 13th, 1844, aged 85.

♣♣♣♣♣♣♣♣♣♣♣

Sydenham.

IT is said by some who are competent to give an opinion, that the compound word "Sydenham" means "Southern house," and may originally have been applied to the House or Temple of God. In regard to Thame such is the geographical position of this village; for it lies almost directly south,—though perhaps a little to the east, at a distance of three and a half miles. From Tettesworth, on the east, it is distant two miles and three quarters. A purely agricultural village, it contains little of interest. In the year 1831, it owned 367 inhabitants; in 1861, 397; in 1871, 377; at the last Census its numbers were only 355, shewing a slight decrease. The Parochial Feast is kept on the last Sunday in August within the Octave of the Feast of the Assumption, O.S.

The following account of the chief building in Sydenham, the House of God, was written about the year 1841. Subsequently to that date, *i.e.* in 1855, the Church was repaired and enlarged, under the direction of Mr. John Billing, architect, F.S.A., at a cost of £647 2s. od., by Giles Holland, builder, of Thame, and solemnly re-opened by Bishop Wilberforce in 1856.

"The Church of Our Blessed Lady of Sydenham consists of a nave and chancel of first-pointed work, with a central tower of wood. Most of the windows are simple lancets: but there are some later insertions of inferior work. The font is circular, first-pointed in style and plain. The chancel arch is of good proportions, but its mouldings have been seriously damaged, and in some parts destroyed. A third-pointed rood-skreen and loft remain, but are disfigured with plaster and whitewash. The doorways are first-pointed in style, with deep mouldings, and their ironwork and hinges are of good and effective design.* There is a small second-pointed cross on the west gable in fair preservation. The buttresses have lost their old character by rude repairs and the insertion of rough brickwork."

* These have all been removed since 1841.

This was a perfectly fair and faithful description of the building at the period specified. It was much out of repair. There had been half an acre of land rented by Mr. Robert Fox in King James I.'s days bequeathed for the reparation of the Church, and a small annual rent-charge left in King Charles II.'s reign, for keeping the same in good condition, by Mr. Robert Monday, a great benefactor to the poor of the parish.* But a few additional facts need to be here put on record. The nave was enlarged by an addition of seven feet to the west end, and an entirely new tower and spire of wood erected at the time specified. To accomplish this a new chancel arch was put up, and a similar arch, corresponding to it, erected at the east end of the nave. The rood-skreen was utterly destroyed. There is a small chantry chapel to the south of the tower; and in the eastern part of the wall of the said chapel an empty niche or tabernacle, cusped in the head, three feet two inches in height and exactly two feet wide. There is also a first-pointed *piscina*, much mutilated, close to this niche on the right hand, in the south wall—the bowl of which is almost destroyed. No doubt there was an altar here originally, most probably dedicated in honour of the patron saint, Our Blessed Lady. The pue, which fills up this chapel, belongs to the farm now owned by the Rev. Canon H. W. Burrows. There is a small vestry to the north in the transept, and above a somewhat awkward staircase to reach the ringing loft and belfry, in which are five bells.

As regards the present dimensions of the building, the chancel is twenty-four feet eight inches in length and nineteen feet ten inches in breadth. It bears slightly to the north, not being exactly parallel with the nave. The length of the latter is forty feet and six inches up to the tower arch,—the space covered by the tower being exactly twelve feet four inches from west to east. Thus the whole length of the Church, from end to end, measured from within, is exactly seventy-seven feet and a half. The roof of the nave is in good preservation, severe and simple in its design: the old roof of the chancel being hidden by a lathe-and-plaster construction of great simplicity and singular ugliness. There is a small organ on the north side of the chancel. The Communion-table, the two choir-pues placed stall-wise, and the cumbersome reading-pue and pulpit, are all vulgar and common-place in their design, poor as to their materials, and, as regards the size of reading-pue and pulpit, utterly out of all proportion to the Church itself. The Communion cup, of silver—seven inches in height and four inches across the bowl, without any marks—is quite plain, but the other plate is not of precious metal and is modern.

The following Inventory from the Record Office shews how effectually this Church also had been cleared of its ancient *ornamenta*, prior to the reign of Edward VI.:—

H. of Lewkno', Syd'nam.

This Inventorye Indentyd made the xxij[th] daye of Maye in the vj[th] yere of the reigne of o[r] Soueraigne Lord Kynge Edward the VIth of all the bells and challyses and surpleses of the chirche aboutsayd delyveryd by S[r] ffraunces Knowles S[r] Will'm Raynsforde Knyghts Thomas bridges Leonard Chamberlayne Edmo'de Asshefylde & Thomas Denton Esquieres unto the custodye of Sir Ric' Stevins, W[m] Cope & Th's ferder safelye to be kept to the use of o[r] Soueraigne lord the Kynge.

ffyrste a challis of sylu'
It[m] iij bells & j sauns bell.

---

* The Will of Robert Monday of Sydenham, yeoman, was made 7 January 1660. Therein he gives a freehold messuage at Kingston Blount and twenty-three acres of arable land in the common fields of Kingston for the poor, the proceeds of which are to be duly distributed on the two feasts of the Annunciation of Our Lady and St. Michael and All Angels. From this bequest twenty shillings a year is to be first taken for the repairs of Sydenham Church. Christopher Stevens and Thomas Cammore were the Overseers.—"Wills of the Peculiar of Thame," etc.

The following Letter, which relates to this bequest, addressed to the ex-Vicar, Mr. Littlejohn, may be suitably reproduced:—

London, 2nd March, 1870.

Sydenham. Robert Munday's Charity.

REVEREND SIR,

For your information I enclose a copy of so much of the Printed *Reports* of the Former Commissioners for inquiring concerning Charities made in 1822 (vol. viii., p. 535) as relates to the above-mentioned parish.

The evidence upon which this Report was made was given on the 18th December 1820 by Mr. Thomas Sheen the Churchwarden, in the presence of the Rev. Timothy Tripp Lee, the Curate [it should be Vicar], and Mr. Wm. Jones, the Overseer.

An Act of Parliament was passed in the year 1831 (2 and 3 Will. IV., cap. 1) for inclosing lands in the Parish of Aston Rowant. It has been referred to and contains a power in general terms only to the two Commissioners to effect exchanges of land, and I must therefore refer you to the award made under the provisions of that Act and to the plan which will be found attached to it.

A duplicate thereof should be in the Parish Chest, or may perhaps be lodged in the custody of some person professionally concerned for the Parish.

The award and plan should be found deposited with the Clerk of the Peace for the County of Oxford. Mr. J. M. Davenport, of Oxford, at present fills that office.

In a *History of the County of Oxford*, Printed and Published by Robert Gardiner in the year 1852, it is stated that "Robert Munday left a house and 30 acres of land in the open fields of Kingston Blount to the poor of this Parish. This property was *exchanged* in 1832 for about 16 acres of land in Sydenham which now let for about £20 per annum. The rents are given to the poor at Christmas."

Reference has also been made to the Documents at the Public Record Office, and an Inquisition of Charitable Uses (23rd April 10 James I.) has been perused, it was found that half an acre of land in the parish of Sydenham then in the tenure of one Robert Fox was given for the maintenance of the Church of Sydenham, and that the rent had been employed accordingly until about ten years then past, and that Fox had received and taken the issues to his own use for the ten years. The decree, however, if any were made, appears to have been lost.

I am, Rev. Sir,
Your obedient Serv't.,
HENRY M. VANE,
Secretary.

The following are the only two monuments remaining in the Church. There were three Purbeck marble slabs in the Chancel, below the old platform of the altar, prior to the year 1841. Of these, two had formerly received brasses: on one were cavities in which a man and his wife had been represented; on the other a single figure, but whether of a woman or of a priest in a cope seems uncertain. Several ancient slabs in the floor, said to have been much worn and broken, were removed in 1855.

North side of Chancel. Freestone.

Near
This Place lieth
interr'd the Body of
JOHN
QUARTERMAINE,
Who died Dec. ye XXVI
MDCCLXXX
Aged LXXIV years.

I in my life afflicted was
With grievous pains full sore;
Yet hope to find a place of rest
With Christ for evermore.

East end of Chancel. Freestone.

NEAR HERE
LIETH ABIGAIL
Y^e WIFE OF ROBT. SEY-
WELL JUN^r AND DAUGH.
OF EDWARD PHILLIPS
OF THAME, DRAP^r. OBIIT
IVNE Y^e 23, 1705.
AGED 33 YEARS
& 9 WEEKS.*

It appears, from the following introductory paragraph, that the ancient Register Books of the Parish† were taken away and lost during the Great Rebellion. A person named Francis Bailey, who had been a brazier of Bedford, never ordained, but who had acted as Preacher to a detachment of the troops of Lord Essex, took forcible possession of the Curate's residence, and under a warrant from Parliament ejected the lawful minister. This is what is set forth and recorded at the commencement of the present oldest book :—

A Register Booke for the
Parishe of Sydenham By
Ffrancis Herne, Minister
there 1663.
Memorandum That in the
tyme of Robothom about the
yeare 1653, there came One
ffrances Bayley &
seized the Minister's place
at Sidnam, & about the
year 1661 he and his whife
run away & took with
them the Register book There
being no Register book kept
This Book was provided
by the Churchwardens of
Sydenham Anno Dom' 1663
RICHARD WEBB and
JOHN NORTH, Churchwardens.

Another volume, of paper, contains this inscription at its commencement :—

A Registar kept by me Richard Clark
of Sidenham from the time [*sic*]
to the Visitation Coart kept at the Red
Lion in Thame on July 9, 1705.

The following names of clergy ministering in the Church under the respective Vicars of Thame are gathered from the Registers which remain :—

Joseph Urmestone was "Minister of Sydenham" in 1665, and is said to have directly succeeded Mr. Francis Hearne.

1752. Richard Hickson,
1772. Samuel Thomas, } Curates.
1777. Robert Style,
1776. E. Williams, Minister.
1785. John Holland,
1789. W. Harrison,
1789. Joseph Rose, } Curates.
1792. Thomas Cripps,
1792. E. Evans,
1792. T. T. Lee, Curate, subsequently Vicar.
1790. J. Williams,
1829. Henry Roberson, } Curates.
1829. Frederick Lee,
1841. James Prosser,
1841. John Stamer, } Ministers.
1841. J. Williams,

* The Will of Robert Sewell, yeoman—the father-in-law of Abigail here commemorated—was made 26 May 1662, and proved 1 June 1676. Therein he leaves to his wife Ann certain houses and lands, as also other legacies to his sons Christopher, Stephen, Robert, and Thomas, to his married daughters Elizabeth Hatton and Eleanor Floyd, and to his single daughters Mary, Prudence, and Hannah. His wife was sole executrix. The Will was witnessed by Joseph Urmestone and Jeffrey North, and the Inventory amounted to £334.—"Wills of the Peculiar of Thame," etc.

† "The Parish Registers here have been little looked after, and seem to have been mostly under the care of the Clerk of the Parish."—Letter to the Author from the Rev. W. D. Littlejohn, 23 Aug. 1877.

About this period Dr. R. B. Slater, of Wycombe, having purchased the advowson of the Mother Church of Thame, with its daughter Chapelries, procured the formal separation of the latter from the former. Sydenham then became an independent benefice, the first Incumbent, who was subsequently made a Vicar, saw the erection of a suitable house of residence for the clergyman and convenient parochial Schools. The benefice is now worth, in gross, about £150.

William Douglas Littlejohn, only son of Colonel Peter Littlejohn of Aberdeen, by Jane Richardson, of Langholm, Dumfriesshire, was born 31 August 1807, graduated B.A. at Corpus College, Cambridge, in 1837, was ordained priest in 1838, married Amelia St. George, daughter of Colonel Arthur Browne, Governor of Charlesfort, Kinsale, Ireland, and has issue three daughters. He was instituted to the Vicarage of Sydenham in 1844, and resigned it in 1878.

Mr. Littlejohn's successor was John Gottfried Heisch, M.A., of Trinity Coll., Cantab., the present Vicar. He was curate of St. Mary's, Islington, from A.D. 1839 to 1841, and subsequently became Vice-Principal of the Islington Mission College. He was instituted to Sydenham in 1878.

The churchyard and the graves are well kept, and the paths about the Church are in good order. Standard roses bloom luxuriantly here and there amongst the graves, and the southern wall of the Church is, in summer, bright with flowers. To the immediate north stands the village School. Though the monumental memorials mainly commemorate persons in humble life, they serve, however, to complete a brief notice of the Parish Church as it at present exists. The names of Unneston, Heybourne,* Almond, Taylor, Tompson, Stevens,† Herne, Cooke, "Piggott, of the Tything of Plomridge," Pimme, Burroughes, White,‡ and Eaton, were visible on some old stones in the year 1841, but these are all now lost. So certain of the remaining inscriptions have been transcribed and are here reproduced:—

In Memory of
JOHN HOLLAND
Who departed this life
May 6th 1832
Aged 61 years.

In Memory of
REBECCA Wife of
JOHN HOLLAND
Who departed this life
Novr 9th 1849
Aged 76 years.

Sacred
to
the Memory of
SARAH Wife of
JOHN HOLLAND
Who died Decr 22nd
1849. Aged 46 years.

My Glass is run, my days are spent,
My life is gone, it was but lent;
And as I am, so must you be,
Therefore prepare to follow me.

In
Affectionate remembrance of
RICHARD HOLLAND
Who departed this Life July 17, 1865
Aged 62 years.

Death little warning to me gave,
But quickly called me to the grave;
Repent in time; make no delay,
For no one knows their dying day.

Sacred
to
the Memory of
BENJAMIN BERNARD
Who fell asleep in Jesus
June 23rd 1861
aged 38 years.
"Believe on the Lord Jesus Christ &
thou shalt be saved."

* The family of Heybourne were in a good position at Sydenham during the seventeenth century. One member of the Thame branch is buried in the choir there. Richard Heybourne, of Sydenham, whose Will was proved 18 June 1677, was a substantial yeoman. Therein he leaves to his wife Agnes "the house I live in for her life and then to cousin William, son of William." But if he dies before Agnes, then the house shall go to my nephew Thomas, brother Thomas's son. To these two last-named a house in Friday Street, Thame, is bequeathed. To his brother Christopher he leaves £10, and £5 each to his children. To his cousin Richard, son of William, and to Mary, wife of Thomas King, £10, to cousin Jane Webb £20, and many other similar legacies. To "Cousin William the drawer-table in the Hall." To William Keen and Jeffrey North, witnesses, 50 shillings each. Rest of goods to Agnes my wife: she and brother Thomas, sole executors. The Inventory amounted to £551 19s.—"Wills of the Peculiar of Thame," etc.

† "Sir Richard Stevens" was curate in the last year of Edward VI.

‡ The Will of "Roger White, of Siddenham Leys, yeoman," was made 5 Sept. 1663. Therein he leaves to his daughter Elizabeth Tompson £100 and two silk coverlids. To John, son of John, to granddaughter Anne, to William and Elizabeth, son and daughter of William, £10 each. Loving brothers William Almond, of Cuddington, and Robert Monday, of Shalford, to be overseers. He also bequeaths legacies to Hugh Willis, Vicar of Thame, and to Francis Hearne, minister of Sydenham. The witnesses are Jerome White and Richard Rastell. The Inventory amounted to £134 9s. The signature of the testator is bold and good, and the Will is sealed with a seal of arms, apparently Gules, a chevron between three goats' heads, couped ar.—"Wills of the Peculiar of Thame," etc.

In affectionate Remembrance
of
SARAH GIBSON
who died May 21, 1866
Aged 42 years.
Also
HARRIET
Daughter of the above
who died January 1858
Aged 16 months.
"Watch, therefore, for ye know not
what hour your Lord doth come."

In affectionate Remembrance
of
JAMES GIBSON
Who died July 11, 1880
Aged 57 years.
Also
SUSANNA GIBSON
Daughter of the above
Who died July 1870
Aged 22 years.
"Blessed are the dead which die
in the Lord."

In Memory of
DAMARIS Wife of
WILL^{m} HOLLIER
Who died Nov. 16th 1855
Aged 80 Years.

Also of Wm HOLLIER
Who died Oct. 29th 1857
Aged 80 years.

And of WILLIAM their Son
Who died Feb 5th 1865
Aged 57 years.

In affectionate Remembrance
of
WILLIAM HOLLIER
who died April 6th 1878
in his 70th year.

Our path is marked by changes,
And strewn with many a care;
We have no Home but Heaven,
So, wherefore seek one here?

South side.

In Memory of ANN
the Wife of JOHN
VEAR, Who departed
this life May the 30th
1741.
Aged 46 Years.

South-west side. On a wooden memorial.

In Memory of SARAH the wife of RICHARD CROTEN
who Died Nov. 12 1839 Aged 83 years.

A tender Mother lieth here,
Consign'd to Native dust;
In hope that she at the last day
May rise among the Just.

In Memory of RICHARD CROTEN
Who died Oct. 19th 1829 Aged 69 years.

East part of Churchyard.

In Loving Memory
of
ADELAIDE,
Daughter of WILLIAM And
MATILDA IVES,
Who Died August 3rd 1875
Aged 14 years.
"Trusting in Jesus."

Sacred to the Memory
of
WILLIAM IVES,
Who Died
September 6th 1880,
Aged 54 years.
"Fell asleep in Jesus."

Also of
ARTHUR,
Son of the Above,
Died September
29th 1880,
Aged 9 Months.

In Memory of
RICHARD KING
who died Dec. 12th 1857
Aged 82 years.
Also of
ESTHER his Wife
who died Aug. 13th 1858
Aged 80 Years.

In affectionate Remembrance
of
HARRY WILD,
Died February 24th 1880,
Aged 61.

May he who unto us proved kind
rest in peace,
While we who here remain behind
live in hope.

In affectionate remembrance
of
PRUDENCE
Second Wife of
EDWARD WITNEY
who departed this Life
July 7, 1878
Aged 50 years.

In affectionate remembrance of
MARY WITNEY
who departed this Life March 24, 1872
Aged 11 years.

The family of Burroughs or Burrows, of Thame, possess certain property at Sydenham, so that their Pedigree, with some account of them, may suitably enough appear here. For much interesting information concerning no less than five generations of his race the Author is indebted to an Oxford Professor who, by some research, and with considerable care, has gathered many historical particulars concerning them, which are on record in a privately-printed and interesting volume of more than two hundred pages.

Its Author thus writes:—

"The Register of Thame Parish Church, which, strangely enough, seems never to have been searched by our family till this present year [A.D. 1877], begins at 1610. It contains no names of our family till 1660, when, and in the three subsequent years, there occur the baptisms of three children of 'George Boroughs,' and the death of one of them, an infant. In these four entries the name is spelt three different ways, twice as above, once Borroghes, and once Bourroughs. They are all evidently meant for the same person; and, indeed, it is certain that there is only one family of this name in the whole Register—our own. The family had only just come into the parish, and the spelling was uncertain. But the first form is soon dropped; for we read, in 1667, of the burial of 'Mrs. Elizabeth Burrowes, wife of Mr. George Burrowes.' She apparently died in childbed, as 'Elizabeth, daughter of Mr. George Burrowes,' is baptized on the same day. From that date the name is always spelt 'Burrowes' (with one accidental exception of 'Borrowes') till 1695. After that a comma is generally substituted for the e, after the manner of contractions then in use, which, however, soon disappears, and the name subsides into 'Burrows.' The same gradual change from 'Burrowes' to 'Burrows,' by the temporary substitution of the comma for e, may be traced in the signatures attached to some family papers which have survived. But the original form, though dropped in the Register, is not quite forgotten; for it occurs in the list of High Sheriffs, when Giles Burroughs' name is so spelt officially.

"While the first entries inform us as to the spelling of the name, the next indicate the condition of the new comers. In 1668 and 1669, within a few months of each other, Richard Burrowes marries Martha Thame, of Thame; and George Burrowes, his brother, marries a second wife, Phyllis Parker, a widow, of Long Crendon. Both are married by license, an exceedingly rare exception during the first hundred and fifty years of the Register, for Thame, though of respectable size, was never a large town. Also George, when mentioned both as husband of his two wives in succession, and father of several of his children, is called 'Mr.' George Burrowes, the prefix hardly ever recurring in other cases. The Stribblehills, Watsons, and two or three more are the rare exceptions.* This distinction continues in the family, and is accorded to George's sons and grandsons, as well as to a member of the family of an older generation, probably the father of the above two brothers, whose burial, in 1693, is thus registered:—'Mr. George Burrowes, Marchant.' Further, Martha Burrowes, when a widow in 1687, is wealthy as well as charitable enough to give £160 to be laid out in land for the poor of Thame. Multiplied by three or four for the difference of value of money, this was a large sum to give away during life, and the inference from these various entries must, I think (independently of the evidence of George Burrowes' Will in 1701), be that the family was one of importance in Thame from its first appearance.

"Whence did they come? They seem to drop from the skies. Our grandfather did not know. Writing in 1762 he tells us:—'How they came there [to Thame], and where they came from, I have never been able to learn.' But wealthy woolstaplers, or 'Marchants,' or drapers, have had a beginning somewhere. The date of their appearance is suggestive. It is the date of the Restoration, the date of a general resettlement after twenty years of anarchy; just the time when a family which had left one place for some reason connected with the universal struggle would migrate to another. Were they persecuted Churchmen, for many years debarred from the old religious rites, now clustering under the walls of a church where their children might be baptized, their sons married, and themselves buried? Who can tell?"†

Tradition affirms that some members at least of the Burrows' family were Jacobites and Nonjurors. When, in order to perpetuate the apostolical succession of the latter, the Rev. Timothy Newmarch, D.D., was consecrated a Bishop at a private chapel in or near Gray's Inn Square, in the eighteenth century, a "Mr. Burrows of Thame," together with a Mr. Calvert and a Mr. Lee, formally witnessed the consecration. The family of Dorrell of Thame, brewers of wealth and position, held the same political and religious convictions, and took a very active part in promoting the interests of Prince James Stuart. The first Earl of Litchfield, Edward Henry Lee, whose lady had witnessed the birth of that

---

* [*Note by the Author.*]—I am bound to observe that the result of my own careful and constant examination of the Registers and Parochial Books does not bear out the Professor's statements in the text, either as regards the use of marriage licences or the prefix "Mr." There are very many examples of both in the earlier records, and still more in those of a later period.

† *History of the Family of Burrows, of Sydenham and Long Crendon*, by Montagu Burrows, R.N., M.A. For Private Circulation only. Pp. 68. Oxford: 1877.

R

Prince of Wales, and who himself had accompanied the King on his retirement from England, though he returned to Ditchley, never attended the House of Lords after the Revolution; became the trusted Oxfordshire leader of this honoured party, and led those hereabouts, who sympathized with the unjustly-exiled race, with tact, boldness, and discretion. Correspondence on that delicate subject, much treasured, still exists. John Dorrell of Thame was tried at Oxford, and hung at Tyburn, as a rebel to the Hanoverian authorities, on the 7th of December, 1715.

The Wollastons and the Burrows, as far as I have been enabled to gather, came to Thame about the period of the Restoration. For prior to this date their names are certainly not found, either in the Church Registers or the Parochial Account-books. Divers migrations took place about that period. The Civil War had wrought endless trouble and great misery for many an old family of the town. From the period in question, for nearly twenty years, a very keen struggle for existence had been going on. Trade languished: several of the farms in the adjoining neighbourhoods were uncultivated. Ruin stared many people in the face. County families, whose members had been leal and loyal to the sovereign and frankly self-sacrificing, were persecuted, harrassed, and down-trodden by those who had secured the whip-handle. Some impoverished families had to dispose of their estates and leave their old homes for ever. Amongst these were the Curzons of Waterperry. The family of Reynolds, which then also arrived, may have already had relations or connections at the adjoining village of Crendon; and it seems certain that some of these latter were originally large graziers and woolstaplers. As Tradition affirms they sprung from Leicester.* The Wollastons likewise came from the same county, and bore the same arms as the gentle family of that name long resident at Shenton. Mr. Samuel Wollaston, surgeon and apothecary of Thame, married, in 1717, Mary, the daughter of Mr. John Burrowes. It seems exceedingly probable, moreover, that the marriage of Thomas, one of the Curzons of Waterperry,† with an Elizabeth Burroughs on the 14th of September, 1654, and the birth of a daughter Elizabeth, in November of the following year, may have turned the attention of George Burroughs or

* See the Pedigree of Reynolds of Notley in Chapter V.

† From the Marriage Register of Waterperry, co. Oxon:

1654. Sept. 14. Tho. Curson arm. and Eliz. Burrough.

This lady was the daughter of William Burrowe or Borrough of Borough, co. Leicester.

From the Baptismal Register of the same place:

1655. Nov. 18. Eliz. fi. Tho. Curson arm. et Eliz. ux. nat.

The following inscriptions appear to relate to this family:—

Here lieth the Body of Mrs Martha Borough
relict of Dr William Borough
Rector of Sapcote in this county,
who departed this life the 18th of March 1726, æt. 87
And near this place the Body of Mr John Borough,
son of the said William and Martha,
who departed this life June 3, 1722, æt. 52

—Collegiate Church of St. Mary-de-Castro, Leicester. Nichols' *History of Leicester*, vol. i., part 2, p. 320.

This family owned property at Bredon on the Hill; where Sampson Burrough held one messuage, 20 acres, etc., and 4 closes called "Burrough Hill," with a messuage, for three lives, paying yearly £2 18s. od., and two capons. His fine was between £50 and £60.—*Ibid.*, p. 487.

The following Pedigree, the substance of which is supplementary to the information of ordinary entries in the *Baronetties*, is from a MS. formerly in the possession of Mr. Nichols, the Historian of Leicestershire:—

CAVE OF LEICESTERSHIRE.

Brian Cave of Ingardsby (son of Richard Cave, by Margaret his 2nd wife, dau. of Thomas Saxby of Northampton), merchant of the Staple of Calais, and owner of Kirkby, co. Rutland, in 1575. [This was a religious house.—F. G. L.] = Bridget, dau. of Sir William Skipwith, Knt. (2nd wife).

Henry Cave, wool-merchant, son and heir, living 1589; sold Kirkby to Ralph Browne of Northampton, Gent. = Elizabeth, dau. of Sir Gregory Isham of Braunston, co. Northampton.

Sir Richard Cave, Knt., son and heir, living 1630. = Mary, dau. of Sir Erasmus Dryden of Canons' Ashby, co. Northampton.

John Cave, 2nd son. Vicar of Great Milton, co. Oxon, and Rector of Middleton Cheney in the same county. = Elennor, widow of Mr. William Davies of Great Milton, Gent., and dau. of Charnell Pettie of Thame and Tetsworth, Gent.

John Cave, M.A., Rector of Cold Overton, co. Leicester. = Mary, dau. of John St. John of Cold Overton aforesaid, Gent. — George Cave.

That which follows is a copy from the same collection, illustrating the alliance recorded in the Registers of Waterperry:—

BOROUGH OF BOROUGH.

William Borough of Borough, co. Leicester, living in 1647. = Mary, born in 1618, dau. of George and Elizabeth Cave, and granddaughter of Christopher Cave, living in 1647.

George Borough, born in 1641. — John Borough, born in 1643. — Thos. Curson of Waterperry. = Elizabeth, born in 1637; m. at Waterperry 14 Sep. 1654.

William Borough, born in 1639. Rector of Sapcote, co. Leicester. Buried at St. Mary's, Leicester. = Martha Reynolds of Leicester, m. in 1669.

John Borough, Gent., died 3 June, 1722; buried at St. Mary's, Leicester.

And that below, not borne out, however, by ordinary genealogical works, relates to the Barons de Burgh:—

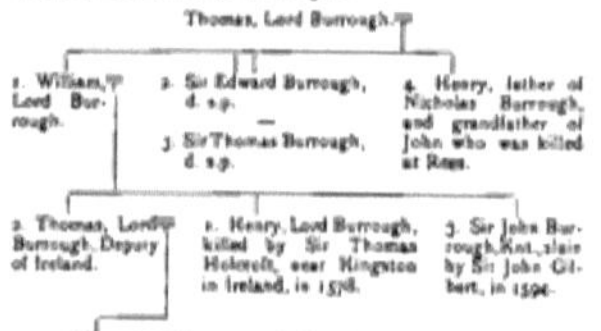
Thomas, Lord Burrough. =

1. William, Lord Burrough. =
2. Sir Edward Burrough, d. s.p.
3. Sir Thomas Burrough, d. s.p.
4. Henry, father of Nicholas Burrough, and grandfather of John who was killed at Rees.

2. Thomas, Lord Burrough, Deputy of Ireland. =
1. Henry, Lord Burrough, killed by Sir Thomas Holcroft, near Kingston in Ireland, in 1578.
3. Sir John Burrough, Knt., slain by Sir John Gilbert, in 1594.

Robert, Lord Burrough, died in 1602. Barony extinct.

Burrowes of Leicestershire to Thame and its locality. Dr. William Borough, the Rector of Sapcote, co. Leicester, had previously married a Martha Reynolds of Leicester (born in 1639), and had had issue a son John, who died forty years after the Restoration in 1722, aged 52, and was buried at St. Mary's, Leicester. He was connected with the knightly race of Cave of Leicestershire, one of whom had been Vicar of Great Milton adjoining, and in 1626 had married a member of the family of Pettie of Thame, whose descendants allied themselves with the families of Parsons of Great Milton and Waterstock, of Dormer and Hester of Thame, and of Cozens of Tettesworth.

Professor Burrows shall continue his narrative. Here is a further extract from it:—

"Mr. George Boroughs had two families. We are descended, by Elizabeth his first wife, surname unknown, from John his second son. His eldest child Elizabeth died an infant in 1661, his eldest son George was baptized in 1662, John in 1663, and another Elizabeth in 1667. This Elizabeth, whose birth was coincident with her mother's death, survived her father, as she is liberally provided for in his Will; but we hear nothing more of her. Over the history of George, the eldest son, hangs a mystery. If the Register is correct, it would seem that he lived for some years at Thame; for the baptism of two of his daughters is registered, that of Martha in 1702, and of Jane in 1708, but there is no register of his marriage, or of the burial of himself or daughters; nor, which is the curious thing, is there any mention of him in his father's Will, which is made in 1701 (about the time he would have married), and proved in 1706. By this Will the father's estate (lands and houses) is left to his son John, with remainder to that son's eldest son, his grandson George. It is of no use to speculate on this circumstance. No tradition about the eldest son, George, and his daughters, has survived, and their existence has only been discovered through the Register. It is quite possible that Martha and Jane have been wrongly registered as his children instead of the children of his brother, whose daughters of the same names have no baptism registered against them, but only their deaths as infants, in 1703 and 1710. If this is a correct guess, it would account for George's marriage not being registered, and suggest that he died, unmarried, before 1701.

"The father married again, as we have seen, Phyllis Parker, widow, of Long Crendon, probably a useful marriage in the way of business, but she brought him no sons. Of the three daughters he had by her, we hear no more of two than their baptisms, Sarah in 1673, and Martha in 1675, and the provision for them in their father's Will; the eldest, baptized in 1671, married 'Christopher Potter, son of —— Potter of Toot Baldon, Esq.,' by which marriage, our grandfather says, 'the Popham family' is connected with ours.

"The Will of this Mr. George Boroughs or Burrowes shews that he was a man of good fortune. The value of the 'lands and houses' left to his son John is not indeed to be gathered from the Will, but his legacy to his daughter Elizabeth amounts to £800, and to Sarah and Martha he leaves £600 apiece, which sums must, as said above, be multiplied by about three for the present value of money. Tables, pictures, and rings are left to his wife, his son John, and his daughters, and a 'golden piece called a guinea' to divers relations and friends. Three persons are nominated to be overseers of the Will, to whom all disputes regarding its interpretation are to be referred, and whose decision is to be final, so that his family may not go to law. Such 'overseers of the Will' may have been customary under the Stuarts. Lord Clarendon names Archbishop Sheldon and Bishop Morley in that capacity.

"The rapidly improving fortunes of the family now tempt them to establish themselves in London, which, upon the death of Mr. George Burrowes, becomes, I think, the main centre of the business, with a branch at Thame.

* * * * *

"They were certainly woolstaplers or dealers in wool, as well as drapers, and it is probably this large way of business, and the rank it gave them at Thame, which prevented their names from being associated with any trade or calling, except that of 'Marchant,' in the parish Register. During the whole of their period the name of the trade is very often attached to the names entered—glover, draper, ironmonger, etc.—but never once to our family. The word 'Marchant' I only remarked once used in the whole Register, besides the case in which it is attached to the name of the old George Burrowes, whom we believe to be the father of the first settler. . . . . Putting all the known facts together, I am inclined to place the family, relatively to the society of that day, very much in the position now held by leading manufacturers. The 'Marchant's' son is a wealthy man of business, whose daughter marries into a gentleman's family, and whose son carries the business to London; that son is styled 'gentleman' on a monument, is a 'citizen of London' and one of the Ironmongers' Company; the two great-grandsons of the 'Marchant' are, one of them a 'wholesale wollendraper' of good fortune in London, and the other High Sheriff of his county.* All are landowners, and we shall see that the stock of mental cultivation they accumulated could not have been small."†

* From papers in possession of the family, it appears that Mr. Giles Burrows bought land at Ludgershall in 1732, that he was styled "gentleman" in the recital of a deed referring to an estate at Chinnor, co. Oxon, in 1743, and in deeds executed in 1755 he is designated "Esquire." He also acquired lands at Walton near Aylesbury, and at Aylesbury, as well as elsewhere. The following is an extract from the Sheriff's Will:—"Also to Mr Thomas Hill of Aylesbury, merchant, the sum of Five guineas, all my laced waistcoats, and also a light colored waistcoat that was laced when I was Sheriff of the county of Bucks, and likewise the lace that was on it and is now taken off. Also I give and bequeath to the Rev. Thomas Brougham, after the decease of my wife, a silver stand with five silver castors for pepper, vinegar, oyl, mustard, and sugar. Also to the Rev. John Kipling the elder . . . . a silver sauce boat and four silver salts with my crest on them . . . . and to Mary Reynolds, the wife of John Reynolds of Notley, the sum of Five guineas and a silver waiter . . . . and to my nephew John Burrows my gold watch, my gold-headed cane and scarlet roquelaine. Where are these memorials? Perhaps some of them may yet be recovered."—*History of the Family of Burrows, etc.*

The Thomas Brougham referred to above was Vicar of Ashendon, co. Bucks, having been inducted thereto 8 May, 1739. He was also Vicar of Haddenham, in the same county, in 1749, and likewise Vicar of Kingsey. He died in 1783.

† *History of the Family of Burrows, etc.*, pp. 12-15.

One other passage from this interesting volume will close the account of their connection with Thame itself:

"Here also we part with those very ancient and somewhat sleepy localities. Their connection with our family dies out with Giles. Besides the visit just noticed, we know but of one other paid them by our grandfather, and that of an earlier date, when he went down to vote for Wenman and Dashwood in 1754—though of course there may have been others. None of our name have ever lived there since those days, and that name would have been long ago forgotten if the Charities of two centuries had not kept it alive among the poor. Possibly some interest in Thame may yet revive in the minds of our descendants if they are privileged to aid in the restoration of the Church where our ancestors worshipped. The day must also come when the fine old village Church at Long Crendon will be restored. It is as yet in, I should think, exactly the same condition as when Giles and his wife marched there in state from the Manor House. The only sign of life about the place is the smart new school which the Education Department, by the agency of a School Board, has forced the inhabitants to build. It seems very much out of place. Not so the figure of the white-headed Vicar,* who has held his preferment for sixty years, and kindly gave me some information. The old court-house, of early Tudor, or even earlier date, still stands close to the Church and manor house. It was there that the tithe-wool was stored. It is still used, I was told, for some public purposes, but it is difficult to imagine anything so lively at Long Crendon as a public purpose. Advancing Civilization has carried off the wool trade to other spots, and the growth of London continually draws off the population from these agricultural districts and small towns. But our family at any rate ought never to regard them with indifference."†

The most distinguished man of this family, of a previous generation—for several of a later day have served God well in Church and State—was the Rev. John Burrows, son of Mr. Burrows, of Lombard Street, and his wife Mary. He was educated, until the year 1747, at Thame Grammar School, under Mr. John Kipling, the Head Master—a scholar and literary man of good repute, who had secured for that School a high and well-deserved character—and eventually entered at Trinity College, Oxford, but removed to Exeter College, where he graduated B.C.L., 27 May, 1762. He was firstly called to the Bar at the Middle Temple, but disliking that profession subsequently received Orders, and became a clergyman of distinction, mixing in the leading literary society of London, and owning considerable reputation.‡ He was the intimate friend, amongst others, of Mrs. Montagu, Mrs. Chapone, Wedderburn, and Dunning, Dr. Richard Price, Mrs. Boscawen, and the Wartons of Winchester. He appears to have been a good scholar, with a taste both for poetry and philosophy, a faithful and efficient teacher, as well as a man of acute observation, who lamented the moral deficiences of his own age and times, and who evidently felt disposed to appreciate the irregular but earnest labours of Whitfield and Wesley in their endeavours to infuse new life into the ranks of the Erastianized clergy of the Hanoverian era. He began writing a "Common Place Book" about the year 1757, and though afterwards he made it a repertory of miscellaneous anecdotes, verses, criticisms, and conversations, it appears to contain many facts, comments, and reflections of great interest, and is still deservedly treasured by his descendants. As strengthening the tradition that some members of the Burrows' family of Thame were Jacobites, it is worthy of notice that Mr. John Burrows supported the two Tory candidates at the celebrated election for Oxfordshire in 1754. Subsequently he married the daughter of Mr. Thomas Smith, of Friday Street, Cheapside, and of Hadley, co. Middlesex, of which village he afterwards became the Rector. Mrs. Chapone, in an "Imitation of Ossian," described the personal appearance and intellectual characteristics of her friend Mr. Burrows, in somewhat grandiloquent language; but the following description of him by his grandson, Professor Burrows, from an existing representation, is at once concise and forcible: "A broad, heavy-built, but well-made man, sitting in the attitude of reading a newspaper, with his legs crossed, and with a bolt-upright, resolute, keen, intelligent air. It is a mere outline . . . . but remarkably well done."* He had been Morning Preacher at St. Anne's, Soho, then a fashionable church, and was also for some time "Lecturer" at Berkeley Chapel, Mayfair, as also Minister of Christ Church, Blackfriars, and Rector of St. Clement Danes, in the Strand. His influence in certain of the literary gatherings of London appears to have been deservedly considerable. He died, aged 54, deeply regretted by a large circle of friends, in 1786, and was buried at Hadley.†

* [*Note by the Author.*]—Thomas Hayton, aged 21, son of John Hayton, of Wigton, co. Cumberland, Gent., matriculated from Queen's College, 13 March, 1815. He was placed in the second class in *literis Humanioribus* in Easter Term 1818, and graduated B.A. 22 Oct. of the same year. He is now Vicar of Crendon.

† *History of the Family of Burrows*, etc., p. 32.

‡ "I wish you were to hear Mr. Burrows preach. There is a simplicity and an earnestness in his manner more affecting than anything I ever heard from the pulpit. His matter is not less admirable than his manner; both seem to speak the true spirit of Christianity.—*Posthumous Works of Mrs. Chapone.* Letter of 31 July, 1763. London: 1804.

* *History of the Family of Burrows*, etc., p. 74.

† There are monuments existing in St. Mary's Church, Hadley, to this clergyman, to his youngest son James, to Mary his wife, who died in 1792, to his sister "Mrs. Amy Burrows," with armorial bearings, and to his only daughter Frances, who died 11 May, 1860. There are also several monuments to their kinsfolk and connections, the Culling Smiths (baronets), the Cotterells, and the Mosses.

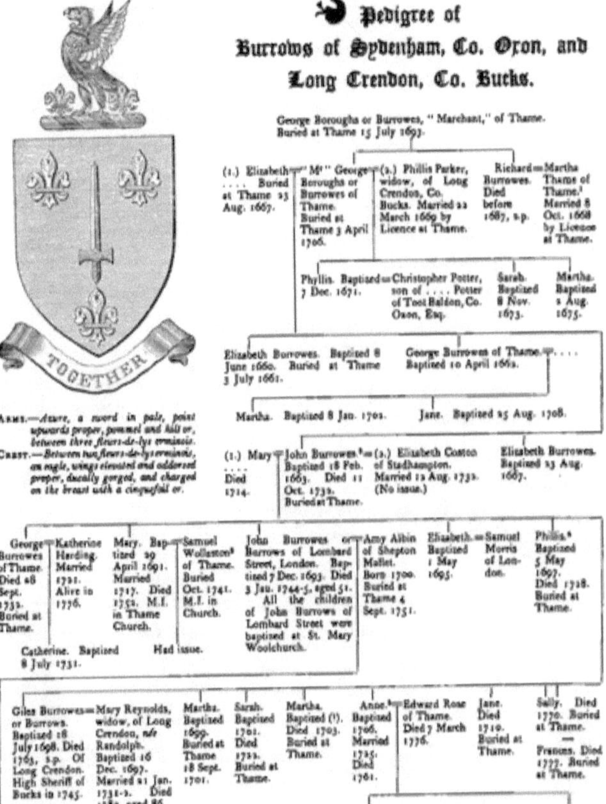

ARMS.—*Azure, a sword in pale, point upwards proper, pommel and hilt or, between three fleurs-de-lys erminois.*
CREST.—*Between two fleurs-de-lys erminois, an eagle, wings elevated and addorsed proper, ducally gorged, and charged on the breast with a cinquefoil or.*

Pedigree of Burrows of Sydenham, Co. Oxon, and Long Crendon, Co. Bucks.

George Boroughs or Burrowes, "Marchant," of Thame. Buried at Thame 15 July 1693.

(1.) Elizabeth .... Buried at Thame 23 Aug. 1667. = Mr "George" Boroughs or Burrowes of Thame. Buried at Thame 3 April 1706. = (2.) Phillis Parker, widow, of Long Crendon, Co. Bucks. Married 22 March 1669 by Licence at Thame.

Richard Burrowes. Died before 1687, s.p. = Martha Thame of Thame.[1] Married 8 Oct. 1668 by Licence at Thame.

Phyllis. Baptized 7 Dec. 1671. = Christopher Potter, son of .... Potter of Toot Baldon, Co. Oxon, Esq.
Sarah. Baptized 8 Nov. 1673.
Martha. Baptized 2 Aug. 1675.

Elizabeth Burrowes. Baptized 8 June 1660. Buried at Thame 3 July 1661.
George Burrowes of Thame. Baptized 10 April 1662. = ...

Martha. Baptized 8 Jan. 1702.
Jane. Baptized 25 Aug. 1708.

(1.) Mary .... Died 1714. = John Burrowes.[2] Baptized 18 Feb. 1663. Died 11 Oct. 1732. Buried at Thame. = (2.) Elizabeth Costeo of Stadhampton. Married 12 Aug. 1732. (No issue.)
Elizabeth Burrowes. Baptized 23 Aug. 1667.

George Burrowes of Thame. Died 28 Sept. 1732. Buried at Thame. = Katherine Harding. Married 1721. Alive in 1776.
Catherine. Baptized 8 July 1731.

Mary. Baptized 29 April 1691. Married 1717. Died 1752. M.I. in Thame Church. = Samuel Wollaston[3] of Thame. Buried Oct. 1741. M.I. in Church.
Had issue.

John Burrowes or Barrows of Lombard Street, London. Baptized 7 Dec. 1693. Died 3 Jan. 1744-5, aged 51. All the children of John Burrows of Lombard Street were baptized at St. Mary Woolchurch. = Amy Albin of Shepton Mallet. Born 1700. Buried at Thame 4 Sept. 1751.

Elizabeth. Baptized 1 May 1695. = Samuel Morris of London.

Phillis.[4] Baptized 5 May 1697. Died 1728. Buried at Thame.

Giles Burrowes or Burrows. Baptized 18 July 1698. Died 1763, s.p. Of Long Crendon. High Sheriff of Bucks in 1745. = Mary Reynolds, widow, of Long Crendon, *née* Randolph. Baptized 16 Dec. 1697. Married 21 Jan. 1731-2. Died 1783, aged 86.

Martha. Baptized 1699. Buried at Thame 18 Sept. 1701.
Sarah. Baptized 1701. Died 1722. Buried at Thame.
Martha. Baptized (?). Died 1703. Buried at Thame.

Anne.[5] Baptized 1706. Married 1725. Died 1761. = Edward Rose of Thame. Died 7 March 1776.
Burrows Rose. Baptized March 1732-3. Buried 1 May 1747. Had issue.
And others.

Jane. Died 1710. Buried at Thame.

Sally. Died 1770. Buried at Thame.
Frances. Died 1777. Buried at Thame.

A

[1] Founded a Charity at Thame in 1687.
[2] Churchwarden of Thame 1699; moved to St. Mary Woolchurch, London, about 1706; bequeathed an Educational Charity to Thame.
[3] Bequeathed an Educational Charity to Thame.
[4] Bequeathed a Charity to Thame.
[5] The Jemmetts and Turners of Thame are descended by the female line from this marriage.

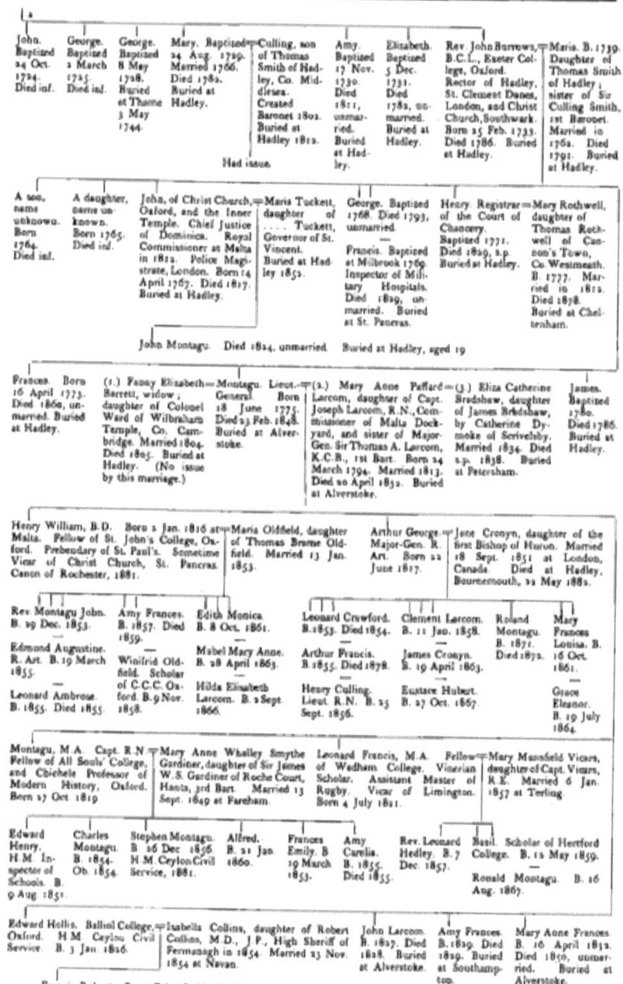

a

John. Baptized 24 Oct. 1724. Died inf.

George. Baptized 2 March 1725. Died inf.

George. Baptized 8 May 1728. Buried at Thame 3 May 1744.

Mary. Baptized 24 Aug. 1729. Married 1766. Died 1782. Buried at Hadley. = Culling, son of Thomas Smith of Hadley, Co. Middlesex. Created Baronet 1802. Buried at Hadley 1812.

Had issue.

Amy. Baptized 17 Nov. 1730. Died 1811, unmarried. Buried at Hadley.

Elizabeth. Baptized 5 Dec. 1731. Died 1782, unmarried. Buried at Hadley.

Rev. John Burrows, B.C.L., Exeter College, Oxford. Rector of Hadley, St. Clement Danes, London, and Christ Church, Southwark. Born 25 Feb. 1733. Died 1786. Buried at Hadley. = Maria. B. 1739. Daughter of Thomas Smith of Hadley; sister of Sir Culling Smith, 1st Baronet. Married in 1762. Died 1791. Buried at Hadley.

A son, name unknown. Born 1764. Died inf.

A daughter, name unknown. Born 1765. Died inf.

John, of Christ Church, Oxford, and the Inner Temple. Chief Justice of Dominica. Royal Commissioner at Malta in 1812. Police Magistrate, London. Born 14 April 1767. Died 1817. Buried at Hadley. = Maria Tuckett, daughter of .... Tuckett, Governor of St. Vincent. Buried at Hadley 1852.

John Montagu. Died 1824, unmarried. Buried at Hadley, aged 19

George. Baptized 1768. Died 1793, unmarried.

—

Francis. Baptized at Millbrook 1769. Inspector of Military Hospitals. Died 1829, unmarried. Buried at St. Pancras.

Henry. Registrar of the Court of Chancery. Baptized 1771. Died 1829, s.p. Buried at Hadley. = Mary Rothwell, daughter of Thomas Rothwell of Cannon's Town, Co. Westmeath. B. 1777. Married in 1812. Died 1878. Buried at Cheltenham.

Frances. Born 16 April 1773. Died 1860, unmarried. Buried at Hadley.

(1.) Fanny Elizabeth Barrett, widow; daughter of Colonel Ward of Wilbraham Temple, Co. Cambridge. Married 1804. Died 1805. Buried at Hadley. (No issue by this marriage.) = Montagu. Lieut.-General. Born 18 June 1775. Died 23 Feb. 1848. Buried at Alverstoke. = (2.) Mary Anne Paffard Larcom, daughter of Capt. Joseph Larcom, R.N., Commissioner of Malta Dockyard, and sister of Major-Gen. Sir Thomas A. Larcom, K.C.B., 1st Bart. Born 24 March 1794. Married 1813. Died 20 April 1832. Buried at Alverstoke. = (3.) Eliza Catherine Bradshaw, daughter of James Bradshaw, by Catherine Dymoke of Scrivelsby. Married 1834. Died s.p. 1838. Buried at Petersham.

James. Baptized 1780. Died 1786. Buried at Hadley.

Henry William, B.D. Born 2 Jan. 1816 at Malta. Fellow of St. John's College, Oxford. Prebendary of St. Paul's. Sometime Vicar of Christ Church, St. Pancras. Canon of Rochester, 1881. = Maria Oldfield, daughter of Thomas Brame Oldfield. Married 13 Jan. 1853.

Rev. Montagu John. B. 29 Dec. 1853.

—

Edmond Augustine. R. Art. B. 19 March 1855.

—

Leonard Ambrose. B. 1855. Died 1855.

Amy Frances. B. 1857. Died 1859.

—

Winifrid Oldfield. Scholar of C.C.C. Oxford. B. 9 Nov. 1858.

Edith Monica. B. 8 Oct. 1861.

—

Mabel Mary Anne. B. 28 April 1863.

—

Hilda Elizabeth Larcom. B. 2 Sept. 1866.

Arthur George. Major-Gen. R. Art. Born 22 June 1817. = Jane Cronyn, daughter of the first Bishop of Huron. Married 18 Sept. 1851 at London, Canada. Died at Hadley, Bournemouth, 22 May 1882.

Leonard Crawford. B. 1853. Died 1854.

—

Arthur Francis. B. 1855. Died 1878.

—

Henry Culling. Lieut. R.N. B. 25 Sept. 1856.

Clement Larcom. B. 11 Jan. 1858.

—

James Cronyn. B. 19 April 1863.

—

Eustace Hubert. B. 27 Oct. 1867.

Roland Montagu. B. 1871. Died 1872.

Mary Frances Louisa. B. 16 Oct. 1861.

—

Grace Eleanor. B. 19 July 1864.

Montagu, M.A. Capt. R.N. Fellow of All Souls' College, and Chichele Professor of Modern History, Oxford. Born 27 Oct. 1819 = Mary Anne Whalley Smythe Gardiner, daughter of Sir James W. S. Gardiner of Roche Court, Hants, 3rd Bart. Married 13 Sept. 1849 at Fareham.

Edward Henry. H.M. Inspector of Schools. B. 9 Aug. 1851.

Charles Montagu. B. 1854. Ob. 1854.

Stephen Montagu. B. 26 Dec. 1856. H.M. Ceylon Civil Service, 1881.

Alfred. B. 21 Jan. 1860.

Frances Emily. B. 19 March 1853.

Amy Carelia. B. 1855. Died 1855.

Leonard Francis, M.A. Fellow of Wadham College. Vinerian Scholar. Assistant Master of Rugby. Vicar of Limington. Born 4 July 1821. = Mary Mansfield Vicars, daughter of Capt. Vicars, R.E. Married 6 Jan. 1857 at Terling.

Rev. Leonard Hedley. B. 7 Dec. 1857.

Basil. Scholar of Hertford College. B. 12 May 1859.

—

Ronald Montagu. B. 16 Aug. 1867.

Edward Hollis. Balliol College, Oxford. H.M. Ceylon Civil Service. B. 3 Jan. 1826. = Isabella Collins, daughter of Robert Collins, M.D., J.P., High Sheriff of Fermanagh in 1854. Married 23 Nov. 1854 at Navan.

Francis Robert. B. 29 Feb. 1856 in Ceylon.

John Larcom. B. 1827. Died 1828. Buried at Alverstoke.

Amy Frances. B. 1829. Died 1829. Buried at Southampton.

Mary Anne Frances. B. 16 April 1832. Died 1850, unmarried. Buried at Alverstoke.

Towersey.

THE Church, as at present existing, consists of nave, chancel, north chantry, and tower over its south porch. It is dedicated to God in honour of St. Katherine, and contains provision for seating nearly three hundred people. From its first foundation it was a chapelry of the Prebendal Church of Thame; served, firstly, under the direction of the Prebendary of Thame, and, subsequently, when the Prebend was suppressed, by the Vicar. It no doubt formed part of one of the charges of St. Birinus of Dorchester. Originally it was of Norman or Romanesque architecture, now it is of later styles. There are excellent school buildings standing to the south-west of the churchyard, and a picturesque modern vicarage in a pleasant garden to the west.

Prior to the "restoration" of the Church, about thirty years ago, in which it is to be feared several objects of archæological interest were removed and lost, there was a bell-turret, twelve feet square, at the west end of the nave. This, however, was taken down, when the Tower was built, as was also a parvise over the old, first-pointed south porch. The present Tower, which was erected by the generosity, and at the sole cost, of the late lord of the manor, Mr. Edward Griffin, is an important and substantial addition to the sacred building. Its chief defect, however, is that the pinnacles by which it is surmounted are a little too stunted, and want both height and elegance. Perhaps, too, if the Tower had been carried up six or eight feet higher, as an architect would no doubt have suggested, it might have harmonized better with the outline and main features of the sacred building, which, on account of the unusual size of its long and broad roof, unrelieved by any break or ornament, is wanting generally in effect. The Belfry, entered from the porch by a ladder, contains a peal of four modern bells and an old Saint's Bell.

The Chancel, measured from within, is thirteen feet wide and twenty feet long, the nave twenty-four feet in width and fifty-six feet in length, thus making the whole length of the building (including the width of the chancel arch) seventy-seven and a half feet.

There is a remarkable square-headed Norman *piscina*, with a projecting pillar and square drain, *circa* 1150, on the south side of the sanctuary, perhaps the most notable detail remaining in the church—shewing that a very old chapel had evidently existed here even as early as the days when Theobald, Archbishop of Canterbury, ruled over the province in the reign of King Stephen. The following engraving of it is most exact. Since the original drawing was made, however, the level of the sanctuary floor has been raised more than two feet; so that at least half the pillar here represented is now buried in the ground.

Ancient Piscina, Towersey Church.
(From a Drawing by Mr. William Twopeny.)

In the north wall of the chancel, near the sanctuary, there is a small recess of freestone—no doubt the original Eastern sepulchre. It is eleven inches high, eight inches broad, and five deep; just sufficient to receive a Pyx or *Ciborium*, with the Blessed Sacrament; and is placed in exactly that position which the ancient rules and customs of the Catholic Church decreed that it should occupy.

Against the north side of the chancel, west of the sanctuary, an altar-tomb to the memory of the ancient family of Heath remains. Its lower part is of freestone, the slab being of marble. This latter is five feet five inches in length, and twenty-one inches broad. The tomb itself is two feet and five inches in height. On the slab a boldly-cut coat of arms, argent, a chevron gules between three embattled towers sable, with the motto, "**In the Lord is all our trust,**" still remains. A similar coat (which does not appear in Sir Bernard Burke's *Armoury*) appears to have been removed from the head of the north lancet window of the chancel adjoining, where (though damaged) it remained in the year 1840.

There are eastern windows on either side of the chancel arch, before which altars anciently stood. These windows of two lights, with a quatrefoil in the head, are of excellent second-pointed work, the mouldings of the mullions being bold and good.

There is also a chantry chapel on the north side of the nave, towards its eastern part, covered by a lean-to roof. The northern window therein, with a wide splay, is of three lights, with appropriate tracery in the head, of an artistic second-pointed character. Forty years ago this window was filled with several curious and interesting fragments of stained glass, amongst others in the central light a figure of our Blessed Lord in the act of benediction. At that time the arms of the Arundells and the Collingridges also remained. This chantry, since the "restoration" of the church, has been skreened off by an oak skreen and is now used as a vestry. Near the pue of this chantry chapel, on the north side of the nave, a Purbeck marble slab, with the following fragmentary inscription, with four shields of brass at the corners, remained within the last forty years. The words in brackets were then wanting :—

Pray for the sowlys of William [de Grenville] and Christian his wife; also for [. . . . .] Arundell and Julyan [his wife] Also for Bartholomew Collingridge & Alys his wife, and William ther sonn that her' lyeth upon whose sowlys o'r Lord Jhu have mercy. Amen.

The windows of the nave are of two lights, second-pointed in character, with flowing tracery in their heads, the west window of the nave being of a specially graceful design—of three lights with quatrefoils of the same style and character up above. There is a north door immediately opposite the south porch. The roof, simple and solid, is of an excellent and dignified pitch.

The font, of hard close-grained freestone—most probably of Norman work—is perfectly plain and circular, with no lining of lead. It stands upon a single step, formerly it was raised on two steps, near the south porch, on the left hand of the door, as one enters; and is protected by a modern carved oak cover of Jacobean character, made apparently to correspond with the pulpit. The iron frame for an hour-glass remained attached to the pulpit, and was a good specimen of early seventeenth-century metal work, until the year 1843, but appears to have been then removed.

The Chancel itself is much dilapidated, and at the east end shews signs of having lost security as regards its foundations. Parts of its external stone work are evidently very old. It has been recently bound together with iron bands, one of which is placed horizontally across the old Romanesque *piscina*. The east window of the sanctuary is of two lights, with a quatrefoil in the head, its mouldings being rich and fine. There were formerly two corbelled brackets in freestone, obviously for images, on the eastern wall, one on either side of the chancel window. And there are still two rude and curious heads in stone, most possibly terminations of the internal hood-mouldings of long-destroyed Norman windows. The north and south windows of the sanctuary are plain lancets. There is a later window of two lights inserted on the south side of the chancel, very commonplace in character. Several old pues in the nave and four ancient oak stalls in the chancel were removed about thirty years ago, and the poppy-heads or carved ends of the latter placed elsewhere, two in the nave and one near the south door.

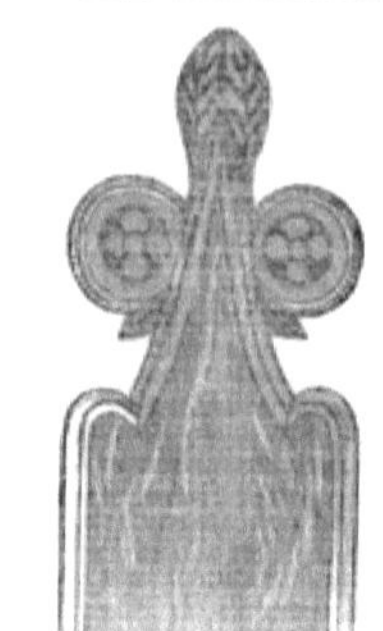

Ancient Stall-head, Towersey Church.

(From a Drawing by the Author.)

The pue in place of the stalls on the south side of the chancel is modern and commonplace.

The solid communion-table of oak—four feet nine inches long, two feet six inches broad, and two feet eight inches high—is covered with an *antependium* and frontal of crimson velvet.

Just outside the chancel arch on the north side stands the old Jacobean pulpit, with a sounding-board; and on the south, to correspond, cumbersome reading-desks, facing westwards, for the minister and clerk.

The Church of old was mainly served by the Prebendaries and Vicars of Thame or their direct deputies. But since the Reformation resident curates, or curates serving two or three parishes, have from time to time ministered here. Sir Laurence Rouby was "parish priest" in the first year of Queen Mary Tudor. William Jones was "clerk"—that is, clerk in Holy Orders—in 1606. Richard Rastall, of a Thame family, was curate in 1629; and Christopher Etherigg, also sprung from Thame, "parson" in 1632. Hugh Willis was curate in 1665, and Edward Fellowes in 1666. John King officiated here in 1702. William Yate was ministering in 1756; John Newborough was curate in 1759; his son, William Newborough, curate in 1769; Thomas Cripps in 1791; Timothy T. Lee in 1792; Thomas Evans in 1794; and the Rev. Joseph Rose at a later period. When the living was separated from Thame Mr. Williams became the perpetual curate for a short period; afterwards the Rev. Samuel W. Barnett, B.A. Cantab., was appointed vicar. He resided here greatly respected for more than thirty years; and, on his resignation, was succeeded by the Rev. Henry Hare, B.A., of Trinity College, Dublin.

This clergyman is the fourth son of William Hare, of the city of Dublin, gent., by Eliza his wife, and was born 4th November, 1807. He was sometime "Impropriate Curate" of Painstown, co. Carlow; subsequently Minister of St. Mary's, Kilkenny; Prebendary of Blackrath in the Cathedral Church of that city, and Chaplain of the Forces. He married Frances-Alicia, second daughter of William Fishbourne, of Carlow, gent., and has issue three sons, William, John, and Joseph; and two daughters, Elizabeth and Sophia-Jane. He was instituted to Towersey in October 1878. The gross value of the benefice, with a vicarage-house, is £146.

The above coat of arms appears on the upper slab, and the following inscription, much worn, remains on the south side of the tomb of the Towers family :—

HERE LIETH THE BODY OF MARY
THE LATE WIFE OF EDWARD HETH
WHO DEPARTED THIS
LIFE 25TH DAY OF IUNE ANNO
DO' 1676 BEING AGED 27
YEARS.

The following entries relating to this lady and her son, courteously furnished to me by the present Vicar, Mr. Hare, occur in the Old Register :—

Mary the wife of Edward Heath deseased the 25th day of June in the year of our Lord God, 1676.

Edward the Son of Edward Heath was baptised the 10th day of June in the year of our Lord God, 1676.

There was also an inscription to the following effect, on a diamond-shaped slab of white marble, but it is now lost :—

Here
Lieth the Bodie
of ALICE ye Daughter of
THOMAS & ANNE PHILLIPS
of Wor'nall. She died an
Infant, Nov. ye 14th
1729.

There is a good example of an Elizabethan Communion Cup, *circa* 1570, of the usual shape and type, and with the ordinary Renaissance engraving, remaining here. It is of silver, marked with (1) a fleur-de-lys, (2) a crowned leopard's head, (3) a lion passant guardant, and (4) the letter "u." Its height is exactly seven inches, and it is three inches and three-quarters across the bowl. The knop, stem, and mouldings are fairly executed, and it is in very good preservation. The other vessels are modern, unremarkable, and not of precious metal.

As in the case of Tettesworth and Sydenham, so in that of Towersey, the triumphant policy of the "robbers of Churches" is on record in the following document, shewing the nakedness of the land :—

Queen's Remembrancer, Miscellanea, Church Goods, Record Office.

[HUNDRED] OF TAME.—Inventory Indentyd & mayd the xvij daye of Maye in the vj yere of the Reygne of Kyng Edward the VJ of all bellis challis & surpleases of the Chyrche of Touzay delyvered by Sr ffrauncs Knollis Sr Will'm Ransfford Knyghts Thomas Burges leonard Chamberlayn Edm'd Asshefeld & Thomas Dent'n Esquieres unto the custody of Sr laurens Rouby curatt John Good thomas Addambis churche wardyns savely to kepe to the use of ou' Soweryn lord the Kyng.

Impa one challes of sylu' wt ought a paten.
Itm thre bells.
laurens Rouby curatt.

The Register Books, on the whole, have been well and carefully kept. The oldest, a vellum volume, small folio in size, commences in the year 1589 and ends in 1729. Another book of Marriages commences in 1756 and ends in 1785. The records of a third volume—inaccurately marked No. 1 on its exterior—begin in 1733 and end in 1752. A fourth volume, containing Baptisms and Burials, begins in 1792 and ends in 1812. The handwriting of the sixteenth and seventeenth centuries is much better, clearer, and more carefully executed than that of later periods. The methods of entry, too, are precise, express, and definite. In many cases, however, the spelling is at once archaic and provincial.

The following extracts from the earlier part of the Ancient Register may be here properly reproduced :—

Extracts from the Register Book of the Chapel of Saint Katherine, Towersey, in the co. of Bucks.

1590. James quatreman the sonne of Nicholas quatreman was christened the 1th of November predict'.

1591. John Alnat the sonne of John Alnat was christened the xvij daye of October anno predict'.

1592. Edmund horseman the sonne of John Horseman was christened the vijth day of Maie An'o p'dict'.

Peter bowden & John bowden the sonnes of Thomas bowden were christened the xxvth of June An'o predict'.

Cristian floyde the daughter of gregory floyde was christened the viij daye of October An'o predict'.

1593\. Alice quatreman the daughter of Nicholas quatereman was baptized the xxvjth daye of August An'o p'dict.

Cornelius horseman the sonne of John Horseman was baptized the xxxth day of December A'no predict.

1595\. William Bowden the sonne of Thomas Bowden was christened the viijth day of June an'o predict.

Agnes horseman the daughter of John Horseman was baptized the second day of November, An'o predict.

1596\. Katherine Horseman the daughter of John Horseman was baptized the xvijth day of November An'o predict'.

John baylye the sonne of John bailey th' elder was christened the xxixth of November An'o p'dict.

Margaret floyd the daughter of gregory floyd was christened the xxixth day of february An'o p'dict'.

1597\. ffrauncs bowden the sonne of thomas Bowden was christened the xviijth of December, A'o p'dict.

1598\. John Collyns the sonne of John Collins was christened the xxjst of December A'o p'dict.

1599\. Christian ffincher the daughter of Robt ffincher, clerke, was borne the xxiijd of June & christened the viijth of Julye followinge.

1604\. Samuell ffincher the sonne of Robert ffincher clerk was baptized the xxixth of Julie A'o p'dict'.

1606\. A'o Dom. Charnell Johnes the sonne of Will: Johnes, Cler: was borne the 5th of June, being thursday between xj and xij a clocke in the night and christened the eleventh daye of the same moneth 1606.

Edmund Belsone the sonne of Steven Belson was christened the seaventh of September 1606.

1608\. fransise Stutfield the daughter of Tho. Stutfield was christened eodem die [i.e. the second of September] an'o p'dict'.

1617\. Will'm Brudnell the sonne of Wm Brudnell gent. was baptized the 17 of August Ao p'dict.

Jeffry Alnut the sonne of John Alnott was baptized the xijth of October in Ao p'dict'.

1618\. alice horseman was buried the 7 of february Ao p'dict.

Agnes the daughter of John Belson was baptized the 26 of Apprill p'edict.

Jeremias Whyte filius Guil'mi Whyte baptizatus erat primi die mensis Octobris in Ao p'dict.

1619\. Alice horseman vid' was Buried the 5 of Maie.

1620\. Phillippe hedges and Ellen Rogers were married the fyrst of Januarie in ao p'dict.

1621\. Robart harison and Anne Smale boyth of Oxon werre married the xxijnd of Apprill.

John Parker and Elizabeth Way the daughter of Thom's Way were married the xxvij of May in ao p'dict.

1622\. John Collins Al's Dayne was Buried the vjth of October in Ao p'dict.

1623\. James the sonne of Edmond horseman was baptized the xjth of May in ao p'dict.

1624\. Margery the daughter of Aaron Collins was baptized the 28th of November in Ao p'dict.

1625\. Cornelius Horseman and Katherin hugges were married the xvij of Jannuarye in Ao p'dict.

George heyborne was Buried the xxjst of January ao p'dict.

1626\. Agnes horsma' the daughter of Edward horsma' was Baptized the 3 of Januarie in ao p'dict.

John Dorrell & Susan hubbard were married the xxth of August ao p'dict.

Gragarie Deane the son of Aaron Deane was baptized the iiij of februarii in ao p'dict.

1627\. Elizabeth Horseman the daughter of Edwarde horseman was baptized the 7th of november in Ao p'dict.

1628\. Matha the daughter of Edward Norwod was baptized the iijd of Marche in ao p'dict.

Rich. Rennell Curat de Towerseye, 1629.

1629\. John Horseman was buryed September 23rd Anno Dom' 1629.

Aaron Deane the sonne of Aaron Deane was baptized Nov. 1 Anno Dom' 1629.

1630\. Petrus Tomlinson et Margareta filia Joh'es Burte de Thame matrimonio coniuncti sunt 8vo die Aprilis An'o Dom' 1630.

1631\. Joh's filius Aaronis Deane bapt' erat 12 Jan. 1631.

Johis filius Edwardi Horseman baptiz' 20o die Jan. 1631.

Christopher Etherigge Curat. de Towersey, 1632.

1633\. Charles Etherigge the sonne of Christopher Etherigge, Clerke, was borne the twentieth day of December being friday at twelve of the clocke at night or there about was baptized the twentie seconde day being Sunday 1633.

Richard the sonne of Aaron Deane and of Rebecca his wife baptized the seauenteenth day of ffebruarie 1633.

1636\. Christopher Deane the son of Aaron Deane and Rebecca his wife was baptized the nineteenth day of november 1635.

1638\. Thomas Deane the sonne of Aaron Deane and of Rebeccha his wife was baptized the second day of December.

1641\. William Hitcheogdon the sonne of Matthew Hitcheadon and of Joane his wife was baptized the twentie seauenth day of December.

Gregory Howlet the sonne of John Howlet was baptized the nineteenth day of Januarie.

1642\. Edmond Belson the sonne of Stephen Belson and of Judith his wife was baptized the twentie second day of Januarie.

1643\. Sibbell Dutton the daughter of Leonard Dutton and of Sibbell his wife was baptized the third day of June.

Thomas Horseman the sonne of John Horseman was baptized the third day of November.

1645\. Edmond Dutton the sonne of Leonard Dutton and of Sibbell his wife, was baptized the seauenteenth day of Aprill an'o p'dict' 1645.

John Woodbridge the sonne of Robert Woodbridge and of Margaret his wife was baptized the twentie sixth day of December anno domini p'dict.

1646\. Mary Belson the daughter of John Belson & Joane his wife was baptized the seaventeenth day of September in the year of our lord God 1646.

1647\. Mary way the daughter of Richard way and of Mary his wife was baptized the second day of November anno p'dicto. Videlicet 1647.

William North the son of William North and Jane his wife was baptised the 4th day of November Anno p'dicto 1647.

1649. Zachary Deane the soone of Zachary Deane & of Alice his wife was baptized the twenty ninth day of October, a'o p'dicto 1649.

Richard Horseman and James Horseman the sonnes of John Horseman & Elizabeth his wife were baptized the first day of December Anno Dom. 1649.

1650. Henry Deane the sonne of Aaron Deane and of Priscilla his wife was baptized the first day of August anno Domini 1650.

1651. Mary Inglish the daughter of Richard Inglish and of Jane his wife was baptised the seaventeenth day of Julie anno predicto 1651.

Mary Deane the daughter of Aaron Deane and Priscilla his wife was baptized the twelfth day of Februarie Anno Domini 1651.

1652. Elizabeth Grubb the daughter of Mr John Grubb & of Bashwell his wife was baptized the fourth day of September anno supra.

John Deane the sonne of Zachary Deane and of Allice his wife was baptized the twentie third day of May.

Burials.

1594. Peter Dorrell was buryede the xvjth day of decemb. An'o p'dict.

1595. Agnes Horseman the daughter of John Horseman was buried the xviijth day of November a^{o} p'dict.

1596. Edward Belson was buried the first day of Maie 1596.

Katherine horseman the daughter of John Horseman was buryed the vjth of Januarye A^{o} p'dict.

1597. ffraunces bowden the sonne of Thomas Bowden was buryed the xxvj of December an'o p'dict.

Maude neweman al's ffoyd widdowe was buryed the xxijth day of februarye a'o p'dict.

1601. Elenor horseman the wife of John Horseman was buryed the xxth of September 1601.

1602. Margaret ffincher the wife of Robert ffincher clark was buryed the viijth of March A^{o} p'dict.

1603. John Deane al's Collynes was buryed ye xvth of Maye 1603.

Marye howllet the daughter of Edmond Howlet was burryed the xxixth of October a'o p'dict.

1604. Joane quatreman the daughter of Nicholas quaterman was burryed the 3 of Julye an'o 1604.

Thomas Tabbatte burryed the 16th of September.

1609. An Burte gentlewoman was buried the xxvth day of Julie 1609.

1634. Gregorie ffloyd was buried the eight day of Aprill.

Rebecca the daughter of Edward Horseman & of Ursula his wife was buried the 10th day of May.

1640. Ellenour the wife of Phillippe Hedges was buried ye sixteenth day of December.

Mary the wife of Thomas howlet was buried the twentieth day of Januarie Anno predicto.

Ann howlet the daughter of Thomas Howlet was buried the twentie fifth day of ffebruarie anno predicto.

1642. Henry deane the sonne of Aaron Deane was buried the second day of October Anno predicti 1642.

1643. Sibell the daughter of Leonard Dutton was buried the tenth day of June.

Thomas Bull of Thame was buried the twentie third day of June Anno p'dict' 1643.

Rebeccha the wife of Aaron Deane was buried the twentie seaventh day of July Anno Dom' 1643.

Isabell the wife of Baldwin Baron was buried the twentie first day of August anno p'dict 1643.

William Alnat iunior was buried the twentie seaventh day of November anno dom' 1643.

1645. Barbara Horseman the wife of James Horseman was buried the thirteenth day of October a^{o} p'dict 1645.

1646. Thomas Howlett the sonne of John Howlet was buried the twenty second day of October anno supradict'.

1647. Mary the wife of Richard Way was buried the fourth day of November Anno Domini 1647.

1650. Margaret Way the wife of Thomas Way, generosus, was buried the twentie eight day of September Anno Dom'n' 1650.

1651. Henry deane the sonne of Aaron deane & of Priscilla his wife was buried the first day of July in the year 1651.

1652. Mary deane the daughter of Aaron Deane and of Priscilla his wife was buried the fifteenth day of July Anno p'dict 1652.

1653. Thomas Way, generosus, was buried the twentie third day of August in the year of our Lord God, 1653.

Baptisms and Marriages.

1648. Zacharie Deane & Allen Ewestace of Bledlow were married the 30th daie of October being mundaie Anno domini 1648.

1668. Richard Deane the soun Zachary Deane & Alice his wife was baptized the 28 daye of Marne An'o Domini 1668.

1674. John Alnat the son of John Alnat was baptized August 22. In the yeare of our Lord 1674.

1651. Richard Way the sonne of Mr Thomas Way and Margarett Mead the daughter of Thomas Mead & of Sibell her mother were married the seaventh day of Aprill anno dom' 1651.

Robert Robotham of Thame and Sarah hebborne widowe of hebborne were married the twentye eighth day of August anno p'dicto 1651.

Richard Atkins the sonne of Richard Atkins of Thame and Jane Llvet (? Lovett) of the same were married the eighteenth day of March anno p'ict 1651.

Thomas Way the sonne of Richard Way and of Margarett his wife was baptized the nineteenth day of August 1652.

Charles Deane the son of Aaron Deane & of Priscilla his wife was baptized the ninth day of June in the year of our Lord God 1653.

Aaron Deane the sone of Zachariah Deane was baptized the 23 November 1654.

Zachary Deane the sonne of Zachary Deane was baptised the 29 day of October 1649.

John Deane the son of Zachary Deane was baptised the 23 day of May 1652.

Mary deane the dafter of Savce deane was baptised the six day of Aprill in the year of our Lord 1662.

Christofer deane the sonne of Serce Deane was baptised the three & twenty day of March in the year of our Lord, 1663.

1664. Henery Deane the sonne of Aaron deane was baptised the first day of December in the year of our Lord 1664.

Marriages.

William Newell & Catherine Tomlinson 13 Nov. 1609.
Thomas Tredway & Mary Way 15 Oct. 1632.
James Beake of Heddenham & Agnes Ballowe, of Thame, *vidua* } 1 Oct. 1633.
James Horseman & Jane Way 16 May 1644.

Death.

Dorothy Deane the wife of Richard Deane deceased the 8 of July 1675.

The Registers of our old churches in general were not so carefully kept during the Commonwealth, when Disorder reigned, services were unsaid, churches wrecked and closed, and the ministers were sometimes slandered, "rabbled" and ruined, and in consequence of this neglect much evidence of interest and value has thus been lost. There are distinct traces of omission and carelessness in the Registers of Towersey at the period in question. An Act had been passed under Cromwell, in 1653, enjoining the ministers to give up the old Parish Registers to some layman to be then appointed "Parish Registrar," who was empowered to take possession of them, and to charge fourpence for the insertion of every subsequent birth and burial, and one shilling for every marriage—celebrated by and before some Justice of the Peace.* Baptisms being repudiated by the Rebels and Revolutionists, save and except the occasional baptism of an ass or a colt in mockery and derision, were not inserted at this period; but, in many cases, were subsequently entered in a batch, when the Nation, sick at heart and weary of its oppressors, threw off the usurped authority of the allies and followers of Cromwell.

The surnames of Quartermain, Horseman, Bowden, Floyd, Dutton, Collins, Belson, Stutfield (or Stutville), Brudenell, Etheridge (or Etherigg), Dutton, Woodbridge, Grubb, Tabbatte (evidently Talbot), Way, Eustace, Lovett, Tredway, and Beake (or Beke), all found in the preceding extracts, are those of gentle-people either of Buckinghamshire or Oxfordshire during the sixteenth and seventeenth centuries. Some are members either of noble or knightly families.

In these extracts it is notable how many old English Christian names are retained, more especially the names of Saints; *e.g.*, Nicholas, Agnes, Jerome, Leonard, Matthew, Stephen, Margaret, Gregory, Peter, Christopher, and John. But the Puritan fancies for Old Testament and Jewish names soon took hold of the popular taste, and sometimes resulted in baptismal eccentricities* of a profane and ridiculous character.

The family of Belson owned lands in Towersey and several of its adjoining parishes, intermarrying, as the following Pedigrees shew, with the Cursons, Horsemans, Tempests, Lovetts,† Francklins, and Bullers (or Bollers), of Kingsey. Of this last-named family, Thomas Boller, by his Will, proved 15 October, 1532, left a legacy to the Church of Towersey.

As regards the tomb on the north side of the choir, the arms on which are given on page 257, it seems extremely probable that they are those of the ancient family of Towers or Tours, from which the place itself is named. The late Mr. Kidman, of Thame, preserving some ancient tradition, maintained this, and took a sketch of a similar coat, on the lancet window to the north of the sanctuary, which coat was in his day imperfect, and appears to have had the word **Towers** on a label above it. It is possible, however, that the family of Heath, or Heth, of Towersey and Thame, having intermarried with some member of the Towers family, proceeded to adopt their armorial bearings, an act for which precedents are not altogether wanting.

As regards the relationship between the Collingridges or Colridges, Arundells and Dormers, it will be set forth on a later page, in the Pedigree of the latter family.

---

* "Maryinge by Justices, election of Registers by parishioners and the use of Ruling Elders, first came into fashion in the time of [the] Rebellion under that Monster of Nature and bludy tyrant, Oliver Cromwell."—*Note inserted in the Parochial Register Book of Elwick, co. Durham.*

"Anno Dni, 1641. Know all men that the reason why little or nothing is registered from this year until the year 1649, was the Civil Warrs between King Charles and his Parliament, which put all into a confusion since then, and neither minister nor people could quietly stay at home for one party or the other."—*Note from the Register Book of Kibworth Beauchamp, co. Leicester.*

"The Ordinances contain no particular directions for the preservation of the Registers, and as they were retained in private hands, and the Registrars were continually changed, most of the records have been lost; in some parishes the entries are found in the old parish book of Registers. With the Restoration this irregular system of Registers ceased."—*Manual for the Genealogist, Topographer, Antiquary, etc.*; by Richard Sims, p. 353, 2nd Ed. London: 1861.

* The following seven examples of such names, which I have noted from time to time, may be worthy of being here recorded:—*Accepted* Frewen (or "*Accepted* Ebor," as he began to sign himself officially when he was made Archbishop of York in 1660), *Kill-sin* Pimple, *Rather-fruit* Foggs, *Never-faint* Dustpenny, *Faint-not* Kennard, *Got-a-shore-heavenward* Bigge, and *Free-gift* Mabbe.

† Of this family Lawrence Lovett married a niece of John, Lord Williams of Thame, *i.e.*, Elizabeth, the eldest daughter of his brother, Reginald Williams, by Elizabeth Fox his wife.

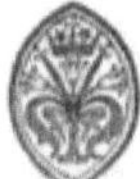

THE two following Pedigrees relate to an Oxfordshire family, which had many members residing at Towersey in the early part of the seventeenth century:—

Pedigree of Belson of Aston Rowant.

No. I.

ARMS.—*Gules, on a chevron engrailed between three greyhounds' heads erased argent, collared or, three hurts.*

[Harl. MSS., British Museum, No. 1412.]

Robert Belson.

Will'm Bellson of the Brill in Com. Buck. = Anne, dau'r to Walter Curson of Waterperry in Com. Oxon.

Augustine Belson of Aston Rohant in Com. Oxon, son'e and heire. = Margaret, dau'r to [Richard] Scarneinge de Com. Warr.

Edward Belson, 2 sonne, of Brill in Com. Bucks; mar. Anne Roce.

Johanne, mar. to Thomas Bullstrode, 1.

Anne, mar. to . . . . Butler, 2.

Robert Belson of Aston Rohant in Com. Oxon. = Anne, dau'r to Robert Tempest of Holmesyde in Com. Durham.

William Belson, 2 sonne, maryed Isabell, dau'r to Abraham Horseman of Hasely in Com. Oxon.

Elianor, 3

Nicholas, 2 sonne.

Augustine Belson of Aston Rohant, sonne and heire, mar. Mildred, dau'r to Edward Gage of Bentley in Com. Sussex.

Katherine, mar. to Wm. Brodgate of Lemmington in Com. Warr.

Margarett, mar. to Francis Lovett of Weston Pinkeney in Com. North'ton.

Elizabeth. — Margarett.

♣♣♣♣♣♣♣♣♣♣♣

Pedigree of Belson of Kingston Blunt.

No. II.

[Harl. MSS., British Museum, No. 1095.]

Will'm Belson of Aston Rohant in Com. Oxon. =

1 Thomas Belson of Aston Rohant.

2 John Belson of Kingston Blunt in Com. Oxon. = Alice, dau'r to John Ficher of Wensley in Com. Oxon.

Will'm. — John.

Agnes, mar. to . . . . Wilson.

Robert Belson of Kingston Blunt in Com. Oxon. = Mary, dau'r of . . . . Franklyn of Brodhinton, widdow of . . . . Wallys.

Amy, maryed to Robert Harris of Healey in Com. Oxon.

Isabell, mar. to John Bullor of Kingsey in Com. Buck.

Margarett, maryed to James Buller.

Sibill, maryed to George Cupper of Stoke.

Richard Belson of Kingston. = Elizabeth, dau'r of John Lechepole of Newbery.

Elianor, mar. to . . . .

1 Bartholomew. 2 Augustine. 3 Thomas. Johanne.

The following inscriptions, remaining in various parts of the churchyard of Towersey, are here reproduced:—

North side. With the arms of Griffin, Whitehouse, and Upjohn.

Sacred
to the memory of
EMILY
the dearly beloved Wife of
JAMES WHITEHOUSE GRIFFIN
of Towersey, Esquire, and second daughter of
William Rouse W. Upjohn
of Guestling Hall, Sussex, Esquire,
Who died April 26th 1874, aged 24 years.

Also of EMILY
the infant daughter of the above
JAMES WHITEHOUSE & EMILY GRIFFIN,
Who was born April 20th, 1874,
and survived her birth but a few hours.

Sacred
to the Memory of
EDWARD GRIFFIN
of Towersey Manor, Esquire,
Who died April 22nd 1879,
Aged 82 Years.

Also of MARY
His dearly-beloved wife
Who died
suddenly on the same day
Aged 66 Years.

"In the midst of life we are in death."
"Lovely and pleasant in their lives
and in their death they were not divided."
2 Samuel i. 23.

South side.

In Pious
And loving Memory
of
THE REV. S. W. BARNETT
30 years Vicar of this Parish,
Died May 16th 1880,
Aged 81 Years.
"Thy Brother shall rise again."

Also of ELIZABETH
Wife of the above
Died June 7th, 1881, Aged 77.
"Blessed are the dead which die in the Lord."
Rev. xiv. 13.

Sacred
To the Memory of
ANNIE FRANCES,
youngest daughter of
THE REVD S. W. BARNETT,
Vicar of Towersey
And Elizabeth His Wife,
Who died April 23rd 1859
Aged 14 years.

"I am the Resurrection and
the Life: he that believeth in
Me though he were dead
yet shall he live." John xi. 25.

South side.

In Memory of
WILLIAM HOLLIER,
of Towersey Grange,
Who died 26th Febry 1817 Aged 63 years.

"This world is vain and full of pain,
With cares and troubles sore;
But they are best who are at rest
With Christ for evermore."

Also of MARY his Wife
who died 23rd Febry 1820, Aged 61 years.

With patience to the last she did submit
And murmured not at what the Lord thought fit,
She with Christian courage did resign
Her soul to God at His appointed time.

North side.

EDWARD,
only son of
THOMAS & EMMA BURNARD,
of Westbrook, Towersey,
Who Died Jan. 10, 1880.

"Blessed are the dead which
die in the Lord from henceforth,
Yea, saith the Spirit, that
They may rest from their
labours; and their works
Do follow them."
Rev. xiv. 13.

South side.

Sacred
To the Memory of
CECILIA ABBOTT,
Daughter of WILLM & ELIZTH
ABBOTT,
Who died Octr 14th 1838
Aged 18 Years.

South side.
Sacred
To the Memory of
ELIZTH Wife of
WILLIAM ABBOTT,
Who died May 6, 1853,
Aged 66 years.

Sacred
to the Memory of
WILLIAM ABBOTT,
Who died Dec. 26th 1847,
Aged 64 years.

Sacred
to the Memory of
TIMOTHY NORTH,
Who departed this life
13th March 1836,
Aged 28 years.

In Memory of
ANN NORTH,
Who departed this Life
January 2nd 1824
Aged 23 yrs.

In Memory of
BETHIA Wife of WILLM NORTH,
Who Died June 3rd
1809
Aged 74 Years.

In Memory of
GEORGE, Son of
WILLM & BETHIA
NORTH,
Who died 9th May 1801,
Aged 13.

In Memory of
HENRY NORTH,
Who departed this Life
August 22nd 1834
Aged 26 years.

In Memory of
WILLIAM NORTH,
Who died June 4th 1842
In the 80th year of his age.

In Memory of
WILLM NORTH,
Who died 1st June
1801, Aged 77.

South side.
In Memory of
ANN, Relict of
WILLIAM NORTH,
Who was burried July 24,
1845
Aged 72 Years.

Sacred
To the Memory of
ANN NORTH,
Who departed this life
February 2nd 1846
Aged 13 Years.
"Since Death cannot be denied,
But will the dearest friends divide;
Lord, grant that we may meet again."

Sacred
To the Memory of
THOMAS HENRY NORTH,
Who departed this life
August the 5th 1846,
Aged 9 years.
"The Lord gave and the Lord hath taken away,
Blessed be the Name of the Lord."

Sacred
To the Memory of
MARIA, Wife of GEOE NORTH,
and Daughter of
WILLIAM & ELIZABETH
ABBOTT,
Who died July 12th 1851
Aged 34 Years.
"Blessed are the dead who die in the Lord."

Sacred
To the Memory of
ELIZTH Daughter of
WILLM & ANN NORTH,
of Towersey,
Who departed this life
30th March 1864.
Aged 18 Years.

Sacred to the Memory of
HARRIET, Wife of
THOMAS MALIN,
Who died Feby 11 1856,
Aged 53 Years.

Sacred to the Memory of
JOHN WHITE,
who died June 20 1855
Aged 61 years.
"I know that my Redeemer liveth."

South side.
Also of HANNAH,
Relict of the Above,
Who died July 18, 1871.
Aged 85 years.

Sacred to the Memory of
JOHN WHITE,
Who died Nov. 7th 1859,
Aged 51 years.

Also of
HENRY HERBERT WHITE,
Son of the above
Who died March 20th
1860. Aged 4 years.

So much for the existing inscriptions. Several monuments remain on which the records of yeomen and husbandmen are defaced by Time, and those persons commemorated are altogether forgotten. Some head-stones are broken, or have sunk into the ground: above the great majority of graves possibly no memorial was ever placed, just as now no hope nor prayer for the departed passes through the mind or from the lips of their surviving friends and kinsfolk.

> "No crosses mark those northern graves.
> No flowers adorn, no yew-tree waves;
> Unknown, uncared-for, there they lie,
> Under the chill of wintry sky,
> Or, under light of July sun,
> Lone and forgotten every one.
> Pass no lone nameless sleeper's bed,
> For once on such Heaven's dew was shed:
> By sudden death, by wasting pain,
> God called them to Himself again:
> Pray then for Souls who longing wait
> To enter Sion's golden gate."*

As regards the old family of Deane of this parish—a family so many of the names of which occur in the Registers—and whose representatives have lived at Stokenchurch and Chalgrove, Tettesworth and Milton; it was a current tradition that one of its best-known Puritan members, Richard Deane, the Regicide and Admiral, was born and baptized here. (*Vide* entry on p. 260.) Such, however, is not the case. *The Life of Richard Deane* has been recently written and published by one of his kindred,† in which his immediate origin has been patiently traced and carefully and most laboriously recorded. He was no doubt of the same family, though of another branch, but his allusion in his Will to his cousin, Anne Collins, of this parish, his intimacy with Cromwellite allies from Buckinghamshire, and his general co-operation with these, indicates as much.

He was born and baptized at Lower Guyting, near Winchcomb, co. Gloucester. Here is a copy of his baptismal record:—

> "1610. Anno D'ni 1610 ye viij daie of Julie was baptized Richard Deane ye sonne of Edward Deane."

His mother was Anne Wasse, or Wace,* of a knightly family of Buckinghamshire. He died by a shot from the Dutch Fleet 2 June, 1653, and from a woodcut engraving of his funeral car in the Bodleian Library, on which the words "ÆTATIS SUAE 42" appear, it is clear that he is the person whose birth is recorded as above. Richard Deane's grandmother was Margaret, daughter of Edward Wykeham, of Swalcliffe, co. Oxon, by Isabel, daughter of Mr. Giles Poulton, from whom the late Baroness Wenman of Thame Park was likewise directly descended.

The Will of "Richard Deane of London, Esquire," was made 31 March, 1653, and proved 20 January 1654. He died seised of the Manor and Grange of Sydenham, co. Oxon, and other property. In his Will he mentions his wife Mary Deane (daughter of John Grimsditch, of Knottingley, co. York, Esq., whom he had married at the Temple Church 21 May, 1647); his mother Anne; his sister Jane Sparrow, widow; his daughters Mary and Hannah, to each of whom he left £1000; and his cousin, Captain Richard Deane, who, with William Robinson, were executors. He was decreed a public funeral, and was buried in Henry the Seventh's Chapel in Westminster Abbey, 24 June, 1653, but exhumed after the Restoration, and his body, with others, cast into a large grave in the churchyard.

---

* *Lyrics of Light and Life*, pp. 141, 142. 2nd Edition. London: 1878.

† *The Life of Richard Deane*, by the Rev. J. Bathurst Deane, M.A., F.S.A. London: 1870.

* I possess the matrix of the seal of Sir Gilbert Wace, or Wasse, of this family, who was Sheriff of Oxfordshire in 1372, and, dying in 1408, was buried in the Abbey Church of Dorchester, co. Oxon.

Seal of Sir Gilbert Wace.

ARMS OF WACE.—Argent, three bars gules, on a canton of the second, a mullet of the first.

Helen Wace, *circa* 1291, married Richard de Louches, Lord of Milton, and was buried under an altar-tomb in Great Milton Church. A pedigree of Wasse, of Wycombe, occurs in the *Visitation of Bucks*, A.D. 1634.

THE family of Deane of Towersey came from an old stock belonging originally to Hampshire. Their kinsfolk, in the later years of Queen Elizabeth's reign, lived at Chalgrove, Tettesworth, Stokenchurch, Kingsey, and Cuxham. In subsequent periods they found themselves settled at and about Reading; and the representatives of Aaron and Christopher, of Towersey, having intermarried with many of the leading families of Berkshire, own a position of rank and repute.

Pedigree of Deane or Dene, of Deanlands or Denelands, Co. Hants.

No. I.

(Harl. MSS. 1544, fol. 199.)

Robert de Dene de Odyham, an'o 4 Henry V. = Isabella, fil. Rad'i Yong.

- Willi'mus at Dene, temp. H. VI. =
  - Matthew at Dene. = Agnes, fil. et hæ. Joh'es Leech.
    - John at Dene de Odiham, ob. s.p.
    - Jacobus at Dene. = Amy ....
      - Joannis at Dene. = Margeria, fil. .... Dunhurst.
        - Anne, d. of .... Hall, 1 wiffe. = Henry Deane, of Deanland. = Allice, ye heire of Thom. Berington of Streightley in Com. Berks, 2 wiffe.
          - 1 John Deane.
          - 2 James Deane of Deanland, m. ffrances, d. of Thomas Barnard of Lockham in Cornwall. = Elizabeth, d. of ffrancis pigott of Colletts in Com. Buck.
            - Henry Deane.
            - Margerett.
            - Elizabeth.
          - 3 Will'm Deane. = ffrances, d. of Thomas Vachell.
          - Elizabeth, m. Thomas Phillip of Rochester.
          - Anne, m. John Baldin of Berchington.
        - Richard Deane. = Bridgett, d. of Thomas Berington of Streightley in Com. Berks, sister of Allice.
      - Christopher & James, s.p.
      - Richard.
      - Elizabeth.
      - Amy.
      - Margery
    - Richard at Dene.

♣♣♣♣♣♣♣♣♣♣♣

Pedigree of Deane of Towersey.

No. II.

ARMS (granted by Dethick, Garter, to Henry Deane of Deanelands *circa* 1585; confirmed by William Camden in 1622).—*Gules, a lion couchant guardant or, in chief argent three crescents gules.*

John Deane, *alias* Collins, of Towersey, yeoman.[1] Presumed to have been grandson of Christopher Deane of Stokenchurch. The said John was buried at Towersey 15 May 1603. Will proved at Thame 13 Feb. 1603-4. Thomas and Francis Deane, *alias* Collins, supervisors of the Will. = Alice, mentioned in her husband's Will.

- John Deane, *alias* Collins, of Towersey aforesaid, Gent., son and heir. Sole executor of his father's Will.
- Edward Deane, *alias* Collins. Under age in 1603.

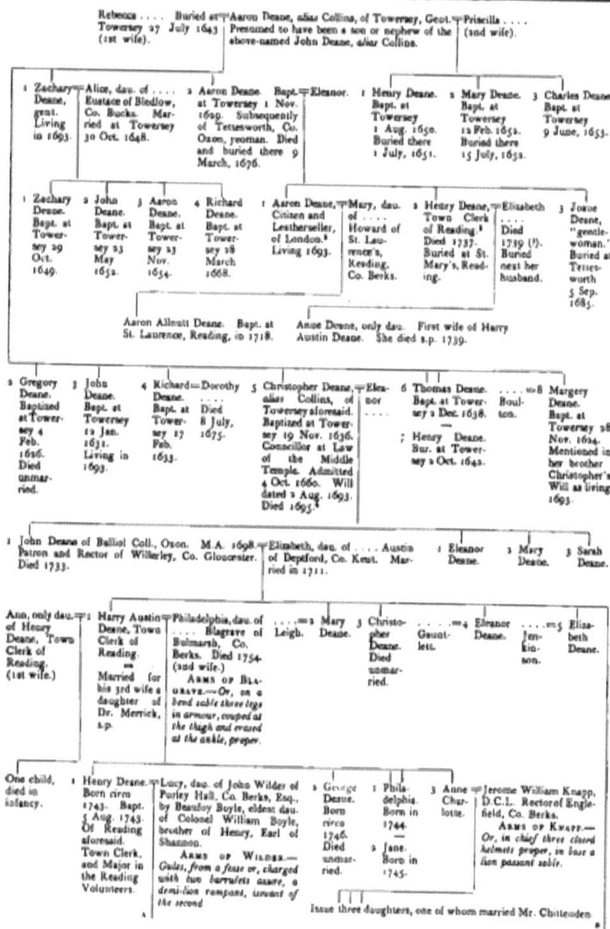
Rebecca .... Buried at Towersey 27 July 1643 (1st wife).
= Aaron Deane, alias Collins, of Towersey, Gent. Presumed to have been a son or nephew of the above-named John Deane, alias Collins.
= Priscilla .... (2nd wife).
1 Zachary Deane, gent. Living in 1693.
= Alice, dau. of .... Eustace of Bledlow, Co. Bucks. Married at Towersey 30 Oct. 1648.
2 Aaron Deane. Bapt. at Towersey 1 Nov. 1629. Subsequently of Tetsworth, Co. Oxon, yeoman. Died and buried there 9 March, 1676.
= Eleanor.
1 Henry Deane. Bapt. at Towersey 1 Aug. 1650. Buried there 1 July, 1651.
2 Mary Deane. Bapt. at Towersey 12 Feb. 1652. Buried there 15 July, 1652.
3 Charles Deane. Bapt. at Towersey 9 June, 1653.
1 Zachary Deane. Bapt. at Towersey 29 Oct. 1649.
2 John Deane. Bapt. at Towersey 23 May 1652.
3 Aaron Deane. Bapt. at Towersey 23 Nov. 1654.
4 Richard Deane. Bapt. at Towersey 18 March 1668.
1 Aaron Deane, Citizen and Leatherseller, of London.[1] Living 1693.
= Mary, dau. of .... Howard of St. Laurence's, Reading, Co. Berks.
2 Henry Deane, Town Clerk of Reading.[?] Died 1737. Buried at St. Mary's, Reading.
= Elizabeth .... Died 1739 (?). Buried next her husband.
3 Joane Deane, "gentlewoman." Buried at Tetsworth 5 Sep. 1685.
Aaron Allnutt Deane. Bapt. at St. Laurence, Reading, in 1718.
Anne Deane, only dau. First wife of Harry Austin Deane. She died s.p. 1739.
2 Gregory Deane. Baptized at Towersey 4 Feb. 1626. Died unmarried.
3 John Deane. Bapt. at Towersey 12 Jan. 1631. Living in 1693.
4 Richard Deane. Bapt. at Towersey 17 Feb. 1633.
= Dorothy .... Died 8 July, 1675.
5 Christopher Deane, alias Collins, of Towersey aforesaid. Baptized at Towersey 19 Nov. 1636. Councillor at Law of the Middle Temple. Admitted 4 Oct. 1660. Will dated 2 Aug. 1693. Died 1695.[?]
= Eleanor ....
6 Thomas Deane. Bapt. at Towersey 2 Dec. 1638.
7 Henry Deane. Bur. at Towersey 2 Oct. 1642.
.... Boulton. = 8 Margery Deane. Bapt. at Towersey 28 Nov. 1624. Mentioned in her brother Christopher's Will as living 1693.
1 John Deane of Balliol Coll., Oxon. M.A. 1698. Patron and Rector of Willerley, Co. Gloucester. Died 1733.
= Elizabeth, dau. of .... Austin of Deptford, Co. Kent. Married in 1711.
1 Eleanor Deane.
2 Mary Deane.
3 Sarah Deane.
Ann, only dau. of Henry Deane, Town Clerk of Reading. (1st wife.)
= 1 Harry Austin Deane, Town Clerk of Reading. = Married for his 3rd wife a daughter of Dr. Merrick, s.p.
= Philadelphia, dau. of .... Blagrave of Bulmarsh, Co. Berks. Died 1754. (2nd wife.)
Arms of Blagrave.—Or, on a bend sable three legs in armour, couped at the thigh and erased at the ankle, proper.
.... Leigh. = 2 Mary Deane.
3 Christopher Deane. Died unmarried.
.... Gauntlett. = 4 Eleanor Deane.
.... Jenkinson. = 5 Elizabeth Deane.
One child, died in infancy.
1 Henry Deane. Born circa 1743. Bapt. 5 Aug. 1743. Of Reading aforesaid. Town Clerk, and Major in the Reading Volunteers.
= Lucy, dau. of John Wilder of Purley Hall, Co. Berks, Esq., by Beauloy Boyle, eldest dau. of Colonel William Boyle, brother of Henry, Earl of Shannon.
Arms of Wilder.—Gules, from a fesse or, charged with two barrulets azure, a demi-lion rampant, issuant of the second
A
2 George Deane. Born circa 1746. Died unmarried.
1 Philadelphia. Born in 1744.
2 Jane. Born in 1745.
3 Anne Charlotte.
= Jerome William Knapp, D.C.L. Rector of Englefield, Co. Berks.
Arms of Knapp.—Or, in chief three closed helmets proper, in base a lion passant sable.
Issue three daughters, one of whom married Mr. Chittenden
B

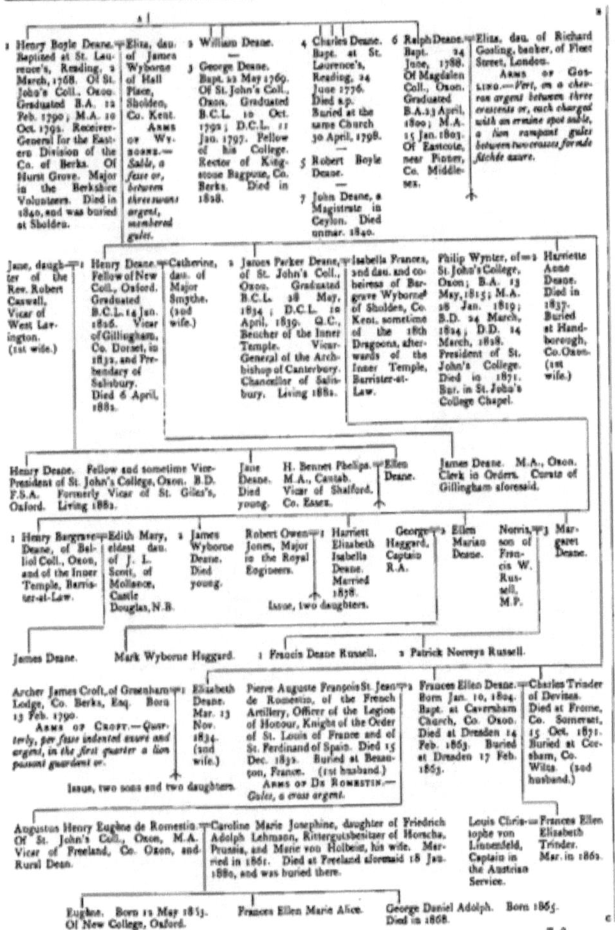

A

1 Henry Boyle Deane. Baptized at St. Laurence's, Reading, 2 March, 1768. Of St. John's Coll., Oxon. Graduated B.A. 12 Feb. 1790; M.A. 10 Oct. 1792. Receiver-General for the Eastern Division of the Co. of Berks. Of Hurst Grove. Major in the Berkshire Volunteers. Died in 1840, and was buried at Sholden. = Eliza, dau. of James Wyborne of Hall Place, Sholden, Co. Kent. ARMS OF WYBORNE.—*Sable, a fesse or, between three swans argent, membered gules.*

2 William Deane.

3 George Deane. Bapt. 22 May 1769. Of St. John's Coll., Oxon. Graduated B.C.L. 10 Oct. 1792; D.C.L. 11 Jan. 1797. Fellow of his College. Rector of Kingstone Bagpuze, Co. Berks. Died in 1828.

4 Charles Deane. Bapt. at St. Laurence's, Reading, 24 June 1776. Died s.p. Buried at the same Church 30 April, 1798.

5 Robert Boyle Deane.

7 John Deane, a Magistrate in Ceylon. Died unmar. 1840.

6 Ralph Deane. Bapt. 24 June, 1788. Of Magdalen Coll., Oxon. Graduated B.A. 23 April, 1800; M.A. 15 Jan. 1803. Of Eastcote, near Pinner, Co. Middlesex. = Eliza, dau. of Richard Gosling, banker, of Fleet Street, London. ARMS OF GOSLING.—*Vert, on a chevron argent between three crescents or, each charged with an ermine spot sable, a lion rampant gules between two crosses formée fitchée azure.*

Jane, daughter of the Rev. Robert Caswall, Vicar of West Lavington. (1st wife.) = 1 Henry Deane. Fellow of New Coll., Oxford. Graduated B.C.L. 14 Jan. 1826. Vicar of Gillingham, Co. Dorset, in 1832, and Prebendary of Salisbury. Died 6 April, 1882. = Catherine, dau. of Major Smythe. (2nd wife.)

2 James Parker Deane, of St. John's Coll., Oxon. Graduated B.C.L. 28 May, 1834; D.C.L. 10 April, 1839. Q.C., Bencher of the Inner Temple. Vicar-General of the Archbishop of Canterbury. Chancellor of Salisbury. Living 1882. = Isabella Frances, 2nd dau. and coheiress of Bargrave Wyborne of Sholden, Co. Kent, sometime of the 18th Dragoons, afterwards of the Inner Temple, Barrister-at-Law.

Philip Wynter, of St. John's College, Oxon; B.A. 13 May, 1815; M.A. 28 Jan. 1819; B.D. 24 March, 1824; D.D. 14 March, 1828. President of St. John's College. Died in 1871. Bur. in St. John's College Chapel. = 3 Harriette Anne Deane. Died in 1837. Buried at Handborough, Co. Oxon. (1st wife.)

Henry Deane. Fellow and sometime Vice-President of St. John's College, Oxon. B.D. F.S.A. Formerly Vicar of St. Giles's, Oxford. Living 1882.

Jane Deane. Died young.

H. Bennet Phelips. M.A., Cantab. Vicar of Shalford, Co. Essex. = Ellen Deane.

James Deane. M.A., Oxon. Clerk in Orders. Curate of Gillingham aforesaid.

1 Henry Bargrave Deane, of Balliol Coll., Oxon, and of the Inner Temple, Barrister-at-Law. = Edith Mary, eldest dau. of J. L. Scott, of Mollance, Castle Douglas, N.B.

2 James Wyborne Deane. Died young.

Robert Owen Jones, Major in the Royal Engineers. = 1 Harriett Elizabeth Isabella Deane. Married 1878. Issue, two daughters.

George Haggard, Captain R.A. = 2 Ellen Marian Deane.

Norris, son of Francis W. Russell, M.P. = 3 Margaret Deane.

James Deane.

Mark Wyborne Haggard.

1 Francis Deane Russell.

2 Patrick Norreys Russell.

Archer James Croft, of Greenham Lodge, Co. Berks, Esq. Born 13 Feb. 1790. ARMS OF CROFT.—*Quarterly, per fesse indented azure and argent, in the first quarter a lion passant guardant or.* = 1 Elizabeth Deane. Mar. 13 Nov. 1834. (2nd wife.) Issue, two sons and two daughters.

Pierre Auguste François St. Jean de Romestin, of the French Artillery, Officer of the Legion of Honour, Knight of the Order of St. Louis of France and of St. Ferdinand of Spain. Died 15 Dec. 1832. Buried at Besançon, France. (1st husband.) ARMS OF DE ROMESTIN.—*Gules, a cross argent.* = 2 Frances Ellen Deane. Born Jan. 10, 1804. Bapt. at Caversham Church, Co. Oxon. Died at Dresden 14 Feb. 1863. Buried at Dresden 17 Feb. 1863. = Charles Trinder of Devizes. Died at Frome, Co. Somerset, 15 Oct. 1871. Buried at Corsham, Co. Wilts. (2nd husband.)

Augustus Henry Eugène de Romestin. Of St. John's Coll., Oxon, M.A. Vicar of Freeland, Co. Oxon, and Rural Dean. = Caroline Marie Josephine, daughter of Friedrich Adolph Lehmann, Rittergutsbesitzer of Horscha, Prussia, and Marie von Holbein, his wife. Married in 1861. Died at Freeland aforesaid 18 Jan. 1880, and was buried there.

Louis Christophe von Linnenfeld, Captain in the Austrian Service. = Frances Ellen Elizabeth Trinder. Mar. in 1862.

Eugène. Born 12 May 1853. Of New College, Oxford.

Frances Ellen Marie Alice.

George Daniel Adolph. Born 1865. Died in 1868.

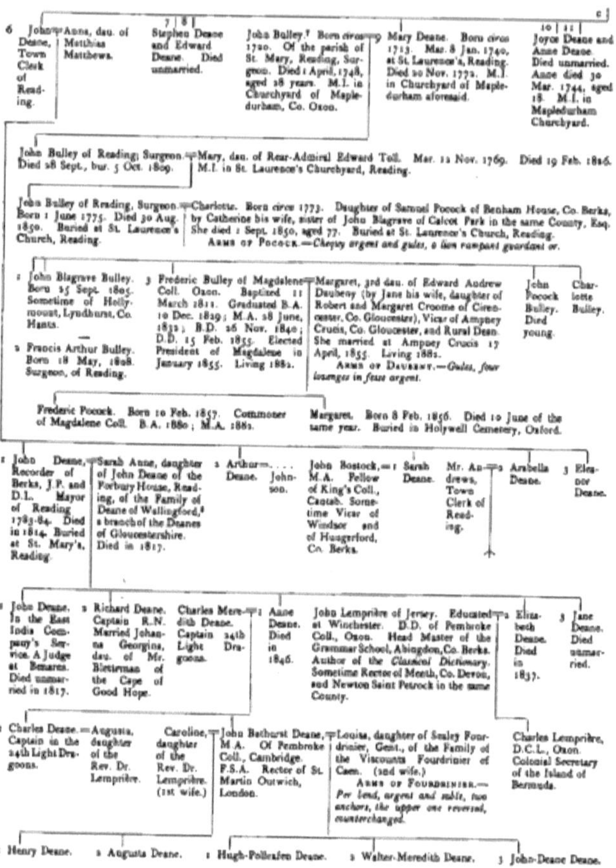

c

6 John Deane, Town Clerk of Reading. = Anne, dau. of Matthias Matthews.

7 | 8 Stephen Deane and Edward Deane. Died unmarried.

John Bulley.[7] Born *circa* 1720. Of the parish of St. Mary, Reading, Surgeon. Died 1 April, 1748, aged 28 years. M.I. in Churchyard of Mapledurham, Co. Oxon. = 9 Mary Deane. Born *circa* 1713. Mar. 8 Jan. 1740, at St. Laurence's, Reading. Died 20 Nov. 1772. M.I. in Churchyard of Mapledurham aforesaid.

10 | 11 Joyce Deane and Anne Deane. Died unmarried. Anne died 30 Mar. 1744, aged 18. M.I. in Mapledurham Churchyard.

John Bulley of Reading; Surgeon. Died 28 Sept., bur. 5 Oct. 1809. = Mary, dau. of Rear-Admiral Edward Toll. Mar. 12 Nov. 1769. Died 19 Feb. 1826. M.I. in St. Laurence's Churchyard, Reading.

John Bulley of Reading, Surgeon. Born 1 June 1775. Died 30 Aug. 1850. Buried at St. Laurence's Church, Reading. = Charlotte. Born *circa* 1773. Daughter of Samuel Pocock of Benham House, Co. Berks, by Catherine his wife, sister of John Blagrave of Calcot Park in the same County, Esq. She died 1 Sept. 1850, aged 77. Buried at St. Laurence's Church, Reading.
ARMS OF POCOCK.—*Chequy argent and gules, a lion rampant guardant or.*

1 John Blagrave Bulley. Born 25 Sept. 1805. Sometime of Hollymount, Lyndhurst, Co. Hants.

2 Francis Arthur Bulley. Born 18 May, 1808. Surgeon, of Reading.

3 Frederic Bulley of Magdalene Coll. Oxon. Baptized 11 March 1811. Graduated B.A. 10 Dec. 1829; M.A. 28 June, 1832; B.D. 26 Nov. 1840; D.D. 15 Feb. 1855. Elected President of Magdalene in January 1855. Living 1882. = Margaret, 3rd dau. of Edward Andrew Daubeny (by Jane his wife, daughter of Robert and Margaret Croome of Cirencester, Co. Gloucester), Vicar of Ampney Crucis, Co. Gloucester, and Rural Dean. She married at Ampney Crucis 17 April, 1855. Living 1882.
ARMS OF DAUBENY.—*Gules, four lozenges in fesse argent.*

John Pocock Bulley. Died young.

Charlotte Bulley.

Frederic Pocock. Born 10 Feb. 1857. Commoner of Magdalene Coll. B.A. 1880; M.A. 1882.

Margaret. Born 8 Feb. 1856. Died 10 June of the same year. Buried in Holywell Cemetery, Oxford.

1 John Deane, Recorder of Berks, J.P. and D.L. Mayor of Reading 1783-84. Died in 1814. Buried at St. Mary's, Reading. = Sarah Anne, daughter of John Deane of the Forbury House, Reading, of the Family of Deane of Wallingford,[8] a branch of the Deanes of Gloucestershire. Died in 1817.

2 Arthur Deane. = ... Johnson.

John Bostock, M.A. Fellow of King's Coll., Cantab. Sometime Vicar of Windsor and of Hungerford, Co. Berks. = 1 Sarah Deane.

Mr. Andrews, Town Clerk of Reading. = 2 Arabella Deane.

3 Eleanor Deane.

1 John Deane. In the East India Company's Service. A Judge at Benares. Died unmarried in 1817.

2 Richard Deane. Captain R.N. Married Johanna Georgina, dau. of Mr. Bletterman of the Cape of Good Hope.

Charles Meredith Deane. Captain 24th Light Dragoons. = 1 Anne Deane. Died in 1846.

John Lemprière of Jersey. Educated at Winchester. D.D. of Pembroke Coll., Oxon. Head Master of the Grammar School, Abingdon, Co. Berks. Author of the *Classical Dictionary*. Sometime Rector of Meeth, Co. Devon, and Newton Saint Petrock in the same County. = 2 Elizabeth Deane. Died in 1837.

3 Jane Deane. Died unmarried.

1 Charles Deane. Captain in the 24th Light Dragoons. = Augusta, daughter of the Rev. Dr. Lemprière.

Caroline, daughter of the Rev. Dr. Lemprière. (1st wife.) = John Bathurst Deane, M.A. Of Pembroke Coll., Cambridge. F.S.A. Rector of St. Martin Outwich, London. = Louisa, daughter of Sealey Fourdrinier, Gent., of the Family of the Viscounts Fourdrinier of Caen. (2nd wife.)
ARMS OF FOURDRINIER.—*Per bend, argent and sable, two anchors, the upper one reversed, counterchanged.*

Charles Lemprière, D.C.L., Oxon. Colonial Secretary of the Island of Bermuda.

1 Henry Deane. 2 Augusta Deane. 1 Hugh-Pollexfen Deane. 2 Walter-Meredith Deane. 3 John-Deane Deane.

SOME EXPLANATORY NOTES OF THE FOREGOING PEDIGREES.

[1] John Deane *alias* Collins, of Towersey, yeoman. Will made 1603. "My body to be buried within the Church or Churchyard of Towersey" aforesaid. Bequeaths to the Church of Towersey 5s., to the Poor of the Parish 3s. 4d. To Alice his wife £50, to be paid within three years next after his decease. To Edward his son £50, when he shall have attained the age of 21. To John Deane *alias* Collins, his son, all the rest of his property, and to be full and sole executor. Thomas and Francis Deane *alias* Collins to be supervisors, and to have 12s. each. Proved at Thame 13 Feb., 1603.—"Wills of the Peculiar of Thame," etc.

The above-named John Deane is supposed to have been grandson to Christopher of Stokenchurch, co. Oxon, who, it appears, was the second son of James Deane, or Dene, of Deanlands, and Amy his second wife.

[2] Christopher Deane, of Stokenchurch, co. Oxon, and his son John, both living in the latter part of the reign of Queen Elizabeth, filed a Bill in Chancery against Thomas Deane, who was asserted to have fraudulently obtained possession of a copyhold estate at Stokenchurch from Christopher Deane—the same copyhold having been settled in tail upon John Deane, son of the aforesaid Christopher; while Wills in the Prerogative Court of Canterbury and the Peculiar of Thame go to shew that the above John Deane, of Towersey, was grandfather of Aaron Deane of the same place.—*Note from the Rev. J. Bathurst Deane, M.A.*

[3] DEANE OF WALLINGFORD.—"A vellum escutcheon thus subscribed:—

"Ye armes & crest of Mr John Deane of Mattingley in hampshire sonn of John Deane of Wallingford in Berkshire gentl'man exemplified ratified and confirmed to him and his posterity with the due difference for ever.

"WILLm CAMDEN,
"Clarencieux King of Arms."

—Harl. MSS. 1544, folio 177b.

"Michaell Paynard one of ye six Clarkes of ye Chancery in H. 7 ob. s.p. His sister Margery ux' to Joh' Deane of Wallingford in co. Berks & had Ann ux' to Rob. Steele of Reading. Alice ux' to Will' Martin of Wickham in com. Bucks, & Margarett mar. to Will' White of Bramley in com. Hamps' & had Jo. White who mar. Elianor da. to Hen. Clarke of Gorync in com. Oxon."—Add. MSS., Brit. Mus., 14284, fol. 53, *Visit. of Berks*, 1665.

Arms of Deane of Wallingford: Vert, on a chevron between three griffins' heads erased or, five mullets sable.—Grants and confirmations of William Camden, College of Arms.

The following inscription on a brass in St. Mary's, Wallingford, is preserved in Symonds' Church Notes, Harl. MSS., Brit. Museum, No. 965:—

Hic jacet Joh'es a Deane et Alicia uxor ejus, qui quidem Joh'es obiit. . . . . Anno D'ni mccc, et p'd'a Alicia obiit yy die Julii A'o D'ni mcccclv quor' animab'e p'p' Deus. Amen.

Sir James Deane built the Alms-houses at Basingstoke, co. Hants. In 1677 his arms were remaining over the principal entrance. He had been buried in St. Olave's, Hart Street, London, where there was a monument to him and his two wives and children. On an old Mill at Freefolk, near Whitchurch, co. Hants, there was, and probably is, a representation in sculpture of the arms of Deane of Deanelands—the last of that name who had property at Freefolk.

[4] EXTRACT FROM THE WILL OF CHRISTOPHER DEANE, A.D. 1693.—"I Christopher Deane of the Middle Temple, London, Gent., this second day of August, in the year of our Lord one thousand six hundred and ninety-three, give, devise, & bequeath unto my brothers Zachary, John, & Richard Deane, my nephew Henry Deane, & sister Margery Boulton & their heirs, & to the Church Wardens & overseers of the Poor of Towersey, in the County of Bucks, where I was born, & their successors for ever, all that my Close of pasture Ground, containing about thirty acres—called Great Breamen, lying in Gaton in the County of Lincoln, now in the occupation of Arthur Lomas, Esqre* at the yearly rent of eight pounds, the same being worth £10 per annum, upon special Trust & confidence that they & their heirs & successors, out of the rents & profits of the said close, shall yearly & every year for ever yield & pay five pounds unto such Minister, Curate, Vicar, or Incumbent, for the time being of the Church of Towersey aforesaid, being a sober, orthodox man, & duly presented, instituted & inducted, & there officiating, preaching, catechising, & reading divine service there according to the Cannons of the Church of England as the best reformed Church, & shall & will from time to time for ever hereafter employ & lay out the residue of the profits & rents received & made by them out of & by the same Close for & towards putting forth & binding poor children born in Towersey aforesaid Apprentices from time to time to some handy craft Trades."

(Extracted from the Registry of the Prerogative Records, 29 Bond, folio 42.)

CHAS DYNELEY,
JOHN IGGULDEN, } Deputy Registers.
W. F. GOSTLING,

[5] Indenture between John Archer, Esq., High Sheriff of the county of Berks, on the one part, and Aaron Deane, of London, Citizen and Leatherseller, of the other part. Dated 1695, 8th June. "Henry Deane, gent.," is mentioned in it as one of the Attorneys of the Court of King's Bench.

[6] The escutcheon of pretence is borne by James Parker Deane in right of Isabella Frances his wife, daughter and coheiress of the late Bargrave, who was eldest and only surviving son of James, Wyborn, of Sholden, co. Kent, and Rebecca his wife, who was the last direct representative of the Bargraves of Eastry Court, co. Kent. The families of Wyborn and Bargrave are now extinct in the male line.

[7] FAMILY OF BULLEY.

From the Register of Baptisms belonging to the Church of St. Laurence, Reading.

1725. May 16. John, son of John and Sarah Bulley.
1770. April 3. Lucy, daughter of John and Mary Bulley.
1773. July 9. Mary, daughter of John and Mary Bulley.
1775. June 1. John, son of John and Mary Bulley.
1777. Jan. 23. Jane Elizabeth, daughter of John and Mary Bulley.
1781. Jan. 9. Ashbournham, son of John and Mary Bulley.
1783. Catherine, daughter of John & Mary Bulley.
1789. July 16. Charles, son of John and Mary Bulley.
1791. Dec. 22. Ann Arabella, daughter of John and Mary Bulley.
1803. Sep. 22. Charlotte, daughter of John and Charlotte Bulley.
1806. Mar. 5. John Blagrave, son of John and Charlotte Bulley.
1808. Oct. 17. Francis-Arthur, son of John and Charlotte Bulley.
1811. Mar. 7. Frederic, son of John and Charlotte Bulley.

From the Register of Marriages of the same Church.

1740. Jan. 8. John Bulley, of St. Mary's, and Mary Dean of this parish.
1769. Nov. 21. John Bulley and Mary Toll.
1820. May 13. Thomas William Thomas, Esq., to Ann Arabella Bulley.
1824. Feb. 24. John Blagrave Bulley to Mary Jarvis Briscoe.

From the Register of Burials of the same.

1727. Aug. 25. John Bulley, senior.
1734. June 19. John Bulley.
1735. Mar. 2. Elizabeth Bulley.
1781. Jan. 4. Jane Bulley, daughter of John and Mary Bulley.
1809. Oct. 5. John Bulley, Alderman.
1841. Nov. 11. John Pocock Bulley, an infant.
Sep. 6. John Bulley [aged] 75 years.
1850. Sep. 6. Charlotte Bulley [aged] 77 years.
1862. Oct. 11. Catherine Bulley, aged 79.

From the Register of Baptisms belonging to the Church of Our Blessed Lady at Reading.

1700. May. John, son of John and Elizabeth Bulley.
1703. Mar. Thomas, son of John and Elizabeth Bulley.

From the Register of Burials belonging to the Parish Church of Mapledurham, co. Oxon.

1744. Nov. 14. Ann Bulley, of St. Laurence's, Reading.
1747. Dec. 9. Thomas Bulley, of Reading.
1748. John Bulley, of Reading.
1752. Oct. 27. Elizabeth Bulley, from Reading.
1772. Nov. 26. Mrs Bulley, from Reading.

* "The present occupier—(it is uncertain when these words were penned)—is Robert Epworth, Esq., Grimblethorp, near Wragby, Lincolns'. The rent is payable at Lady-day and at Michaelmas."—*Note.*

A FEW facts must now be put on record as regards the Manor, or Manors; and here it may be observed that the name of the parish, Towersey, seems to have been derived from the term "Eye" affixed to the family name of certain former Saxon owners of the place, the Tours or Towers—thus, "Towers-eye." The lands are said to have been given to Nigel de Albini, a retainer of William the Conqueror, younger brother of William de Albini, ancestor of the Earls of Arundel (though the fact of this descent is disputed). A certain Ralph Pirot, or Perot, appears to have held them of the de Albinis in 1222; and another Ralph Pirot, possibly his son, died seised of them in 1253. A century later one John of Moreton, in the parish of Thame, and Muriel of Weston (adjoining Moreton) were tenants under the Pirots, who certainly held the aforesaid lands until the year 1341. Nicholas de Touresye, in 1253, owned an interest in certain possessions there, and was a reputed descendant of former owners; while prior to the year 1264 the Abbot and Monastery of Thame had acquired certain tenements and lands of the Manor in the parish of Towersey, which remained unalienated until the dissolution of the Greater Monasteries under Henry VIII. Towersey Manor—then valued at £25 per annum—was granted by Letters Patent, dated 15 September, 1542, to the Dean and Chapter of Oxford.*

Certain other lands in Towersey, as well as parts of the other Manor (as there appear to have been two Manors†), were in the possession of Sir John de Burghersh, of Tythrope, in the adjoining parish of King's-eye, or Kingsey, on his death in 1391.

Alliances between this and certain noble and knightly families connected with Towersey may thus be seen:—

John de Burghersh, of Towersey and Tythrope; died in 1350. = Maude, daughter and coheiress of Edmund Bacon. (Dugdale's *Baronage*, vol. iii., p. 36.)
ARMS OF BACON: *Gules, on a chief argent two mullets sable.*

A

John de Burghersh, of Towersey aforesaid; died in 1391. (2nd husband.) = Ismania Hanham, of . . . . co. of Gloucester. = Sir John Ralegh, of Nettlecombe, co. Somerset, Knt. (1st husband.)

An only daughter, married to Sir John Walesborough, Knt. This Sir John's second daughter, Anne, married, firstly, William, Lord Moleyns; and, secondly, Sir Edmund Hampden, Knt. Sir John's third daughter, Elizabeth, married John Hampden, of Hampden, Esq.*

Sir John Grenville, of . . . . Cornwall, Knt. = Margaret de Burghersh. = Sir John Arundell, of Lanherne, co. Cornwall, Knt. (2nd husband.)

Thomas Chaucer. = Maude de Burghersh.

Elizabeth, daughter of Nicholas Wilford—some authorities write Wyfield—Lord Mayor of London. (2nd wife.) = Henry, first Lord Marny, of Lower Marny, co. Essex, K.G., Keeper of the Privy Seal to Henry VIII.; died 22 May, 1523.
ARMS OF MARNY: *Gules, a lion rampant guardant argent.* = Thomasine Arundell, daughter and coheiress. (1st wife.)

Bartholomew Collingridge, of Towersey, Esq. = Alice Arundell, dau. and coheiress.

Sir Henry Bedingfield, Knt. = Grace Marny.

Geoffrey Dormer, of West Wycombe, co. Bucks, and of Thame. = Ursula Collingridge.

Upon the death of Sir John de Burghersh the properties, both in Kingsey and Towersey, were divided between his two coheiresses, Margaret and Maude, and so passed, the former to the Arundells, Collingridges, and Dormers; and the latter in turn to the Chaucers,†

* At what is often called "the Reformation," certain lands bequeathed long previously to provide lights before the Blessed Sacrament, the Rood, and the image of St. Katherine in the Parish Church of Towersey, were granted by Queen Elizabeth to William Tipper and Robert Dawe; and another acre of land was in 1585 granted to John Walton and John Cresset, on the petition to the Crown of Sir James Croft, Knt., husband of the Dowager Lady Williams, of Thame.

† What is traditionally called "The Old Manor House" stands close to, and directly to the north of, the Churchyard. It is a house possibly built as early as the reign of Richard III., and even now is extremely picturesque. The pitch of the roofs is excellent, the plan simple, the rooms of a fair size are conveniently arranged; while the ancient Soler on the upper floor (now used as a bedroom) contains a curious carved fire-place, and there is an excellently-designed timber window on the north side. The large stack of chimneys to the west, the Hall with its oaken sedilia, and the rude staircase are features of interest; and although the building has been evidently battered, patched, and considerably altered, some of the mouldings of the woodwork bespeak its antiquity. It now belongs to the family of Lupton, of Thame.

* The following descents are also of interest:—

Sir John Hampden, Knt. = Elizabeth Walesborough.

Henry Ferrers, of Baddesley Clinton, co. Warwick. = Catherine Hampden.

Edward Ferrers, only son. = Bridget Windsor, third daughter of William, second Lord Windsor, of Bradenham, K.B., by Margaret his wife. Bridget Ferrers died in 1564.

† The portion of Maud de Burghersh, wife of Thomas Chaucer, was in 1403 settled upon a certain Edmund Hampden. It appears to have passed to his son, Sir Edmund Hampden, Knt., whose son, William Hampden, of Thame, and subsequently of Dinton, by his Will orders the property to be applied towards providing portions for his daughters. Subsequently the Towersey estate passed to the issue of Katherine Hampden's first husband, Henry Ferrers, of Baddesley Clinton, co. Warwick. But it is almost impossible to unravel the intricacies of the descent at this period. A branch of the Hampden family of Bucks was certainly resident in Thame, as early

Hampdens, Ferrerses, and Pyes.* Sir Edmund Pye had married Martha, daughter of Sir Thomas Lucas, Knt., High Sheriff of Essex in 1657, by his wife, Elizabeth Leighton, and sister of John, first Lord Lucas, and upon his death the Towersey estate passed by the marriage of Anne Pye, his eldest daughter, to John, Lord Lovelace, whose youngest daughter, Martha Lovelace, eventually became sole heiress of her grandfather, and was in her own right Baroness Wentworth. She married Sir Henry Johnson, of Triston, co. Suffolk, Knt., a wealthy ship-builder; but, dying without issue in 1745, the title passed to her kinsman, Sir Edward Noel, Bart., whose mother Elizabeth was the daughter of Thomas Rowney, of Oxford, Attorney-at-Law. Thomas, second Viscount Wentworth, in March, 1788, conveyed the Manor and estate to George Bowden, of Radford, co. Oxon, of an old Towersey family, who was succeeded in 1790 by his son George, who dying in 1822, this property then descended to his three daughters and coheiresses, Mary-Elizabeth, Elizabeth, and Anne-Frances, who became joint Ladies of the Manor. The members of this family were Catholics. Subsequently the property was purchased by Mr. Edward Griffin, of Wolverhampton, whose son, the present Lord of the Manor, courteously furnished me with the following too brief information concerning it:—

"The property here consists of Towersey Manor (house and grounds), the 'Walnuts' (house, garden, and orchard), the Grange and Penn Farms, together with several cottages in the village, in all comprising about a third of the acreage of the parish. There is but one Manor here, of which I am Lord, the rental from which is not excessive, for most of the land has been enfranchised."*

as the second year of Henry VII., A.D. 1486, and the following entry occurs in the "Accounts" nearly forty years afterwards:—"1524. It'm rec' for the sepulcre of Will'm Hampden gentilman the iiijth day of January vj s. viij d." In the year 1427, Thomas Chaucer had been Seneschal of the Abbey Lands at Thame, Dorchester, Woburn, and Tyncheliffe, with a fee of £6 a year. (Computus Roll, 5 Henry VI.)

* Lady Katherine Pye, of this family, by an Indenture dated 15 November, 1733, conveyed a Farm in Towersey to certain Trustees to promote the Christian education of twenty boys or girls of Bradenham, Towersey, Princes Risborough, Hughenden, and West Wycombe. The Trustees have always been clergymen and laymen of the Established Church, and the estate now produces about £60 a year.

* Letter of Mr. J. Whitehouse Griffin to the Author, dated 24 July, 1882.

Pedigree of Griffin of Towersey Manor.

ARMS OF GRIFFIN.—*Sable, a griffin rampant argent, beaked or.*

Thomas Griffin of Tenbury, Co. Worcester, who died A.D. 1800. = Ann, daughter of John Benbow of Burraston, Co. Salop.

Sarah, daughter of Thomas Walker, Esq., of Chiddingfold, Co. Surrey. Buried at Wolverhampton. M.I. in St. George's Church. (1st wife.) = Edward Griffin, the youngest son. Born 1797. Joint Lord of the Manor of Towersey, Co. Bucks. Commissioner of Taxes, Co. Bucks. Died 22 April 1879. Buried at Towersey. M.I. in Churchyard. = Mary, eldest daughter and coheiress of James Whitehouse of Willenhall, Co. Stafford, Esq. Born 2 Oct. 1812. Married at Willenhall A.D. 1844. Died 22 April 1879. Buried at Towersey. M.I. in Churchyard. (2nd wife.)

Alfred Edward Griffin, eldest son. Born 13 July 1836. Died 26 Dec. 1873. Married Eliza, daughter of Randall Walker of Wolverhampton. Living, a widow, in 1882. Born at Wolverhampton.
Issue four sons and two daughters.

1. Elizabeth Mary Griffin. Born 5 Dec. 1825. Married, at Wolverhampton in 1844, Sir John Morris (born 1821), Knt., of Elmsdale. J.P. for Co. Stafford. Mayor of Stafford, 1865-7. Knighted in 1866.
Issue a son and two daughters.

2. Emma Griffin. Born 18 Oct. 1829. Married, at Wolverhampton, Frederick Farmer of Bridgewater, Co. Somerset, J.P. M.D. Dublin.
Issue one son.

3. Sarah Matilda Griffin. Living in 1882.

1. James Whitehouse Griffin. Born at Wolverhampton 8 Aug. 1846. Son and heir. Of Towersey Manor and Willenhall aforesaid. Commissioner of Taxes for the Hundred of Ashendon, Co. Bucks. Living 1882. = Emily, second daughter of William Rose Whittingham Upjohn of Guestling Hill, Co. Sussex. Married at Guestling 5 June 1873. Died 26 April 1874. Buried at Towersey. M.I. in Churchyard.

2. Clifton Benbow Griffin, second son, of Willenhall and Towersey aforesaid. Born 19 Jan. 1850. = Isabella Elizabeth, third daughter of George Rogers, M.A., Vicar of Gedney, Co. Lincoln. Married in August 1874 at Gedney.

1. Mary Helen Griffin. Living 1882.

2. Anne Maria Sarah Griffin. Living 1882.

Emily. Died an infant. Buried at Towersey.

1. Mary Isabelle. Living in 1882.

2. Alfred Clifton. Living in 1882.

North Weston.

THE hamlet of North Weston in the Parish of Thame is situated about a mile and three-quarters to the west of the town, having the hamlet of Moreton to the south, Long Crendon to the north, Shabbington to the north-west, and Rycott to the south-west. From the hill of North Weston a large tract of undulating and picturesque country may be seen, both to the north and south. The northern portion is well watered by the river Thame, while in every part the hamlet itself contains some rich grazing land, fairly wooded and sparsely inhabited.

Here in mediæval times, under the Bishop of Lincoln, various persons held the property. Two Manor Houses from time immemorial have stood in the hamlet: one known as the Hall Place, on the hill to the north; the other as Quartermain's Manor, in the valley below looking south. A certain John de Weston held one Manor in the year 1239, Nicholas de Weston in 1375, and Muriel his daughter in 1392. Prior to that date the Quartermains appear to have already owned a mansion and lands, and occupied a position of importance here as well as at Thame and Rycott. There is some evidence to shew that in the early part of the fifteenth century both the Manors in question were in the possession of the Quartermains; and that the south aisle of the Chapel at North Weston was at that time their most ancient burial-place. On the other hand it is certain that long previously they had buried their relations and kinsfolk before the altar of St. Christopher in Thame Church.

The House itself, built in the main, no doubt, by Sir John Clerke, Knt., *circa* 1535, and completed about the time of his death 1539, appears to have been a large and effective specimen of sixteenth-century domestic architecture, with highly-pitched gable roofs. Its ground plan was simple; a long and lofty Hall, bearing an open timber roof, with porch and minstrels' gallery at the east end, formed the chief central part of the mansion, which stood east and west, with an imposing gable-end facing south at each end of the Hall, and with two considerable wings placed towards the south at right angles to the whole, and forming three sides of a square. Parts of the old House appear to have been erected in the reign of Henry VIII.,* on the site of a much older building, out of the proceeds of the ransom of the French Duke; but many changes with the varying tastes of succeeding ages—had from time to time been made in its character, both by owners and tenants. The oaken staircase was broad and massive, and admirably carved. The great Hall was panelled to a height of five feet all around, and entirely panelled with Renaissance canopies of oak at the upper end, where the dais stood, near the large bay-window. In William III.'s reign the long and lofty Tudor windows of the Hall had given place to others of a very inferior character; and four sash-windows were inserted in each of the gable-ends in lieu of broad mullioned lights, with quarries below and armorial bearings in stained glass above. When a taste for classic architecture came in, much destruction of older work was wrought, and many interesting memorials of the past unfortunately perished.

About the year 1750 Mr. Francis Clerke was obliged to sell his estate at North Weston. This was purchased by the then Duke of Marlborough, and subsequently bequeathed to his son Lord Charles Spencer of Wheatfield, co. Oxon, whose son is said to have compelled his father to dispose of it soon after he had come into possession. It was then bought by the Earl of Abingdon of that day, in whose family it still remains.*

The old Manor House was partly taken down about sixty years ago, only the east wing being allowed to remain—which still stands much mutilated, used as a farmhouse. This contains the ancient kitchen and offices to the north, and several spacious but low rooms panelled with oak, but now partially dismantled and painted. The chimneys are massive, and the back portion of the building is exceedingly picturesque though low and irregular. The brewing-house and other outbuildings to the east of this part are of considerable antiquity; and a large high-gabled barn, standing to the south-west, (previously the stables of the House,) still remains. The old garden, surrounded by a high and massive brick wall, lies to the west of the House. In it are three dilapidated, but once exceedingly handsome, freestone alcoves or summer-houses of a classic design, with the arms of Clerke, (with the added canton,) carved in front up above.

The Chapel of North Weston, dedicated to St. James, stood a short distance to the west of the House. Its foundations at the present time can

* "When the principal part of the old house was pulled down, the writer saw a noble beam of Spanish chestnut taken from the front, which extended along the whole of the so-called 'dancing-room' and Hall. It bore a deep cut of the 30th year of Henry VIII." [*i.e.* 1539].—Information given by the late Mr. Harry Lupton of Thame.

* 1754. On June 13th of this year a sale by Mr. Ford of London was held "of the Furniture, China, Watches, Curiosities, and Library of Books of the Right Hon. Bridget, Dowager Lady Bulkeley, deceased, at her ladyship's late dwelling-house at North Weston." This lady, the daughter of James, Earl of Abingdon, by Eleanor, daughter of Sir Henry Lee, third baronet of Dytchley, had married Richard fourth Viscount Bulkeley.

scarcely be traced, and traditions differ somewhat as to its style and character. After a reference to the Church Books of Thame and other authorities, and after much consideration of current traditions, an old and inartistic sketch, and a careful examination of the site, I am disposed to maintain that it consisted of a nave, south aisle, and chancel; and that it possessed anciently at least two altars: one in honour of the Patron Saint, and another in honour of the Blessed Virgin. It also contained an image of St. Hugh in a tabernacle. Thirty years ago some fragments of the stone pillars of the nave were used to support a farm building; but these are now either removed or destroyed.

The following five coats of arms were in the windows when Nicholas Charles, Lancaster Herald, visited it in 1609, and were tricked by him:*—

1. Quartermain of Thame, impaling Englefield of Englefield, co. Berks.
2. Quartermain of Thame, impaling Fitz Ellis of Waterperry.
3. Quartermain of Thame, impaling (1) Danvers, (2) Bruley of Waterstock.
4. Quarterly, Arms of (1) Fowler, (2) Hester, (3) Englefield, (4) Brecknock.
5. Quarterly, Arms of (1) Fowler, (2) Quartermain, (3) Hester, (4) Danvers.

The Chapel field shews some traces of the boundary of the old burial-ground; and a row of lofty elm-trees stands to the west, marking its position in that direction. A child named Diana Susanna, daughter of Mr. Francis Clerke, was baptized there so late as the 8th of July, A.D. 1750, and burials of various folk of the hamlet took place in the latter part of the last century. As at the "Reformation" with regard to monastic burying-places, so now, in reference to destroyed churches, swine grub up the graves around them, the sanctity of the ground is wholly unrecognized, and as a consequence Desolation reigns.

Towards the close of the last century the House was leased by Lord Charles Spencer to the Rev. Thomas Plaskett, on the understanding that the Chapel —which had been long disused, and which nobody cared to repair, the roof being rotten, the walls unsafe, and the windows broken and boarded up—was to be pulled down at the expiration of the lease, and its materials sold. It appears that these included pues, timber and carved mullions, the paving-stones of the building, as well as the vaults and their contents. John Bonner and Joseph Eustace of Thame had authority to remove all the leaden coffins and removed them. The bones and bodies, it may be hoped, were left. An old brass of a priest in eucharistic vestments, which I purchased more than a quarter of a century ago of a dealer in metal, came, as there is some reason for believing, from the chancel floor of this old house of sacrifice and prayer. The stone in which it had been embedded was turned face downwards and used as a fire-hearth; but subsequently—that is about thirty years ago—re-laid, and the figure removed and sold for old metal. This latter is possibly unique as regards the position of the person represented—a priest holding a chalice in his left hand and blessing it with his right.

Memorial Brass of a Priest in Eucharistic Vestments.

There was no inscription attached to it when it came into my possession, nor could I find that any inscription had been found or was recoverable. The stones of the Chapel were used to erect farm buildings and to mend the roads.

A family of yeomen of the name of Carter lived at Weston for many years from the early part of the seventeenth century, and subsequently ranked as gentlepeople and esquires,* making several good matches. They were persons of considerable substance and high character, intermarrying with the Stribblehills, Leavers, and Holts; and were benefactors both to the Church and Parish of Thame.

As may be gathered from the Thame Registers, and as will be set forth in the Pedigree of Knollys farther on, Francis Knollys of Lower Winchendon, co. Bucks, and Elizabeth Stribblehill of Thame were married in North Weston Chapel on the 19th of August, 1696; and the lady of Mr. Francis Clerke was buried in his family vault there, thirty years afterwards,—that is on July 2nd, 1726.

* Lansdowne MSS., British Museum, No. 874.

* One of their kinsfolk, Edward Carter, Esq., was High Sheriff of Oxfordshire in 1708; and the remains of others rest in their vault in the nave of Thame Church. *See* Chapter V.

Pedigree of Quartermain of North Weston and Rycott.

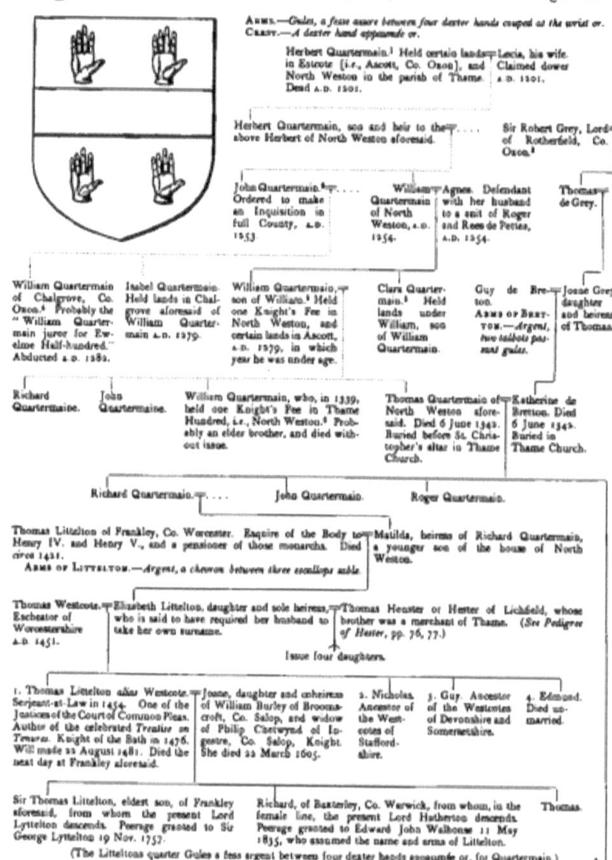

A

Thomas Quartermain[7] of North Weston aforesaid, son and heir. Died 6 May 1399. Buried in Thame Church. (1st husband.) = Joane, daughter, by Margerie his wife, of Sir Robert Fitz-Ellys, Lord of Waterperry, Co. Oxon; Conservator of the Peace; Leader of the Levies of the County; and High Sheriff of Berks and Oxon A.D. 1342; who, in 1382, was possessed of the Manors of Wormingball and Oakley, Co. Bucks, and of Waterperry aforesaid. = John Creedie. (2nd husband.)

ARMS OF FITZ-ELLIS.—*Argent, a bend between six fleurs-de-lys gules.*

John Rycott, Lord of Rycott, Co. Oxon. = Elizabeth, daughter and heiress of Sir John Gernon of Lavington Gernon, Co. Wilts.

Nicholas Clerke *alias* Rycott, Lord of Rycott aforesaid,[11] in right of his wife. = Katherine Rycott, daughter and heiress.

Joane Rycott, daughter and heiress. = Nicholas Englefield of Englefield, Co. Berks, and Lord of Rycott in right of his wife. Clerk of the Green Cloth. Comptroller of the Household to King Richard II. Died 1 April A.D. 1415. Buried at Haseley, Co. Oxon.

ARMS OF ENGLEFIELD.—*Gules, two bars argent, on a chief or a lion passant azure.*

Elizabeth Quartermain, second daughter of Thomas. Coheiress in her issue to her brother Richard. = ... Beke. Probably of the family of Ereley White-Knights, co. Berks.

John Englefield. Born 1411.

Baldwin Butler[12] of Great Haseley, Co. Oxon. = Isabel Englefield. Inscription to herself and husband formerly in the windows of Great Haseley Church aforesaid.

ARMS OF BUTLER.—*Gules, three covered cups or.*

1. Richard Butler. Born 1448.

2. Thomas Butler. Sometime Rector of St. Botolph without Bishopsgate, London, and subsequently by exchange, made 15 May 1472 with Robert Kendall, Rector of Haseley, Co. Oxon. Died in 1494. Buried at Haseley. Memorial Brass in the Church.

Sibill Butler.

Eustace Grenville, of Wootton, co. Bucks. = Elizabeth Butler.

Thomas Walrond or Walron of Culham, Co. Oxon. = 1. Alice Beke. Born A.D. 1421.

ARMS OF WALROND.—*Argent, three bulls' faces sable, in fess point an annulet for difference.*

. . . . Rouse or Rosse. = 2. Joane Beke.

Richard Rouse or Rosse of Thame.

Peter Feteplace, Esq. M.P. for Co. Oxon in 1420, and again in 1433, and 1434. = 3. Margaret Beke.

John Feteplace.

. . . . Moore, 1st husb.; Robert Pointz, 2nd husband; Humphrey Forster, 3rd husb., living in 1478. = 4. Sibill Beke.

3. Richard Quartermain.[8] Born in 1393. Succeeded to North Weston A.D. 1414. M.P. for the County in 1432, 1433, and 1472. High Sheriff of Co. Oxon in 1436, and again in 1454. Refounder, with his wife, of Rycott Chapel. Died without issue 6 Sept. 1478. Buried in Thame Church.[14] = 1. Sibill Englefield.[10] Born A.D. 1400. Heiress of Rycott. Died without issue A.D. 1483.

3. Agnes Englefield.

2. Cecily Englefield. Born 1403. = William Fowler of Buckingham, and Co. Oxon.[13]

ARMS OF FOWLER.—*Ermine, on a canton gules an owl or.*

1. John Quartermain, son and heir.[7] Born at North Weston in 1384. Died without issue in 1409.

2. Guy Quartermain.[8] Born at North Weston in 1388. Died without issue in 1414.

John, son and heir of William Bruley, Lord of Waterstock, Co. Oxon, by Agnes his wife.[15] = 1. Matilda Quartermain, eldest daughter of Thomas. Coheiress in her issue to her brother Richard.

ARMS OF BRULEY.—*Ermine, on a bend gules three chevronells or.*

Sir Walter Mantell of Harford, Co. Northampton. (2nd husband.) = Joane Bruley, daughter and heiress of John of Waterstock aforesaid. = John Danvers, Lord of Ipwell and Banbury, Co. Oxon, whose first wife was Alice, daughter and heiress of William Verney of Byfield, Co. Northampton. (1st husband.)

ARMS OF DANVERS.—*Argent, on a bend gules three martlets vert.*

Thomas Danvers of Waterstock aforesaid. Heir to his grandmother Matilda Quartermain. Knighted. Died without issue. = Sibilla Fowler, daughter of William Fowler and Cecily Englefield, and sister of Richard Fowler.[16]

Joane Danvers. = 1. Richard Fowler of Co. Buckingham and Oxon. Chancellor of the Duchy of Lancaster A.D. 1471–78. Died in 1478.

B

2. Thomas Fowler.

3. Nicholas Fowler.

1. Alice Fowler. Married Thomas Rokes.

2. Sibilla Fowler. Married Sir Thomas Danvers.

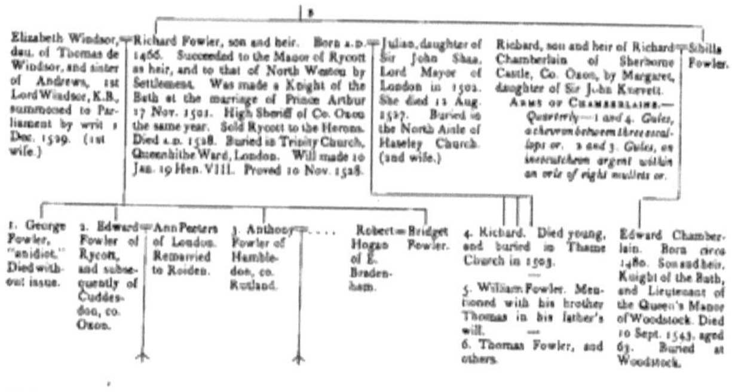

SOME EXPLANATORY NOTES OF THE FOREGOING PEDIGREE.

[1] The following relates to the three earliest Quartermain descents. In the first four descents dotted lines have been used, because the proofs of descent and exact relationship are not absolutely certain from the documents at hand. There can be little doubt, however, of the correctness of this early portion.

In the reign of King Stephen, from A.D. 1135-1154, Herbert Quartermain attested the grants of Robert Danvers, Roger de Begstrop, and Walter de St. Fey to the Abbey of Thame.—*Chartulary of Thame Abbey.*

Oxfordshire Fines, from a MS. volume in the Record Office.

2 King John, *i.e.* A.D. 1201. Estcote [*i.e.* Ascott] and Weston. Inter Lecia' que fuit uxor Herberti Quatremane pet. and Herbert Quatremans ten. of a third part of six hides and three virgates in Estcote and Weston. She claims the said third part as dower of gift of Herbert Quatremain formerly her husband. Finally, on receipt of 20s. she quit-claims to Herbert, and is granted a capital messuage and five virgates in Estcote for life.

38 Henry III., *i.e.* A.D. 1254. Between Roger de Petton and Rose his wife; and William Quartermain and Agnes his wife.

[2] Placitorum Abbreviatio.

Page 132. Michaelmas Term, 37 Henry III., Oxon, *i.e.* A.D. 1253. Alan le Kyngles plaintiff *versus* John Quartermaine and others for not having taken an Inquisition in full county; ordered that he should do so except as to the Liberty of Wallingford.

Page 204. Trinity Term, 10 Edward I., Oxon, *i.e.* A.D. 1272. Geoffrey de Lewknore impleads a number of people for the abduction of the body of William Quatermayne, who holds lands from him by knight service in Chalgrove. (Rot. viii.)

William Quartermain, in the 41 Henry III., *i.e.* A.D. 1257, attested the grant of Roger d'Aumain to the Abbey of Thame, and also that of William Mauduit to the same. In both he is styled "D'nu Willelmus Quartermayne."—*Chartulary of Thame Abbey.*

[3] The following descents of the Greys of Rotherfield are taken mainly from a pedigree in the library of the late Sir Thomas Phillipps of Middle Hill, near Broadway, co. Worcester, of which a copy was courteously furnished to me. A few additions from other acknowledged authorities have been added, so as to set forth the exact relationship between the Greys and the Quartermains. It appears probable from a coat of arms in latten still remaining upon the latest of the two Quartermain tombs at Thame—Arms: Grey of Rotherfield impaling quarterly Quartermain and Bretton—that a daughter of Thomas Quartermain named at the end of the following Pedigree married a son of the House of Grey of Rotherfield.

Grey of Rotherfield, co. Oxon.

John de Grey, a noble Norman, who came to England with William the Conqueror, A.D. 1066. = Adelisa, daughter of William Fitz-osbourne, Earl of Hereford, sister and coheir of Roger de Bretville, Earl of Hereford.

Reginald de Grey, son and heir. Arms of Grey.—*Barry of six argent and azure, a bend gules.* = Joane, daughter and coheiress of James Fouldlarch, of Normandy.

Richard de Grey, alias Waterton of Rotherfield, co. Oxon, and of Codnor, co. Derby, A.D. 1108. = Helen, daughter of Henry, Lord Bohun. Arms of Bohun.—*Azure, a bend argent cotised or, between six lions rampant of the third.*

John de Grey, of Stoke, from whom are descended the Barons of Greystoke.

Henry de Grey, of Thurrock, co. Essex (A.D. 1194), and of Grimston, co. Nottingham (A.D. 1216). = Isolda, niece and heiress of Robert Bardolph.

John Doyley, of Oxfordshire. = Agnes de Grey, sister of Walter the Archbishop of York.

Walter de Grey, Bishop of Worcester, 5 Oct. 1214. Archbishop of York in 1215. Chancellor of England. Died 1 May, 1255. Buried in York Minster.

Robert de Grey, of Rotherfield, co. Oxon, by the gift of his uncle Walter. Died in 1268. Arms of Grey of Rotherfield.—*Barry of six argent and azure, a bendlet gules.* = . . .

John de Grey, of Codnor aforesaid. = Eleanor, daughter of Roger de Clare, third Earl of Hertford (who died in 1173). Arms of de Clare.—*Or, three chevrons gules.*

Robert de Grey, Lord of Rotherfield, died A.D. 1295. = Avicia, or Avice, daughter of William St. Clare alias St. Liz (living A.D. 1294), married circa A.D. 1269.

a

[c] Hundred Roll of Oxfordshire, 7 Edward I., *i.e.* A.D. 1279.

Page 751. William Quartermain is one of the Jurors for the Half Hundred of Ewelme.

Page 769. William Quartermain holds half a virgate of land in Chalgrove for 3s. and 8d. from Theobald de St. Albino, who holds from Margaret Plesset, who holds from the gift of John de Plesset formerly Earl of Warwick.

Page 770. William Quartermain holds in Chalgrove one messuage of Henry de *Swecenden*, and he of Dn' William de Baroof'. He likewise holds one acre of meadow for 1s. of Richard Russell of Clecr', and he of the heirs of Robert Braud. He also holds in the village of Chalgrove one hide of land, etc., which used to be held of the Lord of Cuxham, but now of Dn' Geoffrey Lewknore. Isabel Quartermain likewise holds of the aforesaid William Quartermain one messuage, etc., for life.

Page 821. William Quartermain (under age), son of William Quartermain, holds four virgates belonging to his fee of Weston, and has eleven customars who pay 5s. and give service worth 2s. 6d., and three cottars who pay 1s. 6d. and give service worth 6d.

[d] Page 822. William Quartermain, son of William, has one knight's fee in Weston with fifteen virgates of land in Ascot, held of the Bishop of Lincoln as of the manor of Thame, and seven virgates of land doing for them suit of Hundred in Thame Hundred and scutage; and has the right of fishing on the bank of the river Thame. He also has five customars and three cottars. Clara Quartermain holds from the said William certain virgates at the rent of 1d.

[e] Pleas of the Crown, from a MS. book in the Record Office. 13 Edward II., *i.e.* A.D. 1320, com. Oxon. Thame Hundred. W^s Quatermeyns simul cum dote matris tenet 1 feod. milit. et est plene etatis et nondum miles—ideo in misericordia.

Inquisitiones post mortem. 22 Richard II., *i.e.* A.D. 1399. No. 39. Thomas Quatremayns. Inquisition taken at Watlington on the Saturday in the Feast of St. Matthew in the said year before T. Rochewell, escheator. The jurors are William Hamelton, Richard atte More, etc. John Tame de Henle, etc., who say that Thomas Quartermayns held, by knight service, from Jane, daughter and heiress of Robert de Grey and Rotherfeld chivaler defunct, one messuage and one virgate of land and one orchard in Rotherfeld Greys "et valent per ann' in omnibus exitibus suis ultra repris' xiij s. iv d.," and that Thomas Quartermayns held one messuage with curtilage adjacent in Henle from the heirs of Richard le Molyns chivaler defunct, by the service of suit of court "et valet etc., ultra repris' vj s. viij d.," and that the aforesaid Thomas held 20 acres in Scaldefeld near Henley of the King as of his Manor of Bensington, etc., and one carucate of land in North Weston from the Bishop of Lincoln by knight service et val, etc., ult. repris' lxvj s. viij d., and of the same Bishop one burgage in the parish of Thame at the rent of 8d. per annum, and another in the same parish at vj s. viij d., and five cottages in Stanlake of the heirs of Richard Talbot, Lord of Bampton, by suit of court, 20 shillings. And the said Thomas died on the Tuesday next after that of the Holy Apostles Philip and James last past, and John his son is his nearer heir, aged 15 years.

[Note that in the year 1399 this Feast occurred on Thursday, as that day was the 1st of May. The following Tuesday was the 6th. On the tomb in Thame Church, therefore, the recorded inscription is right as to the day but wrong as to the year.]

[f] 10 Henry IV., *i.e.* A.D. 1409. Inquisition taken at Thame on the day of March next after the Feast of the Annunciation of the Blessed Virgin Mary before John Willicotes, escheator. Jurors: John Tettesworth, John Middlewood, etc. Thomas Bate, John Bate, William Turnpas, Richard Smith of Stanlake, etc., and Peter Mapledurham [sometime Churchwarden of Thame], who say that one messuage with curtilage in Henley and five cottages in Stanlake are held from the heir of Robert Grey of Rotherfeld, as of the Manor of Rotherfeld Greys by knight service into the hands of the King, by reason of the minority of John, son and heir of Thomas Quatremayn, and that they are worth 22s.; that John died on the Vigil of St. Thomas the Apostle, in the fifth year of the King; and that Guy, son of Thomas and brother of John, is the nearer heir of John Quatremayn, and aged 21 years and more.

[g] 11 Henry IV., *i.e.* 1410. The writ to John Willicotes, escheator for Oxon, states that Guy, son of Thomas Quartermain, brother and heir of John, who was son and heir to the said Thomas, was lately under age and in the custody of John de Etton and of Jane, widow of the said Thomas Quartermain.

Inquisition taken at Weston on the day of March next following the Feast of the Apostles Simon and Jude. Jurors: Thomas Chevedon, John Bolleur, William Wrench, John Middlewood, Nicholas Hykkes, Thomas Bate, Robert Nasch, John Bartholomew, William Humphreis, John Ascote, proved and lawful men, who say that Guy Quartermain is aged 21 years and more, was born at North Weston, and baptized in the Chapel of St. James there; and when it was asked how he was found to be of such full age, one of the Jurors, John Bate, said that he was certain that Guy was of full age because he was himself in the said Chapel at the time when the said Guy was baptized by the hands of Stephen Donington, then Rector of Aldebury. On the said day of March, Thomas Chevedon, second juror, of the age of 50 years, John Bolleur, third juror, of the age of 46 years, severally say that it is certain to them that the said Guy is of full age. Thomas Bolleur, fourth juror, aged 40, William Wrench, fifth juror, aged 54, William Walsh, sixth juror, aged 40, severally say that they are certain as to the age of the said Guy, because they were in the said Chapel, and William Bruley is his *compater* (*i.e.* godfather). John Middlewood, seventh juror, aged 32, Nicholas Hykkes, eighth juror, aged 47, severally say that they are certain as to the age of the said Guy, because they were *in cunctis* (*i.e.* restoratione) of the said Chapel, on which day Master John Bockyngham then Bishop of Lincoln "equitavit ad prandium usque villam de Thame." Thomas Bate, ninth juror, aged 48, says that he is certain of the full age of the said Guy, because he was there at the time of the baptism, on which day, "incontinenter postea," Robert, son of the said Thomas Bate, was baptized. Robert Nasch, tenth juror, aged 38 years, John Bartholomew, eleventh juror, aged 50 years, severally say that they are certain of the full age of the said Guy, because they were in the said Chapel and were godfathers to the said Robert, son of Thomas Bate. John Ascott, twelfth juror, aged 60 years, says that he too is certain of the full age of the said Guy son of Thomas Quartermain, because he was there at the time of the baptism to make a convention with one Semstar for making a new window in the said Chapel.

2 Henry V., *i.e.* A.D. 1414. Guy Quartermain. Inquisition taken at Watlington, 16 June, before Robert James, escheator. Jurors: Roger Badele, Richard Pepard, John Hynton, John Thomle, John Deyvile, Richard Gustard, John Orchard, Richard Dyer, John Bartholome, Simon Hatton, etc., who say that Guy Quartermain held in fee of John Lord Darycourt, son and heir of Jane, daughter and heir of Robert Grey de Rothefeld, "chivaler, defunct," one messuage and one virgate in Rotherfeld Grey, one curtilage in Henley of William Molyns "chivaler," 20 acres in Baldefeld, near Henley, of the King as of his manor of Bensington, one carucate, messuage and lands in North Weston, and one burgage in Thame of

Philip Bishop of Lincoln, together with five cottages in Stanlake of the heir of Richard Talbott, Lord of Bampton. Of all these Joanna, wife of John Creedy and widow of Thomas Quartermain, father of Guy, holds a third part in dower; and Guy had, by two indentures, granted to the said John Creedy the other two-thirds, etc., in North Weston, except the 40s. reddit. Guy died 15th May last, and Richard Quartremayne is brother and nearer heir, aged 22 years and more.

* William Dylet, instituted to Rectory of Ickford, co. Bucks, 14 August 1458, on the presentation of Richard Quartermain.

ROT. FIN. 37 Henry VI., *i.e.* A.D. 1459. Sir William la Zouche, born in 1432, married Katherine Lenton. The latter held Chilton, co. Bucks. A fine was passed between Richard Quartermain, Esq., Richard Fowler, Thomas Lovedon, and Henry Pennall, and William Geoffrey and Joane his wife, of messuages and lands in Chilton, supposed to have had relation to the settlement of his estates. Sir William la Zouche died 8 January 1468, seised of the manor of Chilton.

12 June, 6 Edward IV., *i.e.* 1467. Quartermain grants to Peter Feteplace and Margaret his wife (one of Beek's daughters and coheirs) £40 rent. Quartermain grants to Robert Points and Sibil his wife (another daughter and coheir of Beek, and widow of Moore) the manor of Chiswellhampton.—Muniments of Sir Cope Doyley, summarized A.D. 1624.

INQUISITIONES POST MORTEM. 17 Edward IV., *i.e.* A.D. 1478. Richard Quatremayne. 1. Inquisition taken at Aylesbury. 2. Inquisition taken in part in the parish of St. Nicholas Olif in Bred Strete Ward, London, 28 October. The Jurors declare that Richard Quartermain, Esq., was seised of one tenement in the parish of St. Mildred, Brede Street; of another in St. Mary Magdalene's parish in Old Fish Street; of another called "*Adyehouse*" in the parish of St. Peter at Paul's wharf in Temystrete, London, all held of the King in burgage; and that his heirs are Thomas Danvers, son and heir of Johan, only child of Matilda, first sister of Richard Quatermaine, aged 40 years; then Richard Boteler, son of Isabel, eldest daughter of Elizabeth, second sister of Richard Quartermain, aged 30 years; Alice, wife of Thomas Walrond, second daughter of Elizabeth, second sister of Richard Quartermain, aged 57 years; Richard Rous, son of John by the third daughter of the sister of Richard Quartermain, aged 30 years; Margaret, wife of Peter Fetyplace, fourth daughter of the second sister of Richard Quartermain, aged 53 years; and Sibilla, wife of Humphrey Forster, fifth daughter of the second sister of Richard Quartermain. 3. Inquisition taken at Uphaven, co. Wilts, 20 October. 4. Inquisition taken at New Thame, in the county of Oxford. The Jurors say that by letters patent, dated at Hamford 28 July Anno Regni 13, there was granted to Richard Quartermain, William Hampton (Alderman of London), Richard Fowler (Chancellor of the Duchy of Lancaster), John Leyston, and John Beset, *inter alia*, the Manor of Haltone [co. Oxon], lately belonging to William, some time Viscount Beaumont. Richard Quartermain and John Leyston died; and it appears to have come by survivorship to William Hampton, Richard Fowler, and John Beset.

Amongst the Additional Charters in the British Museum is a small indenture, numbered 20,320, made the 5th day of February the 37 year of Henry VI., *i.e.* A.D. 1458, between Richard Quartermain, Esquire, of the one part, and John Barantyne, Esq., relating to the Manor of Chalgrove, to which a small seal—on which appears an open hand, the crest upon a helmet,—and the signature of the said Richard are attached.

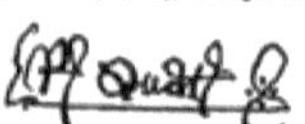

* 1 Richard III., *i.e.* A.D. 1483. Sibilla Quartermayne. Inquisition taken at Oxon die Jovis 29th January. The Jurors say that Sibilla on the day she died held to herself, the heirs of the body of herself and her late husband Richard Quartermayn, the manor of North Weston called Quartermaynes Manor, and six messuages, four cottages, three hundred acres of land, sixty acres of meadow, two hundred acres of pasture, in North Weston, of the gift of John Trevett to Richard and Sibilla, by a certain indented deed which settled them in remainder to Richard Fowler, Jane his wife, daughter of Jane, wife of John Danvers and daughter of Matilda, one sister of Richard Quartermayne, and their heirs male, with remainder to the male heirs of their female heirs, remainder in order to daughters of Richard and Joane Fowler, remainder to Richard Boteler, son and heir of Isabel, etc., and his heirs male, remainder to Thomas Boteler his brother and his heirs male, remainder to Richard Rous and his heirs male, remainder to John son of Margaret Feteplace and his heirs male, remainder to the said Jane who was the wife of John Danvers and her heirs male, remainder to right heirs of Richard Quatermayne. Jane, wife of Richard Fowler, is alive and succeeds to the said manor and lands. And the said manor, etc., worth twenty-one marcs 6s., are held of the Bishop of Lincoln as of his manor of Thame. And Sibilla also held in the same way the manor of Great Ricott, etc., and three hundred acres of pasture, six acres of wood, and 5s. rent of the gift of Robert Burton, who settled them on the heirs of Richard Quatermayne and Sibilla, with remainder to heirs of Sibilla, remainder to said Richard Fowler the son and heir of Cecilie, sister of Sibilla and heirs, then to heirs of body of Cecilie, then to Thomas Boteler, younger son of Baldwin Boteler and Isabel lately his wife, daughter of the said Nicholas Englefeld and Elizabeth his wife, sister of Richard Quartermayne in fee simple, then to Richard Boteler, eldest son of Baldwin Boteler in fee simple, remainder to Sibilla sister of Richard and Thomas Boteler in fee simple, then to Elizabeth wife of Eustace Greenville, Esq., and sister of Richard and Thomas Boteler, in fee simple, and then to right heirs of John de Ricote. Richard, son and heir of Richard Fowler, is alive and succeeds, and the said manor, lands, etc., are worth forty marcs, and were held under Edward V. the Bastard, late King of England, of the manor of Wallingford. Sibilla died 22 May in the first year of Edward V., and Richard Fowler, son of Richard, is her heir and of the age of seventeen years.

* 3 Henry V., *i.e.* A.D. 1416. Nicholas Englefeild. From this it appears that Nicholas Englefeild died on the 1st April last. John is his son and heir; and his three daughters are coheiresses to Nicholas Rycote. The following is proved from his Inquisition:—

Nicholas Rycote, who settled the Manor of Rycott after the death of his wife and daughter. = Katherine, seised with her husband of the Manor in question.

Joanna Rycote, daughter and heiress. = Nicholas Englefeild. =

Sibilla, aged 15 years.
Cecilia, aged 12 years.
Agnes Englefeild, aged 8 years.
John Englefeild, son and heir, aged 4 years.

There is a most elaborate Pedigree of Englefeild, beginning with a member of the family said to have lived in the time of King Edward the Confessor, on folios 208 and 209 of Harl. MSS. No. 4031. Therein it is stated that both Sibilla, wife to Richard Quartermain, Esq., and Cecilia, wife to William Floyler, Esq., are the daughters of John Englefeild and Isabell his wife. But on folio 105 a of this said MS. the deed of settlement of Rycott, summarized in the following note, proves the accuracy of the Pedigree in the text above relating to the issue of Richard and Sibilla.

* The Rycott Settlement Deed, A.D. 1454, Harl. MSS. No. 4031, begins by reciting that Richard Quartermain and William Fowler and their wives had acknowledged that they had conveyed the manor of Great Rycott, etc., to Robert Burton, John Cottismore, Thomas Hensster, David Pryse, and Robert Tong, and that the second, third, and fourth had died seised of the same; and that now in the 32 year of Henry VI. (viz., A.D. 1454) the survivors, Robert Burton and Robert Tong, convey Great Rycott and lands in Little Rycott, Sidenham, co. Oxon, and Appleton, co. Berks, to Richard Quartermain and Sibila his wife, one of the daughters and heirs of Nicholas Ricote, or Rycott, *alias* Clerke, and Catherine his wife, daughter and heiress of John Ricote, and their legitimate issue, with remainder to the legitimate issue of Sibilla Quartermain, to the heirs male of the body of Richard Quartermain, and remainder in succession to Richard, Thomas, Nicholas, Alice, and Sibilla Fowler, the children of the said Sibilla's sister Cecilie, remainder to Thomas Boteler, etc., remainder to Richard Boteler, son and heir of Isabel, etc. Witnesses, Edmund Rede, William Marmion, Robert Fitz-Elys, Thomas Lovedon, etc.

1479, Sep. 27.—Mast' John Coldale, priest, was presented by Sibilla Quartermayne, relict of Richard Quartermayne, deceased, to the Church of Halton (or Holton), by the death of Mast' Edw' Byrt.

—Register of Bishop Rotherham alias Scott, of Lincoln, appointed Bishop of Lincoln in 1472.

1494-5, March 19.—Sir Robert Orcslshawe, priest, was presented by Johanna Fowler, widow, to the Church of Halton, by resignation of Master John de Coldall.—Register of Bishop William Smythe.

* The following, mainly taken from the *Visitation of Oxfordshire* in 1574 by Richard Lee, Portcullis, and Deputy to Robert Cooke, Clarencieux, shews the connection between the Families of Bruley, Quartermain, Danvers, Cottismore, Fowler, and Symeons.

PEDIGREE OF BRULEY AND OTHERS.

William Bruley, Lord of Waterstocke, sixth in descent from Sir Henry Bruley. = Agnes.

ARMS OF BRULEY—*Ermine, on a bend gules three chevronells or.*

John Bruley, son and heire, of Ipwell and Banbury, co. Oxon. (In Waterstocke Church there remained, *circa* 1574, a shield of arms of John Bruley impaling Maude Quartermain; and another of Danvers quarterly with Bruley, over all on a shield of pretence, Quartermain.—See Richard Lee's *Gatherings of Oxfordshire*; Anthony à Wood's MSS., Bodleian Lib., No. 14, D. It is therefore possible, as the *Visitation of Oxfordshire* states, that the first wife of this Thomas Danvers may have been an "Isabell Quartermain." But evidence is against it. A tradition of seventy years may have been easily attenuated or corrupted—though Richard Lee, sometime of Thame, when he recorded the Pedigree, knew the locality well.) = Maude, dau. of Thomas Quartermain of North Weston, in Thame.

Joane Bruley, daughter and heire. = John Danvers of Waterstock, co. Oxon.

Sir Thomas Danvers of Waterstocke, Knt. Died without issue. = Sibilla, dau. of William Fowler, and sister of Richard and Cecilia Englefield his wife.

Joane Danvers. = Richard Fowler of Rycott, Chancellor of the Duchy of Lancaster.

Sir John Cottismore of Baldwin Brightwell, co. Oxon. Lord Chief Justice. Died in 1439. = Amicia Bruley.

ARMS OF COTTISMORE—*Azure, an imperial eagle displayed argent, on his breast an escocheon gules charged with a leopard's face or.*

Sir William Cottismore, Knt., son and heire. = Alice, dau. of . . . . Hall of Ossebridge, in co. Wilts.

Thomas Cottismore. = Elizabeth, dau. of William Symeons or Simonds of Pirton, co. Oxon. Of this family was Robert Symeon of Thame, M.P. for Oxfordshire in 1375, in 1377, and 1378, *i.e.* during the reign of Edward III. and Richard II.

ARMS OF SYMEONS—*Per fesse sable and argent, three trefoils slipped counterchanged.*

* EXTRACT FROM THE "ITINERARY" OF JOHN LELAND (A.D. 1542).

"Ricote longid to one Fulco de Ricote.

"After it cam to one Quatermains.

"The house of the Quatermains in Oxfordshir hath bene famose and of right fair Possessions. Their chief house was at Weston by Ricote, wher Mr. Clerk now dwellith.

"And Shirburne withyn a Mile of Wathelington chirch, wher is a strong Pile or Castelet, longid to Quatremains: sins Fowler: and by Exchaunge now to Chaumbrelain of Oxfordshir.

"About King Henry the vj. Dayes dyvers Brethren dyed of the Quatermains one after another, and by a great onlyheithod al the landes descendid to one Richard, the Yonggest of the Brethren, that was a Marchant of London, and after Custumer there.

"This Richard had a servaunt caullid Thomas Fowler his clerk, a toward felaw that after was Chaunselar of the Duchy of Lancastre.

"Richard Quatermains bare great favor to this Thomas.

"Richard was God-father to Thomas sonne, and namid hym Richard Quatermains Fowler.

"Richard Quatermains lay at Ricote: and causid Thomas Fowler to lay at Weston.

"Richard Quatermains made Richard Thomas Fowler's Sonne heir of most Part of his landes, bycause he had no Children.

"Richard Quatermains God-father to Richard Fowler made a Right goodly large Chapelle of Ease hard without the Manor Place of Ricote, and foundid ther 2. Chauntre Prestes to sing perpetually for his Soule, endewing the Cantuaries with good Landes: and made a fair House for the Prestes therby.

"This fundation was begon in Henry the 6. dayes: and endid yn Edward the 4. Tyme.

"This Richard foundid also a Cantuarie in Tame parochе chirche a 2. miles from Ricote, wher he in a chapelle is buried undre a Marble Stone.

"This Richard foundid ther also an Hospitale by Tame Chirche endowing it by Landes.

"Richard Fowler, heir to Quatremains was a very onthrift, and sold al his Landes leving his children ful smaul lyvinges.

"Syr John Heron, Treasorer of the Chaumbre to Henry the vij. and the viij. boute the reversion of the lordship of Ricote, and Giles his sonne possessid it a while.

"Giles Heron wise in wordes but folisch yn deades, as Syr Richard Fowler was, sold Ricote to John Willyams, now knighte (in 1542)." Vol. ii., pp. 9, 10.—Oxford: 1745.

The following Memorandum remaining in the Church Book seems to bear out Leland's statement, that Sir Richard Fowler was "onthrift:"—"Detts owinge to the Churche. Imprimis, my Lorde of Notteley owith for the rente of a house called Gylberds which hath been unpaid xvij yeres iij^{s} iv^{d}. It'm Do' Richard Flowler owith to the Church for the rent of a ten't called Jenkyn Grenes, & has not paid for vij yeres, xxv^{s} viij^{d}."—*Church Accounts of Thame.*

From the Register of Bishop West, of Lincoln, A.D. 1526, it is clear that the Chapel at Rycott was dedicated in honour of St. Michael and All Angels; and that there were at that period two chaplains then serving it, of which the senior was Thomas Kendall.

1571, Aug. 25.—Roger Quartermayne and Steven Smythe, High Constables of the Half Hundred of Ewelme, made certificate of search for rogues and vagabonds to Sir Edmund Ashfeild, Anthony Carleton, and Thomas Wynchcombe, Esq^{rs}., Justices.—*State Papers.*

1535. VALOR ECCLESIASTICUS.—Wallyngton, Oxon. Roger Quatermayn pays rent.

TURNER AND COXE'S BODLEIAN CHARTERS.—1561, p. 277. Oxon.—Articles of Agreement between the Dean and Chapter of Christ Church and Roger Quatermayn of Chalgrove, yeoman, of one part, and William Standisshe of Oxford, Gent., of other part, dated 16 May, 3 Q. Eliz. To abide the award of Edmund Plowden as to how far the Berro Herlewyn or Bekkharvest tithes in Chalgrove extend.—Ch. 142.

BLUNT *v.* QUATERMAN.—Calendar, vol. i., p. 66, from *Genealogist*, vol. v., p. 296. The Plaintiff's claim is dated 15th October, 1594, and is to avoid the purchase of cottages and lands in Wallington, Oxon, because Christopher Marshall, deceased, who contracted to purchase, had a power of revoking the contract and of demanding back the price paid, viz. £80. This power he exercised on finding that the premises were held not in fee and common socage, but by knight's service of the Queen. The defendant Jerome Quaterman, gentleman, files two answers alleging that the purchase was complete. The plaintiff files a replication. See *Genealogist*, vol. v., pp. 127-8, which shews that Jerome Q. married Mary Marshall at Blewberry in 1558.

CLOSE ROLLS.—Vol. 22. A° 37 Eliz., par. 23. Herein is a reference to an old deed of Richard Quatermayne's of North Weston.

Vol. 30. 16 James, par. 10, No. 47. Danl. Quatermain and Wm. Hobbes.

Vol. 32. 2 Chas. I., par. 21, No. 9. Francis Q. and Sir W. Whitmore.

Vol. 33. 6 Chas. I., par. 3, No. 18. Walt. Q. and Ralph Massy.

Vol. 34. 8 Chas. I., par. 39, No. 42. James Q. and T. Ayshman.

Vol. 36. 13 Chas. I., par. 40, No. 184. Rog. Q. and Dudley Digges.

1654. Par. 51, No. 19. An Indenture between Henry Earl of Kingston of first part, Charlotte Countess Dowager of Darby of second part, and James Quatermaine of Eonham, Oxon, yeoman, of third part. For £55 they grant to him at a rent of 16s. 8d. a house and homestall, containing 1 rood 32 perches in Evensham alias Eonham, Oxon, also parcells of land.

No. 20. A further conveyance from same to same for £60, but he is herein called James Quatermayne, gent.

Lipscombe's Buckinghamshire.—Seaton Quatermain, Rector of Newton Longueville 23 Dec. 1558. Buried 27 July 1613.

Notes and Queries (6th Series, 1881).—Sentorio Quatremanno of Italy, circa 1550. A Poet.

List of Members of Inner Temple.—Ralph Quatermain of Chalgrove admitted to Inner Temple in 16—; died there in 1621, aged 24.

State Papers Domestic.—1640; p. 405. Acts of the Courts of High Commission. April 23, John Vicars, undermaster of Christ Church school, and Roger Quatreman of the borough of Southwark. Vicars appeared and was sworn. Quatreman appeared and was referred to Dr. Fealty to confer about the lawfulness of the oath *ex-officio*, and to report this day fortnight.

P. 416. May 7th, 1640. R. Q. ordered to confer again.

P. 426. June 18th, 1640. R. Q. ordered to confer again.

P. 430. June 25th, 1640. R. Q. ordered to confer again.

Report of Historical MSS. Commission, No. IV., p. 460.

For the county of Oxford there are 379 deeds, from the middle of the twelfth century to 1572, many of which relate to the family of Quatremayn.—*Muniments of Magdalen College, Oxford.*

Report of Historical MSS. Commission, Nos. VI. and VII.

Ormonde Papers. Letters from a Widow Quatermain.

Oxfordshire Poll-book, a.d. 1754. Wotton Hundred.—Eynsham: James Q. of Eynsham voted for Parker and Turner.

Lewknor Hundred.—Chinnor: Benj. Q. of Hogshaw Hill, Bucks, voted for Wenman and Dashwood.

Kingston Blount: Andrew Q. of Kingston Blount voted for Wenman and Dashwood.

Ewelme Hundred.—Cuxham: John Q. of Thame Park voted for Wenman and Dashwood.

Little Haseley: Abraham Q. of Little Haseley voted for Wenman and Dashwood.

* The following was formerly in one of the windows of Great Haseley Church:—

Orate pro an'mabus Radulphi Boteler et Isabel
ux' ejus, et pro bono statu D'ni Tho'e Boteler
. . . . rector istius . . . .

ADDITIONAL NOTES.

Abstracts of Wills, a.d. 1620—1744.

Richard Quartermain of Aston Thropps, in the parish of Blewberry, co. Berks, yeoman. Will made 13 Dec. 1620. Proved 1 Feb. 1620-1. To my brother Christopher Quartermain, £40. To my brother Thomas and to my sister Mary, £10 between them. My brother John Quartermain, my brother-in-law Thomas Bradford, my sisters-in-law Dorothy and Martha Bradford, £4 between them. Mary Pawline my daughter-in-law. Henry White my son-in-law. John White my son-in-law. Mrs. Mary Bradford my mother. Mary my wife, executrix and residuary legatee. Leaves legacies to the poor of "Aston Terrauld," Aston Thropps, and Watlington.—Will Office, Somerset House, Dale 18.

Ralph Quartermayne of Chalgrove, co. Oxon. Will made 2 August 1621. Proved 16 September 1621. The lease of my farm at Chalgrove to my mother Joane Chibnall. £5 to the Church of Chalgrove. £20 to my uncle Thomas Deane. Witnesses: Humphrey and Francis Aylworth and Thomas Deane.—Will Office, Somerset House, Dale 77.

See also the footnotes on p. 92 of this book relating to members of this family.

Walter Quartermain of Shabbington, Bucks. Will made 26 December 1634. To William Quartermain my son and his heirs my two cottages in Warborow, Oxon. To Elizabeth my wife my tenements in Shabbington where I dwell. Remainder of said lease to Walter Quartermain my son, during life of son William. Residue to the above and Elizabeth my daughter. All children under age. Witnesses: Thomas Phillips, Thomas Carter. My loving friend Thomas Phillips of Ickford and my brother Daniel Quartermain, overseers.—Will, proved in 1635, in Will Office, Somerset House, Sadler 11.

Maximilian Quartermain. Will made 26 October 1639. Proved 2 January 1639-40. He leaves £60 amongst "the six children of Henry Owen, clerk, my brother-in-law," of Stad'on (*i.e.* Stadhampton), Oxon. £15 amongst the three children of William Brocooke, dwelling in Oxford. £20 "to my sister-in-law Marie Quartermain." Sarah Franckling, my sister; William, my godson, son of William Ward, of Arnton, Berks. Residue to Henry Owen.—Will Office, Somerset House, Coventry 10.

Andrew Quartermayn of Little Milton, co. Oxon. Will made 11 June 1653. Proved 30 May 1654. Leaves 5s. to Thomas Quartermayne, his eldest son. "£20 to Thomas Clayton, my son-in-law." "Elisabeth Carpenter, my daughter." "Item I give unto my grand-children, being twenty in number, twelve pence apiece." Residue to my two youngest sons John and Ralphe Quartermayne, who are executors.—Will Office, Somerset House, Alchin 74.

Robert Quartermain of Thame. Will made 13 April 1731. Proved 19 March 1744. Leaves his father a legacy. To wife Elisabeth, if with child, £250; if not with child, then £50 to his kinsman Robert Quartermain, son of his uncle Thomas, and £200 to his wife. —"Wills of the Peculiar of Thame."

The following is from an altar-tomb in the churchyard of Little Kimble, co. Bucks:—

Sacred to the Memory of
STEPHEN QUARTERMAINE,
Late of this village,
Third son of BENJAMIN QUARTERMAINE,
of Hogshaw House,
in the Parish of Quainton, and
descendant of the ancient family of
Quartermaines of Oxfordshire,
(Once the possessors of Sherborne Castle
and other estates
in the above County,)
who died January 14th, 1831,
Aged 76 years.

Also to Mary, Widow of the above,
and only child
of John and Susannah Brimer,
who died February 11th, 1839,
Aged 79 years,
After a long and severe illness which was borne with
Christian fortitude and resignation.

Joseph Quartermaine died June 1st, 1870, aged 75.

Sacred to the Memory of
Anne, daughter of
Stephen and Mary Quartermaine,
who died March 2nd, 1783, aged 3 years.

Also of Mr. John Brimer,
Grandfather of the above, of this village;
who died Feby. 22nd, 1792, aged 79.

Also of Susannah, his widow,
who died Sept' 6th, 1798, aged 83.

Also of Stephen, son of
Stephen and Mary Quatermaine,
who died Dec' 26th, 1804, aged 23.

Also of George, their son,
who died at Paris, (where he was buried,)
Aug' 7th, 1819, aged 19 years;
Having been thrown from his horse
which caused his death.

Also of Benjamin, their son,
who died Aug' 18th, 1833, aged 55.

Also of John Brimer, their son,
who died from the effects of a fall,
July 11th, 1839, aged 56.

THOUGH that particular branch of the family of Quartermain, set forth in the Pedigree just recorded, died out in the male line and was merged in the knightly family of Fowler and others, yet there are many members of the Quartermain race existing, who have never recovered the social position which their ancestors of Thame and North Weston owned in the fourteenth and fifteenth centuries. At Chalgrove, Watlington, Oxford, Stokenchurch, Eynsham, Thame, and elsewhere, they have had numerous representatives, but mainly in humble life—some, it may be, of illegitimate descent; but others without any doubt members of an honoured and knightly race, once ranking with, and representing, some of the oldest and noblest families of the land.

They came originally from Normandy—as the character of their name seems to indicate—and it is said that both at Caen and in its neighbourhood residents bearing that name can be traced until the period of the French Revolution. One exiled priest, Michael Quartermain, having fled from France, with others, during the Reign of Terror, resided at Thame towards the close of the last century; and, unlike some of his brethren, lived to return to his native country, Normandy, at the beginning of the present, about 1803.

The arms of Quartermain appear to have come down to them from time immemorial. The tinctures are different in various records. Somewhat similar coat-armour belonged to the ancient family of Tremaine of Cornwall—both races using what are called "canting arms."

In the year 1488—as may be gathered from a "Computus Roll" of Thame Abbey, preserved at Lord Bath's mansion, Longleat, in Wiltshire—one "Richard Quatermaigne" is mentioned as Seneschal of the Abbey: whilst amongst the Churchwardens' Accounts of Thame, of the latter part of the fifteenth century, several allusions to himself, or another person of the same Christian and surname, occur, as early as the year 1465. This man was probably an official of the Court of the Prebendary of Thame, and may have been similarly employed in other ecclesiastical courts. Two entries relating to him have been reproduced on p. 47, in connection with a case before the Dean of Lincoln at a Court, held in the Common Hall of Lincoln College in Oxford. About the same time he was engaged with a "Master Standishe" in collecting Peter's Pence from various places within the ancient Peculiar of Thame and Great Milton; and appears to have resided at some mansion-house,—possibly the Grange belonging to Thame Abbey,—in the parish of Sydenham. The yeoman family of Quartermain, which lived in that village until the year 1780 (see p. 175), are said to have been his lineal descendants.

In the *Memoirs of Samuel Pepys, comprising his Diary*, under the date 24 May 1660, it is on record that its author was on board the ship which was bringing King Charles II. back to England, where there was an "extraordinary press of noble company and great mirth all day," and there "dined with me in my cabin . . . . . Dr. Quartermain and Dr. Clerke, physicians." The former has already been alluded to; the latter was a member of the family of Clerke of Warwickshire.

A Richard Quartermain of Chalgrove, allied to the family of Basse of Moreton in Thame, wrote a curious treatise on Heraldry. It was existing at Thame in MS. in the year 1854, but appears to be lost.

The family of Clerke of Weston now comes directly under consideration. Of the events incident to the war between England and France, in the early years of Henry VIII.'s reign, which secured to John Clerke the dignity of knight banneret, Lord Herbert of Cherbury shall speak :—

"Upon the twelfth of *August* [A.D. 1513] *Maximilian* the Emperor came to the King, in the quality of his souldier, and therefore not *onely* wore the Crosse of Saint *George*, but receiv'd his pay duly, which I find, by some, to have been a hundred Crownes *per diem*. Notwithstanding which, that all due respect might be rendered to his Person, the King gave order to lodge him according to his dignity, in a tent of Cloth of Gold, for the rest most sumptuously entertaining him the space of two dayes that he stayed in the campe. *Therouene* was not yet so streightly besieged, but that on the one side which was toward the river Lys, there was a way open, on which part the French intended to relieve it. The King, therefore, commanded five bridges to be instantly made over the said river, by which himselfe with *Maximilian* (who was now return'd again) and a great part of his army passed. This was scarce done when our light-horse brought word that the French were in sight. Our King thereupon marched toward them. The French at first came as if they meant to fight; but, after a slight skirmish, fled away in much disorder, which seemed the stranger that the fight was between the horsemen only, and many of the bravest of their nation were among them. Our men pursued and tooke *Louis Duc de Longueville*, Marquesse *de Rotelin*, *Bayard*, *Fayette*, *Clermont*, and *Buisse d'Amboise*, and brought them away, together with nine cornets. The *Seigneur de la Palisse* and *Monsieur d'Imbrecourt* were also taken, but agreeing for their ransom upon the place were presently let free, or, as others say, escaped. This Battaile, happning the 16th of *August*, was call'd by the French, *la Journee des Esperons*, because they made little use of anything but their spurs, for the good successe whereof therefore both the King and *Maximilian* the Emperor (wearing still his Badge of the Red-Crosse) did upon the place congratulate with each other, and afterwards assisted at a solemne *Te Deum* for this easie victory."*

* *The Life and Raigne of King Henry the Eighth.* By Edward, Lord Herbert of Cherbury, p. 38. London, 1649.

But to revert for awhile to the Manor. Christopher Edmonds, of North Weston, Esq., afterwards knighted, was a stepson of Sir John Williams, and no doubt obtained the Manor of North Weston from or through his enterprising and successful stepfather. From an existing deed, made on the 23rd February 1563, between this Christopher Edmonds and Francis Alford of London, Gent., it appears that Sir John Williams, Knt., by a previous deed—dated 14 November 1553, to which Nicholas Clerke, Elizabeth Clerke, widow, late wife of Nicholas, William Clerke, Esq., son and heir of the said Nicholas, Henry Norris and Richard Wenman were parties—had granted a lease of the Manor of North Weston to Nicholas Clerke, for three score and five pounds thirteen shillings and four pence.

Three years afterwards, on the 20th of March 1566, an indenture was made between "John Goodwyn of Bishopp's al's Woburne Deincourt," in the county of Bucks, Esq., John Croke of Chilton, Esq., and Edward Martyn of Swallowfield, co. Berks, Gent., on the one part, and Francis Alford of London, Gent., on the other part, which states that whereas Sir John Williams, Knt., granted the Manor of North Weston to the Clerkes, as already set forth, it is now sold to Francis Alford; and the further statement is made that the Manor is then in the tenure of Roger Alford, husband of Elizabeth Clerke.*

There had evidently been some marriage or connection between the Clerkes of Warwickshire and the family of Littelton *alias* Westcott, who appear in the Quartermain pedigree. It may have been that Nicholas Clerke *alias* Rycott formed this link; for soon after the death of Sir John Clerke, Christopher Westcott, (who had married Margaret, one of the daughters of Sir Richard Fowler of Rycott, by Julian his wife,) brought to the Churchwardens of Thame the sum of 40s. which Sir John had bequeathed to the Parish Church; and two years afterwards, in the year 1542, the same Christopher Westcott paid to the Churchwardens of Thame the sum of 12d. for the solemn and consolatury service for the departed at Sir John's year's-mind.

It is clear that Sir John Clerke had three wives. The first, who died young and was buried at Quarrendon, was Jane, daughter of Benedict and the youngest sister of Richard Lee (who in a deed dated 1472 was styled "firmare," and was Constable of Quarrendon from A.D. 1472 to 1485); the second was Elizabeth Ashby, who bore him two sons; and the third Agnes, widow of Nicholas Pyncheon, "cityzen and bocher," sometime Sheriff of London (whose Will was proved in 1533). This last-named lady left her son "John Pynchyon" a legacy.

Sir William Clerke, Knt., of Weston—only son of Nicholas, and grandson of Sir John in question, who is buried at Thame—was certainly a Catholic. His lady, Mary, daughter of Sir John Bourne, of Worcestershire, Knt., (who had been a most earnest supporter of the Old Religion under Queen Mary Stuart,) was also a most devout Catholic, and in 1604 protected the persecuted clergy of the ancient order most boldly.* At that period the Cursons of Waterperry, the Wenmans of Thame Park, the Belsons of Aston, and the family of Phillips of Ickford were likewise Catholics.

The Pedigrees which follow will set forth the history of the Thame and North Weston branch (practically founded in 1513), for nearly three hundred and fifty years, and the descent of the baronetcy which this branch possesses, from the time of its creation to the present day. Sir John Clerke of Thame, as will be seen, came originally from Warwickshire.

Of this family were the Clerkes of Launde Abbey, co. Leicester, one member of which, Clement Clerke, was created a baronet by King Charles II. by Letters Patent dated 18 June 1661. He was descended from Robert Clerke, the younger of the two elder brothers of Sir John of Thame. There were six baronets of Launde Abbey—ancient Church property; but this branch was not prolific, and the title became extinct upon the death of Sir Talbot Clerke, who had married Lucy, daughter of the Rev. Mr. Rogers of Painswick, and died without issue 10 July 1730.

A second baronetcy was granted, 26 October 1774, to the husband of Dorothy Clerke (a daughter of the first baronet), Philip Jennings of Duddlestone, co. Salop, who by Royal Licence dropped his own surname, and took that of Clerke; but he too died without any lawful issue on 22nd April 1788, and this baronetcy likewise became extinct.

Richard Clerke, Chamberlain of London, bore the same arms as those of Sir John of Thame, including the honourable canton. His crest, however, instead of a ram's head, was a swan. John Clerke of Aston, Oxfordshire, descended from Serjeant Clerke of Guilsborough, also bore the same arms, but without the canton; and he had for his crest a dove or pigeon, with expanded wings, and holding three stalks of wheat in its beak. Mr. Clerke Brown of Kingston Blount represents this branch of the Clerkes in the female line.

* *Harleian Charters*, Brit. Museum, 79 F., 26, 30.

* "A.D. 1604. Mr. Owen, a Roman Catholic Priest, was with the Lady Clark, in Oxfordshire, at Weston nigh unto Thame."—It is a tradition, I may here add, that up to the year 1624 the old Catholic services were said in the Chapel of Weston. But what is more probable is that Mass was said in some private chapel in the Manor House.

Pedigree of Clerke of North Weston in Thame, Co. Oxon.

No. I.

Arms.—*Argent, on a bend gules, between three pellets, as many swans proper.*
Crest.—*A ram's head argent, attired or.*
Honourable Augmentation.—*Sinister, a canton azure with a demi-ram salient argent, two fleurs-de-lys or in chief; and over all a dexter baton trunked.* (See Kent's *Abridgment of Guillim's Heraldry*, vol. ii., p. 673: London, 1728.)

Richard Hamond *alias* Clerke of Willoughby, Co. Warwickshire, *temp.* Henry VI. Had the manor and tithes of Willoughby granted to him by lease from Magdalene College, Oxford. = Collet, his wife.

William Clerke of Willoughby aforesaid, son and heir. = Alice, his wife.

William Clerke of Willoughby aforesaid. = Elizabeth, his wife.

William Clerke of Willoughby aforesaid. = Agnes, his wife.

Children:

- 1. Richard Clerke, son and heire.
- 2. Robert Clerke of Willoughby, Co. Warwick. Second son. (*See Pedigree of Clerke, No. II.*) = Elizabeth, daughter of .... Clerke of the Were, Co. Herts.
- Jane Lee. Died 19 Oct. 1516. Buried at Quarrendon, Co. Bucks. (1st wife.) [In the Collections of Nicholas Charles, Lancaster Herald, he describes a gravestone with the Arms of Clerke of Weston (with the honourable canton) impaling the old Arms of Lee, ar. a fesse between three leopards' heads sable, as remaining, A.D. 1611, in the Chapel of Quarrendon, Co. Bucks. The inscription runs thus: "Here lieth buried under this stone the body of Jane Clarke, late the wife of John Clark, wch departed out of this world the 19th day of October the year after the incarnation of our Lord God, 1516, on whose soule Jhesu have mercy. Amen. And for her soul and all Christian soules of your charity every man that shall read this scripture, or hear it read, say devoutly a Pater noster & an Ave." See *Bibl. Lansdowne*, Brit. Museum, 874. Plut. LXXIX. D.] = 3. John Clerke of North Weston, Oxon. Third son. He made Louis, Duke of Longueville, prisoner at the Battle of Spurs, 1513, for which service he was knighted, and had an augmentation to his Arms granted by Thomas Wriothesley, Garter, and Thomas Benolt. He married, for his third wife, Agnes, widow of Nicholas Pyncheon,[1] "citizen and bocher," Sheriff of London 1533, and died 5 April 1539. M.I. in Thame Church.[3] = Elizabeth, daughter of ... Ashby. Buried at Blakesley,[2] Co. Northants. (2nd wife.)

Children of Robert Clerke and Elizabeth:

- 1. Henry Clerke. From whom the Clerkes of Kingsthorpe, Co. Northants, descend, as also the Clerkes of Willoughby.
- 2. William Clerke.
- 3. Clement Clerke. Born in 1546.
- Two daughters.

Children of John Clerke:

- Ambrose Clerke. [See Francis Thynne's *Collectanea Heraldica*, Cleopatra C. III., Brit. Museum, folio 5.]
- Nicholas Clerke, Esq., of North Weston, Co. Oxford, and of Hitcham, Co. Bucks. Died in July 1551. Buried in the Chancel of Hitcham Church.[5] (1st husband.) = Elizabeth, daughter of Thomas Ramsey[4] of Hitcham, Esq., by Parnell, his wife, daughter and coheir of Sir John Baldwin, Knt., of Aylesbury, Co. Bucks. Chief Justice of the Court of Common Pleas A.D. 1535. Arms of Ramsey.—*Argent, a chevron gules between three rams' heads couped proper.* = Roger Alford of the City of London, Gent., and subsequently of Hitcham, Co. Bucks. Tenant of Weston Manor in 1556. He died 16 July 1580.[6] (2nd husband.)

Children of Roger Alford and Elizabeth:

- Edward Alford.
- Edward Pettiplace. = Anne Alford.

Children of Nicholas Clerke and Elizabeth:

- 1. Sir William Clerke, Knt., of Hitcham, son and heir of Nicholas. Died 1 Feb. 1624. Buried at Hitcham. Monument in the Chancel.[7] A = Margaret, one of the daughters of Sir John Bourn of Holt Castle, Co. Worcester, Knt. Sometime Secretary of State to Queen Mary. Arms of Bourn.—*Argent, on a chevron gules, between three lions rampant sable, as many mascles or.*
- 2. Nicholas Clerke. = ...
  - Mary Clerke. Baptized at Thame 9 May 1649.
  - John Clerke. M.A. Cantab. = Mary Winslowe. Married at Thame 31 Oct. 1649.
- 1. Jane Clerke. Died unmarried. Buried at Hitcham.
- 2. Dorothy Clerke. Married first Henry Long of Shingey; and secondly Sir Charles Morrison of Cashiobury, Co. Herts, Knt.

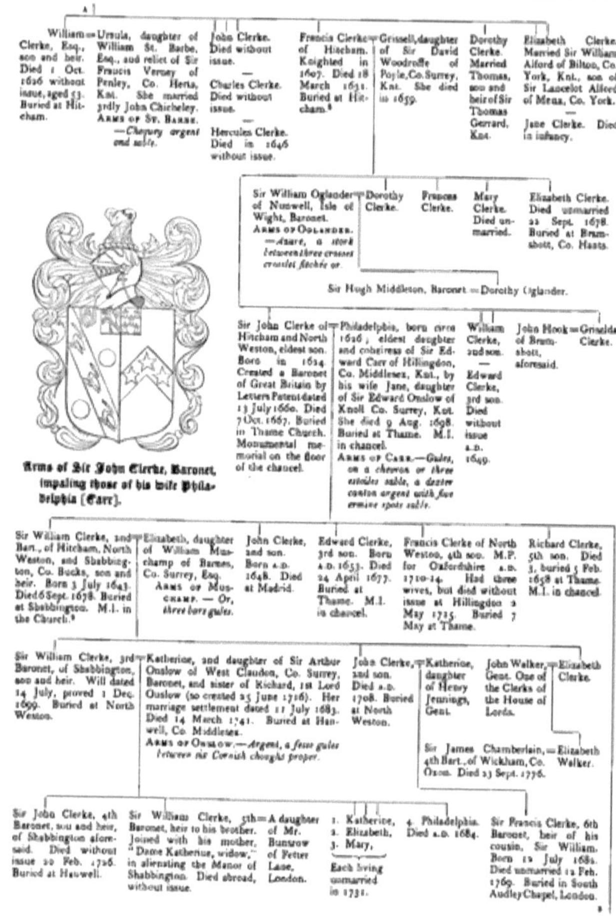

A

William Clerke, Esq., son and heir. Died 1 Oct. 1626 without issue, aged 53. Buried at Hitcham. = Ursula, daughter of William St. Barbe, Esq., and relict of Sir Francis Verney of Penley, Co. Herts, Knt. She married 3rdly John Chicheley. ARMS OF ST. BARBE.—*Chequy argent and sable.*

John Clerke. Died without issue.

Charles Clerke. Died without issue.

Hercules Clerke. Died in 1646 without issue.

Francis Clerke of Hitcham. Knighted in 1607. Died 18 March 1631. Buried at Hitcham.[1] = Grissell, daughter of Sir David Woodroffe of Poyle, Co. Surrey, Knt. She died in 1659.

Dorothy Clerke. Married Thomas, son and heir of Sir Thomas Gerrard, Knt.

Elizabeth Clerke. Married Sir William Alford of Bilton, Co. York, Knt., son of Sir Lancelot Alford of Meux, Co. York.

Jane Clerke. Died in infancy.

Sir William Oglander of Nunwell, Isle of Wight, Baronet. ARMS OF OGLANDER.—*Azure, a stork between three crosses crosslet fitchée or.* = Dorothy Clerke.

Sir Hugh Middleton, Baronet = Dorothy Oglander.

Frances Clerke.

Mary Clerke. Died unmarried.

Elizabeth Clerke. Died unmarried 22 Sept. 1678. Buried at Bramshott, Co. Hants.

Arms of Sir John Clerke, Baronet, impaling those of his wife Philadelphia (Carr).

Sir John Clerke of Hitcham and North Weston, eldest son. Born in 1624. Created a Baronet of Great Britain by Letters Patent dated 13 July 1660. Died 7 Oct. 1667. Buried in Thame Church. Monumental memorial on the floor of the chancel. = Philadelphia, born circa 1626; eldest daughter and coheiress of Sir Edward Carr of Hillingdon, Co. Middlesex, Knt., by his wife Jane, daughter of Sir Edward Onslow of Knoll Co. Surrey, Knt. She died 9 Aug. 1698. Buried at Thame. M.I. in chancel. ARMS OF CARR.—*Gules, on a chevron or three estoiles sable, a dexter canton argent with five ermine spots sable.*

William Clerke, 2nd son.

Edward Clerke, 3rd son. Died without issue A.D. 1649.

John Hook of Bramshott, aforesaid. = Griselda Clerke.

Sir William Clerke, 2nd Bart., of Hitcham, North Weston, and Shabbington, Co. Bucks, son and heir. Born 3 July 1643. Died 6 Sept. 1678. Buried at Shabbington. M.I. in the Church.[2] = Elizabeth, daughter of William Muschamp of Barnes, Co. Surrey, Esq. ARMS OF MUSCHAMP.—*Or, three bars gules.*

John Clerke, 2nd son. Born A.D. 1648. Died at Madrid.

Edward Clerke, 3rd son. Born A.D. 1653. Died 24 April 1677. Buried at Thame. M.I. in chancel.

Francis Clerke of North Weston, 4th son. M.P. for Oxfordshire A.D. 1710-14. Had three wives, but died without issue at Hillingdon 2 May 1715. Buried 7 May at Thame.

Richard Clerke, 5th son. Died 3, buried 5 Feb. 1658 at Thame. M.I. in chancel.

Sir William Clerke, 3rd Baronet, of Shabbington, son and heir. Will dated 14 July, proved 1 Dec. 1699. Buried at North Weston. = Katherine, 2nd daughter of Sir Arthur Onslow of West Clandon, Co. Surrey, Baronet, and sister of Richard, 1st Lord Onslow (so created 25 June 1716). Her marriage settlement dated 11 July 1683. Died 14 March 1741. Buried at Hanwell, Co. Middlesex. ARMS OF ONSLOW.—*Argent, a fesse gules between six Cornish choughs proper.*

John Clerke, 2nd son. Died A.D. 1708. Buried at North Weston. = Katherine, daughter of Henry Jennings, Gent.

John Walker, Gent. One of the Clerks of the House of Lords. = Elizabeth Clerke.

Sir James Chamberlain, 4th Bart., of Wickham, Co. Oxon. Died 23 Sept. 1776. = Elizabeth Walker.

Sir John Clerke, 4th Baronet, son and heir, of Shabbington aforesaid. Died without issue 20 Feb. 1726. Buried at Hanwell.

Sir William Clerke, 5th Baronet, heir to his brother. Joined with his mother, "Dame Katherine, widow," in alienating the Manor of Shabbington. Died abroad, without issue. = A daughter of Mr. Bunstow of Fetter Lane, London.

1. Katherine,
2. Elizabeth,
3. Mary,

Each living unmarried in 1731.

4. Philadelphia. Died A.D. 1684.

Sir Francis Clerke, 6th Baronet, heir of his cousin, Sir William. Born 12 July 1682. Died unmarried 12 Feb. 1769. Buried in South Audley Chapel, London.

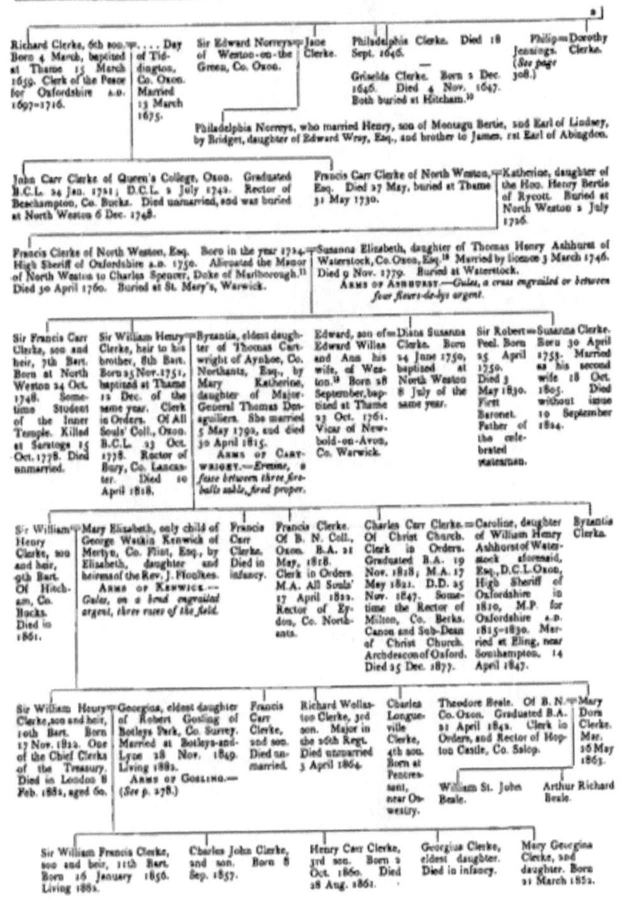

a

Richard Clerke, 6th son. Born 4 March, baptized at Thame 15 March 1659. Clerk of the Peace for Oxfordshire A.D. 1697–1716. = ... Day of Tiddington, Co. Oxon. Married 13 March 1675.

Sir Edward Norreys of Weston-on-the Green, Co. Oxon. = Jane Clerke.

Philadelphia Clerke. Died 18 Sept. 1646.

Griselda Clerke. Born 2 Dec. 1646. Died 4 Nov. 1647. Both buried at Hitcham.[10]

Philip Jennings. (*See page* 308.) = Dorothy Clerke.

Philadelphia Norreys, who married Henry, son of Montagu Bertie, 2nd Earl of Lindsey, by Bridget, daughter of Edward Wray, Esq., and brother to James, 1st Earl of Abingdon.

John Carr Clerke of Queen's College, Oxon. Graduated B.C.L. 24 Jan. 1721; D.C.L. 2 July 1742. Rector of Beachampton, Co. Bucks. Died unmarried, and was buried at North Weston 6 Dec. 1748.

Francis Carr Clerke of North Weston, Esq. Died 27 May, buried at Thame 31 May 1730. = Katherine, daughter of the Hon. Henry Bertie of Rycott. Buried at North Weston 2 July 1726.

Francis Clerke of North Weston, Esq. Born in the year 1724. High Sheriff of Oxfordshire A.D. 1750. Alienated the Manor of North Weston to Charles Spencer, Duke of Marlborough.[11] Died 30 April 1760. Buried at St. Mary's, Warwick. = Susanna Elizabeth, daughter of Thomas Henry Ashhurst of Waterstock, Co. Oxon, Esq.[12] Married by licence 3 March 1746. Died 9 Nov. 1779. Buried at Waterstock.
Arms of Ashhurst.—*Gules, a cross engrailed or between four fleurs-de-lys argent.*

Sir Francis Carr Clerke, son and heir, 7th Bart. Born at North Weston 24 Oct. 1748. Sometime Student of the Inner Temple. Killed at Saratoga 15 Oct. 1778. Died unmarried.

Sir William Henry Clerke, heir to his brother, 8th Bart. Born 25 Nov. 1751, baptized at Thame 12 Dec. of the same year. Clerk in Orders. Of All Souls' Coll., Oxon. B.C.L. 23 Oct. 1778. Rector of Bury, Co. Lancaster. Died 10 April 1818. = Byzantia, eldest daughter of Thomas Cartwright of Aynhoe, Co. Northants, Esq., by Mary Katherine, daughter of Major-General Thomas Desaguiliers. She married 5 May 1792, and died 30 April 1815.
Arms of Cartwright.—*Ermine, a fesse between three fire-balls sable, fired proper.*

Edward, son of Edward Willes and Ann his wife, of Weston.[13] Born 28 September, baptized at Thame 23 Oct. 1761. Vicar of Newbold-on-Avon, Co. Warwick. = Diana Susanna Clerke. Born 24 June 1750, baptized at North Weston 8 July of the same year.

Sir Robert Peel. Born 25 April 1750. Died 3 May 1830. First Baronet. Father of the celebrated statesman. = Susanna Clerke. Born 30 April 1755. Married as his second wife 18 Oct. 1805. Died without issue 10 September 1824.

Sir William Henry Clerke, son and heir, 9th Bart. Of Hitcham, Co. Bucks. Died in 1861. = Mary Elizabeth, only child of George Watkin Kenwick of Mertyn, Co. Flint, Esq., by Elizabeth, daughter and heiress of the Rev. J. Ffoulkes.
Arms of Kenwick.—*Gules, on a bend engrailed argent, three roses of the field.*

Francis Carr Clerke. Died in infancy.

Francis Clerke. Of B. N. Coll., Oxon. B.A. 21 May, 1818. Clerk in Orders. M.A. All Souls' 17 April 1822. Rector of Ecton, Co. Northants.

Charles Carr Clerke. Of Christ Church. Clerk in Orders. Graduated B.A. 19 Nov. 1818; M.A. 17 May 1821. D.D. 25 Nov. 1847. Sometime the Rector of Milton, Co. Berks. Canon and Sub-Dean of Christ Church. Archdeacon of Oxford. Died 25 Dec. 1877. = Caroline, daughter of William Henry Ashhurst of Waterstock aforesaid, Esq., D.C.L. Oxon, High Sheriff of Oxfordshire in 1810, M.P. for Oxfordshire A.D. 1815–1830. Married at Eling, near Southampton, 14 April 1847.

Byzantia Clerke.

Sir William Henry Clerke, son and heir, 10th Bart. Born 17 Nov. 1822. One of the Chief Clerks of the Treasury. Died in London 8 Feb. 1882, aged 60. = Georgina, eldest daughter of Robert Gosling of Botleys Park, Co. Surrey. Married at Botleys-and-Lyne 28 Nov. 1849. Living 1882.
Arms of Gosling.—(*See p.* 278.)

Francis Carr Clerke, 2nd son. Died unmarried.

Richard Wollaston Clerke, 3rd son. Major in the 26th Regt. Died unmarried 3 April 1864.

Charles Longueville Clerke, 4th son. Born at Pentrepant, near Oswestry.

Theodore Beale. Of B. N. Co. Oxon. Graduated B.A. 21 April 1842. Clerk in Orders, and Rector of Hopton Castle, Co. Salop. = Mary Dora Clerke. Mar. 16 May 1863.

William St. John Beale.

Arthur Richard Beale.

Sir William Francis Clerke, son and heir, 11th Bart. Born 16 January 1856. Living 1882.

Charles John Clerke, 2nd son. Born 8 Sep. 1857.

Henry Carr Clerke, 3rd son. Born 2 Oct. 1860. Died 28 Aug. 1861.

Georgina Clerke, eldest daughter. Died in infancy.

Mary Georgina Clerke, 2nd daughter. Born 21 March 1852.

♣♣♣♣♣♣♣♣♣♣♣

Pedigree of Clerke of Willoughby, Co. Warwick.

No. II.

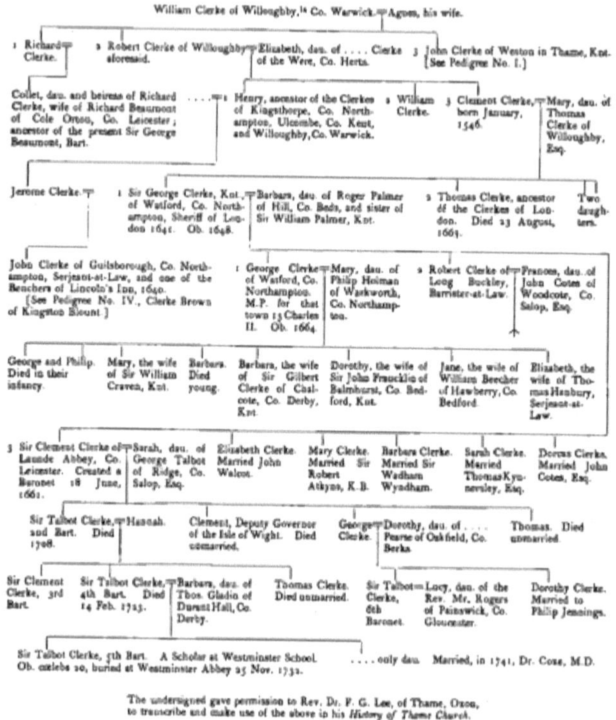

The undersigned gave permission to Rev. Dr. F. G. Lee, of Thame, Oxon, to transcribe and make use of the above in his *History of Thame Church*.

W. H. Clerke.

All the above was copied this 18th day of October, from a MS. Volume belonging to Sir William Henry Clerke, Bart. So I testify.

London, 18 Oct. 1875. Frederick George Lee.

♣♣♣♣♣♣♣♣♣♣♣

Pedigree of Clerke of Oxfordshire and Warwickshire.

No. III.

(From William Camden's Visitation of Warwickshire, A.D. 1619, Harl. MSS. No. 1167.)

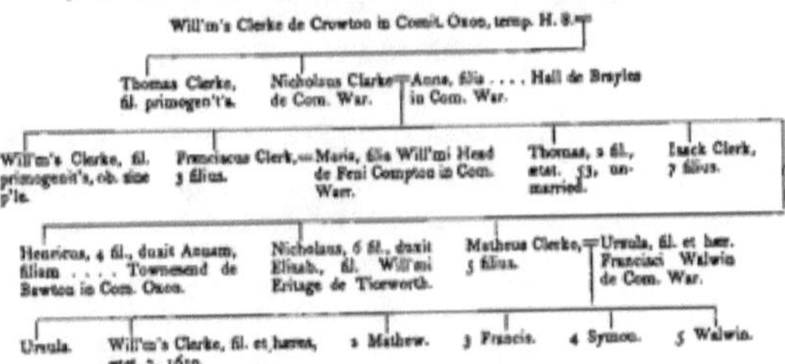

♣♣♣♣♣♣♣♣♣♣♣

Pedigree of Clerke of Aston, Co. Oxon, and of Clerke Brown of Kingston Blount in the same county.

No. IV.

Arms of Clerke Brown: Brown.—*Quarterly: 1st and 4th, gules, a chevron between three fleurs-de-lis or; 2nd and 3rd, sable, three lions passant in bend between two double cotises argent.*
Clerke.—*Argent, on a bend gules, between three pellets, as many swans of the field.*

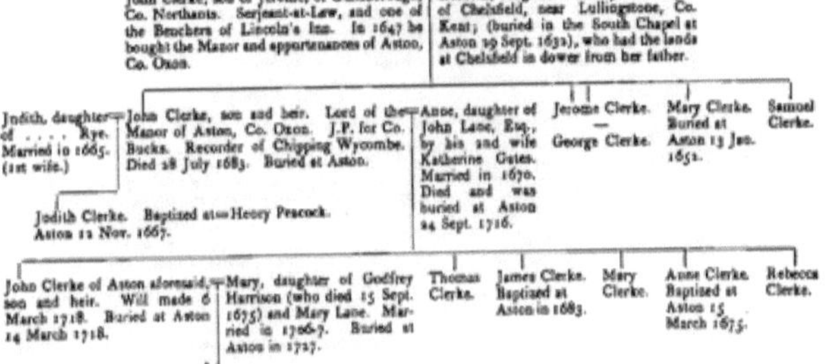

a

Mary, eldest daughter of John Harrison, by Elizabeth Glover his wife. Died and buried at Aston 1 March 1757. (1st wife.) = John Clerke of Henley, Co. Oxon, son and heir. Baptized at Aston 3 June 1709. By his Will, dated 6 Feb. 1764, he gave all his real property and the residue of his personal estate to his nephew John, eldest son of his brother Edward. Buried at Aston 11 Dec. 1771. = Ann, daughter of . . . . Died 8 Jan. 1775. (2nd wife.)

Jane, daughter of John and Elizabeth Harrison of Peryvale, Co. Middlesex. Bapt. at Peryvale 11 Oct. 1716. Married by Licence 31 May 1737. Died and buried at Aston 12 Sept. 1740. (1st wife.) = Edward Clerke, second son. Baptized at Aston 1 June 1714. Of New Inn, Co. Middlesex. Buried 24 Sept. 1780. = Sarah, daughter of John and Elizabeth Harrison. Baptized at Peryvale aforesaid 10 Jan. 1721. Proved her husband's Will 23 Oct. 1780. Buried there 11 Feb. 1792. (2nd wife.)

Mary Clerke. Died unmarried. Buried at Aston 10 March 1727.

John Clerke, son and heir, of Hayes, Co. Middlesex. On 29 May 1787, in default of issue, he settled his estates at Stokenchurch, Co. Oxon, upon Richard Clerke in fee simple. And by his Will, made 24 Nov. 1788, and proved March 1792, confirmed the said settlement in consideration of the marriage of the said Richard Clerke with Mary Foley. Died without issue. Buried at Peryvale 1 March 1792. = Damaris, daughter of . . . . Ford of . . . . . Married 1783. Proved her husband's Will 15 March 1792. Married afterwards Mr. Malpas. Died 20 Aug. 1798.

Lane Clerke. Baptized at Peryvale 27 Aug. 1746. Buried there 13 Sept. of the same year.

Edward Clerke. Baptized at Peryvale 22 Aug. 1747. Buried there 6 Sept. of the same year.

Edward Clerke. Baptized at Peryvale 26 March 1748. Buried there 30 Aug. 1749.

Lane Clerke. Baptized at Peryvale 10 Aug. 1750. Buried there 29 Aug. of the same year.

Richard Clerke. Baptized at Peryvale 2 May 1752. Educated at B.N.C., Oxon. Graduated B.A. 1 July 1773; M.A. 5 July 1776. Barrister-at-Law. Will made 7 Dec. 1804, and proved 1 July 1820. Buried at Aston 27 Jan. 1820. = Mary, second daughter of Thomas, 1st Baron Foley, by Grace Granville, 3rd daughter and coheiress of George, 1st Baron Lansdowne, of Bideford, Co. Devon. Married at St. Marylebone, London, 26 July 1787. She died 8 Dec. 1844. Buried at Aston.

Arms of Foley.—*Argent, a fesse engrailed between three cinquefoils sable, all within a bordure of the last.*

Cranley Lancelot, born *circa* 1765. Son of Lancelot Kerby, Clerk in Orders, of the City of Winchester. Matriculated from New College, Oxon, 2 March 1784. Graduated B.C.L. 10 Oct. 1791. Clerk in Orders. Fellow of New College 1 March 1786, which he resigned in 1793. Rector of Whaddon, Co. Bucks, 1793; of Stoke-Talmache, Co. Oxon, in 1820, and of Bampton in the same County in 1824. Died 19 Sept. 1857. = Mary Clerke. Born 21 April, baptized 11 May 1755. Died 2 March 1832. Buried at Aston.

John, eldest son of Thomas Brown of Grosvenor Street, St. George's, Hanover Square, by Rhoda Browne, of the family of the Marquis of Sligo. Born at Calcutta. Educated at Eton and Christ Church, Oxon. Graduated B.C.L. 21 April 1819. Member of the Supreme Council in India. J.P. and D.L. for Oxon. High Sheriff in 1851. Will made 24 Feb. 1848; proved in 1870. Died 20 March 1870. Buried at Aston. = Mary Elizabeth Clerke. Born 7 Nov., baptized at the Church of St. Marylebone 5 Dec. 1791. Married at Aston 22 May 1821. Buried at Aston 16 Dec. 1844.

John Clerke Brown, eldest son. Born at Kingston Blount, and baptized at Aston 7 May 1825. Died 13, buried there 18 Dec. 1833.

Arthur Henry Clerke Brown, second son, and eventually heir of Kingston Blount, Co. Oxon. Born at Kingston. Baptized at Aston 9 May 1826. Educated at Eton and Christ Church, Oxon. J.P. and D.L. for Oxon. High Sheriff of Oxfordshire in 1878. Living 1882. = Sophia, eldest daughter of John William Fane of Wormsley, Co. Oxon, J.P. and D.L., Colonel in the Oxfordshire Militia, by Catherine, 7th daughter of the late Sir Benjamin Hobhouse, Bart. Married at St. George's, Hanover Square, 29 July 1851.

Arms of Fane.—*Azure, three dexter gauntlets, backs affrontée, or.*

Henry Clerke Brown, eldest son and heir. Born in London 8 May 1852. Educated at Eton and Christ Church. Barrister-at-Law of Lincoln's Inn. Living 1882.

George Clerke Brown, 2nd son. Born at Kingston Grove 1 May 1855. Educated at Christ Church. Living 1882.

John Fane Ballard, Major in the 32nd Foot, only child of the Rev. John Ballard of Rock in Washington, Co. Sussex, by Elizabeth, eldest daughter of John Fane of Wormsley, Co. Oxon, Esq. = Mary Brown, eldest daughter. Born at Kingston Grove 11 Aug. 1853. Married at Aston Rowant 9 May 1877.

William Henry, eldest son of John Henry Ashhurst of Waterstock House, Esq. = Catherine Sophia Brown, 2nd daughter. Born at Kingston Blount 2 March 1857. Married at Aston Rowant 8 July 1882.

Arms of Ashhurst.—*Gules, a cross engrailed or between four fleurs-de-lys argent.*

The above Pedigree, as exemplified by Rev. Dr. F. G. Lee, is true and accurate according to my knowledge and belief. So I testify.

Arthur Henry Clerke Brown.

Kingston Blount, near Aston Rowant.
1 September 1882.

To face pp 319-320.

Various Heraldic Book-plates. No. I.

Lupton. Clerke. Lee. Rose. Wakeman. Staveley

SOME EXPLANATORY NOTES OF THE FOREGOING PEDIGREES.

[1] PEDIGREE OF EMPSON, PYNCHEON, CLERKE, AND OTHERS.

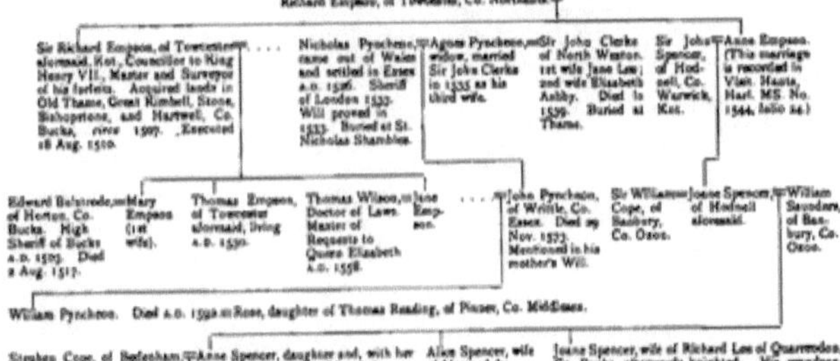

Stephen Cope, of Bedenham, Co. Southampton. = Anne Spencer, daughter and, with her two sisters, coheiress of her father.

Thomas Cope. Other issue.

Alice Spencer, wife of Marmaduke Cooke.

Joane Spencer, wife of Richard Lee of Quarrendon, Co. Bucks, afterwards knighted. His grandson, Sir Anthony Lee, in 1545, and in conjunction with John Croke of Chilton, obtained the grant of the Manor of Saintclere, in Stone, which had belonged to his great-great-uncle, Sir Richard Empson.

[2] The Will of Sir John Clerke was made 20 January 1538, and proved 19 May 1539. It is most devoutly phrased. In it he expresses a desire to be buried in the Church of Thame, and to have a monument erected to his memory. "I will there be made over there as my body shall lye a tombe under an arch over it, with a scripture of my name upon it, not for the pompe of the Worlde, but the rather thereby to move devout people of their charitie to have me remembered in their prayers." He bequeaths 40s. to the Church of Thame, and 20s. to the Church of Blakesley in Northamptonshire. He mentions Agnes his wife (the widow of Pyncheon), and leaves to her a hundred marks, and other specific legacies, confirming the settlement already made by an "indenture of marriage" on the 15 Nov., 25 Henry VIII., *i.e.* in 1534. He leaves various pieces of silver plate with his arms to his sons; the lease of North Weston to his eldest son Nicholas; lands, house, and cattle at Blakesley to his younger son Ambrose (then under age). He also bequeaths to the latter "a pair of beades of gold," and to Elizabeth Clerke, his daughter-in-law, "a flat crosse with a littel chaine." "To William Clerke five marks and a gelding," and similar legacies to his servants, both personal and agricultural. To Robert Dormer, Knight, and to Christopher Westcott, executors, to each of them he bequeaths £10. "I will that a preest sing for my soule and all Xt's soules by the space of vj yeres, and to have yerely £5 6s. 8d." He orders a stone to be laid over Elizabeth his late wife at Blakesley, and imposes the costs thereof upon his younger son Ambrose. The Will, to which there was added a codicil, was witnessed by William Watts, John Bourne, James Tillesey, William Clerke, and others.

[3] The Vicar of Blakesley, near Towcester, courteously wrote to me thus:—"There is no monument or stone erected to the memory of Lady Clerke in the church or churchyard of Blakesley, or I would be very pleased to send you a copy."

[4] The following remains in the Church of Hitcham, co. Bucks:—

Pray for ye soules of Thomas Ramsey & Margaret his wyf, which Thomas decessid the xxx day of Januare the yere of o'r Lord mdlj., on whose soules Jhu have mercy. Amen.

[5] The following remains on an altar-tomb of Sussex marble, in the chancel of Hitcham Church, on a brass plate:—

"Here lieth Nicolas Clarke Esquyer sonne and heyer to Syr John Clarke of Weston Knight that tooke the Duke of Longeuyle prisoner, who married with Elizabeth Ramsey sole Doughter and heyer unto Thomas Ramsey of Hycham Esquyer, by whom he had iiij children, namely, Jane, William, Dorothye, & Jhon: and Dyed of the Sweet in the moneth of Julye, in the yere of our Lord mdcccccli.

"Here allso lyeth by her Father Ann Clarke one of the seyd iiij Children, who Dyed in her tender yeres before marriage, in April Anno D'ni mdccccclxiij."

On a plate of brass the arms of Clerke appear, impaling quarterly, 1. Argent, a chevron gules between three rams' heads. 2. Vaire. 3. A lion rampant within a bordure. 4. A saltire between four eagles displayed. The tinctures are indistinct.

[6] Also the following:—

"Here lieth buried Roger Alford of London and late of Hitcham, Esquire, who married Elizabeth Clark, Widowe, late wife of Nicholas Clark of Weston, Esquire, and daughter and heir of Thomas Ramsey of Hitcham, Esquire, and after they had lived together about twenty years he died the 16th daye of July A° Dni. 1580, et Reg. Eliz. 22, leaving issue behind hym by her Anne and Edward. The said Anne married sins her father's death Edmund Fettiplace of Chorley, Esq[r] and Edward Alford his Son and Heir, who was at his Father's death of the age of 15 years 2 monethis and odd dayes. The said Elizabeth had issue by Mr. Clark her first Husband, who was son and heir of S[r] John Clark of Weston, Knight, 2 sonnes and 2 daughters; Jane, who died before marriage; William, who married Margaret one of the daughters of S[r] John Borne, Kn[t], and Dorothy, who first was married to Henry Long of Shingay, and after to Charles Morrison of Chashiobery, Esquire, and John, a Student and Master of Arts in Cambridge. This monument Elizabeth Alford made in her widowhed for Mr. Alford and for herself, when God shall appoint the tyme."

On a brass plate in Hitcham Church the following likewise remains:—

AN EPITAPH UPPON JANE CLARK.

Lapt in the moulde wherein the father lyes,
The daughter dead, here resteth in her grave,
Fraught erst with thewes and vertues in such wise
As ever yet such tender yeres could have:
But God, Who knewe her meete for Him alone,
Dyd take her hens and left her frendes to mone.

[7] This likewise is in the chancel of the same Church:—

"Here lies Sir William Clarke, Kn[t], sonne and heire to Nicholas Clarke, of North Weston, Esq., & sonne and heire to Elizabeth Ramsey, of Hitcha'. He died y[e] first of February A° D'ni 1624."

[8] The following remains upon a large plate of brass, affixed to a slab in the pavement, within the sanctuary of Hitcham Church :—

"Here lyeth buried Sir Francis Clarke Knight, youngest sonne of Sir William Clarke of Hitcham Knight. Hee married Grisell Daughter of Sr David Woodroofe of Poyle in Surrey Knight by whome he had leave three Sonnes viz. John, William and Edmond; and five Daughters Grisell, Dorothy, Frances, Mary and Elizabeth. He departed this Life the eighteenth of March Anno Domini 1631."

[9] The following remains in the Church of Shabbington, Co. Bucks :—

H. S. E.
GULIELMUS CLERK, BARONETTUS.

JOH'IS CLERK, DE NORTH WESTON IN COM' OXON. BAR. (EX CONJUGE PHILADELPHIA) FILIUS NATU MAX. QUI 6 SEPT. Aº D'NI 1678, ÆTAT' SUAE 35 OBIIT IN AGRO SURRIENSI, UNDE DUXERAT UXOREM ELIZABETHAM GULIELMI MUSCHAMP DE P'ROC' BARNES Arᵍ FILIAM, CUI TRES RELIQUIT LIBEROS, GULIELMUM (PATERNI TITULI HÆR'DEM) JOH'EM & ELIZABETHAM MŒSTAE MATRIS SOLATIO OMNIUM SPEI ET DELITIAS.

[10] And the following upon slabs, in the floor of the same chancel,—

"Here lieth buried yᵉ Body of Gresselda Clarke, Daughter of John Clarke, Esq. & Philadelphia his Wife, who was born the 1ˢᵗ of Dec. 1646, and died yᵉ 4 Nov. 1647.

"Here lieth the body of Philadelphia Clarke, daughter of John Clarke, Esq. and Philadelphia his wife, who departed this life yᵉ 18ᵗʰ of September 1646, aged 9 months od dayes."

[11] The following Abstracts of Deeds relate to a valuable farm at North Weston, which, subsequently to the date of the last of these Deeds, was sold to Messrs. Thomas and William Hedges of an old family of yeomen long resident in that hamlet. On the death of the latter, a moiety of it passed to Mr. Edward Parsons, his nephew, and the other to Mr. Thomas Parsons, sometime of Waterstock, descendants of the Parsons family of Great Milton (see pp. 231, 236), one of whom, Mr. Benjamin Parsons, occupied it for some years. The daughters and coheiresses of Mr. Edward Parsons obtained one portion, while the other was carried by the marriage of Mr. Thomas Parsons' only daughter to the late Mr. Alfred Robert Howland of Thame.

A.D. 1722, 31st May.—Indenture of release made between the Honᵇˡᵉ Jaˢ Bertie the Elder Esqʳ & Thoˢ Rowney Esq. of the first part, Francis Carr Clarke Esqʳ of the second part, Katherine Bertie Spinster of the third part, the Rev. Charles Bertie, Clerk, & Henry Harris Esqʳ of the fourth part, & James Bertie the younger Esqʳ & the Revᵈ Robᵗ Lydall Clerk of the fifth part.

1747, 27th May.—Office Copy of Report of Master Holford in the Cause of Clarke v. Clarke.

1747, 8th & 9th July.—Indentures of Lease and Release, the latter between Francis Clerke Esq. of the one part, and Joseph Cranmer Esqʳᵉ & Jaˢ Cranmer the younger, Gentleman, of the other part.

1747, Nov. 25th & 26th.—Indentures of Lease & Release, the latter made between Francis Clerke Esq. of the first part, John Cranmer, Gentleman, of the second part, & Jaˢ Cranmer the younger of the third part.

Mich' Term, 21st George II.—Exemplification of a Common recovery wherein John Cranmer was Demand'. Jaˢ Cranmer Tenant & Francis Clerke vouchee (Oxfordshire).

1747, 2nd March.—Indenture between Francis Clerke of the one part & Josᵉ Cranmer of the other part.

1748, 26th May.—Indenture between Josʰ Cranmer of the first part, Francis Clerke of the second part, & Cæcilia Scott Spinster of the third part.

1748, 8th August.—Deed Poll under the hand and seal of Francis Clerke Esqʳᵉ.

1749, 10th June.—Indenture between Francis Clerke of the first part, Cæcilia Scott of the second part, and John Scrope Esqʳᵉ of the third part.

Same date.—Deed Poll (indorsed on the Indenture of 26th May, 1748) under the hands and seals of Cæcilia Scott, Francis Clerke, & John Scrope.

1754, 22nd Nov.—Indenture between Francis Clerke of the one part, and Ann Jackson Widow of the other part.

1755, 20th June.—Deed Poll (indorsed on the Indenture of 26th May 1748) under the hands and seals of Joseph Banks, Francis Fane, & Francis Clerke.

1769, 18th May.—Indenture between the Right Honᵇˡᵉ Charles Spencer, commonly called Lord Charles Spencer, and John Spencer his eldest son of the first part, The Right Honbˡᵉ John Lord Viscount Bateman of the second part, The Right Honᵇˡᵉ Sir John Skynner Knt. of the third part, and John Cailland Esqʳᵉ of the fourth part.

[12] WATERSTOCK, CO. OXON. Register No. II., p. 6 :—

"Francis Clerke Esq. of Weston in the Parish of Thame, and Susanna Elizabeth Ashhurst, daughter of the late Thomas Henry Ashhurst Esq. and his wife Diana, were married March the third 1746 per Licence.

"E. LEWIS, Rector."

Note by Rev. J. H. Canon Ashhurst, 31st August, 1882 :—

"There is no entry of the Burial of a Clerke in the Waterstock Register between the years 1770 and 1780; but at the bottom of Page 19 in the Register No. II. there is this entry :—

"Memorandum—Susannah Elizabeth Clerke, widow of Francis Clerke Esq. of Weston in the Parish of Thame, died November 9 1779.

"R. ROBINSON, Rector."

[13] FAMILY OF WILLES.—Some members of this family were tenants of Weston House in the eighteenth century; about the year 1735. Of these were Sir John Willes and Mr. Justice Willes, his second son. Others resided at Thame.

PEDIGREE OF WILLES OF NORTH WESTON AND THAME.

The following Pedigree contains two descents :—

John Willes, educated at Trinity College, Oxon, Rector of Bishop's Itchington, Co. Warwick, and Canon of Lichfield, D.D. 23 Feb. 1684. Died 1700. = Mary, daughter of Sir William Walker, Mayor of Oxford.

John Willes, son and heir, born 29 Nov. 1685. Admitted to Trinity Coll., Oxon, B.A. 23 June 1704; M.A. 9 Dec. 1707; called to the bar 1713; D.C.L. 29 Oct. 1715; K.C. in 1719; M.P. for Launceston in 1722; Lord Chief Justice of the Court of Common Pleas in Jan. 1737. Died, aged 76, on 15 Dec. 1761. Buried at Bishop's Itchington.

He was a person of learning and ability, but intriguing, ambitious, and immoral. In Walpole's *Memoirs*, vol. i., p. 77, a story is told to this effect :—"A grave person," reported to have been Mr. Thornbury, Vicar of Thame, "came to reprove the scandal he gave, and to tell him that the World talked of one of his maid-servants being with child. Willes said, 'What is that to me?' The Monitor answered, 'Oh, but they say it is by your lordship.' 'And what is that to you?' was the reply." = Margaret, daughter and coheiress of Mr. Brewster of the City of Worcester.

Edward Willes, educated at Oriel Coll., Oxon. B.A. 30 Oct. 1712; M.A. 6 July 1715; D.D. 8 July 1726; Bishop of St. David's, 2 Jan. 1743; of Bath 1743. Died 24 Nov. 1773.

John Willes, eldest son, of Thame, and subsequently of Asthropp, Co. Oxon. Hon. D.C.L. Oxon 12 April, 1749.

Edward Willes, second son, of Thame. Entered at Lincoln's Inn in 1740, was called to the bar in 1746, made one of King's Counsel in 1756, and Solicitor-General in 1766; became a Justice of the King's Bench 27 Jan. 1768. He married Anne, daughter of the Rev. Edward Taylor of Sutton, Co. Wilts, and left three sons. His second son, Edward, who was baptized at Thame 23 Oct. 1761, married Diana Susanna, daughter of Mr. Francis Clerke of North Weston. He himself died 14 Jan. 1787, and was buried at Burnham, Co. Bucks.

[14] CLERKS OF WILLOUGHBY.—The following exists in the Register Book of this Parish.

"Whereas the Ancient Registers of Willoughby having miscarried, other true copy cannot be had, that it may give satisfaction to Posterity. These are to certify that Clement Clerke of Willoughby had three sons: Thomas Clerke his eldest, who died at Willoughby; George, his second son, who inherited sometime at Watford, Northamptonshire, Knight and Alderman of London; W. Clerke, his third son, who lived at Honingslaw in Staffordshire. Thomas Clerke, eldest son of Clement Clerke, had four sons: John Clerke, the eldest, merchant of London; George Clerke, merchant of London; Christ. Clerke, merchant of London; and Henry Clerke, fourth son, Doctor of Physic and now President of Magdalene College, Oxford. John, eldest son of Thomas Clerke, had three sons: Thomas, the eldest, now of Willoughby; George the second, Aybury the third, both of them dying young. John Clerke had also two daughters: Anne, his eldest, died young; Eliz^th, the second, married Richard Cayle, Councillor-at-law of Glo'ster. We whose names are subscribed do attest all this to be true.

"THOMAS CLERKE.
"DR. WARD."

"EXTRACTS FROM THE REGISTER OF ASTON, CO. OXON.

1652. Henricus Lee, armiger et dux, sepultus erat vicesimo nono die Septembris.

1652, 13 Jan. Mary Clerke, the daughter of Serjeant Clerke, was buried the thirteenth day of January Anno Dom' 1652.

1658. George, son of John Clerke & Judith his wife.

1663. Thomas, filius Johannes Clerke, arm., sepultus.

1665. Elizabetha, filia Johannis Clerke, armig'. et Judithæ uxoris, baptizata est decimo quinto die Februarii. Compat' Isham, et Comat' Eliz. Tipping et Eliz. Price.

1666. Elizabetha, sepulta est.

1667. Juditha, filia Johannis Clerke, armig'. et Juditha uxoris ejus baptizata est undecimo die Novembris, Comat' Domina Abigaila Busbby et Dom' Eliz. Price, Compatre D'no Henrico Isham.

1667. Maria, filia Johannis Clerke, Armig'. decimo Septimo die Decembris, sepulta est.

1667. Johannis, filius Johannis Clerke, armigeri, et Annæ uxoris, baptizatus decimo tertio die Decembris, Compatribus Do'o Rogero Price, Do'o Johannis Lane, procuri Edmundo Whitwell, Commatre autem D'na Elizabetha Tipping.

1671. Georgius Clerke (Northantoniensis), sepultus est tricesimo die Decembris.

1675. Anna, filia Johannis Clerke, armigeri, et Annæ uxoris ejus, baptizata decimo quinto die Martii, Comat. Jana Eyre vice Georgii Tipping, Johannis Clerke, Oxon.

1675. Gertruda, filia Edwardi Clerke de St. Martin's le Grand, sepulta.

1676. Johannes Clerke, Cantii comitatu natus et beatæ Mariæ Magdalenæ apud Oxonienses artium baccalaureus e variolis laborans hic obiit et sepultus est vicesimo quinto die Maii.

1681. Henricus, filius Johannis Clerke, armigeri, sepultus decimo quinto die Februarii.

1683. Jacobus, filius posthumus Dominæ Annæ Clarke viduæ (relictæ Johannis Clerke, armigeri defuncti) baptizatus est.

♣♣♣♣♣♣♣♣♣♣♣

Chapel of St. Michael and All Angels, Rycott.
(From a Sketch by Mr. P. H. Delamotte.)

Rycott Chapel.

THIS Chapel—dedicated in honour of St. Michael and All Angels—stands to the south-west of what remains of the old Mansion. Though Rycott is in the Parish of Great Haseley, yet the connection of the various families who have lived there with the Church and Town of Thame makes it desirable that some account of the Chapel and Manor should be given here. As far as regards the external appearance of this Chapel, it is little altered since it was restored, or perhaps rebuilt, by Richard and Sibilla Quartermain, and completed at a later period under the supervision of Adrian de Bardis, Prebendary of Thame. Anciently a small square castellated building, containing rooms for two Chaplains or Chantry-priests, stood to the immediate north of its westernmost portion: between the Chapel and the House. The Chapel is more than an average specimen of early third-pointed architecture, both as regards its general plan and details. It consists of a nave and chancel under one roof, with a tower rather less in width than the nave at the west end. The nave measured from within is fifty feet long from the east of the tower to the lower step of the sanctuary; and the sanctuary, raised on two steps, is exactly ten feet deep by nineteen feet in width. Measured externally, and including the buttresses, the Chapel is exactly eighty-five feet long and twenty-eight feet wide.

The Tower, of three stages or stories, is exceedingly well proportioned. The chief entrance, *i.e.* the western doorway, is of good design—an arch, with deep and bold hollow mouldings, and a dripstone above. Immediately over it is a window of three plain lights with cusped heads under an angular arch, also with a dripstone or hood-mould ending in carved shields with the arms of Quartermain and Hester of Thame. In the second stage, immediately over the window just described, is a very picturesque niche or tabernacle over a pedestal, with an effective and foreign-looking pyramidal cap above, evidently intended for an image of St. Michael, but there are no traces of the latter. Above this again, in the third stage, is a window of two lights, corresponding to that below. The buttresses of the tower, of quite a severe type, are set on at the western angles in a diagonal position, and run up almost to the base and string-course of the third stage. There is a small staircase turret, as at Thame and Crendon, at the south-eastern angle, carried up to the top of the castellated battlement which crowns the tower itself. String-courses divide each stage, and there are bold projecting gurgoyles to carry off the water from the roof.

The four buttresses on either side of the Nave are exceedingly solid, with substantial pinnacles crocketted above. The easternmost buttresses, like those at the west end, are placed diagonally, and finished with figures of greyhounds or talbots—probably in reference to the heraldic bearings of the Bretton family, which the Quartermain family represented; or it may be that these figures were added by Sir John Williams when he became possessed of the Mansion and Manor of Rycott.

The doorway, now blocked up, on the western end of the Chapel's north side—that anciently used by the family of the House,—is somewhat curiously constructed with a four-centred arch, having a square label over it, terminating in carved heads and decorated with three plain shields. In the spandrils are effective quatrefoils with an archaic rose carved in the centre of both. The oaken door, with some bold ironwork, still remains. A similar door towards the eastern part of the north side, evidently intended for the chaplain or parson, remains; as also another of the same type in the southern side. The side windows, like those in the tower, have angular arches. They are of two lights,

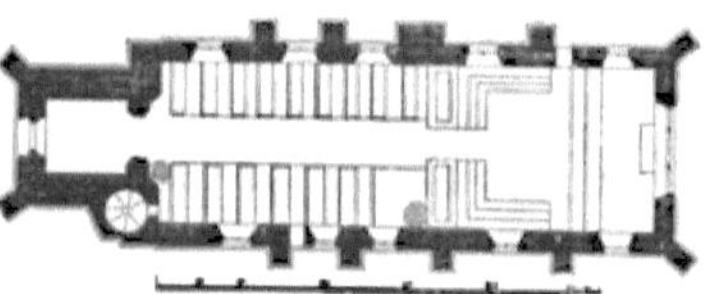

Ground Plan of Chapel of St. Michael and All Angels, Rycott.

with cinquefoils in their heads, and well-designed labels above terminating in plain shields.

The east window of five lights is an admirable specimen of early third-pointed work, owning certain remarkable features; possibly of an earlier date than the Chapel in general. It is cinquefoiled in its head; while each of the five divisions is again sub-divided into two subordinate lights, all of which are trefoiled both above and below. Over the window there is a triangular opening evidently for ventilation, while above is a bold and effective cross flory in stone.

And now to pass into the interior. The roof, which is evidently original, and of the middle or perhaps latter part of the fifteenth century, is vaulted and lined with boards placed concavely. The principal beams, which are bold and well moulded, project as ribs, the portions between them being painted blue with stars in gold. The open seats are simple and convenient—almost exactly like those in the mother church of Great Haseley. At the easternmost part of the nave are two large enclosed pues, one on either side of the entrance into the chancel, erected no doubt during Queen Elizabeth's reign. That on the north side has an almost unique upper story; and is an elaborate specimen of Renaissance wood-work, consisting of arabesque carvings, open trellis work, with here and there elaborate paintings in medallion. That on the south side, though less elaborate, is of the same style, but with a few Gothic features, and no doubt of the same date—possibly a little earlier. Instead of an upper story, however, it is covered with a cumbersome crocketted *cupola*, which rises from its four corners and is surmounted by figures of Our Blessed Lady and Her Divine Child. Tradition asserts that this pue was erected for the use of the Lady Elizabeth when she was a sojourner under Lord Williams' custody and care at Rycott.

The oaken Communion Table is of the same character as the northern pue: the piscina to the north being square-headed with a trefoiled arch beneath. It is said that a portrait of Queen Elizabeth was once placed over the Communion Table, but was subsequently removed to Wytham House. The pulpit, on the south side of the nave at its east end, has a large and dignified canopy or *baldachino* of good proportions.

The font, of third-pointed work, is at the west end, and there was formerly an old sixteenth-century organ much dilapidated. The remains of several tattered banners were to be seen on the walls half a century ago; but these have been lost.* Lord Williams' first wife was buried here; and it was sometime one of the burying-places of the families of Norreys and Bertie.

The following inscription is on a handsome white marble monument on the south wall of the chancel:—

The Rt. Honble James Bertie, Earl of Abingdon, and
Ld Norreys of *Rycot*,
Son of *Mountague* Earl of *Lindsey* (Ld Great Chamberlain of
England), by *Bridget* his
Wife, Baroness *Norreys*, sole daughter & Heir to *Edward*
Wray, Esq., & the Lady *Eliz.*
Norreys, sole Daughter and Heir to *Francis* Ld *Norreys*,
Viscount *Thame* and Earl of
Berkshire, from whom the Barony of Norreys descending
to him, He was for his great
loyalty and services to ye Crown created Earl of
Abingdon by K. Ch. 2, A^o^ D. 1682.
He was Ld Lieut. of this County from the year
1674 to the year 1687, and afterwards
Ld Lieut. and Custos Rotulorum from the 1st of
K. W. & *Qu. Ma.* A^o^ D. 1688 till the year 1697.
And was also Chief Justice in *Eyre* of all the King's
Forests etc. South of Trent.
He married to His 1st wife *Eleanora*
Eldest Daught^r^ & at last Sole Heir to Sr *Hen. Lee* of
Ditchley in this County (by *Anne* his wife Daught^r^
of Sr *John Danvers*, & Sister & Coheir
to Henry Danvers, Esq., Nephew & Heir to Hen. Earl
of Danby) She Dyed 31st Maij A^o^ 1691
& left him 6 Sons, *Montagu* (who succeeded him
in his Honours), *James, Henry, Robert, Pere-*
grine & *Charles*, & 3 Daught^rs^ *Bridget, Anne*
& *Mary*, & lyes here Interred with Him.
In the year 1698 He took to his 2nd Wife,
Catherine Eldest Daught^r^ & coheir to Sr Thomas
Chamberlaine Bart. & Widow of *Richd.* Visc^t^ *Wenman*, who
departed this Life at Westm^r^
on Monday 22^d^ Maij A^o^ 1699 in the 46th year of his age and
to the general Lamentation off
his country, of whose Liberty and Religion he was a
constant & zealous Assertor.

The following is the record preserved by Richard Lee, when he visited Rycott, of the armorial bearings then remaining in the windows of the Chapel:—

In Ricote Church.
In a Pane.

Arg., a chevron between three crescents Sa.
Or, a saltire engrailed Sa. between four garbs Gu.

i. Arg., three wolves' heads erased Gu., within a bordure Az. charged with a semée of castles Or.

ii. Gu., a fess Az. between four dexter hands couped at the wrist Or*: impaling, (1) Arg., a chevron between three escallops Sa.; (2) Arg., a bend Sa., within a bordure engrailed Gu. bezantée.

iii. Quatremayne, impaling Erm., on a bend Or, three chevrons Gu.

iv. Arg., a covered cup having a fleur-de-lys issuant Sa. (Said to belong to ye name of Stretley.—*Wood.*)

v. Arg., a chevron between three martlets Sa., impaling Vairée Arg. and Gu.

vi. Vairée Arg. and Gu.

vii. Barry of six Arg. and Az., a bend Gu.: impaling (1) Arg., two hounds passant, palewise Gu.; (2) Quatremayne as before. (The coats 1 and 2 take up the sinister side of the shield, and are divided per pale.)

viii. Grey of Rotherfield, impaling, Arg. a maunche Sa.

ix. Quarterly:—1 and 4 Gu. a fess checky Arg. and Sa. between six cross crosslets fitchée Or; 2 and 3 Gu. two bends Or.

x. (1) Quatremayne.

xi. (2) Quatremayne, impaling, Barry of six Arg. and Gu., a bend Az. on a chief Or, a lion passant guardant of the third.

Over these coats (10 and 11) is written, Richard and Sibill, he kneling in armor, wth this armes (1) on his bake, and his wife wth his and her one; (2) in a robe on hir back.†

xii. Barry nebulée of six Or and Gu.

xiii. Grey of Rotherfield.

xiv. Lovell, impaling Grey of Rotherfield.

xv. Grey of Rotherfield, impaling, quarterly: 1 and 4, Arg., a chief Gu. over all a bend Az.; 2 and 3, Checky, Or and Gu. a chief Erm.

xvi. Grey of Rotherfield, impaling, Gu. a bar. Arg. . . . . (broken).

xvii. Quatremayne, impaling Bretton.

xviii. Quatremayne, impaling, Arg. a bend between three fleur-de-lys Gu.

On the flowre, not to be sene (19-23).

xix. Erm., on a canton Gu. an owl, impaling, quarterly: 1 and 4, Three martlets on a bend; 2 and 3, Erm., on a bend, three chevrons.

xx. Fowler, impaling a saltire Arg. between twelve cross crosslets Or.

xxi. Az., in chief three crowns Or, ... impeling.

xxii. (Field untinctured) . . . . A chevron between three escallops Or, impaling . . . . (worn out).

xxiii. Fowler, with the bordure as 1.

---

* The following remains, on a diamond-shaped marble slab, in the floor of the nave:—"✠ In Memory of Sir John Collins, who died ye 22nd of June, 1763, In the 75th year of His age. Requiescat in pace."

* I am disposed to conclude that the above is a misdescription of the arms of Quartermain.

† On folio 30 of the Harleian MS. No. 245, there is a representation of Richard Quartermain and Sibilla his wife, as they formerly appeared in these windows. He is in armour, but without a helmet, and wearing his tabard with the arms of his house upon it, and collar of SSS's. The lady wears a tall head-dress, and a long robe on which the Quartermain arms are embroidered. Underneath, on her kirtle, the arms of Englefield are represented. They are both kneeling, and hold between them the representation of a church. Above this rude sketch are the words, "*In Capella de Ricott, in com' Oxon*," and below, "*Orate pro animab' Ric'i Quatermayn's Ar' et Sibilla uxor eiũ fundator' istius Capellae.*"

THE descent of the Manors of Great and Little Rycott from the time of the Conqueror can be learned from the following pedigree of the de Magnavilles or de Mandevilles, who were possessed of the same until the early part of the thirteenth century.

Pedigree of the de Mandevilles, Lords of Great and Little Rycott.

Arms.—*Quarterly or and gules.*

[Originally in the windows of Rycott Chapel, and in those of the Rycott Aisle in the Church of Great Haseley.]

Geoffrey de Mandeville, a follower of the Conqueror, received the Lordships of Great and Little Rycott and other manors by special grant from the King. Buried in Westminster Abbey. = Athelarda. Buried in Westminster Abbey.

William de Mandeville, his son and heir, Lord of Rycott. Founded the Monastery of Black Canons at Stoneley in Huntingdonshire. = Margaret, daughter and heiress of Eudo de Rye, Steward, for the King, of Normandy.

. . . . = Geoffrey de Mandeville, son and heir, Lord of Rycott. Made Custodian of the Tower of London by the Empress Maude. Created Earl of Essex by special charter of King Stephen. Founded the Monastery of Little Walden, Co. Essex. Died excommunicate, 14 Sept. 1144. Buried eventually in the Temple Church, London. = Rohesia, daughter of Alberic de Vere, Earl of Oxford, Chief Justice of England. Arms of de Vere.—*Quarterly gules and or, in the first quarter a star of six points of the second.*

Hugh Talbot. (1st husband.) = Beatrix de Mandeville, sister of the Lord of Rycott. = William de Say. (2nd husband.) Arms of De Say.—*Azure, two bars nebulée argent.*

An only daughter, Alice, who married John de Lacy, Constable of the City of Chester.

Ernulph de Mandeville, eldest son. Died without issue.

Geoffrey de Mandeville. Restored by King Henry II. to possession of the lands of his ancestors, and so became Lord of Rycott. Died, without issue, 12 Nov. 1165. = Eustachia.

Avicia, daughter and heiress of William Le Gros, Earl of Albemarle. = William de Mandeville. Succeeded to the Lordship of Rycott as heir of his brother in 1165. Attended King Henry into France. In 1177 he made a pilgrimage to the Holy Land; and died in 1190, when the Earldom expired. Qy.? buried in the Church of Great Haseley, Co. Oxon. = Christian, daughter of Robert, Lord Fitz Walter, of the Clare family, one of the Barons who extorted the Great Charter from King John. Died in 1219. = Raymond de Burgh.

William de Say, eldest son. =

Geoffrey de Say.

Avelina. (2nd wife.) = Geoffrey Fitz Piers or Fitz-Peter, Justice of England. By a new creation made Earl of Essex, 26 June 1199, at the coronation of King John. Lord of Rycott, and Patron of the Monastery of Walden aforesaid. Had a grant of the Castle and Honor of Berkhampstead, Co. Herts. Died 2 Oct. 1213. Arms of Fitz Piers.—*Quarterly or and gules, a bordure vair.* = Beatrix de Say, grand-niece of the first Earl of Essex. (1st wife.)

William de Bowland. = Maude de Say.

John Fitz Piers, Sheriff of Yorkshire in 1234. Died 23 Oct. 1213. = Isabel sister of John Bigod. Arms of Bigod.—*Or, a cross gules.*

Geoffrey Fitz Piers or de Mandeville, eldest son; Earl of Essex. Succeeded his father in 1213, as Lord of Rycott. One of the 25 Lords selected to enforce the Great Charter. Died without issue in 1216. Buried in the Church of the Priory of the Holy Trinity, Aldgate, London. = Isabella, Countess of Gloucester, the divorced wife of King John.

William Fitz Piers or de Mandeville, heir to, and succeeded, his brother Geoffrey. Died 25 Dec. 1227, on which the Earldom of Essex passed to his sister Maude.

Henry Fitz Piers or de Mandeville, priest. Dean of Wolverhampton.

Robert de Bohun, Earl of Hereford, whose son became Earl of Essex, as heir to his mother Maude. = Maude Fitz Piers or de Mandeville, heiress to her brother William.

In the reign of King Henry III. the Manors of Great and Little Rycott were in the possession of a family which most probably took their surname from the place—de Rycott. Whether these obtained the Manors by purchase or grant appears uncertain. Another family, Pypard* by name, with whom the de Rycotts had intermarried, had long flourished at Haseley;—the earliest known presentation to that benefice, in 1223, having been made by one Roger Pyppard.† It is on record that this race became extinct hereabouts in 1482, when the patronage of the Rectory was given to the Dean and Canons of the College of Windsor. One member of the first-named race, Fulco de Rycott, granted a charter relating to lands in Great Haseley as early as the year 1305,—a copy of which is on record in the Ledger Book of the Preceptory of the Knights Templars at Sandford, co. Oxon, preserved in the Bodleian Library. John, the last of the de Rycotts, whose wife was heiress of the renowned family of Gernon of Wiltshire, died leaving Katherine his own heiress; who, as may be gathered from the Quartermain Pedigree, married Nicholas Englefield of Berkshire. The manors then passed, firstly to the Quartermains, and secondly to the Fowlers; and so subsequently by purchase to the Herons, and again in 1539 by purchase‡ to Sir John Williams, Knt.

The family of Heron, sprung from the ancient baronial race of that name of Ford Castle in Northumberland, had for at least two generations owned lands in Lincolnshire.§ In the latter part of the fifteenth century they were of rank and importance, residing at Hackney, co. Middlesex, where they had considerable possessions and influence.‖ They evidently belonged to an old and noble lineage; and, to judge from the character of the Wills of Sir John Heron and his Lady, and their testamentary bequests, were sincerely attached to the ancient faith.

The Herons lived for several generations at Shacklewell House in the parish mentioned; and both it, as well as Rycott Manor, were no doubt for some time the residences of Cecilia, daughter of Sir Thomas More, and wife of Giles Heron, who became involved in the fate of his father-in-law, and was so unjustly and basely attainted of high treason. The only son of Giles Heron, Thomas Heron, who married Cecilia Jekyll, dying without issue, that direct line became extinct. But others of the family were living in the parish in question, during the sixteenth and seventeenth centuries, and were liberal benefactors both to the church and poor of Hackney. The Herons, however, only held Rycott for about the space of twenty years.

* "Robt. de Wichelord, acolitus, ad Eccl' de Haseley ad pres. Rog' Pyppard, facta prius inquisit' per Archid' Oxon."—Register of Hugo Wells or Wills, Bishop of Lincoln, from 20 Dec. 1209 to 7 Feb. 1235.

† Arms of Pypard: Argent, two bars azure, on a canton of the second a star of five points or.

‡ 1539. An Act for the assurance of the Manor of Rycott to Sir John Williams of Thame was passed this year, the 31st of King Henry VIII.

§ "I will that Giles Heron my sonne & heire, when he shall come to th' age of xxj yeres, shall haue my landes in Lincolnshire that I was born unto & that came to me by inheritance, & also the reversion in Lincolnshire that I have purchased after the decease of Margaret my wife."—*Will of Sir John Heron.*

‖ PEDIGREE OF HERON.

(Taken from the Visitation of Middlesex, A.D. 1572, Harl. MSS. No. 1551, folio 64a, with additions from the Wills of Sir John and Lady Heron.)

ARMS OF HERON.—*Sable, a chevron ermine between three herons close argent.*

John Heron, of Chipchase = ...

- William Heron, came from Ford Castle, Co. Northumberland = ...
  - Sir John Heron, Treasurer of the Chamber to King Henry VIII., Lord of Great and Little Rycott, by purchase of the reversion from Sir Richard Fowler, with mansion-houses at Shaklewell in Hackney, at Aldarbroke, London, and Richmond in Surrey. Will made 2 June, 12 of Henry VIII., *i.e.* 1521; proved 19 May 1525. = Margaret . . . . Will made 24 September 1531; proved 23 October 1532.
    - Giles Heron, son and heir, Lord of Great and Little Rycott. Sole executor of his mother's Will. Sold the Manor and lands of Rycott to Sir John Williams, Knt., *circa* 1539. = Cicely, daughter of Sir Thomas More, Lord High Chancellor of England.
      - Thomas Heron, of Shackelwell. Died without issue. = Cicely, daughter of Bartholomew Jekyll.
    - Edmund Heron.
    - Christopher Heron.
    - Henry Heron.
    - John Heron, of the co. of Hartford. =
      - John Heron the younger.
      - Margaret Heron.
    - Jane Heron. = . . . Dysham.
    - Ursula Heron.
    - Joane Heron.
    - Margaret Heron.

(James Prior of Colchester, co. Essex.)

Sir John Heron, one of the followers of the Conqueror, possessed Ford and acquired Chipchase by marriage with the heiress of its Saxon Lord, Sir William Chipchase. William Heron of Chipchase, who obtained licence to crenellate, was summoned to Parliament as a baron by King Richard II., 13 Nov. 1398; and another William Heron had been so summoned by King Edward III., 8 Jan. 1371. Cuthbert Heron of Chipchase Castle was created a Baronet 20 Nov. 1662. It is said by some that this title became extinct on the death of Sir Thomas Heron 27 May 1801, but this seems doubtful.

Sir John's Will was made 12 June 1521, and proved 19 May 1525. In it he devoutly bequeaths his soul to God. "And I will that after my death xx^{s} be offered unto the Sacrament of Hackney for my oblacions omitted"—a phrase which is remarkable. He then proceeds thus:—

"I will that Sir Richard ffowler be paid yerelie c^{li} at Alhalowentyde during thee yeres to come and a hundred m'rcs at halowentyde anno d'ni m^{l} v^{c} xxiij^{o} in full contentacion and payment of a thowsand m'rcs, vpon foure obligacions of the statute of the Staple remaynING with the forsaid Sir Richard ffowler, for the reuersion of the manor of Grete Reycote and litill Reycott in Buk' and Oxon shires, for the payment whereof thre hundred poundes is to be receyved of Richard Botellers landes, that is to say fourty poundes yerely at mighelmasse at Ester and also xxx^{li} of Sr Thomas Dynh'm londes in Devon and Som'shire, that is to say xl^{li} yerely during thee yeres, whereof xx^{li} was dew at Ester last passed and xx^{li} at Mighelmas next comyng and so yerely after during two yeres, wherof Radclyff hath the dede of feoffement myn indentures and auctoritie to receyve the rent thereof . . . . . . Also I will that Giles Heron my Sonne and heire shalhave the Reu'sion of grete Rycot and litill Rycot when he shall come to th'age of xxj^{ti} yeres, immediately after the decease of Sir Richard ffowler and Dame Julian his Wife."

He certainly owned great possessions, much plate and household stuff; but he was evidently in debt; for he goes on to say that "yf there be not redy money for the payment of my debtes that then a certain porcion of my plate be laid to pledge for the contentacion thereof, until they may be pledged owt again of my reuercions, or owt of such landes as heretofor been appointed therfor, and that mine aray be sold also therfor."

He died in the spring of 1525. His wife survived him exactly six years. Her Will was made 24 September 1531, and proved 23 October 1532. It is that of a thoroughly religious and devout woman, as the following extracts will shew:—

"ffirst and principally above all erthly thinges I bequethe and recomend my Soule to Allmighty God the Father of hevyn my Creatour and Maker, Saviour of all the worlde, and to our blissid Ladye Sainte Mary the moost glorious virgin his Mother, and to all the glorious company of hevin, my bodye to be buryed in the parrishe churche of Hackney beforesaid as nere to my said late husband as it convenyently may be. Item I bequethe to the high aulter in the saide parrishe churche of Hakney in recompence and satisfaction of my tithes forgotten or necligently w'holden indischarge of my conscience xx^{s}. It' I will and bequethe to the reparac'ons of the said Churche of Hackney xx^{s}. Item I give and bequeath to the said Church of Hakney my gowne of tawny velvit furrid wth blacke bouge to make a vestment or coope, the making to be at the charge of the Parrishe. It' I give and bequeathe to the Parrishe Churche of Canfeeld in the Countie of Essex one cope to be made of a piece of tawny damask which I bought but late conteyning vj yardes. And I will that the same coope shalbe made wt'orpheries and embroderid at my cost and charge. It' I will to the Parrishe Churche of Gelson in the Countie of Hertf' one vestment of the price of xl^{s}. Item I gyue and bequethe viij^{li} to a Preest for saying masse at suche tymes as he shalbe disposed in the forsaid Parrishe Churche of Hackney by the space of one hole yere next after my decease. And I will the said Preest be chosen and appointed by Sr John Barowe now vicar of the said church of Hackney. . . . . And I gyve and bequeath vnto the ymage of our blissid Ladye of Walsingham a floure of golde sett with three dyamountes a Rubye and iij peerles. It' I bequeath unto Margaret Heron dowghter of my Sonne John Heron at footes Craye a floure of gold sett with ij balisses and ij peerles. And I will that my iiij Sonnes Edmond X'tofer Henry and John the yonger shallhave all my plate to be eqally devided betwene them according to their Fathers Will. Item I bequethe to Margarete Reed my God daughter xx^{s} Sterlinge. Item I bequethe vnto Sir Richard Bucklers bryther the preest vj^{s} viij^{d}. It' to my said Sonne John Heron the yonger my signet w^{t} armes graven therein of goolde. The residewe of all my goodes, my debtes paid my funeralles and obsequies doon, and this my present testament fulfilled, I hooly give and bequethe to Giles Heron my Sonne whome I ordeyne declare and make my soole Executour of this my present testament and last Will, he to dispose for the welthe of my Soule and all xr'tn soules as God shall put in his mynde and as my special trust is that he will."

Some idea of the plan and character of Rycott House, and its appurtenances and grounds, may be gathered from an old print, of which I possess a proof, drawn in a most masterly and effective style by "L. Knyff," and excellently well engraved by "I. Kip." The plate is thirteen inches and three quarters in height and nineteen inches and a quarter in width. At its foot the following inscription stands:—"*Rycott, in the County of Oxford, one of the Seats of the R^{t} Honble Montagu Earle of Abingdon, Baron Norreys of Rycott,*" with the Arms of the House, consisting of six quarterings of which the last is the arms of Lee. The plate comprises a bird's-eye view of the Mansion and Park, with the hills of Crendon and Brill far off in the distance to the left, and the Church and Town of Thame faintly represented to the right.

Judging from this print, the main part of the Mansion,* which faced southwards, consisted of a large quadrangle containing the chief rooms, with four octagonal turrets at the corners divided by string-courses and capped with depressed crowns of lead. The building, of fine proportions and in the third-pointed style, was of two main stories, with gabled roofs, stepped

* The Mansion described in the text above was probably not of an earlier date than the reign of Henry VII. It had no doubt been erected on the site of a much more ancient and possibly a timber mansion, in which previous possessors of the Manor had dwelt. There is no known evidence to shew that any fortified residence had been in existance at Rycott.

gables, and dormer windows up above. The cornices cresting the walls were embattled. The Hall occupying two stories, with lofty windows, ran the whole length of the northern side of the quadrangle; while the soler, parlours, picture-gallery, and library were on the east, facing the gardens, pleasaunce, and terrace. Other important rooms, the music-hall and council chamber, were placed on the southern side with the state bedrooms above. On the north were the servants' offices, compactly arranged, the kitchen, buttery, bakehouse, common hall for tenants, servants' hall, and brewhouse. To the north of this again were the various fishponds, flanked on either side with plantations, at the commencement of a stately avenue which stretched northwards for a considerable distance towards the old road from Thame to Oxford. The stables, carriage-houses, and dog-kennels stood towards the north-west of the Mansion, and to the south lay two extensive orchards and kitchen gardens, while farther to the west were enclosed closes, and a farm-yard, with barns, cattle-sheds, and rickyards. The whole of this part was walled in; while still farther to the west was the "East India Deer Park." To the east of the Mansion were the lawns, gravel-walks, and flower-gardens, with two large ponds; raised terraces with alcoves, adorned with statues, and flanked with formally-arranged plantations, shrubberies, and woods, with another long terrace still farther to the east. To the south-east stood the Chapel—much as it remains now—with the chaplain's rooms and offices, a building of two stories between the house and the Chapel itself, with separate gardens and enclosure.

Up to the chief entrance, in the centre of the south wing, was a broad walk or avenue flanked with trees, and there were stately and stiff plantations on either side. The Park, which was of considerable size, was well planted, and had a large lake, with an island in the centre and a swannery, in its northern portion. All this is set forth in Knyff's sketch, except a few unimportant facts preserved by common tradition.

Another engraving of Rycott—in size three and three-quarter inches by five inches—appeared in the *European Magazine*, published by J. Sewell, Cornhill, Dec. 1, 1799, but it is remarkably inferior to that already described. The gardens, orchards, and pleasaunces had by that time been destroyed by neglect, the chaplains' residences were gone, most of the outbuildings had been removed, though some still stood on the west side. The southern front of the house remained much in the same state as of old, and the tower of the Chapel is represented to the right. The house itself, however, since then—except a mere fragment of one of the corner turrets, and certain inferior offices—was taken down, and some portion of its contents, and the materials of the building, sold. A handsome staircase and several ancient mahogany doors were introduced into a private residence at Thame, nearly opposite to the lane to Aylesbury in the narrowest part of the High Street; other fittings, carvings, doors, and chimney-pieces, were made use of in a house now belonging to Dr. Herbert Lee, and called "The Moats." I myself possess two portions of ancient pictures, sold when the mansion was dismantled, once the property of the late Rev. Amos Hayton, of Chearsley, one representing Our Blessed Saviour, and the other St. John the Baptist, each meritorious, the last-named of much power and character.

The Chapel, which seems to have been occasionally used when the Earls of Abingdon resided at Rycott, more as a burying-place for the dead however than as a House of Prayer for the living, is in a state of great dilapidation, the internal fittings having become rotten and destroyed, and the roof scarcely water-tight. Many copies of an old and rare edition of the *Book of Common Prayer*, viz., that published in the first year of King James I., remained there within my remembrance, lying tattered upon moth-eaten and inodorous cushions. But their remains are said to have been no long time ago taken to Wytham House.

It is of course sad to see so beautiful a sanctuary given up to desolation and emptiness. It may be that, like its neighbours, the Chapels of North Weston, Moreton, Ascott, Waterperry, the Prebendal House of Thame, Notley Abbey, and Winchendon Priory, it will either remain unrestored, or, in this strictly utilitarian age, its materials in due course be appropriated for mending the highways or repairing dilapidated farm buildings.

Might it not be well, however, considering that the Established Church and the modern sects are hereabouts so well provided with preaching-places, that this Chapel of St. Michael and All Angels should be used once again by those of the Ancient Religion—a mere scattered few, but attached to the Faith—who have no nearer place of worship than the Catholic Churches in Oxford, but who no doubt would be ready and willing to repair the broken-down altar, to kindle anew the Lamp of the Sanctuary, to ostracise the "Abomination of Desolation," and restore the Divine Worship of the de Mandevilles, the Quartermains, and the Herons of old?

Hæc dicit Dominus, Adhuc audietur in loco isto, quem vos dicitis esse desertum. . . . . Vox dicentium Confitemini Domino

exercituum, quoniam bonus Dominus, quoniam in æternum misericordia ejus, et portantium vota in domum Domini.

CHAPTER THE FOURTH.

The Cistercian Abbey of Thame Park, and its Chartulary; with Some Account of the Grammar School of Lord Williams of Thame.

THE original Abbey of Otteley, situated in the village of Ottendune or Oddington,* in the county of Oxford, was founded by Sir Robert le Gait. This Knight was the Lord of the Manor, and owner of a fourth part of the village in question. He petitioned Gilbert, the second Abbot of Waverley, for permission to found the House of Otteley, and, having obtained authority, proceeded to set it up. But the situation, being low and marshy, deeply flooded in winter, and proving to be unhealthy, was abandoned under the advice of Alexander, Bishop of Lincoln, who, with the object of securing a more suitable site, bestowed upon the monks of Otteley his official Manor† and Park of Thame, and certain other lands which had belonged to Nigel Kyre. This change was commenced about the year 1132, and so far completed in a few years, with the aid of Lincoln masons, that the buildings were ready for their occupants, and the Church for consecration, in the spring of the year 1138. Alexander the Munificent solemnly consecrated it on the 21st July of that year, and the Abbey was legally and formally constituted in the following month.*

The monks of this Cistercian order, who preserved a strict silence, went to rest at sunset, rose soon after midnight, and sung the Canonical Hours in choir. Mass was often celebrated as early as four A.M., and those monks who were priests said mass daily.

As regards food, the flesh of quadrupeds was forbidden. They contented themselves with rye or barley bread, with two dishes of vegetables, and a third of fruit and salad. Butter, honey, eggs, milk, cheese, and fish were taken on all days out of Advent and Lent, when vegetables and bread was the appointed diet. St. Benedict allowed a pint of wine daily. Sometimes beer was substituted for wine. From the 14th September until Easter they ate but once a day, at two in the afternoon. During the other part of the year their chief meal was taken at noon, and they partook of bread, fruit, and salad at sunset. The choir monks employed themselves in the farm or garden, at which they worked six hours daily. Some copied MSS., others occupied

* Oddington is in the Hundred of Ploughley and Deanery of Bicester. The Church, dedicated to God in honour of St. Andrew, is of the early second-pointed style, about seventy feet long and twenty broad, with a tower at the west end. This Church is believed to have been erected by the monks during the reign of Edward I.

† This Manor is reputed to have been a part of the possessions of the later Bishops of Dorchester; and is so described in an ancient deed referred to in an abstract of deeds belonging to Sir Cope Doyley, made in the seventeenth century.

* "1138.—Hoc anno Abbatia de Thama fundata est xi. Kal. Augusti."—*Annales de Waverleia*, MS. Cotton, Brit. Museum, Vespasian A., xvi.

special offices. Their churches were in the highest degree simple, severe, plain, and ungaudy.*

Of the value and importance of the Monastic system, both contemplative and practical, there can be no doubt.† The influence of the various Abbeys and religious houses—so long as their inmates faithfully observed their Rules—was beneficial in the highest degree, and both in the natural and supernatural order blessed those who came under its power. It has been well said that, "An order fulfils its mission in proportion as it keeps close to the spirit of its primitive institution. When it departs from the first principles of its foundation, it cannot accomplish its proper work; and its own decay and dissolution are the result of its infidelity."‡ Those who knew Monasticism by experience—the high and noble, as well as the merchant and yeoman, maintained it and admired it. Ever since the Tudor era, its want has been felt: for nothing which has been set up in its place—whether reformatories, dissenting chapels, poor-houses, or lunatic asylums—has adequately supplied the want. No one, of course, would maintain that a life of seclusion is the ordinary vocation for persons in general; yet in all ages there have been exceptional cases of men living apart from the World, in order to consecrate themselves specially to the service of their Maker. In the Old Testament precedents are to be found in the Schools of the Prophets; and St. John the Baptist, from his childhood, dwelt in the desert. In its purest and most perfect form, Christianity, from the outset, has preached a contempt for much which the World values highly; declaring that the highest and holiest kind of life is one of abstinence, seclusion, and self-discipline, in which the soul is free to contemplate heavenly things and the World to come; and the next to that, one in which, for the love of God, and out of pure charity, with no hope of earthly reward, the religious of both sexes instructed the ignorant, fed the hungry, visited the sick, comforted the sorrowful and outcast, and buried the dead.

The importance of the new foundation at Thame Park, and the welcome which the Cistercians received from the chief inhabitants of this locality, is best understood by a study of those deeds which record the gifts of various influential and benevolent donors of the neighbourhood.

Lord Bath's original Register or Chartulary of Thame Abbey, in excellent condition, is in small folio, on vellum, consisting of eighty-seven pages, and its contents are of the thirteenth, fourteenth, and fifteenth centuries. It was rebound some few years ago. I am indebted to Canon J. E. Jackson for the following account of the various instruments and documents contained in it:—

Contents of Thame Register or Chartulary at Longleat.

Otteleia, 1—19.
Mortune, 10—24.
Ottendune, 24—26^a.
Sidenham, 27, 27^a.
Kingston, 27^a.
Morton, 28^a—31^a.
Scypdon, 32—33^a.
Sanctleia Saenteldon, 34—35^a.
Horsendun, 36—37^a.
Stokes, 37^a—39.
Tettesworth, 39^a—43.
Wyfold, 43^a—45^a.
Privilegia Regum, 45^a—47.
Wifold, 47^a—48^a.
Chesterton, 48^a—49^a.
Wendelbury, 50, 50^a.
Craynford, 53^a.
Deed, Rector of Stokenchurch, 55.
Bull, Pope Innocent, 56.
,, ,, Eugenius, 56^a.
,, ,, Alexander, 57^a.
,, ,, ,, 58^a.
,, ,, Lucius, 59.
,, ,, Alexander, 59^a.
,, ,, ,, 59^a.
,, ,, ,, 59^a.
,, ,, ,, 60.
,, ,, Lucius, 60.
,, ,, Innocent, 61.
,, ,, ,, 61^a.
Advowson of Vicarage of Chalgrove, 62.
Tithes of Chalgrove, 62^a.
,, of Colham in Hellingdon, 63, 63^a.
Dean of Wallingford, 63^a.
Edward IV.'s Charter, 64—68^a.

* "With the Cistercians the animating principle of the Order was an austere, extreme simplicity. This may be called 'the Cistercian Idea.' This was the thing that astonished and appalled the World. To become a Cistercian monk was to be bereft of everything that could please the senses, or flatter the pride of the intellect. This was truly leaving the World for the desert. It was like being entombed alive. Yet this very absence of all that could entice or allure was the loadstone of attraction."—*Spirit and Mission of the Cistercian Order*, by the Rev. Henry Collins, M.A., p. 73. London, 1866.

† "A community of pious men, devoted to literature and to the useful arts, as well as to Religion, seems, in those ages, like a green oasis in the desert. Like stars in a moonlight night, they shine upon us with a tranquil ray. If ever there was a man who could truly be called 'Venerable,' it is he to whom that appellation is constantly prefixed—Bede, whose life was passed in instructing his own generation, and preparing records for posterity. In those days the Church offered the only asylum from the evils to which every country was exposed; amidst continual wars the Church enjoyed peace: it was regarded as a sacred realm by men who, though they hated each other, believed and feared the same God. Abused as it was by the worldly-minded and ambitious; and disgraced by the artifices of the designing, and the follies of the fanatic, it afforded a shelter to those who were better than the World in their youth; or weary of it in their age; the wise as well as the timid and the gentle fled to this Goshen of God, which enjoyed its own light and calm amid darkness and storms."—*The Quarterly Review* for December, 1811.

‡ The Rev. Henry Collins.

The MS. volume of Nicholas Charles,—in which a copy of only a portion of the Thame Chartulary is found,—small folio in size, is beautifully written, and other documents therein are illustrated with drawings of seals and coats of arms.*

Those which follow occupy the latter portion of the volume, from p. 287 to p. 304*, which is an acknowledged transcript of the original Chartulary in the possession of the Marquis of Bath.

The charters and documents here reproduced have been carefully compared with those in Lord Bath's MS. by the favour of Canon Jackson.

Incipit Prologus in Cartas Sancte Marie de Tama.

INTER dona præcipua Nature humano generi collata, unum est quod supereminet & superexcellit, literarum habitus usque & fructus: hic namque est, qui nobis brevi quidem & facili suo ministerio archana Dei revelat & secreta celestia. Hic est qui nos fidem docet, spem erigit, infundit caritatem; hic est qui nobis veterum nobilium dicta vel facta laude vel memoratu digna ad imitandum vel ad cavendum ac si sub oculis nostris nunc fiant representata & omnium fere veram quandam presentialem perpetuitatem exhibet: . . . . hic est qui ad posteros nostros quis, quid, ubi, quando, quantum, cui, quomodo, quale dixerit vel fecerit, transmittet. Hinc est quod opere pretium duxi litteris committere fidelibus, qui fuerint Abbatie de Tama Fundatores, quibus eam terris dotaverint, quibus eam cartis & privilegiis munierint. Igitur cum cepissent Abbatie Cisterciensis ordinis per Angliam diffundi, & jam Domus de Waverleia duas generasset filias Gerondoniam† & Fordam, ad petitionem Roberti Gait militis concepit & genuit tertiam quæ nunc dicitur Thama. Hic Robertus Gait, qui in villa de Ottendun quartam partem habuit, ad Abbatem Gilbertum veniens Conventum ad Abbatiam in memorata villa construendum petiit & accepit. Construxitq' ergo ibi Abbatiam, & eam dotavit portione sua modica quidem, videlicet quinque virgatis terræ quæ & ipse quartam partem unius militis faciebat vocavitque eam ex nomine eo adjacentis nemoris Otteleiam. Prima* itaque die, qua Conventus venit Otteleiam Edith filia Forn, uxor videlicet Roberti de Oilli, qui in proximo comanebat, impetivit a marito suo xxxv acras terræ proximas sancte Abbatie & contulit cum magna devotione novo illi Conventui.

Carta Roberti le Gait.

NOTUM sit omnibus Sancte Ecclesie filiis tam presentibus quam futuris, quod Ego Robertus Gait dedi omnem terram de Ottendun & omnia eidem terræ pertinentia, in bosco & plano, prato & pasturis & aquis, liberam & quietam ab omni servitio seculari & consuetudine terrena Deo & Sancta Marie ad abbatiam construenda de Ordine Cisterciensi, in presentia Alexandri Lincolniensis episcopi. Testibus, magistro Osberno de Hache, Roberto de Oilli† Constabulario Regis, Wankelin Wodardo, Rogero de Aumari, Radulpho de Salchei.

Carta Edith uxoris Rob' de Oilli.

NOTUM sit omnibus Sancte Matris Ecclesie filiis tam presentibus quam futuris, quod Ego Edith Roberto de Olli conjugali copula juncta consilio & voluntate ejusdem Roberti mariti mei de Duario meo de Weston dedi in perpetuam elemosynam Deo & Sancte Mariæ & fratribus in Ottelleia secundum institutionem Cistertii viventibus dominum illud, quod extremitate nemoris illorum absque alterius terræ intermiatione continuatur pro salute mariti mei & meâ & filiorum & filiarum & parentum nostrorum, necnon & pro anima Henrici Regis Anglorum. Quod ut ratum sit nec aliqua temporum vicissitudine aut rerum permutatione aut posterorum successione solvatur, mariti mei & filiorum meorum Henrici & Gilberti & filiarum mearum concessione & sigilli mei impressione confirmo. Testibus, Fromand sacerdote, Fulco de Oilli, Herchell, Ranulfo filio Johanni, Fulco Luvell, Henrico filio Roberti filii Aumeri, Roberto Capellano.

Robertus de Oilli confirmat Cartam uxoris suæ.

NOTUM sit cunctis fidelibus Sancte Ecclesie, quod Ego Robertus de Oilli concedo & confirmo idipsum, scilicet quam Edith uxor mea dedit terram de Weston quæ jacet Weston supra parcum Deo & Domino Abbati & fratribus de Ottelleia. Testibus, Fromand sacerdote et Fulco & Nigello de Oilli, Ranulfo fil. Johanne.

NOTUM sit omnibus sancte Ecclesie filiis tam presentibus quam futuris. Quod Ego Henricus de Oilli‡ Constabularius

* Cotton MSS., Brit. Museum, Julius C., vii., folio 287.
† The Abbey of Garendon, near Loughborough, Co. Leicester.

* In Lord Bath's Register these last lines—from "Prima" down to "conventui"—come in after the first charter.

† Robertus de Oilli Const' Regis. Edith filia Forn, uxor.

Henricus Const. Regis. Gilebertus de Oilli.

‡ Henricus de Oilli p'tris sui et m'tris confirmat donation'.

Regis & filius Roberti de Oilli, concedo donationem illam quam pater meus & mater mea Abbati & Conventui de Tama, fecerunt de terra viz. de Weston quæ juxta nemus de Ottelleie Jacet xxxv acr. scilicet post obitum meum Abbatem & Conventum de Tama, eo quod Abbatia de Ottelei apud Tamam transposita sit, inquietare aut disturbare voluerit, liberè & quietè ab omni servitio, quod ad me & heredes meos pertinet, ipsam donationem Abbati de Tama & Conventui sigilli mei appensione confirmare statui. Hujus Donationis & Confirmationis Testes S'tus Ricardus Daumeri Cantor & archidiaconus Lincolnie, Radulfus Daumeri coram sacerdote Thoma Deuval, & multi alii.

Sciant universi sancte Ecclesie filii, quod Ego Reinaldus le Gai dedi & concessi in perpetuam elemosynam Abbati de Tama & fratribus suis totam terram de Ottendun quam Robertus le Gai* pater meus in elemosynam eis dedit pro anima patris sui & matris suæ, pro salute & incolumitate suâ, filiorum suorum amicorumque suorum: de Abbatiâ, quam in illa terre assensu & consensu Comitis Glocestrie fratrumque meorum facere deberent, quietos & liberos in perpetuum esse permitto, ita quod nunquam per me, nec per aliquem aliom hominem vis eis inferatur ut praedicta Abbatia ibi fiat. De rebus suis quas in illa terra, viz. pecorum, frugum, aliarumque rerum, habuerint, volo & concedo ut in Abbatia sit potestate & Monachorum quicquid facere voluerint, vel inde ferre, vel ibi dimittere, ut quicquid aliud agendum decreverint, habeant potestatem. Hujus donationis† & hujus partionis sunt Testes, Prior de Osen', Walchinus Sacerdos de Buldewella, Radulfus Sacerdos de Brac, Robertus de Chesnei, Ansgerius de Lewken', Willelmus de Chesn, Hugo frater ejus, Eustachius de Chesn, Walter Cadell, Engelram de Pende, Paganus de Westbr', Walter de Peri, Hugo Wiethull, Fulco Har', Rogerus Foliot, Philippus de Hamton, Robertus filius Aumari, Fulco Ettenel, Robertus de Suldewella.

In the original Chartulary there is an instrument with this heading :—

Robertus le Gait antecessorum suorum donacionem confirmat.

Notum sit omnibus quod Ego Thoroldus filius Henrici de Ottendun‡ confirmavi totam donationem quam avus meus Thoroldus fecit Monachis de Tama de terra sua in Ottendun vis. quatuor acras, quarum duo sunt super Banda & tertia juxta Greenwaie al' Such & quarta in Lambecote furlunge, & dimidiam acram quam pater meus Henricus cum corpore suo dedit eis, illam scilicet quae jacet juxta portam Grangie Monachorum: Escambium quoque trium acrarum, quod pater meus predictis Monachis fecit, concessi & confirmavi vis. unam acram super Bandam, aliam in Lambecote furlung & tertiam subtus —— Grangie. Ego quoque Thoroldus pro salute anime mee & parentum meorum dedi predictis Monachis quatuor acras & unam buttam, quarum due sunt super Bandam, tertia ad finem Bande in prato, quarta versus Littlemora & le butte in veteri sectun. Hæc autem omnia eis concessi & confirmavi tenenda de me & heredibus meis libera & quieta ab omni servicio in puram & perpetuam elemosynam. His Testibus, Thoma de Dedenton, & Henrico filio ejus, Baldewino, Dracone, Fulcone, fratribus meis.

Notum sit universis Sancte Ecclesie filiis, quod Ego Robertus, filius Radulfi do & concedo & confirmo donationem in perpetuam elemosynam assensu uxoris mee & heredum meorum quam pater meus Radulfus dedit Monachis de Tama, scil' duas acras terre cum prato ad capita illarum, que viciniores sunt terre quam habent ipsi Monachi de dominio Domini mei, solutas & quietas & liberas ab omnibus serviciis & auxiliis que ad me & heredes meos pertinent. Et hæc feci pro salute anime mee & Domini mei Henrici de Oilly & pro animabus patris & matris mee & omnium antecessorum meorum: Et sciendum hujus rei gratiâ ex caritate Domus sue quinque solidos argenti mihi dederunt. His Testibus, Willelmo Preposito, Hakeld Forestano, Willelmo filio Matildis, Rudulfo filio Swartling, Rudulfo le Blund, Henrico filio Thoraldi, Thoma de Ottendun, Roberto de Stoke & Rogero socio ejus.

Notum sit omnibus Ecclesie filiis quod Ego Hugo Pauper* assensu Domini mei Genteschivre Pauperis, dedi & concessi & hac mea carta confirmavi Deo & Ecclesie Sancte Marie de Tama & Monachis ibidem Deo servientibus, cum corpore meo totum pratum meum de Ladene, (quod incipit a fossa de Lacolputte & tendit juxta boscum Genteschivre Pauperis de Ottendun, usque ad boscum Henrici de Oilli de Weston ex una parte & ex alia juxta boscum Radulfi filii Amalrici de Cesterton, sic aque cursum de Wivering decurrens usq' ad predictam fossam de Lacolputte) in puram & perpetuam elemosynam liberè & quietè ab omni servicio & exactione, excepto, quod heredibus meis reddent annuatim duodecim denarios ad festum Sancti Michaelis. Hoc autem feci pro anima patris mei Walteri & Willelmi Pauperis avunculi mei & salute mea & Matildis matris mei & Genteschivre domini & antecessorum meorum & quod predicti Monachi dederunt mihi decem marcas argenti ad relevandam terram meam & liberandum me de manibus Judæorum, et ego & heredes mei predictum pratum Monachis ibidem Deo servientibus warrantizabimus, & Ego & heredes mei si warrantizare non potuerimus, ad valentiam vel in terra arabili vel in prato escambiemus. His Testibus, Rob' de Witefeld, Will' fratre ejus, Rob' Daulmari, Rob' filio ejus, Rob' de Stanford, Walt' de Sancta Fide, Thom. de Jer'lap, Genteschivre domino meo, Math. de Watelele, Hug. de Gersend, Walt. de l'Esche, Will. Bodin, Nichol. Clerico, Rad. Lawvene, Thorold de Ottendun, Wydo de Cherlenton, Fulc. Paupere, Rob. fratre ejus, Walhamet, Hugone, Giliberto & Ricardo fratribus Genteschivre Domini mei, Rob. Gelance, Will. Malcuilvert & multis aliis tum presentibus.

Notum sit omnibus Sancte matris Ecclesie filiis, quod

* Robertus Gait, myles.=
Reinaldus le Gait.=
Robertus le Gait.

† "In the Abbey Book of Godstowe Robert Gay gave half a yard land in Hampton Gay to Godstowe with the consent of Mauld, his wife, and Philip, his heire."

‡ Thoroldus de Ottendun.=
Henricus de Ottendun.=
Thoroldus de Ottendun.=Sara, uxor. Baldwin. Fulc'. Draco.
1. Martin heres Thoroldi, Mabilia uxor ejus. 2. Herbert'. 3. Henric'.

* Walterius Paup'.=Matild', uxor ejus.
Hugo Paup'.

Ego Gentenchivre Pauper filius & heres Willelmi Pauperis de Ottendun concedo & hac presenti carta confirmo Deo & Ecclesie Sancte Mariæ de Tama & Monachis ibidem Deo servientibus donationem quam Hugo Pauper homo meus illis fecit de prato suo de Ladene (scilicet quod incipit a fosse de la colpette & tendit juxta boscum Gentischivre Pauperis de Ottendun, usque ad boscum Henrici de Oilli de Westona ex una parte & ex alia juxta boscum Radulfi filii Amalrici de Casterton sic aquæ cursum decurrens & designata usque ad predictum fossatum,) tenendum liberè & quietè in puram & perpetuam elemosynam, sicut predicti Hugonis Pauperis carta testatur: et hoc feci pro salute animæ meæ & patris mei Willelmi Pauperis & antecessorum meorum & successorum meorum: et ut illius donatio & mea confirmatio rata in perpetuum & stabilita permaneat presens scriptum & sigilli mei munimine roboravi. Testes iidem qui in priori carta.

NOTUM sit universis Sancte Matris Ecclesie filiis quod Ego Gentenchivre Pauper filius Willelmi Pauperis de Ottendun, dedi & concessi assensu heredum meorum quatuor buttas terræ quæ jacent in angulo versus orientem juxta Grangiam & unam perticatam terræ quæ vocatur Adgerd, quæ tendit in moram usque ad aquam currentem ad molendinum meum, Deo & Ecclesie Sancte Marie de Tama & Monachis ibidem Deo servientibus liberè & quietè ab omni servicio et exactione, quod ad me & ad heredes meos pertinet. Predicti vero Monachi debunt unum caponem ad nativitatem Domini. His Testibus, Robᵒ Almari, Willᵒ de Prestecot.

SCIANT presentes & futuri quod Ego Gentenchivre le Poure dedi & concessi & quietum clamavi & presenti carta confirmavi Monachis de Tama in villa mea de Ottendun juxta aquam quam descendit a mora versus Hictenlep de la chenen quam Hugo le Curteis tenuit usque ad parvum vadum, totam quartam partem prati & preterea unam acram terre in Bruoemner quod tenent in villa de Ottendun. Ita scilicet quod nec Ego nec heredes mei in posterum aliquid juris inde clamare poteruimus.

NOTUM sit omnibus Christi fidelibus quod Ego Gentischivre Dominus de Ottendun anno secundo Regis Johannis, coram Magistro de Cennor officiali & omni Clero in Synodo congregato apud Oxoniam jurejurando promisi me in posterum de Tama fidelitatem & indempnitatem in omnibus servitorum & sullsteous deinceps in conversis & famulis in blado aut pratis aut bosco vel quacunque alia re ad predictam Domum pertinentià scienter nociturum.

WILLELMUS Pauper omnibus amicis & Hominibus suis Francis & Anglis salutem. Sciatis quod Ego voluntate & consensu heredum meorum cambivi contra Abbatem de Tama & totum Conventum ejusdem Loci quatuor acras terre, quæ fuerunt ante Grangiam de Otteleia, pro crofta illa quæ jacet ante Domum Radulfi Albi & Wlfrici, Nigelli, & Herberti filiorum Thoraldi in Ottendun, & caput crofte quæ fuit Nigelli Carpenter, et sciendum quod una virgata predicte terre jacet juxta Westune & Ottendun ante Grangiam de Otteleia, & una dimidia acra ad caput hujus virgate, et due acre & una virgata ad hujus dimidie acre virgrotes ad terram de Weston, & una acra ad caput harum duarum acrarum. Testibus Willᵒ de Ease, Rad. Albo, Herberto & Henrico filiis Thoroldi, Walt. Peregrine, Johᵉ Scotto.

SCIANT presentes & futuri quod Ego Gentenchivre le Powere pro salute animæ meæ & Amicie uxoris meæ & pro animabus omnium antecessorum meorum & heredum meorum, dedi & concessi & presenti carta mea confirmavi Deo & Beate Marie & Monachis de Tama in liberam puram & perpetuam elemosynam, quinque acras terre cum pertinentiis suis quas habui in illa cultura quæ se extendit in fossatum Curtis, ipsorum Monachorum scilicet totum pirum & illas sex buttas cum pertinentiis quæ jacent in eadem cultura juxta le Chalvercrofte cum illa parte assarti mei quæ jacet ad caput illarum buttarum usque ad novum fossatum meum, & quod possint fossare & includere totam prefatam terram sicut ipsi voluerint; Tenendas & habendas prefatis Monachis in perpetuum liberè, quietè, integrè, bene & in pace: Et Ego Gentenchivre le Poure* & heredes mei warrantizabimus & defendemus prefatis Monachis totam predictam terram cum pertinentiis & clausuram in perpetuum versus omnes homines & feminas, sicut nostram puram elemosynam. His Testibus, Domino Roberto de Aumari, Domino Hug. de Wistall, Domino Ricᵒ Foliot, Domino Ricᵒ Pirrus, Philippo de Cranford, Thom. de Fishide, Thorald. de Ottendun, Martino filio suo & aliis.

NOTUM sit omnibus Sancte Ecclesie filiis, quod Ego Radulfus Albus de Ottendun assensu Domini sui Gentenchivre Pauperis, dedi & concessi & saisivi & presenti carta confirmavi Deo & Sancte Marie de Tama Monachis decem acras terre arabilis & tres acras prati pro salute animæ meæ & parentum meorum in puram & perpetuam elemosynam solutas & quietas & liberas ab omni servicio & exactione seculari & demanda, salvo servicio Domini Regis quantum pertinet ad quartam partem unius virgate & salvis duobus denariis, quos mihi & heredibus meis reddent annuatim ad festum Sancti Michaelis: Quæ videlicet acre in his culturis de Ottendun continent in Lambescotefurlong ante Grangiam Monachorum unam acram juxta duo acras eorum & in eadem cultura aliam juxta duo alias eorundem, quæ tendit super Havedlond Domini & in Stolling juxta acram Thoraldi, unam acram & post duas acras & dimidiam in eadem cultura, dimidiam acram & in Butte ultra Wivering dimidiam acram quæ tendit super Havedlond Herberti & in Stolling duo dimidias acras quæ tendunt in Putternersdig, ultimas ex parte occidentis preter dimidiam acram & in Bandun unam acram juxta secundam acram Monachorum & aliam in eadem cultura post quatuor acras eorundem & in Chippeneo juxta Grimway unam acram inter acras Thoraldi & Willelmi de Prestet & dimidiam juxta Littleford quæ tendit super latam acram Monachorum & in Stollinge juxta Ealeo dimidiam acram & juxta pontem ex parte occidentis, inter acram Thoraldi & acram Ecclesie, unam acram in Franeford inter acram Thoraldi & acram Monachorum, unam acram prati & in Longelonde juxta acram Monachorum, unam acram & in Wivering inter acram Thoraldi & acram Ecclesie unam acram: Et quia predicti Monachi adjoverunt me in urgentissima mea necessitate de quatuor marcis argenti, Ego & heredes mei predictam terram, erga omnes homines & feminas eisdem Monachis warrantizabimus. His Testibus, Hugo Paupere, Petro filio Symonis, Johᵉ fratre ejus, Hamunde de Sancta Fide, Wid. de Cherleton, Rob. Templario, Thom. filio Will. de Westbr', Thoma juniore, & multis aliis.

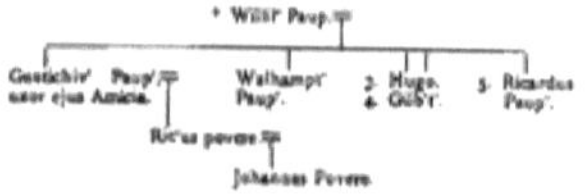

* Willᵐ Paup. =

Gentichiv' Paup' = uxor ejus Amicia. | Walhampt' Paup'. | 2. Hugo. | 4. Gilb't. | 5. Ricardus Paup'.

Ric'us povere =

Johannes Povere

Notum sit omnibus Sancte Matris Ecclesie filiis quod Ego Genteschivre Dominus de Ottendun pro salute anime mee & parentum meorum, concessi & ratum habui & presenti carta confirmavi donationem, quam Radulfus Albus, Homo meus fecit Deo & Monachis de Tama scil. decem acras arabiles & tres acras prati de feudo meo in Ottendun, liberas & quietas & solutas ab omni servicio & exactione seculari, salvo servicio Domini Regis quantum pertinet ad quartam partem unius virgate de Ottendun: ut haec illius donatio & mea confirmatio rata in perpetuum & stabilis preservetur, presentis scripti & sigilli mei munimine roboravi. Hii sunt Testes, Hugo Pauper Ham. de Sancta Fide, Pet. filius Symonis, Joh. frater ejus, Wyd. de Cherleton, Rob. Templaris, Thom. fil. Will. de Westhr', Thomas Junior, & multi alii.

Notum sit omnibus X'ti fidelibus, presentibus & futuris quod Ego Radulfus le Alunar concessi & in escambium dedi & presenti carta mea confirmavi Monachis de Tama illas quatuor buttas quae jacent pro una acra terre & sunt proxime porte Grangie sue de Ottell' ad sinistram sit exitus (*sic*) de porta, tenendum in perpetuum liberas & quietas de omnibus serviciis & rebus ad me & ad heredes meos inde pertinentibus, pro qua acra accepi ab eis unam acram aliam, illam scilicet quae vicinior est domui mee, versus orientem: et sciendum quod Ego & heredes mei, predictis Monachis warrantizabimus illam acram, quam eis escambivimus, contra omnes homines & omnes feminas: vel si eam warrantizare non possumus, illam acram eis reddemus quam ab eis in escambium accessimus. Hoc autem escambium feci eis consensu Domini mei Genteschivre Pauperis. His Testibus, Hugo Paupere, Ham. de Sancta Fide, Torald. de Ottendun, Fulco fratre ejus, Lovell Rog. de Bikestrop, Nic. filio suo, & multis aliis.

Notum sit omnibus Christi fidelibus presentibus & futuris quod Ego Gentenschivre Pauper de Ottendun pro salute anime mee & omnium antecessorum & heredum meorum, concessi & presenti carta mea confirmavi Monachis de Tama illas quatuor buttas que jacent pro una acra terre & sunt proxime Grangie sue de Ottell' scilicet ad sinistram sit exitus (*sic*) de porta. Quam acram Radulfus le Alunar Homo meus eisdem Monachis dedit in escambium pro una alia acra quam ab eis accessit, illa scilicet que vicinior est domui sue, versus orientem. Quare volo quod predict: Monachi teneantur in perpetuum predictam acram terre liberam & quietam de omnibus rebus que ad me & ad heredes meos & ad predictam Radulfum & ad heredes suos inde pertinentibus: Qui Radulfi & heredes sui warrantizabunt predictis Monachis predictam acram contra omnes homines & omnes feminas; vel si eam warrantizare, non possint, illam acram eis reddent, quam ab eis pro alias in escambium acceperunt. His Testibus (iisdem ut in precedenti).

Sciant presentes & futuri Quod Ego Thoraldus de Ottendun dedi & concessi & presenti carta mea confirmavi Deo & Beate Marie & Monachis de Tama in liberam puram & perpetuam elemosynam duo acras prati mei in Ottendun, que jacent in prato quod vocatur Chippeam scilicet que incipiunt ad australe caput culti quod vocatur Bandun & se extendit ad Boreale caput culture, quod vocatur Russefurlung & sunt proxime prato ipsorum Monachorum versus occidentem: & preterea unam perticatam terre que se extendit in Luchlemore & jacet juxta molendinum quod vocatur Backesmille, tenendas prefatis Monachis in perpetuam liberas & quietas ab omni servicio, exactione & consuetudine & de omnibus rebus que de terra exigi possint: Et Ego Thoraldus & heredes mei warrantizabimus prefatis Monachis de Tama prefatas duas acras & prefatam perticatam terre sicut nostram liberam puram & perpetuam elemosynam contra omnes homines & feminas. His testibus, Rob. de Aumari, Ham. de Seinte foi, Rob. de Insula, Joh. Pauper, Thoma Pagnant de Westun, Will. Juvene de Westun, Joh. filio Willelmi, Walt. Ilbert, Adam filio Stephani & aliis.

Sciant presentes & futuri, quod ego Thoraldus de Ottendun dedi & concessi & hac presenti carta mea confirmavi Deo & Beate Marie de Tama pro salute anime mee heredum meorum in puram & perpetuam elemosynam tres acras terre arabilis & unam acram prati in villa de Ottendun cum suis pertinentiis, scilicet unam que se abuttat in Periforlang & aliam acram propinquiorem molendino ad ventum, dictorum Monachorum ex parte occidentali & tertiam acram que jacet in Brokeforlang propinquior la Greenwaye ex parte australi preter duas dimidias acras dictorum Monachorum: dicta vero acra prati jacet in Langelonde propinquior terre arabili ex parte orientali in Eodem forlungo, tenendas & habendas dictis Monachis de me & heredibus meis liberè, quietè & pacificè ab omni exactione seculari & demanda que de terra aliquo modo exigi possit: Et ego Thoraldus & heredes mei warrantizabimus, adquietabimus & defendemus predictas tres acras terre arabilis cum prefata acra prati cum suis pertinentiis prefatis Monachis sicut nostram puram & perpetuam elemosynam in perpetuum contra omnes homines & feminas. In cujus rei testimonium presenti scripto sigillum meum apposui. His Testibus, Hamunde de Sancta Fide, Joh. Paupere, Joh. Pynell, Pet. de Wendlebri, Adam de Blechesden, Walt. Ybert, Will. de la Dene & multis aliis.

Sciant presentes et futuri, quod Ego Thoraldus de Ottendun pro salute anime mee et pro salute animarum omnium antecessorum et heredum meorum dedi & concessi et presenti Carta mea confirmavi Deo et Beate Marie & Monachis de Tama in liberam puram et perpetuam elymosynam unam acram terre arabilis & prati & unam virgatam terre cum pertinentiis suis in villa de Ottendun, videl. illam acram que jacet juxta acram predictorum Monachorum que vocatur Holeredaker & se extendit ultra stagnum molendini de Brakenmulne & illam virgatam terre que se abuttat in fossatum de Periforlange ipsorum Monachorum, tenendas et habendas dictis Monachis liberè & quietè in perpetuum. Et Ego Thoraldus et heredes mei warrantizabimus, adquietabimus et defendimus totam predictam terram cum pertinentiis suis predictis Monachis sicut nostram liberam, puram & perpetuam elemosynam contra omnes homines & feminas in perpetuum. Datum Anno gracie millesimo ducentesimo tricesimo septimo. His testibus, Ham. de Sancta Fide, Gent. Paupere, Ad. de Blechesden, Clerico, Joh. le Poure, Pet. de Wendlebir, Will. de Jovene & multis aliis.

Sciant presentes et futuri, quod Ego Robertus le Gait pro animabus omnium antecessorum meorum & pro salute anime mee & animarum omnium heredum meorum concessi & presenti Carta mea confirmavi Deo et Beate Marie & Monachis de Tama in liberam puram et perpetuam elemosynam totam terram & tenuram cum omnibus pertinentiis suis in omnibus locis & in omnibus rebus quam habeat ex dono antecessorum meorum in Ottendun, & quia locus ille nec idoneus, est nec sufficiens ad Abbatiam faciendam, ad quod terra illa primum fuit assignata, Ego pro me & heredibus meis quietos clamavi predictos Monachos in perpetuum de facienda ibi Abbatia, & concessi quod sine impedimento mei & heredum meorum habeant ibi Grangiam, vel faciant inde quicquid eis placuerit: Et Ego Robertus & heredes mei warrantizabimus totam predictam terram cum omnibus pertinentiis suis predictis Monachis in perpetuum contra omnes homines et feminas & defendemus & adquietabimus predictam terram de omnibus forensecis & aliis serviciis versum Dominum Regem & versus capitales dominos et versus omnes homines, sicut nostram puram elemosynam. Et ut hoc sit in perpetuum ratum et stabile, presentem Cartam meo sigillo roboravi. His Testibus, Gentschivre Paupere, Mat' de Bikestrop, Fulco filio Ricardi, Roger de Stanford, Will' de Anvers, Ric' de Bikestrop, Henrico et Willm fratribus ejus, Thoma filio Rogeri, Will' Poker & aliis.

Sciant presentes & futuri, Quod Ego Martinus, filius & heres Thoraldi de Ottendun pro salute anime mee & uxoris mee & omnium antecessorum & heredum meorum Concessi & remisi & pro me et heredibus meis confirmavi Deo et Beate Marie et Monachis de Tama, totam donationem, venditionem, et escambium, tam de terra arabili quam de pratis pascuis et pasturis & redditibus cum omnibus pertinentiis et aisiamentis suis, quas habeat ex venditione, donatione et escambio patris mei et antecessorum meorum in villa et campo de Ottendun; et insuper remisi eisdem Monachis & pro me et heredibus meis quietum clamavi totum jus et clameum, quod unquam habui, vel habere poti aliquo modo, tam in communa quam in aliis rebus in illa clausura que vocatur le Periforlange; Ita quod nec Ego Martinus nec heredes mei quicquam juris poterimus a modo clamare in prenominatis terris & tenuris in perpetuum. Et Ego Martinus et heredes mei et assignati mei, warrantizabimus, adquietabimus et defendimus omnia predicta, sicut sepius expressum est, cum omnibus pertinentiis suis predictis Monachis de sequilis comitatus et hundredorum, de scutagiis & omnibus demandis et consuetudinibus, tam contra Dominum Regem quam contra omnes homines et feminas: Et ut ista concessio et confirmatio et quieta clamatio stabilis in perpetuum preservetur presenti scripto sigillum meum apposui. His testibus, Rog' de Almar', Hamone de Sancta Fide, Will' de Hamton, Will' de Aerdlei, Ric' de Prescott, Elia de Witfield, Alex' de Camb', Pet' filio Oliveri, Will' de Scalebroke, Rob' de Wicester, Will' Gerun & aliis.

Sciant presentes et futuri, quod Ego Martinus filius & heres Thoraldi de Ottendon et pro salute anime mee et Mabilie uxoris mee, et omnium antecessorum meorum et heredum meorum dedi et concessi et presenti Carta mea confirmavi Deo et Beate Marie & Monachis de Tama in liberam puram et perpetuam elemosynam, undecim acras terre arabilis cum omnibus pertinentiis suis, scil. cum capitibus, pratis, et pascuis in Villa de Ottendun, quarum tres acre jacent in cultura, que se extendit in Bakebroc, et quarta acra jacet in Quarentena, que se extendit in Chippenen juxta acram dictorum Monachorum ex parte occidentali, et dimidia acra jacet in Eldelond, & se extendit in Fulrithie, et alia dimidia acre jacet in Chippenen, in Quarentena, que vocatur Smalcirde, propinquior capitali dimidie acre que fuit Domini Gentichivre, & quinta acra se extendit in longitudine juxta rivulum de Bakkesmulne, & sexta acra jacet in cultura que vocatur Burlingmore, et se extendit in Chippenen, et septima acra se extendit in Luttokestoke & duo acre se extendunt in Drafweie, et dimidia acra, que fuit Drafweie averiis meis; (ita quod Ego et heredes mei habebimus liberum introitum et exitum averiis nostris in pasturam nostram de Brokforlang in eadem dimidia acra vel alibi illi predicti Monachi habebunt introitum et exitum ad averia sua in eandem pasturam) et una virga capitalis que in quadam Quarentena de Backbrok abuttat et alia virga que se extendit in Potesmeadich propinquior viridi vie preter unam virgam que est ipsorum Monachorum. Preterea concessi et presenti carta mea confirmavi eisdem Monachis in liberam, puram et perpetuam elemosynam, quatuor acras et dimidium terre arabilis et tres acras prati cum omnibus pertinentiis suis scil. cum chevesiis pratis et pascuis in eadem villa, videl. unam acram que se abbuttat in Periforlange, et aliam acram que est propinquior molendino ad ventum ipsorum Monachorum ex parte occidentali, et tertiam acram que jacet in Brokeforlange propinquior viridi vie preter duo dimidias acras dictorum monachorum ex parte australi, et quartam acram, que jacet juxta acram predictorum Monachorum, que vocatur Holeredaker, et se extendit ultra stagnum Molendini de Bakesmulne, et unam acram prati que jacet in Langforlange propinquior terre arabili ex parte orientali in eodem furlongo, et duo acras que jacent in prato de Chippenen scil. que incipiunt ad australe caput culture que vocatur Bendun, et se extendunt ad aquilonare caput culture que vocatur Russiforlang, et sunt proxime prato dictorum Monachorum versus occidentem, et unam virgam terre arabilis que se extendit in Litlemore prope molendinum, et aliam virgam, que abuttat in fossatum de Periforlange. Preterea concessi et presenti Carta mea confirmavi eisdem Monachis in liberam, puram et perpetuam elemosynam omnes donationes, venditiones, et escambia que Thoraldus predictus vel aliquis aliis predecessorum meorum predictis Monachis alicubi fecit. Preterea et a me et ab heredibus meis remisi et quietum clamavi eisdem Monachis in perpetuum totum jus et clameum quod habuimus vel habere potuimus in communa pastura, vel aliquo alio modo in cultura ipsorum que vocatur Periforlang. Habenda et tenenda omnia predicta in omnibus locis et rebus sicut supradictum est predictis Monachis in perpetuum libera, salva et quieta ab omni servicio consuetudine, exactione et demanda seculare: Et Ego Martinus et heredes mei warrantizabimus, adquietabimus et defendemus omnia predicta cum omnibus suis pertinentiis, sicut nostram liberam puram et perpetuam elemosynam predictis Monachis tam contra Dominum Regem quam contra omnes homines et feminas in perpetuum: Et ut ista donatio et confirmatio firma sit in perpetuum, presentem Cartam sigilli mei impressione signavi. His testibus, Ham' de Sancta Fide, Will' de Hanton, J. Pynell, Pet' & Roger de Wendlebir, Will' Junive de Westun, Will' Painant de Westun & aliis. Datum anno gracie millesimo ducentisimo quadragesimo, mense Martio.

Sciant presentes et futuri, quod Ego Martinus de Ottendun pro salute anime mee et animarum omnium antecessorum et heredum meorum dedi et concessi et hac presenti Carta mea confirmavi Deo et Beate Marie et Monachis de Tama in liberam, puram et perpetuam elemosynam quatuor acras et unam virgam terre cum pertinentiis suis in villa de Ottendun videl. illas quatuor acras que jacent in cultura que vocatur Brokforlang juxta terra ipsorum Monachorum et illam virgam capitalem que jacet in cultura que vocatur Crofta, habendas et tenendas predictis Monachis & eorum successoribus liberè et quietè de omni servicio consuetudine et demanda in perpetuum. Et Ego Martinus & heredes mei warrantizabimus adquietabimus et defendemus prefatis Monachis & successoribus suis predictam terram cum pertinentiis suis contra omnes homines et feminas, sicut nostram puram elemosynam in perpetuum. In cujus rei confirmationem presentem cartam sigilli mei impressione signavi. His Testibus, Ham' de Sancta Fide, Will' de Hanton, J. Pynell, Pet' & Rog' de

Wendlebir', Will' Jurene de Westun, Will' Peinant de Westun, & Will' de Geoffric' de Westun, & multis aliis.

Sciant presentes & futuri, quod Ego Martinus filius Thoraldi de Ottendun pro salute anime mee & antecessorum et heredum meorum, dedi et concessi & carta mea confirmavi Deo et Beate Marie & Monachis de Teme cum corpore meo, quod post decessum meum apud eos proposui sepeliendum, in liberam puram et perpetuam elemosynam unam acram et unam virgam terre, cum pertinentiis suis in Ottendun, que jacent in Bancumhall & extendunt a Luttenlake in rivum qui fuit subtus Bakenmulne: Preterea quietum clamavi eisdem Monachis totam communam totius pasture pro me et heredibus meis et assignatis meis, a Penniford per Chippesen usque ad dimidiam acram que vocatur Drafwei in Hai et ad eam Drafwei usque ad terram australissimam que fuit Gentechirre in Bancesballe, que jacet a Luttenlake usque ad ductum aque sub dicto Bakenmulne: Et Ego et heredes mei warrantizabimus, adquietabimus et defendemus dictam terram cum pertinentiis suis, et predictam communam pasture predictis Monachis et successoribus suis contra omnes homines et feminas in perpetuum. Ita quod possint easdem terras cum pertinentiis suis quantum ad me, vel ad heredes meos et assignatos meos, pertinet ad culturam aut ad alios profectus suos convertere: sic quod nec Ego nec heredes vel asignati mei, aliquid in communa illa clamare poterimus, in quam omnes alii communicant. His Testibus, Rog' de Aumari, Will' de Hampton, Ham' de Sancta Fide, John Paupere, Petro de Wendlebir', Rog' Clerico, Will' Jurene de Weston, et aliis.

Sciant presentes et futuri, quod Ego Martinus Thoraldus de Ottendun pro salute anime mee et antecessorum meorum et heredum meorum dedi et concessi et hac presenti Carta confirmavi Deo et Beate Marie & Monachis de Tama in liberam, puram et perpetuam elemosynam, duas acras et dimidiam et unam virgam terre arabilis in villa de Ottendun videl: unam acram integram in cultura que vocatur Stoning que, jacet inter terram dictorum Monachorum & terram Johannis le Poore, et unam dimidiam acram in Eldelond, que jacet inter Stollinge Johannis le Poore & terram eorundem Monachorum & unam foveram super le Helle, que jacet pro dimidia acra & unam dimidiam acram in Stoninge, que jacet inter terram dictorum Monachorum ex utraque parte & extendit in Petesmoredich, & unam virgam que jacet juxta crucem Gentechirre inter terram persone de Ottendun, & terram Johannis Petcheto: Et preterea unam portionem prati, que jacet inter Luttenlake versus caput juxta la Blackeyard: habendas et tenendas dictis Monachis et eorum successoribus in perpetuum, cum pertinentiis suis liberè integrè et quietè solutas et quietas ab omni secta, servicio seculari, & omni occasione que possit contingere, in terra vel de terra: Et Ego Martinus & heredes mei warrantizabimus et de omni secta consuetudinibus debitis et exactionibus et rebus aliis adquietabimus et defendemus versus omnes homines et feminas Judaice legis & Christiane sicut nostram puram et perpetuam elemosynam predictam terram & pratum cum pertinentiis predictis Monachis et eorum successoribus in perpetuum. In cujus rei testimonium presenti carte sigillum meum apposui. His Testibus, Joh' le Poore de Cherlton, Joh' Pinell, Joh' filio Widonis, Pet' de Wendleburie, Roger de Wendleburie, clerico, Will' Jurene de Westun, Will' Poignant, & aliis.

Sciant presentes et futuri quod Ego Martinus Thoraldi de Ottendun pro salute anime mee & antecessorum & heredum meorum, dedi et concessi & hac carta mea confirmavi Deo et Beate Marie & Monachis de Tama, in liberam puram et perpetuam elemosynam, unam foveram terre mee, illam videlicet foveram que jacet ad occidentem ville de Ottendun juxta terram dictorum Monachorum, habendam et tenendam dictis Monachis et eorum successoribus liberè, quietè, purè et integrè in perpetuum: Et Ego Martinus et heredes mei warrantizabimus et de omnibus sectis, consuetudinibus debitis et rebus aliis adquietabimus et defendemus predictam foveram terre predictis Monachis et eorum successoribus contra omnes gentes Christiane et Judaice legis, sicut nostram liberam puram et perpetuam elemosynam in perpetuum. Et ut hec mea donatio, concessio, carte confirmatio et warrantia firma sit in perpetuum, presentem cartam sigillo meo roboratam eisdem Monachis feci. His Testibus, Joh' Poore de Cherlton, Peter de Frankelaine de Wendlebir', Will' Juvene de Weston, Will' Swartling de Weston, Will' le Nefe de Itchenlep, Joh' filio Widonis de Cherlton, & aliis.

Sciant presentes et futuri, quod Ego Martinus filius et heres Thoraldi de Ottendun pro salute anime mee et antecessorum & heredum meorum, dedi et concessi et hac presenti carta mea confirmavi Deo et Beate Marie & Monachis de Tama in liberam puram et perpetuam elemosynam, duo acras terre mee arabilis in campo boreali de Ottendun, & duo porciones prati in eodem campo, videl: illam dimidiam acram terre arabilis que jacet juxta la Culputte cum portiuncula prati jacentis ad caput ejusdem dimidie acre, inter terram predictorum Monachorum et terram Johannis le Poure et unam acram terre que jacet in eadem cultura de la Colputte, inter terram predictorum Monachorum et terram Johannis le Poure, et dimidiam acram terre apud le Hulliemed, et illam dimidiam partem supernominati prati, videl: unum sidling apud la Hulliemed, et alteram partem, scilicet unum sidling apud la Colputte, inter terram predictorum Monachorum et terram Johannis le Poure, et preterea unum sidling prati apud Benbroch, inter terram predictorum Monachorum et terram Johannis le Poure et unum sidlinge apud Luttenlake quod se abuttat in la Longehavidland, et preterea dimidiam acram que jacet sub montem, et se extendit in Brunesmere, habenda et tenenda dictis Monachis et eorum successoribus integrè, purè, liberè, et quietè in perpetuum: Et Ego Martinus et heredes mei warrantizabimus, et de omnibus sectis consuetudinibus debitis, et omnibus aliis rebus adquietabimus, et defendemus totam predictam terram et pratum cum omnibus pertinentiis suis predictis Monachis et eorum successoribus, contra omnes gentes in perpetuum. In hujus rei testimonium presenti carte sigillum meum apposui. His Testibus, Joh' le Poure de Ottendun, Joh' le Poure de Cherlton, Joh' Wido, Will' Medico, Pet' de Wendlebir', Will' Jurene de Westun, Will' le Neve de Ychtenlep, et aliis. Actum anno gratie millesimo ducentesimo quinquagesimo, et secundo mense Martii quinto nonarum ejusdem.

Carta Abbatis et Conventus de Oseneya.

Noverint universitas fidelium, quod Ego Johannes Abbas de Oseneye & ejusdem loci Conventus, unanimi consensu remisimus et quietum clamavimus, pro nobis & successoribus nostris, Domino Hillario Abbati de Tama et conventui ejusdem loci et successoribus suis in perpetuum scutagium, quod ab eis petebamus de tenemento suo in Ottel', quod est in parochia de Ottendun, quod habent de dono Roberti le Gelt; Ita quod nos vel successores nostri de cetero de dictis Abbate & Conventu et successoribus suis, ullum scutagium ratione dicti tenementi exigere, non possimus; Sed dicti Abbas et Conventus & successores sui liberi et quieti, in perpetuum de predicto scutagio, quantum ad nos pertinet. Pro hac autem remissione et scutagii quieta clamatione nostra dederunt nobis dicti Abbas et Conventus de Tama, centum solidos esterlingorum: Et ut hec remissio et pro nobis et successoribus nostris quieta clamatio semper stabilis et firma permaneat, huic scripto sigillum nostrum commune apposuimus. His Testibus, Rog' Germano, Rog' de Aumari, Pet' de Esrug, Ballivo Domini Ricardi Comitis Cornubie, Hur' Simeon, Walter de Barthon, Lawrence le Brun, Anketillo Clerico, et aliis.

Universis Christi fidelibus presens scriptum visuris, vel audituris, Johannes le Pouvre filius Ricardi le Pouvre Dominus de Ottendun, salutem in Domino sempiterno. Noverit universitas vestra me cartam Gentischivre avi mei prospexisse, continentem subscripta. Sciant presentes et futuri, quod Ego Gentischivre le Poure, pro salute anime mee et Amicie uxoris mee & pro animabus omnium antecessorum & heredum meorum, dedi et concessi & presenti carta mea confirmavi, Deo et Beate Marie et Monachis de Tama in liberam, puram et perpetuam elemosynam quinque acras terre cum pertinentiis suis que jacent in illa cultura que se extendit in fossato Curtis ipsorum Monachorum, sic contra pirum & illas sex buttas cum pertinentiis, que jacent in eadem cultura, juxta le Chalvercrofte, cum illa parte assarti mei qui jacet ad caput illarum buttarum, usque ad novum fossatum meum & quod possint fossare, & includere totam predictam terram sicut ipsi voluerint; tenendas et habendas prefatis Monachis in perpetuum liberè, quietè, bene et in pace. Et Ego Gentischivre le Poure & heredes mei warrantizabimus et defendemus predictis Monachis totam predictam terram, cum pertinentiis et clausturam in perpetuum versus omnes homines et feminas sicut nostram puram elemosynam. His Testibus, Domino Rob' de Aumari, Domino Hug' de Wistall, Domino Ric' Poliot, Domino Ric' Pirun, Phil' de Cranford, Tho' Fishrid, Thor' de Ottendun, Martino filio suo, et aliis. Hanc donationem Gentischivre avi mei predictis Monachis, Ego Johannes le Poure, pro me et heredibus meis concessi et presenti carta mea confirmavi. Preterea concessi et quietum clamavi pro me et heredibus meis predictis Monachis et successoribus suis, annuum reditum unius caponis quam ab eis aliq' .... exegi. Pro hac autem concessione, confirmatione et quieta clamatione dederunt supradicti Monachi mihi quinque solidos argenti. In hujus rei testimonium presenti carte sigillum meum apposui. His Testibus, Domino Radulph' de Centret, Joh' le Poure de Cherlton, Galfr' de Lecham', Walt' de Borgo, Galf' de Laci, Pet' de Wendlebir', Martin' Thorald', et aliis.

Omnibus ad quos presens scriptum pervenerit Rogerus de Aumari salutem. Noveritis me concessisse & remisisse & quietum clamasse pro me et heredibus nostris Domino Rogero de Marcham, Abbati de Tama & Conventui ejusdem loci totum jus & clameum, quod habui vel aliquo modo habere potui, sine aliquo clameo de me & heredibus meis in omnibus pratis pascuis vel tenementis cum omnibus pertinentiis quae dicti Monachi tenent & tenuerunt de feudo de Weston in campo quod vocatur Westhall unde traxi eosdem Monachos in placitum per breve de recto in curia Domini Regis apud Westmonasterium, coram Justiciariis Domini Regis in Banco. Ita quod nec Ego Rogerus de Aumari, nec heredes mei, nec aliquis pro nobis in predictis terris pratis & tenementis cum pertinentiis aliquod juris sive clamei exigere poterimus. Pro hac concessione & remissione & quieta clamatione dederunt, predicti Monachi quatuor marcas sterlingorum. In cujus rei testimonium presens scriptum sigilli mei munimine roboravi. Datum apud Westmonasterium die medie X'te apud Westmonasterium anno regni Regis Henrici filii Regis XLI. His Testibus, Rad. de Centreton, Joh. le Penne, senescallo domini Regis electi Romanorum, Gilb. de Bracy, Domino Will. Quatremain, Domino Fulco de Rucot, Andrea Croke, Phil. de Wapele, Widone Parage, & aliis.

Notum sit omnibus quod Ego Willelmus Mauduit, filius Thome Mauduit, concessi & presenti carta confirmavi Deo & Beate Marie & Domino Rogero Abbati de Tama & ejusdem loci Conventui omnes terras & tenementa cum pertinentiis, quae habuerunt ex dono Thoraldi de Ottendun & Martini filii ejus, habenda et tenenda eisdem Abbati & Conventui & eorum successoribus in perpetuum liberè & quietè in puram elemosynam, sicut carte, quas inde habent, portant & testantur. Et Ego Willelmus & heredes mei warrantizabimus predictas terras & tenenta cum pertinentiis predictis Abbati et Conventui in perpetuum. In cujus rei testimonium presenti scripto sigillum meum apposui. His Testibus, Rad. de Centreton, Domino Willelmo Quatremaine, Domino Fulco de Rucot, Pet. de Poivick, Will. de Bluntesdon, Joh. le Povre de Cherlton, Will. Juvine de Westun, & aliis.

Memorandum quod ita convenit inter Dominum Hillarium Abbatem & Conventum de Thama ex una parte, et Dominum Rogerum de Turbervill Rectorem Ecclesie de Ottendun ex altera parte, videl: quod dicte partes ad invicem, concesserunt pro se & successoribus suis, non licebit eisdem partibus sine mutuo consensu aliquid in nova cultura redigere in villa de Ottendun. Item concesserunt dicti Abbas & Conventus pro se & successoribus suis quod cheminum illud quod vadit subtus Grangiam suam de Ottel' ex parte occidentali inter Ottendun & Westun ad pedes & ad equos sine bigis aptum remaneat. Item si contigerit aliquem de servientibus dictorum Abbatis & Conventus apud Ottell' manentibus ibidem infirmari & inde deportari ad Abbatiam, propter hoc dicte Ecclesie de Ottendun in primum dicetur quantulum in ipsis est, quod de ipso tamque parochiano, suo sine contradictione ipsorum Abbatis & Conventus jus suum habeat. In cujus rei testimonium presenti scripto in modum chirographi confecto sigilla sua alternatim apposuerunt, anno gracie millesimo ducentesimo quadragesimo sexto, die Sanctorum Crispini & Crispiniani.

Omnibus Christi fidelibus, ad quos presens scriptum pervenerit, Robertus Dei gratia Lincolnie Episcopus salutem in Domino. Noverit universitas vestra nos, interveniente dilectorum filiorum Genteschivre militis Patroni & Rogeri de Turberville Rectoris Ecclesie de Ottendun assensu, concessisse & presenti carta nostra confirmasse, quod dilecti filii Abbas et Conventus de Thame habeant Capellam apud Grangiam suam de Ottell', & divina celebrent in eadem sumptibus ipsorum Abbatis et Conventus, exclusis omnibus parochianis dicte Ecclesie de Ottendun. Ita quod dominicis & festis diebus familia ejusdem Grangie in eadem capella divina non audiat nec panem benedictum nec aquam benedictam nec alia sacramenta in prejudicium matris Ecclesie de Ottendun ibidem percipiat, sed matricem Ecclesiam eisdem diebus debito more, sicut consuevit, visitabit: dicti vero Abbas & Conventus Sacramentum fidelitatis per Monachos & Conversos ibidem manentes exhibebunt scilicet, quod omnes obventiones undecunque in dicta capella pervenient sine diminutione qualibet Ecclesie matrici de Ottendun quam citius restituant; hoc excepto, quod si Episcopus, Comes, Baro, seu persona aliqua, libertatem capelle de consuetudine habens & per parochiam transiens in dicta capella per proprium capellanum divina audierit & oblationem ibidem factam asportaverit, propter haec versus dictum Abbatem & Conventum vel eorum successores, dicte Ecclesie persona vel ejus successorem actionem vel litem movere nequaquam poterunt. Si autem occasione ejusdem capelle quicquid in prejudicium supradicte ecclesie fuerit acceptatum, cessantibus omni appellatione exemptione et privilegio impetrato vel impetrando cessabit auctoritate Ordinarii dicta capella, donec matrici ecclesie super injuria et omnibus subtractis legitimè fuerit satisfactionem. Ordinavimus et de consensu predictorum Patroni et Rectoris, ipsorum Abbatis et Conventus accedente consensu, quod idem Abbas et Conventus immunes sint in perpetuum a prestacionibus omnium decimarum provenientium de cultura illa que vocatur Chalcroft, et de cultura illa que vocatur Petiforlange; que quidem culture clause fuerint fossato versus Grangiam de Ottel' tempore istius compositionis pro quarum decimarum quieta clamantia concesserunt et dederunt dicti Abbas et Conventus dicto Rogero et successoribus suis et ecclesie sue de Ottendun, duo acras terre cum pertinentiis suis, in liberam puram et perpetuam elemosynam videl. unam acram in Bradewesferlange que jacet inter dimidiam acram Domini Gentechirre et dimidiam acram Ysabelle vidue: que quidem acra se extendit super quinque capitales dimidias acras dicti Gentechirre, et aliam acram que se extendit ab oriente in occidentem ex parte boreali domus ipsius Persone de Ottendun, que quidem acra jacet inter acram Willelmi Botte et tres virgas Richardi Herbert, habendas et tenendas dicto Rogero et successoribus suis et Ecclesie de Ottendun liberè, bene et in pace et quietas ab omni servicio et exactione seculari. Concesserunt etiam dicti Abbas et Conventus pro se et successoribus suis dicto Rogero et successoribus suis et Ecclesie de Ottendun liberè, bene et in pace et quietas ab omni servicio et exactione seculari. Concesserunt etiam dicti Abbas et Conventus pro se et successoribus suis dicto Rogero et successoribus suis et Ecclesie sue de Ottendun, quod acram predictam que jacet ut predicitur ex parte boreali domus ipsius Persone, quantum in ipsis est vel ad eos pertinet, claudere possit una cum ceteris acris propinquioribus curie dicte Persone et cum omnibus earum pertinentiis, et quod super eisdem acris cum suis pertinentiis possit edificare, et pro voluntate sua de eisdem disponere: Ita quod in ipsis acris nec communam pasture nec aliquod aliud dummodo clause fuerint, petere possint. Ut quidem ordinatio predicta de partium predictarum assensu per nos facta, salvo in omnibus jure Lincolniensis Ecclesie, matricis et ecclesie de Ottendun, et vicinarum ecclesiarum, et nostri et successorum nostrorum dignitate, perpetuam optineat firmitatem, presenti scripto in modum chirographi confecto sigillum nostrum una cum sigillis ipsarum partium duximus apponendum. His Testibus, Magistro Rog' de Sakesham, Joh' de Byam, Roger Blunde capellanis, Magistris Rog' de Campeden, Rob' de Geden, Rog' de Caveningham, Thoma de Alkebir', Ricardo Clericis, et aliis.

Universis Sancte Matris Ecclesie filiis presentibus et futuris presens scriptum visuris vel audituris de Colchester et de Middlesex archidiaconi et Decanus Sancte Marie de Arcubus Londinis, salutem in Domino. Universitati vestre notum facimus, quod cum Rogerus Rector Ecclesie de Ottendun Abbatem & Conventum de Tama Cisterciensis ordinis super decimis infra nominatis convenisset per Literas Apostolicas ad Decanum Sarisburie suosque conjudices impetratas sub hac forma—'Gregorius, Episcopus, servus servorum Dei, dilectis filiis, Decano, Precentori et Cancellario Sarisburie salutem et apostolicam benedictionem. Rogero Rectore ecclesie de Ottendun accepimus conquerente, quod Abbas et Conventus de Tama Cisterciensis ordinis et quidam alii Lincolniensis et Sarisburiensis dioceseos super decimis et rebus aliis injuriantur eidem: Ideo discretioni vestre per apostolica scripta mandamus, quatenus partibus convocatis audictis causam et appellatione remota fine debito terminetis, facientes quod decreveritis per censuram ecclesiasticam firmiter observari. Testes autem qui fuerint nominati, si se gratia, odio vel timore subtraxerint per censuram eandem, cessante appellatione, cogatis veritati testimonium perhibere. Quod si non omnes hiis exequendis potueritis interesse, duo vestrûm ea nihilominus exequantur. Datum Parisii, decima kalendarium Februarii, Pontificatus Nostri anno secundo.' Formata quidem editione dicti Rogeri in hunc modum:—Dictus Rogerus Persona de Ottendun (dicit) quod decime omnes majores et minores provenientes ex possessionibus, quas Abbas et Conventus de Thama habent in parochia predicta de Ottendun in terris pratis et animalibus, et obventiones omnes alie ecclesiastice hominum dictorum Monachorum in eadem parochia commorantium, Ecclesie prefate debite sunt, cum possessiones terrarum et pratorum infra limites illius parochie site sunt, et animalia in eadem parochia depascantur, et homines in ecclesia memorata, ecclesiastica jura percipiant; in quarum decimarum et obventionum solutione pro parte est per predictos Monachos cessatio. Est autem cessatio in solutione decimarum provenientium de cultura de Stockinge & de nova cultura in Chippenen et de omnibus pratis, quos habent in dicta parochia, de Ottendun & de animalibus et gardino et curia eorum, preterquam in quibusdam obventionibus hominum servientium suorum, quas percipit Ecclesia: pro quâ cessione parochialis ecclesia enormem patitur lesionem: ecclesie cujus interesse ad summam trium marcarum extenditur annuatim, et hoc interesse petit idem Rogerus Persona ipsius ecclesie, et pro tempore, ex quo dicti Monachi in prenominata parochia possessiones antedicta habuerunt, ejusdem ecclesie interesse extenditur ad summam centum marcarum, de quo petit dicte ecclesie satisfieri et intendit petitorium pro hiis decimis & obventionibus quas non percepit; cum antedicta editio sic jacta fuisset ostensis in judicio quibusdam privelegiis dictorum Monachorum deliberativè lectis et inspectis, interlocutum est ipsos Monachos non debere per predictas litteras, nec de jure posse conveniri nec teneri ad respondendum eisdem cessatis exemptionibus contra privilegia dictorum Monachorum propositis, scilicet de enormi lesione & omnibus aliis. Cumque contra dictum interlocutorium ex parte dicti Rogeri fuisset appellatum ad nos sub forma subscripta impetratum fuit: 'Gregorius, Episcopus, servus servorum Dei, dilectis filiis de Colchester et de Middlesex Archidiaconis & Decano de Arcubus Londoniensis diocesos salutem et apostolicam benedictionem. Rector Ecclesie de Ottendun sua Nobis petitione monstravit, quod cum inter ipsum ex una parte et Abbatem et Conventum de Thama Cisterciensis ordinis Lincolniensis diocesos ex altera coram Decano Sarisburie et conjudicibus suis super quibusdam decimis et rebus aliis auctoritate apostolica questio verteretur, idem perperam procedentes in causa iniquam, tulerunt definitivam sententiam contra eum, a qua ipse nostram audientiam appellavit. Ideoque discretioni vestre per Apostolica Scripta mandamus, quatenus in appellatione tam legitima procedatis sententiam confirmare; appellatione remota terminantes sicut de jure fuerit faciendum. Quod si nec omnes hiis exequendis potueritis interesse, duo vestrûm ea nihilominus exequantur. Datum Laterani quarto Iduum Decembris Pontificatus Nostri anno quarto.' Cum et dicti Monachi super injusta vexatione Litteras Apostolicas impetrassent contra dictum Rogerum et Abbatem Sancte Marie Eboraci et suos collegas sub hac forma—'Gregorius, Episcopus, servus servorum Dei, dilectis filiis Abbati Sancte Marie Cantori et Thesaurario Eboraci, salutem et apostolicam benedictionem suam. Nobis dilecti filii Abbas et Conventus de Thame Cisterciensis ordinis insinuationem monstraverunt, quod cum Rogerus de Turberville Rector Ecclesie de Ottendun Lincolniensis diocesis eos super decimis quibusdam, a quarum prestatione per Apostolice Sedis privilegia sunt immunes, coram Decano Sarisburie et conjudicibus suis authoritate apostolica convenisset, qui cognitis Ecclesie Matricis et inspectis eorundum privilegiis et indulgentiarum suarum tenore, eosdem Abbatem et Conventum ob impetitione ipsius Rogeri sententialiter absolvit, procedens contra eandem sententiam temere veniens, nec contentus damnis & gravaminibus prius super hoc illatis eisdem ipsos super decimis ipsis multiplici molestatione fatigat. Quo circa discretioni vestre per Apostolica Scripta mandamus, quatenus super hiis molestationem desistat monitione premissa per censuram apostolicam appellatione remota cogatis. Quod si non omnes hiis exequendis potueritis interesse, duo vestrûm ea nihilominus exequantur. Datum Laterani Idibus Decembris Pontificatus Nostri anno quarto.' Partibus tandem convocatis & in presentia Nostra constitutis post multas altercationes facta renunciatione nobis utrinque omnium dictarum litterarum impetratarum, lis super predictis mota per amicabilem compositionem realem et perpetuam inter ecclesias factam, in hunc modum conquievit; videl. quod predictis Abbas et Conventus pro bono pacis Ecclesie de Ottendun & Rectoribus qui pro tempore fuerint in eadem, de mesuagio quod Lambertus de eis tenuit in Ottendun, quandam partem contulerunt, scilicet in australi parte ejusdem mesuagii latitudinem quinquaginta pedum juxta viam quæ vadit per medium Ville, et eandem latitudinem per medium ipsius Crofte super predicta via usque ad caput in longitudine, et dictam terram dicte Ecclesie garantizabunt. Dictus Rogerus Rector pro se et successoribus suis et ecclesia sua eosdem Abbatem et Conventum immunes et quietos clamavit in perpetuum a petitione & presentatione petitorum, in quorum solutione dicebat per dictos Monachos fuisse cessatum et omnia jura & actus in supra premissis renunciabit, salvis et retentis sibi et successoribus suis et ecclesie sue hiis in quorum possessione erat idem Rogerus et ecclesia sua tempore compositionis. Ad hujus autem compositionis observationem prius impetratis & impetrandis, tam in foro ecclesiastico quam seculari actionibus exceptionibus, appellationibus et omnibus aliis juris remediis contra predictam compositionem facientibus renunciavit. Promisit et ult' p'r' sub juramento solempni, quod dictam compositionem bona fide et firmiter observabit sub pena quinquaginta marcarum solvendarum a parte non observante eam parti illi quæ eam observaverit; nihilominus compositione in ipsa rata manente in perpetuum et servata Nobis et successoribus Nostris, de consensu partium perpetua jurisdictione compellanda eas ad predicte compositionis observationem & dicte pene, si commissa fuerit, solutionem. In cujus rei testimonium facta est scriptura tripartita sigillis nostris & partibus utrinque signata: cujus prima pars residet penes dictum Abbatem et Conventum, et alia pars penes Rectorem Ecclesie de Ottendun, et tertia pars in archivis Ecclesie Sancte Trinitatis Londonia per nos deposita, et nobis et successoribus nostris cum n'tte fuerit, resignanda, ibidemque iterum reponenda. His Testibus, Magistro Willelmo de Westmenister, Magistro Ric' de Westmenister, Magro Joh' de Leona, Magro Jac' de Wiccam, Magro Pet' de Ladenora, Joh' P. de Gersenden, Hugo fratre ejus, Nicolao de Newam, et aliis.

Universis Sancte Matris Ecclesie filiis presens scriptum visuris vel audituris Prior Rading salutem. Noveritis nos mandatum Domini Pape suscepisse in hæc verba. 'Innocentius, Episcopus, Servus servorum Dei, dilecto filio Prior Rading Sarisburiensis Diocesos salutem & apostolicam benedictionem. Ne dilecti filii Abbas & Conventus de Thame Cisterciensis ordinis Lincolniensis diocesos iste contemplacionis ocio, cui se totaliter donaverunt, per solicitudinem bonorum temporalium (in quibus nonnulli, qui nomen domini recipere in vanum non formidant, multipliciter, ut asserunt, inquietantur) desistare compellantur, Nos volentes eorum providere quieti & molestiantium malitiis obviare discretioni tue per Apostolica Scripta mandamus, quatenus ipsis Abbati & Conventui assistens efficaciter non permittas ipsos contra indulta Sedis Apostolice ab aliquibus indebite molestari; molestatores hujus modi per censuram Ecclesiasticam, appellatione preposita, compescendo, presentibus prius triennium minime valitus. Datum Lugduni xvii Aprilis, Pontificatus Nostri anno tertio'. Hujus quidem authoritate mandati cum deposita esset querimonia dictorum Abbatis & Conventus coram nobis contra dictum Rogerum de Turberville Rectorem de Ottendun, scilicet quod eosdem contra indulta privilegiorum suorum decimis quorundam novalium in parochia de Ottendun spoliavit & eis & suis per se & suos multas injurias intulit et inferri fecit, conquerente nihilominus dicto Rectore apud dictis Abbate et Conventu ac suis eidem Rectori nonnullas illatas fuisse injurias; tandem anno gracie mccxlvii, die Sanctorum Crispi & Crispiani partes, interveniente nostra authoritate, amicabiliter in hanc formam consenserunt, videl. quod omnes controversie quacunque occasione seu quocunque tempore diem supradictam precedente, quæ hinc inde mote erant vel poterant moveri per predictas partes nominibus suis vel suorum aut Ecclesiarum suarum, remisse sunt utrinque, & dicti Abbas & Conventus pro bono pacis perpetue, inter utramque Ecclesiam concesserunt dicto Rectori & successoribus suis tres acras terre in villa de Ottendun in furlango quarrarie, habendas & possidendas ab omni servicio liberas & quietas: et dictus Rector pro se & successoribus suis dictis Abbati & Conventui & successoribus suis immunes & quietos clamavit de prestatione decimarum provenientie de omnibus terris suis in Chippesen, usque ad supra-nominatum diem in culturam redactis & de chevesiis duarum virgarum, quæ sunt in Patemadich, in quarum chevescas terra domini de Ottendun se extendit, et jus, si quid habuit, vel habere potuit in decimis predictis nomine Ecclesie predicte pro se & successoribus suis penitus remisit nostra & successoribus suis in perpetuum decimis bladi provenientibus de ceteris culturis dictorum Abbatis & Conventus in eadem parochia de quibus antea nihil fuit compositum. Quod si aliqua causa contigerit, quod aliquod nomine decime de dicta cultura de Chippesen, seu de alio quocunque loco in prefata parochia, ubi decima dari non debuit, sine jussione dictorum Abbatis & Conventus alicui Rectori dicte Ecclesie de Ottendon solvatur, illud prefatis Monachis non prejudicabit. Similiter predicto Rectori vel successoribus suis non debetur prejudicare, si casu aliquo decima fuerit asportata, que sibi & ecclesie sue debuit competere. Quod si futuris temporibus aliquis ex successoribus predicti Rectoris contra hanc presentem venire presumpserit compositionem, liceat predictis Monachis propria auctoritate, dictas tres acras occupare, vel quod predicta compositio authoritate, nostra rite inita rata & firma in perpetuum habeatur, utraque pars jurisdictioni nostre se subierit de consensu partium, perpetua nobis & successoribus nostris potestate reservata, ut partem utramque ad hujus compositionis observationem possimus compellere, si quam earum ab ea, resilire contigerit. Datis nominibus manentibus utrisque compositionibus in perpetuum inter dictos Abbatem et Conventum et successores suos et dictum Rectorem et successores suos tam super ordinationem. Domini Lincolniensis Episcopi inter ipsos facta, quam compositionem coram Archidiacono Colecestre' et suis collegis inita. Et ut hec compositio perpetuum robur obtineat, presenti scripto in modum chirographi confecto sigillum nostrum una cum sigillis partium duximus apponendum. His Testibus, Domino Phillippo Abbate de Biddlesden, Magistro Walter' de Sancto Edmundo, persona de Chirlebir', Domino Henrico de Boscham & Galfrido de Turberville, Magro Walt' de Tubben, Martino Clerico, Ric' Sturdi, & aliis.

Otte lepa.

Here, in the Longleat Chartulary, follows a schedule of gifts by the Benefactors named in preceding deeds, occupying two pages.

Then another long document, on p. 17, occupying six pages, in which occur the names of

Roger, Prior of Thame,
Warin, Abbot of Grace Dieu,
William, Abbot of Osneye, A.D. 1281.

And another dated A.D. 1297, which is an agreement between the Abbot of Osneye and the Abbot of Reuley, near Oxford.

Cartas de Morton.

The following are only abbreviations of the documents which are given at full length in Lord Bath's Chartulary:—

Galfridus filius Osmundi de Mortun dedit Abbatie de Tamam unam hidam et dimidiam terre in Mortun. Testibus, Rog' Kersington, Petro Clerico de Tama, Rob' Chevacheval, Osbert' filio Thuri, Walt' de Sancta Fide, Nigello filio Petro, & aliis.

Godfrey de Morton gives Aitkismore.

Willelmus filius Galfridi de Mortun assensu Walterii filii fratris sui confirmat donationem patris, sui, &c.

Willelmus filius Gaufridi de Mortun reddidit Monachis de Tama mesuagium Lune sororis sue in Mortun assensu Eve uxoris. Testibus, Rob' de Stanford, Thom' de Tademarton, Rog' de Bikestrop, Rogero filio Rogeri, & aliis.

Willelmus filius Gaufredi de Mortun restituit partem suam prati, quod vocatur Lohedemede, assensu Eve uxoris sue & filii Petri et fratris Walteri. Testibus, Simone Presbytero, Will' Presbytero de Whitfeld, Walt' de Vernun, Rob' Chevauchesul, Osberto de Thame, Ada de Cennor, Walt' filio Osberti de Thame, Raulfo de Pudicote.

Walterus de Bickestrop confirmat donationem Gaufridi avunculi sui, quam ipse fecit Deo et Ecclesie Sancte Marie de Tama; videl'—unam hidam et dimidiam quas predictus Galfridus ille dedit in Mortun.

Walterus de Bikestrop exambivit terras in Mortun cum Monachis de Tam'. Hijs Testibus, Alexro Clerico de Midleton, Ada Clerico de Cennor, Rob' de Stanford, Joh' de T're, Ric' de Horsenden, Hugo de Braimustre, Joh' filio Walteri de Bikestrop, Rog' de Bikestrop et aliis.

Rogerus de Bikestrop assensu Domini sui Walteri de Biskestrop concessit Ecclesie Beate Marie de Tama et Monachis ibidem Deo servientibus virgam terre in Mortun. His Testibus, Ric' Talemashe, Walt' de Bikestrop, Mat' et Mil' de Biskestrop, Rob' Marescallo, Rog' filio Turberti, & aliis.

Radulphus de Bikestrop confirmat Monachis de Thama donationem quam Rogerus pater suus eis dedit de una virgata terre in Mortun de feodo de Ottendun, &c. Testibus, Ric' de Thus, Herberto Quatremaines, Henrico de Bikestrop, Will' & Nich' fratribus suis, Rob' Marescallo, Rog' filio Thurberti, et aliis.

Radulphus de Bikestrop dedit Deo et Beate Marie de Tama terras in Mortun. His Testibus, Petro Talemache, Ric' de Turri, Joh' de Oilli, Henr' de Weston, Hug' de Chiselhampton, Ada de Weston, & Rog' de Franc, & aliis.

Hugo de Braimustre, assensu Petronille uxoris sue & Odonis filii sui, confirmat Ecclesie Sancte Marie de Tama unam hidam & dimidiam in Mortun que Galfridus filius Osmundi homo meus illi dedit, &c. His Testibus, Roberto de Stamford, Roberto Constentin, Sein' filio Restwald, Galfr' de Belchamp', Gerold de Braimustre, Alwine de Ettendun, Nich' filio Osin, Rog' filio Roberti de Stanford, Joh' de Cliftonn, Jac' fratre ejus, Edm' de Wivelcford.

Hugo, Lincolnie Episcopi Constabularius, assensu Adelise sue uxoris, confirmat donationem predictam.

Robertus, Lincolnie Episcopus confirmat Ecclesie Sancte Marie de Parco de Thama et Abbati & fratribus et Monachis ibidem, &c., donationem quam Hugo, Alexandri bone memorie Lincolnie Episcopi, Constabularius eis fecit. Testibus, Magistro Gaufrido electo Sancti Asaph', Hugo Lere, Archidiacono, Rob' Oxoniensi Archidiacono, Rob' Cadom, Ric' Dansi, Rad' Moosmensi Canonicis.

Radulphus, filius Rogeri & sponsa sua Adelisa, & Robertus heres, concesserunt Ecclesie Sancte Marie de Tama dimidiam hidam de ejusdem sponse sue matrimonio Mortun, &c. Testibus, Willo presbytero, Rob' de Whitfeld, Hen' et Will' fratribus ejus, Walt' le Thus, & aliis.

On the back of folio 23 of the Longleat Chartulary are deeds of "Johanna filia Osberti" and of "John de Franc de Mortune."

Cartas de Ettendun.

All these deeds are likewise abbreviated.

Sciant, &c. Quod Ego Hugo de Braimustre, quum profectus fui Jerusalem, dedi Hugoni filio meo medietatem terre mee de Anglia ubicunque sit; et feodum Roberti de Sancto Claro, quod est in Braimustre, & viginti acras de feodo Angi, et tres curticulos de eodem feodo, & curticulum Oini Donani et si feodum Angi non sufficiat ad perficiendas viginti acras terre, Odo filius meus competenter ei in Braimustre supplebit, &c. Testibus, R. de Matreval, Racio fratre ejus, Hubert de Braimustre, Pet' filio Hugonis de Masci, Will' de Franc, et aliis.

SCIANT, &c. Quod Ego Herevicus de Fontibus feci heredem meum Hugonem de Braimustre & Petronillam uxorem ejus, sororem meam et pueros eorum, de tota terra mea, quam teneo & quam adquisiero, si heredem habuero de muliere sponsata & pro hac concessu (Hugo) tribuit mihi terram suam de Attendun, &c. Hæc conventio facta fuit anno quarto postquam Rex Henricus filius Matildis Imperatricis primò coronatus fuit. Testibus, Tho' Pagan, Herving, Amfre, Butetarte, Reg' Chive, et aliis.

NOTUM sit quod Hugo Constabularius et Alicia uxor ejus & Hugo de Braimustre et Petronilla uxor ejus partiti sunt terram Fulconis de Fontibus patris predictarum feminarum hoc modo, quòd villa de Blewaton cessit in partem Hugonis Constabularii et uxoris suæ; villa vero de Attendun contigit Hugoni de Braimustre et ejus uxori. Testibus, Rob' de Chevauchesul, Fulc' filio Roberti, Walt' de Bikestrop, Mil' filio ejus, Audoer filio Restwolde, R. de Stanford, Simon Horkedu', Will' de Fane, Rob. filio Godwini.

ODO de Braimustre assensu Hugonis fratris sui dedit terram suam in Attendun videl:—totam medietatem ville, quam Hugo frater ejus tenet in dominico quam in villenagio. Hæc vero concessio facta est anno regni Regis Ricardi ad festum Sancti Martini. His Testibus, Galfridus de Lunar, Hugo de Han', R. de Stanford, Joh' de Turre, Walt' de Bickestrop, Ada de Cennor, & aliis.

EGO Hugo de Braimustre terram de Attendun, scil: medietatem ville quam tenui fratri meo Odoni reddidi, &c. Et concedo quod Monachi de Tama teneant predictam terram de antedicto Odone in perpetuum. His Testibus, Hugo de Age, Galf' de la Mare, Joh' de Turre, Ada de Cennor, Olivero et Savar de Age, Joh' de Sexholt, Simon de Constantin, Will' de Fale, Rob' de Turre, Gilb' de Mapledurham, Walt' de Bykesthorpe, & aliis.

Here, in the Longleat Chartulary, appears a grant by John de Turre to the Monks of Thame.

ODO de Braimustre pro salute animæ suæ et Alicie uxoris suæ dedit Deo & Beate Marie de Tama dimidiam marcam argenti: pro hac donatione susceperunt se & heredes suos in fratres; quando autem de se et de Hugone filio suo inhumanitus contigerit, &c.

NOTUM sit quod Ego Hugo de Braimustre do et concedo Deo & Sancte Marie & Monachis de Tama in perpetuam elemosynam assensu et permissione fratris mei & Domini Odonis & consensu heredum meorum unam acram in Cumba de terra de Attendun.

ODO de Braimustre dedit Henrico de Colville fœdum unius militis in Attendun & in Mortun, reddendo sibi annuatim unam bisantam vel duo solidos; pro hac donatione prefatus Henricus de Colville dedit sibi xxxv marcas sterlingorum. His Testibus, Domino Jocelino Bath' Episcopo, Magro Rogero Lincolnie Decano, Hugo Wellensi Archidiacono, Hugo de Gurney, Gerard de Cavill, Rob' Basset, Rog' Giffarde, Ric' de Turre, & aliis.

HENRICUS de Colville dedit predictam terram Monachis de Thame.

Cartae de Sider'ham.

RICARDUS de Vernun dedit Serloni Abbati et Monachis de Thama duo hidas terre in Side'ham assensu uxoris sue Matildis. Testibus, Walt' de Bulcher, Hug' fratre ejus, Ric' filio Nigelli, Waltero filio ejus, Hugone de Hillesden, Hugo de Fai, & aliis.

WALTERUS Vernun assensu Hubelmie uxoris sue excambivit Monachis de Tama de duobus acris, quas pater suus eis dedit in Syde'ham. His Testibus, Rob' de Whitfeld, Galf' de la Mar, Will' de Ybeston, Will' de Whitfeld, Rob' de Bulcher, Will' de Sauvage, Galf' Foliot, & aliis.

JOHANNES filius Radulphi de Syde'ham dedit Monachis de Tama terras in Syde'ham.

Michael Grimbald gives some land. The deed setting this forth occurs on the back of p. 27 of the Longleat Chartulary.

RICARDUS Abbas de Thama confirmat Guidoni de Crewell falconario, terras in villa de Kingeston. Testibus, Domino de Thoma de Breaut, Domino Alano de Estone, & aliis. Datum apud Crewell, 1274.

Another by the same to the same.

Cartae de Nortun.

ROBERTUS filius Radulphi de Sifrewast dedit unam hidam terre in Oxenfordscire apud Nortun Deo et Ecclesie Sancte Marie de Waverleia, &c. Testibus, Hug' Barat, Willo filio meo, Radulpho presbytero, Willo nepote meo de Joganville, Rob' de Chase, Rad' de Iotrario, Simone nepote meo, Rad' de Chale.

NOTUM sit omnibus Sancte Matris Ecclesie filiis, quod Ego Gilbertus Abbas & omnis Conventus Waverleie concessimus Conventui Ottelleie hidam de Nortun, nobis a Roberto de Sifrewast in elemosynam datam. Quod ut ratum sit, nullaque temporum varietate vel posterorum successione violetur, sigilli nostri impressione confirmavimus.

In the Longleat Chartulary there appears "Carta Ramburge," on p. 280, and on the same page a charter of "Radulph' de Bristol."

WILLELMUS de Sifrewast concessisset Ecclesie Sancte Marie de Tama terram Ernaldi de Nortun videl. unam hidam quam pater suus dedit Conventui de Waverleia. Testibus, Gilberto et Josepho presbyteris, Helia de Chivell, clerico, Sewal' de Chuserug, Will' Tabart, Sim' Punchun, Rob' Warcheis, & aliis.

SCIANT, &c., quod Ego Milisent filia Eustachii de Frecheville & uxoris sue Dionisie & Stephanus filius et heres meus, assensu Milonis qui tunc temporis custodiam nostri et terre nostre habuit, dedimus unam virgatam terre in Nortun Monachis de Tama liberam ab omni servicio, &c., salvo servicio Domini Regis et Bernardi de Sancto Walerico. Datum Anno 1187 ad Pascha proximum postquam Hugo Lincolnie Episcopus consecratus fuit. Testibus, Alured sacerdote, Ric' de Vernon, Rob' Dalmeri, Will' de Cennor, Walt' de Westberi, Rad' Hareng, Rob' Estrop, & multis aliis.

STEPHANUS de Fretwell confirmat donationem quam Milisent mater sua fecit Monachis de Tama de una virgata terre in Nortun. Testibus, Domino Rad' Hareng, Rad' filio ejus, & multis aliis.

ROBERTUS de Estrop dedit Deo et Sancte Marie & Monachis de Thama duo acras terre de dominico suo de Estrop pro salute sua et pro anima Milisent uxoris sue. Testibus, Rob' de Capellano de Nortun, Magro Nic' de Westmonasterio, Rad' filio Gaufridi, Will' le Brun, Rog' filio Bitcher de Estrop.

Willelmus Luvell assensu Isabelle uxoris sue ad firmam finalem Monachis de Tama anno VIII Ric' duo molendina sua tradidit, unum ad bladum molendum, et aliud ad pannos fulendos in villa sua de Mourtra. His Testibus, Will' de Britwell, Joh' herede et filio meo, Ada Clerico, Rad' filio Gaufridi, Rob' de Estrop, Simon de Merton, & aliis.

Here follow, in the Longleat Chartulary, two instruments, recorded on p. 30, of "Milo Arablastarius" and "Willielmus Luvel."

Walterus de Stratford confirmat Abbati de Tama unam virgatam terre in Blescote, quam Simon de Bamton & Matilda ejus uxor dederunt cum Hugone filio suo. Testibus, Rob' filio Radulfi & Will' fratre ejus, Radulfo filio Rogeri, Rob' Estrop, Rob' de Burton, Ric' de Osen'.

Here likewise follow in the Longleat Chartulary charters of Isabel Luvel & Simon de Bamton.

Notum sit, &c., quod Ego Matilda filia Halive uxor Simonis de Bamton, assensu mariti mei & Willelmi de Stratford domini mei, dedi Ecclesie Sancte Marie de Tama totas tres virgatas terre quam tenui jure hereditario in Beleskott. Testes iidem ut supra.

Here are on record in the Chartulary in question charters of John Balet (p. 31) and Gaufridus de la Lee.

Adam filius et heres eorum confirmat eisdem verbis.

Here again stands "Carta de Belescot" (p. 31a).

Concordia apud Westmonasterium Anno Regni Regis Johannis quinto [*i.e.* 1204] coram G. filio Petri, Eustachio de Faucunburg, Johanne de Gelling, Osberto filio Herberti, Godefrido de Insula, Waltero de Crepinge, justiciariis, et aliis baronibus, &c., inter Walterum de Marisco petentem et Willelmum Abbatem de Tama tenentem de una virgata terre in Norton.

Cartae de Sypdun.

Willelmus filius Othonis dedit Everardo Abbati et Monachis de Tama terram suam de Sypdun, &c., Et hoc fecit pro anima uxoris sue Gisle, &c. Testibus, Alexandro Episcopo Lincolnie, Rob' Londonie Episcopo, Rad' Sancti Pauli, Rad' de Monemue, Rog' Daumeri, Ric' filio Goderici, Rad' Dispensatori, Alrom filio Edwini de Gonefeld, & aliis.

Notum sit, &c., quod Nos Willelmus filius Othonis et Otho & Willelmus & Symon filii mei damus totam terram eorum de Sypdun Deo et Abbati & Monachis de Tama. Testibus, Osberto de Santeradone, Nigello filio ejus, Gauf' filio Nigelli, Irvain & Ruelent Malet, Rob' Chevauchesul, Osberto filio Thuri, &c.

Alexandro Dei gratia, Lincolnie Episcopo & omnibus fidelibus Ecclesie et Willelmo filio Othonis, &c Robertus Comes de Ferar salutem. Sciatis me dedisse Sancte Marie et Abbati de Thama totum servicium meum de feodo unius militis in Sypdun. Testibus, Hamon Abbate de Sancto Petroburgens', Hamon Abbate Bardulfo, Rog' Capell', Hen' filio Fulchi, Hugo de Ferrars, Umfrido de Tolca, dapifero, Hen' filio Sewali et Fulch' fratre ejus.

Willelmus Comes de Ferrariis confirmat donationem, quam Robertus Comes de Ferrariis avus suus fecit Abbati de Tama de feodo unius militis in Scypdun. Testibus, Will' de Essex, Fore' de T'uth, Will' de Redware, dapifero, Rob' de Ferrars, & Henrico fratre ejus, et aliis.

A charter of William, son of Robert, appears on p. 32a of the Longleat Chartulary.

Ruelent Malet assensu Irvoi filii et heredis sui dedit terras in Scypdun. Testibus, Galf' de la Mare, Nich' de la Mare, Ada Cennor, Yrvoi Malet.

Notum sit, &c., quod Ego Yrvoi Malet anno octavo Regni Ricardi confirmavi Monachis de Tama donationem quam Pater meus Ruelent Malet eisdem fecerat. Testibus, Will' de Dorton, Will' fil' Nigelli, Galf' de Creindon.

Conventio inter Abbatem de Tama et Roberto persona de Queinton, 1199, anno regni Regis Johannis primo, concedente et prebente domino de Queinton, Yrvoi Malet.

Conventio, secundo anno post quam Rex redit de Alemannia, inter Monachos de Tama et Samson de Pomario & Christianam de Belawe uxorem suam & heredes eorum de fonasto in Scypdun. Testibus, Ric' filio Walteri de Mortun, Yrvoi Malet, Roger de Cranford, Burchardo Forresta, Rad' le King, Fulc' fratre ejus, & aliis.

Conventio apud Scipdun inter Simonem Abbatem de Tama et Robertum Baskervile, pro quibus terris in Scypdun.

Here on p. 33a of the Longleat MS. there are two or three more deeds about Scypdun. And, in another, Alan de Arches gives lands in Weston.

Cartae de Santerleia.

Osbertus de Santerdun dedit Abbatie de Tama terras in Santerleia. Testibus, Joh' sacerdote de Bledlawe, Osberto patre ejus, Rob' sacerdote de Cennor, Ada fratre ejus, Hugo de Horsendun, milite, et aliis.

Notum sit, quod Ego Robertus filius Osberti de Santerdun, assensu Matildis uxoris mee & Johannis fratris mei et ceterorum fratrum meorum Nigell, et Willelmi, concessi Deo et Sancte Marie et Monachis de Tama partem nemoris mei in Santerleia. Testibus, Nigello & Will^{o} fratribus meis, Joh' de Turre, Rob' filio ejus, Rob' de Constentin, Joh' de Blundehale, Alex' de Britwell, Petro de Morton.

Robertus filius Osberti de Santerdun dedit eisdem Monachis cum assensu Matildis uxoris tres croftas terre in Santerleia. Testibus, Ric' de Horsendun, Walt' de Sancta Fide, Ada de Cennor, Ric' et Clementi filiis Osberti de Santerdun.

Johannes filius Osberti de Santerdun confirmat donationem patris sui et fratris Roberti. Testibus, Will' domino de Santerdun, Ada de Cennor, Johanne de Santerdon, Tho' filio ejus, Reg' de Claidun, Ric' de Perhivale, Ric' de Horsendun, Rob' Constentin, Joh' de Turre. Facta est haec confirmatio in die Sancti Michaelis proxima postquam Rex Anglie Ricardus & Baldwinus Cantuarie Archiepiscopus iter arripuerunt versus Jerosolimam.

Here follow, on pp. 34a, 35a, and 35, other charters in the Longleat MS., of "Gaula de Turville," "John de Santerdun," "Henricus Pirrun," "Alexander de la Lee," and "Will' filius Sevari."

Emma uxor Johannis de Santerdun confirmat eandem donationem.

Conventio inter Abbatem de Thama & Rogero de Stanford, pro quibusdam terris in Santerleia. Testibus (inter alios), Gilb' Martel, Will' de Upton, Johanne de Hyda, Rob' Marr' milite.

Cartae de Horsendun.

Notum sit quod Ego Richardus de Horsendun, assensu Johannis fratris mei, dedi Serloni Abbati de Tama quadraginta acras terre in Calwalid, &c. Testibus, Walt' Giffard, comite, Gauf' Comite de Manderville, Ric' de Locy, Regin' de Wareio, Rad' Basset, & aliis.

Ricardus et Johannes de Horsendun, per petitionem matris eorum Matildis, concesserunt Monachis de Tama quandam terras in Horsendun.

Here in the Longleat Chartulary stands a deed of "Robert de Tenerihebras."

Johannes de Horsendun dedit Abbati de Tama totam culturam de dominico suo, quod jacet inter boscum Rog' de Stanford, &c. Pars ejusdem fuit de dote Domine Cecilie uxoris Ricardi fratris sui. Testibus, Johanne Merewerte, Will' de Upton, Rog' de Stanford, Henrico Camerario, Osberto de Bledlawe, Rob' de Laford, Symon Constentin, & aliis.

Robertus de Braibroc confirmat Monachis de Tama donationes Ricardi et Johannis de Horsendun. Testibus, Rog' de Hamden, Ric' de Turre, Herberto de Bolebec, Hen' de Scaccario, Sim' de Bereville, Helia de Wimbervill, Ric' fratre ejus, Galf' Giberwyn, Rog' de Samford, Rob' de Laford.

Henricus de Braibroc confirmat Monachis de Thama omnes terras quas tenent de feodo de Horsendun, quas pater ejus eis concessit.

Cartae de Stoke.

Petrus Talemache dedit Serloni & Monachis de Tama duo hidas & octo acras de terra sua de Stoke, concedente uxori sua Matilda, & matre sua, et fratre Willelmo. Testibus, Will's de Osberto de Hesell, Hugo de Stoke, sacerdote, &c.

Ricardus Talemache confirmat donationem Petri Talemache patris sui Monasterio de Tama. Testibus, Roberto Chevaucheaul, Pet' Pirun, Ric' filio Alaredi, Ada Clerico de Cennor, Will's Danvers, Osberto de Stoke, &c.

Bernardus de Sancto Gwalerico confirmat donationem predictam.

Ego Laurentius de Stoke, assensu Gilberti le Graunt & Galiene uxoris mee, dedi Abbatie de Tama tres dimidias acras terre mee in Stoke. Testibus, Ricardo Talemache, Petro & Roberto filiis ejus, Ric' le Thus, Hen' de Whitfeld, & Ric' Pirun, et aliis.

Notum, &c., quod Ego Willelmus le Grant, assensu domini mei Ricardi Talemache & Gilberti heredis mei, dedi medietatem illam terre mea de Stoke Deo et Ecclesie Sancte Marie de Tama, & confirmo eisdem Monachis unam acram terre, quam genitor meus Laurentius eis dedit. Testibus, Ric' Talemache, Joh' de Latur', Gilbert le Grant filio meo & Godefrido fratre ejus.

Concordia apud Westmonasterium Anno Regis Henrici secundi vicesimo septimo coram Ro' Wintoniensi, G. Eliensi, G. Norviciensi, episcopis, Ranulpho de Glanville & Ricardo Thesaurariis, Will' Basset, Hug' de Moriwic' et Ranulfo de Gedinge, & aliis baronibus, inter Monachos de Tama & Ricardum Talemache de novem acris terre et dimidia in Stoke, sicut Carta Petri patris predicti Ricardi testatur.

On page 380 of the Longleat Chartulary there are some other deeds about Stoke.

Cartae de Tetteswurth.

Notum sit quod Ego Robertus Chevaucheaul dedi Serloni Abbati de Tama, &c., totam terram meam de Horsendun in Tettesword. Testibus, Thom' de Druvall, Hug' de Druvall, Almarico filio Radulphi, Hen' de Oxon, Walter de Sancta Fide, Alano filio Ansf' de Estone, Widon' Parage, Ric' Talemache.

Robertus Chevauchesul, assensu Matildis uxoris sue, dedit residuum terre sue in Horsendun, &c. Testibus, ut antea.

Alexander Lincolnie Episcopus, &c., confirmaverunt Everard' Abbati de Parco Tama illam hidam, quam Robertus Chevaucheaul dedit iis de terra sua in Tetteswurd, videl: illam partem in Horsendun, &c. Testibus, David Archidiacono de Buck', Rog' Dameri, Magist' Hamon, Rob' Foliot, Galf' de Ireby.

Robertus Dei gratia Lincolnie Episcopus, &c., Nos ratam habere donationem Roberti Chevaucheaul quam fecit assensu Mabilie matris sue, & fratris sui Rogeri et omnium sororum suarum, Deo et Everardo Abbati Monasterii Sancte Marie de Tama, silicet: unam hidam de Tetteswurd continentem centum acras in Horsendun. Testibus, Abbate de Dorecastre', Rob' Archidiacono de Oxon, Rob' de Burneham, Baldw' Cada, Rog' de Kernent, Will' Chesei, Will' Basset, Everardo de Cardunvilla.

Sciant, &c., quod Ego Robertus Chevaucheaul assensu heredum meorum, videl. Ricardi Telmache nepotis mei & Mabilie sororis mee, dedi & concessi Alano Clerico & Claricie nep'ti mee pro servicio illorum & pro quinque marcis argenti unam dimidiam hidam in villa mea de Tetteswurd illa, videl: que vocata terra del Hospital, &c. Si forte evenerit quod aliqua pars illius dimidie hide cadat ad dotem Matildis sponse mee, &c.

Notum, &c., quod Ego Alanus Clericus de Tetteswurd & Claricia uxor mea nep'tis Roberti Chevaucheaul assensu domini fundi, videl: Ricardi Talemache quas quo Rex Ricardus mortuus est, dedimus, &c., Deo & Abbatie de Tama cum corporibus nostris unam dimidiam hidam terre in Tetteswurd, quam tenuimus ex dono Roberti Chevaucheaul. Testibus, Ric' Talemache, Will' de Bruges, Ric' le Thus, Ada de Cennor, Gilb' le Thus, Will' Danvers, & Rad' fratre ejus.

Notum sit quod Ego Ricardus Talemache confirmavi Deo et Abbati de Tama totam terram quam Alanus Clericus et Claricia uxor ejus tenuerunt in Tetteswurd ex dono Roberti Chevaucheaul, &c., sicut carta Roberti Chevaucheaul avunculi mei testatur. Testibus, Will's presbytero de Tetteswurd, Ada de Cennor, Ric' le Thus, & Gilb' fratre ejus, et aliis.

Notum sit quod Ego Emma filia Awcheri Chevaucheaul dedi cum corpore meo Deo et Sancte Marie de Tama, duo acras terre in Tetteswurd de heretagio meo pro anima patris et matris mee & fratris Roberti Chevaucheaul. Testibus, Ric' Talemache, Will', Rad', & Walt' Danvers, Helia Daure & Rob' herede meo, qui huic assensum prebuit.

Sciant, &c., quod Ego Ricardus Talemache assensu Petri filii et heredis mei & Amicie uxoris mee dedi Deo & Beate Marie & Monachis de Tama unam virgatam terre in villa de Tetteswurd, &c., predicti vero Monachi pro amore Dei & caritatis intuitu Radulphum filium meum in Monachum promovebunt & Willelmum fratrem meum in Conversum. Testibus, Mag' Ada de Cennor, Simon de Witefeld, Ric' le Thus, Alano de Tetteswurd, Ric' Pirun, Hen' de Witten, Will' de Bruges, Oliverio de Hesele.

Sciant, &c., quod Ego Alanus Clericus de Tetteswurd assensu Claricie uxoris mee dedi cum corpore meo totam illam dimidiam hidam terre, quam tenuimus in Tetteswurd Deo & Beate Marie & Monachis de Tama. Testibus, Ric' Talemache, Will' de Bruges, Ric' le Thus.

Rogerus filius Alani Clerici de Tetteswurd & Claricie uxoris ejus confirmavit donationem patris & matris ejus.

Petrus Talemache dedit Monachis de Tama pasturam ad octo boves & duo equos in dominico suo de Tetteswurd, anno Incarnationis Domini 1207, nonis Martii.

Notum sit, &c., quod Ego Robertus Danvers dedi Deo et Monachis Sancte Marie de Tama unam virgatam terre in Tetteswurd, cujus dimidiam Emma mater mea dederat fratri meo Willelmo Danvers. Testibus, Ricardo Talemache, Will' de Bruges, Rad' Peliot, Ric' filio ejus, Ric' Pirun, Rad' de Colebi, Nicol' de Olli, Herberto Quatremains, Will' Danvers, Rad' Danvers, Alano Clerico, Gilberto ——, Mag^r^ Laur' de Stoke, Mic' Grimbald, Walt' de Chalewrd, Rob' Garante, et aliis.

Notum sit quod Ego Radulfus Danvers assensu domini mei Roberti Danvers, anno regni Regis Ricardi nono, dedi Deo et Abbatie de Tama totam terram meam in villa de Tetteswurd; silic: duo virgatas terre cum messuagiis & croftis, quas Robertus Chevaucheaul eis dedit. Testibus, Ric' Talemache, Petro filio ejus, Will' et Walt' Danvers, Walt' de Bickestrop, Joh' filio ejus.

Notum sit, &c., quod Ego Robertus Danvers confirmavi donationem quam frater meus Radulfus Danvers fecit Deo et Abbatie de Tama. Testibus, ut supra.

Notum sit quod Ego Rogerus Danvers, clericus, dedi Deo & Ecclesie Sancte Marie de Tama unam virgatam terre in Tetteswurd, pro salute anime mee & dilecte genetris mee & avunculi mei Roberti Chevaucheaul, illam scilicet quam Willelmus Bunetun tenuit quam mihi mater mea filia Awcheri Chevaucheaul & frater meus Robertus Danvers pro servitio meo dederant. Testibus, Ric' Talemache, Osmundo sacerdote, Rad' Danvers, Galf' filio Gunne, Ric' filio Umfr'.

Thomas de Sancto Valerico dedit Monachis de Tama octo acras terre in villa de Stoke, quas Petrus Talemache, senior, eis dedit & filius ejus Ricardus eis confirmavit: et unam perticatam, quam Petrus Talemache junior filius predicti Ricardi eis dedit. His Testibus, Ada Abbate de Betlesden, Rad' Hareng, & aliis.

Henricus de Whitfield dedit Monachis de Tama terras in Whitfield, &c., anno regni Regis Johannis tertio & anno Incarnationis 1202 est facta haec carta. Testibus, Ada de Cenner, Pet' Talemache, Ric' Pirun, Alex^m^ de Cumba, Ric' & Rob' fratribus Petri Talemache, & aliis.

Ricardus Taillard dedit Willelmo Rockell dimidiam virgatam terre in Tetteswurd, scilicet, illam quam Willelmus Longus filius Ricardi, filii Umfridi, tenuit.

Willelmus Rokell dedit Monachis de Tama predictam terram. Teste, Rob' Matheo tunc vice-comite Oxenfordscire.

Ricardus Taillard pro salute anime sue & sororis Claricie confirmavit donationem quam Willelmus Rokell fecit Abbatie de Tama. Testibus, Ric' le Thus, Ric' de Pureo, & aliis.

Sciant, &c., quod Ego Petrus Talemache confirmavi Deo et Beate Marie & Monachis de Tama dimidiam illam virgatam quam Ricardus Taillard avunculus meus tenuit de me. Testibus multis.

Sciant, &c., quod Nos Rogerus dictus Abbas de Tama & ejusdem loci Conventus dedimus Johanni de Stoke Talemache & Johanne uxori sue unum messuagium in Villa de Tetteswurd. Testibus, Domino Hen' de Bruley, Nic' de Gangeville, Ric' Danvers, Edm' de Burton, Hug' Pirun, Nic' de Stoke, Rog' de Weston, Rog' filio Johannis, & aliis, Anno regni Regis Edwardi primi quinto.

Edmundus filius Ricardi quondam Regis Alemanie & Comes Cornubie dedit Deo & Ecclesiae Beatae Mariae de Regali loco & Monachis capellanis Ordinis Cisterciensis juxta Oxoniam totam terram suam, quam habuit in villa Willaston & sexaginta solidos sterlingorum omnis redditus, quem de Abbate de Tama in villa de Stoke Talemache. Testibus, Domino Thoma de Bensete, Ric' de Cornubia, Rob' de Alrner, Hen' de Stokesbroke militibus, et aliis.

Margeria quae fuit uxor Edmundi Comitis Cornubie petit versus Abbatem de Tama tertiam partem sexaginta solidorum redditus in Stoke Talemache, ut dotem, &c. Et Abbas dicit quod sine Domino Rege consanguineo & herede predicti Comitis non potest ei respondere. Termino Sancto Michaelis Anno regni Regis Edwardi filii Henrici Regis tricesimo.

Sciant, &c., quod Ego Agnes de Humez pro salute anime mee & Domini mei Baldewini Wac & pro salute filii mei Baldewini Wac dedi Monachis de Tama unam virgatam terre in villa de Winchendun. Testibus, Herberto de Bolebec, Ranulfo Wac, &c.

Cartae de Crainford.

Sciant, &c., quod Ego Philippus de Cranford dedi Deo & Beate Marie de Tama totam illam dimidiam hidam terre in Cranford, quam tenui de Gilberto Sancto Michaele fratre meo. His Testibus, Domino Alano Englefield, Will' filio Almarici, Nic' de Sancto Germano, Will' de Cranford, Hen' Dairell, Ranulfo de Sobwienton.

Sciant, &c., quod Ego Philippus de Cranford dedi Deo & Beate Marie & Monachis de Tama totam illam virgatam terre in Cranford, quam habui ex dono Domini mei Willelmi de Cranford, tenendam prefatis Monachis in perpetuum, de Domino Johanne de Mascay & Domina Avelina uxore sua, qua fuit filia predicti Willelmi de Cranford & de heredibus suis ex Avelina procedentibus. Testibus, ut supra.

Sciant, &c., quod Ego Symon filius et heres Gilberti de Sancto Michaele confirmavi Deo et Beatae Mariae de Tama donationem quam Philippus de Cranford patruus meus eis fecit de illa dimidia hida terre in Cranford quae fuit maritagium Hersentae avie mee, scilicet, matris patris mei. Testibus, Domino Eustachio Londinensi episcopo tunc Domini Regis Thesaurario, Domino Ricardo Sarisbur' & domino Jocelino Bathoniensi Episcopis, Domino Radulfo Cicestriensi Episcopo tunc Domini Regis Cancellari, Domino Ricardo Abbati de Westmonasterio, Mag^r^ Mic' Bellett, & aliis baronibus Scaccarii, Ric' Reinger, tunc Majore Londinensi, Joh' de Mascay, Hen' Buccinte, God' Hascart, Carta illa in rotulo est in Magno Rotulo Regis in Middlesex anno regni Regis Henrici tertii decimo.

Cartae de Wyfaldia.

Omnibus Sancte Matris Ecclesie filius Galfridus de Ivelo salutem. Notum sit me dedisse Ecclesie Sancte Marie de Tama totam terram quam Nigell Chyre tenuit, & Wyfaldiam & Rochemersbegge, quae erant membra de Bensington. Testibus, multis.

Ricardus Dei gratia Rex Angliae, Dux Normanniae & Aquitaniae, Comes Andegaviae, &c. Sciatis nos dedisse et confirmavisse Deo et Ecclesie Sancte Marie de Tama, &c., totam terram de la Wyfaldia & Ruchmarshegge, &c., pro salvatione Domini Henrici Regis patris mei & A. Reginae matris meae & Johannis fratris nostri, &c. Testibus, Hug' Dunelmensi, G. Wintonensi, H. Sarisburiensi, H. Coventrensi et G. Roffensi, episcopis, Rob' de Whitfeld, Will' filio Adel', Gaufrido filio Petri, Hug' Bardulf, Mic' Beleche, Will' de Bendenge, Rob' le Poer. Datum apud Cantuariam, secundo die Decembris per manum Willelmi Eliensis, electi Cancellarii nostri, regni nostri anno primo.

Concordia anno secundo Johannis coram Galfrido filio Petri, Ric' de Her, Simon de Patashull, Joh' de Gestlinge, Eustach' de Fauconberg, Henrico de Wikenton, Godefr' de Insula, Walt' de Creping justiciariis, inter Willelmum Abbatem de Tama petentem & Robertum Marmion tenentem de viginti acres terre in Bensington.

Stephanus Rex Angliae Episcopo Lincolo', &c. Sciatis me dedisse Ecclesiae Sancte Marie de Tama terram quam Nigell Chyre tenuit, & Wifaldiam & Ruchmarshegge quae erant membra de Bensington, & solebant reddere in firma manerii ejusdem viginti tres solidos & quatuor denarios. Testibus, Hug' de Bolebec, Guid' filio, &c., apud Bensington in exercitu.

Henricus Rex Angliae, Dux Normanniae & Aquitaniae, Comes Andegaviae, omnibus Archiepiscopis, &c. Sciatis me concessisse et confirmavisse Ecclesie Sancte Marie de Tama donationem, quam Gaufridus de Ireto illis fecit de terra quam Nigell Chyre tenuit & de Wyfaldia et Ruchmarshegge, quae erant membra de Bensington, &c. Testibus, P. Abbate de Malmburia, Regn' Comite Cornubiae, Ric' de Humet Constabulario, Hugo de la Mara, Hen' Hosato, apud London'.

Henricus Dei gratia Rex Angliae, Dominus Hiberniae, Dux Normanniae & Aquitaniae & Comes Andegaviae, Archiepiscopis, Episcopis, Abbatibus, Prioribus, Comitibus, Baronibus, Justiciariis, Vicecomitibus, Prepositis, Ministris, & omnibus Balliviis et fidelibus suis, scilicet—Inspeximus Cartam Henrici Regis avi nostri in haec verba :—' Henricus Rex Angliae & Dux Normanniae & Aquitaniae & Comes Andegaviae, Archiepiscopis, Episcopis, Abbatibus, Comitibus, Baronibus, Justiciariis, Vicecomitibus, Ministris, & omnibus fidelibus suis totius Angliae Francis & Anglis salutem. Sciatis Nos concessisse et in perpetuam elemosynam confirmasse Ecclesie Sancte Marie de Thama & Monachis ibidem Deo et Sancte Marie servientibus de Ordine Cisterciensi omnes terras et tenuras suas, quae eis rationabiliter date sunt, & concesse sicut donatorum Carte testantur. Ex dono Alexandri Lincolniensis Episcopi ejusdem loci fundatoris ipsum locum & Parcum in quo Abbatia illa fundata est, et terram quae fuit Nigelli Kyre, et Rugmershegge & Wyfaldam ex dono Galfridi de Ivoio. Ex dono Willelmi filii Othonis septem hidas terre in Sibdon. Ex dono Reginaldi le Geyt quinque virgatas terre in Otteleia. Ex dono Roberti de Oyley triginta et sex acras terre in Weston. Ex dono Roberti filii Almarici, terram de Cesterton. Ex dono Petri Talemache duas hidas terre in Stok quae sunt feodo Reginaldi de Sancto Walerico. Ex dono Ricardi de Virnon & Walteri filii ejus duas hidas terre in Sydenham. Ex dono Hugonis Constabularii dimidiam hidam terre in Morton. Ex dono Roberti Chevauchesul unam hidam terre in Tettesworth. Ex dono Hugonis de Hursendon terram quam eis dedit. Ex dono Osberti de Santerdon croftam illam quae vocatur Bocme et Budeham & Dellpec & pannagium triginta porcorum in bosco suo & partem ejusdem bosci, sicut fossae factae sunt. Quare volo & firmiter precipio quod predicta Ecclesia & Monachi predicti habeant & teneant haec omnia predicta cum omnibus pertinentiis suis in bosco et plano, in pratis et pascuis, in aquis et molendinis, & in omnibus locis quieta, de wyr & hundred & murdre & danégeld & hydagio et scutagio & placitis et querelis & operationibus & auxiliis & donis Vice-Comitum & Ministrorum suorum & omni seculari servitio et exactione cum soca et saca & Tol & Theam & Infangthefe & cum omnibus aliis libertatibus & liberis consuetudinibus suis ita bene et in pace liberè et quietè & honorificè sicut Cartae Alexandri Lincolniensis Episcopi & Roberti successoris ipsius & omnium aliorum donatorum suorum eis rationabiliter testantur. Ac prohibeo, ne quis inde eis super haec injuriam vel molestiam faciat. Testibus, Philippo Baiocensi & Arn' Lexoviensi, Episcopis, & T. Cancellario, Ric' de Humet Constabulario & Warin filio Geroldi Camerario & Manas' Biset, dapifero, et Roberto de Dunell apud Westmonasterium. Nosque concessionem & confirmationem predicti Regis gratam et ratam habentes pro nobis et heredibus nostris eam presenti Carta mea confirmamus. Hiis testibus, Eustach' Londoniensi, Petro Wintoniensi, Jocelin Bathoniensi, Ric' Sarisburiensi, Episcopis, H. de Burgo Comite Kancie, Justiciario nostro, Will' de Evreford, Ric' de Argentin, senescallis nostris, Henrico de Capella, Will' de Cantelupe, & aliis. Datum, per manum Venerabilis patris Radulfi Cicestriensis Episcopi Cancellarii nostri, apud Westmonasterium, decimo nono Februarii anno regni nostri undecimo.

Cartae de Crestreton.

Notum sit omnibus Sancte Ecclesie Matris filiis, quod Ego Robertus Almarici filius dedi Deo et Sancte Marie et Monachis de Tama in Otteleia de gentibus illud de Dominico meo quod Curtlington proximum est de terra de Crestreton pro anima patris & matris mee & pro anima Henrici Regis, necnon pro animabus parentum meorum & parentum uxoris mee. Quod ut ratum perpetuo firmetur jugaliter mei & filiorum meorum Willelmi & Roberti concessione & sigilli mei impressione et testium subscriptione consolido. Testibus, Hen' Rerubold & Osberto & Osmundo clericis & Rob' Capellano.

Notum sit omnibus Sancte matris Ecclesie filiis, quam presentibus tam futuris, quod Ego Robertus filius Almarici dedi et concessi in perpetuam elemosynam Serlo in Abbati & Monachis Abbatie Sancte Marie de Tama totum dominicum meum quod vocatur Ulwardeshull, habens sexaginta acras de Inland & similiter totum dominicum meum de Oacheire, scilicet, decem acras de Inland & praeter haec, viginti acras Warland inter Ulwardeshull & Accemanuestrate: istae viginti acrae debent se defendere pro dimidia hida versus Regem & dominum de cujus feodo terra illa est. Illa autem terra de Ulwardeshull & de Oacheire quae est de Inland libera est, & quieta ab omni consuetudine & servicio seculari versus Regem & versus omnes homines. Dedi etiam eis totum pratum, quod est ad caput Ulwardeshull a ponte, per quem iter est ad Boscum usque ad terram Weston, & preter hoc decem acras de prato meo: Dedique eis communam pasture pro trecentum ovibus & sedecim bobus et sex vaccis & centum overa. Deo bosco mei sive vigint carecturas, concedente here de meo & fratribus ejus Radulfo &

Henrico, concedente & Osmundo Clerico & filio ejus & omnibus villanis. Et hoc feci pro anima mea & pro anima uxoris mee Yvice & filiorum meorum & pro salute mea & omnium parentum meorum; filiarum mearum & omnium antecessorum meorum, et pro concessione hujus donationis Abbas & Monachi predicti dederunt Roberto filio meo & herede centum solidos, et fratri ejus quoddam fuscotristum. Testibus, Rob' archidiacono Oxoniensi, Rogero Cantore Lincolniensi, Rad' de Nowers, Rob' filio Isbert', Jocelin Clerico Archid', Osmundo Clerico de Centreton.

Notum sit Universis Sancte Matris Ecclesie filiis tam presentibus quam futuris, quod Ego Robertus filius Roberti, filii Almarici, consensu Radulfi fratris mei, dedi et concessi in puram elemosynam Abbati de Tama & Monachis ibidem Deo servientibus Ordinis Cisterciensis, dimidiam hidam terre, viginti-sex acras et dimidiam acram continentem in Petiforlange, and quadraginta tres per compos versus Midellatone; et totum pratum meum, quod continetur inter parvam Centreton et Wendelbur': Et sciendum sit, quod hæc terra defendere se debet erga me pro dimidia hida; et preterea confirmavi donationem patris mei, quam dedit, sicut ejusdem Carta testatur. Haec itaque omnia feci pro salute mea et pro anima patris mei et matris mee & omnium predecessorum meorum. Testibus, Ric' Basset, Almarico filio Radulphi.

Amalricus filius Radulfi filii Amalrici confirmavit Ecclesie Sancte Marie de Tama, &c., totam terram illam quam Robertus filius Amalrici avunculus suus & Robertus filius ejus illis dederunt. Testibus, Reg'n' de Brattewell & Eustach' de Edewelle presbyteris, & aliis.

Sciant, &c., quod Ego Radulfus filius Roberti filii Amalrici, &c., confirmavi Monasterio Sancte Marie de Tama, &c., donationem quam predictus Robertus pater meus assensu meo confirmavit; et similiter concessi donationem, quam frater meus Robertus eis in elemosynam dedit assensu meo, &c. Testibus, Ric' Winton', Reg' Bathon', Joh' Norwicen', episcopis, Reg' filio Rainfri, Jord' de Clinton, Rob' de Whitefeld, Rob' filio Radulphi.

Haec est finalis Concordia que facta fuit in Curia Domini Regis apud Westmonasterium ad Scaccarium pascha proxima post concordiam inter Papam Alexandrum & Fredericum Imperatorem, coram Ricardo Wintonensi episcopi, Ricardo de Luci, Willelmo Basset, Rogero filio Rainfridi, Radulfo filio Steffi', Roberto Mantell & ceteris justiciariis domini Regis qui tunc ibi aderant, inter Monachos de Tama & Radulfum filium Almarici de quadam Bercaria in Centreton & quodam parvo prato quod est ante portam ipsorum Monachorum.

Cartae de Wendlebury.

Notum, &c., quod Ego Walterus de Sancta Fide dedi Ecclesie Sancte Marie de Tama, &c. Testibus, Walkelino filio Rogeri, Gauf' de Seint Martin, Rob' de Granville, Ric' de Hassington, Sewald' de Sancta Fide, Petro filio Walteri, Joh' filio Walteri, & aliis.

Notum sit, &c., quod Ego Hamund de Sancta Fide, &c., dedi Deo et Ecclesie Sancte Marie de Tama, &c., cum corpore meo & corpore uxoris mee unam virgatam terre in Wendlebur', illam scilicet quam Gilebertus filius Aldewini tenuit. Testibus, Ric' le Thus, tunc Vice-Comiti Oxoniensi, Ric' Talemache, Herberto Quatremains, Ada de Cenner, Helia de Stoke, Hug' Paupere, Petro filio Walteri, & aliis.

Notum, &c., quod Ego Walkelinus filius Rogeri assensu Domini mei Sewall de Osewill dedi, &c., Monachis de Tama totum pratum meum de Baillebenesham & duo buttas terre mee arabilis in Wendlebur'. Hanc concessi anno octavo Regis Ricardi. Testibus, Rob' Dalmari, Rob' filio ejus, Walt' de Sancta Fide & Hamund filio ejus, & Rob' de Sancta Fide.

Innocentius Episcopus, servus servorum Dei, dilecto filio Everardo Monasterii Beatae Mariae de Parco Tame ejusdemque successoribus regulariter substituendis in perpetuum desiderium quod ad religionis propositum et animarum salutem pertinere monstratur Authore Domino sine aliqua est dilatione complendum. Nec enim Deo aliquis gratus famulatus impenditur, nisi ex caritatis radice procedens in religionis puritate confectus fuerit. Ea propter, dilecte in Domino fili Everarde Abbas, tuis rationabilibus postulationibus gratum prebentes assensum, Monasterium Beatae Mariae de Parco Tame, quod Authore Domino presides sub Apostolica Sedis tutela vel protectione suscipimus & presenti privilegio communimus. Imprimis siquidem statuentes ut Ordo monasticus qui secundum Beati Benedicti regulam & formam Cisterciensium fratrum ibidem dinoscitur institutus, perpetuis futuris temporibus in eodem loco inviolabiliter conservetur. Preterea, quascunque possessiones, quecunque bona tam ex dono venerabilis fratris nostri Alexandri Lincolniae Episcopi quam etiam aliorum fidelium in presentiarum justè et legitimè possides, aut in futuro concessione Pontificum, liberaliter Regum vel principium, oblatione fidelium, seu aliis justis modis (auxiliante Domino) poteris adipisci, firma tibi tuis que successoribus et illibata permaneant. Sane decimas laborum vestrorum quos propriis manibus seu sumptibus excolitis vel de nutrimentis vestrorum animalium a vobis nullus exigere presumat. Nulli ergo hominem fas sit eundem Cœnobium temere perturbare aut ejus possessiones auferre, vel oblatas retinere, minuere aut aliquibus vexationibus fatigare, sed omnia integra conserventur eorum pro quorum gubernatione & sustentatione concessa sunt usibus omnimodis profutura. Si qua igitur in futurum ecclesiastica secularisve persona hanc nostrae Constitutionis paginam sciens contra eam temere venire temptaverit, secundo tertiove commonita, si non congruè satisfecerit potestatis honoris que sui dignitate careat & a Sacratissimo Corpore & Sanguine Dei & Domini Redemptoris nostri Jesu Christi aliena fiat, & in extremo examine districtae subjaceat ultioni. Conservantes autem, intervenientibus Beatorum Petri & Pauli . . . . . Omnipotentis Dei gratiam consequantur. Datum Laterani per manum Guidonis Sanctae Romanae Ecclesiae Diaconi Cardinalis & Cancellarii, quinto Iduum Martii, Indictionis tertio, Incarnationis Dominicae anno millesimo centesimo quadragesimo, Pontificatus vero Domini Innocentii II. anno duo decimo.

Ego, Innocentius, Catholicae Ecclesiae Episcopus.

Ego, Conradus, Sabinensis Episcopus.

Ego, Gerardus, presbyter titulo Sanctae Crucis.

Ego, Anselmus, presbyter Cardinalis titulo Sancti Laurentii.

Ego, Guido, Sanctae Romanae Ecclesiae indignus Sacerdos.

Ego, Gregorius, presbyter Cardinalis titulo Calixi.

Ego, Otto, diaconus Cardinalis Sancti Gregorii ad velum aureum.

Ego, Gerardus, Cardinalis diaconus Sanctae Mariae de Dalmatia.

(L. S.) On the seal the words, "S'c's Petrus—S'c's Paulus. Innocentius P. Pa. S'c'd's." Round it, "Deus Salutaris noster adjuva nos."

Eugenius, Episcopus, servus servorum Dei, dilectis filiis Everardo Abbati Monasterii Beatae Mariae, quod in Parco de Tame situm est, ejusque fratribus tam praesentibus quam futuris regularem vitam professis in perpetuum, &c. Statuentes ut quascunque possessiones, quaecunque bona in praesentiarum justè et canonicè possidetis aut in futuro concessione pontificum, liberalitate regum, largitione principum, oblatione fidelium sive aliis justis modis praestante domino poteritis adipisci, firma vobis vestrisque successoribus illibata maneant. In quibus haec propriis duximus exprimenda vocabulis. Ex dono Alexandri Episcopi Lincolniensis quicquid infra ambitum Parci continetur in terra arabili prato nemore & pastura; preterea totam terram quae fuit rusticorum circa parcum: unam culturam quae fuit de dominico ejusdem Episcopi, quae vocatur Somerlese: pratum quoddam quod vocatur Holmed; partem pasturae versus occidentem a porta veteri usque ad pontem petrinum. Ex dono Roberti Chevauchesul unam hidam terrae in Tetteswurd, sicut ejus carta testatur. Ex dono Ricardi de Vernun unam hidam in territorio de Sydenham. Ex dono Gaufridi unam hidam in territorio de Mortun cum prato et pastura eidem hidae pertinentibus. Ex dono Roberti le Gait & concessione filiorum suorum totam terram suam quam habuit in Ottendun in bosco & plano, pratis & pascuis: totam terram quae fuit Willelmi filii Othonis in territorio de Sipdune sicut ejus carta testatur, ex feodo Roberti de Tuttesbury. Ex dono Roberti de Oilli culturam quandam ex dominico suo quod est prope nemus Otteleie. Sane decimas laborum vestrorum quos propriis manibus excolitas seu sumptibus vel de nutrimentis vestrorum animalium a vobis nullus exigere presumat, &c. Datum trans Tiberim per manum Roberti Sanctae Romanae Ecclesiae Presbyteri Cardinalis & Cancellarii, Nonis Februarii, indictionis octavo, Incarnationis Dominicae anno millesimo centesimo quadragesimo sexto, Pontificatus vero Domini Eugenii Papae Tertii anno primo. Testes, quatuor Episcopi, quinque presbyteri & quatuor diaconi.

(L. S.) On the seal the words, "S'c's Petrus. S'c's Paulus. Eugenius P. Pa. Tertius." Round it, "Fac meum signum in bonum."

Alexander, Episcopus, servus servorum Dei, dilectis filiis Serloni Abbati Sancti monasterii de Thame ejusdemque fratribus tam praesentibus quam futuris regularem vitam professis in perpetuum, &c. Statuentes ut quascunque possessiones quaecunque bona in praesentiarum justè et canonicè possidetis vel in futuro concessione pontificum, liberalitate regum, largitione principum, oblatione fidelium sive aliis justis modis (praestante Domino) poteritis adipisci, firma vobis successoribus que vestris illibata maneant. Ex dono Alexandri Episcopi Lincolniensis locum ipsum in quo praescriptum Monasterium situm est qui dicitur Tama cum pertinentiis suis, sicut in Episcopi carta continetur. Ex dono Roberti Episcopi Lincolniensis molendinum & stagnum & pratum quod dicitur Trendell usque ad eum locum, quo duo rivuli per Sydenham decurrentes conveniunt. Ex dono Henrici Grangiam de Wilfeldis, & Kinelong & Rushmershegge cum pertinentiis suis. Ex dono Roberti le Gait Grangiam de Otteleia cum pertinentiis suis. Ex dono Willelmi filii Othonis Grangiam de Seypdun cum pertinentiis suis. Ex dono Roberti de Oilli terram de Westun sicut ejus Carta testatur. Ex dono Petri de Talemache, Grangiam de Stoke cum pertinentiis suis. Ex dono Roberti de Santerdon Grangiam de Santerleia. Ex dono Roberti filii Almarici & ex dono filii ejus Grangiam de Centreton cum pertinentiis suis. Ex dono Ricardi de Vernun terram de Sydenham. Ex dono Roberti de Chevauchesul terram de Tettesward. Ex dono Willelmi de Siffrewast unam hidam terrae in Nortun. Ex dono Gaufridi de Mortun unam hidam et dimidiam in Mortun. Ex dono Radulfi filii Rogeri et Adelizae uxoris ejus dimidiam hidam in Mortun cum pertinentiis suis, sicut cartae eorum testantur. Sane decimas vestrorum laborum, quos propriis manibus seu sumptibus excolitis vel de nutrimentis vestrorum animalium a vobis nullus exigere presumat. Datum Laterani per manum Alberti Sanctae Romanae Ecclesiae Presbyteri & Cardinalis.

On the seal the words, "S'c's Petrus. S'c's Paulus. Alexander P. Pa. Tertius." Round it, "Vias Tuas Domine demonstra mihi."

♣♣♣♣♣♣♣

Nomina Abbatum.

[From the Chartulary, with Additions.]

A.D. 1130. Everardus, primus Abbas.
1148. Serlo, secundus Abbas de Tame.
1184. Willielmus de Ufford.
1205. Simon, Prior de Brueria.
1225. Laurentius, quintus Abbas.
1232. Robertus de Tetteswurd.
1251. Rogerus Marcham.
1259. Ricardus Bartone.
1283. Rogerus Houlton (Howton, or Hutton).
1302. Willielmus Stratton.
1306. Johannes de Thama.
1349. Willielmus de Steyning.
1355. Johannes de Esingdon.
1361. Ricardus de Wath.
1390. John Beke, or Beek.
1445. John Blackthorne.
1509. John Warren.
1527. Robert Kyng, or King.

In addition to those tables of descents which have been printed as footnotes to pp. 344, 345, 346, and 348, the following occur in the margin of the Chartulary, and are here set forth in order:—

Morton:—

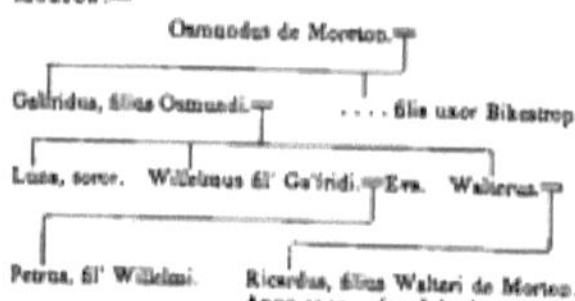

Walterus de Bikestrop. =

Johannes, filius Walteri. Milo, filius Walteri de Bikestrop.

Rogerus de Bikestrop. =

Radulphus. = Adeliza. Nicholas.

Robertus. Willielmus.

ATTENDUN :—

Fulco de Fontibus. =

Herevicius, ob. s.p. Alicia. = Hugo, Constabularius. Hugo de Braimustre. = Petronilla.

Odo, filius Hugonis. = Adeliza. Hugo de Braimustre, fil' Hug'.

SYDENHAM :—

Ricardus de Vernun, A.D. 1148. = Matilda.

Walterus, filius Ricardi. = Aubelma [or Huelmia] uxor ejus.

NORTUN :—

Radulphus de Silrewast. =

Robertus, filius Radulphi. =

Willielmus, filius Roberti.

Eustachius de Frescheville. = Dionysia, uxor.

Mylisent, filia Eustachii & Dionysiæ. =

Stephanus de Fretewell, haeres Milisent'.

Willielmus Lovell de Meostre. = Isabell', uxor ejus.

Johannes, fil' et her' Gulielmo.

Simon de Barnton. = Matilda, filia et heres Haliwæ.

Adam, haeres uxor. Hugo.

STYOUN :—

Otho. =

Willielmus, filius. = Gisle, uxor ejus.

Otho. Willielmus. Simon.

Robertus, Comes de Ferrariis. =

Robertus, Comes de Ferrariis. =

Willelmus, Comes de Ferrariis.

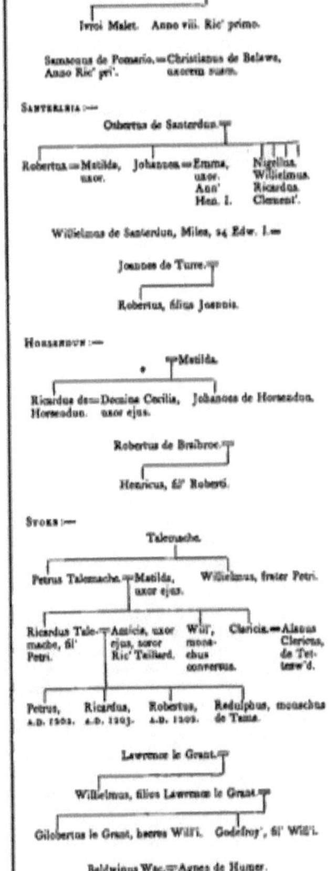

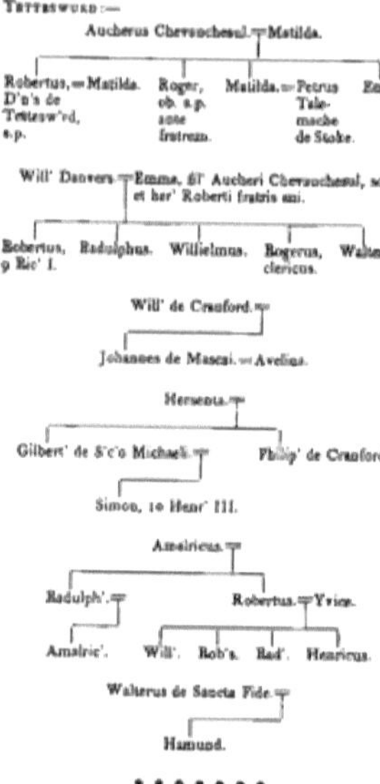

♣♣♣♣♣♣♣

From the above charters and instruments—full of interest to the Christian historian and local genealogist—may be gathered how deep a hold the Monastic system had obtained upon all classes, and how heartily and thoroughly our Catholic ancestors maintained it both by gift and bequest.

Now, in order to understand the religious and social changes which took place at Thame—at the Parish Church and Prebendal House, as well as at the stately and magnificent Abbey of Thame Park, and which enter so directly and considerably into its History—it is necessary to take a brief and faithful survey of public events in general as bearing upon those changes.

And, firstly, let it be remembered that the government of King Henry VIII., when accurately apprehended, presents a deplorable picture of injustice, tyranny, cruelty,* and oppression. His obviously insincere scruples concerning the validity of his marriage with Katherine, brought him into direct collision with the Holy See and all Christian people; while his imperious temper led him to endeavour to weaken that august spiritual authority of the One Church of God which dared to thwart his wishes. It was not Catholic doctrines to which he objected—for these he had defended by his wits and pen—but the Church's authority when fairly and faithfully exercised in the case of monarchs as well as their subjects. It was not, moreover, the supposed vices of the religious orders—regarding which both Lying and Greed, as well as Forgery did so much to help forward the covetous King's designs—but the rich lands, goodly manors, and sacred treasures of the religious, which long lines of self-denying benefactors had from time to time bestowed upon them; not as absolute owners, however, but only as faithful trustees. Old-fashioned Christians, who denied Henry's ridiculous and blasphemous title of "Head of the Church," he simply ordered to be drawn, hung, and quartered; while those who dared to oppose his wishes when he was intent on robbery and sacrilege, or who failed to change their belief as promptly as he changed his, were sent to the block. With a contemptibly servile Parliament he made himself personally absolute—his own outrageous Proclamations having the force of law. But though he plundered the Church without mercy, obtained by theft thousands of gold and silver chalices and other sacred vessels, yet twice without scruple he repudiated his own debts. Having with the consent of Parliament three times settled the succession to the Crown, and on each occasion differently, he was nevertheless permitted subsequently to dispose of it by his last Will and Testament, as though it had been his own private estate. Those who might have withstood his imperious will, and checked his disastrous policy, had long ago passed away from the scene.

Thomas Cromwell had more than once urged upon the King that the influence of the Monks, who were generally opposed to laxity and change, should be curbed by some bold stroke of confiscation (a principle already admitted by Cardinal Wolsey); and at length Cromwell's arguments had their desired effect. Where any monastery was in debt, or its internal affairs were found to be in the least degree mismanaged; where dilapida-

* This great and benevolent monarch ratified and approved of an Act of Parliament, suggested by himself, by which prisoners were ordered to be boiled to death (22 Henry VIII., chapter 19); beggars and vagabonds to be whipped, stocked, pilloried, and have their ears cut off. The opponents of his royal will, from his mistress Anne Boleyne and Sir Thomas More, the upright and high-principled Chancellor, to the meanest monastic lay-brother, found no mercy, and experienced no pity. In truth, he spared neither woman in his lust, nor man in his anger.

tions existed, or any moral weakness of those in authority could be magnified into a crime—confiscation would be easily enough compassed. The work, as Cromwell wisely pointed out, must be done with due art, by degrees, carefully; and in such a manner as to enlist a sufficient number of the impecunious and ignoble nobility upon the side of Robbery and Wrong. Huge bribes, with an ample share of the spoils for the unprincipled co-operators, would no doubt produce the desired result. In many cases such were freely offered and thankfully received. That such a policy, appealing to men's lowest and basest motives, triumphed, History has abundantly shewn.

John Williams, in conjunction with Richard Pollard, Philip Paris and John Smythe (Lord of Willicote, co. Leicester), were amongst the Commissioners appointed in and for the suppression of the Abbeys. They appear to have done their work discreetly and with effect. In a Letter* to Thomas Cromwell concerning the Abbey of Bury St. Edmund's, they admit having taken in gold no less a sum than five thousand marks from that house alone, with other treasures in proportion. Williams was also at Ely, about the same period, where he assisted in the progressive work of suppression and confiscation. In conjunction with Richard Pollard and Thomas Wriothesley, he was likewise at Winchester, from which place he wrote the following characteristic Letter to Lord Cromwell, to which also Thomas Wriothesley and Richard Pollard affixed their signatures. The Letter itself, here reproduced as written, redolent with cant and hypocrisy, occupies two sides of a folio sheet of paper.

"Pleaseth Your Lordship to be advertised, that this Saturdaye in the mornyng aboutes thre of the clok, we made an end of the shryne here, at Wynchestre. There was in it no pece of gold, ne oon ring, or true stone, but al greate counterfaictes. Nevertheles we thinke the sylver alone thereof woll amounte to neere twoo thousand markes. We have also receyved in to our possession the cross of emeraudes, the cross called Hierusalem, an other crosse of gold, a chalices of gold, with some sylver plate, parcel of the portion of the vestrye; but th' old Prior made the plate of the house too thynne, that we can diminish none of it, and leave the Prior anything furnished. We found the Prior and all the convent very conformable; having assistentes with us, at the opening of our charge to the same, the Mayre with 8 or 9 of the best of his brethren, the Bishops chauncelour, Mr. Doctour Craiforde, with a good appearance of honest personages besides, who with oon voyce most hartley gave laude and praise to God and to the Kings Majestye, thinking verily that they do all asmoch rejoice of His Majesties godly and christian purpose herin as can be desired. We have also this morning going to our beddes ward, viewed th' aulter, which we purpose to bring with us. It wolbe worthe the taking down, and nothing thereof seen; but such a pece of work it is, that we think we shall not rid it, doing our best, before Monday night, or Tuesdaye mornyng, which done, we entende both at Hide & St. Maryes, to swepe away all the roten bones that be called reliques; which we may not omytt, lest it should be thought we care more for the treasure, thenne for avoiding of th' abomination of ydolatry. Other thinges, as farre as we canne lerne, there be none for us in those places; which things doon, and our things set outward, we shall attend upon your lordship with diligence."

Williams, in conjunction with Dr. John London, took a leading part in similar work at Reading, at Eynsham, Oxon, at Notley Abbey, Bucks, and at the Priory of Donnington, near Newbury. The plate of the first two was carefully secured; that at Donnington, however, was of such little value as not to have been worth taking away.

The writ for authorizing an enquiry concerning the Oxfordshire Abbey lands—preparatory to carrying out the scheme of seizing and confiscating them—had been dated at Westminster, on the 30th of January in the twenty-sixth year of the reign of Henry VIII., in 1534-5, and was addressed to William Freurs, Mayor of Oxford; to William Tresham, Vice-Chancellor of the University; to William Barentyne, Simon Harcourt, Walter Stonor, John Clerk, Thomas Ellyott, and John Browne, knights; to William Fermor, Thomas Carter, John More, William Raynesford, John Williams, Anthony Cope, John Denton, John Pollard, Richard Greneburst, Thomas Wayneman, gentlemen; and to Robert Huckvale, Henry Combis, Christopher Huckvale, and Richard Cripps, auditors.

It by no means follows that all those therein named were favourers of confiscation, or that all were on the look-out for what they could get. Some were unquestionably men of blood and renown, honest and religious. Others, as events shewed, were only too ready to become subservient to Authority, on the single condition that their own painful labours and ostentatious perseverance were in due course adequately rewarded.

The Report of the Commissioners—in which the few determined and dominant agitators easily overruled the majority—was wholly unworthy of credit. The religious were condemned unheard; while the most loose and slanderous assertions of interested enemies were eagerly taken for truth, repeated and disseminated. The gross violations of justice too often apparent in the proceedings of Parliament; the willingness of the legal authorities to oppress those who appeared disposed to resist the King's will; and the readiness with which the carefully-selected tools of the change-mongers often maintained that white was black and black white—all conducted to the final and deplorable issue. Lying, Injustice, Chicanery, and Oppression, in a compact and active combination tinctured with revolting cant, and

* Cotton MSS., Brit. Museum, Cleopatra, E. IV., fol. 229.

often eloquently using Scripture phrases, did their work directly and efficiently.

Several particulars concerning the state of the Abbey of Thame Park, ten years previously, are embodied in a Report made to the Bishop of Lincoln in the month of February, 1525, from the then Abbot, John Warren, preserved in one of the Register-Books of John Longland, at Lincoln. The nature of this Report, no doubt, led the Bishop of Lincoln to secure the election of Robert King on the death of John Warren, two years afterwards. King, of a Thame family, was evidently a most conscientious dignitary, but of somewhat elastic and flexible principles, and exceedingly well adapted for co-operation in the work already commenced. The Abbey of Thame Park, at the period in question, was rich in sacred vessels. There were nine chalices, three of silver-gilt enamelled, and six of silver partly gilt. There were three large solid altar-crosses, one of gold, adorned with gems, having a foot of silver-gilt, and others of silver encrusted with jewels. There were also three pastoral staves for the Abbot, one of gold and silver, the other two of copper-gilt. There were likewise two silver-gilt thuribles or censers, with incense-boats of the same metal to correspond: a large pair of silver-gilt candlesticks for the High Altar, and a pix of silver-gilt, besides other *ornamenta* of inferior metal.

As regards vestments there appear to have been no less than thirty-eight complete silken sets, of various colours, embroidered by English hands, for Low and High Mass; the former, for the Priest alone, consisting of amice, alb, girdle, stole, chasuble, and maniple; and the latter, for Priest, Deacon, and Subdeacon, consisting, in addition to those for the Priest, of the customary tunics and dalmatics for the appointed assistant-ministers of the altar. There were likewise rich hangings of silk and stuff, embroidered altar-frontals, cere-cloths for the altar-stones; hangings of foreign weaving for the reredoses, canopies, lecterns, and prayer-stools; carpets, cushions, linen cloths and towels, and the usual contents of the Sacristy of a well-ordered monastic Church.

There was also a fair amount of silver and silver-gilt plate for the Refectory, donations to the Abbey by various benefactors, made from time to time, consisting of dishes, drinking-cups, standing-cups, plates, bowls, salt-cellars, and spoons.

The cattle and corn of the Abbey were likewise reckoned up and its amount in various kinds duly set forth.

On the other hand, the debts of the Monastery were considerable, and were thus recorded:—

Firstly, to Mr (subsequently Sir John) Dawns, xxli.
Likewise to the Vicar of Thame, xxxli.
Likewise to David Lewis, xvli.
Likewise to Richard Lambert, xili.
Likewise to Henry Baldwyne, xili.
Likewise to James de Dene, vli.

Mr. Dawnes, a resident at Thame, was connected by office with the Abbey of Notley, being Steward of the demesne lands, and appears to have been sometimes engaged in raising money for the religious of other houses, when, through any misfortune—dangerous floods, a bad harvest, a blight on the corn, or murrain amongst their cattle—they found themselves in any temporary financial difficulty. He also assisted them in pawning their plate to the London goldsmiths, in securing large fines when leases of lands were granted at a small and low rent, and himself managed to benefit by such transactions. He was in alliance with John Williams, John Croke, Roger Lee, Edward Dyer, William Typper, Richard Wenman, and Robert Dawe, a sample of the impecunious worthies, who, like unclean birds scenting from afar approaching death and decomposition, hovered near to feast upon their anticipated prey.

But to proceed with the narrative of facts. So soon as the governors and officials of any religious house—many of whom had been expressly put into authority to betray their sacred trusts—were known to be ready to surrender it, the Commissioners (who had been well supplied with carefully-drawn-up forms to be signed, engrossed on parchment) obtained the needful signatures, and then proceeded to break the official seal of the community, and to assign pensions to its members at once dismissed. On the 4th of December of the year 1539 the Abbey of Eynsham had been suppressed, the authorities having duly surrendered to Sir John Williams and others. Williams had likewise received the surrender of the Prioress and nuns of the Benedictine Nunnery of Studley on the 19th of November, 1539. In the month of August two years previously, this convent, with fifteen other nunneries and five abbeys, had been temporarily spared, because no fault whatsoever had been found, nor could be found, with their inmates; but now the decree for suppression had gone forth, and was to be carried out. In the work of apportioning pensions Sir William Cavendish, Richard Gwent, and John Carleton were associated with Williams, who, having acted as Receiver, had already adroitly secured the grant of the lands. The Prioress, the "Ladye Joane Williams,"* was evidently a kinswoman of the latter, and received for her pension £16 5s. 8d. per annum. Richard Ridge, the last Abbot of Notley, a Berkshire man, seems to have been

* These pensions are set forth on folio 107 of a well-known Pension Book in the Record Office, relating to the Court of Augmentations.

a somewhat pliable cleric. On the 6th of September, 1537, he too acknowledged the new doctrine of the King's supremacy; and two years afterwards, that is on 9th December, 1539, together with thirteen of his monks, surrendered the Abbey to the King, as the Abbot of Eynsham had done, and received a pension of a hundred marks a year, which he enjoyed until his death in 1583. In almost every case the monastic church was at once unroofed and destroyed—under the reasonable and well-grounded fear that, if this were not done promptly, an angry populace might possibly insist on driving off the knightly thieves and legal robbers, and in re-installing the outcast monks in their old homes. The fittings of the church, choir, and chapels, the lead from the roofs, the bells from the steeple, and the cattle and farm produce were sold—the proceeds being paid into the newly-created Augmentation Office.* The plate and the jewels of altar, shrine, and sanctuary were specially reserved for the personal use of the "Supreme Head of the Church."

At Thame Park the Dissolution and Suppression had obviously been temporarily postponed for some good and sufficient cause. The Abbot, Robert King, a shrewd and far-seeing personage of elastic principles, was evidently in favour of Henry VIII.'s policy, and was a temporizer and time-server. His family† had made alliances with the Williamses *alias* Cromwells—all the members of which appear to have been on the look-out for the good things of the present World; and, from the outset of his career, Robert King had been found on the side of the more cautious and calculating innovators. He was indebted to Bishop John Longland, of Lincoln, and to Cardinal Wolsey* for

* The officers of the Court of Augmentations, of which Williams was one, believed it to be their duty to examine with great strictness the terms of any recent grants by the monastic authorities of their official lands and manors. Many of the Visitors or Commissioners, however, had already secured for themselves or their relatives long leases at low rents of various lands and manors, and John Williams was one of these. He was, nevertheless, compelled to disgorge his possessions relating to Notley Abbey; but the leases he had surreptitiously secured from his relation, Robert King, Abbot of Thame Park, after some change and rearrangement, were retained by him with more recent privileges and advantages, and,—though surrendered to the Duke of Somerset for awhile,—were regranted by King James I. to the husband of Williams's daughter Wenman.

† PEDIGREE OF KING, OF THAME AND WORMINGHALL, CO. BUCKS.

Arms of King: *Sable, a lion rampant crowned between three crosslets or.*

John King, yeoman, Churchwarden of Thame in the years 1464, 1465, and 1469.

William King, of Thame, yeoman; born *circa* 1450, living in 1508. =
John King, of Bicester, co. Oxon, vintner, from whom the Kings of the City of London claim descent.

William King, of Thame and Worminghall, co. Bucks, gent. = Anne, daughter of Sir John Williams, of Burghfield, Knt., and sister of "Lady Joane Williams," Prioress of Studley, co. Oxon, and of Sir John Williams, of Thame.

Robert King, Abbot of Bruerne 1515, Abbot of Thame 1527, last Abbot of Oseney, first Bishop of Oxford.

"Hic jacet Robertus Kyng sacre theologie professor et primus Ep'us Oxon. qui obiit quarto die Decembris, 1557."—*Inscription in Ch. Ch. Cathedral, Oxford.*

A

A

Philip King, of Thame and Worminghall, page to King Henry VIII., and subsequently in the service of John, Lord Williams of Thame. Died 12 Jan., 1592. M.I. at Worminghall. = Elizabeth, daughter of Edmund Conquest, of Houghton Conquest, co. Beds.

John King, born at Worminghall aforesaid *circa* 1559; Student of Ch. Ch., 1576; Archdeacon of Nottingham, 13 Aug., 1590; D.D., 1602; Dean of Ch. Ch., 1605; Bishop of London, 1611. Died 30 March, 1621; buried in St. Paul's Cathedral. = Joane, daughter of Henry Freeman, of Staffordshire.

Other issue (twelve children in all).

Henry King, born at Worminghall aforesaid. Baptized 16 Jan., 1591. Educated at Thame Grammar School and at Westminster. Student of Ch. Ch., 1608; Dean of Rochester, 6 Feb., 1638; Bishop of Chichester in 1641. Died 30 Sep., 1669; buried at Chichester. Will dated 14 July 1653, proved 18 Nov., 1669. = Ann, eldest daughter of Robert Berkeley, Esq. Married *circa* 1617. Buried in St. Paul's Cathedral.

John King, Student of Ch. Ch., 1608; Canon of the same, 1624; Canon of Windsor Chapel, 1625; Rector of Remenham, co. Berks. Died 2 Jan., 1638, aged 43. Buried in Ch. Ch. Cathedral, Oxford.

John King, Esq., of Boycote, co. Kent, eldest son of Henry King, Bishop of Chichester, matriculated at Ch. Ch., Oxford, 16 Sep. 1637. He married Anne Hannah Russell, daughter of Sir William Russell, of Strensham, co. Worcester; died 10 March, 1671, and was buried near his father in Chichester Cathedral. Will dated 20th and 24th May, 1670; proved 5th April, 1671.

There are portraits of the Kings, Bishops of London and Chichester, in the Hall of Ch. Ch., and an imaginary representation of Robert King, first Bishop of Oxford, in a cope, with alb, amice, mitre, gloves, and pastoral staff, on stained glass in one of the Cathedral windows.

From the Old Register Book of Worminghall, co. Bucks. "Philippus Kynge Gen. sepultus erat decimo quarto die Januarii, 1592.—1606-7. Elizabetha Kinge, vidua, sepulta erat 21° Martii An'o supradicto."

Philip King, of Worminghall, had a brother, Edward King, of Shabbington, co. Bucks, who married Jane, daughter of William Belson of Brill. His children were—1. William King, of Cadmore, in the parish of Lewknor; 2. Arthur, of Thame; 3. Thomas, of Towersey, who married Susan, daughter of Edmund Powell, of Sandford, co. Oxon.

* "On the 20th January, 1529—(this surmised date is evidently wrong, it should be 1527—F. G. L.)—Dr. John Longland, Bishop of Lincoln, wrote to Cardinal Wolsey, Bishop of Winchester, informing him that the Abbot of the Cistercian Monastery of Thame, in Oxfordshire, had died on the 18th. There was no one in the monastery fit to succeed him, and the house was greatly in debt. The Bishop, as patron of the monastery, being anxious to promote religion there, requested the Cardinal to send a letter to the Abbot of Waverley, the Visitor of the Cistercians, in favour of Dom. Kynge, D.D., Abbot of Bruerne, otherwise the house would be undone.[1] John, Abbot of Waverley, in 1529, was present at the Convocation of the clergy held at St. Paul's Cathedral."[2] [1] State Paper, No. 5,189, Foreign and Domestic Series. [2] *Ibid.*, No. 6,047. —*The Abbey of the Blessed Virgin of Waverley.* By F. J. Baigent, p. 41. London: 1882.

some important preferment. The former, on 15th April, 1535, or as some say seven years previously,* had made him one of his suffragan bishops, with the title of Bishop of Rheon. Without their aid he might have remained in his original obscurity. It is clear, however, that he made everything smooth and easy for the State Authorities, and walked with complacent gratitude into the new and pleasant groove which had been cut out for him. When Thame Abbey was suppressed he became Abbot of Osney, and in due course, *i.e.* 1st Sep., 1542, Bishop of Thame and Osney, and afterwards, *i.e.* 9th June, 1545, Bishop of Oxford.

In the actual Deed of Surrender, dated 16th Nov., 31 Henry VIII., *i.e.* 1540,† the Abbot styles himself "Robartus Kynge, Dei patientia, Reouens' ep'us, Abbasque Monasterii B'te Marie Virginis de Tayme, in Com' Oxon. Cisterciens' ordin'." He and his monks gave up "to the most illustrious and most unconquered Prince and Lord, Henry VIII.," "all and singular their manors, houses, messuages, gardens, curtilages, tofts, lands, tenements," etc. The signatures stand thus:—

Robertus Kynge, Abbas de Tama.
Ricardus Grene, p'or.
William Ovaffile.
Robert's Thomas.
Per Me John' Welsh, subpriorem.
P' Richardus How.

Christofer Brystwyck.*
Henry Bulytmer.
Rychard Brysto'.
Will'mus Forrest.
Will'm' Osburne.
Rychardi Stevyns.
Wyllya' Wylby.

The following signature of the Abbot is taken from another document—a list of persons present at a Convocation of the Clergy in 1535—and is a little bolder and more compact than that of the same dignitary attached to the above Deed of Surrender:—

Robertus Abbas de thama

(Autograph of Robert Kyng, or King, last Abbot of Thame.)

The seal of the Abbey attached to the Deed of Surrender is of red wax, much defaced. It represents under a crocketted canopy a seated figure of Our

* The dates with regard to Robert King's appointment as Bishop of Rheon are very conflicting. The following is from Dr. Maziere Brady's valuable book, *The Episcopal Succession in England, Scotland, and Ireland*, Vol. I., p. 115. Rome: 1876:—"Die 7° Jan., 1527, referente R. D. Card. Campegio, providit ecclesie Reonen' in part. inf. in provincia Constantinopol', certo modo vacanti, de persona D. Roberti Kinge, abbatis Monasterii S'te Mariae de Thame, Lincoln' dioc' concessitque ut possit exercere pontificalia in civitate et diocesi Lincolnen' tantum, cum pensione 50ª marcarum ster' super fructibus Ecclesiae Lincolnen', de consensu episcopi, donec providéatur de tot beneficiis usque ad dictam summam. Et cum retentione Monasterii predicti et dispensatione ad tria secularia et regularia, et quod possit benedicere et dare indulgentias prout alii episcopi. Et quod gaudeat privilegiis Ord' Cisterrcien' non obstante quod sit episcopus," etc.

† The following is the exact text of this Deed:—"Omnibus x'pi fidelibus ad quos p'nts Scriptu' n'rum p'venit Robertus Kynge Dei patientia Reonen' ep'us, Abbasq' Monasterii B'te Marie virginis de Tayme in Com' Oxon' Cistercien' ordinis et eiusd' loci co'ventus Sal'tm in d'no sempiterna'. Noveritis nos prefat' Abb'em et conventu' unanimi co'sensu et assensu n'ris, animis deliberat', Certaq' scie'tia et mero motu n'ris, ex quibusd' ca'is iustis r'onabilib' et l'timis nos a'imas et co'scie'tias n'ras sp'ialit' moven', ultro et sponte dedisse et co'cessisse, ac p' p'n't dam' co'cedim' reddim' deliberam' et co'firmam' Illustriss' et Invictissimo Principi et d'no n'ro Henrico octavo Dei gr'a Anglie et Francie Regi fidei defensori d'no Hib'nie, ac in terris sup'mo eccl'e anglicane sub Ch'r'o capiti totum d'cum monasterio' n'r'm de Tayme pred', ac totu' scitu' fundu' circuitum et preciactu' eiusd' Monasterii de Tayme necnon o'i'a et sing'la maneria domos mesuagia gardina curtilag' toft' terras et ten'ta prata pascua pasturas boscos redditus rev'sio'es s'uic' molendin' passag' feod' milita' ward' maritagia, nativos villanos cu' eor' sequela, co'ias libertates franchesias iur'm officia, cur' let' hundred' vis' franciplag' feria mercat' parcos warren', vivaria aquas piscarias, vias chimina vacuos fundos advocaco'es nominaco'es p'nta'm et donaco'es eccl'iar' vicariar' capellar' ca'tariar' hospitaliu', et alior' b'n'ficior' eccl'iastic' quoru'cu'q' r'ctorias vicarias ca'tarias porc'oes pensio'es annuitates deci'as oblaco'e', ac o'i'a et sing'la emolume'ta p'ficua possessio'es h'editame'ta, et Jura n'ra quecu'q' tam infra d'cum Com' Oxon' q' infra co'itat' Bark' Lincoln' Huntyngton' Buckyngh'm Bedforde et Northehampton', et alibi infra regnu' Anglie, Wallie et H'ibiar' eoru'd' eidem Monasterio de Tayme quoquom° p'tinen' spectan' appendes' sive incumbentium, ac o'imod' chartas evide'tias scripta et munime'ta n'ra, d'co monasterio de Tayme, ac man'iis terris ten'tis et ceteris p'missis cu' p'tin', seu alicui' inde p'celle, quoquom° spectan' aut conc'nentia. H'endum tenend' et gaudend' d'tum Monasteriu' scitu' fundu' circuitum et p'cinctum de Tayme pred' terrasq' ten'ta et cetera p'miss' cu' om'ib' et sing'lis suis p'tinen' prefat' Invictissimo' Principi et d'no n'ro regi hered' et assign' suis in p'petuu' cui in hac p'te ad o'em iuris eff'ctum qui exinde sequi poterit aut potest, Nos et d'cum Monasterio' de Tayme pred', ac o'ia iura nobis qual'rcu'q' acquisit' (ut decet) subiicim' et submittim', Dantes et co'cedentes eidem Regie magestati hered' et assign' suis o'em et o'imod' plena' et libera' facultate' auct'item et p'tatem, Nos et d'cum Monasteriu' de Tayme pred' vna cu' o'ibus et sing'lis maneriis terris ten'tis red'd' rev'sionibus s'uiciis et sing'lis p'miss' cu' suis Jurib' et p'tinen' vniu'sis quibuscu'q' disponend', ac p' suo libero regiae volu'tat' et libito ad quoscu'q' vsus suo maiestati placen' alienand' donand' conu'tend' et transferr'd' h'mo'i dispo'ons alienacio'es donacio'es conu'sio'es et translacio'es p' maiestate' suam quovismodo fiend' extu'c ratificam', rat' et grat', ac p'petuo firm' h'bitur' p'mittim' p' p'nt' et et premissa o'ia et sing'la suu' debitu' sortiri valeant effcum, electio'ib' itaq' nob' et Successo'ib' n'ris necno' o'ibus querelis p'vocac'o'ib' appellac'o'ib' actio'ibus litib' et instantiis aliisq' quibuscu'q' juris remediis et b'neficiis, nobis et successorib' n'ris in ea p'te p'textu dispo'nis alienacio'is translacio'is et conu'sio'is pred' ac ceteror' p'miss' qual'rcumq' co'peten' et co'petitur', o'ibusq' doli erroris metus ignorantie vel alteri' materie siue dispo'nis excep'onib' obiectio'ib' et allegacio'ib' procsus frivolis et deposit', pala' pu'm et expresse, ex cert' n'ra scie'tia animisq' spontaneis renu'tiavim' et cessim' p'ut p' p'nt' renu'tiam' et cedim' et ab eisdem recedim' in hiis scriptis. Et nos pred'ci Abbas et Co'vent' et successores n'ri, d'cm monasterium prediact' scitu' mansio'em et eccl'iam de Tayme pred' ac o'ia et sing'la maneria domos mesuagia gardina curtilag' toft' prat' pascua pastur' boscos subboscos terr' ten'ta ac o'ia et sing'la cetera p'miss' cu' suis p'tinen' univ'a prefat' d'no n'ro regi hered' et assign' suis cont' o'es gentes warra'tizam' imp'petuu' p' p'nt'. In quor' o'ium et sing'lor' fidem et testimo'm nos prefat' Abbas et Co'ventus huic p'nt' scripto sigillu' n'rm co'e apponi fecim'. Dat' in domo n'ra cap'lari Monasterii pred' decimo sexto die mens' Novembris Anno Regni d'ci Illustris d'ni n'ri Henrici octavi tricesimo primo."

* Of this family was Reginald Brystwyck, Churchwarden of Thame in 1497, Christopher Brystwyk in 1515, and another Christopher in 1532 and 1533.

Blessed Lady with her Holy Child, having on either side under smaller canopies two other figures of saints, or, it may be, of angels. At the base there is an arch under which is no doubt a kneeling figure, much obliterated, of Sir Robert Le Gait the founder.

The legend is S' Com'une B' Marie de Tame.

The arms of the Abbey, represented in the woodcut at the head of this Chapter, and also in the left-hand corner of the illustration at its commencement, are—Argent, on a chief sable, two heads of pastoral staves of the first.

Amongst the unarranged deeds remaining in the Bodleian Library is one with the personal seal of Robert Howton, Abbot of Thame, attached. It is of green wax, much defaced and worn. My attention having been called to it by the late Mr. W. H. Turner, I made a drawing of it, from which the accompanying woodcut was produced.

Seal of Robert Howton, Abbot of Thame, A.D. 1283.

At the close of the year 1540, it was found that no less than 665 monasteries—of which 29 had been governed by mitred abbots who sat in Parliament—had been suppressed and their revenues confiscated. In addition to these, 90 well-endowed Colleges with their magnificent Collegiate Churches, 2374 Chantries and free Chapels mainly set up by private munificence, and 110 hospitals for the aged poor and sick, for travellers and lepers, were utterly swept away. Amongst these were the Abbeys of Dorchester, Notley, Osney, Eynsham, Medmenham, Missenden, and Rewley, and, in addition to Chantries, the religious houses of Studley, Nether Winchendon, and Aylesbury, in the more immediate neighbourhood of Thame. Some of the razed Churches of these Houses of Religion were three times or four times as large as the Parish Church of Thame. Those of Rewley, Osney, and Eynsham had been perfectly magnificent both in size and proportions. The enormous spoils in money and plate and the valuable goods seized throughout the kingdom amounted to a very large sum. But these spoils often perished in the hands of the graspers.* Misfortune and Misery tracked their pathway. Though honours and dignities were bestowed upon them in abundance, these soon perished. Their heirs died in youth, and their daughters were smitten with barrenness or wasted away. Their ill-gotten lands were soon taken by strangers, and their hated names silently cursed or forgotten. Monarch, baron, and knight thus alike suffered.

The obvious object of King Henry and his advisers, in this work of destruction, was to break the power and destroy the legitimate and beneficent influence of the religious houses, whose members, with but very few exceptions, were unanimously in favour of preserving the visible unity of the Church, and altogether opposed to the newly-invented Royal Supremacy, as well as to the King's divorce of his lawful wife. In this work of destruction, however, the Monarch's aim was distinctly and directly accomplished.

At this period many of the old families, noble and gentle, had either died out, were sinking steadily to a lower social level, or their surviving members owned neither pluck nor power to resist the innovators, or to repel a small army of half-ruined and impecunious gentlemen and pushing scriveners, who—perceiving the course of events—only waited for a reasonable opportunity to secure their anticipated prey.

* "Since all arguments *à priori* must be, at the best, uncertain, we proceed onwards, and assert that if it be true that at the very commencement of this sacrilege an evil fate seemed to hang over those who were principally concerned in, or who chiefly profited by, it: that the chief actors perished in the most miserable and unusual manners; that of two hundred and sixty gentlemen who reaped the largest profits from their iniquity, scarcely sixty left an heir to their name and estate; that by the scaffold, by murder, by unprecedented accidents, in misery, in poverty, in crime, in contempt, the majority of the Church spoilers ended their mortal existence; that men, at the time, avoided them as accursed persons, or pointed them out as instances of the terrible justice of God; that the same fate, from that time to this, has followed the posterity of the offenders; that of all families, theirs have been the most miserable; that of all fearful judgments, by far the greater part have visited their *descendants*: if it be true that, at this very time, the curse is powerful to their evil; that, to this very day, fire, and robbery, and sickness, in such households, do their work; that male heirs fail; that jealousy springs up between man and wife, that unnatural hatred between parents and children; that a sickly season carries off one, a violent *death* another; that speculations go wrong; that thief consumes, and moth destroys; that the curse evermore broods over its victims with its dry and tearless eyes, crossing them in their best-laid plans, entrapping them in an inextricable web, perplexing, and harassing, and impoverishing, and weakening, and ruining, and only leaving them when the last heir is laid in the family vault; that no analogy of human justice, no appeal to human law, no reference to past tolerance of the Church, no allegations of supposed impossibilities, can shield the offender; that instances of God's hitherto forbearance, alleged by any that would thence deduce the innocence of their sacrilege, prove only that their judgment now of a long time lingereth not, and their condemnation slumbereth not,—then, we say, the infatuation of such as retain these possessions, that wilfully shut their eyes to their dangers, that hazard family and prosperity, wife and children, body and soul, daring God to do His worst, and refusing to own that whom He blesseth is blessed and whom He curseth cursed, is nothing short of judicial."—*The History and Fate of Sacrilege*, by Sir Henry Spelman, Kt. London: Printed for John Hartley over against Gray's Inn in Holborn, 1698.

In the neighbourhood of Thame many an obscure but daring person, thrusting himself to the forefront by art and chicanery, and fawning obsequiously upon those in authority, who were ready to make use of his services, and occasionally to borrow his money, soon gained the object of his desire and hope. The Dormers, though Catholics, secured a large share in the monastic spoils, Wing being a portion of the lands of St. Alban's Abbey, and Lee Grange a part of the possessions of the Abbey of Thame Park; the Lenthalls of Latchford did the same, obtaining Burford Priory. John Pollard* grasped much that was valuable from the proceeds of confiscation and robbery; so likewise did Christopher Edmonds, son of Sir John Williams's† first wife. In truth, the whole of this man Williams's near relations—his two wives' kinsmen, both male and female, his two surviving co-heiresses, his grandfather's numerous descendants, his cousins' children and their uncles, and those political allies who had helped a beggar-on-horseback to mount the saddle—were all generously remembered when the religious houses were robbed. In the age of the Tudors, the great principle of being truly liberal with other people's property was then elevated to a science, and regarded as a noble virtue, and has invariably remained such in the opinion of many, even to the present day. John Croke, a lawyer, secured the Priory of Studley, and its possessions, receiving a grant of the same from King Harry on 26th Feb., 1540; John Williams obtained Notley Abbey, and its site,‡ Thame Park and its Abbey and appurtenances, and numerous other lands and manors.§ Richard Crispe, who had been Auditor of the Priory of Studley, likewise secured several grants—and added to the wealth of his race, at Cobcutt, near Thame, from Church spoils. Lamp-lands, belonging to Thame Church, in the parish of Crendon were given to one person; the possessions of the Chantry of St. Christopher to another.‖ Sometimes the action taken by individuals to benefit themselves was not generally observed; or, if observed, winked at. Ecclesiastical property and the lands of "corporations sole" were so carefully dealt with by exchange, re-arrangement and legal art, under the guidance of "Reformers," that many ancient benefactions to our Catholic ancestors—passing from public to private hands—were absolutely and totally lost. The only gain to anybody fell to the lot of adroit thieves, who, flinging away relic and rosary, piously blessed God for having obtained the "Ten Commandments in English" for the general populace—Commandments, however, which they themselves failed to respect and made but slight efforts to obey.

The Abbey of Thame Park, thus surrendered, was mainly of first-pointed architecture, severe in its style, dignified in its size, and complete in its well-arranged and extensive plan. It is believed to have been arranged in three large squares. It comprised Hall, Frater-House, Dormitory, Lavatory, Chapter-House, Refectory, Cloisters, and Kitchen. There was likewise a special range of buildings in an outer court, towards the north, known as the Guest-House, with servants' apartments, and stables for the horses of strangers. There was also a Burial Ground, and a grand Church. This latter, cruciform in plan, with a Lady Chapel at the east end, was of course its chief feature, towering far above the other Abbey-buildings. Near the chief entrance, outside the gateway, was a Chapel for visitors, strangers, wayfarers, and others who lived near. The Abbot's lodgings, in a later architectural style, were on the south side. Portions of these still remain, mutilated. This picturesque range of buildings, mainly of the fifteenth century, consists of an embattled Tower of three stories, marked out by string-courses, with an octagonal stair-turret at the corner, rising above the cresting of the Tower, and a range of rooms having two double bay-windows of stone, picturesquely placed, in both stories. Another smaller staircase in the south wall of this portion formerly led from the rooms beneath to those above. Including the inferior offices, with farm buildings, granaries, barns, and stables, nearly three acres and a half were covered. These farm buildings, wool-barns, orchards, fishponds, and gardens were also very extensive. But, after the Abbey Church had been cleared out of all its fittings and destroyed, many of the buildings of the adjacent monastery—such, for example, as the Chapter House and the Monks' Dormitory—were allowed to go to ruin. They were not wanted by Sir Richard Wenman and his lady; hence their destruction.

* Ford Abbey, another Cistercian House, mentioned in the Preface to the Thame Chartulary, was situated in the Parish of Thorncombe, co. Devon. The site of this House had been secured by Richard Pollard (a co-Commissioner with John Williams); but his son, Sir John Pollard, one of the Oxfordshire Commissioners, alienated it, and it speedily passed to other owners.

† John Goodwin of Wooburn Deincourt had a son of the same name, who was knighted. The latter married Katherine, daughter of Thomas Bledlowe, one of Sir John Williams's connections, and had a son William, who bought the manor of Nether Winchendon, from Francis, Earl of Bedford, son of John, Lord Russell, one of the most conspicuous and successful of the ruffians of the Reformation.

‡ In 1547, Edward VI. granted to Sir William Paget, his heirs and assigns, the site of Notley Abbey, and reversion of the premises, formerly demised to Sir John Williams and Roger Lee of Thame. *Patent Roll*, 1 Edw. VI. (30 of May).

§ For the details, taken from existing documents, and authentic records, see the personal account of this worthy later on.

‖ In 1549, King Edward VI., on the petition of Sir John Williams, and for the sum of £71 6s. 8d., granted to him certain lands in Crendon, late belonging to a dissolved Chantry or Guild of St. Christopher in Thame Church. The details of lands in Thame, Hughendon and elsewhere, are set forth later on.

The practical loss which the town of Thame and its neighbourhood sustained by the suppression of the Monasteries and the robbery of the Parish Church was far greater than is generally realized. The monks, being merely trustees for life, were reasonable and charitable in the granting of leases and privileges, and made admirable landlords. Often bound to the families who lived near, by ties of kinship, as well as by the fact that the ancestors of these families had often been benefactors of the Abbey, and were sometimes buried in its precincts, these monks were thoroughly devoted to the practice of true religion, measuring all things by a higher standard than that adopted by persons living in the world. Thus their influence was for good. Moreover, their charities were considerable, and their practical care for the poor and infirm quite in harmony with Christian traditions. These latter, as a consequence, were weakened under the guidance of men whose vast and far-reaching revolution was of such a nature that its active evils live and energize and multiply even at the present day. The destructionists of the sixteenth century were the heralds of the Great Rebellion and the Commonwealth, the precursors of the Revolution, and the preparers of the way for the Radicals and Communists of the present period.

Two hundred years after the Surrender much larger portions of the old Abbey—several low, straggling buildings—having become ruinous and dilapidated, were entirely pulled down, *i.e.*, about the year 1745; and many additions made to the House by Philip, 6th Lord Viscount Wenman, soon after that period. These were planned by Mr. Smith, an architect of Coventry, and executed with care and liberality, in accordance with the prevalent taste of the time for classical architecture. The rooms then built are well designed, of good proportions and very conveniently arranged, considering that they had to be adapted to those which were then preserved of the older parts of the House. The new front is effective, though quite out of architectural harmony with the ancient portions of the Abbey. These latter are now so altered and defaced that it is almost impossible to distinguish and describe them. Sufficient fragmentary remains exist, however—built into walls and out-houses—to shew that the older parts of the original monastic building were in a severe first-pointed style—having mouldings and chamfers of the simplest character—and were most probably the work of the celebrated Lincoln masons, carried out under the direction of the Master of the Cathedral fabric. It is said that about a hundred and twenty years ago the foundations of the ancient monastic church—measuring, independent of the Lady-chapel, which extended forty-five feet, eastwards—more than two hundred and thirty feet in length,* by seventy feet in breadth across the nave—could be distinctly traced close to the northern side of the present mansion; and that the position of the bases of the fourteen pillars of the nave, seven on either side, could be easily determined. The present kitchen of the House is thought by some to have been the old sacristy.

The Saloon or chief drawing-room and the Library occupy the main parts of this new building, which is conveniently planned, and comfortable rather than stately or grand. The Library is a handsome room, and contains a tolerable collection of historical, scientific, and miscellaneous books, but nothing of any special literary interest. The Library and collections of the last Lord Viscount Wenman, in which there were several curious MSS., were disposed of and dispersed. Those books now filling the shelves of the room have on no very definite principle been gathered since his death. An apartment is devoted to a large but miscellaneous Collection of China, much of which is curious, some of which is choice, and the whole of which is valuable. The most interesting room is that which is named after the Abbots of the old monastery. Though, like all the rest of the more ancient parts, this has been considerably altered, patched, restored, and re-arranged by various hands, and with varying ideas of good taste, it still possesses several features of interest, and, with the adjoining desolate and dreary Tower, is certainly the most attractive portion of the mansion. The ceiling is of carved oak, the well-moulded chief timbers, which project, crossing each other diagonally. A tradition of doubtful value maintains that the portrait of a gentleman in the dress of the Tudor period, over the mantel-piece, is that of Robert King. If so, he had become entirely secularized. This room contains several coats of arms, amongst others those of the Abbey of Thame; the personal monogram of Robert King, "R. R." (Robertus Reonensis Ep'us), with mitre and pastoral staff, the arms of the Abbey of Waverley in Surrey, both the official and personal arms of John Longland, Bishop of Lincoln, those of Henry VIII., Sir John Williams, Knt., Roger Lee, "Argent, a fesse between three leopards' heads erased sable," Sir John Clerke of Thame, and Sir Richard Wenman of Oxfordshire, the husband of Isabel Williams.

* The red-sandstone Abbey Church of Furness, a Cistercian House, was 275 feet long, and is said to have been of about the same size, and to have been built in the same style, as that of Thame Park. A Report in MS.—which was presented to Pope Julius II., in the early part of the sixteenth century, by William Wood, one of the monks of Thame Park—still amongst the Archives of the Vatican, contains a statement that the Churches of the Cistercian Abbeys of Furness and Thame were nearly of equal dimensions—A.D. 1506-1507. "D'n's Will'mus Wode, monachus de Thame ordinis Cisterciensis xxij Ap'lis."—*Archives of the English College at Rome*, "of Strangers visiting."

Pictures in the Mansion House of Thame Park.*

Gothic Dining Room:—

Half-length portrait of Sir Thomas Wenman, in armour.

Half-length portrait of a Lady of the Wenman family, of the time of Charles the Second.

Half-length portrait of Richard, Lord Viscount Wenman, who died in 1742.

Half-length portrait of King Charles the Second.

Whole-length portrait of Elizabeth Jephson, daughter of Thomas Norris, Esq.

Half-length portrait of Philip, Lord Viscount Wenman.

Half-length portrait of Lady Norris.

Half-length portrait of Thomas, Lord Viscount Wenman, who was born in 1596.

Half-length portrait of a Lady unknown, in the costume of the time of Queen Elizabeth.

A three-quarter portrait of a Gentleman unknown, in a velvet dress trimmed with sable.

Half-length portrait of Sir Francis Wenman of Carswell, Knt.

Half-length portrait of Mr. Francis Wenman, who died in 1657.

Full-length portrait of Isabel, daughter of Lord Williams of Thame, seated.

Portrait of Lord Wenman, in the robes of a Peer.

North Dining Room:—

The School of Athens, after Raphael.

A Gentleman of the Wenman family, in a velvet dress.

Corridors:—

St. Mary Magdalene, after Guido.

A Boar Hunt, in the style of Velasquez.

Judith with the Head of Holofernes, in the style of the Italian School.

Saloon:—

The Rape of the Sabines.

The Horatii and Curiatii, after *Le Brun*.

Drawing Room:—

A three-quarter portrait of a Lady of the Wenman family, of the time of Charles the First.

A three-quarter portrait of Thomas, second Lord Wenman.

Library:—

A Lady with high collar, face to the left, with a fan in her right hand.

A three-quarter portrait of Edward Butler, LL.D., President of Magdalene College, Oxford.

Portrait of Sophia, daughter of Viscount Wenman, who married Humphrey Wykeham of Swalcliffe. Her face to the right, with scarf over a gown of embroidered white satin.

Over one of the mantel-pieces, a portrait of Frances, daughter of Thomas, Lord Viscount Wenman, wife of Thomas Samwell, Esq.

A Lady in white satin, her face to the left, in evening dress.

A Lady in white satin trimmed with blue satin.

A Gentleman of the time of Charles the First, wearing an embroidered doublet with lace collar, with a sword in his left hand.

A full-length portrait of Elizabeth, daughter of Thomas, Lord Viscount Wenman, and wife of Greville Verney, Esq.

Penelope, daughter of Thomas, Lord Viscount Wenman, wife of Sir Thomas Cave of Stanford, Northamptonshire.

Jane, daughter of Sir Thomas Wenman, who married, firstly, Mr. James Cressie, and, secondly, Sir Thomas Tasburgh.

A three-quarter portrait of Philip, fifth Viscount Wenman.

Mary, daughter and coheiress of James Herbert of Tythorpe, by Hudson.

Crimson Bedroom:—

A half-length portrait of a Lady, one of the Wenman family, in the style of Sir Peter Lely.

A half-length portrait of a Gentleman of the Wenman family, with lawn bands.

Bedroom, No. 2:—

A whole-length portrait of a Child with a battledore.

A half-length portrait of a Gentleman, in a black velvet dress and flowing wig, of the time of Charles the First.

Dressing Room, No. 3:—

A half-length portrait of a Lady, in a blue dress, one of the Wenman family.

Pink Room:—

A three-quarter portrait of Richard, Lord Viscount Wenman, 1640.

White Bedroom:—

A three-quarter portrait of a Lady, of the time of Charles the Second.

White Dressing Room:—

A three-quarter portrait of Henrietta Maria, Queen of Charles the First.

Chintz Bedroom:—

A three-quarter portrait of Sir Richard Wenman, in a black dress.

Dressing Room:—

A half-length portrait of a Lady, in a brown dress.

There are some well-preserved specimens of armour, various warlike instruments of mediæval times, and a few curiosities of a miscellaneous character, arranged on either side of a passage in the ancient part of the house. Amongst the armour—some of which is both interesting and curious—is a portion of a Saxon shield which was discovered in a field at Sydenham. In the Hall near to the chief staircase is a quaint painting on panel, dated 1672, of the armorial bearings of Wykeham.

In its centre is a shield with—1st and 4th, the arms of Wykeham; 2nd, those of De Waterville; and

* The Author, not having had an adequate opportunity of examining them, is not responsible for the accuracy of the description of these pictures—which, with a few unimportant additions, is taken from a MS. list existing at Thame Park. It is quite obvious that some of them are misdescribed.

3rd, the arms of Sir John Le Sore; and the crest of Wykeham above, placed upon the helmet of an esquire. These same arms of four quarters are repeated on other smaller shields, impaling—1stly, Houldbeck; 2ndly, those of a daughter of Gyles Poulton; and 3rdly, those of Mary, daughter of Edward Underhill. The arms of Le Sore are:—Or, a chief azure. John Le Sore or Lizours held lands in Warwickshire, 44 Edw. III. Arms of Poulton:—Argent, a fesse gules charged with three plates between three mullets gules. Giles Poulton of Desborough, co. Northampton, was the father of Ferdinando Poulton, a lawyer. Arms of Underhill:—Argent, a chevron sable between three trefoils vert. John Underhill, of this family, was consecrated Bishop of Oxford at Lambeth, 14 Dec. 1589, and died 12 May 1592. Again, Mary, daughter of Edward Underhill, yeoman, lessee (under the renowned family of Shirley) of the Manor of Ettington, co. Warwick, by Margaret Middlemore of Edgbaston, in the same county, married "Humphrey Wykeham of Thame and Swalcliffe, co. Oxon."*

The Chapel near the House, which had remained in a state of dilapidation for many years, was repaired and restored for service about half a century ago, in the year 1836. It was originally the Chapel for externs and strangers. Herein it is believed that Robert King sometimes held his ordinations for some few years after the first foundation of the See of Oxford; for the Abbey Church had been pulled down immediately upon the Suppression; so that, when the Bishop continued to reside here for awhile, this, the "Chapel of the wayfarers," was thus found to be of some practical use. It is a building of second-pointed character, with well-designed windows and some excellent general features. In shape it is a parallelogram, externally buttressed at the angles and elsewhere, with a high-pitched roof, a western bell-cote, and a doorway at the west end. It has a small projecting sanctuary at the east end, under which is a vault where rest the remains of the late Sophia, Baroness Wenman. In the work of reparation, however, too many of the ancient characteristics of the Chapel were either so marred or destroyed that it has lost much of its previous interest. The Chapel was restored before its time, when taste was either imperfect or somewhat degraded; and when the leading idea of restoration was to fill up a small building with coarse, ill-designed, and cumbrous fittings, large enough for a Cathedral. The high pues are ugly to a degree, the pulpit and reading-pue being out of all proportion to the size of the place; while the general arrangements of the interior are quite absurd for a small domestic chapel and only in harmony with what is known as "carpenters' Gothic." There is a small and sweet-toned organ on the south side of the nave, large pues on either side of the sanctuary arch, a few open seats for the servants and tenants at the west end, and a pulpit and reading-pue placed opposite the organ against the north wall. In the sanctuary stands an old-fashioned communion-table, with the customary arm-chairs at either end. There are some very curious and remarkable encaustic tiles remaining in the floor, some of which were discovered under the ruins of the great monastic Church, and placed in the Chapel at the time when it was repaired. Some are apparently as early as of the thirteenth century, others as late as the sixteenth. One of the former has a plain and severe fleur-de-lys on it; another, a ring-dove in a circle; a third, a square intersected by two semi-circles; a fourth, of a later period, a conventional rose; and a fifth, a cross florey between four six-petalled flowers. The still later tiles are perhaps of less excellent designs, though interesting and effective both in combination and contrast. The glass of the windows is poor, and the kneeling figure of the Blessed Virgin in the west window thoroughly inartistic and unsatisfactory. The service of the Church of England, however, is said in the Chapel on Sundays—sweetly and efficiently sung by a Chaplain and a band of surpliced choristers. Around the Chapel are a few graves, under the shadow of beautiful trees; while, when summer is upon us, roses, jessamine, and flowering creepers adorn its sacred walls.

The following monumental inscriptions remain:—

Floor.

Here
lieth ye Body
of Seymour
Wroughton (of
Oakly, in the County of
Berks*) Esq. Who departed
this life the 19th day of
November
1736
Ætatis suæ
47.

Floor.

✠
J. H. S.
BERNARD STAFFORD
died
July 12 1788
Aged 76.

* From information given to me by the late Evelyn P. Shirley, Esq., Lord of Ettington.

* This is a mistake for Bucks.

Floor.

Here
Lieth ye body of
THO^{s} WENMAN, eldest
Sonne of Sr FRAN: WENMAN,
of Carswell, K^{t} & Baronet,
Who deceased ye 5th day
of Sept. 1663.
Aged 11.

Floor.

Here lyeth the Body of *Philip Lord Viscount Wenman* Who was born Nov. 23 1719, and died August 15th 1760
He married *Sophia* Daughter of *James Herbert of Tythorpe*
in the Co. of Oxford Esqr and Coheiress of her Brother *Philip Herbert Esqr.* By her his Lordship had Issue *Philip*
the Present Lord, born April 18th 1742; *Sophia*, born August
17th 1743; *Susanna* born Nov. 10th 1744 who died young and
was buried at Witney; *Thomas Francis* born Nov. 18 1745;
Richard, born Novr 13th 1746, who Died in his Infancy, and
was buried at Witney; *Mary* born March 27 1748 who died young, and *Herbert Henry*, who also died young and
were both buried at Thame Park.

North Wall.

Near this place are deposited the remains of
PHILIP, LORD VISCOUNT WENMAN, BARON TUAM,
of the Kingdom of Ireland.
His Lordship was returned to serve the County of Oxford
In Parliament five successive times.
Being the last of the Family, and dying without Issue, the Title becomes extinct.
This Monument is erected by his Nephew
PHILIP THOMAS WYKEHAM
as a small token of Affection.
His Lordship died March 26th 1800, Aged 58 years.

Floor.

Here Lieth the Body of
SOPHIA, VISCOUNTESS WENMAN,
Who departed this Life
July 19 1787.
Aged 72.

South side.

Sacred
To the Memory of
SOPHIA ELIZABETH, BARONESS WENMAN,
who departed this life
August 9 1870,
Aged 80 Years.

♣♣♣♣♣♣♣

HERE it may not be out of place to diverge for awhile from the subject of the Abbey in general to the person and labours of one of the most remarkable men amongst the religious of the later days of that monastery; who, though too generally unknown, owned literary abilities and poetic taste of no mean character, and whose historical and poetical productions deserve to be rescued from that oblivion into which—because of their thoroughly Christian character—they long ago fell.

William Forrest, no doubt a native of Oxford, and born about the year 1505, was a Cistercian monk of Thame Park at the time of the Suppression. Three hundred years previously a certain Bacchardo Forresta had been one of the witnesses to an agreement relating to land in Scypdun between the monks of Thame and Samson de Pomario. In the parishes of St. Peter's-in-the-Bailey and St. Peter's-in-the-East, in the City of Oxford, members of this family, citizens of repute, had resided from the year 1495* to the year 1600, and some of them had allied themselves in marriage with inhabitants of Thame. Others had secured for themselves appointments about the Court. One, Edward Forrest, was Groom of the Chambers to Queen Katherine in 1517; Miles Forrest held a similar office about the King; while, in 1538, Father John Forrest, Prior of Greenwich and Provincial of the Franciscans in England, who was most cruelly burned at the stake for denying the new dogma of the King's supremacy, was Chaplain to Queen Katherine. At the Surrender and Dissolution of the Abbey of Thame Park, William Forrest, following his superiors, took an official part. Robert King, the Abbot, as is already on record here,

---

* John Forrest was a Councillor and afterwards Chamberlain of the City (29 Sep., 1556). Robert Forrest held the Office of Councillor likewise (29 Sep., 1554), as did also William Forrest (29 Sep., 1555). The Will of the last-named "of St. Peter's in the Baylye," made 10 Sep., 1571, was proved 30 May, 1579. His wife Alice was executrix, and "Sir William Wells, Curate," had been one of the witnesses. See *Selections from the Records of the City of Oxford*, etc. By W. H. Turner. London: 1880.

"John Florest and Jane Kinge of Ailsbury were marryed together the second day of December by vertue of a license from Mr Doctor Smith unto me directed. Anno D'ni, 1602."—*Register of Crendon, Co. Bucks.*

The arms of "Thos. King of Aylesbury, D^{r} in Physic," are given in the Harl. MSS., Brit. Museum, Plate lv., F.

Richard Greene, the Prior, and John White, the Sub-prior, signed the Deed of Surrender, with ten others of the brethren, amongst whose names stands that of William Forrest.

Signature of William Forrest from the Deed of Surrender in the State Paper Office.

He received a small pension,* and was very probably, soon afterwards, engaged as one of the Secretaries of Cardinal Wolsey; for in Forrest's poem on Queen Katherine he describes the building of Cardinal College, now Christ Church, with the power and point of an eye-witness. In 1551 and the following year he was ministering in Thame Church. Probably, too, he was a member of the society of Cardinal College, for on its dissolution his name is found amongst its pensioned fellows or clergy. He appears to have received the sum of £6 annually from the year 1553 to the year 1556. This, however, may have been his pension as a discharged monk. On the 1st July, 1556, he was presented to the Vicarage of Bledlow, Co. Bucks, by Anthony Sampson, and duly instituted, and seems to have remained there until 1576, when his successor was appointed. His precisely-written details of the funeral of Queen Katherine—unnoticed by historians in general—shew that he himself was personally present; while his vigorous denunciations of Dr. Richard Coxe, Dean of Christ Church and Vice-Chancellor of Oxford, are evidently the work of an honest and upright man, who heartily abhorred the double-dealing, heresy, and time-serving, which were the leading characteristics of that Erastian dignitary.

Forrest's chief poem is entitled "Grysilde the Second," under which he gives an account of the Divorce of Henry VIII. from Queen Katherine. The King is represented as "Walter." The volume is preserved amongst Anthony à Wood's MSS. in the Bodleian Library. It is artistically and beautifully written on fine vellum in the author's own handwriting. Proper names and some other words are in red ink, but the text in general is in black. It was anciently bound in satin, but this is now torn and faded. There is a centre boss, and there are other bosses, with brass clasps, on which is engraven—AVE MARIA, GRACIA PLE'A. It sometime belonged to Ralph Sheldon,† of Weston Park, Co. Warwick, Esq., who gave it to Anthony à Wood. Parts of it had been already printed by Sir Frederick Madden and Dr. Philip Bliss; but in 1875 it was well and efficiently edited by the Rev. W. D. Macray, M.A., of Ducklington, for the Roxburgh Club, at Baron Heath's suggestion and expense. This book is in small quarto, and consists of pp. xxviij, 200. In all the leading features and particulars of the poem it bears out the historical facts and statements of Archdeacon Harpsfield's remarkable Treatise on the Divorce; while perhaps the chief merit of Forrest's poem lies in the fact that of several of the details which he so carefully records he himself was an actual eye-witness. The cruelty of Henry in forbidding his daughter Mary to see her mother on her deathbed—without assigning any reason for so doing—is duly chronicled by Forrest, and thus corroborates the categorical statement of Cardinal Pole.

The journey of the King and Queen and their suite through Thame is thus referred to :—

From thense wheare hee came, faste iumpe by his syde,
Accompayned hym the lady *Anne Bulleyne*,
All pleasaunte, fresche and gallaunt that tyde,
Good *Grysilde* following, as one of her trayne,
At whiche manye (that wise weare) did disdayne
So noble a woman to bee forsake,
And in her steade so meane a thing to take.

For thorowe *Thame*, that gentle Market Towne,
The Kynge then issued vpp to *Londonwarde*,
Where dyverse and many their headys henge downe
To see the case with *Grysilde*, how it fared,
Unto their hartys God wote, it went full harde,
And thus did say mutteringe as they stoode still—
"Christe saue good *Grysilde* to His blessed will."

O Lord (they saide, togeather as they stoode),
What meaneth our Kinge good *Grysilde* to forego,
Which hym here followethe withe trobled moode
That better for her weare she weare ferder froe!
In his solacinge she feelethe but woe;
Whoe can her chalenge or bleme in the case,
She to followe an other in her place!

Of the manner in which the King received the news that the Holy Father discountenanced the proposal for a divorce, Forrest writes thus :—

By this the Messengers to the Cowrte came
Voyde of the purpose for whiche they weare sent:
So soone as *Walter* vnderstoode the same
For malencolye hee ynwardelye brent,
And was (throughe malice) moste earnestlye bent
Agaynste the Busshope for sayinge hym naye,
Ragynge as lyon depryued his praye.

Thomas Cromwell, as Cardinal Pole also pointed out, is no doubt referred to in the following stanzas, the

* Soon afterwards he was engaged as a scribe. "1545. It'm p'd to Master Florest for a hymnall, xs." —Churchwarden's "Accounts" of Thame Church.

† Jane, daughter of William, 8th Lord Delawarr, who was the wife of Sir Thomas Wenman, Knt., having on his death secured two other husbands in succession, married as her fourth husband this Mr. Ralph Sheldon.

original suggestor of the new Tudor dogma of the Royal Supremacy:—

At which selfe season one certayne stoode by,
Whois name (thoughe I herde) I will not expresse,
Whoe saide to *Walter* much coragyouslye,
"What shoulde this mateir oughtes vex your highnes?
Ye maye (witheoute doubtinge) it clearlye redresse,
Sithe yee are heere Kynge and lorde of this lande,
Yee dooynge your lyste, whoe dare youe withestande?

Yee, takynge on youe the Supreamacye
As headde of the Churche ouer all Brytayne,
And other youre Domynyons specyallye,
Yee maye (at pleasure) then althinges ordayne,
So foreuermore *Rome Courte* to refrayne;
If yee not sticke to put this in practice,
Whoe is that dare denye youre enterprise!"

Walter this hearynge his harte can reuyue,
Callynge to hym of his Counsell the cheeif,
For the saide mateir with speede to contryue
That hee weare quyeted out of his greeif;
The thynge by Perlyament putten in preeif,
It was condescended after his mynde,
None durste say nay but deathe hee liste to fynde.

In the ninth chapter of the poem is a curious and interesting account of the *reference* of the divorce question to the University of Oxford, where John Longland, Bishop of Lincoln, the King's Confessor, was the Chief Commissioner, and a certain monk, Nicholas, the King's Advocate. Many of the touches and points, unchronicled by others, give value to the testimony of the poet. Forrest thus writes of himself:—

At which trauelynge certaynlye was I,
Attendynge vpon a certayne goode man,
Whearfore in the same I somewhat say can.

As to the one-sidedness of the argument, the danger to which those exposed themselves who were opposed to the divorce, and the excitement of the populace against the King, Forrest is both very precise and very forcible. Five of the seven doctors specially appointed to consider the question, were against the King's wishes, viz., Dr. Richard Maudelay, Archdeacon of Leicester and Prebendary of Thame (for whom no doubt Forrest was acting as clerk and notary), John Moreman, William Mortimer, John Holyman (of Coddington, afterwards Bishop of Bristol), and Robert Cooke. The two in favour of a divorce were Robert Aldridge, and Thomas Charnock, a Dominican.

So angry was the populace with the Bishop of Lincoln, who by his right as Visitor was lodging at Lincoln College, that Forrest believes his life would not have been secure had he gone out unprotected. The women of the city, moreover, seemed to have been specially enraged against one, Friar Nicholas, whom they assaulted in the streets because of his gross and unmanly attack on Queen Katherine, for which offence, as Forrest puts on record, thirty of them were on the morrow locked up in Bocardo.

The result of the repudiation of the Pope's authority—as chief Bishop of the Universal Church—Forrest thus forcibly and truly describes:—

The gloryous perpetuall Virgyn *Marye*
No better esteamed than an other woman;
Each dounngegell as good as the Sanctuarye.
Theire myschelfes, with hundredfold moe, began
At the incummyng of this newe Queen *Anne*,
Who as she was, declared at the laste,
Whom Gode vanyshed with much sodayne blaste.

* * * * * *

For certaynlye, vpon this induction
Entred in this Royalme such innouation
(To the poore mannys vtter destruction)
Raysinge of Rentes in wondreful fashion
From one to fyue in ful numeration,
To cawsynge of dearthe in vytayl and warys
With other sundrye ineuytable carys,

Somuch the bodye not heere molestynge,
But hundredfolde more endaungeringe the sowle;
At Fastynge and Prayinge was made but iesting,
The vile Ignoraunte the clarke to controwle,
All holy ceremonys coniuringe the Mowle,
Each cockynge Cobler and spittyllhowse Proctor
In learnynge taken so goode as the Doctor.

In tokne yeat more of Infidelytee,
Downe went the Crosses in euerye countraye,
Goddys servauntes vsed withe muche crudelytee,
Dysmembred (like beastes) in th'open high waye,
Their inwardys pluckte oute and hartis wheare they laye,
In suche (most greuous) tyranny call sorte
That to to shamefull shamefull (*sic*) weare heere to reporte.

Shorteleye after, to mend the mateir more,
Churches and Monasteries downe they went,
To haue the treasure speciallye therefore,
Althoughe they fayned for other entent,
After this Proverbe, to like consequent,
The Glouer (craftelye) brought this reason yn,
The Dogge to be madde, all to haue his skynne.

Yeat this was not the vttermuste euyl;
Theye nybbed Christe's faithe after their pleasure,
So weare they ledde by their Maister the Deuyl,
For, on the truthe, they lyed out of measure:
The whoale heere to wright I haue no leasure,
But to this ende I haue rehersed this,
What came by enchaunge of good *Grisildis*.

The Colophon stands thus:—

¶ Heere endethe the Historye of *Grysilde* the *Seconde* only meanynge *Queene Catharyne*, Mother to oure most dread soveraigne ladye *Queene Marye*, fynysched the 25 daye of June, the yeare of owre Lorde 1558, by the symple and unlearned Syr *William Forreste* Preeiste, propriâ manu.

There is a MS. "History of Joseph the Chaiste, Part I., His Troubles," in the Library of University College, Oxford (No. 88 of the Manuscripts and rarer books), in the Prologue of which the author styles himself "William Forrest, sometyme chaplayne to the noble Queene Marye." It is handsomely bound in tooled calf with corner bosses. "The History of Joseph, Part II., His Felicity," is preserved in the British Museum. (MSS., Royal Library, 18 C. xiii.) This latter part is dedicated to Thomas Howard, Duke of Norfolk, K.G., and dated as having been finished on the 11th April, 1569, but stated by the author to have been written twenty-four years before, that is in 1545.

A MS. version (Royal Library, Brit. Mus., 17 D. iij) of the treatise called Aristotle's *De Regimine Principum* (whose true author, however, was Ægidius Romanus) exists. It is in quarto, on seventy-eight leaves of vellum, with several interesting additions by Forrest himself. It was evidently made for the Duke of Somerset, or perhaps for the use of the young King. On one page is a drawing by the author, in which he is represented as young, without the tonsure, but with long hair, kneeling at Edward VI.'s throne and offering the King his book. No doubt Forrest came across the Duke when, as was the case, the latter received from the Crown a grant of the buildings and site of Thame Abbey, subsequently re-given to Sir John Williams.

In a MS. Book of Music, oblong quarto in shape, preserved in the Library of the Music School at Oxford—no doubt originally belonging to one of the Royal Chapels; for on the binding is stamped the Pomegranate, the badge of Katherine of Arragon, as well as the arms of England with a Dragon and a Greyhound as supporters, and the Tudor Rose—is written the following inscription—"Will' Forrest' hunc librum jurae (*sic*) possidet, cum quinque aliis eidem p'rtinentibus"—the date "1530" being added in another handwriting.

Another of Forrest's MSS. is preserved in the Royal Library of the British Museum. It is a small MS., on paper of 83 folios (17 A., xxj), inscribed thus:—

> To the most woorthie *Prince Edward Duke of Somerset Protr* unto oure most dredde Souereigne *Lorde, King Edward the* vj bee fauoure in god withe honour & peace in prosperous estate long to contynue so wischethe his humble orato' W. ffforreste.

It has on folio 5 the following title:—

> Certaigne psalmes of Dauyd
> in Meeatre added to Maister
> Sterneholdis and oothers by
> William Fforreste —— 1551.

A Life of the Blessed Virgin, from his pen, containing, amongst others, poems in honour of the joyful mysteries, the Immaculate Conception, the Nativity of Our Lady, and the Assumption. It is a small folio volume on paper—Harleian MSS., No. 1703—on the fly-leaf of which is written "Wm Forrest's Poems to Q. Mary." As a literary work it is of rare merit—very much superior to all his other productions. Its simplicity of language, devotional tone, and beauty of illustration, render it quite delightful reading, and make the student of it marvel that it has not as yet been printed.

The following exquisite poem, standing on folio 113, etc., deserves to be reproduced here:—

O man, for loue I have to thee,
Amonge thy mirthes have mynd on mee.

IN healthe, in welth, in thy welfare,
and what other felicitee,
for sodayne falynge into care,
Amonge thy mirthes, have mynde of mee.

Remember, in thin inwarde thought,
How I thee made of harte most free,
Wherefore of duetye wall thou ought,
Amonge thy mirthes, to think on mee.

I made thee man, remember well,
no aspe, no worme, no stock, no tree,
but smally diffringe from aungell,
Wherfore thou oughtist to think on mee.

I cause for thee all grayne to springe,
And everye thing in theire degree,
both foule and fishe in saye sprynggynge,
Wherfore thou oughtist to think on mee.

Thye playes and pastimes all and some,
With what this worlds felicitee,
Unto an end they soone doth come,
In which them all doth think on mee.

The myrthes that man can here devise
Are but breathings of vanitee,
So take them man yf thou be wyse,
And myrth of heaven seeke thou of mee.

This world's vayne myrths doo not regarde,
before myrthe heavenly I wishe thee,
And I shall thee with myrth rewarde
that endless is, in heaven with mee.

The following devotional poem, as yet unpublished, is also a beautiful example of Forrest's powers. It is here reproduced exactly as it is written; and for theological exactness, apt thought, melody of rhythm, and artistic completeness, deserves high commendation. It compares well with the leading productions of those contemporary writers who were so influenced by the Pagan *renaissance*.

De Assumptione gl'iosissimae Virginis Mariae.

Geve prayse to God above althinge
that is soveraigne of myght:
For his mothers high exaltinge
into his heavinlye sight.
To place wheare ever is peace and rest—
Maria virgo Assumpta est.

OF her pure life double is theare none,
ffor shee (of women) was Alone,
As chyldinge chylde as earst before
She was a Mayden evermore,
She suckled Christe w^t her sweete Brest,
And nowe in heavin *Assumpta est.*

Wheare withe her S'n she is indude
With joyes of passinge magnitude,
Above all Angells, next the Throne,
for her vertues that so high shone,
No Angell so with grace possest
And now in heavin *Assumpta est.*

In ffleshe to lyve as she dyd heere
no fleschelye luste in her t'appeere,
It was a lief Angelycall
beyond the lief of Angells all,
ffor their nu'ber by her encrest,
And nowe in heavin *Assumpta est.*

Though some dothe holde the contrary,
She in the earthe to putryfye,
her fleshe and Chrystys sithe bothe one,
that weare no goode condycyon.
No doubt he dyd as seemd best,
thearfore in heavin—*Assumpta est.*

In things that Reason cannot preeve
we ought Christ's Churche for to beleeve,
whiche holdethe she sowle and boadye
to bee assumpte most certaynlye,
Of long is holde, from east to west,
With whom I holde *Assumpta est.*

If saynets in their Bodyes did Ryse,
When Christe arose, and did certyse
his Resurrection to be true,
& did with hym to heavin ensue,
dyinge agayne their death curse drest,
Then she (as theye) *Assumpta est.*

Her Relyques if in earthe byinge
they shoulde have had some mentyonynge,
As Saincte John's headde at Amyas
And other Saynets each in their place;
She-passinge All, withe grace possest,
No dowbte in heaven *Assumpta est.*

her hono^r sithe y^t dyd excell
farre passinge all anye ca' tell,
to Godds owne S'n to be Mother,
To have then that hath none other,
her sowle in Boadye, nowe to rest,
And in the same *Assumpta est.*

In boathe or anye of the twayne
Sithe neaver synne dyd move or raigne,
And synne of old compaction
cause of all putryfaction,
they the most singularlye blest
In singular wyse *Assumpta est.*

That wombe in which Godd's s'n dyd lye
receaving fleshe bloode & Boadye,
With pappes blessed, as Luke dothe saye,
Althoughe to have a dyinge deye,
To turne to duste had not bene the beste,
Thearfore I saye that *Assumpta est.*

Whyther or not to stande in doubte
Inoughe we have heere bowlted owte,
Let them that lyst on theyr peryll,
Well am I sure God dyd fulfyll
for his mother that seemed best,
Therefore I say *Assumpta est.*

To thee O god ffather of myght,
to S'n and to the holye Spryte,
that art one God in Trynyte,
For her Gracys all praysings be,
Who graunte to us at her requeste
to come Wheare she *Assumpta est.*

At the end of this volume, on folio 153, the following is written:—

ffinis. 27 Octobris 1572
per me Mr Guilelm'm fforrestum.

In the Library of the Society of Antiquaries is an original broadside, being verses on the accession of Queen Mary, entitled, *A New Ballade of the Marigolde. Imprinted at London in Alderegate Street, by Richard Lant.* This, too, was from the pen of Forrest.

In the Library of the Monastery of St. Gregory Downside, co. Somerset, an early-printed volume, entitled "Fortalicium fidei contra judeos, saracenos alios'q: christiane fidei inimicos, ——" printed at Nuremburg in the year 1494, has on the title-page his autograph thus, "Liber Guilelmi fforresti p'b'ri."

In a volume of the Burney MSS., in the British Museum, No. 295, Pluto CXLI. B., a sermon in Latin by St. Augustine of Hippo on the Incarnation, written on vellum, and consisting of 19 folios, has the following in Forrest's handwriting at the beginning:—

Lib' S'c'e Marie d' Thama Qui ho'c abstulerit anathema Sit.

In another book of the same set of MSS., "Opuscula varia," No. 357, Pluto CLXII. B., the following occurs at the end:—

Lib' S'c'e Marie de Thama in quo continentur . . . . .
Qui hunc fraude abstulerit vel deposuerit anathema sit.

And on the last page but one,—

liber Guilielmi fforresti.

I have been unable to find any further particulars of him. It would be useless to speculate as to his end. Though the clergy and religious "of the old sort," as they were termed, were not so bitterly persecuted under Elizabeth as were the "Seminaries"—that is, those priests who had been educated in foreign colleges and seminaries—yet many of the monks lost their promised pensions on the plea that they had become disaffected to the authorities, or had been engaged somewhere to read the "New Service" on a starvation stipend, and very frequently suffered under recently-passed statutes against rogues and vagabonds. Let us hope that so pious and accomplished a man as William Forrest was left to die in peace.

♣♣♣♣♣♣♣

IT is now desirable to give some personal account of Sir John Williams, who was summoned to the House of Lords, by writ dated 2 April 1554, by Queen Mary. He was one of those successful adventurers, who, by his discretion, pliability, vigour, and general disregard for sound and settled principles, rose from comparative indigence and obscurity* to wealth, influence, and rank; and, as he was intimately connected with Thame and its neighbourhood, and certain of the manors and lands he acquired still remain with his descendants in the female line, it is well to set forth more in detail some further particulars of his personal history.

John Williams was undoubtedly of a Welsh family, probably from Glamorganshire, and said to have been sometimes called Morgan, and to have sprung originally from the same stock as, or at all events to have been allied with, Thomas Cromwell of Putney, Co. Middlesex—afterwards Earl of Essex.† John Williams's father, another John Williams and a knight, had married Elizabeth, one of the two coheiresses of Richard More of Burghfield, Co. Berks, and ranking amongst the lesser gentry, filled the office of Sheriff of Berks and Oxon in 1502. It is more than probable that he was a cousin or kinsman of Morgan Williams, who had married Mary, Thomas Cromwell's sister. Two Cromwells, John and Robert, first-cousins of Thomas, were employed at Hampton Court by Cardinal Wolsey to brew beer for the Household. Now, the name of one "John Williams" occurs in the year 1526 amongst the servants of the Cardinal, when Lord High Chancellor, as occupying some inferior position in the Court of Chancery; and it may be that the patronage of this prelate first brought this said John Williams, who appears to have been also Receiver of Thame

* His connection in turn with Cardinal Wolsey; Thomas Cromwell, Lord Essex; John Longland, Bishop of Lincoln (Henry VIII.'s spiritual director), and Edward, Duke of Somerset, led to his regular and steady promotion.

† PEDIGREE OF CROMWELL *ALIAS* WILLIAMS *ALIAS* SMYTHE AND OTHERS.

This Pedigree should be studied in connection with that which has been given in a footnote on page 88, shewing the connection between certain families of Thame and its neighbourhood with each other. Here six previous generations to that in which Henry Williams alias Cromwell and Joane Warren appear are now set forth.

William de Cromwell of Norwell, near Cromwell, and Carlton-on-Trent, Co. Nottingham. Held the Prebendal lands and tenement of Palace Hall on lease, and was grandson of another William of the village of Cromwell.

John de Cromwell, his son, of Norwell aforesaid. Settled at Wimbledon, Co. Surrey, *circa* 1461, and obtained a lease from Archbishop Kempe, Lord of the Manor there, of a fulling-mill, residence, and lands. Living at Wimbledon in 1475. Died and buried there *circa* 1480. = A sister of Walter le Smythe of Norwell aforesaid, who subsequently settled at Putney as a blacksmith, armourer, and brewer, *temp.* 1 Edward IV.

William le Smith alias Smythe, an armourer, who was killed at the Battle of Northampton in 1460. = A daughter of William de Cromwell.

Other issue.

Joane Smythe. Married her cousin John Cromwell, brewer, of Stockwell.

William Smythe, smith and armourer of Putney, to whom Thomas Cromwell, his cousin's son, was apprenticed.

Richard Smythe of Putney. = Died in 1478.

Other issue.

An elder daughter, who died young.

Margaret Smythe. Died in 1501. (1st wife.) = John Williams of Lanishen, Co. Glamorgan. In 1493 acting as Overseer of the Manor of Putney; subsequently of Burghfield, Co. Berks. = Elizabeth More, daughter and coheiress of Richard More of Burghfield, Co. Berks.

(*See Pedigree of Lord Williams*, pp. 415-416.)

John Cromwell alias Smythe, held a brewery under Sir John Leigh, Lord of Stockwell, Co. Surrey, Knt., at Stockwell Green. Will dated 20 May 1523. Died during the same year. Buried at St. Mary's, Lambeth. = Joane Smythe. Sole Executrix of her husband's Will. Living in 1523.

A

Walter Cromwell alias Smythe. Born *circa* 1453. Blacksmith, keeper of a hostelry, and a brewery at Putney, Co. Surrey. Obtained a renewal of the lease which had been granted to his father out of the Manor of Wimbledon. Died in 1516. = . . . daughter of . . . . Glossop of Wirksworth, Co. Derby.

B

William Michell, son of a cloth dyer of the same name, of Wandsworth, Co. Surrey, himself following the same occupation. = Margaret Cromwell, one of the sisters of John and Walter.

C

Other issue.

Abbey,* to the notice of the King, and so obtained the King's patronage.† He was evidently engaged in legal work of some kind—acting as scribe, scrivener, and general agent; and was no doubt a man of considerable natural abilities, a shrewd and unscrupulous‡ personage, ready to serve his superiors faithfully, on condition of himself being sufficiently rewarded for so doing. Upon Cardinal Wolsey's misfortunes and death, he very probably attached himself to the interests of his own kinsman Cromwell, then becoming powerful.

However, in the year 1527, he had already been taken into the service of the Monarch himself, having ten pounds *per annum* granted to him by Letters Patent for the keeping of a greyhound. Early in the year 1535—having no doubt learnt what was expected from him both by Cromwell and his Royal Master—he was appointed one of the Commissioners to inquire into the state of the Abbey lands of Oxfordshire. In the Writ he is styled "gentleman." In the following year, however, he obtained the appointment of Clerk of the King's Jewel House, and soon afterwards that of Treasurer of the same, when he received the honour of knighthood. Later on, the Patent conferring the more exalted position of Treasurer of the Jewel House was surrendered, in order that the office might be shared by Thomas, Lord Cromwell (ennobled in the summer of 1536), and a new Patent obtained, in which it was set forth that the profits were to be equally divided between the baron and the knight, and the survivor was to enjoy them in their totality. The death of Cromwell, Lord Essex, in 1540, left Sir John Williams the sole owner of the office and dignity. In the year 1539 the Manor

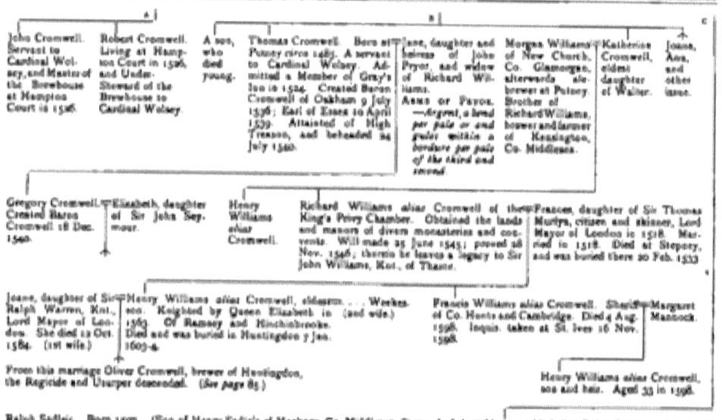

Ralph Sadleir. Born 1507. (Son of Henry Sadleir of Hackney, Co. Middlesex, Steward of the Manor of Cilney in Great Hadham, Co. Essex.) Obtained in 1546 a special Act of Parliament to legitimatise his children. A Privy Councillor to Henry VIII. Made a Knight Banneret under Edward VI., and Chancellor of the Duchy of Lancaster under Queen Elizabeth. Died in 1587. Buried in Standon Church, Hertfordshire.
Arms of Sadleir.—*Or, a lion rampant party per fesse azure and gules, armed and langued argent.*

Margaret Michell. = Ralph Barre or Barry. A foot soldier or pikeman, "who went for divers years to the foreign wars." (1st husband.)

* In the year 1524, at Thame Abbey:—

"Master Richard Eggerley" was the Seneschal, "John Willyams" was the Receiver, and "Robert Perrot" was the Bailiff.

The house, site, and lands of Thame Abbey, with certain lands and tithes in Thame, Sydenham, and Moreton, were granted under the Great Seal to John Williams, Knt., and Elizabeth his wife, 15 March 1542, and subsequently, on 15 September 1543, to the Bishop of Osney.

The House and site of the Abbey, having been apparently surrendered by Williams, or exchanged, were granted, 28 July 1547, to Edward, Duke of Somerset, and are mentioned in the grant as "late parcell of the possessions of Robert Kyng, Bishop of Oxford."

These same were subsequently granted to Richard Wenman of Thame Park, Knt., 2 December 1629, he being the husband of Lord Williams's coheiress.

† "John, Lord Williams of Thame, rose, like most of the great men in K. Henry VIII.'s Court, from a very inconsiderable beginning, for he was only a menial servant to that prince."—*Memoirs of the Cromwell Family*, by Mark Noble, vol. i., p. 237, footnote. Birmingham: 1787.

‡ "This person was deeply engaged in the criminal transactions of that eventful period, and made a distinguished figure in the reigns of Edward VI. and Queen Mary."—*History and Antiquities of the Hundreds of Bullingdon and Ploughley*, vol. i., p. 106. London: 1823.

Furthermore, in 2 Edward VI. (*i.e.* in 1548), Williams was made Steward of all the lands belonging officially to his kinsman Robert, then Bishop of Oxford, the remainder to Francis his son, with an annual salary of six pounds thirteen shillings and four pence for that service.

and lands of Wytham, Co. Berks, which had belonged to Sir Richard Harcourt, were alienated and became the property of Sir John Williams, who about that time obtained for himself a grant of the Stewardship of the Manors of Graffton and Hertwell, in the county of Northampton, together with the office of Keeper of the Parks there, as also grants of the Manors of Weston-on-the-Green* and Botley in Oxfordshire. Of this county he had been appointed High Sheriff in the year 1538. He likewise served the same office in 1553, when he officially attended the execution† of Cranmer, Ridley, and Latimer at Oxford;—a necessary, but very unpleasant duty. In the same year he, together with Sir John Pollard the Speaker, was M.P. for the County of Oxford—a position which he had filled from the year 1542. In fact Fortune favoured him, and being adroit and discreet, he secured considerable political influence and enormous wealth.

The following is taken from one of the several letters relating to the Suppression of the Religious Houses, in the handwriting of Sir John Williams,‡ preserved in the Record Office:—

Autograph of Sir John Williams, Knt.

During Queen Mary's reign, the Princess Elizabeth Boleyne was closely guarded under Sir Henry Bedingfield at Woodstock Park, as she was believed to be in active alliance with the revolutionary religionists of the Continent—many of them traitors, and very daring expounders of lawless and dangerous principles; and some of whom maintained, both by word and writing, that it was lawful to poison a Catholic Queen "because she was an idolater." On one occasion, in Elizabeth's "first day's journey from the Manor of Woodstock to Lord Williams's at Rycott, a violent storm of wind happened, insomuch that her hood and the attire of her head were twice or thrice blown off. On this she begged to retire to a gentleman's house then at hand; but Bedingfield's absurd and superabundant circumspection refused even this insignificant request, and constrained her, with much indecorum, to replace her headdress under a hedge near the road."* Lord Williams is reported to have invariably acted with less severity and greater courtesy, during the time that she resided at Rycott House under his authority.

He had two wives, having married the first (by whom alone he left issue) before he had obtained the honour of knighthood. She was a "Mistress Elizabeth Edmonds," the wealthy widow of a London citizen (Andrew Edmonds, grocer, and sometime Sheriff of London), with a country house in Essex; and was the daughter of a man whose ancestors had come from Bledlow in the neighbourhood of Thame—Thomas de Bledlowe or Bladlowe. A branch of the Mores of Burghfield, whose chief line became extinct in Henry VII.'s time, had been tenants of a house and lands in the village of Bledlow; and one member of this branch, Sir Richard More, Knt., was a Master in Chancery in the seventeenth century, and allied to the Petties of Tettesworth. Hence the connection of Sir John Williams, previously Receiver of Thame Abbey, with the Bledlowes and the Edmondses. His sister Jane had married, for her first husband, John Cheney, merchant of the Staple of Calais, a member of a Buckinghamshire and Bedfordshire family of considerable rank. Her second husband was Sir Gerard Harvey. I possess a deed by which, during the year 1533, he sold to Sir Robert Lee, Knt., certain woods and underwoods in the County of Bucks called "Nernetts." The family of Williams had likewise allied themselves with the Doyleys, a very ancient and respected race which had come to England with the Conqueror. They were of knightly rank, and had owned large possessions at Lewknor, Oxford, and various parts of the county. From a study of the Pedigrees of Williams and Cromwell *alias* Smythe, it will be seen that the innovating party thereabouts had bound themselves by marriage alliances with those upon whom regal Authority then so frequently smiled.

The following Pedigree will serve to illustrate still further the text above:—

* The Advowson of Weston-on-the-Green appears to have been originally included in the grant of the Manor to Osney Abbey, A.D. 1226; for the Abbot undoubtedly exercised the office of patron from that time until the Dissolution. To the ancient tower of the Parish Church a modern nave, in a debased Grecian style, was erected in 1743 by Mr. Norreys Bertie.

† Queen Mary is often unduly blamed for having sanctioned these punishments. Cranmer, it is maintained, had of old been her friend. It should not be forgotten, however, that there is no authority for the assertion that Cranmer's intercession with Mary's furious father saved her life; whereas it is quite certain that the Archbishop both concurred in the cruel and harsh proceedings of Edward VI.'s Council towards the Princess Mary, and joined heartily in the attempt to exclude her from the throne. He had previously pronounced the sentence of divorce against her mother, Queen Katherine; and had also decreed Mary herself to be a bastard. In conjunction with Ridley and other prelatial revolutionists, he had supported the usurpation of Jane Grey, had directly aided in the overthrow of the Old Religion, and was consequently guilty of heresy as well as treason.

‡ It seems doubtful if an authentic portrait of him exists. It is possible, however, that the three-quarter portrait of a "Gentleman," over the mantelpiece of the "Gothic Dining Room" at Thame Park, may represent him.

* *Life of Sir Thomas Pope*, by Thomas Wharton, B.D., p. 76. London: 1772.

Pedigree of John, Lord Williams of Thame.

Arms.—*Azure, an organ-pipe in bend sinister saltirewise, surmounted by another dexter, between four crosses patée argent.*

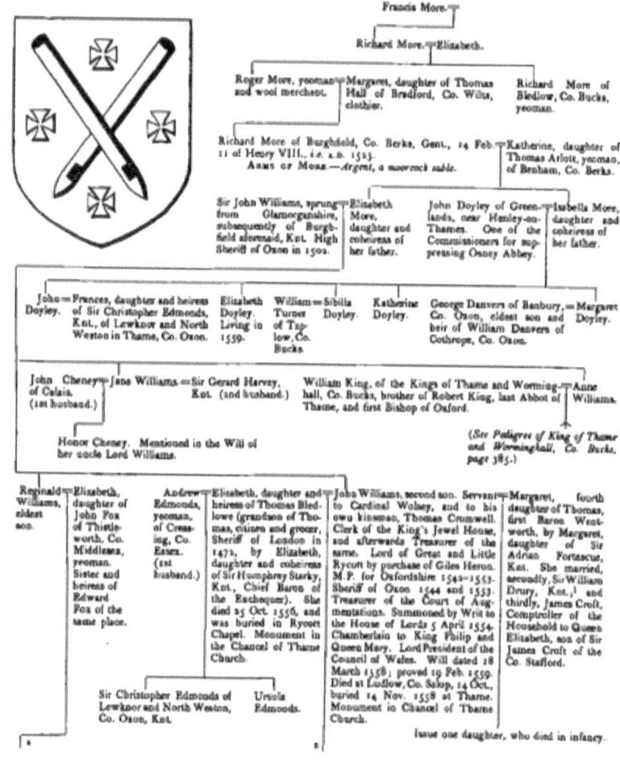

Francis More.
Richard More. = Elizabeth.
Roger More, yeoman and wool merchant. = Margaret, daughter of Thomas Hall of Bradford, Co. Wilts, clothier.
Richard More of Bledlow, Co. Bucks, yeoman.
Richard More of Burghfield, Co. Berks, Gent., 14 Feb. 11 of Henry VIII., i.e. A.D. 1523.
Arms of More.—Argent, a moorcock sable.
= Katherine, daughter of Thomas Arlott, yeoman, of Benham, Co. Berks.
Sir John Williams, sprung from Glamorganshire, subsequently of Burghfield aforesaid, Knt. High Sheriff of Oxon in 1502. = Elizabeth More, daughter and coheiress of her father.
John Doyley of Greenlands, near Henley-on-Thames. One of the Commissioners for suppressing Osney Abbey. = Isabella More, daughter and coheiress of her father.
John Doyley. = Frances, daughter and heiress of Sir Christopher Edmonds, Knt., of Lewknor and North Weston in Thame, Co. Oxon.
Elizabeth Doyley. Living in 1559.
William Turner of Taplow, Co. Bucks. = Sibilla Doyley.
Katherine Doyley.
George Danvers of Banbury, Co. Oxon, eldest son and heir of William Danvers of Cothrope, Co. Oxon. = Margaret Doyley.
John Cheney of Calais. (1st husband.) = Jane Williams. = Sir Gerard Harvey, Knt. (2nd husband.)
William King, of the Kings of Thame and Worminghall, Co. Bucks, brother of Robert King, last Abbot of Thame, and first Bishop of Oxford. = Anne Williams.
Honor Cheney. Mentioned in the Will of her uncle Lord Williams.
(See Pedigree of King of Thame and Worminghall, Co. Bucks, page 385.)
Reginald Williams, eldest son. = Elizabeth, daughter of John Fox of Thistleworth, Co. Middlesex, yeoman. Sister and heiress of Edward Fox of the same place.
Andrew Edmonds, yeoman, of Cressing, Co. Essex. (1st husband.) = Elizabeth, daughter and heiress of Thomas Bledlowe (grandson of Thomas, citizen and grocer, Sheriff of London in 1472, by Elizabeth, daughter and coheiress of Sir Humphrey Starky, Knt., Chief Baron of the Exchequer). She died 25 Oct. 1556, and was buried in Rycott Chapel. Monument in the Chancel of Thame Church.
= John Williams, second son. Servant to Cardinal Wolsey, and to his own kinsman, Thomas Cromwell. Clerk of the King's Jewel House, and afterwards Treasurer of the same. Lord of Great and Little Rycott by purchase of Giles Heron. M.P. for Oxfordshire 1542–1553. Sheriff of Oxon 1544 and 1553. Treasurer of the Court of Augmentations. Summoned by Writ to the House of Lords 5 April 1554. Chamberlain to King Philip and Queen Mary. Lord President of the Council of Wales. Will dated 18 March 1558; proved 19 Feb. 1559. Died at Ludlow, Co. Salop, 14 Oct., buried 14 Nov. 1558 at Thame. Monument in Chancel of Thame Church.
= Margaret, fourth daughter of Thomas, first Baron Wentworth, by Margaret, daughter of Sir Adrian Fortescue, Knt. She married, secondly, Sir William Drury, Knt.,[1] and thirdly, James Croft, Comptroller of the Household to Queen Elizabeth, son of Sir James Croft of the Co. Stafford.
Sir Christopher Edmonds of Lewknor and North Weston, Co. Oxon, Knt.
Ursula Edmonds.
Issue one daughter, who died in infancy.
a
a

A — B

John Williams, son and heir.[4] Died unmarried. Buried at St. Alphege, London Wall, 18 Feb. 1558-9.

Henry Williams, second son.

Francis Williams,[4] third son.

(Henry and Francis:) Both died unmarried during their father's lifetime.

Sir Richard Wenman of Carswell, Co. Oxon, and, by right of his wife, of Thame Park, Knt. = Isabella Williams, eldest daughter and coheiress of her father.

See Pedigree of Wenman and Wykeham.

Sir Henry Norreys, only son of Sir Henry Norreys, Knt., by Mary, daughter of Thomas, Lord Dacre. = Margery Williams, youngest daughter and coheiress of her father.

See Pedigree of Norreys and Bertie.

John Williams, eldest son. Died without issue.

Nicholas Williams, second son. = Mabel, daughter of Richard Staverton of Warfield, widow of Francis Wasterer of London, who, on the death of Nicholas Williams, married as her third husband Sir Read Stafford,[2] Knt.

Sarah Williams.

Richard Williams, third son. One of the Visitors for inquiring into the state of the Monasteries. Died without issue.

Francis Williams, fourth son. Buried at St. Alphege, London Wall, 15 Feb. 1558-9. = A daughter of Ralph Rockley of Kynsbourne, Co. York.

Lawrence Lovett of Sulberry, Co. Bucks. = Elizabeth Williams.

Anthony Foster[3] of Cumnor, Co. Berks. M.P. for Abingdon, Co. Berks, in 1572. Buried at Cumnor. = Anne Williams.

Edmund Odingsells of Itchendon, Co. Warwick. = Edith Williams.

Henry Staverton of Cowley, Co. Southampton, brother of Mabel, and son of Richard aforesaid. = Katherine Williams.

SOME EXPLANATORY NOTES OF THE FOREGOING PEDIGREE.

[1] The following is extracted from the old Register Book of Crendon, Co. Bucks:—1573.—"The xijth day of December was the nativitie of Elizabeth Drury, daughter to the Right Worshipfull Sir William Drury, Knight, and Lady Margery Williams his wife, and baptised the xxixth day of December. Compater Lord Earle of Lecester, Co'mater the Queene's Maiestie and the Ladie Wentworthe, 1573." Note that this "Ladie Wentworthe," wife of the second Baron Wentworth, was Anne, daughter of Sir John Wentworth of Gosfield, Co. Essex, Knt.

[2] Sir Read Stafford, Knt., who died s.p., married Mabel, daughter to Richard Staferton of Warfield, and relict of Nicholas Williams of Burghfield.—*Visitation of Berkshire*, A.D. 1665.

[3] Anthony Foster, or Forrester, was of an old Shropshire family settled in Berkshire. He married Anne, niece of Lord Williams of Thame. Cumnor Hall belonged to Dr. Owen, a physician to the Queen, and Foster first rented it and then purchased it. All his children died. He was a cultivator of the Fine Arts, a musician, a builder, and a planter. In 1572, towards the close of his life, he was returned as M.P. for Abingdon. In Cumnor Church there is a large brass plate to his memory, embellished with coats of arms. He was Chief Comptroller of the household of Lord Leicester. Foster's Will is dated 1572. Mrs. Odingsells, a widow, sister of Mr. Hyde, appears to have lived with the Fosters. See *The Wiltshire Archæological and Natural History Magazine*, No. 49. Devizes: Bull.

[4] "*St. Alphage, London Wall.* Mr. *Francis Williams*, brother's son to the Lord *Williams* of *Thame*, was (Feb. 15, 1558-9) brought from *Fleet Street* and buried here. And three days after, was the corps of Mr. *John Williams*, Heir to the Lord of *Thame*, conducted hither from *Paul's Chain* to be buried, with a Penon of arms and his coat armour, an herald and mourners attending. And twelve gentlemen bare him, twenty clarks before singing. The Funeral Sermon preached by Mr. *Veron* the *French* man."—*Survey of the Cities of London and Westminster*, by John Stow, Book III., p. 75. Corrected by John Strype. London: 1720.

♣♣♣♣♣♣♣♣♣♣♣♣

By his first wife, as will be seen, Sir John had three sons—two of whom, Henry and Francis, grew to manhood, and one other, John, died about the same time as his father and his cousin Francis in 1559. Sir John Williams's two daughters and coheiresses will be referred to later on. His wife had died in the autumn of 1556, and was buried in the Chapel of Rycott. He soon afterwards married Margaret, fourth daughter of Thomas, first Lord Wentworth.* This lady came of distinguished ancestry.* Her mother was Margaret, daughter of Sir Adrian Fortescue, Knt., of the County of Bucks; her grandmother, Anne, daughter of Sir William Stonor, of the County of Oxon; her great-grandmother, Anne, daughter and coheiress of John Neville, Baron of Montacute and Earl of Salisbury. Such a marriage

* Her eldest brother, Thomas, who had taken an active part in supporting Queen Mary, was made by Her Majesty Lord Deputy of Calais and Warden of the Marches thereof. Under him that town was surrendered to the Duke of Guise, having been held by the English for two centuries. Lord Wentworth—whose military action on this occasion resulted in disastrous failure—was tried by his peers on suspicion of treachery and cowardice, but honourably acquitted. The taking possession of Calais by the French is simply but most graphically recorded in the *Chronicles of Grafton*.

* Her sister Cecilia had married Sir Richard Wingfield of Kimbolton, Knt.; her sister Mary, William Cavendish; and her sister Jeane, Henry, first Lord Cheney of Toddington, Co. Bedford, who also was a warm adherent of Queen Mary.

marks the great social advance which Sir John Williams had made since the death of Cardinal Wolsey. Owing to changing circumstances, of which he was evidently a keen observer, he had somewhat veered round in his political and religious policy under Queen Mary; and as Lord Wentworth, Sir Robert Drury, and Lord Windsor* had done the same on the death of Edward VI., his alliance with these, and others who shared their opinions, is easily accounted for. On Mary's death and Elizabeth's accession he veered round again with great discretion.

Lord Williams in his treatment of Elizabeth Boleyne acted with his customary courtesy and far-sightedness. On one occasion, when she expressed a fear that some of her enemies might compass her destruction and take her life, he gallantly declared that he would readily sacrifice his own for her certain security and honour, and that she might absolutely trust herself to him. She was received and entertained at Rycott House on several occasions as a visitor; and for some time, under its Lord's care, at the request of Queen Mary's Council. At that period Elizabeth learnt to confide in Lord Williams, who, though he had a very difficult policy to pursue, managed nevertheless with singular discretion to conceal his own religious predilections if he had any; and, while always securing his own purpose, to remain on good terms with both parties in the State,—the innovators, and those who defended and maintained the Old Religion.

In addition to the possessions already mentioned,—lands and manors, houses and abbey-sites,—which he had obtained, some by lease, and afterwards absolutely by Royal grant or purchase—some by exchange with the other fellow-adventurers† and co-operating land-grabbers, who played into each other's hands—some through mortgages and money-lending,—the following may be put on record, relating to lands belonging to the Counties of Oxon, Bucks, and Wilts:—

* "In this mean season, the Lord Windsor, Sir Edmund Peckham, Sir Robert Drurie, and Sir Edward Hastings, raised the Commoners of the shire of Buckingham; unto whom Sir John Williams, which was afterwards Lord Williams of Thame, and Sir Leonard Chamberlain with the chief power of Oxfordshire. . . . . . These captains with their companies being thus assembled in warlike manner, marched forward toward Norfolke, to the aide of the Lady Marie, and the further they went the more their power increased."—*The Chronicles of England*, by Raphael Hollingshed, pp. 1086-7. London: 1586. See also *The Annals or General Chronicle of England*, by J. Stow, p. 611. London: 1615.

† For example, John Pollard beneficently secured part of the spoils of Thame Abbey in Oddington for John Williams, while John Williams in turn secured a portion of the lands of Dorchester Abbey for John Pollard. The nephew of the last named, another John Pollard, was likewise presented to the Rectory of Lodgershall, 16 Dec. 1557, by Lord Williams of Thame. Of eight other similar cases of like mutual benevolence I have made notes, in which the adventurers duly manipulated other people's properties to their own personal advantage.

In 1543, King Henry VIII. demised to Sir John Williams, Knt., Roger Lee of Thame, gent., and others, about 150 acres of the lands of Notley Abbey, lying in Crendon, and a water-mill on the river Thame, lately belonging to the Monastery.*

On the 29th February, 34 Henry VIII., *i.e.* in 1543, an estate belonging to the Abbey of Thame, in Oddington, was granted to Sir John Williams and Anthony Stringer to hold in fee. [Oddington Grange, now a farm-house, is the site of the old Otteleia Monastery.]

The House of the Sisters of the Order of St. John of Jerusalem at Gosford, in Kiddington, Co. Oxon, was also granted in the 38th year of Henry VIII., *i.e.* in 1547, to Anthony Stringer and Sir John Williams.

In the 2nd and 3rd year of Philip and Mary, *i.e.* in 1555-6, the site and lands of the Monastery or Priory of Little Marlow, Co. Bucks, were alienated by John Titley and Elizabeth Restwold (who had obtained them in the 32nd year of Henry VIII., *i.e.* 1541) to John, Lord Williams of Thame, and Henry Norreys.

Conveyance of Sir John Williams to Richard Warde of the lands called Wood's Grove, in the parish of Hurst, Co. Wilts.—*State Papers*, June 26th, 1552.

Of what the endowments of the Chantry of St. Christopher in the south aisle of Thame Church exactly consisted, may be gathered from the following official and authentic contemporary statement. The details are put forth at length. What the Parish and the Poor lost by the scandalous and unjustifiable confiscation of these endowments to Sir John Williams can scarcely be known. The memory of the original founders, who, by munificence and self-denial, founded this Chantry—the chapel of which is now a mere useless desolation—should certainly be had in remembrance: the memory of the legal thieves who robbed the Parish in distinct execration.

Particulars for Grants of Edward VI. to Sir John Williams.

County of Oxford, Thame. The Chantry or Guild of Saint Christopher in Thame in the County of Oxford aforesaid, founded by Richard Quatremayne as follows, that is to say:—The lands, tenements and possessions to the Chantry or Guild of St. Christopher in Thame aforesaid appertaining, in the County of Oxford aforesaid:—

The rent or farm of one tenement there with two acres of arable land in the fields of Thame aforesaid, demised to Alice Yong by indenture dated the tenth day of May the 37th year of Henry VIII. for the term of fifty-one years, yielding therefore by the year xiij^{s} iiij^{d}.

The rent or farm of one vacant parcel of land there, next the tenement of John Cowper,† demised to the aforesaid Alice by indenture dated 15th of March the 28th year of

* This water-mill, the site and mansion-house of Notley Abbey, and several of the lands here referred to, now belong to the family of Reynolds, whose Pedigree will be found in Chapter V.

† The family of Cowper was allied by marriage to that of Dormer of Thame.

Henry VIII. for term of sixty-one years, yielding therefore by the year viij^{s}.

The rent or farm of one tenement there, next the tenement of Alice Stockdale, demised to Joan Owlefylde by indenture dated the xxvth day of October the 17th year of Henry VIII. for term of twenty-one years, yielding therefore by the year xxj^{s} viij^{d}.

The rent or farm of one tenement in New Thame, next the tenement of Thomas Flome, with one close in the Moore ende and eighteen acres and a half of land in the common fields there, demised to John Isley, otherwise Smythe, by indenture dated the fifth day of April in the 24th year of Henry VIII. for term of sixty years, yielding therefore by the year xxiiij^{s}.

The rent or farm of one tenement there called Fryday's-place, demised to the aforesaid John Isley, by indenture for term of sixty years, yielding therefore by the year xj^{s} viij^{d}.

The rent or farm of one tenement there, next the tene-of Richard Bunse, demised to Simon Synkler, by indenture dated the thirtieth day of May the 26th year of Henry VIII. for term of fifty-one years, yielding therefore by the year xx^{s}.

The rent or farm of one tenement there, next the mansion of Geoffrey Dormer Esquire, demised to Henry Betten by indenture dated the tenth day of May the 19th year of Henry VIII. for term of fifty years, yielding therefore by the year xiij^{s} iiij^{d}.

The rent or farm of one tenement there, next the tenement of Hugh Fletcher, demised to Alexander Pye* by indenture dated 12th day of March 33^{d} year of Henry VIII. for term of seventy-one years, yielding therefore by the year x^{s}.

The rent or farm of one tenement there, demised to Richard Etherygge by indenture dated the 23^{d} day of April in the 36th year of Henry VIII. for term of sixty-one years, yielding therefore by the year 8^{s}.

The rent or farm of one tenement in New Thame, demised to John Collens by indenture dated the 8th day of June in the 37th year of Henry VIII. for term of forty years, yielding therefore by the year 6^{s}.

The rent or farm of one tenement called "The Cage"† demised to James Roose by indenture for term of one hundred years, yielding therefore by the year 8^{s}.

The rent or farm of one tenement, next the tenement of Thomas Roose, demised to Henry Bosaker by indenture dated the 14th day of January in the 36th year of Henry VIII. for term of sixty-seven years, yielding therefore by the year 11^{s} 4^{d}.

The rent or farm of one tenement in New Thame with a garden there, demised to James Roose the elder by indenture dated the xxth of July in the 30th year of Henry VIII. for term of fifty-one years, yielding therefore by the year 7^{s} 10^{d}.

The rent or farm of one tenement there with 7½ acres of arable land in the Prestende ffylde, demised to Joan Mortimer by indenture dated 13th day of May in the 27th year of Henry VIII. for term of twenty-three years, yielding therefore by the year 7^{s}.

The rent or farm of one tenement there, demised to Thomas Persey by indenture dated the 8th day of December in the 34th year of Henry VIII. for term of twelve years, yielding therefore by the year 6^{s}.

The rent or farm of one shop with the appurtenances in the middle of New Thame, demised to John Poude by indenture dated the first day of February in the 26th year of Henry VIII. for term of forty years, yielding therefore by the year 5^{s} 4^{d}.

The rent or farm of one tenement there late in the tenure of Henry Bollars,* demised to the aforesaid John Poude by indenture dated the 20th day of December the 26th year of Henry VIII. for term of fifty-one years, yielding therefore by the year 10^{s}.

The rent or farm of one vacant parcel of land there lying in Fryday strete,† demised to James Watson by indenture (as is said), yielding therefore by the year 16^{d}.

The rent or farm of one tenement in New Thame, next the tenement of Robert Smythe, demised to John Ellys by indenture (as is said), yielding therefore by the year 7^{s}.

The rent or farm of one barn with a vacant parcel of land in ffryday strete, demised to John Lychepole by indenture (as is said), yielding therefore by the year 6^{s} 8^{d}.

The annual rent issuing from the tenement of Katherine Horne in New Thame by the year 12^{d}.

£18 18^{s} 6^{d} (including next).

Ewendon [i.e. Hughendon] in county of Buckingham.

The rent or farm of one messuage, with all lands, meadows, feedings, and pastures to the same appertaining, called Sparlyns, with one dovecote and close there, now in the tenure of Thomas Wycknell, yielding therefore by the year £7 11s.

The rent or farm of three tenements with the appurtenances there, now in the tenure of the aforesaid Thomas Wycknell, yielding therefore by the year 12^{s}.

The rent or farm of one tenement with certain lands there, now in the tenure of Thomas Cannon, yielding therefore by the year 6^{s} 8^{d}.

The rent or farm of one tenement there, now in the tenure of Robert Pawle, yielding therefore by the year 4^{s}.

The rent or farm of one parcel of land with one acre of land there, now in the tenure of John Byrt, yielding therefore by the year 8^{d}.

The rent or farm of certain lands there, now in the tenure of Thomas Wyckson, yielding therefore by the year 2^{s}.

Whereof

Reprises in rents resolute before paid to John Williams Knight as Lord of Thame aforesaid, issuing from the tenements there, videlicet from the tenement of Alice Yonge xij^{d}, from the vacant parcel of land in the tenure of the same Alice 3^{d}, from the tenement of Joan Owlefylde 6^{d}, from the

* This man was a scrivener of Thame, from whom descended the family which rose to opulence and distinction during the Great Rebellion.

† This is now called "The Birdcage," and is a small inn on the southern side of Middle Row. Competent judges of architectural style maintain that this tenement was erected as early as the reign of Edward IV.

* Members of this family, already mentioned in the notes to the Quartermain Pedigree (p. 298), spelt their names variously, thus:—"Bollowes," "Ballour," "Ballores," "Bollour," "Bollars," "Ballowe," "Bollowe," and "Ballowes."

† It will be gathered from the above that the name of Friday Street in Thame has existed for nearly three centuries and a half, and it may be reasonably regretted that modern innovators and change-mongers have endeavoured to alter it.

tenement of John Isley 8^{d}, from the tenement of Simon Synkler 12^{d}, from the tenement of Henry Batten 6^{d}, from the tenement of John Collens 6^{d}, from the tenement of James Rose $2^{s}\ 7^{d}$, from the tenement of Henry Bonaker 6^{d}, from the shop of John Ponde 6^{d}, from the tenement of the same John 12^{d}, from the tenement of John Ellys 6^{d}, in all by the year $9^{s}\ 6^{d}$.

And so remains clear by the year £18 9^{s}.

Whereof paid each week towards the foundation of Richard Quatermayne's five pauper men and one woman pauper, videlicet—John Irysbe, Robert Clare, John Kent, John Hunger, Thomas [*blank in original*], and Agnes Chaterton, each of them 6^{d} in the week, by the year £7 16^{s}. And to the same paupers jointly each week in bread 5^{d}, by the year $21^{s}\ 8^{d}$. In all by the year £8 $17^{s}\ 8^{d}$.

Continued by warrin, &c.

This is perpetually allotted for a Prest to be an ayde to the Vicar of Thame.

Paid also to John Yonge "*Chantarist*" there for his salary allowed by Walter Myldemaye Knight by the year £6.

The Incumbent has the Letters Patent of the King for term of life, &c.

And so remains clear beyond all the charges aforesaid by the year $71^{s}\ 4^{d}$.

Memorandum that the said Town of Tame is a greate Town and hath within the same 800 houseling people; and no other priests* there but only the Vicar of Tame, which Vicarage is a vicarage endowed, and hath for his endowment all privy tithe and all small tithes being scant worth 20 marks by year. And the said Vicar is not able to minister all sacraments and sacramentals to the said parishoners without the aid and help of another priest at the least, which said Chantry Priest hitherto hath been always assistant unto the said Vycar in his ministrations.

Examined by John Maynard, Deputy Surveyor.

The clear yearly value of the premisses over and besides the yearly charges and deductions above rehearsed $71^{s}\ 4^{d}$.

Which the King's Majesty by the advice of his honourable Council is pleased and consented to grant to Sir John Williams Knight and to his heirs for ever.

RICHARD SAKEVYLE.†

There is no evidence existing that Lord Williams was not trusted by Mary, as at the commencement, so at the close of her unfortunate reign; while, on Queen Mary's death, Elizabeth at once somewhat unjustly dismissed Dr. Gilbert Bourne, Bishop of Bath,‡ from the office of Lord President of the Marches of Wales, and conferred that important dignity on Lord Williams of Thame. But the latter did not live long to enjoy it. He was soon to find the end of his tether, and to be judged by a Higher Tribunal than that of his fellow Privy Councillors—the co-operators in his schemes of robbery and self-aggrandisement. In the latter years of his life there were not wanting tokens, steadily accumulating, that punishments for sacrilege do not always tarry. His early patron and a Prince of the Church, Wolsey, had passed to the Unseen World in disgrace in the winter of 1530; ten years afterwards the unscrupulous Lord Essex had been beheaded at Tower Hill. King Henry himself had died in despair a dreadful death in January 1547; five years afterwards the Duke of Somerset had expiated his many crimes on the scaffold; and Henry's only surviving son died in youth. Williams's own sons had likewise died young. His daughter by his second wife had passed away in infancy. Notwithstanding his enormous possessions,* and that he wanted for nothing that this World could give, a remembrance of what had been planned and performed by himself in order to secure those possessions must have been often before him. The Parish Church of Thame had been robbed, rifled, and made empty and desolate. The monks at Thame Abbey, and in hundreds of similar institutions, had been turned out of house and home with only a miserable pittance to support them. The poor of the Parish of Thame had been unjustly defrauded of their lawful rights and privileges. The old pensioners of the Quartermain's Charity had been dismissed, like the monks and monastery servants, to penury and starvation; and were flogged,† stocked, and branded if they complained and

* The Prebend having been suppressed, the Prebendary and his curates had at this time no existence.

† Lord Williams by his Will left a legacy to this man—a legacy which, in his official capacity, he well deserved. He was subsequently knighted.

‡ 1559. The Queen to the Bishop of Bath and Wells, revoking him from the office of Lord President of Wales, having appointed Lord Williams of Thame to be President and Sir Hugh Poulet Vice-President.—*State Papers, Domestic*, Elizabeth, Feb. 1559.

Letter from Lord Paget to Sir W. Cecil, stating that Lord Williams of Thame is very sick and not likely to recover. Solicits his office of Lord President of Wales.—March 17, 1559. Vol. ii., *State Papers, Domestic*, Elizabeth.

John, Lord Williams to Cecil. Has appointed him one of the supervisors of his Will, and left him his interest in Grafton Pastures. Solicits his favour in a controversy between Mr. Harcourt, Mr. Wentworth, and Anth. Docwray.—*Ibid.*

* His lordship's plate is thus described in his Will. I have modernised the spelling:—"I give to my wife these parcels of plate hereafter entering, that is to say, a pair of flagons gilt, weighing 123 ounces; a bowl chased, with a cover gilt, weighing 40 ounces, and a gilt bowl with a cover wherein she used to drink beer. Item a nest of bowls with a cover gilt, weighing 83 ounces. Item two salts four square gilt, weighing 30½ ounces; a standing cup with a cover gilt, given by the Queen's Majesty at the christening of my Lady's child. Item another standing cup with a cover gilt, given at the same time by the Duchess of Norfolk; another standing cup with a cover gilt, given at the same time by the Earl of Bedford; a standing cup with a cover gilt, given to me for a New Year's gift by the Queen's Majesty that now is. Item a pair of flagons parcel gilt, weighing 171 ounces; two pots with their covers parcel gilt, weighing 87½ ounces. Item, I give unto her both my basins and ewers whereof one is gilt and the other parcel gilt. Item four stock salts parcel gilt, weighing 34½ ounces. Item two spoons, weighing 30 ounces, and thirteen spoons weighing twenty-five ounces. Item one pair of the two great pair of white standing pots, weighing both pair together 219 ounces. Item I give unto her three nests of bowls white, with one cover. Item twenty-four silver dishes, marked and engraven with my arms, weighing 128 pounds and 125 ounces; and all my silver trenchers parcel gilt, and the best nest of gilt goblets, with the cover for them."

† "At Thame in Oxfordshire some 'proper stoute abbey-men'—elsewhere called 'abbeye-lubbers'—were convicted of begging and

begged. The solemn services of St. Christopher's Chantry were no longer said. At the same time the two Universities were deserted, Christian education neglected, the lower classes trampled on and degraded, morality undermined, and True Religion banished.

When, in the month of March, the report of Lord Williams's serious illness at Ludlow Castle became known, Lord Paget at once applied, without success, to Sir William Cecil, Elizabeth's Chief Minister, to secure the appointment for himself. On the very day after this application was despatched, Lord Williams, "being sick of body and yet of perfect remembrance," made his last Will and Testament.* The number of his properties was very considerable. He died possessed of the Manor, Town, and Lordship of Thame; the Manors of Rycott, Chalford, Albury, Weston-on-the-Green, Stokenchurch, Beaconsfield, Notley, Crendon, Brill, Gulhampstead, Sheffield, Uffeton, North Hinksey, South Hinksey, Oddington, Chesterton, Wendlebury, Lewknor, Sunningwell, Baiworth, Chiswelhampton, Leistropp, Horton, Beckley, Wytham, Comber in Montgomeryshire, Gresshull, and Burghfield—all of which, with the single exception of the last, which, —mortgaged to his relations the Edmondses—he had inherited from his father, were portions of the spoils of the Church and the property of those trustees who once held it for certain specific religious purposes.

It is quite evident that Lord Williams must have been possessed of considerable natural abilities, clear-headedness, caution, shrewdness, art, and discretion. That he had received the ordinary education of a gentleman, and that in all probability he was originally a lawyer or a scrivener, seems clear. From King Henry's standing-point his Grace had been well served by Williams in all the various offices which he had filled. The latter to have found himself swimming easily with the stream, first under that Monarch, then under his son and the Protector Somerset, and subsequently under Queen Mary, as well as under Queen Elizabeth, evinces the possession of no common powers. As a subservient courtier, an obsequious follower, and a faithful servant, he was probably without an equal. He had evidently been observant of the astonishing events of his own times, and no doubt often readily enough saw or forecast what was not unlikely to happen. His religious opinions, if he owned any, were possibly like easily-fitting clothes—worn without much inconvenience. Though he had no pretensions to being a great statesman, he nevertheless managed to secure for himself a high social position, enormous wealth, and a peerage. He lived to see a considerable circle of aspiring friends, who, like himself, had risen from comparative obscurity, seated at the Council-table or standing near the throne of the Monarch, allied to noble families, and secure in the possession of landed property, which had been not over-scrupulously obtained by them after the complete overthrow of the Old Religion and the monastic system, and the temporal ruin of those few noble Englishmen who had resisted and opposed the innovators.

It may be that Lord Williams, in his latter years, perceiving the increasing evils which these changes had so directly brought about—the decadence of True Religion, the potency of increased selfishness, the pressing need of educational institutions, the inefficiency of the universities, the losses of the agriculturists, and the widespread sufferings of the poor—resolved to make some slight atonement for the systematic robbery in which he had taken so prominent and successful a part, by founding a Grammar School at Thame; or, it may have been, that he saw in the premature deaths of his sons one after the other, and the cutting off of his own reasonable hopes, sure and impressive tokens of Divine vengeance, which he could not altogether disregard, and which his early education in the Religion of his forefathers may have caused him never wholly to forget or to be able to completely put aside.

Of that timely foundation, with the Alms Houses—practically a restoration of the old Charity of Richard Quartermain—particulars will be given later on.

Here it is only necessary to state that Lord Williams, leaving his second wife a widow, died at Ludlow Castle—the official residence of the Lord President of the Council of the Marches of Wales—on the 14th of October, 1559; and, as bearing on the History of the Church, to set forth the details of his funeral in the chancel of Thame Church, which took place a month later.

Amongst the interesting and valuable MSS. of Sir William Dugdale, formerly in the Ashmolean Museum, but now in the Bodleian Library at Oxford, is the following official record of that burial. It is written upon four pages of foolscap paper, and preserved in a volume marked T. 2; in parts the margin and edges are damaged. The funeral was evidently conducted by the Heralds in accordance with recognized customs—though, of course,

punished as vagabonds. Of these it is stated that on September 8th, 1571, "they took their stocking and whipping verie ill. So they were sore bloodied, and one thereafter died, no long while thereupon.'" See also *State Papers, Domestic*, Elizabeth, Vol. lxxx., for documents relating to similar punishments inflicted upon outcasts in Kent and Gloucestershire.

* A Mr. Maunde of Oxford was his local attorney,—one of the Maundes of Chesterton, near Bicester, descended from Simon Maunde, Steward of Ashridge, some of whom subsequently settled at Thame, and lived there and were there buried for six or seven generations. This attorney received the sum of £20 under Lord Williams's Will for having served him well, and he was to receive further 53s. and 4d. annually "by mine executors, so long as they have his help, travail, and furtherance in any matters of mine, or any matters of business touching the performance of my last Will and Testament." The attorneys who drew up this latter were Mr. Robert Nowell or Newell and Mr. Scrope of Lincoln's Inn.

the ancient and most consolatory Catholic rites had been almost everywhere directly abolished.

The Buryall of the Lo' Will'ms of Thame, 1559.

Th' ordre of th' interement and funeral of John Williams, Knight, Barron of Thame, who departyd this *Lyfe* on Satterdaye, the 14 of October, about 2 of the cloke in the mornyng, A'o p'imi Regine Elyzabethe, 1559, within her Ma'tis castle of Lodlowe in the countye of Salope, where he was lately comeo', being apointed Lord presydent of her grace's counsell in the marches ther, and after Brought to Rycote, and fro' thence to Thame, in the myddest chancell of the Parishe Churche, ther he was buryed as followithe :—

It' the said L. had ij wiffes, the fierst was T. late wiffe to Andrew Edmonde, of Essex, douther to Bledloe, by whom he had yssue Henry Williams, *sine prole*, Isabell, Margerye, and another sone, and Ffraunces, *sine prole*.

And by his ijde wiffe Margery *now Lyving*, dought'r to Tomas L' Wentworthe, syster to Thomas L' Wentworthe, that *now* is, and had yssue a doughter w'ch dyed, and left her an honorabill Living. And likewise delt honorably withe all his servants.

It' by his will he apoincted his executers S'r Walter Myldmay, Knights, John Doyley, of Greneland, in the count' of Oxford, Robert Doyley, his Brother, of Marten, in the same countie, gent., and W. Place, gent'man.

And for his offerseers wher appoincted Ffranc's, Erle of Bedforde, S'r William Seycyll, Knyght, Chieffe secretary to the Queen's Ma'tay, Raephe Scrope, of Lincol'sine, and Robert Nowell, of Graysende.

Item, after his body was colde yt was bowelled, tramelled, and wrapped in Lynnen clothe of dyverse foldes, and then put into A coffyn coveryd with blacke, and after that a charyott covered with blacke garnysshed w'th scotcheons was prepared the corps was leyd therin, and so by s'valle Journeys was brought to his house at Rycote, iij *myles* from Thame, in the countie of Oxforde, on Satterdaye, the 28* of the same monthe, wher mydest of the great chamber he was layd, and thereon a large pawle of black velvett cont' 24 yards w'th a crose of white satten of viij yards lyned w'th black boukeram garnisshed w'th scoshios of sarsenett of him and his wiffes. And about yt wher placed the banner and banner Rolles of armes as after dothe appere, w'ch where borne about yt to the churche, and ther in the sayd chamber yt Remayned untill Twysday, the 14 November, that hit was conveyed to Thame, as here after apperethe.

Item, the said great chamber was hanged withe clothe with the halle and others.

Item, the churche of Tame and chancell, and so on bothe sydes w'thout the west dore, was Likewise hangyd and garnyshed, and so was covered ij *fourmes* sett on ether syde about the herse for the executors and assystantes to sytt on, and in the myddes of the sayd chauncell was erected a stronge tymbre herse xix fotte in L. and ix do. in breadt' bourdyd above upon the joyses w'th upper and und'r Raylles, ij trest'es, vij stoles and a table all cov'ed with Brode narrow cotten garnysshed w'th escocheons, xiiij quyshons, vij of velvett and th'other of clothe, and all the grounde strayed with Russhes.

The pyllers fro' the rayles to the *Joyses* were a yarde & q'ter a pece coveryd wth. satten and one eche one eschocheon of mettall wrought on Bouckeram, and round about the Joysts hangyd a valence of sarsenet sett w'th L'res of gold of his wourde *A tous venaur*. And in the myddill of every square, one scoching of armes at w'ch valence hangyd a sylke fourge, and underneathe the Joysts one Ma'tie of sarcenett Lyned with boukeram wrought in the myden w'th his armes and crest, and beasts, in ev'y corner his Badge or crest—a wele. And next about the vallence from pyller to pyller was sett one Barre coveryd with one brode damaste and therappon on eche square two scochins of Boukeram, and on ev'y corner a great scochins of metall wrought on past brode, and above the damaste rounde aboute on the tope of the borde was sett one Gref of payst Boorde* of iiij nayles in Breade all gylt, and in the myddell of every square on the sayd gylde boorder was wrought his armes and creast, w'th Beasts supporting his and his wiffes in pale at the corners; at th'ende hangyd out ij Bannerolles, one of his fathers armes alone, and Bladlowe and Starkey quarterlye.

It' betwene the said gylte wourke and the damaste, and beneathe the damaste, between yt and the vallence, was sett rounde about ij rowes of pencells conteynyng a dossen.

It' on the table was sett the said corps and thereon the pawle of black velvett wheruppon in the mydell was sett his helme and crest, the sword l'ing on the Right syde, the targett on the Left, and the cote armes on the'ede.

And so all thing being in a readynes on twesdaye in the evening, the 14 of November, the corpse was pryvely conveyd by charyott to Thame, to Mr. W'm Dormer's house, wherfore that night he was placyd in the halle, and in the mornyng being Wynsday, the 15 November, about viij of the cloke, the said corpse was conveyed to the Churche as followithe :—

In prymys the ij conductors, Richard Alforde and Mr. Henry Thompson in b. coll. and b. staves.
Then the Prest and Clerke singing.
then Mr. Henry Norreys bering the standart his hode on,
then serton gent'men ij and ij their hodes on their shoulders,
then Mr. Doyley and Will. Place, gent' ij of the executors,
then Mr. John Wake bering the banner of Armes,
then Rouge Dragen off' of armes, bering th' elme and crest,
then Chester bering the targe,
then Clarenc' bering the cotte armour,
then the corps borne by xij of his Yeomen, vj at one tyme and vj at another, at every corner a gent'man with his hode on his heade, for the iiij assistances, viz. :—John Mills, gt., John Goodwyn, gt., W. Dormer, gt., and Thomas Reede, gt.; also at the iiij corners, iiij gent'men bearing the iiij Banerolle of armes, viz. :—Baker, gt., with the hono'r of the deffounct; Anthony Foster, gent., with one of the defuncte, and his wife that nowe is, Ma'gery, douth. to T. L'd Wentworthe, in palle; Anthony Butler, gent., with the iij of the defunct, in pale, w'th his first wiffe the dought. of Bladley, Late wiffe to Andrew Edmonds; and Burlassey, gent., with the iiij of his mother Elysabethe, dough're and heire to John More.
Then Sir Thomas Benger, K., and J. Doyley, esquier,

* This date may be the 26th, 27th, or 28th—for all these various figures seem to have been made and then crossed out in the MS.

* A "Gref of payst Boorde," *i.e.* a figure of a woman weeping.

then Mr. James Wentworthe and — Norreys, gent'man ussher,
And last Henry Norreys and R. Waynemen, esquirs, sons-in-Lawe to the defuncte.
Then the Yeomen in blacke ij and ij
And then all others that woulde.
In w'ch order they proced to the Churche through the stretes where ye corps placyd in the myddyll of the herse, the hatchements thereon, the vij morners w'thin the ryles, the banner and standert w'thout, at the feete the iiij banners holden at the iiij corners, all as after apperythe, and th' executors and assystants placyd—

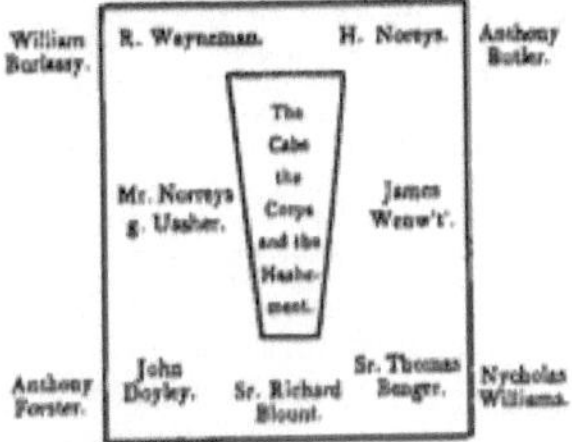

Then Chest' heralde Bade the prayer, w'ch he dyd also at other tymes as often as foll' :—

Blessed be God.

Then the service began, w'ch was the monyall p., but the psalmes wher of prayse and thanksgyving for the departure of the dead in the ff. of cryst. A' the ij chapters wher on out the boke of Job, and th'other the xv of the ffirst Epist' to the Corynthe', w'ch endyd, the com'ynon Began, and at the offering the chieff morner withe the other vj ffollowing him, and th'officers of th' armes before him, p'ceedyd upe to the offering, wheret he offering only a pece of gold for t'head penny, and ret'd to ther places, then at th' heade of herse Mr. Clarencieuex, to Mr. Benger and Mr. Doy' the cote armes, who with Chester before him offeryd upe the same, at whose hands Recyved yt and Layd yt on table of admynystr'con, and they Returned to theyr places.

Then Mr. C. and Mr. Wentw', and Mr. Norreys, the targett, who Lykwyse offeryd the same and returned.

Then Mr. Norreys and Mr. Waynemen rec'd of Mr. C. the sworde, who Likwyse offered the same and returned.

And Last Mr. Benger and Mr. Doyley receved and offeryd lykwyse th' helme and crest, and Returned and toke their places.

Then the chief morner alone, with C. before him, proceyded uppe and offeryd for himselfe alone, and Retourned to his place.

Then Mr. Benger and Mr. Doyley, w'th Chester before him, proceedyd upe, offeryd, and returned.

Then th'other iiij morners offeryd lykewyse ij after ij and returned.

Then offeryd the ij executors w'th Rouge before them and the iij assystants, and then the other gentl'men and the yeomen, and after them the Banner and L. the standred w'th R. before them.

Then the sermon bygan by Doctor——

Wiche ffynysshed, the comm'yon procedyd forward, wher sarten of y'm whent up and Rec'd, and being endyd, the morners departyd fourthe of the church, when the officers of armes and gent' before them in good order to Mr. Dormer's house, fro whense they cam, and ther shyfted them and Ryd to Rycott to dynner.

And they being dep'ted, the corps* was buryed in a vault underneath the herse now made for that purpose, w'ch endyd, everye man departyd to Rycott to dynner and otherwyse at ther leasure.

The dole was gyven at Mr. Dormers house, ij[d] a peece to all person who wher about.

Item, the hatchements Bannerools on the morrowe after was sett up in the walles of the chanchell in order by the heralds, who hade among them for their paynes in Redy mony ffourty marks, besyde the wholl fournitture of the herse as it stode, and their Black for their gownes and cotes, w'ch herse ther stode styll tyll after Crystmasse.

The following is the sentence in Lord Williams's Will† in which he leaves certain properties for the setting up and endowment of a Grammar School at Thame:—

It'm, I will and bequeath the rectories and personages of Brill, Okeley, Burstall, and Eastmeston, to mine Executors for eu'r to the intent that they or the survivor or survivors of them shall within the same erect a Free School in the Towne of Tame, and to fynde and sustaine with the proffitts thereof a Schoolmaster and an Usher for eu'r in such sorte and tyme as my said executors shall think most conveniente for the maintenance of the said Schoole for eu'r.

And the following relates to the rehabilitation and re-endowment of the Quartermain Charity—the possessions of which Williams had himself secured:—

It'm, I will certain landes and tenements in Sid'nam late p'cell of Littelmore to my executors for eu'r for th' intente therewith to augment and encrease the Almeshowse of Tame and the livings of the poor y[e] the same y[e] such sorte and tyme as they shall thinke conveniente.

And the following regarding his Funeral and Tomb:

It'm, I will the mannor of Leistropp and all my landes and tenementes known or called by the name of Leistropp, to be solde by my executors and the money thereof commings to be bestowed on my burial, in makinge of my Toombe at Tame, and in payment of my debtes.

His personal legacies by his Will were very numerous. He bequeathed six hundred sheep at Wytham to his son-in-law Norreys; a lease of a farm at Botley to one of his servants, William Harding, and part of his armour to the Earl of Bedford. He left various horses to Sir Walter Myldmay, Lord Hunsdon, Mr. Drue Drury, William Place and Anthony Butler, two of his

* See footnote on page 170.

† This Will was made 18 March 1558, and proved 19 Feb. 1559, before Dr. Walter Haddon, an official of Queen Elizabeth's "Ecclesiastical" Courts. The document is elaborately engrossed on vellum, and its margin is adorned with the armorial bearings of the deceased peer.

servants, and to Sir Richard Sackville. He left two nags to Mr. Secretary Cecil, and a standing cup and cover of silver-gilt to each of his daughters. To Dr. Bayley of Oxford,* his physician, "my damaske gown last made and furred with coney." To his brother-in-law, Lord Wentworth, "my best gowne furred with sables," and to Sir Ambrose Cave "my gowne of black velvet embroidered, and the cote to the same;" to Lord Robert Dudley, Master of the Horse, a black mare with her colt, "which mare I take to be the best mare in England." Lord Williams left to his niece, Margaret Winslowe, £40, "six feather beds with the bolsters of the same, and two garnishes of pewter vessels,"† and similar legacies to another niece, Elizabeth Doyley. He also left them each £20 (in addition to the sum mentioned above), and a similar legacy to Honor Cheney as a marriage-portion. He left to John Williams *alias* Stafford an interest in "a stock of sheep being upon Brill and Wellfeild," charging his own servant William Place that "he shall honestly find the said John Williams with the profit of the same."‡ To his kinsman Christopher Edmonds he gave "all my interest and inheritance in a certain mead in North Weston called Ham, lying along the river near Shobingdon." Amongst his servants the names of Harding, Sewell, Place, Dockersy, Cowper, Walpole, Lewis, Wiat, and Garland occur—all names of persons living in the neighbourhood who rose to the position of gentlepeople and esquires in a subsequent age. To his nephew Nicholas he left the Manor of Arbor in Berkshire; and to two youths, George and Leonard Williams, the former at school at Winchester, and the other "being now brought up at Brill,"—to each an annuity of £10. To his steward, Rowland Sprot, and other servants he left legacies, and to his physician 20 marks. To the Poor of Thame he bequeathed £20. His servant William Atkins received by his favour certain lands and tenements in Montgomeryshire, and his servant Thomas Webster £20 in money. Both these persons, in addition to others already mentioned, left families in Thame, the former amongst its wealthiest merchants during the seventeenth century.

Before a detailed account is given of the Grammar School—which has proved of such great advantage to the inhabitants of Thame for many generations—it seems desirable to set forth at length the Pedigree of Wenman and Wykeham, as also that of Norreys and Bertie, in order that it may be seen at a glance through what descents the various considerable properties, of which Lord Williams had obtained possession,* have passed, before they reached those favoured persons who now own them. These Pedigrees,—though some collateral branches in both have either been omitted (for brevity's sake) or not amplified,—if studied in connection with that of Lord Williams, will serve to illustrate the text of this book, and to make its historical statements more clear.

In the case of the Wenmans it should be specially noted that they received the honour of an Irish Viscountcy and Barony in the year 1628, which subsequently became extinct; but similar honours in 1683 were again conferred on another member of the same race. These honours, however, again became extinct on the death of Philip, the last Viscount Wenman, who had intermarried with the Berties, and so again connected the divided lines of Lord Williams's two co-heiresses. Furthermore, a Baronetcy had been bestowed upon Sir Francis Wenman, of Carswell, Knt., in 1662; but this dignity likewise became extinct by the decease of the Lord Viscount Wenman already referred to. A third peerage—the fourth hereditary dignity granted in the course of three centuries—was created in the person of Sophia, Baroness Wenman, in the year 1834, but with her death in 1870 it likewise ceased to be:—facts which abundantly serve to bear out the great principles embodied in the remarkable treatise of Sir Henry Spelman already referred to, but which are too often overlooked.

In the following Pedigrees great care has been taken to see that current genealogical errors have been corrected by a reference to Wills, Administrations, and Monumental Inscriptions.

* "Henry Bayley, Doctor of Physicke, married Anne, daughter of Edward Freere of the City of Oxford, Esq. He was buried at All Saints' Church, Oxford. '1556, Dec. 12, Henry Bayley, Med. Dr.'"

† The family of Winslow was connected with the Wenmans, which latter quartered their arms. The former were for some time tenants of Notley Abbey and its lands, and the following early entries in the old Register-book of Crendon relate to them:—

"1561. The xjth day of June Richard Winslowe the Sonne of Mr William Winslowe was baptized.

"1562. The nineteenth day of November William Winslowe ye Sonne of William Winslowe gentleman was baptized.

"1563. The xxth day of ffebruary John Wynslowe ye Sonne of Mr William Winslowe was baptized.

"1567. The vijth day of September Dorothie the daughter of Mr William Winslowe was baptized in Anno D'ni 1567.

"1568. The xxxth daye of Maye oulde Mother Windlowe of Notley was buryed."

The family still exists, and members of it reside at Thame, Prince's Risborough, and elsewhere.

‡ Tradition affirms that this youth was accidentally drowned, and the following extract from the old Register-book of Crendon Church appears to bear this out:—"The xxvjth day of June John Williams of Thame was buryed, the w'ch John was founde drowned in the River betwixt Thame and Crendon the xxiiijth daie of June, Anno Domini 1577."

* "The property of the Church in England has been granted by despots and tyrants to their minions, and has been made the foundation and establishment of powerful families, who, by virtue of that property, and not from any public service of their own, have had for generations a great portion of the government of this country and of its power and patronage."—Speech at High Wycombe, October 30, 1862, by the Right Hon. B. Disraeli, afterwards Earl of Beaconsfield.

Pedigree of Wenman and Wykeham of Thame Park.

ARMS.—1. *Sable, on a fesse argent three lions' heads erased gules between three anchors or.* [WENMAN.] 2. *Azure, a cross flory argent.* [WENMAN.] 3. *Gules, three lions passant argent.* [GIFFARD.] 4. *Ermine, a chief indented gules.* [BASSET.] 5. *Chequy argent and sable, on a chevron azure three roses or.* [VAUX.] 6. *Gyronny of eight or and sable, on a canton gules a covered cup or.* [STRATLEY.] 7. *Ermine, on a chevron engrailed sable three quatrefoils or.* [WINSLOWE.] 8. *Or, a chevron azure between three roses in chief gules, and in base a dolphin naiant gules.* [LANGSTON.] 9. *Argent, on a chevron azure three stags' heads caboshed argent between three lozenges sable.* [STAVELEY.] 10. *Argent, a chevron gules between three eagles displayed sable.* [FRANCIS.] 11. *Azure, a cross flory between four martlets argent.* [BLESSINGTON.] 12. *Argent, a lion rampant azure, depressed by a bend or and sable.* [FAUCONBRIDGE.]

Henry the Wainman or Wenman of Blewbury, Co. Berks. Living 1459. (1st husband.) = Emmota, daughter of Simpkin Hervey of the County of Hertford. = Thomas Fermor, alias Richards, of Witney, Co. Oxon, Wooldealer. M.I. sometime in the Church there. Will proved 9 Sept. 1485. (2nd husband.) = Alice .... Buried at Witney. (1st wife.)

Christian. Died 11 April 1501. M.I. in Witney Church aforesaid. (2nd wife.) = Richard Wainman of Witney, Clothier[1] and Woolstapler. Died in 1500. Buried in Witney Church. M.I. in North Aisle. = Anne Humphrey. (1st wife.)

William Fermor. — Richard Fermor.

Ralph Wainman,[2] a younger son. Under Steward of Pipewell Abbey, Co. Northants, in 1533.

Richard Wainman of Witney,[3] Co. Oxon, Yeoman and Woolstapler. Subsequently Merchant of the Staple of Calais. Died in 1533. Buried in the North Aisle of Witney Church. = Ann, daughter of John Bushe of Northleach, Co. Gloucester, Yeoman. Mentioned in her husband's Will. Living in 1533.

Arms of the Staple of Calais on Richard Wainman's Tomb.

William Wainman, alias Fermor. Died in 1521. Buried in Witney Church. Bequeathed his lands and cattle for religious services for his own soul and for all Christian souls. M.I. remaining in the North Aisle, he being represented full-faced, and in a shroud. = Elizabeth Fermor.

Laurence Fermor, Woolstapler of Witney. = Alice Wainman.

Thomas Wainman or Wenman of Carswell aforesaid, and of Witney, Co. Oxon. Merchant of the Staple of Calais, afterwards Knighted. "Suffered in his goods by the loss of Calais under Lord Wentworth." = Ursula, daughter and heiress of Thomas Giffard[4] of Twyford, Co. Bucks, Esq., by Mary, daughter and heiress of William Staveley of Bignell, Co. Oxon, Esq. Died at Twyford 7 Dec. 1558.

Richard Wenman of Carswell aforesaid, and of Thame Park, Esq., by right of his wife. Godson of his grandfather. Sheriff of Oxon in 1562 and 1570. Died in 1572. (1st husband.) = Isabella, daughter and coheiress of John, Lord Williams of Thame. Died in 1587. = Richard Huddlestone of Little Hasley, son of Anthony Huddlestone and Mary, daughter of Sir William Barentyne, Knt., his wife. He was High Sheriff of Oxon in 1579. (*See Note p. 66.*) (2nd husband.)

Harry. — William. — Thomas. } Living in 1533.

A

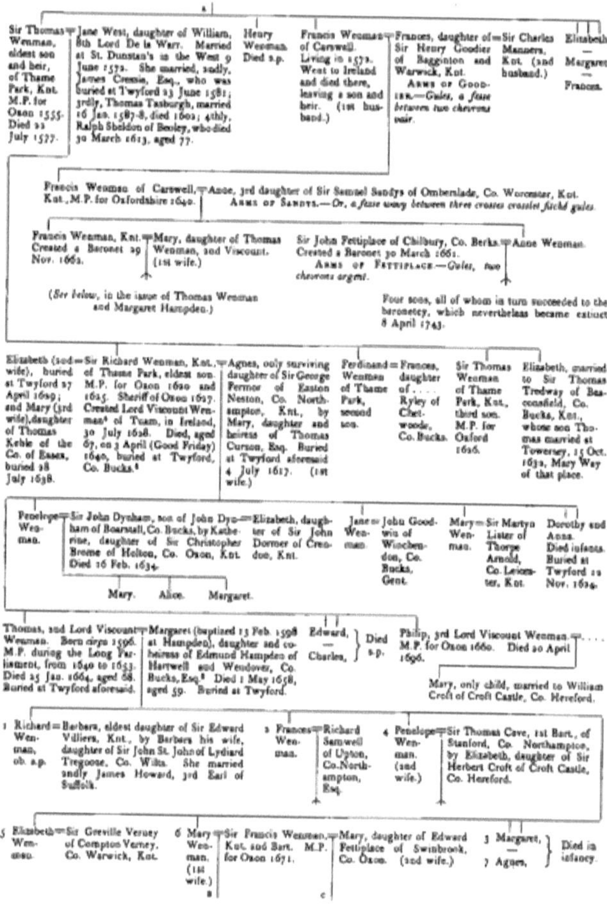
A
Sir Thomas Wenman, eldest son and heir, of Thame Park, Knt. M.P. for Oxon 1555. Died 22 July 1577. = Jane West, daughter of William, 8th Lord De la Warr. Married at St. Dunstan's in the West 9 June 1572. She married, 2ndly, James Cressie, Esq., who was buried at Twyford 23 June 1581; 3rdly, Thomas Tasburgh, married 16 Jan. 1587-8, died 1602; 4thly, Ralph Sheldon of Beoley, who died 30 March 1613, aged 77.
Henry Wenman. Died s.p.
Francis Wenman of Carswell. Living in 1572. Went to Ireland and died there, leaving a son and heir. (1st husband.) = Frances, daughter of Sir Henry Goodier of Bagginton and Warwick, Knt. = Sir Charles Manners, Knt. (2nd husband.)
Arms of Goodier.—Gules, a fesse between two chevrons vair.
Elizabeth. — Margaret. — Frances.
Francis Wenman of Carswell, Knt., M.P. for Oxfordshire 1640. = Anne, 3rd daughter of Sir Samuel Sandys of Omberslade, Co. Worcester, Knt.
Arms of Sandys.—Or, a fesse wavy between three crosses crosslet fitché gules.
Francis Wenman, Knt. Created a Baronet 29 Nov. 1662. = Mary, daughter of Thomas Wenman, 2nd Viscount. (1st wife.)
(See below, in the issue of Thomas Wenman and Margaret Hampden.)
Sir John Fettiplace of Chilbury, Co. Berks. Created a Baronet 30 March 1661. = Anne Wenman.
Arms of Fettiplace.—Gules, two chevrons argent.
Four sons, all of whom in turn succeeded to the baronetcy, which nevertheless became extinct 8 April 1743.
Elizabeth (2nd wife), buried at Twyford 27 April 1629; and Mary (3rd wife), daughter of Thomas Keble of the Co. of Essex, buried 28 July 1638. = Sir Richard Wenman, Knt., of Thame Park, eldest son. M.P. for Oxon 1620 and 1625. Sheriff of Oxon 1627. Created Lord Viscount Wenman[4] of Tuam, in Ireland, 30 July 1628. Died, aged 67, on 3 April (Good Friday) 1640, buried at Twyford, Co. Bucks.[5] = Agnes, only surviving daughter of Sir George Fermor of Easton Neston, Co. Northampton, Knt., by Mary, daughter and heiress of Thomas Curson, Esq. Buried at Twyford aforesaid 4 July 1617. (1st wife.)
Ferdinand Wenman of Thame Park, second son. = Frances, daughter of . . . . Ryley of Chetwoode, Co. Bucks.
Sir Thomas Wenman of Thame Park, Knt., third son. M.P. for Oxford 1626.
Elizabeth, married to Sir Thomas Tredway of Beaconsfield, Co. Bucks, Knt., whose son Thomas married at Towersey, 15 Oct. 1632, Mary Way of that place.
Penelope Wenman. = Sir John Dynham, son of John Dynham of Boarstall, Co. Bucks, by Katherine, daughter of Sir Christopher Brome of Holton, Co. Oxon, Knt. Died 16 Feb. 1634. = Elizabeth, daughter of Sir John Dormer of Crendon, Knt.
Mary. Alice. Margaret.
Jane Wenman. = John Goodwin of Winchendon, Co. Bucks, Gent.
Mary Wenman. = Sir Martyn Lister of Thorpe Arnold, Co. Leicester, Knt.
Dorothy and Anna. Died infants. Buried at Twyford 12 Nov. 1624.
Thomas, 2nd Lord Viscount Wenman. Born circa 1596. M.P. during the Long Parliament, from 1640 to 1653. Died 25 Jan. 1664, aged 68. Buried at Twyford aforesaid. = Margaret (baptized 13 Feb. 1598 at Hampden), daughter and co-heiress of Edmund Hampden of Hartwell and Wendover, Co. Bucks, Esq.[8] Died 1 May 1658, aged 59. Buried at Twyford.
Edward, — Charles, } Died s.p.
Philip, 3rd Lord Viscount Wenman. M.P. for Oxon 1660. Died 20 April 1696. = ...
Mary, only child, married to William Croft of Croft Castle, Co. Hereford.
1 Richard Wenman, ob. s.p. = Barbara, eldest daughter of Sir Edward Villiers, Knt., by Barbara his wife, daughter of Sir John St. John of Lydiard Tregoze, Co. Wilts. She married 2ndly James Howard, 3rd Earl of Suffolk.
2 Frances Wenman. = Richard Samwell of Upton, Co. Northampton, Esq.
4 Penelope Wenman. (2nd wife.) = Sir Thomas Cave, 1st Bart., of Stanford, Co. Northampton, by Elizabeth, daughter of Sir Herbert Croft of Croft Castle, Co. Hereford.
5 Elizabeth Wenman. = Sir Greville Verney of Compton Verney, Co. Warwick, Knt.
6 Mary Wenman. (1st wife.) = Sir Francis Wenman, Knt. and Bart. M.P. for Oxon 1671. = Mary, daughter of Edward Fettiplace of Swinbrook, Co. Oxon. (2nd wife.)
B C
3 Margaret, — 7 Agnes, } Died in infancy.

a | c

Francis Wenman, eldest son and heir. Born *circa* 1652. Died 5 Sept. 1663. Buried at Thame Park. M.I. remaining.

Richard Wenman, 4th Viscount, by a new creation, and of Carswell, Bart. Died *circa* 1691. = Katherine, elder daughter and coheiress of Sir Thomas Chamberlain of Wickam and Northbrook, Co. Oxon, Bart. Married 2ndly, in 1698, James, 1st Earl of Abingdon (who had previously married Eleanor, eldest daughter of Sir Henry Lee, Bart., by Anne Danvers); and 3rdly Francis Wroughton of Heskett, Co. Wilts.

Richard Smith, of the Smiths of Padbury, Co. Bucks. = Dorelina Wenman, only child.

Richard Wenman, 5th Viscount. Died at Thame Park, *non compos mentis*, 28 Nov. 1729. = Susanna, daughter of Seymour Wroughton, who died 19 Nov. 1736, and was buried at Thame Park. (Sister of his mother's 3rd husband.)

Katherine Wenman. = Hon. Robert Bertie, 4th son of the 1st Earl of Abingdon.

A younger daughter. = John Wickstead, Esq.

Philip, 6th Viscount Wenman. Born 23 Nov. 1719, bapt. at St. James's, Westminster, 13 Dec. of the same year. D.C.L. of Oriel Coll. Oxon, 15 April 1741. M.P. for City of Oxford from 1749 to 1754. Died 16 July, buried 23 July 1760, at Thame Park. = Sophia, born *circa* 1715. Daughter and coheiress of James Herbert of Tythorpe, Co. Oxon, Esq. Married 13 July 1741. Died 19 July 1787, aged 72. Buried at Thame Park. M.I. remaining.

Richard Wenman. = Jemima, relict of Colonel Caulfeild.

Philip, 7th Viscount Wenman. Born 18 April 1742. M.P. for Oxon, 1768–1790. M.A. Oriel 29 Oct. 1762. D.C.L. 7 July 1773. Died without issue, aged 58, 26 March 1800.[6] = Lady Anne Eleanor Bertie, daughter of Willoughby, 3rd Earl of Abingdon, by Anna Maria, daughter of Sir John Collins, Knt.

Thomas Francis Wenman. Born 18 Nov. 1745. B.C.L. All Souls 24 Jan. 1771. D.C.L. 7 July 1780.

Richard Wenman. Born 13 Nov. 1746. Died young. Buried at Witney.

Herbert Henry Wenman. Born 18 July 1749. Died young. Buried at Thame Park.

Sophia Wenman. Born 17 Aug. 1743. In her issue the heiress of her father. Married 30 Dec. 1768. Died 1791. = William Humphrey Wykeham of Swalcliffe, Co. Oxon, Esq.[7] Born 1734. Buried at Swalcliffe 2 Oct. 1783.

Arms of Wykeham.—*Argent, two cheveronels sable between three roses gules, seeded or, barbed vert.*

Susanna Wenman. Born 10 Nov. 1744. Died young. Buried at Witney.

Mary Wenman. Died in 1757. Buried at Thame Park.

Miss Hughes. No issue. (2nd wife.) = William Richard Wykeham of Swalcliffe. Born 24 Oct., bapt. 2 Nov. 1769. Died 1 July 1800. = Elizabeth, daughter of Mr. William Marsh. (1st wife.)

William Wykeham. Born in 1791. Died 13 Nov. 1798.

Sophia Elizabeth Wykeham. Born 10 March 1790. Created Baroness Wenman 3 June 1834. Died at Thame Park, unmarried, 9 August 1870. Buried under the Chapel of Thame Park. M.I. remaining. Will made 29 May 1866, proved 13 Oct. 1870.

Eliza, daughter of Fiennes Wykeham-Martin of Leeds Castle, Co. Kent, Esq. Married 24 Jan. 1825. No issue. (2nd wife.) She married 2ndly, 22 Sept. 1836, Edward, 2nd son of Sir John Simeon, Bart., M.P.

Arms of Martin.—*A lion rampant within an orle of mullets and cross-crosslets, alternately, or.*

= Philip Thomas Wykeham.[8] Graduated B.C.L. of All Souls, Oxon, 31 Oct. 1800. Captain of the Thame Volunteers, 1803. Died 5 Sept. 1832. = Hester Louisa, daughter of Fiennes Trotman[9] of Syston Court, Co. Gloucester, Esq. Married 1 Sept. 1806. Died 26 Oct. 1823. (1st wife.)

Sir Edward Johnson. (2nd husband.) = Harriet Wykeham. = Hon. and Rev. Willoughby Bertie. Educated at Trin. Coll. Oxon, where he graduated B.A. 10 Nov. 1778; B.D., All Souls, 5 July 1794. (1st husband.)

Philip Thomas Herbert Wykeham, of Tythorpe House, near Thame, eldest son. Born 9 Sept. 1807. Sometime in the 7th Hussars. J.P. and D.L. for Bucks. High Sheriff of Oxon 1837. Captain of the 8th Oxfordshire Rifles. Died unmarried 21 May 1879. Buried at Thame Park. Will made 26 April 1879, proved 12 July of the same year.

Aubrey Wenman Wykeham,[10] of Chinnor, Co. Oxon, second son. Born 15 April 1809. Educated at Trin. Coll. Oxon, where he graduated B.A. 25 May 1831. Died at Barnsley Park 21 Oct. 1879. = Georgiana, daughter of Sir James Musgrave of Barnsley, Co. Gloucester, Bart., by Clarissa Blackall, his wife. Married 22 June 1836. Died 18 April 1879, at Barnsley. Buried at Thame Park.

Arms of Musgrave.—*Azure, six annulets, three, two, and one.*

Arms of Blackall.—*See* Pedigree of Cozens *of Tetsworth, p.* 229.

Wenman Aubrey Wykeham. Born 24 July 1837. = Jane, 3rd daughter of Admiral the Hon. George Grey.

Philip James Digby Wykeham. Born 12 Oct. 1839. = Georgina Caroline, daughter of Joseph John Henley, Esq.

F F 2

SOME EXPLANATORY NOTES OF THE FOREGOING PEDIGREE.

[1] The second descent in this Pedigree—proved by monumental inscriptions at Witney, once existing but now lost—and by Anthony à Wood's Collections in the Bodleian Library, as well as by existing Wills and Inquisitions after death—is not set forth in the Visitations of Oxfordshire, one of the Richard Wenmans being omitted; while all the printed and received pedigrees of the Viscounts Wenman are full of mistakes and omissions. There can be little doubt, however, that the Heralds of the Tudor and Stuart eras sometimes drew upon their imaginations, and that occasionally in subsequent times too little regard has been had to historical exactness.

[2] "They [the Wenmans] were originally clothiers of Witney; and, being the first that used wains or carts with four wheels to carry their cloth to London, were called 'Wainmen;' or else the first was a driver of a wain."—*Giles's History of Witney*, p. 102. London: 1852.

[3] Richard Wenman of Witney, co. Oxon, "Marchant of the Staple of Caleys." Will made 20 Oct. 1533; proved 18 Dec. 1534. "I Richard Wenman of Witney in the countie of Oxon, marchant of the Staple at Caleys, bequeth my body to be buryed in the Church of Wyttenny." Mentions his wife Anne. Gives to Thomas his son a thousand marks and all his cattle and sheep. To Elisabeth Fermor, the wife of his brother William Fermor, he gives 10 marks. Also to his cousin Richard Humfrey xx*s*, and to Fabyan his son xl*s*. Makes his son Thomas Wenman executor, and his brothers William Fermor and Richard Fermor overseers. Gives to Ursula his daughter, the wife of Thomas Wenman, a juell of v*li*, and to her son Richard Wenman, his godson, xl*li*; and to each of his brethren, Harry, William, and Thomas, xl*li*; and to Ann Wenman and Elisabeth Wenman to each of them c marks.

[4] "Here lyeth buryed the Bodyes of Thomas Giffard of Twiffard in the cou'tye of Buck' esquyer and Marie his wyffe doughter of Wyll'm Staveley of Bignell esquyer, which Thomas deceasyd the xxv day of November in the yere of o'r lorde God MCCCCCL. on whose Soules Jh'u have mercy. Amen."—Brass, South Aisle, Church of the Assumption B.V.M., Twyford, co. Bucks.

Amongst the gifts to the servants of the late Abbey of Pipewell in Northamptonshire, when they were dismissed, were the following:—Rauffe Wenman, 3*s*. 4*d*.; William Farmar, 5*s*. 0*d*.; Thomas Clerke, 3*s*. 4*d*.—Inventory, Court of Augmentations, Public Record Office.

[5] Sir Richard Wenman, Knt., Lord Viscount Wenman of Tuam. Will dated 15 Aug. 1638, a Codicil added in March 1640; proved 30 April 1640 by Sir Thomas Wenman, Knt., son and heir, now Viscount Wenman, sole executor. He desires to be buried in Twyford Church by his wives. Mentions manors, lands, etc., in Oxon and Bucks, and names his son Philip Wenman, and young Edward Sergian, son of Bezaliel Sergian and Elizabeth now his wife. Leaves gifts to the poor of Twyford, Thame, and Brackley. His two sons-in-law, Sir Martyn Lister and Mr. John Goodwin, to be overseers. Witness, William Basse.

[6] The following remains on a monument at Twyford:—

In memory of the
Right Honble Richard Ld Viscount
Wenman (sonne of Tho' Wenman Esqr
& Jane Daught^r of William De La Werre,
The said Thomas being sonne of Sr Richd Wenman
& Isabell eldest Daught^r of John Lord Williams of
Thame, which Sr Richard was sonne of Tho' Wenman
Esqr & Ursula Daughter & heyre of Thomas Giffard
Esqr Lord of this manor) the said Richard Lord Visc^t
Wenman (had to wife Agnes Daughter of Sr George
Fermor of East Neston in ye County Northampton) he
died on Good Fryday A^o Dⁱ 1640 Aged 67 & ye said
Agnes his wife died A^o Dⁱ 1617.
By the care of the Right Honble Thomas Ld Visc^t Wenman
their sonne, this Monument was erected, who deceased
the 25th day of January A^o Dⁱ 1664. Aged 68 yeares
who marryed Margaret Daughter and heire
of Edmund Hampden of Hartwell in the
County of Buckingham Esqr who died
the 1st day of May A^o Dⁿⁱ 1658 aged 59.

Of this first-named peer it has been written that "His lordship zealously promoted the Royal cause during the Civil War, and at his house Dr. Seth Ward, afterwards Bishop of Salisbury, found an asylum, when persecuted for his fidelity to the King."—*Lords Lieutenants and High Sheriffs of Oxfordshire*, by J. M. Davenport, F.S.A. Privately printed. Note on p. 73, dated July 1868.

[7] "In remembrance of my love unto Sir Thomas Weyneman Knight and Dame Margaret his wife, my will is that my Heirs, Executors, Administrators, and Assigns shall pay unto the said Sir Thomas and Dame Margaret his wife and to the longer liver of them the sum of Fifty Pounds yearly at the two usual feasts."—Will of Sir Alexander Hampden of Hartwell, co. Bucks, Knt., made 1 Nov. 1617; proved 24 April 1618.

[8] "The family of Wykeham still possess lands at Swalcliffe near Banbury, which were held by their direct male ancestor Robert the son of Walchelin at the date of the Domesday Survey in 1086."—*History of Leeds Castle*, by Charles Wykeham Martin, M.P., p. 201. London: 1869.

"Mary, daughter of Edward Underhill, lessee of the Manor of Ettington, co. Warwick, by Margaret Middlemore of Edgbaston, married Humphry Wickham of Thame and Swalcliffe, co. Oxon."—From a Note by the late E. P. Shirley, Esq., of Ettington Park.

"Wenman, Viscount Tuam, son and heir of the Lady-dowager Abbington, an ideot, his custody granted to the Visc^t Ryalton, son and heir of the Earl of Godolphin, 23 January 1706-7."—*Memoranda* in Heraldry by Peter Le Neve. This Lady Abingdon was Catherine, daughter of Sir Thomas Chamberlain, and widow of Richard, fourth Viscount Wenman. Viscount Ryalton was M.P. for Oxfordshire in 1708, and was succeeded in that honour by Mr. Francis Clerke.

[9] Bucknell, in Oxfordshire, originally belonged to the Moyles, who sold it to the Ewres or Ewerrs—an old family, some of whom in quite a humble position subsequently resided at Thame. Mr. Edward Ewre, the purchaser of Bucknell, had married Margaret, daughter of Mr. Francis Powre of Bletchingdon, a descendant of the "Pouvres" or "Paupers," who had been such great benefactors to Thame Abbey, and whose names occur so constantly in its Chartulary. From these the Trotmans obtained it for a very small pecuniary consideration, and it subsequently came to Mr. Fiennes Trotman of Syston Court.

[10] "Philip, last Lord Viscount Wenman, and the last of his line, buried at Thame Park, by his Will bequeathed his Estates at Twyford and Charndon to Mr. Philip Thomas Wykeham of Tythorpe House near Thame, who sold the same to pay off various accumulated mortgages, reserving, however, the Manor of Twyford and Charndon and part of Charndon Wood."—Note by Rev. Mr. Lee.

[11] "Mr. Aubrey Wenman Wykeham, the younger brother, married Georgiana, sister of Sir James Musgrave, Bart., of Barnsley Park, Gloucestershire. Sir James was succeeded by the Rev. Sir William Augustus Musgrave, Rector of Chinnor; and on his death, in September 1875, the estate descended to Mr. Wykeham. Under the provisions of Sir James Musgrave's Will, Mr. Aubrey W. Wykeham assumed by Letters Patent the name of Musgrave in addition to his own name, and quartered the arms of Musgrave with his family coat. Mrs. Wykeham Musgrave died, 18 April 1879, at Barnsley Park, and was buried at Thame Park; the Barnsley Estate then vested in her eldest son, Wenman Aubrey Wykeham, who shortly after assumed the additional name and quartered the arms of Musgrave (under the authority of the Patent to his father). On Mr. P. T. H. Wykeham's death (31 May 1879) the Thame Park, Buckinghamshire, and Kent Estates passed (under Lady Wenman's Will) to his brother W. A. Wykeham-Musgrave, whilst the Tythorpe and Emmington Estates were devised by Mr. P. T. Herbert Wykeham's own Will to his second nephew—son of Mr. W. A. Wykeham-Musgrave—Mr. Philip James Digby Wykeham, who has married Miss Georgiana Caroline Henley, granddaughter of our old county member. On Mr. W. A. Wykeham-Musgrave's death, on the 21 October 1879, the Thame Park and other estates subject to the Trusts of Lady Wenman's Will vested in his eldest son, the said Wenman Aubrey Wykeham-Musgrave."—Letter to the Author from Mr. Henry Birch, of Thame, Solicitor.

To face pp. 441-442

Various Heraldic Book-plates. No. II.

Blackall, Deane, Wenman, Ashhurst, Abingdon, Weymouth

Pedigree of Norreys, Bertie, and others,

(including the Dukes of Ancaster, the Earls of Lindsey, and the Earls of Abingdon; as also Francis, Viscount Thame and Earl of Berkshire.)

ARMS OF NORREYS OF BERKS AND OXON.—*Quarterly, argent and gules, in the second and third quarters a fret or, over all a fesse azure.*
DUKE OF ANCASTER AND KESTEVEN.—*Argent, three battering-rams barways in pale proper, headed, armed, and garnished azure.*
EARL OF LINDSEY.—*1st and 4th.* (As arms of Dukes of Ancaster.) *2nd and 3rd. Sable, a shattered castle triple-towered argent.*
EARL OF BERKSHIRE AND VISCOUNT THAME.—*Quarterly, argent and gules, a fesse azure: in the second and third quarters a fret or.*
EARL OF ABINGDON.—(As arms of Earls of Lindsey.)

John Norreys of Yatendon, Co. Berks. Master of the Wardrobe to King Henry VI. Died A.D. 1466. Buried at Bray in the same County.

Isabel, daughter and coheiress of Sir Edmond Ingletthorpe, Knt., and widow of John Nevill, Marquis of Montacute, so created 25 May 1470. (1st wife.) = William Norreys of Yatendon aforesaid, son and heir. Knight of the Body to Edward IV. = Jane de Vere, daughter of John de Vere, 12th Earl of Oxford, by Elizabeth his wife, daughter of Sir John Howard, uncle by the half-blood of John Howard, 1st Duke of Norfolk. (2nd wife.)

Three sons, who died young.

John Langford of Bradfield, Co. Berks. = Isabel Norreys.

John Cheney of Woodbey, Co. Berks. = Joane Norreys.

William Ferrnor of Somerton, Co. Oxon. = Elizabeth Norreys.

Edward Norreys, son and heir of his father. Subsequently Knighted. = Frideswide, daughter and coheiress of Francis, Lord Lovell, by Joane, sister and heiress of William, 2nd Viscount Beaumont.
ARMS OF LOVELL.—*Barry nebulé of six or and gules.*

John Norreys. Esquire of the Body to Henry VIII. Died without legitimate issue. = Elizabeth, daughter of John Braye of Chelsea, Co. Middlesex, and sister of Edmund, 1st Lord Braye of Braye, Co. Bedford.
ARMS OF BRAYE.—*Argent, a chevron between three eagles' legs erased sable.*

Henry Norreys. Usher of the Black Rod, and Gentleman of the Privy Chamber to Henry VIII. Constable of Wallingford Castle. Beheaded 14 May 1536. = Mary, daughter of Thomas, Lord Dacre.

Henry Norreys or Norris. Resided at Wytham, Co. Berks, one of the Manors of his father-in-law. Knighted at Rycott in 1566. Sometime Ambassador to France. Summoned by Writ to the House of Lords, 8 May 1572, as Baron Norreys of Rycott, Co. Oxon. Will dated 24 Sept. 1589. Died in 1600. Buried at Rycott. Monument in Westminster Abbey. = Margery, younger daughter and coheiress of John, Lord Williams of Thame, by whom her husband acquired the Lordships of Rycott and of Priestend in the Parish of Thame.

Henry Norreys. Died, unmarried, of a wound received in battle.

Thomas Norreys. Knighted. Sometime President of the Council of Munster in Ireland. Had a grant of the confiscated Estate of Mallow from Queen Elizabeth. = Elizabeth.

Maximilian Norreys. Slain in Brittany.

Edward Norreys. Sometime Governor of Ostend. Knighted. Died in 1604.

Sir John Jephson of Froyle, Co. Hants, Knt. (Second son of William Jephson by Mary, daughter of John Darell.) Major-General and Privy Councillor in Ireland. = Elizabeth Norreys, only daughter and heiress of her father.

William Norreys. Marshal of the Town of Berwick. Knighted. Died 25 Dec. 1580. = Elizabeth, daughter of Sir Richard Morrison, Knt., by Bridget, daughter of Lord Hussey. She married secondly Lord Clinton.

John Norreys. Knighted and made President of the Council of Munster in Ireland. A celebrated Military Commander. Died there *circa* 1592, unmarried.

Edward Norreys. Governor of Ostend. Knighted. Died there, unmarried.

Francis, only child, who succeeded as the 2nd Baron Norreys. Created Viscount Thame and Earl of Berkshire 28 Jan. 1620. K.B. Died in the same year, when these new creations became extinct, but the Barony of Norreys descended to his daughter Elizabeth. Buried at Rycott. = Bridget de Vere, daughter and coheiress of Edward de Vere, 17th Earl of Oxford, by Anne his 1st wife, daughter of William Cecil, Lord Burleigh.

Edward Wray, 2nd son of Sir William Wray, Bart., of Glentworth, Co. Lincoln. Groom of the Bedchamber to King James I.
Arms of Wray.—*Azure, on a chief or, three martlets gules.*
= Elizabeth Norreys, only daughter and heiress of her father.[1] Married at St. Mary's Aldermary, in the City of London, 27 March 1612. Buried in Westminster Abbey 28 Nov. 1645.

Diana Wray. Died young. Buried at Thame 17 Nov. 1630.

Edward Sackville, 2nd son of Edward, 4th Earl of Dorset. Died in 1646. (1st husband to Bridget Wray.) = Bridget Wray. Born 1627. Second daughter and heiress of her father. (2nd wife to Montagu Bertie.) = Montagu Bertie, 2nd Earl of Lindsey. (2nd husband to Bridget Wray.) = Martha Cockayne. (1st wife.)

(*See* Pedigree B, *pages* 447-8.)

Philadelphia, daughter of Sir Edward Norris of Weston. = Henry Bertie of North Weston and Chesterton, Co. Oxon. Buried at Chesterton 5 Dec. 1734. = A sister of Sir Henry Featherstone, Bart.

Edward Bertie. Died young.

Charles Dormer, Earl of Carnarvon. = Mary Bertie. Died without issue.

James Bertie, eldest son. = Elizabeth, daughter of Mr. Roger Harris of Winchester.

Norris Bertie of North Weston in Thame.

Charles Montagu Bertie. M.A. of Magdalen College, Oxon, 12 March 1718. Rector of Uffington, Co. Lincoln.

Francis Clerke, Esq., of North Weston. = Catherine Bertie.

(*See* Pedigree of Clerke, *pages* 313, 314.)

Eleanor Bertie and Ann Bertie. Both died unmarried.

Eleanora, eldest daughter and co-heiress of Sir Henry Lee of Ditchley, Co. Oxon, Bart., by Anne, daughter of Sir John Danvers of Dauntsey, Co. Wilts, Knt., and sister and co-heiress of Henry Danvers, Esq. (1st wife.) = James Bertie. Born *circa* 1653. Son and heir, and by right of his mother Lord Norreys. Lord Lieutenant of Oxfordshire 1674-97. Created Earl of Abingdon 30 Nov. 1682. Died 22 May 1699, aged 46. Buried at Rycott. M.I. in the Chapel. = Katherine, eldest daughter and coheiress of Sir Thomas Chamberlain, Bart., and widow of Richard, 4th Lord Viscount Wenman.§ Died without issue. (2nd wife.) She married, thirdly, James Wroughton of Estcott, Co. Wilts, and died 9 Feb. 1741.

Robert Bertie. M.P. for Westbury, Co. Wilts. Died without issue 16 Aug. 1710. = Katherine, daughter of Richard, 4th Viscount Wenman of Thame Park.

Peregrine Bertie. Captain R.N. Died unmarried in 1709, being a prisoner of war in France.

Charles Bertie. B.C.L. 1706. D.C.L. 1711. Professor of Natural Philosophy at Oxford. Rector of Kenn, Co. Devon. = Elizabeth, daughter of the Rev. Mr. Kerry, Rector of Treddington, Co. Worcester.

Richard, Viscount Bulkeley. = Bridget Bertie.

Sir William Courtenay, Bart. = Anne Bertie.

Mary Bertie. Died unmarried.

Ann, daughter and heiress to Peter Venables, Baron of Kinderton, by his wife Catherine Shirley, one of the daughters of Sir Robert Shirley. Born 7 May 1674. Married 22 Sept. 1687. Lady of the Bedchamber to Queen Anne. Died without issue 28 April 1715, aged 41. Buried at Rycott. (1st wife.) = Montagu Bertie, eldest son and heir. Constable of the Tower of London. Lord Lieutenant of Oxfordshire in 1702. Died 16 June 1743. = Mary, daughter and sole heiress of James Gould of Dorchester, and widow of General Charles Churchill. Married 13 Feb. 1716-7. Died in 1756. (2nd wife.)

James Bertie, Lord Norreys. Died of the smallpox, in his father's lifetime, 25 Feb. 1717-8.

James Bertie, 2nd son. Born 13 March 1673. Of Stanwell, Co. Middlesex. M.P. for Middlesex. = Elizabeth, only surviving daughter of George, 7th Lord Willoughby of Parham. Born 29 April 1673. Married 5 Jan. 1691. Died in childbed 26 Sept. 1715, aged 42. Buried at Stanwell aforesaid.

Arabella Susanna, daughter of Viscount Glenawly, Co. Fermanagh. Baptized at St. Margaret's, Westminster, 7 Feb. 1666-7. Died without issue 10 Dec. 1708. (1st wife.) = Henry Bertie. Born 4 May 1675. M.P. for Westbury, Co. Wilts. Died in Dec. 1735. = Mary, daughter of Peregrine Bertie, son of Montagu, 2nd Earl of Lindsey.

Charles Bertie. = Susanna Bertie. Baptized at Kensington 18 Jan. 1719.

Henry Bertie.

John Bertie. Clerk in Orders. Rector of Kenn, Co. Devon, and Prebendary of Exeter. = Mary, daughter of Mr. Clerk Nicholas.

Robert Cotymore of Cotymore, Co. Carnarvon, Esq. = Bridget Bertie.

Eight other children, died in infancy.

John. William. Norreys. Each died young.

Willoughby Bertie.

Anne Bertie. — Mary Bertie.

Bridget Bertie. — Elizabeth Bertie.

Frances Mary Bertie.

Eleanor Bertie. — Isabella Bertie.

Mary Bertie. — Sophia Eustachia Bertie.

b

Willoughby Bertie, eldest son. Born at Lindsey House, Westminster, 28 Nov. 1692. Succeeded his uncle as 3rd Earl in 1743. Died 10 June 1760. = Anna Maria, daughter of Sir John Collins, Knt. Married at Florence in August 1727. Died 21 Dec. 1763.

Edward Bertie. 2nd son. Died 21 Sept. 1733.

William Bertie, 3rd son. M.A. of Christ Church, Oxon, 18 March 1729; B.D. 6 March 1741; D.D. 2 May 1752. Perpetual Curate of Long Crendon, Co. Bucks. Rector of Albury, Co. Oxon. =

James Bertie. — Richard Bertie. — Frances Bertie. — Sophia Bertie. — Anne Bertie.

Thomas Clifton of Clifton and Lytham, Co. Lancaster, Esq. Born in 1728. = Jane Bertie. Married 29 Sept. 1760, as his 3rd wife. Died 1791.

Bridget Bertie. Died unmarried 9 Dec. 1760.

Anne Bertie.

Philip, 7th and last Lord Viscount Wenman of Thame Park. = Anne Eleanor Bertie.

Miles Stapleton of Wighill and Clints, Co. York, Esq. = Mary Bertie. Born 1746.
Arms of Stapleton.—*Argent, a lion rampant sable.*

Sophia Bertie. Born 1748. Died unmarried 1760.

James Bertie, eldest son, Lord Norreys. Burnt to death in his bed at Rycott 12 Oct. 1745. Buried at Rycott.

Willoughby Bertie, 2nd son. Born 16 Jan. 1740. Succeeded as 4th Earl of Abingdon in 1760. Died in 1799. = Charlotte, daughter of Admiral Sir Peter Warren, K.B., M.P. for Westminster. Married 7 July 1768. Died 28 Jan. 1799.

Peregrine Bertie, 3rd son. Born 14 March 1741. Died 20 August 1798. = Miss Hutchins. Married 7 May 1790.

Sir John Gallini, Knt. = Elizabeth Bertie.

Peregrine Bertie. Born 30 July 1790. Died 17 Oct. 1849.

Frederick Bertie. Clerk in Orders. Rector of Albury, Co. Oxon. = Georgina Anne Emily, 2nd daughter of Lord Mark Kerr.
Issue, seven sons and three daughters.

Charles John Baillie Hamilton, Esq. M.P. for Aylesbury. Died in 1865. = Caroline Bertie. Married 23 Jan. 1821.

Willoughby Bertie, Lord Norreys. Born 8 Feb. 1779. Died in infancy. Buried at Rycott.

Montagu Bertie. Born 30 April 1784. Succeeded as 5th Earl of Abingdon in 1799. Lord Lieutenant of Berks. High Steward of Abingdon. Created Hon. D.C.L. of Oxford 3 July 1810. Died 16 Oct. 1854. = Emily, 5th daughter of the Hon. Thomas Gage, by Margaret, daughter of Peter Kemble, and sister of Henry, Viscount Gage; her grandmother being Margaret, daughter of the Right Hon. Stephen Van Cortland. Married 27 August 1807. Died 1838.
Arms of Gage.—*Gyronny of four azure and argent, a saltire gules.*

Willoughby. Born 24 June 1787. Of Weston-on-the-Green, Co. Oxon. Capt. R.N. Wrecked in H.M. ship "Satellite" on the Goodwin Sands in 1810. = Catherine Jane, daughter of Mr. Saunders.

Montagu Bertie. Born 19 June 1808. Created Hon. D.C.L., Oxon, 11 June 1834. High Steward of the City of Oxford, and of the Borough of Abingdon. Lord Lieutenant of Berks. Succeeded his father as 6th Earl of Abingdon 16 Oct. 1854. = Elizabeth Lavinia, only daughter of George Granville Vernon-Harcourt, Esq., by his 1st wife, Lady Elizabeth Bingham, eldest daughter of Richard, 2nd Earl of Lucan. Died 16 Oct. 1858.

Montagu Arthur Bertie, Lord Norreys. Born 13 May 1836. = Caroline, eldest daughter of Charles Towneley of Towneley, Co. Lancaster, Esq. Married 10 July 1858.

Francis Leveson Bertie. Born 17 August 1844.

Alberic Edward Bertie. Born 14 Nov. 1846. Clerk in Orders. Rector of Albury, Co. Oxon.

George Aubrey Vere Bertie. Born 1 May 1850.

Charles Claude Bertie. Born 31 August 1851.

Reginald Henry Bertie. Born 26 May 1856.

Elizabeth Emily Bertie.

Lavinia Louisa Bertie.

Evelyn Frances Bertie. A nun in the Catholic Church.

Montagu Charles Francis Bertie. Born 3 Oct. 1860.

Arthur John Bertie. Born 26 Dec. 1861. Died 10 Jan. 1862.

Mary Caroline Bertie.

Ann Josephine Bertie.

Pedigree A.

Richard Bertie.[1] Born *circa* 1518. (Son of Captain Thomas Bertie, Constable and Governor of Hurst Castle in the Isle of Wight.) Of Corpus Christi College, Oxon; graduated B.A. 3 May 1537; Hon. M.A. Cantab. 1564. Died 9 April 1582, aged 64. "This person came out of Kent."[3] = Katherine, sole daughter and heiress of William, Lord Willoughby de Eresby, and widow[2] of Charles Brandon, Duke of Suffolk. Died 19 Sept. 1580.

Peregrine Bertie. Born at Wesel, in the Duchy of Cleves in Germany, 12 Oct. 1555. His Patent of Naturalization dated 2 August 1559. Succeeded through his mother to the dignity of Lord Willoughby de Eresby 11 Nov. 1580. Governor of Bergen-op-Zoom in Brabant. General of Queen Elizabeth's Forces in the Netherlands 10 Nov. 1587. Will dated 17 August 1590. Died at Berwick 25 June 1601, aged 46. Buried at Spilsby, Co. Lincoln. = Mary, daughter of John Vere,[4] 16th Earl of Oxford, Great Chamberlain of England, by Margery, daughter of John Golding of Halstead, Co. Essex, Esq.

Reginald Grey, Earl of Kent. (1st husband.) = Susan Bertie. = Sir John Wingfield, Knt.

Robert Bertie. Born *circa* 1582. Lord Willoughby de Eresby. Lord Great Chamberlain of England in right of his mother. Created Earl of Lindsey 22 Nov. 1626. Elected Knight of the Garter 18 April 1630. Constable of England. Lord High Admiral in 1636. Governor of Berwick 1639. A distinguished and illustrious Royalist. General of the Forces of Charles I. 1640. Wounded fatally at the battle of Edge Hill 23 Oct. 1642, aged 60. Buried at Edenham, Co. Lincoln. = Elizabeth, only daughter of Edward, Lord Montagu of Boughton, Co. Northampton, by Elizabeth, daughter of Sir John Jefferies, Knt., Chief Baron of the Exchequer. Died 30 Nov. 1654.

Peregrine Bertie.

Ambrose Bertie.

Henry Bertie of Fulstowe, Co. Lincoln.

Vere Bertie. Living in 1590.

Roger Bertie. Living in 1590.

Lewis Watson, eldest son of Sir Edward Watson, by Anne, dau'r of Kenelm Digby of Stoke, Co. Rutland. Of Rockingham Castle, Co. Northampton, Knt. Created a Baronet 23 June 1621. A brave and noted Royalist. Afterwards Lord Rockingham, so created 29 Jan. 1645. = Catherine Bertie. Died without issue. (1st wife.)

Arms of Watson.—*Argent, on a chevron engrailed azure between three martlets sable, as many crescents or.*

Sir William Paston, Bart. = Catherine Bertie.

Sir Miles Stapleton of Carleton, Co. York. = Elizabeth Bertie.

Anne Bertie. Died in infancy.[5]

John Hewett, D.D. (1st husband.) = Sophia Bertie. = Sir Abraham Shipman, Knt. (2nd husband.)

Roger Bertie, 2nd son. Knighted. = Ursula, sole daughter and heiress of Sir Edward Lawley of Ercall, Co. Salop, Knt.

Robert Bertie, 3rd son. Died in 1608.

Peregrine Bertie, 4th son, of Evedon, Co. Lincoln. = Anne, daughter of Daniel Harvey of Evedon aforesaid.

Francis Bertie, 5th son. A Captain. Killed in Ireland.

Alice, daughter of Richard Barnard. (1st wife.) = Robert Bertie, 6th son. Born 1619. = Elizabeth, 2nd daughter of Sir Thomas Bennet of Babraham, Co. Cambridge, Knt.

Henry Bertie, 7th son. Killed at the battle of Newbury.

Vere Bertie, 8th son. Died unmarried at Newport, Co. Essex.

Edward Bertie, 9th son. Born 1624.

Martha, 3rd daughter of Sir William Cockayne of Rushton, Co. Northampton, Alderman of London, and widow of John Ramsey, Earl of Holderness. Died July 1661. (1st wife.) = Montagu Bertie, eldest son and heir. Succeeded his father as 2nd Earl of Lindsey in 1642. Captain of the Guards. Gentleman of the Bedchamber to King Charles I. Privy Councillor to King Charles II. K.G. 1 April 1661. Great Chamberlain of England. Died at Kensington 25 July 1666, aged 58. Buried at Edenham aforesaid. = Bridget Wray. (2nd wife.)[1]

(*See pages* 443-4.)

Mary, 2nd daughter and coheiress of J.... Massingberd of .... Co. Lincoln. A Merchant of the City of London. (1st wife.) = Robert Bertie, son and heir. Baron Willoughby. Succeeded to the Earldom of Lindsey as 3rd Earl in 1666. Privy Councillor to King Charles II. Died 8 May 1701. = Elizabeth, only daughter of Philip, 4th Lord Wharton, by Elizabeth, daughter of Sir Rowland Wandesford of Pickhay, Co. York, Knt. (2nd wife.) = Elizabeth, daughter of Thomas Pope, Earl of Downe in Ireland, and widow of Sir Francis Henry Lee of Ditchley, Co. Oxon, 4th Baronet. (3rd wife.)

Arms of Pope.—*Per pale or and azure, on a chevron between three griffins' heads erased, four fleurs-de-lys all counterchanged.*

Thomas Savage, 3rd Earl Rivers. = Arabella Bertie. Died without issue. (2nd wife.)

Philip Bertie. Died 15 April 1728, aged 64.

Norreys Bertie. Educated at Magdalen College, Oxon. Created Hon. M.A. 27 May 1738.

Albemarle Bertie. Graduated B.A. University College, Oxon, 20 April 1689; M.A. 21 Jan. 1691. M.P. for Lincoln 1705; for Cockermouth 1708; for Boston, Co. Lincoln, 1734. Died in 1741.

A B | C

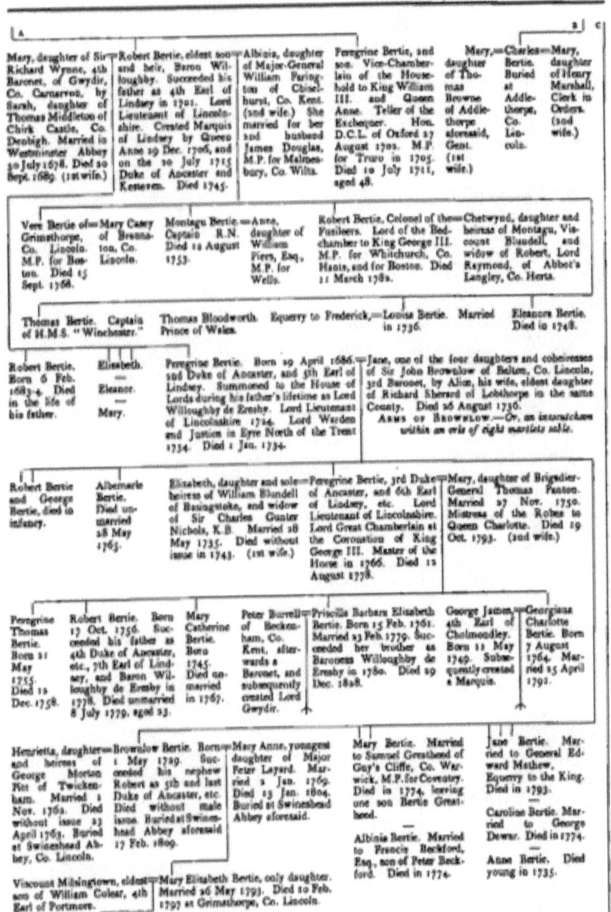

A — B — C

Mary, daughter of Sir Richard Wynne, 4th Baronet, of Gwydir, Co. Carnarvon, by Sarah, daughter of Thomas Middleton of Chirk Castle, Co. Denbigh. Married in Westminster Abbey 30 July 1678. Died 20 Sept. 1689. (1st wife.) = Robert Bertie, eldest son and heir, Baron Willoughby. Succeeded his father as 4th Earl of Lindsey in 1701. Lord Lieutenant of Lincolnshire. Created Marquis of Lindsey by Queen Anne 29 Dec. 1706, and on the 20 July 1715 Duke of Ancaster and Kesteven. Died 1745. = Albinia, daughter of Major-General William Farington of Chiselhurst, Co. Kent. (2nd wife.) She married for her 2nd husband James Douglas, M.P. for Malmesbury, Co. Wilts.

Peregrine Bertie, 2nd son. Vice-Chamberlain of the Household to King William III. and Queen Anne. Teller of the Exchequer. Hon. D.C.L. of Oxford 27 August 1702. M.P. for Truro in 1705. Died 10 July 1711, aged 48.

Mary, daughter of Thomas Browne of Addlethorpe aforesaid, Gent. (1st wife.) = Charles Bertie. Buried at Addlethorpe, Co. Lincoln. = Mary, daughter of Henry Marshall, Clerk in Orders. (2nd wife.)

Vere Bertie of Grimsthorpe, Co. Lincoln. M.P. for Boston. Died 15 Sept. 1768. = Mary Casey of Brannston, Co. Lincoln.

Montagu Bertie, Captain R.N. Died 12 August 1753. = Anne, daughter of William Piers, Esq., M.P. for Wells.

Robert Bertie, Colonel of the Fusileers. Lord of the Bedchamber to King George III. M.P. for Whitchurch, Co. Hants, and for Boston. Died 11 March 1782. = Chetwynd, daughter and heiress of Montagu, Viscount Blundell, and widow of Robert, Lord Raymond, of Abbot's Langley, Co. Herts.

Thomas Bertie. Captain of H.M.S. "Winchester."

Thomas Bloodworth. Equerry to Frederick, Prince of Wales. = Louisa Bertie. Married in 1736.

Eleanora Bertie. Died in 1748.

Robert Bertie. Born 6 Feb. 1683-4. Died in the life of his father.

Elizabeth. — Eleanor. — Mary.

Peregrine Bertie. Born 29 April 1686. 2nd Duke of Ancaster, and 5th Earl of Lindsey. Summoned to the House of Lords during his father's lifetime as Lord Willoughby de Eresby. Lord Lieutenant of Lincolnshire 1724. Lord Warden and Justice in Eyre North of the Trent 1734. Died 1 Jan. 1734. = Jane, one of the four daughters and coheiresses of Sir John Brownlow of Belton, Co. Lincoln, 3rd Baronet, by Alice, his wife, eldest daughter of Richard Sherard of Lobthorpe in the same County. Died 26 August 1736.

Arms of Brownlow.—*Or, an inescutcheon within an orle of eight martlets sable.*

Robert Bertie and George Bertie, died in infancy.

Albemarle Bertie. Died unmarried 28 May 1765.

Elizabeth, daughter and sole heiress of William Blundell of Basingstoke, and widow of Sir Charles Gunter Nichols, K.B. Married 28 May 1735. Died without issue in 1743. (1st wife.) = Peregrine Bertie, 3rd Duke of Ancaster, and 6th Earl of Lindsey, etc. Lord Lieutenant of Lincolnshire. Lord Great Chamberlain at the Coronation of King George III. Master of the Horse in 1766. Died 12 August 1778. = Mary, daughter of Brigadier-General Thomas Panton. Married 27 Nov. 1750. Mistress of the Robes to Queen Charlotte. Died 19 Oct. 1793. (2nd wife.)

Peregrine Thomas Bertie. Born 21 May 1755. Died 12 Dec. 1758.

Robert Bertie. Born 17 Oct. 1756. Succeeded his father as 4th Duke of Ancaster, etc., 7th Earl of Lindsey, and Baron Willoughby de Eresby in 1778. Died unmarried 8 July 1779, aged 23.

Mary Catherine Bertie. Born 1745. Died unmarried in 1767.

Peter Burrell of Beckenham, Co. Kent, afterwards a Baronet, and subsequently created Lord Gwydir. = Priscilla Barbara Elizabeth Bertie. Born 15 Feb. 1761. Married 23 Feb. 1779. Succeeded her brother as Baroness Willoughby de Eresby in 1780. Died 29 Dec. 1828.

George James, 4th Earl of Cholmondeley. Born 11 May 1749. Subsequently created a Marquis. = Georgiana Charlotte Bertie. Born 7 August 1764. Married 25 April 1791.

Henrietta, daughter and heiress of George Morton Pitt of Twickenham. Married 1 Nov. 1762. Died without issue 23 April 1763. Buried at Swineshead Abbey, Co. Lincoln. = Brownlow Bertie. Born 1 May 1729. Succeeded his nephew Robert as 5th and last Duke of Ancaster, etc. Died without male issue. Buried at Swineshead Abbey aforesaid 17 Feb. 1809. = Mary Anne, youngest daughter of Major Peter Layard. Married 2 Jan. 1769. Died 13 Jan. 1804. Buried at Swineshead Abbey aforesaid.

Mary Bertie. Married to Samuel Greatheed of Guy's Cliffe, Co. Warwick, M.P. for Coventry. Died in 1774, leaving one son Bertie Greatheed.
—
Albinia Bertie. Married to Francis Beckford, Esq., son of Peter Beckford. Died in 1774.

Jane Bertie. Married to General Edward Mathew, Equerry to the King. Died in 1793.
—
Caroline Bertie. Married to George Dewar. Died in 1774.
—
Anne Bertie. Died young in 1735.

Viscount Milsingtown, eldest son of William Colear, 4th Earl of Portmore. = Mary Elizabeth Bertie, only daughter. Married 26 May 1793. Died 10 Feb. 1797 at Grimsthorpe, Co. Lincoln.

An only son, Brownlow Charles Colear. Murdered at Rome in 1819.

D

D

Peregrine Bertie, 2nd son. = Susan, daughter of Sir Edward Monins of Waldershare, Co. Kent, Knt.

Richard Bertie. M.P. for Woodstock 1685. Died unmarried 19 Jan. 1685-6.

John, 1st Earl Paulet. Died in 1747. Buried at Hinton, Co. Somerset. = Bridget Bertie.
ARMS OF PAULET.—*Sable, three swords in pile, points in base, pommels and hilts or.*

Anthony Henley of the Grange, Co. Hants, Esq. (1st husband.) = Mary Bertie. = Henry Bertie, 3rd son of James, 1st Earl of Abingdon, and Eleanora Lee his wife. (*See page 444.*) = Arabella Susanna.

Vere Bertie. Created M.A., Oxon, 8 Sept. 1665. Serjeant-at-Law 1675. Justice of the Court of Common Pleas. Died unmarried 17 Feb. 1680.

Charles Bertie of Uffington, Co. Lincoln. Created M.A., Oxon, 8 Sept. 1665. Secretary to the Lord Treasurer. Treasurer of the Ordnance. M.P. for Stamford. Died 13 Jan. 1678-9. = Mary, daughter of Peter Tryon of Harringworth, Co. Northampton, Gent., widow of Sir Samuel Jones of Courtenhall in the same County, Knt.

Baptist Noel, 3rd Viscount Campden, by Juliana, eldest daughter of Sir Baptist Hicks, Knt. Died at Exton, Co. Rutland, 29 Oct. 1682. = Elizabeth Bertie. (4th wife.)
ARMS OF NOEL.—*Or, fretty gules, a canton ermine.*

Sir Thomas Osborne, Knt., only son of Sir Edward Osborne of Kiveton, Co. York, by Anne, daughter of Thomas Walmesley, Esq. Subsequently created Duke of Leeds, and K.G. Died 26 July 1712. = Bridget Bertie.
ARMS OF OSBORNE.—*Ermine and azure, over all a cross or.*

Robert Dormer of Dorton, Co. Bucks, son of Sir Robert Dormer of Duns Tew, Co. Oxon, Knt., and great-grandson of William Dormer of Thame. His second wife was Anne Cotterell. He was buried at Crendon, Co. Bucks, 14 Feb. 1695. = Catherine Bertie. Buried at Crendon 9th June 1659. (1st wife.)

Thomas Bertie. Died in infancy.

Charles Bertie of Uffington aforesaid. M.P. for Stamford from 1685 to 1722. Died in 1730. = Mary, daughter and heiress of John Norborne of Great Stewkley, Co. Hunts.

Eliza Bertie.

Maria Bertie. Died young.

Charles Bertie of Uffington aforesaid. = Bathsheba, daughter of Richard Mead, M.D. Married 14 July 1731. Died 23 Sept. 1749.

Charles Bertie. Died in 1780.

Richard Bertie.

James Bertie.

Montagu Bertie. Clerk in Orders. Rector of Uffington.

Vere Bertie. Died in 1747.

Bathsheba Bertie. Died 1749.

Peregrine Bertie of Lincoln's Inn, Barrister-at-Law. By right of his wife Lord of the Manor of Wooburn Deincourt, Co. Bucks. Died 21 June 1777, aged 68. Buried at Wooburn Deincourt aforesaid. = Elizabeth, daughter of Edward Payne, and niece of John Morse, Lord of the Manor of Wooburn Deincourt, Co. Bucks. Married 23 Dec. 1736. Died 13 March 1765, aged 50. Buried at Wooburn.

Norborne Bertie. Clerk in Orders. Of St. John's College, Oxford; B.A. 21 Jan. 1733; M.A. 18 May 1737.

Edward Hales, 2nd son of Sir Edward Hales of Coventry, by Anne, daughter of Mr. Johnson, Alderman of London. = Susan Bertie. Married in Jan. 1735-6.
ARMS OF HALES.—*Gules, three arrows or, feathered argent.*

Sophia Bertie. Died 23 Jan. 1772, aged 28. Buried at Wooburn.

Fletcher Richardson of Cartmell, Gent. = Louisa Bertie.

George Edmonds of the City of Peterborough, Gent. = Henrietta Bertie.

Peregrine Morse Bertie. Born 4 Nov. 1737. Died 18 Nov. 1738. Buried at Wooburn.

Peregrine Bertie. Born 22 June 1739. Lord of the Manor of Wooburn. Died 12 Oct. 1782. Buried at Wooburn.

Elizabeth Maria, daughter of Mr. William Clay, and widow of Thomas Scrope, Esq. Married 7 May 1794. She died without issue in July 1806. (1st wife.) = Albemarle Bertie. Born 17 Sept. 1744. Colonel of the 89th Regiment. M.P. for Stamford. Sold the Manor of Wooburn to Mrs. Du Pre, and the lands of Notley Abbey to Mr. Reynolds. Succeeded his kinsman and third cousin, Brownlow Bertie, last Duke of Ancaster, as 9th Earl of Lindsey 8 Feb. 1809. Died 17 Sept. 1818. = Charlotte Susanna Eliza, daughter of Charles Peter Layard, D.D., Dean of Bristol. (2nd wife.) She married secondly William Pegus, Clerk in Orders, and died 28 Nov. 1858.

Albemarle George Augustus Frederick Bertie. Born 4 Nov. 1814. Of Uffington House, Stamford, Co. Lincoln. Succeeded his father as 10th Earl of Lindsey.

Montagu Peregrine Bertie.

Charlotte Elizabeth Bertie.

SOME EXPLANATORY NOTES OF THE FOREGOING PEDIGREE.

[1] The Family of Bertie.—"Before Peregrine Lord Willoughby, the Berties were an ancient gentleman's family, but none of them, that I have met with, noble. I dare not assert that they are descended from Queen Berta, whose bones are in the Church of St. Ambrose at Milan, with this inscription, '*Hic Bertae Reginae ossa.*' I shall not enquire whether they came over with the Saxons from Bertiland, or whether there is any such land, or whether one 'Leopold de Bertie' was Constable of Dover Castle in Ethelred's reign. Such a family as this *non eget antecessoribus illis.* There is, doubtless, such a place in Kent as Berstead; if this was originally Bertiestead, and had its name from the Berties; if Thomas Bertie, who, Dugdale, in his *Baronage*, says, was of this Berstead, was also Constable of Hurst Castle under Henry VII., and his son, Richard Bertie, married Catherine, Duchess of Suffolk, and by her had this Peregrine; it is sufficient to prove they were no inconsiderable family when only commoners."—*A Memoir of Peregrine Bertie*, pp. 2, 3. London: 1838.

The allusions of this writer in the words above are to the various romances and statements founded on imagination so current amongst the Tudor Heralds, more especially to the fantastic conceptions with which they had endeavoured to surround the Berties after Peregrine Bertie's alliance with the Duchess of Suffolk.

[2] The Duchess of Suffolk's Husband.—"It must be acknowledged that the Bertie family has been raised by marriages. If Peregrine had not been the son of the Duchess of Suffolk, and heir-apparent to the Barony of Willoughby, his great merit might not have enabled him to be the founder of so great a family. *Magnis virtutibus obstat, &c.* Besides, he had other circumstances of good fortune to set him in a fair light with Queen Elizabeth.

"Charles Brandon was himself a Protestant, and Cranmer's great supporter; and his having never been out of the King's favour is, by the way, a strong argument that Henry VIII. was in his heart a Protestant, and a Papist only in politics.

"Whether the Duchess received these principles from him, she was herself so zealous in them that she became a kind of martyr, and had her first son born in this voluntary exile. Such a birth as this was setting out well for the times.

"After the death of the Duke, the Duchess lived at Grimsthorp, in Lincolnshire.

"This seat has now been inhabited by the Berties about 160 years, which, since Henry VII. gave the nobility a license of alienation, is no inconsiderable time for an estate to remain in the same family; it may be said of too many a nobleman's estate—*Permutat dominos et cedit in altera jura*; changes its lord, and takes a stock-jobber.

"At Grimsthorp, she kept for her chaplain, Latimer, who afterwards died at the stake. When Henry VIII.'s last Queen, Catherine, died in childbed of a daughter, the Protector Somerset sent that daughter to the Duchess at Grimsthorp; from whence she sent him an ingenious letter of complaint—'That he had used her like a courtier, sent her a burthen without a pension.' She married Richard Bertie, son and heir of Thomas Bertie, Constable of Hurst Castle. This Richard Bertie was educated by Wriothesly, Lord Chancellor, and 'his mother (says Gardiner) I know to be as godly a Catholic as any in the land.'

"Her first child by him was Susan, who afterwards married Reginald Grey, Earl of Kent."—*A Memoir of Peregrine Bertie*, pp. 11, 12, 13. London: 1838.

[3] Refuted Arms and Crest of Thomas Bertie of Bersted.—(From MS. Grants by Thomas Hawley, 2 H. 5, fol. 67, in the College of Arms.)—The Armes and Creste of Thomas Bertye of Bersted in the Countye of Kente gentilman and at this p'sente tyme Captayne of Hurste Castell for ye Kings Ma'tie he bereth Silver the fawlcys or mottons the bodyes of Tymb' heddid armed horned asur two above one upon the Tymber a Ryng of the same upon his helme on a Torse silver and sable on a hussok verte a date tree the dates in theire prop' couler leved verte manteled geules dobled silr' as more plain apereth here depicte Gyven by me Thomas Hawley al's Clarenciaulx the xth daye of Julye in the fourthe yere of the Reigne of o' Soveraigne Lorde King Edward the VJth, &c.

Grant of Arms to Thomas Bertie, Gent., A.D. 1551.—(Glover's Collections, A. 41, College of Arms.)—To all nobles and gentilles these present L'res reading heeringe or seeinge Thomas Hawley al's Clarenciaulx principall Herald and King of Armes of the South East and West partes of this realme from the ryver of Trent southward, sendeth humble co'mendacion and greeting. Equitie willeth and reason ordeyneth that men vertuous and of noble courage be by their merites and good renowne rewarded not alonly their persons in this mortall lyf so brief and transitory but also after theim those that shalbe of their bodyes descended to be in all places of honor with other nobles and gentilles accepted and taken by certeyn enseignes and demonstrances of hono' and noblesse, that is to say blason healme and tymber, to th'end that by their ensamples other may the more enforce theim selfes to have perseverance to use their dayes in feates of armes and works vertuous to gett the renowne of auncyent noblesse in their Lignes and posterities. And therefor I Clarenciaulx not alonly by the co'mon renowne, but also by the report and witnesse of dyvers worthy to be taken of word and credence, am plainly advertised and enfourmid that Thomas Bertie of Bersted in the countie of Kent gentleman is descended of an howse undefamed and beinge at this present tyme Capitayne of Hurst Castell for the Kinges Ma'tie and hath of longe tyme used himself in feates of armes and goode workes so that he is well worthy to be in all places of hono' admitted nombred and taken in the company of other nobles and gentill's, and for the remembraunce of the same by the vertue authoritie and power annexed attributed gyven and graunted by the Kinge our Souv'eigne Lordes highnes to me and to my office of Clarenciaulx Kinge of Armes by expresse wordes under his Ma'ties most noble greate seale have devysed ordeyned gyven and graunted to the said Thomas Bertie gentleman and for his posteritie th' Armes and Creast as hereafter followeth, That is to say, Sylver three fawlcys of Mottons the bodys of tymber hedded armed horned asure upon the tymber a ryng of the same two above one. Upon his healme on a torse silver and sable on a hussok vert a date tree and the dates in their proper colour levyd vert, mantelled geules doubled silver, as more playnly apereth depicted in this margent. To have and to hold for him and his posteritie and they it to use and enjoy for evermore. In witnesse whereof I the said Clarenciaulx Kinge of Armes have signed these presentes with my hand and sette thereunto the seale of my Armes with the seale of my office of Clarenciaulx Kinge of Armes. Gyven and graunted at London the xth day of July in the fourth yere of the reigne of our Souv'eigne Lord Edward the Sixt by the grace of God Kinge of England ffraunce and Ireland Defendo' of the faith and of the Church of England and Ireland under Christ in earth the Supreme Head.

Par moy Clarenciaulx
Roy Darmes.

[4] The Family of Vere.—"John Vere erl of Oxford son and heyre of John maryed to his fyrst wyef Dorothe doughter to Raff, Erl of Westm'land & hath issue by her Kateren, wedid to Sr Edward Wyndsor Knight, Lord Wyndsor. After the said John Vere Erl of Oxford wedded to his 2 wyef Margery doughter of John Goldynge of Halsted in the Countie of Essex, esquyer, & hath issue by her Edward de Veer, lord Bulbecke son & heyre, lady Mary."—Add. MSS., British Museum, No. 7098.

[5] Burials at Westminster Abbey.

1660-1. March 22. The Lady Anne Bertue sister to the Earl of Lindsy in St. Michael's Chapel.

1656-7. March 24. The Lady Bridget, Countess of Lyndsy, in St. Andrew's Chapel.

1645. Nov. 28. The Lady Elizabeth Norris wife of Edward Ray, Esq., in St. Nicholas Chapel.

[The following extracts—for which I am indebted to the courtesy of the Hon. and Rev. Alberic Bertie, Rector of Albury—reached me too late for the information contained in them to be embodied in the Bertie Pedigree. They are, however, appropriately reproduced here, as they contain several interesting facts.]

EXTRACTS FROM THE REGISTERS OF THE CHURCH OF ALBURY, CO. OXON.

1678. The Right Honble Charles Earle of Carnarvon and the Right Honble the Lady Mary Bertie (Sister of the Right Honble James Lord Norreys of Rycott) were marryd (by vertue of a License) the fifteenth day of December one thousand six hundred and seventy eight by mee

W. MOORE, Rector of Albery.

1680. The Worshippfull John Cooke of Studley and Mary Norreys (sister to Sir Edmund Norreys of Weston on the Green) were marryd (by virtue of a License) the twelfth of April one thousand six hundred and eighty by mee

W. MOORE, Rector of Albery.

The Births and Christenings of severall of the Children of the Right Honble James Lord Norreys and Elianora his wife Registered by William Moore Clerke, Rector of Albery and Domesticke Chaplain to his Lordship:—

1672-3. Montagu Bertie eldest son of the Right Honble James Lord Norreys of Rycott and Elianora his wife (who was one of the daughters and coheirs of Sir Henry Lee and Dame Anne his wife) was born the 4th of February and Baptized the fifteenth of the same month in the year one thousand six hundred seventy two and three by mee

W. MOORE, Rector de Albery.

1674. James Birtie second son of the sd James Lord Norreys and Elianora was borne the thirteenth of March and Baptis'd the third day of April following in the year of Our Lord one thousand six hundred seventy foure by mee

W. MOORE, Rector de Albery.

1675. Henry Bertie third son of the said James Lord Norreys and Elianora was borne the fourth of May and Baptis'd the tenth of the same month in the year of our Lord one thousand six hundred seventy five by mee W. MOORE.

1676-7. Robert Bertie fourth son of the sd James Lord Norreys and Elianora was borne the eight and twentyth day of February and Baptis'd the fourth of March followinge in the year one thousand six hundred seventy six and seven by mee W. MOORE.

Peregrine Bertie fifth son to the sd James Ld Norreys and Elianora was borne the twelfth and Baptis'd the seven and twentyth of February 1677-8.

Charles Bertie sixth son of the sd James Ld Norreys and Elianora was borne the sixth and Baptis'd the eighteenth of February in the yeare 1678-9.

Bridgett Bertie eldest daughter of the sd James Ld Norreys and Elianora was borne the 17th and Baptis'd the seven and twentyth day of March 1680.

Anne Bertie second daughter of the sd James Ld Norreys and Elianora was borne the seventh and Baptis'd the two and twentyth of March 1680-1. W. MOORE.

The Lady Mary Bertie third daughter of the sd James then Earle of Abingdon and of ye Elianora his Countess was borne on Saturday the foure and twentyth of March 1682-3 and Christ'ned Munday the ninth of April 1683 by the name of Mary by mee

W. MOORE.

1698. April 16. The Right Honble James Earle of Abingdon and Baron Norreys of Rycott was marryd to the Right Honble Katherine Viscountesse Wenman widdow of Richard Lord Wenman and daughter and coheir of Sr Thomas Chamberlaine late of Wickham in this county. 18th April 1698.

1699. The Right Honble James (The Good) Earle of Abingdon Baron Norreys of Rycott and Patron of this Church dyed May the 22nd and was buried in his Chappell at Rycott the 30th, whose Justice, Piety, Charity, Hospitality, Love of his country and Zeale for the Church of England ought never to be forgotten as they will hardly ever be parallelled. W. MOORE.

The Lady Elianora his first and most beloved wife was by his directions (when livinge) removed from Lavington (where she had been interred over 8 years) and deposited by him.

1700. April 19. The Right Honble John Lord Poulett of Hinton St. George in the County of Somersett and Mrs. Bridgett Bertie (eldest daughter and coheir of the Honble Peregrine Bertie Esqre late of Waldershare in the County of Kent) was marry'd by virtue of a License the 14th day of April 1702. This Register'd and the Kings Tax pd in the Parish of St Martin's in the Fields where the Lady lived.

1704. July 20. The Honble Sr William Courtenay of Powderham in the County of Devon, Baront, was marryd to the Right Honble the Lady Anne Bertie (2d daughter of the Rt Honble James late Earle of Abingdon) at Wing in the County of Bucks. The Marriage Registred there 20 July 1704.

The Revd Mr William Moore, M.A., Rector of Albury, and Chaplain to ye Rt Honble the Earl of Abingdon, died on Tuesday Nov. 20 1711, and lies buried in a vault under ye Reading Desk in Rycott Chapel. He left the Rt Honble the Earl of Abingdon his executor, but he accepted it not.

1715. May 12. The Right Honble Ann Countess of Abingdon was interred in Ricot Chapel.

James Lord Norreys was born at Lindsey House Nov. 14 1717, being ye first-born of ye Rt Honble Montague and Mary Earl and Countess of Abingdon.

1716. Feb. 13. The Right Honble Montague Earl of Abingdon was married to Mrs. Mary Churchill of Dorchester in the County of Dorset, Widow, by ye Rev. Mr Fellplake [Qy. Fettiplace], Chaplain to his Lordship.

James Lord Norreys (First Child of the Right Honble Montague and Mary Earl and Countess of Abingdon), died of the small pox at Lindsey House Westminster, Feb. 26 1717, and was brought down and interred in ye vault in Ricot Chapel on the Friday following about 11 o'clock in the morning. 1718. Feb. 28.

1743. Nov. 7. Frances Eleanora daughter of William Bertie Rector of this Parish and Ann his wife baptized, who was born Oct. 15.

1745. April 22. Richard son of William Bertie Rector of this Parish and Anne his wife baptized, who was born April 7.

WM BERTIE, Rector.

1747. Apr. 3. Sophia, Daughter of William Bertie Rector of this Parish and Anne his wife, was baptized who was born March 28.

1751. March 27. Anne, daughter of William Bertie Rector of this Parish and Anne his wife, was baptized who was born March 25.

Burials.

1760. June 16. The Right Honble the Earl of Abingdon in his own Chapel at Rycott.

Oct. 17. The Right Honble Lady Sophia Bertie in the same place.

Dec. 15. The Rt Honble Lady Bridget Bertie in the same place also.

1763. Dec. 30. The Rt Honble Anna Maria Countess of Abingdon at Rycott Chappel.

1794. Feb. 8. Charlotte Countess of Abingdon at Rycott. The Tax Paid.

1818. March 27. Vere Peregrine son of the Earl and Countess of Abingdon in the Family Vault at Rycott, age 3 months.

CHAS. ANNESLEY, Curate.

1825. Feb. 9. Albemarle son of the Earl and Countess of Abingdon in the Family Vault at Ricott, age 13.

W. WILLIAMS, Off. Minister.

1838. The Right Honorable Emily Countess of Abingdon Wytham in the County of Berks, September the sixth in Rycott Chapel, age 62. BULKELEY BANDINEL, Off. Minister.

Nov. 7. Georgina Elizabeth Bertie, Albury, in Rycott Chapel, age 10. S. H. JOHNSON, Off. Minister.

The Right Honble Montagu Fifth Earl of Abingdon, abode Wytham in the County of Berks, October the twenty third in Rycott Chapel, age 70. BULKELEY BANDINEL, Off. Minister.

D Thame Schole, of the foundation of Sir John Williams, Knyght of the rank of the Military Ordre of Knyghthode, & Lorde Williams of Thame.

IT is clear that Lord Williams (probably for reasons already indicated) had not only conceived the plan of setting up a Grammar School some few years before his death, but had actually laid the foundation-stone of the School House,* had seen it completed, inaugurated, and enlarged; and in all probability had witnessed some of those practical benefits which had arisen from its institution. On his lordship's death, his two trustees, John Doyley of Merton, Esq., and Mr. William Place of Ludgershall, Gent., proceeded to take such action as secured its foundation in perpetuity,† on principles which were then recognized as true and useful.‡ With that object the patronage and protection of the Warden and Senior Fellows of St. Mary's College of Winchester in Oxford were secured by Lord Williams's trustees; who, assisted by Mr. Edward Harris of Thame, the first Head Master, prepared Rules and Statutes for the regulation and good governance both of the Grammar School and the Hospital or Alms-houses; while the Warden and Fellows accepted the responsibility of becoming in their official capacity permanent Trustees and Guardians of both.

The following Agreement between the Executors of Lord Williams and the Warden and Fellows of New College ("the College of Our Blessed Lady in Oxford")—the original of which is most artistically illuminated and very beautifully engrossed—indirectly provides much curious and valuable information regarding both the School and Hospital:—

This Indenture, made the first daye of August, in the sevententh yere of the raigne of our Soberreigne Ladie Elizabeth by the grace of God Queene of England, Fraunce, and Ireland, defendour of the faith, &c., Betwene Robert Doilye, of Merton, in the Countye of Oxford, Esquyer, and William Place, of Lurgishall, in the Countye of Buck', gentleman, executours of the last Will and Testament of Sir John Williams, Knyght, late Lorde Williams, of Thame, deceased, of the one partye, and the Wardens and Schollers of the Collidge of our blessed ladye in Oxford, called Saynt Marye College of Wynchester, on thother partye, **Witnesseth,** that whereas the said late Lord Williams, of his good and vertuous disposition toward the good and godlye education of the youth of his countrye, did by his last Will and Testament put in writynge in his lyfe tyme, give certen land, tenement, and hereditament to the said Robert Doylye and William Place, and to others his executours, whose estate and interest therein, the said Robert Doylye and William Place, holye nowe have to thende and intent, that his said executours, or the survyvors or survivor of theym shoulde, in as conveynent tyme as might be after his decease, bestowe and ymploye the same land, tenement, and hereditament, in and upon the mayntenaunce of a free Grammer Schoole, for the education and bringinge uppe of yonge children, and upon other charitable and godlye uses within the Towne of Thame, in the said Countye of Oxford. And whereas, the said Robert Doylye and William Place, sythens the death of the said late Lorde Williams, for the better and more sufficient accomplishement of the good intent and meanynge of the said last Will, have obteyned and purchased to theym and to their heyres, certen Lands, Tenements, and hereditaments, hereafter in this Indenture also menctioned, scituate, lyinge, and beinge in Newe Thame, within the said Countye of Oxford; **Nowe the** said Robert Doylye and William Place, who have ever sythens the decease of the said late Lorde Williams, solye taken upon theym the execution of the said Will, for the true and faythfull executynge, accomplishement, and perfectinge of the said godlye intent and purpose, and for the better discharge of the Truste in theym therein reposed, havinge, upon good advise and deliberation for diverse speciall causes and considerations, chosen the said Warden and Schollers and their successours, in whome they meane to repose the trust for the contynuall ymployinge and bestowynge of the proffits of the said lands, tenements, and hereditaments, accordinge to the mynde and Will of the said late Lord Williams, and accordinge to suche composition as, is, and shall be made for the disposition thereof. The said Robert Doylye and William Place, for theym, their heyres, executours, admynystratours, and assigneis, doe covenannt and grant, to, and with, the said Warden and Schollers and their successors, that they, the said Robert Doylye and William Place, or the survivor of theym, or the heyres, executours, admynystrators, or assigneis of them, or of the survyvor of theym, at their, some of their, proper cost and charg, shall, and will, before the feast of the Natyvitye of our Lorde God next followynge the date hereof, convey, and assure, or cause to be conveyed and assured, with warranty of theym, and their heyres agaynst theym, the said Robert Doylye and William Place, their heyres and assigneis onelye unto the said Warden and Schollers and their successors, all and singuler the mesuag, land, tenement and hereditament,

* It is on record that Lord Williams himself superintended the laying of the foundation-stone, and paid step by step for the erection of the substantial School House; while he liberally provided for the adjoining House of Charity or Hospital, both by annual payments and by special donations, which he was well able to do, seeing that he had long previously secured the lands and possessions of the Quatermain Hospital and Chantry. The buildings still existing are no doubt of the latter part of the sixteenth century, erected in Lord Williams's time.

† The Letters Patent of Queen Elizabeth, authorizing its foundation, were dated 27 January 1575.

‡ Though the old Catholic principle had then quite recently been deliberately abandoned by the Nation,—or, to write more accurately, removed by Henry VIII., Edward VI., and Elizabeth, and their advisers,—yet the Christian principle remained embodied in, and represented by, the National Church. It has been reserved for the present faithless age to deliberately sever the Christian principle from the education of youth both in elementary and Grammar Schools.

hereafter in theis present Indentures mencyoned. That is to saye, all that capitall mesuage or house newlye buylded in Olde Thame, in the said Countye of Oxford, called the Schoole House, with a gardyn and orchard and a curtilage thereunto adjacent and lyinge. And all and singuler buyldinges, edifices, comodityes, easements, watercourses, soyle and hereditament whatsoever to the same capitall mesuage or House belonginge or appertynynge or therewith or thereunto now used or occupyed. And also all that, the rent of thirtye and six pound of good and lawfull mony of England yerelye issuyng and goynge forth of the Mannour of Brylle with the appurtenance in the said Countye of Buck', and forth of the Parsonage or Rectories of Brill, Okeley and Borstall, with their appurtenances in the same Countye of Buck': and forth of one mesuage or tenement with the appurtenance in Brille aforesaid, called Lane's tenement, and forth of dyverse lands, tenements and hereditaments in Borstall, Brylle and Okeley aforesaid. And also all the annuall rent of fourtye two shilling yerelye yssuynge and goynge forth of one mesuage or tenement, with the appurtenance in New Thame in the said Countye of Oxforde, and now or of late in the tenure or occupacion of Johane Robothome, widowe. And also all that mesuage or tenement, with the appurtenance in Newe Thame aforesaid, nowe or late in the tenure or occupacion of Thomas Symeon or his assigneis. And also all that Rectorye and Churche of Eastneston, with the appurtenance, in the Countye of Northampton. And all and singuler houses, edifices, glebes, landes, tenements, rents, tythes, oblacions, obvencions, pentions, portions, proffits, comodities, emolument and hereditament whatsoever, with the appurtenance as well spirituall as temporall scituate, lyinge and beinge in Eastneston aforesaid, orells wheresoever in the said Countye of Northampton, and in the Countye of Bedford, or in the one of theym, to the same Rectory by any manner of meane belonginge or appertayninge, or as member or parcell of the same Rectorye before this at anye tyme esteamed, accompted, knowne, accepted, used, demised, or lett. And all that mesuage or tenement, with the appurtenance, and one yard and a halfe of lande, with the appurtenance, in Syd'nam, in the said Countye of Oxforde, nowe or of late in the tenure or occupacyon of one Walter Northe, or his assigneis. And all that cotage and one Close of lande, contaynynge by estymacyon, one yarde and three acres of errable lande, with the appurtenance in Syd'nam aforesaid, nowe or of late in the tenure or occupacion of John Springholde, or his assigneis. And all that cotage and one Close of lande, conteynynge, by estimacion, one yarde and three acres of errable lande, with the appurtenance in Syd'nam aforesaid, now or late in the tenure or occupacion of Simon Stephans, or his assigneis. And also, all that cotage and one Close of lande, conteynynge, by estimacion, one yarde and three acres of errable lande, with the appurtenance in Syd'nam aforesaid, and nowe or late in the tenure or occupacion of Henrye Gibson, or his assigneis. And all that mesuage and one yarde of lande, comonlye called Chapman's, with the appurtenance in Eastheenrid, in the Countye of Berk', and nowe or late in the tenure or occupacion of William Hyde, or his assigneis. And all that mesuage and one yard of lande, comonlye called Ffynnarmoures, with the appurtenance in Easthenryd aforesaid, and nowe or late in the tenure or occupacion of the said William Hyde, or his assigneis. And also, all that mesuage and halfe yard of lande, with the appurtenance in Easthenryd aforesaid, and nowe or late in the tenure or occupacion of Thomas Holmes, or his assigneis. And all that mesuage and halfe yarde of lande, with the appurtenance in Easthenryd aforesaid, and nowe or late in the tenure or occupacion of Johane Carpenter, or her assigneis. And all that tenement, together with certen landes and tenements to the same tenement apperteynynge, with the appurtenance in Easthenryd aforesaid, and nowe or late in the tenure or occupacion of Robert Whytinge, or his assigneis. And all that Close of lande, comonlye called Royle's Close, conteynynge, by estimation, three roode of lande, with the appurtenance in Easthenryd aforesaid, and nowe or late in the tenure or occupation of Richard Holmes, or his assigneis. All whiche premisses, in Easthenryd aforesaid, were late parcell of the late Priorye of Litilmore, and sometyme collected by Robert Parrott, of Oxforde. And also, all those two mesuages or tenements, with the appurtenance, in Newe Thame aforesaid, sometyme in the tenure of Richard Bunce, and nowe or late in the tenure or occupacion of Robert Phillipps, alias Coxe, or his assigneis. And all that mesuage or tenement, with the appurtenance, in Newe Thame aforesaid, and nowe or late in the tenure or occupacion of Nicholas Stanton or his assigneis. **To have, holde**, perceyve, take and enjoye the aforesaid rents, mesuages, landes, tenements, cotages, rectoryes, and all and singuler other the premysses before expressed and specified, with all and singuler their appurtenance to the foresaid Warden and Schollers and their successors for ever, to the onelye and severall uses, behoofes, intent and purposes hereafter in this Indenture to be specified, declared, expressed and lymyted, and to no other use, behoofe, intent or purpose, in part of the accomplishement of all whiche premisses, and to the ende and intent the said last Will of and concernynge the same premysses, shall and may be duly accomplished and performed accordingly. And for other the considerations aforesaid, the said Robert Doylye and William Place do by these presents give and graunte unto the said Warden and Schollers and their successours, all and singuler deedes, evidences, charters, writings, escripts, court rolles, rentalls, exemplifications of recorde, surveys, terrers and munyment whatsoever touchinge and concernynge onelye the premysses above by theis present mentioned to be bargayned and solde or onelye concernynge any part or parcell of theym. All which dedes, evidences, charters, writings, escripts, courte rolles, rentalls, exemplifications of record, surveys, terrours, and munyments, or as many of theym as the said Robert Doylye and William Place nowe have, or the one of theym nowe hath, in his or their hands, custodye or possession, or whiche nowe be in the hand, custodye or possession of any other person or persons to his or their use or uses, or by his or their delyverye, or whiche the said Robert Doylye and William Place, or the one of theym maye laufulye gett, obtayne or come by without suyte in lawe, together with the true coppye and copies of all other deeds, evidences, charters, writinges, escriptes, court rolles, rentalls, exemplifications of record, surveys, terrours and mynyments, being in the custody or possession of the said Robert Doylye and William Place, or either of theym, or whiche they or either of theym maye laufullye come by without suyte in the lawe, touchinge or concernynge the premises above by theis presents covenanted to be conveyed and assured, or any parte thereof joyntlye with any other lands, tenements or hereditaments; the same copy or copies to be written at the cost and charges of the said Robert Doylye and William Place, or of the survyvour of theym, or the heyres, executours or admynystratours of the survivour of theym, the said Robert Doylye and William Place, for theym, their heyres, executours and admynystratours, do, by these presents covenaunt, promyse and graunte to delyver, or cause to be delyvered to the said Warden, or to the Warden of the said Colledge for the tyme beinge requyringe the same, before the feast of the annunciacion of Our Lady the Virgyn next followynge the date hereof, hole, safe and undefaced. And the said Robert Doylye and William Place, for theym, their heyres, executours and admynystratours, do covenaunte, promyse and graunte to, and with the said Warden and Schollers and their successours by theis presents in manner and form following; That is to say, that they, the said Robert Doylye and William Place, their heyres or assigneis, at all and everye tyme and tymes hereafter, and from tyme to tyme duringe the space of two yeres next comynge the date hereof, at the reasonable request of the Warden of the said Colledge for the tyme being, shall and will do, make, and knowledge and suffer to be done, made and knowledged, with warraunty agaynst theym and their heyres, and agaynst all and every other person and persons havinge or laufullye claymynge to have any right, title, or interest in the premisses or any part thereof, by, from, or under theym, or any of theym, all and every such further laufull and reasonable act and acts, thing and things, devise and devises in the lawe whatsoever, for the further and more better assuringe and sure makinge of all and singuler the premisses, before by theis present covenaunted to be assured and conveyed to the saide Warden and Schollers and their successours for ever, to the uses, behoofes, intent and purposes, accordinge to the true intent, purport and meanyng of this Indenture, as shall be from tyme to tyme reasonably devised, advised and requyred by the Warden of the said Colledge for the tyme beinge, or by his counsell learned in the laws of this realme; be it by fyne, feoffment, recovery with duble or single voucher or vouchers, dede or dedes inrolled, the inrolment of theis presents release, confirmation with warranty of the said Robert Doylye and William Place and their heyres agaynst theym, the said Robert Doylye and William Place and their and either of their hyres, onely or otherwise with lyke warrauntye, or without warraunty, by all the wayes and meanes, or by any or some of theym, or otherwise at the erection, will, and pleasure of the Warden of the said Colledge for the tyme being, and at the proper and onelye cost and charge in the law of the said Robert Doylye and William Place, or the survivor of theym. And further, the said Robert Doyly doth covenaunte, promyse and graunte to, and with, the said Warden and Schollers and their successours by theis presents, that he, the said Robert Doylye shall and will, at all tymes from henceforth, at his owne proper cost and charge, clerely exonerate and discharge, or otherwise upon sufficient notyce and request, save and kepe harmeles, as well the said Warden and Schollers and their successours, as also the said messuages, rent, land, tenement, and all other the premisses by theis presents covenaunted to be assured or conveyed, and every part and parcell thereof, with all and singuler their appurtenaunces of, and from all and all manner of former bargaynes, former sales, guyft, graunt, titles, right, joyntures, dowers, uses, Will, intayles, leases, alyenacions, intrusions, mortgage, forfeitures, conditions, judgement, executions, rent, annuyties, statuts, merchant statuts of the staple recognyzaunces, liveries, ouster-le-mayne, and of and from all other charges, titles, troubles and incumbraunce whatsoever hadd, made or done before the sealying and delyverie hereof by the said Robert Doylye, or by any other person or personnes lawfullye claymynge by, from, or under the said Robert Doylye before the same sealinge and delyverye; except, as hereafter is excepted accordinge to the true intent and meanynge of theis present. And the said William Place for hym, his heyres, executours, admynystratours and assigneis, doth covenaunt, promyse and graunt to, and with the said Warden and Schollers and their successours by these present, that he, and they, shall and will, at all tymes, from henceforth for ever, at his or their owne proper cost and charge, clerelye exonerate and discharge, or otherwise, upon sufficient notyce and request, save and kepe harmeles, as well the said Warden and Schollers and their successours, as also the said messuages, rents, lands, tenements, and all other the premisses by theis presents covenaunted to be assured, or conveyed, and every part and parcell thereof, with all and singuler their appurtenaunc of, and from all and all manner of former bargaynes, former sales, gifts, graunts, titles, rights, joyntures, dowers, uses, willes, intayles, leases, alienations, intrusions, mortgages, forfeitures, conditions, judgements, executions, rents, annuyties, statuts, merchant statuts of the staple recognyzaunces, liveries, ouster-le-mayne, and of and from all other charges, titles, trobles, and incombraunces whatsoever hadd, made, or done before the sealinge and delyverye hereof by the said William Place, or by any other person or persons lawfullye claymynge by, from, or under the said William Place. Exept allwaye out of theis presents, one lease made by Indenture by the said Robert Doylye and William Place to Richard Waye, of Thame, aforesaid, of one messuage or tenement, with the appurtenaunc in New Thame aforesaid, nowe or late in the tenure or occupacion of Thomas Symson, or his assigneis, dated the last daye of Marche, in the seventeenth yere of the reigne of our said soveraigne ladye Queene Elizabeth, for the terme of nynety-nyne yeres, whereupon the yerelye rent of fyve pound two shilling foure pence is reserved, and also excepted the demyse, lease and graunt of suche other messuages, houses, lands, tenements, and hereditaments, with their appurtenaunc, scituate, lyinge and beinge in Syd'nam aforesaid, as bene in and by the same Indenture bearinge date the said last daye of Marche, in the said seventeenth yere mencyoned to be demysed, graunted or leased by the said Robert Doylye and William Place to the said Richard Waye, for and duringe suche yeres, and in suche manner and forme as in the same Indenture is lymyted and expressed. And also, excepted one other lease made by Indenture by the said Robert Doylye and William Place to Henry Gibson, of Syd'nam, aforesaid, of a tenement or cotage, and certen land in Syd'nam, in the said Countye of Oxford, dated the twentith daye of August, in the fourteenth yere of the reigne of our said soveraigne ladye Queene Elizabeth, for the terme of one and thirtye yeres, whereupon the yerelye rent of six shilling eight pence is reserved. And also, excepted one other lease made by Indenture by the said Robert Doylye and William Place to Maulde Stephens, widowe, of a tenement or cotage, and certen land in Syd'nam aforesaid, dated the twentith daye of August, in the fourteenth yere of the reigne of our said soveraigne ladye Queene Elizabeth, for the term of one and twentye yeres, whereupon the yerelye rent of six shilling and eight pence is reserved. And also, excepted one other lease made by Indenture by the said Robert Doylye and William Place to Robert Phillippe, alias Coxe, of two message or tenement in Newe Thame aforesaid, dated the three and twentith daye of Aprill, in the seventeenth yere of the raigne of our said soveraigne ladye Queue Elizabeth, for the term of fiftye-one yeres, whereupon the yereley rent of fortye shilling is reserved. And also, excepted one other lease made by Indenture by the said Robert Doylye and William Place to Phillippe Kinge and the said Richard Waye, of the Rectorye and Personage of Eastneston, in the Countye of Northampton aforesaid, dated the first daye of April, in the said seventeenth yere of the raigne of our said soveraigne ladye Queue Elizabeth, for terme of nynetye-nyne yeres, whereupon the yerelye rent of foure pound is reserved. And also, excepted one other lease made by Indenture by the said Robert Doylye and William Place to Richard Holmes, of a Close in Eastheneyd, in the Countye of Berk'. dated the sixteenth daye of Marche, in the thirteenth yere of the raigne of our said soveraigne ladye Quene Elizabeth, for the terme of one and twenty yeres, whereupon the yerelye rent of twenty pence is reserved. And also excepted one other lease made by Indenture by the said Robert Doyle and William Place to Richard Pytman, of a message or tenement, with the appurtenanne in Newe Thame aforesaid, late in the tenure of Nicholas Stanton or his assigneis, dated the fourth day of Aprill in the said seventeenth yere of the raigne of our said soveraigne ladye Queue Elizabeth, for the terme of nynetye-nyne yeres, whereupon the yerelye rent of fiftye-three shilling four pence is reserved. **In Consideration** of which covenannt, graunt and other conveyaunc to be made as is aforesaid, and to the intent that the said godlye purpose and good meanynge of the aforesaid late Lorde Williams may be in every respect furthered, accomplished, perfected and duly executed, the said Warden and Schollers for theym and their successours do covenaunt, promise and graunt to, and with, the said Robert Doylye and William Place, their heyres, executours and admynystratours by theis present, in manner and forme followynge:—That is to say, that they, the said Warden and Schollers and their successours for ever shall and will, with suche proffitt and comodityes yerely arysinge, growinge or comynge of the premisses, or anye parte thereof, as they or any of theym shall or maye laufullye have, recyve, or take, well and dulye for ever upholde and mayntayne a Free Grammer Schole for the free teachinge and exercise of grammer in the said capitall messuage in Olde Thame aforesaid, there newelye buylded and called the Schole House, and in none other place, except in tyme of plage or other contageious sickness in Thame aforesaid, accordinge to suche statutes, rewles and ordynannces as bene conteyned in one scedule or composition to these present Indentures annexed. And shall and will also with such other proffitt of the premises as is aforesaid for ever fynde, susteyne and mayntyne a schoolemaister and an usher; that is to saye, one honest and discrete person sufficientlye furnyshed and inhabited with learnyng, discretion and other good qualityes for a schoolemaister or cheife teacher, and one other honest and discrete person likewise sufficiently inhabited with learnynge for an usher or under teacher, to instruct, teache, and bringe uppe chyldren and others in the rules of grammer in the said capitall messuage called the Schoole House; except in tyme of plage or other contagious sicknes in Thame aforesaid, for ever, accordinge to the said statuts, rules and ordynannces made, agreed upon and sett fourth as is aforesaid. And shall and will also yerelye and everye yere for ever, with the rent, yssues and proffitt of the premysses, from tyme to tyme, well and trulye paye or cause to be payd to the schoolmaister, usher, and other the persons hereafter mentyoned, the severall somme of monye hereafter in theis present perticulerly expressed, lymyted and declared. That is to say, to every suche scholemaster of the said schole for the tyme beinge, for and in the name of his yerelye salarye, stipend or wage, the somme of twentye-sixe pound thirtene shilling foure pence of good and laufull monye of England, at foure termes in the yere. That is to saye, at the feast of the Natyvitye of our Saviour Christe, of th'annunciation of the Virgyn Marye, of the Natyvitye of Saynt John Baptist, and of Saynt Michaell the Archaungell, or within thirtye dayes next after every of the said feasts by even portions; and to everye suche usher for the tyme beinge, for and in the name of his yerelye salarye, stipend or wage, the somme of thirtene pound sixe shilling eight pence of lyke monye, at the same foure severall feasts, or within thirtye dayes next after every of the same feasts by even porcyons without any deteynynge or witholdinge of any parte or parcell of the said severall sallaries, stipend or wages, or any part or parcell of theym, or anye of theym, from the said schoolemaister or usher, to be due unto hym, theym, or either of theym, or their, or either of their said sallarye, stipend or wages as is aforesaid, otherwise, or in any other manner then as is hereafter mencyoned or declared, and without exactynge of theym any mony for any acquyttannc or other discharge for the payment thereof; **And** further, that they, the said Warden and Schollers and their successours shall and will, at all and every tyme and tymes, and from tyme to tyme for ever, so oft as nede shall requyre, well and sufficiently repayre, uphold, maynteyne and kepe, as well the said capitall messuage or house newly buylded in Old Thame, called the Schoole House, and all manner of buyldinge belonginge to the same, as also the Tombe of the said late Lorde Williams, sett in the chauncell of the Parishe Churche of Thame aforesaid, in all manner of reparacions so farr forth as the surplusage of the yerelye proffitt and commodities of the premises over and above the severall sommes mony by this Indenture, or other composition appoynted to be payd will beare and extend. And moreover, that neither the said Warden and Schollers and their successours, nor any of theym at any tyme hereafter, shall make any gift, graunte, or other assurannce by way of patent, or otherwise to any person or persons for terme or termes of life, lyves, or yeres of the office of the said schoolemaister or usher, or the said severall sallaryes, stipend, or wages appoynted for the said schoolemaister and usher of any part or parcell of them, nor shall do, cause or procure to be done, any act or acts, thinge or things, whereby the said Warden and Schollers for the tyme beinge, or their successours, at any tyme shall, or maye be disabled, at their will and pleasure upon just occasion to expell, remove, or displace any schoolemaister or usher there appoynted to teache, and in his or their place to constitute and appoynte one other or others there to teache accordinge to the true intent and meanynge of the foundation of the said schoole, or accordinge to suche composition and agreament touchinge the same foundation as nowe presentlye is or hereafter shall be sett fourth in writinge by the said Robert Doylye and William Place, or the survivour of theym on the one party, and the said Warden and Schollers on the other partye. And, to the intent that the said schoolemaister and usher for the tyme beinge maye be alwayes the more carefull of their dutyes in the diligent and vertuous exercyse of suche as shall from tyme to tyme be brought up under theym, and that therebye, more fruyt by the good increase of vertue and learnynge maye from tyme to tyme be plentifullye reaped of the foresaid good and godlye purpose and meanynge of the said late Lorde Williams, The said Warden and Schollers for theym and their successours do further promyse, covenannt and graunte to, and with the said Robert Doylye and William Place, their heyres, executours and admynystratours by this present, that the Warden of the said Colledge for the tyme beinge, at some one convenyent tyme every two yere, or at one tyme at the least in everye third yere for ever, shall and will goe and repayre to the said Schoole and then and there shall make a good and diligent visitation, examynation, and serche as well touchinge the good behaviour, diligence and good order in teachinge to be followed, observed and kept by the said schoolemaister and usher for the tyme beinge accordinge to the said composition, and otherwise, at their discretion, to be made for the same School, as also touchinge the profitinge of the Schollers and their severall procedingss in learnynge accordinge to the said rules and ordynannc nowe presentlye made, or to be made as is aforesaid of, or concernynge the same. And Whereas, the said late Lord Williams, in his lyfe tyme hadd an Almes Howse within the said town of Thame, wherein were lodged and maynteyned fyve pore men and one poore woman, by the name of fyve almes men and one almes woman, there to have contynuannce for ever. And whereas, also the said late Lorde Williams, by his last Will and Testament, willed and devised certen land, tenement, parcell of the premyses; That is to saye, two mesuags or tenements in Newe Thame aforesaid, sometyme in the tenure of Richard Bunce, and nowe or late in the tenure of Robert Phillippes, *alias* Cone, and all other the said lands, tenements and hereditaments in Syd'nam and Eastheeryd, beinge of the yerelye rent of seven pound foure shilling nyne pence, for the intent therewith to augment and increase the said Almes House of Thame and the lyvinge of the pore men in the same, and in and by this conveyannce and agreement are ment and intended severallye to go to that intent and purpose, the said Warden and Schollers for the considerations above said for theym and their successours do covenannt, promyse and graunte to, and with the said Robert Doylye and William Place, and their heyres, executours and admynystrators by this present, in manner and forme followynge; That is to say, that they, the said Warden and Schollers, and their successours for ever, with suche proffitt of the last recyted premisses as they maye laufullye receyve, shall and will trulye give, exhibite and pay, or cause to be well and truly given, exhibited and payed yerely for ever to the said fyve almes men and one almes woman in Thame aforesaid, for the tyme beinge, in augmentation of their lyvinge, or ells to the schoolemaister of the said Schoole in Thame aforesaid for the tyme beinge, by him to be paid over to the said almes men and almes woman accordinge to the true intent, purport and meanynge of the said late Lorde Williams, in his last Will and testament expressed and declared, the sum of seven pounds foure shilling nyne pence of good and laufull monye of England, at two termes in the yere; that is to say, at the feast of th'annunciation of Our Ladye, three pound eleven shilling and six pence; and Saynt Michaell the Archaungell, three pound thirtene shilling and three pence, either within two monthes next after either of the said feasts, or ells aforehand wekely, ratably and proportionatelye accordinge to the said somme, as shal be thought most profytable for the releife of the said fyve almes men and one almes woman for the tyme being, for and toward the supplye whereof, as neade shall requyre, the said Robert Doylye and William Place have already delyvered the value of one hole yere's rent beforehande. And also shall and will, from tyme to tyme, agaynst the feast of the birth of our Lorde God, once within everye fourthe yere for ever give and bestowe to and upon everye of the said fyve almes men and one almes woman, in Thame aforesaid, for the tyme beinge, one clothe gowne, to be lyned, faced and readye made in suche sort and after suche rate as hereafter is declared and specified; that is to say, everye one of the gownes for the fyve almes men to conteyne three yarde of lyon tawney cloth, of Readinge making, at sixe shilling eight pence a brode yarde and not above, if suche manner clothe maye convenyently be hadd, and in default, or in want thereof, then suche other clothe of the said price as the said Warden and Schollers and their successours shall thinke and esteme to be most meete for that purpose. And the gowne for the almes woman to contayne two yard and a halfe of lyon tawney clothe, of Readinge making, at sixe shillinge eight pence a broad yarde and not above, if suche manner clothe maye convenyentlye be hadde as above said; and in default, or want thereof, then suche other clothe as the rest of the almes men shall have, and every of the said fyve men's gownes to be faced with blacke lambe, at two shilling sixe pence a face and not above. And the lynynge of every of the said fyve men's gownes to contayne seven yard of white cotton, at eight pence a yarde and not above. And shall and will bestowe upon the makinge and layinge in of the furre of everye of the said men's gownes, three shillinge and not above. And upon the lynynge, furringe, and making of the woman's gowne, six shilling eight pence and not above. And the said Warden and Schollers, for theym and their successours, do covenannte, promyse and graunte to, and with the said Robert Doylye and William Place, their heyres, executours and admynystratours by this present, in manner and forme followinge; That is to say, that they, the said Warden and Schollers and their successours for the tyme beinge, shall and will yerelye and everye yere for ever, paye or cause to be payed to the clerke of the Parishe Churche of Thame aforesaid, for the tyme beinge, for and in the name of a yerelye stipende or wages for the dressinge and cleane kepinge of the Tombe of the saide late Lorde Williams, in the said Churche, the somme of eight shilling of good and lawfull monye of England, at the said foure termes in the yere by even portions; And shall and will also paye, or cause to be payed to the most auncyent almes man, in contynuannce of the said fyve almes men, for and in the name of a yerelye stipend or wage, for the dressinge, scowringe and clene keapinge of the watercourse runynge from the upper ende of the rayles at the corner of the almes house aforesaid, unto the pyrrie at the corner of the orcharde of the said Schoole house, the somme of foure shilling of lyke monye at the said foure termes by even porcyons, if suche almes man will take upon hym so to do, and will and do performe the charge thereof, and if he will not take it, or be negligent in so doynge as is aforesaid, then the said stipend to be bestowed upon anye suche other of the said fyve almes men as the said scholemaiser of Thame schoole aforesaid, for the tyme

H H

beinge, shall thinke most fitt and diligent for that service, provided alwayes that the said Warden and Schollers, nor their successours, nor the former land, tenement or hereditament of the said Warden and Schollers, or their successours, nor theym, shall be burdened, onerated, or charged with, or for the said payment of the said severall sommes mony before in this Indenture, by the said Warded and Schollers, and their successours, covenaunted and promysed to be bestowed and ymployed in and upon the said schoolemaster, usher, almes men, almes women, and other uses before mentioned, or in an composition made or to be made, or in any of theym over and above the value of suche yerelye yssues, proffitt and commodityes of the said rents, messages, lands, tenements, and other the premyses before by theis presents covenaunted to be assured or conveyed, as the said Warden and Schollers, or their successours, for the tyme beinge, shall and may laufullye have, receyve, or take of same any thinge in this Indenture conteyned to the contrarye thereof in any wise notwithstandinge. And provided also, that if it shall happen anye of the said messuages, rents, lands, tenements, and other the premysses, or anye of theym other then the said two tenements in Newe Thame, in the tenure of Robert Phillipps, *alias* Cone, and the landes, tenements and hereditaments in Syd'nam and Easthenryd aforesaid, to be laufullye evicted from the said Warden and Schollers, for the tyme beinge, and their successours, without any fraude, guyle, covyne in theym, or that all the said land, tenement, and other the premyses shall not and maye not be, and for ever contynue of the same yerely value whereof they nowe be over all repryses. That then and from thenceforth it shal be and maye be well and laufull to, and for the said Warden and Schollers, and their successours, for the tyme beinge, ratablye and proportionably to abate, defalke and take out onely of the said severall payment or yerelye sommes of monye of twenty-sixe pound thirtene shilling foure pence, and thirtene pound sixe shilling eight pence, appoynted for the usuall wages of said schoolemaister and usher, so muche onelye as shall be requysite and nedefull to be abated, defalked and taken out for and toward the mayntenannce, performannce and contynuannce of the ordynannc, as is aforesaid, accordinge to the true intent and meanynge of theis presents, or as, is, or shall be specified in the said composition or compositions made, or to be made, as is aforesaid, any thinge in this Indenture conteyned to the contrary thereof in anywise notwithstandinge. **Provided** also, and the said Warden and Schollers, for theym, and their successours, do covenaunt, promyse and graunte to, and with the said Robert Doylye and William Place, and their heyres, executours and admynystratours, by theis presents, that it shall and maye be well and laufull to, and for the said Robert Doylye and William Place, and the longer lyver of theym, at all and everye tyme and tymes, and from tyme to tyme duringe their two lyves and the lyfe of the longer lyver of theym, at his or their will and pleasure, to have the nomynatinge and appoyntinge of the schoolemaister and usher of the said schoole, and by theymselves, or their deputyes to receyve the rents, revenues and proffitts of all and singuler the premisses before by theis presents covenaunted to be conveyed or assured, and to make the severall payments of wages and sommes of monye before by theis presents lymyted to the schoolemaister and usher, almes men and almes women, and to other uses, and to have the orderinge and disposicion of all things touchinge the said schole and almes house in suche sort as they, the said Robert Doylye and William Place nowe have, at the tyme of the sealinge and delyvery of theis presents, So as, and upon this condition, that the said Warden and Schollers, and their successours, be not charged or chargeable by reason of any covenaunt aforesaid touchinge any thinge or thing whatsoever wherewithall the said Robert Doylye and William Place, or the one of theym, or the survivour of theym, shall intermedle by force and vertue of this present proviso, or covenaunt any other thinge in this Indenture conteyned to the contrarye thereof, in any wise notwithstandinge. **And whereas**, there is nowe a writinge indented, annexed to theis presents, conteynynge a composition or ordynannce for the disposition of the said messuages, lands, tenements, and other the premisses, before by theis presents mencyoned, to be conveyed or assured as is aforesaid, and for the governement of the said Schoole, almes house, and other thing whiche the use of tyme hereafter upon occasion maye be thought mete to be altered, changed, or augemented, Therefore, the said Warden and Schollers, for theym, and their successours, do covenaunte, promyse and graunte to, and with the said Robert Doylye and William Place, their heyres, executours and admynystratours, by theis present, That it shall and maye be alwayes laufull to and for the said Robert Doyly and William Place, and the longer lyver of theym, at all and everye tyme and tymes, and from tyme to tyme duringe their lyves and the lyfe of the longer lyver of theym, as he or they shall see occasion, with the consent of the said Warden and Schollers, or their successours, for the tyme beinge, to alter, chaunge, or take awaye anye statut lawes, rules and ordynannc conteyned in the same composition, and likewise with the consent of the said Warden and Schollers, or their successours, for the tyme beinge, to adde, make and create newe statuts, lawes, rules and ordynannces for the better governmment of the same schoole and almes folke, and for the better advauncement of vertue and learnynge, and that they, the said Warden and Schollers, and their successours shall and will, from tyme to tyme, observe, performe, fullyll and kepe, as well all and everye thinge and thing whiche on their part are to be observed, performed, fulfilled and kept, conteyned and specified in the said writinge, indented of composition, annexed to theis presents; and also, all and every other thinge and thing on their part to be performed whiche shal be conteyned in any other writinge, compositions and agreament hereafter to be made betweene the said Robert Doylye and William Place, or the survyvour of theym on the one party, and the said Warden and Schollers, or their successours on the other partye, And shal be left in force at the tyme of the decease of the said Robert Doylye and William Place, or the survivour of theym; **In Witness** whereof, to the one part of theis Indentures remaynynge with the said Warden and Schollers, the aforesaid Robert Doylye and William Place have subscribed their names and sett seales, and to thother part hereof remaynynge with the said Robert Doylye and William Place, the aforesaid Warden and Schollers have sett common seale, proven within the said Colledge, the daye and yere above wrytten.

The Statutes of the School,—full of practical wisdom,—are divided into three parts. Firstly, those which relate to the persons in authority; secondly, those relating to the persons under authority; and thirdly, those concerning the poor inmates of the Hospital and its management.

As regards the election of Head Master, when a vacancy has arisen the names of two fit and proper persons are to be chosen by the Warden and Fellows of the College aforesaid, one of whom is to be selected by the "Lord Henry Norreys" or by "the heirs of the same person if deceased." Candidates are to be Masters of Arts of the University or Bachelor of Laws or of Arts of eight years' standing; and are not to be less than twenty-six years of age or more than sixty. The final selection rests with Lord Norreys or his heir. Then, having read the statute relating to his duties, the elected and approved Head Master is to be formally admitted to his office in the Chapel of the College in question. The Under Master or Usher is to be chosen by the Head Master on the Sunday following his own appointment, in the south Chapel of the Parish Church of Thame, in the presence of the Church Wardens and other responsible inhabitants of the town. The stipend of the Head Master was to be forty marks (£26 13s. 4d.), paid quarterly; that of the Under Master, to be paid at the same time, twenty marks (£13 6s. 8d.). The Head Master was to have the rooms on the right hand of the west entrance of the School House with the bedroom and attics above, and the Under Master the corresponding rooms to the left. They were each forbidden, if married, to have either their wives or children in the School House, or in any apartments of the same. The Head Master, under the direction of the College Authorities, was to pay all stipends, and to give in writing a yearly account of his stewardship. The surplus funds were to be applied to keeping the School House, Masters' Lodgings, and adjoining Hospital in good repair, to maintain the tomb of the Founder, and to pay any necessary legal costs and charges. The Head Master if neglectful of his duties was to be admonished by the Warden and Fellows of St. Mary College, then fined if disregardful, and altogether removed from his office if necessary.

Those Statutes which relate to the practical working of the School are rife with prudence and forethought. For example—

"Moreover, we wish, that that custom be here diligently observed, which is usual in the other famous schools: viz., that on ordinary days the Under Master go to the School to teach at six o'clock a.m., while the Master shall enter about seven o'clock; both of them to perform their duty with proper attention, until a suitable time for dinner. And when this is finished the former shall return to school at once, at one o'clock p.m.; and the latter at two o'clock. And neither of them shall leave (without legitimate excuse) in winter before five o'clock, in summer before six o'clock; unless they have obtained permission to have a holiday, and so can arrange to have the hours altered. While we wish the whole power of granting this indulgence to be in the hands of the Master alone (as long as he is at home), or of his substitute; yet, he may not grant this at random to all of them, nor oftener than once in the same week; nor on any day on which a crowd of persons is wont to gather in the Thame Market Place, for making purchases or holding a market."

As regards the payments to be made by the pupils these were small. A groat was to be given—to be applied to the general purposes of the School—prior to the admission of a pupil; in addition to which entrance fee a shilling a quarter was to be furthermore paid to the Head Master, and sixpence a quarter to the Under Master, in addition to a quarterly fee of twopence from each pupil, which money was to go towards the cleaning of the School twice a week and "to the purchasing of rods." All relations and kinsmen "of the most illustrious lord and heir, our most respected John Williams, and all the sons of his tenants residing either in Old or New Thame, Priestend, North Weston, or Moreton," were to be educated without any charge. And his lordship's relations were to have the privilege of using the larger attic—that is a long dormitory over the School Room, "as a special privilege, before all the other pupils, whosoever they may be," if such relations desired it. All the boys were to assemble at the School House and attend Divine Service every Sunday and Holy Day, sitting in their accustomed places in the chancel*—prior to which they were to be duly instructed in the Church Catechism. The other Rules and Regulations, which mainly relate to discipline and good government, were to be "set forth in Latin Hexameters" and painted up on a board in the School Room.

The old School House is a well-planned, substantial, picturesque, and convenient building of stone in the domestic Tudor style, the chief apartment in which, with mullioned windows, is a large, lofty, and well-proportioned School Room. The western portion and chief front of the house contains the lodgings and rooms of the officials; but this part has been much altered.† The old oaken stair-case, which had been originally placed here, was removed about the year 1842, when considerable alterations and additions were made to the house,‡ and an entire northern wing added,

* It is clear from Dr. Burte's Petition to the Warden of New College, set forth on p. 479, that the Gallery in the south aisle was not erected until the seventeenth century; and that prior to that period the boys occupied the low sedilia in the chancel.

† A List of the Names of the various Schoolmasters, with the dates of their appointments, had been painted on two boards affixed on either side of the window to the east wall of the School Room, but this was removed and is lost. I myself possessed a copy of it, which I took when a boy, and have transferred it to Dr. Sewell the Warden of New College.

‡ At this period the old well-worn oak fittings of the School

together with dormer windows to the west side, a mullioned bay-window to the lower north-west room, a new stair-case, and a thorough internal rearrangement effected. A western gallery and stairs to the attics were removed from the School Room. Externally the pitch of the gabled roof is good, the chimneys are well placed and picturesquely grouped, while the general appearance of the building from every point of view is one of solidity and repose.* In Anthony à Wood's time the following arms remained in the windows of the School Room. His description of them is exactly reproduced :—

Ar'es in the windowes of Thame Schoole, in Com. Oxon, built by ye Executors of Joh' L'd Williams.†

At the opp' end in ye East window.

France & Engl. quartered, with supporters. Qu. Elizab.

A rose g. with a crowne on it.

. . . . Two organ pipes in saltire (the big ends upp'-most) betw. 4 crosses patée (Williams)—impaling, arg. a bird (Cornish chough) sab. rather a morecock or hen (More) parted p' chev. . . . . [?] Arg. 2 greyhounds combitant in ye upp' part, within a bord. . . . . charged with fleur de lise . . . . impaling . . . . broken.

On the north side.

1. Organ pipes quartering Cornish ch. as before—impaling arg. a cheveron betw. 3 maunches or sleeves s'.
2. The said quarterings, impaling or a chev. g. quartering arg. 2 birds sab.
3. Organ pipes quartering ye chough—impaling the 2 Greyhounds combitant quart'ing arg. a Stork‡ sab.

Arg. chev. betw. 3 rooks or eagles heads erased sab. quartering—(1) bendy of 6 or & az. within a bord. g. ; (2) barr. nebuley of 6 or & g. ; (3) azure between (*sic*) billettey or ; (4) arg. Lyon ramp. s. crownd or within a bord. s. ; (5) azure semie de lise . . . . a lyon ra'p. arg. ; (6) az. semie de lise . . . . a lyon ra'p. or ; (7) az. 3 wheat-sheaves or ; (8) az. 3 sfoyles peirced or ; (9) Quarterly g. & ar. an eagle displayed in ye 1 or.

The organ pipes & chough quartered againe.

Sab. fess arg. betw. 3 ankors or—L'd Wainman quartering—(1) parted p' pale az. & g. a cross patée or ; (2) G. 3 lyons passant ; (3) Gironey of 8 pieces S. & or on a cant. g. a cup covered ; (4) Chequy g. & arg. on a chev. az. 3 roses arg. ; (5) Erm. on a chev. . . . . 3 roses or ; (6) or a chev. az. betw. 3 roses & a dolphin naiant gules ; (7) arg. on a chev. az. betw. 3 lozenges sab. as many bucks heads caboshed . . . . ; (8) arg. a chev. betw. 3 spread eagles g. ; (9) az. a cross patone arg. betw. 4 martlets.

Imp. { Arg. a chev. sab. between 3 rooks heads Erased sab. as before.
Quart. organs pipes & chough ut supra. wth 2 quarterings quarter ye 2 greyhounds combitant ut supra.

To the south and south-east of the School House are excellent gardens, both for flowers and fruit, with what was once an orchard to the east. The whole of the premises are enclosed and surrounded by a substantial stone wall, while on the southern side lies a pleasant lawn.

Over the entrance of the chief door, from the School House into the School Room, the following inscription formerly stood—being the well-known injunction set forth at Winchester School—

Aut disce, aut discede,
Manet sors tertia, cædi.

This is said to have been removed and lost during the alterations made about forty years ago.

On the west front, over the chief external doorway, where the armorial bearings of the Founder carved in stone remain, the following inscription cut on brass or latten was placed. It is here exactly reproduced :

Qui legit, et lectas didicit conscribere voces
Nec satis hac doctum se putat arte puer
Si volet hinc latiæ capiat primordia linguæ
Hæc schola gramaticen rhethoriceq; docet

House—fittings coeval with its first foundation—were likewise cast out and destroyed, to make way for others of painted pine-wood. On the school-desks and wall-panelling hundreds of names and devices had been from time to time carved—amongst others those of Hester, John Milton, Rouse, Blount, Quatremain, Symeon, Trowe, Powell, Bale, Spires, Head, Norreys, John Ayres, Hampden, Dormer, George Croke, Hardinge, Belson, Etheridge, Marmyon, Ellis, Temple, Clerke, Francklin, Ballowe, Phillips, Fortescue, Sutton, Holland, Scroope, Tryon, Winslowe, Holte, Herbert, Cannon, Smythe, Knollys, Burnard, Barry, Ingoldsby, Lee, Doyley, Waye, Woodbridge, Kinge, Wenman, Knight, Pope, Marshe, Lenton, Parke, Towers, Sewell, Danvers, Dutton, Shephard, Willis, Stone, Truelove, Chamberlain, Hedges, Harris, Goodwin, Anthony à Wood, Heyboorne, Bertie, Reynolds, Cope, Hearne, Bryan, Brangwyn, Manners, Lovelace, Holt, Fettiplace, Curson, Leaver, and Lupton.

* There is an engraving of the western front, from the pencil of Mr. Buckler, in Carlisle's *Grammar Schools*, and another in Skelton's *Antiquities of Oxfordshire*. A sketch, taken since the additions and alterations of 1842, is also given in Lupton's *History of Thame*.

† Wood MS., 4 D., p. 289 (but p. 1 of the volume), and p. 289ᵃ.

‡ P'haps s' Hearne rather a Stork by ye na's of Storks.

On the outside of the external stone gateway leading to the garden—a gateway immediately opposite to the chief external western doorway—the following inscription, in the same style of art, also cut on brass or latten, formerly stood :—

"Cuja domus? Gulielmiadae. Cui condita? Phoebo.
  Cur Phoebo? Musis praesidet ingenijs.
Quid docet? ut latio pueri sermone loquantur.
  Quo pretio? gratis, laus ea cuja Dei.
Grammaticen quicunque puer vult scire latinam,
  Culte Romano possit ut ore loqui,
Hunc Schola nostra (prius discat modo scribere) gratis.
  Ex Gulielmiadae munere structa docet."

There are few more rare printed volumes than the small quarto book of Latin Prayers of this School. A copy on vellum, quite perfect and in excellent preservation, remains in the Grenville Library of the British Museum. There is also (1) an imperfect copy, on paper, in the King's Library of the same institution; (2) another copy, on paper, wanting the Appendices, at New College, Oxford, in the custody of the Warden; (3) a third copy, on paper, at Thame, in charge of the Head Master; (4) a fourth copy, on paper, was sold at the sale of the Library of the late Dr. Philip Bliss of Oxford; and (5) a fifth copy, on paper, is preserved in the Bodleian Library. This last-mentioned specimen ends on L ii. On the fly-leaf Dr. Richard Rawlinson, the distinguished Non-juring antiquary, has written the following memorandum: "This copy of the Charter Agreement between the Trustees, Latin and English Statutes, belonging to Tame Schole in Oxfordshire, I take to be as scarce and valuable as any MS., and think it should be esteemed as such. R. R., London House, 21 Decem' 1743."

The title-page of the vellum copy in the Grenville Library stands thus :—

SCHOLA
THAMENSIS
EX FVNDATIONE
Iohannis VVilliams Militis
domini Williams de Thame
1575.

The Prayers alone were reprinted on five leaves in 1578, but copies of this reprint are also remarkably rare. A third edition was put forth in the year 1662 under Dr. Henry Beeston, of which a specimen remained, with the autograph of "A. Hampden" on its title-page, bound up with other pamphlets, in the Library of the late Dr. John Lee of Hartwell Park—a collection disposed of by public auction a few years ago.

The following is the text of the *Prayers* :—

Preces Matutinae, in Schola, ante alia exercitia, dicendae.

Deus misereatur.
Gloria Patri.
Sicut erat.
Kyrie eleyson.
Christe eleyson.
Kyrie eleyson.
Pater noster.
Et ne nos inducas in tentationem ;
Sed libera nos a malo. Amen.

Oremus.

CLAMANT primo statim ad Tuam, clementissime Deus, Omnipotentiam miselli, quos condidisti, quasi luteum vasculum ad figulum, quasi errantes oviculae ad pastorem, aut inutilissimi servi ad dominum beneficentissimum ; dignare hodie animis illabi, dignare mentibus illucescere, ignorantiae nebulam detergens, et carnis concupiscentias auferens ut his obstaculis mentes liberatae, liberales disciplinas capere et percipere possint, quarum adminiculis in perfectam Tui cognitionem grandescant, Quem noscere et diligere summa est felicitas. Amen.

OMNIPOTENS Deus, Qui hoc tempore et unanimi voce supplicationes nostras Tibi faciamus, gratiose largitus es : et promisisti si quando duo vel tres in Nomine Tuo congregati fuerint, vota illorum Te concessurum ; exple voluntatem, Domine, petitionesque servorum Tuorum, quemadmodum ex usu illorum maxime futurum est, et annue ut in hoc seculo cognitionem veritatis Tuae, in futuro vitam aeternam habeamus ; per Christum Dominum Nostrum. Amen.

AUDI preces nostras, Aeterna Patris Sapientia, Domine Jesu Christe, Qui humanae naturae docilitatis, memoriae, et intelligentiae commodum addidisti ; adde, quaesumus, ad naturae propensionem auxilium gratiae Tuae, ut liberales disciplinas ac sacras litteras citius perdiscamus, sed gloriae Tuae servituras : quarum adminiculis adjutae mentes nostrae plenius assequantur cognitionem Tui, Quem nosse felicitatis humanae summa est : atque ad Tuae sanctissimae pueritiae exemplum, indies proficiamus aetate, sapientia, et gratia apud Deum et apud homines ; Qui vivis et regnas Unus Deus, cum Patre et Spiritu Sancto, ad omnem aeternitatem. Amen.*

Benedicite. Dominus.
In Nomine Patris, et Filii, et Spiritus Sancti. Amen.

Preces ante decessum a Schola dicendae.

Antiphona canenda ad quemlibet tonum Primi Psalmi Anglici.

Jesu, Redemptor omnium,
Salutis Anchora,
Audi preces clamantium,
et mitis adjuva.
Tu sola Spes, et saucii
Medela cordis es ;
Te, tot malorum conscii,
rogamus supplices ;
Aufer tenebras sensibus,
et lumen ingere ;
Tuum timorem mentibus,
cultumque subjice.
Fac ut voluntas indoli
semper respondeat,
laborque vires ingeni
infractus augeat.
Da sic magistris obsequi
qui nobis imperant,
ne quando ad iram conciti
se nimis torqueant.
Da literis quas discimus,
sic uti in posterum,
ut gloriam, dum vivimus,
Tuam sonent. Amen.

Confitebor Tibi.

Confitebor Tibi, Domine, in toto corde meo : in consilio justorum, et congregatione.

Magna opera Domini : exquisita in omnes voluntates Ejus.

Confessio et magnificentia opus Ejus : et Justitia Ejus manet in seculum seculi.

Memoriam fecit mirabilium Suorum, misericors et miserator Dominus :

Escam dedit timentibus Se. Memor erit in seculum testamenti Sui :

Virtutem operum Suorum annunciabit populo Suo :

Ut det illis hereditatem gentium : opera manuum Ejus, veritas et judicium.

Fidelia omnia mandata Ejus : confirmata in seculum seculi facta in veritate et aequitate.

Redemptionem misit [Dominus] populo Suo : mandavit in aeternum testamentum Suum. Sanctum et terribile Nomen Ejus.

Initium sapientiae timor Domini. Intellectus bonus

---

* A translation of the above three Collects is here provided :—

Most Gracious God, early in the morning, Thy miserable servants cry unto Thine Almighty power, whom Thou hast made, as an earthen vessel to the potter, as wandering sheep to their shepherd, or as most miserable servants to a most kind master ; vouchsafe to enter their hearts this day, and to send Thy light into their minds, dispelling the mist of ignorance, and taking away from them all fleshly lusts, that their minds being freed from such hindrances they may be able to hear and receive such sound learning, so that they may grow to a perfect knowledge of Thee, Whom to know and to love is the greatest happiness. Amen.

Almighty God, Who hast given us grace at this time with one accord to make our common supplications unto Thee ; and dost promise, that when two or three are gathered together in Thy Name Thou wilt grant their requests : Fulfil now, O Lord, the desires and petitions of Thy servants, as may be most expedient for them ; granting us in this world knowledge of Thy truth, and in the world to come life everlasting. Amen.

O Lord Jesus Christ, Eternal Wisdom of the Father, Who hast added to man's nature the benefit of teachableness, memory, and understanding, hear our prayers ; and grant the help of Thy grace to our own natural endeavours, that we may the more readily acquire true knowledge and sacred learning, to Thy greater glory ; so that our minds, being strengthened by such help, may attain to a fuller knowledge of Thee, Whom to know is the highest human happiness ; and that, following the example of Thine Own most Sacred Childhood, we may daily increase in years, and in wisdom and favour with God and man ; Who with the Father and the Holy Ghost livest and reignest one God, for ever and ever. Amen.

omnibus facientibus eum: laudatio Ejus manet in seculum seculi.

Gloria Patri.
Sicut erat.
Kyrie eleyson.
Christe eleyson.
Kyrie eleyson.

Pater noster.
Et ne nos inducas in tentationem;
Sed libera nos a malo. Amen.

Oremus.

TIBI, Omnipotens Deus, Coelestis Pater, in Cujus miseratione fidelium animae requiescunt, gloria, laus, et honor; Qui, pro ineffabili dilectione, famulum Tuum *Johannem Williams* Fundatorem nostrum, tot et tantis in terra beasti muneribus, ut quamplurimos ad aedificationem Ecclesiae omni seculorum memoria produceret; mitte clementissime Deus de coelis sanctis Tua charismata, quae in aliis ita operentur, ut ejus exemplo novos foetus ad Nominis Tui gloriam formare studeant; per Christum Dominum nostrum. Amen.*

Benedicamus Domino. Deo gratias.

As regards the restored Hospital or Alms-house, consisting of six separate residences, five men were to be admitted and one woman. These were to be poor persons belonging to the Town, of good character; and were specially enjoined to bear themselves at all times and on all occasions with propriety and decorum. When the Statutes were drawn up, the appointment of each to the privileges of the Hospital was to rest with Henry, Lord Norreys, the son-in-law of the Founder, and afterwards with his heirs. Each of the appointed inmates was to have a weekly gift of money, according to the proceeds of the endowment;† proper under-clothing, "made of black lambskin wool," and long black cloth cloaks reaching to the ankle, to be provided every year, adorned with "military silver buttons of the most honorable lord, John Williams," and to be distributed by the Steward of the Hospital on Christmas Eve. In addition to this, a scarlet cloak, adorned with a stout silver plate, on which the armorial bearings of the Founder had been impressed, was delivered to the inmates once in four years, to be worn at Christmas, Easter, Pentecost, Trinity Sunday, the Epiphany, Circumcision, the Purification and Annunciation of the B. Virgin Mary, the Feasts of St. John the Baptist, St. Mark, St. Luke, St. Michael and All Saints; and whenever Royalty passed through the Town; or when special commemorations of the foundation of the School and Hospital were held; or when the Visitor, the Warden of New College, came. These cloaks were to be carefully preserved, not torn up nor converted into common use, and were to be kept in the Hospital. Attendance at daily, morning, and evening prayer at the Parish Church (when such prayers were said*) was expected of them, "as far as their infirmities will permit them."† On Sundays and festivals this became a duty, and was not to remain unperformed. "They must attend at the usually-assigned seats in the Chancel of the aforesaid Parish Church;" and there, either standing or kneeling before and beside Lord Williams's Tomb, having appointed places assigned to them according to their seniority, devoutly join in the public devotions and common prayers.

All notorious irregularities of life were to be noticed—firstly, by suitable admonition; and, secondly, by fines. But the testimony of two or three townsmen of undoubted respectability and character was required to make proof of an accusation, and before any punishment was decided on or inflicted. This Hospital has proved a great temporal benefit to many throughout the last three centuries. Recently, however, it has been altogether recast in its plan and provisions; while many needless changes have been made in a valuable and valued institution which was originally based on a religious principle—now entirely wiped out and totally obscured.

For seventy years after its foundation, the School attracted the sons of the neighbouring nobility and gentry, who received in it a substantial education in grammar, and were thoroughly well grounded in classical knowledge. It produced from time to time several renowned and distinguished scholars, and maintained its original reputation as a useful and

* A translation of the above Collect is here provided:—

O Almighty God and Heavenly Father, in whose mercy the souls of the faithful repose, we render Thee glory, praise and honor, for Thine ineffable love who didst endue thy servant, *John Williams* our Founder, with so many and such excellent temporal gifts, that he provided for the edification of the living Church as a remembrance for all generations. Send down from Thy Holy Throne, Most Gracious God, the dew of Thy heavenly blessing; and so in like manner influence others, that, after his example, they may study to produce fresh fruits, to the Glory of Thy Name, through Christ our Lord. Amen.

† In the early part of the present century the funds of the Charity enabled those who distributed them to grant seven shillings and sixpence a week to each of the six inmates, and special donations of five shillings at Christmas and Easter. The "New Scheme," by which the Charity has been fundamentally changed, is set forth amongst the Appendices.

* There can be exceedingly little doubt that Public Prayers were greatly neglected, and almost universally left unsaid, during the latter part of Elizabeth's reign; and that, as a consequence, indifference and godlessness largely increased. Thame was no exception to the general rule in regard to the decay of True Religion.

† "No excuse shall be admitted as legitimate for the absence of any one from the aforesaid Prayers, save and except infirm bodily health, or some serious business-matter which cannot be conveniently performed at any other time or properly postponed."—*Ancient Statutes of the Hospital at Thame.*

excellent school. On some later pages a brief account will be given of certain of its more remarkable pupils.

During the Great Rebellion, however, it suffered severely, as did every similar institution thereabouts. There are few greater curses than a bitter and prolonged Civil War. This evil existed in an active form throughout the more inhabited parts of Oxfordshire and Buckinghamshire. At Aylesbury and Boarstall, at Chalgrove and Crendon, the clang of battle had been heard. Skirmishes were of frequent occurrence. Thame for some time was the centre of important military operations, while for eighteen months on one occasion, and for thirteen on another, it was garrisoned by rebel musters; so that agriculture decayed, trade was at a standstill, taxation became almost unbearable, and the greatest misery for the multitude, as a consequence, ensued. In a previous century, however, the Religious Houses had been destroyed, God's sanctuaries (their churches and chapels) razed to the ground, True Religion and Liberty abolished by a most cruel Despotism; and Persecution had been rampant for at least two generations. Thus in the great drama of religious change and destruction, it cannot cause wonder that as the altars were first thrown down under the Tudors, the throne was overturned a century afterwards under the Stuarts. Huge national crimes, as History so truly testifies, seldom go unpunished.

Though Dr. Burte was connected by marriage with the chief Puritanical families of the neighbourhood, he was unable to stem the tide of destruction and profanity which the Civil War had brought in. The flood-gates of Rebellion had been long previously opened. The rejection of lawful Authority over the National Church had soon been followed by its repudiation in the State. The following Petition—presented between the month of November 1647 and August 1648—only too clearly depicts the situation:—

The humble Request of Willi'a Burte late School M^{r} of Thame Schoole unto ye right W^{ll} Mr Dr Stringer* Warden of New College in Oxon & the 3 Senior Fellowes of ye same College.

That whereas Hee ye sayd Willi'a Burte hath beene 16 yeeres Schoolem^{r} of ye sayd Schoole; yet notwithstanding his great paynes therein for soe many yeeres, by his many Expenses in & for ye Schoole, & by ye miserye of ye Times, being very much disabled in his Estate; as—

1. by Suffering in ye Erection of ye Gallerye in ye Church soe beneficiall for ye Schollers; to which ye Com'on Chest contributed not any thing.

2. by paym^{ts} for his 20th p't v^{li}.

3. by plunders of his goodes about 22^{li}.

4. by Losses at one time by ye Parliam^{t} Army about 50^{li}.

5. by ye dissepation of All his Schollers uppon ye Accesse of ye Army, & general Infection of ye whole Towne: for a long time ye Schoole shutt quite up, & ever since but slowlye increasing from ye lowest Ebb.

6. by Many great & continuall Taxes to divers Garrisons, not only for his p'sonall Estate, but allsoe out of his bare Stipend, for ye Schoole.

7. by often & long q'rtring of Souldiers, wch hee suffered ye more in his owne house to his great charge, to p'serve & redeeme ye Schoole, wch sometimes had beene turned into an Hospitall, sometimes into a Courte of guard, sometimes into a Garrison; had not Hee to his manifest danger & detrim^{t}, opposed.

8. by ye long Sickenes of his wife taken at first by a fright in ye Schoole, about wch hee hath expended about 60^{li}.

9. And since hee freely left ye Schoole, desiring ye Advancement thereof by an Able Successor; by many & great Charges Hee hath beene putt to for Repara'ons of his house & otherwise.

All wch concurring in these difficult & expensive times have very much cast him behind hand & engulft him into Debt, even to ye Morgaging of that little hee hath.

Hee therefore humbly Requesteth, that ye p'mises Especially those incident unto him in & for his Rela'on to ye Schoole, his constant residence in these sad times, & great paynes there, may be taken into y^{r} considera'on: soe farr at least as to give him full discharge of ye Remaynder of his finall Accountes: viz. xxxi^{li} vii^{s} x^{d} ob. for some Recompense of his many losses. And withall that his 2 bonds wch. hee sealed at his first Admiss'n to ye place may be both p'sently canceld. For wch hee shall Remayne

Y^{r} W^{ps} obliged in all love
to serve you
W. Burte.

Thirteen years afterwards, the official Visitor of the School thus recorded the state of affairs soon after the restoration of the lawful king:—

A Memorandum by Dr Michael Woodward,* Warden of New College, of What was done when he visited the School of Thame, May 16, 1661.

From keeping a Court at Weedon by Ailebury I went to visitt ye Schoole of Thame; where I viewed all ye Buildings of ye Schoole, & Almeshouse there, wth ye Walls & Out-houses; wch were all very safe & in good repaire, being lately new mended, Lathed & Tiled. I went also & saw ye Lord Williams his Tombe in ye Church of Thame, in one of ye Iles there, that is very much mangled, & broken. I resolved to speak unto Mr Jackson ye Stone-cutter to mend it if hee had such Materialls, (viz. Alabaster) to mend it with all. The Plate of Brasse wth ye Inscriptio thereon is in the hands of ye Schoolemaster Mr Willis; ye other, as tis said, in ye keeping of my Lord of Lyndsey, who in behalfe of his Lady is Successour unto ye aforesaid Lord Williams. Mr Jackson goeing over unto Thame to view ye said Tombe, & to value ye Charge of ye repaire of it, conceived it to be £32 14s. 00d. But this being conceived too high a Rate by my Selfe, & ye 3 Senio'rs, was referred ye choise of ye worke-

* Dr. Stringer was elected Warden of New College 19 Nov. 1647, and was ejected by an order of the Parliamentary Visitors of Oxford 1 August 1648.

* Dr. Michael Woodward was Warden of New College from A.D. 1658 to 1675. He succeeded Dr. George Marshall, who had been elected Warden in 1649.

man to my Lord of Lynsey himselfe, to imploy in that Businesse whom he pleased; The Chest of Thame in yᵉ College disbursing yᵉ Charge of it.

The Tombe heretofore was covered over with a sheet of Canvas, to keep off yᵉ dust &c.; but yᵉ Souldiers who mangled the Tombe stole that away. When yᵉ Tombe is in repaire, I shall cause another Sheet to be bought, & layed uppon yᵐ. In yᵉ Schoole one of yᵉ Schollers made a Speech unto mee. The Almes-people also (five men & one woman) p'sented yᵐselves unto me in their Scarlett Gownes; unto whom, with yᵉ Scholler, I gave their respective Gratuities.

I told Mʳ Willis of his haveing a wife & familie in yᵉ School Lodgings (that being agᵗ yᵉ Statutes) requireing him, in a short convenient time, to provide for his wife & familie elsewhere.

The following documents will be read with interest. They contain sufficient accurate information to enable the reader to judge of the devastation which the Rebels had committed. The destruction effected in the interior of the Church was considerable. Some of the vaults were rifled for the sake of the leaden coffins within them, while almost every fragment of stained glass and stone carving was smashed to atoms.

The Estimate for repairs to Lord Williams' Tomb.

The Estimate in the handwriting of Mr. Jackson.

	£	s.	d.
"The 2 pare of handes lost "The ladyes Nose Brused "his and her garments defaced "The 2 creasts broke at the feete which was yᵉ Unicorne & Grahound	6	12	6
"The ledges all Broke except 7 or 8 foot which is brused "the 2 Tabells of Inscription lost with the Compartement & winges of the broken Cheeribins heades defaced	15	11	6
"The new pollishing all the Alabaster worke and glasinge it anew	10	10	00
Summa	32	14	00

"This was yᵉ Charge of mending yᵉ Lord Williams his Tombe in Thame Church as Valued or Computed by Mʳ Jackson, Sculptoʳ."

(Dʳ Woodward's Note on the preceding Estimate itself.)

The actual Bills for the work executed were as follows:—

June 25, 1662. The Bill of Wᵐ Byrde Sculptor (as receipted by him).

	£	s.	d.
"The repayering of 2 figures - - - -	03	10	00
"2 New Supporters at foote of the figures—a lion & a Grayhound - - -	07	10	00
"The Couch repayering and 16 foote of new ffringe - - - - -	02	06	00
"Two new Co'partiments yᵗ are abought yᵉ brase Tables - - - - -	03	10	00
"Fast'ning up the brase Tables - -	01	10	00
"Repayering yᵉ Coates of Armes - -	01	10	00
"The Carriage of worke to Thame - -	00	04	00
Totall Some -	20	00	00

The Bill of Richᵈ Hawkins, for painting & gilding Lᵈ Williams' Tomb (as receipted by him May 13, 1663).

	£	s.	d.
"For paintinge and gildinge of the Lord Williams his monument with the severall matches and quarteringe being gilded and painted in their proper colours being all done in oyle - - - -	10	0	0
"Then there was the grate painted and gilded besides, there are 46 flowerdelucea gilded on both sides at 8ᵈ a peice - - -	1	10	8
"Then there are 92 spikes gilded at a peony a peice, cometh to - - - -	0	7	8
"there is 8 corners gilded at 6ᵈ a peice - -	0	4	0
"for those 8 corners yirons coloured at 3ᵈ a peice cometh to - - - - -	0	2	0
"for 16 broad reyles at 2ᵈ a peice - -	0	2	8
"for 184 barres coloured at a peony a peice cometh to - - - - -	0	15	4
"for 46 flower delucea done with throwing blew at a peony a peice - - - -	0	3	10
The whole -	13	6	2

Here it may be well to set forth a few personal and official particulars, which have been gathered by research and enquiry, concerning the various Head Masters of the School, from its first foundation to the present time. The difficulty in collecting facts, such as those required for reliable biographical notices, however, can only be properly realized by those who have made the attempt.

Head Masters of Thame Grammar School.

1. Edward Harris, born about the year 1534; matriculated at Oxford 20 Feb. 1564; was appointed the first Head Master in 1574. He graduated M.A., and was a Fellow of New College. A native of Thame, he was a kinsman of the last Prior of Notley Abbey, Valentine Bownde. In the plans adopted for setting up the Grammar School he gave such excellent advice to the Executors of Lord Williams that he received from them a grant of the Mastership for life.* Under his tuition the School began

* "We have thought it in accordance with strict justice and but reasonable that the enjoyment of this office of Master should be given in preference to all others, as a sort of special benefaction, by way of reward for his labour to the man who has assisted us in an especial manner before all others with all his energies in forming this School for learning, to wit Edward Harris, who has attained the position of Master of Arts, who has now been for eight years Head of this School, to his own credit and to the advantage of his pupils alike. . . . . . For this purpose our Letters, which they call Letters Patent, have been added, enabling him to retain the aforesaid rights unimpaired, with no interference from any person whatsoever,

to flourish. He died 3 Nov. 1597, aged almost 63 years, and was buried in the choir of Thame Church, where there is a monument to his memory erected by William Ballowe.

2. Richard Boucher, son of Richard Boucher, Bouchier, or Butcher, and Agnes his wife, of Handborough,* Co. Oxon, baptized 7 Oct. 1561, was admitted to Winchester College in 1577. He became a Bachelor of Laws of Oxford and Fellow of New College, 28 Nov. 1583. He was appointed Head Master of Thame School in 1597. He died 14 July 1627, was buried two days afterwards, and a marble monument was erected to his memory in the choir by his brother Thomas. He left a legacy of £4 to the Church, which was laid out in the repair of the fabric.

3. Hugh Evans, of Harlech, Co. Merioneth, was admitted to Winchester College in 1613; matriculated from New College, Oxford, 10 Oct. 1617, aged 19; Fellow of New College, 28 Aug. 1619; sometime a Schoolmaster at Southampton. Appointed Head Master of Thame School in 1627. He died and was buried at Thame 5 Jan. 1631.

4. William Burte, of the parish of St. Laurence, Winchester, son of William Burte of Thame,† *gent.*; Mus. Doct., and one of the choir of Winchester Cathedral; admitted to Winchester College in 1618; elected Fellow of New College, 16 Sept. 1627; Head Master of Thame School, 1631-1647; Head Master of Winchester College, 1653-1658; Warden of Winchester, 28 August 1658; Rector of Wheatfield, Co. Oxon; and Canon of Winchester, 22 Sept. 1664. He died 3 July 1679; and was buried in the choir of the College Chapel at Winchester, on the epistle side of the altar. He married at Thame, 26 Jan. 1636, Elizabeth, daughter of Maximilian Petty of Thame,* Esq., by Elizabeth, daughter of Robert Waller of Beaconsfield, Co. Bucks, Esq., and left issue a son and four daughters.

5. William Atliffe, admitted to Winchester College in 1632; Fellow of New College, 27 Aug. 1640; S.C.L.; appointed Head Master of Thame School in 1647, and so remained until 1655; Vicar of Ambrosden near Bicester in 1655. Died by leaping out of a window at Ambrosden Vicarage, 28 April 1664.†

6. Henry Beeston,‡ of Titchfield, Co. Hants, admitted to Winchester College in 1644; Fellow of New College, 1648; appointed Head Master of Thame School in May 1655; Rector of Wallop, Co. Hants; married Elizabeth, daughter of the Rev. Dr. Burte, by Elizabeth, daughter of Maximilian Petty of Thame, Esq.; Head Master of Winchester School, 1658; D.C.L., Oxon, 12

either the Warden or the Fellows of the aforesaid College, so long as he chooses to perform the duties of the aforesaid office."—Chap. X., Appendix of Agreement between Robert Doyley, Esq., and William Place, Gent., and the Warden of the College of the Blessed Mary in Oxford.

* This family, long seated at the Manor House, a fine Elizabethan mansion, partly destroyed, was of considerable antiquity and influence. One member of it, William Bouchier, was President of C.C.C. Oxford in 1559. Another, Thomas Bouchier, was Fellow of All Souls' College, Oxford, and Regius Professor of Civil Law in 1672, and was appointed Principal of St. Alban Hall in 1678. He was also Official Principal of the Peculiar and Exempt Jurisdictions of Thame and Milton for many years. James Bouchier, of the same stock, was made Principal of St. Alban Hall in 1723. The Registers of Handborough contain numerous entries relating to this family; amongst others the following:—" 1561. Richardus Butcher filius Johannis Butcher, baptizatus erat septimo die [Octobris]." There are several monuments to Bouchiers in the Church of Handborough. A large mausoleum which stood at the north-west corner of the churchyard over their vault, having become ruinous, was taken down.

† This family was of great antiquity at Thame. Edward Burte, of this parish, was Rector of Holton, Co. Oxon, and died in 1479. A William Burte was educated at Winchester College, A.D. 1497. A branch of the family lived for several generations at Shabbington, Co. Bucks. Philip Byrde or Byrte was Churchwarden of Thame in 1567, and other members of the family resided at Crendon.

* Maximilian Petty of the Place House, Thame, Esq. = Elizabeth, daughter of Robert Waller of Beaconsfield, Co. Bucks, Esq.

Elizabeth Petty, eldest daughter. M.I. in Thame Choir. = William Burte, D.D., of Thame, Head Master of Thame School; afterwards Warden of Winchester College.

1. Maximilian Petty Burte; admitted to Winchester College in 1654.
2. Elizabeth Burte. = Rev. Henry Beeston, D.C.L., Rector of Wallop, Head Master of Thame School, and subsequently Warden of New College.
3. Anne Burte. = Robert Hawkins, D.D., a Wiltshire man.
4. Judith Burte. = Henry Bradshaw, D.D., Prebendary of Winchester.
5. Mary Burte. = Rev. Mr. Brooks.

Mr. Maximilian Petty of Thame "in contempt for his fee to the Heralds."—Visit. Oxon, A.D. 1634.

† "1664. 28 April.—Will. Ayliffe, LL.Bac., sometime Fellow of New Coll., and a founder's kinsman there, now Vicar of Amersden [Ambrosden] near to Bister in Oxfordshire, and lately Schoolmaster of Thame School (but began to teach there after A. W. had left that School), leaped naked out of his window, belonging to the Vicaridge of Amersden, and broke several parts of his body, and died soon after. He had married a young rich widow, lived high, and had severall children by her; but she dying in the prime of her yeares, and leving him and the children little or nothing of her estate, and her joynture going away with her life, he grew exceedingly discontented thereupon, and made away with himself."—*Life of Anthony à Wood*, p. 139. London: 1848.

"August 1650. Bridgett ye wife of Mr Wm Allife buried 20th."—Register of Burials, Thame Church.

‡ One son of this clergyman—matriculated from New College, 30 March 1683, aged 14—Henry Beeston, afterwards of the Inner Temple, Esq., born *circa* 1669, was Recorder of Woodstock from 1709 to 1743. He died 16 July 1743, aged 76, and was buried at Wootton, Co. Oxon, where there is M.I. on the floor of the chancel to his memory.

Feb. 1660; Canon of Winchester, 5 Oct. 1664; Warden of New College, Oxford, 7 Aug. 1679; Commissary of Oxford, 1680; one of the first Members of the Chemical Society of Oxford. Died 12 May 1701; buried in the Ante-Chapel of New College. M.I. on the floor, "H. B. obt. 12 Maii, 1701."

7. Hugh Willis. (See List of Vicars, p. 144.) Appointed Head Master of Thame School in 1655, and so remained until 1675.

8. Thomas Middleton, born *circa* 1644, son of Thomas Middleton of St. Clement's, London, *gent.* Admitted to Winchester College in 1660; matriculated at Oxford from New College, 13 November 1663, aged 19; graduated B.A., 17 April 1667; M.A., 14 January 1670; Fellow of New College; and Vicar of Chesterton, Co. Oxon,

Signature of Thomas Middleton.

which he resigned on being appointed Head Master of Thame School in 1675; Vicar of Wilsford,* Co. . . . . ; Vicar of Long Crendon, Co. Bucks, 24 April 1682. Died 22 April 1694, aged 51. He married and had issue. A son, Thomas, is buried in the Choir of Thame Church. His daughter Anne, who married the Rev. James Buerdsell,† M.A., Fellow of B.N.C., lived to an advanced age. Her M.I. is in the Choir of Thame Church.

9. Henry Bruges, born *circa* 1669, son of Robert Bruges of Winchester, *pleb.* Admitted to Winchester College, 1681; matriculated at Oxford, from St. Mary Hall, 3 October 1687, aged 18; elected Fellow of New College, 2 May 1690; graduated B.A., 14 January 1691; appointed Head Master of Thame School, 1694; graduated M.A., 21 October 1697. He married and had issue, Henry,* Katherine, and Anne. Buried at Thame, 6 May 1727. His brother Robert was admitted to Winchester School in 1685, his brother John in 1689. The latter became Fellow of C.C.Coll. Oxon, in 1691; B.A., 5 Dec. 1695; M.A., 2 March 1698; and B.D., 17 July 1708.

10. William Lamplugh, born *circa* 1700, son of the Rev. Dr. Thomas Lamplugh of Kensington, Co. Middlesex, *cler.*, Vicar of St. Martin's-in-the-Fields, and afterwards Bishop of Oxford. He was admitted Scholar of New Coll., 14 July 1719, and matriculated from that Society, 15 July 1719, aged 19; graduated B.A., 24 April 1723; M.A., 14 January 1726; was appointed Head Master of Thame School, 10 June 1727, but resigned his position within a few weeks. He was subsequently presented by the Warden and Fellows of New Coll. to the Rectory of Alton Barnes (or Berners), 1 Aug. 1728.

11. James Fussell, born at Winchester, 17 Dec. 1699, second son of John Fussell of Winchester, *gent.* Educated at Winchester School; matriculated at Oxford, from New College, 17 July 1719; graduated B.A., 24 April 1723; Fellow of New College; M.A., 14 January 1726; appointed Head Master of Thame School, 27 July 1727; Vicar of Whaddon, Co. Bucks, 5 Dec. 1728; afterwards Vicar of Swalcliffe, Co. Oxon, which he quitted for that of Hardwicke, Co. Bucks—to the Rectory of which he was instituted 19 Aug. 1738. He died at Bath, 29 January 1760. His Will, dated 8 May 1753, was proved at London, 11 August 1760. There is a M.I. on the north side of the Chancel of Hardwicke, with the following inscription, thus:—"In memory of the Rev. James Fussell, A.M., twenty-two years Rector of this Parish, who departed this life, greatly lamented by all that knew him, Jany 29th in the *year of* Our Lord 1760, and in the 60th year of his age, with an entire resignation to the Divine Will; in sure and

* I am uncertain whether Mr. Middleton was Vicar of Wilsford in the diocese of Lincoln, or of that in the diocese of Salisbury.

† This clergyman, born *circa* 1670, matriculated at Oxford from B.N.Coll., 10 April 1685, and graduated B.A., 17 Oct. 1688, and M.A., 15 April 1692, was the author of a small volume, foolscap 8vo in size, pp. 224, entitled "Discourses and Essays on several Subjects relating chiefly to the Controversies of these Times, especially with the Socinians, Deists, Enthusiasts, and Sceptics." Oxford: Printed by Leonard Lichfield, 1700. It is dedicated to William Lloyd, Lord Bishop of Worcester, Lord Almoner to the King. The book, which treats of the doctrine of Sacrifice and the Resurrection of the Body, contains five Sermons and three Essays. They are all interesting and readable, and the whole volume is remarkable for its logical power, piety, and devout suggestions. The author writes of Our Lady as "the Blessed above all women, the Holy and Immaculate Virgin" (p. 172); and was evidently a sincere sympathiser with the Non-Jurors. He died young. A monument with the following inscription stands on the east wall of the middle cloister of B.N.Coll., Oxon:—"H. S. E. Vir desideratiss. Jac. Buerdsell, A.M. et hujus Coll. Socius; Qui varias admodum naturæ dotes nobiliori Literaturæ humanioris proventu auxit. Cujus tam morum probitatem tam vitæ per omnia sanctimoniam superstites (qua possint) penitus æmulentur! Ob. 9no Oct. Æræ Chr. 1700, Ætat. suæ 30."

* This Henry, who was of Corpus Christi Coll. Oxon, graduated M.A. 3 July 1722. He was instituted to the Rectory of Pitchcott, Co. Bucks, 27 Nov. 1724, on the presentation of Thomas Saunders of Brill, Co. Bucks, Esq., which he resigned in 1727.

certain hope of a joyful resurrection to a glorious immortality through the merits of his Blessed Redeemer, Christ Jesus."

12. Robert Wheeler, matriculated from University College, Oxford, 10 Dec. 1722, *pleb. filius*; graduated B.A., 1 March 1726; M.A. at New College, 18 June 1729. He was Head Master of Thame School for only a short period.

13. John Kipling, born 1695, son of John Kipling of Tackley, Co. Durham, *pleb.*; matriculated at Oxford, from Magdalen Hall, 1 Dec. 1713, aged 18; graduated at Ch. Ch., B.A., 1 Feb. 1717; M.A., 11 July 1720; appointed Head Master of Thame School in 1729. Married at Thame, 4 August of that year, Elizabeth Deeley.* Instituted Perpetual Curate of Chearsley, Co. Bucks, in 1721. The following is from the Chearsley Register:—"John Kipling, A.M., Enter'd upon ye Cure of Chersley ye 11th June 1721." He died, aged 76, 23 April 1769, and was buried in the Chancel at Chearsley, where there is a monumental memorial with the following inscription to his memory: "Hic jacet Joh' Kipling, A.M. Scholæ Thamensis quadraginta annos magister; hujusce ecclesiæ quadraginta septem annos curio: obdormivit Aprilis 23 Anno Domini 1769, ætatis 76."

14. John Hook, born *circa* 1739, son of Luke Hook of the City of Gloucester, *gent.*; matriculated at Oxford, from New College, 30 July 1757, aged 18; graduated B.C.L. at New College, of which he was a Fellow, 10 July 1765; appointed Head Master of Thame School in 1768.† He resigned this for the Head Mastership of Bedford School in 1773, when he vacated his fellowship. He had been presented to the Vicarage of Heckfield, Co. Hants, in 1770, but resigned the living in 1772.

15. William Cooke, born *circa* 1746, son of William Cooke of Enford, Co. Wilts, *cler.*; matriculated at Oxford, from New College, 7 Feb. 1765, aged 19; graduated B.A., 10 Oct. 1768; M.A., 14 January 1774; appointed Head Master of Thame School, 16 Nov. 1773. Married at Thame by licence, 8 July 1774, Elizabeth Clerke of Upminster, Co. Essex. Presented by Edward Horne of Bevis-Mount, Co. Hants, Esq., to the Vicarage of Worminghall, Co. Bucks, to which he was inducted 8th October 1783. Chaplain to the Marquis of Tweeddale. He died in 1795. His publications were: "The Conquest of Quebec, a Poem, occasioned by the Premium offered by the Right Hon. [George Henry Lee] Earl of Litchfield, Chancellor of the University of Oxford," quarto, 1769; "The Way to the Temple of True Honor and Fame by the Paths of Heroic Virtue, exemplified," etc., in four volumes duodecimo, Devizes, 1773; "Poetical Essays on Several Occasions." Dedicated to the Lady Catherine Hay. Quarto, London: 1774. Amongst the names of the subscribers to the latter are the Author's father, the Rev. Mr. Cooke, Enford, and the following persons belonging to Thame: Mr. Richard Way, Mr. James Way, Mr. Th. Dorrington, Mr. Rose, and Mr. Richard Smith.

16. William Stratford, born *circa* 1747, son of Robert Stratford of the City of Oxford, *pleb.*; matriculated at Oxford, from Corpus Christi College, 16 July 1763, aged 16; graduated B.A.,

* The following Pedigree of Kipling of Thame is here appended:—

Kipling of Thame.

John Kipling of Tackley, Co. Durham. =

John Kipling, born *circa* 1695. Perpetual Curate of Chearsley, 1721; Head Master of Thame School in 1729. Died 23 April 1769. M.I. at Chearsley. = Elizabeth Deeley, m. at Thame 4 August 1729.

1. John, baptized at Thame 2 Nov. 1730; died an infant.

2. John, born *circa* 1733. Admitted to Winchester School in 1746; B.A. Ch. Ch., 17 Dec. 1755; M.A., 30 June 1758; Vicar of Oakley, Co. Bucks.

3. Charles, of Thame, born *circa* 1734. Matriculated from Wadham Coll., 28 March 1751; Fellow of Wadham Coll.; M.A., 7 July 1759; Vicar of Oakley, and Perpetual Curate of Chearsley; of Oakley, 23 Jan. 1790. Died 30 April 1800. M.I. at Chearsley. = Penelope, born *circa* 1739; died 29 July 1820, aged 81. M.I. at Chearsley.

1. John Kipling, born *circa* 1767. Scholar of Lincoln Coll., Oxon, 1784; B.A., 7 June 1787; M.A., 14 April 1790; Vicar of Oakley and Nether-Winchendon, Co. Bucks; J.P. for that county. He was also Vicar of Chilton in the same county, which he resigned in 1829. = Catherine, born 3 August 1773; died 2 August 1802.

2. Charles, born *circa* 1769, of Wadham Coll., Oxon; B.C.L., 8 July 1809; Vicar of Stoney-Stratford, Co. Bucks, and subsequently Rector of Colston, Co. Leicester.

Elizabeth Penelope, buried at Chearsley, 28 Feb. 1776. M.I. at Chearsley.

† Dr. Sewell, the Warden of New College, in answer to inquiries, most courteously wrote thus:—"I have a note which I found attached to Hook's name in a List of Members of the College, 'Scholæ Thamensis Ludi magister,' and in the Master's *Book of Accounts*, though there is no mention of the Master's name, the handwriting for the year from 1769 to 1773 is different from the handwriting of the previous or the following years. I find no record of Hook's actual appointment or vacation of office."

18 Nov. 1768; M.A., 19 January 1770; appointed Head Master of Thame School in 1783; was instituted Rector of Holton, Co. Oxon, in 1794. He was also Rector of Easington in the same county in the year 1809, and died in the year 1814.

17. Timothy Tripp Lee. (See List of Vicars, p. 147.) Appointed Head Master in 1814, and so remained until his death in 1840.

18. Thomas Broadley Fooks or Foorks, eldest son of Thomas Broadley Fooks of Dartford, Co. Kent, Esq., by Maria Penelope Cracroft of Hackthorne, Co. Lincoln, born *circa* 1809; matriculated from New College, Oxford, 22 January 1828, aged 19; graduated B.A., 27 June 1833; B.C.L., 11 March 1841; D.C.L., 9 June of the same year; appointed Head Master of Thame School in 1841. He married, *circa* 1834, Maria Susanna, daughter of George Valentine Cox, M.A., of New College, Esquire-Bedell; and having resigned his position as Head Master, and retired on a pension, died at Clapham, Co. Surrey, 1 Nov. 1874, aged 66.

19. George Plummer, born at Penzance, Co. Cornwall, 15 September 1846; educated at the Grammar School, Penzance, and under private tuition; graduated B.A. of the University of London in 1869, and M.A. in 1876; held the office of Head Master of the Wellingborough Grammar School from 1870 to 1879; was appointed Head Master of Thame Grammar School in 1879. He married, 3 July 1872, Sarah Jane, youngest daughter of William Blenkinsop Pollard, and has issue four children.

AMONGST the School's distinguished scholars*—of certain of whom some account will be given in the next Chapter, when the general character of the Town and its inhabitants is under consideration—will be found the following: Sir George Croke, Dr. Ballowe (Prebendary of St. Paul's Cathedral, London), Bishop John Fell, John Godwin of Lower Winchendon, Lord Chief Justice Holt, Sir John Dynham, Edmund Waller, Anthony à Wood and his brothers, Bishops Henry King and John King, collateral relations of the last Abbot of Thame, Dr. Edward Pocock, John Cave, Shakerley Marmion, and Sir George Etheridge, Knt., dramatists, John Hampden, Richard Ingoldsby, and John Wilkes, Dr. Richard Powell—of the family of Milton's connections—Francis Willis, William Basse, and Henry Temple, poets, Dr. Joseph Rose, of Trinity College, Oxford, Dr. Croke, Rector of Amersham, Thomas Phillips, Author of the "Life of Cardinal Pole," and George, Marquis of Buckingham.

For some years during the latter part of the seventeenth century the School regained a large part of that reputation which it had so invariably enjoyed prior to the Great Rebellion; and it held an excellent position in the county up to the beginning of the present century. Evidence of this will be found set forth either directly or indirectly in the next Chapter. But the changed circumstances of the times, the want of fresh and more elastic Rules to be sanctioned and issued by Authority for the management of the School, the growing local indifference to the need and profit of a strictly classical education, and the increase in influence of superior schools elsewhere, led to a state of somnolency on the part of its Governors, Trustees, and Officers, which, on the whole, can neither be excused nor defended.

About the year 1842, however, considerable and important changes were made. The old School House was re-arranged internally, much altered and considerably added to—the stipends of the Masters being trebled. Independent of the changes already mentioned, several rooms were erected on the north side of the building. The School in truth obtained a new start; it owned numerous pupils of a good social position, who did credit to its teaching both at Oxford and Cambridge; but this change for the better was not destined to last long: while the fact that some of the original Statutes and regulations had obviously become obsolete, led eventually to still more startling and fundamental changes later on. The agitation of a small minority of resolute doctrinaires which resulted in the secularization of our ancient Universities, and eventually secured an universal system of atheistic elementary education for the lower classes, likewise brought about many important alterations in the endowed Grammar Schools of England. This was certainly* the case at Thame.

In the year 1878 the Scheme for the future management of the School† under the Endowed Schools' Act having been approved by the Queen in Council, it was understood that the Head Master then to be elected held his office subject to the provisions of that Scheme. It was at the same time determined that the School

* Amongst the earlier pupils competent to write Latin verses were the following: R. Gibbings, J. Blount, S. Blount, J. Hester, S. Benson, W. Hester, Blackynton, T. Alnutt, C. Spire, S. Lawson, Griffin, and S. Hester. Some of their MS. exercises still exist.

* "Religious opinions"—by which the Atheistic doctrinaires in question mean a repudiation of the Christian Religion—"or attendance or non-attendance at any particular form of religious worship shall not in any way affect the qualification of any person for being a Governor under this Scheme."—*Scheme for the Management of Thame School.*

† This "Scheme" is set forth at length amongst the Appendices. It will be noticed that women-governors are allowed—a notion which was not even contemplated or entertained under Queen Elizabeth.

should be a Day and Boarding School for boys between the ages of eight and seventeen years; and that the subjects of instruction should be reading and writing, arithmetic and mathematics, geography and history, natural science, English grammar, composition and literature, Latin and at least one foreign European language, drawing and vocal music; and that Greek might be taught as an extra.

The Head Master, who was not required to be a Clerk in orders, was to receive a fixed salary of £150, and an annual capitation fee of not less than £2, nor more than £4, for each boy, and to be allowed to take boarders at a charge of not more than £35 per annum.

About the same time the old School House, which, though it had served its purpose for three centuries, was condemned as no longer suitable nor sufficient, together with the adjacent Alms-houses, and other properties in Thame belonging to the School Estate, were disposed of, either by private sale or public auction; and plans in the meantime were prepared for the erection of a new School House and buildings on an eminence in Priest End to the south of the road to Oxford, and looking towards the Chiltern Hills.

These School Buildings, which were planned and designed by Mr. W. Wilkinson of Oxford, were arranged to accommodate 120 Scholars, including at least 50 Boarders; and comprized a suitable Residence for the Head Master, free from rates and taxes. A Notice to Builders desiring to tender for the erection of these buildings, dated 3 April 1877, and signed by Mr. William Parker, Clerk to the Governors, was issued; soon after which arrangements were completed with Messrs. Taylor and Grist of Bierton to proceed with their erection. This, with the aid of an efficient Clerk of the Works, and in a reasonable period, was done to the satisfaction of the Governors; and the School, without any public ceremony, was in due course opened.

For the alms-people, residence in the buildings of the old Hospital was by the new Scheme no longer required; while attendance at Church was dispensed with. The exact requirements and new conditions are set forth in the Scheme to be found amongst the Appendices.

The following is an extract from an interesting explanatory Letter of the Architect to the Author:—

"The amount authorised to be expended by the Charity Commissioners on the School at Thame was barely sufficient to provide even in a plain way the required accommodation. Therefore the building itself scarcely deserves more than a passing notice in your Book. It is an unpretending red-brick building with Bath-stone dressings on the model of St. Edward's School near Oxford, which was built by me about five years ago. It contains a Residence for the Head Master, rooms for the Second Master, School Room 50 feet by 22 feet, Dining Hall 45 feet by 20 feet, Dormitories for 50 Boarders, Bath Rooms, Lavatories, and the usual Domestic Offices for such an establishment."*

The new buildings, carefully planned and grouped with some art, are certainly not unpicturesque from the south side,† but may, perhaps, be a little disappointing to the critical spectator—when first seen from the high road. Their disadvantage lies in the fact that the inferior domestic portions come first into view, while the main part is hidden. But few modern buildings look well from every standing-point—their leading and chief contrast to old buildings. When the adjacent young trees and plantations grow up, the general effect of the new School will no doubt be heightened.

The plea for the practical abolition of Religion in Endowed Schools is founded on the disastrous but obvious fact that there are now so many new religions of all sorts and kinds energizing—each one come into existence since "the Reformation"—that universal toleration must be granted by the State to each and all, as also to Atheism. By consequence the outcome is that no religion of any value or importance is taught at all; while few religious obligations are either required or undertaken. The Tudor changes, as all allow, involved the deliberate putting aside of Catholicism by the Nation;—while more recent reforms, as events before our eyes shew, threaten eventually to obliterate the Christian principle altogether. It may be found out after all,—but possibly when too late to avert the evil consequences,—that the matured wisdom of our ancestors ought to have been far preferred before the rashness and insanity of our restless and short-sighted contemporaries.

* *Letter from the Architect to the Author, dated Oxford, 15 Nov.* 1878.

† A vigorous and picturesque sketch in perspective of the new buildings from this point of view, shewing the Master's House, Dining Hall, School Room, and Dormitories, together with the Ground Plan, and a Plan of the First Floor, were published in the *Builder* of 2 April 1881.

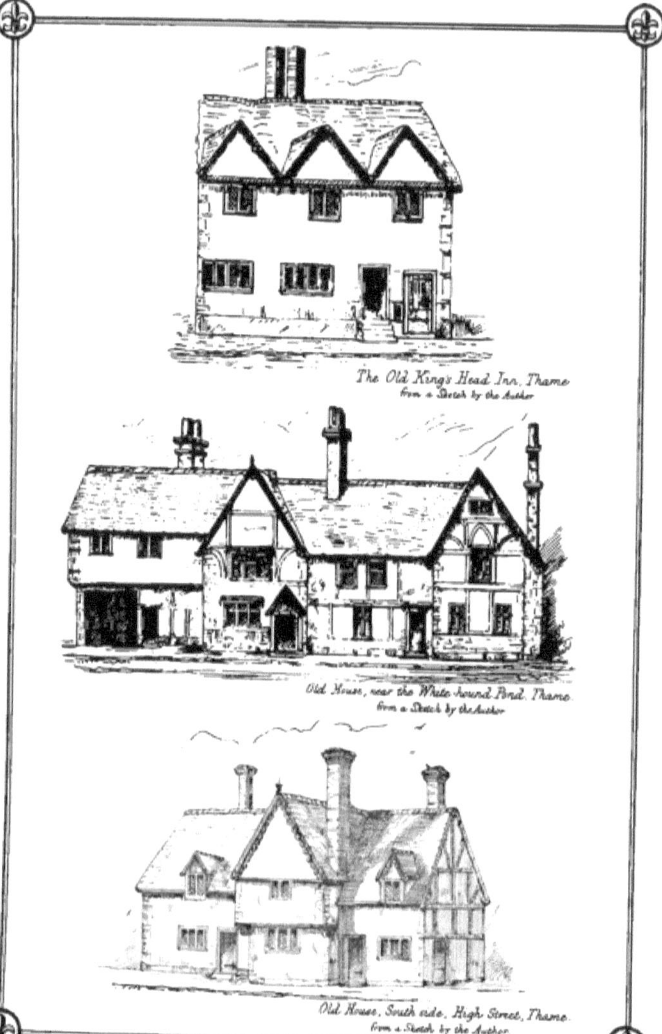

The Old King's Head Inn, Thame
from a Sketch by the Author

Old House, near the White-hound Pond, Thame.
from a Sketch by the Author

Old House, South side, High Street, Thame.
from a Sketch by the Author

CHAPTER THE FIFTH.

The Town of Thame and its Inhabitants.

ON the suppression of the religious houses—greatly impoverishing and injuring the localities of such institutions—and* the notable changes in Religion which ensued under the Tudors, corresponding social changes very generally took place throughout England. The Town of Thame of course was no exception to the general rule. And although it may be that the social changes which necessarily followed the religious took some time to be effected, they were made on a considerable scale, and soon began to exercise a direct and very widespread influence. Ignorance, Disaffection, want of religious principle, and Injustice were combinedly rampant.

The influence of the Church in previous centuries had always been considerable at Thame, and invariably beneficial throughout the whole kingdom; indeed the clergy as a body stood between the strong and the weak, neither flattering the former nor taking advantage of the latter. To the nobles as well as to the monarch they were true and faithful in their warnings against injustice; to the poor they were found to be both valued protectors under trials, and from the cradle to the grave firm and faithful friends.* As early as the tenth century the Town had become of a sufficient size and importance to have been styled "a burgh," and it is said to have received a Charter some centuries earlier, viz., from Wulfhere, King of Mercia (A.D. 661–675). It was certainly comprised in the ancient See of Dorchester, to which Oskytel, afterwards Archbishop of York, had been originally consecrated. It is chronicled that he died at Thame A.D. 970, and that his kinsman Thurkytyl, Abbot at Bedford, bore the corpse to that town for the rites of burial. The occasional residence of a Bishop in or near the Town of Thame would have added to its privileges. In great probability Thame Park originally belonged to the See of Dorchester, and the manor and lands were conveyed to the Bishop of Lincoln when the change of the Bishop's seat from Dorchester to Lincoln was completed. Anyhow, the following passage translated from

* Those who wish to study bare facts and dry details on the subject may consult the following volume—*Account of the Monastic Treasures Confiscated at the Dissolution of the various Houses in England*, by Sir John Williams, Knight, late Master of the Jewels to His Majesty King Henry VIII. Quarto, pp. 118. Edinburgh: Printed for the Abbotsford Club, 1836.

As to plate at Godstowe and Thame, the following is on record:—

"The said Sir William Cavendishe Knight one of the Commissioners at Godstowe in the County of Oxforde, in gilte plate cxij oz. in p'cell gilte plate iiij^{xx}xiij oz. and in white plate cxxj oz. Thame in the saide countye in p'cell gilte plate ciiij^{xx} oz. and in white plate clvij oz." (p. 37).

* King Henry II. held his Court at Brill, when the Chancellor Thomas à Becket, Archbishop of Canterbury, presided. At this Court the King, at the Archbishop's instigation, granted free warren to the Abbot and Monks of Thame Abbey.

that part of *Domesday Book* relating to Oxfordshire, is conclusive as to ownership at the period of the Norman Conquest :—

"The Bishop [of Lincoln] himself holds Thame. There are sixty hides there. Of these he has thirty-seven hides in his own farm; and his knights have the others. There is land to thirty-four ploughs. Now in demesne are five ploughs and five bondmen; and twenty-seven villanes with twenty-six bordars have nineteen ploughs. There is a mill there of twenty shillings. From meadows sixty shillings. In King Edward's time, it was worth twenty pounds; when received, sixteen pounds; now, thirty pounds."*

A Market and two annual Fairs† appear to have been held here by licence of the Lord Bishop as early as the time of Walter of Coutances (A.D. 1183–1186), but a century later, in Bishop Oliver Sutton's days (A.D. 1280–1299), the grant of a Market to the adjoining village of Haddenham, made in 1294, was withdrawn at the demand of another prelate, and the Market itself at the latter place discontinued,* because it had proved detrimental to the lawful rights of the Bishops of Lincoln and the interests of his people at Thame.

These rights had been already abundantly secured to them by royal confirmation, for a Charter for the Thame Market had been formally granted by King John to Hugh Wallis, Bishop of Lincoln (A.D. 1209–1235), in the early part of the episcopate of the latter; so that the ancient customs in regard both to Market and most probably to annual Fairs likewise were thus authoritatively approved and confirmed by regal authority.

Thame previously formed a portion of the old Hundred of Dorchester. It is now itself a Hundred, and comprises the parishes of Great and Little Milton, Great and Little Haseley, Waterstock, Waterperry,

House of the Striblehills at Priestend in Thame (circa 1648).

(From a Sketch by the Author taken in 1841.)

Tettesworth, Stoke Talmache, Shirburn, Lewknor, Wheatfield, South Weston, Postcombe, Crowell, Sydenham, Emmington, Easington, Warpsgrove, Chalgrove, Ascott, Tiddington, and Albury.

The Town itself consists mainly of one long and broad main street, remarkably wide about the middle, and bearing a somewhat foreign appearance, owing to its breadth and numerous gable-roofed, picturesque houses here and there still remaining. This street begins at Priestend in the west, at right angles with the road to Oxford—where stands the old house of the Striblehills looking up the street eastwards—and ends towards the east of the Town in what was formerly known as "Brick-kiln Lane," now called "Park Street." In the midst of the Town stand several groups of somewhat ancient buildings known as

* I am indebted to my friend Mr. James Parker of Oxford for the above translation. Much of course depends on the punctuation of the original. It is evidently not quite clear, however, where the terse sentences descriptive of the various ranks and gradations begin and end.

† These are held on the Tuesday in Easter week, in the Spring, and on Old Michaelmas Day, the 11th October, in the Autumn. To the Earl of Abingdon as Lord of the Manor, by right of descent from Lord Williams's coheirs, belong the profits of the Fairs and Markets, *e.g.*, stallage, package, and the customary tolls and duties.

* This was John of Alderby (A.D. 1300–1320), who raised an action against the Prior of Rufford, and obtained a decree in his favour.

"Middle Row"—the most ancient probably being The Birdcage Inn, facing the Spread Eagle. Another example, on the south side of the High Street, of which a sketch is provided—the old King's Head, immediately east of the Wesleyan meeting-house, is an excellent specimen of a mediæval timber Hostel; as likewise are some other picturesque Inns, the Swan (newly faced with brick, *circa* 1710), the Six Bells towards Priestend, the Saracen's Head* in the Butter Market, with several others of an inferior character in Friday Street and elsewhere. The old Red Lion, on the south of the High Street (it existed when Henry VIII. passed through the Town at Michaelmas 1530), an Inn where the Bishops of Lincoln of the seventeenth century (Dr. Thomas Barlow in 1688, and Dr. Thomas Tenison in 1692, for instance), put up, with their official retinue, when they held their Visitation, has been pulled down. Therein the Archdeacons of Buckingham and the Commissaries of the Dean and Chapter of Lincoln for several generations met their clergy at an official dinner once in three years; therein their Archidiaconal-Visitation Courts were likewise held,† probably from the time when the local Prebend was suppressed and the Prebendal Court abolished in the sixteenth century.

These old houses, framed of well-grown English oak, erected on stone or brick foundations, were often put together, as regards their main supports, frames and roofs, near to those woods in which the oaks made use of had slowly grown; and then brought down on low carriages with wheels. To the north of the Town, Bernewode Forest and Crendon Park—the latter noted in *Domesday Book*; to the South, Thame Park and the thickly wooded slopes of the Chiltern Hills from Stokenchurch to the two Kimbells, formerly rich in timber, were the places at which such oak could be obtained and such house-frames constructed. The upper portions overhung the lower, and so protected them from rain and damp. Gable roofs—in lieu of the flat, inconvenient, costly impostures of recent times—served to throw off the rain and snow. The windows had external water-boards preventing the rain from drifting in, while the projecting gables, ornamented with barge-boards, obviously protected the pargetted walls from any ill effects of the weather. Independent of the King's Head, two fair specimens of domestic architecture are represented. Nails appear to have been seldom or never used in the making of these oaken-frames, only stout oak pegs. The joints were constructed with some art, great patience and much honest work; the chamfers of the beams and the mouldings being generally of good design. In the days that are gone, such houses were made for comfort and convenience, mainly to live in, and not primarily to sell.* So that such were almost invariably well and strongly constructed, arranged with forethought and art; while many of them, in the main portions of their features, as may be seen, have lasted for three and four centuries.

The Hostels and Shops had their symbols, signs, or armorial bearings—the arms of the Grocers, Mercers, or Merchant Taylors: the various tenements and mansion-houses, streets, and lanes had their customary designations.

In times gone by, for many generations, the names of old families and benefactors connected with the place and other remembrances have been preserved in the designations of certain localities; for example—Bates's Leys, Cottismore Wells, Dormer's Leys, Allen's Lane, Friday's Street, May's Elms, Etheridge's, Rook's Lane, Place House,† Baker's Lane, Whitehound Pond,

* A Saracen's Head appears to have been the crest of the Oxfordshire branch of the Marmions, and its adoption for the sign of this Inn may possibly serve to shew that the mansion-house of the family in question at Thame originally stood towards the north of Middle Row. Under this Inn is a groined cellar or crypt of considerable size, evidently of early third-pointed work, and possibly a portion of the mansion-house of the Marmions. Its roof rests on stone pillars much mutilated; but, here and there, sufficient portions of certain of the mouldings remain to enable its probable age to be determined. It is possible, though not probable, that a similar crypt under an old house at the south-west corner of Friday Street, recently pulled down, may have been originally a part of that under the Saracen's Head.

† See p. 236.

* The following, having reference to houses belonging to the Church, and taken from certain old Accounts of the year 1465, will serve to indicate the cost both of materials and labour at that period:—

It' we have payde to ye Carpunters for mendyng of ye Chirch howse y^t Baker dwellyth in, xj^d.

It' we payde for stods to ye Wallys, ij^d ob.

It' we payde for lathis, ij^d ob.

It' we payde for lathnayle, j^d.

It' we payde oth^r naylis to set on stods and twists of ye dors, ob.

It' we payde for iij Carteful white erth, iij^d.

It' we payde for dawbyng of ye Wallys and mendyng of a twist and a hoke, v^d.

It' we payde for Rodds, ij^d ob.

It' we payde for iiij pesis of Oke, j^d ob.

It' we payde for hey to make ye mort^r, ob.

It' we payde for stonys, j^s j^d ob.

It' we payde for ground pynnyng and mete and drynke, iv^d.

It' we payde for John Kyngs labor abowte ye sam howse, ij^d ob.

It' we payde for dawbyng of ye howse y^t was Longs, v^d.

It' we payde for Rodds to ye sam howse, iv^d.

It' we payde for stods to ye sam howse, ij^d.

It' we payde for naylys to set on stods and oth^r thyngs, ob.

It' we payde for white erthe to dawbe ye wallys, viij^d.

It' John Kyng stodyd hit hymself, for his lab^r we how [owe] hym, j^s.

It' we payde for straw to make ye mort^r, ob.

It' we have payde for M tyle, iij^s vj^d.

It' we have payde for Raftur loggs and a port, vij^d ob.

It' we have payde for hewyng of them and for mete and drynke, iij^d.

† The House of the Dormers stood in a garden in Friday's Street, and in old documents is called "Maister Dormer's House." No doubt the adjacent lands both to the east and north belonged to it.

Court Close, Court Well Brook (corrupted to Cuttle Brook), Lashlake (formerly Lash-brook and Lasher-brook), and Butwell Leys, where the archers of old practised at the Butts. Court Close and Courtwell were no doubt appurtenances to Baldington's Court—the exact situation of which seems uncertain; the Moats to the destroyed mansion of the Dormers, probably the site of Baldington's Court.

Of late years—upon utilitarian principles, if any, or possibly as the outcome of a mere craze for change, by which so many restless persons are so strangely affected—the streets of Thame have been re-named. We have now Upper High Street, the Corn Market, and Lower High Street, with North Street instead of Friday Street, Pound Street instead of Pound Lane, Southern Road instead of Allen's Lane, Park Street instead of Brick-kiln Lane; Priestend Road, East Street, and One Bell Lane; Rook's Lane retaining its old designation.

It is of course quite impossible to set forth a tithe of the information which has been gathered regarding the various families of the Town and neighbourhood, though indirectly much information is here provided; while sufficient leading facts, names, and dates may be found to enable any special researches concerning particular families to be made with greater ease, and it may be hoped with some secured clue to accuracy.

In many cases the old families of esquires and gentlepeople (whom the Wars of the Roses had impoverished, and whose attachment to the old order of things, both in politics and religion, had perhaps hastened their decadence and temporal ruin), were pushed aside by others of a lower grade, who reasonably enough availed themselves of the opportunities offered such to mount the social ladder.* These latter at Thame, as elsewhere, often secured for their children alliances with the ancient gentry: so that the strain of change was felt less keenly; and in some instances its steady progress may have been occasionally almost imperceptible. The younger sons of the nobility of every order are found to have been not unfrequently allied to the gentlepeople of a rank below them; while some of knightly position, like the Heusters or Hesters of Litchfield and the Bekes of Berkshire, allies of the De Mandevilles, became merchants. Under Elizabeth one of the Wenmans found a mine of wealth by becoming "an adventurer" in Ireland; for he obtained from that Queen large tracts of land out of the confiscated estates of the conquered and oppressed Irish nobility and chieftains. One of the Marmions accompanied Sir Francis Drake in his explorations; a nephew of Cannon of Thame, one of the religious of Notley Abbey, was a follower of Sir Walter Raleigh. William Basse, sen., a yeoman of Moreton, and a tenant under the Wenmans and Norreyses, became a distinguished poet of a later Elizabethan era; and his son, of the same name, followed in his father's footsteps.

As those who examine the Pedigrees set forth may learn, the Wenmans, like the Baldingtons* and the Deanes, owned two coats of arms as belonging to their name—the one coat extremely dissimilar to the other. The marriage in the sixteenth century of Thomas Wenman (whose father had been a Merchant of the Staple of Calais or "Stapler") with Ursula, heiress of Thomas Giffard or Gifford of Twyford, connected these successful Witney wool-dealers with one of the most ancient Buckinghamshire families. Nine quarterings came to their descendants by this advantageous alliance. The last of the Barentynes had married Anthony

Geoffrey Dormer had inherited Baldington Court through an heiress of the Baldingtons. When the elder grandsons of Geoffrey Dormer left Thame for Ascott, Peterley, and Eythorpe, their House was inhabited by Mr. William Place, executor of Lord Williams's Will, and appears to have been termed "Place House" or "The Place House;" but subsequently, after having had various tenants, it fell into a state of dilapidation and was taken down in the early part of the present century.

* The following extract from a very ably-written treatise on Heraldry will enable the reader to follow many of the remarks in the text. Formerly the various divisions of rank were most strictly fenced in and carefully hedged round. So that those who would measure the past by the levelling and dangerous processes and notions of the present, may find themselves astray and in ignorance of the elementary principles of ancient social life:—

"Some others there are that number up nine several sorts of *Gentlemen*. First, those of *Ancestry*, which must be *Gentlemen* of *Blood*. Secondly, those of *Blood* and not of Ancestry, as when he is in the second degree descended from the first. Thirdly, *Gentlemen* of *Coat Armour* and not of *Blood*, as when he beareth a device given him by the *Heralds*, and then he and his issue are so styled to the third descent, who are *Gentlemen* of *Blood*. Fourthly, *Gentlemen* of Coat Armour and not of blood, as when the King gives them and their Heirs a *Lordship* by vertue thereof they may bear the *Coat Armour* of the old *Lord*, the *Heralds* approving thereof, and provided the said old Lords *Family* is extinct. Fifthly, a *Christian Soldier* that in the *Service* of *God* and his *Prince* killeth a *Heathen Gentleman* he shall bear his Arms, and if he hath issue to the third *Degree*, then they are Gentlemen of blood; but note that no *Christian Soldier* may bear another *Christian Coat* although vanquished by him in *Battle*, but may bear his Coat in the sinister *Quarter* with the proper Coat of such a Gentleman that he killed or put to flight, provided it be done in an *Army Royal*. Sixthly, if the *King* Knight a *Yeoman*, he is then adjudged a *Gentleman* of blood. Seventhly, when a *Yeoman's Son* is advanced to *Spiritual Dignity* he is then a Gentleman, but not of *Blood*, except he be a Doctor of the Civil *Laws*. Eighthly, or such that are brought up in a *Cathedral* or *Abbey* there serving in good office, or such as are of near kin to the *Bishop* or *Abbot*. And, ninthly, such as serve a *Prince* as a *Page*: and afterwards by their diligent and faithful service are advanced to higher places, although without badge by *Birth*, are esteemed Gentlemen."—*The Art of Heraldry*, pp. 254, 255. London: 1693.

* It is believed that Henry Collingridge, one of the Coleridges or Collingridges of Towersey, in the second year of Henry VI., *i.e.* 1423, had married Agnes, another heiress of the Baldingtons of Albury and Thame, and had adopted their more ancient armorial bearings—a custom of old not unfrequently followed. In Sir Bernard Burke's *Armory* he gives, Or, three fleurs-de-lys azure, for Collingridge.

Huddlestone, whose son Richard in turn married Isabel, daughter of Lord Williams and widow of Sir Richard Wenman. Sir John Dormer of Crendon and Dorton married a lady of the same house, but of another branch—the Giffards of Chillington. The Wenmans, one of whom did wisely by his marriage with Lord Williams's coheiress, were subsequently allied by Doselina Wenman's marriage to the Smiths of Padbury, (a family ruined by the bursting of the South Sea Bubble,* who in their turn were connected by a similar alliance with the Chesters of Chicheley); as also by Elizabeth Wenman's marriage to the Tredways, a knightly family of Beaconsfield; these again wedded with the Ways of Towersey and the Belsons of Brill and Aston Rowant. The Hesters of Thame, merchants, represented the old family of Marmion and a junior branch of the Englefields of Englefield—having married the heiresses of certain branches of both houses. The Ballowes, another very old family of merchants, became wealthy, and gave several sons to serve God in Church and State. The Dynhams of Boarstall and Eythorpe—a very ancient race—intermarried with the Wenmans and Dormers, the Dormers in turn with the Berties, the Berties with the Wrays of Glentworth, and one, the third Earl of Lindsey, with the widow of Sir Francis Henry Lee; the Wenmans again with the Hampdens, the Hampdens with the family of Waller the poet, and the Wallers with the Burtes and other residents in Thame. So it was in the seventeenth century with the Barrys of Thame and the Scropes of Wormsley, and with the Petties and Caves of Great Milton and Waterstock—such intermarriages were very numerous, while families of varying ranks were thus allied.

The following curious and interesting account of life at Thame Park in the seventeenth century, relating to Lady Wenman the first wife of Sir Richard, is taken from a recent publication of the Rev. John Morris, S.J.:—

"It happened on one occasion when I was in this lady's house, and was sitting with her after dinner, the servants having gone down to get their own dinner, that suddenly a guest was shewn up who had just arrived. This was an Oxford Doctor of Divinity, a heretic of some note and a persecutor of Catholics; his name was Dr. Abbot. He had just before this published a book against Father Southwell, who had been executed, and Father Gerard, who had escaped from the Tower, because these two had defended the doctrine of equivocation, which he chose to impugn. After this publication the good man had been made Dean of Winchester, a post which brought him in a yearly income of eight thousand florins (£800). This man then, as I said, was shewn up, and entered the dining-room, dressed in a sort of silk soutane coming down to his knees, as is the manner of their chief ministers. We were in appearance sitting at cards, though when the servants had all left the room we had laid the cards down to attend to better things. Hearing, however, this gentleman announced, we resumed our game, so that he found us playing with a good sum of money on the table.

"I may here mention that when I played thus with Catholics, with the view of maintaining among a mixed company the character in which I appeared, I always agreed that each one should have his money back afterwards, but should say an *Ave Maria* for each piece that was returned to him. It was on these terms that I frequently played with my brother Digby and other Catholics where it appeared necessary, so that the bystanders thought we were playing for money, and were in hot earnest over it.

"So also this minister never conceived the slightest suspicion of me, but after the first courtesies began to talk at a pretty pace: for this is the only thing those chattering ministers can do, who possess no solid knowledge, but by the persuasive words of human wisdom lead souls astray, and subvert houses, teaching things which are not convenient. So he, after much frivolous talk, began to tell us the latest news from London; how a certain Puritan had thrown himself down from the steeple of a church, having left it in writing that he knew himself to be secure of his eternal salvation. About this writing, however, the learned Doctor said nothing, but I had heard the particulars myself from another quarter.

"'Wretched man!' said I, 'what could induce him thus to destroy body and soul by one and the same act?'

"'Sir,' said the Doctor, learnedly enough and magisterially, 'we must not judge any man.'

"'True,' I replied, 'it is just possible that as he was falling he repented of his sin, *inter pontem et fontem*, as they say: but this is extremely improbable, since the last act of the man of which we have any means of judging was a mortal sin and deserving of damnation.'

"'But,' said the Doctor, 'we cannot know whether this was such a sin.'

"'Nay,' I replied, 'this is not left to our judgment; it is God's own verdict, when he forbids us under pain of Hell to kill any one; a prohibition which applies especially to the killing of ourselves, for charity begins from oneself.'

"The good Doctor being here caught, said no more on this point, but turned the subject, and said smiling, 'Gentlemen must not dispute on theological matters.'

"'True,' said I, 'we do not make profession of knowing theology; but at least we ought to know the law of God, though our profession is to play cards.'

"The lady with whom I was playing, hearing him speak to me in this way, could scarce keep her countenance, thinking within herself what he would have said if he had known who it was he was answering. The Doctor, however, did not stay much longer. Whether he departed sooner than he first intended, I know not; but I know that we much preferred his room to his company.

"The lady, in whose house Father Gerard met Dr. Abbot, must have been Agnes, Lady Wenman, wife of Sir Richard Wenman of Thame Park, not far from Oxford. Sir Richard was knighted in 1596 for his conduct at Cadiz, and attained the object of his ambition very long after this was written; for he was made a peer of Ireland in 1628 as Baron and Viscount Wenman. Agnes his wife came of a Catholic family, being the daughter of Sir George Fermor of Easton Neston in Northamptonshire."—*The Life of Father John Gerard*, 3rd edition, pp. 345-348. London: 1881.

* "Richard Smith of Padbury Manor, grandson of Doselina Wenman, settled a fourth part of the Stoke Hammond property and lands on his marriage with Penelope, upon that lady, one of the daughters of Sir John Chester of Chicheley, Baronet."—*Note from the late Colonel J. L. Chester.*

THE following Pedigrees of the Dormers of Thame etc., and of the Cottrell-Dormers of Rousham are suitably set forth here:—

Pedigree of Dormer of Thame, Ascott, and Great Milton, Co. Oxon, and of Crendon, Winge, and Peterley, Co. Bucks, and elsewhere,

(including the Earls of Carnarvon and Barons Dormer.)

ARMS OF DORMER.[1]—*1st and 4th, Azure, ten billets, four, three, two, and one, or, on a chief of the second a demi-lion issuant sable, armed and langued gules*; 2nd [DORRE alias CHOBBE or CHUBBE], *Gules, a chevron argent, charged with three shovellers sable between three chubbs argent, on a chief indented or three escallops gules* (one old Pedigree, dated 1622, makes the chief argent); 3rd [BALDINGTON], *Argent, three fleurs-de-lys azure.* (Note that other Arms of BALDINGTON of Oxfordshire are, *Argent, on a chevron sable, between three pellets, as many roses of the field*: and another Coat, *Azure, three fleurs-de-lys or.*)

CREST OF DORMER.—*A fox passant proper between two wings endorsed argent.*

ANOTHER CREST OF DORMER.—*A fox passant proper.*

CREST USED BY THE BARONS DORMER.—*A glove fesswise, thereon a falcon, wings inverted argent, belled and beaked or.*

Geoffrey Dormer of West Wycombe in Co. Bucks, Gent. = Margaret [another MS., dated 1640, in Lord Dormer's possession, has "Eleanor"], daughter and heiress of Thomas Dorre alias Chobbe.

Geoffrey Dormer, eldest son and heir, of West Wycombe aforesaid, and by right of his wife Lord of the Manor of Baldington in Thame. = Judith, daughter and heiress of Robert Baldington,[2] Lord of Baldington in Thame, Esq.

Other issue.

ARMS OF BALDINGTON OF THAME.—*Azure, three fleurs-de-lys or.*

Margaret. She bore her husband five sons and eight daughters. (1st wife.) = Geoffrey Dormer of the Parish of St. Laurence in West Wycombe, and of Old Thame, son and heir.[3] Merchant of the Staple of Calais. Will made 10 Oct. 1502. Part of it only recorded in one of the Register Books of the Registry at Canterbury, marked "Reg. F." Therein he bequeaths the Manor of Baldington's Court in Old Thame, with his lands and tenements, etc., in Old Thame, New Thame, Moreton, Priest End, and Attington to his son Geoffrey, and his heirs male. Died 9 March 1502-3. Buried in the Trinity Aisle at Thame. = Alice [Lord Dormer's Pedigree, and the alliance on page 284 of this Volume, have "Ursula"], daughter and heiress of Bartholomew Collingridge of Towersey, Esq., by Alice his wife. [See previous descents recorded on page 284.] She bore her husband seven sons and five daughters. (2nd wife.)

Other issue. Amongst which was William Dormer,[4] M.P. for Wycombe in 1542.

(Arms of Staple of Calais.)

(Autograph of Geoffrey Dormer.)

A

B

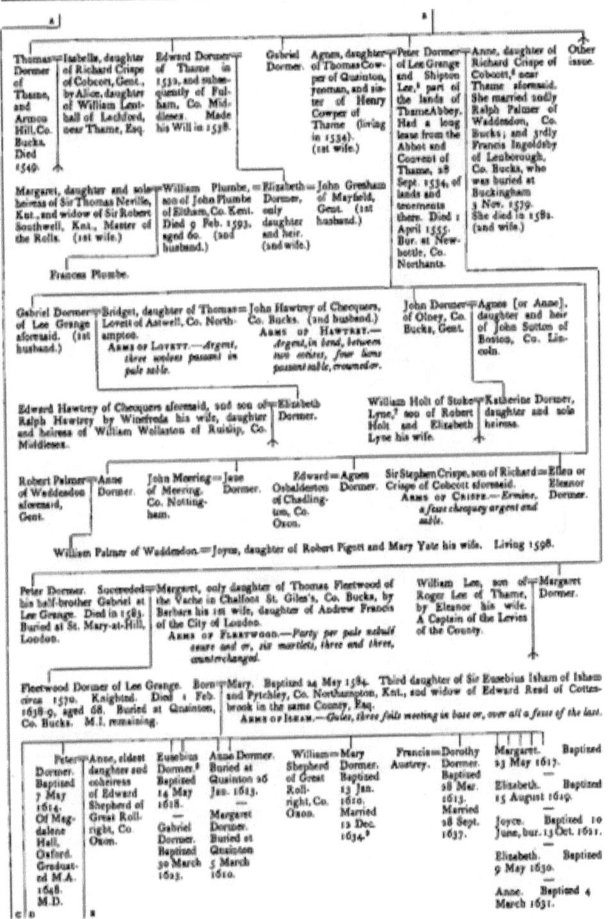
A
B
Thomas Dormer of Thame, and Armon Hill, Co. Bucks. Died 1549. = Isabella, daughter of Richard Crispe of Cobcott, Gent., by Alice, daughter of William Lenthall of Lechford, near Thame, Esq.
Edward Dormer of Thame in 1532, and subsequently of Fulham, Co. Middlesex. Made his Will in 1538.
Gabriel Dormer.
Agnes, daughter of Thomas Cowper of Quainton, yeoman, and sister of Henry Cowper of Thame (living in 1534). (1st wife.) = Peter Dormer of Lee Grange and Shipton Lee,[5] part of the lands of Thame Abbey. Had a long lease from the Abbot and Convent of Thame, 28 Sept. 1534, of lands and tenements there. Died 1 April 1555. Bur. at Newbottle, Co. Northants. = Anne, daughter of Richard Crispe of Cobcott,[6] near Thame aforesaid. She married 2ndly Ralph Palmer of Waddesdon, Co. Bucks; and 3rdly Francis Ingoldsby of Lenborough, Co. Bucks, who was buried at Buckingham 3 Nov. 1579. She died in 1582. (2nd wife.)
Other issue.
Margaret, daughter and sole heiress of Sir Thomas Neville, Knt., and widow of Sir Robert Southwell, Knt., Master of the Rolls. (1st wife.) = William Plumbe, son of John Plumbe of Eltham, Co. Kent. Died 9 Feb. 1593, aged 60. (2nd husband.) = Elizabeth Dormer, only daughter and heir. (2nd wife.) = John Gresham of Mayfield, Gent. (1st husband.)
Frances Plumbe.
Gabriel Dormer of Lee Grange aforesaid. (1st husband.) = Bridget, daughter of Thomas Lovett of Astwell, Co. Northampton.
Arms of Lovett.—Argent, three wolves passant in pale sable. = John Hawtrey of Chequers, Co. Bucks. (2nd husband.)
Arms of Hawtrey.—Argent, in bend, between two cotises, four lions passant sable, crowned or.
John Dormer of Olney, Co. Bucks, Gent. = Agnes [or Anne], daughter and heir of John Sutton of Boston, Co. Lincoln.
Edward Hawtrey of Chequers aforesaid, and son of Ralph Hawtrey by Winefreda his wife, daughter and heiress of William Wollaston of Ruislip, Co. Middlesex. = Elizabeth Dormer.
William Holt of Stoke Lyne,[7] son of Robert Holt and Elizabeth Lyne his wife. = Katherine Dormer, daughter and sole heiress.
Robert Palmer of Waddesdon aforesaid, Gent. = Anne Dormer.
John Meering of Meering, Co. Nottingham. = Jane Dormer.
Edward Osbaldeston of Chadlington, Co. Oxon. = Agnes Dormer.
Sir Stephen Crispe, son of Richard Crispe of Cobcott aforesaid.
Arms of Crispe.—Ermine, a fesse chequy argent and sable. = Ellen or Eleanor Dormer.
William Palmer of Waddesdon. = Joyce, daughter of Robert Pigott and Mary Yate his wife. Living 1598.
Peter Dormer. Succeeded his half-brother Gabriel at Lee Grange. Died in 1583. Buried at St. Mary-at-Hill, London. = Margaret, only daughter of Thomas Fleetwood of the Vache in Chalfont St. Giles's, Co. Bucks, by Barbara his 1st wife, daughter of Andrew Francis of the City of London.
Arms of Fleetwood.—Party per pale nebulé azure and or, six martlets, three and three, counterchanged.
William Lee, son of Roger Lee of Thame, by Eleanor his wife. A Captain of the Levies of the County. = Margaret Dormer.
Fleetwood Dormer of Lee Grange. Born circa 1570. Knighted. Died 1 Feb. 1638-9, aged 68. Buried at Quainton, Co. Bucks. M.I. remaining. = Mary. Baptized 24 May 1584. Third daughter of Sir Eusebius Isham of Isham and Pytchley, Co. Northampton, Knt., and widow of Edward Reed of Cottesbrook in the same County, Esq.
Arms of Isham.—Gules, three foils meeting in base or, over all a fesse of the last.
Peter Dormer. Baptized 7 May 1614. Of Magdalene Hall, Oxford. Graduated M.A. 1648. M.D. = Anne, eldest daughter and coheiress of Edward Shepherd of Great Rollright, Co. Oxon.
Eusebius Dormer.[8] Baptized 14 May 1618.
—
Gabriel Dormer. Baptized 30 March 1623.
Anne Dormer. Buried at Quainton 26 Jan. 1613.
—
Margaret Dormer. Buried at Quainton 5 March 1610.
William Shepherd of Great Rollright, Co. Oxon. = Mary Dormer. Baptized 13 Jan. 1610. Married 12 Dec. 1634.[9]
Francis Austrey. = Dorothy Dormer. Baptized 28 Mar. 1613. Married 28 Sept. 1637.
Margaret. Baptized 23 May 1617.
—
Elizabeth. Baptized 15 August 1619.
—
Joyce. Baptized 10 June, bur. 13 Oct. 1621.
—
Elizabeth. Baptized 9 May 1630.
—
Anne. Baptized 4 March 1631.
C D E

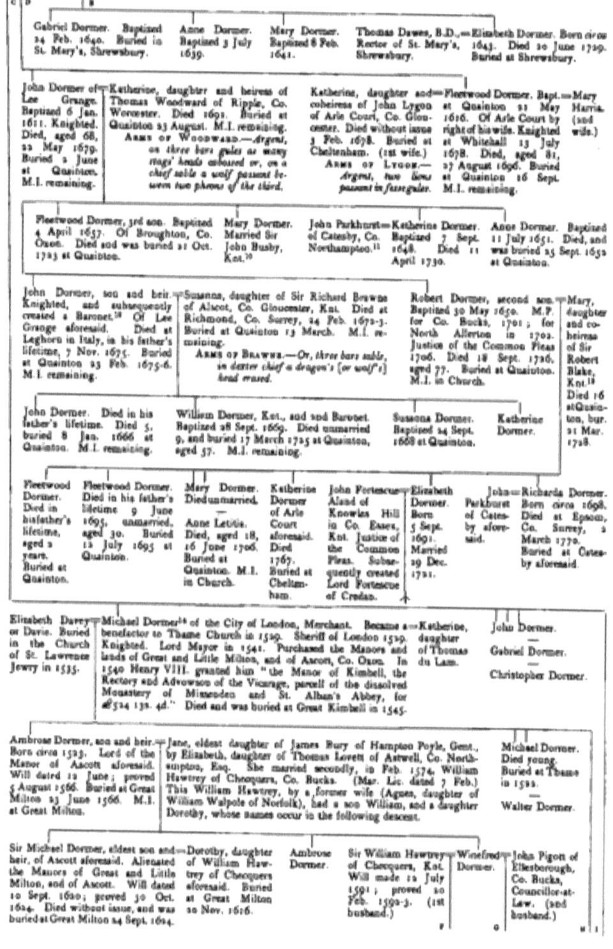

C | D | E

Gabriel Dormer. Baptized 24 Feb. 1640. Buried in St. Mary's, Shrewsbury.

Anne Dormer. Baptized 3 July 1639.

Mary Dormer. Baptized 8 Feb. 1641.

Thomas Dawes, B.D., Rector of St. Mary's, Shrewsbury. = Elizabeth Dormer. Born *circa* 1643. Died 20 June 1729. Buried at Shrewsbury.

John Dormer of Lee Grange. Baptized 6 Jan. 1611. Knighted. Died, aged 68, 22 May 1679. Buried 2 June at Quainton. M.I. remaining. = Katherine, daughter and heiress of Thomas Woodward of Ripple, Co. Worcester. Died 1691. Buried at Quainton 23 August. M.I. remaining.
Arms of Woodward.—*Argent, on three bars gules as many stags' heads cabossed or, on a chief sable a wolf passant between two pheons of the third.*

Katherine, daughter and coheiress of John Lygon of Arle Court, Co. Gloucester. Died without issue 3 Feb. 1678. Buried at Cheltenham. (1st wife.)
Arms of Lygon.—*Argent, two lions passant in fesse gules.* = Fleetwood Dormer. Bapt. at Quainton 21 May 1616. Of Arle Court by right of his wife. Knighted at Whitehall 13 July 1678. Died, aged 81, 27 August 1696. Buried at Quainton 16 Sept. M.I. remaining. = Mary Harris. (2nd wife.)

Fleetwood Dormer, 3rd son. Baptized 4 April 1657. Of Broughton, Co. Oxon. Died and was buried 21 Oct. 1723 at Quainton.

Mary Dormer. Married Sir John Busby, Knt.[10]

John Parkhurst of Catesby, Co. Northampton.[11] = Katherine Dormer. Baptized 7 Sept. 1648. Died 11 April 1730.

Anne Dormer. Baptized 11 July 1651. Died, and was buried 25 Sept. 1652 at Quainton.

John Dormer, son and heir. Knighted, and subsequently created a Baronet.[12] Of Lee Grange aforesaid. Died at Leghorn in Italy, in his father's lifetime, 7 Nov. 1675. Buried at Quainton 23 Feb. 1675-6. M.I. remaining. = Susanna, daughter of Sir Richard Browne of Alscot, Co. Gloucester, Knt. Died at Richmond, Co. Surrey, 24 Feb. 1672-3. Buried at Quainton 13 March. M.I. remaining.
Arms of Browne.—*Or, three bars sable, in dexter chief a dragon's [or wolf's] head erased.*

Robert Dormer, second son. Baptized 30 May 1650. M.P. for Co. Bucks, 1701; for North Allerton in 1702. Justice of the Common Pleas 1706. Died 18 Sept. 1726, aged 77. Buried at Quainton. M.I. in Church. = Mary, daughter and coheiress of Sir Robert Blake, Knt.[13] Died 16 at Quainton, bur. 21 Mar. 1728.

John Dormer. Died in his father's lifetime. Died 5, buried 8 Jan. 1666 at Quainton. M.I. remaining.

William Dormer, Knt., and 2nd Baronet. Baptized 28 Sept. 1669. Died unmarried 9, and buried 17 March 1725 at Quainton, aged 57. M.I. remaining.

Susanna Dormer. Baptized 24 Sept. 1668 at Quainton.

Katherine Dormer.

Fleetwood Dormer. Died in his father's lifetime, aged 2 years. Buried at Quainton.

Fleetwood Dormer. Died in his father's lifetime 9 June 1695, unmarried, aged 30. Buried 12 July 1695 at Quainton.

Mary Dormer. Died unmarried.
—
Anne Letitia. Died, aged 18, 16 June 1706. Buried at Quainton. M.I. in Church.

Katherine Dormer of Arle Court aforesaid. Died 1767. Buried at Cheltenham.

John Fortescue Aland of Knowles Hill in Co. Essex, Knt. Justice of the Common Pleas. Subsequently created Lord Fortescue of Credan. = Elizabeth Dormer. Born 5 Sept. 1691. Married 29 Dec. 1721.

John Parkhurst of Catesby aforesaid. = Richarda Dormer. Born *circa* 1698. Died at Epsom, Co. Surrey, 2 March 1770. Buried at Catesby aforesaid.

Elizabeth Davey or Davie. Buried in the Church of St. Lawrence Jewry in 1535. = Michael Dormer[14] of the City of London, Merchant. Became a benefactor to Thame Church in 1529. Sheriff of London 1529. Knighted. Lord Mayor in 1541. Purchased the Manors and lands of Great and Little Milton, and of Ascott, Co. Oxon. In 1540 Henry VIII. granted him "the Manor of Kimbell, the Rectory and Advowson of the Vicarage, parcell of the dissolved Monastery of Missenden and St. Alban's Abbey, for £524 13s. 4d." Died and was buried at Great Kimbell in 1545. = Katherine, daughter of Thomas du Lam.

John Dormer.
—
Gabriel Dormer.
—
Christopher Dormer.

Ambrose Dormer, son and heir. Born *circa* 1523. Lord of the Manor of Ascott aforesaid. Will dated 12 June; proved 5 August 1566. Buried at Great Milton 23 June 1566. M.I. at Great Milton. = Jane, eldest daughter of James Bury of Hampton Poyle, Gent., by Elizabeth, daughter of Thomas Lovett of Astwell, Co. Northampton, Esq. She married secondly, in Feb. 1574, William Hawtrey of Chequers, Co. Bucks. (Mar. Lic. dated 7 Feb.) This William Hawtrey, by a *former* wife (Agnes, daughter of William Walpole of Norfolk), had a son William, and a daughter Dorothy, whose names occur in the following descent.

Michael Dormer. Died young. Buried at Thame in 1522.
—
Walter Dormer.

Sir Michael Dormer, eldest son and heir, of Ascott aforesaid. Alienated the Manors of Great and Little Milton, and of Ascott. Will dated 10 Sept. 1620; proved 30 Oct. 1624. Died without issue, and was buried at Great Milton 24 Sept. 1624. = Dorothy, daughter of William Hawtrey of Chequers aforesaid. Buried at Great Milton 20 Nov. 1616.

Ambrose Dormer.

Sir William Hawtrey of Chequers, Knt. Will made 12 July 1591; proved 20 Feb. 1592-3. (1st husband.) = Winefred Dormer. = John Pigott of Ellesborough, Co. Bucks, Councillor-at-Law. (2nd husband.)

F | G | H | I

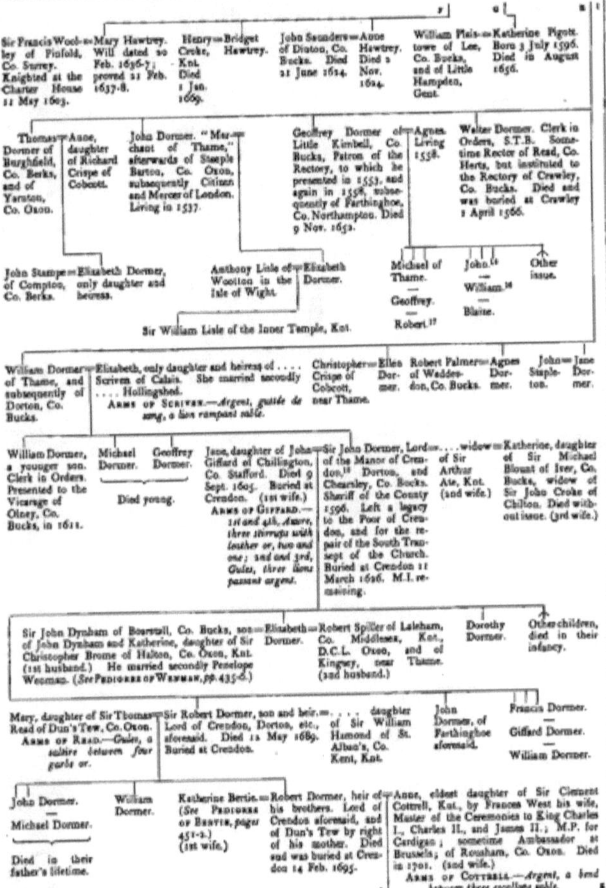

Sir Francis Woolley of Pinfold, Co. Surrey. Knighted at the Charter House 11 May 1603. = Mary Hawtrey. Will dated 20 Feb. 1636-7; proved 21 Feb. 1637-8.

Henry Croke, Knt. Died 1 Jan. 1669. = Bridget Hawtrey.

John Saunders of Dinton, Co. Bucks. Died 21 June 1624. = Anne Hawtrey. Died 2 Nov. 1624.

William Plaistowe of Lee, Co. Bucks, and of Little Hampden, Gent. = Katherine Pigott. Born 3 July 1596. Died in August 1656.

Thomas Dormer of Burghfield, Co. Berks, and of Yarnton, Co. Oxon. = Anne, daughter of Richard Crispe of Cobcott.

John Dormer. "Merchant of Thame," afterwards of Steeple Barton, Co. Oxon, subsequently Citizen and Mercer of London. Living in 1537.

Geoffrey Dormer of Little Kimbell, Co. Bucks, Patron of the Rectory, to which he presented in 1553, and again in 1558, subsequently of Farthinghoe, Co. Northampton. Died 9 Nov. 1652. = Agnes. Living 1558.

Walter Dormer. Clerk in Orders, S.T.B. Sometime Rector of Read, Co. Herts, but instituted to the Rectory of Crawley, Co. Bucks. Died and was buried at Crawley 1 April 1566.

John Stampe of Compton, Co. Berks. = Elizabeth Dormer, only daughter and heiress.

Anthony Lisle of Wootton in the Isle of Wight. = Elizabeth Dormer.

Sir William Lisle of the Inner Temple, Knt.

Michael of Thame. — Geoffrey. — Robert.[17]

John.[15] — William.[16] — Blaise.

Other issue.

William Dormer of Thame, and subsequently of Dorton, Co. Bucks. = Elizabeth, only daughter and heiress of .... Scriven of Calais. She married secondly .... Hollingshed.
Arms of Scriven.—*Argent, guttée de sang, a lion rampant sable.*

Christopher Crispe of Cobcott, near Thame. = Ellen Dormer.

Robert Palmer of Waddesdon, Co. Bucks. = Agnes Dormer.

John Stapleton. = Jane Dormer.

William Dormer, a younger son. Clerk in Orders. Presented to the Vicarage of Olney, Co. Bucks, in 1611.

Michael Dormer. Geoffrey Dormer. Died young.

Jane, daughter of John Giffard of Chillington, Co. Stafford. Died 9 Sept. 1605. Buried at Crendon. (1st wife.)
Arms of Giffard.—*1st and 4th, Azure, three stirrups with leather or, two and one; 2nd and 3rd, Gules, three lions passant argent.*

= Sir John Dormer, Lord of the Manor of Crendon,[18] Dorton, and Chearsley, Co. Bucks. Sheriff of the County 1596. Left a legacy to the Poor of Crendon, and for the repair of the South Transept of the Church. Buried at Crendon 11 March 1626. M.I. remaining.

= .... widow of Sir Arthur Ate, Knt. (2nd wife.)

= Katherine, daughter of Sir Michael Blount of Iver, Co. Bucks, widow of Sir John Croke of Chilton. Died without issue. (3rd wife.)

Sir John Dynham of Boarstall, Co. Bucks, son of John Dynham and Katherine, daughter of Sir Christopher Brome of Halton, Co. Oxon, Knt. (1st husband.) He married secondly Penelope Wenman. (See Pedigree of Wenman, pp. 435-6.) = Elizabeth Dormer. = Robert Spiller of Laleham, Co. Middlesex, Knt., D.C.L. Oxon, and of Kingsey, near Thame. (2nd husband.)

Dorothy Dormer.

Other children, died in their infancy.

Mary, daughter of Sir Thomas Read of Dun's Tew, Co. Oxon.
Arms of Read.—*Gules, a saltire between four garbs or.*

= Sir Robert Dormer, son and heir. Lord of Crendon, Dorton, etc., aforesaid. Died 12 May 1689. Buried at Crendon.

= .... daughter of Sir William Hamond of St. Alban's, Co. Kent, Knt.

John Dormer, of Farthinghoe aforesaid.

Francis Dormer. — Giffard Dormer. — William Dormer.

John Dormer. — Michael Dormer. Died in their father's lifetime.

William Dormer.

Katherine Bertie. (See Pedigree of Bertie, pages 451-2.) (1st wife.) = Robert Dormer, heir of his brothers. Lord of Crendon aforesaid, and of Dun's Tew by right of his mother. Died and was buried at Crendon 14 Feb. 1695. = Anne, eldest daughter of Sir Clement Cottrell, Knt., by Frances West his wife, Master of the Ceremonies to King Charles I., Charles II., and James II.; M.P. for Cardigan; sometime Ambassador at Brussels; of Rousham, Co. Oxon. Died in 1701. (2nd wife.)
Arms of Cottrell.—*Argent, a bend between three escallops sable.*

1 2

John Dormer of Rousham, Co. Oxon. Born 16 Jan. 1669. Buried at Crendon 7 April 1719. His daughter Diana[19] married General Piercy Kirke.

Charles Dormer. Born 15 Feb. 1670.

William Dormer. Born 13 Feb. 1671.

Robert Dormer. Born 16 Oct. 1676. Died, and bur. 29 Dec. 1736.

Philip Dormer. Born 25 Nov. 1677. Died without issue.

James Dormer. Born 16 March 1679. Lord of the Manor of Crendon, Captain and Colonel of the 1st Horse Grenadier Guards, subsequently a General. Died 24 Dec. 1741. Buried at Crendon 2 Jan. 1741-2. Devised his estates at Chearsley to his cousin Cotrell.

Clement Dormer. Born 14 Feb. 1684. Died, and was buried at Crendon 22 June 1697.

Sir Samuel Daniel, Knt.[20] = Frances Dormer. Born 9 March 1681. Married 12 April 1709.

Anne Dormer.

Catherine Dormer. Died young.

Geoffrey Dormer, son and heir. Inherited Baldington's Manor. Had a grant of Arms from Thomas Wriothesley, Garter, in 1523. Made his Will in 1526. Died without issue, and was buried at Thame. = Elizabeth Jordan of Thame. Buried at Thame.

William Dormer of West Wycombe, heir of his brother Geoffrey. Will made 12 Sept. 1506; proved 7 Oct. 1506. = Jane, daughter of Sir John Launcelyn[21] of Launcelynsbury.

Arms of Launcelyn.—*Argent, on a fesse sable three mullets of the field.*

John Godwin of Wooburn Deincourt, Co. Bucks. Gave "a payre of vestments of grene sattyne" to Thame Church in 1544. = Elizabeth Dormer. Died before 1547.

Arms of Godwin.—*Per pale or and gules, a lion rampant between three fleurs-de-lys counterchanged.*

Judith Dormer.

Mary Dormer.

Richard Cowley of Thame, yeoman. = Margaret Dormer.

Other issue.

. . . . Aldborough of Bromwell. = Joane Dormer.

William Baldwin of Aylesbury. Father of Sir John Baldwin. = Agnes Dormer.

Bridget Dormer. Married 1st to . . . . Brittayne of London, and 2ndly to . . . . Collingbourne.

Robert Dormer, only son and heir. Sheriff of Bucks and Beds. Knighted 18 Oct. 1537. Secured the Manor of Winge, Co. Bucks, part of the possessions of the Abbey of St. Albans. Will dated 20 June 1552; proved 20 Oct. 1552. = Jane, daughter of John Newdigate of Hatfield, Serjeant-at-Law, and of Amphelicia his wife, sole daughter and heiress of John Nevill, brother to William Nevill of Holt, Co. Leicester, Esq.

Arms of Newdigate.—*Gules, three lions' gambs erased argent.*

Thomas Deane of Wargrave, Co. Bucks. = Margaret Dormer.

Mary, daughter of Sir William Sidney, Knt., by Anne, daughter of Hugh Pagenham (ancestor to the late Earls of Leicester). (1st wife.)

Arms of Sidney.—*Or, a pheon azure.*

= William Dormer of Ascot, Co. Oxon, and of Eythorpe, Co. Bucks. K.B. Knight of the Shire for Bucks 6 Edw. VI., and 4 and 5 Philip and Mary, and 13 of Elizabeth. Died 17 May 1575. = Dorothy, daughter of Anthony Catesby of Whiston, Co. Northants, Esq. (2nd wife.) Remarried to Sir William Pelham, Knt., Master of the Ordnance, and Lord Deputy of Ireland.

Arms of Catesby.—*Argent, two lions passant sable, crowned or.*

Thomas Dormer and Roger Dormer, both died young.

Anne Dormer. = Sir William Hungerford, Knt., of Farley Castle, son and heir to Walter, Baron Hungerford.

Jane Dormer. Maid of Honour to Queen Mary Tudor. = Don Gomez Suarez de Figueroa y Cordova, Duke of Feria.

Edward Hungerford. Ob. s.p.

Susan Hungerford. = Michael Earnley of Cannings, Co. Wilts, Gent.

Lucy Hungerford. = Sir John St. John of Lydyard Tregooze.

Jane Hungerford. = Sir John Kerne of Wenny, Co. Glamorgan, Knt.

---

1. Katherine Dormer.[22] Died 23 March 1614. Buried in St. Michael's Chapel, Westminster Abbey. = John, Lord St. John of Bletsoe.

Arms of St. John.—*Argent, on a chief gules two mullets or.*

Anthony, eldest son of Anthony Browne, 1st Viscount Montagu. Died 29 June 1592. = 2. Mary Dormer. = Sir Edward Uvedale, Knt., 2nd son of Francis Uvedale of Horton, Co. Dorset. Sir Edward died 6 April 1606. Buried in Wimborne Minster; after which his widow married Sir Thomas Gerard of Bryn, Knt.

3. Margaret Dormer. = Sir Henry Constable of Burton Constable, Co. York, Knt.

Elizabeth Browne, daughter of Anthony, 1st Viscount Montagu, K.G., by Magdalene, his 2nd wife, daughter of William, Lord Dacres of Gillesland.

Arms of Browne.—*Sable, three lions passant in bend between two double cotises argent.*

2

= Robert Dormer, son and heir. Knighted 1591. Created a Baronet 10 June 1615, and a Peer of England 30 June 1615, by the title of Baron Dormer of Winge, Co. Bucks. Master of the King's Falcons. Died 8 Nov. 1616. Inq. post mortem taken at Aylesbury 19 Jan. 1616-7.

Richard Dormer, 2nd son.

Francis Dormer, 3rd son.

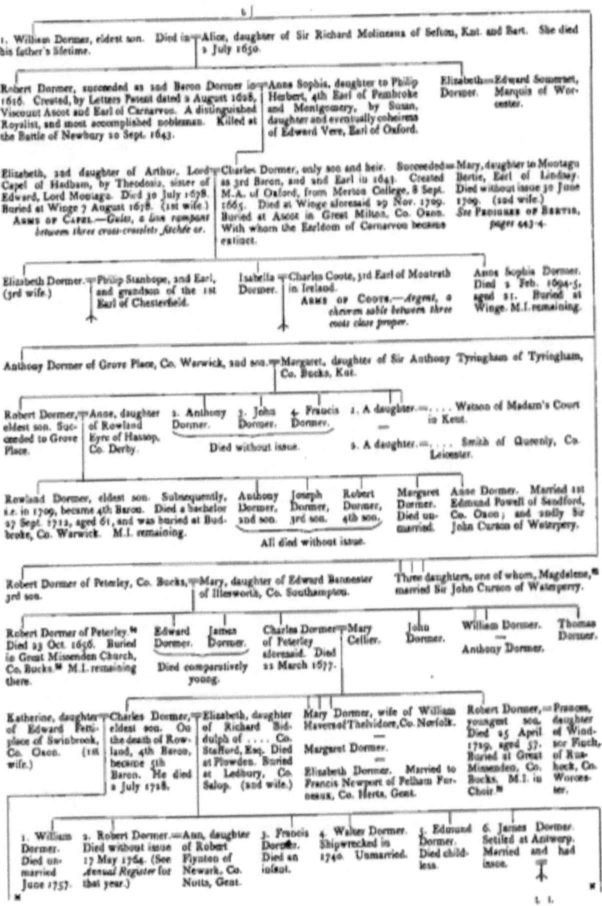

b

1. William Dormer, eldest son. Died in his father's lifetime. = Alice, daughter of Sir Richard Molineaux of Sefton, Knt. and Bart. She died 2 July 1650.

Robert Dormer, succeeded as 2nd Baron Dormer in 1616. Created, by Letters Patent dated 2 August 1628, Viscount Ascot and Earl of Carnarvon. A distinguished Royalist, and most accomplished nobleman. Killed at the Battle of Newbury 20 Sept. 1643. = Anna Sophia, daughter to Philip Herbert, 4th Earl of Pembroke and Montgomery, by Susan, daughter and eventually coheiress of Edward Vere, Earl of Oxford.

Elizabeth Dormer. = Edward Somerset, Marquis of Worcester.

Elizabeth, 2nd daughter of Arthur, Lord Capel of Hadham, by Theodosia, sister of Edward, Lord Montagu. Died 30 July 1678. Buried at Winge 7 August 1678. (1st wife.)
Arms of Capel.—*Gules, a lion rampant between three cross-crosslets fitchée or.*
= Charles Dormer, only son and heir. Succeeded as 3rd Baron, and 2nd Earl in 1643. Created M.A. of Oxford, from Merton College, 8 Sept. 1665. Died at Winge aforesaid 29 Nov. 1709. Buried at Ascot in Great Milton, Co. Oxon. With whom the Earldom of Carnarvon became extinct.
= Mary, daughter to Montagu Bertie, Earl of Lindsey. Died without issue 30 June 1709. (2nd wife.) *See* Pedigree of Bertie, *pages* 643-4.

Elizabeth Dormer. (3rd wife.) = Philip Stanhope, 2nd Earl, and grandson of the 1st Earl of Chesterfield.

Isabella Dormer. = Charles Coote, 3rd Earl of Montrath in Ireland.
Arms of Coote.—*Argent, a chevron sable between three coots close proper.*

Anna Sophia Dormer. Died 2 Feb. 1694-5, aged 21. Buried at Winge. M.I. remaining.

Anthony Dormer of Grove Place, Co. Warwick, 2nd son. = Margaret, daughter of Sir Anthony Tyringham of Tyringham, Co. Bucks, Knt.

Robert Dormer, eldest son. Succeeded to Grove Place. = Anne, daughter of Rowland Eyre of Hassop, Co. Derby.

2. Anthony Dormer. 3. John Dormer. 4. Francis Dormer. Died without issue.

1. A daughter. = ... Watson of Madam's Court in Kent.
—
2. A daughter. = ... Smith of Queenly, Co. Leicester.

Rowland Dormer, eldest son. Subsequently, *i.e.* in 1709, became 4th Baron. Died a bachelor 27 Sept. 1712, aged 61, and was buried at Budbroke, Co. Warwick. M.I. remaining.

Anthony Dormer, 2nd son. Joseph Dormer, 3rd son. Robert Dormer, 4th son. All died without issue.

Margaret Dormer. Died unmarried.

Anne Dormer. Married 1st Edmund Powell of Sandford, Co. Oxon; and 2ndly Sir John Curson of Waterpery.

Robert Dormer of Peterley, Co. Bucks, 3rd son. = Mary, daughter of Edward Bannester of Illesworth, Co. Southampton.

Three daughters, one of whom, Magdalene,* married Sir John Curson of Waterperry.

Robert Dormer of Peterley.* Died 23 Oct. 1656. Buried in Great Missenden Church, Co. Bucks.* M.I. remaining there.

Edward Dormer. James Dormer. Died comparatively young.

Charles Dormer of Peterley aforesaid. Died 22 March 1677. = Mary Cellier.

John Dormer.

William Dormer.
—
Anthony Dormer.

Thomas Dormer.

Katherine, daughter of Edward Fettiplace of Swinbrook, Co. Oxon. (1st wife.) = Charles Dormer, eldest son. On the death of Rowland, 4th Baron, became 5th Baron. He died 2 July 1728. = Elizabeth, daughter of Richard Biddulph of .... Co. Stafford, Esq. Died at Plowden. Buried at Ledbury, Co. Salop. (2nd wife.)

Mary Dormer, wife of William Haverse of Thelvidore, Co. Norfolk.
—
Margaret Dormer.
—
Elizabeth Dormer. Married to Francis Newport of Pelham Furneaux, Co. Herts, Gent.

Robert Dormer, youngest son. Died 25 April 1719, aged 57. Buried at Great Missenden, Co. Bucks. M.I. in Choir.* = Frances, daughter of Windsor Finch, of Rushock, Co. Worcester.

1. William Dormer. Died unmarried June 1757.

2. Robert Dormer. Died without issue 17 May 1764. (See *Annual Register* for that year.) = Ann, daughter of Robert Flynton of Newark, Co. Notts, Gent.

3. Francis Dormer. Died an infant.

4. Walter Dormer. Shipwrecked in 1740. Unmarried.

5. Edmund Dormer. Died childless.

6. James Dormer. Settled at Antwerp. Married and had issue.

* *

L L

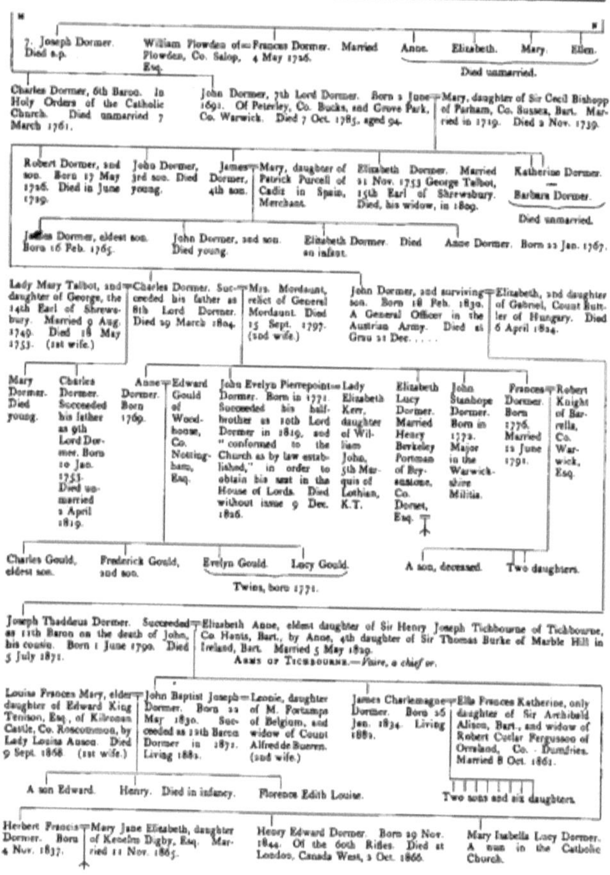
7. Joseph Dormer. Died s.p.
William Plowden of Plowden, Co. Salop, Esq.
Frances Dormer. Married 4 May 1726.
Anne. Elizabeth. Mary. Ellen.
Died unmarried.
Charles Dormer, 6th Baron. In Holy Orders of the Catholic Church. Died unmarried 7 March 1761.
John Dormer, 7th Lord Dormer. Born 2 June 1691. Of Peterley, Co. Bucks, and Grove Park, Co. Warwick. Died 7 Oct. 1785, aged 94.
Mary, daughter of Sir Cecil Bishopp of Parham, Co. Sussex, Bart. Married in 1719. Died 2 Nov. 1739.
Robert Dormer, 2nd son. Born 17 May 1726. Died in June 1729.
John Dormer, 3rd son. Died young.
James Dormer, 4th son.
Mary, daughter of Patrick Purcell of Cadiz in Spain, Merchant.
Elizabeth Dormer. Married 21 Nov. 1753 George Talbot, 15th Earl of Shrewsbury. Died, his widow, in 1809.
Katherine Dormer.
Barbara Dormer.
Died unmarried.
James Dormer, eldest son. Born 16 Feb. 1765.
John Dormer, 2nd son. Died young.
Elizabeth Dormer. Died an infant.
Anne Dormer. Born 22 Jan. 1767.
Lady Mary Talbot, 2nd daughter of George, the 14th Earl of Shrewsbury. Married 9 Aug. 1749. Died 18 May 1753. (1st wife.)
Charles Dormer. Succeeded his father as 8th Lord Dormer. Died 29 March 1804.
Mrs. Mordaunt, relict of General Mordaunt. Died 15 Sept. 1797. (2nd wife.)
John Dormer, 2nd surviving son. Born 18 Feb. 1830. A General Officer in the Austrian Army. Died at Grau 21 Dec. . . . .
Elizabeth, 2nd daughter of Gabriel, Count Butler of Hungary. Died 6 April 1824.
Mary Dormer. Died young.
Charles Dormer. Succeeded his father as 9th Lord Dormer. Born 10 Jan. 1753. Died unmarried 2 April 1819.
Anne Dormer. Born 1769.
Edward Gould of Woodhouse, Co. Nottingham, Esq.
John Evelyn Pierrepoint Dormer. Born in 1771. Succeeded his half-brother as 10th Lord Dormer in 1819, and "conformed to the Church as by law established," in order to obtain his seat in the House of Lords. Died without issue 9 Dec. 1826.
Lady Elizabeth Kerr, daughter of William John, 5th Marquis of Lothian, K.T.
Elizabeth Lucy Dormer. Married Henry Berkeley Portman of Bryanstone, Co. Dorset, Esq.
John Stanhope Dormer. Born in 1772. Major in the Warwickshire Militia.
Frances Dormer. Born 1776. Married 22 June 1791.
Robert Knight of Barrella, Co. Warwick, Esq.
Charles Gould, eldest son.
Frederick Gould, 2nd son.
Evelyn Gould. Lucy Gould.
Twins, born 1771.
A son, deceased.
Two daughters.
Joseph Thaddeus Dormer. Succeeded as 11th Baron on the death of John, his cousin. Born 1 June 1790. Died 5 July 1871.
Elizabeth Anne, eldest daughter of Sir Henry Joseph Tichbourne of Tichbourne, Co. Hants, Bart., by Anne, 4th daughter of Sir Thomas Burke of Marble Hill in Ireland, Bart. Married 5 May 1829.
Arms of Tichbourne.—Vaire, a chief or.
Louisa Frances Mary, elder daughter of Edward King Tenison, Esq., of Kilronan Castle, Co. Roscommon, by Lady Louisa Anson. Died 9 Sept. 1868. (1st wife.)
John Baptist Joseph Dormer. Born 22 May 1830. Succeeded as 12th Baron Dormer in 1871. Living 1882.
Leonie, daughter of M. Fortamps of Belgium, and widow of Count Alfred de Buerren. (2nd wife.)
James Charlemagne Dormer. Born 25 Jan. 1834. Living 1882.
Ella Frances Katherine, only daughter of Sir Archibald Alison, Bart., and widow of Robert Cutlar Fergusson of Orroland, Co. Dumfries. Married 8 Oct. 1862.
A son Edward.
Henry. Died in infancy.
Florence Edith Louise.
Two sons and six daughters.
Herbert Francis Dormer. Born 4 Nov. 1837.
Mary Jane Elizabeth, daughter of Kenelm Digby, Esq. Married 11 Nov. 1865.
Henry Edward Dormer. Born 29 Nov. 1844. Of the 60th Rifles. Died at London, Canada West, 2 Oct. 1866.
Mary Isabella Lucy Dormer. A nun in the Catholic Church.

♣♣♣♣♣♣♣♣♣♣♣

Pedigree of Cottrell-Dormer of Rousham, Co. Oxon.

(Setting forth the alliance of Anne Cottrell with Robert Dormer, great-grandson of William Dormer of Thame.)

ARMS OF COTTRELL.—*Argent, a bend between three escallops sable.*

Thomas Cottrell. Living at South Repps, Co. Norfolk, in Queen Elizabeth's reign. = Mary, daughter of Mr. Iuglos of South Repps aforesaid.

Issue:

- Clement Cottrell. Born at Wilsford, Co. Lincoln, in 1585. Was Groom Porter to King James I. Knighted in 1607. Died in 1631. = Anne, daughter of Henry Alleyne of Wilsford, Co. Lincoln.
- Nicholas Cottrell.
- Francis Cottrell.
- Margaret Cottrell.
- Other issue.

Issue of Clement Cottrell and Anne Alleyne:

- Charles Cottrell. Born *circa* 1618. Educated at Cambridge. A noted Royalist. Hon. D.C.L. of Oxford 20 Dec. 1670. Succeeded Sir John Finet, Knt., as Master of the Ceremonies. M.P. for Cardigan. Ambassador to the Court of Brussels. Knighted at Oxford after the Battle of Edge Hill. Master of Requests to Charles II., and an Author of repute. Died in 1701. = Frances, daughter of Edmund West of West Place in Marsworth, Co. Bucks, Esq.
  ARMS OF WEST.—*Argent, on a fesse indented sable three tigers' faces jessant fleur-de-lys or.*
- Sir Thomas Clayton. Warden of Merton College, Oxon, Knt. Died in 1693. = Bridget Cottrell.
  - Issue: James Clayton of Chalfont St. Giles, Co. Bucks. Died without issue 28 Nov. 1714, aged 64. Buried at Chalfont. = Mary, daughter of Sir Joseph Alston, Bart. (2nd wife.)
- Sir Richard Higham of Stratford-le-Bow, Co. Middlesex, Knt. = Anne Cottrell. Died without issue.

Issue of Charles Cottrell and Frances West:

- Robert, 3rd son and eventually heir of Sir Robert Dormer of Crendon, Knt., and great-grandson of William Dormer of Thame. = Anne Cottrell, eldest daughter.
  Issue, seven sons and three daughters. The sixth son, General James Dormer, who was sometime British Minister to the Court of John V. of Portugal, and had served under the Duke of Marlborough, dying in 1741, bequeathed his lands at Chearsley and Rousham to his cousin Clement Cottrell.*
- Frances Cottrell, 2nd daughter. Died in infancy.
- Clement Cottrell, eldest son and heir. Born 1650. A Midshipman under the Earl of Sandwich. Killed by an explosion in the vessel 'Royal James' off the coast of Sussex. Buried in Westminster Abbey.
- Elizabeth Burwell, daughter and co-heiress of James Burwell of Rougham, Co. Suffolk, Esq., and brother of Sir Geoffrey Burwell, Knt. (1st wife.) = Charles Lodowick Cottrell. Born at The Hague. God-son of the Queen of Bohemia. Gentleman Commoner of Merton College, Oxon. In 1686 appointed Master of the Ceremonies in succession to his father, and Knighted 18 Feb. of that year. Died in 1711. = Elizabeth, daughter of Chaloner Chute of The Vine, Co. Hants, Esq., son of Chaloner Chute, Speaker of the House of Commons, and Dorothy, his wife, daughter of Lord North.
  ARMS OF BURWELL.—*Or, a chevron ermine between three oak-leaves vert.*
  Issue (by second wife), the Cottrells of Hadley and Barnet, Co. Middlesex.
- William Trumbell. Born *circa* 1641. Son of William Trumbell of Easthampstead, Co. Berks. Knighted at Whitehall 21 Nov. 1684. Doctor of Laws. One of the Secretaries of State. The friend and patron of Alexander Pope the Poet. = Elizabeth Cottrell. God-daughter to the Queen of Bohemia. Died without issue in 1704. (1st wife.)

Issue of Charles Lodowick Cottrell and Elizabeth Burwell:

- Charles Cottrell, Esq., eldest son. Born *circa* 1683. Died unmarried in 1707.
- Henry Cottrell, 2nd son. Assistant to his father. Died unmarried.
- Bridget, daughter of Davenant Shirbourne of the Strand in the City of Westminster, and grand-daughter of William Shirbourne, D.D., Oxon, Rector of Pembridge, and Chancellor of Llandaff (by Alice, sister of Sir William Davenant, Knt.). = Clement Cottrell, 3rd son, but subsequently heir to his father, and to his uncle Clement. Knighted at Kensington Palace by Queen Anne 24 July 1710. Made Master of the Ceremonies to King George II. 6 Sept. 1727. Vice-President of the Society of Antiquaries. Assumed the name of Dormer by Royal Licence on inheriting his cousin's properties. Died 13 Oct. 1758 at Rousham, Co. Oxon. = Elizabeth Allen. Died 12 May 1731.
- Other issue. Died young.

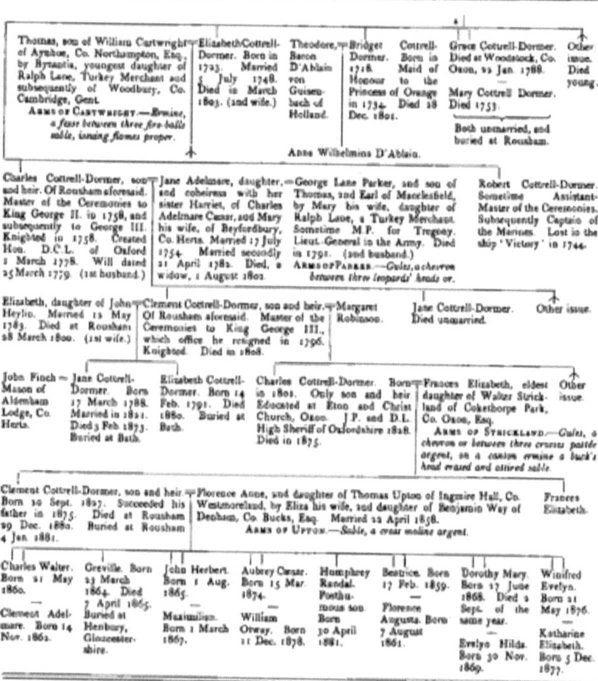

Thomas, son of William Cartwright of Aynhoe, Co. Northampton, Esq., by Byzantia, youngest daughter of Ralph Lane, Turkey Merchant and subsequently of Woodbury, Co. Cambridge, Gent. Arms of Cartwright.—*Ermine, a fesse between three fire-balls sable, issuing flames proper.* = Elizabeth Cottrell-Dormer. Born in 1723. Married 5 July 1748. Died in March 1803. (2nd wife.)

Theodore, Baron D'Ablain von Guisenbach of Holland. = Bridget Cottrell-Dormer. Born in 1718. Maid of Honour to the Princess of Orange in 1734. Died 28 Dec. 1801.

Anna Wilhelmina D'Ablain.

Grace Cottrell-Dormer. Died at Woodstock, Co. Oxon, 22 Jan. 1788.

Mary Cottrell Dormer. Died 1753.

Both unmarried, and buried at Rousham.

Other issue. Died young.

Charles Cottrell-Dormer, son and heir. Of Rousham aforesaid. Master of the Ceremonies to King George II. in 1758, and subsequently to George III. Knighted in 1758. Created Hon. D.C.L. of Oxford 1 March 1778. Will dated 25 March 1779. (1st husband.) = Jane Adelmare, daughter, and coheiress with her sister Harriet, of Charles Adelmare Cæsar, and Mary his wife, of Beyfordbury, Co. Herts. Married 17 July 1754. Married secondly 21 April 1782. Died, a widow, 1 August 1802. = George Lane Parker, 2nd son of Thomas, 2nd Earl of Macclesfield, by Mary his wife, daughter of Ralph Lane, a Turkey Merchant. Sometime M.P. for Tregony. Lieut.-General in the Army. Died in 1791. (2nd husband.) Arms of Parker.—*Gules, a chevron between three leopards' heads or.*

Robert Cottrell-Dormer. Sometime Assistant-Master of the Ceremonies. Subsequently Captain of the Marines. Lost in the ship 'Victory' in 1744.

Elizabeth, daughter of John Heylin. Married 12 May 1783. Died at Rousham 28 March 1800. (1st wife.) = Clement Cottrell-Dormer, son and heir. Of Rousham aforesaid. Master of the Ceremonies to King George III., which office he resigned in 1796. Knighted. Died in 1808. = Margaret Robinson.

Jane Cottrell-Dormer. Died unmarried.

Other issue.

John Finch Mason of Aldenham Lodge, Co. Herts. = Jane Cottrell-Dormer. Born 17 March 1788. Married in 1821. Died 3 Feb. 1873. Buried at Bath.

Elizabeth Cottrell-Dormer. Born 14 Feb. 1791. Died 1880. Buried at Bath.

Charles Cottrell-Dormer. Born in 1801. Only son and heir. Educated at Eton and Christ Church, Oxon. J.P. and D.L. High Sheriff of Oxfordshire 1828. Died in 1875. = Frances Elizabeth, eldest daughter of Walter Strickland of Cokethorpe Park, Co. Oxon, Esq. Arms of Strickland.—*Gules, a chevron or between three crosses pattée argent, on a canton ermine a buck's head erased and attired sable.*

Other issue.

Clement Cottrell-Dormer, son and heir. Born 30 Sept. 1827. Succeeded his father in 1875. Died at Rousham 29 Dec. 1880. Buried at Rousham 4 Jan. 1881. = Florence Anne, 2nd daughter of Thomas Upton of Ingmire Hall, Co. Westmoreland, by Eliza his wife, 2nd daughter of Benjamin Way of Denham, Co. Bucks, Esq. Married 22 April 1858. Arms of Upton.—*Sable, a cross moline argent.*

Frances Elizabeth.

Charles Walter. Born 21 May 1860.

Clement Adelmare. Born 14 Nov. 1862.

Greville. Born 23 March 1864. Died 7 April 1865. Buried at Henbury, Gloucestershire.

John Herbert. Born 1 Aug. 1865.

Maximilian. Born 1 March 1867.

Aubrey Cæsar. Born 15 Mar. 1874.

William Otway. Born 11 Dec. 1878.

Humphrey Randal. Posthumous son. Born 30 April 1881.

Beatrice. Born 17 Feb. 1859.

Florence Augusta. Born 7 August 1861.

Dorothy Mary. Born 17 June 1868. Died 2 Sept. of the same year.

Evelyn Hilda. Born 30 Nov. 1869.

Winifred Evelyn. Born 21 May 1876.

Katharine Elizabeth. Born 5 Dec. 1877.

SOME EXPLANATORY NOTES OF THE FOREGOING PEDIGREES.

Miscellaneous Notes Relating to the Family of Dormer and their Alliances.

[1] Arms of Dormer.

The arms of Dormer occur in the *Visitation of Bucks*, A.D. 1634, by John Withy, MS. Philpot, 49, folio 58, in the College of Arms. The crest in this is a fox sable between two wings, and it is said to belong to Geoffrey Dormer of Thame, in Com. Oxon, Esq. A similar crest is given in Vincent's *Visitation of Bucks*, in the same office, No. 138, folio 28. On folio 77[d] of 1st C. 26, *Visitation of Bucks*, by Richard St. George, occurs an interesting variation of the Dormer crest, viz., An Arctic fox argent, differenced by a mullet. The entry is attested by "Fletewood Dormer."

There is also the record of a grant by Segar to Dummer—apparently made up by a combination from the old arms of Baldington and Dormer: Azure, three fleurs-de-lys or, on a chief of the second a demi-lion of the first.—*From information given me by C. A. Buckler, Esq., Surrey Herald.*

In Harl. MS., No. 1139, folio 101, the arms and crest of Dormer are represented. The shield is of four quarters—1 and 4, Dormer; 2, Chobbe; 3, Baldington. The animal, whatever it be, of the crest, probably a fox, is winged. The Author possesses a coloured representation of the arms on paper, painted in the sixteenth century.

[2] 1411–1474. William Baldington was Lord of Albury, Aldeburgh, or Oldbury, Co. Oxon, in 1411 and in 1431.

The following sets forth a descent:—

Thomas Baldington. (A.D. 1437, 15 Henry VI.) = Agnes, daughter of Sir John Danvers.

Geoffrey Yate, living 1474 (2nd husband.) = Agnes Baldington, heiress of her father. = William Brome. (1st husband.)

Geoffrey Dormer, of Thame and West Wycombe, married Judith,

daughter of Thomas Baldingdon, or Baldington, of Baldington's Court, in Thame.

16 and 17 Rich. II., Inquisit. post mortem Aliciæ quæ fuit uxor Johannis Baldyngton.

4 and 5 of Henry V. William Baldington, Escheator of the King.

14 and 15 Henry VI., Inquisit. post mortem Thomæ Baldyngdon.

Rectors and Patrons of Albury, Co. Oxon.

Rectores de Albery:—John Anneys [?] pres. by Thomas Baldyngton, Lord of Albury.

John Kendall pres. by Will. Brome 17 Jan. 1459.

John Bowes pres. by Sir Geoffrey Yate and Agnes his wife 6 July 1474.

Inquisitions set forth that Sir Geoffrey Yate married Agnes, widow of William Brome, gent., deceased, and daughter and heiress of Thomas Baldyngton, Esq., former Patron.

Extracts from the Church Books of Thame.

1446. It' rec. of Geffrey Dorm' for settyng of ij setes in the Try'te lle und'nete the organ loft, iiij[d].

Amongst the Accounts for 1454, when William Yong and Thomas Tabarde were Churchwardens, the following occur:—

1454. It' re' of M[r] Dormer for hys wyvys sepultre, vj[s] viij[d].

1503. It' rea' of Alen Dormer for the beryng of her husband, vj[s] viij[d].

1505. It' re' of M[r] Dorm' for hys wyvys sepultur, vj[s] viij[d].

1512. It'm for beriing of Mast'r Dormer in the chourche, vj[s] viij[d].

1537. It'm Rec'd of Maystress Dormer for the sepultur of Maister Dormer her late husband, vj[s] viij[d].

It'm Receued of the same Maistress Dormer for the waste of wax, 2[d].

1542. William Dormer represented Chipping Wycombe in Parliament in the 33rd year of Henry VIII. [*i.e.* in 1542].

Monument to Peter Dormer.

On the north side of Newbottle Church, Co. Northants, within the sanctuary, over an altar-tomb of Purbeck marble, in the renaissance style, is an arch surmounted by an entablature of freestone. Within this arch, upon an incised brass, are the representations of a man between his two wives—behind one of whom are nineteen children. On the front of the altar-tomb stand three black shields, and over the figures three brass shields—1. Arms of Dormer of Thame; 2, Arms of the Staple of Calais (see pp. 503, 504); and, 3, Dormer impaling Baldington of Thame. The inscription stands thus:—

Hic jacet
Petrus Dormer de Lee Grange in comitatu
Buckinghamiensi, filius Galfridi
Dormer de West Wiccombe, in eodem
Comitatu, armigeri, Dominus hujus
Manerii: conjuges duxit duas ex
quibus filiorum filiarumque vicenario
numero pater factus: fatis concessit
primo die Aprilis anno domini 1555.

Crispe and Dormer.

Sir Stephen Crispe, son of Richard = Elianor, daughter of Peter Crispe, of Cobcott, near Thame. | Dormer, of Thame, and of Lee, Co. Bucks.

Peter Dormer, of Newbottle, = Anne Crispe, daughter of . . . . Co. Northampton. | Crispe, of Cobcott, near Thame.

"It is clear that Kingsey, Towersey, and Tythorpe descended from Peter Dormer of Thame to his sons and grandsons."—*Note by E. E. Estcourt, M.A., Canon of Birmingham.*

1580. Dormer and Holte.

W[m] Holte of Stoke Lyne; died 7 Jan[y] 1580. = Katherine, d[r] and sole heiress of John Dormer, of Owlsey, Co. Bucks, gent.

Thomas. William. Ann. Bridget. Frances. Katherine.

—*Note from a monument at Stoke Lyne, Co. Oxon.*

From the Register of St. Dionis Backchurch, London.

Marriages. 1620. June 25. John Wise of St. Buttolphes without Aldersgate and Thomasine Dormer of the same. By lic.

1646-7. March 11. Eusebius Dormer and Susan Harbert.

1634. Mary, daughter of Sir Fleetwood Dormer, Knt. (and sister of Sir John, below), married William Sheppard, of Rowland Wright Magna, Co. Oxon., A.D. 1634.

Busby and Dormer.

Judith, d[r] of Sir W[m] Mainwaring. (1st wife.) = Sir John Busby, of Stratton Audley, near Bicester, Co. Oxon. = Mary, d[r] of John Dormer, of Lee Grange, Co. Bucks, Esq. (2nd wife.)

Hester. | Thos. Busby, LL.D., Lord of the Manor of Addington, Co. Bucks.

Lady Arabella Dormer was the second daughter and coheiress of Charles, second Earl of Carnarvon.

1680. Parkhurst and Dormer.

John Parkhurst, of Catesby, Co. Northampton. = Katherine, d[r] of John Dormer, of Lee Grange, Co. Bucks (afterwards a Baronet).

Nathaniel Parkhurst. = Althamia Smith, of Kensington, Co. Middlesex. Mar. 10 Feb. 1699-1700, at Westminster Abbey.

1661. Sir John Dormer, of Lee Grange, Co. Bucks, was knighted at Whitehall 10 July 1661, and created a baronet 23 of the same month and year. He married Susan, daughter and coheiress of Sir Richard Browne, of Allscott, Co. Gloucester, by whom he had issue a son, William, who succeeded to the title, but died unmarried 9 March 1725-6, when it became extinct, and a daughter Susan, wife of Francis Sheldon, of Abberton, Co. Worcester, Esq.

1678. Fleetwood Dormer, of Arle Court, Co. Gloucester, brother of the above Sir John Dormer, Bart., was knighted at Whitehall 13 July 1678. He subsequently emigrated to Virginia.

1683. Blake and Dormer.

Sir Richard Blake, Knt.; died 26 Aug. 1683, aged 69; buried in the Savoy Church in the Strand. = Elizabeth, d[r] of John Bathurst, gent.

(1) Elizabeth Blake. = Robert Berkeley, of Spetchley, Co. Worcester, Esq. | Robert, 2nd son of John Dormer, of Lee Grange, Co. Bucks, Esq., by Katherine, daughter of Thomas Woodward, of Ripple, Co. Worcester, Esq. = (2) Mary Blake.

From the Registers of Great Milton, Co. Oxon.

Marriage. 1552. June 20. Stephen Dormer and Margaret Leicester.

Baptism. 1631. March 31. William Dormer, sonne of S[r] Robert Dormer, Knt., borne 15th day.

Burials. 1616. Nov. 20. Lady Dorothie Dormer, wife of S[r] Michael Dormer.

1624. Sept. 24. S[r] Michael Dormer, Knt.

1636-7. March 23. Michael, son of Sir Michael Dormer, Knt.

1639. March 29. Lady Mary, wife of S[r] Robert Dormer of Ascot, Knt.

1619. Will of John Dormer, of Thame, yeoman, made 7 July 1609. He bequeaths to the Church of Thame 10s., to the alms-men 6d. a year, and to the poor 3s. 4d. To M[r] Michael Saunders certain lands and houses which are to be sold to pay his debts. Mentions his wife Elizabeth and his son Robert. Also "Martha Towne, daughter of my sister Katherine Towne," and "Samuel Yates, son of my sister Ann Yates." The overseers of the Will are M[r] Mich. Saunders, M[r] Hester, and John Burt, and it was "published in the presence of John Trinder, W[m] Cussens, John Burte, and Edward Towne."—*Wills of the Peculiar of Thame.*

From the Register of St. Peter's, Cornhill, London.

Burials. 1665. Oct. 17. Samuell, sonne of William Dormer; pitt in the cloysters.

1665. Nov. 1. John, sonne of William Dormer; pitt in the cloysters.

1668. April 7. Elizabeth Dormer, servant and kinswoman to —— Gerrard; in the east yard.

1603. Robert Dormer, of Thame, witnessed John Whitney's Will, which was proved at Thame 13 Feb. 1603.

INSCRIPTIONS FROM COFFIN-PLATES IN CRENDON CHURCH.

Copies from the inscriptions on the Plates of the coffins in the vault of Sir John Dormer in Crendon Church, Co. Bucks, made by the Rev. Thomas Hayton, B.A., Vicar of Crendon, in October 1860.

John Dormer, Esqre, died April 3rd 1719, aged 48 y^{rs}.

Robert Dormer, Esqr, died 22 Dec. 1737, aged 64 y^{rs}.

Anne, wife of the late Robert Dormer of Rowsham, obit July the 16th 1695, Ætatis 47.

Robert Dormer of Dorton, Esqr, son of Robert Dormer, Esqr, who married the Right Honorable Catharine Beatrice, third daughter of Montague, Earl of Lindsey, Great Chamberlain of England, which said Robert the son married Martha Penelope Noel, daughter of Baptist, Lord Viscount Campden. He died without issue 1 July 1694, Ætatis 35.

Here lyes the body of the Lady Catharine Dormer, daughter of ye Right Honble Montague, Earl of Lindsey, and wife to Robert Dormer, Esqr, which said Lady Catharine Dormer dyed ye 3^{d} of June and in the 19th year of her age 1659.

The Honorable Lieutenant-General Dormer died Dec. 24th 1741 in the 62^{d} year of his age.

The slab stone on the monument shews the dates of death of Dame Jane and Sir John Dormer.

Additional Note by the Vicar.—A Mr William Dormer was buried 23^{d} Dec. 1705. (*Vide* Parish Register.) Also a Mr Robert Dormer of Dorton, "one of the Lords of the Manor of Crendon," was buried 12th May 1689.

1710–1743. Mrs Diana Dormer, born 17 April, baptized 10 May 1710, at St. Martin's in the Fields; buried in Westminster Abbey 3 March 1742-3. Will dated 18 Dec. 1742; proved 23 Feb. 1742-3. She was daughter of John Dormer, of Rousham, Co. Oxon, by Diana, d^{r} of Lieut.-General Piercy Kirke.

1709. DANIELL AND DORMER.

Samuel Daniell, of Over Tabley, Co. Chester, Esq., Knighted at St. James's Monday 21 Feb. 1708-9. = Frances, only d^{r} of Robert Dormer, of Rousham, Co. Oxon. Mar. 12 April 1709. Sister of John, Robert, and James Dormer.

1709. "Sir Samuel Daniell, of Over Tabley, Cheshire, Knt., married to Frances Dormer, only d^{r} (two sons living) of Robert Dormer, of Rousham, Oxon, and Anne, d^{r} of Sir Charles Cotterell, Thursday, 12 of April 1709."—Peter Le Neve's *Memoranda*.

1501. DORMER AND LAUNCELEYNS.

The following is from two sixteenth-century MSS.—

John Launceleyn, of Launceleynsbury, Co. Hunts, and Cople, Co. Beds. = Margaret . . . .

Sir John Launceleyn, Knt. = ...

(1) Benedicta or Benet, dau. and coheir. = Thomas Grey.

Sir Wm. Ouseubridge, 1st husband. = (2) Anne, d^{r} and coheir. = Sir Walter Luke, Knt.; died 1544.

Nicholas Luke, buried at Cople 1563.

Wm. Dormer, of Wycombe, Co. Bucks. = (3) Jane, d^{r} and coheir.

Geoffrey Dormer, of Thame, Merchant of the Staple of Calais. —Harl. MSS. 1563, fol. 17^{b}, and Lansdowne MSS. 863, fol. 156.

1614. Lady Katherine Dormer, of the family of St. John of Bletsoe, died 23 March 1614-5, and was buried 25 March. Will dated 26 Aug. 1609. Proved, 22 May 1615, by her only child Lady Anne Howard.

1600. DORMER AND CURSON.

Sir John Curson of Waterpery. = Magdalene, 2nd d^{r} of Sir Robt. Dormer, of Winge.

Robert, bap. 23 June 1604. Thomas, bap. 3 April 1603.

FROM THE REGISTER OF GREAT MISSENDEN, BUCKS.

[The following are abstracts and not exact copies.]

Burials. Robert, son of Robert Dormer, Esq., 18 Nov. 1640.

Robert, son of Lord Dormer, 29 Oct. 1656.

Baptisms. Robt., son of Charles Dormer, Esq., and Elizth his wife, baptized by their own Priest 3 Nov. 1696.

Ann, dau. of Cha. Dormer, Esq., and Elizth his wife, baptized by their own Popish Priest 30 Nov. 1697.

Francis, son of Charles Dormer, Esq., and Elizth his wife, bapt. by their own Popish Priest 10 April 1700.

Mrs Catherine, d^{r} of ye Honble John Dormer and Mary his wife, was born at Peterley 16 July, and baptized the same day by ye own Priest, 1727.

John, son of the Hon. John Dormer, Esq., and Mary his wife, born att Peterley 18 Feb. 1730, and baptized ye same day by ye Romish Priest.

Ann Barbara, d^{r} of the Hon. John Dormer, etc., etc., 13 Sept. 1731.

James, son of the Hon. John Dormer, etc., etc., born at Peterley 21 May 1733, and baptized the same day by ye Romish Priest.

William, etc., etc., 27 Sept. 1733.

Mary, d^{r}, etc., etc., 28 Aug. 1736.

Mary, d^{r} of the Hon. Cha. Dormer and Lady Mary his wife, 21 May 1750.

George, etc., etc., 13 May 1751.

Charles, etc., etc., 10 Jan. (N.S.) 1752.

Frances, d^{r} of the Hon. Cha. Dormer and Elizth his wife, 9 Aug. 1774.

Hugh, etc., etc., 26 July 1775.

Burials. The Rt. Hon. Cha. Lord Dormer, Baron of Wing, 4 July 1728.

The Hon. Mary Dormer, wife of John Dormer, Esq., 1 Nov. 1739.

Lady Mary Dormer, wife of Chas. Dormer, Esq., of Peterley, 20 May 1753.

Charles Dormer, son of the Hon. Chas. Dormer, 14 March 1761.

Hon. Robert Dormer, 24 May 1763.

Mary Dormer, inft. dau. of the Hon. James Dormer, 6 March 1769.

INSCRIPTIONS ON MONUMENTS IN GREAT MISSENDEN CHURCH, CO. BUCKS, 1656–1729.

Hic jacet corpus Roberti Dormer de Peterley, Armigeri, filii nate tertii Roberti Dormer Baronis de Wing. Obiit die 23 Octobris Anno 1656. Cujus animæ propitietur Deus.—*Choir floor*.

Near this place lieth inter'd the Body of the Honble Robert Dormer, Esq., second brother to Charles late Lord Dormer of Wenge, who departed this life the 25th day of April An^{o} Dom^{i} 1729, in the 58th year of his age. He took to wife, with whom he lived happily 31 years, Mrs Frances Finch, sole daughter of Windsor Finch of Rushock, in Worcestershire, Esq., who in memory of her beloved husband caused this monument to be erected. "He was beloved by rich and poor. May his soul rest for evermore."—*Choir*.

FAMILY PORTRAITS AT ROUSHAM.

Sir John Dormer, of Dorton, in the Hall at Rousham.

He is represented wearing the costume of the time of James I., and 70 years of age—the date of the picture 1626. His hair is cut close, he has a moustache and short beard. He wears a black doublet and hose, a black ribbon gold-edged, tied in a bow round his leg below the knee. The doublet, trimmed with bows at the waist, has a plait on the shoulders, but the sleeves are tight, and the lawn cuffs are edged with lace. His right hand rests on a plan of Dorton House, placed upon a table covered with red cloth, a green curtain hangs behind. It is a vigorous painting by an unknown artist.

Jane Dormer, Duchess of Feria.

Anne, daughter of Sir Peter Vanlore, first wife of Sir Charles Cæsar.

Sir Julius Cæsar, Master of the Rolls.

Sir Robert Dormer, Knt.

Robert Dormer, Esq., by Sir Peter Lely.

John Dormer, by Sir Godfrey Kneller.

Charles Dormer.

William Dormer, by Commins.
Robert Dormer.
Philip Dormer, who fell at the Battle of Blenheim.
James Dormer.
Clement Dormer.
General Dormer, by Vanloo.
Sir Charles Cottrell, by Dobson.
Sir Clement Cottrell, by Vandyke.
Sir Charles Cottrell, by Sir Godfrey Kneller.
Sir Charles Lodowick Cottrell, by Sir Godfrey Kneller.
Sir Clement Cottrell Dormer, by Hudson.
Sir Charles Cottrell Dormer, by West.
Sir Clement Cottrell Dormer, by West.
Anne Alleyne, wife of Sir Clement Cottrell.
Frances West, wife of Sir Charles Cottrell, by Dobson.
Elizabeth Burwell, 1st wife, and Elizabeth Chute, 2nd wife, of Sir C. L. Cottrell.
Bridget Shirburne, wife of Sir Clement Cottrell Dormer.
Jane Cæsar Adelmare, wife of Sir Charles Cottrell Dormer, by Sir Joshua Reynolds.

♣♣♣♣♣♣♣♣♣♣♣

PRIOR to the year 1447 "John Crouche," as he is called in one entry, but "JohnCrooke" in another, had given a suit of vestments to the Church of Thame, and under the name of "John Croke" had likewise provided "steyned clothes ffor the lecternes." Of this family, "Isabell Chapman, otherwise called Crokk," had also given a "vestment of blew damaske, wt orfray of cloth of gold." These benefactors were members of a race of yeomen and gentlepeople resident in the town and neighbourhood; and the John Croke in question was probably grandfather of the person of the same names who so benefited himself by the Tudor changes, and obtained such a considerable share in the monastic spoils.

This last-named John Croke was in Holy Orders, and had become one of the six Clerks in Chancery as early as 1522, when he, with others, petitioned King Henry VIII. to be allowed to marry. In 1529 he purchased an estate at Chilton in Bucks, having previously lent a substantial sum of money upon it. In 1539, by the aid of John Williams, he secured the site and lands of Studley Priory in Oxfordshire for a comparatively small sum. He also bought the Manor of Canon's Court in Crendon,* parcel of the dissolved Monastery of Notley, in 1541. In conjunction with Sir Anthony Lee, he obtained, in 1545, a grant of the Rectory of Stone, Co. Bucks, and the Manor and lands of Saint Clere's in that parish. He was elected M.P. for Chippenham in 1547, and appointed one of the Masters in Chancery in 1549. He married Prudence, daughter of Mr. Richard Cave, gent., by Margaret Saxby, of the town of Northampton, and sister of Henry Cave, woolstapler, of Kirkby, Co. Rutland, and also of Sir Ambrose Cave, Chancellor of the Duchy of Lancaster. John Croke's Will* was made 11 June 1554, and proved 18 Oct. 1555. He died 2 Sept. 1554, and was buried at Chilton. His wife had predeceased him.

His eldest son, John Croke, born in 1530, who was the sole executor of his father's Will, married Elizabeth, daughter of Sir Alexander Unton, of Checquers, Co. Bucks, Knt., from whom descended a considerable race, now widely scattered.

Charles Croke, third son of Sir John Croke, the Judge—to whom further reference will be made on a succeeding page—was educated at Thame School under Mr. Richard Boucher. He subsequently entered Ch. Ch., Oxford, 5 January 1603, graduated B.A. 16 April 1608, and received two higher degrees later on; secured ordination, was afterwards made Professor of Rhetoric in Gresham College, London; became Rector of Waterstock; graduated D.D. 20 June 1625; and was likewise Rector of Amersham, Co. Bucks, in 1625, and Chaplain to King Charles I.

George Croke, another member of this family, was

* Canon Court Manor Farm in Crendon had been alienated by the Crokes on or before the year 1699 to George Burrows of Thame, Esq., who, in 1708, also purchased other lands in Crendon. These descended to his son John Burrows of Thame, but in 1747 were in the hands of Thomas Kersey of Chilton, Esq., Sheriff of Bucks in that year.

* In his Will there is no reference whatsoever to his supposed name of "Blount," nor is there in his monumental inscription still remaining in Chilton Church. In a deed in my possession relating to Saint Clere's Manor in Stone—by which he obtained a joint interest with Sir Anthony Lee—he signs himself simply "J. Croke." The Blount connection appears like a genealogical romance of some imaginative Tudor Herald. The following, however, stands in a MS. volume written in the later years of Queen Elizabeth's reign:—

Nicholas le Blount al's Croke = Agnes . . . .
Ricardus Croke, filius et heres de Agnes = ... filia.
Johannes Croke, fil' et heres de Richard'. = ... filia de Cave.

—*Pedigrees of English Nobility*, Harl. MS. 1074. [illegible] 3. British Museum.

The inscription in question stands thus:—

"✠ Here lyeth buried John Croke, the Elder, Knyght, sum tyme one of the six Clerkys of the Kynges Courte of the Chauncery, and after ward one of the Maisters of the seid Chauncery. He departed the second day of September in the yere of oure Lorde God mcccccliiij. ✠"—Chilton with Easington Co. Bucks.

also educated at Thame under the same master, and subsequently was matriculated from Ch. Ch. Sometime before the year 1615 he purchased the estate of Waterstock of his kinsman, Sir William Cave.

At a later period others of the Croke race were educated at the same school. This was the case with Alexander, born 24 Feb. 1704, the eldest son of Alexander Croke, Rector of Hartwell. He married, at the age of twenty-two, Elizabeth, daughter of Richard Barker, Esq. (whose wife was Ann Peck of Thame), and lived at Dinton. Another Alexander Croke, eldest son of the above-named Alexander and Elizabeth, born at Dinton, 27 Nov. 1728, subsequently an attorney at Aylesbury, had for his contemporary at Thame School Lord Cobham, afterwards Earl Temple.

The following descents (see also footnote p. 145) will shew the connection between the families of Croke, Heath, Fanshawe, and Noel:—

Paulus Ambrosius Croke, of Thame, son of John Croke. = Frances, dau. of Francis Wellesborne, of Hanny, Co. Berks, Esq. She died 10 July 1605, aged 22. (1st wife.)

Sir Robert Heath, Lord Chief Justice of the King's Bench, a cousin of Robert Heath, of Thame. (See page 122.) = Margaret Croke.

Margaret Heath. = Sir Thomas Fanshawe, of Jenkins, Co. Essex, Knt.

Susanna Fanshawe. = Baptist Noel, of Luffenham, Co. Rutland.

Baptist Noel, 3rd Earl of Gainsborough.

The family of Etheridge—spelt also Etherege, Edryche, Ederiche, Easkrigge, and Etherigge—resided at Thame for some generations. Some of them lived at Priest End. Thomas Etherigge, yeoman, was churchwarden in 1520. In 1550, William Etheridge, gentleman, bought the canopy of the High Altar for twenty-six shillings and eightpence (no doubt to preserve it from profanation), and is mentioned in the Church Accounts in 1554 and again in 1557. Three generations later, Christopher Etheridge, born at Thame in Elizabeth's reign, a clerk in Orders, was Curate of Towersey in 1632, and had a son Charles. Nearly a century afterwards, Richard Eskrigge, of Fulmer, his great-nephew, was High Sheriff of Bucks in 1741. The two most distinguished members of the family, however, were Dr. George Etheridge,* Regius Professor of Greek at Oxford in Queen Mary's reign, the intimate friend of John Leland the antiquary, Rector of Great Haseley; and Sir George Etheredge the dramatist and diplomatist of the seventeenth century.

The former, born at Thame, and educated first at Thame Abbey, was admitted to Corpus Christi College, Oxford, in 1534, of which he was elected a Fellow in 1539. So distinguished an author and so excellent a Greek scholar did he become that he was made Regius Professor of Greek in 1553. His commendable zeal for the Old Religion, however, was such as that it counterbalanced all else, and he was unjustly deprived of his office when Elizabeth came to the throne. Upon this, he is said to have practised Medicine with great success at Oxford, and to have educated several sons of the old nobility in their ancient Faith. Amongst others of his pupils was William Giffard, of the family of the Giffards of Crendon, Co. Bucks, afterwards Archbishop of Rheims. Anthony à Wood notes that

* The following is Anthony à Wood's valuable record:—"George Ethryg, or *Etheridge*, or, as he writes himself in Latine, *Edrycus*, was born in a mercate town in *Oxfordshire* called Thame, admitted *Scholar* of C.C. Coll. in *Nov.* 1534, being then put under the tuition of *John Sheprove*, and in *Feb.* 1539 was made Probationer-Fellow. In 1543 he was licensed to proceed in Arts, and two years after was admitted to the reading of any of the Books of Aphorismes of *Hyppocrates*. At length being esteemed by all to be a most excellent Grecian, he was made the King's Professor of that language in the University about 1553, and kept that lecture till some time after *Qu. Elizab.* came to the Crown; and then, because he had been a forward Person against the Protestants in *Qu. Maries* Reign, was forced to leave it. So that following the practice of his faculty of Medicine with good success in, and near, Oxon, especially among those of his opinion, gained a considerable stock of wealth. He mostly lived, and kept a Family in an antient decayed place of literature called *Georges* hall opposite almost to the South end of *Catstreet* in St. *Maries* Parish in *Oxon*, in which he took to him (in the condition of Sojourners) the Sons of divers Catholick Gentlemen to be instructed in several arts and sciences; among whom was *Will. Gifford* afterwards Archbishop of *Rheims*, who received from him rudiments in Grammar, Musick, and partly in Logick. He constantly adher'd to the R. Catholick Religion, wherein he had been zealously educated, for which he suffer'd at the reformation by losing his lecture (perhaps his Fellowship too) and by continual imprisonments to the great impoverishment of his health and estate. In a word, he was esteemed by most Persons, especially by those of his opinion, a noted Mathematician, well skill'd in vocal and instrumental Musick, an eminent Hebrician, Grecian, and Poet, and above all an excellent Physician, as it appears in certain books of his composition, the titles of which follow.

Musical compositions }
Diversa Carmina } MS.

Acta Henrici octavi, carmine Graec. Presented in MS. to Qu. *Elizabeth* when she was in Oxon 1566.

Hypomnemata quaedam in aliquot libros Pauli Æginetæ, seu observationes medicamentorum quae hâc aetate in usu sunt. Lond. 1588. Oct. He also turn'd the *Psalmes of David* into a short form of Hebrew verse, and translated most, if not all, of the works of *Justin Martyr* from Greek into Latin, with other things, which I have not yet seen. He was living an antient Man in fifteen hundred eighty and eight, but when, or where he died, I know not, nor where buried unless in the yard of St. *Maries* Church in *Oxon*, in which his Father and Mother were before buried. *John Leland* who was his familiar friend did celebrate his memory by verse while he lived, and told him thus.

Scripsisti juvenis multâ cum laude libellos,
Qui Regi animis per placuere meo."

—*Athenæ Oxonienses*, vol. i., pp. 191, 192. London: 1691.

Etheridge "was reckoned a very sincere man, and adhered to the last to the Catholic Religion, though he suffered exceedingly by it." The same trustworthy author states that "he was living an ancient man in 1588," but gives no record of his death.

The latter, of the same name, who was born *circa* 1635, was educated at Thame Grammar School under Dr. Burte, and afterwards studied Law in London, proceeding to France to finish his education. There he found a welcome by Charles II., for Etheredge was a staunch loyalist, and—seeing the misery and ruin which had overtaken his country—a determined hater of the sour and canting Puritans. It has been remarked of him that he "virtually founded English comedy, as it was necessarily understood by Congreve, Goldsmith, and Sheridan." In 1664 he published, in quarto, "The Comical Revenge, or Love in a Tub," dedicated to Charles Sackville, Lord Buckhurst, afterwards 6th Earl of Dorset, and acted during that year at the Duke of York's Theatre in Lincoln's Inn Fields. In 1668 he published "She Would if she Could," and eight years afterwards "The Man of Mode, or Sir Fopling Flutter." This latter at once passed through several editions (one of which appeared as late as 1693), while the acting of the play itself created some sensation. It was dedicated to Mary of Modena, Queen of James II., prior to her marriage, and had a considerable sale. Sir Carr Scroope wrote the Prologue, John Dryden the Epilogue; and, amid much applause, it was acted for several months by the best performers of the day, including Betterton and the beautiful Mrs. Barry, who, by the way, for some time was Etheredge's mistress, and by whom he had a daughter, and upon her he settled six thousand pounds, but she died young. He entered the diplomatic service, was appointed Envoy Extraordinary at The Hague and afterwards at Ratisbon—some say to Constantinople,* married and was knighted, but did not live on very good terms with his wife. He is reported to have been a great favourite with King Charles II., and was a leader amongst those whose brilliant wit and sarcasm were at that time so remarkable. He grew somewhat loose in morals, however, and dissipated in bearing.

At the Revolution, in the spring of 1689, Etheredge fled to Paris, and is said to have died about the year 1693, but where and when remain somewhat uncertain.

But to continue the facts and records.

The following, from an original MS. of the Tudor era, shews certain alliances by which it may be that the Ashhursts first became connected with Oxfordshire families:—

A.D. 1577.

Georgius Grey, generosus, de Thame in Co. Oxon. =

- Ricardus Grey, Vice-comes Civitatis London.
- Maria Grey, nupta Henrico Rookes, generoso. =

Oliverus Delalyne, 2 filius [of William Delalyne, of the Co. of Salop, arm., and Margaret, dau. of John Ashhurst of Co. Lancaster, ar.]. = Agnes, filia Henrici Rookes.

- Thomas, primogenitus, supers' 1577.
- Cuthbertus, 2 filius, supers' 1577.

—Miscellaneous Pedigrees, Harl. MSS. No. 4031, Brit. Museum, folio 71.

The ancient and renowned family of Marmion, as has been already shewn,* had representatives living at Thame during the fourteenth and fifteenth centuries. One of these, Shakerley Marmion, a dramatist of the reign of Charles I., was educated at Thame School. The following sets forth his immediate ancestry:—

Rowland Shakerley of London, gent. Purchased the Manor of Aynhoe, Co. Northants, in 1544. = Ann . . . . ., his wife. Buried 16 April 1571. Will proved 11 May of the same year.

Thomas Marmion of Thame, Councillor-at-Law, of Lincoln's Inn, and subsequently of Aynhoe aforesaid. Buried 24 Aug. 1583. = Mary Shakerley, only daughter and heiress of her father.

Shakerley Marmion of Aynhoe, Esq. Baptised 23 Nov. 1575. = Mary, only daughter of Bartrobe Lukin, gent. Marriage Settlement dated 1 June 1600; living in 1615.

Shakerley Marmion, the younger. Baptised 21 Jan. 1602; educated at Thame School; of Wadham Coll., Oxon, M.A. 1624; died in 1639.

He wrote three plays, which at the time of their publication became very popular:—"Holland's Leaguer: a Comedy," quarto, 1632; "A Fine Companion," quarto, 1633; and a third, published after his death, "The Antiquary," quarto, 1641. They all indicate art, feeling, and the possession of much dramatic taste and ability. He likewise published a poem entitled "Cupid and Psyche," and died at the early age of 37 in 1639.

* *The Letter Book of Sir George Etheredge*—relating to work done during his sojourn at Ratisbon—is preserved in the MS. Room of the British Museum.

* This family, already referred to (see footnote, p. 174), was also connected with Ewelme, Co. Oxford:—

Manor of Ewelme. In the reign of Queen Elizabeth John Marmion complained that Thomas Brasier of Bensyndon and others had forcibly entered his Close and House called "Cottismore," parcel of the said Manor of Ewelme; but, failing to produce his title, judgment was given on behalf of the defendants.—Exchequer Pleas, 1578-1579.

Cecilia, daughter of John Marmion, who was the son of Anthony, was the sole daughter and heiress of William Slythurst, late of Ewelme.

Sir Richard Ingoldsby—second son of Sir Richard of Lenthenborough, Co. Bucks, by Elizabeth, daughter of Sir Oliver Cromwell of Hinchinbrook, Co. Hunts, Knt.—being of the Founder's kin, was also educated at this School, and became a Captain in John Hampden's Regiment. This family was nearly related to the Hampdens of Thame, to the Lees of Quarrendon,—in the Chapel of which House their armorial bearings were set up, as Nicholas Charles has put on record,—and to the Lovelaces of Berkshire. It is said that, being a weak man, Richard Ingoldsby was drawn into a course of rebellion against legitimate Authority by the influence of his Puritanical and disorderly connections, but that, seeing the practical miseries of Civil War and the evils of unchecked rebellion and blasphemous cant, repented sincerely of his errors, and subsequently received the Monarch's pardon.

♣♣♣♣♣♣♣

IT may be well to reproduce here a Certificate which is preserved in the Record Office in regard to the Robbery of the Church which took place in 1548. It appears obvious that this Certificate was made in response to an official enquiry from the King's Council, asking what had become of the plate and Church goods—to which the Council in question maintained the Monarch owned a personal right.

Now between the years 1542 and 1549 (see p. 155) the "Church Accounts" are very deficient, and the names of certain of the Churchwardens are, in some instances, likewise wanting. The following document happily supplies certain of those deficiencies. "Abraham" evidently stands for "Abraham Metcalfe." His colleague, Henry Cowper, was the husband of Agnes Dormer. The next "reforming" Churchwardens (*circa* 1544) were Edward Collins and John Hester—the former a brother of John Collins, the ex-chantry priest of the Parish Church; the latter, a member of the old family of Hester of Thame. The others were Buns, Spencer, and Mynchard,—led on by John Smythe, who had been Churchwarden as early as the year 1529. Their superiors in rank, as should be noted, had already so benevolently robbed the monastic churches, and obtained the monastic manors and lands, that the Churchwardens themselves no doubt thought it both shortsighted and "ungodly" not to imitate their betters, and so proceeded to rob the Parish Church. They, at all events, had as good a right to the chalices, crosses, canopies, and hangings as the King—who was so anxious to obtain them "for Our own personall use and behoof." Moreover it is quite possible that certain of the Church *ornamenta* may have been removed to preserve them from desecration.

A Certificate concerning the Robbery of the Church.

Tame in the County of Oxon (*circa* 1548).

(*From the State Paper Office.*)

A CERTIFICATH made to the kyngs ma'tie & hys hon'able counsell by the most p'te of the Inhabitants & p'ry'sonor[s] there of soche Churche goods guelte plate & other ornaments of the said Churche as hath be'n sold & dem' fyve yeres last past by the p'sons hereafter namyd.

ffyrst iiij chalecys of sylver.
It' ij crossys of sylu' & gylte.
It' a fote for the grete crosse of sylu' & gylt.
It' ij basyns of sylu'.
It' ij sensers of sylu'.
It' ij shypps of sylu'.
It' ij candelstycks of sylu'.
It' a pax of sylu' & gylt.
It' a pycks of sylu' & gylt.
It' the grett bell.
It' the fore bell.
It' the hangyngs of the hygh altare of fyne sylk.
It' the hangyngs of the sepulcre of sylk.
It' a A canapie y[t] cost viij[li] besyde vestments &c.

The ffyrst churchwardens that began to sell the sayd churche goods were Abraham & Henry Cooper.

The next churche wardens Edward Collyns & John Hester.

The next to them Rychard Buns, Spenser, & Wyll[m] Mynshare the w[ch] thre p'sons hawe spoyled all & haue left almost noo thyngs, for when the Alters were taken down they caryed awey the stones by nyght. And they haue m'de none akompte to the pyr'she by the space of thre yeres & more last past.

And the chyeff counceller & doer of all thyngs aforeseyd y[s] one John Smyth of Tame aforseyd.

Also All the kyngs ma' trewe & faythfull subjects there thynk that All the seyd goods juells plate & ornaments soo sold Amounted to thre hundred pounds & more the w[ch] was devyded amongst the p'sons before menc'y'd & they threten to pun'she ys poore subiects & haue punyshed them that speake of the sam' so that they stand in feare to declare the trewthe theren.

♣♣♣♣♣♣♣

THE paving of the Market Place—the site of the old Market Cross—was done soon afterwards, in 1550; and a new causeway at the White Hound style was made at the same time. The cost of this seems enormous—no less than £28 13s. 3d. Part of this sum appears to have been obtained by the sale of certain pieces of the church plate. In the following year the two churchwardens John Spencer and Richard Bunce expended still larger sums for digging gravel and carting it, and "for pavyng about the Com'on Well in the Markett Place," £51 18s. 4d. At the same time the whole of the church money and receipts—certain portions of which had been lent to Mr. William Dormer and then repaid by him—were expended thus: "Payde for the dyggynge and caryinge of stones and gravell, and for makynge of ye hyewayes ffrom Crendon Brigs alonge by the Vicarage and soe uppe the layne by Iohn Striblehill's dore, and also ye hyewaies from Priest End Elmes along the strete by Etheriggs, and soe through't Alyn's Lane, as it dothe appere by the Boke of reckenings, brought into this accompte—xxxiij^{li} xv^{s} ix^{d}."

THE following is a record of one year's receipts and expenditure of the Surveyors of the Highways. The presents of wine and pepper to Mr. Belson, a justice, for his services in approving of the method of expenditure will be noted:—

Th' Accompt of John Spens' phillippe Byrde and henry Grenod surueyours and orderers of the works for Amendment of the high wayes in the p'yrish of Thame for one hole yere ended the Tewsday in Ester Weke, Anno D'ni' 1560 et Anno Regni Elizabethe Dei gra' Anglie ffrancie et hib'nie Regine fidei defensoris &c. secundo.

Receipts.

	s.	d.
IN PRIMIS Receauyd of Will'm Bekynsfeld ...	xx	
It'm of Edmond lawson		xvj
It'm of Manerll		xij
It'm of John leif		xvj
It'm of Thomas Page	ij	
It'm of Will'm Smythe		xx
It'm of Rayfe pollen		xvj
It'm of Robt. Cone al's philipps	ij	
It'm of Richard Bolde		xiiij
It'm of Margarett Nedam wid.		xvj
It'm of Thomas Andefeld	ij	
It'm of Will'm Bradley		viij
It'm of Thomas Barnard		xvj
It'm of Thomas Symeons	ij	
It'm of Nicholas Stanton		xij
It'm of Robt. Tame		iiij
It'm of John Childe		xij
It'm of John Morley Bucher		xvj
It'm of Robt. parks		iiij
It'm of Will'm prest		xiiij
It'm of Thomas Hibbart		xij
It'm of Richard Worsley		xij
It'm of Nicholas Cowper		xij
It'm of John helyer		x
It'm of Will'm Haywood		xvj
It'm of Cornelyse		ij
It'm of Rayfe Willmot		xiij
It'm of Symon Syncler	ij	
It'm of Luke Saunders		viij
It'm of John Tatnell	ij	
It'm of John Bedforde		xvj
It'm of Robt. Spryngolde		xvj
It'm of Thom^{s} Bendell		xvj
It'm of M'ris Dormer wid.		xix ob.
It'm of Richard Benson		xij
It'm of Will'm thomson		vj
It'm of Richard Cotton		xvj
It'm of Richard ffellow		xiiij
It'm of John huckett		xij
It'm of Will'm Turneley		viij
It'm of Awsten shomaker		xij
It'm of Culle		xij
It'm of Benet		viij
It'm of Adams		xij
It'm of Powell		xvj
It'm of Will'm Byles		xx
It'm of porter		viij
It'm of John Morley senior		xvj
It'm of Richard pitman	ij	
It'm of Nicholas Wrigge		viij
It'm of Water Tame		xx
It'm of Will'm Pollyngton	ij	vj
It'm of Olyu' Boller		xvj
It'm of Thomas Banester		xij
It'm of John Person		xij
It'm of Robt. Aley		xij
It'm of John Cawkett	ij	
It'm of John Kerby		xij
It'm of thomas hunt	iij	vj
It'm of Will'm Mynnard	xl	
It'm of Olyu' Rowbothome	iij	iv
It'm of Gyles lewen		iij
It'm of Roose		iij

S^{m} pay' ... vj^{li} xij^{s} ij^{d} ob.

Payments.

	s.	d.
IN P'M' payd for wyne gevyn to Mr. Belson ...		xij
It'm payd to the pariers for the last yere ...	x	
It'm p'd for j^{li} of pepe' gevyn to Mr. Belson ...	iij	
It'm p'd to iij laborers for iij Dayes worke ...		xx
It'm p'd to one laborer for ij dayes ...		xij
It'm p^{d} to hoore for selvynes [qy.] the mattok ...		ij
It'm p^{d} for the dyggynge of lxxiiij lood of stonne ...	xix	
It'm p^{d} for ye cariage of vj lood ...	iiij	
It'm p^{d} for the dyggynge & cariage of iiij lood ...	iiij	
It'm p^{d} to ij laborers for one daye ...		xv
It'm p^{d} to John Whellars for mendynge of the Mattock ...		xvj

Sum ... v^{li} xix^{s} ix^{d}

Summa totalis Recept' ... vj li. xij s. ij d. ob.
Summa in expens' ... v li. xix s. ix d.
Sum'a Remanens de claro ... xj s. iiij d. ob.

AND so ys elect for the hyeways men for this year ffolowyng by the consent of the p'risconars.

Will'm Pollington, Richard Pitman, John Benet jun. } for New Thame.
Will'm Mynchard for olde Thame.
Thom's Garnett for prestend.
Edmund hendy for morton.

♣♣♣♣♣♣♣

Ave Maria gratia plena.

IN the eleventh year of Queen Elizabeth's reign no chalice nor paten of precious metal remained in the Church for the administration of the Lord's Supper. All the old sacred vessels "savouring of superstition" had been disposed of or removed—their actual destination being extremely uncertain. It was necessary, therefore, to procure at least two "covered cups;" and two of the ordinary Elizabethan type, slightly engraven, were then provided. These still remain. The largest of silver-gilt is exactly eight inches and a quarter in height, and three inches and a half in width. It has a tightly-fitting cover, which when reversed served as a plate or paten. On this latter the date "1570" and the letters "N. T." (New Thame) are engraven. The smaller is exactly six inches in height, of precisely the same type, with a corresponding cover. Neither is very solid. Most probably this latter was provided by the residents in Old Thame. The two silver candlesticks for the Holy Table, given by a member of the Thynne family, *circa* 1706, were stolen. Amongst the present plate, of the early part of the eighteenth century, is a very solid and substantial silver-gilt flagon, eleven inches in height, with the following inscription engraved upon it:—

Domino
et
Ecclesiæ Parochiali de Thame
in Com. Oxon.
Thomas Carter, Arm'
D.D.D.
Anno Domini
1715.

And there is also a large solid silver paten, eight inches and a half in diameter, on a foot or stand, with "M. H. 1705" engraved thereon, together with the arms of Holt impaling those of Striblehill—the gift of Madam Martha Holt.

THE disintegrating and disastrous principle which, under the Tudors, the continental Communists and foreign preachers had brought into the country, and had seen applied so ruthlessly,—by which True and Lawful Spiritual Authority had been set aside,—was still farther put into practice a century later under King Charles I. The active spirit of insubordination and rebellion had been steadily growing—fostered as well by the complex miseries which the Tudor changes had directly brought about, as by the unscrupulous arts of aggressive and ambitious* demagogues,—and eventually broke out in England into active rebellion. Those who watched and waited for their opportunity secured it when the subject of Ship Money came under consideration.

If the nation was to be defended by one efficient fleet, if the *dominium maris* was to be recovered,—and surely the Monarch who ruled† and was the acknowledged Head of the nation was the best judge of what was required,—the costs of making and maintaining such a fleet must be met as of old. Under adequate necessity, and when dangers to the body politic threatened, writs had been frequently issued by English monarchs compelling the dwellers in ports and maritime counties to provide ships. That precedent was reasonably enough followed; and, when more extended defences were to be created, it was by no means improperly applied to all the shires. This gave great offence to many already heavily-enough burdened. Though a considerable sum was thus raised, which was duly and carefully devoted to the very necessary purpose for which it had been distinctly demanded, and a fleet of more than sixty wisely-manned and well-armed vessels had been provided, yet certain of the dissatisfied and fanatical denied altogether the Monarch's right to levy the money at all. Of course, where the good and safety of the whole kingdom was concerned, it was only reasonable and fair that the whole nation should fairly and equally share the burden, and not alone the ports and adjacent parts.

To obtain the matured opinion of those competent to give it, the two following questions were formally put to the Judges—"First, Whether in cases of danger to the good and safety of the kingdom in general, the King could not impose Ship Money for its defence and safeguard; and by law compel payment from those who refused. Secondly, Whether He were not the sole judge both of the danger and how it was to be prevented."

* The following avowal, from Hampden's mother to a confidential friend, is at least frank and sincere. She desires a peerage for him, and hopes he may secure it.—"If ever my sonn will seek for his honor, tell him nowe to come; for heare is multitudes of lords a makinge—Viscount Mand'vile Lo' Threasorer, Viscount Dunbar which was Sr Hr' Constable, Viscount Faukland which was Sr Harry Carew. These two last of Scotland, of Ireland divers, the Deputy a Vicount, and one Mr Fitzwilliams a Barron of Ingland, Mr Villers a Vicount, and Sr Will. Filding a Barron . . . . I am ambitious of my sonn's honor, which I wish were nowe conferred upon hime, that he might not come after so many new creations."—*Harleian MSS.*, Letter, dated *circa* 1621, from Mistress Elisabeth Hampden, second daughter of Sir Henry Cromwell, and aunt of the Usurper, to Mr. Anthony Knyvett.

† Persons who are dependent for their information upon the untrustworthy statements and direct perversions of fact by modern Radical Historians should study a remarkable treatise, based on the wisdom of Aristotle and the masterly dissertations of Thomas Aquinas, from the pen of the Rev. Dr. F. H. Laing, entitled *Whence does the Monarch get his Right to Rule?* London: 1872.

Ten of the Judges affirmed the truth, equity, and reasonableness of these crucial questions. But John Hampden of Hampden and Thame—for in Thame Church several of his ancestors and kinsmen had been buried—demurred to the proceedings which appeared to many people to have settled the point raised, and suffered imprisonment rather than pay his share of the demand,—exactly twenty shillings. The point at issue, raised once again in a slightly different form, was argued before the twelve Judges, seven of whom pronounced in favour of the King's reasonable and ancient prerogative, and five in favour of the appellant Hampden; only two of the five Judges, however, had the temerity to deny the ancient right of the Crown.

These pages are no place in which to enter into details as to the origin of the Civil War and Great Rebellion. Nor, except as far as regards occurrences which took place at Thame and in its immediate neighbourhood, need the progress of that disastrous conflict be followed.* It was obviously a well-deserved punishment for the impieties and wickednesses of the previous century—for the sins of one generation are often visited on those who come after. It gave a taste to the People of England in general of what rampant fanaticism and rejection of all authority invariably bring about. Oliver Cromwell, the brewer of Huntingdon, under the false plea of securing the People from tyranny, himself became a cruel, malicious, and bloodthirsty tyrant; rampant with the most repulsive cant, and terrible because of his fearful injustice and frightful cruelties. He, with his despicable coadjutors, eventually secured the murder of the Lord's Anointed. A pretended trial was arranged at which "Charles Stuart, late King of England"—as His Majesty was insolently and absurdly termed—"was accused of the treasone of levying war against the Parliament and People of England," found guilty, and executed as "a traitor, a tyrant, a murderer, and the Enemy of the English people." When the so-called "Warrant" was signed—"Downes, one of the military judges burst into tears. 'Are we men,' he exclaimed, 'or have we hearts of stone?' and in spite of Cromwell's efforts to silence him, he refused to give his voice with the others. The Warrant for the King's execution was signed by twenty-six persons; Cromwell, as he set his name, expressing his coolness and indifference by a brutal exhibition of buffoonery. He smeared his inky pen in Henry Marten's face, caught Ingoldsby by the arm, and, amid shouts of laughter, forced the pen into his hand and affected to guide it. Twelve of those who signed the paper afterwards asserted that they did so only under the threat of death." This was one of the gravest issues of Rebellion. It is with John Hampden and his death,* however, that we are now mainly concerned.

Early in 1643 Hampden had been sent for from Wycombe, where he commanded a regiment, by Mr. Richard Grenville, the High Sheriff of the County, also a Rebel, in order to attack the King's forces at Brill Hill and Boarstall House, a post of considerable strategic importance held by Sir Gilbert Gerard for his Majesty. But the Rebels were totally unsuccessful, and, after several ineffectual attempts to carry the lines of defence by storm, were compelled to retire with great loss.

Later on, in the spring of 1643, Prince Rupert so effectually harassed the Rebels in the neighbourhoods of Thame and Wycombe, that the impotence and inactivity of Lord Essex their Commander, whose head-quarters were at Thame, became a cause of deep dissatisfaction. The dashing and heroic Prince, whose zeal never slumbered, did his work well; while the nature of the country round about was found to be admirably suited for such persistent activity. Captain Urrie, sometime disloyal, having acknowledged his

* "The whole kingdom at this period exhibited a most melancholy spectacle. No man was suffered to remain neuter. Each county, town, and hamlet was divided into factions, seeking the ruin of each other. All stood upon their guard, while the most active of either party sought the opportunity of despoiling the lands, and surprising the persons of their adversaries."—*History of England*, by John Lingard, D.D., vol. viii., chap. i., pp. 6, 7. London: 1874.

"Even things inanimate, which appeal to Remembrance only, crowd in with their numberless associations, to tell us how unnatural a state of man is Civil War. The village street barricaded; the house deserted by all its social charities, perhaps occupied as the stronghold of a foe; the Church where lie our parents' bones become a battery of cannon, an hospital for wounded, a stable for horses, or a keep for captives;—the accustomed paths of our early youth beset with open menace or hidden danger, its fields made foul with carnage and the imprecations of furious hate, or the supplications of mortal agony, coming to us in our own language, haply in the very dialect of our peculiar province—these are among the familiar and frequent griefs of Civil War."—*Some Memorials of John Hampden*, etc., by Lord Nugent, vol. ii., pp. 163, 164. London: 1832.

* For certain of the details in the text, I am indebted to *A True and Faithful Narrative of the Death of Master Hampden, etc.*, by Edward Clough. London: 1643.

Inscription on Monument in Chalgrove Field.—Here In this field of Chalgrove, John Hampden, after an able and strenuous But unsuccessful resistance In Parliament, And before the Judges of the Land, To the Measures of an arbitrary Court, First took arms, Assembling the Voices of the associated counties of Buckingham and Oxford In 1642; and Here, within a few paces of this spot, He received the wound of which he died While fighting in defence of the free Monarchy And antient liberties of England June 18th 1643. In the two hundreth year from that day this Stone was raised In reverence to his memory.

Inscription on Monument at Stoke Mandeville, Co. Bucks.—*For these lands in Stoke Mandeville John Hampden Was assessed in twenty shillings Ship Money, Levied by command of the King, Without authority of law The 4th of August, 1635. By resisting the claim of the King, In legal strife, He upheld the rights of the People Under the law, And became entitled to grateful remembrance: His work on earth ended After the conflict in Chalgrove Field, The 18th of June, 1643, And he rests in Great Hampden Church.* W. E., 1863. (*i.e.*, Sir William Erle.)

error and returned to his proper allegiance, in conjunction with Prince Rupert, planned an attack upon the Parliamentarian soldiers, after the retreat of the latter at Islip. The King's forces, skilfully led, went out from Oxford on Saturday morning, 18 June 1643, crossed Chiswelhampton Bridge, and, after having authoritatively heard the results of a skirmish at Chinnor, met the enemy coming in force from that village and Tettesworth by way of Easington and Golder's Hill, so as by effect of numbers to overpower Prince Rupert, whose forces were then ably drawn up, in Chalgrove Field. This was early on the morning of the following day. Hampden, the leader of the Rebels, was soon wounded in the conflict. If the examination of a body which was rudely and unwarrantably exhumed in 1828 in the Chancel of Great Hampden Church by the late Lord Nugent and others, was an examination of the corpse of John Hampden, it is probable that the latter was disabled at the Chalgrove fight by the bursting of a pistol, as was recorded by his son-in-law, Sir Robert Pye. Being himself thus wounded; finding, moreover, that the expected troops of Lord Essex had not come up to his support; unable to resist with any effect the spirited and repeated charges of the Cavaliers; out-generalled in tactics, and his republican followers defeated in a fair fight and scattered, he eventually made the best of his way to Thame. A local tradition, quite worthy of respect, asserts that he was first observed riding in the direction of Pyrton, the residence of his father-in-law, Mr. Symeons.* But, upon being threatened by some Royalist horse-soldiers, who were moving in that direction, he himself rode off, his head bending down and his hands resting on his horse's neck, towards the headquarters of the Rebel Commander. Being well acquainted with the roads and byeways thither, and most probably preferring to take the latter rather than the former; he rode towards Stoke Talmache, then across the Haseley meadows, cleared the little river which there meanders along at a narrow point by a single leap; and so, having ridden nearly ten miles in intense pain, reached the Town of Thame. He rode straight for the Greyhound Inn, an old Hostel in the middle of the Town on the north side of the street, which he had no doubt known well from boyhood. There his wounds† were dressed by a local surgeon, Mr. Ezekiel Brown, and there he died from the combined effects of the wound and the general shock to his system, on the 24th June. The house in which his death took place—regarding which the local tradition is unvarying—was of the old type of country Inns—a large Tudor archway of timber leading into the courtyard, with rooms below on either side, and an external staircase leading to the sleeping apartments above, the doors of which opened on to a gallery running round. But its internal features were greatly changed when the building was newly fronted with brick in the reign of James II., and still greater alterations have been effected since. Forty years ago it was still an Inn, with its old sign; but it has been subsequently altered into two houses, the front making the buildings appear far less ancient than is actually the case with those old portions which still remain.

The noble generosity of King Charles I. is made manifest by the following words of Sir Philip Warwick: "The King, being informed of Mr. Hampden's being wounded, would have sent him over any chirurgeon of his, if he had been wanting, for he looked upon his interest, if he could gain his affection, as a powerful means of begetting a right understanding between him and the two Houses."

On his deathbed Hampden (though he soon learnt that his wound was mortal—for no doubt the wrench to his system, as well as the actual damage done to himself, served to forbid the surgeon who tended him from raising false hopes),—does not appear to have in any way repented of the sin of rebellion. A certain Dr. Giles of Chinnor, and a Presbyterian minister named Spurstow, fortified him in his political obstinacy and religious errors, and gave him what they termed "the Lord's Supper." Even in his death-agony he shewed himself in his true colours, when he could send up to the Throne of the Great King of the whole earth the following astonishing petition:—"Confound and level in the dust those who would rob the People of their liberty and lawful prerogative. Let the King see his errors, and turn the hearts of his wicked Counsellors from the malice and wickedness of their designs." If Authority comes from the Mob, of course such a prayer may be read with some patience; but if, on the other hand, true kingly authority is directly derived from the King of kings, the obvious impiety of such petitions is plainly apparent.

Hampden died in a town where he had received his

* From information given by Mr. Francklin, of Easington Manor, to his kinsmen of Haddenham and Westlington House, and given to me by the late Mr. John Francklin, of Dinton. Independent testimony to the same effect was recorded by the late Mr. John Blackall, of Haseley, whose ancestors had lived in that neighbourhood for many generations.

† There can be little doubt that the general impression of his contemporaries was that he was wounded in the shoulder by two carbine balls, which broke the bone; and to this opinion Lord Nugent, in his *Some Memorials of John Hampden*, adhered. One tradition asserts that he fell off his horse, as an immediate consequence of such wound, when riding towards Pyrton; and other local Tradition points out that a Tree, still flourishing, was soon afterwards planted to mark the spot. This, of course, may have occurred. Anyhow (as is set forth in the text above) Hampden soon afterwards rode off through Haseley in the direction of Thame, where, in less than a week, he died and was carried off for burial.

early education under Dr. Richard Boucher, and where some of his ancestors long previously had resided.

On the Sunday following his death, attended by such of the Rebel soldiery as could be conveniently assembled, the corpse of Hampden was carried from the Market Place at Thame to its resting-place amongst the Chiltern Hills. Through the adjacent village of Kingsey towards Princes Risborough, and then along the old Icknield Way up to Great Hampden, with arms reversed, and to the sound of muffled drums, they bore their burden. He was buried in the chancel of Great Hampden Church. Those who followed as mourners sang the Ninetieth Psalm, *Domine refugium*, as they carried the corpse into church, and *Judica me Deus*, the Forty-third Psalm, on leaving the grave.*

Little did those imagine who had marched and prayed, that the leaden coffin containing their leader's remains, which they had seen deposited in the old vault of the Hampdens, would in less than two centuries be opened and rifled, under the guidance of persons in a superior station of life; in order to gratify a morbid curiosity and to serve no good purpose whatsoever—the corpse partly taken out of its coffin, and propped up in a sitting position by a shovel, and then hacked about by a peer with a barrister's pocket penknife.† It may be reasonably enough pointed out that the Rector and Churchwardens of the Parish should, on every ground, as Custodians of the Church and its appurtenances, have opposed such proceedings on the part of a gang of well-dressed and polite resurrection-men.* Nor was it creditable to the representative of the Hampden family that such an outrage on decency should have been winked at and tolerated.

The late Mr. Grace of Wardrobes, who was present when the vault was opened, wrote that the corpse "had a beautiful face." Some persons asserted that it was, after all, the body of a woman. But a servant at Hampden House, named Robertson, who appears to have represented his absent master, Lord Buckinghamshire, and who was a witness of the whole proceedings wrote—"The first time I went upstairs after the exhumation, a portrait†

* "1643. John Hampden, esquier, Lord of Hampden, buried June xxv—Robert Lenthall, Rector."—*From the Parish Register of Great Hampden.*

† I am indebted to the late Mr. W. J. Bernhard Smith, barrister-at-law, for the following:—"On Saturday the 19th of June 1828, I left London with Lord Nugent and Mr. Denman (then Common-Serjeant of London, afterwards Lord Denman). We halted at Chalfont to see the Church and the house where Milton had for a time resided; thence to Amersham and Aylesbury, where we visited the county jail; and upon that occasion I made my first, and I hope my last, appearance on the treadmill, in company with the future Lord Chief-Justice of England. We arrived in the evening at Lilies, Lord Nugent's residence, and on the following Monday morning started early for Great Hampden, where, at the church door, we were met by the Rev. Mr. Brooks, the rector; Mr. Grace, Lord Buckingham's land steward; Mr. C. Moore, the eminent sculptor; Mr. Coventry, and one or two other gentlemen. After the inscriptions on several coffins had been examined, one was found about four feet from the surface, on the right-hand (south ?) side of the communion table, on which no letters were legible, and as the plate was not much decayed, it seemed probable that there never had been any inscription. It was immediately determined that this should be opened. It was cut open, and the lead rolled back; the body was laid in a wooden shell, and upon removing the sawdust, was found to be enveloped in very numerous folds of cerecloth, which would, perhaps, account for its remarkable preservation; the flesh was white and firm, but with no other odour than that of the surrounding earth. The features were much compressed by the weight of the bandages; the eyes were covered with a white film; the beard had been shaven, but there appeared a growth of about a sixteenth of an inch. The hair was long and flowing, as represented in the portraits of Hampden; it had been collected and tied with a black riband at the back of the head. In colour it corresponds with the description given by Mrs. Grote. I cut off a lock, which is still in my possession. As there was no surgeon present, Lord Nugent descended into the grave, and endeavoured to ascertain whether there was any wound upon or near the left shoulder, but it being found impossible then to make a satisfactory examination, the coffin was raised and set upon trestles in the middle of the chancel. The Body was placed in a sitting posture, with a shovel to support the head. The shoulders and arms were then carefully inspected, and the result proved that Lord Nugent's 'foregone conclusion'—that Hampden's death was occasioned by a gunshot wound in the shoulder—was at once dissipated. There did not appear any discolouration or the slightest injury to the shoulders or arms; but in order to be perfectly satisfied, Lord Nugent himself, with a small pocket-knife, borrowed from me at the instant, made several incisions in the parts adjacent to the shoulder joint, without finding any fracture or displacement of the bones. Lord Nugent was evidently disappointed; he did not care to establish the fact that Hampden's death was occasioned in any other manner than by a shot from the King's troops. My own opinion rather leaned to the tradition related by *Sir Robert Pye* (Hampden's son-in-law), that his right hand was shattered by the bursting of his pistol, and that death probably ensued from lockjaw, arising out of extensive injury to the nervous system. When I took up the right hand it was contained in a sort of funeral glove, like a pocket. On raising it I found it was entirely detached from the arm; the bones of the wrist and of the hand were much displaced, and had been evidently splintered by some violent concussion; only the ends of the fingers were held together by the ligaments. The two bones of the *forearm*, for about three inches above the wrist, were without flesh or skin, but there were no marks of amputation; both the bones perfect. The left hand was in a similar glove, but it was firmly attached to the arm, and remained so when the glove was drawn away. There were slight portions of the flesh upon the hand; the bones were complete, and still held in their places by the ligaments which supported them. This remarkable difference in the condition of the hands sufficiently proves the truth of *Sir Robert Pye's* relation of the cause of Hampden's death."

The following is Sir Robert Pye's account of Hampden's death:—"That in the action of Chalgrove Field, his pistol burst, and shattered his hand in a terrible manner. He, however, rode off and got to his quarters, but finding the wound mortal, he sent for Sir Robert Pye, then a Colonel in the Parliamentary army, and who had married his eldest daughter, and told him that he looked on him in some degree accessory to his death, as the pistols were a present from him. Sir Robert assured him that he bought them in Paris of an eminent maker, and had proved them himself. It appeared on examining the other pistol, that it was loaded to the muzzle with several supernumerary charges, owing to the carelessness of a servant who was ordered to see that the pistols were loaded every morning, which he did, but without drawing the former charge."

* In the case of the removal of the late Earl of Crawford's remains a chief delinquent, when detected and convicted, was sentenced to five years' penal servitude.

† The Author formerly possessed a portrait of Hampden, with flowing hair and in armour—now belonging to G. J. R. Gordon of Ellon Castle in Aberdeenshire, Esq. It is said to be extremely like that at Hampden House, here referred to.

which hung on the best staircase appeared to be looking at me; and I immediately recognized the face and the figure of the man I had seen in the grave at Hampden Church. The sight I shall never forget as long as I live. On the arrival of my late employer, Lord Buckinghamshire, from France, I told him the impression on my mind that the portrait on the staircase must be that of the patriot Hampden. He immediately gave me orders to have it taken down and examined; and, on removing a piece of old canvas, we found the patriot's name written on the canvas of the painting in a very legible hand thus—'*John Hampden 1640, A Present to Sr William Russel, and afterwards given to John, Lord Russel.*' "

The actual state of affairs at Thame during the period immediately following this event will be better realized by quotations from the writings* of those who knew it by personal experience, than by any disquisitions of the author. A striking incident; a graphically-described event; the record of some grave inconvenience or gross injustice, impresses the memory and illustrates History. Both Dr. Bruno Ryves† and Anthony à Wood owned unusual facilities for actual observation and accurate knowledge. The former, a warm supporter of Authority in Church and State, and a dutiful subject and servant of King Charles, was subsequently Rector of the adjacent Parish of Haseley from 1661 to 1667: the latter a boy at school at Thame. Their respective narratives are here quoted as written:—

[A.D. 1644.] "While A. Wood and his brother Christopher continued at Thame, you cannot imagine, what great disturbances they suffer'd by the soldiers of both parties, sometimes by the parliament soldiers of Aylesbury, sometimes by the King's from Borstall house, and sometimes from the King's at Oxon, and at Wallingford. The chiefest disturbances and affrightments, that they and the family, wherein they lived, endured, were these:—

"On the 27 of January, being Munday, An. 1644. Colonel Tho. Blagge, governour of Wallingford-castle, roving about the country very early with a troop of stout horsmen, consisting of 70 or 80 at most, met with a partie of parliamentairs or rebells, of at least 200, at Long Crendon, about a mile northward from Thame: which 200 belong'd to the Garrison of Aylesburie, and being headed by a Scot, called Colonel Crafford, who, as I think, was Governour of the Garrison there, they pretended, that they were looking out quarters for them. I say, that Col. Blagge and his partie, meeting with these Rebells at Long Crendon, fought with, and made them run, till his men following them too eager were overpower'd with multitudes, that afterwards came in to their assistance, (almost treble his number) at which time he himself with his stout Captaine —— Walter (they two only) fought against a great many of the Rebells for a long while together; in which encounter the brave Colonel behaved himself as manfully with his sword, as ever man did, slashing and beating so many fresh Rebells with such courage and dexterity, that he would not stirr, till he had brought off all his owne men, whereof the rebells kill'd but two (not a man more) tho' they took sixteen, who stayed too long behind. Captain Walter had six rebells upon him, and, according to his custome, fought it out so gallantly, that he brought himself off with his colonel, and came home safe to Wallingford with all their men, except 18. Col. Blagge was cut over the face, and had some other hurts, but not dangerous.

"After the action was concluded at Crendon, and Blagge and his men forced to fly homeward, they took part of Thame in their way. And A. W. and his fellow-sojourners being all then at dinner in the parlour with some strangers there, of whome their master Burt and his wife were of the number, they were all alarum'd with their approach: and by that time they could run out of the house into the backside, to look over the pale that parts it from the common road, they saw a great number of horsemen posting towards Thame over Crendon bridge, about a stone's cast from their house (being the out and only house on that road, before you come into Thame) and in the head of them was Blagge with a bloody face, and his party with Capt. Walter following him. The number, as was then guessed by A. W. and those of the family, was 50 or more, and they all rode under the said pale and close by the house. They did not ride in order, but each made shift to be foremost; and one of them riding upon a shelving ground, opposite to the dore, his horse slip'd, fell upon one side, and threw the rider (a lusty man) in A. Wood's sight. Colonel Crafford, who was well hors'd and at a pretty distance before his men in pursuite, held a pistol to him; but the trooper crying quarter, the rebells came up, rifled him, and took him and his horse away with them. Crafford rode on without touching him, and ever or anon he would be discharging his pistol at some of the fag-end of Blagg's horse, who rode thro' the west end of Thame, called Priest-end, leading towards Ricot.

"Whether Crafford and his men followed them beyond Thame in truth I cannot now tell: but I think they did not,

---

* *The Diarie of the Life of Anthony à Wood, Historiographer and Antiquarie of the Most famous Universitie of Oxford. In which are intermix'd severall Memorials relating to his neare Allies, Kindred and others; as also certaine publick Actions of His time, which may be useful hereafter to Historians.*

In addition to Anthony, several members of the gentle family of à Wood of Oxford—sprung out of Lancashire—were educated at Thame School, under the care of their kinsman, Thomas Henant the Vicar. Amongst others, John, Thomas, Robert, and Christopher. The author quoted in the text above was that laborious and accomplished compiler of the *Athenæ Oxonienses*, who has given in his *Life* so many interesting particulars of his own family and contemporaries—and in his great work has gathered so much valuable information relating to the distinguished authors and churchmen of the university.

† Dr. Ryves records a successful skirmish in the following sentences:—[A.D. 1643.] "*July the 1st* The Earl of *Essex* being with his Army at *Tame* in *Oxfordshire*, sent Colonel *Middleton* with 500 horse and Dragoons to *Padbury* to waylay Prince *Rupert* and his Forces from returning from *Buckingham* to *Oxford*, while *Essex* with his Army fell on the Prince, but *Sir Charles Lucas* by his Scouts discovered the Rebels' design, and accordingly met them with three troops of his own Regiment wherewith he routed all *Middleton's* 400 horse and Dragoons, pursued them to their pass at *Worthillbrook*, followed them through the foard (in despight of all their Musquettiers there), slew above 100, took 40 Prisoners, and prevented the Rebels' hopeful design."—*Mercurius Belgicus—Memorable Occurrences in* 1643. London: 1685.

but went into the towne, and refreshed themselves, and so went to Aylesbury."*

Fourteen months afterwards, a vigorous skirmish is thus graphically described :—

[A.D. 1645.] "The next great disturbance, whereby A. W. and his fellow sojournours were alarum'd at Thame, was this :—In the latter end of Apr. 1645, a famous Buckinghamshire commander, called capt. —— Phips the ragman, was in Thame with 20 horse and dragoons, to guard their committee for the excise (the chief of which committee were Goodman Heywood and Goodman the butcher his servant) and tarrying there two dayes or more, Sr Will. Campion, governour of Borstall house, having received notice of them, sent out his captaine lievetenant, called capt. —— Bunce, with a partie of 20 horse, who instantly marching thither over Grendon Bridg, as it seems, and so by the Vicaridge House, drove them thro the towne of Thame. Whereupon Phips and his committee flying pretty fast, till they came to the bridg below Thame mill (which is eastward and a little by north about a stone's-cast from the vicar's house) they faced about, hoping to make good the bridg with their dragoons. But this valiant captaine Bunce, after he had receiv'd a volley from Phips and his partie (which touched only one common soldier slightlie) charged over the bridg, and with his pistols shot one of them dead, and beat them off the bridg, so as they all ran away, but lost just half their number; for besides him that was killed, there were nine taken, whereof two were Cap. Phips himself and his lievtenant, ten only escaping, most of which had marks bestowed on them."

Five months afterwards the following skirmish likewise took place :—

"Another great alarme to the juvenile muses in the Vicaridge House, particularly to A. W., was this. Colonel Rich. Greaves, a most confiding presbyterian, laying couchant for a considerable time in Thame with a great partie of horse (upon what account I can not tell) in the beginning of Sep. 1645, it was knowne among the chief officers in Oxon. Whereupon Col. Will. Legge the governour thereof, resolving to beat up him and his partie, he sent 400 horse from Oxon. commanded by Col. David Walter (high-sheriff of the countie) and Col. Rob. Legge the governour's brother. These, with 60 musquetiers of the governour's regiment (commanded by Captaine —— Burgh) marched forth from Oxon. in the afternoon of Saturday Sept. 6, and before they came to Thame, they divided into two bodies, the van headed by Col. Walter and the reer by Col. R. Legge. They found the towne very strongly barricaded at every avenue: notwithstanding which, Major —— Medcalf (maj. to col. Rob. Legge) charged the rebells' guards, so as Maj. Medcalfe with 7 troopers leapt from their horses, and removing the carts opened the avenue. This done, the two gallant Majors charged the rebells up thro the street, doing execution at the way to the Marketplace, where Col. Greaves himself stood with about 200 horse drawn up; but Col. Walter being ready with the other troops (viz. his owne, that of Col. Tooker and that of Major Trist) gave the rebels such a charg, as made them fly out of the towne; and after pursuing the fugitive rebels, drove them above half a mile from Thame. In the meane while Col. Legge, who with the reere guarded the towne and avenews, least other of the rebells (being in all 800) should break in and desert the whole, now drew into the towne, that others might have secure time to search houses and stables. Orders were given, and 'twas done accordingly. After which they all drew out of the towne, and marched away with their horses and prisoners.*

"Before they had gone two miles, at least 200 rebels were got in their reere, but then col. Legge charged them so gallantly, that the rebels ran back, much faster than they came on. Yet farr had they not gone, before these vexed rebels came on againe, and then also col. Legge beat them so farr back, that they never attempted to come on againe. In this last charge that most hopeful yong gentleman capt. Hen. Gardiner (son of Sr Tho. Gardiner, his majestie's sollicitor gen.) was unfortunately shot dead; a youth of such high incomparable courage, mix'd with such abundance of modesty and sweetness, that wee cannot easily match him unless with his brave brother, yong Sr Thomas Gardiner, which two are now buried both in one grave in the cathedral of Christ Church in Oxon. whether they were brought with much universal sorrow and affection.

"Besides this gallant gentleman, no officer was killed, only 3 common soldiers, nor scarce any hurt, only Maj. Medcalfe shot in the arme. The rebels dropt plentifully in the streets and in the fields, and Col. Greaves escaped very narrowly, being run into the body, and at first thought to have been slaine. The rebells being thus beaten, his Majestie's forces brought away those prisoners they had taken, which, besides common troopers, were 27 officers: among whome were their adjutant-general —— Puide, their provost-general marshall (or prov. marshal general) and their chief engineer, four captaines, as capt. Hanson, Joh. Thornhill, James the elder &c., seven lievtenants, viz. Wilmot, Hughes, Bagnall, Lampert, Canoe, Wilson, Crompton, and three cornets, Bradshaw, Brooks and Symons. There were also taken 13 sergeants, quartermasters and corporalls, and a great deal of money was found in the rebels' pockets (having lately received advance-money). Many armes also were taken, and between two and three hundred good horse, besides three colours, two whereof had mottos. The one was, *Non Rros Res*, and the other was, *Patria poscente paratus*.

"This alarm and onset was made by the Cavaliers from Oxon. about break of day on Sunday morning Sept. 7 before any of the rebels were stirring. But by the alarm taken from the sentinel, that stood at that end of the towne leading to Oxon. many of them came out of their beds into the marketplace without their doublets; whereof adj. gen. Puide was one, who fought in his shirt. Some that were quarter'd near the church as in Vincent Berry's house between it and the School, and those in the Vicar's house

* *Life of Anthony à Wood, etc., in loco.*

* Dr. Bruno Ryves gives the following brief independent account of this skirmish :—"*Sept. 6th.* His Majesties Forces From *Oxford* beat up the Rebels Quarters at *Tame*, kill'd divers, took Prisoners Adjutant General *Puide*, with divers other Officers and common Soldiers. They also took 3 Colours and above 200 Horse, and this done with the loss only of Captain *Gardiner* a gallant young Gentleman, and some few more on His Majesties part."—*Mercurius Belgicus—Memorable Occurrences in 1645.* London: 1685.

(where A. W. then sojourn'd) fled into the Church (some with their horses also) and going to the top of the tower, would be peeping thence to see the cavaliers run into the houses, where they quarter'd, to fetch away their goods.

"There were about 6 of the parliament soldiers (troopers) that quarter'd in the Vicar's House, and one being slow and careless, was airing and warming his boots, while they were fighting in the Towne: and no sooner he was withdrawne, into the garden I think, but some of the Cavaliers, who were retiring with their spoyle towards Borstall (for they had separated themselves from those that went to Oxon.) ran into the Vicar's House, and seized on cloaks and goods of the rebels, while some of the said rebels (who had lock'd themselves up in the church) were beholding out of the ch. windows what they were doing.

"On the day before (Saturday) some of the said rebels, that lodg'd in the said house, had been progging for venison in Thame Park I think, and one or two pasties of it were made, and newly put into the oven before the Cavaliers entered into the house. But so it was, that none of the said rebels were left at eleven of the clock to eat the said pasties, so their share fell among the school-boyes, that were sojournours in the said house.

"As for the beforemention'd Adj.-Gen. Puid, he had leave within 3 days after he was brought to Oxon. to depart upon his parol; yet wanted the civility, either to returne himself, or to release the gentleman, (or any other) that he had promised in exchange for him. Such, and no better, is the faith and humanity of the Rebels.

"Besides these, were other alarms and skirmishes, which being frequent and of little concern, yet much to the school-boyes, who were interrupted thereby, I shall forbeare the recital of them. They had also several times troopers from Borstal, who would watch and be upon the guard in the Vicaridge House (the out-house northward from Thame, as I have before told you) and continue there a whole night together, while some of their partie were upon London road neare Thame, to lay in wait for provision or wine that came from London towards Aylesbury, or to any persons thereabouts that took part with the Rebells. Some of these Troopers would discourse with the school-boyes, that lived in the house (being of the number of six, or sometimes more) while they were making their exercise in the Hall against the next day. Some of them A. W. found to have grammar learning in them, as by the questions they proposed to the boys; and others having been, or lived, in Oxon. knew the relations of A. W. which would make them shew kindness to him and his brother. But that which A. W. observ'd, was, that the Vicar and his wife were alwaies more kind to the Parl. Soldiers or Rebells, than to the Cavaliers, as his master W. Burt* and his wife were, having been alwaies acquainted with and obliged to the families of the Ingoldesbies and Hamdens in Buckinghamshire, and other puritanical and factious families in the said countie; who, while yong, had been mostly bred in the said school of Thame, and had sojourned either with the Vicar or Master: but as for the usher Dav. Thomas, a proper stout Welshman, A. W. alwaies took him to be a good loyalist, as indeed he was.

"Wednesday Jun. 10, the garrison of Borstall was surrendered for the use of the parliament. The school-boys were allowed by their Master a free libertie that day, and many of them went thither (4 miles distant) about 8 or 9 of the clock in the morning to see the form of surrender, the strength of the garrison, and the soldiers of each partie. They, and particularly A. W., had instructions given to them before they went, that not one of them should either tast any liquor, or eat any provision in the garrison; and the reason was, for feare the royal partie, who were to march out thence, should mix poyson among the liquor or provision that they should leave there. But as A. W. remembered, he could not get into the garrison, but stood, as hundreds did, without the works, where he saw the governour S[r] Will. Campion, a little man, who upon some occasion or other layd flat on the ground on his belly, to write a letter, or bill, or form of a pass, or some such thing."

Dr. Bruno Ryves, in his valuable publication issued in the Monarch's interest, put on record the following additional particulars. Some of his details, having reference to the immediate locality and the sufferings of certain persons, are extremely interesting:—

"While the Rebels' Army lay at *Tame* sending out parties, by chance they lighted on some of the Kings Souldiers, and amongst them there was one, who touched in Conscience for so grievous a Sin as lifting up his hand against his lawful Sovereign, 'the Lord's Anointed,' forsook the Rebels' Army, and was entertained in his Majestie's pay: and being in their power, they resolve instantly to hang him: but with such Circumstances as in the murther of the Subject they evidently manifest their malitious rebellious hearts towards their Sovereign. Nothing will serve to hang him on, but the sign-post of the *Kings Head* in *Tame*;* the poor man being ready to be thrown from the Ladder, prayed very fervently, and cried out *Lord Jesus receive my Soul.* The Rebels standing about him, instead of joyning with him in his Devotions, made a confused noise, and laughed at him. They that had so little mercy for his Soul, were not likely to draw out any bowels of Compassion towards his body. No, they will not only murther him, but murther him by lingering Torment; they will not afford him the favour of a running knot quickly to obstruct the Throat, and totally deprive him of breath, but the halter is tyed so fast, that he hanged gasping for breath, not drawing so much as to maintain life, nor so little as suddenly to lose it: having in this torment hanged a while, a barbarous inhuman Villain stept to him, and fearing he should give up his vexed Ghost too soon, he puts his hands under his feet and lifted him up to give some scope of Respiration, but even in this unchristian usage of a poor wretch, he did not forget to *Blaspheme* his *Lord* and *King*: for having lifted him up, he turned the dying man's face towards the sign it self of the Kings Head, and jeeringly said, *Nay, Sir you must speak one word with the King before you go, you are*

* Dr. Burte, like many others, lived to find out his mistake. The utter ruin into which the Country was brought by the overthrow of all lawful authority, in due course brought the infatuated Nation to its senses. But not until Misery and Suffering had devastated the land, and thoroughly sickened the populace of their Puritan masters.

* The old King's Head, as will be seen from the sketch provided, is extremely little altered from the appearance it no doubt bore when the Cavalier in question was so inhumanly hung from its sign-post. Its more ancient parts are no doubt of the age of Henry VII.

blindfold, and he cannot see, and by and by you shall both come down together! Let the World if it can now give us a parallel of so undutiful, so high a contempt of Regal Authority; or tell us whether any of the several Spawns of Hell but only an Atheistical Puritan could possibly commit such devilish Cruelties against his fellow Subject, or belch out such venome against his Sovereign. Amongst those many Sins which call for our publick humiliation and our earnest zeal to purge the land from the guilt which hath polluted it, certainly Contempt and Scorn of so good, so gracious a King is none of the least."*

And the following is worthy of being reproduced, for it shews the hardships† which even the admirers of Rebellion and its votaries had eventually to endure :—

"There is one *Beale* dwelling at *Haseley* (as I take it) in *Oxfordshire*: a Man much devoted to the Proceedings of the two Houses of Parliament, yet it was his chance to fall into their hands who *weaken the wicked*: some of the Rebels under the command of the Earl of Essex, Plundered him of two Horses: upon complaint made unto the Earl, he gives *Beale* command to attend him at *Tame*, and there he should have them again: according to the directions given him by the Earl (accompanied by his *Brother*) he comes to *Tame*, hoping to have his Horses restored; being come thither, Beale is apprehended and committed to Prison; and his Horse, together with that which his Brother rode on, are both seized for the Earls use; nor can either Man or Horse be released, unless he will pay down twenty pound in ready mony. Having continued in Prison four days, at last his Mother (for fear if she rode she might have been Prisoner for her Horses' sake, as her Son was) comes to *Tame* on foot, and brings twenty pound with her to redeem her Son out of Prison; upon receipt of the Money, being a Debt so justly due and so truly paid, his Excellency released him out of his Imprisonment, and restored him the two worst Horses of the four, and wisely kept the two best for himself, which, with a very little help, may serve to explain the mystery of his *Motto*, Cave adsum, i.e., *Where I come, look well to your Money and Horses*."‡

♣♣♣♣♣♣♣♣♣♣♣

THE following Accounts, relating to lands and "Town stock," serve to shew both the value of the properties leased or let to the chief people of the Town, in the early part of the seventeenth century, as well as the amounts received from others, to whom the said "stock" had been lent :—

June 1609.—Grounds behinde at Midsommer next :—

	s.	d.
Sr Wm Clark 2 quarters	v	
Mr Yorke	vj	
Mr Pawlin	iiij	vj
Mr Simeons	xviij	
Walter Lake for Hall cope	ij	
Jo. Hester for Bishops lease	xij	
Jo. Bigg & Augn Striblehill	ix	

The Towne stocke remayning in these meanes hands hereunder written the xjth of Maye 1609 :—

	li.	s.	d.
Augustian Striplinge	xij	x	
Cowsellous Cawden		xliiij	
Wm Heabourne in yt churchwardenns hands	x	x	
Mr Pinnock		xxxviij	vj
Walter Jemott	v	x	
Mr Trender		xliiij	
For the use of Walter Jemots five pounds received		x	
It'm for the use of vli yt Wm Springall recd		x	
For the use of Mr Pynnocks monie		iij	vj
For the use of Cornelis his monie yt he hath of the pore		iiij	
In the hands of Peter Willmot		xx	

To the above is attached the following with other signatures :—

Mich. Dormer

(Autograph of Michael Dormer of Thame.)

Here follow Pedigrees of Ballowe and Beke of Thame. Of the former family there were representatives in Thame as early as the reign of Henry IV. (See p. 298.) From the latter Tradition maintains that Thomas Beck, consecrated Bishop of Lincoln 7 July, 1342, at Avignon, by Pope Clement VI. (Pierre de Roger), was of the Family of Beke or Beck of Berkshire and Thame.

* *Mercurius Rusticus, etc.*, pp. 129, 130. London: 1685.

† A considerable number of the local Puritans helped themselves to the lands, goods, and chattels of their Royalist neighbours, as the following document abundantly shews :—"The members of the Committee for the County of Buckingham had often been changed, and still the succeeding ones continued to heap up vast estates for themselves out of the sequestered estates in this county; nor could any of them ever be brought to account for the great sums of money received by them, none of which was ever returned for the use of the State." The above is a "Note" appended to a Letter, signed "Simon Mayne, F. Fleetwood, C. Fenn, Chr. Egleton, Hen. Beke; John Deverill, *Trevor*"; dated Aylesbury 21 Sep. 1648, declining to give information, and implying that there were no proceeds in hand.—Add. MSS., Brit. Museum, 5490-2.

‡ *Mercurius Rusticus, etc.*, p. 91. London: 1685.

Pedigree of Ballowe of Thame in alliance with Beke of Haddenham, Co. Bucks.

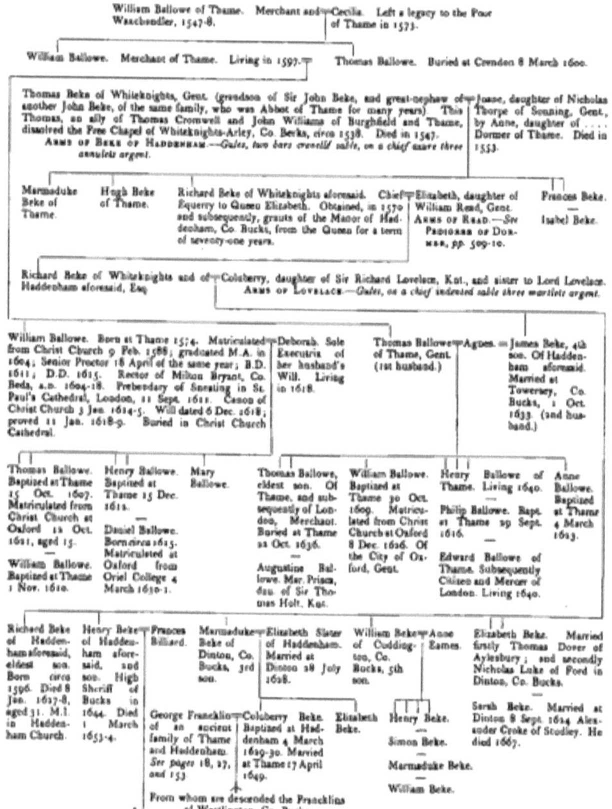

Lavinia, youngest daughter of Roger Whitstone of Whittlesea in the Isle of Ely, by Catherine, daughter of Robert Cromwell, and sister of the Regicide. Married at White Hall. Died without issue soon afterwards, 7 Feb. 1655. (1st wife.) = Richard Beke of Haddenham aforesaid. Baptized there 8 Sept. 1630. M.P. for Peterborough. Major in one of the Rebel Regiments. Knighted by Richard Cromwell 6 Dec. 1658. Obtained a Pardon from Charles II. 2 Jan. 1660-1. Died at Dinton, intestate, aged 78, 29 Nov. 1707. Buried there 2 Dec. of the same year. = Elizabeth, youngest daughter of Sir Thomas Lee of Hartwell, Co. Bucks, Bart., K.B. Baptized at Hartwell 28 July 1662. Died a widow 30 May 1737. Buried at Dinton. (2nd wife.)

Anne Beke. Elizabeth Beke. Mary Beke.

Three coheiresses.

NOTE TO THE FOREGOING PEDIGREE.

EXTRACTS FROM THE DONATION REGISTER OF THE BODLEIAN LIBRARY.

Don'i Gvil' Ballow Academiæ Procuratoris.

Anno MDCIII., vol. i., pages 91-2.—Augustin' de non iurando, fo. MS. De trib. hostibus ho'ium impugna'tib'. De verbis Domini & Apostoli. Ad fratres in Eremo. Epistola ad Julianu' Comitem. De igne purgatorij. De 10 plagis et de 10 preceptis. De gaudio & supplicio damnatoru'. Stimulus conscientiæ. Sermo Aug. de tremendo Judicio. De ebrietate. De fuga mulierum. Sermo ad parochianos. Epistolæ variæ Hieronymi ad diversos. Notabilia excerpta de epistolis Hieronymi. Aug. de perfectione iustitiæ. De vita Christiana. Eiusdem meditationes de dilectione Dei. De decimis reddendis. Expositio S. Bernardi super Magnificat. Sermo de laude B. Mariæ. Distinctiones bonæ per Alphabetum. Aug. sup' Gen. ad literam, fo. MS. Boetius de hebdomadib'. Aug. de Trinitate. De vera religione. De libero arbitrio. De natura boni. De natura et gratia. Liber retractationu'. De presentia Dei ad Dardanum. De fide ad Petrum. De predestinatione. De gratia & libero arbitrio. Ad inquisitiones Januarij. De fide & symbolo. Sermo ad iuvenes. De cura gerenda pro mortuis. De moribus Ecclesiæ et Manichæorum. Hypognost. Contra Epistola' Manichæi. De mendacio. Contra mendacium. De duabus animab'. De videndo Deo'. Ad Macedonium. Soliloq. De assumptione B. Virginis. Ep. ad Volusian'. De virginit'. Sermo Ambrosij de assumptione. Sermones in monte. De adulterinis coniugijs. De utilitate credendi. De natura & origine animæ. De oper' Monachorum.

Sermones Aug. diversi, fo. MS.
Epistolæ B. Aug., fo. MS.
Aug. de Civitate Dei, fo. MS.
Secunda quinquagena Aug. in Psalm, fo. MS.
Aug. sup' Epist. Canon Johannis.
Haymo in epistolas Pauli, fo. MS.
Epistolæ B. Bernardi, fo. MS.
Stephanus in expositionem Ecclesiastici, fo. MS.
Cassiodorus in psalterium, fo. MS.
Meldensis distinctiones cum sermonibus de festis. Ars predicandi. Sermones optimi. Odo sup' Euangelia ab Ascensione domini usq' ad Adve'tum, fo. MS.
Will. Wodeford contra Wickleffum, fo. MS.
Historia scholastica P. Comestoris, fo. MS.
Partitiones quæda' Theologicæ ab incerto auctore, 4to MS.

Donum alterum Gvil. Ballow, Procuratoris Academiæ.

Anno MDCV., vol. i., p. 94.—De vita S. Germani, MS. Sulpitius Severus de vita S. Martini. Vitæ et passiones S. Nicolai, St. Clementis, et S. David, MS. fo. Holcot Distinctiones, MS. Pastorale B. Gregorij, MS. Pastorale B. Ambrosij, MS. Anselmi opuscula quædam, MS. Isidorus de summo bono, MS. P. Blesensis super Job, MS. B. Aug. de penitentia, MS. fo.

Quidam Postillator super Job, MS. Hugo de Vienna in lib. Sapientiæ et Cant' Cantic', MS. fo.

Flores super diversos libros Augustini, MS.

♣♣♣♣♣♣♣♣♣♣♣♣

SIR George Croke, educated at Thame Grammar School, was the third son of John Croke, and a Councillor-at-Law, descended from the old race of that name of Thame. His advance in his profession was rapid. In 1575 he was admitted to the Inner Temple, called to the bar during Hilary term of 1584, became a bencher 5 Nov. 1597, was appointed Autumn Reader in 1599 and again in Lent 1618, having in the interim filled the office of Treasurer. The year 1597 witnessed the commencement of his Parliamentary career as Member for Beralston, and King James I. knighted him when he became Serjeant-at-Law and King's Serjeant in June 1623. He purchased in 1615 the estate of Waterstock near Thame from Sir William Cave, and later on, in 1621, Studley Priory from his nephew. On 11 Feb. 1625 he was appointed Justice of the Court of Common Pleas, and was made a Judge of the King's Bench on 9 Oct. 1628. Sir George was one of the Judges who in Hampden's case gave his decision against the Crown, and soon afterwards sent in his resignation to the King and retired to his seat at Waterstock, where he spent the remainder of his life. He died there 16 Feb. 1641-2, in the 82nd year of his age. He married, in 1604, Mary, daughter of Sir

Thomas Bennet, Lord Mayor of London. She died 1 Dec. 1651, leaving one son and three daughters. The son Thomas died without issue. The eldest daughter married Sir Harbottle Grimston, Bart. The second daughter, Elizabeth, was firstly wife of Thomas Lee, Esq., of Hartwell, Co. Bucks, and secondly of Sir Richard Ingoldsby, already referred to. Croke's third daughter, Frances, became the wife of Richard Jervois, Esq. His acts of charity and munificence were numerous. At Studley he erected a Chapel in his mansion-house, and settled £20 a year on a clergyman to minister there. He also founded an Alms' House for four poor men and four poor women, and gave £100 to the Library of Sion College. His property at Waterstock was left to his nephew, Dr. Henry Croke, also educated at Thame School, the son of his brother Henry; whose son, Sir George, dying without male issue, the mansion-house and several farms and tenements there were sold to Sir Henry Ashhurst. The family of Croke was connected by marriage with that of Beke, as already set forth. It was also allied to the Lees and Walpoles of Thame in the sixteenth century; as well as to the Hawtreys of Checquers Court, on the slopes of the Chiltern Hills.

♣♣♣♣♣♣♣♣♣♣♣

THE following Pedigrees will suitably appear here. Although collateral alliances have been omitted, the main stem is set forth, so that enquirers as to details, and the investigators of particular branches of the two noble families in question, may find their labours lightened by studying them :—

Pedigree of Lee and Walpole of Thame.

No. I.

Arms of Lee of Cheshire.—*Argent, a chevron between three leopards' heads erased sable.*

John Lee of Lee in the Parish of Wibunbury, Co. Chester. = Margaret, daughter of Sir Ralph Hocknell.

Henry Lee, 4th son, of Aston, Co. Stafford. Elder brother of Benedict Lee of Quarrendon, Co. Bucks. =

Anthony Lee, 3rd son, of Aston aforesaid. =

Anthony. =

Roger Lee of Aston aforesaid; of Winchcombe, Co. Gloucester; of Panlersbury, Co. Herts; and of Thame, Co. Oxon.[1] Had a grant of the lands of Notley Abbey, Co. Bucks, from Henry VIII. = Eleanor, daughter of John Bull of Madestock and Sheldon, Co. Warwick.

Arms of Lee of Quarrendon, Co. Bucks.—*Argent, a fesse between three crescents sable.*

Henry de Walpole,[2] son and heir of Sir Henry de Walpole, Lord of Houghton. Knight of the Shire 7 Edward III. = Joane.

Henry Walpole of Houghton aforesaid, Esq. Will proved at Norwich 27 of June 1442. (*Test. Vetus.*, p. 243.) = ... daughter of Sir Oliver le Crosse of Crostwick, Co. Norfolk, and of Essex. Died before her husband. Buried at Houghton.

a a

A B

Henry Walpole of Houghton, Esq. = Margaret, daughter of Sir John Harsicke of Southacre, Co. Norfolk, Knt., by Agnes, daughter and coheiress of Sir William Caley of Oby, Knt.

Robert Walpole, 2nd son, of South Eddes, Co. Huntingdon. =

John Walpole of Houghton, son and heir. Died 12 April 9 Henry VII. Inq. post mortem taken at Westacre 24 Oct. 10 Henry VII. = Elizabeth, daughter of Robert Shaa or Shaw of Derby, Esq.

Issue, Walpoles of Houghton of Whaplode, Co. Lincoln, and Walpoles, Earls of Orford.

Arms of Walpole of Thame Park.—*Or, on a fesse between two chevrons sable, three crosses-crosslet of the first.* (See Harleian MSS. No. 1092, fol. 107-8.)

1. Elizabeth Lee, eldest daughter. Married to Hugh Withenhall of Co. Norfolk.

2. Ann Lee,[2] 2nd daughter. Married firstly to John Colley[3] of Edgcott, Co. Bucks; secondly to Robert Marriott; and thirdly to John Robins of Cobcott.

3. Ellen Lee, 3rd daughter.[4] Will dated 21 June 1592; proved as "widow of Thomas Walpole of Thame Park" 1 June 1597. = Thomas Walpole, 2nd son, of Thame Park. Died before 1592. Mentioned in the Will (dated 18 March 1557) of Sir John Williams, Knt.

George Walpole, eldest son, of Thame Park. Churchwarden of Thame in 1603. Sole executor of his mother's Will. =

Henry Walpole, 2nd son. =

Edward Cutler. Deceased before 1592. = Elizabeth Walpole, eldest daughter. Living in 1592.

Thomas Barnard of Co. Essex. = Frances Walpole, 2nd daughter. Living in 1592.

Margaret Walpole, 3rd daughter. Married John Cannon[6] of Thame. Living in 1592.

Dorothy Walpole, 4th daughter. Married Thomas Warrene.

Jane Walpole. Baptized at Thame 1 April 1606.

Francis Walpole.

Elizabeth Walpole.

Joane, daughter of .... Hurst. (1st wife.) = John Lee of Thame,[7] son and heir. Godson of John Williams. Afterwards Knighted. = Anne Croke of Chilton. (2nd wife.)

Richard Lee, 2nd son, of Thame. Born *circa* 1531. Clarencieux King of Arms.[8] Died 23 Sept. 1597. Buried at St. Alphege, London Wall.

William Lee, 3rd son, of Thame. A Captain of the Levies of the County. Churchwarden of Thame in 1554. = Margaret, daughter of Peter Dormer of Thame, Gent.

Anthony Lee, 4th son, of Thame. Scribe and Secretary of Sir John Williams, Knt. Mentioned in his Will.

Richard Lee of Thame. Churchwarden of Thame in 1624. = Anne, daughter of ....

Robert Collingridge or Colridge. = Margaret Lee. Married at Thame 26 April 1606.

Richard Lee. Baptized at Thame 23 Jan. 1622.

Anthony Lee. Baptized at Thame 2 March 1624.

Anne Lee. Baptized at Thame 2 Feb. 1625.

Eleanor Lee. Baptized at Thame 17 Feb. 1628.

Elizabeth Lee. Baptized at Thame 20 Nov. 1634.

SOME EXPLANATORY NOTES OF THE FOREGOING PEDIGREE.

The following Pedigree, which sets forth a few collateral alliances, is extracted from Harl. MS. No. 1486, folio 96 b, a Visitation taken by Robert Glover, *Somerset Herald*, and William Flower, Norroy, in the year 1580; and from Harl. MS. No. 1505, folio 100 (another copy of the same Visitation).

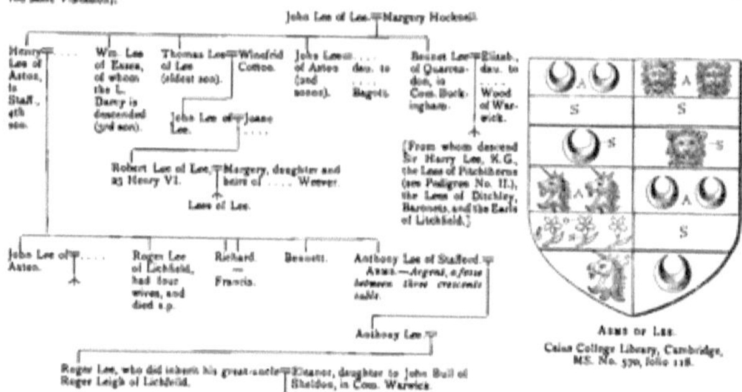

ARMS OF LEE.
Caius College Library, Cambridge, MS. No. 570, folio 118.

¹ King Edward VI. granted to Sir William Paget, father of the Lady of Sir Henry Lee, K.G., his heirs and assigns, the site of Notley Abbey, about 250 acres in Crendon, and the reversion of premises formerly devised by the late King his father in 1542 to Sir John Williams and Roger Lee, gent.—Patent Roll, 1 Edward VI. (Test. 30 May.)

² See the alliances between the Dormers, Hawtreys, and Walpoles recorded in the Pedigree of Dormer, pp. 507–8 of this volume. For the recorded Pedigrees of Walpole, see Harl. MS. No. 1550, folio 83 *b*, and *Papers of the Norfolk Archæological Society*, vol. viii. Printed Visitation, pp. 363-410.

³ "I bequeath to Anne Lee a tablett of golde, with a pommaunder in it."—Will of John Croke the elder, of Chilton, Co. Bucks, made 11 June 1554.

⁴ Amy, eldest daughter of James Chetwode, Esq., of Oakley, Co. Stafford, married Roger Colley of Edgcott.—MS. Pedigree of Chetwode.

⁵ Ellen Walpole of Thame Park, widow of Thomas Walpole of Thame Park, gentleman. Will dated 21 June 1592, proved by George Walpole, eldest son and executor, 1 June 1597. To be buried by my late husband in the Chapel of Thame Park; my son Henry W., my daughter Elizabeth, late the wife of Edward Cutler, deceased. Frances my daughter, now wife of Thomas Barnard of Essex. Margaret my daughter, wife to John Cannon of Thame; my brother Richard Lee; my youngest daughter Dorothy, now wife to Thomas Warren; Francis and Elizabeth Walpole, son and daughter to my son Henry Walpole.—From the Will Office, Somerset House (Cobham, 62).

George Walpull, Churchwarden of Thame in 1603, present at the taking of an Inventory, which he signed, of the goods of Thomas Clarke of Moreton.

William Walpole married Ann, daughter of Henry Croke of Chilton, Co. Bucks.—Lipscombe's *History and Antiquities of Bucks*, vol. i., p. 132.

Agnes, daughter of William Walpole, married (*circa* 1554) William Hawtrey of Chequers.—*Ibid.*, vol. ii., p. 192.

⁶ The Cannons of Thame and Crendon, a family of gentlepeople, occupied a good position hereabouts for some centuries. Memorials of them, both in stone and brass, remain in the Church of Crendon.

⁷ WALPOLE OF THAME PARK.

"Henrie Walpoole maried . . . . . ., daughter to Creset of Essex, and had issue by her,—Henry Walpoole, his sonne and heire, who married Margaret, daughter to Sir Edmund Harsicke of Southacre; and Thomas his second son.

"Henrie Walpoole, sonne and heire of Henrie aforesaid, had issue by Margaret his wife two sonnes,—John, his sonne and heire, who maried Elisabeth, daughter of Robert Shaa of Darbishire, that bore for his arms a chevron between three lozes peasant, and Robert Walpoole, his second sonne, that was of St. Eddes in the Countie of Huntington or Cambridge, which Robert had issue Thomas Walpoole, his second son, of Thame Park, in the Countie of Oxford, who married Ellen, third daughter to Roger Lee, first of Aston in the Countie of Stafford, after of Paulesbury in the Countie of Northampton, and of Eleanor, daughter to John Bull of Madestocke, in the Countie of Leicester vel Warwick; which Roger Lee had issue, three sons and three daughters,—John Lee, his sonne and heire, married two wives, the first was Joane, daughter to Horst *al's* Serst, that beareth three starres; his second wief was . . . . . ., daughter of . . . . .; his second sonne was Richard Lee, the pursuivant of Armes by the name of Porticullis after created Richmond Heraold of Armes A° 1585, and before his death created Clarencieulx King of Armes; William Lee, third sonne; Elizabeth married to Hugh Withenall, and had manie children; Anne, second daughter of Roger Lee, first married to John Colly of Edgcott, secondly to Robt. Marryott, and lastly to John Robins of Cowcott, and had issue by them all three; and Alice, third daughter to Roger Lee, was first married to John Houghton, after to Christopher Winslow, and had issue."—Harl. MSS., Brit. Museum, No. 1092, fol. 107–108.

⁸ "Camden esteemed and admired him: he calls Lee, *vir clarus*. When Porticullis and Richmond he visited, but never for himself. He died 23 September 1597, aged 66, at his residence in Philpot Lane, London. He was buried on the twenty-seventh following at St. Alphege, London Wall. His arms were:—Argent, a fesse between three crescents sable, a fleur-de-lys gules for a difference. This is the same arms as the Lees of Quarrendon, of Buckinghamshire, used, created baronets in 1611 by James I."—*History of the College of Arms*, by Rev. Mark Noble, p. 171. London: 1805.

Pedigree of Lee of Cos. Chester, Bucks, and Oxon.

No. II.

(From the original Vellum Roll in the possession of the Author.)

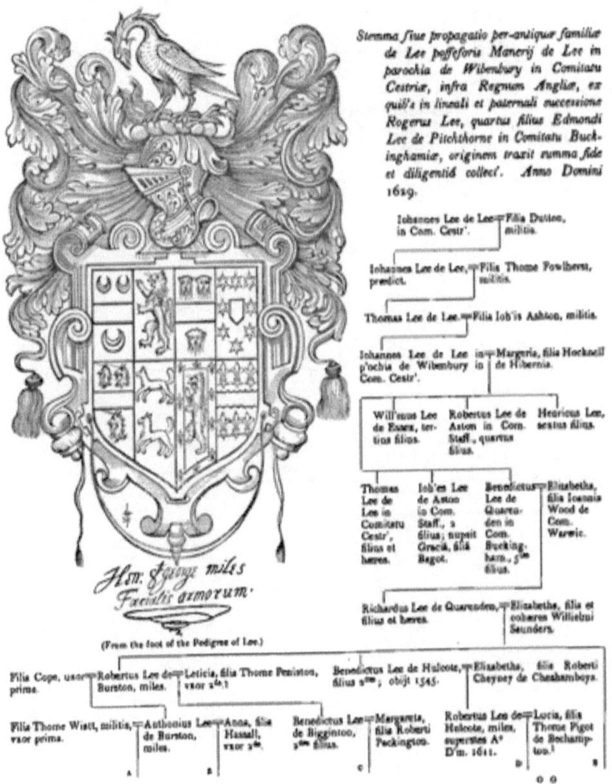

(From the foot of the Pedigree of Lee.)

Stemma siue propagatio per-antiquæ familiæ de Lee possessoris Manerij de Lee in parochia de Wibenbury in Comitatu Cestriæ, infra Regnum Angliæ, ex quib's in lineali et paternali successione Rogerus Lee, quartus filius Edmondi Lee de Pitchthorne in Comitatu Buckinghamiæ, originem traxit summa fide et diligentiâ collect'. Anno Domini 1619.

Iohannes Lee de Lee in Com. Cestr'. = Filia Dutton, militis.

Iohannes Lee de Lee, prædict. = Filia Thome Fowlherst, militis.

Thomas Lee de Lee. = Filia Ioh'is Ashton, militis.

Iohannes Lee de Lee in p'ochia de Wibenbury in Com. Cestr'. = Margeria, filia Hocknell de Hibernia.

Children: Will'mus Lee de Essex, tertius filius. — Robertus Lee de Aston in Com. Staff., quartus filius. — Henricus Lee, sextus filius. — Thomas Lee de Lee in Comitatu Cestr', filius et hæres. — Ioh'es Lee de Aston in Com. Staff., 2 filius; nupsit Graciâ, filiâ Bagot. — Benedictus Lee de Quarenden in Com. Buckingham., 5^tus filius. = Elizabetha, filia Ioannis Wood de Com. Warwic.

Richardus Lee de Quarenden, filius et hæres. = Elizabetha, filia et cohæres Willielmi Saunders.

Filia Cope, uxor prima. = Robertus Lee de Burston, miles. = Leticia, filia Thome Peniston, vxor 2da.[1]

Benedictus Lee de Hulcote, filius 2^dus; obijt 1545. = Elizabetha, filia Roberti Cheyney de Cheshamboys.

Filia Thome Wiatt, militis, vxor prima. = Anthonius Lee de Burston, miles. = Anna, filia Hassall, vxor 2da. A B

Benedictus Lee de Bigginton, 3us filius. = Margareta, filia Roberti Peckington. C

Robertus Lee de Hulcote, miles, superstes A° D'ni. 1611. = Lucia, filia Thome Pigot de Bechampton.[1] D E

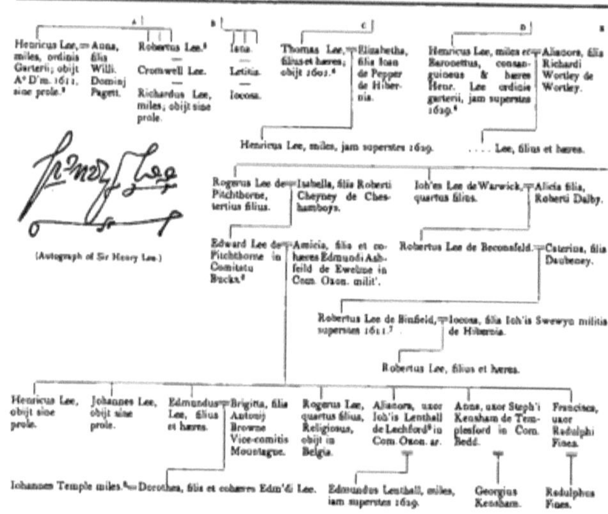

(Autograph of Sir Henry Lee.)

SOME EXPLANATORY NOTES ON THE FOREGOING PEDIGREE.

[1] For the Family of Pigott of Beachampton, Co. Bucks, see fol. 125, Harl. MSS. 5181, 1391, Brit. Museum. Pluto, lvi. D. In these, Robert Lee of Hellcote is styled "Robert Lee of Wedon in Buck."

[2] For arms of Sir Harry Lee, see fol. 118, MS. No. 570, Caius Coll. Library, Cambridge. Also his Garter Plate at St. George's Chapel, Windsor.

[3] For the pedigree and issue of Robert Lee, Esq., of Hatfield, Co. York, brother of Sir Henry Lee, K.G., see p. 177 of Hunter's *South Yorkshire;* also Dugdale's "Visitation of Yorkshire," under heads of "Hungate of Saxton," "Lee of Pinchinthorpe," and "Morton of Spouthouse." Also for arms, Bibl. Lansdn. 865. Pluto, lxxix. D.

[4] As regards Thomas Lee, who married Elizabeth Pepper of Ireland, the Harl. MS. No. 1533, folio 77a, states that he "a Captain, dyed attainted of treason in the rising Rob't Erle of Essex temp. Q. Elizabeth;" and that he had issue "Henry Lee" and "Margarett." This Margaret married Sir Charles Manners, younger brother of Henry Manners, second Earl of Rutland, K.G., by Theodosia, daughter of Sir Thomas Newton, Knt.

[5] For the brothers and sisters, as well as the issue of Sir Henry Lee, first Baronet, see Harl. MS. No. 1533, fol. 78.

[6] For the issue of Lee and Ashfeld, see Harl. MS. 5966, fol. 25.

[7] For the issue of Robert Lee of Binfield, Co. Berks, Esq., and Joyce his wife, see "Visitation of Berks," A.D. 1665.

[8] Sir Peter Temple, eldest son of this John, was of Stowe, Co. Bucks (now the seat of the Duke of Buckingham), and married Eleanor, daughter of Sir Timothy Tyrrell of Oakley, Bucks, who took for her second husband Richard Grenville of Wootton, Esq. Sir Peter Temple was the author of a devout book, *Man's Masterpiece*, 12mo, London, 1658. I possess the Author's own copy, with his MS. corrections and additions for a reprint. It probably came through Mr. Henry Temple of the Irish branch of that family. It also contains portraits of Sir Peter and Lady Temple of extreme rarity. In the corner are the arms of Lee and Temple quartered, impaling those of Tyrrell of Thornton, Co. Bucks.

[9] Lachford is a manor in the parish of Haseley in the county of Oxford, four miles south of Thame. It belonged to the Lenthalls for two hundred years. The mansion is now mainly destroyed, but a portion of it still serves as a farmhouse. See Leland's *Itinerary*, vol. ii., folios 7, 8.

♣♣♣♣♣♣♣♣♣♣♣

SOME account of William Basse, sen., and of his son of the same name, may now be given. A local tradition asserts that the former came from Norfolk with the Walpoles of Thame Park, and settled thereabouts in Elizabeth's reign. It may be that his son, William Basse, jun., was a native of Moreton, and possibly a retainer of Sir Richard Wenman, Knt., afterwards Viscount Wenman in the peerage of Ireland. The father seems afterwards to have been connected with the noble family of Norreys of Rycott; for he addressed some verses to Francis, Lord Norreys and Earl of Berkshire. It is by no means clear, however, when the elder died, or when the younger first flourished, or which poems belong to each. It is certain that the two following were from the pen of the elder Basse:—

Three Pastoral Elegies of Anander, Anetor, and Muridella, in the Library of Winchester College. By William Bas, 4to. London, printed by V. S. for J. B., and are to be sold at his Shop in Fleet Street at the Sign of the Great Turk's Head, 1602.

Sword and Buckler or Serving-Man's Defence, by William Bas, 4to. At London: Was printed for M. L., and are to be sold at his Shop in S. Dunston's church-yard: 1602. This volume is dedicated in five stanzas of six lines each, "To the honest and faithful Brotherhood of True-hearts, all the old and young serving-men of England, health and happiness."

The same man also wrote certain lines *On William Shakespeare, who died in April*, 1616, which appeared in the volume of poems by the latter in 1640, and are reprinted in Malone's and other editions of Shakespeare. (See Malone's Collections in the Bodleian Library at Oxford.)

Mr. J. Payne Collier, who has published one of the MS. volumes of William Basse, jun., courteously wrote to me thus in 1877:—"Probably you have seen what I said of William Basse .... I daresay you have also seen the reprint of his *Great Brittaine's Sunnes-set*, made two or three years ago.* I have an imperfect copy of the original impression; but I have nothing more. It would give me great pleasure to be of use to you; but as I am now in my 89th year, I have not much time to spare; and the edition of Shakespeare, upon which I am daily employed, necessarily occupies much of my attention."

To Mr. Payne Collier's account I am indebted for certain information and criticism, which, almost in his own words, I here reproduce:—

"As stated in my *Bibliographical Account*, etc. (8vo, 1865, vol. i., p. 57), there must have been two writers of poems of the name of William Basse. One of them published two productions in 1602, and the other (whom I take to have been his son) solicited pardon for his 'young Muse' in 1613, when he printed an elegy on the death of Prince Henry, under the title of *Great Brittaine's Sunnes-set*. It is of the latter, who seems to have survived the Civil Wars, and of his MS. poems (long lost* and recently recovered), that I am about to speak. I do not refer to his 'Polyhymnia'†—also existing only in manuscript and well known—but to an entirely different and much superior collection, which has come into the possession of a very liberal and tasteful friend of mine, Mr. F. W. Cosens, who has permitted me to print it in my 'Yellow Series' of tracts in verse and prose of the reigns of Elizabeth and her successor. It is the very manuscript Thomas Warton used one hundred and eight years ago (when he quoted the lines by Bathurst), and of which until now, I believe, nothing has been seen or heard.

"As I have not the book at hand, I do not recollect Warton's reasons for assigning the commendatory poem to Bathurst. It is only subscribed 'R. B.'; and those initials point as well to Richard Brathwayte, who was one of the friends of the younger William Basse, and whose playful and pleasant style of composition it seems to resemble. Izaak Walton appears also to have been acquainted with Basse; and the small folio in my hands, besides bearing out Basse's claim as a 'smooth' versifier, shews a degree of power, originality, and variety hardly to be looked for after Walton's description of the Author's merits. Here we have three distinct productions, carefully prepared for publication, and certainly of a date anterior to 1612, because they are dedicated to Prince Henry, who died in November of that year. Still, they were not transcribed and put together for the press until 1653, when Basse was yet living. He perhaps died soon afterwards.

* *Great Brittaine's Sunnes-set, Bewailed with a shower of Teares.* By William Basse. At Oxford, Printed by Joseph Barnes, 1613. Facsimiled by W. H. Allnutt, Oxford, 1872.

* This MS. was never lost. It belonged to the late Mr. Harry Lupton of Thame, and still has his autograph on the fly-leaf before the title-page. Whether he inherited it from his ancestors in the Town, whether it came to him by bequest from Mr. J. M. Kidman, or whether by gift from Mrs. Martha Maria Smith (daughter of Mr. Richard Talbot, a direct descendant of William Basse), remains uncertain. Anyhow Mr. Lupton gave it, or lent it, for an archæological exhibition (with an old grant of arms of the Lee family, procured from the late Mr. Hollier of Thame, who was not its owner), to a Mr. T. J. Pettigrew, a surgeon of London; from whom the MS. passed to the Rev. Mr. Corser of Stand, near Manchester, and the grant of arms to the father of Mr. W. J. Thoms, sometime Sub-Librarian of the House of Lords. When Mr. Corser's library was sold, Mr. Ellis, a bookseller in Bond Street, purchased Basse's Poems for £29. This MS. now belongs to Mr. F. W. Cosens, F.S.A., of 27 Queen's Gate, who kindly presented me with a special copy of Mr. Payne Collier's reprint of it. The printed book is made up as follows:—Introduction pp. iv. The Pastorals and other Workes of William Basse. Never before imprinted. "*Dat fromdem frondi singula Musa meae*," 1653. Printed at Oxford, etc. Are to be Sold, etc. It contains verses "To Mr. William Basse, upon the now publishing of his Poems;" "Clio, or The First Muse, in 9 Eclogues in honour of 9 Vertues," dedicated "To the right honorable Sr Richard Wenman, K^nt, Baron of Kilmainham, Lord Vis-Count of Tuham, my much honored Lord and Master;" "Urania, the Woman in the Moone, in Foure Cantoes, or Quarters," dedicated "To the honorable, vertuous, and renowned Lady, the Lady Penelope Dynham;" "The Metamorphosis of the Wallnutt-tree of Borestall, in an Eglogue and 3 cantos, between Jasper and Jefferye." It occupies exactly pp. 130.

† *Polyhymnia*, a Poem, Written by William Basse, gent. Original MS., quarto, no date, *circa* 1650.

"At this time the printer and publisher of the volume had not been decided upon, and therefore we read, underneath the above, 'Imprinted at Oxford, etc. Are to be Sold, etc.'

"The first poem, *Clio*, is considerably the longest, and consists of nine pastorals. They were originally intended to be seven, and are named after the days of the week; but Basse added two others afterwards, and inscribed them to nine several 'virtues,' viz., Chaste Love, Gratitude, Contentment, Worthy Memory, Temperance, Patience, Hospitality, Constancy, and Humility. In an introduction he thus mentions Spenser and his *Shepherd's Calendar*:—

"'The famous Shepheard Collin, whom we looke
Never to match (though follow him we may,
That follow sheep and carry scrip and booke),
By just advantage of his time and way,
Has plac'd the Moneths in his eternall booke,
All in their owne due order and array—
A Kalendar to last, we cannot say
For one yeare, but as long as yeares shall be;
Yet of the Weeke has left me every day,
Vertues to sing, though in *more* low degree.'

"So that Basse avowedly starts with Spenser for his model, and in the commencement, as the author of *The Shepherd's Calendar* had called himself by the pastoral name of Collin, Basse assumes that of Collinet, which he preserves till near the end, when, for the purpose chiefly of introducing a marriage song on the union of his patron, Lord Wenman of Thame, he changed it to Jeffrey. It would be almost profane to say that these Pastorals are as good as those of Spenser, but they are certainly equal to those of Basse's contemporaries, Browne, Wither, or Brooke, and they are moreover free from personality, while they pleasantly and easily refer to some of the peculiarities and incidents of the time; they have none of the satirical pungency of Spenser, which compelled him not to own his pastorals in any way after their first publication in 1579. Basse is by no means deficient in harmony, but he sometimes wants strength and vigour in his versification. Like his great prototype, he invariably adds characteristic mottoes in Latin, English, or French at the end of several eclogues. I may here add a passage from the last pastoral, where Basse thus laments the lighter and more youthful productions of his muse:

"'O Hobbinoll! we may not still pursue
The path of youth, nor walke besides the line
That from false joyes should leade us to the true.
I now those wanton virelayes doe *rue*,
The fancyes of my light phantastique dayes,
Wherein to Swaynes and Nymphes more prais than due,
The more I sang I lessen'd mine owne praise,
With olive twine now twisted in my bayes.'

"Such passages as the above we may suppose to have been inserted when the Author had arrived at more mature years than when he wrote the main portion of his pastorals. Nevertheless, it is quite clear that the second part of the volume in my hands was the production of Basse's 'phantastique dayes'; for throughout it is a very lively and agreeable, semi-satirical, classical invention of the elevation of a woman to the skies; who, when she arrived at the court of Jove and Juno, set all the gods and goddesses at odds, the male deities falling in love with her, and the female maddened by jealousy. The consequence was, that Jupiter was obliged to banish the woman to the Moon, where she is still seen—the sex of the supposed occupant of that sphere having been all along mistaken. The leading idea of this production is, of course, not new, but the treatment of it in our language was a considerable novelty; while the versification and some of the expressions may lead to the belief that the poem called 'Britain's Ida,' which was formerly imputed to Spenser, and has usually been inserted among his works, was really by Basse. The whole of his 'Urania' is in six-line stanzas of very easy construction, as may be seen from the following speech of the Fates, when they are urging 'the Cloud-compeller' to drive the woman out of heaven:—

"'Down with the woman, down with her againe
To sinfull earth, as low as she was borne!
Unless thou art dispos'd, great soveraigne,
To make thy glorious realme to men a scorne,
By everlasting jarres and breach of lawes,
Which her proud spirit eternally will cause

If thou wilt needs doe her base world that grace
As to detain her here, then send us thither;
For thou shalt finde that state in cursed case
Where Fates and Women domineer together:
Where we are, Jove, there needs no such as she;
Where she is needs no other destinie.'

"For the facility of the verse, indeed, much of the production might have been written yesterday, and by some of the best living masters of our language, and the thoughts are generally as sprightly as the measure is attractive.

"If the second piece in Mr. Cosens' MS. makes a demand upon the imagination of the poet, the third production makes even a more imperative claim upon the imagination of the reader; it requires him to believe that a raven flies about the country, through Oxfordshire, Berkshire, Surrey, and Kent, to summon all nut-bearing trees to the funeral of an ancient Walnut-tree at Boarstall; and, after all, when they arrive they do not bury their dead friend, but have him cut up by sawyers in order that he may form planks and wainscoting for the pew of Lady Dynham in Boarstall Church. This is not a very happy local invention, but nevertheless the reader is carried merrily onward, and all the trees invited are brought to the appointed place by the Orphean Magic of the Muse's lyre. It is not long, but still rather too long; and although it may have been welcomed by the inmates of Thame Park, the reader of our own time has some reason to complain that his fancy is too severely taxed when he is called upon to believe that an Oak of four centuries' growth moved his unwieldy form, by the aid of a Gravesend barge and turnpike-roads, all the way from near Maidstone to Thame in Oxfordshire. No man but one of considerable ability and poetical talent could have at all reconciled us to the transference or transmigration. However, it gratified those for whom the poem was composed; and as it is very well written, I am sure that it will be thought worth printing with the other and superior productions by the same pen."

♣♣♣♣♣♣♣♣♣♣♣

Pedigree of Herbert of Tythorpe, near Thame.

Arms of Herbert.—*Per pale azure and gules, three lions rampant argent.*

Henry Spiller of Blackfriars, Co. Surrey, Distiller. Purchased in 1619 of the Crown the Manor and Lordship of Kingsey alias Rose Kingsey, commonly called "Tythorpe Farm" and "Rollris, *cum pertinentiis*," etc., and was living in 1620. =

Sir Robert Spiller of Laleham, Co. Middlesex, and of Kingsey aforesaid, Knt. = Elizabeth, daughter of Sir John Dormer of Creadon and Dorton, Knt., and widow of Sir John Dynham, Knt. Carried an Estate at Kingsey to her husband.

Hon. James Herbert, 6th son of Philip, 4th Earl of Pembroke, K.G., 1st Earl of Montgomery, and Chancellor of the University of Oxford, by Susan, his first wife, 3rd daughter and coheiress of Edward Vere, 17th Earl of Oxford. In right of his wife of Kingsey aforesaid. M.P. for Malmesbury. Buried at Thame 13 April 1677. Will dated 2 April 1677, proved 2 May of the same year. = Jane, only daughter and heiress of her father. Married at St. Peter's, Paul's Wharf, London, 3 August 1646. Living in 1677.

Thomas Herbert. Succeeded his father as Lord of Kingsey, etc., but dying without issue was buried at Thame 21 Jan. 1711-2.

James Herbert. Succeeded his brother as Lord of Tythorpe and Kingsey. M.P. for Malmesbury 1685; for Aylesbury 1702. Died in 1709. = Catherine Osborne, 4th daughter of Thomas, 1st Earl of Danby, subsequently created Duke of Leeds, by Bridget, daughter of Montagu Bertie, Earl of Lindsey. Died in 1702. Buried at Chenies, Co. Bucks.
See Pedigree of Bertie, *page* 451-2.

William Herbert. By right of his father's bequest Lord of the Manor of Rumpney, Co. Monmouth.

James Herbert of Tythorpe and Kingsey, son and heir. Sometime M.P. for Queensborough. "Was found drowned in a pond near his seat at Kingsey 27 April 1720." Buried at Thame 4 May following. = Maria, daughter of James Hallest of Edgeware, Co. Middlesex. Married 15 Sept. 1710. Buried at Thame 30 June 1729.

James Herbert, eldest son, of Tythorpe and Kingsey aforesaid. M.P. for Oxford 1739, 1741, and 1747.

Philip Herbert, brother and heir of James of Kingsey. Died 22 July 1759 without issue. Buried at Thame. = Mary, sole daughter and heiress of Edward Butler, D.C.L., President of Magdalen College, M.P. for the University of Oxford.

Hallest Herbert. Buried at Thame 2 April 1719.

Philip, 6th Viscount Wenman. *See* Pedigree of Wenman and Wykeham, *page* 437-8. = Sophia Herbert. Born *circa* 1715. Eventually coheiress with her sister Anne of their father. Died, a widow, 19 July 1787, aged 72.

Katherine Herbert. Buried at Thame 11 July 1718.

Anne Herbert. Born *circa* 1718. Youngest daughter and eventually coheiress with her sister, Viscountess Wenman, of their father. Died 30 Jan. 1810. Left £100 to the Poor of Kingsey.

Jane Herbert. Mentioned in her father's Will as being under age. Living in 1677.

Dormer Herbert. Mentioned in his father's Will, from whom he received a legacy of certain houses in St. Giles's-in-the-Fields, Co. Middlesex.

Colonel Philip Herbert, younger son. Mentioned in his father's Will, from whom he inherited certain rents and emoluments in Co. Bucks, formerly belonging to Sir Philip Palmer, Bart. Died 12 March, buried in Westminster Abbey 18 March 1715-6. = Marianne, daughter of William, Lord Maidstone, by Elizabeth, daughter of Thomas Wyndham of Felbrigg, Co. Norfolk, Esq. Died intestate, aged 47. Buried in Westminster Abbey 2 March 1717-8.

Penelope Herbert. Baptized at St. Margaret's, Westminster, 2 Dec. 1651.

Edward Herbert. Born *circa* 1693. Of Fryers, near Cardiff, Co. Glamorgan. Died at Clapham, Co. Surrey, 18 Sept., buried 24 Sept. 1715, aged 22. (1st husband.) = Elizabeth Herbert, eldest daughter. Buried 9 Nov. 1718 in Westminster Abbey. = James Jeffreys, Esq., of St. James's, Westminster. Marriage Licence dated 14 Oct. 1717. Resident for the King at the Court of the Czar of Muscovy. (2nd husband.)

Robert Garrard of St. Bride's, Fleet Street, Druggist. = Marianne Herbert. Married at St. Bride's, London, 31 March 1718. Died, aged 25, 8 Jan. 1723. Buried 13 Jan. in Westminster Abbey.

Thomas Herbert, only son. Baptized at St. Margaret's, Westminster, 27 Oct. 1713.

♣♣♣♣♣♣♣♣♣♣♣

Pictures in the Mansion-House of Tythorpe.

THE following List of Pictures and Family Portraits of the Herberts and Wykehams at Tythorpe House will suitably succeed the Herbert Pedigree. The List in question is taken from a MS. volume courteously lent to the Author by the present owner of Tythorpe.*

Dining Room:—

Large half-length painting of a Philosopher in his Study reading, by Adrian Ostade, 1668.

Dead Partridges, Pigeons, etc., by Van Alen, 1651–1690.

Cock, Hen, and Chickens, by Van Alen, 1651–1690.

Crayon portrait of Lord Wenman, in blue dress. [The last Viscount.]

Eleven portraits of "The Herbert Family" in one picture, by Sir Godfrey Kneller.

A Race Horse, Groom, etc., by G. Stubbs, 1740–1806.

Chestnut-coloured Horse.

Mrs. Herbert Wykeham, whole-length, on a sofa, terrace scene, by John Linnell, 1819.

Large half-length painting, young Lady with a Guitar and young Gentleman with Music-book (Sir Peter Lely and his wife), by Sir Peter Lely, 1677–1680.

Large half-length portrait of Philip, Earl of Pembroke and Montgomery, when old, in a yellow dress, staff and sword, by Sir Anthony Vandyke.

Half-length portrait of King Charles I., in white coat, sword, stick (old copy), by Old Stone.

Saloon:—

Two Landscapes, with Cattle and Figures. Barker.

Gipsy Girl with Water Pitcher, by Barker, 1806.

Painting on panel, portrait of King Charles I.

Painting on panel, portrait of Queen Henrietta Maria.

Painting on copper, portrait of Mary, Queen of Scotland, in a red dress, worked and jewelled.

Mr. and Mrs. H. Wykeham, two Sons, and an elderly Lady, by John Linnell, 1817.

On copper, Madonna, Our Blessed Saviour, and St. John the Baptist.

Don John of Austria, 1629–1679.

Landscape with Cows, Sheep and Goat. Flemish.

On copper (allegorical), "The Triumph of the Church," by Rubens. Represented by a female seated in a magnificent car drawn by three white horses, holding in her hands a pix containing the consecrated host; two angels are behind her, one of whom holds the train of her robe, the other a mitre over her head; three females (emblems of Justice, Mercy, and Truth) guide the spirited animals, on the nearest one of which is an angel bearing the symbolic keys; three other angels float in air above their heads; two figures personifying Ignorance and Superstition are chained to the car, the wheels of which are passing over the bodies of Envy and Falsehood; numerous other figures contribute to perfect the allegory.

A Boy reading by candle-light, by Rembrandt.

Interior of a mansion with portraits, the Earl of Pembroke receiving King Charles I. and Queen Henrietta Maria.

On copper, an Interior with Lady and Gentleman. Conversation, by Teniers.

Portrait of King Charles I. on horseback, copy after Vandyke.

Old Gipsy Woman with a Pipe, by Barker.

Old Beggarman with Dog, by C. Biedermann, 1809.

Small whole-length portrait of Lord Charles Howard, Earl of Nottingham, installed Knight of the Garter 24th April 1574, and having been appointed by Queen Elizabeth Commander-in-Chief of the Fleet fitted out to oppose the Spanish Armada in 1588, his Lordship had the high honour of preserving the shores of his country inviolable by dispersing and totally destroying that powerful armament. On the 22nd October 1596 Lord Howard was created Earl of Nottingham, after the Accession of James I. (at whose Coronation he officiated as Lord High Steward of England). There is a coat of Arms of Howard, with coronet and a garter at the top, and an anchor on the ground. His Lordship died at the advanced age of 87, 14th December 1624.

Small whole-length portrait of Robert, Earl of Essex, K.G., 1601, in gilt frame; beheaded 25th February 1601, aged 34. [This and the previous picture are archaic and out of drawing, but are curious and interesting contemporary portraits.—F. G. L.]

Portrait of the Earl of Pembroke.

A Pony.

A Pony, larger.

Small Drawing Room:—

On a panel, Lord Wenman (a copy from a crayon drawing). [The last Viscount.]

On a panel, Holy Family and Angels.

Portrait of Jerome Weston, Earl of Portland.

Portrait of Miss Jane Spiller, by Sir Peter Lely.

Portrait of Hester Louisa Trotman, by E. Biedrw, 1809.

Painting on panel of Anne Clifford, Countess of Pembroke, by Cornelius Jansen.

Portrait of W. H. Wykeham, by J. Cotes, R.A., 1769.

Old Lady in velvet head-dress. [Qy., the "Old Countess of Desmond."]

Portrait of William, Earl of Pembroke, by D. Mytens.

Portrait of Sophia Wykeham, by Toffany, 1765–1772.

Portrait of Robert, Earl of Lindsey, in armour, Vandyke.

Portrait of Mary, Queen of Scotland. [Qy.—F. G. L.]

Staircase:—

Portrait of Lord Wenman, with Dog and Bow, by Sir Godfrey Kneller.

Portrait of Lady in pink dress, with white roses, by Sir P. Lely.

Portrait, Boy, fancy mantle, black velvet cap, and white feather, with dog and parrot.

* The Author is not responsible for the accuracy of their description, but puts on record the List as describing one of the most interesting and important in the county.

The Library:—

Portrait of Lord Wenman, in blue dress, with fawn, by Sir Godfrey Kneller.

Large whole-length portrait of Bishop King, last Abbot of Osney and Thame, first Bishop of Oxford. [This picture is obviously not earlier than the middle of the seventeenth century, and almost exactly corresponds with that in stained glass in Oxford Cathedral.—F. G. L.]

Prints:—

Battle of the Boyne.
Lord Howe's Victory.
Death of General Wolfe.
Dead Christ and Mary.
Battle of La Hogue.
Admiral Duncan's Victory.
Penn's Treaty with the Indians.
Moses raising the Brazen Serpent.
Christ healing the Sick.
Landscape after Claude.
Isles L'Archepel, after Vernet.

Fossil Room:—

The Right Hon. and Rev. John Lord Viscount Tracey, D.D., Warden of All Souls' College.
Sir John Aubrey.
Two Siston Court Views.
Bishop King of Thame and Osney.
Miniature on ivory: Rev. Thomas Brougham, Vicar of Kingsey, A.D. 1749–1783.
On an oak panel, The Salutation, by Coypel.

The Gallery round the Hall:—

Large whole-length painting of Herbert Wykeham and wife, by C. Biedermann, 1806.
Philip Herbert, 4th son, afterwards Earl of Pembroke, by Vandyke; half-length.
Lady in black satin dress, by Vandyke; half-length.
Half-length portrait of Lord Charles Herbert, son of Earl of Pembroke, by Vandyke.
Eleven family portraits, by Sir Godfrey Kneller.
William Herbert, 5th son of the Earl of Pembroke; half-length.
John Herbert, 7th son of the Earl of Pembroke; half-length.
Portraits of James Herbert, 6th son of Philip, Earl of Pembroke, and Jane Spiller his lady.

Bedroom (carving over Fireplace):—

Half-length portrait of a Gentleman, blue coat and wig.

Dressing Room (to ditto):—

Half-length portrait of a Lady, in pink robe, with white roses (like one on the Staircase).

The Hall:—

Half-length portrait of a Lady, in blue dress, red mantle, with dog.
Half-length portrait of James Herbert, 6th son of Philip, Earl of Pembroke, by Sir Peter Lely.
Half-length portrait of Jane Spiller, the Lady of James Herbert, Esq., in a blue and white satin dress, by Sir Peter Lely.
Half-length portrait of Philip, Lord Wenman, 1748, in a black and gold coat, a blue and gold waistcoat.
Half-length portrait of Ann Herbert, 1748, in a white satin dress, with a wreath of flowers.
Half-length portrait of a Gentleman in armour, with long hair, and a camp in the distance.
Landscape with figures, Flemish. Ammunition Train attacked by Cavalry, by A. F. Van der Meulin.

Miniatures:—

A small circular portrait of an old Gentleman, in a black dress, wearing a ruff of the time of James I.
Small circular portrait of a Lady, in a black silk dress with ruff to match.
Charles, Earl of Carnarvon.
Charles Bertie, son of Montague, Earl of Lindsey, on ivory.
A Lady, on ivory (long oval shape), taking an arrow out of a quiver.
Portrait, oval, on copper, of a Gentleman, time of Charles I.
Small portrait of a Lady, in black and brown velvet dress, ruff, gold chain, 1572.
Italian coloured drawing in distemper, Venus and Cupids.
Italian coloured drawing in distemper, Diana Sleeping, attended by Cupids.
Rape of the Sabines, on ivory, oval.
Five oval portraits on ivory.
Catherine, Empress of Russia.
Lady Mary Bertie and Lady Wykeham, by Bernard Lens, R.A., 1769.
Five miniatures on ivory.
Prince James Edward Stuart, born 10th June 1688, obt. 12th January 1766, by N. S. A. Belle; a French miniature, 1674–1734, oval.
Miss Herbert, Tythorpe House.
Miss Herbert, to match.
A Lady in a black dress, holding a ring, oval.
A miniature on ivory of Richard Bertie, fifth son of the Hon. James Bertie, second son of James, Earl of Abingdon, by Elizabeth, daughter of George, Lord Willoughby of Param.
A miniature on ivory of a Lady, with blue mantle, holding a cornucopia with flowers.

♣♣♣♣♣♣♣♣♣♣♣

THE Prebendal House, which stood in ruins* for more than a century, *i.e.*, from 1710 to 1835, has been so much altered of late years that little remains of those parts which were erected when the Prebend was first founded about the middle of the thirteenth century.† It was no doubt planned, and the plans carried out, by Lincoln masons. The remaining mouldings and certain carved details are very like much of the ancient work at Lincoln Minster. Parts of Aylesbury Church, and the tower of Ickford Church in the County of Bucks, were no doubt being built at the same time. The buildings generally of the Prebendal House were originally arranged in the form of a quadrangle, the Chapel being placed at the south-east corner, and the Great Hall to the north of the chapel standing north and south. On the southern side large portions of picturesquely-designed thirteenth-century work remain; but many interesting features have been greatly obscured or altered; while some architectural remains of interest, including two large mantel-pieces of freestone,‡ are altogether lost. There still remains a curious first-pointed circular chimney§ in the southern part of the building adjoining the kitchen garden, no doubt of the same age as the chapel. This latter is an extremely good example of a small domestic chapel.‖ Its height is twenty-four feet and a half to the wall-plates,

* Dates differ as to when the buildings first became untenanted, possibly during the Civil Wars. Prior to that period the mansion-house had been inhabited by some of its owner's family—in 1605 by "Mr. Thyne," in 1691 by "J. Thyne," and later by a Mrs. Leaver, "Maystris Thynne's kinswoman."

† Local tradition affirms that Prebendary Adrian de Bardis built the Mansion-house in the fifteenth century. No doubt he practically *rebuilt* and improved it; but of course the older parts, including the chapel, had been erected at least two centuries before he was born.

‡ Drawings of these were taken by Mr. William Twopenny, a skilful draughtsman and architect, about forty years ago.

§ This chimney is extremely like one of the same architectural style at Sherborne Abbey, and another of a similar type remaining at Aydon Castle, Co. Northumberland.

‖ "Some years ago, before the ancient Prebendal-house of Thame, Oxon, was adapted for a modern dwelling-place, the Chapel of that building, in its principal features, remained almost as it had been at the time of the Reformation. In the refectory of the above building there stood a small cupboard, in great probability the ancient tabernacle from the chapel [or possibly that which had been provided for the parish church in Queen Mary's reign, perhaps removed hither for security's sake.—F. G. L.]. Since then this has been lost or destroyed. It was somewhat over a foot in height, rounded at the top, and opened by a panelled door. The moulding had been painted in vermilion and gold, but was much worn and defaced. There was no sacramental device on any part of it, but the symbol of the Holy Trinity inlaid above the door, with the letters A and Ω on either side the device. The material was oak, or some wood very like oak."—*Glossary of Liturgical and Ecclesiastical Terms*, p. 397. London: 1877.

of which ten feet are taken off by an original apartment below—possibly the sacristy—of exactly that height. The floor between the two is of boards on rafters. Above, there are two lancet windows on either side, and below, one on each side with a long lancet window at the west end, now bricked up. The present entrance is by an arched doorway ten feet from the ground, reached by a ladder. Originally the chapel was entered by a direct communication with the now-destroyed apartments of the Prebendary. The chief features of the chapel are the lancet windows, with delicate and beautiful mouldings, arranged in a triplet at the east end. The internal splays are deep, and there are small detached pillars of dark marble polished, with appropriate bases and carved capitals on either side.

The property previously surrendered to the Crown—*i.e.*, "all manors, lands, chantries, glebe-lands, courts, liberties, etc., in Thame, Weston, Tettesworth, Towersey, Sydenham, Priestend, Moreton, Emmington, and elsewhere, in Co. Oxon, being reputed parcell of the said Prebend"—passed from George Heneage, the last Prebendary, to Sir John Thynne and Robert Keilway on 16 Nov. 1547.* Two years afterwards there was a dispute in law between Thynne and Keilway on the one part, and Edward, Duke of Somerset, and Sir John Williams and his lady, on the other part, with regard to the above, it being also claimed by the latter. The capital messuage or mansion-house† was then in the occupation of Robert Coape (Churchwarden in 1556), and this it appears was then legally transferred by the Duke, etc., to Sir John Thynne and his heirs, Henry Holbeach, Bishop of Lincoln, on 16 Feb. 2 Edward VI., confirming the said transfer. It remained with the family of Thynne until the middle of the eighteenth century. In 1610 John, youngest son of the second Sir John Thynne, had it in lieu of an annuity of £100, and probably granted a short lease of it to some member of the Catholic family of Curson of Waterperry. It was surrendered to Sir James Thynne in 1663, and forty years afterwards the Prebendal lands were leased by "Madam Jane Thynne of Egham" to Mr. John Rose of New Thame, and to Mr. Leaver of "Priestend and Moreton Parsonage." The Prebendal mansion-house, sometimes called "the Parsonage," with the Prebend and advowson, were sold by Lord Carteret, brother to Lord Viscount Weymouth, to Mr. John Blackall of Haseley, through whom, with other properties, they passed to Mr. Walter Long of Preshaw, Co. Hants, of whom it was

* See pp. 138-140 of this volume, where an abstract of existing deeds is set forth.

† I believe that Mass was said there during James I.'s reign; as also at Thame Park and at Waterperry; possibly, too, during the early part of the reign of King Charles I.

Old Town Hall, Thame.

Prebendal House, Thame.

Old Grammar School, Thame.

To face pp. 575, 576

subsequently purchased by Miss Wykeham of Thame Park, afterwards Baroness Wenman, who, in turn, sold the House, and about sixteen acres of land adjoining, *circa* 1835, to Mr. Charles Stone of Thame, a retired merchant, brother to a local banker. At that period it had been used for nearly a century and a half as a farm-house, and its appurtenances for farm buildings.* It had fallen into a state of great dilapidation, but the hall, refectory, kitchen, and chapel remained practically intact, though Ruin had done a vast amount of work in general. The old house was then restored under the advice of Mr. H. B. Hodson, and turned into a private residence; the large hall was cut up and separated into sitting and sleeping rooms, the interior being generally rearranged. The gable end of the refectory remained, and still remains covered with ivy; while the chapel, once a granary, subsequently a jockey's sleeping-room, afterwards a place for lumber, is in a state of emptiness and desolation. Mr. Charles Stone soon died, and the property was then purchased by Mr. John Stone, J.P., of the Manor House, Crendon (of another race), who enlarged it, with whose family it still remains.

* A small engraving of the Prebendal House in this state may be found in Skelton's *Antiquities of Oxfordshire*, under the account of Thame. And I myself possess copies of two uniform lithographic views of the same, from drawings by Mr. G. Childs, in size, including the margin, 15 by 11½ inches. They are both lettered thus: "The Prebendal House, Thame, Oxfordshire, founded in the thirteenth century. This building, after remaining upwards of two hundred years subsequent to the Reformation in a dismantled state, appropriated to agricultural purposes, was restored and converted into a private residence, in 1837, by Charles Stone, Esq. (the proprietor), according to the designs and under the superintendence of H. B. Hodson, Architect, published by H. B. Hodson, 13 New Ormond Street, Bedford Row, and may be had at Ackerman and Co., 96 Strand, Weale, 59 High Holborn, and Bradford, at Thame."

♣♣♣♣♣♣♣♣♣♣♣

Pedigree of Warner, Way, and Stone.[1]

Arms of Warner.—*Vert, a cross engrailed or.*

Henry Warner of Thame. (Sprung from a family of that name of Farmingham, Co. Suffolk.) Born *circa* 1680. Attorney-at-Law. Died 17 Feb., buried at Thame 23 Feb. 1750. = Elizabeth. Born *circa* 1680. Eldest daughter of Thomas Hodgkins of Stoke Goldington, Co. Bucks, Gent. (by Sarah his wife, daughter of Thomas and Mary Hooton of the same place). She died 30 May 1733, aged 53, and was buried at Stoke Goldington.

(Autograph of Henry Warner from a Letter.)

Henry Warner of Thame aforesaid, and of Towersey, Co. Bucks, Gent. Born 1710. Died 5 June 1746, aged 36. Buried at Thame. = Esther, daughter of Thomas Newell of Postcombe, Co. Oxon.[2] Married at Thame 5 Jan. 1739-40. Died 19 Feb. 1765, aged 58. Buried at Thame.

Thomas Warner. Born 1713. Died unmarried 20 Dec. 1734, aged 21. Buried at Thame.

Sarah Warner. Born 1712. Died unmarried 27 Nov. 1771, aged 59.

James, son of James Way of Thame, Gent. Born 26 Feb. 1747-8. Attorney-at-Law. Died 18 Sept. 1791. He was younger brother of Richard Way of Thame, Gent., and Coroner for the County of Oxon.[3] = Sarah Warner, only child and heiress. Born 16 July 1746. Married by Licence at Thame 27 July 1768. Died 9 Sept. 1825.

1. James Warner Way. Born 1 June 1769. Died 2 Sept., and buried at Thame 4 Sept. of the same year.

2. Henry Warner Way. Born 11 Jan. 1774. Died 26, and buried at Thame 31 March of the same year.

1. Sarah Way. Born 27 May 1770. Died 29 Feb. 1849, aged 79. Bur. at Thame.

Abraham Favenc of Throgmorton Street, London, Merchant. = 2. Charlotte Way. Born 18 July 1771. Died 22 Dec., and buried at Thame 27 Dec. 1823.

1. Abraham Favenc. Born 11, died 14 Oct. 1793.

2. John Favenc. Born 9, died 10 Oct. 1794.

Both buried in a small vault between two windows in the Churchyard of St. Bartholomew the Less, behind the Royal Exchange.

3. James Way. Born 6 Feb. 1775. Matriculated from Pembroke College, Oxon, 2 November 1792.[4] Graduated B.A. 26 May 1796; M.A. 9 May 1799. Rector of Adwell, Co. Oxon, 1802, and for sometime Curate in charge of Lapworth, Co. Warwick. Died 11, buried 20 Nov. 1816 at Lapworth. = Elizabeth Garrett Ross Crosbie. Born 10 Oct. 1777. Sole surviving daughter of John Crosbie of the Island of Antigua, Merchant. "Descended out of the King's County, and kinsman of the Earls of Glandore, in the Kingdom of Ireland." Married 10 Oct. 1805 at Queen's Square Chapel, Bath. Died 16, buried 23 May 1810, at Lapworth.

Arms of Crosbie.—*Argent, a lion rampant sable, in chief two dexter hands couped and erect gules.*

4. Warner Way. Born 14 Sept. 1777. Died at the Hot Wells, Bristol, 25 Oct. 1786. Buried at Thame.

A

a

Ralph Stone of the Manor House, Crendon, Co. Bucks, yeoman. Born *circa* 1672. Died 25 Sept. 1758, aged 86. Buried at Crendon. M.I. in the Chancel. = Eliza Margaretta, born *circa* 1685, 4th daughter of John Davies, M.A., Rector of Saunderton, Co. Bucks, by presentation of Charles Dormer. She died 26 May 1751, aged 66. Buried at Crendon. M.I. in the Chancel.

Ralph Stone of Crendon aforesaid, Gent. Born *circa* 1717. Died 18 August 1776, aged 59. Buried at Crendon. M.I. in the Chancel. = Anne, born *circa* 1733, daughter of Mr. Hicks of Stinchcombe, Co. Gloucester. Died 15 Jan. 1818, aged 85. Buried at Crendon. M.I.

William Stone of Crendon aforesaid, Gent. Born *circa* 1754. Died 21 Feb. 1824, aged 70. Buried at Crendon. = Anne, born *circa* 1757, daughter of William Smith of Dorton, Co. Bucks, yeoman, by Jane,[8] born 1734, daughter of Mr. Quartermain of Thame (which Jane married secondly Mr. Hedges of North Weston, and died 14 July 1802, aged 68). Died 29 March 1801, aged 44. Buried at Crendon.

Two sons. Both died in infancy. The younger born 19 June 1809.

Sarah Frances Warner Way. Born 6 Jan. 1807. Only surviving child and heiress. Married at St. James's, Piccadilly, 6 Jan. 1829. Died at Oxford 7 Dec. 1871. Buried at Crendon. M.I. in Chancel. = John Stone.[6] Born *circa* 1790. Eldest surviving son. Of the Manor House, Crendon, aforesaid, and of the Prebendal House, Thame, Esq. J.P. and D.L. for Bucks. Died at Hastings, Co. Sussex, 2 Nov., and buried at Crendon 9 Nov. 1861.[7] M.I. in Chancel.

William Stone. Born *circa* 1786. Died 27 March 1800, aged 14. Buried at Crendon.

John, son of Captain Colin Campbell, R.N. Was himself a Captain in the Service of the Hon. East India Company, and on the Staff. Died s.p. = Jane Stone. Born 1 May 1796. Married at the Spa Episcopal Chapel, Gloucester, *circa* 1831. Living 1882.

Robert Juggins Sheldon. Born at Holton, Co. Oxon, 28 March 1784. Of Rycott, in the same Co., Gent. Died at Clevedon, Co. Somerset, May 1871. = Anne Stone. Died at Clevedon aforesaid Feb. 1868.

1. William Way Stone of the Prebendal House, Thame, aforesaid. Born 11 Nov. 1829. Died in Great Ormond Street, London, 19 April 1867. Buried at Kensal Green Cemetery. = Edith Lucy (daughter of William Fletcher, M.A., of St. John's College, Cambridge, Vicar of Stone, Co. Bucks, by Mary, daughter of John Studd of Snaffeld Hall, Co. Suffolk, Esquire). Married 15 Feb. 1853 at St. Mary's, Compton Parva, Co. Berks. Living 1882.

2. Robert Warner Stone of the Manor House, Crendon, aforesaid. Born 2 Oct. 1833. Educated first at Thame Grammar School. Entered subsequently at Rugby 2 Oct. 1849. Ensign 23 July 1858. Captain 80th Foot 15 May 1872. Major 1 July 1881. Living 1882.

1. Frances Sophia Sarah Stone. Born 2 Dec. 1834. Deceased. Buried at Thame.

Alexander John Clark. Sometime Lieutenant in the Indian Navy. Living 1882. = 2. Jane Mary Stone. Born 8 April 1836. Married at Feltham, Co. Middlesex, 20 August 1878. Living 1882.

Issue, a daughter.

1. John William Stone, only son. Born 15 Dec. 1853.

1. Edith Mary Stone Born 29 Jan. 1855.

2. Lucy Harriet Stone. Born 4 Feb. 1856.

All living 1882.

James Thomas Hopwood of Lincoln's Inn, Esq. (son of John Stephen Spindler Hopwood of Montagu Place, Russell Square, by Mary Ann his wife). Called to the Bar 30 Jan. 1851. Living 1882. = 3. Anna Ellen Stone. Born 19 March 1838. Married at St. James's, Paddington, 21 April 1860. Died 22 Jan. 1873. Buried at Kensal Green Cemetery.

1. Francis John Stephen Hopwood. Born 2 Dec. 1860. Living 1882.

2. Frederick Flowers Hopwood. Born 25 Nov. 1867. Living 1882.

3. Charles Daniel Hopwood. Born 4 Oct. 1871. Living 1882.

1. Mary Ethel Hopwood. Born 24 April 1863. Died 5 Jan. 1881.

2. Henrietta Hopwood. Born 27 Oct. 1864. Died 28 July 1865.

3. Kate Hopwood Hopwood. Born 23 May 1869. Living 1882.

James Taylor of New College, Oxon, Mus. B., Gent. Born 25 June 1833. Only surviving son of William Taylor of the City of Gloucester, by Sarah his wife, youngest daughter of Thomas Smith of Matson in the said County. Living 1882. = 4. Eliza Anne Stone. B. 5 Feb. 1840. Married at St. Stephen's, Westbourne Park, 7 April 1863. Living 1882.

1. Stuart Campbell Taylor. Born 2 June 1872.

2. Leonard Campbell Taylor. Born 12 Dec. 1874.

3. Reginald Campbell Taylor. Born 11 July 1878.

4. Colin Moncrieff Campbell Taylor. Born 21 Feb. 1881.

1. Leila Campbell Taylor. Born 9 July 1867.

2. May Campbell Taylor. Born 8 Nov. 1870.

All living 1882.

a

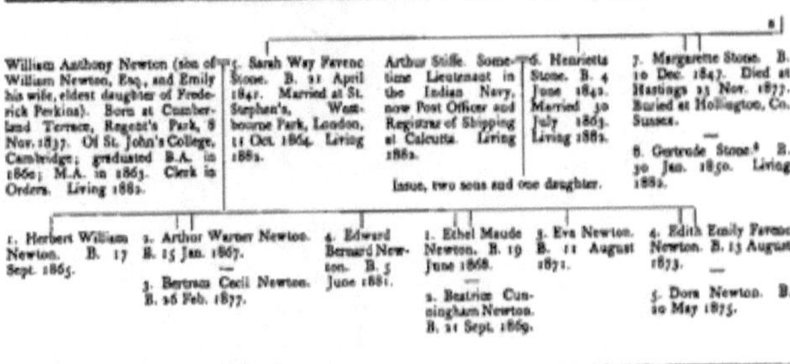
William Anthony Newton (son of William Newton, Esq., and Emily his wife, eldest daughter of Frederick Perkins). Born at Cumberland Terrace, Regent's Park, 8 Nov. 1837. Of St. John's College, Cambridge; graduated B.A. in 1860; M.A. in 1863. Clerk in Orders. Living 1882. = 5. Sarah Way Favenc Stone. B. 21 April 1841. Married at St. Stephen's, Westbourne Park, London, 11 Oct. 1864. Living 1882.

Arthur Stiffe. Sometime Lieutenant in the Indian Navy, now Post Officer and Registrar of Shipping at Calcutta. Living 1882. = 6. Henrietta Stone. B. 4 June 1842. Married 30 July 1863. Living 1882.

Issue, two sons and one daughter.

7. Margarette Stone. B. 10 Dec. 1847. Died at Hastings 23 Nov. 1877. Buried at Hollington, Co. Sussex.

8. Gertrude Stone.[4] B. 30 Jan. 1850. Living 1882.

1. Herbert William Newton. B. 17 Sept. 1865.

2. Arthur Warner Newton. B. 15 Jan. 1867.

3. Bertram Cecil Newton. B. 26 Feb. 1877.

4. Edward Bernard Newton. B. 5 June 1881.

1. Ethel Maude Newton. B. 19 June 1868.

2. Beatrice Cuningham Newton. B. 21 Sept. 1869.

3. Eva Newton. B. 11 August 1871.

4. Edith Emily Favenc Newton. B. 13 August 1873.

5. Dora Newton. B. 20 May 1875.

SOME EXPLANATORY NOTES TO THE FOREGOING PEDIGREE.

[1] The 22j[th] day of July John Stone of Moorton and Ellenor Stratton of Longe Crendon were married together, 1573.—Registers of Crendon, Co. Bucks.

INSCRIPTIONS IN THE CHURCH OF STOKE GOLDINGTON, CO. BUCKS.

Floor of the Nave.

Sarah the wife of Thomas Hodgkins. She departed this life ye 1st of November 1710, aged 55 years.

Near this place lye the Bodies of Thomas Hodgkins of this Parish, Gent., who was buried Sep. 25, 1720; Sarah his wife (daughter of Thomas & Dorothy Hooton), Nov. 26th 1710; and Sarah Hodgkins their youngest daughter June 12th 1738 aged 55 years. Elizabeth, their eldest daughter, married Henry Warner of Thame, Oxon, Gent., & is here interred.

Here lieth y[e] Body of Thomas, the Son of Thomas & Mary Hooton. He departed this life the 6th of January 1710, in the 22nd year of his age.

[2] Of this family was William Newell, B.A., who was instituted to the Rectory of Horsenden, Co. Bucks, 2 August 1592, and who married at Towersey, 13 Nov. 1609, Catherine Tomlinson of Thame, and died Rector of Horsendon in 1632. William Newell of Adwell, Esq., was High Sheriff of Oxfordshire in 1695. Another William Newell, M.A. Ch. Ch. Oxford, was appointed Rector of Ickford, 27 Feb. 1737, and Samuel Newell, B.A., was presented to the same Rectory by Esther Newell, widow, and inducted 9 July 1776. He was also Rector of Adwell, Co. Oxon, and Chaplain to George Henry Lee, third Earl of Litchfield. He died in 1802 at Dinton, Co. Bucks, and was succeeded by the Rev. James Way of Thame.

[3] The following descents of the Family of Way of Thame and Towersey are taken from Registers and Wills:—

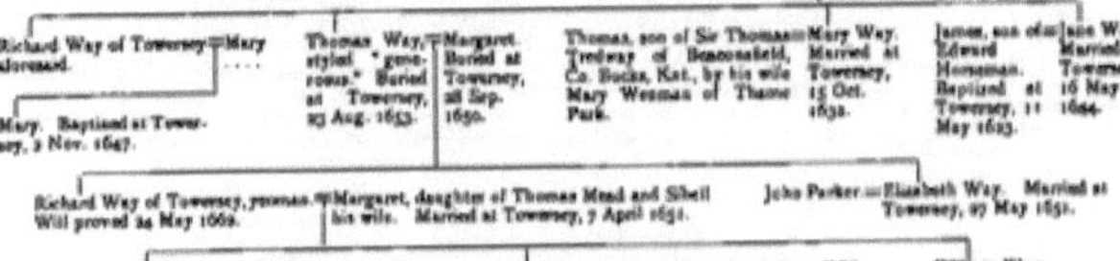
Richard Way (grandson of Richard, who was Churchwarden of Thame in 1532, 1533) of Towersey, yeoman, A.D. 1597. = Mary ....

Richard Way of Towersey aforesaid. = Mary ....

Mary. Baptized at Towersey, 2 Nov. 1647.

Thomas Way, styled "generosus." Buried at Towersey, 23 Aug. 1653. = Margaret. Buried at Towersey, 28 Sep. 1650.

Thomas, son of Sir Thomas Tredway of Beaconsfield, Co. Bucks, Knt., by his wife Mary Wenman of Thame Park. = Mary Way. Married at Towersey, 15 Oct. 1632.

James, son of Edward Horseman. Baptized at Towersey, 11 May 1623. = Jane Way. Married at Towersey, 16 May 1644.

Richard Way of Towersey, yeoman. Will proved 24 May 1669. = Margaret, daughter of Thomas Mead and Sibell his wife. Married at Towersey, 7 April 1651.

John Parker = Elizabeth Way. Married at Towersey, 27 May 1651.

Thomas Way. Baptized 19 Aug. 1652.

Richard Way. Mentioned in his father's Will.

William Way.

The Will of Richard Way of Towersey, Co. Bucks, yeoman, was proved 24 May 1660. He bequeaths to his son Thomas a black cow, his best feather bed and bedstead, etc. To his son Richard his second best bed and bedstead, and his best chest, and one cow after the decease of his wife Margaret. To his son William his other chest and one cow. All the rest of his goods and chattels to his wife.—"Wills of the Peculiar of Thame," etc.

The Will of William Way of Moreton, in the parish of Thame, yeoman, was made 22 June 1742. He leaves legacies to his daughter Mary, wife of James Norris, and to his son William. The rest of his goods and chattels to his wife Rebecca, sole executrix, and to his five children. Witnessed by Thomas and Arabella Prickett.—"Wills of the Peculiar of Thame," etc.

Thame Register—*Burials*.

1778. April 19. Mary, wife of Richard Way, Gent., Coroner.

1784. Dec. 3. Richard Way, Coroner.

Sarah, the daughter of Richard Way, Gent., and Mary his wife, married, by licence at Thame, William Simeons, Junr. They had issue four sons, viz., (1) Richard Way, (2) William, (3) Alfred Way, and (4) James Way, and three daughters, (1) Caroline, (2) Harriett Philadelphia, and (3) Clarissa. This family of Simeons, related to the Hampdens, succeeded the family of Bethom at Adwell. The arms of the latter are—Ermine, a chevron between three boars' heads passant sable (Harl. MSS. No. 1095, fol. 27).

[4] From the Register of Matriculations of the University of Oxford.

1792 Nov[bris] 2[o] Jacobus Way, 17, Jacobi Way de Thame Com. Oxon. Arm. Fil.
Coll. Pemb.

[5] In Dorton Church, Co. Bucks, there are inscriptions to the memory of Jane Hedges, who died 14 July 1802, aged 68; and to Jane, daughter of William and Jane Smith, who died 5 June 1771, aged 16.

[a] Chancel, Crendon Church, Co. Bucks.
Sacred
to the Memory of
William Stone,
who departed this life
on the 21st of February, 1824,
in the 70th year of his age.
Also of
Ann Stone Sheldon
his granddaughter,
who died in her infancy.
Also of
John Stone,
son of the above William Stone,
Deputy-Lieutenant and Magistrate
for this County,
who died at Hastings
on the 2nd of November, 1861,
aged 71 years.
Also of
Sarah Frances Warner his wife
who died 7th Dec. 1874, aged 64 years.

[1] The following notice of Mr. Stone appeared in the newspapers:—

John Stone, Esq.—We regret to have to record the decease of an active magistrate and kind-hearted, upright man, Mr. John Stone, well known and much respected in the part of the country where he resided. All his life, until recently, living on his property, first at Crendon, Bucks, and afterwards at Thame, Oxon, he set an example worthy of imitation, as a magistrate, of unwearied assiduity, of firmness and kindness combined; as a landlord, liberal and indulgent to his tenants; as a man, of sincere and unaffected friendship and open-hearted charity. In his own parish he was ever active in doing good, and in his desire to promote the interest and welfare of those around him, he would neither evade nor refuse to serve any parochial office, whatever were the responsibilities, trouble, or difficulty attendant upon the performance of the duties. Unobtrusive and retiring, yet his excellent qualities had in a long and useful life secured to him respect and regard by no means limited to his immediate neighbourhood. Highly esteemed by the noble house of Chandos in its days of splendour, its misfortunes found him still its firm adherent. He lived to see what he hoped was the dawn for it of a brighter day. Chosen by his fellow magistrates and county men to be one of the trustees in whom the property of the famous Chandos memorial was vested, he has outlived all of them but one. His early life was spent in times and circumstances which now happily are matters of history. First as a Volunteer in the old days, afterwards as a Captain in the Militia, he was active and of service when serious agricultural riots required courage for their repression. He was offered by the General of the district, in recognition of his soldierly qualities, a commission in the line, but declined it. He was for many years a magistrate and deputy-lieutenant of the county of Buckingham. A ripe old age, seventy-three years, found him still active, happy, cheerful, and hospitable, when he was seized with the malady which proved fatal. He died at St. Leonard's on Saturday the 2nd instant, and in pursuance of his earnest wish, will this day (Saturday the 9th) be gathered to his fathers at Crendon Church. Need we add that such a man was kind and affectionate to wife and children. They, knit together by the ties of love, which it was his care to cherish, will in mutual affection and remembrance of his many virtues, find the best consolation for his loss.

[a] Miss Gertrude Stone possesses a small quarto copy of the New Testament, printed in black letter in the year 1612 by "Robert Barker, Printer to the King's Most Excellent Majestie," whose pedigree has been given on p. 146 of this work. After the New Testament is a copy, also in black letter, of "The whole Booke of Psalmes, collected into English meeter by Thomas Sternhold, John Hopkins, and others. Printed for the Companie of Stationers 1620." The volume is especially remarkable for its curious and interesting binding with silver ornaments—a very fine specimen of English work. The clasps are wanting. It is bound in choice calf-leather, with, originally, seven silver *plaques* most efficiently engraved on either side of the cover. One is lost from the front, but the others are complete. It is believed to have belonged to Pierse, son of Sir Thomas Crosbie, for it has the letters P. C. in silver both on front and back. In the middle of the front, which is adorned with stamped flowers, very artistically arranged—roses, lilies, pinks, tulips, and marigolds, is the Resurrection of Our Lord, with the Apostles Philip, Bartholomew, Matthew, Simon, and James around; while on the back is the Adoration of the Magi (turned upside down) and the Apostles Peter, Thomas, Andrew, Jude, and SS. Mark and Luke. At the end of the book there is a somewhat repulsive prayer, also in black letter, rife with questionable statements, and reeking with the spirit of persecution and Erastianism. It is a part of the Book of Psalms officially put forth, and stands thus:—"As Moses, Ezechias, Jonas, and other good Rulers purged the Church of God from superstition and idolatry, so the defence of Christ's Church against all idolators and heretickes, as Papists, Anabaptists, with such like lims of Antichrist to roote out all doctrine of Divels and men, as the Mass, Purgatory, *Limbus patrum*, prayers to saints and for the dead, free-will, distinction of meats, apparell, and daies, vowes of single life, presence of Idoll service, man's merits, with such like, which draw us from the society of Christ's Church, wherein standeth only remission of sinnes purchased by Christ's blood to all them that believe, whether they be Jewes or Gentiles, and lead us to vain confidence in creatures and trust in our own imaginations; the punishment whereof, although God oftentimes deferreth [*it*] in this life, yet after the general Resurrection, when our souls and bodies shal rise againe to immortality, they shall be damned to unquenchable fire."

♣♣♣♣♣♣♣♣♣♣♣

BEFORE the local Tradesmen's Tokens are described, I may mention that several English coins of interest have been from time to time discovered at Thame, with a considerable number of Abbey Tokens, a few coins of Calais, and some Anglo-Gallic deniers of Queen Eleanor. Amongst the former I possess silver pennies of William the Conqueror, Henry I., King Stephen, and Henry II. (both of the first and second coinage). I own, likewise, examples found in the Town and neighbourhood of the silver pennies of Henry III., Edward I., and Edward II., and some fine examples of groats and half-groats of Edward III., Henry V., Henry VI., Edward IV., and Henry VII. Many later specimens of the coinage of the Tudors have been occasionally found, but none, as far as I am aware, of any remarkable excellence—save and except a very fine shilling of Philip and Mary, found near the site of the Place House. A gold coin of the Emperor Honorius, in rare preservation, was discovered on the land of the late Mr. Harry Lupton, and a gold coin of Cunobelin, with the horse and wheatear, was ploughed up at Priestend in 1843.

Tradesmen's Tokens of Thame.

THE origin of seventeenth-century Tradesmen's Tokens was as follows:—

In the absence of any adequate national representation of either the half-penny or the farthing,*—a remarkable and very practical inconvenience to the lower classes, for small change was exceedingly scarce;—quite an unlimited number of Tradesmen's Tokens obtained currency during the seventeenth century—coined, of course, at the cost and risk of those who issued them. Some were of copper, others of brass, others again of mixed metals. They were often designed and executed by itinerant coiners, whose headquarters were in London. The name of the person whose they were, and who first circulated them, was commonly placed on one side—the obverse, with his initials in the centre; and his designation, his personal coat of arms, or the arms of his guild or company on the other or reverse. The initial of the Christian name of the man's wife who had the Token designed and coined was also frequently introduced on one side of the Token in conjunction with his own initials. These were often separated by a star, or a fleur-de-lys, or a small rose. The leading tradesmen of any town, or sometimes those of several towns in a county or particular locality, agreed to take, and afterwards to interchange, each other's Tokens. This was done once in three months, after the two or three annual local fairs, or at other times agreed upon; so that private enterprise effected a relief to the inconvenience of the want of half-pence and farthings, which for so considerable a period had been left unremedied by Authority.

No Tradesman's Token of any locality, either in town or country, appears to bear an earlier date than 1648. Of those issued in Thame the earliest that is known is dated 1653, and the latest 1669.

Some of the specimens of Thame Tokens, worn and battered, are exceedingly imperfect and indistinct, and it is not easy to procure better. Those in my collection, of Robert Crewes, John Gurdon, Richard Hearne, Hugh Hester, Edward Leaver, and Richard Rastell, are all good examples and come out well in the accompanying woodcuts.

Six of these Tokens have various representations of armorial bearings upon them, as follow:

The Arms of the Mercers' Company (incorporated in 1394), confirmed by St. George, Richmond Herald, in 1634, are, Gules, a demi-virgin couped below the shoulders, issuing from clouds all proper, vested or, crowned with an Oriental crown of the last, her hair dishevelled and wreathed round the temples with roses of the second.

The Arms of the Grocers' Company (granted 23 Henry VIII.) are, Argent, a chevron gules between nine cloves sable, three, three, and three.

The Arms of the Drapers' Company (incorporated 17 Henry VI.) are, Azure, three clouds proper, radiated in base or, each surmounted with a triple crown or.

The arms of the Merchant Taylors' Company (incorporated in 1466) are, Argent, a royal tent between two parliament robes gules, lined ermine, the tent garnished or, tent staff and pennant of the last, on a chief azure a lion passant guardant or.

The only person who used his personal crest on his token—an unicorn—appears to have been Mr. John Burges.

The following eighteen specimens—three, those of William Atkins, Dorothy Burges, and Isaac Weekes, were half-pence; the others farthings—are all that I have been able to discover:—

1. Obv. Richard Adkin=The Grocers' Arms.
   Rev. In Thame 1669=R. S. A.

2. Obv. The Blacke Lion 1669=A lion rampant.
   Rev. William Adkens of Thame*=His Half Peny.

3. Obv. Ruth Akers=R. A.
   Rev. Of Thame=R. A.

* The Earl of Arundel, Lord Marshal, secured from James I. a patent for the exclusive coining of small copper money. The Mint-house, from which in the earlier part of the seventeenth century the authorised farthings had been issued, was on the north side of Lothbury, in the City of London—hence, and still, called Tokenhouse Yard.

* To a William Atkins (possibly grandfather to the above-named), who was servant to Lord Williams, and to his heirs for ever, were bequeathed certain lands, rents, and reversions, in the county of Montgomery, under his Lordship's Will.

4. Obv. Dorothy Burgis* in Thame = A lion rampant.
Rev. Her Halfe Penny = D. B. 1669.

5. Obv. Iohn Burgess = A unicorn.
Rev. In Thame 1653 = I. B.

6. Obv. Will : Cope Grocer in = W. C.
Rev. Tame in Oxfordshir = I. A. C.

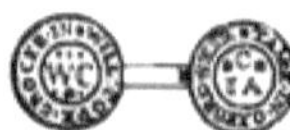

7. Obv. Robert Creswell = A stick of candles.
Rev. Of Thame 1668 = R. F. C.

8. Obv. Iohn Daniel, Hater = A hat.
Rev. In Tame 1669 = I. R. D.

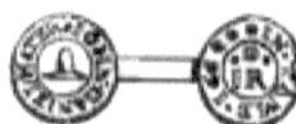

9. Obv. Iohn Gyrdon = 1657.
Rev. In Thame 57 = I. G.

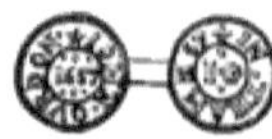

10. Obv. Iohn Harris at the = A lion rampant.
Rev. Read Lyon in Thame = I. H.

11. Obv. Richard Hearne = The Drapers' Arms.
Rev. Of Thame 1669 = R. H.*

12. Obv. Hugh Hester = The Grocers' Arms.
Rev. In Thame 1657 = H. H.

13. Obv. Richard Rastell = The Mercers' Arms.
Rev. In Thame = R. R.

14. Obv. William Tripp = A stick of candles.
Rev. In Thame Chandler = W. E. T.

15. Obv. Mathew Walters = The Mercers' Arms.
Rev. Of Thame Mercer = M. W.

16. Obv. Isaac Weeks 1667 = A tree.
Rev. Gardener in Thame = His Halfe Penny.

17. Obv. Edward Leaver = Arms of the Merchant Taylors.
Rev. Of Thame = E. I. L.

* The Will of Thomas Burges was made 24 Feb. 1663, proved 6 April 1665. His "loving wife Dorothy" was "sole executrix." He left substantial legacies to his sons William and Richard, and to his daughters Eleanor and Dorothy. His other children named therein were Thomas, John, Symon, and Jonathan; Mary and Elizabeth. The Inventory amounted to £134 0s. 9d.—"Wills of the Peculiar of Thame," etc.

* "A golden token of Richard Hearne of Thame, weighing twenty-three grains, has been brought to me. . . . . . It was found in digging a well at Milton, where I recollect some of the family residing. . . . . . I never recollect seeing any previous tradesman's token, excepting of brass, copper, or silver."—*History of Thame and its Hamlets*, by Harry Lupton, Surgeon, etc., p. 25. Thame: (Dedication dated) 1860.

18. Obv. William Iemet=A hat.
Rev. Of Thame 1669=W. I. I.

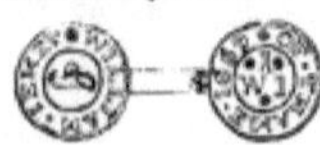

A Proclamation, dated 1672, giving the first blow to the favourers of Tokens, enjoined that certain recently coined farthings of the King "were current from and after this date, in all payments under the value of sixpence and not otherwise."* These farthings were issued in large numbers, though many of the country people—possibly unacquainted with the Proclamation in question—still retained the use of the private Tokens, to which for twenty years they had been accustomed—for some time preferring the latter to the former.

Hence another Proclamation was issued two years afterwards. Complaints had been made that the people were sometimes defrauded by the use of private Tokens. It is clear that many of such pieces of money were of little intrinsic value, yet, in sad and turbulent times, they had proved a great convenience to the country people and others who needed small change; and though some interested persons maintained that "vast profit attended these Tokens, for which the utterers thereof chose to run any hazards of the law, rather than quiet the hopes of their own private lucre," the credit of respectable and reputable tradesmen in their own particular localities still sufficed to render their own Tokens acceptable. By direction of the High Sheriff, Sir Thomas Curson of Waterperry, Bart., the Proclamation was enclosed to the Constables of Thame, with directions to have copies of it posted up in various parts of the Town, and with an order to the Town Crier or Bellman to proclaim it at the Town Hall on three successive market-days.

Here are its exact terms:—

"A Proclamation enjoining the Prosecution of all such Persons as shall make or utter any Farthings, Half-pence, or Pence of brass, or utter base metals with private stamps.

"CHARLES R.

"Whereas His Majesty, having by His Royal Proclamation of the 16th of August [1672], in the twenty-fourth year of His reign, forbidden the use of all private farthings, did cause sufficient quantities of copper farthings and half-pence, of the intrinsic value, to be coined for the general good and convenience of his subjects: nevertheless, His Majesty hath been informed, that several persons and corporations remote from London have forborne to call in their private farthings, and do still presume to make use of and utter the same; whereby they continue not only to violate the laws of this kingdom, and defraud His Majesty's good subjects, but hinder the vending of those half-pence and farthings which are provided for necessary exchange, which would have been ere this time dispersed in those parts, if the said abuses of stamping and uttering of private farthings had been duly suppressed. His Majesty, therefore, to the end that all offenders to the premises, who are now left without excuse, may know the danger they daily incur, and desist from any further proceeding in the like kind, hath thought fit by this his royal proclamation to publish and declare his royal will and pleasure to be, that a strict and severe inquiry shall be made off all persons that shall, after the 2d day of February [1674-5], next ensuing, stamp, vend, utter, or in any way make use of in payment or exchange, any half-pence, farthings, or pieces of brass, copper, or other base metals whatsoever, other than the half-pence and farthings by His Majesties royal proclamation authorized and allowed; and whosoever shall be found culpable therein shall be severely punished. And for that purpose, His Majesty doth hereby will and command all his judges, justices of assise, justices of the peace, and all other inferior officers and ministers of justice whatsoever, that they take care at their several and respective courts, assizes, quarter-sessions, and other inferior courts, that have or may have cognizance or punishment of the said offences, that after the 2d day of February they cause all such as shall offend in the premises to be proceeded against, and punished as they shall deserve.

"Given at our Court at Whitehall, the 5th day of December [1674], in the twenty-sixth year of our reign."

In due course, and by degrees, this official action, combined with the interference and directions of local authorities, caused the circulation of such Tokens to decrease and eventually to come to an end.

♣♣♣♣♣♣♣

I NOW proceed to set forth a Pedigree of Knollys, a family of distinction which rose to remarkable eminence under the Tudors; several members of which became honourable officers of State, and persons of note, in later periods. The family had its origin in the City of London. The heiress of Robert Knollys of North Mymms married a Frowick, whose second daughter, Isabell, became an ancestress of Sir John Williams of Thame. Subsequently the Family of Knollys was duly ennobled, and a branch of it resided at Lower Winchendon. In the eighteenth century another member, Francis Knollys, whose immediate ancestors had been connected with Thame for several generations, was created a Baronet, but the title on his death became extinct. I also give the direct line of the Earls of Banbury down to the present representative, Sir William Knollys, K.C.B.:—

* *London Gazette*, Monday, 19 Aug. 1672.

Pedigree of Knollys, Earls of Banbury, and Knollys of Thame.

Arms of Knollys.—1. *Semée of cross-crosslets, a cross moline or, voided throughout of the field.* 2. *Gules, on a chevron argent three roses of the field.* (These Arms are often borne quarterly. In some old examples there appears a dexter canton ermine.)

Thomas Knollys (son of Sir Thomas Knollys, citizen and grocer, twice Lord Mayor of London, viz. in 1399 and 1410, who was buried in St. Antholin's Church, Budge Row). He had eighteen brothers and sisters. = Joane.

Thomas Knollys of North Mymms, Co. Herts, citizen and grocer. Will dated 7 and 8 Feb. 1445, proved 18 Feb. of the same year. Died 8 Feb. 1445. Buried at St. Antholin's. = Isabell. Predeceased her husband.

William Knollys of Bristol, merchant. Will dated 2 Sept., proved 10 Sept. 1442. = Katherine. = ... Alice.

John Chicheley, Chamberlain of the City of London. Second son of Alderman William Chicheley, and nephew of Archbishop Chicheley. = Margaret Knollys.

Robert Knollys, son and heir, of North Mymms. Buried there. = Elizabeth, daughter and heiress of William Troutbeck. She died 28 Nov. 1458. Monumental Brass at North Mymms.

Richard Knollys, second son. Aged 21 in 24 Henry VI., *i.e.* 1446. = Margaret, daughter of William Doyley of Eweden in Hambledon, Co. Bucks. Died in 1449.

John Knollys, Prior of Coxford, Co. Norfolk, in 1463. Rector of Harpbey in 1474. Died 1478.

Beatrice Knollys, a nun at Dartford.

—

Joane Knollys, wife of William Baron.

—

Isabell Knollys.

Henry Frowick. = Anne Knollys.

Robert (or Thomas) Knollys. 36 Henry VI., *i.e.* in 1458. Living = Elizabeth. Buried in the Churchyard of St. Helen's, Bishopsgate, as her son's Will indicates.

Thomas Frowick. Died without issue.

Thomas Bledlowe of London, whose descendant married Sir John Williams of Thame, Knt. (See pp. 415, 416.) = Isabell Frowick.

John Coningsby. = Elizabeth Frowick.

Robert Knollys, Gentleman Usher to King Henry VIII. Obtained a lease of the Manor of Rotherfield Greys 25 Jan. 1517-18. Died in 1521. Will dated 13 Nov. 1520, proved 10 June 1521. Buried in the Churchyard of St. Helen's, Bishopsgate, aforesaid. = Lettice, second daughter of Sir Thomas Peryston, Knt., by Alice his wife, daughter of Richard Bulstrode of Hedgerley, Co. Bucks. She married, secondly, Robert Lee of Quarrendon, knighted in 1526; and thirdly Sir Thomas Tresham. Her Will dated 28 June 1557, proved 11 June 1558.

A

Francis Knollys of Rotherfield Greys aforesaid. Born *circa* 1514. Had the Lordship of Rotherfield Greys in fee from Henry VIII. Vice-Chamberlain of the Household to Queen Elizabeth. Treasurer of the Household 7 January 1570. K.G. 23 April 1593, installed 25 June. Custos Rotulorum of the Co. Oxon. Died 19 July 1596. Buried at Rotherfield Greys 18 August. Will dated 22 March 1595-6, proved 15 Sept. 1596. Inq. post mortem taken at Reading 8 April 1597. = Catherine, daughter of William Carey, Esq., by Lady Mary Boleyne, one of the daughters and heiresses of Thomas Boleyne, Earl of Wiltshire, and sister to Anne Boleyne, concubine to King Henry VIII. Died at Hampton Court 15 Jan. 1568. Buried in St. Edmund's Chapel, Westminster Abbey.

Henry Knollys. Represented Reading in Parliament 1563, and was subsequently M.P. for Guildford and Christ Church. Will dated 27 July 1582, proved 2 Sept. 1583. His "dear brother Sir Francis K. and his nephew William K. his executors."

Mary Knollys.

Sir Richard Wingfield of Kimbolton Castle, Knt. = Jane Knollys.

Henry Knollys, son and heir, of Kingsbury, Co. Warwick. M.P. for Reading. Educated at Magdalene College, Oxon. Accompanied the Earl of Essex to Ireland. Esquire of the Body to Queen Elizabeth. Will dated 21 Dec. 1582, proved 14 May 1583. = Margaret, born *circa* 1549, daughter and heiress of Sir Ambrose Cave, Knt., Chancellor of the Duchy of Lancaster, by Margaret his wife, daughter and coheiress of William Willington of Barcheston, Co. Warwick. Married before 11 April 1568. Sole executrix of her husband's Will. Her own Will dated 19 June 1602, proved 15 Nov. 1606. She died 15 Aug. 1606. Buried at Hadley, near Barnet.

Sir Henry Willoughby of Risley, Co. Derby, Knt. Created a Baronet 29 June 1611. Died without male issue in 1649. = Elizabeth Knollys, eldest daughter. Died before 1632.

Arms of Willoughby.—*Or, two bars gules, each charged with three water-bougets argent.*

William, 4th Lord Paget. Died 20 August 1629. = Letitia Knollys, youngest daughter.

From whom, in the female line, comes the Marquis of Anglesey.

Dorothy, fifth daughter of Edmund, Lord Bray, and widow of Edmund Brydges, Lord Chandos. Died, without issue, in 1605. (First wife.) = William Knollys, second son, but eventually heir. Knight Banneret in 1586. Comptroller of the Household to Queen Elizabeth 1596. Created Baron Knollys of Rotherfield Greys 13 May 1603. Treasurer of the Household to King James I. Elected K.G. 24 April 1615. Viscount Wallingford 7 Nov. 1617. Earl of Banbury 18 Aug. 1626. Will dated 13 and 19 May 1630, proved 2 July 1632. Died in Paternoster Row, London, 25 May 1632, aged 88. Buried at Rotherfield Greys. In an Inquisition p.m. taken at Burford, Co. Oxon, 11 April 1633, he is said to have left "no issue,"—a statement directly contradicted by a subsequent Inquisition. = Elizabeth Howard, daughter of Thomas, Earl of Suffolk. Died in 1658. (Second wife.) Married to Lord Vaux two months after Lord Banbury's death, *i.e.* in July 1632. = Edward, 4th Lord Vaux, of Harrowden, Co. Northants. Died 6 Oct. 1661. (Second husband.)

Edward Knollys, 1st son. Born at Rotherfield Greys. Baptized 11 August 1627. 2nd Earl of Banbury. Killed in a duel in 1645, and was buried at Calais, unmarried.

Isabella, daughter of Mountjoy Blount, Earl of Newport. (First wife.) = Nicholas Knollys, 2nd son, born 3 Jan. 1630-1, at Harrowden. In Oct. 1646 his step-father Edward, 4th Lord Vaux, settled Harrowden in Northamptonshire on this Nicholas. Took his seat as 3rd Earl of Banbury in the Convention Parliament in June 1660. Died 14 March 1673-4. Buried at Boughton, Co. Northants. = Anne, daughter of William, Lord Sherard of Leitrim. Married in 1655. (Second wife.)

Anne, only child. Married firstly to Charles Fry, Esq., and secondly to John Brisco, subsequently a Knight.

Elizabeth, daughter of Edward Lister of Burwell, Co. Leicester. = Charles Knollys, baptized at Boughton aforesaid 3 June 1662, and there registered as "Viscount Wallingford." 4th Earl of Banbury in 1673-4. Died in 1740. Buried in France. = Mary, daughter of Thomas Woods of London, merchant, and Mary his wife. Died at Bath. Buried there 12 May 1762.

Other issue.

William Knollys, who died in his father's lifetime in 1740. Buried in South Audley Street Chapel 14 June 1740. = Mary Catherine, daughter of John Law. Died without issue 14 Oct. 1790. Buried beside her husband. Will dated 25 Dec. 1784, proved 27 Oct. 1790.

Charles Knollys, Clerk in Orders. Vicar of Burford. 5th Earl of Banbury in 1740. Died 13 and buried 19 March 1771, at Burford, Co. Oxon. = Martha Hughes of Southampton. Died 9 Sept., buried beside her husband 16 Sept. 1771.

B C

a | c

William Knollys, son and heir. Born 21 Oct. 1726. Died unmarried 29 Aug. 1776. Buried at Burford aforesaid.

Thomas Woods Knollys, heir of his brother. Born 16 Dec. 1727. 6th Earl of Banbury. Died 18 March 1793. Buried at Winchester. = Mary, daughter of William Porter of Winchester. Married by licence at St. Thomas's, Winchester, 30 March 1761. Died 23 March 1798. Buried at Winchester.

Charles and Cyprian, died unmarried. — Other issue.

Samuel Knollys. — Francis Knollys.

William Knollys, son and heir.[8] Baptized at St. Thomas's, Winchester, 2 March 1763. Of the 3rd Regt. of Foot Guards. 7th Earl of Banbury. = Charlotte Martha, daughter of Ebenezer Blackwell of Winchester.

William Thomas Knollys. Born 1 Aug. 1797. Of the Scots Guards. General in the Army 1866. K.C.B. 1867. P.C. 1872. Hon. D.C.L. Oxon. Gentleman Usher of the Black Rod 1877. Of Blount's Court, Co. Oxon. D.L. Living in 1883. Claimant of the Earldom of Banbury. = Elizabeth, fifth daughter of Sir John St. Aubyn, Bart., by Juliana his wife. Married in 1830. Died in Feb. 1878. Buried in Highgate Cemetery.

William Frederick Erskine Knollys, M.A. Merton Coll., Oxon. Clerk in Orders. Rector of Wrotham, Co. Kent, 1879. Married and has issue. Living in 1883.

Other issue.

William Wallingford Knollys, eldest son. Married and has issue.

Francis Knollys, C.B., second son. Private Secretary to the Prince of Wales.

Henry Knollys, third son.

Frederick Robert Knollys, fourth son.

Arthur Cyprian Knollys, fifth son.

Captain Grey. = Mirabel Knollys.

Archibald Augustus Knollys, Clerk in Orders. M.A. B.N. Coll., Oxon, 1878. = Constance Knollys.

Charlotte Knollys. Living unmarried in 1883.

Edward Knollys, third son. M.P. for the City of Oxford 2 April 1571. Died circa 1580.

Robert Knollys, fourth son. Keeper of Syon House 1560. M.P. for Co. Brecon 7 Queen Elizabeth. Usher of the Mint in the Tower 5 Feb. 1578. Knight of the Bath 24 July 1603. Died in Jan. 1625. = Katherine, daughter and coheiress of Sir Rowland Vaughan of Porthample, Knt.

Richard Knollys, fifth son, of Stanford in the Vale, Co. Berks. M.P. for Wallingford in the Parliament which ended 14 Sept. 1586. Died and was buried at Rotherfield 21 Aug. 1596. = Joane, daughter of John Higham of Cliffords, Co. Sussex, and sister of John Higham of Stanford. She married, secondly, Francis Winchcombe of Bucklebury, Co. Berks. Buried at Rotherfield Greys aforesaid 10 Oct. 1631.

Robert Knollys of Rotherfield Greys aforesaid. Knighted 12 Jan. 1612-13. Buried 26 June 1659. = Joanna, daughter of Sir John Wolstenholme of Nostell Priory, Co. York, Knt., by his wife, Katherine Fanshawe of Thame. Buried at Rotherfield Greys 29 Dec. 1660.

Henry Knollys. Bapt. at Rotherfield Greys 20 Jan. 1586. Died without issue.

Mary, daughter of Sir Charles Wiseman, Knt. = Francis Knollys of Stanford aforesaid. Died 4 Aug. 1640. = Alice, daughter of Sir William Becher, Knt.

Issue two sons and one daughter.

Other issue.

William Knollys, son and heir, of Rotherfield aforesaid. Buried there 4 Sept. 1664. = Margaret, daughter of John Saunders of Thame. Married 23 May 1642. Buried at Rotherfield 20 Dec. 1659.

Other issue.

Robert Knollys. M.P. for Co. Oxon. Died without issue in April 1670.

William Knollys. Died unmarried in March 1664.

Margaret Knollys. Buried at Rotherfield 2 Oct. 1667.

Walter Kennedy. = Letitia Knollys.

Robert Haldanby of Yorkshire. = Katherine Knollys.

Sir Francis Knollys, sixth son.[4] Had a lease from the Crown of the site of the Manor of Battel, near Reading, Co. Berks, and of the farm called Battel Farm, for life. M.P. for the City of Oxford and for the Co. Berks. In 1596 made a Deputy Lieutenant for Berkshire. Will proved 5 May 1648. = Lettice, daughter of John Barrett of Hanham, Co. Gloucester, and of Essex.

Sir Francis Knollys, Knt., son and heir. Resided at Reading, and subsequently at Thame. A Justice of the Peace for Berks, Bucks, and Oxon. = Ellen, daughter and heiress of Richard Millis of Lower Winchendon, Co. Bucks. Married at St. Lawrence's, Reading, 26 Dec. 1611. Buried there 7 Oct. 1629.

Other issue.

Richard Knollys, of Chichester, Co. Sussex, Esq. Died at Lower Winchendon 2 January, buried at Reading 9 January 1655. = Mary, daughter of John Bellingham of Everingham, Co. Sussex, Gent., sister and heiress of her brother Henry.

Other issue.

b

D

Francis Knollys of Thame, Esq. = Ann, daughter and coheiress of . . . . Bateman of Cumnor, Co. Berks. — Other issue.

Francis Knollys of Thame, Esq., son and heir. Educated at the Grammar School. M.P. for Reading. Died in 1701. = Elizabeth, youngest daughter, and coheiress with her sisters Martha and Frances, of John Striblehill of Thame, Gent., by Frances, daughter of Thomas Carter of North Weston, Esq.[5] Baptized at Thame 30 Nov. 1678. Married at Weston 19 April 1696. Died in 1701. Buried at St. Lawrence's, Reading, 6 Aug. 1701.

Sir Francis Curson of Waterperry. = Elizabeth Knollys.

A son, who died young at St. Omer's.

Francis Knollys of Thame, Esq., son and heir. Educated at the Grammar School. M.P. for Oxford. Died unmarried 24 June 1757.

Elizabeth, daughter and coheir of Humphrey Thayer, Commissioner of Excise, of Theydon, Co. Essex. (First wife.) = Richard Knollys of Thame, and subsequently of Mortlake. He married, thirdly, Anne, daughter of John Taylor, Treasurer of Bridewell and Bethlehem Hospitals. = Hannah, daughter of Theophilus Sallwey of Stratford, Co. Essex. Married at Somerset House Chapel in the year 1735. (Second wife.)

Cecilia Knollys. Born in 1699. Died in 1700.

John Knollys. Born in 1701. Died at school at Eton in 1717.

Francis Knollys of Thame, and of Fern Hill,[6] near Cranbourne Lodge, in Windsor Forest, son and heir. Educated at Thame Grammar School, and St. John's Coll. Oxford. Made M.A. 19 April 1744. Created a Baronet 1 April 1754. Hon. D.C.L. of Oxford 8 July 1756. Sheriff of Oxfordshire in 1757. M.P. for Reading in 1761. Died without issue 29 June 1772. Will made 22 June of that year, proved 10 July. = Mary, born *circa* 1728, daughter and heiress of Robert Kendall Cater, third son of John Kendall of Basingbourne Hall, Co. Essex, and of Kempston, Co. Bedford. Married 24 April 1756. Died 19 Dec. 1791, aged 63.

SOME EXPLANATORY NOTES TO THE FOREGOING PEDIGREE.

[1] Thomas Knolles was buried in St. Antholin's Church, and on his tomb the following:—

Here lyth graven under this ston
Thomas Knolles, both flesh and bon,
Grocer and Alderman yeres fortye,
Sheriff, and this Maire truly:
And for he shuld not ly alone
Here lyth with him his good wyff Jone:
They weren togeder sixty yere,
And nineteen chyldren they had in fere;
Now ben they gon we them misse:
Christ hathe them brought to heven blisse.
Amen.

[2] Thomas Knolles lyeth undre this ston
And his wyff Isabell flesh and bon;
They weren togeder nyntene yere
And x chyldren they had in fere.
His Fader and he to this Church
Many good dedys they did wurch.
Example by him ye may see
That this world is but vanitie;
For whether he be smal or gret
All shall turne to wormys mete.
This sayd Thomas was leyd on bere
The eighth day the moneth Februar,
The date of Jesu Crist truly
An' M.CCCC. five and forty.
We may not prey; hertily prey ye
For our Sowlys Pater Noster and Ave,
For sooner of our peynes lessid to be
Grant us the holy Trinitie. Amen.
—*St. Antholin's, Budge Row, London.*

These two quotations from the old Knollys tombs occur on folio 240 of Cotton MS., Julius C., vii.

[3] The Committee for Privileges, upon a division of twenty-one to thirteen, on 11 March 1813, Resolved to report that they had come to the following resolution:—"Resolved that it is the opinion of this Committee that the Petitioner hath not made out his Claim to the title, dignity, and honor of the Earl of Banbury." Of the twenty-one peers who formed the majority, four were spiritual lords who had never attended the proceedings, ten only attended even occasionally, and more than one never until the day on which they gave their vote. A formal Protest against the decision was drawn up, and is a most ably-written document. It was signed by ten peers.

[4] FROM THE REGISTER OF MARRIAGES, ST. LAURENCE'S, READING.

1611. Dec. 26. Mr. Francis Knowles and Mrs. Helena Milles.
1615. July 31. John Knowles and Alice Knight.

FROM THE REGISTER OF BURIALS OF THE SAME CHURCH.

1618. Sep. 20. Mr. William Knowles.
1629. Oct. 7. Elena Knollys, domina.
1643. May 17. Sir Francis Knollis, jun., knight.
1655. Jan. 9. Richard Knowles, Esq.
1669. April 14. Mrs. Marie Knowles, widow.
1672. Oct. 11. Mrs. Lettice Knollis.
1676. Mar. 13. Mrs. Cecilia Knollis.
1677. Sep. 12. The Ladie Cecilia Knollis.
1689. Oct. 8. Francis Knollys, Esq.
1690. Feb. 21. Mrs. Elizabeth Knollys, widow.
1700. . . . . . Cecilia, daughter of Francis and Elizabeth.
1701. July 23. Francis Knollys, Esq., of Nether Winchendon, in the County of Bucks.

FROM THE REGISTER OF BURIALS OF ST. GILES'S, READING.

1656. April 21. A son of Mr. Robert Knollys, still-born.
1677. . . . . . The honoured Lady Cecilia Knollys.

[5] The Will of John Carter of North Weston, made 22 July 1643, was proved 16 Sep. of the same year. To son William, £20. To daughters Margaret, Mary, and Katherine, £10 apiece. Brothers, Thomas and Samuel. To wife all residue of my goods and chattels. Inventory, £201 12s. 8d.—From "Wills of the Peculiar of Thame," etc.

[6] I am indebted to Sir William Knollys, K.C.B., for the following transcript of an original list of Portraits of members of his family:—

Family Pictures at Lady Knollys's, Fern Hill, near Windsor, Berkshire.

1. The Rt. Honble. Sir Fras. Knollys, father to the Earl of Banbury, aged 72. He was Lord Treasurer to the Queen Elizabeth, and died in 1596.

2 and 3. There are two pictures in the drawing-room of the Lord Treasurer, and a Sir Fras. Knollys, supposed to be his son—but

hanging high could not discover any dates thereon. They appear much in years, and the dress of the times makes them look older.

4. "Katherine, wife of the Lord Treasurer, 1567, aged 36." She died at Hampton Court, Jan. 15th, 1568, and was buried in Westminster Abbey. By her monument it appears she had sixteen children, eight sons and eight daughters; but how many survived her is not mentioned.

5. "Sir Robt. Knowls, cousin-german of Queen Elizabeth, created Knight of the Bath at Coronation of King James I., July 20th, 1603." A whole-length in armour, a fine picture, but not framed. The late *Sir* Francis accidentally saw it, and exchanged a Scripture painting for it. He was son to the Lord Treasurer, and brother to the first Earl of Banbury. When he died I know not, but think he was buried in the Church of Southmims in Midsex. A handsome monument is there, bearing the family arms, but the inscriptions having been on brass are taken off. I believe he left no son, but had a daughter by whom the estate at Northmims came to the Duke of Leeds, the present possessor.

6. "Sir Fras. Knollys, 1624." He was probably another son of the Lord Treasurer, and a brother of the Earl, who lived six or seven years after this picture was drawn. There is no picture of the first Earl, but an old print taken when he was Lord Wallingford, which Lady Knollys made a present of to the Hon. and Rev. F. Knollis, and is now at Burford in Oxon.

7. "Cecilia Knollys, daughter to the Lord Treasurer, afterwards Lady Laughton, 1580." No further account of her.

8. "Letitia Knollys, now Lady Leicester." She was daughter to the Lord Treasurer, and widow of the unfortunate Earl of Essex. No date taken from this picture.

9. "Ann Knollys, now Lady Delawar, 1592." Another daughter of the Lord Treasurer.

10. "Walter Devereux, Earl of Essex, married Letitia Knollys."

11. "Earl of Leicester." A fine portrait.

12. "Fras. Knollys, Esq., married Ann Bateman." Probably a son of No. 6, and father of the following.

13. "Fras. Knollys, 1699." He lived at Thame, and was uncle to Sir Francis.

14. "Richard Knollys, 1699." Lived and died at Mortlake, and was father to Sir Francis. There are two good portraits of these last drawn, when they were men (these having been taken when children); and also

15. "Sir Fras. Knollys, Bart." A handsome picture of the late Sir Francis hangs in the drawing-room.

The Arms are the cross-crosslets quartering the three roses, and one of the lady's has the roses singly.

♣♣♣♣♣♣♣♣♣♣♣

THE first of the family of Phillips of Thame appears to have been Robert Coxe *alias* Phillips, who was living in Queen Elizabeth's reign. He was a tenant and retainer of Sir John Williams, who had possibly brought him there from Glamorganshire or Worcestershire. Certain of the family became subsequently well-to-do merchants, occupying a good position in the Town during the seventeenth century. Several of them held various offices of trust and responsibility; for instance, members of this family were Churchwardens in 1568, 1569, 1630, 1668, 1669, 1703, 1704, 1732, and in 1747; and, having in due course acquired considerable property by commerce, obtained the social position of gentlepeople—subsequently intermarrying with certain families of rank and repute, *e.g.* Crosse, Leaver, and Fienes Trotman. Some members of the family of Phillips settled at Ickford, Forest Hill, Shabbington, and Crendon. At the first-named village, in the year 1634, they were obviously then only of the rank of yeoman; for, in the Buckinghamshire Visitation of that year, under the "Hundred of Ashendon," the following occurs: "Phillips of Ickford no gent." (Harl. MSS., Brit. Museum, No. 1533); but Thomas Phillips, attorney-at-law, of the next generation, became a very wealthy man. He was a Catholic,* as were his children, and his grandson of the same name, sometime a member of the Society of Jesus, became a distinguished author. Another branch of the same family was allied to that of John Milton the poet, whose ancestors had lived at Thame in the fifteenth and sixteenth centuries.

Thomas Phillips, of the Society of Jesus, wrote the *History of Reginald, Cardinal Pole*,* which was published at Oxford in quarto in 1764. It is a pleasantly-written and very truthful work, in which the various mis-statements of Erastian and prejudiced historians concerning the Tudor changes and "reforms" are quietly and effectively opposed. The Author's account of the Sacred Council of Trent is exceedingly valuable; while the whole book, the style of which is dignified and simple, is scholarly, interesting, and meritorious.

He also wrote the following:—

Philemon, in 8vo, printed in 1761, but without a Publisher's name.

Competent critics affirm this to be a record of his own life. There are some severe comments in it upon

* Being Roman Catholics and Nonjurors, their own clergy baptized and married them, though at funerals they were no doubt compelled to have the official services of the parochial minister. Amongst other Nonjurors of the county and neighbourhood at that period were Maurice Belson of Aston Rowant, Elizabeth Winslowe of Haseley, Matthew Haskey of Pyrton, Sir John Curson and Frances Curson of Waterperry, Charles Greenwood of Thame and Easington, and Henry Seymour of Thame.

* It was originally published in 1764 in two parts. The first part contains 460 pages, the second part 247 pages. Of these only a limited edition appears to have been issued. But the intense opposition which it excited, and the numerous answers it received, caused a second edition to be demanded, which was published in two volumes in 1767.

The following were some of the publications in reply:—

Letter to Mr. Phillips, containing some Observations on his History of the Life of Reginald Pole; by Richard Tillard, M.A., 8vo. 1765.

Review of Mr. Phillips's History of the Life of Reginald Pole; by Gloucester Ridley, LL.B., 8vo. 1766.

Animadversions upon Mr. Phillips's History of the Life of Cardinal Pole; by Timothy Neve, D.D., Rector of Middleton Stoney, Oxfordshire, 8vo. 1766.

Remarks upon the History of the Life of Reginald Pole; by Edward Stone, Clerk, A.M., and late Fellow of Wadham College, Oxford, 8vo. 1766.

the general state of English education at that period; and an indirect condemnatory reference to the Thame Grammar School.

The Study of Sacred Literature, fully Stated and Considered in a Discourse to a Student in Divinity, published at Liege, the first edition in 1756, the second in 1758, and the third in 1765.

He was also no mean poet, having not only translated several of the Latin Hymns of the Church, but penned several tasteful and touching original productions. The following lines may be suitably quoted:

To the Right Reverend & Religious Dame, Elizabeth Phillips, on Her Entering the Religious Order of St. Bennet in the Convent of English Dames of the same Order at Gant.

* * * * * *

"Do you my ways direct, my steps attend,
At once my guide, companion, and my friend;
O teach me, teach me heavenly joys to prize,
Myself to conquer and the World despise:
Prompt to my view each blissful scene display,
And charm my sight with gleams of endless day:
Thus, when this frame shall shake with ready death,
And my lips tremble with their latest breath,
My parting soul, in seas of pleasure drown'd,
By saints surrounded, and by angels crown'd,
From earth, on wings of seraphs borne, shall fly,
And mount triumphant to its native sky;
There, thron'd in glory, shall we ever shine,
And friendly spirits place my seat with thine."*

Phillips was held in great respect by many. He went to Rome, where he was introduced by Father Henry Sheldon, S.J., to Prince James Edward, son of King James II., who received him most kindly, and through whose influence he was made Canon of Tongres. He was sometimes in friendly communication with the Nonjurors of Oxfordshire, with Lord Litchfield, Anthony Cope, Lord Wenman, Bishops Newmarch and Spinckes, the Tippings of Wheatfield, Thame, and Ewelme, the Trotmans of Bucknell and Shelswell, and others. In the later years of his life he was highly regarded by the third Earl of Litchfield, Chancellor of the University of Oxford, who presented him with one of the rarest and most precious MSS. in existence—a transcript of St. John's Gospel, in Latin, upon vellum, which Dr. Thomas Lee, one of the Monastic Visitors under Henry VIII., had stolen from the Shrine of St. Cuthbert in Durham Cathedral, when that shrine was so sacrilegiously rifled,—which MS. had no doubt been carefully preserved at Ditchley since the sixteenth century.

The following inscription stands upon a fly-leaf opposite the first page of the text of that manuscript:—

Evangelium Joh'is quod inventum fuerat ad caput beati patris nostri Cuthberti in sepulchro jacens, anno translac'onis ipsius.

Pasted against the cover at the end, with no fly-leaf intervening between it and the last page of the text, is a paper, the writing on which runs thus:—

Hunc Evangelii Codicem
Dono accepit
ab [Georgio] Henrico Comite de Litchfield,
et dono dedit
Patribus Societatis Jesu,
Collegii Anglicani
Leodij; Anno 1769;
Rectore ejusdem Collegij
Joanne Howard:
Thomas Phillips, Sac. Can. Ton.

In a case, along with the MS., which is now preserved at Stonyhurst College in Lancashire, is a Letter in the same handwriting as that of the above inscription, of which a copy follows this. The signature has been cut off, as also the lower right-hand corner of the paper, which is a single sheet, has been accidentally torn off and lost, leaving *lacunæ* at the ends of the three last lines of the letter. One of the *lacunæ* certainly contained the word "Cuthbert," and no more. They are all of the same length.

30th June (no place).

My dear and honored Father,

I desire your Reverence to accept of the MS. which this note accompanies, for your Library. You will see by the short inscription at the beginning, how and when and where it came to be discovered: and I have every reason to think it is Saint Cuthbert's handwriting, from the concurring evidence of these circumstances.

I showed it to the Society of Antiquaries in London, and they said they could .... me so far as to its being of the age in which S .... lived: the letter M being formed as it is in this .... that only.

[In another hand.] Thomas Phillips to
Father J. Howard.

The character of the Phillips family for intelligence, integrity, and benevolence can be easily gathered from records which still remain. The Fathers of the Society of Jesus, (who educated several of their children,) invariably found in them firm and generous friends; and this when Prejudice and Ignorance were even more potent than is the case at the present day. The Catholic line has come to an end.

Representatives of the family of Phillips, however, still remain at Thame and in adjacent parts.

* Brit. Museum, 4to, No. 1346, b. 18, a volume which contains autographs of "Wm. Cole, Coll. Regal., Cantab., A.M., 1748," and of "James Bindley, 1787." See also the *European Magazine* for 1796, the *Catholic Miscellany* for October 1822, pp. 433-5, the *Catholic Magazine* for March 1833, pp. 223-232, and the same serial for March 1834.

Pedigree of Blancks, Crosse, and Phillips, of Thame and Ickford, Co. Bucks.

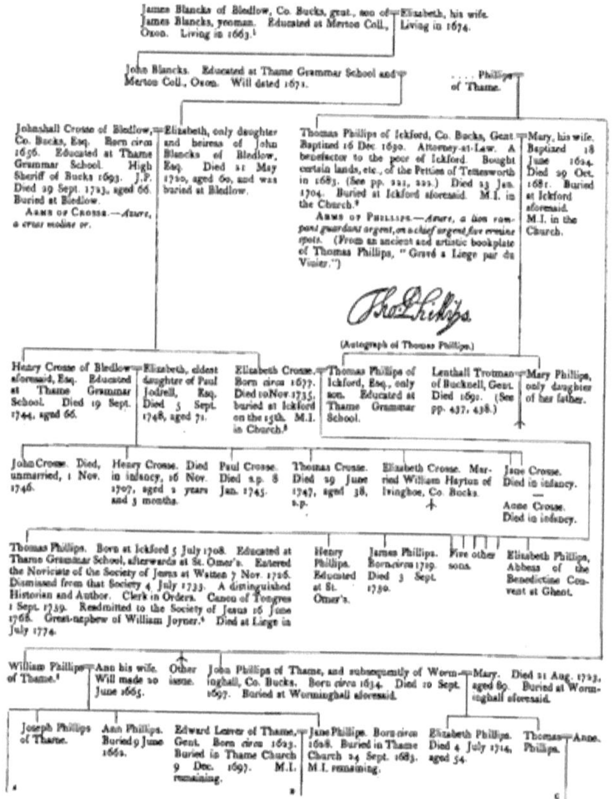

William Leaver. Baptized at Thame 20 Jan. 1658. Buried 1 Oct. 1662.

Richard Leaver of Thame, Gent. Born *circa* 1655. Died 30 Aug. 1733, buried in Thame Church 2 Oct. of the same year. M.I. remaining. = Anne, born *circa* 1656, youngest daughter of Thomas Carter of North Weston, Esq. Buried in Thame Church 9 Nov. 1710. M.I. remaining.

(Leaver impaling Carter.)

Alice. Died an infant 14 Nov. 1729. Buried at Towersey.

Edward Phillips of Thame. Born *circa* 1633. Sole executor of his mother's Will. Died 5 May, buried 8 May 1719, aged 86. = Abigail. Born *circa* 1627. Died 11 May 1689.

William Phillips of Thame. Buried at Thame 10 Dec. 1729. = Elizabeth. Born *circa* 1607. Died 7 Oct. 1703. M.I. in Thame Church.

Edward Phillips, eldest son, of Thame, Gent. Will made 13 May 1792, proved 24 June 1795.

Anne Phillips. Buried 9 June 1662.

Robert Seywell of Sydenham, jun. = Abigail Phillips. Died 23 June 1705. M.I. in Sydenham Church.

William Phillips. Bapt. at Thame 16 Nov. 1662.

William Phillips.

Frances Phillips. Born *circa* 1698. Died 30 July 1724.

SOME EXPLANATORY NOTES TO THE FOREGOING PEDIGREE.

[1] Family of Blanckes.—"James Blanks, a hansome yong man, and contemporarie with A. W. in Mert. Coll., being sent for home to keep his Christmas, A. W. went with him to the house of his father James Blanks, gent., impropriator of Bledlow in Bucks, neare to Thame in Oxfordshire, where he continued more than a week."—Anthony à Wood's *Life* (under the year 1649).

[2] Phillips Monuments at Ickford, Co. Bucks.

Neare this place lye Thomas Phillips Gent. & Mary his only wife. He was liberal to the poor of this parish, and She a person of eminent piety. He was baptized 10^{ber} 16, 1630 & died Jany 23rd 1704. She was baptized June 18, 1624 & died Oct. the 29, 1681. They left one son and one daughter, viz., Thomas and Mary.—South Aisle, Mural Monument, Ickford Church, Bucks. Arms: Phillips impaling Ermine, a lesse gules between three eagles displayed.

In memory of Mrs. Elizabeth Phillips, the only Wife of Thomas Phillips, Gent., who by her had eight sons and one daughter. She was a person of great virtue and true piety, charitable to the poor, and, besides the accomplishments peculiar to her sex, she had all Christian perfections in a very eminent degree. She was sole daughter of Johnshall Crosse, Esq., and departed this life the tenth day of November, in the year of our Lord God 1735, aged 58.—North Aisle. Arms of Phillips impaling Crosse.

Thomas Phillips, of Ickford, in 1697, settled by deed a rent-charge out of his estate there, on the Minister and six trustees, to provide annually three coats, three gowns, and other clothes for poor persons to be distributed at Christmas.

His son Thomas, in 1733, by another deed augmented his father's benefaction, and settled £10 a year on a Schoolmaster to instruct poor children, but it is said that this additional legacy was never received.

[3] From the Registers of Ickford, Co. Bucks.

Marriages.

1738. Oct. 13. Mr. Thomas Phillips and Mrs. Sarah Handley this day owned that they were married the 22nd day of October, in the year 1737: this account was sent in writing, signed by Mrs. Thomas Phillips, the 16th day of October, 1738, to me, John Ryley, Curate.
1764. ... .. Samuel Phillips & Mary Roberts.
1770. ... .. Samuel Phillips & Elizabeth Wheeler.
1795. ... .. Joseph Phillips & Elizabeth Johnson.

Baptisms.

1766. April 7. Ann, daughter of Samuel & Mary Phillips.
1766. Dec. 12. Thomas, son of Samuel & Mary Phillips.
1767. Nov. 26. Thomas, son of Samuel & Mary Phillips.

Burials.

1735. Nov. 15. Elizabeth, wife of Thomas Phillips, Esq.
1742. Sep. 4. Thomas Phillips, gentleman.
1766. April 23. Ann Phillips, infant.
1766. Dec. 22. Thomas Phillips, infant.
1767. Dec. 11. Thomas Phillips, infant.
1768. May 20. Mary, the wife of Samuel Phillips, victualler.
1780. Nov. 26. Elizabeth Phillips.

[4] Family of Joyner of Oxfordshire.

Anne, daughter, by Alice his wife, of Richard Beauforest (who purchased the Abbey Church of Dorchester at the Dissolution of the Monasteries), married Robert Lyde *alias* Joyner of Dorchester.—Visitation of Oxford, 1574, etc., MS. Queen's Coll., H. 33, fo. 7 and 96.

Dorcas, daughter of Leonard Perrott of Drayton, Co. Oxford, by Dorothy, daughter of Thomas Skipwith of St. Alban's, married William Lyde *alias* Joyner of Dorchester, Co. Oxon.

John Joyner of Horsepath disclaimed arms and gentry at Oxford in Sep. 1634.—Visitation of Oxfordshire, Harl. MSS. No. 1533.

3 July 1654. Edward Lyde *alias* Joyner of Horsepath parish and Dorothy, one of the daughters of John Robinson of Whately, yeoman, were married by and with the consent of the said Jo' Robinson, in this parish before Unton Croke, Justice of the Peace, according to the statute. Unton Croke.—Register of Marriages, Marston, near Oxford.

William Lyde *alias* Joyner, a distinguished Fellow of Magdalene Coll., Oxon, and author of *The Roman Empress*, a Tragedy, 4to, 1671, and of some original Hymns on the Blessed Sacrament, etc., died 14 Sep. 1706. He was of an old Oxfordshire family, and great-uncle of Thomas Phillips of Ickford, S.J.

[5] Family of Phillips.—Will of Ann, widow of William Phillips, made 20 June 1665. To son William, £15. To son Joseph, "four-score and tenn pownds." To son-in-law Edward Leaver, £15, "& green say curtains & vallences, & four wrought cushions which I bought of Mrs. Horwood." To grandchildren John and Dorothy Neville, £20 apiece. "To cosin Thomas Phillips of Ickford and my cosin John Phillips of Wor'sall, twenty shillings apiece to buy each of them a ring, whom I do make overseers. All the rest and residue to Edward Phillips, sole executor." Inventory, £327 5s. 0d. Witnesses, James Ross, Mary Ross.

Will, made 17 July 1780, of Thomas Phillips, late of Oakley, Co. Bucks, now of Thame. To brother Richard, a freehold cottage at Oakley and £40; to sister Mary Williams, £40.

Will of Edward Phillips of Thame, gent. Made 13 May 1792; proved 24 June 1795. To Mr. Joseph Burnard of Thame, glover, and Mrs. Sarah Moreton, all household goods and personal estate.—"Wills of the Peculiar of Thame," etc.

As early as 1446 the family of Rose resided in Thame. The name of William Rose occurs in that year, his funeral having then taken place, when the customary charge was made for the use of the funeral lights. Richard Rose married Jean, daughter of Richard Quartermain of North Weston. Thomas Rose, of Thame, was one of the representatives of the borough of Wallingford, Co. Berks, in the Parliament summoned at Westminster A.D. 1472. Nicholas Rouse or Rose is mentioned in 1498; William was Churchwarden in 1507. James Rose the younger was Churchwarden in 1542; and other members of the same family are mentioned from time to time during the last three centuries—John in 1688, and Thomas in 1721. From Thame they passed, at different periods, to Haddenham, Cuddington, Waddesdon, and Wycombe.

Pedigree of Rose of Waddesdon, Co. Bucks.[1]

No. I.

[Visitation of Bucks, A.D. 1634, British Museum, Harl. MSS. No. 1533, Pluto LVI. B., folio 114.]

ARMS.—*Azure, a chevron ermine between three water-bougets argent.*
CREST.—*A buck trippant argent.*

Thomas Rose of Waddesdon in Com. Buckingham. = Allice, d^r Thomas Parsons of Melton Magna [i.e. Great Milton.] in Com. Oxon. [*See p. 232 of this book for* PEDIGREE OF PARSONS.]

- John Rose of Waddesdon, pleader [Qy.] in y^e Inner Temple in London 1598, ob. s.p., was of Waddesdon.
- Thomas Rose of Waddesdon in Com. Bucks. 1634. = Mary, dau'r of Richard Blount of Blounthall in Com. Stafford.
  - William Rose of Dadbrooke in [the Parish of Cuddington] Com. Bucks. = Allice, d^r of Duncombe of Tringe [Qy.].
    - Thomas Rose, now living, 1634.
    - John Rose, 2nd sonne.

♣♣♣♣♣♣♣♣♣♣♣♣

Pedigree of Rose of Thame and Rayners, Co. Bucks.

No. II.

John Rose. Baptized at Thame 10 Dec. 1623. Son of Thomas and grandson of James Rose, who was Churchwarden of Thame in the reign of Henry VIII., was kinsman of Richard Quartermain, Seneschal of Thame Abbey, and held lands at Priestend, under the Abbot of Thame. = ...

William Rose of Thame, Gentleman. Buried there in 1638. M.I. remaining. = ...
- Thomas Rose. Baptized at Thame 12 Feb. 1633.
- Other issue.

(From a gravestone at Thame dated A.D. 1658.)

Issue of John Rose:

- John Rose of Thame. Born *circa* 1649. Churchwarden of Thame 1688, 1689. Lessee of the Prebendal House and lands in Old Thame by grant of Madam Jane Thynne of Egham, Co. Surrey, widow of John Thynne, Esq. Died 7 Feb. 1726, aged 75 years and 11 months. Buried in the South Transept of Thame Church. M.I. remaining. = Elizabeth . . . . Born *circa* 1652. Died 3 April 1690, aged 37 years and 11 months. Buried in the South Transept of Thame Church. M.I. remaining.
  - Thomas Rose, son and heir, of Thame aforesaid. Churchwarden of Thame in 1721. Will made 6 May 1746, and codicils added in 1747 and 1756. = Mary, daughter of William Peck of Thame and Dorothy his wife. Married by licence at Chearsley, Co. Bucks, 1 Sept. 1698.[2] Probate of her husband's Will granted to her 21 April 1758.
    - 4
  - Other issue.
- Other issue.

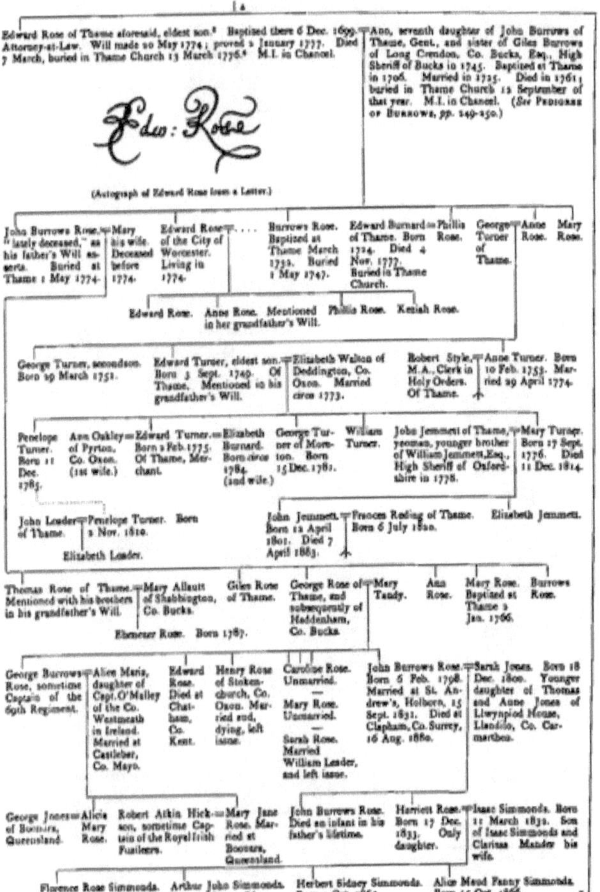

a

Edward Rose of Thame aforesaid, eldest son.[8] Baptised there 6 Dec. 1699. Attorney-at-Law. Will made 20 May 1774; proved 2 January 1777. Died 7 March, buried in Thame Church 13 March 1776.[9] M.I. in Chancel. = Ann, seventh daughter of John Burrows of Thame, Gent., and sister of Giles Burrows of Long Crendon, Co. Bucks, Esq., High Sheriff of Bucks in 1745. Baptised at Thame in 1706. Married in 1725. Died in 1761; buried in Thame Church 12 September of that year. M.I. in Chancel. (*See* Pedigree of Burrows, *pp.* 249-250.)

(Autograph of Edward Rose from a Letter.)

John Burrows Rose, "lately deceased," as his father's Will asserts. Buried at Thame 1 May 1774. = Mary his wife. Deceased before 1774.

Edward Rose of the City of Worcester. Living in 1774. = ...

Burrows Rose. Baptised at Thame March 1732. Buried 1 May 1747.

Edward Burnard of Thame. Born 1724. Died 4 Nov. 1777. Buried in Thame Church. = Phillis Rose.

George Turner of Thame. = Anne Rose.

Mary Rose.

Edward Rose. Anne Rose. Mentioned in her grandfather's Will. Phillis Rose. Keziah Rose.

George Turner, second son. Born 29 March 1751.

Edward Turner, eldest son. Born 3 Sept. 1749. Of Thame. Mentioned in his grandfather's Will. = Elizabeth Walton of Deddington, Co. Oxon. Married *circa* 1773.

Robert Style, M.A., Clerk in Holy Orders. Of Thame. = Anne Turner. Born 10 Feb. 1753. Married 29 April 1774.

Penelope Turner. Born 11 Dec. 1785.

Ann Oakley of Pyrton, Co. Oxon. (1st wife.) = Edward Turner. Born 2 Feb. 1775. Of Thame, Merchant. = Elizabeth Burnard. Born *circa* 1784. (2nd wife.)

George Turner of Moreton. Born 15 Dec. 1781.

William Turner.

John Jemmett of Thame, yeoman, younger brother of William Jemmett, Esq., High Sheriff of Oxfordshire in 1778. = Mary Turner. Born 17 Sept. 1776. Died 11 Dec. 1814.

John Leader of Thame. = Penelope Turner. Born 2 Nov. 1810.

Elizabeth Leader.

John Jemmett. Born 12 April 1801. Died 7 April 1883. = Frances Reding of Thame. Born 6 July 1820.

Elizabeth Jemmett.

Thomas Rose of Thame. Mentioned with his brothers in his grandfather's Will. = Mary Allautt of Shabbington, Co. Bucks.

Ebenezer Rose. Born 1787.

Giles Rose of Thame.

George Rose of Thame, and subsequently of Haddenham, Co. Bucks. = Mary Tandy.

Ann Rose.

Mary Rose. Baptised at Thame 2 Jan. 1766.

Burrows Rose.

George Burrows Rose, sometime Captain of the 69th Regiment. = Alice Maria, daughter of Capt. O'Malley of the Co. Westmeath in Ireland. Married at Castlebar, Co. Mayo.

Edward Rose. Died at Chatham, Co. Kent.

Henry Rose of Stokenchurch, Co. Oxon. Married and, dying, left issue.

Caroline Rose. Unmarried.
—
Mary Rose. Unmarried.
—
Sarah Rose. Married William Leader, and left issue.

John Burrows Rose. Born 5 Feb. 1798. Married at St. Andrew's, Holborn, 15 Sept. 1831. Died at Clapham, Co. Surrey, 16 Aug. 1880. = Sarah Jones. Born 18 Dec. 1800. Younger daughter of Thomas and Anne Jones of Llwynpiod House, Llandilo, Co. Carmarthen.

George Jones of Boonara, Queensland. = Alicia Mary Rose.

Robert Atkin Hickson, sometime Captain of the Royal Irish Fusiliers. = Mary Jane Rose. Married at Boonara, Queensland.

John Burrows Rose. Died an infant in his father's lifetime.

Harriett Rose. Born 17 Dec. 1833. Only daughter. = Isaac Simmonds. Born 11 March 1832. Son of Isaac Simmonds and Clarissa Mander his wife.

Florence Rose Simmonds. Born 20 June 1862.

Arthur John Simmonds. Born 22 Sept. 1863.

Herbert Sidney Simmonds. Born 2 Oct. 1865.

Alice Maud Fanny Simmonds. Born 15 Oct. 1866.

a

R R

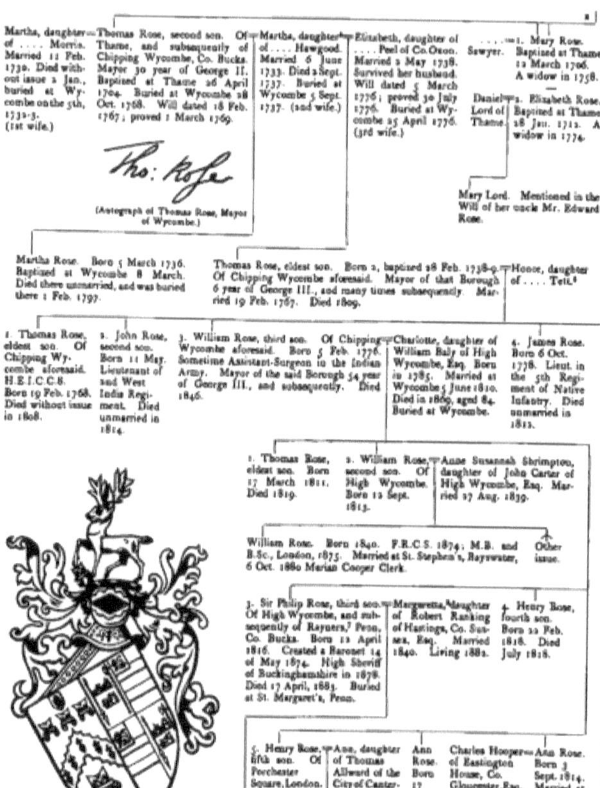

Martha, daughter of .... Morris. Married 11 Feb. 1730. Died without issue 2 Jan., buried at Wycombe on the 5th, 1732-3. (1st wife.) = Thomas Rose, second son. Of Thame, and subsequently of Chipping Wycombe, Co. Bucks. Mayor 30 year of George II. Baptized at Thame 26 April 1704. Buried at Wycombe 28 Oct. 1768. Will dated 18 Feb. 1767; proved 1 March 1769. = Martha, daughter of .... Hawgood. Married 6 June 1733. Died 2 Sept. 1737. Buried at Wycombe 5 Sept. 1737. (2nd wife.) = Elizabeth, daughter of .... Peel of Co. Oxon. Married 2 May 1738. Survived her husband. Will dated 5 March 1776; proved 30 July 1776. Buried at Wycombe 25 April 1776. (3rd wife.)

.... Sawyer. = 1. Mary Rose. Baptized at Thame 12 March 1706. A widow in 1758.

Daniel Lord of Thame. = 2. Elizabeth Rose. Baptized at Thame 28 Jan. 1712. A widow in 1774.

Mary Lord. Mentioned in the Will of her uncle Mr. Edward Rose.

Tho: Rose

(Autograph of Thomas Rose, Mayor of Wycombe.)

Martha Rose. Born 5 March 1736. Baptized at Wycombe 8 March. Died there unmarried, and was buried there 1 Feb. 1797.

Thomas Rose, eldest son. Born 2, baptized 28 Feb. 1738-9. Of Chipping Wycombe aforesaid. Mayor of that Borough 6 year of George III., and many times subsequently. Married 19 Feb. 1767. Died 1809. = Honor, daughter of .... Tett.[6]

1. Thomas Rose, eldest son. Of Chipping Wycombe aforesaid. H.E.I.C.C.S. Born 19 Feb. 1768. Died without issue in 1808.

2. John Rose, second son. Born 11 May. Lieutenant of 2nd West India Regiment. Died unmarried in 1814.

3. William Rose, third son. Of Chipping Wycombe aforesaid. Born 5 Feb. 1776. Sometime Assistant-Surgeon in the Indian Army. Mayor of the said Borough 54 year of George III., and subsequently. Died 1846. = Charlotte, daughter of William Baly of High Wycombe, Esq. Born in 1785. Married at Wycombe 5 June 1810. Died in 1869, aged 84. Buried at Wycombe.

4. James Rose. Born 6 Oct. 1778. Lieut. in the 5th Regiment of Native Infantry. Died unmarried in 1812.

1. Thomas Rose, eldest son. Born 17 March 1811. Died 1819.

2. William Rose, second son. Of High Wycombe. Born 12 Sept. 1813. = Anne Susannah Shrimpton, daughter of John Carter of High Wycombe, Esq. Married 27 Aug. 1839.

William Rose. Born 1840. F.R.C.S. 1874; M.B. and B.Sc., London, 1875. Married at St. Stephen's, Bayswater, 6 Oct. 1880 Marian Cooper Clerk.

Other issue.

3. Sir Philip Rose, third son. Of High Wycombe, and subsequently of Rayners,[7] Penn, Co. Bucks. Born 12 April 1816. Created a Baronet 14 of May 1874. High Sheriff of Buckinghamshire in 1878. Died 17 April, 1883. Buried at St. Margaret's, Penn. = Margaretta, daughter of Robert Ranking of Hastings, Co. Sussex, Esq. Married 1840. Living 1882.

4. Henry Rose, fourth son. Born 22 Feb. 1818. Died July 1818.

5. Henry Rose, fifth son. Of Porchester Square, London. Born 23 April 1825. = Ann, daughter of Thomas Allward of the City of Canterbury, Esq. Married 20 March 1851.

Ann Rose. Born 17 July 1812. Died 5 Feb. 1813.

Charles Hooper of Eastington House, Co. Gloucester, Esq., who died without issue, and was buried at Eastington 22 Sept. 1869. = Ann Rose. Born 3 Sept. 1814. Married at Wycombe 7 Jan. 1858.

Henry Rose. Born 3 Sept. 1853.

Other issue.

Probitate ac Virtute.

Arms of Sir Philip Rose, Bart.—*Azure, a chevron invected erminois between three water-bougets in chief and one in base.*

Crest.—*A stag argent and resting the dexter foreleg on a water-bouget azure.*

C

D

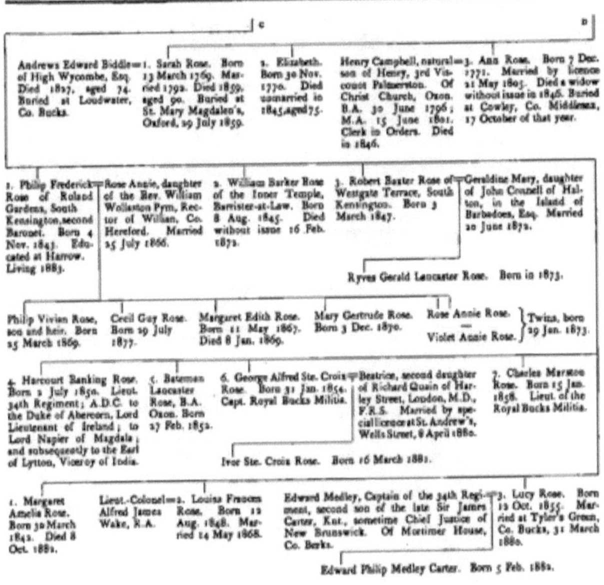

SOME EXPLANATORY NOTES TO THE FOREGOING PEDIGREE.

[1] FROM THE REGISTERS OF WADDESDON CHURCH, CO. BUCKS.

Baptisms.

1603. Samuel, son of Anthony Rosse.
1605. Thomas, son of Anthony Rosse.
1608. July 10. William, son of Anthony Rosse.
1612. July 7. Martha, daughter of John Rosse.
1614. March 19. John, son of Anthony Rosse.
1616. Dec. 13. Alicia, daughter of John Rosse.
1619. March 18. Jone, daughter of John Rosse.
1621. July 18. Mary, daughter of Anthony Rosse.

Marriages.

1612. John Rosse and Margaret Bennet.
1636. April 25. Gabriell Turpin and Ann Rosse.

Burials.

1614. Sept. 7. Thomas Rosse.
1615. Feb. 22. Thomas Rosse.
1616. April 24. John, son of Anthony Rosse.
" Feb. 10. Ann, wife of Mr. Thomas Rosse.
1617. May 14. Martha, daughter of John Rosse.

May 18, 1617. { Thomas Ross. James Ross. Elizabeth Ross.

1642. Dec. 2. Jane, wife of Anthony Ross de Waddesdon.

[2] FROM THE REGISTER OF MARRIAGES, CHEARSLEY CHURCH, CO. BUCKS.—"Thomas Rose and Marie Peck, both of Thame, were married in the Parish Church of Chersley by Licence Sept. 1, 1698."

[3] On folio 195a of the *Visitation of Bucks*, A.D. 1634 (Harl. MSS. No. 1533), stands a coat of four quarters, of which the last is that of Rose of Co. Bucks and Oxon, and another that of Darrell of Lillingstone Darrell.

[4] MR. EDWARD ROSE, GENT., OF THAME.—Will made 20 May 1774, proved 2 January 1777. In it he leaves his lands, woods, and house and cottages at Bledlow Ridge, held of Eton College, to Richard and James Way of Thame, executors, for trust purposes; also freehold properties at Ickford, Towersey, New Thame, Priestend, Old Thame, Pound Lane, and elsewhere. Bequeaths £200 to his son Edward, and a similar sum to his daughter Phillis Burnard; and to his granddaughter Nancy Style half of a copyhold estate at Priestend,

and to all his grandchildren £150 apiece. Mourning rings to Mr. Richard Style and others. He also bequeathe legacies to his servants. His body to be interred in the Chancel of Thame Church, in his family vault.

[3] A large table-tomb remains in Wycombe Churchyard to the memory of the Hawgoods. Mrs. Rose's sister, Miss Hawgood, was Embroideress to Queen Caroline; and a present to her from the Queen is still retained at Rayners.

[4] THE EARL OF SHELBURNE'S "LIFE."—After describing a dance at Wycombe Abbey in January 1768, the following occurs:—"Amongst our ladies was a very pretty bride, the wife of the Mayor, Mr. Rose. Lord Clare divided his compliments between her and Miss Kitty Shrimpton." (*Life of William, Earl of Shelburne, etc.*, vol. ii., p. 178.) A copy of a portrait in oils of this Mrs. Rose (Honor Tett) is at Rayners, the original being in the possession of the Biddle family, kinsfolk of the Hoptons of Canons' Frome, Co. Hereford.

[5] The Collection of Miniatures, etc., at Rayners, numbering 333, is large and remarkably fine,—possibly one of the most complete, if not the best, in the county. It is full of historical portraits, both English and foreign, of singular interest, and contains a choice and almost complete series of the Royal Stuarts, and of the House of Hanover. There are likewise many distinguished statesmen, by eminent artists, together with many beautiful representations of saints, numerous valuable examples of sacred and legendary art, and several family miniatures. Two descriptive Catalogues which I possess have been privately printed,—one, containing 48 pages, describing 260 objects of interest; the second, containing 180 pages, dated "March 1882," and entitled *Rayners: Collection of Miniatures, Enamels, Pictures, and Miscellaneous Articles belonging to Sir Philip Rose, Bart.*

[6] This lady is the daughter of Robert Ranking of Hastings, Esq., son of John Jackson Ranking (born in 1758, died in 1830) by Mary (born in 1763, died in 1846), one of the three daughters and coheiresses of John Lancaster (a baronial race) of the Ringhouse and Low Moss in Furness. The Rankings themselves are a Border family of considerable antiquity, and claim descent from "Gabriel Rankeine, Marchant and Burgess of Edinburgh, A.D. 1600," as set forth in their certified armorial chart.

♣♣♣♣♣♣♣♣♣♣♣

Pedigree of Reynolds of Notley Abbey and Thame.

ARMS.—*Azure, a chevron embattled ermine, charged with four cross-crosslets fitchée gules.*
CREST.—*A portcullis sable, chained azure.*

Henry Reynolds. Baptized 5 July 1671. Said to have been "descended from an ancient family in the town of Leicester." Living at Thame in 1739. Buried at Crendon 7 May 1743. = Grace Hyde. Married *circa* 1697.
ARMS OF HYDE.—*Gules, two chevrons argent.*

Henry Reynolds, eldest son. Bapt. 26 March 1699. Of Thame, and was Tenant of Notley Abbey. Died in Jan. 1729. = Mary, born *circa* 1697, daughter of Edward Randolph of Long Crendon, Co. Bucks, yeoman. She remarried, 21 Jan. 1731, Giles Burrows[2] of Thame, Esq., High Sheriff of Bucks A.D. 1745 (who died in 1763), and she died, aged 86, in 1783, and was buried at Crendon. M.I. in the churchyard. *See* PEDIGREE OF BURROWS, pages 249-250.

John Reynolds, 2nd son.[1] = Mary, daughter of .... Burte of Chilton, Co. Bucks, and afterwards of Easington, Co. Oxon, yeoman. Married at Crendon 26 July 1744. She received a legacy of money and plate from her connection, Mr. Giles Burrows in 1763.
ARMS OF BURTE.—*Argent, a chevron gules, charged with three cross-crosslets or between three bugle-horns stringed sable.*

William Gibson of Crendon aforesaid. = Grace Reynolds. Married at Crendon by Licence 1 May 1744.

Other issue.

Henry Reynolds, Gent. Baptized 22 May 1745. Bought Notley Abbey from General Bertie afterwards Earl of Lindsey.[3] Died 10 July 1806. = Ann, baptized at Thame in March 1746, daughter of Richard and Sarah Head of North Weston. Married at Thame by Licence 14 Dec. 1771. Buried at Crendon 10 Jan. 1802.
ARMS OF HEAD.—*Sable, a chevron between three unicorns' heads erased argent.*

Other issue.

John Reynolds of Notley Abbey and Thame, Gent. Baptized 5 March 1774. Died 21 Oct. 1839. Buried at Crendon. = Arabella, daughter of William Winter of Thame and Elizabeth his wife (who died 24 April 1811, aged 60). Married at Thame by Licence 23 June 1808. Buried at Crendon.

Henry Reynolds of Thame, Attorney-at-Law. Born 31 August 1777. Died 14 May, buried at Crendon 21 May 1806. M.I. in Thame Church. = Elizabeth, only daughter of Edward Wells of Wallingford, Co. Berks, Esq., J.P. Married 18 April 1801. Remarried to Harry Lupton of Thame, Surgeon.
ARMS OF WELLS.—*Argent, a chevron voided azure between three flames proper.*

Other issue.

1. Henry Reynolds, son and heir. Born *circa* 1814. Of Notley Abbey, aforesaid, Gent. Living 1882. = Harriett, daughter of Peter Hughes of Walton Hill, Aylesbury, Co. Bucks, Gent. Living 1882.

2. John Reynolds. Born *circa* 1820. Buried at Cuddington 22 Sept. 1865. = Mary, daughter of John Baker of Cuddington, Co. Bucks, yeoman. He died 15 Nov. 1864, aged 83.

3. William Reynolds. Died unmarried at Crendon Nov. 1881. Buried at Crendon.

A | B

1. Harriett Reynolds, eldest daughter. Living unmarried at Crendon 1882.

Lewis Lovegrove. = 2. Arabella Reynolds. Baptized at Crendon 8 Sept. 1811.

Issue, three sons.

3. Ann Reynolds. Died young. Buried at Crendon.

Other issue.

Anne, born circa 1810, 4th daughter of Edward Wells of Wallingford, Co. Berks, J.P., Esq., by Mary his wife. Married at Thame by Licence as a minor, with consent of her Guardians, 17 August 1829. Died and buried at Thame, aged 36, 28 July 1846. M.I. in Thame Church. (1st wife.) = 1. Henry Wells Reynolds. Born 29 July 1802. Of The Hollies, Thame. Surgeon, M.R.C.S. 1843. Sometime Surgeon to the Bucks Yeomanry Cavalry. Died 12 Jan. 1875. Buried at Thame. Monumental window and Inscription in the Choir there. = Anne, born in 1814, 5th daughter of Richard Holloway of Arlescote, Co. Warwick, Esq. Married 29 August 1850. Living 1882. (2nd wife.)

2. Edward Reynolds. Born at Thame in 1804. Settled at Wallingford, of which town he was sometime the Mayor. Died 1 Dec. 1865. = Hannah, 2nd daughter of Edward Wells of Wallingford aforesaid, by Mary his wife. Married 15 Oct. 1829.

Edward Wells Reynolds of Thame, Gent., only son. Born at Thame 24 Nov. 1836. Gazetted Lieutenant Royal Oxfordshire Volunteer Rifle Corps 7 April 1862. Living 1882. = Harriett, born in 1842, only surviving child of James Giles of Woodstock, Co. Oxon, Gent., and niece of Richard Giles of Oxford, M.D. Married at St. Peter's in the East, Oxford, 6 Feb. 1877. Living 1882.

1. Edith Mary Reynolds. Born 19 June 1879.

2. Henrietta Millicent Reynolds. Born 6 June 1880.

1. Henrietta Margaret Reynolds. Born at Thame 10 August 1835. Died in April 1850. Buried at Thame.

Matthew Hale Humphreys of Thame, Surgeon. Born 1 Oct. 1836. Fourth son of Thomas Humphreys of the City of London, Attorney-at-Law, and Lucy Jacks his wife. M.R.C.S. 1861. Living 1882. = 2. Anne Emily Reynolds. Born at Thame 17 April 1844. Married at Thame 5 July 1866. Living 1882.

1. Richard Humphreys. Born 28 Feb. 1868.

2. Matthew Hale Humphreys. Born 8 Oct. 1871. Died 19 Feb. 1873.

3. Frederic Augustus Humphreys. Born 30 August 1876.

4. George Jacks Humphreys. Born 19 Feb. 1878.

1. Janet Humphreys. Born 12 May 1869.

2. Rose Humphreys. Born 25 Oct. 1870.

3. Alice Humphreys. Born 6 April 1873.

4. Lucy Jacks Humphreys. Born 19 June 1875. Died 11 Dec. of the same year.

5. Florence Humphreys. Born 3 Feb. 1880.

SOME EXPLANATORY NOTES TO THE FOREGOING PEDIGREE.

[1] From the Register of Baptisms belonging to the Church of Crendon, Co. Bucks.

1745. May 22. Henry, ye son of Jno & Mary Reynolds, baptized.
1746. Jan. 31. James, ye son of Jno & Mary Reynolds, baptized.
1749. Dec. 20. Charles, ye son of Jno & Mary Reynolds, baptized.
1809. Dec. 11. Mary Ann, daughter of John & Hashlough Reynolds.
1811. Sep. 8. Harabello, daughter of John and Harabello Reynolds.

From the Register of Marriages of the same place.

1744. May 1. Wm Gibson & Grace Reynolds, marry'd by Lic'.
1744. July 26. Jno Reynolds & Mary Birt of Chilton, marry'd.

From the Register of Burials of the same place.

1743. May 7. Henry Reynolds, buried.
1747. Aug. 28. Tho' Winter of Thame, bury'd.
1747. Oct. 9. The widow Winter of Thame, bury'd.
1799. July 22. John Reynolds, farmer.
1802. Jan. 10. Ann, wife of Henry Reynolds.
1806. May 21. Henry Reynolds the younger, notley abey, attorney.
1806. July 15. Henry Reynold the elder, noteley abey.
1809. Oct. 17. Hirreat, dr of Jno & Harabella Reynolds, notley abey.
1811. May 1. Eliz', wife of Wm. Winter of thame, oxon.
1811. Nov. 17. Mary Ann, daughter Jno & Harabella Reynolds.
1824. Nov. 15. Mary Reynolds, aged 73, buried by Tho. Hayton.

[2] "The family of Burgh or Borrough of Leicester (possibly left-handed kinsfolk of the Barons of that name)—who held a good position, and intermarried with the Cosens or Corsons of Oxfordshire and Derby; the Caves, Baronets; and the Puritan Haslriggs—had been enriched by grants of Church lands, and might furnish some notable facts to a modern Spelman."—Letter from the late Mr. John Gough Nichols, F.S.A., to the Author, dated 8 June 1870.

[3] "My own relations were brought by the Duke of Ancaster from Leicestershire to Notley Abbey. General Bertie, who became Earl of Lindsey on the death of the last Duke, sold Notley to my grandfather on account of the long connection which had existed between the families. We were an old Leicestershire family, some members of which had been Mayors of Leicester. . . . . . . It is curious that in Crendon there were two families of the name of Reynolds, not related to each other—the one, not mine, the oldest, traceable to the days of Henry VI. One of the last members of that race was married to the Rev. Dr. Gerard, Rector of Monks' Risborough, leaving two daughters who lived to be very old women, and died four or five years since."—Letter from the late Mr. Henry Wells Reynolds to the Author, dated 7 March 1874.

IN the reign of Henry VIII. Chesterton Manor House, near Bicester, was occupied by "John Maunde, Gent.,* Bailiff and Steward of the Estate

ARMS OF MAUNDE.

belonging to the College of Ashridge." He had a family of seven sons and daughters. John Maunde of this race, whether son or nephew of the above, seems uncertain, was knighted, and his son Simon became one of the Yeomen of the Guard to Queen Elizabeth. They had intermarried with the Warwickshire families of Clinton and Bushell,—both of which had been equally earnest in promoting the spoliation of the religious houses under the Tudors. Other members of the Maunde family settled at Witney, Wendlebury, Wheatfield, and in the parishes of St. Mary and St. Michael at Oxford. Entries of their Births, Marriages, and Deaths may be found in the various Registers of those Parishes. A branch likewise settled at Thame at the beginning of the reign of Charles I., and another batch of their kinsmen arrived there from Chesterton about the close of the Civil War—a period of considerable change and migration—and flourished for about a century. Robert Maunde was Churchwarden in 1636, William in 1668, another Robert in 1710, and Timothy in 1749. Nicholas Maunde, Curate of Thame in 1714, died Rector of Wheatfield. Their names often occur in the Registers of Thame; and there are freestone monuments still existing at the outside of the west end of the Church to their memory, somewhat defaced by Time. In earlier years they had occupied a good social position; but subsequently fell into the lower ranks, while some came to penury. But at Thame this race, like so many others which attained distinction and affluence through the appropriation of Church spoils, is now extinct.

William—grandson of William Harding of Thame, who was one of the personal attendants of Lord Williams, and is mentioned in his Will—aged 17 in 1641, and at that time a Fellow of St. John's College, Oxford, was an ardent Royalist, having taken up arms for his King and country. He had by his zeal rendered himself most unpopular with the Parliamentarians hereabouts, during the occupation of the Town by the troops of Lord Essex; and was obliged to leave his home at Thame to avoid condign punishment. He suffered severely for his sturdy loyalty, both in mind, body, and estate.

On July 29, 1645, Sir Thomas Gardiner of Cuddesdon, son of the Recorder of London, and a Captain of Horse under King Charles I., who, knowing the neighbourhood well, had taken a most active and efficient part in the various fights and skirmishes in and about Thame, and was greatly beloved by his soldiers; on his death, was buried in Christ Church Cathedral under Alexander Gerard's monument. He had been knighted by his Majesty while he sat at dinner, upon the delivery of the news of Prince Rupert's success against the Rebels who had besieged Newark, in March 1643-4. The arms of Gardiner are, Party per pale gules and or, a fesse between three hinds trippant counterchanged: a label for difference.

* MAUNDE OF CHESTERTON.

John Maunde of Chesterton, in Com. Oxon, gen. = Sibill, dau. of Tho. Clynton of Castle in Co. . . . . . , gen. (Qy. Clinton of Coleshill, Co. Warwick.)

Symon Maunde of Chesterton, pd. yeo. of the guarde to Queen Elizabeth.

—Harl. MS. No. 808, folio 29.

William Maunde. Died 1612. =

Isabel Maunde, his heiress. = John Maunde of Witney.

Of your charity pray for the souls of John Maunde & X'tian his wife which John deceased the vii day of February in the year of our Lord God MVXXX on whose soules & all Christians Jesu have mercy. Amen.

(Under it seven boys.)

Under the hope of the resurrection lyeth buryed here the body of William Maunde Gent. & Anne his wife: the said William lived the age of 67 years & dyed the xxix Day of May Anno Do'ni 1612 & the said Anne dyed . . . . Anno do'ni . . . . both of them living & dying in credit & good reputation in ye country.

Here lieth the body of George Maunde of Chesterton, who died 21st July 1648.

Heare lieth the Body of Richard Maunde the Son of George Maunde who dec'ed the 26 of July at the age of 17 years 1665.

On a diamond stone, "M.M. 1690."

MAUNDE OF OXFORD.

Nicholas Maunde of Oxford, apothecary. Born *circa* 1646; died 10 Nov. 1681, aged 35. Buried in St. Mary's Church, Oxford. = Mary. Born *circa* 1650; died 8 Nov. 1684, aged 34. Buried in St. Mary's Church, 11 Nov.

Elizabeth. Bap. 19 Sep. 1672; bur. 26 Aug. 1673.
—
Ann. Bap. 5 March 1673-4; bur. 4 Sep. 1678.

Nicholas. Bap. 14 May 1675. Matriculated from Oriel Coll. 19 March 1691-2. Aged 16.

John. Bap. 5 July 1677.
—
Thomas. Bur. 13 June 1683.

Ancher. Bap. 4 March 1679-80. Bur. 25 March 1680.

—From Parochial Registers and Monumental Inscriptions.

Margaret, dau. of Edw. Bussell of Brodmerston, Co. Warwick. = ... Maunde of Chesterton.

Simon Maunde. Anne Maunde. Isabell Maunde. = Edw. Porter.

Giles Porter.

—Abstract from William Camden's *Visitation of Warwickshire*, Harl. MSS. No. 1167.

Henry Gardiner, "a most noble and valiant man," a Captain of Horse, the second son of Sir Thomas, was killed in the High Street at Thame, Sep. 7, 1645, when "the Cavaliers beat up the quarters of the Parliamentarians there;" but was borne away and buried near his father, "amid the lamentations and regret of all good townsmen thereabouts."

In 1654, as Anthony à Wood relates in his *Life*, "Hussey and .... Peck, two gentlemen that were lately officers in the King's Army, were hanged in the Castle Yard in Oxon, to the great reluctancy of the generous royalists then living in Oxon. They were out of commission and employ, had no money to maintain them, which made them rob on the highway. After a tedious imprisonment in the jayle in Oxon they were condemn'd to dye by that inveterate enemy to the royal partie, John Glynn, Serjeant-at-Law, who this year went Oxford circuit."

William Mordaunt of Turvey, Co. Beds (ancestor of L'Estrange Mordaunt, created a Baronet 29 June 1611), married Margaret, daughter of John Peck of Cople, Co. Beds, whose son of the same name had settled at Thame in the reign of King Henry VII., founding a family there of yeomen and merchants. The name of Peck is frequently found both in the Churchwardens' and Parochial Accounts. Many of their sons were educated at the Grammar School, and memorials of other members of this race still remain in the Church.

A few particulars of some other of the more remarkable persons educated at Thame School must now be given:—

Edward, son of Edward Pocock, of St. Peter's in the East, Oxford, and Fellow of Magdalene College, born 8 Nov. 1604, was educated under Mr. Richard Boucher, after which he entered Magdalene Hall. Subsequently migrating to Corpus Christi College he there graduated, and in 1629 was ordained Priest by Corbet, Bishop of Oxford. He went as English Chaplain to Aleppo in the following year, gaining much information and valuable experience, and became Professor of Arabic at Oxford, 10 Aug. 1636. He was also appointed Canon of Christ Church and Regius Professor of Hebrew; but was ejected by the Cromwellites. He married Mary Burdett of Thame, and died 10 Sep. 1691, remarkable for his learning, piety, and high character, and was buried in Christ Church Cathedral.*

John Fell, born at Longworth, Co. Berks, was the son of Dr. Samuel Fell, some of whose relations lived at Thame, by Margaret his wife, daughter of Thomas Wyld of Worcester. He was educated at Thame School under Dr. Burte; and in 1636 became a student of Christ Church and Chaplain to the King, but was turned out by the allies of the Usurper during the Great Rebellion. Later he was made, firstly, Canon, then Dean of Christ Church, Vice-Chancellor of Oxford from 1666 to 1669, and six years afterwards Bishop of Oxford. He died greatly respected in 1686, and was buried in Christ Church Cathedral; regarded by all as a staunch Churchman, a divine of eminence, and a man of integrity, piety, and great consistency of character.

John Holt, eldest son of Sir Thomas Holt, by Susan, daughter of John Peacock,* born at Thame 30 Dec. 1642, was educated at the Grammar School under Mr. Ayliffe; then entered at Oriel College under the Rev. Francis Barry of Thame; graduated and was called to the Bar 27 Feb. 1663; he was made Serjeant 22 April 1686, and also Recorder of London. He was knighted and appointed Lord Chief Justice of the Court of King's Bench 17 April 1689, which he held for twenty-one years. He died in Bedford Row, London, the 5, and was buried the 10 of March 1709-10, aged 67, at Redgrave, Suffolk. His portrait was painted by Sir Godfrey Kneller, and engraved by R. White in 1689.

John Wilkes, born 17 Oct. 1727, second son of Israel Wilkes, a distiller of Clerkenwell, sprung from a family of that name at Leighton Buzzard, was also educated at Thame School under Mr. Kipling, and afterwards at the University of Leyden. Wilkes was evidently a man of ability and decision, and made himself felt in public affairs,—being supposed by some to have advanced "the cause of Liberty;" though certain of his contemporaries maintained that much of his so-called "patriotism" was mere vapour, and that his twin ruling passions were selfishness and ambition. The cheap popularity of the Rabble, of course, never counts for much; for it is invariably only fleeting and worthless. Wilkes was, however, undoubtedly well read, though no great scholar, brilliant in conversation,

* Arms of Pocock impaling Burdett: Chequy argent and gules, a lion rampant guardant or; Azure, two bars or, on the upper bar three martlets gules.—From the Monument in Ch. Ch. Cathedral, Oxford.

* John Holt, the grandfather of Sir Thomas Holt, is believed "to have come out of Lancashire," and to have been the fifth son of Francis Holt of Grizelhurst in that county, by Ellen, daughter of Sir John Holcroft, Knt. There are pedigrees of the family of Holt of Stoke Lyne, Co. Oxon, in Harl. MS. No. 4170, folio 75; as also in MSS. Nos. 5966, 5812, folio 151 a. Arms of Holt (granted in 1567), Argent, on a bend engrailed sable three fleurs-de-lys of the field.—See also a *Life of Sir John Holt*, etc., by a Gentleman of the Inner Temple. London: 1764. The Lord Chief Justice's brother, Rowland Holt, married Prisca Ballowe of Thame; and of a subsequent generation Charles Holt of Stoke Lyne (who had married Martha, daughter of John Stribblehill of Thame, Esq., by Frances, daughter of Thomas Carter of North Weston, Esq.), was High Sheriff of Oxfordshire in 1721. (See p. 535.)

an artful political tactician, a firm friend, somewhat fond of display, and exceedingly entertaining in company. After a chequered political life, full of turmoil, Wilkes died, somewhat neglected by the Public, at his daughter's residence in Grosvenor Square, 26 Dec. 1797, and was buried in the Chapel of South Audley Street.

Richard Powell, born at Thame about the close of the year 1766, the son of Joseph Powell, Gent., by Francis his wife, sister of Richard Smith, Esq., was likewise educated first at the Grammar School, but subsequently on the Foundation at Winchester, where he distinguished himself by his accurate scholarship and painstaking energy. He matriculated at Pembroke College, Oxford, 19 January 1785, but, removing to Merton, graduated B.A. 23 October 1788; M.A. 31 October 1791; B.M. 12 July 1792; and M.D. 20 January 1795. In the following year he became a Fellow of the Royal College of Physicians of London, and in 1803 was appointed one of the Physicians of St. Bartholomew's Hospital. Three years previously he had been made by the Government a Commissioner for Licensing and Inspecting Lunatic Asylums. He was Censor of the College of Physicians for some time; and in 1808 was selected to deliver the Harveian Oration—in his hands a thoughtful, scholarly, and elegant composition. He contributed six papers to the *Transactions* of the College. He was also a Fellow of the Society of Antiquaries, to which, on 17 November 1817, he communicated a learned paper, entitled "An Account of a Deed granted by the Prior and Convent of St. Bartholomew, Smithfield," which was printed in vol. xix. of the *Archæologia*. For many years he was one of the leading London physicians, and his advice was much sought after. He was held in respect both by the profession and the public. He died at his residence, York Terrace, Regent's Park, on the 18th August 1834. A portrait of him may be found in Pettigrew's *Medical Portrait Gallery*; and Sir Henry Halford, in delivering the Harveian Oration, spoke of him with great praise.

For the silver medal of Thame School, of which an illustration is here given, I am indebted to the kindness of the Rev. Edward Marshall, of the Manor House of Sandford St. Martin, Oxon. It was struck about the year 1783, for it was near that time bestowed as an honourable distinction upon Nicholas Marshall,* born in 1768, who afterwards became the Rev. Nicholas Marshall Hacker, of Enstone, Oxon, who had received his early education at the Grammar School

Medal of Thame Grammar School.

under the Rev. William Cooke. Another medal, in yellow metal, was obtained by the same scholar, and is preserved by Mr. Marshall.

May this School, in the future, send forth worthy successors to those, known and unknown, who, having benefited by, and done credit to, its teaching, have finished their work here and passed away.

Of the families which belonged to the Town in the middle of the sixteenth century, there are still representatives of the following:—Annesley,* Saunders, Phillips, Cope, Jemott or Jemmett, Watson, Ayres,† Arnott, Cotton, Cowley, Eeles, Green, Wheeler, Stone, Thame, Way, Page, Winslowe, Burte or Byrde, Greenwood, Francklin, and some others.

♣♣♣♣♣♣♣

I NOW proceed to set forth a Pedigree of Lupton of Thame—an old north-country family, a member of which settled here in Oxfordshire during the eighteenth century. Canon Phelps of Ridley, Co. Kent, informs me that his uncle, Mr. Harry Lupton of Thame, had established his claim to be of kin to Dr. Roger Lupton, the celebrated Provost of Eton. Other members of the family were distinguished both in divinity and general literature, and served God faithfully both in Church and State.

* He was the son of Nicholas Marshall, Esq., D.L., by Eleanor, daughter of John Coxwell of Ablington House, co. Gloucester, Esq. He graduated from St. Alban's Hall, Oxford, as B.A., 30 May, 1793. A black marble slab covering his tomb remains at Church Enstone, co. Oxon, on the floor of the north aisle, with the following inscription:—"Underneath this pew lieth the body of the Rev. Nicholas Marshall Hacker, M.A., who departed this life March 11th, 1827, aged 58 years." There is also a marble monument to his memory on the north wall.

* "William Annesley, Esq., elder son to Thomas of Roddington (Co. Notts), married Mabel, daughter of . . . . English, and had issue five sons and four daughters, viz., Sir Hugh of Mapledurham, in Oxfordshire, who left three coheirs."—*Peerage of Ireland*, by Mr. Lodge, vol ii., p. 272. Dublin: 1754.

See references to this family on pp. 69, 72, 78. One of the Snapes, allied to the Petties, married an Annesley of Thame and Mapledurham. See p. 215.

† Philip Ayres of Thame, an author of some repute, wrote *Emblemata Amatoria, in Four Languages, Dedicated to the Ladys*, 8vo. London: 1683. Also *Lyric Poems, Made in Imitation of the Italians*, by Philip Ayres, Esq., 8vo. London: 1687. A descendant of the above, Philip Bernard Ayres of Thame, M.D., a quarter of a century ago, held a high position as a Physician at Charing Cross Hospital and in London; but died comparatively young and much regretted.

(Arms of Lupton. From eighteenth-century stained glass at Sedbergh.)

Pedigree of Lupton of Thame.

Arms of Lupton.—*Argent, a chevron sable charged with three white lilies, leaves vert, between as many wolves' heads erased of the second, langued or, on a chief of the last a Tau of St. Anthony between two escallops or.*

Crest.—*A wolf's head erased sable.*

John, son of Christopher Lupton of the township of Lupton, Co. Westmoreland, a kinsman of Roger Lupton, Clerk in Orders. D.D. Founder of the Free School of Sedbergh, Co. York, and afterwards Provost of Eton. = Joane or Jane, daughter of Robert Middleton of Middleton Hall, Co. Westmoreland. Living 1660. Arms of Middleton.—*Argent, a saltire engrailed sable.*

Issue:

- Thomas Lupton, son of John. A Councillor-at-Law, and one of the Benchers of Lincoln's Inn. = Mary, daughter of Henry Tempest of Stella, Co. Durham. Arms of Tempest.—*Argent, a bend engrailed between six martlets sable.*
- Other issue.

Sackville Bale of Albemarle Street, London. Living 1755.

Issue of Sackville Bale:

- Mary Bale, eldest daughter. Resided as a widow at North Weston, near Thame. = Richard Brudenell Exton, M.D., son of William Exton and the Hon. Mary Brudenell. Arms of Exton.—*Azure, a cross argent between twelve crosses-crosslet fitchée or.*
- Letitia Charlotte Bale, 2nd daughter. Buried in Thame Church. = Thomas Lupton. A younger son of Thomas.
- Jane Theodosia Bale, 3rd daughter. Died at Thame 21 Sept. 1806. Buried beside her husband. = Henry Style. Born *circa* 1709. Youngest son of Robert Style, Clerk in Orders, sometime Curate of Thame, subsequently Rector of Towcester, Co. Northants, and eventually heir of his father, and Lord of the Manor of Syresham in the same County. Of Thame. Died 8 Dec. 1798, aged 89. Buried in the north transept of Thame Church. M.I. remaining.

Issue of Henry Style and Jane Theodosia Bale:

- Harry Style.
- Jane Theodosia Style. Buried 27 Oct. 1756.
- Henrietta Frances Style. Baptized 10 Feb. 1763. Buried 21 Jan. 1765.
- Robert Style. Born *circa* 1754. Matriculated from Pembroke College, Oxon, 13 June 1770. Clerk in Orders. Curate of Thame 1777. = Ann, born 10 Feb. 1753, daughter of George Turner of Thame by Anne his wife, daughter of Edward Rose, Attorney-at-Law. Married at Thame by Licence 29 April 1774. *See* Pedigree of Burrows, *page* 250.
- Jane Theodosia Style. Baptized at Thame 27 Oct. 1756. Died 7 Jan. 1834. Buried in the chancel of Thame Church. [A miniature on ivory of this lady, exquisitely painted, is in the possession of Mrs. Chard of Thame, her grand-daughter.] = Sackville Bale Lupton, only son. Of Thame. Surgeon. Born 22 Oct. 1755. Died 3 June 1840. Buried in the chancel of Thame Church. M.I. remaining.
- Charlotte Theodosia Sackville Style. Bapt. 23 March 1758. Died without issue. Buried in Thame Church. = John Holland. Born *circa* 1759. (Son of John Holland, who matriculated from Balliol College, Oxon, 7 July 1737; M.A. 26 Jan. 1743; subsequently Clerk in Orders; himself son of John Holland of Ludlow, Co. Salop, Gent.) Matriculated from Pembroke College, Oxon, 15 Dec. 1778. Graduated B.A., Balliol, 25 May 1780; M.A. 4 Dec. 1783. Clerk in Orders. Curate of Thame 1782. Vicar of Aston Rowant with Stokenchurch, Co. Oxon.
- Other issue.

Issue of Robert Style and Ann Turner:

- Joseph Gascoigne Style. Baptized 9 Sept., buried 9 Oct. 1777.
- Theodosia Charlotte Style. Baptized 3 June 1779.
- Frances Henrietta Style. Born 3, baptized 4 March 1782.

Issue of Sackville Bale Lupton and Jane Theodosia Style:

- Thomas Lupton. Born at Thame 12, baptized 13 Sept., 1782. Assistant Surgeon in the Oxfordshire Militia. Died 25 May 1810. Buried at Thame.
- Harry Lupton. Born at Thame 1 Dec. 1785. Baptized 2 March 1786. Died at Thame 18 June 1861. = Elizabeth, daughter of Edward Wells of Wallingford, Co. Berks, Gent. (by Mary Prouse his wife), and widow of Henry Reynolds of Thame, Attorney-at-Law. Died 7 March 1848. Buried at Thame 13 of the same month.
- Sackville Lupton. Baptized at Thame 31 March 1784. Died young.
- William Lupton. Died young.
- Arthur Lupton. Born 20 March 1790. Died two days afterwards.
- William Lupton. Born 27 August 1791. Died 29 Dec. 1792.
- Arthur Style Lupton. Born 2 Oct. 1792. Died the following day.

A

Elizabeth Lupton. Born 25 Sept. 1815.

Marian Lupton. Born 1 April 1818. Died 21 Oct. of the same year.

Matilda Dorothea Lupton.

Charles Henry, son of George William James Chard of Winchester, Mus. Doct., by Amelia, daughter of the Rev. Mr. Burdon, M.A., Oriel College, Oxon. Of Winchester. = Jane Lupton. Born in 1812. Married by Licence at Thame 7 April 1830. Living 1882.

Harry Lupton, eldest son. Born 3 Aug. 1820. Died unmarried in London 26 Sept. 1853. Buried at Thame.

Sackville Lupton, 2nd son. Born 11 Dec. 1823. Surgeon. Of Thame. Died there 28 Jan. 1856. (1st husband.) = Ellen, daughter of Thomas Hearne Seymour of Thame, by Arabella Stone his wife. A kinsman of Thomas Hearne, M.A. 3 July 1703, the learned and distinguished Oxford Antiquary. Married at St. Pancras, London, 18 March 1851. = John Wilkinson Edwards. Clerk in Orders. Educated at B.N. Coll., Oxon. Graduated B.A. 21 May 1834. Rector of Beddiley, Co. Chester. Mar. at Thame 7 May 1861. (2nd husband.)

B

John Hendley, of a family long resident in Kent. Deputy Surgeon-General, and C.B. Mr. Hendley has seen much active service. He took part in certain operations on the Western Coast of Africa in 1854-5. In Nov. 1854 he was engaged against rebellious tribes; also in July and August 1855 with a combined force of English and French troops against the Mahometans of Combo, River Gambia, when he was wounded. In 1863 he was on duty in the North-Western portion of India. In the Afghan campaign of 1878-9 he was the principal medical officer of the Western Afghanistan Field Force; and was mentioned with commendation in despatches. = Elizabeth Amelia Janet Chard, only daughter. Married at Thame 9 Jan. 1856.

Sackville Lupton, 2nd son. Born 2 March 1854. Of Leamington, Co. Warwick. Living 1882.

Harry Lupton, eldest son. Born 13 May 1852. Licentiate of the Royal Coll. of Physicians of London. Of Stratford-on-Avon, Co. Warwick. = Clara Maria. Born at Sulhampstead, Co. Berks. Daughter of John Dewe of Benson, Co. Oxon, Gent., of an old Oxfordshire family of Bampton, etc. Married at St. Helen's, Abingdon 12 Nov. 1874.

Ellen Seymour Edwards. Born 16 Feb. 1862.

Montagu Stone Edwards. Born 14 Jan. 1865.

Nevill Perine Edwards. Born 4 Nov. 1866.

Harry Lupton, eldest son. Born 13 Aug. 1875.

Sackville Lupton, 2nd son. Born 19 Aug. 1876.

Clara Hayton Lupton. Born 2 Oct. 1877.

Alice Lupton. Born 25 Aug. 1879.

John Lupton Hendley.

Charles Edward Hendley.

Arthur Gervase Hendley.

Walter Hendley.

Bessie Hendley.

Edith Alice Hendley.

Ethel Mary Hendley.

Margaret Gertrude Hendley.

C

Letitia Charlotte Lupton, eldest daughter. Born 26 May, baptized 6 July 1781. Died and was buried at Lamberhurst, Co. Sussex.

Matilda Dorothea. Born 19 Jan. 1799. Bapt. 23 April 1800.

Thomas Prankerd. Born in 1781. Second son of Thomas Phelps, M.A., Hertford College, Oxon, Clerk in Orders, Vicar of Haddenham, Co. Bucks, by Elizabeth, daughter of Henry Dampier, first cousin of Sir Henry Dampier, K.B., and of his brother Thomas Dampier, D.D., Lord Bishop of Rochester; of the Dampiers of East Hall, Co. Somerset. Vicar of Tarrington, Co. Hereford. Died in 1854, and was bur. there.

Arms of Phelps.—*Paly of five argent and sable, semée of cross-crosslets or.*

= Jane Theodosia Lupton. Born 21 April 1788. Baptized 24 July 1789. Married 10 July 1809. Died at Birling Vicarage, Co. Kent, 22 June 1857. Buried beside her husband at Tarrington.

Anna Maria Hollier. Married at Thame 29 June 1818. (1st wife.) = Jacob Watson of Thame, and subsequently of London, Co. Oxon. Of the 14th Regiment of Foot. Subsequently Major and Lieut.-Colonel of the same. Younger brother of Gen. Sir James Watson, K.C.B. Died and was buried at Wendover, Co. Bucks in 1859. = Diana Style Lupton. Born 7 June 1794. Married by Licence at Thame 26 June 1835. Died at Thame 13 Feb. 1873. (2nd wife.)

Decima Holland Lupton. Born 8 Jan. 1796.

Henry Dampier Phelps, eldest son. Born 1811. Graduated M.A., Wadham College, Oxon, 28 April 1836. Clerk in Orders. Vicar of Birling, Co. Kent. Died without issue in 1864. = Frances Jane Brown.

Thomas Prankerd Phelps, 2nd son. Born 1814. Graduated B.A., Worcester College, Oxon, 6 June 1838. Clerk in Orders. Rector of Ridley, Co. Kent, and owner of East Hall aforesaid. Hon. Canon of Rochester and Rural Dean. = Laura, 4th daughter of Sir Percival Hart Dyke of Horeham, Co. Sussex, Bart., by Anne, eldest daughter of Robert Jenner of Chislehurst, Co. Kent, Esq. Married 9 Feb. 1847.

Arms of Dyke.—*Or, three cinquefoils sable.*

Matilda, daughter of the Rev. William Goodall of Berkhampstead, Co. Herts, and subsequently, by right of his wife, of Dinton Hall, Co. Bucks. Brother of the Provost of Eton. Died without issue. (1st wife.)

Arms of Goodall.—*Gules, an eagle displayed argent, armed or, on a canton of the second a chaplet gramine vert.*

= Sackville Phelps, 3rd son. Born 1821. = Jane Scott Darlington. (2nd wife.)

Henry George Hart Phelps. Born 1849.

Hubert Dampier Phelps. Born 1851. In the Royal Navy.

Lancelot Ridley Phelps. Born 1853. M.A., Oxon. Clerk in Orders. Fellow of Oriel College, Oxford.

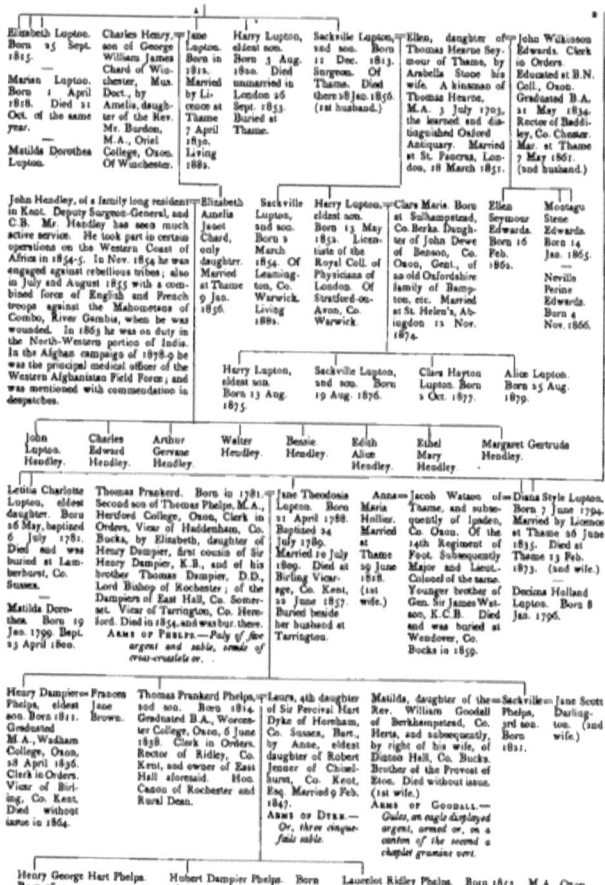

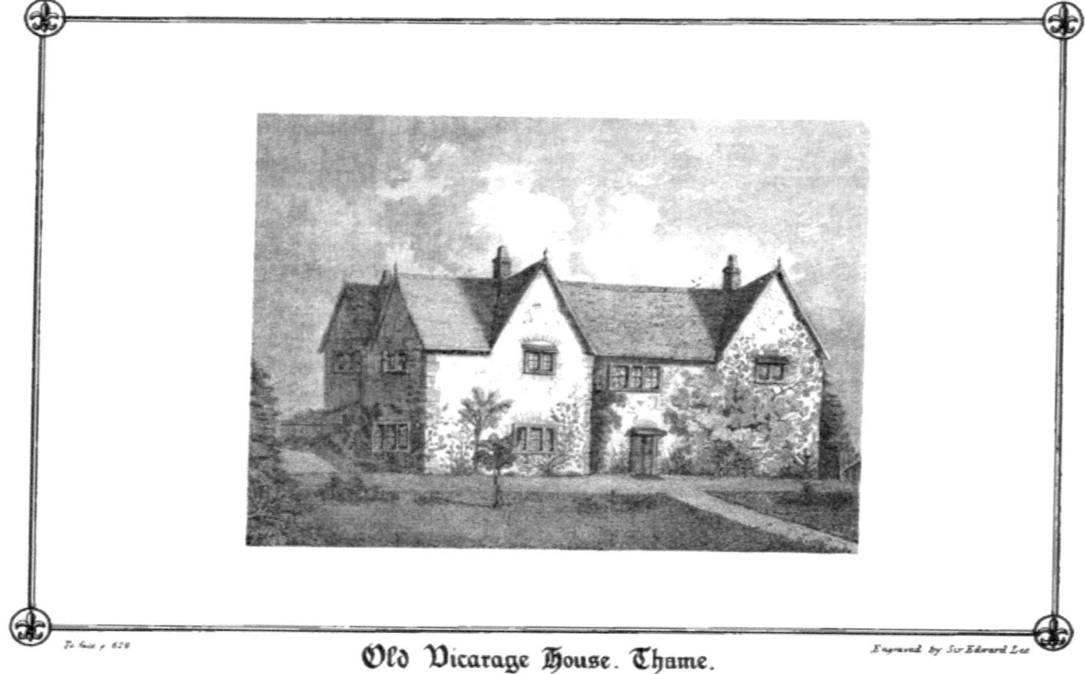

To face p. 629

Old Vicarage House. Thame.

Engraved by Sir Edward Lee.

Pedigree of Patten, Rose, Talbot, and others.

Catherine, daughter of Randle Fielding or Fielden of Blackburne, Co. Lancaster, by Mary Bolton his second wife. Married 3 July 1716. Died 1731, aged 39. (1st wife.) = Jonathan Patten of Manchester, Merchant. Born 13 April 1695. A younger brother of Thomas Patten of Bank Hall, Warrington, Co. Lancaster, Esq., Lord of Winmarleigh. Of the family of William Patten of Waynflete, Bishop of Winchester from A.D. 1447 to 1486. = Jane, daughter of John Sydall of Green, and relict of John Green of Holcombe, Co. Lancaster. Married 1732. Died 1745. (2nd wife.)

Arms of Patten of Winmarleigh.—(John Wilson Patten, created Baron Winmarleigh 16 March 1874.)—*Paully ermine and sable, a canton gules.* Thomas Patten, of this family, born 22 Feb. 1770, died 7 Dec. 1827, took the surname of Wilson in compliance with the testamentary injunction of his kinsman Thomas Wilson, D.D., Bishop of Sodor and Man.

Letitia Patten. Born in 1737. = Joseph Rose of Foster Lane, London, Merchant, and subsequently of Tottenham, Co. Middlesex, Esq.
Arms of Rose.—*Gules, three water-bougets argent.*

Thomas Crews of Thame, Merchant. Born *circa* 1687. Died 26 Jan. 1727, aged 60. = Sarah, daughter of Matthew Loder of Thame, Naval Surgeon. (*See p.* 121.)

(Arms of Loder of Thame.)

Giles Prickett. = Mary Crews. Married at Thame by Licence 30 April 1759.

Richard Wyndowe, Surgeon, of Islington, Co. Middlesex. (1st husband.) = Anne Crews. = Richard Talbot of Thame, Merchant, son of Richard Talbot, sen., and Mary Basse his wife, and grandson of Robert and Anne Basse of Thame. Married by Licence at Thame 30 May 1760. (2nd husband.)
Arms of Talbot.—*Gules, a lion rampant within a bordure engrailed.*

Matthew. Died 25 Dec. 1778, an infant.

Other issue.

Other issue.

Joseph Rose. B.A. Trinity College, Oxon, 12 May 1789. Clerk in Orders. Sometime Curate of Thame. Minister of the Chapel of Ease, Islington. Hon. D.D. Founder's kin, through his mother, at All Souls and St. Mary Magdalene Colleges, Oxford. Died 17 June 1830. M.I. in Chapel of Ease aforesaid. = Bett Talbot, eldest daughter. Died 13 May 1846. M.I. in Chapel of Ease aforesaid.

Thomas Richard Talbot of Thame, only son. Died *circa* 1842. Buried in Thame Church.

Mary Penelope Talbot, 3rd daughter. Died unmarried.

John Smith of Thame, Surgeon. = Martha Maria Talbot, 4th daughter. Died, a widow, 1859.

Francis Smith. Died an infant. Buried at Thame.

Thomas Prickett of Thame. Born *circa* 1761. Attorney-at-Law. Died 26 Aug. 1816, aged 55. M.I. in Thame Church. = Sarah Smith Talbot, 2nd daughter.

Joseph Rose. Born 31 Dec. 1791. Of Islington. Surgeon. Died unmarried 1 April 1865.

Holtom George Bennett. Born 25 Dec. 1792. Brother of the Rev. John Townsend Bennett, M.A., Sub-Dean of St. Paul's Cathedral. Died without issue 21 July 1854. = Mary Anne Rose, 2nd daughter. Born 28 April 1800. Living 1882.

Frederick Charles, son of Captain Frederick Thomas of the Tower Hamlets Militia, and of the Inland Revenue Office. Died in 1852. Buried in the yard of the Chapel of Ease, Islington. = Elizabeth Talbot Rose, eldest daughter. Born 23 Aug. 1794. Died at Islington 1853. Buried in the yard of the Chapel of Ease, Islington.

William Wootton. Born 22 Oct. 1802. Of Harrold, Co. Beds. Surgeon. Died 9 April 1866. = Letitia Patten Rose, 3rd daughter. Born 23 Jan. 1803.

Frederick John Thomas. Born 9 Jan. 1832. Of Swaffham, Co. Norfolk. Surgeon. Living 1882. = Letitia Patten Rose Wootton, eldest daughter of William and Letitia. Married at Harrold aforesaid 17 July 1856. Living 1882.

Joseph Rose Thomas. Elizabeth Eleanor Thomas. Charles George Thomas. Died unmarried.

Augustus William Thomas. Born 30 Aug. 1858.

Edwin Harrold Thomas. Born 25 March 1861.

John Erichsen Thomas. Born 22 March 1868.

Percival James Thomas. Born 6 June 1871.

Henry Chichele Thomas. Frederick Talbot Thomas. Died young.

Florence Thomas. Born 13 May 1857.

Gertrude Thomas. Born 15 March 1860.

William Wootton, eldest son.	Holtom Bennett Wootton, 2nd son. Died in the Mauritius 11 Aug. 1877. = Marie Lidone de la Martin.	Letitia Patten Rose Wootton, eldest daughter. Born 24 May 1830. Married her first cousin.	Mary Anne Jane Wootton, 2nd daughter. Born 1 Sept. 1832. Died unmarried.	James Broad, 2nd son of Thomas Hacker Bodilly of Penzance, Co. Cornwall, by Ann Broad his wife. Surgeon. Of Harrold, Co. Beds. Died 26 Aug. 1874. Buried at Highgate Cemetery. =	Louisa Elizabeth Wootton, 3rd daughter. Born 11 July 1837. Married at St. Pancras, London, 28 May 1864. Living 1883.

Reginald Thomas Hacker Bodilly, only son. Born at Harrold, Co. Beds, 16 Feb. 1865. Educated at King's College, London.

♣♣♣♣♣♣♣♣♣♣♣

TO the immediate north of the Church, the old Vicarage House,* a substantial construction of solid oak, brick, and lathe-and-plaster, with gabled roofs and massive chimneys, was pulled down about the year 1841, and a new House built in its stead. The former, though much dilapidated, was curious, picturesque, and interesting. Traces of effective pargetting on its west side remained, like that on the House of the Striblehills. Parts of the old Vicarage were no doubt as ancient as the reign of Henry VII. The main portion consisted of a Hall standing north and south in the centre, with a large panelled parlour and oaken staircase to the south; kitchens, cellars, and domestic offices to the north; with numerous sleeping chambers, some low and some lofty, also panelled in oak and with open-timbered ceilings, above. In the Hall there had been a large broad fireplace in its north wall, with stone sediles on either side, and five carved quatrefoils containing shields of arms, a mitre, and a Tudor rose up above; but this had been long previously bricked up and obscured. Round the cornice of the parlour was an artistically carved oaken ornament, with sentences from the Latin Psalter. The broad rectangular staircase of three flights, placed in the south-west corner of the House, was also of oak, with substantial railings of early sixteenth-century work. The mouldings of all the beams and the oaken window frames and divisions were very artistic; several flowered quarries were to be seen amongst the diamond-panes, and there were carved pent-boards on external projecting supports to protect the windows. Fragments of Tudor barge-boards likewise remained under some of the gables.

* There is an extremely rude woodcut of the old Vicarage, taken from the south-west, in William Hone's *Year Book*, pp. 705, 706. The engraving opposite, made about twenty years ago by my brother, Sir Edward Lee, was taken from a drawing, not in very good perspective, from the pencil of the late Mr. J. M. Kidman of Thame,—the same local artist who supplied Mr. Hone with the sketch from which the engraving referred to above was taken.

On the east side of the House was a lawn and flower garden: to the north-east a kitchen garden abutting on to the adjacent meadow to the south of the River Thame.

When the enclosure of Priestend Fields was carried out in 1823, an allotment there in lieu of tithes was made, consisting of about one hundred and twenty-one acres; and another allotment in the Common Fields of Thame, near Cottismore Wells, of about eighteen acres.

By the valuation under Pope Nicholas, the Vicarage of Thame and its adjoining Chapelries was returned as worth 12 marks; but in Henry VIII.'s day at £48. The gross annual value of the benefice (not including the Chapelries, now separate Parishes) at the present time is £300.

The new Vicarage House, built at a cost of nearly £1800, of stone with freestone dressings, in a quasi-Tudor style of architecture, is a commodious and convenient residence, containing the usual characteristics of a clergyman's house, and is placed away from the road several yards eastward of the site of the old Vicarage.

The following Poem, penned at Thame Vicarage, by the Rev. William Lisle Bowles, was written on the occasion of a meeting which had just taken place at Cheltenham by several old school and college friends: amongst others, the Rev. William Howley, afterwards Archbishop of Canterbury; Mr. Lee, the Vicar of Thame, who had gone to school at Winchester in August 1782; and Mr. Cranley Lancelot Kerby, subsequently Rector of Stoke Talmache:—

"Here the companions of our careless prime,
Whom Fortune's various ways have severed long
Since that fair dawn when Hope her vernal song
Sung blithe,—with features mark'd by stealing Time,
At these restoring springs are met again!
We, young adventurers on Life's opening road
Set out together. To their last abode
Some have sunk silent; some awhile remain;
Some are dispersed. Of many growing old
In Life's obscurer bourne, no tale is told.

Here, ere the shades of the long Night descend,
And all our wanderings in oblivion end,
The parted meet once more, and pensive trace
(Marked by that Hand unseen, whose iron pen
Writes *mortal change* upon the fronts of men,)
The creeping furrows in each other's face.

"'Where shall we meet again?' Reflection sighs,
'Where?' 'In the dust,' Time, rushing on, replies.
Then hail the hope which lights the pilgrim's way,
Where come nor Change, nor Darkness, nor Decay."

It seems more probable that the first draft of it was made at Cheltenham, and that it was amended, polished, and put on paper at Thame. Its Author, son of the Rev. William Thomas Bowles, by Bridget his wife, second daughter of the Rev. Richard Grey, was first educated at Thame, but went to Winchester School in 1776, and became Head-boy in 1781. Subsequently he entered Trinity Coll., Oxon, graduating B.A. 21 Feb. 1786 and M.A. 24 May 1792. His "Sonnets" were first published in 1789. He was Vicar of Bremhill, Co. Wilts, and married Magdalene, daughter of the Rev. Charles Wake, Prebendary of Westminster. In 1803 he was made Prebendary of Sarum. There is a very expressive pencil-sketch of him by Daniel Maclise amongst the Forster bequests in the South Kensington Museum.

The Trustees of the four benefices of Thame, Towersey, Tettesworth, and Sydenham were, in the first instance, upon Dr. Slater's death—who bought the advowson from the family of Blackall of Haseley—Sir Walter Farquhar, Bart., the Rev. F. W. Rice (subsequently Lord Dynevor), the Rev. John Wing, and the Rev. James Prosser.

At the present time they are the Rev. James Slater, the Rev. Alfred Peache, the Rev. Thomas D. Canon Bernard, and the Rev. W. H. Barlow.*

There are four dissenting meeting-houses in the Town—two of which, on the south side of Upper High Street, those used respectively by the Wesleyans and Congregationalists, are somewhat pretentious in their architecture; in the other two, humbler structures, the Baptists and Methodists assemble. During the past fifty years, here as elsewhere, the Established Church appears to have steadily lost both followers and power. Dissent, however, being almost exclusively negative, exercises little else than a disastrous influence; for indifference, heretical sentiments, and democratic dreams—even in combination—and with a boasted "open Bible,"† cannot make up for the loss of the Old Religion, or fill the gaping void in men's hearts created by its abolition.

There are several ancient Houses of the same type and age as the old Vicarage remaining, and many substantially-built and commodious Houses of the seventeenth and last century in the Town, well suited for the residence of gentlepeople. In addition to the Prebendal and the old Grammar School, there are "The Elms," "The Moats," the residence of Mrs. Chard—belonging to the family of Lupton—and the Houses of Mr. William Parker, Mrs. Holloway, Mrs. Reynolds, Mr. Toovey, Mr. Harding Smith,* Mr. Birch, Mr. Humphrey, etc. The private residences at Lashlake, built in Queen Anne's time, are well placed and convenient in arrangement.

The Mansion House† and grounds where Sir Francis Knollys resided—on the south side of the High Street, upon his death passed from his executors to Alcock, then to John Jones, then to Hedges; then in turn to Thomas Stone, Edward Payne, and George Wakeman, and so to its present owner, Mr. James Marsh, Founder of the Oxford County Middle-Class School.

As far as I can discover there is no record of the original erection of a Town or Market Hall. The Market Cross is alluded to as early as the reign of Edward V., and this no doubt remained until the Tudor changes, when all crosses—whether in market-places, churchyards, burial-grounds, or highways—were deliberately and of purpose destroyed. It is exceedingly probable that a Market Hall was put up in Edward VI.'s time—for an existing representation appears to indicate that such was its age. It was originally a single room, of timber, pargetting and with a tiled roof, erected on posts, with a kind of pent-house or shed around it on each side. Later the latter was removed, and the main building rebuilt. Quite recently it was altered and repaired, while a singular excrescence in the roof was added on the north side to contain the works of the Town Clock.

A Pedigree of another branch of the Family of Lee now follows:—

* From information courteously supplied to me, in January 1883, by Sir Walter Farquhar, Bart.

† One is reminded, by the existing state of affairs, of the following verse regarding the Bible:

Hic liber est, in quo quærit sua dogmata quisque,
Invenit, et pariter dogmata quisque sua.

Which has been thus put into English:

One day at least, in every week, the sects of every kind
Their doctrines here are sure to seek, and just as sure to find.

* This House belonged to a person named Kitteridge in 1678, but in 1717 it was sold to Matthew Wilkins, Gent., whose widow in 1724 sold it to Thomas Ward, who in 1741 disposed of it to George Townsend. He in turn sold it to Martha Doughty. It then passed successively to Thomas Yeate, to Yeate's widow, Richard Way, Job Payne, William Claridge, William Claridge Harding, and so to Mr. Harding Smith, its present owner.

† In the Entrance Hall there is a bas-relief of John Hampden's face, reputed to have been copied from a more ancient specimen—which local Tradition asserted to be a correct likeness, originally taken just after his death.

Pedigree of Lee of Thame.

Francis Henry Lee. Born 23 April 1665. Entered at Trinity Coll., Oxon, August 1680. Admitted to the Middle Temple 6 August 1684. Councillor-at-Law. Died of small-pox at Chelsea. Buried at Spelsbury, Co. Oxon, 24 June 1698. Administration granted to his widow 14 July 1699.

= Abigail, daughter of Edmund Williamson of Westminster, Esq., by Ann his wife. Married circa 1686. Residing at Isleworth, Co. Middlesex, in 1700. Buried at Spelsbury aforesaid 13 August 1703. Will made 29 June 1703, proved 7 Aug. of the same year.

your friend and servant
Francis Henry Lee.

(From a Letter.)

George Henry Lee, Gent. Died young, and was buried at St. Luke's, Chelsea, 17 June 1698, but reinterred with his father 24 June 1698.

Francis Lee. Baptized 17 Nov. 1692. In the King's Navy, under Captain Francis Blewo, and in the "Litchfield" man-of-war *circa* 1711.

= Sarah, daughter of John Dolman Tripp, and niece of Robert Tripp, Gentleman Usher and Carver[1] to the King, of Somerset House. Married 14 Sept. 1709. Buried 4 Aug. 1748. Will made 3 July 1748. Administration granted to her son John 5 Feb. 1749.

Francis Henry Lee. Baptized 7 Jan. 1695. Master of the King's Revels 1725. Lieut.-Colonel of the 4th Foot 31 March 1727. Died at Somerset House, London. Buried 29 March 1730 at the New Church in the Strand. (1st husband.)

= Elizabeth Lee. Born 26 May 1693. Married firstly, at Clewer, 31 Aug. 1717, and secondly 27 May 1731. Buried at Welwyn 29 Jan. 1739. Administration granted to her husband 28 March 1741. M.I. in the Church of Welwyn.

= Edward, son of Edward Young, B.C.L. of New College, Oxford, Dean of Salisbury, and Rector of Upham, Co. Hants. Educated at Winchester and Oxford. Fellow of All Souls 1706. Graduated B.C.L. 22 Nov. 1714; D.C.L. 10 June 1719. Chaplain to George II. in 1728. Rector of Welwyn, Co. Herts, 1730. Author of *Night Thoughts* and other works. Died 5 April 1765. Buried at Welwyn. M.I. in the Church.[2] (2nd husband.)

Frederick Young, only son. Living in 1766.

Ann Elizabeth Lee. Bapt. 22 Sept. 1687 at the Lodge in Woodstock Park by Mr. Rowlandson, Rector of Wootton, Co. Oxon.

Charlotte Lee. Baptized 31 Oct. 1689. Buried in the Vault under the Chapel of Somerset House 21 Aug. 1720.

Abigail Lee. Baptized 3 April 1691.

Charles Henry Lee of the parish of St. George, Hanover Square. Succeeded his father as Master of the King's Revels, by appointment of the Duke of Grafton, 22 Oct. 5 of George II., *i.e.* A.D. 1732. Died without issue in 1744. Adm'on granted, 24 July 1744, of his goods and chattels to Elizabeth Deranda, widow, the mother and curatrix and guardian lawfully assigned to Martha Lee, widow, a minor.

= Martha, daughter of Paul Deranda of Putney, Co. Surrey, Merchant, and Elizabeth his wife. Married at Richmond, Co. Surrey, by Dr. Young, 29 Sept. 1743.

Jane, daughter of Sir John Barnard, Knt., Lord Mayor of London. Married in 1738. (2nd wife.)

= Henry Temple, eldest son of Henry, 1st Viscount Palmerston, by Anne, daughter of Abraham Houblon.

= Elizabeth Lee. Married 18 June 1735. Died without issue at Lyons in 1736. Buried in the Swiss Protestant Cemetery of that City 10 Oct. 1736. M.I. remaining.[3] (1st wife.)

Arms of Haviland.—*Argent, three towers triple-turretted sable.*

Caroline Lee. Married 5 July 1748. Died without issue. (1st wife.)

= William Haviland of Penn, Co. Bucks. Colonel of the 45th Infantry; subsequently a General. Died 16 Sept. 1784. Buried at Penn aforesaid. M.I. in the Church.[4]

= Salusbury, daughter and coheiress of Thomas Aston of Beaulieu, Co. Louth, Esq., by Abigail, daughter of Henry Bellingham of Castle Bellingham in the same County, Esq. Married 11 Dec. 1752. Died at Beaconsfield, Co. Bucks, 30 Oct. 1807. Buried there. (2nd wife.)

A B

a

b

Thomas Haviland. = Mary Cecilia, daughter of Patrick French, and niece and representative of the Right Hon. Edward Burke.

Samuel Ruston Fitzherbert = Mary Haviland. Died 13 Sept. 1786. M.I. in Penn Church.
of Swinnerton, Co. Meath.

John Lee, eldest son. Born 5 July 1710. Of Pocklington, Co. York, Gent. Died 23 Dec., and buried 28 Dec. 1771. Will made 18 July 1770; proved 14 May 1772. M.I. "eldest son of Francis Lee, Esq., of Spelsbury." = Charlotte Crowe. Born in 1708. Of a family residing at Kipplin, near Bolton-on-Swale, Co. York. Living in the "Precincts of the Savoy" in 1744.

George Lee. Living in 1741. Sole executor and residuary legatee of his mother's Will. On 8 Nov. 1748 administration of his own effects granted to his brother John. M.I. remaining.[8]

William Lee.

John Lee, only surviving son. Of Pocklington aforesaid, Gent. Educated under Rev. John Page, M.A., Vicar of Penn. Student in the Temple in 1744. Sole executor of his father's Will. Living 1772. = Mary, daughter of Timothy Newmarch, D.D., Clerk in Orders, a Nonjuror,[f] sometime of Penn, Co. Bucks, by Mary his wife, daughter of William Tipping of Wheatfield, Co. Oxon.[1] Affidavit made at Aylesbury for Marriage Licence of Mary, under age, with "John Lee a minor, son of John Lee," dated 10 Dec. 1744. Died before 1770.

Arms of Newmarch.—*Gules, five fusils in fesse or.*

George Henry Lee. A child. "Buried in the New Church in the Strand."

Charlotte Lee. Died in infancy.

Timothy Newmarch Lee, eldest son. Born 10 Nov., baptized 18 Nov. 1745. Of Thame. Died 20 Nov. 1795; buried 26th of the same in the south transept of Thame Church. M.I. in the chancel. = Elizabeth, eldest daughter of William Simeons of Thame, by Ann his wife. Born 20 Jan. 1747. Married by Licence 27 Sept. 1768. Buried in the south transept of Thame Church 2 Nov. 1804.

Francis Lee, second son. Baptized 22 Feb. 1749. Twice mentioned, with his elder and younger brothers, in his grandfather's Will.

Thomas Lee, third son. Baptized 17 Nov. 1752.

Elizabeth Lee. Baptized 23 April 1748. Goddaughter to "Squire Duncum" of Helmsley, Co. York, and brother to Mrs. Crowe of Kipplin. Buried 22 Sept. of the same year.

Abigail Lee. Privately baptized by Mr. Willcocks 3 Jan. 1754. Died in March of the same year.

Timothy Tripp Lee, only son. Born at Thame 22 Dec. 1769. Educated at Winchester College; graduated B.A. Pembroke Coll., Oxon, 23 June 1791. Instituted to the Vicarage of Thame, with the Chapelries of Towersey, Tetsworth, and Sydenham, 1795. Honorary Chaplain of the Thame Volunteers 1803. Appointed Head Master of the Grammar School in 1814. Purchased Dell's Manor Farm in the parish of Lewknor Uphill, and other estates in Haddenham, Co. Bucks. Died at Thame 29 Dec. 1840. Buried in the sanctuary of the Church 6 Jan. 1841. M.I. in the chancel. = Elizabeth, third daughter of Richard Smith of Thame, Esq., J.P. and D.L. for Bucks, by Mary his wife. Born 16, baptized at Thame 20 Feb. 1775. Married at St. Mary's, Islington, 2 Feb. 1792. Died at Thame 25 Jan. 1854. Buried at Thame. M.I. in the chancel.

Charlotte Lee. Baptized at Thame 16 May 1771. Died unmarried, and buried 17 Dec. 1816 in the south transept of Thame Church.

Abigail Lee. Died in infancy. Buried in the south transept of Thame Church. M.I. in the chancel.

Timothy Lee, eldest son. Born at Thame 26 Nov. 1792. Assistant Receiver-General of H.M. Customs, London. Died at Barnsbury Park 13 April 1874. Buried at Thame. Will made 25 Mar. 1860; proved by his widow and sole Executrix 13 May 1874. = Sophia, born 18 Feb. 1801, eldest daughter of Joseph Wood by Sophia his wife. Married at Islington 6 May 1820. Died without issue at Barnsbury Park 13 March 1878. Buried at Thame. Will made 29 April 1874; proved 2 April 1878.

Cornelius Lee, 2nd son. Born at Thame 7 Nov. 1796. Educated at Christ Church, Oxford. Resident at Headington, Co. Oxon, but died at Thame without surviving issue 10 Feb., buried 17 Feb. 1843 in the south transept of Thame Church. Adm'on granted to his brother Timothy Lee, Esq., 17 March 1843. M.I. in the chancel. = Charlotte Louisa, younger daughter and heiress of William Wykes by Catherine his wife. Married by Licence at Islington 17 Oct. 1827, and having had two children, Abigail, and a son, who both died in infancy, she died 15 May 1830. M.I. in the Church of St. Sepulchre, London.

Frederick Lee, 3rd son. Born at Thame 4 Dec. 1798. Educated at Magdalene and Merton Colleges, Oxford. Graduated B.A. 9 June 1821; M.A. 1 Feb. 1823. Rector of Easington, Co. Oxon, 6 Nov. 1832, and Vicar of Stantonbury, Co. Bucks, 11 Aug. 1838. Died at Thame 4 Nov. 1841. Buried on the 11th, in the sanctuary of Thame Church. M.I. in the chancel. = Mary, born 1 Nov. 1803, only daughter and heiress of George Ellys and Lydia Clifford his wife. Marriage settlement dated 8 Feb. 1831. Married by Licence at Aylesbury 10 Feb. 1831. Died 27 May 1853. Buried at Thame. M.I. in the chancel.

c

11

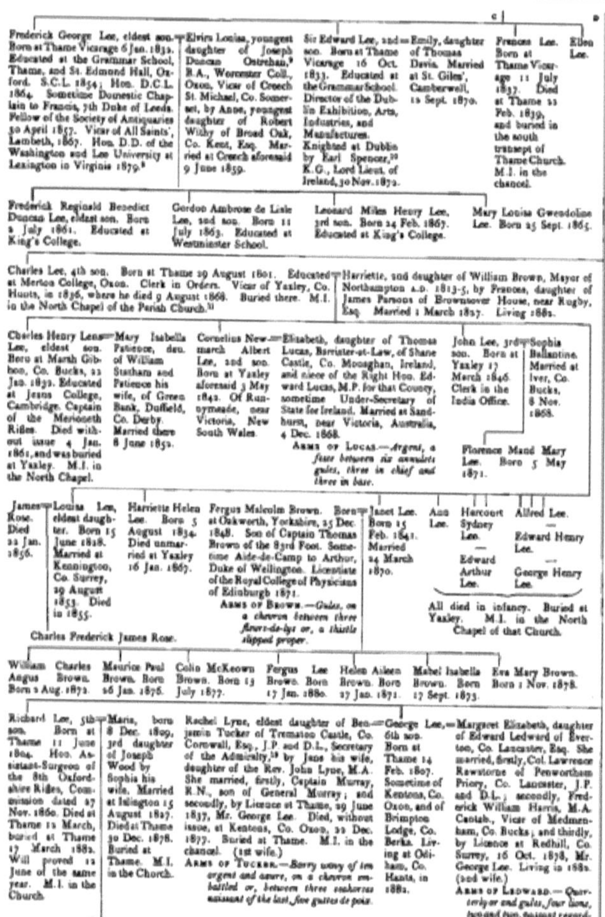

c a

Frederick George Lee, eldest son. Born at Thame Vicarage 6 Jan. 1832. Educated at the Grammar School, Thame, and St. Edmond Hall, Oxford. S.C.L. 1854; Hon. D.C.L. 1864. Sometime Domestic Chaplain to Francis, 7th Duke of Leeds. Fellow of the Society of Antiquaries 30 April 1857. Vicar of All Saints', Lambeth, 1867. Hon. D.D. of the Washington and Lee University at Lexington in Virginia 1879.[8] = Elvira Louisa, youngest daughter of Joseph Duncan Ostrehan,[9] B.A., Worcester Coll., Oxon, Vicar of Creech St. Michael, Co. Somerset, by Anne, youngest daughter of Robert Withy of Broad Oak, Co. Kent, Esq. Married at Creech aforesaid 9 June 1859.

Sir Edward Lee, 2nd son. Born at Thame Vicarage 16 Oct. 1833. Educated at the Grammar School. Director of the Dublin Exhibition, Arts, Industries, and Manufactures. Knighted at Dublin by Earl Spencer,[10] K.G., Lord Lieut. of Ireland, 30 Nov. 1872. = Emily, daughter of Thomas Davis. Married at St. Giles', Camberwell, 12 Sept. 1870.

Frances Lee. Born at Thame Vicarage 11 July 1837. Died at Thame 22 Feb. 1839, and buried in the south transept of Thame Church. M.I. in the chancel.

Ellen Lee.

Frederick Reginald Benedict Duncan Lee, eldest son. Born 2 July 1861. Educated at King's College.

Gordon Ambrose de Lisle Lee, 2nd son. Born 11 July 1863. Educated at Westminster School.

Leonard Miles Henry Lee, 3rd son. Born 24 Feb. 1867. Educated at King's College.

Mary Louisa Gwendoline Lee. Born 25 Sept. 1865.

Charles Lee, 4th son. Born at Thame 29 August 1801. Educated at Merton College, Oxon. Clerk in Orders. Vicar of Yaxley, Co. Hunts, in 1836, where he died 9 August 1868. Buried there. M.I. in the North Chapel of the Parish Church.[11] = Harriette, 2nd daughter of William Brown, Mayor of Northampton A.D. 1813-5, by Frances, daughter of James Parsons of Brownsover House, near Rugby, Esq. Married 1 March 1827. Living 1882.

Charles Henry Lens Lee, eldest son. Born at Marsh Gibbon, Co. Bucks, 22 Jan. 1832. Educated at Jesus College, Cambridge. Captain of the Merioneth Rifles. Died without issue 4 Jan. 1861, and was buried at Yaxley. M.I. in the North Chapel. = Mary Isabella Patience, dau. of William Statham and Patience his wife, of Green Bank, Duffield, Co. Derby. Married there 8 June 1852.

Cornelius Newmarch Albert Lee, 2nd son. Born at Yaxley aforesaid 3 May 1842. Of Runnymeade, near Victoria, New South Wales. = Elizabeth, daughter of Thomas Lucas, Barrister-at-Law, of Shane Castle, Co. Monaghan, Ireland, and niece of the Right Hon. Edward Lucas, M.P. for that County, sometime Under-Secretary of State for Ireland. Married at Sandhurst, near Victoria, Australia, 4 Dec. 1868.

Arms of Lucas.—*Argent, a fesse between six annulets gules, three in chief and three in base.*

John Lee, 3rd son. Born at Yaxley 17 March 1846. Clerk in the India Office. = Sophia Ballantine. Married at Iver, Co. Bucks, 8 Nov. 1868.

Florence Maud Mary Lee. Born 5 May 1871.

James Rose. Died 22 Jan. 1856. = Louisa Lee, eldest daughter. Born 15 June 1828. Married at Kennington, Co. Surrey, 29 August 1853. Died in 1855.

Charles Frederick James Rose.

Harriette Helen Lee. Born 5 August 1834. Died unmarried at Yaxley 16 Jan. 1867.

Fergus Malcolm Brown. Born at Oakworth, Yorkshire, 25 Dec. 1848. Son of Captain Thomas Brown of the 83rd Foot. Sometime Aide-de-Camp to Arthur, Duke of Wellington. Licentiate of the Royal College of Physicians of Edinburgh 1871. = Janet Lee. Born 15 Feb. 1841. Married 24 March 1870.

Arms of Brown.—*Gules, on a chevron between three fleurs-de-lys or, a thistle slipped proper.*

Ann Lee.

Harcourt Sydney Lee. — Edward Arthur Lee. — Alfred Lee. — Edward Henry Lee. — George Henry Lee.

All died in infancy. Buried at Yaxley. M.I. in the North Chapel of that Church.

William Charles Angus Brown. Born 2 Aug. 1872.

Maurice Paul Brown. Born 26 Jan. 1876.

Colin McKeown Brown. Born 13 July 1877.

Fergus Lee Brown. Born 17 Jan. 1880.

Helen Aileen Brown. Born 27 Jan. 1871.

Mabel Isabella Brown. Born 17 Sept. 1873.

Eva Mary Brown. Born 1 Nov. 1878.

Richard Lee, 5th son. Born at Thame 11 June 1804. Hon. Assistant-Surgeon of the 8th Oxfordshire Rifles, Commission dated 27 Nov. 1860. Died at Thame 12 March, buried at Thame 17 March 1882. Will proved 12 June of the same year. M.I. in the Church. = Maria, born 8 Dec. 1809, 3rd daughter of Joseph Wood by Sophia his wife. Married at Islington 15 August 1827. Died at Thame 30 Dec. 1878. Buried at Thame. M.I. in the Church.

b

Rachel Lyne, eldest daughter of Benjamin Tucker of Trematon Castle, Co. Cornwall, Esq., J.P. and D.L., Secretary of the Admiralty,[12] by Jane his wife, daughter of the Rev. John Lyne, M.A. She married, firstly, Captain Murray, R.N., son of General Murray; and secondly, by Licence at Thame, 29 June 1837, Mr. George Lee. Died, without issue, at Kentons, Co. Oxon, 22 Dec. 1877. Buried at Thame. M.I. in the chancel. (1st wife.) = George Lee, 6th son. Born at Thame 14 Feb. 1807. Sometime of Kentons, Co. Oxon, and of Brimpton Lodge, Co. Berks. Living at Odiham, Co. Hants, in 1882. = Margaret Elizabeth, daughter of Edward Ledward of Everton, Co. Lancaster, Esq. She married, firstly, Col. Lawrence Rawstorne of Penwortham Priory, Co. Lancaster, J.P. and D.L.; secondly, Frederick William Harris, M.A. Cantab., Vicar of Medmenham, Co. Bucks; and thirdly, by Licence at Redhill, Co. Surrey, 16 Oct. 1878, Mr. George Lee. Living in 1882. (2nd wife.)

Arms of Tucker.—*Barry wavy of ten argent and azure, on a chevron embattled or, between three seahorses naissant of the last, five guttes de poix.*

Arms of Ledward.—*Quarterly or and gules, four lions, two and two, passant regardant proper.*

y

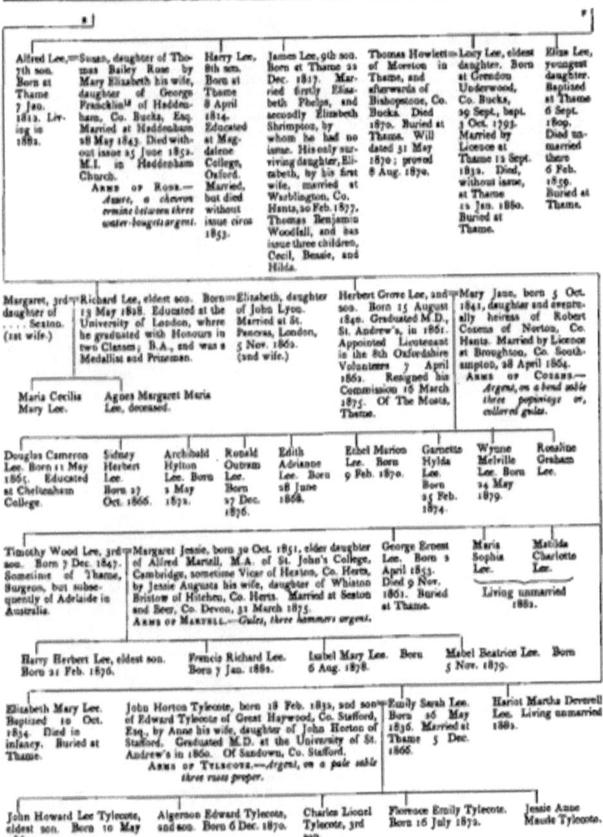

Alfred Lee, 7th son. Born at Thame 7 Jan. 1812. Living in 1882. = Susan, daughter of Thomas Bailey Rose by Mary Elizabeth his wife, daughter of George Francklin[12] of Haddenham, Co. Bucks, Esq. Married at Haddenham 28 May 1843. Died without issue 25 June 1852. M.I. in Haddenham Church.
ARMS OF ROSE.—*Azure, a chevron ermine between three water-bougets argent.*

Harry Lee, 8th son. Born at Thame 8 April 1814. Educated at Magdalene College, Oxford. Married, but died without issue circa 1853.

James Lee, 9th son. Born at Thame 22 Dec. 1817. Married firstly Elizabeth Phelps, and secondly Elizabeth Shrimpton, by whom he had no issue. His only surviving daughter, Elizabeth, by his first wife, married at Warblington, Co. Hants, 20 Feb. 1877, Thomas Benjamin Woodfall, and has issue three children, Cecil, Bessie, and Hilda.

Thomas Howlett of Morton in Thame, and afterwards of Bishopstone, Co. Bucks. Died 1870. Buried at Thame. Will dated 31 May 1870; proved 8 Aug. 1870. = Lucy Lee, eldest daughter. Born at Grendon Underwood, Co. Bucks, 29 Sept., bapt. 3 Oct. 1793. Married by Licence at Thame 12 Sept. 1832. Died, without issue, at Thame 12 Jan. 1880. Buried at Thame.

Eliza Lee, youngest daughter. Baptized at Thame 6 Sept. 1809. Died unmarried there 6 Feb. 1859. Buried at Thame.

Margaret, 3rd daughter of . . . . Sexton. (1st wife.) = Richard Lee, eldest son. Born 13 May 1828. Educated at the University of London, where he graduated with Honours in two Classes; B.A., and was a Medallist and Prizeman. = Elizabeth, daughter of John Lyon. Married at St. Pancras, London, 5 Nov. 1862. (2nd wife.)

Maria Cecilia Mary Lee.

Agnes Margaret Maria Lee, deceased.

Herbert Grove Lee, 2nd son. Born 15 August 1840. Graduated M.D., St. Andrew's, in 1861. Appointed Lieutenant in the 8th Oxfordshire Volunteers 7 April 1862. Resigned his Commission 16 March 1875. Of The Moats, Thame. = Mary Jane, born 5 Oct. 1841, daughter and eventually heiress of Robert Cozens of Norton, Co. Hants. Married by Licence at Broughton, Co. Southampton, 28 April 1864.
ARMS OF COZENS.—*Argent, on a bend sable three popinjays or, collared gules.*

Douglas Cameron Lee. Born 11 May 1865. Educated at Cheltenham College.

Sidney Herbert Lee. Born 27 Oct. 1866.

Archibald Hylton Lee. Born 2 May 1872.

Ronald Outram Lee. Born 27 Dec. 1876.

Edith Adrianne Lee. Born 28 June 1868.

Ethel Marion Lee. Born 9 Feb. 1870.

Garnette Hylda Lee. Born 25 Feb. 1874.

Wynne Melville Lee. Born 24 May 1879.

Rosaline Graham Lee.

Timothy Wood Lee, 3rd son. Born 7 Dec. 1847. Sometime of Thame, Surgeon, but subsequently of Adelaide in Australia. = Margaret Jessie, born 30 Oct. 1851, elder daughter of Alfred Martell, M.A. of St. John's College, Cambridge, sometime Vicar of Hexton, Co. Herts, by Jessie Augusta his wife, daughter of Whiston Bristow of Hitchen, Co. Herts. Married at Seaton and Beer, Co. Devon, 31 March 1875.
ARMS OF MARTELL.—*Gules, three hammers argent.*

George Ernest Lee. Born 2 April 1853. Died 9 Nov. 1861. Buried at Thame.

Maria Sophia Lee. Matilda Charlotte Lee. Living unmarried 1882.

Harry Herbert Lee, eldest son. Born 21 Feb. 1876.

Francis Richard Lee. Born 7 Jan. 1882.

Isabel Mary Lee. Born 6 Aug. 1878.

Mabel Beatrice Lee. Born 5 Nov. 1879.

Elizabeth Mary Lee. Baptized 10 Oct. 1834. Died in infancy. Buried at Thame.

John Horton Tylecote, born 18 Feb. 1832, 2nd son of Edward Tylecote of Great Haywood, Co. Stafford, Esq., by Anne his wife, daughter of John Horton of Stafford. Graduated M.D. at the University of St. Andrew's in 1860. Of Sandown, Co. Stafford. = Emily Sarah Lee. Born 26 May 1836. Married at Thame 5 Dec. 1866.
ARMS OF TYLECOTE.—*Argent, on a pale sable three roses proper.*

Hariot Martha Deverell Lee. Living unmarried 1882.

John Howard Lee Tylecote, eldest son. Born 10 May 1869.

Algernon Edward Tylecote, 2nd son. Born 6 Dec. 1870.

Charles Lionel Tylecote, 3rd son.

Florence Emily Tylecote. Born 16 July 1872.

Jessie Anne Maude Tylecote.

♣♣♣♣♣♣♣♣♣♣♣♣

SOME EXPLANATORY NOTES TO THE FOREGOING PEDIGREE.

[1] ROBERT TRIPP. (*From the Original.*)

These are to require you to swear and admit Robert Tripp Esq[re] into the Place and quality of Gentleman Carver in Ordinary to His Majesty. To Have Hold, exercise & enjoy the said Place, together with all Rights, profitts, priviledges and advantages thereunto belonging, in as full & compleat a manner as any Carver formerly held, or of right ought to have held and enjoyed the same. And, etc.

Given, etc., this twenty-first day of August 1727, in the first year of His Majesty's Reign.

To the Gentlemen Ushers, etc.

(Signed) GRAFTON.

See also Chamberlain's *State of England* (Part II., page 58) for 1727 and (Part II., page 62) for 1728.

[2] FROM THE CHANCEL OF WELWYN CHURCH, CO. HERTS.

M.S.
Optimi Parentis
EDVARDI YOUNG, LL.D.
Hujus Ecclesiæ Rect.
et
ELIZABETHÆ
Fœm. prænob.
conjugis ejus amantissimæ
pio et gratissimo animo,
Hoc marmor posuit
F. Y.
filius superstes
1766.

[3] FROM THE SWISS PROTESTANT CEMETERY OF LYONS.

Hic jacet
ELIZABETH TEMPLE, ex parte patris
FRANCISCI LEE, Regiæ Legionis
Tribuni, necnon ex parte
Matris, ELIZABETH LEE
Nobilissimorum *Comitum*
De Litchfield consanguinea.
Avum habet, EDVARDUM LEE
Comitem de Litchfield
Proavum CAROLUM II.
Magnæ Britanniæ
Regem. In memoriam
Conjugis carissimæ,
Peregrinis in oris (ita
Sors acerba voluit,) hunc
Lapidem mœrens posuit
HENRICUS TEMPLE, filius
Vicecomitis de
Palmerston. Obiit
Die 8 Oct[ris] A.D. 1736. Ætat. 18.

LINES WRITTEN BY MR. TEMPLE AT LYONS, IN 1736, ON THE DEATH OF HIS WIFE, THE NARCISSA OF YOUNG'S "NIGHT THOUGHTS."

(*From the Original.*)

"Forgive, kind Heaven, this lavish waste of tears,
Whilst sins unwept remain in vast arrears;
Fain would I stop their too, too rapid course,
Or owe their flowing to a nobler source;
But ah! whilst yet the beauteous corse I view,
Smiling in death, and take my last adieu,
Th' impetuous streams no reasoning can restrain,
Unchecked they run and scorn the stoick rein;
What tho' her present state no sorrow knows,
My heart adopts imaginary woes;
Her griefs, her anguish, and her restless pain,
Still tear my breast and throb through every vein;
My listening ear each moment hears her moan,
And troubled Fancy forms as oft a groan."

FROM THE PEERS' ENTRIES IN ULSTER'S OFFICE.

The Right Hon'ble Henry Temple, Viscount Palmerston, died in June 1757. He married first Anne, daughter of Abraham Houblon, Esq., by whom he had five children, Henry, Jane, Elizabeth, John, and Richard, who all died before him. He afterwards married Isabella, daughter of Sir Francis Gerrard, of Harrow on the Hill, in Middlesex, Bart., widow of Sir John Fryer, Bart., by whom he had no issue. The eldest son, Henry, married first the daughter of Colonel Lee, by Lady Elizabeth Lee, daughter of the Earl of Litchfield; who dying without issue, he married Jane, daughter of Sir John Barnard, Knt., by whom he had one son, Henry, now Viscount Palmerston. The truth of all which is attested by the said Lord, this 1st day of May 1767. Pursuant to a Standing Order of the House of Lords, dated this 12th of August 1707.

(Signed) PALMERSTON.
W. HAWKINS, Ulster.

Arms: 1 and 4, Or, an eagle displayed sable; 2 and 3, Argent, two bars sable each charged with three martlets or. *Supporters*: A lion passant and a horse argent, maned, tailed, and hoofed or, both regardant. *Crest*: On a wreath, a hound sejant sable, collared or. *Motto*: Flecti non frangi.

[4] FROM THE SOUTH AISLE OF HOLY TRINITY CHURCH, PENN, CO. BUCKS.

Here rest the remains of General William Haviland, late Colonel of the 45th Regt. of Infantry; an experienced and successful Commander without ostentation; a firm friend without profession; a good man without pretence. He died Septr 16th, 1784, aged 67.

On an atchievement formerly on the south side of the nave:— Arms of Haviland: Argent, three castles embattled sable; impaling those of Aston: Argent, a fesse sable, in chief three lozenges of the last.

[5] FROM THE CHURCHYARD OF POCKLINGTON, CO. YORK.

Fide et constantiâ.

Here rests the Bodye of George Lee, Gent. . . . . . 1748.
For him whose corps reposeth here
Pray we to Him Who heareth prayer;
Give, Lord, thy peace in Abraham's breast,
Grant light divine, Eternal Rest.
Thus all who pray, through Jesus' sake
Shall see His Face when they awake. Amen.
The memory of ye just is blest.

[6] DR. NEWMARCH THE NONJUROR.

"Mr. Dr. Timothy Newmarch was raised to y[e] Apostolick Order in Mr. Blackbourne's Chapple scituate within Graye's Inn uppon Sundaye y[e] twenty-ninth day of May, 1726, by Mr. Henry Hall and Dr. Richard Weltone, in the presence of Mr. Thomas Martyn, Mr. Lee, Mr. Calvert, Mr. Burrows from Thame, and divers others." "He died in Holland."

Dr. Welton was sometime Rector of Whitechapel, but was deprived, and it is presumed had been consecrated a Bishop by Ralph Taylor in 1723. He had put up an altar-piece in his Church representing the Lord's Supper, in which a portrait of Bishop Gilbert Burnet, the Erastian, or (as some say) of White Kennett, was introduced as Judas Iscariot, which of course gave great offence. In 1726 Welton retired to Portugal and there died.

The Mr. Calvert above mentioned is probably Benedict Leonard Calvert, second son of Benedict Leonard George, fourth Lord Baltimore, by his wife Lady Charlotte Lee. He was born 7 Sept. 1700, appointed Governor of Maryland in 1727, and died at sea on his passage home 1 June 1732. Lady Baltimore on becoming a widow married Mr. Christopher Crowe of Yorkshire. "So far as I can ascertain," wrote the late Dean of York, the Hon. Augustus Duncombe, in 1873, "the marriage between Crowe and Miss Duncombe, whose mother was daughter of Sir Henry Slingsby, is accurately stated; and the 'Squire Duncum,' who, in 1747, was godfather to Elizabeth Lee (of Pocklington) was Thomas Duncombe, Esq., brother to Mrs. Crowe, whose father Thomas died in 1746."

The "Mr. Burrows" was either John or George of Thame. (See p. 242.)

John Blackburne, M.A. Trin. Coll., Camb., and Henry Hall had been made Bishops by Nathanael Spinkes, Henry Gandy, and Henry Doughty. Blackburne died 17 Nov. 1741, aged 58, and was buried at Islington. Anthony Cope, Turkey merchant, second son of Sir

John Cope, fifth Bart., married Anne, daughter of Nathanael Spinckes, a Nonjuring Bishop, whose portrait is preserved at Bramshill, Co. Hants.

A Mr. Peck of Thame was sent to Scotland on behalf of Bishop Jeremy Collier and other Nonjurors to procure a synodical judgment as to certain restored Catholic "usages," as they were termed.

[7] Pedigree of Tipping of Co. Oxon.

Arms: *Or, on a bend engrailed vert three pheons of the field.*

Tipping of Tipping Hall in Com. Lanc., Esq.

William Tipping of Merton in Com. Oxon, gent., son and heir. = Agnes, dau. and heire to Thomas Burte of Shabington in Com. Bucks.		Alice, mar. to .... Harte of Blackthorne, Com. Oxon, gent.

John Tipping, son and heire. — Thomas Tipping, 2nd son, of Draycott. — Leonard Tipping, 3rd son.	Margarett, mar. to Richard Deane of Merton.	second husband, Thomas Vickers of Horton in Com. Oxon.	Alice, mar. to John Brown of Shabington.

—Harl. MSS. No. 1412, fol. 13.

Of this family, George Tipping was High Sheriff of Oxfordshire in 1604, Thomas Tipping in 1641, and William Tipping in 1716. (See pp. 325, 326.)

The Tippings of Thame and Wheatfield intermarried with the Doyleys of Merton, with the family of Borlacy of Little Marlow, with the knightly family of Pigott, with the Winters of Thame, with the Copes of Banbury, and one of them with Thomas the first Lord Sandys.—George Tipping, Clerk in Orders, who had been "Reader at Somerset House Chapel in ye Strande," kinsman of Mrs. Newmarch, was Instituted Vicar of Haddenham near Thame, "cum capellâ de Cudsdon," in April 1732. (See also p. 79.)

[8] Lee Portraits, etc.

Oil-paintings of Eleanor, Lady Lee, wife of Sir Henry Lee, Bart.; Francis Harry Lee, Councillor-at-Law; Richard Lee; George Lee; Charlotte Louisa Wykes; Rev. T. T. Lee; Sir Francis Harry Lee, Bart.; Sir Henry Lee, K.G. (a copy on mahogany); George Henry Lee, third Earl of Litchfield (after Huddesford of New Coll., Oxon); Edward Young, D.C.L.; and Rev. Edward Lee of Merton Coll.

Miniatures of King Charles the Second; Lucius Carey, Viscount Falkland; George Henry Lee, second Earl of Litchfield; the Rev. T. T. Lee, when young, aged 22, and of the same aged about 50; Cornelius Lee; Rev. Frederick Lee; Elvira Duncan; and Prince Charles Edward Stuart.

[9] Family of Duncan.—Alexander Duncan of Lundie, Co. Angus, married Isabella, daughter of Sir Peter Murray of Aughtertyre, Bart., and had issue Alexander his heir, grandfather of Adam Duncan, the great naval commander, who, 30 Oct. 1797, was created Baron Duncan of Lundie and Viscount Duncan of Camperdown. This peer's uncle, William Duncan, created a baronet 14 August 1754, married Lady Mary Tufton, eldest daughter of Sackville, seventh Earl of Thanet, by Lady Mary Savile, youngest daughter and coheiress of William, Marquis of Halifax, but dying without issue in September 1774 the baronetcy became extinct. The great-niece of Sir William, and the niece of the first Viscount, Elvira Duncan,—daughter of Haldane Duncan of Lundie aforesaid by Elvira Dunlop his wife,—married Joseph Ostrehan of St. Michael's in the Island of Barbadoes, Esq., grandfather of Mrs. Lee.

[10] Office of Arms, Dublin Castle,
30 November, 1872.

This day, on the occasion of the closing of the Dublin Exhibition of Arts, Industries, and Manufactures, His Excellency the Lord Lieutenant was pleased to confer the honor of Knighthood on Edward Lee, Esq., Manager of the said Exhibition.

J. Bernard Burke,
Ulster.

—*Dublin Gazette*, Tuesday, Dec. 3, 1872.

[11] From the North Chapel of the Church of Yaxley, Co. Hunts.

Sacred to the Memory
of the
REV. CHARLES LEE, M.A.,
thirty-two years Vicar of this Parish.
He was born Aug. 29th 1801, the fourth son of
the Rev. T. T. Lee, B.A., Vicar of Thame, of the ancient
family of Lee of Pocklington, Co. York, and
of Quarrendon, Co. Bucks.
He died August 9, 1868.

This Monument is of marble and alabaster (with arms of four quarters and crest of Lee carved above).

Sacred
to the Memory of
Charles Henry Lens Lee,
(late Captain of the Merioneth Rifles,)
eldest son of the Rev. Charles Lee,
Vicar of this Parish,
who died January 4th 1861
in the 29th year of his age.

To the Memory of
Edward Arthur Lee,
who died Decr 16, 1842,
in the 4th year of his age.

Also of
Edward Henry Lee,
who died in his infancy,
sons of the
Rev. Charles Lee, Vicar of this Parish.

[12] From the Church of Paddington, Co. Middlesex.

In the Vault under this Tablet
are deposited the remains of
JANE
the Daughter of the Rev. John Lyne,
of Liskeard in the County of Cornwall,
and Wife of Benjamin Tucker
of Saltash in the same County.
She was born on the 9th of September 1768
and died on the 17th of October 1809.
Optima mulierum.

Near the remains of his wife Jane
are deposited the remains of
BENJAMIN TUCKER, ESQ.,
of Trematon Castle in the County of Cornwall.
Having, in the Navy, gained by industry & talent,
The patronage and unceasing confidence
of the Earl St. Vincent,
He became His lordship's Private Secretary,
A Commissioner in the Navy, & Secretary to the
Admiralty during Three Administrations;
And subsequently, for twenty years,
Surveyor General of the Duchy of Cornwall,
In which situation he died 11th Dec. 1829
Aged 63 years and 11 months.

[13] George Francklin of Haddenham, Esq., was Sheriff of Bucks in 1729; Joseph Francklin was Sheriff of the same County in 1803; and Richard Rose of "The Chesnuts," Aylesbury, was Sheriff in 1872.

♣♣♣♣♣♣♣♣♣♣♣

A FEW Miscellaneous Notes of some interest may here be now recorded.

Nov. 1, 1732. A numerous meeting of gentlemen and ministers of the counties of Oxon and Bucks assembled this day at Thame about the Repeal of the Test Act, the Lord Viscount Barrington, chairman, when seven Resolutions were passed in favour of the measure, which are given at length (on page 1116) in the *Gentleman's Magazine* for 1732.

A certain "Widow Phill"—born at Thame, "of an ancient race there living," but afterwards of the Parish of St. Paul, Covent Garden—in her Will, dated 15 February 1743, which was proved 4 March 1744, left the large sum of £1000 for the Relief of the Widows of Clergymen. She died at Hackney. Her executors were Mary Wilson, widow, and William Wilson. The bequest was received by Mr. Giles Vincent, at that time Treasurer of the Corporation of the Sons of the Clergy.

Having regard to dates relating to the middle of this century, it is necessary to bear in mind that the Julian, or Old Style, which made the year to commence on the 25th of March, was used until the 1st of January 1752, on which day the New Style commenced.

I find a local record in which the following is preserved:—"Oct. 28, 1766. On this day at Thame the mob rose and regulated the Prices of Bread, Cheese, Butter, and Bacon."

For the curious record concerning the disparking of Rycott, here reproduced, I am indebted to the kindness of the late Evelyn Philip Shirley, Esq., of Ettington Park:—

"Deer parks, duly enclosed by Royal Licence, are exempt from the payment of tithe, but this immunity is lost if the ground be ploughed up and the deer killed. At Rycott, when the family left for Wytham, the grass was let to a farmer; but, to keep the land tithe free, two deer were penned up in a corner. This went on for years, until some children gave the creatures the boughs of a noxious tree to eat. The wanting link could never be secured; the land was disparked, and Lord Abingdon now pays tithe."

James Figg,* a native of Thame, as is on record, "was a master of the noble art of self-defence," in which science he taught numbers of gentlemen in his amphitheatre in the Oxford Road, Marylebone, where he was largely patronized. Sutton, the pipe-maker of Gravesend, was his rival; so, too, were Thomas Buck and Robert Stokes. Figg died on 7 December 1734. He is said to have only been defeated once—when he was in ill health—and then by Sutton, a celebrated boxer. Figg's portrait was painted by Ellis and engraved by Faber. I have seen another, a contemporary oil-painting, not unlike the work of Hogarth.

The Pedigree of Wakeman of Thame is now set forth:—

Pedigree of Wakeman of Thame.

ARMS OF WAKEMAN. (Granted in 1586.)—*Vert, a saltire wavy ermine.*

Henry Wakeman of Doddington, Co. Northampton, Gent. Reputed to have sprung from a brother of John Wakeman, first Bishop of Gloucester, residing at Woodrow, Co. Worcester. Died 17 April 1747. = Ann, daughter of William Whitworth, Clerk in Orders.

Issue:

- Henry Wakeman, eldest son. Died without issue.
- Herbert Wakeman, 2nd son. Born 23 Jan. 1714. Clerk in Orders. Vicar of Buckden, Co. Huntingdon, and Prebendary of Lincoln. Died in 1773. Buried at Buckden. = Mary, daughter of George Cooper of Holywell in Oxford, Gent. Died in 1764.
- Sarah Wakeman. Married John Cherry, and died without issue in 1786.

Issue of Herbert Wakeman:

George Wakeman, son and heir. Born 20 June 1760. Clerk in Orders. A.B. of Emmanuel College, Cambridge. Vicar of Bishopstone, Co. Wilts. Died 29 June 1816. Buried at Bishopstone. = Mary, daughter of John Goodhall of Market Harborough, Co. Leicester, Gent. Married 28 June 1787. Died 24 July 1813.

Issue:

- George Wakeman, son and heir. Born 29 July 1788. Of Thame. Surgeon. Owner of the Mansion House of Sir Francis Knollys. Died 14 June 1868. Buried at Thame. = Sarah Jane, daughter of Edward Payne of Lashlake in Thame, Gent., and Hannah his wife. Born 5 April 1788. Married by Licence at Thame 10 Oct. 1815. Died 22 Nov. 1867. Buried at Thame.
- Mary Sophia Wakeman. Born 16 Nov. 1789. Died unmarried 6 Dec. 1859. Buried at Cheltenham.
- Eliza Susannah Wakeman. Born 12 Feb. 1791. Died unmarried 11 June 1823. Buried at Thame.

* See Noble's *Continuation of Granger's Biographies*, vol. iii., p. 479, and *Reliquiæ Hearnianæ*, edited by Rev. Philip Bliss, under the year 1734.

A

George Wakeman, son and heir. Born 11 July 1826. Educated at Thame Grammar School, and St. John's College, Cambridge. Died 18 Aug. 1845. Buried at Thame.

Thomas, born 5 Sept. 1815, 2nd son of John Greenwood of Easington Manor House, Co. Oxon, Gent. (by Anne his wife, eldest daughter of John Deane, Gent.), Lord of the Manor of Easington. Living 1883. = Jane, eldest daughter. Born 17 June 1827. Married at Cheltenham by Licence 17 July 1862. Died 29 June 1880. Buried at Easington.

Edward Payne Wakeman, 2nd son. Born 20 March 1829. Educated at Thame Grammar School. Died 17 Dec. 1842. Buried at Thame.

Thomas Fairthorne Greenwood, eldest son. Born 27 April 1864. | John Wakeman Greenwood, 2nd son. Born 3 June 1865. | Frank Greenwood, 3rd son. | Herbert Greenwood, 4th son.

Benjamin John Holloway of Thame, Attorney-at-Law. Younger son of Richard Holloway of Arlescote, Co. Warwick, Esq. Died 26 May 1871. = Hannah Mary Wakeman. Born 7 May 1830. Married at Thame 12 Dec. 1857.

Susan Wakeman, 3rd daughter. Born 4 May 1832. Died 12 Sept. 1847. Buried at Thame.

William Holloway. Born 4 June 1859. | Mary Holloway. Born 2 June 1861. | Richard Holloway. Born 28 Nov. 1862. | Hannah Holloway. Born 24 March 1864. | Margaret Holloway. Born 6 Sept. 1865. | Alice Holloway. Born 8 Sept. 1867. | George Holloway. Born 12 March 1869. | Lilian Holloway. Born 28 Aug. 1870.

Herbert John Wakeman, 3rd son, but eventually heir of his father and elder brothers. Born 6 Oct. 1833. Educated at Thame Grammar School. Of Warminster, Co. Wilts. Attorney-at-Law. Living 1883. = Ellen, daughter of Luke Thomas Crossley of Hankelow Hall, Co. Chester, Esq. Married 11 Aug. 1863.

George Herbert Wakeman. Born 15 June 1866. | Maurice Reginald Wakeman. Born 8 Aug. 1872. | Henry Wakeman and Maude Wakeman. Died in their infancy. | Hugh Alexander Wakeman. Born 7 Oct. 1876. | Helena Wakeman. Born 22 July 1864. | Alice Wakeman. Born 14 June 1865. | Constance Wakeman. Born 23 March 1868. | Evelyn Wakeman. Born 6 Feb. 1871.

♣♣♣♣♣♣♣♣♣♣♣

OXFORDSHIRE had been a stronghold of Tory and Jacobite principles ever since the Restoration. Cromwell, Hampden, and Pym, Grenville, Temple, and Ingoldsby, in the seventeenth century, had given the good people hereabouts more than a taste of the pestilential policy of Rebellion and the disastrous practical evils of Civil War. So, when the lawful Monarch was restored, there was an almost general reversion to the principle of authority. The repulsive cant of Sectarianism and the self-willed lawlessness of Republicans had become alike distasteful. "Fear God and Honour the King" was a maxim widely accepted. Later on, James the first Earl of Abingdon promoted the Revolution under Dutch William. On the accession of George I., however, there was a remarkable demonstration in Thame at the Michaelmas Fair of 1714 in favour of the exiled Stuarts—said to have been quietly pre-arranged by certain noble members of the "Constitution Club," which had its headquarters at Oxford, and by other enthusiastic Nonjurors, already referred to, who lived in the Town and neighbourhood of Thame. But it was not until the celebrated County election of April 1754, when sick and even dying voters were polled, and which lasted six days, that the Whigs* gained a secure footing in Oxfordshire.† At Thame at the election in question they were in a distinct minority, as the actual voting, set forth in the Appendices, conclusively shews.

* "The Mob that espoused the 'New Interest' (*i.e.* the Whigs) were on some occasions most tumultuous and indecent. Among other enormities they got into one of the churches at Oxford, and, mounting the pulpit, drank damnation to the last 'Blue Parson' that preached in that 'Blue Pulpit.'"—*Oxfordshire Annals*, by J. M. Davenport, p. 97. Privately Printed, 1869.

† The following amusing electioneering squib, which I believe has never been published (from the pen of Henry, 2nd Viscount Palmerston, who had been educated at Thame, and had espoused the Whig cause, whose father Henry had first married Elizabeth, one of the daughters of Colonel Lee), was, in 1841, found amongst my grandfather's MS. papers:—

THE OLD INTEREST.

A SONG BY AN OXFORDSHIRE FREEHOLDER (April 1754).

First in support of Interest Old,
From Ditchley, staggers Litchfield bold—
A hardy chief for drinking:
His glass he fills up to the brim,
And thinks, by making his head swim,
He keeps his Cause from sinking.

Pedigree of Hedges of Thame and Wallingford.

ARMS OF HEDGES. (Granted 25 Nov. 1687.)—*Azure, three swans' heads erased argent.*

CREST.—*A swan's head erased proper.*

[These Arms are represented on a white marble monument in the Church of Cublington, Co. Bucks.]

Robert Hedges of North Weston in Thame, Gent., subsequently of Haddenham, Co. Bucks, of an old Family of Oxford, Thame, Towersey, and Weston. Will made 23 May 1817. Died 7 Oct. 1817. = Cassandra, daughter of John Woodbridge of Haddenham aforesaid, Gent., by Mary his wife, sister of Richard Smith of Thame, Esq., J.P. and D.L. Died 18 Nov. 1804.

ARMS OF WOODBRIDGE. (From a tomb and hatchment at Haddenham, Co. Bucks.)—*Argent, on a bend gules three chaplets of roses proper.*

Edward Hedges of Thame. Died 5 May 1833. Buried at Thame.

Robert Hedges of Thame. = Phillippa Field. Died without issue 20 April 1829. Buried at Thame. Will made 14 March 1829; proved 16 Oct. of the same year.

Mary Hedges. Baptised at Thame 18 Aug. 1769. Died 25 Jan. 1843.

Thomas Winslowe of Kingsey, near Thame, Gent. Died July 1825. Buried at Princes Risborough. = Elizabeth Hedges. Died 3 March 1824.

ARMS OF WINSLOWE.—*Ermine, on a chevron engrailed sable three quatrefoils or.* (*See pp.* 433-4.)

Robert Winslowe, son of Thomas and Elizabeth. Died 19 March 1868. Buried at Princes Risborough aforesaid. = Fanny, daughter of John Eeles of Thame by Judith his wife, daughter of Thomas Cozens of Tetsworth. Married by Licence at Thame 4 April 1821. (*See* PEDIGREE OF COZENS, *pp.* 227-8, *etc.*)

Robert Winslowe. Born 13 Feb. 1822. Of Risborough aforesaid. Died 29 Nov. 1843. = Emma, daughter of William Cox and Olive Cozens his wife.

Frances Winslowe.

John Hedges. Born at Thame *circa* 1766. Of Wallingford, Co. Berks. Attorney-at-Law. Thrice Mayor of Wallingford. Died 19 March 1826. M.I. in St. Mary's, Wallingford. = Jane, born *circa* 1764, daughter of John Allnatt of Wallingford, Co. Berks, Attorney-at-Law, Mayor of Wallingford. Died 1 June 1813. M.I. in St. Mary's, Wallingford. [A fine portrait of this gentleman remains in the Town Hall.]

Thomas Hedges. Born 24 March 1767. Of Thame. Died 7 May 1847. Buried at Thame. M.I. in Church. = Sophia, born *circa* 1780, daughter of William Cox of Tattenhoe, Co. Bucks, Gent., by Sophia Deverell his wife. Died 29 Jan. 1861, aged 81. Buried at Thame. M.I. in Church.

Sophia Cassandra Hedges, only daughter. Born at Thame 7 March 1816.

John Allnatt Hedges. Born *circa* 1787. Of Wallingford aforesaid, Gent. Died 22 Aug. 1854. Buried at Wallingford. M.I. in St. Mary's Church there. = Maria, born *circa* 1780, daughter of John Kirby of South Moreton, Co. Berks, Gent. Married at Cholsey, Berks. Died 25 Sept. 1854. M.I. in St. Mary's Church, Wallingford.

A

Charles Hedges. Died young.

B

Next comes an almost unknown Lord,
For Fiddle, Lute, and Harpsichord,
And Songs more famed than Bounty;
His lyre he strikes, invokes Apollo,
And wonders no more Brutes will follow
The Orpheus of the County.

But who comes next with mighty noise
And bellows forth with clamorous Voice?—
Come Jemmy and we'll crown ye;
Or he is one beneath your note,
"A bottle in a human coat"—
'Tis only drunken Rowney.

Fain would I stop, for to write ought
Of one who scarce deserves a thought,
Implies an idle penman:
But, as the dupe of all this crew,
And as a sample of "True Blue,"
I can't omit Lord Wenman.

These are the men who claimed a right
To Parliament to send our Knight,
Nor thought our votes worth asking;
'Till Parker and 'till Turner came
To fix an almost doubtful claim,
And make our rights more lasting.

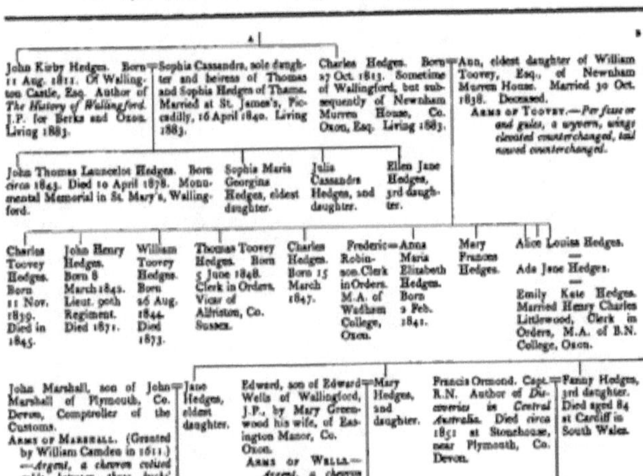

♣♣♣♣♣♣♣♣♣♣♣

During the Reign of Terror in France—the atrocities and horrors of which are not generally known, or their characteristics exactly appreciated by the present generation;—after the aristocracy, the clergy became the objects of the greatest abhorrence on the part of the frenzied and diabolically-inspired Mob.

This is what took place: In the name of Equality the Revolutionists established a band of permanent assassins; in the name of Liberty they transformed the cities of France into bastilles; in the name of Justice they everywhere created a tribunal to consummate murders; in the name of Humanity they poured forth everywhere rivers of blood. Robbery was unpunished, spoliation decreed, divorce encouraged, prostitution pensioned, irreligion lauded, falsehood rewarded, tears interdicted. An eye wet with pity led to the scaffold. Infancy, old age, grace, beauty, genius, worth, were alike conducted to the guillotine. A general torpor paralyzed France; the fear of death froze every heart; its name was inscribed on every door.

At the same time the cathedrals and parish churches were stripped of their ornaments and taken possession of by the Rabble. Out of consecrated chalices degraded women drank strong wine until they became intoxicated, in honour, as themselves avowed, of Humanity and Liberty; and, while the images of our Blessed Lord and His Immaculate Mother were thrown down, smashed, and trampled under foot, busts of the most repulsive and blaspheming Republicans were elevated and honoured in their places. Public utterances were thoroughly revolting. One man ostentatiously remarked that, though he had lived the victim of Superstition, he would no longer be its slave. "I know," he exclaimed, "no other worship than that of Liberty; no other religion but the love of Humanity and of Country." Hébert maintained that God did not exist, and that the worship of Reason was to be substituted in His stead. Jean Baptiste Gobel, the apostate Bishop of Paris, declared, "I submit to the Omnipotent Will of the People. There ought to be no national worship at all, except that of Liberty and Sacred Equality, as the Sovereign People wish it to be. From henceforth, therefore, I renounce and repudiate the Christian Religion." Another, Monvel, a comedian, went to the verge of impiety, when, amid the rapturous applause of the base creatures who surrounded him, he dared to cry out in the Church of St. Roch: "God Almighty, if you exist avenge your injured Name. I am here to deny you utterly. I bid you doe and deliberate defiance. Launch forth your thunders if you are able. . . . After your silence, what human fool, O God, will acknowledge your existence!" As a direct consequence of such utter blasphemy and national impiety, Sunday was abolished; the church bells were silenced; children remained unbaptized; marriage, as a sacrament or Christian rite,* was abolished; the sick received no sacred consolation in their sorrow and extremity; the dead no religious rites. Instead of the Catholic sacraments, licentious women performed degrading and disgusting rites in the ancient churches. Drunken artizans, wild in their license, and shameless prostitutes, profaned the sacred aisles most grossly by their filthy orgies.

The clergy were persecuted, abused, seized, imprisoned, and put to death. No words can duly depict the horrors of that awful Reign of Terror. One consequence was that no less than eight thousand of the French clergy, bishops, dignitaries, and parish priests, escaped to England, impoverished, ruined, starving. Our good and high-principled King, George III., gave up his Palace at Winchester to house nine hundred of these exiled ecclesiastics; and means were found to provide them with food and other necessaries of life. As many as fifty were received and secured a refuge at Thame, residing in the Mansion House which had previously belonged to Sir Francis Knollys. While the hatred of ruffianly cut-throats and detestable French Revolutionists for England and William Pitt, our great Minister, was intense, the noble bearing and gratitude of the French clergy to our English King and people were remarkable. The presence here of these ecclesiastics tended, in a large degree, to soften British prejudice against the Faith of our forefathers; to benefit those of the English clergy with whom they came into contact; and indirectly to pave the way for the Oxford Revival of half a century later, and for the movement for Corporate Reunion of the present day.

At Thame they had a temporary Chapel in their house-of-sojourning, where Mass was duly said. On a few special occasions—one was a Public Thanksgiving—some of them attended Divine Service in the Parish Church; during which, seated in the stalls of the Chancel in their soutanes, they said their own Breviary-office in Latin. My grandfather, the then Vicar of Thame, was intimate with many; and his father-in-law, Mr. Richard Smith, besides putting aside for several years a substantial sum of money towards their maintenance and aid, procured many benefactions from George, Marquis of Buckingham; and himself always exercised towards them a liberal and generous hospitality.*

The anointed bodies of many of the exiled clergy were laid to rest in the old burial-grounds of England, and under the shadows of sacred churches. An Archdeacon and Vicar-General of Dol, in Brittany, Michael Thoumin Desvalpon, D.D.,† who had died at Overies,

* "Marriage was declared a civil contract, binding only during the pleasure of the contracting parties. Divorce immediately became general; the corruption of manners reaching a pitch unknown. . . . So indiscriminate did concubinage become, that by a decree of the Convention, bastards were declared entitled to an equal share of the succession with legitimate children."—*History of Europe*, by Sir Archibald Alison, Bart. Ninth Edition, vol. iii., p. 24. London: 1854.

* In 1796 the University of Oxford printed at its own expense two hundred copies of the Vulgate for distribution amongst the exiled French clergy, and the Marquis of Buckingham did the same. Fifty copies of the latter were distributed at Thame, by Mr. Richard Smith and the Vicar.

† To the Memory of the Rev.
Michael Thoumin Desvalpon
Aged 62
D.D. & C.L. Arch Deacon and Vicar
General of Dol in britany
A Man conspicuous for his Deep
Knowledge and his Moral Virtues
Exiled since 1792 for his Religion
and his King, favourably Received
by the English Nation
Deceased at Overy March 2nd 1798
greatly indebted to the Family of
Mr Davey, and Interred in this
Church at the Request and Expence
of the Revd Dr Gauntelett Warden
of New College Oxon.
R.I.P.
—Dorchester Cathedral Church, Oxon.

was buried in the ancient Church of Dorchester, at the cost of Dr. Gauntlett, Warden of New College. Two of them were also buried at Thame. The entries stand thus:

Burials.—Jan. 18, 1796. Rev. Wm Chandermerle, French Priest of the Parish of St. Thurian, Town of Quintin, Diocese of St. Brieux, Province of Brittany, aged 69.* [This should be 59.]

1797. ... .. Rev. John Benign Le Bihan, French Priest, Rector of St. Martin des Pres, Diocese of Quimper, Province of Brittany, aged 60.

The following tells its own story:

"Before those who returned home left the Town, they publicly thanked God in the prayers of the Church of England on a day set apart, for His mercies and blessings to them, and acknowledged the hospitalities of the English people. The Vicar preached on the occasion of this occurrence, and a beautiful and touching sermon it was. The French priests revered him greatly. He had buried some of their number in the churchyard, when the services were very solemnly done; and they left him memorials of their affection and respect, both as a friend and as the Clergyman of the Parish."

In the early part of the present century, when an invasion of England was contemplated by the French, here as elsewhere the patriotic and martial spirit of the people was practically manifested. The Thame Volunteers, consisting of three companies of sixty men each, were enrolled, drilled, and trained. Their uniform consisted of a scarlet swallow-tailed coat, with white tufted epaulettes, and white facings. The shakoes, high and large, were surmounted by a white and red feather. Their muskets had flint locks. Under Colonel Wykeham they became exceedingly efficient, and not only merited but gained high praise from the military authorities.

Napoleon's attempt at an invasion, however, failed. Abroad the British arms, after some difficulties and reverses, were triumphant. No demand upon the bravery of the local volunteers was made. On the contrary, the French, demoralized and ruined by the Reign of Terror, were not only defeated, but several prisoners taken in war—about one hundred and thirty—were received and provided for in Thame, one of the appointed depôts. Amongst these were General Villaret de Joyeuse, Governor of Martinique.

Four of the French prisoners so interned were married in the Parish Church, viz.:—

1. François Robert Boudin, officer on parole, to Hannah Elizabeth Bone, after banns, 11 January 1813.

2. Jacques Terrier, French prisoner on parole, and Mary Green, after banns, 7 July 1813.

3. Prevost de la Croix, French prisoner on parole, to Elizabeth Hill, by license, 22 July 1813.

4. Louis Amedée Conte, French prisoner on parole, to Mary Simmonds, by license, 24 April 1816.

IN the early part of the last century legacies were occasionally left towards rendering the education of the children of the poor of Thame more efficient. The family of Burrows, by two of its members, had bequeathed £150, Mr. Samuel Wollaston £50, Mr. Matthew Crews £200, and Montagu, Earl of Abingdon, £200. Certain of these sums had been invested, and the proceeds in hands of Trustees served to provide a Master for the instruction of poor children. The education was no doubt both limited and imperfect; but it is by no means certain that the present system of educating the young for stations superior to that in which they were born, and rendering them indisposed to earn an honest livelihood as their fathers before them have done, is practically any better. It is more than doubtful, too, if the present race is any happier or more contented than the despised children of the last century, who often, under excellent religious influences, were simply taught to love and fear God and to do their duty to their neighbours.

About the year 1837 the system of "British Schools,"—as they were termed,—was introduced into Thame, and a building for children of both sexes was erected on the south side of Brick Kiln Lane. This institution, mainly promoted by Radicals, Dissenters of various sects, and political opponents of the State Church, has done much to maintain and consolidate the Democratic and "Nonconforming interest" in the Town. It was, however, speedily met by a counter-move.

On the 17th of November 1838, under the Presidentship of the then Vicar of Thame, a meeting was held in the Town Hall to set on foot National Schools for Boys and Girls. The gathering consisted of the most influential persons in the Town and neighbourhood. Six formal Resolutions were proposed and carried, by which it was determined that the proposed Schools should be in connection with the Established Church, and that the children should duly be present at Divine Service. About ninety persons contributed

* The following is a translation of the Register of this clergyman's birth, for which I am indebted to the courtesy of M. Charles Hettier, of 27 Rue Guilbert, Caen, and to the Mayor of Quintin:—"No. 92. William Francis born on this date, legitimate son of Mr John Chandermerle and of Miss Saint Le Nouvel, his wife, was baptised in the Collegiate Church of Quintin. The godfather was Peter Augustus Chandermerle, the godmother Miss Frances Richard. 21 May 1738."

funds for the scheme.* Lord Abingdon generously gave an acre of land, known as the site of the Old Hog Fair; Mr. Abraham, an architect, without fees or charge, kindly contributed plans; and Isaac Stone, a local builder, was appointed to erect the Schools at a cost of about £855. In 1842 an Infant School in the Third Pointed style was built immediately to the north of those already existing, from the design of Messrs. Scott and Moffatt, at a cost of about £300,—institutions greatly to the advantage and benefit of the many children who have received an elementary education therein.

On Monday, October 24, 1864, the Railway from Oxford to Thame was opened, thus directly connecting those places with Aylesbury, Wycombe, and London, as also with the west of England. Since that period the Town has increased somewhat in a southern direction; though no buildings of any importance, save the Grammar School, have been erected. Mere villas in a somewhat vulgar style have been built, with a few terraces of red-brick houses faced with freestone.

In the year 1873, at the suggestion and through the active labours of Mr. Richard Lee, a new organ, built by Conacher and Co. of Huddersfield, at a cost of £300, was obtained for the Parish Church.† It is placed on an elevated frame of wood in the north transept, almost exactly in the same position which an old organ in the sixteenth century occupied. Special Services were held on Wednesday, 29 October 1873, when this new organ was first used, the Bishop of the Diocese, Dr. J. F. Mackarness, preaching in the morning, and the Ven. Charles Carr Clerke, Archdeacon of Oxford, in the evening. The tone of the organ is sweet and melodious. Considering, however, the almost entire absence of colour and warmth in the Church generally, the organ's polychromatic decoration is, perhaps, a little too pronounced.

As regards the Parish Church itself, it is to be hoped that wise and efficient means may soon be taken to effect its much needed repair and restoration. The unjust abolition of Church Rates has thrown upon the worshippers within its walls, instead of upon the whole Parish as heretofore, the pleasant burden of keeping the fabric in repair. At Chipping-Wycombe and Monks' Risborough on the one side, however, and at Cuddington and Worminghall in other directions, the Parish Churches have been thoroughly well restored by voluntary offerings of the respective parishioners. May zeal and energy, self-denial and liberality combined, speedily accomplish what is so obviously wanting at Thame! An experienced architect would no doubt seek to undo several of the disastrous changes of forty years ago, and aim at bringing the building more into harmony with its ancient features as they existed in the ages of Faith and good works. *Fiat, in Nomine Domini, fiat!*

And now I bring my task to an end, and lay down my pen. I may be allowed, in conclusion, to express a hope that the information and facts already recorded, while, perhaps, of direct interest only to those connected with Thame, may not be altogether unacceptable to a wider circle, as a humble contribution to the History of the County, though it has had for its immediate subject only the Parish Church of a mere country Town.

* The late Mr. Charles Dorrington of Thame, whose wife was a Miss Kirby of South Moreton, bequeathed £500 to these Schools; Miss Winslow of Thame £50.

† Amongst the chief contributors were Mr. Corbett, the Vicar, Lord Dynevor, Mr. Herbert Wykeham, and Mr. Richard Lee, who each gave £10; and the following donors of £5 each:—Mr. S. Lacey, Mr. Charles Ellis, Mr. T. S. Sutton, Sir Walter Farquhar, Bart., Dr. Herbert Lee, Mr. A. R. Howland, Mr. J. Marsh, Mr. Edward Griffin, Rev. Dr. F. G. Lee, Mr. Smith, Rev. W. Toovey, Mr. Samuel Field, jun., Mr. William Parker, Mr. and Mrs. Lee of Barnsbury Park, Miss Field, "A Well-wisher," and "X. Y. Z."

APPENDICES.

No. I. EXTRACTS FROM THE REGISTERS OF THE CHURCH OF OUR BLESSED LADY OF THAME.

Baptisms, Marriages, and Burials.*

A.D. 1601-1668.

1601. July. Ann Brasey the first day christened.
1602. Sep. Margaret Philipps the xij day christened.
Nov. Thomas Bryan the viij day buryed.
1603. Mar. Thomas Dorrell the xxij day buryed.
May. Joane Quarterman the same day [*i.e.* the 13th] baptized.
Sep. Edward Petty the same day [*i.e.* the 11th] baptized.
Feb. A pore minister yt sometime dwelt at broad Ryngton in Glo'rshire the second day buryed.
1604. Sep. Robert Pecke the seconde day baptized.
1605. Apr. Mary Lea the daughter of Thomas Lea the xiiij day baptized.
May. John Hester the sonne of Richard Hester the xvij day baptized.
July. John Simons the first day buryed.
Aug. Leonard Burte and Margaret Bryan the xxv day maryed.
Oct. Walter Jemett and Isabel Surman ye xvj day maryed.
Nov. Vincent Hester ye xxij day buryed.
Dec. Thomas Tybbard the xiiij day buryed.
Jan. Mary Hester ye daughter of Will'm Hester ye first day baptized.
Feb. Thomas Bigge the sonne of Leonard Bigg the third day baptized.
1606. Mar. Winnefrint Jemott the daughter of John Jemott the xxviij day baptized.
Apr. Robert Collingridge and Margery Lee the same day marryed [*i.e.* the 26th].
July. William Burt ye sonne of John Burte ye xvij day baptized.
July. Leonard Towne and Katherine Dormer the same day maryed [*i.e.* the 31st]
Nov. Humfry Jemott and Ales Groome the vj day maryed.
Jan. Margaret Hester ye daughter of Wm Hester the xiij day baptized.
1607. Apr. Jane Wallpolle ye daughter of George Wallpoole ye same day baptized [*i.e.* the 1st].
May. Susann Lea the daughter of Thomas Lea the xxviij baptized.
June. Richard Stribblehill the xxvij buried.
July. Joane Hester ye daughter of Richard Hester ye xxviij day baptized.
Aug. Will'm Burte the ix day buryed.

* These Registers are evidently copies only. The originals, which were in Latin, and from which Dr. Rawlinson, the Antiquary of St. John's College, Oxford, made extracts, are apparently lost. See *Rawlinson's Collections for Oxfordshire* in the Bodleian Library.

1607. Sep. Richard Laughton and Joane Striblehill the xiij day marryed.
Oct. Thomas Ballowe ye xv day baptized.
Oct. Henry Jemott ye sonne of Walter Jemott ye xxv day baptized.
Feb. Joane Hester ye daughter of William Hester the iiij day baptized.
1608. Dec. Elizabeth Bryan ye x day baptized.
Dec. Richard Stribblehill ye xxiv day baptized.
1609. Oct. Jane Petty the iij day baptized.
Oct. William Atkins and Margt Ffrancklin the xxij day married.
Oct. Will'm Ballowe the xxx day baptized.
Nov. Thomas Wallpole the xix day baptized.
1610. Apr. Walter Jemot ye xxviij day baptized.
May. John Hester the xvij day buryed.
Nov. Will'm Ballowe ye son of Mr William Ballowe the first day baptized.
Nov. Henry Ballowe ye sonne of Mr Wm Ballowe ye xv day baptized.
1612. Dec. Mr Michael Saunders and Mrs ffrancis Barry ye xxj day married p' licentia.
1613. Dec. Edmund Trowe ye v day baptized.
1614. July. John Hester ye xxx day baptized.
Aug. Elizabeth Saunders ye daughter of Mr Richard Saunders ye xxviij day baptized.
Nov. Samuel Saunders the sonne of Marmaduke Saunders the second day baptized.
Nov. Nicholas Almond and Elizabeth Ellis the xvij day married.
1615. July. Thomas Hester the sonne of Mr Will'm Hester the xxiij day baptized.
Oct. Richard Atkins and Alice Neighbor the ix day married.
Dec. Mr Thomas Ballowe ye xxj day buryed.
Jan. Richard Saunders the sonne of Mr Michael Saunders the 7 day baptized.
Jan. Richard Dormer the x day buryed.
Feb. Francis Carter the xix day baptized.
1616. Sep. Phillip Ballowe the xxix day baptized.
Dec. Bennedict Dormer ye xiiij day baptized.
1617. Jan. Henry Simons and Mary Reddinge ye xj day married.
1618. Apr. John Stribblehill the xx day buried.
Apr. Robert Dormer the xix day buried.
Apr. Mr Blase Goodwine ye xx day buried.
Nov. John Simons and Margaret Rogers the viij day married.
Nov. Richard Dormer the xv day baptized.
Nov. Margery Dormer the xix day buried.
1619. July. John Dormer the vj day buried.
Aug. Susann Pecke the xviij day baptized.
Sep. John Hester and Mary Ffrancklin ye xxiij day married.

1620. May. Baldwin Dormer ye xxx day baptized.
Oct. Katherine Hester the xv day baptized.
Oct. Ann Hester the daughter of John Hester the xxij day baptized.
Dec. Thomas Stribblehill the xxiij day baptized.
Feb. Elizabeth Dormer the xxj day baptized.
Feb. Gilbert Trowe the xxviij day baptized.
1621. Oct. William Powell and Elizabeth Atkins the fifthe day married.
Dec. William Pecke the xij day baptized.
Dec. Richard Smith the xxij day boried.
Jan. Elizabeth Petty the x day baptized.
1622. Apr. Elizabeth Robotham the third day baptized.
Apr. Agnes Holt the vij day baptized.
Apr. Dorothie Hester the xxvij day baptized.
June. Elizabeth Simons the xij day baptized.
June. Anne Petty the daughter of Robert Petty the xxiiij day baptized.
Oct. Mary Smith the daughter of John Smith same day baptized [i.e. the 3rd].
Dec. Anne Dormer the xxviij day baptized.
Jan. Anne Warner the daughter of a Londoner the sixth day baptized.
Jan. Maximilian Petty the vij day baptized.
Jan. Rich'd Lea the xxiij day baptized.
1623. Apr. John Powell and Elizabeth ffrancklin the xiiij day married.
July. John Powell the soune of John Powell and Joane was baptized the xvj day.
Oct. Jane Basse the daughter of W'm Basse the second day baptized.
Oct. Mr Ffrancis Bartlet the xxv day buried.
Dec. John Rose the x day baptized.
Dec. Richard Smith the xxiij day baptized.
Jan. Henry Hester the x day baptized.
Feb. Ann Simons the xvj day buried.
Mar. Ann Ballowe ye daughter of Thomas Ballowe the iv day baptized.
Mar. Jane Powell ye daughter of Jo. Powell of Priestend the xxj day baptized.
1624. Apr. Gabriel Atkins the sonne of Will'm Atkins baptized the iiij day.
Apr. Raphe Pecke the soun of John Pecke the 21 day baptized.
July. Jane Hester the xxj day baptized.
July. Susanna Stribblehill the daughter of Thomas Stribblehill the same day baptized.
Sep. Thomas Rose and Grace Grimborowe this day [19th] were maryed.
Dec. Gabriel Hester the son of John Hester the fourth day baptized.
Jan. Samuel Talbot the sonne of Thomas Talbott the first day baptized.
Jan. Margaret Simons the daughter of John Simons the sixth day baptized.
Feb. Ann Holte the 12 day baptized.
Feb. Blanch Holt the 21 day buried.
Mar. Anthonie Lea ye son of Mr Richard Lee the 2 day baptized.
Mar. Robert Pettie the son of Mr Maximilian Pettie the vj day baptized.
Mar. Elizabeth Petty ye daughter of Robert Petty the xxij day baptized.
1625. Aug. John Hester the sonne of Mr William Hester the vij day baptized.
Sep. Christopher Walklin ye xij day buried.
Sep. Elizabeth Peck the 22 day baptized.
Sep. William Trippe and Jane Burgess the 26 day married.
Sep. Hugh Robotham the son of Mr Hugh Robotha' the 28 day baptized.
Nov. Elizabeth Trowe the xj day buried.
Nov. Elizabeth Basse the xx day baptized.
Feb. John Burton the first day buried.
Feb. Ann Lea the second day baptized.

1627. July. Mr Richard Butcher the xvj day buried.
Dec. William Trippe the 9 day baptized.
Jan. John Pecke the x day buryed.
Robert Pettie the xxiij day baptized.
1628. Apr. Walter Robotham the xvij day buried.
Sep. Thomas Burte and Joane Lovell the x day married.
Nov. Mary Hester ye daughter of Mr William Hester the xiij day baptized.
Nov. Ann Brian ye daughter of Thomas Bryan ye same day baptized.
Nov. Richard Carter ye sonne of Jo. Carter ye xvj day baptized.
Feb. El'nor Lea the daughter of Richard Lea ye xvij day baptized.
1629. June. John Burt the xxv day buried.
Nov. Mr John Trender, vicker, buried ye v day.
Nov. William Maunde ye sonn of Robert Maunde baptized ye 26 day.
Dec. Anne Tripp ye daughter of William Trippe bapt. ye first day.
Feb. Edmund Walpoole ye sonne of John Walpoole baptized ye iiij day.
1630. July. William Dormer was buried 25.
Aug. Richard the sonne of Rich. Lee baptized 1.
Aug. Francis Simons and An'e Davis were married 19 by banes.
Nov. Diana the daughter of Edward Wray, Esq., buried 17.
Dec. Jerome ye son of John Simons baptized 31.
Jan. Tho. Hennant, vicar, and Elizabeth Petty were married at Tetsworth 17 by license.
Feb. Jane ye daughter of Robert Petty baptized 5.
Feb. Jane ye daughter of Robert Petty buried 7.
Feb. Lettice Petty was buried 19.
Mar. Katherine the daughter of Tho. Crum was baptized 6.
1631. Apr. John Symons was buried 21.
Aug. John Ellis, clark, and Rebekah Petty were married 24 by license.
Sep. Robert Petty and Anne Holly were married 26 by banns.
Oct. Rich'd Hester and Elizabeth Smith were married 26 by banns.
Nov. Mrs Rebekah Ellis was buried 7.
Jan. Mr Hugh Evans was buried 5.
Jan. John ye sone of Mr Max' Petty buried 15.
Mar. Richard ye sone of William Tripp baptized 18.
1632. May. Christopher ye son of Mr John Petty baptized 3.
May. ffrancis ye son of Mr Vincent Barry baptized 10.
June. Eleanor ye daughter of Robert Petty baptized 29.
Oct. Richard the son of Richard Hester baptized 11.
Nov. Elizabeth ye wife of Wm Powell was buried 28.
Feb. Maria ye daughter of ye Ladie Pigott buried 24.
1633. Aug. Richard ye sonn of Rich. Smith baptized 11.
Sep. William Borte and Elizabeth Woodbridge were married 19 by license.
Feb. Thomas ye son of Wm Rose baptized 22.
1634. Apr. Roger Fanshawe and Anne Towne were married 10 by license.
Apr. Thomas Powell and Alice Woodbridge were married 17 by banns.
Sep. Jane ye daughter of William Basse buried 10.
Sep. Thomas ye sone of Mr William Hester buried 21.
Oct. Alice ye daughter of John Cousin buried 8.
Oct. Robert Colingridge was buried 14.
Nov. Robert Robinson and Christian Burges were married 20 by license.
Nov. Elizabeth ye daughter of Richd Lee baptized 20.
Dec. Thomas Smith of Morton was buried 14.
Feb. Adrian ye son of Mr Vincent Barry baptized 12.
1635. Aug. Sarah ye daughter of Hugh Hester baptized 30.
Oct. Wm the son of Mr Wm Hester was buried 27.
1636. Oct. Thomas Ballowe, marchant, was buried 22.
Jan. Wm Burt, clerk, and Elizabeth Petty married 26.

1637. June. Elizabeth ye daughter of Mr Vincent Barry baptised 7.
Aug. Francis Robotham and Elizabeth Hester were married 29 by license.
Sep. Helinor ye wife of Willia' Basse buried 23.
Oct. John Ffigg and Ellinor Burton were married 15 by license.
Nov. William Adkins was buried 17.
Dec. Gilbert Trowe buried 27.
Jan. Henry ye son of Henry Tripp baptised 11.
Feb. Robert ye sone of Robert Maunde baptised 26.
Mar. Elizabeth ye daughter of Hugh Hester buried 8.
1638. May. Susannah ye daughter of John Ffigge baptised 6.
June. Wm ye son of Mr William Burt baptised 13.
June. Mrs Elizabeth Hester was buried 27.
July. Richd ye sone of Richard Lee baptised 14.
Oct. Joane Petty buried 10.
1639. June. Elizabeth ye daughter of Mr Vincent Barry was buried 17.
1640. Oct. Sarah ye daughter of Mr Vincent Barry baptised 29.
Nov. Edmund Maunde and Jane Benson married 10.
1641. Apr. Jo. the sone of Robt Maunde baptised 16.
Apr. Anne ye daughter of a Rich'd Lee baptised ye same day [i.e. 18th].
July. Anne the daughter of Hugh Hester baptised 25.

* * * * * *

1646. May. Widow Dormer buried 8.
July. Luke Burnha' and Isabell Jutson, and Robert Greene and Elizabet Langston, married 16.
July. Tho. Smith and Ann Petty married 29.
Nov. Tho. Jem'ott and John Trinder buried 29.
Jan. Ann ye daughter of John Wilmott baptised ye same day [i.e. 21st].
Mar. Judith ye daughter of Wm Burte, clerke, baptised 11.
1647. May. Wm Typpin and Mary Winter married 11.
Aug. Tho. ye sone of Thomas Dorrell, Jane ye daughter of Benedict Corner, baptised 19.
1648. Apr. Ye wife of John Carter buried 28.
May. Steven Cousin was buried ye same day [i.e. 15th].
Nov. Rich. ye sone of Tho. Waine baptised ye same day.
Mar. Mr Edward Oakley and Mrs Margarett Barry maried 1.
1649. Mar. Mary ye daughter of Mr Tho. Holt baptised 30.
Apr. George Ffranklin and Colliberry Beake were maried 17.
May. Mary ye daughter of Nicholas Clerke baptized 9.
May. Ann ye daughter of Mr Wm Herewood buried ye same day [i.e. 16th].
July. Wm Lee and Ann Woodbridge were married 15.
Oct. Jo. Clerke and Mary Wenlow married 31.
Dec. Edward ye sone of John Higgons baptised 12.
Dec. — Philpott, a souldier, buried 18.
Mar. Richard Lee was buried ye first day.
Mar. Jone ye daughter of Charnell Jones baptized 19.
1650. May. Alexander ye sone of Mr Richard Crooke baptized 1.
May. John Dorrell was buried 3.
May. Quince ye sone of Captain Rose baptised 29.
July. Tho. ye sone of Buckingha' and Elizabeth ye daughter of Tho. Sterbbihill baptized 24.
Aug. Bridgett ye wife of Mr Wm Ailife buried 20.
Mar. Isabell ye daughter of Henry Beck baptised 5.
1651. Mar. Ffrances ye daughter of Mr Wm Harrward buried 25.
Apr. Elizabeth ye daughter of Mr Edward Oakley baptized 10.
Apr. James ye sone of John Ffigg baptised 17.
Apr. Ffrancis ye sone of Mr David Thomas baptised 23.
July. Grace ye daughter of Robert Peck baptised 30.
Oct. Edward Toovy and Joane Bayley married 7.
1651. Jan. Robert Belsone and Mary Stone married 26.
1652. June. Mr Nicholas Alman buried 16.
June. Jo. Randolph and Jane Staunton married 27.
June. Elizabeth ye daughter of John Egerton baptised ye same day.
Nov. Jo. ye sone of Tho. Striblehill baptised 18.

Ffrom November 1653 to Maye 1657 the order was they should be Registred in the Tole Booke.

1657. June. Mr Willia' Hull was buried 18.
Oct. Sarah ye daughter of Robert Belson baptized 1 day.
Jan. Mary ye daughter of John Ballowe baptised 7.
1658. Apr. Richard Lloyde, clerke, buried 7.
Apr. Elizabeth ye daughter of John Carter baptised 16.
Aug. Mrs Elizabeth Petty was buried 16.
Aug. Mrs An'e Brian was buried 26.
Nov. John Typping and Elizabeth Maior maried 30.
Dec. Mrs Hull was buried ye second day.
Dec. Widdowe Peck was buried 5.
Jan. Willia' ye sonne of Edward Leaver baptised 20.
Feb. Richard ye son'e of John Clarke, Esq., of North Weston, buried 5.
Mar. Dulcebilla ye daughter of Mr Hugh Willis baptized 11.
Mar. Richard ye son'e of Jo. Clark, Esq., of Northweston, baptized 17.
1659. Apr. Mr Leonard Petty buried 9.
May. John ye son'e of Mr John Eustace baptised 5.
June. Peter Tomlinson and Meary Burt were married 21.
Aug. Mrs Katherine Barry buried 19.
Aug. John Carter buried ye same day.
Mar. Hugh ye son'e of Mr Hugh Willis baptized 8.
1660. Mar. Robert Maund was buried 28.
Apr. Hugh the son of Mr Hugh Willis buried 20.
Apr. Tho. Staveley and Elizabeth Smith were married 25.
Apr. Peter the son of Peter Tomlinson, and Sarah the daughter of John Dobbinson, were baptised ye same day [i.e. 25th].
Apr. Elizabeth ye daughter of Roger Keyble baptized 26.
Apr. Jane ye wife of John Randolph buried ye same day.
June. Elizabeth ye daughter of George Boroughs baptized 8.
Sep. Tho. Stribilhill was buried 5.
Sep. Ffraunces ye daughter of Robert Belson baptized 20.
Oct. Marmaduke Price and Mary Horwoode married 7.
Oct. Margaret daughter of Wm Maund baptised 18.
Nov. Edmund Maunde and Elizabeth Field married 15.
Dec. John Boroughe buried 26.
Feb. Elizabeth ye daughter of Edmund Philips baptized 7.
Feb. Nicholas ye sone of John Horrowrd baptized 28.
1661. June. Anthony Fforde and Amee Towersie married 19.
July. Widow Davie and Elizabeth Boroughes were buried 3.
Aug. Captain Goddard's wife buried 18.
Sep. Edmund Maunde buried ye first day.
Sep. Christopher Hyde buried 27.
Oct. Mr Charles Quarles buried ye second day.
Nov. John Bewe and Elizabeth Crewes married ye third by license.
Nov. Elizabeth ye daughter of Mr Hugh Willis baptized 23.
Jan. Ffrancis ye sone of Mr Vincent Barry, jun., baptised 3.
Feb. Matthew ye sone of Matthew Crewes baptized 13.
1662. Apr. George ye sone of George Boroughs baptized 10.
June. An'e ye daughter of Edward Philips buried 9.

1662. Aug. Ffrancis ye son'e of Mr Vincent Barry buried 5.
Oct. Willis' ye son'e of Edward Leaver buried ye first day.
Nov. Wm ye sone of Edward Philips baptized 16.
Jan. Augustine ye son' of Tho. Stribbhill buried 14.
Jan. Ffrancis ye sonne of Mr Hugh Willis baptized 18.
Feb. John Randolph and Jane Cock married 25 by license.
1663. Feb. John ye son'e of George Burroughs baptized 18.
1665. June. Robert Cruse & Ffrances Smarte marryed by license.
June. Henry Tripp ye younger and Anne Carpenter marryed by license at ye same time.
1666. Apr. William ye son and Elizabeth ye daughter of William Pecke, being twinnes, were baptized privately 15.
July. Vincent Barry of Thame, Esquire, buried ye 21.
Oct. Robt ye son of Robert Cruse baptized privately ye 6.
Dec. Thomas ye son of Mathew Cruse baptized ye 23.
Feb. Anne ye daughter of Mr Hugh Dorrell baptized ye 4.
Mar. Elizabeth and Ffrances being twines ye 2 daughters of Mr John Stribblehill, junior, were baptized 10; (buried ye 16).
1667. May. Mr Jacob Watson and Mrs Mary Burnham marryed by license 2.
May. Mr William Stratfold and Mrs Mary Winter of Chaseley marryed by license upon Sunday, being ye 12.
May. Anne ye daughter of Mr Phillips buried ye 17.
Aug. Mrs Elizabeth Burrowes ye wife of Mr George Burrowes buried ye 23 day.
Aug. Elizabeth ye daughter of Mr George Burrowes baptized ye same day.
Oct. Robert ye son of Robert Maune was baptized ye 10 day.
Oct. Sir John Clarke, Knight and Baronett, was buried ye 10 day.
Nov. Christopher ye son of Mr Christopher Maunde baptized 22.
Dec. Mrs Heather ye wife of Mr Thomas Heather was buried in ye church ye 2 day.
Dec. Richard Lake and Ursula Tomlinson marryed by lic' 31.
Jan. John Edwards and Mary Stribblehill maryed by lic' 1.
1668. July Mr Nathanael Yynter [i.e. Wynter] and Mrs Sarah Barry were marryed by lic' 23 day.
July The wife of Rev. Robt Heath was buried ye same day [i.e. 24th].
Oct. Richard Burrowes and Martha Thame were marryed by lic' 8 day.
Oct. A stranger, beinge a ffooteboy to Sr William Clarke, was buried ye 28.
Dec. Thomas ye son of Matthew Cruse was baptized ye 30 day.

Baptisms, Marriages, and Burials,

A.D. 1713–1733.

1713. Mar. Dorothy ye wife of William Peck buryed j day.
1714. July. Ann ye wife of Mathew Loader buryed ye 9 day.
Aug. Mary ye daughter of John Stribblehill of London buryed 22 day.
Dec. William ye son of Robert Maund baptiz'd ye 15 day.
Feb. Rich'd Adkins, sen., buryed 23 day.
1715. Apr. William Peck, sen., buryed ye 14 day.
Apr. Elizabeth ye daughter of Will. Peck, jun., baptized 19 day.
May. Ffrancis Clerk of North Weston, Esq., buryed ye 7 day.
1715. June. William Maund buryed ye 19 day.
Aug. John ye son of Thomas Smyth baptized ye 9 day.
Oct. Richard Wollaston, Esq., and Mrs Anne Knott marryed ye 5 day by banns.
Jan. Widow Maund buryed ye 2 day.
Jan. George ye son of Tho. Smyth baptized ye 2 day.
Feb. Penelope ye daughter of Mathew Loader baptized ye 13 day.
1716. July. Joseph Tripp of St. Andrew's, London, buryed ye 11 day.
Nov. Will. Deely and Ann Simonds marry'd 17 day by license.
Dec. Mary Crews, widow, buryed ye 13 day.
1717. Sep. Ann ye daughter of Robert Maund, jun., baptized ye 4 day.
Sep. William Peck, sen., buryed ye 16 day.
1718. Apr. John Pierce ye son of Mathew Loader baptized ye 24 day.
June. Katherine ye daughter of ye Right Honble James Herbert buryed ye 12 day.
Dec. Sarah ye daughter of Tho. Smyth baptized ye 27 day.
Dec. Mathew ye son of Tho. Crewes buryed ye 27 day.
Jan. John Peirce Loader ye son of Mathew Loader buryed 3 day.
Mar. Mary ye daughter of Mr Wollaston baptized ye 18 day.
1719. Apr. Halleat ye son of ye Honble James Herbert buryed ye 2 day.
May. Mr Edward Phillips, sen., buryed ye 8 day.
May. Alice ye daughter of Tho. Fanshawe, Esq., born ye 3, baptized ye 25 day.
June. Jone ye wife of Mr William Clerke, minister, buryed ye 24 day.
July. Alice ye daughter of Thomas Fanshawe, Esq., buryed ye 24 day.
Philip Wenman son of Richard Lord Wenman & Lady Sus. born Nov. 23 in ye year of our Ld. 1719 and baptized ye 13 of December following, St. James', Westminster.
Jan. Timothy ye son of Robert Maund baptized ye 30 day.
1720. May. The Widow Simmons buryed ye same day [i.e. the 2nd].
June. ffrances ye daughter of Thomas Fanshawe, Esq., baptized 23.
Dec. ffrances ye daughter of Mathew Loader baptized ye 22 day.
May. The Honble James Herbert of Kingsey buryed ye 4 day.
1721. Nov. William Symons and Elizabeth Peck married ye 9 day by license.
Jan. Mr William Clerk, minister, buried ye 10 day.
Jan. Thomas ye son of Thomas Ffanshear, Esq., born ye 4 day and baptized ye 28 day.
Jan. Thomas Crews buried ye 29 day.
1722. Mar. Ann ye daughter of Henry Simons baptized ye 26 day.
Apr. Mr Wilkins buried ye 11 day.
May. The daughter of ye Rev. Mr Ward buried ye 4 day.
May. John Stribilhill buried ye 21 day.
June. Frances ye daughter of Robert Maund baptized ye 6 day.
June. Philip Herbert of Kingsey, Esq., buried the 29 day.
Oct. Madam Stribblehill buried ye 13 day.
Feb. John Maund buried ye 2 day.
Feb. The Rev. Mr Thomas Horwood and Mrs Eliz. Clerke were married ye 23 day by license.
1723. May. ffrances ye daughter of Robert Maund buried ye 4 day.
June. Elizabeth ye daughter of Thomas Smith baptized ye 12 day.

1723. July. Samuel ye son of John Powell baptised ye 2 day.
Aug. William ye son of William Symons baptised ye 21 day.
Sep. Mr Richard Leaver buried ye 2 day.
Oct. George ye son of Samuel Wollaston baptised ye 7 day.
Dec. Mrs Ann Wollaston buried ye 5 day.
Feb. Mrs Middleton buried ye 29 day.
1724. Apr. John ye son of Henry Symons baptised ye 22 day.
May. Edward ye son of ye Rev. Mr Peter Walldo buried ye 23 day.
Aug. Christian Symmons buried ye 14 day.
Aug. Frances ye daughter of ye Rev. Mr Robert Hughes baptised ye 26 day.
1725. Apr. Frances ye daughter of Robert Maund baptised ye 28.
Dec. Jos ye son of Mr Wm Simons baptised ye 23.
Feb. Mary ye daughter of Tho. Smith, jun., baptised ye 5.
1726. July. The wife of Francis Clerk, Esq., buried at North Weston ye 9.
July. John ye son of Wm Simons buried ye 25.
Aug. Moses ye son of ye Rev. Mr Robert Hewes bury'd ye 28.
Dec. The Widow Maund bury'd ye 16.
Jan. Robert Maund son bury'd ye 18.
Feb. Frances Powel, widow, bury'd ye 15.
Mar. Catherine ye daughter of Robert Maund baptised ye 2.
Mar. Amey daughter of Tho. Smith, jun., baptis'd ye 11.
1727. Apr. Mr Gilbert Trow of Crendon bury'd ye 14.
May. The Rev. Mr Henry Bruges bury'd ye 6.
July. Ann ye daughter of Tho. Smith bury'd ye 22.
1728. Apr. Frances ye daughter of ye Rev. Mr Hewes bury'd ye 5.
Apr. Thomas ye son of Tho. Smith, jun., baptised ye 17.
Apr. Elis. ye daughter of Wm Symons bury'd ye 29.
Mar. Frances ye daughter of Tho. Smith baptised ye 23.
1729. Apr. The Widow Smith bury'd ye 30.
June. Mrs Maria Herbert of Kingsey bury'd ye 30.
Sep. Susannah ye wife of Jos Simons bury'd ye 12.
Dec. Mr William Phillips, sen., bury'd ye 10.
Dec. Wm Tripp, sen., bury'd ye 19.
Mar. Mathew ye son of Mathew Loader bury'd ye 20.
1730. May. Francis Carr Clerke of North Weston, Esq., died on Wednesday ye 27, and was buryed on Sunday the 31.
Nov. Jos ye son of the Rev. Mr Kipling baptis'd ye 2, bury'd ye 13.
Nov. Mary ye daughter of Henry Simons baptis'd ye 15.
1731. Sep. Rich'd ye son of Tho. Smith baptis'd ye 10.
Dec. Tho. ye son of Graveley Stribblehill baptis'd ye 27.
Dec. Widow Simons buryed ye 30.
1733. July. Frances ye daughter of Thos. Stribblehill buryed 21.
Oct. Jenny ye daughter of Henry Simons baptised ye 7.

Burials, A.D. 1735-1751.

1734/5. Feb. 7. Ann ye wife of Henry Simons.
1737. Oct. 17. Frances ye wife of Tho. Smith.
1739. Jan. 7. Christopher Petty Esq.
Dec. 13. Widow Petty.
1740. Apr. 3. Mr Peregrine Herbert of Kingsey.
Nov. 28. James Herbert, Esq., of Kingsey.
1741. Aug. 14. Thomas Smith.
Oct. 4. Mr Samuel Wollaston.
1742. July 13. Peregrine ye son of Israel Bull.
1743. Apr. 17. Edward ye son of Thos. and Mary Smith.
Dec. 15. The Rev. Mr Robert Heath.
1744. Dec. 9. Mary Heath, widow of ye Rev. Robt Heath.
Apr. 18. Israel Bull.
1746. June 11. Henry Warner, gent., from Towersey, Bucks.
Aug. 9. Robert ye son of Rob't Maund from Henley.
Oct. 10. Mr Robert Maund.
Oct. 12. Frances Powell.
Oct. 29. William ye son of Mr Rob't Maund from Crendon.
1747. May 1. Burrows ye son of Edward Rose, gent.
1748. Dec. 6. The Rev. Jo. Clerke, LL.D., Rector of Beachhampton in Bucks, buried at North Weston.
1749. July 31. Philip Herbert, Esq., from Kingsey.
1750. May 5. Elizabeth Simmons widow.
Feb. 23. Mrs Henry Warner.
1751. July 15. The Rev. Saml Thornbury, vicar.

Baptisms, A.D. 1735-1756.

1735. Aug. 28. Sophia daughter of Israel Bull.
1737. Jan. 7. Sarah ye daughter of Henry and Mary Simons.
1738. May 27. Peregrine son of Israel and Mary Bull.
May 27. Edward son of Tho. and Elis. Smith.
May 27. Henry ye son of Henry and Mary Simons.
1740. Feb. 1. Wm ye son of Henry and Sarah Simons.
Oct. 15. Edwd ye son of Tho. and Mary Smith.
1743. Oct. 28. Hannah ye daughter of Henry and Mary Simons.
Jan. 25. Jos ye son of Thomas and Mary Smith.
1744. Nov. 1. John ye son of Rich'd and Mary Head of Weston.
Mar. 11. Jos son of Tho. and Elis. Smith.
Mar. 24. James ye son of Wm and Mary Smith.
1746. Mar. 2. Ann ye daughter of Rich'd and Sarah Head of Weston.
June 15. William ye son of Thomas and Elis. Smith.
1747. July 11. Elisabeth ye daughter of William and Ann Simons.
Oct. 4. William ye son of William and Elizabeth Simons.
1748. Aug. 26. Ann ye daughter of Wm and Ann Simons.
1749. Aug. 2. William ye son of William and Ann Simons.
1749/50. Mar. 25. Mary ye daughter of ye Rev. John Newborough and Catherine his wife baptised, born ye 2.
July 8. Diana Susanna daughter of Francis Clarke, Esq., baptised at Weston.
July 31. Elisth ye daughter of Richd and Sarah Head of Weston.
Oct. 17. Elis. daughter of Thomas and Elis. Smith.
1751. May 22. Richd son of John and Elith Tripp.
Dec. 12. William Henry son of Francis and Susanna Clarke of North Weston was baptized.
Dec. 14. Kitty ye daughter of the Rev. John Newborough and Catherine his wife.
1752. Apr. 7. John son of Willm and Ann Simons.
1753. Sep. 7. Barbara Susanna daughter of John and Catherine Newborough.
1754. Feb. 18. Mary daughter of William and Ann Simons.
Mar. 11. Robert son of Mr Harry Style and Theodosia his wife.
July 4. Elisabeth daughter of John and Elisabeth Tripp.
1755. Apr. 25. John and Robert sons of Thomas and Elisabeth Smith.
Nov. 5. Mary daughter of John and Elisth Tripp.
Dec. 19. Richard Needham son of John and Catherine Newborough.
1756. Feb. 20. Richd son of William and Ann Simons.
Oct. 27. Jane Theodosia daughter of Mr Harry and Theodosia Style.

Burials, A.D. 1752–1756.

1752. Aug. 11. Mrs Mary Wollaston.
1754. May 3. Mrs Loder wife of Mr Mathew Loder.
1755. May 3. Robert son of Thomas and Eliz. Smith.
1756. Feb. 4. Richd Nedham son of John and Cath. Newborough.
Feb. 20. Richd son of William and Ann Simons.
Oct. 27. Jane Theodosia daughter of Mr Harry and Theodosia Style.
Sep. 6. Mary wife of Henry Simons.

Baptisms, A.D. 1757–1784.

1757. June 29. William son of John and Elizabeth Tripp.
Oct. 18. Ann daughter of the Rev. John Newborough and Catherine his wife.
1758. Mar. 23. Charlote Sackville daughter of Mr Harry and Theodosia Style.
July 16. William son of John and Mary Simons.
1760. Jan. 28. Thomas son of Mr Giles Prickett.
Mar. 2. Mary daughter of John Simons.
Mar. 24. Rebecca daughter of John and Elizth Tripp.
Oct. 16. Sarah daughter of John and Jane Tripp.
1761. Oct. 23. Edward Willes son of Edward Willes, Esq., and Ann his wife of Weston, who was born Sep. 28, 1761.
1762. Jan. 31. Rich'd son of John and Mary Simons.
1763. Feb. 10. Henrietta Frances daughter of Mr Harry and Theodosia Style.
Nov. 2. John son of Thomas and Elizabeth Smith.
1766. Jan. 2. Mary daughter of Mr John and Mary Rose.
1767. May 11. Richard son of Joseph and Fanny Powell.
1769. Aug. 18. Mary daughter of Mr Robert and Cassandra Hedges.
Oct. 4. John son of Mr Edward Prickett.
Oct. 4. Elizabeth daughter of Mr Edward Prickett.
Dec. 26. Timothy Tripp son of Mr Timothy and Elizabeth Lee.
1771. Jan. 26. Penelope Needham daughter of the Rev. Charles and Penelope Kipling.
May 16. Charlotte daughter of Timothy Newmarch and Elizabeth Lee.
Nov. 23. Fanny daughter of Richd and Mary Smith.
1773. Aug. 22. Thomas James son of Richd and Mary Smith.
Sep. 15. Ann daughter of Richard and Anne Stone.
1774. May 12. Nanny daughter of John and Elizth Simons.
1775. Feb. 20. Elizabeth daughter of Rich'd and Mary Smith.
1776. Feb. 19. Elizabeth Ann daughter of the Rev. Wm and Elizth Cooke.
Apr. 20. William son of William and Sarah Simons.
July 18. Elizabeth Tripp daughter of Rich'd and Ann Stone.
1777. Feb. 25. Richard son of Richard and Mary Smith.
Sep. 9. Joseph Gascoigne son of the Rev. Robert and Ann Style.
Sep. 23. Carolina daughter of William and Sarah Simons.
1777. Dec. 14. Richard son of Richard and Ann Stone.
1779. Feb. 8. Alfred Way son of William and Sarah Simons.
June 3. Theodosia Charlotte daughter of the Rev. Robert Style and Ann his wife.
Aug. 24. Lucy daughter of Richard and Mary Smith.
1780. Mar. 14. Hariot Philadelphia daughter of William and Sarah Simons.
Nov. 2. Spencer son of Richard and Mary Smith.
Nov. 19. Samuel son of John and Elizabeth Simons.
1781. July 6. Letitia Charlotte daughter of Mr Sackville Beal Lupton and Jane Theodosia his wife.
Sep. 9. Richard Way son of William and Sarah Simons.
1782. Mar. 4. Frances Henrietta daughter of the Rev. Robert and Nanny Style born the 3 and baptized 4.
Sep. 13. Thomas son of Sackville Beal Lupton and Theodosia his wife.
1783. Jan. 4. Juliana daughter of Richard and Mary Smith.
Mar. 16. Clarissa daughter of William and Sarah Simons.
1784. Mar. 31. Sackville son of Sackville and Jane Theodosia Lupton.
Oct. 4. James son of William and Sarah Simons.

Burials, A.D. 1758–1784.

1758. Apr. 22. Mr Peck.
June 9. Henry Simons.
Oct. 22. Richard Stone.
1759. July 13. Mr William Simons, sen.
July 29. Mr Maund.
1760. June 26. Thomas Smith, sen.
July 23. The Right Hon. Philip Lord Viscount Wenman in the Chapel of Thame Park.
1761. Sep. 12. Ann wife of Mr Edward Rose.
1763. Jan. 5. Mr Giles Burrows.
Oct. 31. Mr Matthew Loder.
1764. July 9. Mr Thomas Smith.
Sep. 25. Mr William Simons.
1765. Jan. 21. Henrietta Frances daughter of Mr Harry and Theodosia Style.
Feb. 2. Mr Robert Heath from Crendon.
1768. May 30. Mrs Ann Crews, sen.
1769. May 15. Mrs Mary Smith.
1777. May 12. Sarah Bull.
Oct. 19. Joseph Gascoigne son of the Rev. Robert and Anne Style.
1778. Apr. 19. Mary wife of Richard Way, gent., coroner.
1780. Nov. 17. Mrs Elizabeth Rose.
1781. Oct. 8. Mrs Thomas Yate.
1784. Feb. 21. Mrs William Eaton.
Apr. 16. Mr Edmund Prickett.
Oct. 9. Ann Newborough daughter of the Rev. John Newborough.
Dec. 3. Richard Way, coroner.

No. II. LITANY OF THE SAINTS. (From a Lincoln Horæ B.V.M. in my possession.)

Kyrie eleison.
Christe eleison.
Kyrie eleison.
Christe audi nos.
Christe exaudi nos.
Pater de cœlis Deus: miserere nobis.
Fili Redemptor mundi Deus: miserere nobis.
Spiritus Sancte Deus: miserere nobis.
Sancta Trinitas, Unus Deus: miserere nobis.
Sancta Maria: Ora pro nobis.
Sancta Dei genitrix: Ora.
Sancta Virgo virginum: Ora.
Sancte Michael: Ora.
Sancte Gabriel: Ora.
Sancte Raphael: Ora.
Omnes sancti Angeli et Archangeli Dei: Orate pro nobis.
Omnes sancti beatorum Spirituum ordines: Orate pro nobis.
Sancte Joannes Baptista: Ora.
Omnes sancti Patriarchæ et Prophetæ: Orate.
Sancte Petre: Ora.
Sancte Paule: Ora.

Sancte Andrea: Ora.
Sancte Johannes: Ora.
Sancte Jacobe: Ora.
Sancte Thoma: Ora.
Sancte Philippe: Ora.
Sancte Jacobe: Ora.
Sancte Matthæe: Ora.
Sancte Bartholomæe: Ora.
Sancte Simon: Ora.
Sancte Thadæe: Ora.
Sancte Matthia: Ora.
Sancte Barnaba: Ora.
Sancte Marce: Ora.
Sancte Luca: Ora.
Omnes sancti Apostoli et Evangelistæ: Orate.
Omnes sancti discipuli et innocentes: Orate.
Sancte Stephane: Ora.
Sancte Line: Ora.
Sancte Clete: Ora.
Sancte Clemens: Ora.
Sancte Fabiane: Ora.
Sancte Sebastiane: Ora.
Sancte Cosma: Ora.
Sancte Damiane: Ora.
Sancte Prime: Ora.
Sancte Feliciane: Ora.
Sancte Dionysi cum sociis tuis: Orate.
Sancte Victor cum sociis tuis: Orate.
Omnes sancti martyres: Orate pro nobis.
Sancte Sylvester: Ora.
Sancte Leo: Ora.
Sancte Hieronyme: Ora.
Sancte Augustine: Ora.
Sancte Isidore: Ora.
Sancte Juliane: Ora.
Sancte Gildarde: Ora.
Sancte Medarde: Ora.
Sancte Albane: Ora.
Sancte Eusebi: Ora.
Sancte Swithune: Ora.
Sancte Birine: Ora.
Omnes sancti confessores: Orate pro nobis.
Omnes sancti monachi et eremitæ: Orate.
Sancti Maria Magdalena: Ora pro nobis.
Sancta Maria Ægyptiaca: Ora pro nobis.
Sancta Margareta: Ora.
Sancta Scolastica: Ora.
Sancta Petronella: Ora.
Sancta Genovefa: Ora.
Sancta Praxedis: Ora.
Sancta Sotheris: Ora.
Sancta Prisca: Ora.
Sancta Tecla: Ora.
Sancta Afra: Ora.
Sancta Editha: Ora.
Omnes sanctæ Virgines: Orate pro nobis.
Omnes sancti: Orate.

No. III. POEMS BY WILLIAM BASSE OF THAME.

Great Brittaines Sunnes-set: bewailed with a show of Teares.*

By WILLIAM BASSE.

At Oxford: Printed by Joseph Barnes, 1613.

A Soule ore-laden with a greater Summe
Of ponderous sorrow then she can sustaine,
(Like a distressed sayle that labours home)
Some obiect seekes, whereto she may complaine.
Not that (poore soule) hir obiect can draw from
Hir groaning breast th'occasion of hir paine:
But overcharg'd with Teares shee (widow-like) bestowes
Vpon hir best friends eares, some children of her woes.

Not (like as when some triviall discontents
First taught my raw and lucklesse youth to rue)
Doe I to Flockes, now vtter my laments,
Nor choose a tree, or streame, to mourne vnto:
My weightier sorrow now (*Deare Sir*) presents
These her afflicted features to your view.
Whose free and noble mind (were not this griefe your owne)
Would to my plaints be kind, if I complain'd alone.

But such true arguments of inward woe
In your sad face, I lately haue beheld,
As if your teares (like floods that overflowe
Their liquid shores) alone, would haue excell'd
This generall *Deluge* of our eies, that so
Sea-like our earth-like cheekes hath overswell'd
As if your heart would send forth greatest lamentation,
Or strive to comprehend our universall passion.

And as th'occasion (*Sir*) may iustly moue
To maid-like sorrow the most man-like heart:
So may your griefe (to your beholders) proue
The iustice of His grace, and your desert.
For teares and sighs are th'issues of true loue:
Our present woes our former ioies imparte.
He loues the living best, who for the dead mournes most:
He merits not the rest, who not laments the lost.

To you I therefore weepe: To you alone
I shew the image of your teares, in mine;
That mine (by shewing your teares) may be show'n
To be like yours, so faithfull, so divine:
Such, as more make the publique woe their owne,
Then their woe publique such as not confine
The'selues to times, nor yet formes fro' examples borrow:
Where loue is infinite, there boundlesse is the sorrow.

O let us (Muse) this heavynesse (that no
Just heare, vnclest, at one time can sustaine)
By fittes, and preparations undergoe:
Let's feare, let's hope: tremble; and hope againe.
O, let vs this dysastrous truth ne're know;
But rather deafe and stupefied remaine:
For happier much it were, the hearing sence to loose
Then loose all sence to heare such an vnhappy newes.

Like to a changeling (in his sleepes) become
Rob'd of his sexe, by some prodigious cause
I am turn'd woman: warrish feares benumbe
My Heart: my Masculine existence thawes
To teares, wherein I could againe entombe
His tombe, or penetrate hir marble iawes:
But, O, why should I twice entombe him! O what folly
Were it to pierce (with sighes) a monument so holy!

Here then run forth thou River of my woes
In cease-lesse currents of complaining verse:
Here weepe (young Muse) while elder pens compose
More solemne Rites vnto his sacred Hearse.
And, as when happy earth did, here, enclose
His heav'nly minde, his Fame then Heav'n did pierce:
Now He in Heav'n doth rest, now let his Fame earth fill;
So, both him then possess'd: so both possesse him still.

Or, like a *Nymph* distracted or vndone
With blubber'd face, hands wrong, neglected haire,
Run through moist Valleys, through wide deserts run
Let speech-lesse *Eccho* eccho thy dispaire.
Declare th'vntimely *Set* of *Brittaines Sun*
To sorrowing Shepheards: To sad *Nymphes* declare
That such a night of woes, his *Occident* doth follow
That *Day* in darknes clothes, and mourner makes *Apollo*.

* At the back of the titlepage stands the following dedication: "To His Honourable Master, Sr Richard Wenman, Knight."

But of his partes thinke not t'expresse the least
Whom Nature did the best in all things forme.
First, borne a *Prince* (next to his FATHER) best;
Then, Fram'd a Man, to be, as he was borne:
Beauty his youth beyond all others blest,
Vertues did him beyond his youth aborne.
What Muse, what voice, what pen, ca' giue the all thy duties!
O Prince of Princes, me': youth, wisdo', deeds, and beauties.

Fates, that so soone beheld his Fame enrould,
Put to his golden thred their envious sheeres:
Death fear'd his magnanimitie to behold,
And (in his sleepe) basely reveng'd hir feares.
Time, looking on his wisdom, thought him old,
And laid his rash Sythe to his Primest years.
Stars that (in loue) did long t'embrace so faire a myrrhour
Wink'd at *Fates* envious wrong, *Death's* treason and *Times* errour.

O *Fates*, O *Time*, O *Death*, (But you must all
Act the dread will of your Immortall GVIDE)
O *Fates*, How much more life did you appaule,
When you his liuely texture did divide!
O *Time*, when by thy sythe this *Flow'r* did fall
How many thousands did'st thou wound beside!
O *Death*, how many deathes, is of that life compacted,
That from all living breathes, his only death extracted.

How many brave Deedes ha's the wounded wombe
Of Hope, miscarryed, now, before their time!
How many high designes haue seene their doome
Before their birth, Or perish'd in their Prime?
How many beauties drown'd are in his tombe?
How many glories, with him, heav'ns do clime!
How many sad cheekes mourne, Him laid in Earth to see,
As they to earth would turne, his Sepulcher to be.

Like a high Pyramis, in all his towers
Finish'd this morning, and laid prostrate soone;
Like as if *Nighte's* blacke and incestuous bowers
Should force *Apollo's* beauty before Noone:
Like as some strange change in the heav'nly powers
Should in hir *Full* quench the refulgent *Moone*:
So HE, his daies, his light, and his life (here) expir'd
New-built, most (*Su'*-like) bright Ful Mo', & most admir'd.

But HEAV'NS, Disposers of all *Life* and *Death*,
That our pied pride, and wretched liues mislike,
Took HIM that's gone (from vs) to better breath
Vs that remaine, with (death from him) to strike.
His flower-like youth here, there more flourisheth,
His graces then, are now more Angel-like.
Those glories that in Him, so shone, now thine much more,
Our glories now are dim, that shin'd in him before.

And thou faire *He*, whose three-fold beauties face
Enchants the Three-fork'd *Scepter* of thy *Lover*
That with thine owne eies drown'st thy lap, the place
That his enamour'd armes and streames would cover:
Make true and two-fold vse of griefe, That grace
May with affliction now itself discouer.
These teares thou dost begin, to shed for HENRYES sake,
Continue for thy sinne, which made Heau'n *Henry* take.

That thy iust JAMES, who hitherto hath sway'd
Thy Scepter Many-fold, and ample Frame,
Many more ages, yet, may live obay'd
T'enlarge thy glories, and to yeeld the same
Divine examples unto CHARLES that made
HENRY so noble, and so great in Fame.
For who but such a King, as *He*, can such another
In place of *Henry* bring? Who match him but a BROTHER?

And neighbour Lands to whome our moanes we lent
May to our greater losse now lend vs theirs.
Florence hir old *Duke* mourn'd but we lament
A *greater* then a *Duke* in flowring yeares.
Spaine for a *Queene* hir eies sad moisture spent:
We for a Prince (and for a Man) shed teares.
But *France* whose cheek's still wet, nearest our griefe hath smarted;
For she from *Henry* Great; wee from Great *Henry* parted.

And thus, As I haue seene an even, showre,
(When *Phœbus* to *Joues* other splendent heyres
Bequeath'd the Day) down from *Olympus* powre,
When Earth in teares of Trees, and Trees in teares
Of Mountaines wade: Like some neglected flowre
(Whose sorrow is scarce visible with theirs)
Downe to my silent brest my hidden face I bow:
My *Phœbus* in his Rest, hath hid his heav'nly brow.

William Basse

(Autograph from an Original Document.)

A Morning after Mourning.

Let me no longer Presse your gentle eies,
Be'ing of themselues franke of religious teares:
But stanch these streames with solace from the Skies;
Whence *Hymen* deck'd in Saffron robes appeares.
Let *Henry* now rest in our memories,
And let the *Rest*, rest in our eies and eares.
Now He hath had his Rites, Let Those haue their adorning
By whose bright beames our Night of mourning ha's a morning.

And now (my *Muse*) vnmasque thee: And see how
A second *Sonne* in *Henries* place doth shine
See *Five* great *Feastes* all meete in one Day, now
Our MAKER keepes his *Sabaoth* most divine.
Isis and *Rhene* are ioyn'd in sacred vow;
And faire *Eliza's Fredericke's Valentine*.
The *Court* in ioy attires hir splendent brow;
The *Country* shrowes; And all in mirth combine.
Five-times be hallowed, The Day, wherein, GOD rests,
Saints triumph, Princes wed: and Court and Cou'try feaste's.

No. IV. OXFORDSHIRE CHRISTMAS MIRACLE PLAY.

(From "Notes and Queries," Fifth Series, 26 December 1874.)

PERHAPS the following may be of sufficient interest to appear in your Christmas number. The text of the play was taken down by myself from the lips of one of the performers in 1853. I first saw it acted in the Hall of the old Vicarage House at Thame, in the year 1839, by those whose custom it had been, from time immemorial, to perform it at the houses of the gentlepeople of that neighbourhood at Christmas, between St. Thomas's Day and Old Christmas Eve, January 5. These performers (now long scattered, and all dead but one, as I am informed), claimed to be the "true and legitimate successors" of the mummers who, in previous centuries, constantly performed at the "Whitsun" and "Christmas Church Ales," records of which are found on almost every page of the "Stewards' and Churchwardens' Books of the Prebendal Church of our Blessed Lady of Thame."

In Mr. Lupton's *History of Thame* some account of these performances is given; while, in the "Address" prefixed to his privately-printed and curious tract, *Extracts from the Accounts of the Proctors and Stewards, etc.*, of that town, he refers to the exceeding great popularity of the mumming for many years. In Lord Wenman's time, *i.e.* 1790, the performances were annually given at Thame Park; and at the Baronial Hall of Brill, Bucks, about 1808-14, the entertainment was attended by the nobility and gentry for miles round, and is reported to have been produced on a scale of considerable magnificence.

The man from whom I took down the following in my note-book had performed at Brill in the year 1807, and his father had done the same at Thame Park in the previous century. I do not profess to be able to explain the text of the play, nor can I quite admire all its points. Its coarseness, too, is not to my taste. Least of all can I comprehend its purport. Its anachronisms will be patent to all. But at least its action is vigorous, and, when I was a boy, I confess that I thought the performance most delightful and impressive. As the late Mr. Lupton (a local antiquarian and a gentleman of excellent taste and high character) informed me of so much that is here set forth, I may add that he, at the same time, expressed his conviction that my version of the play is most probably the *only one* that had ever been committed to paper; for the dialogue was purely traditional, and handed down from father to son. Nothing whatsoever has been altered or added by myself. I have only ventured to put the directions in italics in a little more concise and intelligible language than that in which they were dictated to me.

FREDERICK GEORGE LEE, D.C.L.

All Saints' Vicarage, Lambeth.

DRAMATIS PERSONÆ.

King Alfred.
King Alfred's Queen.
King William.
Old King Cole (with a wooden leg).
Giant Blunderbore.
Little Jack.
Old Father Christmas.
St. George of England.
The Old Dragon.
The Merry Andrew.
Old Doctor Ball.
Morres-Men.

All the mummers come in singing, and walk round the place in a circle, and then stand on one side.

Enter King Alfred and his Queen, arm-in-arm.

I am King Alfred, and this here is my Bride;
I've a crown on my pate and a sword by my side.
[*Stand apart.*

Enter King Cole.

I am King Cole, and I carry my stump.
Hurrah for King Charles! down with old Noll's Rump!
[*Stands apart.*

Enter King William.

I am King William of blessed me-mo-ry,
Who came and pulled down the high gallows-tree,
And brought us all peace and pros-pe-ri-ty.
[*Stands apart.*

Enter Giant Blunderbore.

I am Giant Blunderbore, fee, fi, fum,
Ready to fight ye all—so I says "Come."

Enter Little Jack (Blunderbore continues).

And this here is my little man Jack,
A thump on his rump and a whack on his back.
[*Strikes him twice.*

I'll fight King Alfred, I'll fight King Cole,
I'm ready to fight any mortal soul;
So here I, Blunderbore, takes my stand,
With this little devil, Jack, at my right hand,
Ready to fight for mortal life. Fee, fi, fum.
[*The Giant and Little Jack stand apart.*

Enter St. George.

I am St. George of Merry Eng-land;
Bring in the morres-men, bring in our band.
[*Morres-men come forward and dance to a tune from fife and drum. The dance being ended, St. George continues.*

These are our tricks. Ho! men, ho!
These are our sticks,—whack men so.
[*Strikes the Dragon, who roars, and comes forward.*

The Dragon speaks.

Stand on head, stand on feet,
Meat, meat, meat for to eat.
[*Tries to bite King Alfred.*

I am the Dragon, here are my jaws;
I am the Dragon, here are my claws.
Meat, meat, meat for to eat.
Stand on my head, stand on my feet.
[*Turns a somersault and stands aside.*

All sing, several times repeated.

Ho! ho! ho!
Whack men so.

[*The drum and fife sound. They all fight, and after general disorder fall down.*

Enter Old Doctor Ball.

I am the Doctor, and I cure all ills,
Only gullup my portions [? potions] and swallow my pills;
I can cure the itch, the stitch, the palsy, and the gout,
All pains within and all pains without.
Up from the floor, Giant Blunderbore!
[*Gives him a pill, and he rises at once.*

Get up, King; get up, Bride;
Get up, Fool, and stand aside.
[*Gives them each a pill, and they rise.*

Get up, King Cole, and tell the gentlefolks all,
There never was a doctor like Mr. Doctor Ball.
Get up, St. George, Old England's Knight.
[*Gives him a pill.*

You have wounded the Dragon, and finished the fight.
[*All stand aside but the Dragon, who lies in convulsions on the floor.*

Now kill the old Dragon, and poison old Nick,
At Yule-tyde both o' ye, cut your stick.
[*The Doctor forces a large pill down the Dragon's throat, who thereupon roars, and dies in convulsions.*

Then enter Father Christmas.

I am Father Christmas! hold, men, hold!
Be there loaf in your locker, and sheep in your fold,
A fire on the hearth, and good luck for your lot,
Money in your pocket, and a pudding in the pot.

He sings.

Hold, men, hold!
Put up your sticks,
End all your tricks;
Hold, men, hold!

Chorus (all sing, while one goes round with a hat for gifts).

Hold, men, hold!
We are very cold,
Inside and outside,
We are very cold.
If you don't give us silver,
Then give us gold
From the money in your pockets—
[*Some of the performers shew signs of fighting again.*
Hold, men, hold!

Song and chorus.

God A'mighty bless your hearth and fold,
Shut out the wolf, and keep out the cold;
You gev [have given] us silver, keep you the gold,
For 'tis money in your pocket.—Hold, men, hold!

Repeat in chorus.

God A'mighty bless, etc.
[*Exeunt omnes.*

No. V. THE FIGHT AT CHINNOR AND CHALGROVE.

The following rare contemporary Tract, written in the interest of the Rebels—and therefore not wholly to be relied on—is here reproduced:

A true Relation of a gret Fight between the King's Forces and the Parliament's, at Chinner neer Tame on Saturday last, with the manner how the King's Forces made the assault, and by what meanes they were forced to retreat. Also in what manner Colonell Hampden is wounded, with the names of the chiefe Commanders that were killed and taken prisoners on both sides. As also the firing and burning of the Towne of Chinner, by the King's Forces, and many other remarkable passages concerning the said fight. London, printed by B. A. for Robert Wood and John Greenesmith.

Vpon Munday last it was informed by divers letters and several persons that came from the Army, to this effect, viz., That on Saturday night last, three or foure troops of the King's forces having wheeled from Abington to Wallingford, and from thence towards Stoken Church, under the Hills neere unto Tetsworth, they came unto a towne three miles from Tame, called Chinner, at which place the Lord Generall with his Maine Forces (consisting, as it is credibly informed, of very neer thirty thousand able fighting men), were quartered, it being upon the edge of Buckinghamshire, at which place were quartered about four hundred of the Parliament's Forces, the greatest part whereof were forces that lately came to assist his Excellencie in the Parliament's service, which came out of Bedfordshire and Essex, and missing the Parliament's Scouts they came to the said Towne, and gave a sodden assault against the Parliament's Forces there, and cut off some of their Centinels and entered the towne, and according to their barbarous and destructive manner, fired the same in divers places. But before I proceed in the further relation of this businesse, I may not forget the valour and courage of the Parliament's Forces which were in this towne, for they charged the enemy with as much courage and resolution as could be expected or performed by men being unexpectedly assaulted, and continued fight with them many houres. And upon this assault of the enemy, an alarm was given to the Lord General's quarters at Tame, upon which divers troops of horse were designed to sally forth upon this expedition. And amongst those Colonels and Commanders that were at an instant willing to hazard their lives upon this designe, Colonell Hampden (who is a Gentleman that hath never been wanting to adventure his life and fortunes for the goodwill and welfare of his King and Countrey) may not be forgotten, who finding of a good troop of Horse (whose Captaine was at that time willing) desired to know whether they would be commanded by him upon this designe. Whereupon the officers and common souldiers freely and unanimously consented, and proffered to adventure their lives with this noble Gentleman, and shewed much cheerfulness that they should have the honour to be led by so noble a Captaine. And so the said Colonell Hampden and some other Colonels and Captains came with a considerable party of horse with all expedition to assist the rest of their forces, which, as aforesaid, were quartered at Chinner. And as soone as the Cavaliers perceived that some of the Lord General's Forces were come in from Tame, they presently fled from Chinner back againe towards Tetsworth, and were then pursued by Colonell Hampden and the rest of the Lord General's forces that came upon this designe, about two miles; in which pursuit there were many of the King's Forces killed and taken prisoners, in which retreat this is observable, that the Cavaliers (as it appeared afterward) had plotted in a perfidious manner to have intrapped the Parliament's Forces, and to have killed and taken them all prisoners, but it pleased God to prevent their plot: for on the way Prince Rupert, with about 1000 Horse, lay in ambush ready to fall upon the Parliament's forces; and although the Earle of Essex forces were scarcer ten for one, that were at this time in the battell, yet they gave them a brave volley of shot, and slew many of the enemy's forces as well at this place, which was neer Tetsworth, as at Chinner, and for some time, it being Sunday morning, held them fight without the losse of many men. But at last the enemy having intelligence that some regiments of foot were coming from Tame of the Lord General's forces, they retreated towards Abington, and durst not fight till they came in: for the foot forces are a great amazement unto them. Having thus farre, in a generall manner, declared the truth of this businesse, it rests in the next place that I enter into some particulars concerning the same for the better satisfaction of the Kingdome whose expectation thirsteth after the same. I dare not to delude with false and fabulous matter, and therefore I shall (being the first relater hereof) ommit uncertaine reports, than committ that to writing which hereafter may be questionable, and therefore I shall be more sparing therein and write onely those things which are authenticke, which that I may doe, first—it is certain that Colonell Hampden, that noble and valiant gentleman, received a shot with a bullet behind in the shoulder, which struck between the bone and the flesh, but is since drawne forth, and himself very cheerful and hearty, and is (through God's mercy) more likely to be a badge of honour than being danger of life. Serjant-Major Gunter, a gent. of the Parliament's side, was slaine, and Capt. Buller (as it is thought) taken prisoner. Some of the prisoners were taken on the Parliament's side; but in regard the particulers of the fight were not known when the intelligence came from the army. I shall omit to particulerize any more of them. On the enemies' side was slain Capt. Legge (who was once taken prisoner by the Parliament's forces and made an escape); and it is said that Col. Hurrey, which was heretofore employed in the Parliament's service and was last week in London, is either killed or taken prisoner; the L. Thomas Howard is also taken prisoner by the Parliament's forces, with divers other gent. of quallity, besides common souldiers. The certaine number that were slaine on either side I shall not at this time relate, for that it was not knowne in the Army when the Post that brought these tydings came from thence; but it is reported that there was an equall losse on both sides, there being about 400 slayne on both sides. A great part of the Town of Chinner was burnt by the King's forces, by which doings, compared with what had beene certified out of other parts, we may see that killing, burning, and destroying of all that is deare to us, is the Religion, Lawes and property of the subject they seeke for.

♣♣♣♣♣♣♣♣♣♣♣

No. VI. EXTRACTS FROM THE POLL OF FREEHOLDERS OF OXFORDSHIRE.

Taken at Oxford, on the 17th of April 1754, by Thomas Blackall, Esq., High Sheriff.

Relating to Thame and its Chapelries.

In the Hundred of Thame :—

Thame.

Name	Abode	W.	D.	P.	T.
Barnard, Vincent, jun.	Thame	W.	D.		
Bayley, John	Thame	W.	D.		
Bayley, Ralph	Thame	W.	D.		
Bell, Anthony	Aylesbury	W.	D.		
Benham, Tomlins	Stow on the Would			P.	T.
Boreham, John	Thame	W.	D.		
Bouler, Edward	Thame	W.	D.		
Burroughs, John, Esq.	Temple, London	W.	D.		
Callis, Richard	Thame	W.	D.		
Cashin, Daniel	Thame			P.	T.
Childs, Obadiah	Thame	W.	D.		
Clark, Richard	Thame	W.	D.		
Cook, Ambrose	Leighton Buzzard			P.	T.
Cox, Wm. (writ Long Crendon, Bucks, and as living in Thame)				P.	T.
Deely, Thomas	Thame	W.	D.		
Dobinson, Richard	Thame	W.	D.		
Dudley, Samuel	Thame	W.	D.		
Eeles, Wm.	Thame	W.	D.		
Edgerton, Peter, Esq.	Chalgrove	W.	D.		
Elliot, William	Stanton St. John			P.	T.
Eversitch, James	Thame	W.	D.		
Eustace, Daniel	Thame	W.	D.		
Eustace, Joseph	Thame	W.	D.		
Gibbins, ——; clerk	Thame	W.	D.		
Gilbert, Wm.; clerk	Berkstone, Lincolnshire			P.	T.
Hedges, Thomas	North Weston	W.	D.		
Hewet, Owen	Thame	W.	D.		
Howes, Joseph	London			P.	T.
Howland, Robert	Thame	W.	D.		
Humphrey, Henry	Thame	W.	D.		
Humphrey, John	Thame	W.	D.		
Hyott, Wm.	Thame	W.	D.		
Jackson, John	Chersley	W.	D.		
Jemmett, Henry	Thame	W.	D.		
Jemmett, Robert	Aylesbury	W.	D.		
Kent, Thomas	Thame	W.	D.		
Knollys, Francis, Esq.	Thame	W.	D.		
Ledwell, Wm., Esq.	Studley	W.	D.		
Lester, Benjamin	Charles Street, West'	W.	D.		
Letsom, Samson; clerk	Maddox St., Lond.	W.			T.
Loder, Matthew	Thame	W.		P.	
Looseley, William	Thame	W.	D.		
Messenger, Leonard	Thame	W.	D.		
New, Edward	Tetsworth	W.	D.		
Ostridge, Simon	Thame	W.	D.		
Page, William	Thame			P.	T.
Payne, Francis	Thame	W.		P.	
Payne, Henry	Chasfont by Sidnam	W.	D.		
Payne, William	Thame	W.	D.		
Peck, Samuel	Thame	W.	D.		
Phillips, Edward	Thame	W.	D.		
Prickett, Henry	Thame	W.	D.		
Prickett, John	Garsington	W.	D.		
Read, Thomas	Moreton	W.	D.		
Reeve, Benjamin	Thame	W.	D.		
Rose, Edward	Thame	W.	D.		
Seywell, Edward	Agmondesham Her.	W.	D.		
Simmons, Wm., jun.	Thame	W.	D.		
Steadman, Thomas	Lambeth Hill, Lon.	W.	D.		
Stephens, John	Thame	W.	D.		
Stone, Edward	Thame	W.	D.		
Stubbs, James	Ashborne in the Peak	W.	D.		
Taylor, John	Hampstead, Midds.	W.	D.		
Tomlinson, Edm.	Thame	W.	D.		
Tomlinson, Thomas	Tower Street, Lond.			P.	T.
Turner, John	Thame	W.	D.		
Trencher, John	Oxford	W.	D.		
Unwin, James, Esq.	Castle Yard, Holborn	W.	D.		
Wakelin, Baliol	Thame	W.	D.		
Wakelin, Richard	Thame	W.	D.		
Ward, Thomas	Green Arber Court	W.	D.		
Webb, John	Moreton	W.	D.		
Weedon, William	Gr. Marlow, Bucks	W.	D.		
West, Thomas	Thame	W.	D.		
Wheeler, John	Thame	W.	D.		
Williams, John	Thame	W.	D.		
Whitmill, John	Thame	W.	D.		
Winter, Thomas, sen.	Wornall			P.	T.
Winter, Thomas	Wornall, Bucks	W.	D.		
Yate, Thomas	Thame	W.	D.		

North Weston.

Name	Abode	W.	D.	P.	T.
Clark, Francis, Esq.	Warwick	W.	D.		

Moreton.

Name	Abode	W.	D.	P.	T.
Child, Richard	Goring	W.	D.		
Cosins, Richard	Tetsworth	W.	D.		
Orepenyer, John	Hanwell Heath, Midd.	W.	D.		

Tetsworth.

Name	Abode	W.	D.	P.	T.
Allen, Robert	Tetsworth			P.	
Francklin, John	Hurley, Berks			P.	T.
Hale, John	Tetsworth			P.	T.
Hartley, John, Esq.	Chipping Wicomb			P.	T.
Haydon, Daniel	Wooburn, Bucks			P.	T.
Hobday, Edward	Tetsworth	W.	D.		
Hobday, William, sen.	Tetsworth	W.	D.		
King, Edward	Chipping Wicomb	W.	D.		
Lane, John	Tetsworth	W.	D.		
Low, Nicholas	Tetsworth	W.	D.		
Snagg, Richard	Old Bailey, London			P.	T.
Young, Thomas	Hawhatch, Bucks			P.	

In the Hundred of Lewknor :—

Siddenham.

Name	Abode	W.	D.	P.	T.
Stephens, James	Siddenham	W.	D.		
Stephens, Henry	Siddenham	W.	D.		
Vardery, Henry	Towersey, Bucks	W.	D.		
Webb, Thomas	Stoke Talmage			P.	T.
Wheeler, Robert	Fulham, Middlesex	W.	D.		
White, Charles	Chalford	W.	D.		

Final Numbers:			Plumpers:
Wenman	2033.		W. 2.
Dashwood	2014.		D. 3.
Parker	1919.		P. 6.
Turner	1890.		T. 2.

No. VII. THE BELLS OF THE CHURCH.

A new Peal of Bells for the Prebendal Church of the Blessed Virgin Mary of Thame. MDCCCLXXVI.

In Dr. Rawlinson's MSS. in the Bodleian Library, that learned antiquary has recorded a visit he made to Thame Church two centuries ago—to examine monuments, records, and bells—when Mr. William Clark, Vice-Principal of Hart Hall, Oxford, was Vicar, having been instituted to his sacred office by Barlow, Bishop of Lincoln, October 29, 1675. Of this visit the following account is given:—"The Bishop of Lincoln "only institutes, for the Vicaridge is a peculiar to the "Deanery of Lincoln, and the Dean is Visitor solely [not y^e "Bp. of Oxon] being a Prebendary belonging to the Church "of Lincoln. The Church, *cum membris*, were appropriated "to the Abbey of Thame and bought of Henry VIII. by the "family of the Thynnes, of which the late Ld Weymouth "was the last, who gave it by will to the late Ld Carteret. "The Church is very fine, 6 bells, and had an organ, till the "Earl of Essex's Soldiers in ye Rebellion, pulled them down, "and went tooting about the Town with the pipes. . . . . "Mr. Clark, of Thame, was very courteous as to intelligence; "gave us a good account of the place, but no victuals nor "drink."

The six bells referred to here are those which have recently been recast. The following were their respective inscriptions and weights:—

I AS TREBL BE GIN—six hundred-weight.
I AS SECOND SING—seven hundred-weight.
I AS THIRD WILL RING—eight hundred-weight.
I AS FORTH IN MY PLACES—ten hundred-weight.
I AS FIFT WILL SOVND—twelve hundred-weight.
RICHARD KEENE CAST ME 1667—seventeen hundred-weight and a half.

The tenor bell came from the Woodstock Foundry, carried on for many years by Richard Keene and James Keene of that town, probably from A.D. 1626 to 1686. The other bells, including the Sanctus or Priest's bell (now rung just before service), were no doubt of the early or middle part of the sixteenth century; and were probably cast either by J. Wallis of Salisbury, or at Hawlwood's Foundry at Reading.* One of these bells had been cracked for several years, and a second received a similar injury about ten years ago. None of them were coeval with the building of the Church, nor was either of very great antiquity.

An attempt, therefore, was made to obtain funds for their recasting, by the issue of a Circular containing the following words, signed by me:—

"An earnest Appeal is made to all who are connected with the "old Parish Church of St. Mary, Thame, Oxon, in order that the "Bells of the Church may be re-arranged, two of them now cracked "to be re-cast, and the whole of them re-hung. It is both hoped and "believed that, by earnest co-operation and steady endeavours, the "sum required may, in due course, be raised. An Appeal, therefore, "is made to all, and of every class and and rank. While it is desirable that those who possess good means should give of their abundance for so excellent a purpose, the offerings of the poor, no matter "how small, will be heartily welcomed. And it is hoped that many "of those who once belonged to the Town, but are now removed "from it, may be induced to lend a helping hand in completing so "excellent and necessary a work. This Appeal has the direct sanction "of the Rev. the Vicar, as also of the Churchwardens, who will "gladly receive donations."

The result of this Appeal was, that the sum of £240 19s. having been collected, I, after having taken counsel with the Vicar, Churchwardens, and others, gave an order to Messrs. Mears and Stainbank of Whitechapel, to recast the old bells, and provide a new peal of eight. This, in due course, was satisfactorily done; and in the month of July, they were successfully hung by Messrs. White and Son of Besselsleigh.

The weights of the new bells are as follows: treble $4\frac{1}{2}$ cwt., second 5 cwt., third $5\frac{1}{2}$ cwt., fourth $6\frac{1}{2}$ cwt., fifth $7\frac{1}{2}$ cwt., sixth 9 cwt., seventh 11 cwt., tenor 14 cwt.

The only inscription placed on them, stands thus:—

REV. F. B. CORBETT, Vicar.

WILLIAM EDDEN, RICHARD BERRY, } Churchwardens. 1876.

The note of the old bells was E natural; that of the new is F natural.

In the *Oxford Journal* of August 19th the following occurs:—

"The task of opening the new peal was assigned to the 'Appleton Society of Change Ringers,' who visited Thame on the 11th, "and discoursed excellent music on the bells for upwards of three "hours, during which time the whole peal of 5040 changes was "obtained in the grandsire method. The ringers were as follows: "Hedman White, treble; E. Hollifield, 2; B. Barrett, 3; W. Bennett, "4; G. Hollifield, 5; Rev. F. E. Robinson, 6; F. White, 7; and T. "Bennett, tenor. The peal was composed by F. White, and conducted by the Rev. F. E. Robinson. The ringers were kindly and "hospitably entertained at Mr. Lee's expense, and the proceedings of "the day gave great satisfaction to all concerned in them."

The following inscription on brass for the interior of the Church will not unsuitably commemorate a work which, by God's blessing, and the co-operation of townspeople, friends, and neighbours, has been thus happily brought to a satisfactory termination:—

[This inscription is already given on p. 99.]

In forwarding a copy of this to all who have aided, I take the opportunity of expressing my hearty acknowledgments for their respective gifts, and my sincere congratulations on the accomplishment of the work completed.

RICHARD LEE.

Thame, Oxfordshire, October, 1876.

* It appears from the Churchwardens' Accounts, that two of the bells were certainly recast at Reading in 1530, at a cost of ten pounds. The following, relating to others recast fifteen years afterwards, is of interest:—

A.D. 1545. Itm. Payd to *Simon Synclere* for his labore and th' Horse Rydynge to Redynge to see the casting of the Bellis .... xvj^d
Itm. Pd. for the hyer of horse for Richd Chylde to Redynge for the space of iij days and for horse bred .... xij^d
Itm. Pd. for the costes of Richd Chylde and Simon Synclere Rydynge to Redynge for to see the weight And cartynge of the Bellis, By the space of ij days and ij Nightts for their Horses and theire selfs .... v^s viij^d
Itm. Pd. for Ale to them y^t helpyd to have the said Bellis downe and uppe into the steple .. vj^d
Itm. Pd. to John Miller for hanging the said Bellis .... xvj^d
Itm. Pd. for Mete and Drynke for the same John And his Sone by the space of ij dayes for his Sone and iij days for hymselffe .... v^d
Itm. Pd. to the Bellfoundyrs as doth appere by a Byll indented .... iiij^{li} xiij^s iv^d
Itm. Pd. to the Carter for Carriage of the Bellis .... xxvj^s viij^d

♣♣♣♣♣♣♣♣♣♣♣

No. VIII. STATUTES OF THAME SCHOOL.

SCHEME for the Management of the "Thame School of the Foundation of Sir John Williams, Knight, Lorde Williams of Thame," and of the Almshouses of Lord Williams united therewith at Thame, in the County of Oxford.

PART I.—GENERAL SCOPE OF TRUST.

1. The object of this Foundation or Trust shall be—

(a) To supply a liberal and practical education by means of a School or Schools at Thame, or otherwise;

(b) To serve other charitable uses.

And from the date of this Scheme all the particulars which by the Endowed Schools Acts, 1869 and 1873, are capable of being hereby repealed and abrogated, shall, so far as relates to the management of this endowment, be repealed and abrogated.

2. Subject to the provisions of Part IV. of this Scheme for the benefit of certain Almspeople and for other purposes, the endowment of this Trust shall be applied wholly for the educational object stated in sub-section (a) of the foregoing clause.

PART II.—CONSTITUTION OF GOVERNING BODY AND MANAGEMENT.

3. The Governing Body, hereinafter called the Governors, shall, when completely formed and full, consist of 13 persons, of whom three shall be ex-officio Governors, three nominated, four representative or elective, and three co-optative.

4. The Ex-officio Governors shall be—the owner of the Manor of Rycote in the County of Oxford, if of full age; the Warden of New College, Oxford, or some person to be nominated by him for the term of five years; and the Chairman of the Board of Guardians for the Poor Law Union of Thame.

5. The Nominated Governors shall be nominated—one by the Members of Parliament for the county of Oxford; and two by the Warden and Fellows of New College aforesaid.

6. The Representative Governors shall be elected—three by the Vestry of Thame; and one by the Board of Guardians for the Poor Law Union of Thame.

7. The Co-optative Governors shall, except as hereinafter provided, be appointed by the Governors, by a resolution to be forthwith notified by them, with all proper information to the Charity Commissioners for England and Wales at their office in London; but no such appointment shall be valid until it has been approved by the said Commissioners, and their approval certified under their official seal.

8. The Governors, other than ex-officio, shall be appointed to office as follows: the Nominated and Representative Governors each for the term of five years, and the Co-optative Governors each for the term of eight years. The first nomination and first election of Nominated and Representative Governors shall take place as soon after the date of this Scheme as conveniently may be. The first Co-optative Governors shall be—the Earl of Macclesfield, Hugh Hamersley of Pyrton Manor, and Philip Thomas Herbert Wykeham of Thame Park.

9. If during his term of office any Governor, other than ex-officio, becomes bankrupt, or incapacitated to act, or expresses to the Governors in writing his wish to retire, or omits for the space of two years to attend any meeting, the Governors shall cause a record of the fact to be entered in their books, and upon such record being entered the Governor to whom it applies shall forthwith cease to be a Governor.

10. Each vacancy in the office of Governor, other than ex-officio, shall, as soon as can conveniently be managed, be filled by the appointment of a new Governor, in manner hereinbefore prescribed, by the body entitled on such vacancy to nominate, elect, or appoint a new Governor, as the case may be. On each vacancy in the office of Nominated or Representative Governor notice thereof shall be given by the Governors to the proper nominating or electing body.

11. Women may be Governors.

12. No Master of the School shall be a Governor.

13. Religious opinions or attendance or non-attendance at any particular form of religious worship shall not in any way affect the qualification of any person for being a Governor under this Scheme.

14. Every Governor shall, at or before the first meeting which he attends in that character, sign a memorandum declaring his acceptance of the office of Governor, and his willingness to do his duty as such, and to act in the Trusts of this Scheme. And until he has signed such a declaration he shall not be entitled to discharge the functions of a Governor.

15. The Governors shall hold meetings in some convenient place in Thame or elsewhere, as often as may be found necessary for the management of the Trust, and at least twice in each year, on some convenient days to be appointed by themselves.

16. The Governors shall, at their first meeting in each year, elect one of their number to be Chairman of their meetings for that year, and make regulations for supplying his place whenever he is absent.

17. A quorum shall be constituted whenever five Governors are present. Whenever any decision is carried by the votes of less than a majority of the whole existing number of Governors, any two Governors may, within 14 days from the day of the decision, demand that the decision shall be once reconsidered at a special meeting.

18. Any two Governors may at any time summon a special meeting for any cause that seems to them sufficient.

19. All special meetings shall be convened by notice in writing to the Governors, specifying the object of the meeting. And it shall be the duty of the Clerk to give such notice when required by any Governors having a right to summon such meeting.

20. All matters and questions shall be determined by the majority of the Governors present at any meeting; and in case of equality of votes, the Chairman shall have a second or casting vote.

21. If a sufficient number of Governors to form a quorum are not present at any meeting, or if the business at any meeting is not fully completed, those present may adjourn the meeting to a subsequent day.

22. A minute-book and proper books of account shall be provided by the Governors, and kept in some convenient and secure place of deposit to be provided or appointed by them for that purpose, and minutes of the entry into office of every new Governor, and of all proceedings of the Governors, shall be entered in such minute-book and duly signed.

23. Full accounts shall be kept of the receipts and expenditure of the Governors, and such accounts shall be stated for each year, and examined and passed annually at the first meeting in the ensuing year, and signed by the Governors then present.

24. The Governors shall cause sufficient abstracts of the accounts to be published annually in two local newspapers. Such abstracts may be in the form appended to this Scheme, unless any form is prescribed by the Charity Commissioners, in which case the form so prescribed shall be followed.

25. The Governors shall make such arrangements as they may find most fitting for the custody of all muniments, title-deeds, and other documents belonging to the Trust, for deposit of money, for drawing cheques, and for the appointment of agents for the conduct of their business. If any such agent be himself a Governor he shall not be entitled to a salary.

26. All lands and hereditaments, not being copyhold, belonging to the Trust, and all terms, estates, and interests therein, shall from the date of this Scheme vest in the Official Trustee of Charity Lands and his successors. And all stock in the public funds and other securities belonging to the Trust shall be transferred to and vest in the Official Trustees of Charitable Funds, by whom the dividends and income arising therefrom shall be from time to time paid to the Governors or their order.

27. The Governors may from time to time, when and as favourable opportunity offers, if the Charity Commissioners deem it to be for the permanent benefit of the Trust, and with their sanction, sell such real estates of the Trust as are not required to be used for the objects of this Scheme; and shall, with the like sanction, invest the proceeds in the names of the Official Trustees of Charitable Funds in such mode as the Court of Chancery, in exercise of its statutory powers, or as any Act of Parliament, may authorise for the investment of Trust Funds in general.

28. All the estates and property of the Trust remaining unsold, and not required to be retained or occupied for the purposes thereof, shall be let or otherwise managed by the Governors, or by their officers acting under their orders, according to the general law applicable to the management of property by the Trustees of Charitable Foundations.

29. From the date of this Scheme all rights and powers reserved to, belonging to, or claimed by, or capable of being exercised by the Warden of New College, or any person other than Her Majesty as Visitor of this Trust, shall be transferred to Her Majesty, and all such rights and powers, and also any like rights and powers vested in Her Majesty on the 2nd day of August 1869, shall be exercised only through and by the Charity Commissioners for England and Wales.

30. From the date of this Scheme all jurisdiction of the Ordinary relating to or arising from the licensing of any Master under this Trust shall be abolished.

PART III.—THE SCHOOL AND ITS MANAGEMENT.

31. The School shall be a Day and Boarding School.

32. As soon as practicable after the date of this Scheme the Governors shall provide, on or near the site of the present School and Almshouses, School Buildings suitable for 120 scholars or thereabouts, including at least 60 boarders, with a residence for the Head Master, and arranged so as to admit of convenient extension. Such buildings shall be according to plans and estimates approved by the Endowed Schools Commissioners, or, after their powers have ceased, by the Charity Commissioners. For these purposes the Governors may pull down the Almshouses when vacated by the present Almspeople, and may purchase land for a playground or as additional site for the School Buildings, and may spend a sufficient sum of money to be raised out of the accumulated capital of the Trust, or by sale or mortgage under the directions of the Charity Commis-

sioners of real estate belonging to the Trust, but not exceeding £5000, unless with the consent of the Charity Commissioners.

33. No person shall be disqualified for being a Master in the School by reason only of his not being, or not intending to be, in Holy Orders.

34. The Governors shall appoint the Head Master at some meeting to be called for that purpose, as soon as conveniently may be after the occurrence of a vacancy, or after notice of an intended vacancy. The Master shall be a Graduate of some University within the British Empire. The circumstance that he has taken or made, or omitted to take or make, any oath or declaration on obtaining a degree shall not affect his qualification. In order to obtain the best candidates, the Governors shall for a sufficient time before making any appointment give public notice of the vacancy and invite competition by advertisements in newspapers, or other methods as they may judge best calculated to secure the object. The first appointment of a Head Master under this Scheme may be made at such time as the Governors think fit, being not later than the time at which the new school buildings are completed and ready for use.

35. The Governors may dismiss the Head Master without assigning cause, after six calendar months' written notice, given to him in pursuance of a resolution passed at two consecutive meetings held at an interval of at least fourteen days, and duly convened for that express purpose, such resolution being affirmed at each meeting by not less than two-thirds of the Governors present.

36. For urgent cause the Governors may, by resolution passed at a special meeting duly convened for that express purpose, and affirmed by not less than two-thirds of the whole existing number of Governors, declare that the Head Master ought to be dismissed from his office, and in that case they may appoint another special meeting to be held not less than a week after the former one, and may then, by a similar resolution, affirmed by as large a proportion of Governors, wholly and finally dismiss him. And if the Governors assembled at the first of such meetings think fit at once to suspend the Head Master from his office until the next meeting, they may do so by resolution affirmed by as large a proportion of Governors. Full notice and opportunity of defence at both meetings shall be given to the Head Master.

37. Every Head Master, previously to entering into office, shall be required to sign a declaration, to be entered in the Minute Book of the Governors, in the following from :—

"I, declare that I will always, to the best of my "ability, discharge the duties of Head Master of Lord Williams' "School at Thame during my tenure of the office, and that if I am "removed by the Governors, according to the constitution of the "said School, I will acquiesce in such removal, and will thereupon "relinquish all claim to the mastership and its future emoluments, "and will deliver up to the Governors, or as they direct, possession "of all their property then in my possession or occupation."

38. The Head Master shall dwell in the residence assigned for him. He shall have the occupation and use of such residence and of any other property of the Trust of which he becomes occupant, in respect of his official character and duties, and not as tenant, and shall, if removed from his office, deliver up possession of such residence and other property to the Governors, or as they direct. He shall not, except with the permission of the Governors, permit any person to occupy such residence or any part thereof.

39. The Head Master shall give his personal attention to the duties of the School. During his tenure of office he shall not accept or hold any benefice having the cure of souls, or any office or appointment which, in the opinion of the Governors, may interfere with the proper performance of his duties as Head Master.

40. Neither the Head Master nor any Assistant Master shall receive or demand from any boy in the School, or from any person whomsoever on behalf of any such boy, any gratuity, fee, or payment, except such payments as are prescribed or authorised by this Scheme.

41. Within the limits fixed by this Scheme the Governors shall prescribe the general subjects of instruction, the relative prominence and value to be assigned to each group of subjects, the division of the year into term and vacation, the payments of scholars, the number and payments of boarders, and the number of holidays to be given in the term. They shall take general supervision of the sanitary condition of the School buildings and arrangements. They shall determine what number of Assistant Masters shall be employed. They shall every year assign the amount which they think proper to be paid out of the income of the Trust for the purpose of maintaining Assistant Masters and a proper plant or apparatus for carrying on the instruction given in the School.

42. Before making any regulations under the last preceding clause the Governors shall consult the Head Master, in such a manner as to give him full opportunity for the expression of his views.

43. Subject to the rules prescribed by or under the authority of this Scheme, the Head Master shall have under his control the choice of books, the methods of teaching, the arrangement of classes and school hours, and generally the whole internal organisation, management, and discipline of the School: Provided that if he expels a boy from the School he shall forthwith make a full report in writing of the case to the Governors.

44. The Head Master shall have the sole power of appointing, and, subject to appeal to the Governors, of dismissing all Assistant Masters, and shall determine, subject to the approval of the Governors, in what proportions the sum assigned by the Governors for the maintenance of Assistant Masters and of plant or apparatus shall be divided among the various persons and objects for which it is assigned in the aggregate. And the Governors shall pay the same accordingly, either through the hands of the Head Master or directly, as they think best.

45. The Head Master may from time to time submit proposals to the Governors for making or altering regulations concerning any matter within their province, and the Governors shall consider such proposals and decide upon them.

46. The Head Master shall receive a fixed stipend of £150 a year. He shall also receive head money calculated on such a scale, uniform or graduated, as may be agreed upon between him and the Governors, being at the rate of not less than £2 or more than £4 yearly for each boy. These payments shall be made terminally or quarterly as the Governors think fit.

47. The Governors shall make such regulations as they think right for the reception of boarders either into the houses of any Master upon terms sufficiently profitable to the Master, or upon the system generally known as the hostel system, under which the pecuniary and domestic arrangements of the boarding-house are regulated by persons directly accountable to the Governors, and the profit, if there is any, accrues to the credit of the Trust. Or if they think it best they may combine both systems.

48. All boys, except as hereinafter provided, shall pay such entrance and tuition fees as the Governors shall fix from time to time, provided that no such entrance fee shall exceed £1, and that no such tuition fee shall be less than £4 or more than £10 a year. No difference in respect of these fees shall be made between any scholars on account of place of birth or residence, or of being or not being boarders. The payments for a boarder apart from the tuition fee shall not exceed the rate of £35 a year. No extras of any kind shall be allowed without the sanction of the Governors, and written consent on behalf of the scholar concerned.

49. All payments for entrance or tuition shall be made in advance to the Head Master, or to such other person as the Governors shall from time to time determine, and shall be accounted for by the person receiving them to the Governors, and treated by them as part of the general income of the Trust.

50. No boy shall be admitted into the School unless he has attained the age of 8 years. No boy shall remain in the School after the end of the term in which he has attained the age of 19 years.

51. Subject to the provisions established by or under the authority of this Scheme, the School and all advantages of the School shall be open to all boys who are of good character and sufficient health, and who are residing with their parents, guardians, or next friends, or in some boarding-house established under the sanction of the Governors. No boy not so residing or boarding shall be admitted to the School unless he has previously obtained the express permission of the Governors.

52. Applications for admission to the School shall be made to the Head Master, or to some other person named by the Governors, according to a printed form to be approved of by the Governors, and delivered to all applicants.

53. The Head Master or other person named by the Governors shall keep a register of applications showing the date at which every application is made for the admission of a boy, the date of his admission, withdrawal, or rejection, the cause of rejection, and the age of the boy at the date of the application. Provided that every person requiring an application to be entered shall pay such fee as the Governors may fix, not exceeding five shillings.

54. Every applicant for admission shall be examined by or under the direction of the Head Master, who shall appoint convenient times for that purpose and give reasonable notice to the parents of those whose turn is arriving. No boy shall be admitted to the School except after undergoing such examination and being found fit for admission. Those who are so found fit shall, if there is room for them, be admitted in order according to the dates of their application, but the Governors may direct that if there is not room their priority shall be determined by competitive examination.

55. The examination for admission shall be graduated according to the age of the boy, but it shall never fall below the following standard, that is to say: Reading easy narrative; small text handwriting; the first four rules of aritmetic; the outlines of the geography of England. The Governors may raise the minimum standard from time to time if they deem it advantageous for the School.

56. The parent or guardian of or person liable to maintain or having the actual custody of any day scholar may claim, by notice in writing addressed to the Head Master, the exemption of such scholar from attending prayer or religious worship, or from any lesson or series of lessons on a religious subject, and such scholar shall be exempted accordingly, and a scholar shall not, by reason of any exemption from attending prayer or religious worship or from any lesson or series of lessons on a religious subject, be deprived of any advantage or emolument in this School or out of this Trust to which he would otherwise have been entitled. If any teacher, in the course

of other lessons at which any such scholar is in accordance with the ordinary rules of the School present, teaches systematically and persistently any particular religious doctrine, from the teaching of which any exemption has been claimed, as in this clause before provided, the Governors shall, on complaint made in writing to them by the parent, guardian, or person liable to maintain or having the actual custody of such scholar, hear the complainant, and inquire into the circumstances, and if the complaint is judged to be reasonable, make all proper provisions for remedying the matter complained of.

57. The Governors and Head Master shall, within their respective departments, as hereinbefore defined, and subject to the provisions of this Scheme, make proper regulations for the religious instruction to be given in the School.

58. No alteration in any regulations made by the Governors respecting the religious instruction to be given in the School shall take effect until the expiration of not less than one year after notice of the making of the alteration is given.

59. The subjects of secular instruction shall be as follows: Reading and writing, arithmetic and mathematics, geography and history, natural science, English grammar, composition, and literature, Latin, and at least one foreign European language, drawing and vocal music. The boys shall be instructed in the foregoing subjects according to the classification and arrangements made by the Head Master. Greek may be taught as an extra at an additional fee of not less than £3 a year for each boy.

60. There shall be once in every year an examination of the scholars by an Examiner or Examiners appointed for that purpose by the Governors, and paid by them, but otherwise unconnected with the School. The Examiners shall report to the Governors on the proficiency of the scholars, and on the position of the School as regards instruction and discipline, as shown by the results of the examination. The Governors shall communicate the report to the Head Master.

61. The Head Master shall make an annual Report in writing to the Governors on the general condition of the School, and on any special occurrences during the year. He also may mention the names of any boys who in his judgment are worthy of praise or substantial reward, having regard both to proficiency and conduct.

62. By way of Exhibitions tenable at the School, the Governors may grant exemptions from the payment of tuition fees for such periods and on such conditions as they think fit. All such exemptions shall be given as the reward of merit only, and shall be assigned, in the case of candidates for admission on the result of the examination for admission, and in the case of boys already attending the School on the Reports of the Examiners and Head Master, and no exemption shall be granted to any such boy if the Head Master reports that he is rendered undeserving of it by ill-conduct. The Governors may, under these conditions, exempt boys from the payment of the whole or of one-half of the tuition fee, but such exemption shall in every case be liable to forfeiture in the event of misconduct or failure to maintain a reasonable standard of proficiency. Boys so exempted shall be called and ranked as Foundation Scholars, and the degrees of exemption shall be further distinguished if the Governors think fit. Not more than 10 per cent. of the boys shall be wholly exempt, and no further exemptions shall be allowed when the exemptions, total and partial, reach the proportion of one in every five boys in the School.

63. Of these Exhibitions one-half shall be competed for in the first instance by boys who have for not less than two years been educated at the Public Elementary Schools in the parishes in the Poor Law Union of Thame; and the Governors shall make such arrangements as seem to them best adapted to secure the double object of attracting good scholars to the School, and applying a stimulus to the said Public Elementary Schools. In cases of equal merit on the part of any candidates for this class of Exhibitions, preference shall be given to such as are of kin to the founder or are inhabitants of Old or New Thame, Priest End, or the liberties of North Weston, Moreton, or Thame Park. None of this class of Exhibitions shall be thrown open to all comers until the Head Master has reported that there are not enough boys from the said Public Elementary Schools who on examination prove worthy to take them. Subject to the preference given by this clause, the Exhibitions established under this Scheme shall be freely and openly competed for.

64. The Governors may also, if the state of the funds will admit, establish Exhibitions tenable at other places of education, and to be awarded by open competition among the boys who have been educated at the School for such time previous to the grant of the Exhibition as the Governors may prescribe.

65. The Exhibitions established under this Scheme shall be tenable only for the purposes of education. If the holder dies, his representatives shall be entitled only to the next instalment whenever payable. If the holder is guilty of gross misconduct or idleness the Governors may determine the Exhibition.

66. The Governors may, if the state of the funds admits, establish in Thame a School for girls of the same general character as is hereinbefore prescribed for the Boys' School. For this purpose they shall apply to the Endowed Schools Commissioners, or, after the powers under the Endowed Schools Acts, 1869 and 1873, have expired, to the Charity Commissioners, for a Scheme establishing such a Girls' School.

PART IV.—TRUSTS FOR THE ALMSPEOPLE AND OTHER OBJECTS.

67. The Almspeople shall be five men and one woman appointed in the same manner and subject, except so far as otherwise hereby provided, to the same regulations as heretofore, but in lieu of residence and the allowances hitherto customary shall receive out of the endowment the sum of £33 6s. 8d. each yearly by as nearly as may be equal weekly payments. The present Almspeople shall become entitled to such payment from the time of their respectively vacating the Almshouses, and in the meantime shall each have the weekly allowance of 7s. 6d. and right of residence and other rights hitherto customary: Provided that after six months from the date of this Scheme the Governors may make such arrangements as the Charity Commissioners think proper for housing or lodging elsewhere in Thame any present Almsperson who has not then agreed to accept such yearly sum of £33 6s. 8d. in lieu of all other rights, and on such arrangements being made such present Almsperson shall have no further right of residence in the present Almshouses.

68. The Governors shall keep in repair the tomb of the Founder.

69. The Governors shall continue the payment to the late Head Master, the Rev. Thomas Bradley Fookes, D.C.L., during his life of the pension lately granted to him on his retirement.

PART V.—APPLICATION OF INCOME.

70. The Governors shall, as soon as funds are available for the purpose, place the sum of £1000 Consols to a separate account in the name of the Official Trustees of Charitable Funds, entitled "Repairs and Improvements." The income shall be paid to the Governors, and applied by them in ordinary repairs or improvements of the School site and buildings, and if not wanted for that purpose shall be accumulated by them to the same account. The Governors shall draw upon the accumulations at their discretion for the purpose of any such repairs or improvements, but shall not encroach upon the capital, except for the purpose of substantial improvements or extraordinary repairs or renewal of such property, and then not without the consent of the Charity Commissioners, and under such conditions of replacing the capital as that Board may think right.

71. Until the Repairs and Improvements Fund is provided the Governors shall treat the sum of £30 a year as applicable to the same purposes as the Repairs and Improvements Fund, except that they may lay by any surplus in the ordinary way, and need not pay it over to the Official Trustees of Charitable Funds.

72. After defraying the expenses of management and of any ordinary repairs or improvements which the income of the Repairs and Improvements Fund may be insufficient to answer, and payment of any legal claims on the Governors which may be due, the Governors shall make any payments directed or authorized in Part IV. of this Scheme, and shall then employ the income in paying the Head Master as hereinbefore prescribed, in paying the amount assigned for the Assistant Masters and School plant or apparatus, and paying the Examiner or Examiners, and in providing for such Scholarships, Exhibitions, and Prizes as they may have adjudged.

73. The Governors may also, if they think fit and the funds suffice for the purpose, agree with the Head Master for the formation of a fund in the nature of a Pension or Superannuation Fund, the main principle of such agreement being that the Head Master and the Trust Fund shall each contribute annually for a period of 20 years such sums as may be fixed on; that these contributions shall accumulate at compound interest; that in case the Head Master serves his office 20 years he shall on his retirement be entitled to the whole fund; that in case he retires earlier on account of permanent disability from illness he shall also be entitled to the whole fund; that in all other cases he shall, on his ceasing to be Master, be entitled to the amount produced by his own contributions.

74. If there is any residue of income the Governors may employ it in increasing the stipend of the Head Master, or the Fund applicable to the payment of Assistant Masters and School plant or apparatus, in improving the accommodation of the School buildings, in aiding the games of the scholars, or generally in promoting the spirit and efficiency of the School. Whatever they do not think fit to spend in these ways they shall on passing the yearly accounts state as Unapplied Surplus, and shall deposit it in a bank; and if the sum so deposited rise to £300 they shall invest the same in the manner hereinbefore directed to the general credit of the Trust.

PART VI.—GENERAL.

75. The Governors may receive any additional donations or endowments for the general purposes of the School. They may also receive donations or endowments for any special objects directed by the donors, provided that such objects are certified by the Charity Commissioners to be for the general benefit of the Schools or either of them, and not calculated to give privileges to any scholar on any other ground than that of merit, and not otherwise inconsistent with or calculated to impede the due working of the provisions of this Scheme.

76. If any doubt or question arises among the Governors as to the proper construction or application of any of the provisions of this Scheme, the Governors may apply to the Charity Commissioners for their opinion and advice thereon, which opinion and advice when given shall be binding on the Governors.

77. The Charity Commissioners may from time to time in the exercise of their ordinary jurisdiction frame Schemes for the alteration of any provisions of this Scheme or otherwise for the government or regulation of the Trust, provided that such Schemes be not inconsistent with Clause 1 of this Scheme, or with any thing contained in the Endowed Schools Acts, 1869 and 1873.

78. This Scheme shall be printed and a copy given to every person who shall become a Governor, and to every Master or Assistant Master appointed to the School, and copies shall be sold at a reasonable price to all persons who may wish to buy.

79. The date of the Scheme shall be the day on which Her Majesty by Order in Council declares her approbation of it.

No. IX. DOCUMENTS RELATING TO THE ABBEY OF THAME, ETC.

Patent Roll (12th of December), 26 Henry VI., part ii., membrane 8. A licence to found Quatermayne's Chantry in Thame Church to John Archbishop of Canterbury, William Bishop of Lincoln, Humphrey Duke of Buckingham, William Earl of Suffolk, Sir William Lovell, Knt., Sir Ralph Cromwell, Knt., Sir Ralph de Sudeley, Knt., and Drugo Barentyne and Richard Quatremayne, Esqs.

The provisions of this foundation are set forth in detail in the Particulars for Grants, Edward VI., to Sir John Williams.

Chantry Certificates, County of Oxford. Roll xxxviij, No. 8. Relating to the Chantry of St. Christopher, founded by Richard Quatermayne, Esq.

Status Mon' de Thame, etc. (A.D. 1525). On folio 42 of the Register of John Longland, Bishop of Lincoln.

Patent Roll, 33 Henry VIII., part vii., membrane 8 (27). For Sir John Williams, Knt., concerning a grant to him and his heirs of the Manor of Sydenham and the Grange, etc. etc.

Particulars of Grants, Henry VIII., to the Bishop of Oseney.

Patent Roll, 34 Henry VIII., part i., membrane 11 (16). For the Bishop of Oxford, a grant of the Manors of Medley, etc., and the site, enclosure, circuit, and precinct of the late Monastery of Thame, etc.

Patent Roll, 1 Edward VI., part iv., membrane 36 (15). To Edward, Duke of Somerset, granted to him and his heirs the Manor of Mildenhall, and the site of the late Monastery of Thame, etc. To be held, in *capite*, by the service of the fortieth part of one knight's fee.

Particulars for Grants, Edward VI., section 3. Edward Pease and James Wilson. A. 4. Thame in the County of Oxford. The rent or farm of eight acres of land called Butwell Leyse, and a certain meadow called Wyde-mead, granted for the sustaining of a certain light. In free socage, at 24 years' purchase, £9 12s. od.

Patent Roll (30 day of April), 29 Elizabeth, part ii., membrane 36. Concerning a special grant to Theophilus Adams and Thomas Butler, gentlemen, of certain lands, tithes, tenements, etc., in Sydenham, Thame, Shepcotes, and Moreton, parcel of the possessions of the late Monastery of Thame, etc.

Patent Roll (30 day of March), 34 Elizabeth, part iv., membrane 21. Concerning a grant to William Typper and Robert Dawe and others, for life, of certain lands, tenements, etc., in Thame, Goring, and Rewlaye, etc.

Patent Roll, sixth year of James I., part ix., no. 5. Wenman, headed, "Concerning a grant to him and his heirs, for Sir Richard Wenman, Knt.," in return for the sum of one hundred and two pounds and sixpence.

No. X. THE LEES OF BUCKS AND OXON AND THE LEES OF VIRGINIA.

At the particular request of several members of the Family of Lee of Virginia, I reproduce the following which I contributed to the *Standard* some years ago.

An American book—*Genealogical History of the Lee Family of Virginia and Maryland*, by Edward C. Meade; New York, 1868—is so full of the most obvious and egregious errors, that it is all the more necessary to place on record the following facts:

1. Richard Lee, the first English settler in Virginia, was the seventh son of Sir Robert Lee, Knight, of Hulcott, Bucks, son of Benedict Lee of the same place, by Elizabeth, daughter of Robert Cheyne of Chesham Bois in the same county. Sir Robert Lee was born at Helsthorpe, Bucks, 15 June 1545, and married Lucy, daughter of Thomas Pigott of Beachampton; dying at Stratford Langton in Essex, he was buried in the chancel of Hardwick, Bucks, 20 August 1616, aged 78. (See Pedigree, pp. 561, 562.) His monument still exists. His eldest son, Henry, was the first baronet of Quarrendon. The Will of the abovenamed Richard Lee, who calls himself "Colonel," is dated 1663, and he describes himself in it "of Stratford Langton in the County of Essex, Esquire."

2. Richard Lee, his second son, was born in Virginia A.D. 1646, and was sent to England to be educated. He married Letitia, the eldest daughter of Henry Corbin; obtained a large property in the American State of Westmoreland, where he built a residence, naming it "Ditchley," after the chief Oxfordshire mansion of his English relations. On his monument it is stated, "In magistratum obeundo boni publici studiosissimi, in literis Græcis et Latinis et aliis humanioris literaturæ disciplinis versatissimi." He died 12 March 1714, aged 68. This Richard Lee left five sons, viz., Richard, Philip, Francis, Thomas, and Henry. I am concerned with the last named.

3. Henry Lee, born in Virginia, was a member of the early councils of that colony, and married a Miss Bland, daughter of "Richardus Bland, armiger." (See Campbell's *History of Virginia*, p. 161.) Of this marriage there were two sons—Richard and Henry—and a daughter.

4. Henry Lee, the second son, married Lucy Grymes, granddaughter of General Thos. Grymes, at Spring Green, on Saturday, 1 December 1753. Spring Green was the residence of President Lee. An interesting description of the old mansion is given in the *Virginia Historical Register*. This Henry Lee, by Lucy his wife, had six sons and five daughters.

5. Their eldest son, Henry, who was a general in the army, and was known by the sobriquet of "Light Horse Harry," was the well-known ally and distinguished friend of General Washington. He it was who, in 1799, pronounced the great eulogium in the American Congress upon Washington, and is remembered as one of the most remarkable men of his day. He married, as his second wife, Ann, daughter of Charles Carter, Esq., and had three sons and two daughters. He died 25 March 1818.

6. Of these sons, the youngest, Robert Edward, is the general whose death has recently taken place. General Lee married Mary, daughter of George Washington Park Custis, and has issue three sons and four daughters.

I have thus briefly traced, from family documents in my possession and other sources, the pedigree of this illustrious man, connecting him by undoubted proofs with the Buckinghamshire and Oxfordshire Lees. The very fact that in the new colony of Virginia the names of their family's old homes in England were given to the residences they erected—"Ditchley," "Lee's Rest," and "Stratford"—is, in conjunction with the Wills and monumental inscriptions existing, a clear proof of their descent from an old English family of note and reputation.

And I add to it the following touching Poem which my contemporary at Oxford, the late Mr. Philip Stanhope Worsley, with a copy of his graceful and scholarly Translation of the *Iliad*, wrote to the late General Lee :—

The grand old Bard that never dies,
  Receive him in our English tongue;
I send thee, but with weeping eyes,
  The story that he sung.

Thy Troy is fallen, thy dear land
  Is marred beneath the spoiler's heel;
I cannot trust my trembling hand
  To write the things I feel.

Ah! realm of tears! but let her bear
  This blazon to the end of time—
No Nation rose so pure and fair,
  None fell so pure of crime.

The widow's moan, the orphan's wail,
  Rise round thee; but in truth be strong:
Eternal Right, though all else fail,
  Can never be made wrong.

An angel's pen, an angel's mouth,
  Not Homer's could alone for me,
Hymn well the great Confederate South,
  Virginia first and—Lee!

ERRATA, ADDENDA, ET CORRIGENDA.

Page 17, line 1, *for* pede *read* Rede.
" 32, line 12, *for* lavon *read* lavon.
" 44, line 18, *for* lyre *read* lyne.
" 56. SIR JOHN DAUNCE OR DAWNE OF THAME.—See *Proceedings of the Society of Antiquaries*, second series, vol. viii., pages 98, 270, in which a brief account is given of certain Rolls containing official records of disbursements in the reign of Henry VIII., signed by Sir John, which Rolls are now in the possession of Colonel Smyth of Welwyn.
" 65, line 41, *for* offices *read* officers.
" 75, in the fifth line from the bottom omit "that."
" 83, line 16, *for* Whitsunde *read* Whitsuntide.
" 99. William Harvey, Esq., Clarencieux King at Arms, so created 21 Nov. 1557, died at Thame 27 Feb. 1566-7, and was buried there. Francis Thynne, of the same College, visited Thame Church officially in Sept. 1582. Anthony à Wood, under the date of 20 Aug. 1661, as he himself puts on record, "was at Thame; continued there one or more nights; transcrib'd all the monumental inscriptions in the church, armes in the windowes, and the armes in the windowes of the Free School."—Wood's MSS., Bodleian Library, 8518, 2.
" 139, line 4, *for* Emsworth *read* Tetsworth.
" 154, line 24, *for* Anger *read* Anger.
" 160, in the tenth line from the bottom, for *Protestanibus* read *Protestantibus*.
" 192, in the third line from the bottom, "1" has dropped out.
" 197, in the second line from the bottom, *for* "Thomas" *read* "William." [In this I was misled by a mistake in the late Mr. Davenport's *High Sheriffs of Oxfordshire*.]

Pages 215, 216. FAMILY OF PETTY.—We whose names are underwritten do testify that being with Mr George Petty on Monday ye 7 day of Feb. 1630, & askinge him howe he would bestowe his estate, his answer was that he left it to his two brothers, Mr Leonard Petty, and Mr Maximilian Petty to be divided equally between them.

WILL'M SELLAR. ALEXANDER FISHER.

Administration granted 3 March 1630.

Maximilian Pettye, æt. 15. }
Christopher Pettye, æt. 13. } Matriculated at B.N.C., 13 Oct. 1598. — Matriculation Register.
George Pettye, æt. 11. }

Page 244. FAMILY OF BOROUGH.—The following, which may indicate ancestors of the race of Burrows of Leicestershire, and of Thame, Crendon, and Sydenham, was transcribed by me from a note-book of the late Mr. J. Gough Nichols, which had belonged to his father:—

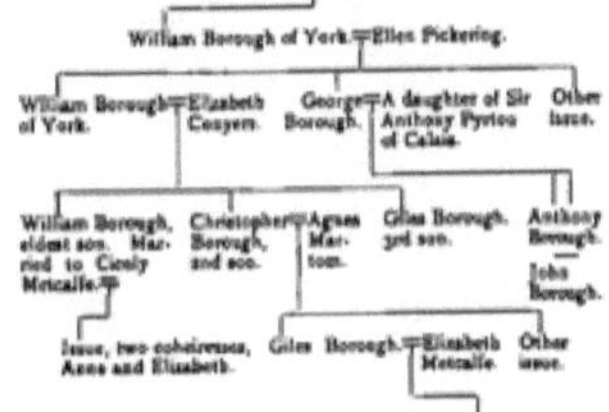

Page 253, line 38, *for* Saint's Bell *read* Saints' Bell.
" 254, line 7, *for* Eastern *read* Easter.
" 281. FAMILY OF DEANE.—Here lieth the Body of Mary Deane, widow of John Deane Esq. late of Mattingley, in com' South'ton. Obiit 5 Mar. Anno Dom' 1706, ætatis suæ 81.—St. Laurence's Church, Reading.
" 314, in the eleventh line from the bottom, *for* B. N. Co. Oxon, *read* B. N. Coll. Oxon.
" 398. FATHER BERNARD STAFFORD, S.J., THAME PARK.—A member of the Society of Jesus known as "Father Cassidy." In 1764 he resided at Warkworth, Co. Northampton, which belonged to the Holman family, and in subsequent years at Thame Park. One of the Squires of Warkworth had married the Lady Anastasia Stafford, a kinswoman of Father Bernard's. It is most improbable that this priest would have been buried in his assumed name.—*Records of the Society of Jesus*, by H. Foley, vol. vii., page 1452. London: 1883.

Pages 411, 412. FAMILY OF CROMWELL.—"The Cromwells, the most opulent family in Huntingdonshire, after a gradual decline, totally expired, and their great estates fell into various other hands: Ramsey, the richest, into those of the celebrated Colonel Titus, by purchase. What this monastery was may be guessed by the value of such appendages as were held by the Cromwells, which would now let for, perhaps, upwards of £80,000 per annum; but the estate had been so lessened that this Mr. Cromwell *alias* Williams had only £2000 per annum, and that probably much encumbered."—*Memoirs of the Cromwell Family*, vol. i., page 73. Birmingham: 1787.

Page 417. Here the reference to note 4 on the second line should be to Francis Williams on the tenth line.
" 433. WYKEHAM OF TYTTEGROVE.—See *The Noble and Gentle Men of England*, etc., pages 176, 177; and *The Topographer and Genealogist*, vol. iii., page 49.
" 437, line 5, *for* 1691 *read* 1697.
" 495. THE ORDNANCE SURVEY.—The parish of Thame is included in fifteen sheets, on the scale of 25 inches to the mile. Each sheet is about 20 inches by 40, and comprises a tract of country, one mile from north to south, and one and a half mile west to east (960 acres). The adjoining parishes are Shabbington, Long Crendon, Haddenham, Bucks; Kingsey, Oxon.; Towersey, Bucks; Sydenham, Attington, Tettesworth, Great Haseley, and Albury, Oxon. A large portion of each of the above parishes is included in the maps. The altitude above the sea-level is specified at the various "bench marks" on buildings, posts, etc.; the one on the Parish Church of Thame being 226 feet. The area may be briefly stated as follows:—Land 5051, roads 108, water 44, railway 26, total 5229 acres. The parish is in the Hundred of Thame, in the county of Oxford.
" 496. I find that the actual date remaining on the House of the Striblehills is 1647, a year earlier than that mentioned below the illustration of it.
" 514, *for* Thelvidore *read* Thelvedon.
" 515, *for* Herbert Francis *read* Hubert Francis.
" 530, in the third line from the bottom, *for* daughter *read* wife.
" 555. WALPOLE OF THAME PARK.—"Reginald de Walpole, in the time of Henry I., seems to have been lineal ancestor of the House."—*The Noble and Gentle Men of England*, etc., pages 142, 143. London: 1860. Blomefield's *History of Norfolk*, vol. iii., page 796; and vol. iv., page 708.
" 614. DARRELL OF LILLINGSTONE DARRELL.—"A very ancient and honourable family of Norman descent, who came over with the Conqueror, and seated themselves at Lillingstone before the year 1200."—*The Noble and Gentle Men of England*, by Evelyn P. Shirley, p. 7. London: 1860.
" 629. PATTEN OF BANK HALL.—"Richard Patten, who appears to have flourished before the reign of Henry III., by his marriage with a coheiress of Dagenham became possessed of the Court of that name in the county of Essex."—*The Noble and Gentle Men of England*, etc., page 124. London: 1860.

INDEX.

A

B

C

D

E

I

J

K

L

M

Q

R

S

T

U

V

W

LIST OF SUBSCRIBERS.

The following is the Original List of the Subscribers to this Book:—

The Most Noble the Marquis of Bath, Longleat, Warminster.
The Most Noble the Marquis of Bute, K.T., 83 Eccleston Square, S.W.
The Right Honourable the Earl Beauchamp, M.A., F.S.A., 13 Belgrave Square, S.W.
The Right Honourable the Earl of Carnarvon, President of the Society of Antiquaries, 43 Portman Square, W.
The Right Honourable the Earl of Beaconsfield, K.G. (the late), Hughendon Manor, High Wycombe.
The Right Honourable Lord Ardilaun, 11 Carlton House Terrace, S.W.
Sir Alfred Slade, Bart., 3 Lyall Street, Belgrave Square, S.W.
Sir W. H. Clerke, Bart. (the late), 10 South Eaton Place, S.W.
Sir Philip Rose, Bart. (the late), Rayners, Penn, Bucks.
Sir Philip Frederick Rose, Bart., Rayners, Penn, Bucks.
Sir Edward Lee, F.S.A., 10 Chalcot Crescent, Regent's Park, N.W.
Sir Albert W. Woods, F.S.A., College of Arms, Queen Victoria Street, E.C.
Right Hon. J. W. Henley, M.P., Waterperry House, Oxfordshire.
Ven. Archdeacon Clerke, D.D. (the late), Christ Church, Oxford.
William Rose, Esq., J.P., High Wycombe, Bucks.
George A. Sainte Croix Rose, Esq., 6 Victoria Street, Westminster, S.W.
Henry Rose, Esq., 8 Porchester Square, Hyde Park, W.
Granville Leveson Gower, Esq., F.S.A., Titsey Place, Limpsfield.
W. E. Biscoe, Esq., J.P., D.L., Holton Park, Oxford.
Henry Barnett, Esq., J.P., D.L., Glympton Park, Woodstock, Oxon.
Sackville Lupton, Esq., The Brewery, Leamington.
George Lindsey, Esq., Hope Cottage, Small Heath, Birmingham.
Mrs. E. A. Sheppard, Great Milton House, Tettesworth, Oxon.
Rev. Canon J. H. Ashhurst, M.A., Waterstock Rectory, Oxford.
G. E. Cokayne, Esq., F.S.A., College of Arms, Queen Victoria Street, E.C.
T. B. Grove, Esq., Watercroft, Penn, Bucks.
Montagu Burrows, Esq., M.A., F.S.A., Norham House, Oxford.
Rev. S. W. Barnett, B.A. (the late), Newbury Villa, Thame, Oxon.
A. H. Clerke Brown, Esq., J.P., D.L., Kingston Blount, Tettesworth, Oxon.
J. P. Deane, Esq., Q.C., 16 Westbourne Terrace, Hyde Park, W.
Gordon Dayman, Esq., Solicitor, Oxford.
Clement Upton Cottrell Dormer, Esq., J.P. (the late), 22 Berkeley Square, W.
Mr. William Downing, 74 New Street, Birmingham.
A. Lisle March Phillipps de Lisle, Esq. (the late), Garendon Park, Loughborough, Leicestershire.
J. G. Godwin, Esq., 76 Warwick Street, Pimlico, S.W.
William Harrison, Esq., F.S.A. (the late), Samlesbury Hall, Preston, Lancashire.
Herbert G. Lee, Esq., M.D., The Moats, Thame, Oxon.
Rev. F. C. Hingeston-Randolph, M.A., Ringmore Rectory, near Kingsbridge, Devon.
Harry Lupton, Esq., Chapel Street, Stratford-on-Avon.
William Cozens, Esq., Bishop's Court, Dorchester, Oxfordshire.
Rev. F. Bulley, D.D., President of Magdalene College, Oxford.

J. D. Chambers, Esq., M.A., F.S.A., 16 Prince's Gardens, Hyde Park, W.
Mr. J. Newman, 235 High Holborn, W.C.
H. Hucks Gibbs, Esq., J.P., D.L., Aldenham House, Elstree, Herts.
W. N. Skillicorne, Esq., J.P., D.L., 9 Queen's Parade, Cheltenham.
M. H. Humphreys, Esq., Thame, Oxon.
E. Story-Maskelyne, Esq., Hatt House, Box, Wilts.
Miss E. Loader, 112 High Street, Thame.
H. J. Wakeman, Esq., Warminster, Wiltshire.
Henry Lee, Esq., Boston, U.S.A.
Mr. Roger W. Rose, Grenville Manor Place, Haddenham, Bucks.
Major Robert Warner Stone, The Curragh, Ireland.
Mrs. William Way Stone, The Glen, Cookham Dean, near Maidenhead.
B. W. Greenfield, Esq., 4 Cranbury Terrace, Southampton.
J. Kirby Hedges, Esq., J.P., Wallingford Castle, Berks.
Colonel Bulwer, Quebec House, East Dereham.
F. J. Morrell, Esq. (the late), Broughton Grange, Banbury.
G. Ambrose de Lisle Lee, Esq., 148 York Road, Lambeth, S.E.
G. E. Street, Esq., R.A. (the late), 14 Cavendish Place, W.
H. Wells Reynolds, Esq. (the late), The Hollies, Thame, Oxon.
George Lee, Esq., Wheatley Manor House, Alton, Hants.
J. H. Parker, Esq., C.B., Oxford.
Library of the Science and Art Department, South Kensington, S.W.
Library of New College, Oxford.
Library of the Society of Antiquaries, Burlington House, Piccadilly, W.
Herbert Wykeham, Esq. (the late), Tythorpe House, near Thame.
Frederick Reginald B. D. Lee, Esq., All Saints' Vicarage, Lambeth, S.E.
Evelyn Philip Shirley, Esq. (the late), Ettington Park, Stratford-on-Avon.
F. A. Crisp, Esq., Inglewood House, Grove Park, S.E.
V. D. H. Cary-Elwes, Esq., Billing Hall, Northampton.
Guildhall Library, Guildhall, E.C.
George Graham Stone, Esq., Eastcote, Red Hill Common, Surrey.
Edward G. Stone, Esq., 18 Marloes Road, Kensington, W.
Timothy Lee, Esq. (the late), Barnsbury Park, N.
James T. Hopwood, Esq., 10 Old Square, Lincoln's Inn, W.C.
Royal Library, Windsor Castle.
Miss Cottrell Dormer, Danes' Dyke, Flamborough, Hull.
Philip J. D. Wykeham, Esq., J.P., Tythorpe House, near Thame.
Thomas Briggs, Esq., J.P., Stoneleigh House, Salford.
Rev. W. J. Blew, M.A., 16 Warwick Street, Pall Mall, S.W.
J. T. Peacock, Esq., Sudbury House, Hammersmith, W.
Thomas M. Davenport, Esq., M.A., County Hall, Oxford.
Henry Boddington, Esq., The Cove, Silverdale, Carnforth.

London: Mitchell and Hughes, Printers, 140 Wardour Street, W.

www.ingramcontent.com/pod-product-compliance
Lightning Source LLC
Chambersburg PA
CBHW051243300426
44114CB00011B/864
* 9 7 8 3 3 3 7 2 0 1 8 6 9 *